A

STUDENT'S HISTORY OF ENGLAND

A

STUDENT'S

HISTORY OF ENGLAND

FROM THE EARLIEST TIMES TO 1885

BY

SAMUEL R. GARDINER, D.C.L., LL.D.

FELLOW OF MERTON COLLEGE, OXFORD

ETC.

NEW EDITION

LONDON

LONGMANS, GREEN, AND CO.

AND NEW YORK

1895

PREFACE

THE PRESENT WORK is intended for such students as have already an elementary knowledge of the main facts of English history, and aims at meeting their needs by the use of plain language on the one hand, and by the avoidance, on the other hand, of that multiplicity of details which is apt to overburden the memory.

At the close of the book I have treated the last eleven years, 1874 to 1885, in a manner which precludes all expression of my own views, either on the characters of the actors or on the value of the work performed by them ; and something of the same reticence will be observed in the pages dealing with the years immediately preceding 1874 We have not the material before us for the formation of a final judgment on many points arising in the course of the narrative, and it is therefore better to abstain from the expression of decided opinion, except on matters so completely before the public as to leave no room for hesitation. Especially is this rule to be observed in a book addressed to those who are not yet at an age when independent investigation is possible.

I hope it will be understood that in my mention of various authors I have had no intention of writing a history of literature, however brief. My object has been throughout to exhibit that side of literature which connects itself with the general political or intellectual movement of the country, and to leave unnoticed the purely literary or scientific qualities of the writers mentioned. This will explain, for instance, the total omission of the name of Roger Bacon, and the brief and, if regarded from a different point of view, the very unsatisfactory treatment of writers like Dickens and Thackeray.

Those of my readers who have complained that no maps were to be found in the book may now be referred to a 'School Atlas of English History,' recently edited by me for Messrs. Longmans & Co. To include an adequate number of maps in this volume would have increased its size beyond all fitting limits.

In the spelling of Indian names I have not adopted the modern and improved system of transliteration. Admirable as it is when used by those who are able to give the right sound to each letter, it only leads to mispronunciation in the mouths of those who are, as most of the readers of this volume will be, entirely in the dark on this point. The old rough method of our fathers at least ensures a fair approximation to the true pronunciation.

My warmest thanks are due to Mr. GEORGE NUTT, of Rugby, and to the Rev. W. HUNT. Mr. NUTT not only looked over the proof-sheets up to the death of Edward I. with excellent results, but gave me most valuable advice as to the general arrangement of the book, founded on his own long experience of scholastic teaching. The Rev. W. HUNT looked over a considerable portion of the remaining proof-sheets, and called my attention to several errors and omissions which had escaped my eye.

The illustrations have been selected by Mr. W. H. ST. JOHN

HOPE, Assistant-Secretary of the Society of Antiquaries. He wishes to acknowledge much valuable assistance given to him in the choice of portraits by GEORGE SCHARF, Esq., C.B., F.SA., who is recognised as the highest authority on the subject.

I am indebted to Her Majesty the QUEEN for permission to engrave two of the portraits appearing in the following pages —viz., those of Bishop Fisher, on p. 393, and the Duke of Norfolk, on p. 410—the originals in both cases being at Windsor Castle.

I have to thank Earl SPENCER for permission to engrave the portrait on p. 362 ; the Earl of ESSEX for that on p. 476 ; the Earl of WARWICK for that on p. 403 ; the Earl of CARLISLE for that on p. 459 ; the Viscount DILLON, F.S.A., for that on p. 376 ; the Hon Sir SPENCER PONSONBY-FANE, K.C.B., for that on p. 365 ; Sir JOHN FARNABY LENNARD, Bart., for that on p. 463 ; Dr. EVANS for those on pp. 2, 4, 6 ; EDWARD HUTH, Esq., for that on p. 387 ; Mrs. DENT, of Sudeley, for that on p. 395 ; H. HUCKS GIBBS, Esq., for that on p. 419 ; T. A. HOPE, Esq., for that on p. 487 ; E. B. NICHOLSON, Esq., for the portrait of Lord Burghley in the Bodleian Library, Oxford, engraved at p. 479 ; the authorities of the University of Cambridge for that on p. 477 ; of Jesus College, Cambridge, for that on p. 414 ; and of Sidney Sussex College, Cambridge, for that on p. 567 ; and the Treasurer of Christ's Hospital, London, for the portrait of Charles II. on p. 579. I have also to thank Mr. JOHN MURRAY for permission to engrave the figures on pp. 130, 150, 160, 166, 177, 188, 260 ; Messrs. PARKER & CO., Oxford, for those on pp. 19, 51, 75, 91, 107, 128, 170, 192, 197, 230, 245, 246, 247, 253, 409, 451 ; Mr. W. NIVES for those at pp. 381, 409, 451 ; Mr. J. G. WALLER for those on pp. 219, 229, 292, 298, 515 ; Mr. BRUCE for those on pp. 17, 18, 21 ; Messrs. POULTON & SONS, Lee, for those on pp. 7,

132 ; Mr. G. A. Nichols, Stamford, for those on pp. 311, 316 ; Mr. G. T. Clarke, for that on p. 74 ; Messrs. Carl Norman & Co., Tunbridge Wells, for that on p. 171 ; Mr. R. Keene, Derby, for that on p. 318 ; the Rev. H. H. Henson, Vicar of Barking, Essex, for the photograph of the monument of Sir Charles Montague on p. 507 ; the Science and Art Department for those on pp. 371, 440, 518, 612 ; Mr. W. H. Wheeler, of Oxford, for those on pp. 319, 384 ; Messrs. Valentine & Sons, Dundee, for those on pp. 109, 206, 213, 238, 244, 276, 355, 378, 485, 662, 666, 668, 683, 907, 919, 937, 942 ; and Mr. R. Keene, Derby, for those on pp. 466, 467, 469, 471.

CONTENTS

PART I

ENGLAND BEFORE THE NORMAN CONQUEST

CHAPTER I

PREHISTORIC AND ROMAN BRITAIN

	PAGE
1. Palæolithic Man of the River-Drift	1
2. Cave-dwelling Palæolithic Man	2
3. Neolithic Man	3
4. Celts and Iberians	5
5. The Celts in Britain	6
6. Goidels and Britons	6
7. Phœnicians and Greeks	7
8. Gauls and Belgians in Britain	8
9. Culture and War	9
10. Religion of the Britons	10
11. The Romans in Gaul B.C. 55	10
12. Cæsar's First Invasion. B.C. 55	11
13. Cæsar's Second Invasion. B.C. 54	11
14. South-eastern Britain after Cæsar's Departure. B.C. 54–A.D. 43	12
15. The Roman Empire	12
16. The Invasion of Aulus Plautius. A.D. 43	12
17. The Colony of Camulodunum	13
18. The Conquests of Ostorius Scapula	14

	PAGE
19. Government of Suetonius Paullinus. 58	14
20. Boadicea's Insurrection. 61	15
21. The Vengeance of Suetonius	15
22. Agricola in Britain. 78–84	16
23. Agricola's Conquests in the North	16
24. The Roman Walls	17
25. The Roman Province of Britain	19
26. Extinction of Tribal Antagonism	21
27. Want of National Feeling	22
28. Carausius and Allectus. 288–296	22
29. Constantius and Constantine. 296–337	22
30. Christianity in Britain	23
31. Weakness of the Empire	23
32. The Picts and Scots	23
33. The Saxons	24
34. Origin of the Saxons	24
35. The Roman Defence	24
36. End of the Roman Government. 383–410	25

CHAPTER II

THE ENGLISH SETTLEMENTS

		PAGE			PAGE
1.	Britain after the Departure of the Romans. 410–449 ?	26	12.	The Township and the Hundred	31
2.	The Groans of the Britons	26	13.	Weregild	32
3.	The Conquest of Kent. 449 ?	27	14.	Compurgation and Ordeal	32
4.	The South Saxons. 477	27	15.	Punishments	32
5.	The West Saxons and the East Saxons	28	16.	The Folk-moot	33
6.	The Anglian Settlements	28	17.	The Kingship	33
7.	Nature of the Conquest	28	18.	The Legend of Arthur	33
8.	The Cultivators of the Soil	29	19.	The West Saxon Advance	34
9.	Eorls, Ceorls, Gesiths	29	20.	Repulse of the West Saxons	35
10.	The Gesiths and the Villagers	30	21.	The Advance of the Angles	36
11.	English and Welsh	31	22.	The Kymry	36
			23.	Britain at the End of the Sixth Century	37

CHAPTER III

THE STRIFE OF THE ENGLISH KINGDOMS

1.	England and the Continent	37	17.	Oswald and Aidan	47
2.	Æthelberht's Supremacy	38	18.	Oswald's Greatness and Overthrow	47
3.	Gregory and the English	38	19.	Penda's Overthrow	48
4.	Augustine's Mission. 597	39	20.	The Three Kingdoms and the Welsh	48
5.	Monastic Christianity	39	21.	The English Missionaries	49
6.	The Archbishopric of Canterbury	40	22.	Dispute between Wilfrid and Colman. 664	49
7.	Death of Æthelberht. 616	41	23.	Archbishop Theodore and the Penitential System	50
8.	The Three Kingdoms opposed to the Welsh	41	24.	Ealdhelm and Cædmon	51
9.	Æthelfrith and the Kymry	41	25.	Bede. 673–735	52
10.	Æthelfrith's Victories	42	26.	Church Councils	52
11.	The Greatness of Eadwine	43	27.	Struggle between Mercia and Wessex	52
12.	Eadwine's Supremacy	44	28.	Mohammedanism and the Carolingian Empire	54
13.	Character of the later Conquests	44	29.	Ecgberht's Rule. 802–839	54
14.	Political Changes	45			
15.	Eadwine's Conversion and Fall	46			
16.	Oswald's Victory at Heavenfield	47			

CHAPTER IV

THE ENGLISH KINGSHIP AND THE STRUGGLE WITH THE DANES

1.	The West Saxon Supremacy	55	3.	The English Coast Plundered	57
2.	The Coming of the Northmen	56	4.	The Danes in the North	57

PAGE

5. Ælfred's Struggle in Wessex.
871–878 58
6. The Treaty of Chippenham,
and its Results. 878 . 59
7. Ælfred's Military Work . 60
8. His Laws and Scholarship . 60
9. Eadward the Elder. 901–
925 62
10. Eadward's Conquests . . 62

PAGE

11. Eadward and the Scots . 63
12. Æthelstan. 925–940 . . 63
13. Eadmund (940–946) and
Eadred (946–955) . . 63
14. Danes and English . . 64
15. Eadwig. 955–959 . . 64
16. Dunstan 65
17. Archbishop Oda . . . 65
18. Eadwig's Marriage . . 67

CHAPTER V

EADGAR'S ENGLAND

1. Eadgar and Dunstan. 959–
975 67
2. The Cession of Lothian . 68
3. Changes in English Institutions 69
4. Growth of the King's Power 69
5. Conversion of the Freemen
into Serfs 69
6. The Hundred-moot and the
Lord's Court . . . 72

7. The Towns 72
8. The Origin of the Shires . 73
9. The Shire-moot . . . 73
10. The Ealdormen and the
Witenagemot . . . 73
11. The Land 75
12. Domestic Life . . . 75
13. Food and Drink . . . 75

CHAPTER VI

ENGLAND AND NORMANDY

1. Eadward the Martyr. 975–
979 78
2. Æthelred's Early Years. 979
–988 79
3. The Return of the Danes.
984 79
4. The Norman Dukes. 912–
1002 80
5. Political Contrast between
Normandy and England . 81
6. Svend's Conquest. 1002–
1013 81
7. Æthelred Restored. 1014–
1016 82
8. Eadmund Ironside. 1016 . 83
9. Cnut and the Earldoms.
1016–1035 . . . 83
10. Cnut's Empire . . . 84
11. Cnut's Government . . 84
12. The Sons of Cnut. 1035–
1042 85

13. Eadward the Confessor and
Earl Godwine. 1042–1051 85
14. The Banishment of Godwine.
1051 87
15. Visit of Duke William. 1051 88
16. William and the Norman
Church 88
17. The Return and Death of
Godwine. 1052–1053 . 89
18. Harold's Greatness. 1053–
1066 89
19. Harold and Eadward. 1057
–1065 90
20. Death of Eadward. 1066 . 90
21. Harold and William. 1066. 91
22. Stamford Bridge 1066 . 93
23. The Landing of William.
1066 96
24. The Battle of Senlac. 1066. 96
25. William's Coronation. 1066. 98

PART II

THE NORMAN AND ANGEVIN KINGS

CHAPTER VII

WILLIAM I. 1066—1087

		PAGE			PAGE
1.	The First Months of the Conquest. 1066-1067	101	7.	Ecclesiastical Organisation.	106
2.	The Conquest of the West and North. 1067-1069	102	8.	Pope Gregory VII.	107
			9.	William and Gregory VII.	108
3.	The Completion of the Conquest. 1070	103	10.	The Rising of the Earls. 1075	110
4.	Hereward's Revolt and the Homage of Malcolm. 1070-1072	103	11.	The New Forest	110
			12.	Domesday Book. 1085-1086	111
5.	How William kept down the English	104	13.	William's Great Councils	112
6.	How William kept down the Normans	105	14.	The Gemot at Salisbury. 1086	113
			15.	William's Death. 1087	114

CHAPTER VIII

WILLIAM II. 1087—1100

1.	The Accession of the Red King. 1087	114	8.	William and Scotland. 1093-1094	119
2.	The Wickedness of the Red King	115	9.	Mowbray's Rebel ion. 1095.	120
3.	Ranulf Flambard	116	10.	The First Crusade. 1095-1099	120
4.	Feudal Dues	116			
5.	Archbishop Anselm	117	11.	Normandy in Pledge. 1096.	121
6.	The Council of Rockingham 1095	118	12.	The Last Years of the Red King	121
7.	William II. and his Brothers	118	13.	The Death of the Red King. 1100	122

CHAPTER IX

HENRY I. AND STEPHEN

HENRY I, 1100—1135. STEPHEN, 1135—1154.

1.	The Accession of Henry I. 1100	122	4.	The Battle of Tinchebrai. 1106	124
2.	Invasion of Robert. 1101.	124	5.	Henry and Anselm. 1100-1107	125
3.	Revolt of Robert of Bellême. 1102	124	6.	Roger of Salisbury	126

PAGE

7. Growth of Trade . . 127
8. The Benedictines . . 128
9. The Cistercians . . . 129
10. The White Ship . . . 129
11. The Last Years of Henry I. 131
12. Stephen's Accession. 1135 131
13. Civil War 133
14. Stephen's Quarrel with the Clergy. 1139 . . 134

PAGE

15. Anarchy. 1139 . . . 134
16. The End of the War. 1141–1148 135
17. Henry, Duke of the Normans. 1149 . . . 136
18. The Last Days of Stephen. 1153–1154 . . . 137

CHAPTER X

HENRY II. 1154—1189

1. Henry's Accession. 1154 . 138
2. Pacification of England . 138
3. Henry and Feudality . . 140
4. The Great Council and the Curia Regis . . . 141
5. Scutage 141
6. Archbishop Thomas. 1162 142
7. Breach between Henry and Thomas 143
8. The Constitutions of Clarendon. 1164 . . . 143
9. The Persecution of Archbishop Thomas. 1164 . 145
10. The Assize of Clarendon. 1166 146
11. Recognitions . . . 147
12. The Germ of the Jury . . 147
13. The Itinerant Justices Revived 148
14. The Inquisition of the Sheriffs. 1170 . . 148

15. The Nobles and the Church 149
16. The Coronation of Young Henry. 1170 . . . 149
17. The Return of Archbishop Thomas. 1170 . . 149
18. Murder of Archbishop Thomas. 1170 . . 149
19. Popular Indignation. 1171 151
20. State of Ireland . . . 151
21. Partial Conquest of Ireland. 1166–1172 . . . 152
22. Young Henry's Coronation and the Revolt of the Barons. 1172–1174 . 153
23. The Assize of Arms. 1181 . 154
24. Henry II. and his Sons . 155
25. The Fall of the Kingdom of Jerusalem. 1187 . . 156
26. The Last Years of Henry II. 1188–1189 . . . 157
27. The Work of Henry II. 157

CHAPTER XI

RICHARD I. 1189—1199

1. Richard in England. 1189 159
2. William of Longchamps. 1189–1191 . . . 159
3. The Third Crusade. 1189–1192 161
4. The Return of Richard 1192–1194 . . . 161
5. Heavy Taxation . . . 162
6. The Administration of Hubert Walter. 1194–1198 163

7. Death of Richard. 1199 . 165
8. Church and State under the Angevin Kings . . 165
9. Growth of Learning . . 167
10. The University of Oxford . 167
11. Country and Town . . 168
12. Condition of London . . 169
13. Architectural Changes . 170

PART III

THE GROWTH OF THE PARLIAMENTARY CONSTITUTION. 1199—1399

CHAPTER XII

JOHN. 1199—1216

	PAGE
1. The Accession of John. 1199	173
2. John's First War with Philip II. 1199-1200	173
3. John's Misconduct in Poitou 1200-1201	174
4. The Loss of Normandy and Anjou. 1202-1204	174
5. Causes of Philip's Success	176
6. The Election of Stephen Langton to the Archbishopric of Canterbury. 1205	176
7. Innocent III. and Stephen Langton. 1206	177
8. John's Quarrel with the Church. 1206-1208	178
9. England under an Interdict. 1208	178

	PAGE
10. John Excommunicated. 1209	178
11. The Pope threatens John with Deposition. 1212-1213	179
12. John's Submission. 1213	180
13. The Resistance of the Barons and Clergy. 1213	180
14. The Battle of Bouvines. 1214	181
15. The Struggle between John and the Barons. 1214-1215	181
16. Magna Carta. 1215	182
17. War between John and the Barons. 1215-1216	184
18. Conflict between Louis and John. 1216	184

CHAPTER XIII

HENRY III. 1216—1272

	PAGE
1. Henry III. and Louis. 1216-1217	185
2. The Renewal of the Great Charter. 1216-1217	185
3. Administration of Hubert de Burgh. 1219-1232	186
4. Administration of Peter des Roches. 1232-1234	188
5. Francis of Assisi	190
6. St. Dominic	190
7. The Coming of the Friars. 1220-1224	191
8. Monks and Friars	191
9. The King's Marriage. 1236	192

	PAGE
10. The Early Career of Simon de Montfort. 1231-1243	193
11. Papal Exactions. 1237-1243	194
12. A Weak Parliamentary Opposition. 1244	194
13. Growing Discontent. 1244-1254	195
14. The Knights of the Shire in Parliament. 1254	196
15. Fresh Exactions. 1254-1257	196
16. The Provisions of Oxford. 1258	198

		PAGE			PAGE
17	The Expulsion of the Foreigners. 1258	199	22.	The Battle of Lewes. 1264	201
18.	Edward and the Barons. 1259	199	23.	Earl Simon's Government. 1264–1265	201
19.	The Breach amongst the Barons. 1259–1261	199	24.	The Battle of Evesham. 1265	203
20.	Royalist Reaction and Civil War. 1261	200	25.	The Last Years of Henry III. 1265–1272	204
21.	The Mise of Amiens. 1264	200	26.	General Progress of the Country	206

CHAPTER XIV

EDWARD I. AND EDWARD II.

EDWARD I., 1272—1307.   EDWARD II., 1307—1327

1.	The First Years of Edward I. 1272–1279	208	15.	Wallace's Rising. 1297–1304	221
2.	Edward I. and Wales. 1276–1284	210	16.	The Second Conquest of Scotland. 1298–1304	221
3.	Customs Duties. 1275	210	17.	The Incorporation of Scotland with England. 1305	222
4.	Edward's Judicial Reforms. 1274–1290	212	18.	Character of Edward's Dealings with Scotland	222
5.	Edward's Legislation. 1279–1290	212	19.	Robert Bruce. 1306	223
6.	Edward as a National and as a Feudal Ruler	212	20.	Edward's Third Conquest of Scotland and Death. 1306–1307	224
7.	The Scottish Succession. 1285–1290	214	21.	Edward II. and Piers Gaveston. 1307–1312	224
8.	Death of Eleanor of Castile. 1290	214	22.	Success of Robert Bruce. 1307–1314	226
9.	The Award of Norham. 1291–1292	215	23.	Lancaster's Government. 1314–1322	228
10.	Disputes with Scotland and France. 1293–1295	216	24.	A Constitutional Settlement. 1322	228
11.	The Model Parliament. 1295	218	25.	The Rule of the Despensers. 1322–1326	228
12.	The First Conquest of Scotland. 1296	219	26.	The Deposition and Murder of Edward II. 1327	229
13.	The Resistance of Archbishop Winchelsey. 1296–1297	220			
14.	The 'Confirmatio Cartarum.' 1297	220			

CHAPTER XV

FROM THE ACCESSION OF EDWARD III. TO THE

TREATY OF BRETIGNI. 1327—1360

1.	Mortimer's Government. 1327–1330	231	3.	Troubles in Scotland. 1331–1336	232
2.	The French Succession. 1328–1331	232	4.	Dispute with France. 1336–1337	234

PAGE

5. Edward's Allies. 1337–1338 235
6. Chivalry and War . . 235
7. Commerce and War . . 236
8. Attacks on the North of France. 1338–1340 . 237
9. Battle of Sluys. 1340 . 239
10. Attacks on the West of France. 1341–1345 . 240
11. The Campaign of Creçy. 1346 240
12. The Tactics of Creçy. 1346 241
13. The Battle of Creçy. August 26, 1346 . . 242
14. Battle of Nevill's Cross, and the Siege of Calais. 1346–1347 . . 242
15. Constitutional Progress. 1337–1347 . . . 243

PAGE

16. Edward's Triumph. 1347. 246
17. The Black Death. 1348 . 248
18. The Statute of Labourers. 1349 248
19. The Statute of Treasons. 1352 250
20. The Black Prince in the South of France. 1355 . 251
21. The Battle of Poitiers. 1356 251
22. The Courtesy of the Black Prince 252
23. Misery of France. 1356–1359 252
24. Edward's Last Invasion. 1359–1360 . . . 252
25. The Treaty of Bretigni. 1360 253

CHAPTER XVI

REIGN OF EDWARD III. AFTER THE TREATY OF BRETIGNI

1360—1377

1. The First Years of Peace. 1360–1364 . . . 254
2. The Spanish Troubles. 1364–1368 . . . 254
3. The Taxation of Aquitaine. 1368–1369 . . 256
4. The Renewed War. 1369–1375 256
5. Anti Papal Legislation. 1351–1366 . . . 257
6. Predominance of the English Language . . 258
7. Piers the Plowman. 1362 . 258
8. The Anti Clerical Party. 1371 259

9. The Duke of Lancaster. 1374–1376 . . . 260
10. John Wycliffe. 1366–1376 261
11. Lancaster and the Black Prince. 1376 . . . 261
12. The Good Parliament. 1376. 262
13. The Last Year of Edward III. 1376–1377 . . 262
14. Ireland from the Reign of John to that of Edward II. 264
15 The Statute of Kilkenny. 1367 265
16. Weakness of the English Colony. 1367–1377 . 265

CHAPTER XVII

RICHARD II. AND THE SOCIAL REVOLUTION

1377—1381

1. The First Years of Richard II. 1377–1378 . 266
2. Wycliffe and the Great Schism. 1378–1381 . 266
3. The Poll Taxes. 1379–1381 267
4. The Peasants' Grievances . 268
5. The Peasants' Revolt. 1381 268

6. The Suppression of the Revolt 269
7. Results of the Peasants' Revolt 269
8. Chaucer's 'Canterbury Tales' 270
9. The Prologue of the 'Canterbury Tales' . . 270

	PAGE			PAGE
10. Chaucer and the Clergy	271	14. Alehouses		274
11. Roads and Bridges	272	15. Wanderers		274
12. Modes of Conveyance	273	16. Robbers and Criminals		275
13. Hospitality and Inns	274	17. Justices of the Peace		277

CHAPTER XVIII

RICHARD II. AND THE POLITICAL REVOLUTION

1382—1399

1. Progress of the War with France. 1382–1386 . 278

2. Richard's Growing Unpopularity. 1385–1386 . 278

3. The Impeachment of Suffolk and the Commission of Regency. 1386 . . 279

4. The Lords Appellant and the Merciless Parliament. 1387–1388 . . . 279

5. Richard's Restoration to Power. 1389. . . 280

6. Richard's Constitutional Government. 1389–1396 280

7. Livery and Maintenance. 1390 281

8. Richard's Domestic Policy. 1390–1391 . . . 281

9. Richard's Foreign Policy. 1389–1396 . . . 282

10. Richard's Coup d'Etat. 1397 282

11. The Parliament of Shrewsbury. 1398 . . 283

12. The Banishment of Hereford and Norfolk. 1398 . 283

13. Richard's Despotism. 1398–1399 283

14. Henry of Lancaster in England. 1399 . . 284

15. The Deposition of Richard and the Enthronement of Henry IV. 1399 . 285

16. Nature of the Claim of Henry IV. . . . 286

PART IV

LANCASTER, YORK, AND TUDOR. 1399–1509

CHAPTER XIX

HENRY IV. AND HENRY V.

HENRY IV., 1399—1413.　HENRY V., 1413—1422

1. Henry's First Difficulties. 1399–1400 . . . 289

2. Death of Richard II. 1400 291

3. Henry IV. and the Church . 291

4. The Statute for the Burning of Heretics. 1401 . . 292

5. Henry IV. and Owen Glendower. 1400–1402 . 292

6. The Rebellion of the Percies. 1402–1404 . 293

7. The Commons and the Church. 1404 . . 294

8. The Capture of the Scottish Prince. 1405. . 295

9. The Execution of Archbishop Scrope. 1405 . 296

10. France, Wales, and the North. 1405–1408 . 296

11. Henry, Prince of Wales, 1409–1410 . . . 297

c　　　　　　　　　　　　　　　　a

	PAGE			PAGE
12. The Last Years of Henry IV. 1411–1413	298	18. Henry's Diplomacy. 1416–1417		303
13. Henry V. and the Lollards. 1413–1414	299	19. Henry's Conquest of Normandy. 1417–1419		303
14. Henry's Claim to the Throne of France. 1414	300	20. The Murder of the Duke of Burgundy and the Treaty of Troyes. 1419–1420		304
15. The Invasion of France. 1415	301			
16. The March to Agincourt. 1415	302	21. The Close of the Reign of Henry V. 1420–1422		306
17. The Battle of Agincourt. October 25, 1415	302			

CHAPTER XX

HENRY VI. AND THE LOSS OF FRANCE. 1422—1451

1. Bedford and Gloucester. 1422	307	10. The Defection of Burgundy. 1435	313
2. Bedford's Success in France. 1423–1424	307	11. The Duke of York in France. 1436–1437	313
3. Gloucester's Invasion of Hainault. 1424	308	12. The English Lose Ground. 1437–1443	313
4. Gloucester and Beaufort. 1425–1428	308	13. Continued Rivalry of Beaufort and Gloucester. 1439–1441	314
5. The Siege of Orleans. 1428–1429	309	14. Beaufort and Somerset. 1442–1443	317
6. Jeanne Darc and the Relief of Orleans. 1429	310	15. The Angevin Marriage Treaty. 1444–1445	317
7. The Coronation of Charles VII. and the Capture of the Maid. 1429–1430	311	16. Deaths of Gloucester and Beaufort. 1447	318
8. The Martyrdom at Rouen. 1431	312	17. The Loss of the French Provinces. 1448–1449	318
9. The Last Years of the Duke of Bedford. 1431–1435	312		

CHAPTER XXI

THE LATER YEARS OF HENRY VI. 1450—1461

1. The Growth of Inclosures	320	York's Second Protectorate	324
2. Increasing Power of the Nobility	321	9. Discomfiture of the Yorkists. 1456–1459	325
3. Case of Lord Molynes and John Paston	321	10. The Battle of Northampton and the Duke of York's Claim to the Throne. 1460	326
4. Suffolk's Impeachment and Murder. 1450	322		
5. Jack Cade's Rebellion. 1450	322	11. The Battle of Wakefield. 1460	327
6. Rivalry of York and Somerset. 1450–1453	323	12. The Battle of Mortimer's Cross and the Second Battle of St. Albans. 1461	328
7. The First Protectorate of the Duke of York. 1453–1454	323		
8. The First Battle of St. Albans and the Duke of		13. The Battle of Towton and the Coronation of Edward IV. 1461	328

CHAPTER XXII

THE YORKIST KINGS. 1461—1485

		PAGE
1.	Edward IV. and the House of Commons. 1461	329
2.	Loss of the Mediæval Ideals	330
3.	Fresh Efforts of the Lancastrians. 1462–1465	331
4.	Edward's Marriage. 1464.	331
5.	Estrangement of Warwick. 1465–1468	332
6.	Warwick's Alliance with Clarence. 1469–1470	332
7.	The Restoration of Henry VI. 1470	333
8.	Edward IV. recovers the Throne. 1471	334
9.	Edward IV. prepares for War with France. 1471–1474	334
10.	The Invasion of France. 1475	336

		PAGE
11.	Fall and Death of Clarence. 1476–1478	336
12.	The Last Years of Edward IV. 1478–1483	336
13.	Edward V. and the Duke of Gloucester. 1483	337
14.	Fall of the Queen's Relations. 1483	338
15.	Execution of Lord Hastings	338
16.	Deposition of Edward V. 1483	340
17.	Buckingham's Rebellion. 1483	341
18.	Murder of the Princes. 1483	342
19.	Richard's Government. 1484–1485	342
20.	Richard Defeated and Slain at Bosworth. 1485	343

CHAPTER XXIII

HENRY VII. 1485—1509

		PAGE
1.	The First Measures of Henry VII. 1485–1486	343
2.	Maintenance and Livery	345
3.	Lovel's Rising. 1486	346
4.	Lancaster and York in Ireland. 1399–1485	346
5.	Insurrection of Lambert Simnel. 1487	347
6.	The Court of Star Chamber. 1487	348
7.	Henry VII. and Brittany. 1488–1492	348
8.	Cardinal Morton's Fork. 1491	349
9.	The Invasion of France. 1492	349
10.	Perkin Warbeck. 1491–1494	350
11.	Poynings' Acts. 1494	350
12.	Perkin's First Attempt on England. 1495	351
13.	The Intercursus Magnus. 1496	351

		PAGE
14.	Kildare Restored to the Deputyship. 1496.	352
15.	Perkin's Overthrow. 1496–1497	352
16.	European Changes. 1494–1499	352
17.	Execution of the Earl of Warwick. 1499	354
18.	Prince Arthur's Marriage and Death. 1501–1502	354
19.	The Scottish Marriage. 1503	356
20.	Maritime Enterprise	356
21.	Growth of the Royal Power	356
22.	Empson and Dudley	357
23.	Henry and his Daughter-in-law. 1502–1505	357
24.	The Last Years of Henry VII. 1505–1509	357
25.	Architectural Changes and the Printing Press	358

PART V

THE RENASCENCE AND THE REFORMATION
1509—1603

CHAPTER XXIV

HENRY VIII. AND WOLSEY. 1509—1527

	PAGE		PAGE
1. The New King. 1509 .	361	10. 'The Utopia.' 1515-1516.	367
2. Continental Troubles. 1508-1511 . . .	363	11. More and Henry VIII. .	368
3. The Rise of Wolsey. 1512	363	12. The Contest for the Empire. 1519	369
4. The War with France. 1512-1513 . . .	364	13. The Field of the Cloth of Gold. 1520 . . .	369
5. Peace with France. 1514 .	364	14. The Execution of the Duke of Buckingham. 1521 .	369
6. Wolsey's Policy of Peace. 1514-1518 . . .	364	15. Another French War. 1522-1523 . . .	369
7. Wolsey and the Renascence	366	16. The Amicable Loan. 1525	372
8. The Renascence in England . . .	367	17. Closing Years of Wolsey's Greatness. 1525-1527 .	372
9. The Oxford Reformers .	367		

CHAPTER XXV

THE BREACH WITH THE PAPACY. 1527—1534

1. The Papacy and the Renascence . . .	374	14. The King's Supreme Headship acknowledged by the Clergy. 1531 . .	386
2. Wolsey and the Papacy .	375	15. The Submission of the Clergy. 1532. .	386
3. Wolsey's Legatine Powers .	375	16. Sir Thomas More and the Protestants. 1529-1532.	386
4. Henry VIII. and the Clergy	377	17. Resignation of Sir Thomas More. 1532 . . .	388
5. German Lutheranism .	377	18. The First Act of Annates. 1532	383
6. Henry's Controversy with Luther . . .	379	19. The King's Marriage and the Act of Appeals. 1533	388
7. Queen Catharine and Anne Boleyn . . .	379	20. Archbishop Cranmer and the Court at Dunstable. 1533 . . .	389
8. Henry's Demand for a Divorce. 1527-1528 .	382	21. Frith and Latimer. 1533 .	389
9. The Legatine Court. 1529 .	382	22. Completion of the Breach with Rome. 1533-1534.	390
10. The Fall of Wolsey. 1529-1530	383		
11. The House of Commons and the Clergy. 1529 .	385		
12. The Universities Consulted. 1530 . . .	385		
13. The Clergy under a Præmunire. 1530-1531 .	385		

CHAPTER XXVI

THE ROYAL SUPREMACY. 1534—1547

PAGE

1. The Act of Succession. 1534 392
2. The Acts of Treason and Supremacy. 1534 . . 392
3. The Monks of the Charterhouse. 1534 . . . 393
4. Execution of Fisher and More. 1535 . . . 394
5. The Dissolution of the Smaller Monasteries. 1536 394
6. The Execution of Anne Boleyn. 1536 . . 395
7. The Ten Articles. 1536 . 395
8. The Translation of the Bible authorised. 1536 . 396
9. The Pilgrimage of Grace. 1536-1537 . . . 396
10. Birth of a Prince. 1537 . 397
11. The Beginning of the Attack on the Greater Monasteries. 1537-1538 397
12. Destruction of Relics and Images. 1538 . . 398
13. The Trial of Lambert. 1538 . . . 399

PAGE

14. The Marquis of Exeter and the Poles. 1538 . . 399
15. The Six Articles. 1539 . 399
16. Completion of the Suppression of the Monasteries. 1539-1540 . . . 400
17. Anne of Cleves and the Fall of Cromwell. 1539-1540 400
18. Catherine Howard and Catherine Parr. 1540-1543 . . . 401
19. Ireland. 1534 . . . 401
20. The Geraldine Rebellion. 1534-1535 . . . 402
21. Lord Leonard Grey. 1536-1539 402
22. Henry VIII. King of Ireland. 1541 . . . 404
23. Solway Moss. 1542 . . 404
24. War with Scotland and France. 1542-1546 . 405
25. The Litany and the Primer. 1544-1545 . . . 409
26. The Last Days of Henry VIII. 1545-1547 . . 410

CHAPTER XXVII

EDWARD VI. AND MARY

EDWARD VI., 1547—1553. MARY, 1553—1558.

1. Somerset becomes Protector. 1547 . . . 412
2. The Scotch War. 1547-1548 412
3. Cranmer's Position in the Church of England. 1547 413
4. Ecclesiastical Reforms. 1547-1548 . . . 414
5. The First Prayer Book of Edward VI. 1549 . . 415
6. The Insurrection in the West. 1549 . . . 415
7. Ket's Rebellion. 1549 . 415
8. The Fall of Somerset. 1549 416
9. Warwick and the Advanced Reformers. 1549 416
10. Latimer's Sermons. 1548-1550 417

11. Warwick and Somerset. 1550-1552 . . . 417
12. The Second Prayer Book of Edward VI. 1552 . . 418
13. The Forty-two Articles. 1553 419
14. Northumberland's Conspiracy. 1553 . . 421
15. Lady Jane Grey. 1553 . 421
16. Mary restores the Mass. 1553 422
17. Mary's First Parliament. 1553 422
18. Wyatt's Rebellion. 1554 . 423
19. The Queen's Marriage. 423
20. The Submission to Rome. 1554 424
21. The Beginning of the Persecution. 1555 . . 424
22. Death of Cranmer. 1556 . 425

PAGE   PAGE

23. Continuance of the Persecution. 1556-1558 . . 426
24. The Queen's Disappointment. 1555-1556 . . 426

25. War with France and the Loss of Calais. 1557-1558 . . . 427
26. Death of Mary. 1558 . 427

CHAPTER XXVIII

THE ELIZABETHAN SETTLEMENT IN CHURCH AND STATE
1558—1570

1. Elizabeth's Difficulties. 1558 428
2. The Act of Uniformity and Supremacy. 1559 . . 429
3. The new Bishops and the Ceremonies. 1559-1564 429
4. Calvinism . . . 430
5. Peace with France. 1559 . 431
6. The Reformation in Scotland. 1559 . . . 432
7. The Claims of Mary Stuart. 1559 432
8. The Treaty of Edinburgh. 1560 433
9. Scottish Presbyterianism. 1561 434
10. Mary and Elizabeth. 1561 435
11. The French War. 1562-1564 436

12. End of the Council of Trent. 1563 . . . 436
13. The Jesuits . . . 436
14. The Danger from Scotland. 1561-1565 . . . 437
15. The Darnley Marriage. 1565 438
16. The Murder of Rizzio. 1566 438
17. The Murder of Darnley. 1567 439
18. The Deposition and Flight of Mary. 1567-1568 . 439
19. Mary's Case before English Commissioners. 1568-1569 440
20. The Rising in the North. 1569 441
21. The Papal Excommunication. 1570 . . . 441

CHAPTER XXIX

ELIZABETH AND THE EUROPEAN CONFLICT.
1570—1587

1. The Continental Powers. 1566-1570 . . . 442
2. The Anjou Marriage Treaty and the Ridolfi Plot. 1570-1571 . . . 443
3. Elizabeth and the Puritans. 444
4. Elizabeth and Parliament. 1566 444
5. A Puritan Parliament. 1571 445
6. The Duke of Norfolk's Plot and Execution. 1571-1572 445
7. The Admonition to Parliament. 1572 . . . 446
8. Mariners and Pirates . . 446
9. Westward Ho ! . . . 447
10. Francis Drake's Voyage to Panama. 1572 . . 448
11. The Seizure of Brill, and the Massacre of St. Bartholomew. 1572 . . 449

12. The Growth of the Dutch Republic. 1572-1578 . 449
13. Quiet Times in England. 1572-1577 . . . 450
14. Drake's Voyage. 1577-1580 450
15. Ireland and the Reformation. 1547 451
16. Ireland under Edward VI. and Mary. 1547-1558 . 451
17. Elizabeth and Ireland. 1558-1578 . . . 452
18. The Landing at Smerwick, and the Desmond Rising. 1579-1583 . . . 452
19. The Jesuits in England. 1580 453
20. The Recusancy Laws. 1581 454
21. Growing Danger of Elizabeth. 1580-1584 . . 454

PAGE		PAGE
22. The Association. 1584–1585 . . . 456	Trial of Mary Stuart. 1586 . . . 457	
23. Growth of Philip's Power. 1584–1585 . . . 456	25. Execution of Mary Stuart. 1587 . . . 458	
24. Babington's Plot, and the		

CHAPTER XXX

ELIZABETH'S YEARS OF TRIUMPH. 1587—1603

1. The Singeing of the King of Spain's Beard. 1587. 458
2. The Approach of the Armada. 1588 . . . 458
3. The Equipment of the Armada. 1588 . . . 459
4. The Equipment of the English Fleet. 1588 . 460
5. The Defeat of the Armada. 1588 . . . 462
6. The Destruction of the Armada. 1588 . . . 462
7. Philip II. and France. 1588–1593 . . . 464
8. Maritime Enterprises. 1539–1596 . . . 464
9. Increasing Prosperity . . 464
10. Buildings 465
11. Furniture . . . 465
12. Growing Strength of the House of Commons . 468
13. Archbishop Whitgift and

the Court of High Commission. 1583 . . 468
14. The House of Commons and Puritanism. 1584 . 470
15. The Separatists . . . 470
16. Whitgift and Hooker . . 472
17. Spenser, Shakspere, and Bacon 473
18. Condition of the Catholics. 1588–1603 . . . 475
19. Irish Difficulties. 1583–1594 . . . 475
20. O'Neill and the Earl of Essex. 1595–1600 . . 475
21. Essex's Imprisonment and Execution. 1599–1601 . 476
22. Mountjoy's Conquest of Ireland. 1600–1603 . . 478
23. Parliament and the Monopolies. 1601 . . . 478
24. The Last Days of Elizabeth. 1601–1603 . . 479

PART VI

THE PURITAN REVOLUTION. 1603—1660

CHAPTER XXXI

JAMES I. 1603—1625

1. The Peace with Spain. 1603–1604 . . . 481
2. The Hampton Court Conference. 1604 . . 481
3. James and the House of Commons . . . 482
4. Gunpowder Plot. 1604–1605 483
5. The Post-nati. 1606–1607. 483
6. Irish Difficulties. 1603–1610 483

7. Bate's Case and the New Impositions. 1606–1608. 484
8. The Great Contract. 1610–1611 484
9. Bacon and Somerset. 1612–1613 486
10. The Addled Parliament. 1614 486
11. The Spanish Alliance. 1614–1617 . . . 488

PAGE

12. The Rise of Buckingham.
    1615–1618 . . . 488
13. The Voyage and Execution
    of Raleigh. 1617–1618 . 489
14. Colonisation of Virginia
    and New England. 1607–
    1620 489
15. The Beginning of the
    Thirty Years' War. 1618–
    1620 490
16. The Meeting of James's
    Third Parliament. 1621 490
17. The Royal Prerogative.
    1616–1621 . . . 492
18. Financial Reform. 1619 . 492
19. Favouritism and Corrup-
    tion 494

PAGE

20. The Monopolies Con-
    demned. 1621 . . 494
21. The Fall of Bacon. 1621 . 495
22. Digby's Mission, and the
    Dissolution of Parlia-
    ment. 1621 . . . 496
23. The Loss of the Palatinate.
    1622 497
24. Charles's Journey to Madrid.
    1623 497
25. The Prince's Return. 1623 498
26. The Last Parliament of
    James I. 1624 . . 500
27. The French Alliance . . 501
28. Mansfeld's Expedition, and
    the Death of James I.
    1624–1625 . . . 501

CHAPTER XXXII

THE GROWTH OF THE PERSONAL GOVERNMENT OF CHARLES I.
1625—1634

1. Charles I. and Buckingham. 1625 . . . 502
2. Charles's First Parliament.
   1625 502
3. The Expedition to Cadiz.
   1625 503
4. Charles's Second Parliament. 1626 . . . 503
5. The Forced Loan. 1626 . 505
6. The Expedition to Ré.
   1627 506
7. The Five Knights' Case.
   1627 506
8. Wentworth and Eliot in
   the Third Parliament of
   Charles I. 1628 . . 508
9. The Petition of Right. 1628 508
10. Tonnage and Poundage.
    1628 509
11. Buckingham's Murder. 1628 510
12. The Question of Sovereignty.
    1628 510
13. Protestantism of the House
    of Commons. 1625–1628 511

14. Religious Differences. 1625–
    1628 511
15. The King's Declaration.
    1628 512
16. The Second Session of the
    Third Parliament of
    Charles I. 1629 . . 512
17. Breach between the King
    and the Commons. 1629 513
18. The Constitutional Dispute.
    1629 513
19. The Victory of Personal
    Government. 1629–1632 514
20. Star Chamber Sentences.
    1630–1633 . . . 514
21. Laud's Intellectual Position.
    1629–1633 . . . 515
22. Laud as the Upholder of
    Uniformity . . . 516
23. The Beginning of Laud's
    Archbishopric. 1633–
    1634 517
24. Laud and Prynne. 1633–
    1634 519

CHAPTER XXXIII

THE OVERTHROW OF THE PERSONAL GOVERNMENT
OF CHARLES I. 1634—1641

1. The Metropolitical Visitation. 1634–1637 . . 520
2. Prynne, Bastwick, and Burton. 1637 . . . 521

3. Financial Pressure. 1635–
   1637 521
4. Ship-money. 1634–1637 . 523
5. Hampden's Case. 1637–1638 523

PAGE

6. Scottish Epi.copacy. 1572–1612 524
7. The Scottish Bishops and Clergy. 1612–1637 . 525
8. The Riot at Edinburgh and the Covenant. 1637–1638 525
9. The Assembly of Glasgow, and the Abolition of Episcopacy. 1638. . 526
10. The First Bishops' War. 1639 526
11. Wentworth in Ireland. 1633–1639 . . . 527

PAGE

12. The Proposed Plantation of Connaught . . . 528
13. The Short Parliament. 1640 528
14. The Second Bishops' War. 1640 529
15. The Meeting of the Long Parliament. 1640 . . 529
16. The Impeachment of Strafford. 1641 . . . 530
17. Strafford's Attainder and Execution . . . 530
18. Constitutional Reforms. 1641 531

CHAPTER XXXIV

THE FORMATION OF PARLIAMENTARY PARTIES AND THE FIRST YEARS OF THE CIVIL WAR. 1641—1644

1. The King's Visit to Scotland. 1641 . . . 532
2. Parties formed on Church Questions. 1641 . . 532
3. Irish Parties. 1641 . . 533
4. The Irish Insurrection. 1641 533
5. The Grand Remonstrance. 1641 534
6. The King's Return. 1641 . 534
7. The Impeachment of the Bishops. 1641 . . 535
8. The Impeachment of the Five Members. 1642 . 535
9. The Attempt on the Five Members. 1642 . . 536
10. The Commons in the City. 1642 536
11. The Struggle for the Militia. 1642 536
12. Edgehill and Turnham Green. 1642 . . . 537
13. The King's Plan of Campaign. 1643 . . . 537
14. Royalist Successes. 1643 . 538

15. The Siege of Gloucester. 1643 538
16. The First Battle of Newbury. 1643 539
17. The Eastern Association. 1643 539
18. Oliver Cromwell. 1642–1643 539
19. The Assembly of Divines. 1643 540
20. The Solemn League and Covenant. 1643 . . 540
21. The Irish War. 1641–1643 541
22. Winceby and Arundel. 1643–1644 . . . 542
23. The Committee of Both Kingdoms. 1644 . . 542
24. The Campaign of Marston Moor. 1644 . . . 542
25. Presbyterians and Independents. 1644 . . . 543
26. Essex's Surrender at Lostwithiel. 1644 . . . 544
27. The Second Battle of Newbury. 1644 . . . 544

CHAPTER XXXV

THE NEW MODEL ARMY. 1644—1649

1. The Self-denying Ordinance and the New Model. 1645 545
2. Milton's 'Areopagitica.' 1644 545
3. The Execution of Laud. 1645 546

4. Montrose and Argyle. 1644 546
5. Montrose and the Highlands. 1644–1645 . . 547
6. The New Model Army in the Field. 1645 . . 547
7. The Battle of Naseby. 1645 548

PAGE

8. The Results of Naseby.
   1645 . . . 548
9. Charles's Wanderings. 1645 549
10. Glamorgan in Ireland.
    1645–1646 . . 549
11. The King's Flight to the
    Scots. 1646 . . 550
12. Charles at Newcastle. 1646 551
13. The Removal of the King
    to Holmby. 1647 . . 553
14. Dispute between the Presby-
    terians and the Army.
    1647 . . . 553
15. Cromwell and the Army.
    1647 . . . 554
16. The Abduction of the King.
    1647 . . . 554

PAGE

17. The Exclusion of the Eleven
    Members. 1647 . . 555
18. The Heads of the Proposals.
    1647 . . . 555
19. The King's Flight to the
    Isle of Wight. 1647 . 556
20. The Scottish Engagement,
    and the Vote of No Ad-
    dresses. 1647–1648 . 556
21. The Second Civil War.
    1648 . . . 556
22. Pride's Purge. 1648 . . 557
23. The High Court of Justice.
    1649 . . . 557
24. The King's Trial and Exe-
    cution. 1649 . . . 559
25. Results of Charles's Execu-
    tion. 1649 . . . 560

CHAPTER XXXVI

THE COMMONWEALTH AND THE PROTECTORATE. 1649—1660

1. Establishment of the Commonwealth. 1649 . . 561
2. Parties in Ireland. 1647–
   1649 . . . 562
3. Cromwell in Ireland. 1649–
   1650 . . . 562
4. Montrose and Charles II. in
   Scotland. 1650 . . 563
5. Dunbar and Worcester.
   1650–1651 . . . 563
6. The Navigation Act. 1651 564
7. The Dutch War. 1652–
   1653 . . . 565
8. Unpopularity of the Parliament. 1652–1653 . . 565
9. Vane's Reform Bill. 1653 . 566
10. Dissolution of the Long
    Parliament by Cromwell.
    1653 . . . 566
11. The so-called Barebone's
    Parliament. 1653 . . 566
12. The Protectorate, and the
    Instrument of Govern-
    ment. 1653 . . . 568
13. Character of the Instrument
    of Government . . 568
14. Oliver's Government. 1653–
    1654 . . . 569

15. The First Protectorate
    Parliament. 1654–1655 . 570
16. The Major-Generals. 1655 570
17. Oliver's Foreign Policy.
    1654–1655 . . . 571
18. The French Alliance.
    1655 . . . 572
19. Oliver's Second Parliament,
    and the Humble Petition
    and Advice. 1656 . . 572
20. The Dissolution of the Se-
    cond Protectorate Parlia-
    ment. 1658 . . . 573
21. Victory Abroad and Failure
    at Home. 1657–1658 . 573
22. Oliver's Death. 1658 . . 574
23. Richard Cromwell. 1658–
    1659 . . . 574
24. The Long Parliament Re-
    stored. 1659 . . . 575
25. Military Government. 1659 575
26. Monk and the Rump. 1660 575
27. End of the Long Parliament.
    1660 . . . 576
28. The Declaration of Breda.
    1660 . . . 576

PART VII

THE POLITICAL REVOLUTION. 1660—1689

CHAPTER XXXVII

CHARLES II. AND CLARENDON. 1660—1667

	PAGE
1. Return of Charles II. 1660	578
2. King and Parliament. 1660	579
3. Formation of the Government. 1660	580
4. The Political Ideas of the Convention Parliament. 1660	580
5. Execution of the Political Articles of the Declaration of Breda. 1660	581
6. Ecclesiastical Debates. 1660	583
7. Venner's Plot and its Results. 1661	584
8. The Cavalier Parliament, and the Corporation Act. 1661	585
9. The Savoy Conference, and the Act of Uniformity. 1661–1662	585
10. The Dissenters. 1662	585
11. The Parliamentary Presbyterians. 1662	586
12. Profligacy of the Court. 1662	586
13. Marriage of Charles II. and Sale of Dunkirk. 1662	587

	PAGE
14. The Question of Toleration Raised. 1662–1663	587
15. The Conventicle Act. 1664	588
16. The Repeal of the Triennial Act. 1664	588
17. Growing Hostility between England and the Dutch. 1660–1664	589
18. Outbreak of the First Dutch War of the Restoration. 1664–1665	589
19. The Plague. 1665	590
20. The Five Mile Act. 1665	590
21. Continued Struggle with the Dutch. 1665–1666	590
22. The Fire of London. 1666	592
23. Designs of Louis XIV. 1665–1667	592
24. The Dutch in the Medway, and the Peace of Breda. 1667	593
25. Clarendon and the House of Commons. 1667	593
26. The Fall of Clarendon. 1667	594
27. Scotland and Ireland. 1660	595

CHAPTER XXXVIII

CHARLES II. AND THE CABAL. 1667—1674

1. Milton and Bunyan	596
2. Butler and the Dramatists	596
3. Reason and Science	598
4. Charles II. and Toleration. 1667	598
5. Buckingham and Arlington. 1667–1669	599
6. The Triple Alliance. 1668	599
7. Charles's Negotiations with France. 1669–1670	600
8. The Treaty of Dover. 1670	600
9. The Cabal. 1670	602
10. Ashley's Policy	602
11. Buckingham's Sham Treaty. 1671	603
12. The Stop of the Exchequer. 1672	603

13. The Declaration of Indulgence. 1672	604
14. The Second Dutch War of the Restoration. 1672	605
15. 'Delenda est Carthago.' 1673	606
16. Withdrawal of the Declaration of Indulgence. 1673	606
17. The Test Act. 1673	606
18. Results of the Test Act. 1673	607
19. Continuance of the Dutch War. 1673	607
20. The Duke of York's Marriage and Shaftesbury's Dismissal. 1673	608
21. Peace with the Dutch. 1674	608

CHAPTER XXXIX

DANBY'S ADMINISTRATION AND THE THREE SHORT PARLIAMENTS. 1675—1681

PAGE

1. Growing Influence of Danby. 1675 . . . 610
2. Parliamentary Parties. 1675 . . . 610
3. The Non-Resistance Bill. 1675 . . . 611
4. Charles a Pensionary of France. 1675-1676 . 611
5. Two Foreign Policies. 1677 612
6. The Marriage of the Prince of Orange. 1677 . . 613
7. Danby's Position. 1677 . 613
8. The Peace of Nymwegen. 1678 . . . 614
9. The Popish Plot. 1678 . 615
10. Growing Excitement. 1678 615
11. Danby's Impeachment and the Dissolution of the Cavalier Parliament. 1678-1679 . . . 616

PAGE

12. The Meeting of the First Short Parliament. 1679 616
13. The Exclusion Bill and the Habeas Corpus Act. 1679 617
14. Shaftesbury and the King. 1679 . . . 617
15. Shaftesbury and Halifax. 1679 . . . 618
16. The Divine Right of Kings. 1679 . . . 619
17. The Highland Host. 1677-1678 . . . 619
18. Drumclog and Bothwell Bridge. 1679 . . 619
19. Petitioners and Abhorrers. 1680 . . . 620
20. The Second Short Parliament. 1680-1681 . 620
21. The Third Short Parliament. 1681 . . . 621

CHAPTER XL

THE LAST YEARS OF CHARLES II. 1681—1685

1. Tory Reaction. 1681 . 622
2. 'Absolom and Achitophel.' 1681 . . . 623
3. The Scottish Test Act and the Duke of York's Return. 1681-1682 . . 623
4. The City Elections. 1682 . 623
5. Flight and Death of Shaftesbury. 1682-1683 . . 624
6. The Attack on the City. 1682-1683 . . . 624
7. The Remodelling of the Corporations. 1683-1684 625
8. The Rye House Plot. 1683 625
9. The Whig Combination. 1683 . . . 625
10. Trial and Execution of Lord Russell. 1683 . . 625

11. Execution of Algernon Sidney. 1683 . . 626
12. Parties at Court. 1684 . 626
13. Death of Charles II. 1685 627
14. Constitutional Progress. 1660-1685 . . . 627
15. Prosperity of the Country . 628
16. The Coffee Houses . . 630
17. The Condition of London . 631
18. Painting 631
19. Architecture . . . 631
20. Science 632
21. Difficulties of Communication 632
22. The Country Gentry and the Country Clergy . . 633
23. Alliance between the Gentry and the Church . . 633

CHAPTER XLI

JAMES II. 1685—1689

1. The Accession of James II. 1685 634
2. A Tory Parliament. 1685 . 636
3. Argyle's Landing. 1685 . 636

4. Monmouth's Landing. 1685 637
5. The Bloody Assizes. 1685 637
6. The Violation of the Test Act. 1685 . . . 638

PAGE

7. Breach between Parliament and King. 1685 . . 638
8. The Dispensing Power. 1686 638
9. The Ecclesiastical Commission. 1686 . . . 639
10. Scotland and Ireland. 1686–1687 639
11. The Fall of the Hydes. 1686–1687 . . . 640
12. The Declaration of Indulgence. 1687 . . . 640
13. The Expulsion of the Fellows of Magdalen. 1687 641
14. An Attempt to pack a Parliament. 1687 . . 641
15. A Second Declaration of Indulgence. 1688 . . 642

PAGE

16. Resistance of the Clergy. 1688 642
17. The Trial of the Seven Bishops. 1688 . . 643
18. Invitation to William of Orange. 1688 . . 643
19. Landing of William. 1688 644
20. William's March upon London. 1688 . . 645
21. A Convention Parliament Summoned. 1688 . . 646
22. The Throne Declared Vacant. 1689 . . 646
23. William and Mary to be Joint Sovereigns. 1689 . 647
24. Character of the Revolution. 647

PART VIII

THE RISE OF CABINET GOVERNMENT. 1689–1754

CHAPTER XLII

WILLIAM III. AND MARY II.

WILLIAM III. 1689—1702.   MARY II. 1689—1694.

1. The new Government and the Mutiny Act. 1689 . 649
2. The Toleration Act and the Nonjurors. 1689 . . 650
3. Locke's Letters on Toleration. 1689 . . . 652
4. Establishment of Presbyterianism in Scotland. 1689 652
5. Killiecrankie. 1689 . . 652
6. The Pacification of the Highlands. 1691–1692 . 653
7. The Massacre of Glencoe. 1692 654
8. The Siege of Londonderry. 1689 654
9. The Irish Parliament. 1689 655
10. Schomberg sent to Ireland. 1689 655
11. The Bill of Rights and the Dissolution of the Convention Parliament. 1689–1690 . . . 656

12. Settlement of the Revenue. 1690 656
13. The Conquest of Ireland. 1690–1691 . . . 656
14. War with France. 1689–1690 657
15. Disgrace of Marlborough. 1691–1692 . . . 657
16. La Hogue, Steinkirk, and Landen. 1692–1693 . 658
17. Beginning of the National Debt. 1692 . . . 658
18. Disorder in the Government. 1693 659
19. The Whig Junto. 1693–1694. 659
20. The Junto the Beginning of the Modern Cabinet . 660
21. The Bank of England. 1694 660
22. The Place Bill. 1694 . . 661
23. The Second Triennial Act. 1694 661
24. Death of Mary. 1694 . 661

CHAPTER XLIII

WILLIAM III. (*alone*). 1694—1702

	PAGE			PAGE
1. The Liberty of the Press. 1695	663	11. The Darien Expedition. 1698–1700		671
2. The Surrender of Namur. 1695	663	12. The Second Partition Treaty. 1700		671
3. The Restoration of the Currency and the Treason Trials Act. 1696	664	13. Deaths of the Duke of Gloucester and of the King of Spain. 1700		671
4. Ministerial Corruption. 1695–1696	664	14. A Tory Ministry. 1700–1701		672
5. The Assassination Plot. 1696	664	15. The Act of Settlement and the Succession. 1701		672
6. The Peace of Ryswick. 1697	667	16. The Act of Settlement and the Crown. 1701		672
7. Reduction of the Army. 1698–1699	667	17. The Act of Settlement and the Ministers. 1701		673
8. Signature and Failure of the First Partition Treaty. 1698–1699	667	18. The Tory Foreign Policy. 1701		674
9. Break-up of the Whig Junto. 1699	669	19. The Kentish Petition. 1701		674
		20. The Grand Alliance. 1701		675
10. The Irish Grants and the Fall of Somers. 1700	670	21. Death of James II. 1701		675
		22. Death of William. 1702		676

CHAPTER XLIV

ANNE. 1702—1714

	PAGE			PAGE
1. Marlborough and the Tories. 1702	676	12. The Union with Scotland. 1702–1707		685
2. Louis XIV. and Marlborough. 1702	678	13. The Irish Penal Laws		686
3. Marlborough's First Campaign in the Netherlands. 1702–1703	678	14. Irish Commerce Crushed		686
4. The Occasional Conformity Bill. 1702–1703	680	15. Gradual formation of a Whig Ministry. 1705–1708		687
5. Progress of the War in Italy, Spain, and Germany. 1702–1703	680	16. Progress of Cabinet Government. 1708		687
6. Ministerial changes. 1703–1704	680	17. Progress of the War. 1707–1708		689
7. The Campaign of Blenheim. 1704	682	18. The Conference at the Hague and the Battle of Malplaquet. 1709		690
8. Operations in Spain. 1704–1705	682	19. The Sacheverell Trial. 1710		690
9. A Whig Parliament. 1705–1706	684	20. The Fall of the Whigs. 1710		691
10. The Campaign of 1706 in the Netherlands and in Italy. 1706	684	21. A Tory Parliament and Ministry. 1710		691
11. Campaign of 1706 in Spain. 1706	684	22. Brihuega and Villa Viciosa. 1710.		692
		23. Overtures to France. 1710–1711		692
		24. Literature and Politics. 1710		692
		25. Jonathan Swift		693

		PAGE				PAGE
26.	The Imperial Election. 1711	695		Utrecht on International relations .	.	697
27.	The Occasional Conformity Act and the Creation of Peers. 1711 .	695	31.	England as a sea-power. 1713 .	.	697
28.	The Armistice and the Treaty of Utrecht. 1712– 1713 .	696	32.	Position of the Tories. 1711– 1713 .	.	699
29.	Terms of the Treaty of Utrecht. 1713 .	696	33.	The Last Days and Death of Anne. 1714	.	699
30.	Effect of the Treaty of		34.	Politics and Art .	.	701

CHAPTER XLV

TOWNSHEND, SUNDERLAND, AND WALPOLE. 1714—1737

						PAGE
1.	George I. and the Whigs. 1714 .	702	15.	'Quieta non movere'.	.	716
2.	The Whigs and the Nation. 1714 .	704	16.	The Prime Ministership	.	716
3.	The Whigs and Parliament. 1715 .	704	17.	Walpole and Carteret. 1723 –1724 .	.	718
4.	Mar's Rising. 1715-1716.	705	18.	Wood's Halfpence. 1724 .		718
5.	The Septennial Act. 1716	706	19.	The Last Years of George I. 1724-1727 .	.	718
6.	England and France. 1716	707	20.	George II. and Walpole. 1727 .	.	718
7.	The Whig Schism. 1716– 1717 .	708	21.	Breach between Walpole and Townshend. 1730 .	.	720
8.	The Quadruple Alliance. 1718-1720 .	709	22.	Bolingbroke as Organiser of the Opposition. 1726– 1732 .	.	720
9.	The Relief of the Dissenters, and the Peerage Bill. 1719	710	23.	The Excise Bill. 1733 .		722
10.	The South Sea Bubble. 1720	711	24.	The Defeat of the Excise Bill. 1733 .	.	724
11.	The Bursting of the Bubble. 1720-1721 .	712	25.	Disruption of the Opposition. 1734-1735 .	.	724
12.	Walpole cal'ed to the Rescue. 1721-1722 .	712	26.	The Family Compact. 1773		724
13.	Corruption under Walpole .	713	27.	Dissensions in the Royal Family. 1737 .	.	725
14.	Walpole and Corruption .	714				

CHAPTER XLVI

WALPOLE, CARTERET, AND THE PELHAMS. 1737—1754

						PAGE
1.	The Reign of Common Sense .	726	8.	Carteret and Newcastle. 1742		732
2.	Smuggling in the West Indies .	726	9.	Beginning of the War of the Austrian Succession. 1740-1742 .	.	732
3.	Walpole and Spain .	728	10.	Carteret's Diplomacy. 1742– 1744 .	.	735
4.	William Pitt. 1738 .	728	11.	Carteret and the Family Compact. 1743-1744 .		737
5.	Impending War. 1738– 1739 .	729	12.	Carteret's Fall. 1744 .	.	738
6.	The Spanish War and the Resignation of Walpole. 1739-1742 .	730	13.	The Broad-bottomed Administration. 1744 .		739
7.	The New Administration. 1742 .	730	14.	The Young Pretender in Scotland. 1745 .	.	739

		PAGE			PAGE
15.	The March to Derby. 1745	740	18.	End of the War. 1746–	
16.	Falkirk and Culloden. 1746	740		1748 . . .	743
17.	The Pelhams and the King.		19.	End of Henry Pelham's	
	1745 . . .	743		Ministry. 1748–1754 .	743

PART IX

THE FALL OF THE WHIGS AND THE RISE OF THE NEW TORYISM. 1754–1789

CHAPTER XLVII

NEWCASTLE AND PITT. 1754—1760

1.	Butler, Wesley, and White-field. 1736–1754 . .	745	16.	The Conquest of Canada. 1759–1760 . . .	755
2.	Fielding and Hogarth	746	17.	The War in Europe ; Naval	
3.	Newcastle, Pitt, and Fox. 1754–1755 . . .	746		Successes. 1759 . .	756
4.	The French in America.		18.	Progress of the War in Germany. 1759 . .	756
	1754	747	19.	The East India Company.	
5.	Newcastle's Blundering. 1754–1756 . . .	748		1600–1698 . . .	758
6.	The Loss of Minorca. 1756	749	20.	Break-up of the Empire of the Great Mogul. 1658–	
7.	Beginning of the Seven Years' War. 1756 . .	749		1707	758
8.	Ministry of Devonshire and		21.	The Mahratta Confederacy. 1707–1744 . . .	759
	Pitt. 1756–1757 . .	749	22.	Le Bourdonnais and Du-pleix. 1744–1750 . .	760
9.	Pitt's Dismissal. 1757 .	750	23.	Dupleix and Clive. 1751–	
10.	Nature of Pitt's Popularity. 1757	750		1754	761
11.	Coalition between Pitt and Newcastle. 1757 . .	751	24.	The Black Hole of Calcutta. 1756	762
12.	Military Disasters. 1757 .	752	25.	The Battle of Plassey. 1757	762
13.	Pitt and Frederick the Great. 1757–1758 . . .	752	26.	The Battle of Wandewash and the capture of Pondi-	
14.	Fighting in France and America. 1757–1758 .	753		cherry. 1760–1761 .	764
15.	The Campaign in Canada. 1759	753	27.	Death of George II. 1760 .	764

CHAPTER XLVIII

THE BREAK-UP OF THE WHIG PARTY. 1760—1770

1.	Character of George III. 1760	765		and the Peace of Paris. 1762–1763 . . .	766
2.	The Fall of Pitt. 1761 .	766	4.	The King and the Tories.	
2.	Resignation of Newcastle			1762–1763 . . .	767

	PAGE		PAGE

5. The King's Friends . . 767
6. The Three Whig Parties.
   1763 768
7. Grenville and Wilkes. 1763–
   1764 769
8. George III. and Grenville.
   1763–1764 . . . 770
9. The Stamp Act. 1765 . 770
10. The Rockingham Ministry
    1765 771
11. The Rockingham Ministry
    and the Repeal of the
    Stamp Act. 1766 . . 771

12. Pitt and Burke. 1766 . 772
13. The Chatham Ministry.
    1766–1767 . . . 773
14. American Import Duties.
    1767 773
15. The Middlesex Election.
    1768–1769 . . . 774
16. 'Wilkes and Liberty.'
    1769 774
17. Lord North Prime Minister.
    1770 776

CHAPTER XLIX

THE STRUGGLE FOR AMERICAN INDEPENDENCE. 1770—1783

1. North and the Opposition.
   1770 777
2. North and the Tea Duty.
   1770 778
3. The Freedom of Reporting.
   1771 779
4. Continued Resistance in
   America. 1770–1772 . 780
5. The Boston Tea Ships. 1773 780
6. Repressive Measures. 1774 780
7. The Congress of Philadelphia
   and the British Parliament. 1774 . . . 782
8. Lexington and Bunker's
   Hill. 1775 . . . 782
9. Conciliatory Efforts. . 1775 783
10. George Washington in Com-
    mand. 1775 . . . 783
11. Progress of the War. 1775–
    1776 784
12. The Declaration of Indepen-
    dence and the Struggle in
    New Jersey. 1776–1777 784
13. French Assistance to America.
    1776–1777 . . . 786
14. Brandywine and Saratoga.
    1777 786
15. The French Alliance with
    America and the Death
    of Chatham. 1778 . 786
16. Valley Forge. 1777–1778 787

17. George III. and Lord North.
    1779 787
18. The French in the Channel.
    1779. 788
19. English Successes in America
    1779–1780 . . . 788
19A. Economical Reform. 1779–
    1780 789
20. Parliamentary Reform and
    the Gordon Riots . . 789
21. The Gordon Riots. 1780 . 790
22. The Armed Neutrality.
    1780 792
23. The Capitulation of York-
    town. 1781 . . . 792
24. American Success. 1781 . 794
25. The Last Days of North's
    Ministry. 1781–1782 . 794
26. The Rockingham Ministry.
    1782 795
27. Irish Religion and Com-
    merce. 1778 . . . 795
28. The Irish Volunteers. 1778–
    1781 796
29. Irish Legislative Indepen-
    dence. 1782 . . . 796
30. The Shelburne Ministry and
    the Peace of Paris. 1782–
    1783 796
31. Terms of the Treaty of Paris.
    1783 798

CHAPTER L

PITT AND FOX. 1782—1789

1. The Younger Pitt. 1782–
   1783 799
2. Resignation of Shelburne.
   1783 799

3. The Coalition Ministry.
   1783 800
4. The English in Bengal.
   1757–1772 . . . 801

c   b

		PAGE			PAGE
5.	Warren Hastings, Governor of Bengal. 1772-1774	802	18.	French Commercial Treaty. 1786	810
6.	The Regulating Act and its Results. 1773-1774	802	19.	Trial of Warren Hastings. 1786-1795	811
7.	Hastings and Nuncomar. 1775	803	20.	The Regency Bill. 1788-1789	811
8.	War with the Mahrattas and Hyder Ali. 1777-1779	803	21.	Thanksgiving at St. Paul's. 1789	812
9.	Cheyt Singh and the Begums of Oude. 1781-1782	803	22.	Growth of Population. 1700-1801	813
10.	Restoration of Peace. 1781-1782	805	23.	Improvements in Agriculture	813
11.	Hastings as a Statesman. 1783	805	24.	Cattle-breeding	813
12.	The India Bill of the Coalition. 1783	806	25.	The Bridgewater Canal. 1761	813
13.	The Fall of the Coalition. 1783	806	26.	Cotton-spinning. 1738	814
14.	Pitt's Struggle with the Coalition. 1783-1784	807	27.	Hargreaves' Spinning-jenny. 1767	815
15.	Pitt's Budget and India Bill. 1784	808	28.	Arkwright and Crompton. 1769-1779	815
16.	Pitt's Reform Bill. 1785	808	29.	Cartwright's Power-loom. 1785	816
17.	Failure of Pitt's Scheme for a Commercial Union with Ireland. 1785	810	30.	Watt's Steam-engine. 1785	816
			31.	General Results of the Growth of Manufactures	817

PART X

THE CONFLICT WITH DEMOCRACY. 1789—1827

CHAPTER LI

ENGLAND AND THE FRENCH REVOLUTION. 1789—1795

1.	Prospects of Pitt's Ministry. 1789	819	9.	Pitt and the Slave Trade. 1788-1792	823
2.	Material Antecedents of the French Revolution	820	10.	Rise of a Warlike Feeling in France. 1791-1792	824
3.	Intellectual Antecedents of the French Revolution	820	11.	The French Republic. 1792	824
4.	Louis XVI. 1772-1789	821	12.	Breakdown of Pitt's Policy of Peace. 1792-1793	825
5.	The National Assembly. 1789	821	13.	French Defeats and the Reign of Terror. 1793	826
6.	England and France. 1789-1790	822	14.	French Successes. 1793	826
7.	Fox, Burke, and Pitt. 1789-1790	822	15.	Progress of the Reign of Terror. 1793-1794	827
8.	Clarkson and the Slave Trade. 1783-1788	823	16.	Reaction in England. 1792-1793	827

PAGE

17. End of the Reign of Terror. 1794 828
18. Coalition between Pitt and the majority of the Whigs. 1794 828

PAGE

19. The Treaties of Basel. 1795 829
20. The Establishment of the Directory in France. 1795 829
21. The Treason Act and the Sedition Act. 1795 . 830

CHAPTER LII

THE UNION WITH IRELAND AND THE PEACE OF AMIENS.

1795—1804

1. The Irish Government and Parliament. 1785–1791 . 831
2. The United Irishmen and Parliamentary Reform. 1791–1794 . . . 832
3. The Mission of Lord Fitzwilliam. 1794–1795 . 832
4. Impending Revolution. 1795–1796 . . . 833
5. Bonaparte in Italy. 1796–1797 834
6. Pitt's First Negotiation with the Directory. 1796 . 834
7. Suspension of Cash Payments. 1797 . . . 835
8. Battle of St. Vincent. 1797 835
9. Mutiny at Spithead. 1797 . 836
10. Mutiny at the Nore. 1797 . 836
11. Pitt's second Negotiation with the Directory. 1797 836
12. Bonaparte's Expedition to Egypt. 1798 . . . 837
13. The Battle of the Nile. 1798 838
14. Bonaparte in Syria. 1799 . 838

15. Foundation of the Consulate. 1799–1800 . . . 838
16. An Overture for Peace. 1799 840
17. The Campaign of Marengo and the Peace of Lunéville 1800–1801 . . . 840
18. The Irish Rebellion. 1798 840
19. An Irish Reign of Terror. 1798–1799 . . . 841
20. The Irish Union. 1800 . 842
21. Pitt's Resignation. 1801 . 842
22. The Addington Ministry. 1801 843
23. Malta and Egypt. 1800 . 843
24. The Northern Confederacy and the Battle of Copenhagen. 1801 . . . 844
25. The Treaty of Amiens. 1802 846
26. Rupture of the Treaty of Amiens. 1803 . . 846
27. The last Months of the Addington Ministry. 1803–1804 848

CHAPTER LIII

THE ASCENDENCY OF NAPOLEON. 1804—1807

1. The Napoleonic Empire. 1804 849
2. A Threatened Invasion. 1804–1805 . . . 851
3. The Trafalgar Campaign. 1805 851
4. The Battle of Trafalgar. 1805 854
5. The Campaign of Austerlitz. 1805 854
6. Pitt's Death. 1806 . . 854
7. The Ministry of All the Talents. 1806 . . 855
8. The Overthrow of Prussia. 1806 856

9. The End of the Ministry of All the Talents. 1807 . 857
10. The Treaty of Tilsit. 1807 . 858
11. The Colonies. 1804–1807 . 858
12. The Overthrow of the Mahrattas. 1802–1806 . 859
13. Wellesley's Recall. 1805 . 859
14. The Continental System. 1806–1807 . . . 859
15. Effects of the Continental System. 1807 . . 860
16. The Bombardment of Copenhagen. 1807 . . 860

CHAPTER LIV

THE DOWNFALL OF NAPOLEON. 1807—1814

PAGE

1. Napoleon and Spain. 1807–1808 . . . 862
2. The Dethronement of Charles IV. 1808 . 863
3. The Capitulation at Baylen. 1808 . . . 863
4. Battle of Vimeiro and Convention of Cintra. 1808. 863
5. Sir John Moore's Expedition and the Battle of Corunna. 1808–1809 . 864
6. Aspern and Wagram. 1809. 865
7. Walcheren and Talavera. 1809 . . . 865
8. Torres Vedras. 1810–1811 . 867
9. The Regency and the Assassination of Perceval. 1811–1812 . . . 867
10. Napoleon at the Height of Power. 1811. . . 868

PAGE

11. Wellington's Resources. 1811 868
12. Wellington's Advance. 1811–1812 . . . 869
13. The Battle of Salamanca. 1812 869
14. Napoleon in Russia. 1812. 870
15. Napoleon driven out of Germany and Spain. 1813 . 871
16. The Restoration of Louis XVIII. 1814 . . 871
17. Position of England. 1814 872
18. War with America. 1812–1814 872
19. The Congress of Vienna. 1814–1815 . . . 873
20. The Hundred Days. 1815. 874
21. The Waterloo Campaign . 874
22. The Second Restoration of Louis XVIII. . . 875

CHAPTER LV

ENGLAND AFTER WATERLOO. 1815—1827

1. The Corn-Law and the Abolition of the Property Tax. 1815–1816 . . . 875
2. Manufacturing Distress. 1816 876
3. The Factory-System. 1815–1816 876
4. The Radicals. 1816–1817. 877
5. Suspension of the Habeas Corpus Act. 1817–1818 . 877
6. A Time of Prosperity. 1818–1819 879
7. Renewal of Distress. 1819. 879
8. The 'Manchester Massacre.' 1819 879
9. The Six Acts. 1819 . . 880
10. Death of George III. and the Cato-Street Conspiracy. 1820 . . . 880
11. Queen Caroline. 1820–1821 881

12. The Southern Revolutions. 1820–1823 . . . 882
13. Castlereagh and Canning. 1822–1826 . . . 882
14. National Uprising in Greece. 1821–1826 . . 884
15. Peel as Home Secretary. 1821–1827 . . . 884
16. Criminal Law Reform. 1823 885
17. Huskisson and the Combination Laws. 1824–1825 885
18. Robinson's Budgets. 1823–1825 886
19. The end of the Liverpool Ministry. 1826–1827 . 887
20. Burns, Byron, and Shelley . 887
21. Scott and Wordsworth . 889
22. Bentham 890

PART XI

THE GROWTH OF DEMOCRACY

CHAPTER LVI

CATHOLIC EMANCIPATION AND PARLIAMENTARY REFORM

1827—1832

		PAGE
1.	Questions at Issue. 1827 .	891
2.	Canning Prime Minister. 1827	892
3.	The Battle of Navarino and the Goderich Ministry. 1827	892
4.	Formation of the Wellington Ministry. 1828 .	893
5.	Lord John Russell and Parliamentary Reform. 1819–1828	894
6.	Repeal of the Test and Corporation Acts. 1828 .	894
7.	Resignation of the Canningites. 1828 . . .	895
8.	The Catholic Association. 1823–1828 . . .	895
9.	O'Connell's Election. 1828	896
10.	Catholic Emancipation. 1829	896
11.	Death of George IV. 1830	898

		PAGE
12.	William IV. and the Second French Revolution. 1830	898
13.	The End of the Wellington Ministry. 1830 . .	900
14.	Lord Grey's Ministry. 1830	901
15.	The Reform Bill. 1831 .	902
16.	The Bill Withdrawn. 1831	902
17.	The Reform Bill Re-introduced. 1831. . .	903
18.	Public Agitation. 1831 .	903
19.	The Reform Bill becomes Law. 1831–1832 . .	905
20.	Character of the Reform Act. 1832 . . .	905
21.	Roads and Coaches. 1802–1820	905
22.	Steam Vessels and Locomotives. 1811–1825 .	906
23.	The Liverpool and Manchester Railway. 1825–1829	907

CHAPTER LVII

THE REFORMERS IN POWER. 1832—1841

		PAGE
1.	Liberals and Conservatives. 1832	909
2.	Irish Tithes. 1831–1833 .	909
3.	Abolition of Slavery. 1833	910
4.	The First Factory Act. 1833	911
5.	The New Poor Law. 1834	911
6.	Break-up of the Ministry. 1834	912
7.	Foreign Policy of the Reformers. 1830–1834 .	912
8.	Peel's First Ministry. 1834–1835	913
9.	Beginning of Melbourne's Second Ministry. 1835–1837	913

		PAGE
10.	Queen Victoria. 1837 .	914
11.	Canada. 1837–1841 . .	914
12.	Ireland. 1835–1841 . .	916
13.	The Bedchamber Question. 1839	918
14.	Post Office Reform. 1839 .	918
15.	Education. 1833–1839 .	920
16.	The Queen's Marriage. 1840	920
17.	Palmerston and Spain. 1833–1839 . . .	920
18.	Palmerston and the Eastern Question. 1831–1839 .	921
19.	Threatened Breach with France. 1839–1841 .	922

	PAGE			PAGE
20. Condition of the Poor. 1837–1841	922		22. The Anti-Corn-Law League. 1838–1840	924
21. The People's Charter. 1837–1840	923		23. The Fall of the Melbourne Ministry. 1841	925

CHAPTER LVIII

FREE TRADE. 1841—1852

	PAGE		PAGE
1. Peel's New Ministry. 1841	926	15. Irish Emigration. 1847	933
2. Peel's First Free-trade Budget. 1842	926	16. Landlord and Tenant in Ireland. 1847	933
3. Returning Prosperity. 1843–1844	926	17. The Encumbered Estates Act. 1848	933
4. Mines and Factories. 1842–1847	927	18. European Revolution. 1848	934
5. Aberdeen's Foreign Policy. 1841–1846	927	19. Renewed Trouble in Ireland. 1848	935
6. Peel and O'Connell. 1843	928	20. The Chartists on Kennington Common. 1848	935
7. Peel's Irish Policy. 1843–1845	928	21. European Reaction. 1848–1849	936
8. Peel's Second Free-trade Budget. 1845	929	22. The Decline of the Russell Ministry. 1848–1851	936
9. Peel and Disraeli. 1845	929	23. The Great Exhibition. 1851	937
10. Spread of the Anti-Corn-Law League. 1845	930	24. The End of the Russell Ministry. 1851–1852	938
11. The Irish Famine. 1845	931	25. The First Derby Ministry. 1852	938
12. The Abolition of the Corn Law. 1845–1846	931	26. The Burial of Protection. 1852	938
13. The Close of Peel's Ministry. 1846	931		
14. The Russell Ministry. 1846–1847	932		

CHAPTER LIX

THE CRIMEAN WAR AND THE INDIAN MUTINY. 1852—1858

	PAGE		PAGE
1. Expectation of Peace. 1852	939	11. Resolution of the Allies. 1854	944
2. Church Movements. 1827–1853	940	12. Alma and Sebastopol. 1854	945
3. Growth of Science. 1830–1859	940	13. Balaclava and Inkerman. 1854	946
4. Dickens, Thackeray, and Macaulay. 1837–1848	940	14. Winter in the Crimea. 1854–1855	946
5. Grote, Mill, and Carlyle. 1833–1856	941	15. The Hospital at Scutari. 1855	947
6. Tennyson. 1849	943	16. The Palmerston Ministry. 1855	947
7. Turner. 1775–1851	943	17. The Fall of Sebastopol and the End of the War. 1855–1856	947
8. The Beginning of the Aberdeen Ministry. 1852–1854	943	18. India after Wellesley's Recall. 1806–1823	948
9. The Eastern Question. 1850–1853	943	19. The North-Western Frontier. 1806–1835	948
10. War between Russia and Turkey. 1853—1854	944		

	PAGE			PAGE
20. Russia and Afghanistan. 1835–1838	949	27. Lord Dalhousie's Administration. 1848–1856		951
21. The Invasion of Afghanistan. 1839–1842	949	28. The Sepoy Army. 1856–1857		952
22. The Retreat from Cabul. 1842	950	29. The Outbreak of the Mutiny. 1857		953
23. Pollock's March to Cabul. 1842	950	30. Cawnpore. 1857		953
24. Conquest of Sindh. 1842	950	31. The Recovery of Delhi and the Relief of Lucknow. 1857		953
25. The First Sikh War. 1845–1846	951	32. The End of the Mutiny. 1857–1858		954
26. The Second Sikh War 1848–1849	951			

CHAPTER LX

ANTECEDENTS AND RESULTS OF THE SECOND REFORM ACT.

1857—1874

	PAGE			PAGE
1. Fall of the First Palmerston Ministry. 1857–1858	955	and the Second Reform Act. 1866–1868		961
2. The Second Derby Ministry and the Beginning of the Second Palmerston Ministry. 1858–1859	956	15. Irish Troubles. 1867		962
		16. The Gladstone Ministry and the Disestablishment of the Irish Church. 1868–1869		962
3. Italian War of Liberation. 1859	956	17. The Irish Land Act. 1870		962
4. The Kingdom of Italy. 1859–1861	957	18. The Education Act. 1870		963
5. The Volunteers. 1859–1860	957	19. The War between Prussia and Austria. 1866		963
6. The Commercial Treaty with France. 1860	957	20. War between France and Germany. 1870–1871		963
7. The Presidential Election in America. 1860	958	21. Abolition of Army-Purchase. 1871		965
8. England and the American Civil War. 1861–1862	958	22. The Ballot Act. 1872		965
9. The 'Alabama.' 1862	959	23. Foreign Policy of the Ministry. 1871–1872		965
10. The Cotton Famine. 1861–1864	959	24. Fall of the First Gladstone Ministry. 1873–1874		966
11. End of the American Civil War. 1864	960	25. Colonial Expansion. 1815–1874		966
12. The Last Days of Lord Palmerston. 1865	960	26. The North-American Colonies. 1841–1874		967
13. The Ministry of Earl Russell. 1865–1866	960	27. Australasia. 1788–1874		967
14. The Third Derby Ministry		28. South Africa		968

Summary of Events. 1874—1885

	PAGE			PAGE
1. The Disraeli (Beaconsfield) Ministry. 1874–1880	969	2. The Second Gladstone Ministry. 1880–1885		970

INDEX 973

LIST OF ILLUSTRATIONS

———— ◆◆◆ ————

FIG.   PAGE

1. Palæolithic flint scraper from Icklingham, Suffolk . . . 2
2. Palæolithic flint implement from Hoxne, Suffolk . . . 2
   (From Evans's 'Ancient Stone Implements')
3. Engraved bone from Cresswell Crags, Derbyshire . . . 3
   (From the original in the British Museum)
4. Neolithic flint arrow-head from Rudstone, Yorks . . . 3
5. Neolithic celt or cutting instrument from Guernsey . . . 3
6. Neolithic axe from Winterbourn Steepleton, Dorset . . . 4
   (From Evans's 'Ancient Stone Implements')
7. Example of early British pottery 4
8, 9. Examples of early British pottery 5
   (From Greenwell's 'British Barrows')
10. Bronze celt from the Isle of Harty, Kent 6
11. Bronze lance-head found in Ireland 6
12. Bronze caldron found in Ireland 6
   (From Evans's 'Ancient Bronze Implements')
13. View of Stonehenge 7
   (From a photograph)
14. Part of a British gold corselet found at Mold, now in the British
   Museum 9
   (From the 'Archæologia')
15. Bust of Julius Cæsar 10
   (From the original in the British Museum)
16. Commemorative tablet of the Second Legion found at Halton
   Chesters on the Roman Wall 17
17. View of part of the Roman Wall 18
18. Ruins of a mile-castle on the Roman Wall . . . 18
   (From Bruce's 'Handbook to the Roman Wall,' 2nd edition)
19. Part of the Roman Wall at Leicester . . . 19
   (From Rickman's 'Gothic Architecture,' 6th edition, by J. H. Parker)
20. Pediment of a Roman Temple found at Bath . . 20
   (Reduced from the 'Archæologia')
21. Roman altar from Rutchester 21
   (From Bruce's 'Handbook to the Roman Wall,' 2nd edition)
22. Plan of the city of Old Sarum 34
   (From the Ordnance Survey Plan)

FIG.   PAGE

23. View of Old Sarum   35
    (*Reduced from Sir R. C. Hoare's* 'History of Modern Wiltshire.
    Old and New Sarum')

24. Saxon church at Bradford-on-Avon, Wilts   51
    (*From Rickman's* 'Gothic Architecture,' 6th edition, by J. H. Parker)

25. Saxon horsemen   53

26. Group of Saxon warriors   53
    (*From Harl. MS.* 603)

27. Remains of a viking ship from Gokstad . . .   56
    (*From a photograph of the original at Christiana*) .

28. Gold ring of Æthelwulf   57

29. Gold jewel of Ælfred found at Athelney . . .   59
    (*From* 'Archæological Journal')

30. An English vessel   60

31. A Saxon house   61
    (*From Harl. MS.* 603)

32. A monk driven out of the King's presence . . .   66
    (*From a drawing belonging to the Society of Antiquaries*)

33. Rural life in the eleventh century. January to June . .   70

34. Rural life in the eleventh century. July to December . .   71
    (*From Cott. MS. Julius A. vi.*)

35. Plan and section of a burh of the eleventh century at Laughton-en-
    le-Morthen, Yorks   74
    (*From G. T. Clark's* 'Mediæval Military Architecture')

37. Glass tumbler   76

38. Drinking-glass   76

39. Comb and case of Scandinavian type found at York . .   77
    (*From the originals in the British Museum*)

40. Martyrdom of St. Edmund by the Danes . . .   82
    (*From a drawing belonging to the Society of Antiquaries*)

41. First Great Seal of Eadward the Confessor (obverse) . .   86
    (*From an original impression*)

42. Hunting. (From the Bayeux Tapestry) . . .   87
    (*Reduced from* 'Vetusta Monumenta,' vol. vi.)

43. Tower in the earlier style, church at Earl's Barton . .   91

44. Tower in the earlier style, St. Benet's church, Cambridge .   91
    (*From Rickman's* 'Gothic Architecture,' 6th edition, by J. H. Parker)

45. Building a church in the later style   92
    (*From a drawing belonging to the Society of Antiquaries*)

46. Normans feasting; with Odo, bishop of Bayeux, saying grace.
    (From the Bayeux Tapestry)   93

47. Harold swearing upon the relics. (From the Bayeux Tapestry) .   94

48. A Norman ship. (From the Bayeux Tapestry) . .   95

49. Norman soldiers mounted. (From the Bayeux Tapestry) .   95

50. Group of archers on foot. (From the Bayeux Tapestry) .   96

51. Men fighting with axes. (From the Bayeux Tapestry) .   97

52. Death of Harold. (From the Bayeux Tapestry) . .   98
    (*Reduced from* 'Vetusta Monumenta,' vol. vi.)

53. Coronation of a king, *temp.* William the Conqueror . .   99
    (*From a drawing belonging to the Society of Antiquaries*)

54. Silver penny of William the Conqueror, struck at Romney . .   101
    (*From an original specimen*)

FIG.   PAGE

55. East end of Darenth church, Kent 107
(*From Rickman's* 'Gothic Architecture,' 6th edition, by J. H. Parker)

56. Part of the nave of St. Alban's abbey church . . . 109
(*From a photograph by Valentine & Sons, Dundee*)

57. Facsimile of a part of Domesday Book relating to Berkshire . 112
(*From the original MS. in the Public Record Office*)

58. Henry I. and his queen Matilda 123
(*From Hollis's* ' Monumental Effigies')

59. Seal of Milo of Gloucester, showing mounted armed figure in the
reign of Henry I. 125
(*From an original impression*)

60. Monument of Roger, bishop of Salisbury, died 1139 . . 127
(*From Stothard's* 'Monumental Effigies')

61. Porchester church, Hampshire, built about 1135 . . . 128
(*From Rickman's* 'Gothic Architecture,' 7th edition, by J. H. Parker)

62. Part of the nave of Durham cathedral, built about 1130 . 130
(*From Scott's* 'Mediæval Architecture,' London, J. Murray)

63. Keep of Rochester castle, built between 1126 and 1139 . . 132
(*From a photograph by Poulton & Sons, Lee*)

64. Keep of Castle Rising, built about 1140–1150 . . . 133
(*From a photograph*)

65. Tower of Castor church, Northamptonshire, built about 1145 . 136
(*From Britton's* ' Architectural Antiquities')

66. Effigies of Henry II. and queen Eleanor 139
(*From Stothard's* ' Monumental Effigies')

67. Ecclesiastical costume in the twelfth century . . . 142
(*From Cott. MS. Nero C. iv. f. 37*)

68. A bishop ordaining a priest 144

69. Small ship of the latter part of the twelfth century . . 146
(*From* ' Harley Roll,' Y. 6)

70. Part of the choir of Canterbury cathedral, in building 1175–1184 . 150
(*From Scott's* ' Mediæval Architecture,' London, J. Murray)

71. Mitre of Archbishop Thomas of Canterbury, preserved at Sens . 153
(*From Shaw's* ' Dresses and Decorations')

72. Military and civil costume of the latter part of the twelfth century . 154
(*From* ' Harley Roll,' Y. 6)

73. Royal arms of England from Richard I. to Edward III. . . 159
(*From the wall arcade, south aisle of nave, Westminster Abbey*)

74. The Galilee or Lady chapel, Durham cathedral, built by bishop
Hugh of Puiset, between 1180 and 1197 160
(*From Scott's* ' Mediæval Architecture,' London, J. Murray)

75. Effigy of a knight in the Temple church, London, showing armour
of the end of the twelfth century 162
(*From Hollis's* ' Monumental Effigies')

76. Effigies of Richard I. and queen Berengaria . . . 164
(*From Stothard's* ' Monumental Effigies')

77. Part of the choir of Ripon cathedral, built during the last quarter of
the twelfth century 166
(*From Scott's* ' Mediæval Architecture,' London, J. Murray)

78. Lay costumes in the twelfth century 168

79. Costume of shepherds in the twelfth century . . . 168
(*From Cott. MS. Nero C. iv. ff. 11 and 16*)

80. Hall of Oakham castle, Rutland, built about 1185 . . . 170
(*From Hudson Turner's* ' Domestic Architecture')

FIG.   PAGE
81. Norman house at Lincoln, called the Jews' House 171
        (*From a photograph by Carl Norman, Tunbridge Wells*)
82. Effigies of king John and queen Isabella   175
        (*From Stothard's* 'Monumental Effigies')
83. Effigy of bishop Marshall of Exeter, died 1206   .   .   . 177
        (*From Murray's* 'Handbook to the Southern Cathedrals')
84. Parsonage house of early thirteenth-century date at West Dean,
        Sussex   179
        (*From Hudson Turner's* 'Domestic Architecture')
85. Effigy of a knight in the Temple church, London, showing armour
        worn between 1190 and 1225   182
        (*From Stothard's* 'Monumental Effigies')
86. Silver penny of John, struck at Dublin   184
        (*From an original example*)
87. Effigy of Henry III.   (From his tomb at Westminster)   .   . 186
88. Effigy of William Longespée, earl of Salisbury, died 1227, from his
        tomb at Salisbury, showing armour worn from about 1225 to 1250 . 187
        (*From Stothard's* 'Monumental Effigies')
89. Effigy of Simon, bishop of Exeter, died 1223   .   .   . 188
        (*From Murray's* 'Handbook to the Southern Cathedrals')
90. Beverley Minster, Yorkshire, the south transept; built about 1220–
        1230 189
        (*From Britton's* 'Architectural Antiquities')
91. Longthorpe manor-house, Northamptonshire, built about 1235   . 192
        (*From Hudson Turner's* 'Domstic Architecture')
92. A ship in the reign of Henry III.   193
93. A bed in the reign of Henry III.   196
        (*From Cott. MS. Nero D. i. ff. 21 and 22 b*)
94. Barn of thirteenth-century date at Raunds, Northamptonshire   . 197
        (*From Hudson Turner's* 'Domestic Architecture')
95. A fight between armed and mounted knights of the time of Henry
        III.   201
        (*From Cott. MS. Nero D. i. f. 4*)
96. Seal of Robert Fitzwalter, showing a mounted knight in complete
        mail armour; date about 1265   202
        (*From an original impression*)
97. Effigy of a knight at Gosperton, showing armour worn from about
        1250 to 1300; date about 1270   203
        (*From Stothard's* 'Monumental Effigies')
98. Building operations in the reign of Henry III., with the king giving
        directions to the architect 204
        (*From Cott. MS. Nero D. i. f 23 b*)
99. East end of Westminster abbey church; begun by Henry III. in
        1245 205
        (*From a photograph*)
100. Nave of Salisbury cathedral church, looking west; date, between
        1240 and 1250   206
        (*From a photograph by Valentine & Sons, Dundee*)
101. A king and labourers in the reign of Henry III.   .   .   . 207
        (*From Cott. MS. Nero D. i. f. 21 b*)
102. Great Seal of Edward I. (slightly reduced)   209
        (*From an original impression*)
103. Group of armed knights and a king in ordinary dress; date, *temp.*
        Edward I.   211
        (*From Arundel MS. 83, f. 132*)

FIG. PAGE

104. Nave of Lichfield cathedral church, looking east ; built about 1280 . 213
    (*From a photograph by Valentine & Sons, Dundee*)

105. Effigy of Eleanor of Castile, queen of Edward I., in Westminster
    abbey 215
    (*From Stothard's* 'Monumental Effigies')

106. Cross erected near Northampton by Edward I. in memory of queen
    Eleanor 217
    (*From a photograph*)

107. Sir John d'Abernoun, died 1277, from his brass at Stoke Dabernon ;
    showing armour worn from about 1250 to 1300 . . . 219
    (*From Waller's* 'Monumental Brasses')

108. Edward II. from his monument in Gloucester cathedral . . 225
    (*From Stothard's* 'Monumental Effigies')

109. Lincoln cathedral, the central tower ; built about 1310 . . 227
    (*From Britton's* 'Architectural Antiquities')

110. Sir John de Creke, from his brass at Westley Waterless, Cambridge-
    shire ; showing armour worn between 1300 and 1335 or 1340 ;
    date, about 1325 229
    (*From Waller's* 'Monumental Brasses')

111. Howden church Yorkshire, the west front 230
    (*From Rickman's* 'Gothic Architecture,' 7th edition, by J. H. Parker)

112. Effigies of Edward III. and queen Philippa, from their tombs in
    Westminster abbey 233
    (*From Blore's* 'Monumental Remains')

113. A knight—Sir Geoffrey Luttrell, who died 1345—receiving his helm
    and pennon from his wife ; another lady holds his shield . . 236
    (*From the Luttrell Psalter,* 'Vetusta Monumenta')

114. William of Hatfield, second son of Edward III., from his tomb in
    York Minster 237
    (*From Stothard's* 'Monumental Effigies')

115. York Minster, the nave, looking west 238
    (*From a photograph by Valentine & Sons, Dundee*)

116. Royal arms of Edward III., from his tomb 239
    (*From a photograph*)

117. Shooting at the butts with the long bow 241

118. Contemporary view of a fourteenth-century walled town . . 243
    (*From the Luttrell Psalter,* 'Vetusta Monumenta')

119. Gloucester cathedral church, the choir, looking east . . 244
    (*From a photograph by Valentine & Sons, Dundee*)

120. The lord's upper chamber or solar at Sutton Courtenay manor-house
    date, about 1350 245

121. Interior of the hall at Penshurst, Kent ; built about 1340 . . 246

122. A small house or cottage at Meare, Somerset ; built about 1350 . 247

123. Norborough Hall, Northamptonshire ; built about 1350 . . 247
    (*From Hudson Turner's* 'Domestic Architecture')

124. Ploughing 248

125. Harrowing ; and a boy slinging stones at the birds . . 248

126. Breaking the clods with mallets 249

127. Cutting weeds 249

128. Reaping 249

129. Stacking corn 250

130. Threshing corn with a flail 250
    (*From the Luttrell Psalter,* 'Vetusta Monumenta')

FIG.   PAGE

131. West front of Edington church, Wilts ; built about 1360 . . 253
     (*From Rickman's* 'Gothic Architecture,' 7th edition, by J. H. Parker)

132. Gold noble of Edward III. 255
     (*From an original example*)

133. Effigy of Edward the Black Prince ; from his tomb at Canterbury . 256
     (*From Stothard's* 'Monumental Effigies')

134. William of Wykeham, bishop of Winchester, 1367–1404 ; from his
     tomb at Winchester
     (*From Murray's* 'Handbook to the Southern Cathedrals')   260

135. Tomb of Edward III. in Westminster abbey . . . 263
     (*From Blore's* 'Monumental Remains')

136. Figures of Edward the Black Prince and Lionel duke of Clarence ;
     from the tomb of Edward III.
     (*From Hollis's* 'Monumental Effigies') 264

137. Richard II. and his first queen, Anne of Bohemia ; from their tomb
     in Westminster abbey 267
     (*From Hollis's* 'Monumental Effigies')

138. Portrait of Geoffrey Chaucer 270
     (*From Harl. MS.* 4866)

139. A gentleman riding out with his hawk 271

140. Carrying corn, a cart going uphill 272

141. State carriage of the fourteenth century 273

142. Bear-baiting 275
     (*From the Luttrell Psalter*, 'Vetusta Monumenta')

143. West end of the nave of Winchester cathedral church . . 276
     (*From a photograph by Valentine & Sons, Dundee*)

144. Meeting of Henry of Lancaster and Richard II. at Flint . . 284

145. Henry of Lancaster claiming the throne 285
     (*From Harl. MS.* 1319)

146. Effigy of a knight at Clehonger, showing development of plate
     armour ; date about 1400
     (*From Hollis's* 'Monumental Effigies') 287

147. Henry IV. and his queen Jo n of Navarre ; from their tomb in
     Canterbury cathedral church
     (*From Stothard's* 'Monumental Effigies') 290

148. Royal arms as borne from about 1408 to 1603 . . . 291
     (*From a fifteenth-century seal*)

149. Thomas Cranley, archbishop of Dublin ; from his brass at New
     College, Oxford, showing the archiepiscopal costume . . 292
     (*From Waller's* 'Monumental Brasses')

150. The Battle of Shrewsbury 294

151. Fight in the lists with poleaxes 297
     (*From Cott. MS.* Julius E. iv. ff. 4 and 7)

152. Costume of a judge about 1400 ; from a brass at Deerhurst . . 298
     (*From Waller's* 'Monumental Brasses')

153. Henry V. 300
     (*From an original portrait belonging to the Society of Antiquaries*)

154. Effigy of William Phelip, lord Bardolph ; from his tomb at Den-
     nington, Suffolk
     (*From Stothard's* 'Monumental Effigies') 304

155. Marriage of Henry V. and Catherine of France . . . 305
     (*From Cott. MS.* Julius E. iv. f. 22)

156. Henry VI. 308
     (*From an original picture in the National Portrait Gallery*)

FIG.   PAGE

157. Fotheringay church, Northamptonshire ; begun in 1434   .   311
     (*From a photograph by G. A. Nichols, Stamford*)

158 and 159. Front and back views of the gilt-latten effigy of Richard
Beauchamp, earl of Warwick, died 1439 ; from his tomb at Warwick 314, 315
     (*From Stothard's '*Monumental Effigies ')

160. Tattershall castle, Lincolnshire ; built between 1433 and 1455   .   316
     (*From a photograph by G. A. Nichols, Stamford*)

161. Part of Winfield manor-house, Derbyshire ; built about 1440   .   318
     (*From a photograph by R. Keene, Derby*)

162. The Divinity School, Oxford ; built between 1445 and 1454   .   319
     (*From a photograph by W. H. Wheeler, Oxford*)

163. A sea-fight   325
     (*From Cott. MS. Julius E. iv. f. 18 b*)

164. Effigy of Sir Robert Harcourt, K.G., showing armour worn from
about 1445 to 1480   326
     (*From Stothard's '*Monumental Effigies ')

165. Edward IV.   330
     (*From an original portrait belonging to the Society of Antiquaries*)

166. A fifteenth-century ship   333
     (*From Harl. MS. 2278, f. 16*)

167. Large ship and boat of the fifteenth century   .   .   .   339
     (*From Cott. MS. Julius E. iv. f. 5*)

168. Richard III.   341
     (*From an original portrait belonging to the Society of Antiquaries*)

169. Henry VII.   344

170. Elizabeth of York, queen of Henry VII.   .   .   345
     (*From original pictures in the National Portrait Gallery*)

171. Tudor Rose ; from the chapel of Henry VII., Westminster   .   346

172. Tower of St. Mary's church, Taunton ; built about 1500   .   353
     (*From Britton's '*Architectural Antiquities ')

173. King's College Chapel, Cambridge ; interior, looking east .   355
     (*From a photograph by Valentine & Sons, Dundee*)

174. Henry VIII.   362
     (*From a painting by Holbein about 1536, belonging to Earl Spencer*)

175. Cardinal Wolsey   365
     (*From an original picture belonging to the Hon. Sir Spencer Ponsonby-
Fane, K.C.B.*)

176. The embarkation of Henry VIII. from Dover, 1520 .   .   370
     (*From the Society of Antiquaries' engraving of the original picture
at Hampton Court*)

177. Silver-gilt cup and cover, made at London in 1523 ; at Barber
Surgeons' Hall, London   .   .   .   371
     (*From Cripps's '*College and Corporation Plate ')

178. Part of Hampton Court ; built by Cardinal Wolsey ; finished in 1526   373
     (*From a photograph*)

179. Portrait of William Warham, Archbishop of Canterbury, 1503–1532,
showing the ordinary episcopal dress, with the mitre and archiepiscopal cross   376
     (*From a painting by Holbein, belonging to Viscount Dillon, F.S.A.,
dated 1527*)

180. Tower of Fountains Abbey church ; built by Abbot Huby, 1494–
1526   378
     (*From a photograph by Valentine & Sons, Dundee*)

181. Catharine of Aragon   .   .   .   380
     (*From a painting in the National Portrait Gallery*)

FIG.   PAGE

182. The gatehouse of Coughton Court, Warwickshire ; built about 1530   381
      (*From Niven's ' Illustrations of Old Warwickshire Houses'*)

183. Hall of Christchurch, Oxford ; built by Cardinal Wolsey ; finished
      in 1529   384
      (*From a photograph by W. H. Wheeler, Oxford*)

184. Sir Thomas More, wearing the collar of SS.   387
      (*From an original portrait painted by Holbein in 1527, belonging to
      Edward Huth, Esq.*)

185. John Fisher, Bishop of Rochester, 1504–1535   .   .   .   393
      (*From a drawing by Holbein in the Royal Library, Windsor Castle*)

186. Edward Seymour, Earl of Hertford, brother of Jane Seymour, after-
      wards Duke of Somerset, known as ' the Protector,' at the age of
      28, 1507–1552   395
      (*From a painting at Sudeley Castle*)

187. Henry VIII.   403
      (*From a painting by Holbein, belonging to the Earl of Warwick*)

188. Angel of Henry VIII., 1543   405
      (*From an original example*)

189. Part of the encampment at Marquison, 1544, showing military
      equipment in the time of Henry VIII.   406

190, 191. Part of the siege of Boulogne by Henry VIII., 1544, showing
      military operations 407, 408
      (*From the Society of Antiquaries' engravings, by Vertue, of the now
      destroyed paintings formerly at Cowdray House, Sussex*)

192. Armour as worn in the reign of Henry VIII. ; from the brass of John
      Lymsey, 1545, in Hackney church   409

193. Margaret, wife of John Lymsey ; from her brass in Hackney church,
      showing the costume of a lady *circa* 1545   .   .   .   409
      (*From Haines's ' Manual of Monumental Brasses'*)

194. Thomas Howard, third Duke of Norfolk, 1473 (?)–1554   .   410
      (*From a painting by Holbein at Windsor Castle*)

195. Thomas Cranmer, Archbishop of Canterbury, 1533–1556   .   414
      (*From a painting by Holbein dated 1547, at Jesus College, Cambridge*)

196. Nicholas Ridley, Bishop of London, 1550–1553   .   .   417
      (*From the National Portrait Gallery*)

197. King Edward VI.   419
      (*From a picture belonging to H. Hucks Gibbs, Esq.*)

198. Queen Mary Tudor   422
      (*From a painting by Lucas de Heere, dated 1554, belonging to the
      Society of Antiquaries*)

199. Hugh Latimer, Bishop of Worcester, 1535–1539, burnt 1555   .   425
      (*From the National Portrait Gallery*)

200. A milled half-sovereign of Elizabeth, 1562–1568   .   .   435
      (*From an original example*)

201. Silver-gilt standing cup made in London in 1569–70, and given to
      Corpus Christi College, Cambridge, by Archbishop Parker   .   440
      (*From Cripps's ' College and Corporation Plate '*)

202. Sir Francis Drake in his forty-third year   .   .   .   448
      (*From the engraving by Elstracke*)

203. Armour as worn during the reign of Elizabeth ; from the brass of
      Francis Clopton, 1577, at Long Melford, Suffolk   .   .   451
      (*From Haines's ' Manual of Monumental Brasses'*)

204. Hall of Burghley House, Northamptonshire, built about 1580   .   455
      (*From Drummond's ' Histories of Noble British Families '*)

205. Sir Martin Frobisher, died 1594   459
      (*From a picture belonging to the Earl of Carlisle*)

FIG. PAGE

206. The Spanish Armada. Fight between the English and Spanish
fleets off the Isle of Wight, July 25, 1588 . . . 461
 (*From Pine's engravings of the tapestry formerly in the House of
 Lords*)

207. Sir Walter Raleigh (1552–1618), and his eldest son Walter at the
age of eight 463
 (*From a picture dated 1602, belonging to Sir J. F. Lennard, Bart.*)

208. A mounted soldier at the end of the sixteenth century . . 465
 (*From a broadside printed in 1596, in the Society of Antiquaries'
 collection*)

209. Wollaton Hall, Nottinghamshire ; built by Thorpe for Sir Francis
Willoughby, about 1580–1588 466
 (*From a photograph by R. Keene, Derby*)

210. Hardwick Hall, Derbyshire ; built by Elizabeth, Countess of Shrewsbury, about 1597 467
 (*From a photograph by R. Keene, Derby*)

211. E-shaped house at Beaudesert, Staffordshire ; built by Thomas, Lord
Paget, about 1601 469
 (*From a photograph by R. Keene, Derby*)

212. Ingestre Hall, Staffordshire ; built about 1601 . . . 471
 (*From a photograph by R. Keene, Derby*)

213. Coaches in the reign of Elizabeth 473
 (*From 'Archæologia,' vol. xx. pl. xviii.*)

214. William Shakspere 474
 (*From the bust on his tomb at Stratford-on-Avon*)

215. Robert Devereux, second Earl of Essex. K.G., 1567–1601 . . 476
 (*From a painting by Van Somer, dated 1599, belonging to the Earl of Essex*)

216. Queen Elizabeth, 1558–1603 477
 (*From a painting belonging to the University of Cambridge*)

217. William Cecil, Lord Burghley, K.G., 1520–1591 . . . 479
 (*From a painting in the Bodleian Library, Oxford*)

218. Royal arms borne by James I. and succeeding Stuart sovereigns . 482
 (*From Boutell's 'English Heraldry'*)

219. North-west view of Hatfield House, Herts ; built for Robert Cecil,
first Earl of Salisbury, between 1605 and 1611 . . . 485
 (*From a photograph by Valentine & Sons, Dundee*)

220. Thomas Howard, Earl of Suffolk 487
 (*From a painting belonging to T. A. Hope, Esq.*)

221. King James I. 491
 (*From a painting by P. Van Somer, dated 1621, in the National
 Portrait Gallery*)

222. Civil costume, about 1620 492
 (*From a contemporary broadside in the collection of the Society of
 Antiquaries*)

223. The banqueting-hall of the Palace of Whitehall (from the north-
east) ; built from the designs of Inigo Jones, 1619–1621 . . 493
 (*From a photograph*)

224. Francis Bacon, Viscount St. Alban, Lord Chancellor . . 495
 (*From a painting by P. Van Somer in the National Portrait Gallery*)

225. Costume of a lawyer 497
 (*From a broadside dated 1623, in the collection of the Society of
 Antiquaries*)

226. The Upper House of Convocation 498

227. The Lower House of Convocation 499
 (*From a broadside dated 1623, in the collection of the Society of
 Antiquaries*)

FIG.   PAGE

228. King Charles I.   504
       (*From a painting by Van Dyck*)

229. Queen Henrietta Maria, wife of Charles I.   505
       (*From a painting by Van Dyck*)

230. Tents and military equipment in the early part of the reign of
    Charles I.   507
       (*From the monument of Sir Charles Montague (died in 1625), in the
          church of Barking, Essex*)

231. George Villiers, first duke of Buckingham, 1592–1628   509
       (*From the painting by Gerard Honthorst in the National Portrait
          Gallery*)

232. Sir Edward and Lady Filmer ; from their brass at East Sutton,
    Kent, showing armour and dress worn about 1630.   515
       (*From Waller's* ' Monumental Brasses ')

233. Archbishop Laud   517
       (*From a copy in the National Portrait Gallery by Henry Stone, from
          the Van Dyck at Lambeth*)

234. Silver-gilt tankard made at London in 1634–5 ; now belonging to
    the Corporation of Bristol   518
       (*From Cripps's* 'College and Corporation Plate ')

235. The ' Sovereign of the Seas,' built for the Royal Navy in 1637   522
       (*From a contemporary engraving by John Payne*)

236. Soldier armed with a pike   527

237. Soldier with musket and crutch   527
       (*From a broadside printed about 1630, in the collection of the Society
          of Antiquaries*)

238–243. Ordinary civil costume, *temp.* Charles I., viz. :—

          A gentleman and a gentlewoman   550

          A citizen and a citizen's wife .   551

          A countryman and a countrywoman.   552
       (*From Speed's map of* ' The Kingdom of England,' 1646)

244. View of the west side of the Banqueting-House, Whitehall, dated
    1713, showing the window through which Charles I. is said to have
    passed to the scaffold   558
       (*From an engraving by Terasson*)

245. Execution of King Charles I., January 30, 1649   559
       (*From a broadside in the collection of the late Richard Fisher Esq.,
          F.S.A.*)

246. A coach in the middle of the seventeenth century   564
       (*From an engraving by John Dunstall*)

247. Oliver Cromwell   567
       (*From the painting by Samuel Cooper, at Sidney Sussex College, Cam-
          bridge*)

248. Charles II.   579
       (*From the portrait by Sir Peter Lely in Christ's Hospital, London*)

249. Edward Hyde, first Earl of Clarendon, 1608–1674   581
       (*From an engraving by Loggan*)

250. A mounted nobleman and his squire   582
       (*From Ogilby's* ' Coronation Procession of Charles II.')

251. Dress of the Horseguards at the Restoration.   583
       (*From Ogilby's* ' Coronation Procession of Charles II.)

252. Yeoman of the Guard   583
       (*From Ogilby's* ' Coronation Procession of Charles II.')

253. Shipping in the Thames, *circa* 1660 .   584
       (*From Pricke's* ' South Prospect of London ')

FIG.   PAGE

254. Old St. Paul's, from the east, showing its condition just before the
     Great Fire 59¹
         (*From an engraving by Hollar*)

255. John Milton in 1669 597
         (*From the engraving by Faithorne*)

256. Temple Bar, London, built by Sir Christopher Wren in 1670   . 601
         (*From a photograph*)

257. Anthony Ashley-Cooper, first Earl of Shaftesbury, 1621–1683   604
         (*From the painting by John Greenhill in the National Portrait Gallery*)

258. Ordinary dress of gentlemen in 1675 611
         (*From Loggan's 'Oxonia Illustrata'*)

259. Cup presented, 1676, by King Charles II. to the Barber Surgeons'
     Company   612
         (*From Cripps's 'College and Corporation Plate'*)

260. Steeple of the church of St. Mary-le-Bow, London, built by Sir
     Christopher Wren between 1671 and 1680 614
         (*From a photograph*)

261. Dress of ladies of quality   628
         (*From Sandford's 'Coronation Procession of James II.'*)

262. Ordinary attire of women of the lower classes   .   . 628
         (*From Sandford's 'Coronation Procession of James II.'*)

263. Coach of the latter half of the seventeenth century   .   . 629
         (*From Loggan's 'Oxonia Illustrata'*)

264. Waggon of the second half of the seventeenth century   .   . 629
         (*From Loggan's 'Oxonia Illustrata'*)

265. Reaping and harvesting in the second half of the seventeenth cen-
     tury   630
         (*From Loggan's 'Cantabrigia Illustrata'*)

266. Costume of a gentleman   632
         (*From Sandford's 'Coronation Procession of James II.'*)

267. James II.   635
         (*From the painting by Sir Godfrey Kneller in 1684–5 in the National
         Portrait Gallery*)

268. Yeomen of the Guard 636
         (*From Sandford's 'Coronation Procession of James II.'*)

269. Dress of a bishop in the second half of the seventeenth century   . 642
         (*From Sandford's 'Coronation Procession of James II.'*)

270. William III. 650

271. Mary II. 651
         (*From engravings after portraits by J. H. Brandon*)

272. Royal arms as borne by William III.   652

273. 1, Bayonet as made in 1686 653
     2, Bayonet of the time of William and Mary   .   .   . 653
         (*From 'Archæologia,' vol. xxxviii.*)

274. Part of Greenwich Hospital.   Built after the design of Sir Christo-
     pher Wren   662
         (*From a photograph by Valentine & Sons, Dundee*)

275. Front of Hampton Court Palace ; built by Sir Christopher Wren for
     William III.   665
         (*From a photograph*)

276. Part of Hampton Court ; built for William III. by Sir Christopher
     Wren   666
         (*From a photograph by Valentine & Sons, Dundee*)

277. West front of St. Paul's Cathedral Church ; built by Sir Christopher
     Wren   668
         (*From a photograph by Valentine & Sons, Dundee*)

FIG.   PAGE

278. Queen Anne ; from a portrait by Sir Godfrey Kneller   .   . 677
     (*From an engraving after Sir Godfrey Kneller*)

279. The first Eddystone Lighthouse, erected in 1697 ; destroyed in 1703 . 679
     (*From an engraving by Sturt*)

280. Steeple of St. Bride's, Fleet Street, London ; built by Sir Christopher
     Wren, 1701–1703 681
     (*From an original engraving*)

281. Part of Blenheim ; built by Vanbrugh in 1704   .   .   . 683
     (*From a photograph by Valentine & Sons, Dundee*)

282. Royal arms, as borne by Anne 685

283. Sarah, Duchess of Marlborough ; from a portrait by Sir G. Kneller,
     belonging to Earl Spencer, K.G. 688

284. John Churchill, Duke of Marlborough ; from a portrait belonging to
     Earl Spencer, K.G. 689
     (*Both from Dibdin's ' Ædes Althorpianæ '*)

285. Jonathan Swift, D.D., Dean of St. Patrick's, Dublin   . 694
     (*From a painting by C. Jervas in the National Portrait Gallery*)

286. Henry St. John, Viscount Bolingbroke ; from an engraving after a
     picture by Sir Godfrey Kneller 698
     (*From Lodge's ' British Portraits '*)

287. The Choir of St. Paul's Cathedral Church, looking west, as finished
     by Sir Christopher Wren 700
     (*From an engraving by Trevit, about 1710*)

288. George I. 703
     (*From an engraving by Vertue*)

289. A coach of the early part of the eighteenth century .   . 706
     (*From an engraving by Kip*)

290. An early form of steam-pump for mines .   .   . 708
     (*From an engraving dated 1717*)

291. Group showing costumes and sedan-chair about 1720   . 711

292. View of the Game of Pall-Mall 712
     (*Both from Kip's ' Prospect of the City of London, Westminster, and
     St. James's Park '*)

293. The interior of St. Martin's-in-the-Fields, London ; built by James
     Gibbs, 1722–1726 715
     (*From a contemporary engraving*)

294. Ploughing with oxen in the eighteenth century   .   . 716

295. Mowing grass in the eighteenth century .   .   . 717
     (*Both from Hearne's ' Ectypa Varia,' 1737*)

296. Church of St. Mary Woolnoth, London ; finished in 1727 from the
     designs of Nicholas Hawksmoor 719
     (*From a photograph*)

297. Sir Robert Walpole 721
     (*From the picture by Van Loo in the National Portrait Gallery*)

298. Vessels unloading at the Custom House, at the beginning of the
     eighteenth century 723
     (*From an original engraving*)

299. George II. 727
     (*From the portrait by Thomas Hudson in the National Portrait
     Gallery*)

300. Coach built for William Herrick, of Beaumanor, in 1740   . 729
     (*From a lithograph*)

301. A sitting in the House of Commons in 1741–42   .   . 731
     (*From an engraving by Pine*)

302. Election Scenes—The Canvass .   .   . 733

FIG.   PAGE

303. Election Scenes—The Poll 734

304. Election Scenes—The Chairing of the Member . . . 735

305. Election Scenes—The Election Dinner . . . 736
      (*From engravings after the pictures by Hogarth*)

306. Grenadier of the First Regiment of Footguards, 1745 . . 738

307. Uniform of the Footguards, 1745 738
      (*Both from Sir S. Scott's* ' History of the British Army ')

308. The March to Finchley, 1745 741
      (*From the engraving by Luke Sullivan after the painting by Hogarth*)

309. The Right Hon. William Pitt, Paymaster of the Forces, afterwards
      Earl of Chatham 742
      (*From the mezzotint by Houston after a painting by Hoare*)

310. A view of Cape Diamond, Plains of Abraham, and part of the town
      of Quebec and the river St. Lawrence; drawn by Lieutenant
      Fisher 754
      (*From an engraving in the British Museum*)

311. Wolfe 755
      (*From the painting by Schaak in the National Portrait Gallery*)

312. A naval engagement; defeat of the French off Cape Lagos, August
      1759 757
      (*From a picture by R. Paton*)

313. Officer with fusil and gorget 758
      (*From Sir S. Scott's* ' History of the British Army ')

314. Uniform of Militia, 1759 759
      (*From Raikes's* ' First Regiment of Militia ')

315. Uniform of a Light Dragoon, about 1760 . . . 760
      (*From Grose's* ' Military Antiquities ')

316. The third Eddystone Lighthouse; built by Smeaton in 1759 . 763
      (*From* ' European Magazine,' vol. xix.)

317. Silver coffee-pot belonging to the Salters' Company, 1764 . . 769
      (*From Cripps's* ' College and Corporation Plate ')

318. Edmund Burke 772
      (*From a painting by Reynolds in the National Portrait Gallery*)

319. George III. in 1767 775
      (*From a painting by Allan Ramsay in the National Portrait Gallery*)

320. Lord North 778
      (*From the engraving by Burke after a painting by Dance*)

321. Distribution of His Majesty's Maundy 781
      (*From the engraving by Basire, 1773*)

322. Part of Somerset House; built by Sir William Chambers, 1776–80 . 785
      (*From a photograph*)

323. Charles James Fox as a young man 790
      (*From Watson's mezzotint after a painting by Reynolds*)

324. The Gordon Riots, 1780 791
      (*From an engraving by Heath after the picture by Wheatley*)

325. Newgate Prison; rebuilt in 1782 after the Gordon Riot . . 793
      (*From a photograph*)

326. The Siege of Gibraltar, 1781 797
      (*From* ' European Magazine,' vol. ii.)

327. Costumes of persons of quality, about 1783 . . . 800
      (*From* ' European Magazine,' vol. v.)

328. Costumes of gentlefolk, about 1784 807
      (*From* ' European Magazine,' vol. v.)

329. Society at Vauxhall 809
      (*From an aquatint after T. Rowlandson, 1785*)

FIG.		PAGE
330.	Regulation musket, 1786, popularly known as Brown Bess .	811
	(*From Sir S. Scott's* ' History of the British Army ')	
331.	Pitt speaking in the House of Commons	812
	(*From Hickel's painting in the National Portrait Gallery*)	
332.	Lock on a Canal	814
	(*From Elmes's* ' Metropolitan Improvements,' 1827)	
333.	James Brindley	815
	(*From the portrait by Parsons engraved in Taylor's* 'National Biography')	
334.	Arkwright	816
	(*From a painting by Wright of Derby in the National Portrait Gallery*)	
335.	Crompton	817
	(*From a painting by Allingham engraved in Taylor's* 'National Biography')	
336.	Uniform of sailors about 1790	829
	(*From a caricature by Rowlandson, and a broadside of* 1790)	
337.	Head-dress of a lady (Mrs. Abington) about 1778 . .	839
	(*From* ' European Magazine,' vol. xxxiii.)	
338.	The Union Jack in use since 1801	842
	(*From Boutell's* ' English Heraldry ')	
339.	William Pitt	843
	(*From the bust by Nollekens in the National Portrait Gallery*)	
340.	Royal arms as borne from 1714 to 1801 . . .	844
341.	Royal arms as borne from 1801 to 1816 . . .	844
342.	Royal arms as borne from 1816 to 1837 . . .	844
343.	Greathead's lifeboat, 1803	845
	(*From* ' European Magazine,' vol. xliii.)	
344.	The Old East India House in 1803	846
	(*From* ' European Magazine,' vol. xliii.)	
345.	The old Houses of Parliament and Westminster Abbey, 1803	847
	(*From a contemporary engraving*)	
346.	The King in the House of Lords, 1804 . . .	850
	(*From* ' Modern London ')	
347.	Napoleon's medal struck to commemorate the invasion of England	851
	(*From a cast in the British Museum*)	
348.	Hyde Park on a Sunday, 1804	852
	(*From* ' Modern London ')	
349.	Lord Nelson	853
	(*From the picture by L. F. Abbott in the National Portrait Gallery*)	
350.	Fox	856
	(*From his bust by Nollekens in the National Portrait Gallery*)	
351.	The taking of Curaçao in 1807	861
	(*From an engraving of* 1809)	
352.	The Court of King's Bench in 1810	866
	(*From Pennant's* ' Some Account of London ')	
353.	Grenadier in the time of the Peninsular War . . .	870
	(*From Raikes's* ' First Regiment of Militia ')	
354.	Waterloo Bridge ; opened June 18, 1817, built by Rennie .	878
	(*From Elmes's* ' Metropolitan Improvements ')	
355.	George III. in old age	881
	(*From C. Turner's mezzotint*)	
356.	George IV.	883
	(*From an unfinished portrait by Lawrence in the National Portrait Gallery*)	

FIG.   PAGE

357. Lord Byron 886
(From an engraving after a painting by Sanders)

358. Sir Walter Scott 888
(From a photograph of a painting by Colvin Smith in Scott Memorials)

359. Wordsworth at the age of 28 889
(From a drawing by R. Hancock in the National Portrait Gallery)

360. Canning ; from Stewardson's portrait . . . 892
(From Taylor's ' National Biography ')

361. Apsley House, the residence of the Duke of Wellington, in 1829 . 897
(From Elmes's ' Metropolitan Improvements ')

362. William IV. ; from a portrait by Dawe . . . 899
(From Taylor's ' National Portrait Gallery ')

363. The Duke of Wellington 900
(From a bust by J. Francis in the National Portrait Gallery)

364. Earl Grey 901

365. Viscount Melbourne 902

366. Lord Palmerston 904
(All from Hayter's picture of ' The Meeting of the First Reformed Parliament, Feb. 5, 1833,' in the National Portrait Gallery)

367. An early steamboat 906
(From the ' Instructor ' of 1833)

368. Engine employed at the Killingworth Colliery, familiarly known as ' Puffing Billy ' 907
(From a photograph by Valentine & Sons, Dundee)

369. No. 1 Engine of the Stockton and Darlington Railway . 907
(From a photograph by Valentine & Sons, Dundee, of the original at Gateshead)

370. St. Luke's, Chelsea, designed by Savage, and built in 1824 . 908
(From Elmes's ' Metropolitan Improvements ')

371. Banner of the Royal arms as borne since 1837 . . 914
(From Boutell's ' English Heraldry ')

372. Queen Victoria : after a portrait by Lane . . 915
(From the engraving by Thompson)

373. Lord John Russell 917
(From a painting by Sir F. Grant)

374. The New Houses of Parliament . . . 919
(From a photograph by Valentine & Sons, Dundee)

375. Sir Robert Peel 932
(From the bust by Noble in the National Portrait Gallery)

376. The Britannia Tubular Railway Bridge, opened in 1850 . 937
(From a photograph by Valentine & Sons, Dundee)

377. St. George's Hall, Liverpool, completed in 1859 . 942
(From a photograph by Valentine & Sons, Dundee)

378. The Victoria Cross, instituted in 1856 . . . 947
(From Boutell's ' English Heraldry ')

GENEALOGICAL TABLES

I

ENGLISH KINGS FROM ECGBERHT TO HENRY I.

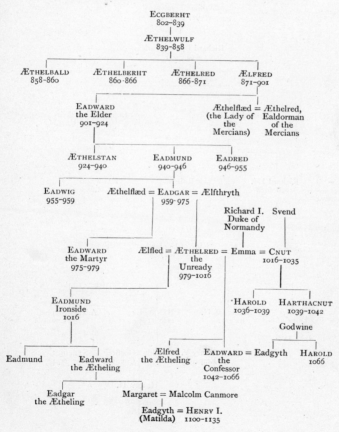

ECGBERHT
802–839

ÆTHELWULF
839–858

ÆTHELBALD 858–860 · ÆTHELBERHT 860–866 · ÆTHELRED 866–871 · ÆLFRED 871–901

EADWARD the Elder 901–924 · Æthelflæd (the Lady of the Mercians) = Æthelred, Ealdorman of the Mercians

ÆTHELSTAN 924–940 · EADMUND 940–946 · EADRED 946–955

EADWIG 955–959 · Æthelflæd = EADGAR = Ælfthryth 959–975

Richard I. Duke of Normandy · Svend

EADWARD the Martyr 975–979 · Ælfled = ÆTHELRED the Unready 979–1016 = Emma = CNUT 1016–1035

EADMUND Ironside 1016 · HAROLD 1036–1039 · HARTHACNUT 1039–1042

Godwine

Eadmund · Eadward the Ætheling · Ælfred the Ætheling · EADWARD the Confessor 1042–1066 = Eadgyth · HAROLD 1066

Eadgar the Ætheling · Margaret = Malcolm Canmore

Eadgyth (Matilda) = HENRY I. 1100–1135

II

GENEALOGY OF THE NORMAN DUKES AND OF THE KINGS OF ENGLAND FROM THE CONQUEST TO HENRY VII.

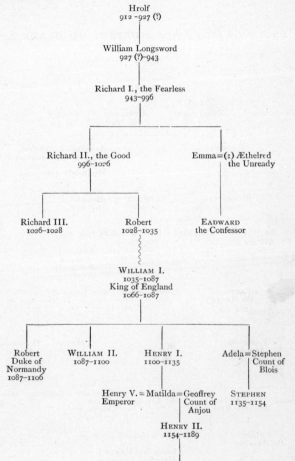

Hrolf
912–927 (?)

William Longsword
927 (?)–943

Richard I., the Fearless
943–996

Richard II., the Good   Emma=(1) Æthelred
996–1026   the Unready

Richard III.   Robert   EADWARD
1026–1028   1028–1035   the Confessor

WILLIAM I.
1035–1087
King of England
1066–1087

Robert   WILLIAM II.   HENRY I.   Adela=Stephen
Duke of   1087–1100   1100–1135   Count of
Normandy   Blois
1087–1106

Henry V.=Matilda=Geoffrey   STEPHEN
Emperor   Count of   1135–1154
                    Anjou

HENRY II.
1154–1189

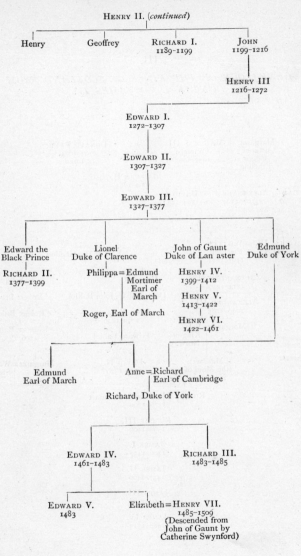

HENRY II. (*continued*)

Henry   Geoffrey   RICHARD I.   JOHN
                       1189-1199   1199-1216

HENRY III
1216-1272

EDWARD I.
1272-1307

EDWARD II.
1307-1327

EDWARD III.
1327-1377

Edward the   Lionel   John of Gaunt   Edmund
Black Prince   Duke of Clarence   Duke of Lan aster   Duke of York

RICHARD II.   Philippa=Edmund   HENRY IV.
1377-1399   Mortimer   1399-1412
                            Earl of
                            March   HENRY V.
                                         1413-1422
                    Roger, Earl of March
                                         HENRY VI.
                                         1422-1461

Edmund   Anne=Richard
Earl of March   Earl of Cambridge

Richard, Duke of York

EDWARD IV.   RICHARD III.
1461-1483   1483-1485

EDWARD V.   Elizabeth=HENRY VII.
1483   1485-1509
                              (Descended from
                              John of Gaunt by
                              Catherine Swynford)

III

GENEALOGY OF THE KINGS OF SCOTLAND FROM DUNCAN I. TO JAMES IV.

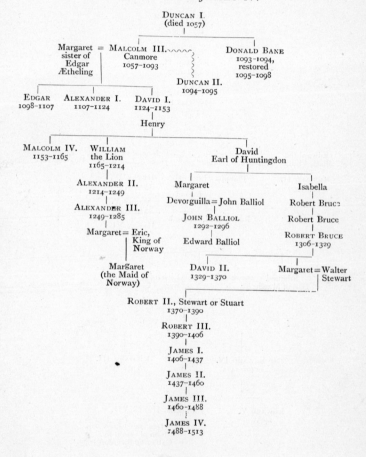

IV

KINGS AND QUEENS OF ENGLAND (AFTER 1541 OF ENGLAND AND IRELAND) FROM HENRY VII. TO ELIZABETH.

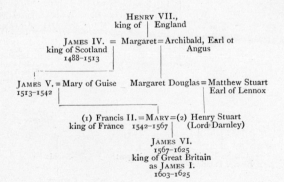

HENRY VII. = Elizabeth
1485–1509   of York

Arthur = Catharine = HENRY VIII. = (2) Anne Boleyn = (3) Jane Seymour
Prince of   of Aragon   1509–1547
Wales

MARY I.   ELIZABETH   EDWARD VI.
1553–1559   1558–1603   1547–1553

V

KINGS OF SCOTLAND FROM JAMES IV. TO JAMES VI.

HENRY VII.,
king of | England

JAMES IV. = Margaret = Archibald, Earl of
king of Scotland   Angus
1488–1513

JAMES V. = Mary of Guise   Margaret Douglas = Matthew Stuart
1513–1542   Earl of Lennox

(1) Francis II. = MARY = (2) Henry Stuart
king of France   1542–1567   (Lord Darnley)

JAMES VI.
1567–1625
king of Great Britain
as JAMES I.
1603–1625

VI

KINGS OF GREAT BRITAIN AND IRELAND FROM JAMES I. TO GEORGE I.

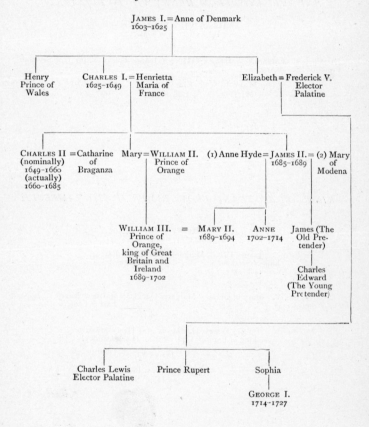

VII

KINGS AND QUEENS OF GREAT BRITAIN AND IRELAND
FROM GEORGE I. TO VICTORIA

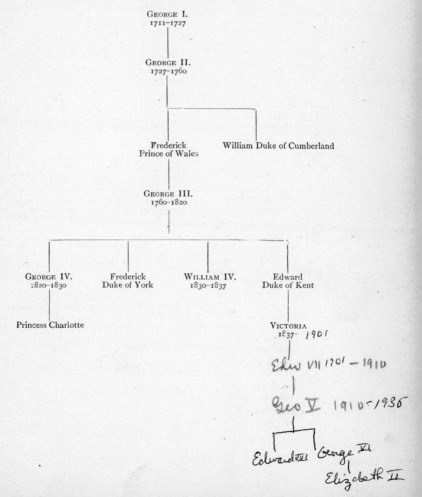

GEORGE I.
1711–1727

GEORGE II.
1727–1760

Frederick
Prince of Wales   William Duke of Cumberland

GEORGE III.
1760–1820

GEORGE IV.   Frederick   WILLIAM IV.   Edward
1820–1830   Duke of York   1830–1837   Duke of Kent

Princess Charlotte   VICTORIA
1837– *1901*

Edw VII 1701 – 1910

Geo V 1910–1935

Edward VIII   *George VI*

Elizabeth II

VIII

GENEALOGY OF THE KINGS OF FRANCE FROM HUGH CAPET TO LOUIS XII.

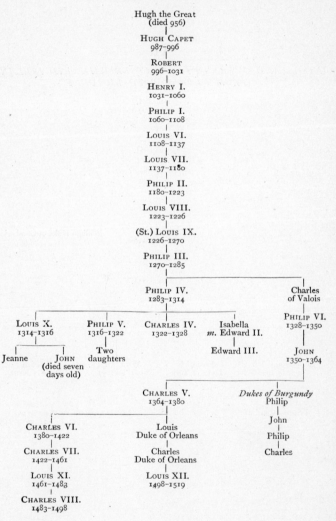

Hugh the Great
(died 956)
|
HUGH CAPET
987–996
|
ROBERT
996–1031
|
HENRY I.
1031–1060
|
PHILIP I.
1060–1108
|
LOUIS VI.
1108–1137
|
LOUIS VII.
1137–1180
|
PHILIP II.
1180–1223
|
LOUIS VIII.
1223–1226
|
(St.) LOUIS IX.
1226–1270
|
PHILIP III.
1270–1285

PHILIP IV.   Charles
1283–1314   of Valois

LOUIS X.   PHILIP V.   CHARLES IV.   Isabella   PHILIP VI.
1314–1316   1316–1322   1322–1328   *m.* Edward II.   1328–1350

Jeanne   JOHN   Two   Edward III.   JOHN
       (died seven daughters   1350–1364
        days old)

CHARLES V.   *Dukes of Burgundy*
1364–1380   Philip

CHARLES VI.   Louis   John
1380–1422   Duke of Orleans
CHARLES VII.   Charles   Philip
1422–1461   Duke of Orleans
LOUIS XI.   LOUIS XII.   Charles
1461–1483   1498–1519
CHARLES VIII.
1483–1498

IX.

GENEALOGY OF THE KINGS OF FRANCE FROM LOUIS XII. TO LOUIS XIV., SHOWING THEIR DESCENT FROM LOUIS IX.

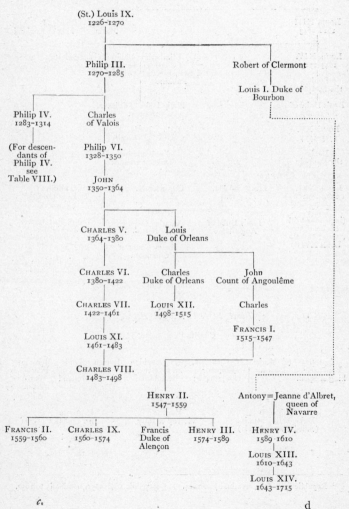

(St.) Louis IX.
1226–1270

Philip III.
1270–1285

Robert of Clermont

Louis I. Duke of Bourbon

Philip IV.
1283–1314

Charles
of Valois

(For descendants of Philip IV. see Table VIII.)

Philip VI.
1328–1350

JOHN
1350–1364

CHARLES V.
1364–1380

Louis
Duke of Orleans

CHARLES VI.
1380–1422

Charles
Duke of Orleans

John
Count of Angoulême

CHARLES VII.
1422–1461

LOUIS XII.
1498–1515

Charles

LOUIS XI.
1461–1483

FRANCIS I.
1515–1547

CHARLES VIII.
1483–1498

HENRY II.
1547–1559

Antony = Jeanne d'Albret, queen of Navarre

FRANCIS II.
1559–1560

CHARLES IX.
1560–1574

Francis
Duke of Alençon

HENRY III.
1574–1589

HENRY IV.
1589–1610

LOUIS XIII.
1610–1643

LOUIS XIV.
1643–1715

X

KINGS OF FRANCE FROM HENRY IV. TO LOUIS PHILIPPE

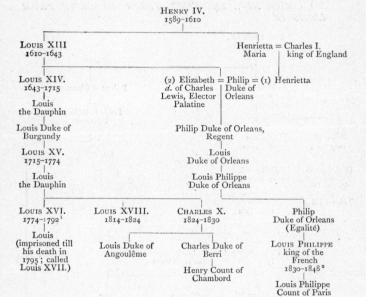

HENRY IV.
1589–1610

LOUIS XIII
1610–1643

Henrietta = Charles I.
Maria │ king of England

LOUIS XIV.
1643–1715

(2) Elizabeth = Philip = (1) Henrietta
d. of Charles │ Duke of
Lewis, Elector │ Orleans
Palatine

Louis
the Dauphin

Louis Duke of
Burgundy

Philip Duke of Orleans,
Regent

LOUIS XV.
1715–1774

Louis
Duke of Orleans

Louis
the Dauphin

Louis Philippe
Duke of Orleans

LOUIS XVI.
1774–1792 [1]

LOUIS XVIII.
1814–1824

CHARLES X.
1824–1830

Philip
Duke of Orleans
(Egalité)

Louis
(imprisoned till
his death in
1795; called
Louis XVII.)

Louis Duke of
Angoulême

Charles Duke of
Berri

LOUIS PHILIPPE
king of the
French
1830–1848 [2]

Henry Count of
Chambord

Louis Philippe
Count of Paris

XI

THE BONAPARTE FAMILY

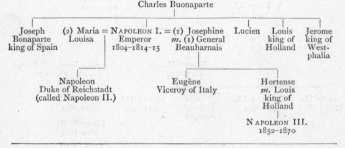

Charles Buonaparte

Joseph
Bonaparte
king of Spain

(2) Maria = NAPOLEON I. = (1) Josephine
Louisa │ Emperor │ *m.* (1) General
│ 1804–1814–15 │ Beauharnais

Lucien

Louis
king of
Holland

Jerome
king of
West-
phalia

Napoleon
Duke of Reichstadt
(called Napoleon II.)

Eugène
Viceroy of Italy

Hortense
m. Louis
king of
Holland

NAPOLEON III.
1852–1870

---

[1] Republic 1792–1799, nominally to 1804.   [2] Republic 1848–1851, nominally to 1852.

XII

GENEALOGY OF THE KINGS OF SPAIN FROM FERDINAND AND ISABELLA TO CHARLES II.

Maximilian I.
Emperor

FERDINAND = ISABELLA
king of Aragon   queen of
1479-1516   Castile
                  1474-1504

PHILIP I. = Juana   Catharine = (1) Arthur, Prince of Wales
Archduke of   (2) Henry VIII. king of England
Austria,
king of Castile
1504-1506

CHARLES I.   Ferdinand I.
(the Emperor Charles V.)   Emperor
king of Castile, 1506-1556,
king of Aragon, 1516-1556

PHILIP II.
1556-1598

PHILIP III.
1598-1621

PHILIP IV.
1621-1665

CHARLES II.
1665-1700

XIII

KINGS OF SPAIN FROM PHILIP V.

PHILIP V.
1700–1724 (abdicates)
(resumes the crown) 1725–1746

LUIS 1724–1725	FERDINAND VI. 1746–1759	CHARLES III. 1759–1783

CHARLES IV.
1788–1808

FERDINAND VII.
1814–1833

ISABELLA
1833–1868 [1]

Alfonso XII
1874–1885

Alfonso XIII.
1886–

XIV

GENEALOGY OF THE GERMAN BRANCH OF THE HOUSE OF AUSTRIA FROM FERDINAND I. TO LEOPOLD I.

(The dates given are those during which an archduke was emperor.)

FERDINAND I.
1536–1564

MAXIMILIAN II.   Charles
1564–1576   Duke of Styria

RUDOLPH II. 1576–1612	MATTHIAS 1612–1619	FERDINAND II. 1619–1635

FERDINAND III.
1635–1658

LEOPOLD I.
1658–1705

[1] Provisional Government 1868
  Regency of Marshal Serrano 1869
  King AMADEO 1870–73
  Republic 1873–74

XV

THE GERMAN BRANCH OF THE HOUSE OF AUSTRIA FROM LEOPOLD I.

(The dates given are those during which an archduke was emperor.)

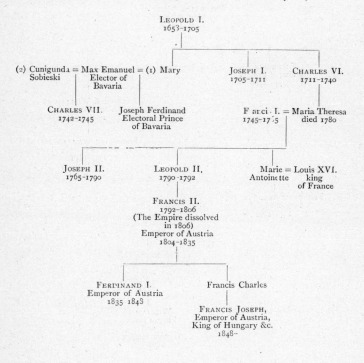

LEOPOLD I.
1653–1705

(2) Cunigunda = Max Emanuel = (1) Mary   JOSEPH I.   CHARLES VI.
Sobieski   Elector of   1705–1711   1711–1740
        Bavaria

CHARLES VII.   Joseph Ferdinand   Francis I. = Maria Theresa
1742–1745   Electoral Prince   1745–1765   died 1780
       of Bavaria

JOSEPH II.   LEOPOLD II.   Marie = Louis XVI.
1765–1790   1790–1792   Antoinette   king
                                  of France

FRANCIS II.
1792–1806
(The Empire dissolved
in 1806)
Emperor of Austria
1804–1835

FERDINAND I.   Francis Charles
Emperor of Austria
1835 1848

FRANCIS JOSEPH,
Emperor of Austria,
King of Hungary &c.
1848–

XVI

KINGS OF PRUSSIA AND GERMAN EMPERORS

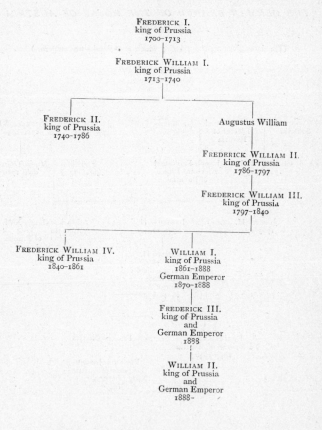

FREDERICK I.
king of Prussia
1700–1713

FREDERICK WILLIAM I.
king of Prussia
1713–1740

FREDERICK II.
king of Prussia
1740–1786

Augustus William

FREDERICK WILLIAM II.
king of Prussia
1786–1797

FREDERICK WILLIAM III.
king of Prussia
1797–1840

FREDERICK WILLIAM IV.
king of Prussia
1840–1861

WILLIAM I.
king of Prussia
1861–1888
German Emperor
1870–1888

FREDERICK III.
king of Prussia
and
German Emperor
1888

WILLIAM II.
king of Prussia
and
German Emperor
1888–

XVII

KINGS OF ITALY

Charles Albert
king of Sardinia
1831–1849

Victor Emmanuel
king of Sardinia
1849–1861
king of Italy
1861–1878

Humbert
king of Italy
1878–

XVIII

THE TZARS OR EMPERORS OF RUSSIA FROM ALEXIS

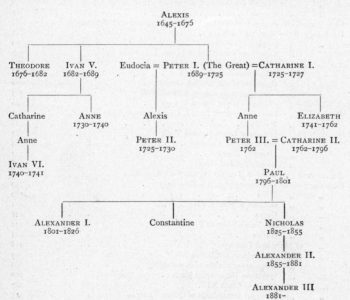

Alexis
1645–1675

Theodore 1676–1682   Ivan V. 1682–1689   Eudocia = Peter I. (The Great) 1689–1725 = Catharine I. 1725–1727

Catharine   Anne 1730–1740   Alexis   Anne   Elizabeth 1741–1762

Anne   Peter II. 1725–1730   Peter III. 1762 = Catharine II. 1762–1796

Ivan VI. 1740–1741

Paul 1796–1801

Alexander I. 1801–1826   Constantine   Nicholas 1825–1855

Alexander II. 1855–1881

Alexander III 1881–

XIX

GENEALOGY OF THE PRINCES OF ORANGE FROM WILLIAM I. TO WILLIAM III.

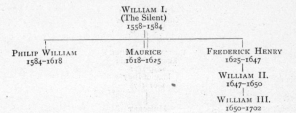

WILLIAM I.
(The Silent)
1558–1584

PHILIP WILLIAM   MAURICE   FREDERICK HENRY
1584–1618   1618–1625   1625–1647

WILLIAM II.
1647–1650

WILLIAM III.
1650–1702

SHORTER AND SOMETIMES MORE DETAILED GENEALOGIES
will be found in the following pages.

		PAGE
Genealogy of the principal Northumbrian kings	. . . . .	41
,, ,, English kings from Ecgberht to Eadgar	. . . .	56
,, ,, English kings from Eadgar to Eadgar the Ætheling	. .	78
,, ,, Danish kings	. .	83
Genealogical connection between the Houses of England and Normandy	. .	84
Genealogy of the Mercian Earls	. .	85
,, ,, family of Godwine . .	. .	89
,, ,, Conqueror's sons and children	. . .	131
,, ,, sons and grandchildren of Henry II.	. . .	156
,, ,, John's sons and grandsons . .	. . .	208
,, ,, claimants of the Scottish throne	. . .	216
,, ,, more important sons of Edward III.	. . .	265
,, ,, claimants of the throne in 1399 .	. . .	286
,, ,, kings of Scotland from Robert Bruce to James I.	. . .	295
,, ,, Nevills	. .	324
,, ,, Houses of Lancaster and York .	. . .	327
,, ,, Beauforts and Tudors . . .	. .	335
,, ,, House of York	. .	337
,, ,, Woodvilles and Greys . . .	. .	338
Abbreviated genealogy of Henry VII. and his competitors	. . .	344
Genealogy of the Houses of Spain and Burgundy .	. . .	349
,, ,, Poles	. .	399
,, ,, children of Henry VIII. .	. . .	411
,, ,, Greys	. .	421
,, ,, last Valois kings of France .	. . .	433
,, ,, Guises	. .	435
,, of Mary and Darnley	. .	438
,, of the descendants of Charles I. .	. . .	609
,, ,, claimants of the Spanish monarchy	. . .	669
,, ,, first three Hanoverian kings .	. .	702
,, ,, family of Louis XIV. . .	. .	707
,, ,, principal descendants of Queen Victoria	. .	925

HISTORY OF ENGLAND

———◆◆———

PART I

ENGLAND BEFORE THE NORMAN CONQUEST

———

CHAPTER I

PREHISTORIC AND ROMAN BRITAIN

LEADING DATES

Cæsar's first invasion	B.C. 55
Invasion of Aulus Plautius	A.D. 43
Recall of Agricola	84
Severus in Britain	208
End of the Roman Government	410

1. **Palæolithic Man of the River-Drift.**—Countless ages ago, there was a period of time to which geologists have given the name of the Pleistocene Age. The part of the earth's surface afterwards called Britain was then attached to the Continent, so that animals could pass over on dry land. The climate was much colder than it is now, and it is known from the bones which have been dug up that the country was inhabited by wolves, bears, mammoths, woolly rhinoceroses, and other creatures now extinct. No human remains have been found amongst these bones, but there is no doubt that men existed contemporaneously with their deposit, because, in the river drift, or gravel washed down by rivers, there have been discovered flints sharpened by chipping, which can only have been produced by the hand of man. The men who used them are known as Palæolithic, or the men of ancient stone, because these stone implements are rougher and therefore older than others which have

B

been discovered. These Palæolithic men of the river drift were a race of stunted savages who did not cultivate the ground, but lived on the animals which they killed, and must have had great difficulty in procuring food, as they did not know how to make handles for their sharpened flints, and must therefore have had to hold them in their hands.

Palæolithic flint scraper from Icklingham, Suffolk. (Evans.)

2. **Cave-dwelling Palæolithic Man.**—This race was succeeded by another which dwelt in caves. They, as well as their predecessors, are known as Palæolithic men, as their weapons were still very rude. As, however, they had learnt to make handles for them, they could construct arrows, harpoons, and javelins. They also made awls and needles of stone ; and, what is more remarkable, they possessed a decided artistic power, which enabled them to indicate by a few vigorous scratches the forms of horses, mammoths, reindeer, and other animals. Vast heaps of rubbish still exist in various parts of Europe, which are found to consist of the bones, shells, and other refuse thrown out by these later Palæolithic men, who had no reverence for the dead, casting out the bodies of their relations to decay with as little thought as they threw away oyster-shells or

Palæolithic flint implement from Hoxne, Suffolk.

reindeer-bones.   Traces of Palæolithic men of this type have been found as far north as Derbyshire.   Their descendants are no longer to be met with in these islands.   The Eskimos of the extreme north

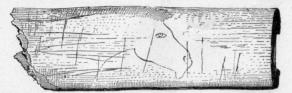

Engraved bone from Cresswell Crags, Derbyshire, now in the British Museum (full size).

of America, however, have the same artistic faculty and the same disregard for the dead, and it has therefore been supposed that the cave-dwelling men were of the race to which the modern Eskimos belong.

3. **Neolithic Man.**—Ages passed away during which the climate became more temperate, and the earth's surface in these regions sank to a lower level.   The seas afterwards known as the North Sea and the English Channel flowed over the depression ; and an island was thus formed out of land which had once been part of the con- tinent.   After this process had taken place, a third race appeared, which must have crossed the sea in rafts or canoes, and which took the place of the Palæolithic men.   They are known as Neo-

Neolithic flint arrow-head from Rudstone, Yorks.   (Evans.)

Neolithic celt or cutting instrument from Guernsey.
(Evans.)

lithic, or men of the new stone age, because their stone implements were of a newer kind, being polished and more efficient than those of their predecessors.   They had, therefore, the advantage of supe-

rior weapons, and perhaps of superior strength, and were able
to overpower those whom they found in the island.　With their

stone axes they made
clearings in the woods
in which to place their
settlements.　They
brought with them do-
mestic animals, sheep
and goats, dogs and
pigs.　They spun
thread with spindle
and distaff, and wove
it into cloth upon a
loom.　They grew corn
and manufactured a

Neolithic axe from Winterbourn Steepleton, Dorset.
(Evans.)

rude kind of pottery.　Each tribe lived in a state of war with its
neighbours.　A tribe when attacked in force took shelter on the
hills in places of refuge, which were surrounded by lofty mounds
and ditches.　Many of these places of refuge are still to be seen,
as, for instance, the one which bears the name of Maiden Castle,
near Dorchester.　On the open hills, too, are still to be found the

Early British Pottery.

long barrows which the Neolithic men raised over the dead.　There
is little doubt that these men, whose way of life was so superior to
that of their Eskimo-like predecessors, were of the race now known

as Iberian, which at one time inhabited a great part of Western Europe, but which has since mingled with other races. The Basques of the Pyrenees are the only Iberians who still preserve anything like purity of descent, though even the Basques have in them blood the origin of which is not Iberian.

4. Celts and Iberians. — The Iberians were followed by a swarm of new-comers called Celts. The Celts belong to a group of races sometimes known as the Aryan group, to which also belong Teutons, Slavonians, Italians, Greeks, and the chief ancient races of Persia and India. The Celts were the first to arrive in the West, where they seized upon lands in Spain, in Gaul, and in Britain, which the Iberians had occupied before them. They did not, however, destroy the Iberians altogether. However careful a conquering tribe may be to preserve the purity of its blood, it rarely succeeds in doing so. The con-

Early British Pottery

querors are sure to preserve some of the men of the conquered race as slaves, and a still larger number of young and comely women who become the mothers of their children. In time the slaves and the children learn to speak the language of their masters or fathers. Thus every European population is derived from many races.

5. **The Celts in Britain.**—The Celts were fair-haired and taller than the Iberians, whom they conquered or displaced. They had the advantage of being possessed of weapons of bronze, for which even the polished stone weapons of the Iberians were no match. They burned instead of burying their dead, and raised over the ashes those round barrows which are still to be found intermingled with the long barrows of the Iberians.

6. **Goidels and Britons.**—The earliest known name given to this island was Albion. It is uncertain whether the word is of Celtic or of Iberian origin. The later name Britain is derived from a second swarm of Celts called Brythons or Britons, who after a long interval followed the first Celtic immigration. The descendants of these first immigrants are distinguished from the new-comers by the name of Goidels, and it is probable that they were at one time settled in Britain as well as in Ireland, and that they were pushed across the sea into Ireland by the stronger and more civilised Britons. At all events, when history begins Goidels were only to be found in Ireland, though at a

Bronze celt from the Isle of Harty, Kent (⅓).

Bronze lance-head found in Ireland.

Bronze caldron found in Ireland.

later time they colonised a part of what is now known as Scotland, and sent some offshoots into Wales. At present the languages derived from that of the Goidels are the Gaelic of the Highlands, the Manx of the Isle of Man, and the Erse of Ireland. The only language now spoken in the British Isles which is derived from that of the Britons is the Welsh ; but the old Cornish language, which was spoken nearly up to the close of the eighteenth century, came from the same stock. It is therefore likely that the Britons pushed the Goidels northward and westward, as the Goidels had

View of Stonehenge. (From a photograph.)

formerly pushed the Iberians in the same directions. It was most likely that the Britons erected the huge stone circle of Stonehenge on Salisbury Plain, though it is not possible to speak with certainty. That of Avebury is of an earlier date and uncertain origin. Both were probably intended to serve as monuments of the dead, though it is sometimes supposed that they were also used as temples.

7. **Phœnicians and Greeks.**—The most civilised nations of the ancient world were those which dwelt round the Mediterranean Sea. It was long supposed that the Phœnicians came to Britain

from the coast of Syria, or from their colonies at Carthage and in the south of Spain, for the tin which they needed for the manufacture of bronze. The peninsula of Devon and Cornwall is the only part of the island which produces tin, and it has therefore been thought that the Cassiterides, or tin islands, which the Phœnicians visited, were to be found in that region. It has, however, been recently shown that the Cassiterides were most probably off the coast of Galicia, in Spain, and the belief that Phœnicians visited Britain for tin must therefore be considered to be very doubtful. The first educated visitor who reached Britain was Pytheas, a Greek, who was sent by the merchants of the Greek colony of Massalia (*Marseilles*) about **330** B.C. to make discoveries which might lead to the opening across Gaul of a trade-route between Britain and their city. It was probably in consequence of the information which he carried to Massalia on his return that there sprang up a trade in British tin. Another Greek, Posidonius, who came to Britain about two centuries after Pytheas, found this trade in full working order. The tin was brought by land from the present Devon or Cornwall to an island called Ictis, which was only accessible on foot after the tide had ebbed. This island was probably Thanet, which was in those days cut off from the mainland by an arm of the sea which could be crossed on foot at low water. From Thanet the tin was carried into Gaul across the straits, and was then conveyed in waggons to the Rhone to be floated down to the Mediterranean.

8. **Gauls and Belgians in Britain.**—During the time when this trade was being carried on, tribes of Gauls and Belgians landed in Britain. The Gauls were certainly, and the Belgians probably, of the same Celtic race as that which already occupied the island. The Gauls settled on the east coast as far as the Fens and the Wash, whilst the Belgians occupied the south coast, and pushed northwards towards the Somerset Avon. Nothing is known of the relations between the new-comers and the older Celtic inhabitants. Most likely those who arrived last contented themselves with mastering those whom they defeated, without attempting to exterminate them. At all events, states of some extent were formed by the conquerors. Thus the Cantii occupied the open ground to the north of the great forest which then filled the valley between the chalk ranges of the North and South Downs : the Trinobantes dwelt between the Lea and the Essex Stour : the Iceni occupied the peninsula between the Fens and the sea which was afterwards known as East Anglia (*Norfolk* and

Suffolk) ; and the Catuvellauni dwelt to the west of the Trinobantes, spreading over the modern Hertfordshire and the neighbouring districts.

9. **Culture and War.**—Though there were other states in
Britain, the tribes which have been named had the advantage of
being situated on the south-eastern part of the island, and therefore
of being in commercial communication with the continental Gauls
of their own race and language. Trade increased, and brought with
it the introduction of some things which the Britons would not have
invented for themselves. For instance, the inhabitants of the south-
east of Britain began to use gold coins and decorations in imita-

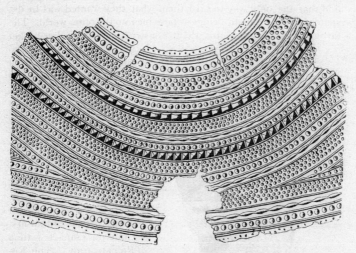

Part of a British gold corselet found at Mold.

tion of those which were then common in Gaul. Yet, in spite
of these improvements, even the most civilised Britons were still
in a rude and barbarous condition. They had no towns, but dwelt
in scattered huts. When they were hard pressed by an enemy
they took refuge in an open space cleared in the woods, and
surrounded by a high earthwork crowned by a palisade and
guarded by felled trees. When they went out to battle they dyed
their faces in order to terrify their enemies. Their warriors made
use of chariots, dashing in them along the front of the enemy's
line till they espied an opening in his ranks. They then leapt
down and charged on foot into the gap. Their charioteers in the

meanwhile drove off the horses to a safe distance, so as to be ready to take up their comrades if the battle went against them.

10. **Religion of the Britons.**—The Celtic races worshipped many gods. In Gaul, the Druids, who were the ministers of religion, taught the doctrine of the transmigration of souls, and even gave moral instruction to the young. In Ireland, and perhaps in Britain, they were conjurers and wizards. Both in Gaul and Britain they kept up the traditional belief which had once been prevalent in all parts of the world, that the gods could only be appeased by human sacrifices. It was supposed that they needed either to drink human blood or to be supplied with human slaves, and that the only way to give them what they wanted was to despatch as many human beings as possible into the other world. The favourite way of doing this was to construct a huge wicker basket in the shape of a man, to cram it with men and women, and to set it on fire. At other times a Druid would cut open a single human victim, and would imagine that he could foretell the future by inspecting the size and appearance of the entrails.

Julius Cæsar. (From a bust in the British Museum.)

11. **The Romans in Gaul.** B.C. **55.**—In the year 55 B.C. the Celts of south-eastern Britain first came in contact with a Roman army. The Romans were a civilised people, and had been engaged for some centuries in conquering the peoples living round the Mediterranean. They possessed disciplined armies, and a regular government. By the beginning of the year the Roman general, Gaius Julius Cæsar, had made himself master of Gaul. Then, after driving back with enormous slaughter two German tribes which had invaded Gaul, he crossed the Rhine, not because he wished to conquer Germany, but because he wished to strike

terror into the Germans in order to render them unwilling to renew
their attack. This march into Germany seems to have suggested
to Cæsar the idea of invading Britain. It is most unlikely that he
thought of conquering the island, as he had quite enough to do in
Gaul. What he really wanted was to prevent the Britons from
coming to the help of their kindred whom he had just subdued,
and he would accomplish this object best by landing on their
shores and showing them how formidable a Roman army was.

12. **Cæsar's First Invasion.** B.C. **55.**—Accordingly, towards
the end of August, Cæsar crossed the straits with about 10,000
men. There is some uncertainty about the place of his landing,
but he probably first appeared off the spot at which Dover now
stands, and then, being alarmed at the number of the Britons who
had crowded to defend the coast, made his way by sea to the site
of the modern Deal. There, too, his landing was opposed, but he
managed to reach the shore with his army. He soon found, however, that the season was too advanced to enable him to accomplish anything. A storm having damaged his shipping and driven
off the transports on which was embarked his cavalry, he returned
to Gaul.

13. **Cæsar's Second Invasion.** B.C. **54**—Cæsar had hitherto
failed to strike terror into the Britons. In the following year he
started in July, so as to have many weeks of fine weather before
him, taking with him as many as 25,000 foot and 2,000 horse.
After effecting a landing he pushed inland to the Kentish Stour,
where he defeated the natives and captured one of their stockades.
Good soldiers as the Romans were, they were never quite at home
on the sea, and Cæsar was recalled to the coast by the news that
the waves had dashed to pieces a large number of his ships. As
soon as he had repaired the damage he resumed his march. His
principal opponent was Cassivelaunus, the chief of the tribe of
the Catuvellauni, who had subdued many of the neighbouring
tribes, and whose stronghold was a stockade near the modern
St. Albans. This chief and his followers harassed the march
of the Romans with the rush of their chariots. If Cassivelaunus
could have counted upon the continued support of all his warriors,
he might perhaps have succeeded in forcing Cæsar to retreat, as the
country was covered with wood and difficult to penetrate. Many
of the tribes, however, which now served under him longed to free
themselves from his rule. First, the Trinobantes and then four
other tribes broke away from him and sought the protection of
Cæsar. Cæsar, thus encouraged, dashed at his stockade and

carried it by storm.   Cassivelaunus abandoned the struggle, gave
hostages to Cæsar, and promised to pay a yearly tribute.   On this
Cæsar returned to Gaul.   Though the tribute was never paid,
he had gained his object.   He had sufficiently frightened the British
tribes to make it unlikely that they would give him any annoyance
in Gaul.

14. **South-eastern Britain after Cæsar's Departure.** B.C. **54**—
A.D. **43.**—For nearly a century after Cæsar's departure Britain
was left to itself.   The Catuvellauni recovered the predominance
which they had lost   Their chieftain, Cunobelin, the original of
Shakspere's Cymbeline, is thought to have been a grandson of
Cassivelaunus.   He established his power over the Trinobantes
as well as over his own people, and made Camulodunum, the
modern Colchester, his headquarters.   Other tribes submitted to
him as they had submitted to his grandfather.   The prosperity
of the inhabitants of south-eastern Britain increased more rapidly
than the prosperity of their ancestors had increased before Cæsar's
invasion.   Traders continued to flock over from Gaul, bringing
with them a knowledge of the arts and refinements of civilised
life, and those arts and refinements were far greater now that
Gaul was under Roman rule than they had been when its Celtic
tribes were still independent.   Yet, in spite of the growth of trade,
Britain was still a rude and barbarous country.   Its exports were
but cattle and hides, corn, slaves, and hunting dogs, together with
a few dusky pearls.

15. **The Roman Empire.**—The Roman state was now a monarchy.   The Emperor was the head of the army, as well as the
head of the state.   Though he was often a cruel oppressor of the
wealthy personages who lived in Rome itself, and whose rivalry he
feared, he, for the most part, sought to establish his power by giving
justice to the provinces which had once been conquered by Rome,
but were now admitted to share in the advantages of good government which the Empire had to give.   One consequence of the conquest of nations by Rome was that there was now an end to cruel
wars between hostile tribes.   An army was stationed on the frontier
of the Empire to defend it against barbarian attacks.   In the interior the Roman peace, as it was called, prevailed, and there was
hardly any need of soldiers to keep order and to maintain obedience.

16. **The Invasion of Aulus Plautius.** A.D. **43.**—One question
which each Emperor had to ask himself was whether he would attempt to enlarge the limits of the Empire or not.   For a time each
Emperor had resolved to be content with the frontier which Cæsar

had left. There had consequently for many years been no thought of again invading Britain. At last the Emperor Claudius reversed this policy. There is reason to suppose that some of the British chiefs had made an attack upon the coasts of Gaul. However this may have been, Claudius in 43 sent Aulus Plautius against Togidumnus and Caratacus, the sons of Cunobelin, who were now ruling in their father's stead. Where one tribe has gained supremacy over others, it is always easy for a civilised power to gain allies amongst the tribes which have been subdued. Cæsar had overpowered Cassivelaunus by enlisting on his side the revolted Trinobantes, and Aulus Plautius now enlisted on his side the Regni, who dwelt in the present Sussex, and the Iceni, who dwelt in the present Norfolk and Suffolk. With their aid, Aulus Plautius, at the head of 40,000 men, defeated the sons of Cunobelin. Togidumnus was slain, and Caratacus driven into exile. The Romans then took possession of their lands, and, stepping into their place, established over the tribes chieftains who were now dependent on the Emperor instead of on Togidumnus and Caratacus. Claudius himself came for a brief visit to receive the congratulations of the army on the victory which his lieutenant had won. Aulus Plautius remained in Britain till 47. Before he left it the whole of the country to the south of a line drawn from the Wash to some point on the Severn had been subjugated. The mines of the Mendips and of the western peninsula were too tempting to be left unconquered, and it is probably their attraction which explains the extension of Roman power at so early a date over the hilly country in the west.

17. **The Colony of Camulodunum.**—In 47 Aulus Plautius was succeeded by Ostorius Scapula. He disarmed the tribes dwelling to the west of the Trent, whilst he attempted to establish the Roman authority more firmly over those whose territory lay to the east of that river. Amongst these later were the Iceni, who had been hitherto allowed to preserve their native government in dependence on the Roman power. The consequence was that they rose in arms. Ostorius overpowered them, and then sought to strengthen his hold upon the south-east of Britain by founding (51) a Roman colony at Camulodunum, which had formerly been the headquarters of Cunobelin. Roman settlers—for the most part discharged soldiers—established themselves in the new city, bringing with them all that belonged to Roman life with all its conveniences and luxuries. Roman temples, theatres, and baths quickly rose, and Ostorius might fairly expect that in Britain, as in Gaul, the native chiefs

would learn to copy the easy life of the new citizens, and would settle their quarrels in Roman courts of law instead of taking arms on their own behalf.

18. **The Conquests of Ostorius Scapula.**—Ostorius, however, was soon involved in fresh troubles.   Nothing is more difficult for a civilised power than to guard a frontier against barbarous tribes. Such tribes are accustomed to plunder one another, and they are quick to perceive that the order and peace which a civilised power establishes offers them a richer booty than is to be found elsewhere. The tribes beyond the line which Ostorius held were constantly breaking through to plunder the Roman territory, and he soon found that he must either allow the lands of Roman subjects to be plundered, or must carry war amongst the hostile tribes.   He naturally chose the latter alternative, and the last years of his government were spent in wars with the Ordovices of Central Wales, and with the Silures of Southern Wales.   The Silures were not only a most warlike people, but they were led by Caratacus, who had taken refuge with them after his defeat by Aulus Plautius in the east.   The mountainous region which these two tribes defended made it difficult to subdue them, and though Caratacus was defeated (**50**), and ultimately captured and sent as a prisoner to Rome, Ostorius did not succeed in effectually mastering his hardy followers.   The proof of his comparative failure lies in the fact that he established strong garrison towns along the frontier of the hilly region, which he would not have done unless he had considered it necessary to have a large number of soldiers ready to check any possible rising.   At the northern end of the line was Deva (*Chester*), at the southern was Isca Silurum (*Caerleon upon Usk*), and in each of which was placed a whole legion, about 5,000 men.   Between them was the smaller post of Uriconium, or more properly Viriconium (*Wroxeter*), the city of the Wrekin.

19. **Government of Suetonius Paullinus. 58.**—When Suetonius Paullinus arrived to take up the government, he resolved to complete the conquest of the west by an attack on Mona (*Anglesey*). In Mona was a sacred place of the Druids, who gave encouragement to the still independent Britons by their murderous sacrifices and their soothsayings.   When Suetonius attempted to land (**61**), a rabble of women, waving torches and shrieking defiance, rushed to meet him on the shore.   Behind them the Druids stood calling down on the intruders the vengeance of the gods.   At first the soldiers were terrified and shrunk back.   Then they recovered courage, and put to the sword or thrust into the flames the priests

and their female rout. The Romans were tolerant of the religion of the peoples whom they subdued, but they could not put up with the continuance of a cruel superstition whose upholders preached resistance to the Roman government.

20. **Boadicea's Insurrection. 61.**—At the very moment of success Suetonius was recalled hurriedly to the east. Roman officers and traders had misused the power which had been given them by the valour of Roman soldiers. Might had been taken for right, and the natives were stripped of their lands and property at the caprice of the conquerors. Those of the natives to whom anything was left were called upon to pay a taxation far too heavy for their means. When money was not to be found to satisfy the tax-gatherer, a Roman usurer was always at hand to proffer the required sum at enormous interest, after which the unhappy borrower who accepted the proposal soon found himself unable to pay the debt, and was stripped of all that he possessed to satisfy the cravings of the lender. Those who resisted this oppression were treated as the meanest criminals. Boadicea, the widow of Prasutagus, who had been the chief of the Iceni, was publicly flogged, and her two daughters were subjected to the vilest outrage. She called upon the whole Celtic population of the east and south to rise against the foreign tyrants. Thousands answered to her call, and the angry host rushed to take vengeance upon the colonists of Camulodunum. The colonists had neglected to fortify their city, and the insurgents, bursting in, slew by the sword or by torture men and women alike. The massacre spread wherever Romans were to be found. A Roman legion hastening to the rescue was routed, and the small force of cavalry attached to it alone succeeded in making its escape. Every one of the foot soldiers was slaughtered on the spot It is said that 70,000 Romans perished in the course of a few days.

21. **The Vengeance of Suetonius.**—Suetonius was no mean general, and he hastened back to the scene of destruction. He called on the commander of the legion at Isca Silurum to come to his help. Cowardice was rare in a Roman army, but this officer was so unnerved by terror that he refused to obey the orders of his general, and Suetonius had to march without him. He won a decisive victory at some unknown spot, probably not far from Camulodunum, and 80,000 Britons are reported to have been slain by the triumphant soldiery. Boadicea committed suicide by poison. The commander of the legion at Isca Silurum also put an end to his own life, in order to escape the punishment which he deserved.

Suetonius had restored the Roman authority in Britain, but it was to his failure to control his subordinates that the insurrection had been due, and he was therefore promptly recalled by the Emperor Nero. From that time no more is heard of the injustice of the Roman government.

22. **Agricola in Britain. 78– 84.**—Agricola, who arrived as governor in 78, took care to deal fairly with all sorts of men, and to make the natives thoroughly satisfied with his rule. He completed the conquest of the country afterwards known as Wales, and thereby pushed the western frontier of Roman Britain to the sea. Yet from the fact that he found it necessary still to leave garrisons at Deva and Isca Silurum, it may be gathered that the tribes occupying the hill country were not so thoroughly subdued as to cease to be dangerous. Although the idea entertained by Ostorius of making a frontier on land towards the west had thus been abandoned, it was still necessary to provide a frontier towards the north. Even before Agricola arrived it had been shown to be impossible to stop at the line between the Mersey and the Humber. Beyond that line was the territory of the Brigantes, who had for some time occupied the position which in the first years of the Roman conquest had been occupied by the Iceni—that is to say, they were in friendly dependence upon Rome, without being actually controlled by Roman authority. Before Agricola's coming disputes had arisen with them, and Roman soldiers had occupied their territory. Agricola finished the work of conquest. He now governed the whole of the country as far north as to the Solway and the Tyne, and he made Eboracum, the name of which changed in course of time into York, the centre of Roman power in the northern districts. A garrison was established there to watch for any danger which might come from the extreme north, as the garrisons of Deva and Isca Silurum watched for dangers which might come from the west.

23. **Agricola's Conquests in the North.**—Agricola thought that there would be no real peace unless the whole island was subdued. For seven years he carried on warfare with this object before him. He had comparatively little difficulty in reducing to obedience the country south of the narrow isthmus which separates the estuary of the Clyde from the estuary of the Forth. Before proceeding further he drew a line of forts across that isthmus to guard the conquered country from attack during his absence. He then made his way to the Tay, but he had not marched far up the valley of that river before he reached the edge of the Highlands. The Caledonians, as the Romans then called the

inhabitants of those northern regions, were a savage race, and the mountains in the recesses of which they dwelt were rugged and inaccessible, offering but little means of support to a Roman army. In 84 the Caledonians, who, like all barbarians when they first come in contact with a civilised people, were ignorant of the strength of a disciplined army, came down from their fortresses in the mountains into the lower ground. A battle was fought near the Graupian Hill, which seems to have been situated at the junction of the Isla and the Tay. Agricola gained a complete victory, but he was unable to follow the fugitives into their narrow glens, and he contented himself with sending his fleet to circumnavigate the northern shores of the island, so as to mark out the limits of the land which he still hoped to conquer. Before the fleet returned, however, he was recalled by the Emperor Domitian. It has often been said that Domitian was jealous of his success ; but it is possible that the Emperor really thought that the advantage to be gained by the conquest of rugged mountains would be more than counterbalanced by the losses which would certainly be incurred in consequence of the enormous difficulty of the task.

24. **The Roman Walls.**—Agricola, in addition to his line of forts between the Forth and the Clyde, had erected detached forts at the mouth of the valleys which issue from the Highlands, in order to hinder the Caledonians from plundering the lower country. In 119 the Emperor Hadrian visited Britain. He was more disposed to defend the Empire than to extend it, and though he did not abandon Agricola's forts, he also built further south a continuous earth work between the Solway and the Tyne. This wall, which formed a far stronger line of defence than the more northern forts, was

Commemorative tablet of the Second Legion found at Halton Chesters on the Roman Wall.

intended to serve as a second barrier to keep out the wild Caledonians if they succeeded in breaking through the first. At a later time a lieutenant of the Emperor, Antoninus Pius, who afterwards became Emperor himself, connected Agricola's forts between

C

View of part of the Roman Wall.

Ruins of a Turret on the Roman Wall.

the Forth and Clyde by a continuous earthwork.   In **208** the Emperor Severus arrived in Britain, and after strengthening still further the earthwork between the Forth and Clyde, and adding a stone wall to the more southern work of Hadrian, attempted to carry out the plans of Agricola by conquering the land of the Cale-donians.   Severus, however, failed as completely as Agricola had failed before him, and he died soon after his return to Eboracum.

25. **The Roman Province of Britain.**—Very little is known of the history of the Roman province of Britain, except that it made considerable progress in civilisation.   The Romans were great road-makers, and though their first object was to enable their

Part of the Roman Wall at Leicester.

soldiers to march easily from one part of the country to another, they thereby encouraged commercial intercourse.   Forests were to some extent cleared away by the sides of the new roads, and fresh ground was thrown open to tillage.   Mines were worked and country houses built, the remains of which are in some places still to be seen, and bear testimony to the increased well-being of a population which, excepting in the south-eastern part of the island, had at the arrival of the Romans been little removed from savagery.   Cities sprang up in great numbers.   Some of them were at first garrison towns, like Eboracum, Deva, and Isca Silurum. Others, like Verulamium, near the present St. Albans, occupied the sites of the old stockades once used as places of refuge by the Celts,

or, like Lindum, on the top of the hill on which Lincoln Cathedral
now stands, were placed in strongly defensible positions. Aquæ
Sulis, the modern Bath, owes its existence to its warm medicinal
springs. The chief port of commerce was Londinium, the modern
London. Attempts which have been made to explain its name by
the Celtic language have failed, and it is therefore possible that an
inhabited post existed there even before the Celts arrived. Its importance was, however, owing to its position, and that importance
was not of a kind to tell before a settled system of commercial inter-

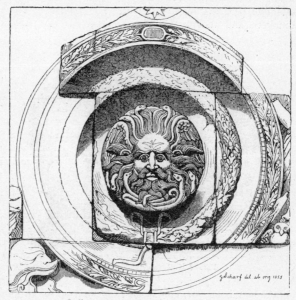

Pediment of a Roman temple found at Bath.

course sprang up. London was situated on the hill on which St.
Paul's now stands. There first, after the Thames narrowed into a
river, the merchant found close to the stream hard ground on which
he could land his goods. The valley for some distance above and
below it was then filled with a wide marsh or an expanse of water.
An old track raised above the marsh crossed the river by a ford at
Lambeth, but, as London grew in importance, a ferry was established where London Bridge now stands, and the Romans, in
course of time, superseded the ferry by a bridge. It is, therefore,

no wonder that the Roman roads both from the north and from the south converged upon London.   Just as Eboracum was a fitting centre for military operations directed to the defence of the northern frontier, London was the fitting centre of a trade carried on with the Continent, and the place would increase in importance in proportion to the increase of that trade.

26. **Extinction of Tribal Antagonism.** — The improvement of communications and the growth of trade and industry could not fail to influence the mind of the population.   Wars between tribes, which before the coming of the Romans had been the main employment of the young and hardy, were now things of the past. The mutual hatred which had grown out of them had died away, and even the very names of Trinobantes and Brigantes were almost forgotten.   Men who lived in the valley of the Severn came to look upon themselves as belonging to the same people as men who lived in the valleys of the Trent or the Thames.   The active and enterprising young men were attracted to the cities, at first by the novelty of the luxurious habits in which they were taught to indulge, but afterwards because they were allowed to take part in the management of local business.   In the time of the Emperor Caracalla, the son of Severus, every freeman born in the Empire was declared to be a Roman citizen, and long before that a large number of natives had been admitted to citizenship.   In each district a council was formed of the wealthier and more prominent inhabitants, and this council had to provide for the building of temples, the holding of festivals, the erection of fortifications, and the laying out

Roman altar from Rutchester.

of streets.   Justice was done between man and man according to the Roman law, which was the best law that the world had seen, and the higher Roman officials, who were appointed by the Emperor, took care that justice was done between city and city.   No one therefore, wished to oppose the Roman government or to bring back the old times of barbarism.

27. **Want of National Feeling.** – Great as was the progress made, there was something still wanting. A people is never at its best unless those who compose it have some object for which they can sacrifice themselves, and for which, if necessary, they will die. The Briton had ceased to be called upon to die for his tribe, and he was not expected to die for Britain. Britain had become a more comfortable country to live in, but it was not the business of its own inhabitants to guard it. It was a mere part of the vast Roman Empire, and it was the duty of the Emperors to see that the frontier was safely kept. They were so much afraid lest any particular province should wish to set up for itself and to break away from the Empire, that they took care not to employ soldiers born in that province for its protection. They sent British recruits to guard the Danube or the Euphrates, and Gauls, Spaniards, or Africans to guard the wall between the Solway and the Tyne, and the entrenchment between the Forth and the Clyde. Britons, therefore, looked on their own defence as something to be done for them by the Emperors, not as something to be done by themselves. They lived on friendly terms with one another, but they had nothing of what we now call patriotism.

28. **Carausius and Allectus. 288 – 296.** – In 288 Carausius, with the help of some pirates, seized on the government of Britain and threw off the authority of the Emperor. He was succeeded by Allectus, yet neither Carausius nor Allectus thought of making himself the head of a British nation. They called themselves Emperors and ruled over Britain alone, merely because they could not get more to rule over.

29. **Constantius and Constantine. 296 – 337.** — Allectus was over-thrown and slain by Constantius, who, however, did not rule, as Carausius and Allectus had done, by mere right of military superiority. The Emperor Diocletian (285—305) discovered that the whole Empire, stretching from the Euphrates to the Atlantic, was too extensive for one man to govern, and he therefore decreed that there should in future be four governors, two principal ones named Emperors (*Augusti*), and two subordinate ones named Cæsars. Constantius was first a Cæsar and afterwards an Emperor. He was set to govern Spain, Gaul, and Britain, but he afterwards became Emperor himself, and for some time established himself at Eboracum (*York*). Upon his death (306), his son Constantine, after much fighting, made himself sole Emperor (325), overthrowing the system of Dio-

cletian.   Yet in one respect he kept up Diocletian's arrangements.
He placed Spain, Gaul, and Britain together under a great officer
called a Vicar, who received orders from himself and who gave orders
to the officers who governed each of the three countries.   Under
the new system, as under the old, Britain was not treated as an independent country.   It had still to look for protection to an officer
who lived on the Continent, and was therefore apt to be more
interested in Gaul and Spain than he was in Britain.

30. **Christianity in Britain.**—-When the Romans put down the
Druids and their bloody sacrifices, they called the old Celtic gods
by Roman names, but made no further alteration in religious usages.
Gradually, however, Christianity spread amongst the Romans on
the Continent, and merchants or soldiers who came from the Continent introduced it into Britain.   Scarcely anything is known of
its progress in the island.   Alban is said to have been martyred
at Verulamium, and Julius and Aaron at Isca Silurum.   In **314**
three British bishops attended a council held at Arles in Gaul.
Little more than these few facts have been handed down, but there
is no doubt that there was a settled Church established in the island.
The Emperor Constantine acknowledged Christianity as the religion of the whole Empire.   The remains of a church of this period
have recently been discovered at Silchester.

31. **Weakness of the Empire.**—The Roman Empire in the
time of Constantine had the appearance rather than the reality of
strength.   Its taxation was very heavy, and there was no national
enthusiasm to lead men to sacrifice themselves in its defence.
Roman citizens became more and more unwilling to become soldiers
at all, and the Roman armies were now mostly composed of barbarians.   At the same time the barbarians outside the Empire were
growing stronger, as the tribes often coalesced into wide con-
federacies for the purpose of attacking the Empire.

32. **The Picts and Scots.**—The assailants of Britain on the
north and the west were the Picts and Scots.   The Picts were the
same as the Caledonians of the time of Agricola.   We do not know
why they had ceased to be called Caledonians.   The usual derivation of their name from the Latin *Pictus*, said to have been given
them because they painted their bodies, is inaccurate.   Opinions
differ whether they were Goidels with a strong Iberian strain,
or Iberians with a Goidelic admixture.   They were probably
Iberians, and at all events they were more savage than
the Britons had been before they were influenced by Roman
civilisation.   The Scots, who afterwards settled in what is

now known as Scotland, at that time dwelt in Ireland. Whilst the Picts, therefore, assailed the Roman province by land, and strove, not always unsuccessfully, to break through the walls which defended its northern frontier, the Scots crossed the Irish Sea in light boats to plunder and slay before armed assistance could arrive.

33. **The Saxons.** — The Saxons, who were no less deadly enemies of the Roman government, were as fierce and restless as the Picts and Scots, and were better equipped and better armed. At a later time they established themselves in Britain as conquerors and settlers, and became the founders of the English nation ; but at first they were only known as cruel and merciless pirates. In their long flat-bottomed vessels they swooped down upon some unde-fended part of the coast and carried off not only the property of wealthy Romans, but even men and women to be sold in the slave-market. The provincials who escaped related with peculiar horror how the Saxons were accustomed to torture to death one out of every ten of their captives as a sacrifice to their gods.

34. **Origin of the Saxons.**—The Saxons were the more dan-gerous because it was impossible for the Romans to reach them in their homes. They were men of Teutonic race, speaking one of the languages, afterwards known as Low German, which were once spoken in the whole of North Germany. The Saxon pirates were probably drawn from the whole of the sea coast stretching from the north of the peninsula of Jutland to the mouth of the Ems, and if so, there were amongst them Jutes, whose homes were in Jutland itself ; Angles, who inhabited Schleswig and Holstein ; and Saxons, properly so called, who dwelt about the mouth of the Elbe and further to the west. All these peoples afterwards took part in the conquest of southern Britain, and it is not unlikely that they all shared in the original piratical attacks. Whether this was the case or not, the pirates came from creeks and inlets outside the Roman Empire, whose boundary was the Rhine, and they could therefore only be successfully repressed by a power with a good fleet, able to seek out the aggressors in their own homes and to stop the mischief at its source.

35. **The Roman Defence.**—The Romans had always been weak at sea, and they were weaker now than they had been in earlier days. They were therefore obliged to content themselves with standing on the defensive. Since the time of Severus, Britain had been divided, for purposes of defence, into Upper and Lower Britain. Though there is no absolute certainty about the matter,

it is probable that Upper Britain comprised the hill country of the west and north, and that Lower Britain was the south-eastern part of the island, marked off by a line drawn irregularly from the Humber to the Severn.[1]   Lower Britain in the early days of the Roman conquest had been in no special need of military protection. In the fourth century it was exposed more than the rest of the island to the attacks of the Saxon pirates.   Fortresses were erected between the Wash and Beachy Head at every point at which an inlet of the sea afforded an opening to an invader.   The whole of this part of the coast became known as the Saxon Shore, because it was subjected to attacks from the Saxons, and a special officer known as the Count of the Saxon Shore was appointed to take charge of it.   An officer known as the Duke of the Britains (*Dux Britanniarum*) commanded the armies of Upper Britain ; whilst a third, who was a civilian, and superior in rank over the other two, was the Count of Britain, and had a general supervision of the whole country.

36. **End of the Roman Government. 383—410.**—In 383 Maximus, who was probably the Duke of the Britains, was proclaimed Emperor by his soldiers.   If he could have contented himself with defending Britain, it would have mattered little whether he chose to call himself an Emperor or a Duke.   Unhappily for the inhabitants of the island, not only did every successful soldier want to be an Emperor, but every Emperor wanted to govern the whole Empire.   Maximus, therefore, instead of remaining in Britain, carried a great part of his army across the sea to attempt a conquest of Gaul and Spain.   Neither he nor his soldiers ever returned, and in consequence the Roman garrison in the island was deplorably weakened.   Early in the fifth century an irruption of barbarians gave full employment to the army which defended Gaul, so that it was impossible to replace the forces which had followed Maximus by fresh troops from the Continent.   The Roman Empire was in fact breaking up.   The defence of Britain was left to the soldiers who remained in the island, and in 409 they proclaimed a certain Constantine Emperor.   Constantine, like Maximus, carried his soldiers across the Channel in pursuit of a wider empire than he could find in Britain.   He was himself murdered, and his soldiers, like those of Maximus, did not return.   In 410 the Britons implored the Emperor Honorius to send them help.   Honorius had enough

---

[1] There were also four smaller divisions, ultimately increased to five.   All that is known about their position is that they were not where they are placed in our atlases.

to do to ward off the attacks of barbarians nearer Rome, and announced to the Britons that they must provide for their own defence. From this time Britain ceased to form part of the Roman Empire.

CHAPTER II

THE ENGLISH SETTLEMENTS

LEADING DATES

Landing of the Jutes in Thanet	A.D.	449 ?
The West Saxons defeated at Mount Badon	.	520
The West Saxons take Sorbiodunum	.	552
Battle of Deorham	.	577
The West Saxons defeated at Faddiley	.	584

1. **Britain after the Departure of the Romans. 410—449?**—After the departure of the Romans, the Picts from the north and the Scots from Ireland continued their ravages, but though they caused terrible misery by slaughtering or dragging into slavery the inhabitants of many parts of the country, they did not succeed in making any permanent conquests. The Britons were not without a government and an armed force ; and their later history shows that they were capable of carrying on war for a long time against enemies more formidable than the Picts and Scots. Their rulers were known by the British title Gwledig, and probably held power in different parts of the island as the successors of the Roman Duke of the Britains and of the Roman Count of the Saxon Shore. Their power of resistance to the Picts and the Scots was, however, weakened by the impossibility of turning their undivided attention to these marauders, as at the same time that they had to defend the Roman Wall and the western coast against the Picts and Scots, they were exposed on the eastern coast to the attacks of the Saxon pirates.

2. **The Groans of the Britons.**—In their misery the thoughts of the Britons turned to those Roman legions who had defended their fathers so well. In **446** they appealed to Aëtius, the commander of the Roman armies, to deliver them from their destroyers. "The groans of the Britons" was the title which they gave to their appeal to him. "The barbarians," they wrote, "drive us to the sea ; the sea drives us back to the barbarians ; between them we are

exposed to two sorts of death : we are either slain or drowned." Aëtius had no men to spare, and he sent no help to the Britons. Before long the whole of Western Europe was overrun by barbarian tribes, the title of Emperor being retained only by the Roman Emperor who ruled from Constantinople over the East, his authority over the barbarians of the West being no more than nominal.

3. **The Conquest of Kent. 449** ?—It had been the custom of the Roman Empire to employ barbarians as soldiers in their armies, and Vortigern, the British ruler, now followed that bad example. In or about **449** a band of Jutish sea-rovers landed at Ebbsfleet, in the Isle of Thanet. According to tradition their leaders were Hengist and Horsa, names signifying the horse and the mare, which were not very likely to have been borne by real warriors. Whatever may have been the names of the chiefs, Vortigern took them into his service against the Picts, giving them the Isle of Thanet as a dwelling-place for themselves. With their help he defeated the Picts, but afterwards found himself unable to defend himself against his fierce auxiliaries. Thanet was still cut off from the mainland by an arm of the sea, and the Jutes were strong enough to hold it against all assailants. Their numbers rapidly increased as shiploads of their fellows landed, and they crossed the strait to win fresh lands from the Britons on the mainland of Kent. In several battles Vortigern was overpowered. His rival and successor, Ambrosius Aurelianus, whose name makes it probable that he was an upholder of the old Roman discipline, drove back the Jutes in turn. He did not long keep the upper hand, and in **465** he was routed utterly. The defeat of the British army was followed by an attack upon the great fortresses which had been erected along the Saxon Shore in the Roman times. The Jutes had no means of carrying them by assault, but they starved them out one by one, and some twenty-three years after their first landing, the whole of the coast of Kent was in their hands.

4. **The South Saxons. 477.**—The conquests of the Jutes stopped at the inlet of the sea now filled by Romney Marsh. To the south and west was the impenetrable Andred's Wood, which covered what is now known as the Weald. At its eastern extremity stood by the sea the strong fortified town of Anderida, which gave its name to the wood, the most westerly of the fortresses of the Saxon Shore still unconquered by the Jutes. It was at last endangered by a fresh pirate band—not of Jutes but of Saxons—which landed near Selsey, and fought its way eastwards, conquering the South Downs and the flat land between the South Downs and the sea, till it reached

Anderida. Anderida was starved out after a long blockade, and the Saxons, bursting in, 'slew all that dwelt therein, nor was there henceforth one Briton left.' To this day the Roman walls of Anderida stand round the site of the desolated city near the modern Pevensey. Its Saxon conquerors came to be known as the South Saxons, and their land as Sussex.

5. **The West Saxons and the East Saxons.**—Another swarm also of Saxons, called Gewissas, landed on the shore of Southampton Water. After a time they were reinforced by a body of Jutes, and though the Jutes formed settlements of their own in the Isle of Wight and on the mainland, the difference of race and language between them and the Gewissas was not enough to prevent the two tribes from coalescing. Ultimately Gewissas and Jutes became known as West Saxons, and established themselves in a district roughly corresponding with the modern Hampshire. Then, having attempted to penetrate further west, they were defeated at Mount Badon, probably Badbury Rings in Dorsetshire. Their overthrow was so complete as to check their advance for more than thirty years. Whilst the coast line from the inlet of the sea now filled by Romney Marsh to the western edge of Hampshire had thus been mastered by Saxons, others of the same stock, known as East Saxons, seized upon the low coast to the north of the Thames. From them the land was called Essex. Neither Saxons nor Jutes, however, were as yet able to penetrate far up the valley of the Thames, as the Roman settlement of London, surrounded by marshes, still blocked the way.

6. **The Anglian Settlements.**—The coast-line to the north of the East Saxons was seized at some unascertained dates by different groups of Angles. The land between the Stour and the great fen which in those days stretched far inland from the Wash was occupied by two of these groups, known as the North folk and the South folk. They gave their names to Norfolk and Suffolk, and at some later time combined under the name of East Anglians. North of the Wash were the Lindiswara—that is to say, the settlers about the Roman Lindum, the modern Lincoln, and beyond them, stretching to the Humber, were the Gainas, from whom is derived the name of the modern Gainsborough. To the north of the Humber the coast was fringed by Angle settlements which had not yet coalesced into one.

7. **Nature of the Conquest.**—The three peoples who effected this conquest were afterwards known amongst themselves by the common name of English, a name which was originally equivalent

to Angle, whilst amongst the whole of the remaining Celtic population they were only known as Saxons. The mode in which the
English treated the Britons was very different from that of the
Romans, who were a civilised people and aimed at governing a
conquered race. The new-comers drove out the Britons in order
to find homes for themselves, and they preferred to settle in the
country rather than in a town. No Englishman had ever lived in a
town in his German home, or was able to appreciate the advantages
of the commerce and manufacture by which towns are supported.
Nor were they inclined to allow the inhabitants of the Roman
towns to remain unmolested in their midst. When Anderida was
captured not a Briton escaped alive, and there is good reason to
believe that many of the other towns fared no better, especially
as the remains of some of them still show marks of the fire by
which they were consumed. What took place in the country cannot be certainly known. Many of the British were no doubt killed.
Many took refuge in fens or woods, or fled to those portions of the
island in which their countrymen were still independent. It is difficult to decide to what extent the men who remained behind were
spared, but it is impossible to doubt that a considerable number of
women were preserved from slaughter. The conquerors, at their
landing, must have been for the most part young men, and when
they wanted wives, it would be far easier for them to seize the
daughters of slain Britons than to fetch women from the banks
of the Elbe.

8. **The Cultivators of the Soil.**—When the new-comers planted
themselves on British soil, each group of families united by kinship
fixed its home in a separate village or township, to which was given
the name of the kindred followed by ' ham ' or ' tun,' the first word
meaning the home or dwelling, the second the earthen mound
which formed the defence of the community. Thus Wokingham
is the home of the Wokings, and Wellington the ' tun ' of the Wel-
lings. Each man had a homestead of his own, with a strip or
strips of arable land in an open field. Beyond the arable land was
pasture and wood, common to the whole township, every villager
being entitled to drive his cattle or pigs into them according to
rules laid down by the whole township.

9. **Eorls, Ceorls, Gesiths.**—The population was divided into
Eorls and Ceorls. The Eorl was hereditarily distinguished by
birth, and the Ceorl was a simple freeman without any such distinction. How the difference arose we do not know, but we do
know that the Eorl had privileges which the Ceorl had not. Below

the Ceorls were slaves taken in war or condemned to slavery as criminals. There were also men known as Gesiths, a word which means 'followers,' who were the followers of the chiefs or Ealdormen (*Eldermen*) who led the conquerors. The Gesiths formed the war-band of the chief. They were probably all of them Eorls, so that though every settler was either an Eorl or a Ceorl, some Eorls were also Gesiths. This war-band of Gesiths was composed of young men who attached themselves to the chief by a tie of personal devotion. It was the highest glory of the Gesith to die to save his chief's life. Of one Gesith it is told that, when he saw a murderer aiming a dagger at his chief, he, not having time to seize the assassin, threw his body between the blow and his chief, and perished rather than allow him to be killed. It was even held to be disgraceful for a Gesith to return from battle alive if his chief had been slain. The word by which the chief was known was Hlaford (*Lord*), which means a giver of bread, because the Gesiths ate his bread. They not only ate his bread, but they shared in the booty which he brought home. They slept in his hall, and were clothed in the garments woven by his wife and her maidens. A continental writer tells how a body of Gesiths once approached their lord with a petition that he should take a wife, because as long as he remained unmarried there was no one to make new clothes for them or to mend their old ones.

10. **The Gesiths and the Villagers.**—At the time of the English settlement, therefore, there were two sorts of warriors amongst the invaders. The Ceorls, having been accustomed to till land at home, were quite ready to till the lands which they had newly acquired in Britain. They were, however, ready to defend themselves and their lands if they were attacked, and they were under the obligation of appearing in arms when needed for defence. This general army of the villagers was called the Fyrd. On the other hand, the Gesiths had not been accustomed to till land at home, but had made fighting their business. War, in short, which was an unwelcome accident to the Ceorl, was the business of life to the Gesith. The exact relationship between the Gesiths and the Ceorls cannot be ascertained with certainty. It is not improbable that the Gesiths, being the best warriors amongst their countrymen, sometimes obtained land granted them by their chiefs, and were expected in consequence to be specially ready to serve the chief whom they had followed from their home. It was from their relation to their chief that they were called Gesiths, a name gradually abandoned for that of Thegns, or servants, when they—as was soon the case—

ceased to live with their chief and had houses and lands of their own, though they were still bound to military service. How these Thegns cultivated their lands is a question to which there is no certain answer. In later days they made use of a class of men known as bondmen or villeins. These bondmen were not, like slaves, the property of their masters. They had land of their own, which they were allowed to cultivate for themselves on condition of spending part of their time in cultivating the land of their lords. It has been supposed by some writers that the Thegns employed bondmen from the earliest times of the conquest. If, however, this was the case, there arises a further question whether the bondmen were Englishmen or Britons. The whole subject is under investigation, and the evidence which exists is excessively scanty. It is at least certain that the further the conquest progressed westwards, the greater was the number of Britons preserved alive.

11. **English and Welsh.**—The bulk of the population on the eastern and southern coasts was undoubtedly English. English institutions and English language took firm root. The conquerors looked on the Britons with the utmost contempt, naming them Welsh, a name which no Briton thought of giving to himself, but which Germans had been in the habit of applying somewhat contemptuously to the Celts on the Continent. So far as British words have entered into the English language at all, they have been words such as *gown* or *curd*, which are likely to have been used by women, or words such as *cart* or *pony*, which are likely to have been used by agricultural labourers, and the evidence of language may therefore be adduced in favour of the view that many women and many agricultural labourers were spared by the conquerors.

12. **The Township and the Hundred.**—The smallest political community of the new settlers was the village, or, as it is commonly called, the township, which is still represented by the parish, the parish being merely a township in which ecclesiastical institutions have been maintained whilst political institutions have ceased to exist. The freemen of the township met to settle small questions between themselves, under the presidency of their reeve or headman. More important cases were brought before the hundred-moot, or meeting of the hundred, a district which had been inhabited, or was supposed to have been inhabited, either by a hundred kindred groups of the original settlers or by the families of a hundred warriors. This hundred-moot was held once a month, and was

attended by four men and the reeve from every township, and also by the Eorls and Thegns living in the hundred. It not only settled disputes about property, but gave judgment in criminal cases as well.

13. **Weregild.**—In early days, long before the English had left their lands beyond the sea, it was not considered to be the business of the community to punish crime. If any one was murdered, it was the duty of the kinsmen of the slain man to put to death the murderer. In course of time men got tired of the continual slaughter produced by this arrangement, and there sprang up a system according to which the murderer might offer to the kinsmen a sum of money known as weregild, or the value of a man, and if this money was accepted, then peace was made and all thought of vengeance was at an end. At a later time, at all events after the arrival of the English in this country, charges of murder were brought before the hundred-moot whenever the alleged murderer and his victim lived in the same hundred. If the accused person did not dispute the fact the moot sentenced him to pay a weregild, the amount of which differed in proportion to the rank of the slain man, not in proportion to the heinousness of the offence. As there was a weregild for murder, so there was also a graduated scale of payments for lesser offences. One who struck off a hand or a foot could buy off vengeance at a fixed rate.

14. **Compurgation and Ordeal.**—A new difficulty was introduced when a person who was charged with crime denied his guilt. As there were no trained lawyers and there was no knowledge of the principles of evidence, the accused person was required to bring twelve men to be his compurgators—that is to say, to hear him swear to his own innocence, and then to swear in turn that his oath was true. If he could not find men willing to be his compurgators he could appeal to the judgment of the gods, which was known as the Ordeal. If he could walk blindfold over red-hot ploughshares, or plunge his arm into boiling water, and show at the end of a fixed number of days that he had received no harm, it was thought that the gods bore witness to his innocency and had as it were become his compurgators when men had failed him. It is quite possible that all or most of those who tried the ordeal failed, but as nobody would try the ordeal who could get compurgators, those who did not succeed must have been regarded as persons of bad character, so that no surprise would be expressed at their failure.

15. **Punishments.**—When a man had failed in the ordeal there was a choice of punishments. If his offence was a slight one, a

fine was deemed sufficient.   If it was a very disgraceful one, such as secret murder, he was put to death or was degraded to slavery. in most cases he was declared to be a ' wolf's-head '—that is to say, he was outlawed and driven into the woods, where, as the protection of the community was withdrawn from him, anyone might kill him without fear of punishment.

16. **The Folk-moot.**—As the hundred-moot did justice between those who lived in the hundred, so the folk-moot did justice between those who lived in different hundreds, or were too important to be judged in the hundred-moot.   The folk-moot was the meeting of the whole folk or tribe, which consisted of several hundreds.   It was attended, like the hundred-moot, by four men and the reeve from each township, and it met twice a year, and was presided over by the chief or Ealdorman.   The folk-moot met in arms, because it was a muster as well as a council and a court.   The vote as to war and peace was taken in it, and while the chief alone spoke, the warriors signified their assent by clashing their swords against their shields.

17. **The Kingship.**—How many folks or tribes settled in the island it is impossible to say, but there is little doubt that many of them soon combined.   The resistance of the Britons was desperate, and it was only by joining together that the settlers could hope to overcome it.   The causes which produced this amalgamation of the folks produced the king.   It was necessary to find a man always ready to take the command of the united folks, and this man was called King, a name which signifies the man of the kinship or race at the head of which he stood.   His authority was greater than the Ealdorman's, and his warriors were more numerous than those which the Ealdorman had led.   He must come of a royal family— that is, of one supposed to be descended from the god Woden. As it was necessary that he should be capable of leading an army, it was impossible that a child could be king, and therefore no law of hereditary succession prevailed.   On the death of a king the folk-moot chose his successor out of the kingly family.   If his eldest son was a grown man of repute, the choice would almost certainly fall upon him.   If he was a child or an invalid, some other kinsman of the late king would be selected.

18. **The Legend of Arthur.**—Thirty-two years passed away after the defeat of the West Saxons at Mount Badon in **520** (see p. 28) before they made any further conquests.   Welsh legends represent this period as that of the reign of Arthur.   Some modern inquirers have argued that Arthur's kingdom was in the north, whilst others have argued that it was in the south.   It is quite

D

possible that the name was given by legend to more than one
champion; at all events, there was a time when an Ambrosius,
probably a descendant of Ambrosius Aurelianus (see p. 27), protected the southern Britons.   His stronghold was at Sorbiodunum,
the hill fort now a grassy space known as Old Sarum, and his great
church and monastery, where Christian priests encouraged the
Christian Britons in their struggle against the heathen Saxons, was
at the neighbouring Ambresbyrig (*the fortress of Ambrosius*), now

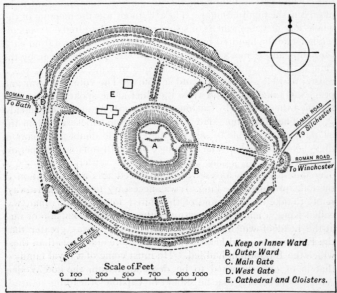

A. *Keep or Inner Ward*
B. *Outer Ward*
C. *Main Gate*
D. *West Gate*
E. *Cathedral and Cloisters.*

Walker & Boutall sc.

Plan of the city of Old Sarum, the ancient *Sorbiodunum*.   The Cathedral is of
later date.

modernised into Amesbury.   Thirty-two years after the battle of
Mount Badon the kingdom of Ambrosius had been divided amongst
his successors, who were plunged in vice and were quarrelling with
one another.

19. **The West Saxon Advance.**—In **552** Cynric, the West
Saxon king, attacked the divided Britons, captured Sorbiodunum,
and made himself master of Salisbury Plain.   Step by step he
fought his way to the valley of the Thames, and when he had
reached it, he turned eastwards to descend the river to its mouth.

Here, however, he found himself anticipated by the East Saxons, who had captured London, and had settled a branch of their people under the name of the Middle Saxons in Middlesex. The Jutes of Kent had pushed westwards through the Surrey hills, but in **568** the West Saxons defeated them and drove them back. After this battle, the first in which the conquerors strove with one another, the West Saxons turned northwards, defeated the Britons in **571** at Bedford, and occupied the valleys of the Thame and Cherwell and the upper valley of the Ouse. They are next heard of much further west, and it has been supposed that they turned in that direction because they found the lower Ouse already held by Angle tribes.

Old Sarum from an engraving published in 1843, showing mound. (It is now obscured by trees from this point of view.)

However this may have been, they crossed the Cotswolds in **577** under two brothers, Ceawlin and Cutha, and at Deorham defeated and slew three kings who ruled over the cities of Glevum (*Gloucester*), Corinium (*Cirencester*), and Aquæ Sulis (*Bath*). They seized on the fertile valley of the Severn, and during the next few years they pressed gradually northwards. In **584** they destroyed and sacked the old Roman station of Viriconium. This was their last victory for many a year. They attempted to reach Chester, but were defeated at Faddiley by the Britons, who slew Cutha in the battle.

20. **Repulse of the West Saxons.**—After the defeat at Faddiley the West Saxons split up into two peoples. Those of them who

settled in the lower Severn valley took the name of Hwiccan, and joined the Britons against their own kindred. This alliance could hardly have taken place if the Hwiccan, in settling in the Severn valley, had destroyed the whole, or even a considerable part, of the Celtic population, though there can be little doubt that there was still slaughter when a battle was fought or a town taken by storm ; as it is known that the magnificent Roman buildings at Bath were standing in ruins and the city untenanted many years after the capture of the city. At all events, the Britons, now allied with the Hwiccan, defeated Ceawlin at Wanborough. After this disaster, though the West Saxon kingdom retained its independence, it was independent within smaller limits than those which Ceawlin had wished to give to it. If he had seized Chester he would have been on the way to gain the mastery over all England, but he had tried to do too much in a short time. His people can hardly have been numerous enough to occupy in force a territory reaching from South-ampton Water to Bedford on one side and to Chester on another.

21. **The Advance of the Angles.**—Whilst the West Saxons were enlarging their boundaries in the south, the Angles were gradually spreading in the centre and the north. The East Anglians were stopped on their way to the west by the great fen, but either a branch of the Lindiswara or some new-comers made their way up the Trent, and established themselves first at Nottingham and then at Leicester, and called themselves the Middle English. Another body, known as the Mercians, or men of the mark or border-land, seized on the upper valley of the Trent. North of the Humber the advance was still slower. In **547**, five years before the West Saxons attacked Sorbiodunum, Ida, a chieftain of one of the scattered settlements on the coast, was accepted as king by all those which lay between the Tees and the Forth. His new kingdom was called Bernicia, and his principal fortress was on a rock by the sea at Bamborough. During the next fifty years he and his successors enlarged their borders till they reached that central ridge of moorland hill which is sometimes known as the Pennine range. The Angles between the Tees and the Humber called their country Deira, but though they also united under a king, their progress was as slow as that of the Bernicians. Bernicia and Deira together were known as North-humberland, the land north of the Humber, a much larger territory than that of the modern county of Northumberland.

22. **The Kymry.**—It is probable that the cause of the slow advance of the northern Angles lay in the existence of a strong

Celtic state in front. Welsh tradition speaks of a ruler named Cunedda, who after the departure of the Roman legions governed the territory from the Clyde to the south of Wales, which formed the greater part of what had once been known as Upper Britain. (See p. 25.) This territory was inhabited by a mixed population of Britons and Goidels, with an isolated body of Picts in Galloway. A common danger from the English fused them together, and as a sign of the wearing out of old distinctions, they took the name of Kymry, or Comrades, the name by which the Welsh are known amongst one another to this day, and which is also preserved in the name of Cumberland, though the Celtic language is no longer spoken there.

23. **Britain at the End of the Sixth Century.**—During the sixth century the Kymry ceased to be governed by one ruler, but the chieftains of the various territories all acknowledged the supremacy of a descendant of Cunedda. For purposes of war they combined together, and as the country which they occupied was hilly and easily defended, the northern English discovered that they too must unite amongst themselves if they were to overpower the united resistance of the Kymry.

CHAPTER III

THE STRIFE OF THE ENGLISH KINGDOMS

LEADING DATES

Augustine's mission	597
Æthelfrith's victory at Chester	613
Penda defeats Eadwine at Heathfield	633
Penda's defeat at Winwæd	655
Theodore Archbishop of Canterbury . . .	668
Offa defeats the West Saxons at Bensington . .	779
Ecgberht returns to England	800
Death of Ecgberht	839

1. **England and the Continent.**—Whatever may be the exact truth about the numbers of Britons saved alive by the English conquerors, there can be no doubt that English speech and English customs prevailed wherever the English settled. In Gaul, where the German Franks made themselves masters of the country, a different state of things prevailed. Roman officials continued to govern the country under Frankish kings, Roman bishops con-

verted the conquerors to Christianity, and Roman cities maintained, as far as they could, the old standard of civilisation. All commercial intercourse between Gaul, still comparatively rich and prosperous, and Britain was for some time cut off by the irruption of the English, who were at first too rude and too much engaged in fighting to need the products of a more advanced race. Gradually, however, as the English settled down into peaceful industry along the south-eastern shores of the island, trade again sprang up, as it had sprung up in the wild times preceding the landing of Cæsar. The Gaulish merchants who crossed the straits found themselves in Kent, and during the years in which the West Saxon Ceawlin was struggling with the Britons the communications between Kent and the Continent had become so friendly that in 584, or a little later, Æthelberht, king of Kent, took to wife Bertha, the daughter of a Frankish king, Charibert. Bertha was a Christian, and brought with her a Christian bishop. She begged of her husband a forsaken Roman church for her own use. This church, now known as St. Martin's, stood outside the walls of the deserted city of Durovernum, the buildings of which were in ruins, except where a group of rude dwellings rose in a corner of the old fortifications. In these dwellings Æthelberht and his followers lived, and to them had been given the new name of Cantwarabyrig or Canterbury (*the dwelling of the men of Kent*). The English were heathen, but their heathenism was not intolerant.

2. **Æthelberht's Supremacy.**—Æthelberht's authority reached far beyond his native Kent. Within a few years after his marriage he had gained a supremacy over most of the other kings to the south of the Humber. There is no tradition of any war between Æthelberht and these kings, and he certainly did not thrust them out from the leadership of their own peoples. The exact nature of his supremacy is, however, unknown to us, though it is possible that they were bound to follow him if he went to war with peoples not acknowledging his supremacy, in which case his position towards them was something of the same kind as that of a lord to his gesiths.

3. **Gregory and the English.**—Æthelberht's position as the overlord of so many kings and as the husband of a Christian wife drew upon him the attention of Gregory, the Bishop of Rome, or Pope. Many years before, as a deacon, he had been attracted by the fair faces of some boys from Deira exposed for sale in the Roman slave-market. He was told that the children were Angles. " Not Angles, but angels," he replied. " Who," he asked, " is their

king?" Hearing that his name was Ælla, he continued to play
upon the words. "Alleluia," he said, "shall be sung in the land
of Ælla." Busy years kept him from seeking to fulfil his hopes,
but at last the time came when he could do something to carry
out his intentions, not in the land of Ælla, but in the land of
Æthelberht. He became Pope. In those days the Pope had far
less authority over the Churches of Western Europe than he afterwards acquired, but he offered the only centre round which they
could rally, now that the Empire had broken up into many states
ruled over by different barbarian kings. The general habit of looking to Rome for authority, which had been diffused over the whole
Empire whilst Rome was still the seat of the Emperors, made men
look to the Roman Bishop for advice and help as they had once
looked to the Roman Emperor. Gregory, who united to the tender-
heartedness of the Christian the strength of will and firmness of
purpose which had marked out the best of the Emperors, now sent
Augustine to England as the leader of a band of missionaries.

4. **Augustine's Mission.** **597.**—Augustine with his companions
landed at Ebbsfleet, in Thanet, where Æthelberht's forefathers had
landed nearly a century and a half before. After a while Æthelberht
arrived. Singing a litany, and bearing aloft a painting of the
Saviour, the missionaries appeared before him. He had already
learned from his Christian wife to respect Christians, but he was
not prepared to forsake his own religion. He welcomed the new-
comers, and told them that they were free to convert those who
would willingly accept their doctrine. A place was assigned to
them in Canterbury, and they were allowed to use Bertha's church.
In the end Æthelberht himself, together with thousands of the
Kentish men, received baptism. It was more by their example
than by their teaching that Augustine's band won converts. The
missionaries lived 'after the model of the primitive Church, giving
themselves to frequent prayers, watchings, and fastings ; preaching
to all who were within their reach, disregarding all worldly things
as matters with which they had nothing to do, accepting from
those whom they taught just what seemed necessary for livelihood,
living themselves altogether in accordance with what they taught,
and with hearts prepared to suffer every adversity, or even to die,
for that truth which they preached.'

5. **Monastic Christianity.**—These missionaries were monks as
well as preachers. The Christians of those days considered the
monastic life to be the highest. In the early days of the Church,
when the world was full of vice and cruelty, it seemed hardly

possible to live in the world without being dragged down to its wickedness. Men and women, therefore, who wished to keep themselves pure, withdrew to hermitages or monasteries, where they might be removed from temptation, and might fit themselves for heaven by prayer and fasting. In the fifth century Benedict of Nursia had organised in Italy a system of life for the monastery which he governed, and the Benedictine rule, as it was called, was soon accepted in almost all the monasteries of Western Europe. The special feature of this rule was that it encouraged labour as well as prayer. It was a saying of Benedict himself that 'to labour is to pray.' He did not mean that labour was good in itself, but that monks who worked during some hours of the day would guard their minds against evil thoughts better than if they tried to pray all day long. Augustine and his companions were Benedictine monks, and their quietness and contentedness attracted the population amidst which they had settled. The religion of the heathen English was a religion which favoured bravery and endurance, counting the warrior who slaughtered most enemies as most highly favoured by the gods. The religion of Augustine was one of peace and self-denial. Its symbol was the cross, to be borne in the heart of the believer. The message brought by Augustine was very hard to learn. If Augustine had expected the whole English population to forsake entirely its evil ways and to walk in paths of peace, he would probably have been rejected at once. It was perhaps because he was a monk that he did not expect so much. A monk was accustomed to judge laymen by a lower standard of self-denial than that by which he judged himself. He would, therefore, not ask too much of the new converts. They must forsake the heathen temples and sacrifices, and must give up some particularly evil habits. The rest must be left to time and the example of the monks.

6. **The Archbishopric of Canterbury.**—After a short stay Augustine revisited Gaul and came back as Archbishop of the English. Æthelberht gave to him a ruined church at Canterbury, and that poor church was named Christ Church, and became the mother church of England. From that day the Archbishop's See has been fixed at Canterbury. If Augustine in his character of monk led men by example, in his character of Archbishop he had to organise the Church. With Æthelberht's help he set up a bishopric at Rochester and another in London. London was now again an important trading city, which, though not in Æthelberht's own kingdom of Kent, formed part of the kingdom of Essex, which was dependent on Kent. More than these three Sees Augustine was

unable to establish. An attempt to obtain the friendly co-operation of the Welsh bishops broke down because Augustine insisted on their adoption of Roman customs ; and Lawrence, who succeeded to the archbishopric after Augustine's death, could do no more than his predecessor had done.

7. **Death of Æthelberht. 616.**—In **616** Æthelberht died. The over-lordship of the kings of Kent ended with him, and Augustine's church, which had largely depended upon his influence, very nearly ended as well. Essex relapsed into heathenism, and it was only by terrifying Æthelberht's son with the vengeance of St. Peter that Lawrence kept him from relapsing also. On the other hand, Rædwald, king of the East Anglians, who succeeded to much of Æthelberht's authority, so far accepted Christianity as to worship Christ amongst his other gods.

8. **The Three Kingdoms opposed to the Welsh.**—Augustine's Church was weak, because it depended on the kings, and had not had time to root itself in the affections of the people. Æthelberht's supremacy was also weak. The greater part of the small states which still existed—Sussex, Kent, Essex, East Anglia, and most of the small kingdoms of central England—were no longer bordered by a Celtic population. For them the war of conquest and defence was at an end. If any one of the kingdoms was to rise to permanent supremacy it must be one of those engaged in strenuous warfare, and as yet strenuous warfare was only carried on with the Welsh. The kingdoms which had the Welsh on their borders were three—Wessex, Mercia, and North-humberland, and neither Wessex nor Mercia was as yet very strong. Wessex was too distracted by conflicts amongst members of the kingly family, and Mercia was as yet too small to be of much account. North-humberland was therefore the first of the three to rise to the foremost place. Till the death of Ælla, the king of Deira, from whose land had been carried off the slave-boys whose faces had charmed Gregory at Rome, Deira and Bernicia had been as separate as Kent and Essex. Then in **588** Æthelric of Bernicia drove out Ælla's son and seized his kingdom of Deira, thus joining the two kingdoms of Deira and Bernicia (see p. 36) into one, under the new name of North-humberland.[1]

9. **Æthelfrith and the Kymry.**—In **593**, four years before the landing of Augustine, Æthelric was succeeded by his son Æthelfrith. Æthelfrith began a fresh struggle with the Welsh. We

---

[1] Genealogy of the principal Northumbrian kings :—[*Note.*—The names of kings are in capitals. The figures denote the order of succession of those who

know little of the internal history of the Welsh population, but what we do know shows that towards the end of the sixth century there was an improvement in their religious and political existence. The monasteries were thronged, especially the great monastery of Bangor-iscoed, in the modern Flintshire, which contained 2,000 monks. St. David and other bishops gave examples of piety. In fighting against Æthelfrith the warriors of the Britons were fighting for their last chance of independence. They still held the west from the Clyde to the Channel. Unhappily for them, the Severn, the Dee, and the Solway Firth divided their land into four portions, and if an enemy coming from the east could seize upon the heads of the inlets into which those rivers flowed he could prevent the defenders of the west from aiding one another. Already in **577**, by the victory of Deorham (see p. 35), the West Saxons had seized on the mouth of the Severn, and had split off the West Welsh of the south-western peninsula. Æthelfrith had to do with the Kymry, whose territories stretched from the Bristol Channel to the Clyde, and who held an outlying wedge of land then known as Loidis and Elmet, which now together form the West Riding of Yorkshire.

10. **Æthelfrith's Victories.**—The long range of barren hills which separated Æthelfrith's kingdom from the Kymry made it difficult for either side to strike a serious blow at the other. In the extreme north, where a low valley joins the Firths of Clyde and Forth, it was easier for them to meet. Here the Kymry found an ally outside their own borders. Towards the end of the fifth century a colony of Irish Scots had driven out the Picts from the modern Argyle. In **603** their king, Aedan, bringing with him a vast army, in which Picts and the Kymry appear to have taken part, invaded the northern part of Æthelfrith's country. Æthelfrith defeated him at Degsastan, which was probably

ruled over the whole of North-humberland. Those whose names are followed by a B. or D. ruled only over Bernicia or Deira respectively.]

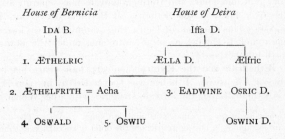

House of Bernicia   *House of Deira*

```
      IDA B.                          Iffa D.
        |                               |
        |                    +----------+----------+
  1. ÆTHELRIC              ÆLLA D.            ÆLFRIC
        |                     |                  |
        |            +--------+--------+         |
  2. ÆTHELFRITH = Acha    3. EADWINE  OSRIC D.
     +----------+----------+                     |
     |                     |                     |
  4. OSWALD            5. OSWIU             OSWINI D.
```

Dawstone, near Jedburgh. 'From that time no king of the Scots durst come into Britain to make war upon the English.' Having freed himself from the Scots in the north, Æthelfrith turned upon the Kymry. After a succession of struggles of which no record remains, he forced his way in **613** to the western sea near Chester. The Kymry had brought with them the 2,000 monks of their great monastery Bangor-iscoed, to pray for victory whilst their warriors were engaged in battle. Æthelfrith bade his men to slay them all. 'Whether they bear arms or no,' he said, 'they fight against us when they cry against us to their God.' The monks were slain to a man. Their countrymen were routed, and Chester fell into the hands of the English. The capture of Chester split the Kymric kingdom in two, as the battle of Deorham thirty-five years before had split that kingdom off from the West Welsh of the south-western peninsula. The Southern Kymry, in what is now called Wales, could no longer give help to the Northern Kymry between the Clyde and the Ribble, who grouped themselves into the kingdom of Strathclyde, the capital of which was Alcluyd, the modern Dumbarton. Three weak Celtic states, unable to assist one another, would not long be able to resist their invaders.

11. **The Greatness of Eadwine.**—Powerful as Æthelfrith was, he was jealous of young Eadwine, a son of his father's rival, Ælla of Deira. For some years Eadwine had been in hiding, at one time with Welsh princes, at another time with English kings. In **617** he took refuge with Rædwald, the king of the East Angles. Æthelfrith demanded the surrender of the fugitive. Rædwald hesitated, but at last refused. Æthelfrith atacked him, but was defeated and slain near the river Idle, at some point near Retford. Eadwine the Deiran then became king over the united North-humberland in the place of Æthelfrith the Bernician, whose sons fled for safety to the Picts beyond the Forth. Eadwine completed and consolidated the conquests of his predecessors. He placed a fortress, named after himself Eadwinesburh, or Edinburgh, on a rocky height near the Forth, to guard his land against a fresh irruption of Scots and Picts, such as that which had been turned back at Degsastan. He conquered from the Kymry Loidis and Elmet, and he launched a fleet at Chester which added to his dominions the Isle of Man and the greater island which was henceforth known as Anglesea, the island of the Angles. Eadwine assumed unwonted state. Wherever he went a standard was borne before him, as well as a spear decorated with a tuft of feathers, the ancient sign of Roman authority. It has been thought by some that his meaning was that

he, rather than any Welshman, was the true Gwledig, the successor of the Duke of the Britains (*Dux Britanniarum*), and that the name of Bretwalda, or ruler of the Britons, which he is said to have borne, was only a translation of the Welsh Gwledig. It is true that the title of Bretwalda is given to other powerful kings before and after Eadwine, some of whom were in no sense rulers over Britons ; but it is possible that it was taken to signify a ruler over a large part of Britain, though the men over whom he ruled were English, and not Britons.

12. **Eadwine's Supremacy.**—Eadwine's immediate kingship did not reach further south than the Humber and the Dee. But before **625** he had brought the East Angles and the kingdoms of central England to submit to his over-lordship, and he hoped to make himself over-lord of the south as well, and thus to reduce all England to dependence on himself. In **625** he planned an attack upon the West Saxons, and with the object of winning Kent to his side, he married Æthelburh, a sister of the Kentish king. Kent was still the only Christian kingdom, and Eadwine was obliged to promise to his wife protection for her Christian worship. He was now free to attack the West Saxons. In **626**, before he set out, ambassadors arrived from their king. As Eadwine was listening to them, one of their number rushed forward to stab him. His life was saved by the devotion of Lilla, one of his thegns, who threw his body in the way of the assassin, and was slain by the stroke intended for his lord. After this Eadwine marched against the West Saxons. He defeated them in battle and forced them to acknowledge him as their over-lord. He was now over-lord of all the English states except Kent, and Kent had become his ally in consequence of his marriage.

13. **Character of the later Conquests.**—Eadwine's over-lordship had been gained with as little difficulty as Æthelberht's had been. The ease with which each of them carried out their purpose can only be explained by the change which had taken place in the condition of the English. The small bodies of conquerors which had landed at different parts of the coast had been interested to a man in the defence of the lands which they had seized. Every freeman had been ready to come forward to defend the soil which his tribe had gained. After tribe had been joined to tribe, and still more after kingdom had been joined to kingdom, there were large numbers who ceased to have any interest in resisting the Welsh on what was, as far as they were concerned, a distant frontier. Thus, when Ceawlin was fighting to extend the West Saxon frontiers

in the valley of the Severn, it mattered little to a man whose own allotted land lay on the banks of the Southampton Water whether or not his English kinsmen won lands from the Welsh near Bath or Gloucester. The first result of this change was that the king's war-band formed a far greater proportion of his military force than it had formed originally. There was still the obligation upon the whole body of the freemen to take arms, but it was an obligation which had become more difficult to fulfil, and it must often have happened that very few freemen took part in a battle except the local levies concerned in defending their own immediate neighbourhood. A military change of this kind would account for the undoubted fact that the further the English conquest penetrated to the west the less destructive it was of British life. The thegns, or warriors personally attached to the king, did not want to plough and reap with their own hands. They would be far better pleased to spare the lives of the conquered and to compel them to labour. Every step in advance was marked by a proportionately larger Welsh element in the population.

14. **Political Changes.**—The character of the kingship was as much affected by the change as the character of the population. The old folk-moots still remained as the local courts of the smaller kingdoms, or of the districts out of which the larger kingdoms were composed, and continued to meet under the presidency of ealdormen appointed or approved by the king. Four men and a reeve, all of them humble cultivators, could not, however, be expected to walk up to York from the shores of the Forth, or even from the banks of the Tyne, whenever Eadwine needed their counsel. Their place in the larger kingdoms was therefore taken by the Witenagemot (*The moot of the wise men*), composed of the ealdormen and the chief thegns, together with the priests attached to the king's service in the time of heathendom, and, in the time of Christianity, the bishop or bishops of his kingdom. In one way the king was the stronger for the change. His counsellors, like his fighting force, were more dependent on himself than before. He was able to plan greater designs, and to carry out military enterprises at a greater distance. In another way he was the weaker for the change. He had less support from the bulk of his people, and was more likely to undertake enterprises in which they had no interest. The over-lordships of Æthelberht and Eadwine appear very imposing, but no real tie united the men of the centre of England to those of Kent at one time, or to those of North-humberland at another. Eadwine was

supreme over the other kings because he had a better war-band than they had. If another king appeared whose war-band was better than his, his supremacy would disappear.

15. **Eadwine's Conversion and Fall.**—In 627 Eadwine, moved by his wife's entreaties and the urgency of her chaplain, Paulinus, called upon his Witan to accept Christianity. Coifi, the priest, declared that he had long served his gods for naught, and would try a change of masters. ' The present life of man, O king,' said a thegn, ' seems to me in comparison of that time which is unknown to us like to the swift flight of a sparrow through the room wherein you sit at supper in winter, with your ealdormen and thegns, and a good fire in the midst, and storms of rain and snow without. . . . So this life of man appears for a short space, but of what went before or what is to follow we are utterly ignorant. If therefore this new doctrine contains something more certain, it seems justly to deserve to be followed.' On this recommendation Christianity was accepted. Paulinus was acknowledged as Bishop of York. The new See, which had been originally intended by Pope Gregory to be an archbishopric, was ultimately acknowledged as such, but as yet it was but a missionary station. Paulinus converted thousands in Deira, but the men of Bernicia were unaffected by his pleadings. Christianity, like the extension of all better teaching, brought at first not peace but the sword. The new religion was contemptible in the eyes of warriors. The supremacy of Eadwine was shaken. The men of East Anglia slew their king, who had followed his over-lord's example by accepting Christianity. The worst blow came from Mercia. Hitherto it had been only a little state on the Welsh border. Its king, Penda, the stoutest warrior of his day, now gathered under him all the central states, and founded a new Mercia which stretched from the Severn to the Fens. He first turned on the West Saxons, defeated them at Cirencester, and in 628 brought the territory of the Hwiccas under Mercian sway. On the other hand, East Anglia accepted Eadwine's supremacy and Christianity. Penda called to his aid Cædwalla, the king of Gwynnedd, the Snowdonian region of Wales. That he should have done so shows how completely Æthelfrith's victory at Chester, by cutting the Kymric realm in two, had put an end to all fears that the Kymry could ever make head against England as a whole. The alliance was too strong for Eadwine, and in 633, at the battle of Heathfield—the modern Hatfield, in Yorkshire—the great king was slain and his army routed.

16. Oswald's Victory at Heavenfield.—Penda was content to split up Bernicia and Deira into separate kingdoms, and to join East Anglia to his subject states. Cædwalla had all the wrongs of his race to avenge. He remained in North-humberland burning and destroying till **635,** when Oswald, who was a son of Æthelfrith and of Eadwine's sister, and therefore united the claims of the rival families, gathered the men of Bernicia round him, overthrew Cædwalla at Heavenfield, near the Roman Wall, and was grate-fully accepted as king by the whole of North-humberland.

17. Oswald and Aidan.—In the days of Eadwine, Oswald, as the heir of the rival house of Bernicia, had passed his youth in exile, and had been converted to Christianity in the monastery of Hii, the island now known as Iona. The monastery had been founded by Columba, an Irish Scot. Christianity had been intro-duced into Ireland by Patrick early in the fifth century. Ireland was a land of constant and cruel war between its tribes, and all who wished to be Christians in more than name withdrew them-selves into monasteries, where they lived an even stricter and more ascetic life than the monks did in other parts of Western Europe. Bishops were retained in the monasteries to ordain priests, but they were entirely powerless. Columba's monastery at Hii sent its missionaries abroad, and brought Picts as well as Scots under the influence of Christianity. Oswald now requested its abbot, the suc-cessor of Columba, to send a missionary to preach the faith to the men of North-humberland in the place of Paulinus, who had fled when Eadwine was slain. The first who was sent came back reporting that the people were too stubborn to be converted. "Was it their stubbornness or your harshness?" asked the monk Aidan. "Did you forget to give them the milk first and then the meat?" Aidan was chosen to take the place of the brother who had failed. He established himself, not in an inland town, but in Holy Island. His life was spent in wandering amongst the men of the valleys opposite, winning them over by his gentleness and his self-denying energy. Oswald, warrior as he was, had almost all the gentleness and piety of Aidan. 'By reason of his con-stant habit of praying or giving thanks to the Lord he was wont whenever he sat to hold his hands upturned on his knees.' On one occasion when he sat down to a feast with Aidan by his side, he sent both the dainties before him and the silver dish on which they had been served to be divided amongst the poor. "May this hand," exclaimed the delighted Aidan, "never grow old!"

18. Oswald's Greatness and Overthrow.—As a king Oswald

based his power on the acknowledgment of his over-lordship by all the kingdoms which were hostile to Penda. In 635 Wessex accepted Christianity, and the acceptance of Christianity brought with it the acceptance of Oswald's supremacy. Penda was thus surrounded by enemies, but his courage did not fail him, and in 642 at the battle of Maserfield he defeated Oswald. Oswald fell in the battle, begging with his last words for God's mercy on the souls of his followers.

19. **Penda's Overthrow.**—After Oswald's fall Bernicia was ruled by his brother Oswiu. Deira, again divided from it, was governed first by Eadwine's cousin Osric, and then by Osric's son, Oswini, who acknowledged Penda as his over-lord. Oswini was a man after Aidan's own heart. Once he gave a horse to Aidan to carry him on his mission journeys. Aidan gave it away to the first beggar he met. " Is that son of a mare," answered Aidan to the reproaches of the king, " worth more in your eyes than that son of God?" Oswini fell at the bishop's feet and entreated his pardon. Aidan wept. " I am sure," he cried, " the king will not live long. I never till now saw a king humble." Aidan was right. In 651 Oswini was slain by the order of King Oswiu of Bernicia, who had long engaged in a struggle with Penda. Penda had for some years been burning and slaughtering in Bernicia, till he had turned a quarrel between himself and Oswiu into a national strife. Oswiu rescued Bernicia from destruction, and after Oswini's murder joined once more the two kingdoms together. Oswini was the last heir of Ælla's house, and from that time there was but one North-humberland. In 655 Oswiu and Penda met to fight, as it seemed for supremacy over the whole of England, by the river Winwæd, near the present Leeds. The heathen Penda was defeated and slain.

20. **The Three Kingdoms and the Welsh.**—For a moment it seemed as if England would be brought together under the rule of Oswiu. After Penda's death Mercia accepted Christianity, and the newly united Mercia was split up into its original parts ruled by several kings. The supremacy of Oswiu was, however, as little to be borne by the Mercians as the supremacy of Penda had been borne by the men of North-humberland. Under Wulfhere the Mercians rose in 659 against Oswiu. All hope of uniting England was for the present at an end. For about a century and a half longer there remained three larger kingdoms—North-humberland, Mercia, and Wessex, whilst four smaller ones—East Anglia, Essex, Kent, and Sussex—were usually attached either to Mercia or to Wessex. The failure of North-humberland to maintain the power

was, no doubt, in the first place owing to the absence of any common danger, the fear of which would bind together its populations in self-defence. The northern Kymry of Strathclyde were no longer formidable, and they grew less formidable as years passed on. The southern Kymry of Wales were too weak to threaten Mercia, and the Welsh of the south-western peninsula were too weak to threaten Wessex. It was most unlikely that any permanent union of the English states would be brought about till some enemy arose who was more terrible to them than the Welsh could any longer be.

21. **The English Missionaries.**—Some preparation might, however, be made for the day of union by the steady growth of the Church. The South Saxons, secluded between the forest and the sea, were the last to be converted, but with them English heathenism came to an end as an avowed religion, though it still continued to influence the multitude in the form of a belief in fairies and witchcraft. Monasteries and nunneries sprang up on all sides. Missionaries spread over the country. In their mouths, and still more in their lives, Christianity taught what the fierce English warrior most wanted to learn, the duty of restraining his evil passions, and above all his cruelty. Nowhere in all Europe did the missionaries appeal so exclusively as they did in England to higher and purer motives. Nowhere but in England were to be found kings like Oswald and Oswini, who bowed their souls to the lesson of the Cross, and learned that they were not their own, but were placed in power that they might use their strength in helping the poor and needy.

22. **Dispute between Wilfrid and Colman.   664.**—The lesson was all the better taught because those who taught it were monks. Monasticism brought with it an extravagant view of the life of self-denial, but those who had to be instructed needed to have the lesson written plainly so that a child might read it. The rough warrior or the rough peasant was more likely to abstain from drunkenness, if he had learned to look up to men who ate and drank barely enough to enable them to live ; and he was more likely to treat women with gentleness and honour, if he had learned to look up to some women who separated themselves from the joys of married life that they might give themselves to fasting and prayer. Yet, great as the influence of the clergy was, it was in danger of being lessened through internal disputes amongst themselves. A very large part of England had been converted by the Celtic missionaries, and the Celtic missionaries, though their life and teaching was in the main the same as that of the Church of Canterbury and of the Churches of the Continent, differed from them in the shape of

E

the tonsure and in the time at which they kept their Easter.   These things were themselves unimportant, but it was of great importance that the young English Church should not be separated from the Churches of more civilised countries which had preserved much of the learning and art of the old Roman Empire.   One of those who felt strongly the evil which would follow on such a separation was Wilfrid.   He was scornful and self-satisfied, but he had travelled to Rome, and had been impressed with the ecclesiastical memories of the great city, and with the fervour and learning of its clergy. He came back resolved to bring the customs of England into conformity with those of the churches of the Continent.   On his arrival, Oswiu, in **664**, gathered an assembly of the clergy of the north headed by Colman, Aidan's successor, to discuss the point. Learned arguments were poured forth on either side.   Oswiu listened in a puzzled way.   Wilfrid boasted that his mode of keeping Easter was derived from Peter, and that Christ had given to Peter the keys of the kingdom of heaven.   Oswiu at once decided to follow Peter, lest when he came to the gate of that kingdom Peter, who held the keys, should lock him out.   Wilfrid triumphed, and the English Church was in all outward matters regulated in conformity with that of Rome.

23. **Archbishop Theodore and the Penitential System.** — In **668**, four years after Oswiu's decision was taken, Theodore of Tarsus was consecrated Archbishop of Canterbury at Rome by the Pope himself.   When he arrived in England the time had come for the purely missionary stage of the English Church to come to an end. Hitherto the bishops had been few, only seven in all England.   Their number was now increased, and they were set to work no longer merely to convert the heathen, but to see that the clergy did their duty amongst those who had been already converted.   Gradually, under these bishops, a parochial clergy came into existence.   Sometimes the freemen of a hamlet, or of two or three hamlets together, would demand the constant residence of a priest.   Sometimes a lord would settle a priest to teach his serfs.   The parish clergy attacked violence and looseness of life in a way different from that of the monks. The monks had given examples of extreme self-denial.   Theodore introduced the penitential system of the Roman Church, and ordered that those who had committed sin should be excluded from sharing in the rites of the Church until they had done penance.   They were to fast, or to repeat prayers, sometimes for many years, before they were readmitted to communion.   Many centuries afterwards good men objected that these penances were only bodily actions, and

did not necessarily bring with them any real repentance. In the seventh century the greater part of the population could only be reached by such bodily actions. They had never had any thought that a murder, for instance, was anything more than a dangerous action which might bring down on the murderer the vengeance of the relations of the murdered man, which might be bought off with the payment of a weregild of a few shillings. The murderer who was required by the Church to do penance was being taught that a murder was a sin against God and against himself, as well as an offence against his fellow-men. Gradually—very gradually— men would learn from the example of the monks and from the discipline of penance that they were to live for something higher than the gratification of their own passions.

Saxon church at Bradford-on-Avon, Wilts.

24. **Ealdhelm and Cædmon.**—When a change is good in itself, it usually bears fruit in unexpected ways. Theodore was a scholar as well as a bishop. Under his care a school grew up at Canterbury, full of all the learning of the Roman world. That which distinguished this school and others founded in imitation of it was that the scholars did not keep their learning to themselves, but strove to make it helpful to the ignorant and the poor. They learnt architecture on the Continent in order to raise churches of stone in the place of churches of wood. One of these churches is still standing at Bradford-on-Avon. Its builder was Ealdhelm, the abbot of Malmesbury, a teacher of all the knowledge of the time. Ealdhelm, learned as he was, let his heart go forth to the unlearned. Finding that his neighbours would not listen to his sermons, he sang to them

on a bridge to win them to higher things. Like all people who cannot read, the English of those days loved a song. In the north, Cædmon, a rude herdsman on the lands of the abbey which in later days was known as Whitby, was vexed with himself because he could not sing. When at ale-drinkings his comrades pressed him to sing a song, he would leave his supper unfinished and return home ashamed. One night in a dream he heard a voice bidding him sing of the Creation. In his sleep the words came to him, and they remained with him when he woke. He had become a poet—a rude poet, it is true, but still a poet. The gift which Cædmon had acquired never left him. He sang of the Creation and of the whole course of God's providence. To the end he was unable to compose any songs which were not religious.

25. **Bede.** *673—735.*—Of all the English scholars of the time Bæda, usually known as 'the venerable Bede,' was the most remarkable. He was a monk of Jarrow on the Tyne. From his youth up he was a writer on all subjects embraced by the knowledge of his day. One subject he made his own. He was the first English historian. The title of his greatest work was the Ecclesiastical History of the English Nation. He told how that nation had been converted, and of the fortunes of its Church; but for him the Church included the whole nation, and he told of the doings of kings and people, as well as of priests and monks. In this he was a true interpreter of the spirit of the English Church. Its clergy did not stand aloof from the rulers of the state, but worked with them as well as for them. The bishops stepped into the place of the heathen priests in the Witenagemots of the kings, and counselled them in matters of state as well as in matters of religion.

26. **Church Councils.**—Bede recognised in the title of his book that there was such a thing as an English nation long before there was any political unity. Whilst kingdom was fighting against kingdom, Theodore in **673** assembled the first English Church council at Hertford. From that time such councils of the bishops and principal clergy of all England met whenever any ecclesiastical question required them to deliberate in common. The clergy at least did not meet as West Saxons or as Mercians. They met on behalf of the whole English Church, and their united consultations must have done much to spread the idea that, in spite of the strife between the kings, the English nation was really one.

27. **Struggle between Mercia and Wessex.**—Many years passed away before the kingdoms could be brought under one king. North-humberland stood apart from southern England, and during

the latter half of the seventh century Wessex grew in power. Wessex had been weak because it was seldom thoroughly united.

Each district was presided over by an Ætheling, or chief of royal blood, and it was only occasionally that these Æthelings, submitted to the king. From time to time a strong king compelled the obedience of the Æthelings and carried on the old struggle with the western Welsh. It was not till **710** that Ine succeeded in driving the Welsh out of Somerset, and about the same time a body of the West Saxons advancing through Dorset

Saxon horsemen. (Harl. MS. 603.)

reached Exeter. They took possession of half the city for themselves, and left the remainder to the Welsh. Ine was, however, checked by fresh outbreaks of the subordinate Æthelings, and in **726** he gave up the struggle and went on a pilgrimage to Rome. Æthelbald, king of the Mercians, took the opportunity to invade Wessex, and made himself master of the country and over-lord of all the other kingdoms south of the Humber. In **754** the West Saxons rose against him and defeated him at Burford. After a few years his successor, Offa, once more took up the task of making the Mercian king over-lord of southern England. In **775**, after a long struggle, he brought Kent as well as Essex under his sway. In **779** he defeated the West Saxons at Bensington, and pushed the Mercian

Group of Saxon warriors. (Harl. MS. 603.)

frontier to the Thames. Further than that Offa did not venture to go, and, great as he was, the West Saxons within their shrunken limits continued to be independent of him.   He turned his arms upon the Welsh, and drove them back from the Severn to the embankment which is known from his name as Offa's Dyke.   The West Saxons, being freed from attack on the side of Mercia, overran Devon.   Then there was a contest for the West Saxon crown between Beorhtric and Ecgberht.   Beorhtric gained the upper hand, and entered into alliance with Offa by taking his daughter to wife. Ecgberht fled to the Continent.

28. Mohammedanism and the Carolingian Empire.—A great change had passed over Europe since the days when a Frankish princess, by her marriage with the Kentish Ethelberht, had smoothed the way for the introduction of Christianity into England.   In the first part of the seventh century Mohammed had preached a new religion in Arabia.   He taught that there was one God, and that Mohammed was his prophet.   After his death his Arab followers spread as conquerors over the neighbouring countries.   Before the end of the century they had subdued Persia, Syria, and Egypt, and were pushing westwards along the north coast of Africa.   In **711** they crossed the Straits of Gibraltar.   All Spain, with the exception of a hilly district in the north, soon fell into their hands, and in **717** they crossed the Pyrenees.   There can be little doubt that, if they had subdued Gaul, Mohammedanism and not Christianity would for a long time have been the prevailing religion in Europe.   From this Europe was saved by a great Frankish warrior, Charles Martel (*the Hammer*), who in **732** drove the invaders back at a great battle between Tours and Poitiers.   Charles's son, Pippin, dethroned the reigning family and became king of the Franks.   Pippin's son was Charles the Great, who before he died ruled over the whole of Gaul and Germany, over the north and centre of Italy, and the north-east of Spain.   His rule was favoured both by the Frankish warriors and by the clergy, who were glad to see so strong a bulwark erected against the attacks of the Mohammedans.   At that time the Roman Empire, which had never ceased to exist at Constantinople, fell into the hands of Irene, the murderess of her son.   In **800** the Pope, refusing to acknowledge that the Empire could have so unworthy a head, placed the Imperial crown on the head of Charles as the successor of the old Roman Emperors.

29. Ecgberht's Rule. 802—839.—Though Charles did not directly govern England, he made his influence felt there.   Offa had claimed his protection, and Ecgberht took refuge at his court.   Ecgberht doubtless learned something of the art of ruling from him, and in **802** he returned to England.   Beorhtric was by this time dead,

and Ecgberht was accepted as king by the West Saxons.   Before
he died, in **839**, he had made himself the over-lord of all the other
kingdoms.   He was never, indeed, directly king of all England.
Kent, Sussex, and Essex were governed by rulers of his own family
appointed by himself.   Mercia, East Anglia, and North-humberland
retained their own kings, ruling under Ecgberht as their over-lord.
Towards the west Ecgberht's direct government did not reach beyond
the Tamar, though the Cornish Celts acknowledged his authority, as
did the Celts of Wales.   The Celts of Strathclyde and the Picts and
Scots remained entirely independent.

CHAPTER IV

THE ENGLISH KINGSHIP AND THE STRUGGLE WITH
THE DANES

LEADING DATES

First landing of the Danes 787
Treaty of Wedmore 878
Dependent alliance of the Scots with Eadward the Elder . 925
Accession of Eadgar 959

1. The West Saxon Supremacy.—It was quite possible that
the power founded by Ecgberht might pass away as completely
as did the power which had been founded by Æthelfrith of North-
humberland or by Penda of Mercia.   To some extent the danger
was averted by the unusual strength of character which for six
generations showed itself in the family of Ecgberht.   For nearly a
century and a half after Ecgberht's death no ruler arose from his
line who had not great qualities as a warrior or as a ruler.   It was
no less important that these successive kings, with scarcely an
exception, kept up a good understanding with the clergy, and
especially with the Archbishops of Canterbury, so that the whole of
the influence of the Church was thrown in favour of the political
unity of England under the West Saxon line.   The clergy wished
to see the establishment of a strong national government for the
protection of the national Church.   Yet it was difficult to establish
such a government unless other causes than the goodwill of the
clergy had contributed to its maintenance.   Peoples who have had
little intercourse except by fighting with one another rarely unite

heartily unless they have some common enemy to ward off, and some common leader to look up to in the conduct of their defence.[1]

Remains of a Viking ship, from a cairn at Gokstad. (Now in the University at Christiania.)

2. The Coming of the Northmen.

—The common enemy came from the north. At the end of the eighth century the inhabitants

[1] Genealogy of the English kings from Ecgberht to Eadgar:—

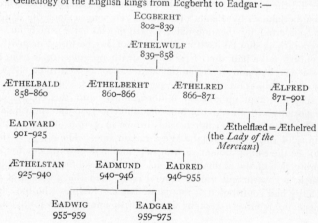

ECGBERHT
802–839

ÆTHELWULF
839–858

ÆTHELBALD   ÆTHELBERHT   ÆTHELRED   ÆLFRED
858–860   860–866   866–871   871–901

EADWARD   Æthelflæd = Æthelred
901–925   (the *Lady of the*
                                       Mercians)

ÆTHELSTAN   EADMUND   EADRED
925–940   940–946   946–955

EADWIG   EADGAR
955–959   959–975

of Norway and Denmark resembled the Angles and Saxons
three or four centuries before. They swarmed over the sea as
pirates to plunder wherever they could find stored-up wealth along
the coasts of Western Europe. The Northmen were heathen
still, and their religion was the old religion of force. They loved
battle even more than they loved plunder. They held that the
warrior who was slain in fight was received by the god Odin in
Valhalla, where immortal heroes spent their days in cutting one
another to pieces, and were healed of their wounds in the evening
that they might join in the nightly feast, and be able to fight again
on the morrow. He that died in bed was condemned to a chilly
and dreary existence in the abode of the goddess Hela, whose name
is the Norse equivalent of Hell.

3. **The English Coast Plundered.**—Since Englishmen had settled
in England they had lost the art of seamanship. The Northmen
therefore were often able to plunder and sail away. They could
only be attacked on land, and some time would pass before the
Ealdorman who ruled the district could
gather together not only his own war-band,
but the fyrd, or levy of all men of fighting
age. When at last he arrived at the spot
on the coast where the pirates had been
plundering, he often found that they were
already gone. Yet, as time went on, the
Northmen took courage, and pushed far
enough into the interior to be attacked
before they could regain the coast. Their
first landing had been in **787**, before the
time of Ecgberht. In Ecgberht's reign
their attacks upon Wessex were so persis-
tent that Ecgberht had to bring his own war-band to the succour
of his Ealdormen. His son and successor, Æthelwulf, had a still
harder struggle. The pirates spread their attacks over the whole
of the southern and the eastern coast, and ventured to remain
long enough on shore to fight a succession of battles. In **851** they
were strong enough to remain during the whole winter in Thanet.
The crews of no less than 350 ships landed in the mouth of the
Thames sacked Canterbury and London. They were finally defeated by Æthelwulf at Aclea (*Ockley*), in Surrey. In **858** Æthelwulf died. Four of his sons wore the crown in succession ; the two
eldest, Æthelbald and Æthelberht, ruling only a short time.

Gold ring of Æthelwulf.

4. **The Danes in the North.**—The task of the third brother,

Æthelred, who succeeded in 866, was harder than his father's. Hitherto the Northmen had come for plunder, and had departed sooner or later. A fresh swarm of Danes now arrived from Denmark to settle on the land as conquerors. Though they did not themselves fight on horseback, they seized horses to betake themselves rapidly from one part of England to the other. Their first attack was made on the north, where there was no great affection for the West Saxon kings. They overcame the greater part of North-humberland. They beat down the resistance of East Anglia, and, fastening its king, Eadmund, to a tree, shot him to death with arrows. His countrymen counted him a saint, and a great monastery arose at Bury St. Edmunds in his honour. Everywhere the Danes plundered and burnt the monasteries, because the monks were weak, and their houses were rich with jewelled service books and golden plate. They next turned upon Mercia, and forced the Mercian under-king to pay tribute to them. Only Wessex, to which the smaller eastern states of Kent and Sussex had by this time been completely annexed, retained its independence.

5. **Ælfred's Struggle in Wessex. 871—878.**—In Wessex Æthelred strove hard against the invaders. He won a great victory at Æscesdun (*Ashdown*, near Reading), on the northern slope of the Berkshire Downs. After a succession of battles he was slain in **871**. Though he left sons of his own, he was succeeded by Ælfred, his youngest brother. It was not the English custom to give the crown to the child of a king if there was any one of the kingly family more fitted to wear it. Ælfred was no common man. In his childhood he had visited Rome, and had been hallowed as king by Pope Leo IV., though the ceremony could have had no weight in England. He had early shown a love of letters, and the story goes that when his mother offered a book with bright illuminations to the one of her children who could first learn to read it, the prize was won by Ælfred. During Æthelred's reign he had little time to give to learning. He fought nobly by his brother's side in the battles of the day, and after he succeeded him he fought nobly as king at the head of his people. In **878** the Danish host, under its king, Guthrum, beat down all resistance. Ælfred was no longer able to keep in the open country, and took refuge with a few chosen warriors in the little island of Athelney, in Somerset, then surrounded by the waters of the fen country through which the Parret flowed. After a few weeks he came forth, and with the levies of Somerset and Wilts and of part of Hants he utterly defeated Guthrum at Ethandun (? *Edington*, in Wiltshire), and stormed his camp.

6. **The Treaty of Chippenham, and its Results. 878.**—After this defeat Guthrum and the Danes swore to a peace with Ælfred at Chippenham. They were afterwards baptised in a body at Aller, not far from Athelney. Guthrum with a few of his companions then visited Ælfred at Wedmore, a village near the southern foot of the Mendips, from which is taken the name by which the treaty is usually but wrongly known. By this treaty Ælfred retained no more than Wessex, with its dependencies, Sussex and Kent, and the western half of Mercia. The remainder of England as far north as the Tees was

Gold jewel of Ælfred found at Athelney. (Now in the Ashmolean Museum, Oxford.)

surrendered to the Danes, and became known as the Danelaw, because Danish and not Saxon law prevailed in it. Beyond the Tees Bernicia maintained its independence under an English king. Though the English people never again had to struggle for its very existence as a political body, yet, in **886,** after a successful war, Ælfred wrung from Guthrum a fresh treaty by which the Danes surrendered London and the surrounding district. Yet, even after this second treaty, it might seem as if Ælfred, who only ruled over a part of England, was worse off than his grandfather, Ecgberht, who had ruled over the whole. In reality he was better off. In the larger kingdom it would have been almost impossible to produce the national spirit which alone could have permanently kept the whole together. In the smaller kingdom it was possible, especially as there was a strong West Saxon element in the south-west of Mercia in consequence of its original settlement by a West Saxon king after the battle of Deorham (see p. 35). Moreover, Ælfred, taking care not to offend the old feeling of local independence which still existed in Mercia, appointed his son-in-law, Æthel-red, who was a Mercian, to govern it as an ealdorman under himself.

7. Ælfred's Military Work.—Ælfred would hardly have been able to do so much unless his own character had been singularly attractive. Other men have been greater warriors or legislators or scholars than Ælfred was, but no man has ever combined in his own person so much excellence in war, in legislation, and in

An English vessel. (Harl. MS. 603.)

scholarship. As to war, he was not only a daring and resolute commander, but he was an organiser of the military forces of his people. One chief cause of the defeats of the English had been the difficulty of bringing together in a short time the 'fyrd,' or general levy of the male population, or of keeping it long together when men were needed at home to till the fields. Ælfred did his best to overcome this difficulty by ordering that half the men of each shire should be always ready to fight, whilst half remained at home. This new half-army, like his new half-kingdom, was stronger than the whole one had been before. To an improved army Ælfred added a navy, and he was the first English king who defeated the Danes at sea.

8. His Laws and Scholarship.—Ælfred was too great a man to want to make every one conform to some ideal of his own choosing. It was enough for him to take men as they were, and to help them to become better. He took the old laws and customs, and then, suggesting a few improvements, submitted them to the approval of his Witenagemot, the assembly of his bishops and warriors. He knew also that men's conduct is influenced more by what they think than by what they are commanded to do. His whole land was steeped in ignorance. The monasteries had been the schools of learning ; and many of them had been sacked by the Danes, their books burnt, and their inmates scattered, whilst others were deserted, ceasing to receive new inmates because the first duty of Englishmen had been to defend their homes rather than to devote themselves to a life of piety. Latin was the language in which the services of the Church were read, and in which books like Bede's Ecclesiastical History were written. Without a knowledge of Latin there could be no intercourse with the learned men of the Continent, who used that language still amongst themselves. Yet when the Danes departed from Ælfred's kingdom, there were but very few priests who could read a page of Latin. Ælfred did his best to remedy the evil. He called learned men to him wherever they could be found. Some of these were English; others, like Asser, who wrote Ælfred's life, were Welsh; others again were Germans from beyond the sea. Yet Ælfred was not content. It was a great thing that there should be again schools in England for those who could write and speak Latin, the language of the learned, but his heart yearned for those who could not speak anything but their own native tongue. He set himself to be the teacher of these.

A Saxon house. (Harl. MS. 603.)

He himself translated Latin books for them, with the object of imparting knowledge, not of giving, as a modern translator would do, the exact sense of the author. When, therefore, he knew anything which was not in the books, but which he thought it good for Englishmen to read, he added it to his translation. Even with this he was not content. The books of Latin writers which he translated taught men about the history and geography of the Continent. They taught nothing about the history of England itself, of the deeds and words of the men who had ruled the English nation. That these things might not be forgotten, he bade his learned men bring together all that was known of the history of his people since the day when they first landed as pirates on the coast of Kent. The Chronicle, as it is called, is the earliest history which any European nation possesses in its own tongue.

Yet, after all, such a man as Ælfred is greater for what he was than for what he did. No other king ever showed forth so well in his own person the truth of the saying, ' He that would be first among you, let him be the servant of all.'

9. **Eadward the Elder. 901—925.**—In 901 Ælfred died. He had already fortified London as an outpost against the Danes, and he left to his son, Eadward, a small but strong and consolidated kingdom. The Danes on the other side of the frontier were not united. Guthrum's kingdom stretched over the old Essex and East Anglia, as well as over the south-eastern part of the old Mercia. The land from the Humber to the Nen was under the rule of Danes settled in the towns known to the English as the Five boroughs of Derby, Leicester, Lincoln, Stamford, and Nottingham. In the old Deira or modern Yorkshire was a separate Danish kingdom. Danes, in short, settled wherever we now find the place-names, such as Derby and Whitby, ending in the Danish termination ' by ' instead of in the English terminations ' ton ' or ' ham,' as in Luton and Chippenham. Yet even in these parts the bulk of the population was usually English, and the English population would everywhere welcome an English conqueror. A century earlier a Mercian or a North-humbrian had preferred independence to submission to a West Saxon king. They now preferred a West Saxon king to a Danish master, especially as the old royal houses were extinct, and there was no one but the West Saxon king to lead them against the Danes.

10. **Eadward's Conquests.**—Eadward was not, like his father, a legislator or a scholar, but he was a great warrior. In a series of campaigns he subdued the Danish parts of England as far north as the Humber. He was aided by his brother-in-law, Æthelred, and after Æthelred's death by his own sister, Æthelred's widow, Æthelflæd, the Lady of the Mercians, one of the few warrior-women of the world. Step by step the brother and sister won their way, not contenting themselves with victories in the open country, but securing each district as they advanced by the erection of ' burhs ' or fortifications. Some of these ' burhs ' were placed in desolate Roman strongholds, such as Chester. Others were raised, like that of Warwick, on the mounds piled up in past times by a still earlier race. Others again, like that of Stafford, were placed where no fortress had been before. Towns, small at first, grew up in and around the ' burhs,' and were guarded by the courage of the towns-men themselves. Eadward, after his sister's death, took into his own hands the government of Mercia, and from that time all

southern and central England was united under him. In **922** the Welsh kings acknowledged his supremacy.

11. **Eadward and the Scots.**—Tradition assigns to Eadward a wider rule shortly before his death. In the middle of the ninth century the Picts and the intruding Scots (see p. 42) had been amalgamated under Keneth MacAlpin, the king of the Scots, and the new kingdom had since been welded together, just as Mercia and Wessex were being welded together by the attacks of the Danes. It is said that in **925** the king of the Scots, together with other northern rulers, chose Eadward 'to father and lord.' Probably this statement only covers some act of alliance formed by the English king with the king of Scots and other lesser rulers. Nothing was more natural than that the Scottish king, Constantine, should wish to obtain the support of Eadward against his enemies ; and it was also natural that if Eadward agreed to support him, he would require some acknowledgment of the superiority of the English king ; but what was the precise form of the acknowledgment must remain uncertain. In **925** Eadward died.

12. **Æthelstan. 925—940.**—Three sons of Eadward reigned in succession. The eldest, of illegitimate birth, was Æthelstan. Sihtric, the Danish king at York, owned him as over-lord, and on Sihtric's death in **926**, Æthelstan took Danish North-humberland under his direct rule. The Welsh kings were reduced to make a fuller acknowledgment of his supremacy than they had made to his father. He drove the Welsh out of the half of Exeter which had been left to them, and confined them to the modern Cornwall beyond the Tamar. Great rulers on the Continent sought his alliance. The empire of Charles the Great had broken up. One of Æthelstan's sisters was given to Charles the Simple, the king of the Western Franks ; another to Hugh the Great, Duke of the French and lord of Paris, who, though nominally the vassal of the king, was equal in power to his lord, and whose son was afterwards the first king of modern France. A third sister was given to Otto, the son of Henry, the king of the Eastern Franks, from whom, in due time, sprang a new line of Emperors. Æthelstan's greatness drew upon him the jealousy of the king of the Scots and of all the northern kings. In **937** he defeated them all in a great battle at Brunanburh, of which the site is unknown. His victory was celebrated in a splendid war-song.

13. **Eadmund (940—946) and Eadred (946—955).**—Æthelstan died in **940**. He was succeeded by his young brother, Eadmund, who had fought bravely at Brunanburh. Eadmund had to meet a

general rising of the Danes of Mercia as well as of those of the north. After he had suppressed the rising he showed himself to be a great statesman as well as a great warrior. The relations between the king of the English and the king of the Scots had for some time been very uncertain. Little is definitely known about them, but it looks as if they joined the English whenever they were afraid of the Danes, and joined the Danes whenever they were afraid of the English. Eadmund took an opportunity of making it to be the interest of the Scottish king permanently to join the English. The southern part of the kingdom of Strathclyde had for some time been under the English kings. In **945** Eadmund overran the remainder, but gave it to Malcolm on condition that he should be his fellow-worker by sea and land. The king of Scots thus entered into a position of dependent alliance towards Eadmund. A great step was thus taken in the direction in which the inhabitants of Britain afterwards walked. The dominant powers in the island were to be English and Scots, not English and Danes. Eadmund thought it worth while to conciliate the Scottish Celts rather than to endeavour to conquer them. The result of Eadmund's statesmanship was soon made manifest. He himself did not live to gather its fruits. In **946** an outlaw who had taken his seat at a feast in his hall slew him as he was attempting to drag him out by the hair. The next king, Eadred, the last of Eadward's sons, though sickly, had all the spirit of his race. He had another sharp struggle with the Danes, but in **954** he made himself their master. North-humberland was now thoroughly amalgamated with the English kingdom, and was to be governed by an Englishman, Oswulf, with the title of Earl, an old Danish title equivalent to the English Ealdorman, having nothing to do, except philologically, with the old English word Eorl.

14. **Danes and English.**—In **955** Eadred died, having completed the work which Ælfred had begun, and which had been carried on by his son and his three grandsons. England, from the Forth to the Channel, was under one ruler. Even the contrast between Englishmen and Danes was soon, for the most part, wiped out. They were both of the same Teutonic stock, and therefore their languages were akin to one another and their institutions very similar. The Danes of the north were for some time fiercer and less easily controlled than the English of the south, but there was little national distinction between them, and what little there was gradually passed away.

15. **Eadwig. 955—959.**—Eadred was succeeded by Eadwig, the

eldest son of his brother Eadmund. Eadwig was hardly more than fifteen years old, and it would be difficult for a boy to keep order amongst the great ealdormen and earls. At his coronation feast he gave deep offence by leaving his place to amuse himself with a young kinswoman, Ælfgifu, in her mother's room, whence he was followed and dragged back by two ecclesiastics, one of whom was Dunstan, Abbot of Glastonbury.

16. **Dunstan.**— Dunstan in his boyhood had been attached to Eadmund's court, but he had been driven off by the rivalry of other youths. He was in no way fitted to be a warrior. He loved art and song, and preferred a book to a sword. For such youths there was no place amongst the fighting laymen, and Dunstan early found the peace which he sought as a monk at Glastonbury. Eadmund made him abbot, but Dunstan had almost to create his monastery before he could rule it. Monasteries had nearly vanished from England in the time of the Danish plunderings, and the few monks who remained had very little that was monastic about them. Dunstan brought the old monks into order, and attracted new ones, but to the end of his days he was conspicuous rather as a scholar than as an ascetic. From Glastonbury he carried on the work of teaching an ignorant generation, just as Ælfred had done in an earlier time. Ælfred, however, was a warrior and a ruler first, and then a teacher. Dunstan was a teacher first, and then a ruler. Eadred took counsel with him, and Dunstan became thus the first example of a class of men which afterwards rose to power — that, namely, of ecclesiastical statesmen. Up to that time all who had governed had been warriors.

17. **Archbishop Oda.**—Another side of the Church's work, the maintenance of a high standard of morality, was, in the time of Eadred, represented by Oda, Archbishop of Canterbury. The accepted standard of morality differs in different ages, and, for many reasons, it was held by the purer minds in the tenth century that celibacy was nobler than marriage. If our opinion is changed now, it is because many things have changed. No one then thought of teaching a girl anything, except to sew and to look after the house, and an ignorant and untrained wife could only be a burden to a man who was intent upon the growth of the spiritual or intellectual life in himself and in others. At all times the monks, who were often called the regular clergy, because they lived according to a certain rule, had been unmarried, and attempts had frequently been made by councils of the Church to compel the parish priests, or secular clergy, to follow their example. In England, however,

F

A monk driven out of the King's presence.   (From a drawing belonging to the Society
of Antiquaries.)

and on the Continent as well, these orders were seldom heeded, and a married clergy was everywhere to be found. Of late, however, there had sprung up in the monastery of Cluny, in Burgundy, a zeal for the establishment of universal clerical celibacy, and this zeal was shared by Archbishop Oda, though he found it impossible to overcome the stubborn resistance of the secular clergy.

18. **Eadwig's Marriage.**—In its eagerness to set up a pure standard of morality, the Church had made rules against the marriage of even distant relations. Eadwig offended against these rules by marrying his kinswoman, Ælfgifu. A quarrel arose on this occount between Dunstan and the young king, and Dunstan was driven into banishment. Such a quarrel was sure to weaken the king, because the support of the bishops was usually given to him, for the sake of the maintenance of peace and order. The dispute came at a bad time, because there was also a quarrel among the ealdormen and other great men. At last the ealdormen of the north and centre of England revolted and set up the king's brother, Eadgar, to be king of all England north of the Thames. Upon this, Oda, taking courage, declared Eadwig and his young wife to be separated as too near of kin, and even seized her and had her carried beyond sea. In 959 Eadwig died, and Eadgar succeeded to the whole kingdom.

CHAPTER V

EADGAR'S ENGLAND

1. **Eadgar and Dunstan. 959—975.**—Eadgar was known as the Peaceful King. He had the advantage, which Eadwig had not, of having the Church on his side. He maintained order, with the help of Dunstan as his principal adviser. Not long after his accession Dunstan became Archbishop of Canterbury. His policy was that of a man who knows that he cannot do everything and is content to do what he can. The Danes were to keep their own laws, and not to have English laws forced upon them. The great ealdormen were to be conciliated, not to be repressed. Everything was to be done to raise the standard of morality and knowledge. Foreign teachers were brought in to set up schools. More than this Dunstan did not attempt. It is true that in his time an effort was

made to found monasteries, which should be filled with monks living after the stricter rule of which the example had been set at Cluny, but the man who did most to establish monasteries again in England was not Dunstan, but Æthelwold, Bishop of Winchester. Æthelwold, however, was not content with founding monasteries. He also drove out the secular canons from his own cathedral of Winchester and filled their places with monks. His example was followed by Oswald, Bishop of Worcester. Dunstan did not introduce monks even into his own cathedrals at Worcester and Canterbury. As far as it is now possible to understand the matter, the change, though it provoked great hostility, was for the better. The secular canons were often married, connected with the laity of the neighbourhood, and living an easy life. The monks were celibate, living according to a strict rule, and conforming themselves to what, according to the standard of the age, was the highest ideal of religion. By a life of complete self-denial they were able to act as examples to a generation which needed teaching by example more than by word. How completely monasticism was associated with learning is shown by the fact that the monks now established at Worcester took up the work of continuing the Chronicle which had been begun under Ælfred (see p. 61).

2. **The Cession of Lothian.**—It is said that Eadgar was once rowed by six kings on the river Dee. The story, though probably untrue, sets forth his power not only over his own immediate subjects but over the whole island. His title of Peaceful shows that at least he lived on good terms with his neighbours. There is reason to believe that he was able to do this because he followed out the policy of Eadmund in singling out the king of Scots as the ruler whom it was most worth his while to conciliate. Eadmund had given over Strathclyde to one king of Scots. Eadgar, it is said—and probably with truth—gave over Lothian to another. Lothian was then the name of the whole of the northern part of Bernicia stretching from the Cheviots to the Forth. In Eadred's time the Scots had occupied Eadwinesburh (*Edinburgh*), the northern border fortress of Bernicia (see p. 43), and after this the land to the south of that fortress must have been difficult to defend against them. It is therefore likely that the story is true that Eadgar ceded Lothian to Kenneth, who was then king of the Scots, especially as it would account for the peaceful character of his reign. Kenneth in accepting the gift no doubt engaged to be faithful to Eadgar, though it is impossible to say what was the exact nature of his obligation. It is of more importance that a Celtic king ruled thenceforward over an

English people as well as over his own Celtic Scots, and that ultimately his descendants became more English than Celtic in
character, through the attraction exercised upon them by their
English subjects.

3. **Changes in English Institutions.**—The long struggle with
the Danes could not fail to leave its mark upon English society.
The history of the changes which took place is difficult to trace ;
in the first place because our information is scanty, in the second
because things happened in one part of the country which did not
happen in another. Yet there were two changes which were widely
felt : the growth of the king's authority, and the acceleration of the
process which was reducing to bondage the ceorl, or simple freeman.

4. **Growth of the King's Power.**—In the early days of the
English conquest the kings and other great men had around them
their war-bands, composed of gesiths or thegns, personally attached to themselves, and ready, if need were, to die on their lord's
behalf. Very early these thegns were rewarded by grants of land
on condition of continuing military service. Every extension of
the king's power over fresh territory made their services more important. It had always been difficult to bring together the fyrd,
or general army of the freemen, even of a small district, and it
was quite impossible to bring together the fyrd of a kingdom
reaching from the Channel to the Firth of Forth. Ælfred's
division of the fyrd into two parts, one to fight and the other
to stay at home, may have served when all the fighting had to
be done in the western part of Wessex. Æthelstan or Eadmund
could not possibly make even half of the men of Devonshire
or Essex fight in his battles north of the Humber. The kings
therefore had to rely more and more upon their thegns, who in
turn had thegns of their own whom they could bring with them ;
and thus was formed an army ready for military service in any part
of the kingdom. A king who could command such an army was
even more powerful than one who could command the whole of
the forces of a smaller territory.

5. **Conversion of the Freemen into Serfs.**—It is impossible to
give a certain account of the changes which passed over the English
freemen, but there can be little doubt that a process had been for
some time going on which converted them into bondmen, and that
this process was greatly accelerated by the Danish wars. When
a district was being plundered the peasant holders of the strips
of village land suffered most, and needed the protection of the
neighbouring thegn, who was better skilled in war than themselves,

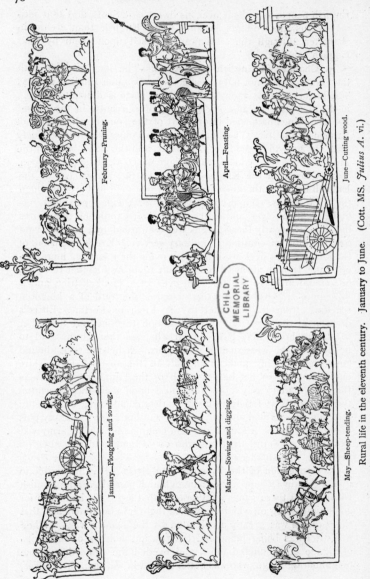

February—Pruning.

April—Feasting.

June—Cutting wood.

January—Ploughing and sowing.

March—Sowing and digging.

May—Sheep-tending.

Rural life in the eleventh century. January to June. (Cott. MS. *Julius A. vi.*)

August—Harvesting.

October—Hawking.

December—Threshing and Winnowing.

July—Mowing.

September—Feeding swine.

November—Making a bonfire.

Rural life in the eleventh century.   July to December.   (Cott. MS.   *Julius A. vi.*)

and this protection they could only obtain on condition of becoming bondmen themselves—that is to say, of giving certain days in the week to work on the special estate of the lord. A bondman differed both from a slave and from a modern farmer. Though he was bound to the soil and could not go away if he wished to do so, yet he could not be sold as though he were a slave ; nor, on the other hand, could he, like a farmer, be turned out of his holding so long as he fulfilled his obligation of cultivating his lord's demesne. The lord was almost invariably a thegn, either of the king or of some superior thegn, and there thus arose in England, as there arose about the same time on the Continent, a chain of personal relationships. The king was no longer merely the head of the whole people. He was the personal lord of his own thegns, and they again were the lords of other thegns. The serfs cultivated their lands, and thereby set them free to fight for the king on behalf of the whole nation. It seems at first sight as if the English people had fallen into a worse condition. An organisation, partly military and partly servile, was substituted for an organisation of free men. Yet only in this way could the whole of England be amalgamated. The nation gained in unity what it lost in freedom.

6. **The Hundred-moot and the Lord's Court.**—In another way the condition of the peasants was altered for the worse by the growth of the king's power. In former days land was held as 'folkland,' granted by the people at the original conquest, passing to the kinsmen of the holder if he died without children. Afterwards the clergy introduced a system by which the owner could grant the 'bookland,' held by book or charter, setting at nought the claim of his kinsmen, and in order to give validity to the arrangement, obtained the consent of the king and his Witenagemot (see p. 45). In time, the king and the Witenagemot granted charters in other cases, and the new 'bookland' to a great extent superseded the old 'folkland,' accompanied by a grant of the right of holding special courts. In this manner the old hundred-moots became neglected, people seeking for justice in the courts of the lords. Yet those who lived on the lord's land attended his court, appeared as compurgators, and directed the ordeal just as they had once done in the hundred-moot.

7. **The Towns.**—The towns had grown up in various ways. Some were of old Roman foundation, such as Lincoln and Gloucester. Others, like Nottingham and Bristol, had come into existence since the English settlement. Others again gathered round monasteries, like Bury St. Edmunds and Peterborough. The

inhabitants met to consult about their own affairs, sometimes in dependence on a lord. Where there was no lord they held a court which was composed in the same way as the hundred-moots outside. The townsmen had the right of holding a market. Every sale had to take place in the presence of witnesses who could prove, if called upon to do so, that the sale had really taken place, and markets were therefore usually to be found in towns, because it was there that witnesses could most easily be found.

8. **The Origin of the Shires.**—Shires, which were divisions larger than the hundreds, and smaller than the larger kingdoms, originated in various ways. In the south, and on the east coast as far north as the Wash, they were either old kingdoms like Kent and Essex, or settlements forming part of old kingdoms, as Norfolk (the north folk) formed part of East Anglia, and Dorset or Somerset, the lands of the Dorsætan or the Somersætan, formed part of the kingdom of Wessex. In the centre and north they were of more recent origin, and were probably formed as those parts of England were gradually reconquered from the Danes. The fact that most of these shires are named from towns—as Derbyshire from Derby, and Warwickshire from Warwick—shows that they came into existence after towns had become of importance.

9. **The Shire-moot.**—Whilst the hundred-moot decayed, the folk-moot continued to flourish under a new name, as the shire-moot. This moot was still attended by the freemen of the shire though the thegns were more numerous and the simple freemen less numerous than they had once been. Still the continued existence of the shire-moot kept up the custom of self-government more than anything else in England. The ordeals were witnessed, the were-gild inflicted, and rights to land adjudged, not by an officer of the king, but by the landowners of the shire assembled for the purpose. These meetings were ordinarily presided over by the ealdorman, who appeared as the military commander and the official head of the shire, and by the bishop, who represented the Church. Another most important personage was the sheriff, or shire-reeve, whose business it was to see that the king had all his rights, to preside over the shire-moot when it sat as a judicial court, and to take care that its sentences were put in execution.

10. **The Ealdormen and the Witenagemot.**—During the long fight with the Danes commanders were needed who could lead the forces of more than a single shire. Before the end of Eadred's reign there were ealdormen who ruled over many shires. One of them for instance, Æthelstan, Ealdorman of East Anglia, and of

the shires immediately to the west of East Anglia, was so powerful
that he was popularly known as the Half-King. Such earldormen
had great influence in their own districts, and they also were very
powerful about the king. The king could not perform any important act without the consent of the Witenagemot, which was

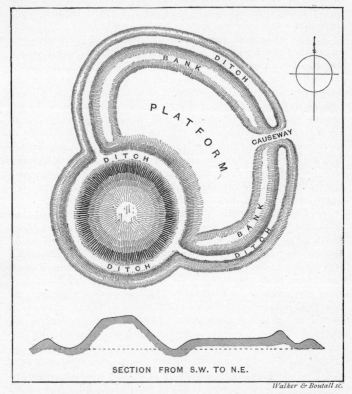

Walker & Boutall sc.

Plan and section of a burh of the eleventh century at Laughton-en-le-Morthen, Yorks.

made up of three classes—the Ealdormen, the Bishops, and the
greater Thegns. When a king died the Witenagemot chose his
successor out of the kingly family; its members appeared as witnesses whenever the king 'booked' land to any one; and it even,
on rare occasions, deposed a king who was unfit for his post. In

the days of a great warrior king like Eadward or Eadmund, members of the Witenagemot were but instruments in his hands, but if a weak king came upon the throne, each member usually took his own way and pursued his own interest rather than that of the king and kingdom.

11. **The Land.**—The cultivated land was surrounded either by wood or. by pasture and open commons. Every cottager kept his hive of bees, to produce the honey which was then used as we now use sugar, and drove his swine into the woods to fatten on the acorns and beech nuts which strewed the ground in the autumn. Sheep and cattle were fed on the pastures, and horses were so abundant that when the Danish pirates landed they found it easy to set every man on horseback. Yet neither the Danes nor the English ever learnt to fight on horseback. They rode to battle, but as soon as they approached the enemy they dismounted to fight on foot.

12. **Domestic Life.**—The huts of the villagers clustered round the house of the lord. His abode was built in a yard surrounded for protection by a mound and fence, whilst very great men often established themselves in burhs, surrounded by earthworks, either of their own raising or the work of earlier times. Its principal feature was the hall, in which the whole family with the guests and the thegns of the lord met for their meals. The walls were covered with curtains worked in patterns of bright colours. The fire was lighted on the hearth, a broad stone in the middle, over which was a hole in the roof through which the smoke of the hall escaped. The windows were narrow, and were either unclosed holes in the wall, or covered with oiled linen which would admit a certain amount of light.

13. **Food and Drink.**—In a great house at meal-time boards were brought forward and placed on tressels. Bread was to be had in plenty, and salt butter. Meat too, in winter, was always salted, as turnips and other roots upon which cattle are now fed in winter were wholly unknown, and it was therefore necessary to kill large numbers of sheep and oxen when the cold weather set in. There were dishes, but neither plates nor forks. Each man took the meat in his fingers and either bit off a piece or cut it off with a knife. The master of the house sat at the head of the table, and the lady handed round the drink, and afterwards sat down by her husband's side. She, however, with any other ladies who might be present, soon departed to the chamber which was their own apartment. The men continued drinking long. The cups or

glasses which they used were often made with the bottoms rounded so as to force the guests to keep them in their hands till

Glass tumbler. (British Museum.)

they were empty. The usual drink was mead, that is to say, fermented honey, or ale brewed from malt alone, as hops were not

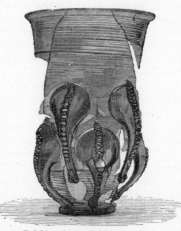

Drinking glass. (British Museum.)

introduced till many centuries later. In wealthy houses imported wine was to be had. English wine was not unknown, but it was so sour that it had to be sweetened with honey. It was held to be disgraceful to leave the company as long as the drinking lasted, and drunkenness and quarrels were not unfrequent. Wandering minstrels who could play and sing or tell stories were always welcome, especially if they were jugglers as well, and could amuse the company by throwing knives in the air and catching them as they fell, or could dance on their hands with their legs in the air. When the feast was over, the guests and dependents slept on the

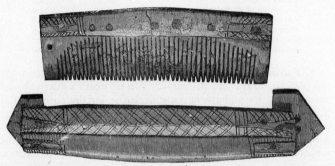

Comb and case of Scandinavian type, found at York. (Now in the British Museum.)

floor on rugs or straw, each man taking care to hang his weapons close to his head on the wall, to defend himself in case of an attack by robbers in the night. The lord retired to his chamber, whilst the unmarried ladies occupied bowers, or small rooms, each with a separate door opening on to the yard. Their only beds were bags of straw. Neither men nor women wore night-dresses of any kind, but if they took off their clothes at all, wrapped themselves in rugs.

CHAPTER VI

ENGLAND AND NORMANDY

LEADING DATES

Death of Eadgar	975
Accession of Æthelred	979
Accession of Cnut	1016
Accession of Eadward the Confessor	1035
Banishment of Godwine	1051
Accession of Harold and Batt'e of Senlac	1066

1. **Eadward the Martyr. 975—979.**—Eadgar died in 975, leaving two boys, Eadward and Æthelred.[1] On his death a quarrel broke out amongst the ealdormen, some declaring for the succession of Eadward and others for the succession of Æthelred. The political quarrel was complicated by an ecclesiastical quarrel. The supporters of Eadward were the friends of the secular clergy ; the supporters of Æthelred were the friends of the monks. Dunstan, with his usual moderation, gave his voice for the eldest son, and Eadward was chosen king and crowned. Not only had he a strong party opposed to him, but he had a dissatisfied step-mother in Ælfthryth, the mother of Æthelred, whilst his own mother, who had probably been married to Eadgar without full marriage rites, had been long since dead. After reigning for four years Eadward was

---

[1] Genealogy of the English kings from Eadgar to Eadgar the Ætheling :—

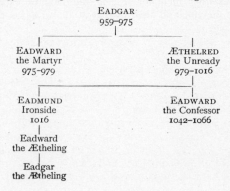

murdered near Corfe by some of the opposite party, and, as was commonly supposed, by his step-mother's directions.

2. Æthelred's Early Years. 979—988.—Æthelred, now a boy of ten, became king in 979. The epithet the Unready, which is usually assigned to him, is a mistranslation of a word which properly means the Rede-less, or the man without counsel. He was entirely without the qualities which befit a king. Eadmund had kept the great chieftains in subordination to himself because he was a successful leader. Eadgar had kept them in subordination because he treated them with respect. Æthelred could neither lead nor show respect. He was always picking quarrels when he ought to have been making peace, and always making peace when he ought to have been fighting. What he tried to do was to lessen the power of the great ealdormen, and bring the whole country more directly under his own authority. In 985 he drove out Ælfric, the Ealdorman of the Mercians. In 988 Dunstan died, and Æthelred had no longer a wise adviser by his side.

3. The Return of the Danes. 984.—It would have been difficult for Æthelred to overpower the ealdormen even if he had had no other enemies to deal with. Unluckily for him, new swarms of Danes and Norwegians had already appeared in England. They began by plundering the country, without attempting to settle in it. In 991 Brihtnoth, Ealdorman of the East Saxons, was defeated and slain by them at Maldon. Æthelred could think of no better counsel than to pay them 10,000*l.*, a sum of money which was then of much greater value than it is now, to abstain from plundering. It was not necessarily a bad thing to do. One of the greatest of the kings of the Germans, Henry the Fowler, had paid money for a truce to barbarians whom he was not strong enough to fight. But when the truce had been bought Henry took care to make himself strong enough to destroy them when they came again. Æthelred was never ready to fight the Danes and Norwegians at any time. In 994 Olaf Trygvasson, who had been driven from the kingship of Norway, and Svend, who had been driven from the kingship of Denmark, joined forces to attack London. The London citizens fought better than the English king, and the two chieftains failed to take the town. 'They went thence, and wrought the greatest evil that ever any army could do, in burning, and harrying, and in man-slaying, as in Essex, and in Kent, and in Sussex, and in Hampshire. And at last they took their horses and rode as far as they could, and did unspeakable evil.' The plunderers were now known as 'the army,' moving about where they would. Æthelred this time

gave them 16,000*l*. He got rid of Olaf, who sailed away and was
slain by his enemies, but he could not permanently get rid of Svend.
Svend, about the year 1000, recovered his kingship in Denmark,
and was more formidable than he had been before. Plunderings
went on as usual, and Æthelred had no resource but to pay money
to the plunderers to buy a short respite. He then looked across
the sea for an ally, and hoped to find one by connecting himself
with the Duke of the Normans.

4. **The Norman Dukes. 912—1002.**—The country which lies
on both sides of the lower course of the Seine formed, at the beginning of the tenth century, part of the dominions of Charles the
Simple, king of the West Franks, who had inherited so much of
the dominions of Charles the Great as lay west of a line roughly
drawn from the Scheldt to the Mediterranean through the lower
course of the Rhone. Danes and Norwegians, known on the Continent as Normans, plundered Charles's dominions as they had plundered England, and at last settled in them as they had settled in
parts of England. In 912 Charles the Simple ceded to their leader,
Hrolf, a territory of which the capital was Rouen, and which became
known as Normandy—the land of the Normans. Hrolf became
the first Duke of the Normans, but his men were fierce and rugged,
and for some time their southern neighbours scornfully called him
and his descendants Dukes of the Pirates. In process of time a
change took place which affected both Normandy and other
countries as well. The West Frankish kings were descended from
Charles the Great ; but they had failed to defend their subjects
from the Normans, and they thereby lost hold upon their people.
One of their dependent nobles, the Duke of the French, whose chief
city, Paris, formed a bulwark against the Normans advancing
up the Seine, grew more powerful than themselves. At the same
time the Normans were becoming more and more French in
their speech and customs. At last an alliance was made between
Hugh Capet, the son of Hugh the Great, Duke of the French
(see p. 63), and Richard the Fearless, Duke of the Normans.
The race of Charles the Great was dethroned, and Hugh became
king of the French. In name he was king over all the territory
which had been governed by Charles the Simple. In reality
that happened in France which Æthelred had been trying to
prevent in England. Hugh ruled directly over his own duchy of
France, a patch of land of which Paris was the capital. The great
vassals of the crown, who answered to the English ealdormen,
only obeyed him when it was their interest to do so. The most

powerful of these vassals was the Duke of the Normans. In **1002** the duke was Richard II.—the Good—the son of Richard the Fearless. In that year Æthelred, who was a widower, married Richard's sister, Emma. It was the beginning of a connection with Normandy which never ceased till a Norman duke made himself by conquest king of the English.

5. **Political Contrast between Normandy and England.**—The causes which were making the English thegnhood a military aristocracy acted with still greater force in Normandy. The tillers of the soil, sprung from the old inhabitants of the land, were kept by their Norman lords in even harsher bondage than the English serfs. The Norman warriors held their land by military service, each one being bound to fight for his lord, and the lord in turn being bound, together with his dependents, to fight for a higher lord, and all at last for the Duke himself. In England, though, in theory, the relations between the king and his ealdormen were not very different from those existing between the Norman duke and his immediate vassals, the connection between them was far looser. The kingdom as a whole had no general unity. The king could not control the ealdormen, and the ealdormen could not control the king. Even when ealdormen, bishops, and thegns met in the Witenagemot they could not speak in the name of the nation. A nation in any true sense hardly existed at all, and they were not chosen as representatives of any part of it. Each one stood for himself, and it was only natural that men who during the greater part of the year were ruling in their own districts like little kings should think more of keeping up their own almost independent power at home than of the common interests of all England, which they had to consider when they met—and that for a few days only at a time—in the Witenagemot. Æthelred at least was not the man to keep them united.

6. **Svend's Conquest. 1002—1013.** —Æthelred, having failed to buy off the Danes, tried to murder them. In **1002**, on St. Brice's Day, there was a general massacre of all the Danes—not of the old inhabitants of Danish blood who had settled in Ælfred's time—but of the new-comers. Svend returned to avenge his countrymen. Æthelred had in an earlier part of his reign levied a land-tax known as the Danegeld to pay off the Danes—the first instance of a general tax in England. He now called on all the shires to furnish ships for a fleet ; but he could not trust his ealdormen. Some of the stories told of these times may be exaggerated, and some may be merely idle tales, but we know enough to be sure that England was

G

a kingdom divided against itself. Svend, ravaging as he went, beat down resistance everywhere. In 1012 the Danes seized Ælfheah, Archbishop of Canterbury, and offered to set him free if he would pay a ransom for his life. He refused to do so, lest he should have to wring money from the poor in order to pay it. The drunken Danes pelted him with bones till one of the number clave his skull with an axe. He was soon counted as a martyr. Long afterwards one of the most famous of his successors, the Norman Lanfranc, doubted whether he was really a martyr, as he had not died for the faith. ' He that dies for righteousness,' answered the gentle Anselm, ' dies for the faith,' and to this day the name of Ælfheah is retained as St. Alphege in the list of English saints. In 1013 Svend appeared no longer as a plunderer but as a conqueror. First the old Danish districts of the north and east, and then the Anglo-Saxon realm of Ælfred—Mercia and Wessex—submitted to him to avoid destruction. In 1013 Æthelred fled to Normandy.

Martyrdom of St. Edmund by the Danes. (From a drawing belonging to the Society of Antiquaries.)

7. **Æthelred Restored. 1014—1016.**—In 1014 Svend died suddenly as he was riding at the head of his troops to the attack of the monastery of Bury St. Edmunds. A legend soon arose as to the manner of his death. St. Edmund himself, the East Anglian king Eadmund who had once been martyred by Danes (see p. 58), now appeared, it was said, to protect the monastery founded in his honour. ' Help, fellow soldiers !' cried Svend, as he caught sight of the saint. ' St. Edmund is coming to slay me.' St. Edmund, we are told, ran his spear through the body of the aggressor, and

Svend died that night in torments. His Danish warriors chose his son Cnut king of England.[1] The English Witenagemot sent for Æthelred to return. At last, in **1016**, Æthelred died before he had conquered Cnut or Cnut conquered him.

8. **Eadmund Ironside.   1016.**—Æthelred's eldest son—not the son of Emma—Eadmund Ironside, succeeded him. He did all that could be done to restore the English kingship by his vigour. In a single year he fought six battles ; but the treachery of the ealdormen was not at an end, and at Assandun (? *Ashington*), in Essex, he was completely overthrown. He and Cnut agreed to divide the kingdom, but before the end of the year the heroic Eadmund died, and Cnut the Dane became king of England without a rival.

9. **Cnut and the Earldoms.   1016—1035.**—Cnut was one of those rulers who, like the Emperor Augustus, shrink from no barbarity in gaining power, but when once they have acquired it exercise their authority with moderation and gentleness. He began by outlawing or putting to death men whom he considered dangerous, but when this had once been done he ruled as a thoroughly English king of the best type. The Danes who had hitherto fought for him had come not as settlers, but as an army, and soon after Eadmund's death he sent most of them home, retaining a force, variously stated as 3,000 or 6,000, warriors known as his House-carls (*House-men*), who formed a small standing army depending entirely on himself. They were not enough to keep down a general rising of the whole of England, but they were quite enough to prevent any single great man from rebelling against him. Cnut therefore was, what Æthelred had wished to be, really master of his kingdom. Under him ruled the ealdormen, who from this time were known as Earls, from the Danish title of Jarl (see p. 64), and of these Earls the principal were the three who governed Mercia, North-humberland, and Wessex, the last named now including the old kingdoms of Kent and Sussex. There was a fourth in East Anglia, but the limits of this earldom varied from time to time, and

---

[1] Genealogy of the Danish kings :—

Svend
|
(1) Ælfgifu = CNUT = (2) Emma
| 1016–1035 |
| |
HAROLD   HARTHACNUT
Harefoot   1040–1042
1035–1040

there were sometimes other earldoms set up in the neighbouring shires, whereas the first-named three remained as they were for some time after Cnut's death.   It is characteristic of Cnut that the one of the Earls to whom he gave his greatest confidence was God-wine, an Englishman, who was Earl of the West Saxons.   Another Englishman, Leofwine, became Earl of the Mercians.   A Dane obtained the earldom of the North-humbrians, but the land was barbarous, and its Earls were frequently murdered.   Sometimes there was one Earl of the whole territory, sometimes two.   It was not till after the end of Cnut's reign that Siward became Earl of Deira, and at a later time of all North-humberland as far as the Tweed.   The descendants of two of these Earls, Godwine and Leofwine, leave their mark on the history for some time to come.

10. **Cnut's Empire.**—Beyond the Tweed Malcolm, king of the Scots, ruled.   He defeated the North-humbrians at Carham, and Cnut ceded Lothian to him, either doing so for the first time or repeating the act of Eadgar, if the story of Eadgar's cession is true.   At all events the king of the Scots from this time ruled as far south as the Tweed, and acknowledged Cnut's superiority. Cnut also became king of Denmark by his brother's death, and king of Norway by conquest.   He entered into friendly relations with Richard II., Duke of the Normans, by marrying his sister Emma, the widow of Æthelred.[1]

11. **Cnut's Government.**—Cnut had thus made himself master of a great empire, and yet, Dane as he was, though he treated English-men and Danes as equals, he gave his special favour to Englishmen He restored, as men said, the laws of Eadgar—that is to say, he kept peace and restored order as in the days of Eadgar.   He

---

[1] Genealogical connection between the Houses of England and Nor-mandy :—

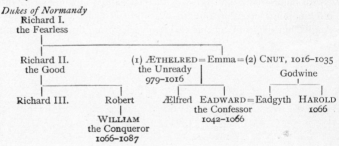

Dukes of Normandy
Richard I.
the Fearless

Richard II.   (1) ÆTHELRED = Emma = (2) CNUT, 1016-1035
the Good   the Unready   Godwine
                    979-1016

Richard III.   Robert   Ælfred   EADWARD = Eadgyth   HAROLD
                                        the Confessor   1066
                  WILLIAM   1042-1066
                  the Conqueror
                  1066-1087

reverenced monks, and once as he was rowing on the waters of
the fens, he heard the monks of Ely singing.   He bade the boatmen
row him to the shore that he might listen to the song of praise and
prayer.   He even went on a pilgrimage to Rome, to humble himself
in that city which contained the burial places of the Apostles Peter
and Paul.   From Rome he sent a letter to his subjects.   ' I have
vowed to God,' he wrote, ' to live a right life in all things ; to rule
justly and piously my realms and subjects, and to administer just
judgment to all.   If heretofore I have done aught beyond what is
just, through headiness or negligence of youth, I am ready, with
God's help, to amend it utterly.'   With Cnut these were not mere
words.   It is not likely that there is any truth in the story how his
flattering courtiers told him to sit by the sea-shore and bade the in-
flowing tide refrain from wetting his feet, and how when the waves
rose over the spot on which his chair was placed he refused to wear
his crown again, because that honour belonged to God alone, the
true Ruler of the world.   Yet the story would not have been
invented except of one who was believed to have been clothed with
real humility.

12. **The Sons of Cnut. 1035—1042.**—Cnut died in **1035**.   Godwine and the West Saxons chose Harthacnut, the son of Cnut and
Emma to take his father's place, whilst the north and centre,
headed by Leofwine's son, Leofric,[1] Earl of the Mercians, chose
Harold, the son of Cnut by an earlier wife or concubine.   Godwine
perhaps hoped that Harthacnut would make the West Saxon earldom the centre of the empire which had been his father's.   Cnut's
empire was, however, breaking up.   The Norwegians chose
Magnus, a king of their own race, and Harthacnut remained in
Denmark to defend it against the attacks of Magnus.   In Normandy
there were two English Ethelings, Ælfred and Eadward, the sons
of Æthelred by Emma, who seem to have thought that the absence
of Harthacnut gave them a chance of returning to England.   Ælfred
landed, but was seized by Harold.   He was blinded with such

---

[1] Genealogy of the Mercian earls :—

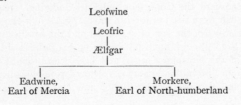

Leofwine
|
Leofric
|
Ælfgar
|

| Eadwine, | Morkere, |
| Earl of Mercia | Earl of North-humberland |

cruelty that he died. His death was, truly or falsely, attributed to Godwine. As Harthacnut still remained in Denmark, the West Saxons deposed him and gave themselves to Harold, since which time England has never been divided. In 1040 Harold died, and Harthacnut came at last to England to claim the crown. He brought with him a Danish fleet, and with his sailors and his house-carls he ruled England as a conquered land. He raised a Danegeld to satisfy his men, and sent his house-carls to force the people to pay the heavy tax. Two of them were killed at Worcester, and he burnt

First Great Seal of Eadward the Confessor (obverse).

Worcester to the ground. In 1042 he died 'as he stood at his drink' at a bridal.

13. **Eadward the Confessor and Earl Godwine. 1042—1051.**— The English were tired of foreign rulers. 'All folk chose Eadward king.' Eadward, the son of Æthelred and the brother of the murdered Ælfred, though an Englishman on his father's side, was also the son of the Norman Emma, and had been brought up in Normandy from his childhood. The Normans were now men of French speech, and they were more polite and cultivated than English-

men. Eadward filled his court with Normans. He disliked the
roughness of the English, but instead of attempting to improve them
as the great Ælfred had formerly done, he stood entirely aloof from
them. The name of the Confessor by which he was afterwards
known was given him on account of his piety, but his piety was
not of that sort which is associated with active usefulness. He
was fond of hunting, but was not active in any other way, and he
left others to govern rather than himself. For some years the
real governor of England was Earl Godwine, who kept his
own earldom of Wessex, and managed to procure other smaller
earldoms for his sons. As the Mercia over which Leofric ruled
was only the north-western part of the old kingdom, and as
Siward (see p. 84) had enough to do to keep the fierce men of North-
humberland in order, Godwine had as yet no competitor to fear.
In **1045** he became the king's father-in-law by the marriage of
Eadward with his daughter, Eadgyth. Eadward, however, did his
best for his Norman favourites, and appointed one of them, Robert

Hunting. (From the Bayeux Tapestry.)

of Jumièges, to the bishopric of London, and afterwards raised him
to the Archbishopric of Canterbury. Between Godwine and the
Normans there was no goodwill, and though Godwine was himself
of fair repute, his eldest son, Swegen, a young man of brutal nature,
alienated the goodwill of his countrymen by seducing the Abbess
of Leominster, and by murdering his cousin Beorn. Godwine,
in his blind family affection, clung to his wicked son and insisted
on his being allowed to retain his earldom.

14. **The Banishment of Godwine. 1051.**—At last, in **1051**, the
strife between the king and the Earl broke out openly. Eadward's
brother-in-law, Eustace, Count of Boulogne, visited England. On
his return his men made a disturbance at Dover, and in the riot
which ensued some of the townsmen as well as some of his own men
were slain. Eadward called on Godwine, in whose earldom Dover
was, to punish the townsmen. Godwine refused, and Eadward
summoned him to Gloucester to account for his refusal. He came
attended by an armed host, but Leofric and Siward, who were
jealous of Godwine's power, came with their armed followers to
support the king. Leofric mediated, and it was arranged that the

question should be settled at a Witenagemot to be held in London. In the end Godwine was outlawed and banished with all his family. Swegen went on a pilgrimage to Jerusalem and died on the way back.

15. **Visit of Duke William. 1051.**—In Godwine's absence Eadward received a visit from the Duke of the Normans, William, the bastard son of Duke Robert and the daughter of a tanner of Falaise. Robert was a son of Richard II., and William was thus the grandson of the brother of Eadward's mother, Emma. Such a relationship gave him no title whatever to the English throne, as Emma was not descended from the English kings, and as, even if she had been, no one could be lawfully king in England who was not chosen by the Witenagemot. Eadward, however, had no children or brothers, and though he had no right to give away the crown, he now promised William that he should succeed him. William, indeed, was just the man to attract one whose character was as weak as Eadward's. Since he received the dukedom he had beaten down the opposition of a fierce and discontented nobility at Val-ès-dunes (**1047**). From that day peace and order prevailed in Normandy. Law in Normandy did not come as in England from the traditions of the shire-moot or the Witenagemot, where men met to consult together. It was the Duke's law, and if the Duke was a strong man he kept peace in the land. If he was a weak man, the lords fought against one another and plundered and oppressed the poor. William was strong and wily, and it was this combination of strength and wiliness which enabled him to bear down all opposition.

16. **William and the Norman Church.**—An Englishman, who saw much of William in after-life, declared that, severe as he was, he was mild to good men who loved God. The Church was in his days assuming a new place in Europe. The monastic revival which had originated at Cluny (see p. 67) had led to a revival of the Papacy. In **1049**, for the first time, a Pope, Leo IX., travelled through Western Europe, holding councils and inflicting punishments upon the married clergy and upon priests who took arms and shed blood. With this improvement in discipline came a voluntary turning of the better clergy to an ascetic life, and increased devotion was accompanied, as it always was in the middle ages, with an increase of learning. William, who by the strength of his will brought peace into the state, also brought men of devotion and learning into the high places of the Church. His chief confidant was Lanfranc, an Italian who had taken refuge in

the abbey of Bec, and, having become its prior, had made it the central school of Normandy and the parts around. With the improvement of learning came the improvement of art, and churches arose in Normandy, as in other parts of Western Europe, which still preserved the old round arch derived from the Romans, though both the arches themselves and the columns on which they were borne were lighter and more graceful than the heavy work which had hitherto been employed. Of all this Englishmen as yet knew nothing. They went on in their old ways, cut off from the European influences of the time. It was no wonder that Eadward yearned after the splendour and the culture of the land in which he had been brought up, or even that, in defiance of English law, he now promised to Duke William the succession to the English crown.

17. **The Return and Death of Godwine. 1052—1053.**—After William had departed Englishmen became discontented at Ead-ward's increasing favour to the Norman strangers. In **1052** Godwine and his sons—Swegen only excepted—returned from exile. They sailed up the Thames and landed at Southwark. The foreigners hastily fled, and Eadward was unable to resist the popular feeling. Godwine was restored to his earldom, and an Englishman, Stigand, was made Archbishop of Canterbury in the place of Robert of Jumièges, who escaped to the Continent. As it was the law of the Church that a bishop once appointed could not be deposed except by the ecclesiastical authorities, offence was in this way given to the Pope. Godwine did not long outlive his restoration. He was struck down by apoplexy at the king's table in **1053**. Harold, who, after Swegen's death, was his eldest son, succeeded to his earldom of Wessex, and practically managed the affairs of the kingdom in Eadward's name.[1]

18. **Harold's Greatness. 1053—1066.**—Harold was a brave and energetic man, but Eadward preferred his brother Tostig, and on the death of Siward appointed him Earl of North-humberland. A little later Gyrth, another brother of Harold, became Earl of East Anglia, together with Bedfordshire and Oxfordshire, and a

---

[1] Genealogy of the family of Godwine :—

Godwine

| Swegen | Harold 1066 | Tostig | Leofwine | Gyrth | Wulfnoth | Eadgyth = Eadward the Confessor |

fourth brother, Leofwine, Earl of a district formed of the eastern shires on either side of the Thames. All the richest and most thickly populated part of England was governed by Harold and his brothers. Mercia was the only large earldom not under their rule. It was now under Ælfgar, the son of Leofric, who had lately died:

19. **Harold and Eadward. 1057—1065** —It became necessary to arrange for the succession to the throne, as Eadward was childless, and as Englishmen were not likely to acquiesce in his bequest to William. In **1057** the Ætheling Eadward, a son of Eadmund Ironside, was fetched back from Hungary, where he had long lived in exile, and was accepted as the heir. Eadward, however, died almost immediately after his arrival. He left but one son, Eadgar the Ætheling (see genealogy at p. 78), who was far too young to be accepted as a king for many years to come. Naturally the thought arose of looking on Harold as Eadward's successor. It was contrary to all custom to give the throne to any one not of the royal line, but the custom had been necessarily broken in favour of Cnut, the Danish conqueror, and it might be better to break it in favour of an English earl rather than to place a child on the throne, when danger threatened from Normandy. During the remainder of Eadward's reign Harold showed himself a warrior worthy of the crown. In **1063** he invaded Wales and reduced it to submission. About the same time Ælfgar died, and was succeeded by his son, Eadwine, in the earldom of the Mercians. In **1065** the men of North-humberland revolted against Tostig, who had governed them harshly, and who was probably unpopular as a West Saxon amongst a population of Danes and Angles. The North-humbrians chose Eadwine's brother, Morkere, as his successor, and Harold advised Eadward to acquiesce in what they had done. Northamptonshire and Huntingdonshire were committed to Waltheof, a son of Siward (see p. 84), and the modern Northumberland was committed to a native ruler, Oswulf.

20. **Death of Eadward. 1066.**—England was therefore ruled by two great families. Eadwine and Morkere, the grandsons of Leofric, governed the Midlands and almost the whole of North-humberland. Harold and his brothers, the sons of Godwine, governed the south and the east. The two houses had long been rivals, and after Eadward's death there would be no one in the country to whom they could even nominally submit. Eadward, whose life was almost at an end, was filled with gloomy forebodings. His thoughts, however, turned aside from the contemplation of earthly things, and he was only anxious that the great abbey church

of Westminster, which he had been building hard by his own new palace on what was then a lonely place outside London, should be consecrated before his death. The church, afterwards superseded by the structure which now stands there, was built in the new and lighter form of round-arched architecture which Eadward had learned to admire from his Norman friends. It was consecrated on December 28, **1065,** but the king was too ill to be present, and

Tower in the earlier style. Church at Earl's
Barton.
(The battlements are much later.)

Tower in the earlier style. St
Benet's Church, Cambridge.

on January 5, **1066,** he died, and was buried in the church which he had founded. Harold was at once chosen king, and crowned at Westminster.

21. **Harold and William. 1066.**—William, as soon as he heard of his rival's coronation, claimed the crown. He was now even mightier than he had been when he visited Eadward. In **1063** he had conquered Maine, and, secure on his southern frontier, he was able to turn his undivided attention to England. Accord-

ing to the principles accepted in England, he had no right to
it whatever ; but he contrived to put together a good many reasons which seemed, in the eyes of those who were not Englishmen, to give him a good case.   In the first place he had been

Building a church in the later style.   (From a drawing belonging to
the Society of Antiquaries.)

selected by Eadward as his heir.   In the second place the deprivation of Robert of Jumièges was an offence against the Church law
of the Continent, and William was therefore able to obtain from
the Pope a consecrated banner, and to speak of an attack upon

England as an attempt to uphold the righteous laws of the Church. In the third place, Harold had at some former time been wrecked upon the French coast, and had been delivered up to William, who had refused to let him go till he had sworn solemnly, placing his hand on a chest which contained the relics of the most holy Norman saints, to do some act, the nature of which is diversely related, but which Harold never did. Consequently William could speak of himself as going to take vengeance on a perjurer. With some difficulty William persuaded the Norman barons to follow him, and he attracted a mixed multitude of adventurers from all the neighbouring nations by promising them the plunder of Eng-

Normans feasting ; with Odo, Bishop of Bayeux, saying grace.
(From the Bayeux Tapestry.)

land, an argument which every one could understand. During the whole of the spring and the summer ships for the invasion of England were being built in the Norman harbours.

22. Stamford Bridge. 1066.—All through the summer Harold was watching for his rival's coming. The military organisation of England, however, was inferior to that of Normandy. The Norman barons and their vassals were always ready for war, and they could support on their estates the foreign adventurers who were placed under their orders till the time of battle came. Harold had his house-carls, the constant guard of picked troops which had been instituted by Cnut, and his thegns, who, like the Norman

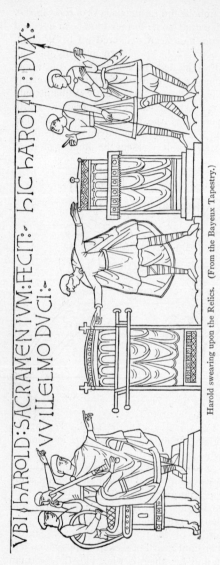

Harold swearing upon the Relics.   (From the Bayeux Tapestry.)

barons, were bound to serve their lord in war. The greater part of his force, however, was composed of the peasants of the fyrd, and when September came they must needs be sent home to attend to their harvest, which seems to have been late this year. Scarcely were they gone when Harold received news that his brother Tostig, angry with him for having consented to his deposition from the Northumbrian earldom, had allied himself to Harold Hardrada, the fierce sea-rover, who was king of Norway, and that the two, with a mighty host, after wasting the Yorkshire coast, had sailed up the Humber. The two Northern Earls, Eadwine and Morkere, were hard pressed. Harold had not long before married their sister, and, whatever might be the risk, he was bound as the king of all England to aid them. Marching swiftly northwards with his house-carls and the thegns who joined him on the way, he hastened to their succour. On

the way worse tidings reached him.   The Earls had been defeated,
and York had agreed to submit to the Norsemen.   Harold hurried
on the faster, and came upon the invaders unawares as they lay

A Norman ship.   (From the Bayeux Tapestry.)

heedlessly on both sides of the Derwent at Stamford Bridge.   Those
on the western side, unprepared as they were, were soon overpowered.   One brave Norseman, like Horatius and his comrades

Norman soldiers mounted.   (From the Bayeux Tapestry.)

in the Roman legend, kept the narrow bridge against the army, till
an Englishman crept under it and stabbed him from below through
a gap in the woodwork.   The battle rolled across the Derwent, and

when evening came Harold Hardrada, and Tostig himself, with the bulk of the invaders, had been slain. For the last time an English king overthrew a foreign host in battle on English soil.

23. The Landing of William. 1066.—Harold had shown what an English king could do, who fought not for this or that part of the country, but for all England. It was the lack of this national spirit in Englishmen which caused his ruin. As Harold was feasting at York in celebration of his victory, a messenger told him of the landing of the Norman host at Pevensey. He had saved Eadwine and Morkere from destruction, but Eadwine and Morkere gave him no help in return. He had to hurry back to defend Sussex without a single man from the north or the Midlands, except those whom he collected on his line of march. The House of Leofric bore no goodwill to the House of Godwine. England was a kingdom divided against itself.

Group of archers on foot. (From the Bayeux Tapestry.)

24. The Battle of Senlac. 1066.—Harold, as soon as he reached the point of danger, drew up his army on the long hill of Senlac on which Battle Abbey now stands. On October 14 William marched forth to attack him. The military equipment of the Normans was better than that of the English. Where the weapons on either side are unlike, battles are decided by the momentum—that is to say, by the combined weight and speed of the weapons employed. The English fought on foot mostly with two-handed axes ; the Normans fought not only on horseback with lances, but also with infantry, some of them being archers. A horse, the principal weapon of a horseman, has more momentum than an armed footman, whilst an arrow can reach the object at which it is aimed long before a horse, and Harold was therefore obliged to attempt to lessen the danger by defensive contrivances. He had in his favour the slope of the hill up which the Normans would have to ride, and he raised near the top of it a wooden palisade to keep off the enemy's cavalry from sweeping away his footmen. Strong as this defence was, it was immovable, and therefore made it impossible for Harold to change his arrangements as the fortunes of the day might need. William, on the other hand, had not only a better armed force, but a more flexible one. He had to attack, and, versed as he was in all the operations of war, he could move his men from place to place and make use of each opportunity as it arrived. The English were brave enough, but William was a more intelligent leader than Harold, and his men were better under control. Twice after the battle had begun the Norman horsemen charged up the hill only to be driven back. The wily William, finding that the dyke was not to be stormed by a

Men fighting with axes.　(From the Bayeux Tapestry.)

direct attack, met the difficulty by galling the English with a shower of arrows and ordering his left wing to turn and fly. The stratagem was successful. Some of the English rushed down the hill in pursuit. The fugitives faced round and charged the pursuers, following them over the dyke. The English on the hill were thus left unguarded; but they held out stoutly, and as the Norman horsemen now in occupation of one end of the hill charged fiercely along its crest, they locked their shields together and fought desperately for life, if no longer for victory. Slowly and steadily the Normans pressed on, till they reached the spot where Harold, surrounded by his house-carls, fought beneath his standard. There all their attacks were in vain, till William, calling for his bowmen, bade them shoot their arrows into the air. Down came the arrows in showers upon the heads of the English warriors, and

H

one of them pierced Harold's eye, stretching him lifeless on the ground.   In a series of representations in worsted work, known as the Bayeux Tapestry, which was wrought by the needle of some unknown woman and is now exhibited in the museum of that city, the scenes of the battle and the events preceding it are pictorially recorded.

25. **William's Coronation.   1066.**—William had destroyed both the English king and the English army.   It is possible that England, if united, might still have resisted.   The great men at London chose for their king Eadgar the Ætheling, the grandson of Eadmund Ironside.   Eadwine and Morkere were present at the election, but left London as soon as it was over.   They would look

Death of Harold, who is attempting to pull the arrow from his eye.
(From the Bayeux Tapestry.)

after their own earldoms ; they would not join others, as Harold had done, in defending England as a whole.   Divided England would sooner or later be a prey to William.   He wanted, however, not merely to reign as a conqueror, but to be lawfully elected as king, that he might have on his side law as well as force.   He first struck terror into Kent and Sussex by ravaging the lands of all who held out against him.   Then he marched to the Thames and burnt Southwark.   He did not, however, try to force his way into London, as he wanted to induce the citizens to submit voluntarily to him, or at least in a way which might seem voluntary.   He therefore marched westwards, crossed the Thames at Wallingford, and wheeled round to Berkhampstead.   His presence there made

Coronation of a king, *temp.* William the Conqueror.
(From a drawing in the possession of the Society of Antiquaries.)

H 2

the Londoners feel utterly isolated.   Even if Eadwine and Morkere
wished to do anything for them, they could not come from the
north or north-west without meeting William's victorious army.
The great men and citizens alike gave up all thought of resistance,
abandoned Eadgar, and promised to take William for their king.
On Christmas Day, 1066, William was chosen with acclamation
in Eadward's abbey at Westminster, where Harold had been
chosen less than a year before.   The Normans outside mistook
the shouts of applause for a tumult against their Duke, and set
fire to the houses around.   The English rushed out to save their
property, and William, frightened for the only time in his life,
was left alone with the priests.   Not knowing what was next to
follow, he was crowned king of the English by Ealdred, Archbishop of York, in an empty church, amidst the crackling of flames
and the shouts of men striving for the mastery.

Books recommended for further study of Part I.

DAWKINS, W. Boyd.   Early Man in Britain.
RHYS, J.   Early Britain.
ELTON, C. J.   Origins of English History.
GUEST, E.   Origines Celticæ.   Vol. ii. pp. 121–408.
FREEMAN.   History of the Norman Conquest.   Vols. i.–iii.
GREEN, J. R.   The Making of England.
————————   The Conquest of England.
————————   History of the English People.   Vol. i. pp. 1–114.
BRIGHT, W.   Chapters of English Church History.
STUBBS, W.   The Constitutional History of England.   Chaps. I.–IX.
CUNNINGHAM, W.   The Growth of English Industry and Commerce
                 during the Early and Middle Ages, pp. 1–128.

PART II

THE NORMAN AND ANGEVIN KINGS

CHAPTER VII

WILLIAM I. 1066—1087

LEADING DATES

William's coronation	1066
Completion of the Conquest	1070
The rising of the Earls	1075
The Gemot at Salisbury	1086
Death of William I.	1087

1. **The First Months of the Conquest. 1066–1067.**—Though at the time when William was crowned he had gained actual possession of no more than the south-eastern part of England, he claimed a right to rule the whole as lawful king of the English, not merely by Eadward's bequest, but by election and coronation. In reality, he came as a conqueror, whilst the Normans by whose aid he gained the victory at Senlac left their homes not merely to turn their Duke into a king, but also to acquire lands and wealth for themselves. William could not act justly and kindly to his new subjects even if he wished. What he did was to clothe real violence with the appearance of law. He gave out that as he had been the lawful king of the English ever since Eadward's death, Harold and all who fought under him at Senlac had forfeited their lands by their treason to himself as their lawful king. These lands he distributed amongst his Normans. The English indeed were not entirely

A silver penny of William the Conqueror, struck at Romney.

dispossessed.   Sometimes the son of a warrior who had been slain was allowed to retain a small portion of his father's land.   Sometimes the daughter or the widow of one of Harold's comrades was compelled to marry a Norman whom William wished to favour. Yet, for all that, a vast number of estates in the southern and eastern counties passed from English into Norman hands.   The bulk of the population, the serfs—or, as they were now called by a Norman name, the villeins—were not affected by the change, except so far as they found a foreign lord less willing than a native one to hearken to their complaints.   The changes which took place were limited as yet to a small part of England.   In three months after his coronation William was still without authority beyond an irregular line running from the Wash to the western border of Hampshire, except that he held some outlying posts in Herefordshire.   It is true that Eadwine and Morkere had acknowledged him as king, but they were still practically independent.   Even where William actually ruled he allowed all Englishmen who had not fought on Harold's side to keep their lands, though he made them redeem them by the payment of a fine, on the principle that all lands in the country, except those of the Church, were the king's lands, and that it was right to fine those who had not come to Senlac to help him as their proper lord.

2. **The Conquest of the West and North. 1067—1069.**—In March 1067 William returned to Normandy.   In his absence the Normans left behind in England oppressed the English, and were supported in their oppression by the two regents appointed to govern in William's name, his half-brother, Odo, Bishop of Bayeux, whom he had made Earl of Kent, and William Fitz-Osbern, Earl of Hereford.   In some parts the English rose in rebellion.   In December William returned, and after putting down resistance in the south-eastern counties, set himself to conquer the rest of England.   It took him more than two years to complete his task. Perhaps he would have failed even then if the whole of the unconquered part of the country had risen against him at the same time. Each district, however, resisted separately, and he was strong enough to beat them down one by one.   In the spring of **1068** he besieged and took Exeter, and subdued the West to the Land's End. When this had been accomplished he turned northwards against Eadwine and Morkere, who had declared against him.   William soon frightened them into submission, and seized on York and all the country to the south of York on the eastern side of England.   In **1069** the English of the North rose once more and summoned to

their aid Svend, king of Denmark, a nephew of the great Cnut. Svend sent a Danish fleet, and the Danes were joined by Eadgar the Ætheling and by other English chiefs. They burnt and plundered York, but could do no more. Their great host melted away. The Danes went off with their booty to their ships, and the English returned to their homes. William found no army to oppose him, and he not only regained the lands which he had occupied the year before, but added to them the whole country up to the Tweed.

3. **The Completion of the Conquest. 1070.**—William was never cruel without an object, but there was no cruelty which he would not commit if it would serve his purpose. He resolved to make all further resistance impossible. The Vale of York, a long and wide stretch of fertile ground running northwards from the city to the Tees, was laid waste by William's orders. The men who had joined in the revolt were slain. The stored-up crops, the ploughs, the carts, the oxen and sheep were destroyed by fire. Men, women, and children dropped dead of starvation, and their corpses lay unburied in the wasted fields. Some prolonged life by feeding on the flesh of horses, or even of men. Others sold themselves into slavery, bowing their heads, as was said, in the evil days for meat. "Waste! waste! waste!" was the account given long afterwards of field after field in what had once been one of the most fertile districts in England. William's work of conquest was almost over. Early in 1070 he crossed the hills amidst frost and snow, and descended upon Chester. Chester submitted, and with it the shires on the Welsh border. The whole of England was at last subdued.

4. **Hereward's Revolt and the Homage of Malcolm. 1070— 1072.**—Only one serious attempt to revolt was afterwards made, but this was no more than a local rising. The Isle of Ely was in those days a real island in the midst of the waters of the fens. Hereward, with a band of followers, threw himself into the island, and it was only after a year's attack that he was driven out. When the revolt was at its height, Eadwine and Morkere fled from William's court to join the insurgents. Eadwine was murdered by his own attendants. Morkere reached Ely, and when resistance was at an end was banished to Normandy. No man ever deserved less pity than these two brothers. They had never sought any one's advantage but their own, and they had been faithless to every cause which they had pretended to adopt. Before Hereward was overpowered, Malcolm, king of the Scots, ravaged northern England, carrying off with him droves of English slaves. In 1072 William,

who had by that time subdued Hereward, marched into Scotland
as far as the Tay.   Malcolm submitted to him at Abernethy, and
acknowledged him to be his lord.   Malcolm's acknowledgment was
only a repetition of the acknowledgment made by his predecessors,
the Scottish kings, to Eadward and Cnut (see pp. 63, 84) ; but
William was more powerful than Eadward or Cnut had been, and
was likely to construe the obligation more strictly.

5. **How William kept down the English.**—William, having
conquered England, had now to govern it.   His first object was to
keep the English in subjection.

(*a*) *The Confiscation of Land.*—In the first place he continued
to treat all who had resisted him as rebels, confiscating their land
and giving it to some Norman follower.   In almost every district
there was at least one Norman landowner, who was on the watch
against any attempt of his English neighbours to revolt, and who
knew that he would lose his land if William lost his crown.

(*b*) *Building Castles.*—In the second place William built a
castle in every town of importance, which he garrisoned with his
own men.   The most notable example of these castles is the Tower
of London. ·

(*c*) *The Feudal Army.*—In the third place, though the diffusion
of Norman landowners and of William's castles made a general
revolt of the English difficult, it did not make it impossible, and
William took care to have an army always ready to put down a revolt
if it occurred.   No king in those days could have a constantly paid
army, such as exists in all European countries at the present day,
because there was not much money anywhere.   Some men had
land and some men had bodily strength, and they bartered one for
the other.   The villein gave his strength to plough and reap for his
lord, in return for the land which he held from him.   The fighting
man gave his strength to his lord, to serve him with his horse and
his spear, in return for the land which he held from him.   This
system, which is known as feudal, had been growing up in England
before the Conquest, but it was perfected on the Continent, and
William brought it with him in its perfected shape.   The warrior
who served on horseback was called a knight, and when a knight
received land from a lord on military tenure—that is to say, on condition of military service—he was called the vassal of his lord.
When he became a vassal he knelt, and, placing his hands between
those of his lord, swore to be his man.   This act was called doing
homage.   The land which he received as sufficient to maintain
him was called a knight's fee.   After this homage the vassal was

bound to serve his lord in arms, this service being the rent payable for his land. If the vassal broke his oath and fought against his lord, he was regarded as a traitor, or a betrayer of his trust, and could be turned out of his land. The whole land of England being regarded as the king's, all land was held from the king. Sometimes the knights held their fees directly from the king and did homage to him. These knights were known as tenants in chief (*in capite*), however small their estates might be. Usually, however, the tenants in chief were large landowners, to whom the king had granted vast estates ; and these when they did homage engaged not merely to fight for him in person, but to bring some hundreds of knights with them. To enable them to do this they had to give out portions of their land to sub-tenants, each engaging to bring himself and a specified number of knights. There might thus be a regular chain of sub-tenants, A engaging to serve under B, B under C, C under D, and so on till the tenant-in-chief was reached, who engaged to bring them all to serve the king. Almost all the larger tenants-in-chief were Normans, though Englishmen were still to be found amongst the sub-tenants, and even amongst the smaller tenants-in-chief. The whole body, however, was preponderantly Norman, and William could therefore depend upon it to serve him as an army in the field in case of an English rising.

6. **How William kept down the Normans.**—William was not afraid only of the English. He had cause to fear lest the feudal army, which was to keep down the English, might be strong enough to be turned against himself, and that the barons—as the greater tenants-in-chief were usually called—might set him at naught as Eadwine and Morkere had set Harold at naught, and as the Dukes of Normandy had set at naught the kings of France. To prevent this he adopted various contrivances.

(*a*) *Abolition of the great Earldoms.*—In the first place he abolished the great earldoms. In most counties there were to be no earls at all, and no one was to be earl of more than one county. There was never again to be an Earl of the West Saxons like Godwine, or an Earl of the Mercians like Leofric.

(*b*) *The Estates of the Barons scattered.*—Not only did William diminish the official authority of the earls, he also weakened the territorial authority of the barons. Even when he granted to one man estates so numerous that if they had been close together they would have extended at least over a whole county, he took care to scatter them over England, allowing only a few to be held by a single owner in any one county. If, therefore, a great baron took it into his head to levy war against the king, he would have to collect his vassals from the most distant counties, and his intentions would thus be known before they could be put in practice.

(*c*) *The Fyrd kept in readiness.*—Still more important was William's resolution to be the real head of the English nation. He had weakened it enough to fear it no longer, but he kept it strong enough to use it, if need came, against the Norman barons. He won Englishmen to his side by the knowledge that he was ready to do them justice whenever they were wronged, and he could therefore venture to summon the fyrd whenever he needed support, without having cause to fear that it would turn against him.

7. Ecclesiastical Organisation.—Before the Conquest the English Church had been altogether national. Its bishops had sat side by side with the ealdormen or earls in the shire-moots, and in the Witenagemot itself. They had been named, like the ealdormen or earls, by the king with the consent of the Witenagemot. Ecclesiastical questions had been decided and ecclesiastical offences punished not by any special ecclesiastical court, but by the shire-moot or Witenagemot, in which the laity and the clergy were both to be found. William resolved to change all this. The bishops and abbots whom he found were Englishmen, and he replaced most of them by Normans. The new Norman bishops and abbots were dependent on the king. They looked on the English as barbarians, and would certainly not support them in any revolt, as their English predecessors might have done. Thurstan, indeed, the Norman Abbot of Glastonbury, was so angry with his English monks because they refused to change their style of music that he called in Norman archers to shoot them down on the steps of the altar. Such brutality, however, was exceptional, and, as a rule, even Norman bishops and abbots were well disposed towards their English neighbours, all the more because they were not very friendly with the Norman nobles, who óften attempted to encroach on the lands of the Church. Many a king in William's position would have been content to fill the sees with creatures of his own, who would have done what they were bidden and have thought of no one's interest but his. William knew, as he had already shown in Normandy, that he would be far better served if the clergy were not only dependent on himself but deserving the respect of others. He made his old friend Lanfranc (see p. 88) Archbishop of Canterbury. Lanfranc had, like William, the mind of a ruler, and under him bishops and abbots were appointed who enforced discipline. The monks were compelled to keep the rules of their order, the canons of cathedrals were forced to send away their wives, and though the married clergy in the country were allowed to keep theirs, orders were given that in future no priest should marry. Everywhere the Church gave signs of new vigour. The monasteries became again the seats of study and learning. The sees of bishops were transferred from villages to populous towns, as when the Bishop of Dorchester, in Oxfordshire, migrated to Lincoln, and the Bishop of Thetford to Norwich. New churches were built and old ones restored after the new Continental style, which is known in England as Norman, and which Eadward had introduced in his abbey of Westminster. The Church, though made dependent on William, was independent, so far as its spiritual

rights were concerned, of the civil courts. Ecclesiastical matters were discussed, not in the Witenagemot, but in a Church synod, and, in course of time, punishments were in- flicted by Church courts on ecclesiastical offenders. The power of William was strength- ened by the change. That power rested on three supports —the Norman conquerors, the English nation, and the Church, and each one of these three had reason to distrust the other two.

8. **Pope Gregory VII.**— The strength which William had acquired showed itself in his bearing towards the Pope.

East end of Darenth Church, Kent.
Built about 1080.

In **1073** Archdeacon Hildebrand, who for some years had been more powerful at Rome than the Popes themselves, himself became Pope under the name of Gregory VII. Gregory was as stern a ruler of the Church as William was of the State. He was an uncom- promising champion of the Cluniac reforms (see p. 67). His object was to moderate the cruelty and sinfulness of the feudal warriors of Europe by making the Church a light to guide the world to piety and self-denial. As matters stood on the Continent, it had been impossible for the Church to attain to so high a standard. The clergy bought their places and fought and killed like the laymen around them. The Cluniac monks, therefore, thought it best to separate the clergy entirely from the world. In the first place they were to be celibate, that they might not be entangled in the cares of life. In the second place they were to refrain from simony, or the purchase of ecclesiastical preferment, that they might not be dependent on the great men of the world. A third demand was added later, that bishops and abbots should not receive from lay-men the ring and staff which were the signs of their authority—the ring as the symbol of marriage to their churches ; the staff or crozier, in the shape of a shepherd's crook, as the symbol of their pastoral authority. The Church, in fact, was to be governed by its own laws in perfect independence, that it might become more pure itself, and thus capable of setting a better example to the laity. As might have been expected, though the internal condition of the Church was greatly improved, yet when Gregory attempted entirely to free ecclesiastics from the influence and authority of the State, he found himself involved in endless quarrels. Clergy and laity alike resisted him, and they were supported by the Emperor Henry IV., whose rule extended over Germany and the greater part of Italy. Gregory next claimed the right of excommunicating kings and emperors, and of deposing them if they did not repent after excommunication. The State, he declared, was as the moon, re-ceiving light from the Church, which shone like the sun in heaven. The whole of the remainder of Gregory's life was spent in a struggle with the Emperor, and the struggle was carried on by the successors of both.

9. **William and Gregory VII.**—It is remarkable that such a Pope as Gregory never came into conflict with William. William appointed bishops and abbots by giving them investiture, as the presenting of the ring and staff was called. He declared that no Pope should be obeyed in England who was not acknowledged by himself, that no papal bulls or letters should have any force till he had allowed them, and that the decrees of an ecclesiastical synod should bind no one till he had confirmed them. When, at a later time, Gregory required William to do homage to the see of Rome, William refused, on the ground that homage had never been ren-dered by his predecessors. To all this Gregory submitted. No doubt Gregory was prudent in not provoking William's anger ; but that he should have refrained from even finding fault with William may perhaps be set down to the credit of his honesty. He claimed to make himself the master of kings because as a rule they did not care to advance the purity of the Church. William did care to

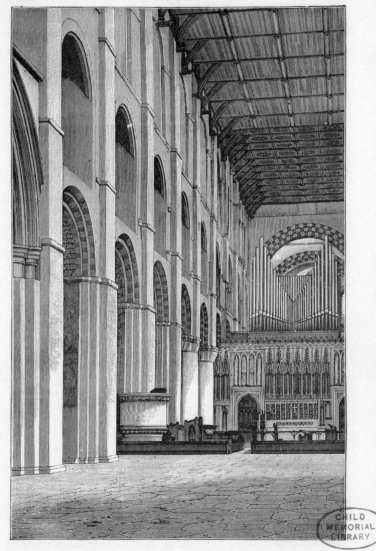

Part of the nave of St. Alban's Abbey Church.   Built by Abbot Paul between
1077 and 1093.

advance it. He chose virtuous and learned bishops, and defended the clergy against aggression from without and corruption within. Gregory may well have been content to leave power over the Church in the hands of a king who ruled it in such a fashion.

10. **The Rising of the Earls. 1075.**—Of the three classes of men over which William ruled, the great Norman barons imagined themselves to be the strongest, and were most inclined to throw off his yoke. The chief feature of the reigns of William and of his successors for three generations was the struggle which scarcely ever ceased between the Norman barons on the one side, and the king supported by the English and the clergy on the other. It was to the advantage of the king that he had not to contend against the whole of the Normans. Normans with small estates clung for support, like their English neighbours, to the crown. The first of many risings of the barons took place in **1075**. Roger, Earl of Hereford, in spite of William's prohibition, gave his daughter in marriage to Ralph of Wader, Earl of Norfolk, who, though of English birth on his father's side, had fought for William at Senlac, and may practically be counted as a Norman. As the chronicler expressed it :

> There was that bride-ale
> To many men's bale.

The two earls plotted a rising against William and the revivals of the old independent earldoms. They took arms and were beaten. Ralph fled the country, and Roger was condemned to perpetual imprisonment. His followers were blinded or had their feet cut off. It was the Norman custom not to put criminals to death. To this rule, however, William made one exception. Waltheof, the last earl of purely English race, had been present at the fatal bride-ale, but though he had listened to the plottings of the conspirators, he had revealed all that he knew to William. His wife, Judith, a niece of the Conqueror, accused him of actual treason, and he was beheaded at Winchester. By the English he was regarded as a martyr, and it was probably his popularity amongst them which made William resolve upon his death.

11. **The New Forest.**—Only once did William cause misery amongst his subjects for the sake of his own enjoyment. Many kings before him had taken pleasure in hunting, but William was the first who claimed the right of hunting over large tracts of country exclusively for himself. He made, as the chronicler says, ' mickle deer-frith '—a tract, that is to say, in which the deer might

have peace—'and laid laws therewith that he who slew hart or hind that man should blind him. . . . In sooth he loved the high deer as though he were their father.' He forbade, in short, all men, except those to whom he gave permission, to hunt within the limits of the royal forests. In the south-west of Hampshire, near his favourite abode at Winchester, he created the New Forest. The soil is poor, and it can never have been covered by cultivated fields, but here and there, by the sides of streams, there were scattered hamlets, and these were destroyed and the dwellers in them driven off by William's orders, that there might be a 'mickle deer-frith.' We may be sure that there was not nearly as much misery caused by the making of the New Forest as was caused by the harrying of the Vale of York, but popular tradition rightly held in more abhorrence the lesser cruelty for the sake of pleasure than the greater cruelty for the sake of policy. It told how the New Forest was accursed for William's family. In his own lifetime a son and a grandson of his were cut off within it by unknown hands, probably falling before the vengeance of some who had lost home and substance through the creation of the Forest, and in due time another son, who succeeded him on the throne, was to meet with a similar fate.

12. **Domesday Book. 1085—1086.**—It was to William's credit that his government was a strong one. In William's days life and property and female honour were under the protection of a king who knew how to make himself obeyed. Strong government, however, is always expensive, and William and his officers were always ready with an excuse for getting money. " The king and the headmen loved much and overmuch covetousness on gold and on silver, and they recked not how sinfully it was gotten, if only it came to them. . . . They reared up unright tolls, and many other unright things they did that are hard to reckon." Other men, in short, must observe the law; William's government was a law to itself. It was, however, a law, and not a mere scramble for money. Though there were no Danish invaders now, William continued to levy the Danegeld, and he had rents and payments due to him in many quarters which had been due to his predecessors. In order to make his exactions more complete and more regular, he resolved to have set down the amount of taxable property in the realm that his full rights might be known, and in 1085, " He sent over all England into ilk shire his men, and let them find out how many hundred hides were in the shire, or what the king himself had of land or cattle in the land, or whilk rights he ought to have. . . . Eke he let write how mickle of land his archbishops had, and his bishops,

and his abbots and his earls, and what or how mickle ilk man had that landholder was in England in land and in cattle, and how mickle fee it was worth. So very narrowly he let speer it out that there was not a single hide nor a yard of land, nor so much as —it is a shame to tell, though he thought it no shame to do— an ox nor a cow nor a swine was left that was not set in his writ." The chronicler who wrote these words was an English monk of Peterborough. Englishmen were shocked by the new regularity

Reduced facsimile of part of Domesday Book.

of taxation. They could hardly be expected to understand the advantages of a government strong enough through regular taxation to put down the resistance of rebellious earls at home and to defy invasion from abroad. The result of the inquiries of the king's commissioners was embodied in Domesday Book, so called because it was no more possible to appeal from it than from the Last Judgment.

13. **William's Great Councils.**—Though William was himself

the true ruler of England, he kept up the practice of his predecessors in summoning the Witenagemot from time to time. In his
days, however, the name of the Witenagemot was changed into
that of the Great Council, and, to a slight extent, it changed its
nature with its name. The members of the Witenagemot had attended because they were officially connected with the king, being
ealdormen or bishops or thegns serving in some way under him.
Members of the Great Council attended because they held land
in chief from the king. The difference, however, was greater in
appearance than in reality. No doubt men who held very small
estates in chief might, if they pleased, come to the Great Council,
and if they had done so the Great Council would have been much
more numerously attended than the Witenagemot had been. The
poorer tenants-in-chief, however, found that it was not only too
troublesome and expensive to make the journey at a time when
all long journeys had to be made on horseback, but that when they
arrived their wishes were disregarded. They therefore stayed at
home, so that the Great Council was regularly attended only by
the bishops, the abbots of the larger abbeys, and certain great
landowners who were known as barons. In this way the Great
Council became a council of the wealthy landowners, as the
Witenagemot had been, though the two assemblies were formed
on different principles.

14. **The Gemot at Salisbury. 1086.**—In 1086, after Domesday
Book had been finished, William summoned an unusually numerous
assembly, known as the Great Gemot, to meet at Salisbury. At this
not only the tenants-in-chief appeared, but also all those who held
lands from them as sub-tenants. "There came to him," wrote the
chronicler, ". . . all the landowning men there were over all England,
whose soever men they were, and all bowed down before him and
became his men, and swore oaths of fealty to him, that they would
be faithful to him against all other men." It was this oath which
marked the difference between English and Continental feudalism,
though they were now in other respects alike. On the Continent
each tenant swore to be faithful to his lord, but only the lords
who held directly from the crown swore to be faithful to the king.
The consequence was that when a lord rebelled against the
king, his tenants followed their lord and not the king. In
England the tenants swore to forsake their lord and to serve
the king against him if he forsook his duty to the king. Nor
was this all. Many men break their oaths. William, however,
was strong enough in England to punish those who broke their

I

oaths to him, whilst the king of France was seldom strong enough to punish those who broke their oaths to him.

15. **William's Death. 1087.**—The oath taken at Salisbury was the completion of William's work in England. To contemporaries he appeared as a foreign conqueror, and often as a harsh and despotic ruler. Later generations could recognise that his supreme merit was that he made England one. He did not die in England. In 1087 he fought with his lord, the king of France, Philip I. In anger at a jest of Philip's he set fire to Mantes. As he rode amidst the burning houses his horse shied and threw him forward on the pommel of his saddle. He was now corpulent and the injury proved fatal. On September 9 he died. When the body was carried to Caen for burial in the abbey of St. Stephen, which William himself had reared, a knight stepped forward and claimed as his own the ground in which the grave had been dug. It had been taken, he said, by William from his father. "In the name of God," he cried, "I forbid that the body of the robber be covered with my mould, or that he be buried within the bounds of my inheritance." The bystanders acknowledged the truth of his accusation, and paid the price demanded.

CHAPTER VIII

WILLIAM II. 1087—1100

LEADING DATES

Accession of William II.	1087
Norman rebellion against William II. . . .	1088
Anselm, Archbishop of Canterbury . . .	1093
The Council of Rockingham, and the First Crusade .	1095
Conquest of Jerusalem by the Crusaders . . .	1099
Death of William II.	1100

1. **The Accession of the Red King. 1087.**—In Normandy the Conqueror was succeeded by his eldest son, Robert. Robert was sluggish and incapable, and his father had expressed a wish that England, newly conquered and hard to control, should be ruled by his more energetic second son, William. To the third son, Henry, he gave a sum of money. There was as yet no settled rule of succession to the English crown, and William at once crossed the sea and was crowned king of the English at Westminster, by Lan-

franc. William Rufus, or the Red King, as men called him, feared not God nor regarded man. Yet the English rallied round him, because they knew that he was strong-willed, and because they needed a king who would keep the Norman barons from oppressing them. For that very reason the more turbulent of the Norman barons declared for Robert, who would be too lazy to keep them in order. In the spring of 1088 they broke into rebellion in his name. William called the English people to his help. He would not, he said, wring money from his subjects or exercise cruelty in defence of his hunting grounds. On this the English rallied round him. At the head of a great army he marched to attack the rebels, and finally laid siege to Rochester, which was held against him by his uncle Odo, Bishop of Bayeux, whom he had released from the imprisonment in which the Conqueror had kept him. William called upon yet greater numbers of the English to come to his help. Every one, he declared, who failed him now should be known for ever by the shameful name of *Nithing*, or worthless. The English came in crowds. When at last Odo surrendered, the English pleaded that no mercy should be shown him. "Halters, bring halters!" they cried; "hang up the traitor bishop and his accomplices on the gibbet." William, however, spared him, but banished him for ever from England

2. **The Wickedness of the Red King.**—William had crushed the Norman rebels with English aid. When the victory was won he turned against those who had helped him. It was not that he oppressed the English because they were English, but that he oppressed English and Normans alike, though the English, being the weaker, felt his cruelty most. He broke all his promises. He gathered round him mercenary soldiers from all lands to enforce his will. He hanged murderers and robbers, but he himself was the worst of robbers. When he moved about the country with the ruffians who attended him, the inhabitants fled to the woods, leaving their houses to be pillaged. William allowed no law to be pleaded against his own will. His life, and the life of his courtiers, was passed in the foulest vice. He was as irreligious as he was vicious. It was in especial defiance of the Christian sentiment of the time that he encouraged the Jews, who had begun to come into England in his father's days, to come in greater numbers. They grew rich as money-lenders, and William protected them against their debtors, exacting a high price for his protection. Once, it is said, he invited the Jewish rabbis to argue in his presence with the bishops on the merits of their respective creeds, and promised to become

a Jew if the rabbis had the better of the argument. His own mouth was filled with outrageous blasphemies. " God," he said, " shall never see me a good man. I have suffered too much at His hands."

3. **Ranulf Flambard.**—The chief minister of the Red King was Ranulf Flambard, whom he ultimately made Bishop of Durham. He was one of the clerks of the king's chapel. The word 'clerk' properly signified a member of the clergy. The only way in which men could work with their brains instead of with their hands was by becoming clerks, the majority of whom, however, only entered the lower orders, without any intention of becoming priests or even deacons. Few, except clerks, could read or write, and whatever work demanded intelligence naturally fell into their hands. They acted as physicians or lawyers, kept accounts, and wrote letters. The clerks of the king's chapel were the king's secretaries and men of business. These ready writers had taken a leading part in the compilation of Domesday Book, and they were always active in bringing in money. Under the Conqueror they were expected to observe at least something of the rules of justice. Under the Red King they were expected to disregard them entirely. Of all the clerks Ranulf Flambard was the most unscrupulous ; therefore he rose into the greatest favour. The first William had appointed high officers, known as Justiciars, to act in his name from time to time when he was absent from England, or was from any cause unable to be present when important business was transacted. Flambard was appointed Justiciar by the second William, and in his hands the office became permanent. The Justiciar was now the king's chief minister, acting in his name whether he was present or absent. Flambard used his power to gather wealth for the king on every side. " He drave the king's gemots," we are told, " over all England ; " that is to say, he forced the reluctant courts to exact the money which he claimed for the king.

4. **Feudal Dues.**—It was Flambard who systematised, if he did not invent, the doctrine that the king was to profit by his position as supreme landlord. In practice this meant that he exacted to the full the consequences of feudal tenure. If a man died who held land by knight service from the crown, leaving a son who was a minor, the boy became the ward of the king, who took the profits of his lands till he was twenty-one, and forced him to pay a relief or fine for taking them into his own hands when he attained his majority. If the land

fell to an heiress the king claimed the right of marrying her to whom he would, or of requiring of her a sum of money for permission to take a husband at her own choice, or, as was usually the case, at the choice of her relations. Under special circumstances the king exacted aids from his tenants-in-chief. If he were taken prisoner they had to pay to ransom him from captivity. When he knighted his eldest son or married his eldest daughter they had to contribute to the expense. It is true that this was in accordance with the principle of feudality. Neither a boy nor a woman could render service in the field, and it was therefore only fair that the king should hold the lands at times when no service was rendered to him for them ; and it was also fair that the dependents should come to their lord's help in times of special need, especially as all that the king took from them they in turn took from their own sub-tenants. Flambard, however, did not content himself with a moderately harsh exaction of these feudal dues. The grievance against him was that he made the king 'to be every man's heir, whether he were in orders or a layman,' that is to say, that Flambard so stripped and exhausted the land belonging to the king's wards as to make it almost worthless, and then demanded reliefs so enormous that when the estate had at last been restored, all its value had passed into the hands of the king. When a bishop or an abbot died, the king appointed no successor, and appropriated the revenues of the vacant see or monastery till some one chose to buy the office from him. The king alone grew rich, whilst his vassals were impoverished.

5. **Archbishop Anselm.**—In 1089 Lanfranc died, and the arch-bishopric of Canterbury was then left vacant for nearly four years. The Archbishop of Canterbury was more than the first of English bishops. He was not only the maintainer of ecclesiastical discipline, but also the mouthpiece of the English people when they had com-plaints to make to the king. Men turned their thoughts to Anselm, the Abbot of Bec. Anselm was a stranger from Aosta, on the Italian side of the Alps. He was the most learned man of the age, and had striven to justify the theology of the day by rational arguments. He was as righteous as he was learned, and as gentle as he was righteous. Tender to man and woman, he had what was in those days a rare tenderness to animals, and had caused astonishment by saving a hunted hare from its pursuers. In 1092 the king's vassals assembled in the Great Council urged William to choose a successor to Lanfranc, and asked him to allow prayers to be offered in the churches that God might move his heart to select a worthy

chief pastor. " Pray as you will," said the king, scornfully. " I shall do as I think good ; no man's prayers will do anything to shake my will ! " In the spring of **1093** William fell sick. Believing himself to be a dying man, he promised to amend his life, and named Anselm archbishop. On his refusal to accept the nomination, Anselm was dragged to the king's bedside, and the pastoral staff, the symbol of the pastoral office of a bishop, was forced into his hands by the bystanders.

6. **The Council of Rockingham. 1095.**— To this well-meant violence Anselm submitted unwillingly. He was, he said, a weak old sheep to be yoked with an untamed bull to draw the plough of the English Church. Yet, gentle as he was, he was possessed of indomitable courage in resistance to evil. William recovered, and returned to his blasphemy and his tyranny. In vain Anselm warned him against his sins. A fresh object of dispute soon arose between the king and the new archbishop. Two Popes claimed the obedience of Christendom. Urban II. was the Pope acknowledged by the greater part of the Church. Clement III. was the Pope supported by the Emperor. Anselm declared that Urban was the true Pope, and that he would obey none other. William asserted that his father had laid down a rule that no Pope should be acknowledged in England without the king's assent, and he proposed to act upon it by acknowledging neither Clement nor Urban. His object was, perhaps, to prevent the enforcement of ecclesiastical discipline by temporarily getting rid of the papal authority. Anselm wanted the authority of the Pope to check vice and disorder. The question was set aside for a time, but in **1095** Anselm, tired of witnessing William's wicked actions, asked leave to go to Rome to fetch from Urban the pallium, a kind of scarf given by the Pope to archbishops in recognition of their office. William replied that he did not acknowledge Urban as Pope. A Great Council was summoned to Rockingham to discuss the question. The lay barons, who liked to see the king resisted, were on Anselm's side. The bishops, many of whom were creatures of William, appointed from amongst his clerks, took the side of the king. Anselm stated his case firmly and moderately, and then, caring nothing for the angry king, retired into the chapel and went quietly to sleep. The king, finding that the barons would give him no support, was unable to punish Anselm. Two years later, in **1097**, Anselm betook himself to Rome, and William at once seized on his estates.

7. **William II. and his Brothers.**—Normandy under Robert was even worse off than England under William. William was

himself a tyrant, but in Normandy there were at least a hundred tyrants because Robert was too easy-tempered to bring any one to justice. The land was full of violence. Each baron made war on his neighbour, and, as usual, the peasant suffered most. Robert's own life was vicious and wasteful, and he was soon in debt. He sold the Cotentin and the territory of Avranches to his youngest brother, Henry. Henry was cool-headed and prudent, and he kept order in his new possession better than either of his elder brothers would have done. The brothers coveted the well-ordered land, and in **1091**, two years before Anselm became archbishop, they marched together against Henry. Henry was besieged on St. Michael's Mount, a rocky island surrounded by the sea at high water. After a time water ran short. The easy-tempered Robert sent in a supply. "Shall we let our brother die of thirst?" he said to William. Henry was in the end forced to surrender, and the land which he had purchased was lost to him for a time. In **1095** Henry was again in Normandy. Robert of Bellême, the lord of Domfront, was the most cruel of the cruel barons. Once he had torn out with his own hands the eyes of his godson, merely because the child's father had displeased him. The people of Domfront called on Henry to deliver them from such a monster. Henry seized Domfront, ruled its people with justice, and soon recovered the possessions from which his brothers had driven him.

   8. **William and Scotland.** 1093—1094.—William's attention was at this time drawn to the North. Early in his reign he annexed Cumberland, and had secured it against the Scots by fortifying Carlisle, which had been desolate since the Danish invasion in the reign of Ælfred. Malcolm, king of the Scots, was a rude warrior who had been tamed into an outward show of piety by his saintly wife, Margaret, the sister of Eadgar the Ætheling. Though he could not read her books of devotion, he liked to look at the pictures in them and to kiss the relics which she honoured. Margaret gathered Englishmen round her, and spread abroad something of southern piety and civilisation amongst the fierce Celtic warriors of her husband. She could not teach them to change their natures. In **1093** Malcolm burst into Northumberland, plundering and burning, till an Englishman slew him at Alnwick. Queen Margaret died broken-hearted at the news, and was before long counted as a saint. For the moment the Scottish Celts were weary of the English queen and her English ways. They set up Malcolm's brother, Donald Bane, as their king, refusing to be

governed by any of Margaret's sons. Donald at once 'drave out all the English that before were with King Malcolm.' In **1094** Duncan, Margaret's step-son, gained the crown from Donald with the aid of a troop of English and Norman followers. The Celts soon drove out his followers, and after a while they slew him and restored Donald.

9. **Mowbray's Rebellion. 1095.**—William had as yet too much to do at home to interfere further in Scotland. The Norman barons hated him, and in **1095** Robert of Mowbray, Earl of Northumberland—the name was now confined to the land between the Tweed and the Tyne—refused obedience. William at once marched against him, and took from him the new castle which he had built in **1080,** and which has ever since been known as Newcastle-on-Tyne. Robert held out long in his stronger fortress of Bamborough, which was only taken at last by fraud. He was condemned to a lifelong imprisonment, and it is even said that the Pope, seeing his case hopeless, allowed his wife to marry again as though her husband had been dead. Mowbray's rebellion, like the conspiracy of the Earls against the Conqueror, shows how eagerly the Norman barons longed to shake off the yoke of the king, and how readily Englishmen and the less powerful Normans supported even a tyrannical king rather than allow the barons to have their way.

10. **The First Crusade. 1095—1099.**—These petty wars were interrupted by a call to arms from the Pope. For centuries Christians had made pilgrimages to Bethlehem and Jerusalem, the holy places where their Lord had been born and had been crucified. When the Arabs conquered the Holy Land, Mohammedans as they were, they gave protection to the pilgrims from the West. The Turks, who were also Mohammedans, had lately obtained the mastery over the Arabs, and had secured dominion over the Holy Land. They were fierce warriors, ignorant and cruel, who either put the pilgrims to death or subjected them to torture and ill-usage. In **1095** Pope Urban II. came to Clermont to appeal to the Christians of the West to set out on a Crusade—a war of the Cross—to deliver the Holy City from the infidel. After he had spoken the multitude burst out with the cry, " It is the will of God ! " Men of every rank placed on their garments a cross, as the sign of their devotion to the service of Christ. In **1096** a huge multitude set forth under Peter the Hermit, who had been active in urging men to take part in the Crusade. They believed it to be unnecessary to take money or food, trusting that God would supply His warriors.

All these perished on the way. A better-equipped body of knights and nobles set out later under Godfrey of Bouillon. They fought their way through Asia Minor and Syria to Jerusalem, and in 1099 the Holy City was taken by storm. Godfrey, though he became its first Christian king, refused to be crowned. "I will not," he said, "wear a crown of gold where my Saviour wore a crown of thorns." The piety of the Christian warriors was not accompanied by mercy to the vanquished. Holding Mohammedans to be the special enemies of God, they treated them as no better than savage beasts. There was a terrible butchery when Jerusalem was taken, and Christian men fancied that they did God service by dashing out the brains of Mohammedan babes against the walls.

11. **Normandy in Pledge. 1096.**—Robert was amongst the Crusaders. To raise money for his expedition he pledged Normandy to his brother William. William had no wish to take part in a holy war, but he was ready to make profit out of those who did. Normandy was the better for the change. It is true that William oppressed it himself, but he saved the people from the worse oppression of the barons.

12. **The Last Years of the Red King.**—The remaining years of William's reign were years of varying success. An English force set up Eadgar, the son of Malcolm and Margaret, as king of the Scots, and Eadgar consented to hold his crown as William's vassal. William's attempts to reduce the Welsh to submission ended in failure, and he was obliged to content himself with hemming them in with castles. In 1098 the wicked Robert of Bellême succeeded his brother as earl of Shrewsbury. Robert robbed and tortured Englishmen as he had robbed and tortured Normans. He was a great builder of castles, and at Bridgenorth he raised a fortress as the centre of a group of strong places which could defy the Welsh and form the basis of his operations against them. In the same year William captured Le Mans, the capital of Maine, which had recovered its independence from Robert, which was held against him by Helie de la Flêche, one of the few unselfish men of the day. Unlike his father, the Red King often began enterprises which he did not finish. In 1099 he had all his work to do over again. He was hunting in the New Forest when he heard that Helie had regained Le Mans. He rode hard to Southampton, and, leaping on board a vessel, bade the sailors put to sea. A storm was raging, and the sailors prayed him to wait till the wind fell. "I never heard," he answered, "of a king being drowned." The next morning he was in Normandy. He

recovered Le Mans, but returned to England without conquering Maine.

13. The Death of the Red King. 1100.—On August 2, **1100**, the Red King went out to hunt in the New Forest. In the evening his body was found pierced by an arrow. Who his slayer was is unknown. The blow may have been accidental. It is more likely to have been intentional. In every part of England were men who had good cause to hate William, and nowhere were his enemies in greater numbers than round the New Forest. Whoever was his slayer, the body of the tyrant was borne to the cathedral of Winchester and buried as the corpse of a wild beast, without funeral rites or weeping eyes. When, after a few years had passed, the tower above the unhallowed tomb fell in, men said that it had fallen because so foul a body lay beneath it.

CHAPTER IX

HENRY I. AND STEPHEN

HENRY I, 1100—1135. STEPHEN, 1135—1154

LEADING DATES

The Accession of Henry I.	1100
Battle of Tinchebrai	1106
Death of Henry I. and Accession of Stephen	1135
The Civil War	1139
Treaty of Wallingford	1153
Death of Stephen	1154

1. The Accession of Henry I. 1100.—When the news spread that the Red King had been slain in the New Forest, his younger brother, Henry, hastened to Winchester, where he was chosen king by the barons who happened to be there. At his coronation at Westminster he swore to undo all the evil of his brother's reign. The name by which he came to be known—the Lion of ·Justice— shows how well he kept his promise. He maintained order as his father had done, and his brother had not done. Flambard, the wicked minister of the Red King, was imprisoned in the Tower, and Anselm, the good archbishop, recalled to England. Henry's chief strength lay in the support of the English. To please them he married Eadgyth, the daughter of Malcolm and Margaret, the descendant through her mother of the old English kings. Through

Eadgyth the blood of Alfred and Ecgberht was transmitted to the later kings. It was, however, necessary that she should take another

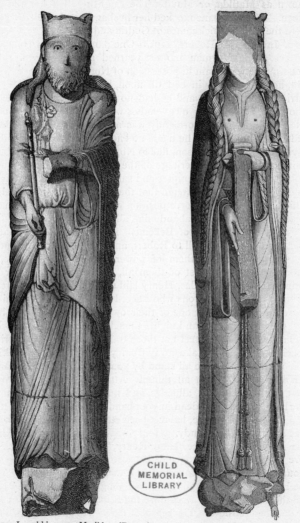

Henry I. and his queen Matilda. (From the west front of Rochester Cathedral.)

name. Every one at Henry's court talked French, and 'Eadgyth' was unpronounceable in French. The new queen was therefore known as Matilda, or Maud. The English called her the good queen. The Normans mocked her husband and herself by giving them the English nicknames of Godric and Godgifu.

2. **Invasion of Robert. 1101.**—One danger at least Henry had to face. The Norman barons yearned after the weak rule of Robert, who was again in possession of Normandy. Once, we are told, he had to stay in bed till noon, because his favourites had carried off his clothes, and he had no others to put on. A duke, who could not keep his own clothes was not likely to be able to rule his duchy, and Normandy was again the scene of fightings and plunderings which he made no effort to suppress. Flambard, having escaped from prison, fled to Normandy, and urged Robert to claim England as the heritage of the eldest son of the Conqueror. Robert listened to the tempter and sailed for England. When he landed at Porchester he found that the Church and the English had rallied to Henry. Robert's position was hopeless, and he made a treaty with his brother, abandoning all claim to the crown.

3. **Revolt of Robert of Bellême. 1102.**—Henry knew that the great barons wished well to Robert, and on one pretext or another he stripped most of them of power. Robert of Bellême, the strongest and wickedest of them all, rose in revolt. After capturing many of his castles, Henry laid siege to his great fortress at Bridgenorth. The barons who served under Henry urged him to spare a rebel who was one of their own class. The Englishmen and the inferior Norman knights thought otherwise. " Lord King Henry," they cried, "trust not those traitors. They do but strive to deceive you, and to take away from you the strength of kingly justice. . . . Behold, we all stand by you faithfully ; we are ready to serve and help you in all things. Attack the castle vigorously ; shut in the traitor on all sides, and make no peace with him till you have him alive or dead in your hands." Bridgenorth was taken, and Robert of Bellême, having been stripped of his English land, was sent off to Normandy. Henry was now, in very truth, king of the English. " Rejoice, King Henry," ran a popular song, " and give thanks to the Lord God, because thou art a free king since thou hast overthrown Robert of Bellême, and hast driven him from the borders of thy kingdom." Never again during Henry's reign did the great Norman lords dare to lift hand against him.

4. **The Battle of Tinchebrai. 1106.**—It was impossible for Henry to avoid interference in Normandy. Many of his vassals in

England possessed lands in Normandy as well, where they were exposed to the violence of Robert of Bellême and of others who had been expelled from England. The Duke of the Normans would do nothing to keep the peace, and Henry crossed the sea to protect his own injured subjects.

Duke Robert naturally resisted him, and at last, in **1106**, a great battle was fought at Tinchebrai, in which Robert was utterly defeated. Duke Robert was kept for the remainder of his life a prisoner in Cardiff Castle, where he died after an imprisonment of twenty-eight years. Henry became Duke of the Normans as well as king of the English, and all Normandy was the better for the

Seal of Milo of Gloucester, showing mounted armed figure in the reign of Henry I.

change. Robert of Bellême was thrown into prison, and the cruel oppressor thus shared the fate of the weak ruler whose remissness had made his oppressions possible.

5. **Henry and Anselm. 1100—1107.**—Though Anselm had done everything in his power to support Henry against Robert of Bellême, he was himself engaged in a dispute with the king which lasted for some years. A bishop in Anselm's time was not only a great Church officer, whose duty it was to maintain a high standard of religion and morality amongst the clergy. He was also one of the king's barons, because he was possessed of large estates, and was therefore bound like any other baron to send knights to the king when they were needed. Consequently, when Anselm became archbishop he had not only received investiture from William II. by accepting from him the ring and the staff which were the signs of ecclesiastical authority, but also did homage, thus acknowledging himself to be the king's man, and obliging himself, not indeed to fight for him in person, but to send knights to fight under his orders. When, however, Henry came to the throne, and asked Anselm to repeat the homage which he had done to William,

Anselm not only refused himself to comply with the king's request, but also refused to consecrate newly-chosen bishops who had received investiture from Henry. During the time of his exile Anselm had taken part in a council of the Church, in which bishops and abbots had been forbidden by the Pope and the council either to receive investiture from laymen or to do homage to them. These decrees had not been issued merely to serve the purpose of papal ambition. At that time all zealous ecclesiastics thought that the only way to stop the violence of kings in their dealings with the Church was to make the Church entirely independent. Anselm's experience of the Red King's wickedness must have made him ready to concur with this new view, and there can be no doubt that it was from the most conscientious motives that he refused to do homage to Henry. On the other hand, Henry, wishing to rule justly, thought it very hard that the archbishop should insist upon the independence of the bishops, especially as in consequence of their large estates they had so many knights to send into the field. Though the dispute was a hot one, it was carried on without any of the violence which had characterised the dispute between Anselm and the Red King, and it ended in a compromise. Henry abandoned all claim to give the ring and the pastoral staff which were the signs of a bishop's or an abbot's spiritual jurisdiction, whilst Anselm consented to allow the new bishop or abbot to render the homage which was the sign of his readiness to employ all his temporal wealth and power on the king's behalf. The bishop was to be chosen by the chapter of his cathedral, the abbot by the monks of his abbey, but the election was to take place in the king's presence, thus giving him influence over their choice. Whether this settlement would work in favour of the king or the clergy depended on the character of the kings and the clergy. If the kings were as riotous as the Red King and the clergy as self-denying as Anselm, the clergy would grow strong in spite of these arrangements. If the kings were as just and wise as Henry, and the clergy as wicked as Ralph Flambard, all advantage would be on the side of the king.

6. **Roger of Salisbury.**—After the defeat of the Norman barons the Great Council ceased for a time to have any important influence on the government. Henry was practically an absolute king, and it was well that he should be so, as the country wanted order more than discussion. Henry, however, loved to exercise absolute power in an orderly way, and he chose for his chief minister Roger, whom he made Bishop of Salisbury. Roger had first attracted his notice when he was going out hunting, by saying mass in a shorter time

than any other priest, but he retained his favour by the order and
system which he introduced into the government. A special body
of officials and councillors was selected by the king—perhaps a
similar body had been selected by his predecessor—to sit in judgment over cases in which tenants-in-chief were concerned, as well
as over other cases which were, for one reason or another, transferred to it from the Baronial Courts. This council or committee
was called the *Curia Regis* (the
King's Court). The members of this
Curia Regis met also in the Exchequer, so called from the chequered
cloth which covered the table at
which they sat. They were then
known as Barons of the Exchequer,
and controlled the receipts and out-
goings of the treasury. The Justiciar
presided in both the *Curia Regis*
and the Exchequer. Amongst those
who took part in these proceedings
was the Chancellor, who was then
a secretary and not a judge, as well
as other superior officers of the
king. A regular system of finance
was introduced, and a regular system of justice accompanied it. At
last the king determined to send
some of the judges of his court to
go on circuit into distant parts of the
kingdom. These itinerant Justices
(*Justitiarii errantes*) brought the
royal power into connection with
the local courts. Their business
was of a very miscellaneous character. They not only heard the cases
in which the king was concerned—
the pleas of the crown, as they
were called—but they made assessments for purposes of taxation,
listened to complaints, and conveyed the king's wishes to his
people.

Monument of Roger, Bishop of Salisbury (died 1139), in his cathedral
church.

7. **Growth of Trade.**—Though Henry's severe discipline was
not liked, yet the law and order which he maintained told on the
prosperity of the country, and the trade of London flourished so

much as to attract citizens from Normandy to settle in it. Flemings too, trained in habits of industry, came in crowds, and with the view of providing a bulwark against the Welsh, Henry settled a colony of them in South Pembrokeshire, which has since been known as Little England beyond Wales. The foreigners were not popular, but the Jews, to whom Henry continued the protection which William had given them, were more unpopular still.

Porchester Church, Hampshire.   Built about 1135.

8. **The Benedictines.**—In the midst of this busy life the Bene-dictine monasteries were still harbours of refuge for all who did not care to fight or trade. They were now indeed wealthier than they had once been, as gifts, usually of land, had been made to the monks by those who reverenced their piety. Sometimes these gifts took a shape which afterwards caused no little evil. Landowners who had churches on their lands often gave to a monastery the tithes which had hitherto been paid for the support of the parish priest, and the monastery stepped into the place of the parish priest,

sending a vicar to act for it in the performance of its new duties. As the monks themselves grew richer they grew less ascetic. Their life, however, was not spent in idleness. They cared for the poor, kept a school for the children, and managed their own property. Some of their number studied and wrote, and our knowledge of the history of these times is mainly owing to monastic writers. When Henry I. came to the throne the Chronicle was still being written in the English tongue by the monks of Worcester, and for some years after his death was still carried on at Peterborough. The best historical compositions were, however, in Latin, the language understood by the clergy over all Western Europe. Amongst the authors of these Latin works, the foremost was William of Malmesbury.

9. **The Cistercians.**—Useful as the Benedictines were, there were some monks who complained that the extreme self-denial of their founder, St. Benedict, was no longer to be met with, and the complainants had lately originated a new order, called the Cistercian, from Cîteaux, in Burgundy, the site of their first abbey. The Cistercians made their appearance in England in **1128**. Their buildings and churches were simpler than those of the Benedictines, and their life more austere. They refused to receive gifts of tithes lest they should impoverish the parish clergy. They loved to make their homes in solitary places far from the haunts of men, and some of the most beautiful of the abbeys which remain in ruins —those, for instance, of Fountains and Tintern—were Cistercian abbeys. They are beautiful, not because the Cistercians loved pleasant places, but because they loved solitude, whilst the Benedictines had either planted themselves in towns or had allowed towns to grow up round their monasteries.

10. **The White Ship.**—Henry, in consequence of the possession of Normandy, had been frequently involved in war with France. Robert's son, William Clito, claimed Normandy, and his claim was supported by Louis VI. the Fat, who was styled king of France, though the territory which he actually ruled was no larger than Normandy. In these wars Henry was usually successful, and at last, in **1127**, William was killed, and Henry freed from danger. His own son, also named William, had already been drowned on the voyage between Normandy and England in **1120**. The ship in which he sailed ran upon a rock, and the young man was placed in a boat, and might have escaped if he had not returned to save his half-sister, the Countess of Perche, who was still on board. As soon as he approached the sailors and passengers crowded into the boat and swamped it. Only one man, a butcher, was saved, by clinging

K

to the mast of the ship when it sank. The captain, who was with
him on the mast, threw himself off as soon as he learned that the
king's son had been drowned, and perished in the water. It is said

Part of the nave of Durham Cathedral. Built about 1130.

that no man dared to tell Henry that his son was drowned, and that at last a little child was sent to inform him of his misfortune.

11. **The Last Years of Henry I.**—Henry had many illegitimate children, but after William's death the only lawful child left to him was Matilda. She had been married as a child to the Emperor Henry V., but her husband had died before she was grown up, and she then returned to her father, as the Empress Matilda. There had never been a queen in England, and it would have been very hard for a woman to rule in those times of constant war and blood-shed. Yet Henry persuaded the barons to swear to accept her as their future sovereign. He then married her to Geoffrey, Count of Anjou, who came of a brave and active race, and whose lands, which lay to the south of Normandy, would enlarge the French possessions of Henry's descendants. In 1135 Henry died. The great merit of his English government was that he forsook his brother's evil ways of violence, and maintained peace by erecting a regular administrative system, which kept down the outrages of the barons. One of the English chroniclers in recording his death prayed that God might give him the peace that he loved.[1]

12. **Stephen's Accession. 1135.**—Among the barons who had sworn to obey Matilda was Stephen of Blois, a son of the Conqueror's daughter Adela, and a nephew of Henry I. As soon as Henry's death was known Stephen made his way to London, where he was joyfully received as king. The London citizens felt that their chief interest lay in the maintenance of peace, and they thought that a man would be more likely than a woman to secure order. The barons chose Stephen king at Winchester, where his brother, Henry of Blois, was the bishop. Shortly afterwards some of these very barons rose against him, but their insurrection was soon repressed. More formidable was the hostility of David,

----

[1] Genealogy of the Conqueror's sons and grandchildren :—

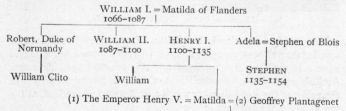

William I. = Matilda of Flanders
1066–1087

Robert, Duke of Normandy — William II. 1087–1100 — Henry I. 1100–1135 — Adela = Stephen of Blois

William Clito — William — Stephen 1135–1154

(1) The Emperor Henry V. = Matilda = (2) Geoffrey Plantagenet

Henry II.
1154–1189

king of the Scots. David was closely connected with the family
of Henry I., his sister having been Henry's wife, the Empress
Matilda being consequently his niece. He also held in right of
his own wife the earldom of Huntingdon. Under the pretext of
taking up Matilda's cause he broke into the north of England.
Though he himself carried on the work of introducing English

Keep of Rochester Castle.   Built between 1126 and 1139.

civilisation into Scotland, his Celtic followers were still savage,
and massacred women and infants. In **1137** Stephen drove David
back. In **1138** David reappeared, and this time the aged Thurstan,
Archbishop of York, sent the levies of the North against him. In
the midst of the English army was a cart bearing a standard, at the
top of which the banners of the three great churches of St. Peter's
of York, St. John of Beverley, and St. Wilfrid of Ripon, waved round

the consecrated Host. The battle which ensued, near Northallerton, has consequently been known as the battle of the Standard. The Scots were completely defeated, but Stephen, in spite of the victory gained for him, found himself obliged to buy peace at a heavy price. He agreed that David's son, Henry, should hold Northumberland, with the exception of the fortresses of Bamborough and of New-castle, as a fief of the English Crown. David himself was also allowed to keep Cumberland without doing homage.

Keep of Castle Rising. Built about 1140-50.

13. **Civil War.**—It would have been well for Stephen if he had learnt from the men of the North that his strength lay in rallying the English people round him against the great barons, as the Red King and Henry I. had done when their right to the crown had been challenged by Robert. Instead of this, he brought over mer-cenaries from Flanders, and squandered treasure and lands upon his favourites so as to have little left for the hour of need. He made friends easily, but he made enemies no less easily. One of the most powerful of the barons was Robert, Earl of Gloucester, an illegitimate son of Henry I., who held the strong fortress of

Bristol, and whose power extended over both sides of the lower course of the Severn. In 1138 Stephen, who distrusted him, ordered his castles to be seized. Robert at once declared his half-sister Matilda to be the lawful queen, and a terrible civil war began. Robert's garrison at Bristol was a terror to all the country round. He, too, gathered foreign mercenaries, who knew not what pity was. Other barons imitated Robert's example, fighting only for themselves whether they nominally took the part of Stephen or of Matilda, and the southern and midland counties of England were preyed upon by the garrisons of their castles.

14. **Stephen's Quarrel with the Clergy. 1139.**—Evil as were the men who fought on either side, it was to Stephen and not to Matilda and Robert that men as yet looked to restore order. The port towns, London, Yarmouth, and Lynn, clung to him to the last. Unfortunately Stephen did not know how to make good use of his advantages. The clergy, like the traders, had always been in favour of order. Some of them, with the Justiciar, Roger, Bishop of Salisbury, at their head, had organised the Exchequer of Henry I., had gathered in the payments due to the Crown, or had acted as judges. Yet with all their zeal in the service of the Crown, they had not omitted to provide for their own interests. Roger in particular had been insatiable in the pursuit of wealth for himself and of promotion for his family. One of his nephews, Nigel, Bishop of Ely, was Treasurer, whilst another, Alexander, was Bishop of Lincoln, and his own illegitimate son, Roger, was Chancellor. In 1139 Stephen, rightly or wrongly, threw him into prison with his son and Alexander of Lincoln. The other nephew, Nigel, escaped to his uncle's castle at Devizes, in which was the younger Roger's mother, Matilda of Ramsbury. Stephen brought her son before the castle, and put a rope round his neck to hang him unless the castle was surrendered. The unhappy mother could not bear the sight, and opened the gates to Stephen. It might have been wise to deprive a too ambitious bishop of his castle, but it was not wise personally to maltreat the clergy. Every priest in England turned against Stephen. His own brother, Henry, Bishop of Winchester, declared against him, and Stephen was obliged to do penance for his offence. The administration of the Exchequer was shattered, and though it was not altogether destroyed, and money was brought to it for the king's use even in the worst times, Stephen's financial resources were from henceforth sadly diminished.

15. **Anarchy. 1139.**—The war now lapsed into sheer anarchy. The barons on either side broke loose from all restraint. " They

fought amongst themselves with deadly hatred ; they spoiled the
fairest lands with fire and rapine ; in what had been the most
fertile of counties they destroyed almost all the provision of
bread." All goods and money they carried off, and if they suspected any man to have concealed treasure they tortured him to
oblige him to confess where it was. "They hanged up men by
the feet and smoked them with foul smoke ; some were hanged
up by their thumbs, others by their head, and coats of mail were
hung on to their feet. They put knotted strings about men's heads,
and twisted them till they went to the brain. They put men into
prisons where adders and snakes and toads were crawling ; and
so they tormented them. Some they put into a chest, short and
narrow and not deep, and that had sharp stones within ; and forced
men therein, so that they broke all their limbs. In many of the
castles were hateful and grim things called neckties, which two or
three men had enough to do to carry. This instrument of torture
was thus made : it was fastened to a beam, and had a sharp iron
to go about a man's neck and throat, so that he might no way sit
or lie or sleep, but he bore all the iron. Many thousands they
starved with hunger. . . . Men said openly that Christ and His
saints were asleep."

16. **The End of the War. 1141—1148.**—In the autumn of
1139, Matilda appeared in England, and in **1141** there was a battle
at Lincoln, in which Stephen was taken prisoner. Henry of Winchester (see p. 131) acknowledged Matilda as queen, and all England
submitted to her, London giving way most reluctantly. Her rule
did not last long. She was as much too harsh as Stephen was too
good-natured. She seized the lands of the Church, and ordered
the Londoners to pay a heavy fine for having supported Stephen.
On this the Londoners rang their bells, and the citizens in arms
swarmed out of their houses 'like bees out of a hive.' Matilda fled
to Winchester before them. Bishop Henry then turned against
her. Robert of Gloucester was taken prisoner, and after a while
Matilda was obliged to set free King Stephen in exchange for her
brother. Fighting continued for some time. On all sides men
were longing for peace. The fields were untilled because no man
could tell who would reap the harvest. Thousands perished of
starvation. If peace there was to be, it could only come by
Stephen's victory. It was now known that Matilda was even less
fit to govern than Stephen. Stephen took one castle after another.
In **1147** Earl Robert died, and in **1148** Matilda gave up the struggle
and left England.

17. Henry, Duke of the Normans.   1149.—Whilst Matilda had
been losing England her husband had been conquering Normandy,

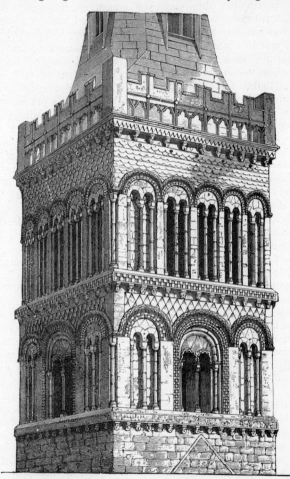

Tower of Castor Church, Northamptonshire.   Built about 1145.
(The parapet and spire are later.)

and for a little while it seemed possible that England and Normandy
would be separated ; England remaining under Stephen and his

heirs, and Normandy united with Anjou under the Angevin Geoffrey and his descendants. That the separation did not yet take place was partly owing to the different character of the two heirs. Stephen's son, Eustace, was rough and overbearing. Geoffrey's son, Henry, was shrewd and prudent. Henry had already been in England when he was still quite young, and had learnt something of English affairs from his uncle, Robert of Gloucester. He returned to his father in **1147**, and in **1149** Geoffrey gave up to him the duchy of Normandy. He was then sent to try his fortune in England in his mother's stead, but he was only a boy of sixteen, and too young to cope with Stephen. In **1150** he abandoned the struggle for a time. In his absence Stephen had still rebels to put down and castles to besiege, but he had the greater part of the kingdom at his back, and if Henry had continued to leave him alone he would probably have reduced all his enemies to submission.

18. **The Last Days of Stephen. 1153—1154.**—In **1150** Geoffrey died, and Henry became Count of Anjou as well as Duke of Normandy. Before long he acquired a much wider territory than either Anjou or Normandy. Louis VII. of France had to wife Eleanor, the Duchess of Aquitaine, and through her had added to his own scanty dominions the whole of the lands between the Loire and the Pyrenees. Louis, believing that she was unfaithful to him, had divorced her on the pretext that she was too near of kin. Henry was not squeamish about the character of so great an heiress, and in **1152** married the Duchess of Aquitaine for the sake of her lands. Thus strengthened, he again returned to England. He was now a young man of nineteen ; his vigour was as great as that of Stephen, and his skill greater. He won fortress after fortress. Before the end of **1153** Eustace died, and Stephen had no motive for prolonging the strife if his personal interests could be saved. It was arranged by the treaty of Wallingford that Stephen should retain the crown for life, and that Henry should be his heir. The castles which had sprung up during the civil war without the licence of the king—the 'adulterine castles,' as they were called—and there were no less than 365[1] of them—were to be destroyed, and order and good government were to return. For five months Henry remained in England. The robber barons could not hold out against the two rivals now united. Many of the castles were demolished, and ' such good peace as never was here ' was established. In **1154** Stephen died, and young Henry ruled England in his own name.

[1] The number usually given, ' 1,115,' is probably an error.

CHAPTER X

HENRY II. 1154—1189

LEADING DATES

Accession of Henry II. 1154
Thomas, Archbishop of Canterbury 1162
The Constitutions of Clarendon 1164
Murder of Archbishop Thomas 1172
The Assize of Arms 1181
Fall of the Kingdom of Jerusalem 1187
Death of Henry II. 1189

1. **Henry's Accession. 1154.**—Henry II. was but twenty-one when he returned, after Stephen's death, to govern England. He had before him the difficult task of establishing order where anarchy had prevailed, but it was a task for which he was specially suited. His frame was strong and thick-set, and he was as active as he was strong. His restlessness was the dismay of his courtiers. Eager to see everything for himself, and having to rule a territory extending from the Pyrenees to the Scottish border, he was always on the move. His followers were not allowed to know till he started in the morning where he intended to sleep at night, and he frequently changed his mind even after he had set out. He was as busy with his mind as he was with his body, as fond of a book as of a horse, and ready to chat with any one of whatever rank. Even when he was at mass he either drew pictures to amuse himself or conversed in whispers with his neighbours. His ceaseless energy was combined with a strong will, a clear perception of the limits beyond which action would be unwise, a good eye for ability in others, and a power of utilising their ability in his own service. On the Continent his sagacity appeared in his resolution to be content with the dominions which he had acquired without making further conquests. In England his main object was the same as that of his predecessors, to establish the king's authority over the great barons. What especially distinguished him was his clear perception of the truth that he could only succeed by securing, not merely the passive goodwill, but the active co-operation of those who, whether they were of Norman or of English descent, were inferior in wealth and position to the great barons.

2. **Pacification of England.**—Henry's first year was spent in completing the work which he had begun after the treaty of Wallingford. He sent Stephen's mercenaries over the sea and

Effigies of Henry II. and Queen Eleanor at Fontevrault.

completed the destruction of the 'adulterine castles.' One great rebel after another was forced to submit and have his strong walls pulled down. There were to be no more dens of robbers in England, but all men were to obey the king and the law. What castles remained were the king's, and as long as they were his rebellions would not be likely to be successful. Henry even regained from Malcolm IV., king of the Scots, Northumberland and Cumberland, which had been surrendered by Stephen (see p. 133). In his government Henry did his best to carry out the plans of his grandfather, Henry I. It was perhaps because he was afraid that one Justiciar would be too powerful, that he appointed two, Richard de Lucy and the Earl of Leicester, to see that justice was executed and the government maintained whether the king were absent or present. The old Bishop Nigel of Ely was reappointed Treasurer, and presided over the Exchequer at Westminster. Thomas of London, known in later times by the name of Becket,[1] an active and vigorous man, fifteen years older than the king, who had been ordained a deacon, but had nothing clerical about him except the name, was made Chancellor. Thomas was the king's chosen friend, and the two together delighted in the work of restoring order. Thomas liked sumptuous living, and the magnificence of his housekeeping and of his feasts was the talk of the whole country. Yet though he laughed and jested in the midst of his grandeur, he kept himself from every kind of vice. Henry was fond of horseplay, and once on a bitter winter's day, when he was riding with Thomas, he snatched at a fine new scarlet mantle from the Chancellor's neck to throw to a beggar. Thomas struggled hard, and the two men nearly pulled one another off their horses, but in the end the beggar got the mantle.

3. **Henry and Feudality.**—It was principally with Thomas the Chancellor that Henry consulted as to the best means of establishing his authority. He resolved not only to renew but to extend the administrative system of Henry I. The danger which threatened him came from the great barons, and as the great barons were as dangerous to the lesser ones and to the bulk of the people as they were to the king, Henry was able to strengthen himself by winning the affections of the people. Feudality in itself was only a method of owning land ; but it was always threatening to pass into a method of government. In France the great feudal

[1] His father's name was Becket, but at that time hereditary surnames had not come into use. He was once called Thomas Becket in his lifetime by one of his murderers as an insult.

lords ruled their own territories with very little regard for the wishes of the king, and the smaller feudal lords had their own courts in which they hanged and imprisoned their villeins. In Stephen's time an attempt had been made to introduce this system into England, with evil consequences both to king and people. Before the Conquest great landowners had often received permission from the king to exercise criminal jurisdiction in the Manor Courts on their own estates, whilst the vast extent of their landed property gave them a preponderant voice in the proceedings of the shire-moots, now known by the Normans as County Courts. Henry resolved to attack the evil at both ends : in the first place to make the barons support the king's government instead of setting up their own ; in the second place, to weaken the Manor and County Courts and to strengthen courts directly proceeding from himself.

4. **The Great Council and the Curia Regis.**—Henry in the early years of his reign revived the importance of the Great Council, taking care that it should be attended not only by the great barons, but by vassals holding smaller estates, and therefore more dependent on himself. He summoned the Great Council oftener than his predecessors had done. In this way even the greater barons got the habit of sharing in the government of England as a whole, instead of seeking to split up the country, as France was split up, into different districts, each of which might be governed by one of themselves. It was in consequence of the increasing habit of consulting with the king that the Great Council, after many changes, ultimately grew into the modern Parliament. It was of no less importance that Henry II. strengthened the *Curia Regis*, which had been established in the reign of Henry I. (see p. 127) to collect the king's revenue, to give him political advice, and to judge as many questions as it could possibly get hold of. It was especially by doing justice that the *Curia Regis* was likely to acquire strength, and the strength of the *Curia Regis* was in reality the strength of the king.

5. **Scutage.**—If Henry was to carry out justice everywhere it would be necessary for him to weaken still further the power of the barons. Before long he hit upon a plan which had the double merit of strengthening the king upon the Continent and of weakening the barons in England. Henry needed an army to defend his Continental possessions against the king of France. The fyrd, or general levy of Englishmen, was not bound to fight except at home, and though the feudal vassals were liable to serve abroad, they could only be made to serve for forty days in the

year, which was too short a time for Henry's purposes. He accordingly came to an agreement with his vassals. The owner of every knight's fee was to pay a sum of money known as scutage (*shield-money*) in lieu of service. Both parties gained by the arrangement. The king got money with which he paid mercenaries abroad, who would fight for him all the year round, and the vassal escaped the onerous duty of fighting in quarrels in which he took no interest. Indirectly the change weakened the feudal vassals, because they had now less opportunity than before of acquiring a military training in actual war.

Ecclesiastical costume in the twelfth century.

6. **Archbishop Thomas. 1162.**—Henry, who meditated great judicial reforms, foresaw that the clergy would be an obstacle in his way. He was eager to establish one law for his whole kingdom, and the clergy, having been exempted by the Conqueror from the jurisdiction of the ordinary law courts in all ecclesiastical matters, had, during the anarchy of Stephen's reign, encroached on the royal authority, and claimed to be responsible, even in criminal cases, only to the ecclesiastical courts, which were unable to inflict the penalty of death, so that a clerk who committed a murder could not be hanged like other murderers. As large numbers of clerks were only in the lower orders, and as many of them had only taken those orders to escape from the hardships of lay life, their morals were often no better than those of their lay neighbours. A

vacancy occurring in the Archbishopric of Canterbury, Henry, who wished to make these clerks punishable by his own courts, thought that the arrangement would easily be effected if Thomas, who had hitherto been active as a reformer in his service, were Archbishop as well as Chancellor. It was in vain that Thomas remonstrated. "I warn you," he said to Henry, "that, if such a thing should be, our friendship would soon turn to bitter hate." Henry persisted in spite of the warning, and Thomas became Archbishop.

7. Breach between Henry and Thomas.—The first act of the new Archbishop was to surrender his Chancellorship. He was unable, he said, to serve two masters. It is not difficult to understand his motives. The Church, as the best men of the twelfth century believed, was divinely instituted for the guidance of the world. It was but a short step for the nobler spirits amongst the clergy to hold it necessary that, in order to secure the due performance of such exalted duties, the clergy should be exempted from the so-called justice of laymen, which was often only another name for tyranny, even if the exemption led to the infliction upon wicked clerks of lesser punishments than were meet. In this way the clergy would unconsciously fall into the frame of mind which might lead them to imagine it more to the honour of God that a wicked clerk should be insufficiently punished than that he should be punished by a layman. Of all men Archbishop Thomas was the most likely to fall into this mistake. He was, as Chancellor, prone to magnify his office, and to think more of being the originator of great reforms than of the great reforms themselves. As Archbishop he would also be sure to magnify his office, and to think less, as Anselm would have thought, of reconciling the true interests of the kingdom with the true interests of the Church, than of making the Archbishop's authority the centre of stirring movement, and of raising the Church, of which he was the highest embodiment in England, to a position above the power of the king. All this he would do with a great, if not a complete, sincerity. He would feel that he was himself the greater man because he believed that he was fighting in the cause of God.

8. The Constitutions of Clarendon. 1164.—Between a king eager to assert the rights of the crown and an archbishop eager to assert the rights of the clergy a quarrel could not be long deferred. Thomas's first stand, however, was on behalf of the whole country. At a Great Council at Woodstock he resisted the king's resolution to levy the old tax of Danegeld, and in consequence Danegeld was never levied again. Henry had for some time been displeased because, without consulting him, the Archbishop had seized on lands which he claimed as the property of the see of Canterbury, and had excommunicated one of the king's tenants. Then a clerk who had committed a rape and a murder had been acquitted in an ecclesiastical court. On this, Henry called on the bishops to promise to obey the customs of the realm. Thomas, being told that the king merely wanted a verbal promise to save his dignity,

A bishop ordaining a priest.   (From a MS. of the latter part of the twelfth century.)

with some reluctance consented. He soon found that he had been tricked. In 1164 Henry summoned a Great Council to meet at Clarendon, and directed some of the oldest of his barons to set down in writing the customs observed by his grandfather. Their report was intended to settle all disputed points between the king and the clergy, and was drawn up under sixteen heads known as the Constitutions of Clarendon. The most important of them de-

clared that beneficed clergy should not leave the realm without the
king's leave ; that no tenant-in-chief of the king should be excommunicated without the king's knowledge ; that no villein should
be ordained without his lord's consent ; that a criminous clerk
should be sent to the ecclesiastical court for trial, and that after
he had been there convicted or had pleaded guilty the Church should
deprive him and leave him to the lay court for further punishment.
It was for the *Curia Regis* to determine what matters were properly to be decided by the ecclesiastical courts; and no appeal to
Rome was to be allowed without its permission. To all this Thomas
was violently opposed, maintaining that the sentence of deprivation,
which was all that an ecclesiastical court was empowered to inflict,
was so terrible, that one who had incurred it ought not to be sentenced to any further penalty by a lay court. After six days' struggle
he left the Council, refusing to assent to the Constitutions.

9. **The Persecution of Archbishop Thomas. 1164.**— Unluckily
for himself, Henry could not be content firmly and quietly to
enforce the law as it had been declared at Clarendon. He had
in his character much of the orderly spirit of his grandfather,
Henry I., but he had also something of the violence of his great-
uncle, William II. A certain John the Marshal had a suit against
the archbishop, and when the archbishop refused to plead in a
lay court, the king's council sentenced him to a fine of 500*l.* Then
Henry summoned the archbishop to his castle at Northampton to
give an account of all the money which, when he was Chancellor,
he had received from the king—a claim which is said to have
amounted to 30,000*l.*, a sum equal in the money of these days to not
much less than 400,000*l.* now. Thomas, with the crucifix in his hand,
awaited in the hall the decision of Henry, who with the council
was discussing his fate in an upper chamber. When the Justiciar
came out to tell him that he had been declared a traitor he refused
to listen, and placed himself under the Pope's protection. Hot
words were bandied on either side as he walked out of the hall.
" This is a fearful day," said one of his attendants. " The Day of
Judgment," replied Thomas, " will be more fearful." Thomas made
his way to the coast and fled to France. Henry in his wrath banished
no less than four hundred of the archbishop's kinsmen and friends.
Thomas found less help in France than he had expected. There
were once more two rival Popes—Alexander III., who was acknowledged by the greater part of the clergy and by the kings of
England and France, and Calixtus III., who had been set up by
the Emperor Frederick Barbarossa. Alexander was too much afraid

lest Henry should take the part of Calixtus to be very eager in
supporting Thomas. He therefore did his best to effect a reconciliation between Henry and Thomas, but for some years his efforts
were of no avail.

10. **The Assize of Clarendon. 1166.**—Henry, being temporarily
disembarrassed of Thomas's rivalry, was able to devote his time
to carrying out still further the judicial organisation of the country.

Small ship of the latter part of the twelfth century.

In 1166 he held a Great Council at Clarendon, and with its approval
issued a set of decrees known as the Assize of Clarendon. By this
assize full force was given to a change which had for some time
been growing in the judicial system. The old English way of
dealing with criminals had been by calling on an accused person
to swear to his own innocence and to bring compurgators to swear
that his oath was true. If the accused failed to find compurgators
he was sent to the ordeal. According to the new way there was to

be in each county juries consisting of twelve men of the hundred
and of four from each township in it to present offences—felonies,
murders, and robberies—and to accuse persons on common report.
They were sworn to speak the truth, so that their charges were
known as verdicts (*verè dicta*). No compurgators were allowed,
but the accused, after his offence had been presented, had to go to
the ordeal, and even if he succeeded in this he was, if his character
was notoriously bad, to abjure the realm—that is to say, to be
banished, swearing never to return. If he came back he was held to
be an outlaw, and might be put to death without mercy by any one.

11. **Recognitions.**—A very similar system to that which was thus
adopted in criminal cases had already in the early part of Henry's
reign been widely extended in civil cases. When, before the
Conquest, disputes occurred amongst the English as to the possession of property, each party swore to the justice of his own case,
brought compurgators, and summoned witnesses to declare in his
favour. There was, however, no method of cross-examination, and
if the hundred or shire court was still unsatisfied, it had recourse to
the ordeal. The Normans introduced the system of trial by battle,
under the belief that God would intervene to give victory to the
litigant whose cause was just. This latter system, however, had
never been popular with the English, and Henry favoured another
which had been in existence in Normandy before the Conquest, and
was fairly suited to English habits. This was the system of recognitions. Any freeholder who had been dispossessed of his land
might apply to the *Curia Regis*, and the *Curia Regis* ordered the
sheriff of the county in which was the land in dispute to select four
knights of that county, by whom twelve knights were chosen to
serve as Recognitors. It was the business of these Recognitors
to find out either by their own knowledge or by private inquiry the
truth of the matter. If they were unanimous their verdict was accepted as final. If not, other knights were added to them, and when
at last twelve were found agreeing, their agreement was held to
settle the question.

12. **The Germ of the Jury.**—Thus, whilst in criminal cases
the local knowledge of sworn accusers was treated as satisfactory
evidence of guilt, in civil cases a system was growing up in which
is to be traced the germ of the modern jury. The Recognitors
did not indeed hear evidence in public or become judges of the fact,
like the modern jury ; they were rather sworn witnesses, allowed
to form an opinion not merely, like modern witnesses, on what they

had actually seen or heard, but also on what they could gather by private inquiry.

13. **The Itinerant Justices Revived.** — To carry out this system Henry renewed his grandfather's experiment of sending members of the *Curia Regis* as itinerant justices visiting the counties. They held what were called the pleas of the crown—that is to say, trials which were brought before the king's judges instead of being tried either in the county courts or the manorial courts. Both these judges and the king had every interest in getting as much business before their courts as possible. Offenders were fined and suitors had to pay fees, and the best chance of increasing these profits was to attract suitors by administering justice better than the local courts. The more thronged were the king's courts, the more rich and powerful he became. The consequent growth of the influence of the itinerant justices was no doubt offensive to the lords of the manor, and especially to the greater landowners, as diminishing their importance, and calling them to account whenever they attempted to encroach on their less powerful neighbours.

14. **The Inquisition of the Sheriffs. 1170.**—It was not long before Henry discovered another way of diminishing the power of the barons. In the early part of his reign the sheriffs of the counties were still selected from the great landowners, and the sheriff was not merely the collector of the king's revenue in his county, but had, since the Conquest, assumed a new importance in the county court, over which in the older times the ealdorman or earl and the bishop had presided. Since the Conquest the bishop, having a court of his own for ecclesiastical matters, had ceased to take part in its proceedings, and the earl's authority, which had been much lessened after the Conquest, had now disappeared. The sheriff, therefore, was left alone at the head of the county court, and when the new system of trial grew up he as well as the itinerant justices was allowed to receive the presentments of juries. When, in the spring of **1170**, the king returned to England after an absence of four years, he held a strict inquiry into the conduct of them all, and deposed twenty of them. In many cases, no doubt, the sheriffs had done things to displease Henry, but there can be no doubt that the blow thus struck at the sheriffs was, in the main, aimed at the great nobility. The successors of those turned out were of lower rank, and therefore more submissive. From this time it was accepted by the kings of England as a principle of government that no great noble should serve as sheriff.

15. **The Nobles and the Church.**—Henry knew well that the great nobles were indignant, and that it was possible that they might rise against him, as at one time or another they had risen against every king since the Conquest. He knew too that his predecessors had found their strongest support against the nobles in the Church, and that the Church was no longer unanimously on his side. He could indeed count upon all the bishops save one. Bishops who were or had been his officials, bishops envious of Thomas or afraid of himself, were all at his disposal, but they brought him no popular strength. Thomas alone amongst them had a hold on the imagination of the people through his austerities and his daring. Moreover, as the champion of the clergy, he was regarded as being also the champion of the people, from whose ranks the clergy were recruited.

16. **The Coronation of Young Henry. 1170.**—At the moment of Henry's return to England he had special need of the Church. He wished the kingdom of England to pass at his death to his eldest son, Henry, and since the Conquest no eldest son had ever succeeded his father on the throne. He therefore determined to adopt a plan which had succeeded with the kings of France, of having the young Henry chosen and crowned in his own lifetime, so that when he died he might be ready to step into his father's place. Young Henry was chosen, and on June 14, **1170**, he was crowned by Roger, Archbishop of York ; but on the day before the coronation Roger received from Thomas a notice of his excommunication of all bishops taking part in the ceremony, on the ground that it belonged only to an Archbishop of Canterbury to crown a king, and this excommunication had been ratified by the Pope. It was therefore possible that the whole ceremony might go for nothing.

17. **The Return of Archbishop Thomas. 1170.**—To obviate this danger Henry again sought to make peace with Thomas. An agreement was come to on the vague terms that the past should be forgotten on both sides. Henry perhaps hoped that when Thomas was once again in England he would be too wise to rake up the question of his claim to crown the king. If it was so he was soon disappointed. On December 1, **1170**, Thomas landed at Sandwich and rode to Canterbury amidst the shouts of the people. He refused to release from excommunication the bishops who had taken part in young Henry's coronation unless they would first give him satisfaction for the wrong done to the see of Canterbury, thus showing that he had forgotten nothing.

18. **Murder of Archbishop Thomas. 1170.**—The aggrieved

bishops at once crossed the sea to lay their complaint before Henry. "What a parcel of fools and dastards," cried Henry impatiently, "have I nourished in my house, that none of them can be found to

Part of the choir of Canterbury Cathedral (in building from 1175-1184).

avenge me on one upstart clerk!" Four of his knights took him
at his word, and started in all haste for Canterbury. The Archbishop before their arrival had given fresh offence in a cause more
righteous than that of his quarrel with the bishops. Ranulf de Broc
and others who had had the custody of his lands in his absence
refused to surrender them, robbed him of his goods, and maltreated
his followers. On Christmas Day he excommunicated them and
repeated the excommunication of the bishops. On December 29
the four knights sought him out. They do not seem at first to have
intended to do him bodily harm. The excommunication of the
king's servants before the king had been consulted was a breach of
the Constitutions of Clarendon, and they bade him, in the king's
name, to leave the kingdom. After a hot altercation the knights
retired to arm themselves. The archbishop was persuaded by
his followers to take refuge in the church. In rushed the knights
crying, "Where is the traitor? Where is the archbishop?" "Behold me," replied Thomas, "no traitor, but a priest of God." The
assailants strove to lay hands upon him. He struggled and cast
forth angry words upon them. In the madness of their wrath they
struck him to the ground and slew him as he lay.

19. **Popular Indignation. 1171.**—Archbishop Thomas did not die
as a martyr for any high or sacred cause. He was not a martyr for
the faith, like those who had been thrown to the lions by the Roman
emperors. He was not a martyr for righteousness, like Archbishop
Ælfheah. He was a martyr for the privileges of his order and of his
see. Yet if he sank below the level of the great martyrs, he did
not sink to that lowest stage at which men cry out for the preservation of their own privileges, after those privileges have ceased
to benefit any but themselves. The sympathy of the mass of the
population shows the persistence of a widespread belief that in
maintaining the privileges of the clergy Thomas was maintaining
the rights of the protectors of the poor. This sentiment was only
strengthened by his murder. All through Europe the news was
received with a burst of indignation. Of that indignation the Pope
made himself the mouthpiece. In the summer of 1171 two Papal
legates appeared in Normandy to excommunicate Henry unless he
was able to convince them that he was guiltless of the murder.
Henry was too cautious to abide their coming. He crossed first to
England and then to Ireland, resolved to have something to offer
the Pope which might put him in a better humour.

20. **State of Ireland.**—In the domain of art, Ireland was inferior
to no European nation. In metal-work, in sculpture, and in the

skilful illumination of manuscripts it surpassed them all. It had no mean school of music and song. In political development it lagged far behind. Ireland was still in the tribal stage, and had never been welded into unity by foreign conquerors, as Gaul had been welded into unity by the Romans, and as England had been welded into unity by the Normans. Tribe warred with tribe and chief with chief. The efforts of chiefs to attain supremacy over the whole island had always ended in partial or complete failure. The Danes had made settlements in Dublin, Wexford, Waterford, Cork, and Limerick, but though the native Celtic population was not strong enough to expel them, neither were they strong enough to conquer the Celts. The Church was as disorganised as the State, and there was little discipline exercised outside the monasteries. For some time the Popes and the Archbishops of Canterbury had been anxious to establish a better regulated Church system, and in 1154 Adrian IV.—the only Englishman who was ever Pope—hoping that Henry would bring the Irish Church under Papal order, had made him a present of Ireland, on the ground that all islands belonged to the Pope.

21. **Partial Conquest of Ireland. 1166—1172.**—Henry, however, had too much to do during the earlier years of his reign to think of conquering Ireland. In 1166 Dermot, king or chief of Leinster, having been driven out of his dominions, appealed to Henry for aid. Henry gave him leave to carry over to Ireland any English knights whom he could persuade to help him. On this a number of knights from South Wales, of whom the most important was Richard de Clare, afterwards known as Strongbow, flocked across the Irish Sea (1169—1170). They fought and conquered, and Strongbow, who married Dermot's daughter, gave himself the title of Earl of Leinster. The rule of these knights was a rule of cruelty and violence, and, what was more, it might well become dangerous to Henry himself. If feudal nobles established themselves in Ireland, they might soon be holding out a hand to help the feudal nobles who were Henry's worst enemies in England. When Henry landed in Ireland in 1171 he set himself to restore order. The Irish welcomed him because he alone could bridle the invaders, and the invaders submitted to him because they dared not resist him. He gathered a synod of the clergy at Cashel, and arranged for the future discipline of the Church. Unhappily he could not remain long in Ireland, and when he left it the old anarchy and violence blazed up again. Though Henry had not served Ireland, he had gained his own personal ends. He had frightened Strongbow and his followers, and had

shown the Pope, by his proceedings at Cashel, that his friendship was worth having.

22. Young Henry's Coronation and the Revolt of the Barons. 1172—1174.—In the spring of **1172** Henry was back in Normandy. The English barons were longing to take advantage of his quarrel with the Church, and his only chance of resisting them was to propitiate the Church. He met the Papal legates at Avranches, swore that he was innocent of the death of Thomas, and renounced the Constitutions of Clarendon. He then proceeded to pacify Louis VII., whose daughter was married to the younger Henry, by having the boy recrowned in due form. Young Henry was a foolish lad, and took it into his head that because he had been crowned his father's reign was at an end. In **1173** he fled for support to his father-in-law and persuaded him to take up his cause. "Your master," said Louis to the ambassadors of the father, "is king no longer. Here stands the king of the English." These words were the signal for a general attack on the elder king. Headed by Louis, his neighbours and discontented subjects took arms against him, and it was not till September that he prevailed over them. In July the great English barons of the north and centre rose in insurrection, and William the Lion, king of the Scots, joined them. De Lucy, the Justiciar, stood up for Henry ; but, though he gained ground, the war was

Mitre of Archbishop Thomas of Canterbury preserved at Sens.

still raging in the following year, **1174**. In the spring of that year the rebels were gaining the upper hand, and the younger Henry was preparing to come to their help. In July the elder Henry landed in England. For the first and only time in his life he brought to England the mercenaries who were paid with the scutage money. At Canterbury he visited the tomb of Thomas, now ac-

knowledged as a martyr, spent the whole night in prayer and
tears, and on the next morning was, at his own request, scourged
by the monks as a token of his penitence. That night he was
awakened by a messenger with good news. Ranulf de Glanvile had won for him a great victory at Alnwick, had dispersed the
barons' host, and had taken prisoner the Scottish king. About the
same time the fleet which was to bring his son over was dispersed

Military and civil costume of the latter part of the twelfth century.

by a storm. Within a few weeks the whole rebellion was at an end.
It was the last time that the barons ventured to strive with the
king till the time came when they had the people and the Church
on their side. William the Lion was carried to Normandy, where,
by the treaty of Falaise, he acknowledged himself the vassal of the
king of England for the whole of Scotland.

23. **The Assize of Arms. 1181.**—In September **1174** there was
a general peace. In **1181** Henry issued the Assize of Arms,

organising the old fyrd in a more serviceable way. Every English freeman was bound by it to find arms of a kind suitable to his property, that he might be ready to defend the realm against rebels or invaders. The Assize of Arms is the strongest possible evidence as to the real nature of Henry's government. He had long ago sent back to the Continent the mercenaries whom he had brought with him in the peril of 1174, and he now entrusted himself not to a paid standing army, but to the whole body of English freemen. He was, in truth, king of the English not merely because he ruled over them, but because they were ready to rally round him in arms against those barons whose ancestors had worked such evil in the days of Stephen. England was not to be given over either to baronial anarchy or to military despotism.

24. **Henry II. and his Sons.**—In England Henry ruled as a national king over a nation which, at least, preferred his government to that of the barons. The old division between English and Norman was dying out, and though the upper classes, for the most part, still spoke French, intermarriages had been so frequent that there were few amongst them who had not some English ancestress and who did not understand the English language. Henry was even strong enough to regain much that he had surrendered when he abandoned the Constitutions of Clarendon. In his Continental possessions there was no such unity. The inhabitants of each province were tenacious of their own laws and customs, and this was especially the case with the men of Aquitaine, the country south of the Loire, who differed in habits, and even in language, from the Frenchmen of Normandy and Anjou. They therefore found it difficult to give a share of the allegiance which they owed to their own duchess, Eleanor, to her Angevin husband, the king of England. Henry in 1172 having appointed his eldest son, Henry, as the future ruler of Normandy and Anjou as well as of England, thought it wise to recognise this feeling by giving to his second son, Richard, the immediate possession of Eleanor's duchy of Aquitaine. In 1181 he provided for his third son, Geoffrey, by a marriage with Constance, the heiress of Brittany, over which country he claimed a feudal superiority as Duke of the Normans. Yet, though he gave away so much to his sons, he wished to keep the actual control over them all. The arrangement did not turn out well. He had set no good example of domestic peace. His sons knew that he had married their mother for the sake of her lands, that he had subsequently thrown her into prison and had been faithless to her with a succession of mistresses. Besides this, they were

torn away from him by the influence of the men whom they were set to rule. Richard was dragged away from his father by the interests and feelings of the men of Aquitaine, Geoffrey by the interests and feelings of the men of Brittany. John, the fourth son, who was named Lackland from having no territory assigned to him, was, as yet, too young to be troublesome.[1] Both Richard and Geoffrey had taken part with their brother Henry in the great revolt of **1173.** In **1177** they were again quarrelling with their father and with each other. " Dost thou not know," was the message which Geoffrey sent to his father, " that it is our proper nature, planted in us by inheritance from our ancestors, that none of us should love the other, but that ever brother should strive with brother and son against father? I would not that thou shouldst deprive us of our hereditary right nor vainly seek to rob us of our nature." Henry loved his children, and could never bring himself to make war very seriously against them. Henry died young in **1183,** and Geoffrey in **1185.** Richard was now the heir of all his father's lands, from the Tweed to the Pyrenees. Henry made an effort to provide for John in Ireland, and in **1185** he sent the youth— now eighteen years old—to Dublin to rule as king of Ireland. John soon showed his incompetence. He was rude to the English barons, and still ruder to the Irish chiefs, amusing himself by laughing at their dress and pulling the hairs out of their beards. Before the end of the year his father was obliged to recall him.

25. **The Fall of the Kingdom of Jerusalem. 1187.**—The divisions in Henry's family were stirred up afresh by the new king of France, Philip II., who had succeeded his father, Louis VII., in **1179.** Philip was resolved to enlarge his narrow dominions at the expense of Henry. He was Henry's feudal lord, and he was crafty enough to know that by assisting Henry's sons he might be able to convert his nominal lordship into a real power. News, however, arrived in the midst of the strife which for a little time put an end to the discords

[1] Genealogy of the sons and grandchildren of Henry II. :—

Philip Augustus

		HENRY II.	
		1154–1189	
Henry	RICHARD	Geoffrey	JOHN = (1) Avice of
m. Margaret of	1189–1199	m. Constance of	1199–1216 Gloucester
France	m. Berengaria of	Brittany	(2) Isabella of
	Navarre		Angoulême
		Arthur	HENRY III.
			1216–1272

of men and peoples. The Latin kingdom of Jerusalem, which had been established after the first crusade, had only maintained itself because the Mahommedan rulers of Egypt were the rivals and enemies of the Mahommedan rulers of Syria. Yet even with the advantage of divisions amongst their enemies, the Christians had only defended themselves with difficulty. A second crusade which had gone out to relieve them in Stephen's reign, under the Emperor Conrad III. and Louis VII. of France, had accomplished nothing. Their real defenders were two bodies of soldiers, known as the Knights Templars and the Knights of St. John, who were bound, like monks, to vows of celibacy, so that they might always be free to defend Jerusalem. At last a great Mahommedan warrior, Saladin, arose, who ruled both Egypt and Syria, and was therefore able to bring the united forces of the two countries against the Christian colony. In 1187 he destroyed the Christian army at Tiberias, and in the same year took Jerusalem and almost every city still held by the Christians in the East. Tyre alone held out, and that, too, would be lost unless help came speedily.

26. **The Last Years of Henry II. 1188 – 1189.**—For a moment the rulers of the West were shocked at the tidings from the East. In 1188 Philip, Henry, and Richard had taken the cross as the sign of their resolution to recover the Holy City from the infidel. To enable him to meet the expenses of a war in the East, Henry imposed upon England a new tax of a tenth part of all movable property, which is known as the Saladin tithe, but in a few months those who were pledged to go on the crusade were fighting with one another—first Henry and Richard against Philip, and then Philip and Richard against Henry. At last, in 1189, Henry, beaten in war, was forced to submit to Philip's terms, receiving in return a list of those of his own barons who had engaged to support Richard against his father. The list reached him when he was at Chinon, ill and worn out. The first name on it was that of his favourite son John. The old man turned his face to the wall. "Let things go now as they will," he cried bitterly. "I care no more for myself or for the world." After a few days of suffering he died. The last words which passed his lips were, "Shame, shame upon a conquered king."

27. **The Work of Henry II.**—The wisest and most powerful ruler can only assist the forces of nature ; he cannot work against them. Those who merely glance at a map in which the political divisions of France are marked as they existed in Henry's reign, cannot but wonder that Henry did not make himself master of the

small territory which was directly governed, in turn, by Louis VII. and Philip II. A careful study of the political conditions of his reign shows, however, that he was not really strong enough to do anything of the kind. His own power on the Continent was purely feudal, and he held authority over his vassals there because they had personally done homage to him. Henry, however, had also done homage to the king of France, and did not venture, even if he made war upon his lord, the king of France, to push matters to extremities against him, lest his sons as his own vassals might push matters to extremities against himself. He could not, in short, expel the king of France from Paris, lest he should provoke his own vassals to follow his example of insubordination and expel him from Bordeaux or Rouen. Moreover, Henry had too much to do in England to give himself heart and soul to Continental affairs, whilst the king of France, on the contrary, who had no foreign possessions, and was always at his post, would be the first to profit by a national French feeling whenever such a feeling arose. England under Henry II. was already growing more united and more national. The crown which Henry derived from the Conqueror was national as well as feudal. Henry, like his predecessors, had two strings to his bow. On the one hand he could call upon his vassals to be faithful to him because they had sworn homage to him, whilst he himself, as far as England was concerned, had sworn homage to no one. On the other hand, he could rally round him the national forces. To do this he must do justice and gain the goodwill of the people at large. It was this that he had attempted to do, by sending judges round the country and by improving the law, by establishing scutage to weaken the power of the barons, and by strengthening the national forces by the Assize of Arms. No doubt he had little thanks for his pains. Men could feel the weight of his arm and could complain of the heavy fines exacted in his courts of justice. It was only a later generation, which enjoyed the benefits of his hard discipline, which understood how much England owed to him.

CHAPTER XI

RICHARD I. 1189—1199

LEADING DATES

Accession of Richard I. 1189
Richard's Return to England from the Crusade . . 1194
Death of Richard I. 1199

1. Richard in England. 1189.—Richard was accepted without dispute as the master of the whole of the Angevin dominions. He was a warrior, not a statesman. Impulsive in his generosity, he was also impulsive in his passions. Having determined to embark on the crusade, he came to England eager to raise money for its expenses. With this object he not only sold offices to those who wished to buy them, and the right of leaving office to those who wished to retire, but also, with the Pope's consent, sold leave to remain at home to those who had taken the cross. Regardless of the distant future, he abandoned for money to William the Lion the treaty of Falaise, in which William had engaged to do homage to the English king.

Royal arms of England from Richard I. to Edward III. (From the wall arcade, south aisle of nave, Westminster Abbey.)

2. William of Longchamps. 1189—1191.—To secure order during his absence Richard appointed two Justiciars—Hugh of Puiset, Bishop of Durham, and William of Longchamps, Bishop of Ely. At the same time he attempted to conciliate all who were likely to be dangerous by making them lavish grants of land, especially giving what was practically royal authority over five shires to his brother John. Such an arrangement was not likely to last. Before the end of **1189** Richard crossed to the Continent. Scarcely was he gone when the populace in many towns turned savagely on the Jews and massacred them in crowds. The Jews lived by money-lending, and money-lenders are never

The Galilee or Lady Chapel, Durham Cathedral. Built by Bishop Hugh of Puiset between 1180 and 1197.

popular. In York they took refuge in the castle, and when all hope of defending themselves failed, slew their wives and children, set fire to the castle, and perished in the flames. The Justiciars were too much occupied with their own quarrels to heed such matters. Hugh was a stately and magnificent prelate. William was lame and misshapen, quick of wit and unscrupulous. In a few weeks he had deprived his rival of all authority. His own power did not last long. He had a sharp tongue, and did not hesitate to let all men, great and small, know how meanly he thought of them. Those whom he despised found a leader in John, who was anxious to succeed his brother, and thought that it might some day be useful to have made himself popular in England. In the autumn of 1191 William of Longchamps was driven out of the country.

3. **The Third Crusade.** 1189 — 1192. — Richard threw his whole heart—his lion's heart, as men called it—into the crusade. Alike by sea and by land, he knew better than any other leader of his age how to direct the operations of war. He was too impetuous to guard himself against the intrigues and personal rancour of his fellow-Crusaders. At Messina he quarrelled with the wily Philip II. of France, while he gave offence to all Germans by upholding the claims of Tancred to the crown of Sicily, which was also claimed by the German king, who afterwards became the Emperor Henry VI. In the spring of 1191 Richard sailed from Sicily for the Holy Land, conquering Cyprus on the way, where he married Berengaria of Navarre. Passing on to the coast of Syria, he found the Crusaders besieging Acre, and his own vigour greatly contributed to its fall. When Acre was taken Philip slipped home to plot against Richard, and Richard found every French Crusader and every German Crusader banded together against him. When he advocated the right of Guy of Lusignan to the crown of Jerusalem, they advocated the claim of Conrad of Montferrat. Jerusalem was not to be had for either of them. Twice Richard brought the Crusading host within eight miles of the Holy City. Each time he was driven to retreat by the failure of the Crusaders to support him. The last time his comrades invited him at least to reach a spot from which a view of the city could be gained. Richard refused. If he was not worthy, he said, to regain the city, he was not worthy to look on it.

4. **The Return of Richard.** 1192—1194.—In 1192 there was nothing for it but to return home. Enemies were watching for him on every shore. Landing at the head of the Adriatic, he attempted to make his way in disguise through Germany. With characteristic want of reflection, he roasted his meat at a village inn near Vienna with a jewelled ring on his finger. Attention was aroused, and he was arrested and delivered up to Leopold, Duke of Austria, who had been his bitter antagonist in the Holy Land, and Leopold delivered him up to his own feudal superior, the Emperor, Henry VI.

M

Effigy of a knight in the Temple Church, London, showing armour of the end of the twelfth century.

The imprisonment of Richard was joyful news to Philip and John. John did his best to get into his hands all the English and Continental dominions of his brother. His meanness was, however, by this time well known, and he was repelled on all sides. At last in **1193** the Emperor consented to let Richard go on payment of what was then the enormous ransom of 150,000 marks, or 100,000*l*. "Beware," wrote Philip to John when he heard that the Emperor's consent had been given; "the devil is loose again." Philip and John tried to bribe the Emperor to keep his prisoner, but in February **1194** Richard was liberated, and set out for England.

5. **Heavy taxation.**—Before Richard reappeared in England each tenant-in-chief had to pay the aid which was due to deliver his lord from prison (see p. 117), but this was far from being enough. Besides all kinds of irregular expedients the Danegeld had been practically revived, and to it was now given the name of carucage, a tax of two shillings on every ploughland. Another tax of a fourth part of all movable goods had also been imposed, for which a precedent had been set by Henry II. when he levied the Saladin tithe (see p. 157). Richard had now to gather in what was left unpaid of these

charges. Yet so hated was John that Richard was welcomed with every appearance of joy, and John thought it prudent to submit to his brother. Philip, however, was still an open enemy, and as soon as Richard had gathered in all the money that he could raise in England he left the country never to return. On the Continent he could best defend himself against Philip, and, besides this, Richard was at home in sunny Aquitaine, and had no liking for his English realm.

6. **The Administration of Hubert Walter. 1194—1198.**—For four years the administration of England was in the hands of a new Justiciar, the Archbishop of Canterbury, Hubert Walter. He was a statesman of the school of Henry II., and he carried the jury system yet farther than Henry had done. The immense increase of taxation rendered it the more necessary to guard against unfairness, and Hubert Walter placed the selection of the juries of presentment (see p. 147) in the hands of four knights in every shire, who, as is probable, were chosen by the freeholders in the County Court, instead of being named by the sheriff. This was a further step in the direction of allowing the counties to manage their own affairs, and a still greater one was taken by the frequent employment of juries in the assessment of the taxes paid within the county, so as to enable them to take a prominent part in its financial as well as in its judicial business. In **1198** there was taken a new survey of England for taxable purposes, and again elected juries were employed to make the returns. In this year Archbishop Hubert retired from the Justiciarship, and was succeeded by Geoffrey Fitz-Peter. Archbishop Hubert's administration marks a great advance in constitutional progress, though it is probable that his motive was only to raise money more readily. The main constitutional problem of the Norman and Angevin reigns was how to bring the national organisation of the king's officials into close and constant intercourse with the local organisation of the counties. Henry I. and Henry II. had attacked the problem on one side by sending the judges round the country to carry the king's wishes and commands to each separate county. It still remained to devise a scheme by which the wishes and complaints of the counties could be brought to the king. Hubert Walter did not contrive that this should be done, but he made it easy to be done in the next generation, because before he left office he had increased the powers of the juries in each county and had accustomed them to deal independently with all the local matters in which the king and the county were both interested. It only remained to bring these juries together in one place where they might join in making the king aware of the

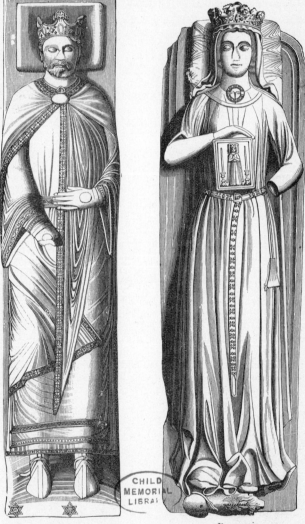

Richard I.
From his tomb at Fontevrault.

Berengaria.
From her tomb at Espan.

wishes and complaints of all counties alike.   When this had been accomplished there would, for the first time, be a representative assembly in England.

7. **Death of Richard. 1199.**—It was not only Richard's love for his old home which fixed him on the Continent.   He knew that the weakest part of his dominions was there.   His lands beyond sea had no natural unity.   Normans did not love Angevins, neither did Angevins love the men of Poitou or Guienne.   Philip was willingly obeyed in his own dominions, and he had all the advantage which his title of king of the French could give him.   Richard fought desperately, and for the most part successfully, against the French king, and formed alliances with all who were opposed to him. He built on a rock overhanging the Seine above Les Andelys a mighty fortress—the Château Gaillard, or Saucy Castle, as he called it in jest.   With characteristic haste he completed the building in a few months.   " How fair a child is mine ! " he called to his followers, " this child but a twelvemonth old."   Other child he had none, and he had but the miserable John to look to to hold his dominions after he was gone.   He did not live long enough to see whether his new castle could stand a siege.   A peasant dug up a treasure on the land of the lord of Châlus in the Limousin.   Richard claimed it as his right because he was the over-lord.   On the refusal of the lord to surrender it he laid siege to Châlus.   An arrow from the castle struck him on the shoulder.   The wound rankled, and mortification followed.   As Richard lay dying the castle surrendered, and the man who had aimed the fatal shot was brought before him.   " What have I done to thee," asked Richard, " that thou shouldest slay me ? "   " Thou hast slain my father and two of my brothers with thy own hand," said the prisoner, " and thou wouldest fain have killed me too.   Avenge thyself upon me as thou wilt.   I will gladly endure the greatest torments thou canst devise, since I have seen thee on thy deathbed." Richard, generous to the last, bade his attendants set the prisoner free.   They kept him till Richard was dead, and then tortured him to death.

8. **Church and State under the Angevin Kings.**—During the forty-five years of the reigns of Richard and his father the chief feature of English history is the growth of the power of the state. There was more justice and order, and also more taxation, at the end of the period than at the beginning.   During the same period the influence of the Church grew less.   The character of Thomas's resistance to the king was lower than that of Anselm, and not long

after Thomas's murder Henry indirectly regained the power which he had lost, and filled the sees with officials and dependents who cared little for the higher aims of religion. The evil consequences

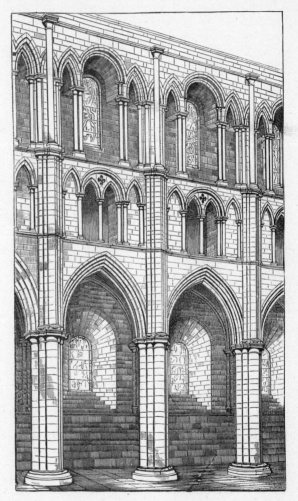

Part of the choir of Ripon Cathedral:
built during the last quarter of the twelfth century.

of making the Church dependent on the king were at least as great as those of freeing the political and social life of the clergy from the control of the State. Even monasticism ceased to afford a strong example of self-denial. The very Cistercians, who had begun so well, had fallen from their original purity. They were now owners of immense tracts of pasture-land, and their keenness in money-making had become notorious. They exercised great influence, but it was the influence of great landlords, not the influence of ascetics.

9. **Growth of Learning.**—The decay of asceticism was to some extent brought about by the opening of new careers into which energetic men might throw themselves. They were needed as judges, as administrators, as councillors. A vigorous literature sprung up in the reign of Henry II., but at the end of the reign most of it was connected with the court rather than with the monasteries. Henry's Justiciar, Ranulf de Glanvile, wrote the first English law-book. His Treasurer, Richard Fitz-Nigel, set forth in the *Dialogus de Scaccario* the methods of his financial administration, and also produced ' The Deeds of King Henry and King Richard.' William of Newburgh, indeed, the best historian of these reigns, wrote in a small Yorkshire monastery, but Roger of Hoveden and Ralph de Diceto pursued their historical work under the influence of the court. Still more striking is the universality of the intellectual inquisitiveness of Walter Map. On the one hand, in his *De Nugis Curialium* he chattered over the manners of his contemporaries, and in his satirical poems scourged the greed and vices of the clergy, whilst on the other hand he took a principal part in spreading a knowledge of the legend of the high-souled King Arthur and of the quest of the Holy Grail. Giraldus Cambrensis again, or Gerald of Wales, wrote on all sorts of subjects with shrewd humour and extensive knowledge.

10. **The University of Oxford.**—There was already in England a place where learning was cherished for its own sake. For some time there had been growing up on the Continent gatherings for the increase of learning, which ultimately were known as universities, or corporations of teachers and scholars. One at Bologna had devoted itself to the study of the civil or Roman law. Another at Paris gave itself to the spread of all the knowledge of the time. In these early universities there were no colleges. Lads, very poor for the most part, flocked to the teachers and lodged themselves as best they could. Such a university, though the name was not used till later, had been gradually forming at Oxford. Its origin and

early history is obscure, but in **1186** Giraldus, wishing to find a cultivated audience for his new book on the topography of Ireland, read it aloud at Oxford, where, as he tells us, 'the clergy in England chiefly flourished and excelled in clerkly lore.' It appears that there were already separate faculties or branches of study, and persons recognised as doctors or teachers in all of them.

11. **Country and Town.**—Intellectual progress was accompanied by material progress. In the country the old system of cultivation by the labour service of villein-tenants still prevailed, but in many parts the service had been commuted, either for a money payment or for payments in kind, such as payments of a fixed number of eggs or fowls, or of a fixed quantity of honey or straw. Greater progress was made in the towns. At the time of the Conquest there were about eighty towns in England, most of them no larger than villages. The largest towns after London were Winchester, Bristol, Norwich, York, and Lincoln, but even these had not a population much above 7,000 apiece. In the smaller towns trade was sufficiently provided for by the establishment of a market to which country people brought their grain or their cattle, and where they provided themselves in turn with such rude household necessaries as they required. Even before the Conquest port towns had grown up on

Lay costumes in the twelfth century.

Costume of shepherds in the twelfth century.

the coast, but foreign trade was slight, imports being almost entirely confined to luxuries for the rich. The order introduced by the Normans and the connection between England and the king's Continental possessions was followed by an increase of trade, and there arose in each of the larger towns a corporation which was known as the Merchant Gild, and which was, in some instances at least, only a development of an older association existing in the times before the Conquest. No one except the brothers of the Merchant Gild was allowed to trade in any article except food, but any one living in the town might become a brother on payment of a settled fee. The first Merchant Gild known was constituted in **1093**. A little later, Henry I. granted charters to some of the towns, conferring on them the right of managing their own affairs ; and his example was followed, in far greater profusion, by Henry II. and Richard I. Though the organisation of the Merchant Gild was originally distinct from the organisation of the town, and the two were in theory kept apart, the Merchant Gild, to which most of the townsmen belonged, usually encroached upon the authorities of the town, regulated trade to its own advantage, and practically controlled the choice of officers, the principal officer being usually styled an Alderman, with power to keep order and generally to provide for the well-being of the place. In this way the trades-men and merchants of the towns prepared themselves uncon-sciously for the time when they would be called on to take part in managing the affairs of the country. Even in these early times, however, the artisans in some of the trades attempted to combine together.

12. **Condition of London.**—Of all the towns London had been growing most rapidly in wealth and population, and during the troubles in which John had been pitted against William of Long-champs it had secured the right of being governed by a Mayor and Aldermen of its own, instead of being placed under the jurisdiction of the King's sheriff. The Mayor and Aldermen, however, did not represent all the townsmen. In London, though there is no evidence of the existence of a Merchant Gild, there was a corporation com-posed of the wealthier traders, by which the city was governed. The Mayor and Aldermen were chosen out of this corporation, as were the juries elected to assess the taxes. Artisans soon came to believe that these juries dealt unfairly with the poor. One of the Aldermen, William Longbeard, made himself the mouthpiece of their complaints and stirred them up against the rest. Hubert Walter sent a messenger to seize him, but William Longbeard slew the

messenger and fled into the church of Mary-at-Bow. Here, according to the ideas of his age, he should have been safe, as every church was considered to be a sanctuary in which no criminal could be arrested. Hubert Walter, however, came in person to seize him, set the church on fire, and had him dragged out. William Longbeard was first stabbed, and then tried and hanged, and for the time the rich tradesmen had their way against the poorer artisans.

13. **Architectural Changes.**—Even in the most flourishing towns the houses were still mostly of wood or rubble covered

Hall of Oakham Castle, Rutland : built about 1185.

with thatch, and only here and there was to be found a house of stone. So slight, indeed, were the ordinary buildings, that it was provided by the Assize of Clarendon that the houses of certain offenders should be carried outside the town and burnt. Here and there, however, as in the case of the so-called Jews' house at Lincoln, stone houses were erected. In the larger houses the arrangements were much as they had been before the Conquest, the large hall being still the most conspicuous part, though another apartment, known as the solar, to which an ascent was made by steps from the outside, and which served as a sitting-room for the master of the house, had usually been added. The castles reared by the king or the barons were built for defence alone, and it was in the great cathedrals and churches that the skill of the architect was shown. An enormous number of parish churches of stone were raised by Norman builders to supersede earlier buildings of wood. For some time the round-arched Norman architecture which had been introduced by Eadward the Confessor was alone followed, such

Norman House at Lincoln, called the Jews' House. Built about 1140.
The square windows are of later date.

as may be studied in the Galilee of Durham (see p. 160) the nave of St. Albans (see p. 109) and the tower of Castor (see p. 136). Gradually the pointed arch of Gothic architecture took its place, and after a period of transition, of which the nave of Durham, and the choirs of Canterbury and of Ripon afford examples (see pp. 130, 150, 166), the graceful style now known as Early English was first used on a large scale in 1192 in the choir of the cathedral of Lincoln.

Books recommended for further study of Part II.

STUBBS, W. (Bishop of Oxford).   Constitutional History of England.
        Vol. i. chaps. ix.–xiii.

FREEMAN, E. A.   History of the Norman Conquest.   Vols. iv. and v.
————   History of William Rufus.

GREEN, J. R.   History of the English People.   Vol. i. pp. 115–189.

NORGATE, Miss K.   England under the Angevin Kings.   Vols. i. and
        ii. pp. 1–388.

CUNNINGHAM, W.   Growth of English Industry and Commerce during
        the Early and Middle Ages, pp. 129–173.

WAKEMAN, H. O., and HASSALL, A.   Constitutional Essays.

PART III

THE GROWTH OF THE PARLIAMENTARY CONSTITUTION. 1199—1399

CHAPTER XII

JOHN. 1199—1216

LEADING DATES

Accession of John	1199
Loss of Normandy	1204
England under an Interdict	1208
Magna Carta	1215
Death of John	1216

1. **The Accession of John. 1199.**—After Richard's death there were living but two descendants of Henry II. in the male line—John, Richard's only surviving brother, and Arthur, the young son of John's elder brother, Geoffrey. The English barons had to make their choice between uncle and nephew, and, as had been done in the days of Ælfred, they preferred the grown man to the child. It was the last time when that principle of election was confessedly acted on. Archbishop Hubert in announcing the result used words which seem strange now : " Forasmuch," he declared to the people assembled to witness John's coronation, "as we see him to be prudent and vigorous, we all, after invoking the Holy Spirit's grace, for his merits no less than his royal blood, have with one consent chosen him for our king." In reality, John was of all men most unworthy. He was without dispute the worst of the English kings. Like William II. he feared not God nor regarded man. Though William indeed was more vicious in his private life, John's violence and tyranny in public life was as great as William's, and he added a meanness and frivolity which sank him far below him.

2. **John's First War with Philip II. 1199—1200.**—On the Con-

tinent John had a difficult game to play. Normandy and Aquitaine submitted to him, but Anjou and its dependent territories declared for Arthur, who was Duke of Brittany in right of his mother. Philip II., who had long been the rival of Richard, now took the field in **1199** as the rival of John in support of Arthur ; but for the moment he ruined his chance of success by keeping in his own hands the castles which he took from John instead of making them over to Arthur. Arthur's supporters took offence, and in **1200** Philip made peace with John. Philip acknowledged John as Richard's heir, but forced him in return to pay a heavy sum of money, and to make other concessions.

3. **John's Misconduct in Poitou. 1200—1201.**—John did not know how to make use of the time of rest which he had gained. Being tired of his wife, Avice of Gloucester, he persuaded some Aquitanian bishops to divorce him from her, though he took care to keep the lands which he had received from her at her marriage. He then married Isabella of Angoulême, though she was betrothed to a Poitevin noble, Hugh of Lusignan. Hugh was enraged, and, together with many of his neighbours, took arms against John. In **1201** John charged all the barons of Poitou with treason, and bade them clear their character by selecting champions to fight with an equal number of English and Norman knights.

4. **The Loss of Normandy and Anjou. 1202—1204.**—The Poitevin barons, instead of accepting the wager of battle, appealed to Philip as John's over-lord, and in **1202** Philip summoned John to answer their complaints before his peers. John not only did not appear, but made no excuse for his absence ; upon which the peers adjudged him to have forfeited all the lands held by him as Philip's vassal. After this Philip, in alliance with Arthur, invaded Normandy. John's aged mother, Eleanor, who was far more able and energetic than her son, took up his cause against her grandson Arthur. She was besieged by Arthur at Mirebeau when John came to her help, and not only raised the siege, but carried off Arthur as a prisoner. Many of his vassals rose against him, and finding himself unable to meet them in the field he wreaked his vengeance on his helpless prisoner. A little before Easter **1203** Arthur ceased to live. How the boy died has never been known, but it was generally believed that he was drowned in the Seine near Rouen— some said by his uncle's own hands. The murderer was the first to suffer from the crime. Philip at once invaded Normandy The Norman barons had long ceased to respect John, and very few of them would do anything to help him. Philip took castle after castle. John was indeed capable of a sudden outbreak of violence,

Effigy of King John
on his monument in Worcester Cathedral

Isabella, wife of King John.
From her monument at
Fontevrault.

but he was incapable of sustained effort. He now looked sluggishly on, feasting and amusing himself whilst Philip was conquering Normandy. " Let him alone," he lazily said; " I shall some day win back all that he is taking from me now." His best friends dropped off from him. The only fortress which made a long resistance was that Château Gaillard which Richard had built to guard the Seine. In 1204 it was at last taken, and before the end of that year Normandy, Maine, Anjou, and Touraine, together with part of Poitou, had submitted to Philip.

5. **Causes of Philip's Success.**—It was not owing to John's vigour that Aquitaine was not lost as well as Normandy and Anjou. Philip had justified his attack on John as being John's feudal lord, and as being therefore bound to take the part of John's vassals whom he had injured. Hitherto the power of the king over his great vassals, which had been strong in England, had been weak in France. Philip made it strong in Normandy and Anjou because he had the support there of the vassals of John. That these vassals favoured him was owing partly to John's contemptible character, but also to the growth of national unity between the inhabitants of Normandy and Anjou on the one hand and those of Philip's French dominions on the other. Normans and Angevins both spoke the same language as the Frenchmen of Paris and its neighbourhood. Their manners and characters were very much the same, and the two peoples very soon blended with one another. They had been separated merely because their feudal organisation had been distinct, because the lord over one was John and over the other was Philip. In Aquitaine it was otherwise. The language and manners there, though much nearer to those of the French than they were to those of the English, differed considerably from the language and manners of the Frenchmen, Normans, and Angevins. What the men of Aquitaine really wanted was independence. They therefore now clung to John against Philip as they had clung to Richard against Henry II. They resisted Henry II. because Henry II. ruled in Anjou and Normandy, and they wished to be free from any connection with Anjou and Normandy. They resisted Philip because Philip now ruled in Anjou and Normandy. They were not afraid of John any longer, because they thought that now that England alone was left to him, he would be too far off to interfere with them.

6. **The Election of Stephen Langton to the Archbishopric of Canterbury. 1205.**—In England John had caused much discontent by the heavy taxation which he imposed, not with the regularity of Henry II. and Hubert Walter, but with unfair inequality. In

1205 Archbishop Hubert Walter died. The right of choosing a new archbishop lay with the monks of the monastery of Christchurch at Canterbury, of which every archbishop, as the successor of St. Augustine, was the abbot. This right, however, had long been exercised only according to the wish of the king, who practically named the archbishop. This time the monks, without asking John's leave, hurriedly chose their sub-prior Reginald, and sent him off with a party of monks to Rome, to obtain the sanction of the Pope. Reginald was directed to say nothing of his election till he reached Rome ; but he was a vain man, and had no sooner reached the Continent than he babbled about his own dignity as an archbishop. When John heard this he bade the monks choose the Bishop of Norwich, John de Grey, the king's treasurer ; and the monks, thoroughly frightened, chose him as if they had not already made their election. John had, however, forgotten to consult the bishops of the province of Canterbury, who had always been consulted by his father and brother, and they too sent messengers to the Pope to complain of the king.

7. **Innocent III. and Stephen Langton. 1206.**—The Pope was Innocent III., who at once determined that John must not name bishops whose only merit was that they were good state officials. Being an able man, he soon discovered that Reginald was a fool.

Bishop Marshall of Exeter, died 1206 ; from his tomb at Exeter, showing a bishop vested for mass.

He therefore in **1206** sent for a fresh deputation of monks, and, as soon as they arrived in Rome, bade them make a new choice in the name of their monastery. At Innocent's suggestion they chose Stephen Langton, one of the most pious and learned men of the day, whose greatness of character was hardly suspected by anyone at the time.

N

8. **John's Quarrel with the Church. 1206—1208.**—The choice of an archbishop in opposition to the king was undoubtedly something new. The archbishopric of Canterbury was a great national office, and a king as skilful as Henry II. would probably have succeeded in refusing to allow it to be disposed of by the Pope and a small party of monks. John was unworthy to be the champion of any cause whatever. In 1207, after an angry correspondence with Innocent, he drove the monks of Christchurch out of the kingdom. Innocent in reply threatened England with an interdict, and in the spring of 1208 the interdict was published.

9. **England under an Interdict. 1208.**—An interdict carried with it the suppression of all the sacraments of the Church except those of baptism and extreme unction. Even these were only to be received in private. No words of solemn import were pronounced at the burial of the dead. The churches were all closed, and to the men of that time the closing of the church-doors was like the closing of the very gate of heaven. In the choice of the punishment inflicted there was some sign that the Papacy was hardly as strong in the thirteenth as it had been in the eleventh century. Gregory VII. had smitten down kings by personal excommunication ; Innocent III. found it necessary to stir up resistance against the king by inflicting sufferings on the people. Yet there is no evidence of any indignation against the Pope. The clergy rallied almost as one man round Innocent, and songs proceeded from the monasteries which mocked the few official bishops who took John's side as money-makers who cared more for marks than for Mark, and more for lucre than for Luke, whilst John de Grey was branded with the title of ' that beast of Norwich.' John taking no heed of the popular feeling, seized the property of the clergy who obeyed the interdict. Yet he was not without fear lest the barons should join the clergy against him, and to keep them in obedience he compelled them to entrust to him their eldest sons as hostages. One lady to whom this order came replied that she would never give her son to a king who had murdered his nephew.

10. **John Excommunicated. 1209.**—In 1209 Innocent excommunicated John himself. John cared nothing for being excluded from the services of the Church, but he knew that if the excommunication were published in England few would venture to sit at table with him, or even to speak with him. For some time he kept it out of the country, but it became known that it had been pronounced at Rome, and even his own dependents began to avoid his company. He feared lest the barons whom he had wearied with heavy fines

and taxes might turn against him, and he needed large sums of money to defend himself against them. First he turned on the Jews, threw them into prison, and after torturing those who refused to pay, wrung from them 40,000*l.* The abbots were next summoned before him and forced by threats to pay 100,000*l.* Besides this the wealthy Cistercians had to pay an additional fine, the amount of which is uncertain, but of which the lowest estimate is 27,000*l* In **1211** some of the barons declared against John, but they were driven from the country, and those who remained were harshly treated. Some of their sons who had been taken as hostages were hanged or starved to death.

11. **The Pope threatens John with Deposition. 1212—1213.**—In

Parsonage house of early thirteenth-century date at West Dean, Sussex.

1212 Innocent's patience came to an end, and he announced that he would depose John if he still refused to give way, and would transfer his crown to his old enemy, Philip II. The English clergy and barons were not likely to oppose the change. Philip gathered a great army in France to make good the claim which he expected Innocent to give him. John, indeed, was not entirely without resource. The Emperor Otto IV. was John's sister's son, and as he too had been excommunicated by Innocent he made common cause with John against Philip. Early in **1213** John gathered an army of 60,000 men to resist Philip's landing, and if Otto with his

Germans were to attack France from the east, a French army would hardly venture to cross into England, unless indeed it had no serious resistance to fear. John, however, knew well that he could not depend on his own army. Many men in the host hated him bitterly, and he feared deposition, and perhaps death, at the hands of those whom he had summoned to his help.

12. **John's Submission. 1213.**—Under these circumstances John preferred submission to the Pope to submission to Philip or his own barons. He invited Pandulf, the Pope's representative, to Dover. He swore to admit Stephen Langton as Archbishop of Canterbury, to restore to their rights all those of the clergy or laity whom he had banished, and to give back the money which he had wrongfully exacted. Two days later he knelt before Pandulf and did homage to the Pope for England and Ireland. He was no longer to be an independent king but the Pope's vassal. In token of his vassalage he agreed that he and his successors should pay to Innocent and his successors 1,000 marks a year, each mark being equal to 13s. 4d., or two-thirds of a pound. Innocent had reached his aim as far as John was concerned. In his eyes the Papacy was not merely the guide of the Church, it was an institution for controlling kings and forcing them to act in accordance with the orders of the Popes. It remained to be seen whether the Pope's orders would be always unselfish, and whether the English barons and clergy would submit to them as readily as did this most miserable of English kings.

13. **The Resistance of the Barons and Clergy. 1213.**—At first John seemed to have gained all that he wanted by submission. Pandulf bade Philip abandon all thought of invading England, and when Philip refused to obey, John's fleet fell upon the French fleet off the coast of Flanders and destroyed it. John even proposed to land with an army in Poitou and to reconquer Normandy and Anjou. His subjects thought that he ought to begin by fulfilling his engagements to them. John having received absolution, summoned four men from each county to meet at St. Albans to assess the damages of the clergy which he had bound himself to make good. The meeting thus summoned was the germ of the future House of Commons. It was not a national political assembly, but it was a national jury gathered together into one place. The exiled barons were recalled, and John now hoped that his vassals would follow him to Poitou. They refused to do so, alleging their poverty and the fact that they had already fulfilled their feudal obligation of forty days' service by attending him at Dover. They had, in

fact, no interest in regaining Normandy and Anjou for John. Though the English barons still spoke French, and were proud of their Norman descent, they now thought of themselves as Englishmen and cared for England alone. John turned furiously on the barons, and was only hindered from attacking them by the new Archbishop, who threatened to excommunicate everyone who took arms against them. It was time for all Englishmen who loved order and law to resist John. Stephen Langton put himself at the head of the movement, and at a great assembly at St. Paul's produced a charter of Henry I., by which that king had promised to put an end to the tyranny of the Red King, and declared amidst general applause that it must be renewed by John. It was a memorable scene. Up to this time it had been necessary for the clergy and the people to support the king against the tyranny of the barons. Now the clergy and people offered their support to the barons against the tyranny of the king. John had merely the Pope on his side. Innocent's view of the situation was very simple. John was to obey the Pope, and all John's subjects were to obey John. A Papal legate arrived in England, fixed the sum which John was to pay to the clergy, and refused to listen to the complaints of those who thought themselves defrauded.

14. **The Battle of Bouvines. 1214.**—In 1214 John succeeded in carrying his barons and their vassals across the sea. With one army he landed at Rochelle, and recovered what had been lost to him on the south of the Loire, but failed to make any permanent conquests to the north of that river. Another army, under John's illegitimate brother, the Earl of Salisbury, joined the Emperor Otto in an attack on Philip from the north. The united force of Germans and English was, however, routed by Philip at Bouvines, in Flanders. "Since I have been reconciled to God," cried John, when he heard the news, "and submitted to the Roman Church, nothing has gone well with me." He made a truce with Philip, and temporarily renounced all claims to the lands to the north of the Loire.

15. **The Struggle between John and the Barons. 1214—1215.** When John returned he called upon all his vassals who had remained at home to pay an exorbitant scutage. In reply they met at Bury St. Edmunds. The charter of Henry I., which had been produced at St. Paul's the year before, was again read, and all present swore to force John to accept it as the rule of his own government. John asked for delay, and attempted to divide his antagonists by offering to the clergy the right of free election to bishoprics and abbacies. Then he turned against the barons. Early

Effigy of a knight in the Temple Church, London, showing armour worn between 1190 and 1225.

in 1215 he brought over a large force of foreign mercenaries, and persuaded the Pope to threaten the barons with excommunication. His attempt was defeated by the constancy of Stephen Langton. The demands of the barons were placed in writing by the archbishop, and, on John's refusal to accept them, an army was formed to force them on the king. The army of God and the Holy Church, as it was called, grew rapidly. London admitted it within its walls, and the accession of London to the cause of the barons was a sign that the traders of England were of one mind with the barons and the clergy. John found that their force was superior to his own, and at Runnimede on June 15, 1215, confirmed with his hand and seal the articles of the barons, with the full intention of breaking his engagement as soon as he should be strong enough to do so.

16. **Magna Carta. 1215.**—*Magna Carta*, or the Great Charter, as the articles were called after John confirmed them, was won by a combination between all classes of freemen, and it gave rights to them all.

(*a*) *Its Concessions.*—The Church was to be free, its privileges were to be respected, and its right to free elections which John had granted earlier in the year was not to be infringed on. As for the laity, the tenants-in-chief were to pay only fixed reliefs when they entered on their estates. Heirs under age were to be the king's wards, but the king was to treat them fairly, and do nothing to injure their land whilst it was in his hands. The king might continue to find husbands for heiresses and wives for heirs, but only amongst those of their own class. The tenants-in-chief again were bound to pay aids to the king when he needed ransom from imprisonment, or money to enable him to bear the expenses of knighting his eldest son or of marrying his eldest daughter. For all other purposes the king could only demand supplies from his tenants-in-chief with the consent of the Common Council of the realm. As only the tenants-in-chief were concerned, this Common Council was the Great Council of tenants-in-chief, such as had met under the Norman and Angevin kings. A fresh attempt, however, was made to induce the smaller tenants-in-chief to attend, in addition to the bishops, abbots, and barons, by a direction that whilst these were to be summoned personally, the sheriffs should in each county issue a general summons to the smaller tenants-in-chief. Though the sub-tenants had no part in the Common Council of the realm, they were relieved by a direction that they should pay no more aids to their lords than their lords paid to the king, and by a general declaration that all that had been granted to their lords by the king should be allowed by their lords to them. The Londoners and other townsmen had their privileges assured to them ; and all freemen were secured against heavy and irregular penalties if they committed an offence.

(*b*) *Its Securities.*—Such were the provisions of this truly national act, which Englishmen were for ages engaged in maintaining and developing. The immediate question was how to secure what had been gained. The first thing necessary for this purpose was to make the courts of law the arbitrators between the king and his subjects. In a series of articles it was declared that the sworn testimony of a man's peers should be used whenever fines or penalties were imposed, and this insistence on the employment of the jury system as it then existed was emphasised by the strong words to which John placed his seal : "No freeman may be taken, or imprisoned, or disseised, or outlawed, or banished, or in any way destroyed, nor will we go against him, or send against him, except by the lawful judgment of his peers, or by the law of the land. To none will we sell or deny or delay right or justice." It was a good security if it could be maintained, but it would avail nothing against a king who was willing and able to use force to set up the old tyranny once more. In the first place John must dismiss all his foreign mercenaries. So little, however, was John trusted that it was thought necessary in the second place to esta-

blish a body of twenty-five—twenty-four barons and the Mayor of
London—which was to guard against any attempt of the king to
break his word.   If John infringed upon any of the articles of the
Charter the twenty-five, with the assistance of the whole community
of the kingdom, had the right of distraining upon the king's lands
till enough was obtained to make up the loss to the person who
had suffered wrong.   In other words, there was to be a permanent
organisation for making war upon the king.

17. **War between John and the Barons. 1215—1216.**—John
waited for the moment of vengeance.   Not only did he refuse to
send his mercenaries away, but he sent to the Continent for large
reinforcements.   Pope Innocent declared the barons to be wicked
rebels, and released John from his oath to the Great Charter.   War
soon broke out.   John's mercenaries were too strong for the barons,
and in the beginning of 1216 almost all England with the exception
of London had been overrun by them.   Though the Pope laid
London under an interdict, neither the citizens nor the barons
paid any attention to it.   They sent to Louis, the eldest son of
Philip of France, to invite him to come and be their king in John's
stead.   Louis was married to John's niece, and might thus be
counted as a member of the English royal family.   The time had
not yet come when a man who spoke French was regarded as
quite a foreigner amongst the English barons.   On May 21, 1216,
Louis landed with an army in the Isle of Thanet.

18. **Conflict between Louis and John. 1216.**—John, in spite of
his success, found himself without sufficient money to pay his mercenaries, and he therefore retreated to Winchester.   Louis entered
London in triumph, and afterwards drove John out of Winchester.
Innocent indeed excommunicated Louis, but no one took heed of
the excommunication.   Yet John was not without support.   The

A silver penny of John, struck at Dublin.

trading towns of the East, who probably regarded Louis as a
foreigner, took his part, and many of his old officials, to whom the
victory of the barons seemed likely to bring back the anarchy of

Stephen's time, clung to him. One of these, a high-spirited and strong-willed man, Hubert de Burgh, held out for John in Dover Castle. John kept the field and even won some successes. As he was crossing the Wash the tide rose rapidly and swept away his baggage. He himself escaped with difficulty. Worn out in mind and body, he was carried on a litter to Newark, where on October **19, 1216,** he died.

CHAPTER XIII

HENRY III.   1216—1272

LEADING DATES

Accession of Henry III.	1216
The Fall of Hubert de Burgh	1232
The Provisions of Oxford	1248
Battle of Lewes	1264
Battle of Evesham	1265
Death of Henry III.	1272

1. **Henry III. and Louis. 1216—1217.**—Henry III., the eldest son of John, was but nine years old at his father's death. Never before had it been useful for England that the king should be a child. As Henry had oppressed no one and had broken no oaths, those who dared not trust the father could rally to the son. The boy had two guardians, one of whom was Gualo, the legate of Pope Honorius III., a man gentler and less ambitious than Innocent III., whom he had just succeeded ; the other was William the Marshal, Earl of Pembroke, who had been constant to John, not because he loved his evil deeds, but because, like many of the older officials, he feared that the victory of the barons would be followed by anarchy. These two had on their side the growing feeling on behalf of English nationality ; whereas, as long as John lived, his opponents had argued that it was better to have a foreign king like Louis than to have a king like John, who tyrannised over the land by the help of foreign mercenaries. Henry's followers daily increased, and in **1217** Louis was defeated by the Marshal at Lincoln. Later in the year Hubert de Burgh, the Justiciar, sent out a fleet which defeated a French fleet off Dover. Louis then submitted and left the kingdom.

2. **The Renewal of the Great Charter. 1216—1217.**—The

Effigy of Henry III. ;
from his tomb in Westminster Abbey.

principles on which William the Marshal intended to govern were signified by the changes made in the Great Charter when it was renewed on the king's accession in 1216, and again on Louis's expulsion in 1217. Most of the clauses binding the king to avoid oppression were allowed to stand ; but those which prohibited the raising of new taxation without the authority of the Great Council, and the stipulation which established a body of twenty-five to distrain on John's property in case of the breach of the Charter, were omitted. Probably it was thought that there was less danger from Henry than there had been from John ; but the acceptance of the compromise was mainly due to the feeling that, whilst it was desirable that the king should govern with moderation, it would be a dangerous experiment to put the power to control him in the hands of the barons, who might use it for their own advantage rather than for the advantage of the nation. The whole history of England for many years was to turn on the difficulty of weakening the power of a bad king without producing anarchy.

3. **Administration of Hubert de Burgh. 1219—1232.**—In 1219 William the Marshal died. For some years the government was mainly in the hands of Hubert de Burgh, who strenuously maintained the authority of the king over the barons, whilst at the same time he set himself distinctly at

the head of the growing national feeling against the admission of foreigners to wealth and high position in England. As a result of the disturbances of John's reign many of the barons and of the leaders of the mercenaries had either fortified their own castles or had taken possession of those which belonged to the king. In **1220** Hubert demanded the surrender of these castles as Henry II. had done in the beginning of his reign. In **1221** the Earl of Aumale was forced to surrender his castles, and in **1224** Faukes de Breauté, one of the leaders of John's mercenaries who had received broad lands in England, was reduced to submission and was banished on his refusal to give up his great castle at Bedford. As long as Hubert ruled, England was to belong to the English. His power was endangered from the very quarter from which it ought to have received most support. In **1227** Henry declared himself of age. He was weak and untrustworthy, always ready to give his confidence to unworthy favourites. His present favourite was Peter des Roches, Bishop of Winchester. The bishop was a greedy and unscrupulous Poitevin, who regarded the king's favour as a means of enriching himself and his Poitevin relatives and friends. Henry was always short of money, and was persuaded by Peter that it was

Effigy of William Longespée, Earl of Salisbury (died 1227) ; from his tomb in Salisbury Cathedral : showing armour worn from about 1225 to 1250.

Hubert's fault. In **1232** Hubert was charged with a whole string of crimes and dismissed from office.

4. Administration of Peter des Roches. 1232—1234.—Henry was now entirely under the power of Peter des Roches. In **1233** he ordered Hubert to be seized. Though Hubert took sanctuary in a chapel, he was dragged out, and a smith was ordered to put him in fetters. The man refused to obey. " Is not this," he said, " that most faithful and high-souled Hubert who has so often saved England from the ravages of foreigners, and has given England back to the English ? " Hubert was thrown into the Tower, and was never again employed in any office of state. As long as Peter des Roches ruled the king it would be hard to keep England for the English. Poitevins and Bretons flocked over from the Continent, and were appointed to all the influential posts which fell vacant. The barons had the national feeling behind them when they raised complaints against this policy. Their leader was Earl Richard the Marshal, the son of the Earl William who had governed England after the death of John. Without even the semblance of trial Henry declared Earl Richard and his chief supporters guilty of trea-son. At a Great Council held at Westminster some of the barons remonstrated. Peter des Roches replied saucily that there were

Simon, Bishop of Exeter (died 1223); from his tomb at Exeter, showing rich mass-vestments.

no peers in England as in France, meaning that in England the barons had no rights against the king. Both Henry and Peter could, however, use their tongues better than their swords. They failed miserably in an attempt to overcome the men whom they had unjustly accused, till in **1234** Peter stirred up some of the English lords in Ireland to seize on Earl Richard's possessions there. The Earl hurried over to defend his estates. Amongst his followers were many of Peter's confidants, who, treacherously deserting him in the first battle, left him to be slain by his enemies. Peter at least gained nothing by his villainy. Edmund Rich, a saintly man, who had recently become Archbishop of Canterbury, protested against his misdeeds. All England was behind the Archbishop,

Beverley Minster, Yorkshire—the south transept ; built about 1220–1230.

and Henry was compelled to dismiss Peter and then to welcome back Peter's enemies and to restore them to their rights. It was of no slight·importance that a man so devoted and unselfish as Edmund Rich had put himself at the head of the movement. It was a good thing, no doubt, to maintain that wealth should be in the hands rather of natives than of foreigners ; but after all every contention for material wealth alone is of the earth, earthy. No object which appeals exclusively to the selfish instincts can, in the long run, be worth contending for. Edmund Rich's accession to the national cause was a guarantee that the claims of righteousness and mercy in the management of the national government would not altogether be forgotten, and fortunately there were new forces actively at work in the same direction. The friars, the followers of St. Francis and St. Dominic, had made good their footing in England.

5. **Francis of Assisi.**—Francis, the son of a merchant in the Tuscan town of Assisi, threw aside the vanities of youth after a serious illness. He was wedded, he declared, to Poverty as his bride. He clothed himself in rags. When his father sent him with a horseload of goods to a neighbouring market, he sold both horse and goods, and offered the money to build a church. His father was enraged, and summoned him before the bishop that he might be deprived of the right of inheriting that which he knew not how to use. Francis stripped himself naked, renouncing even his clothes as his father's property. " I have now," he said, " but one Father, He that is in heaven." He wandered about as a beggar, subsisting on alms and devoting himself to the care of the sick and afflicted. In his heroism of self-denial he chose out the lepers, covered as they were with foul and infectious sores, as the main objects of his tending. Before long he gathered together a brotherhood of men like-minded with himself, who left all, to give not alms but themselves to the help of the poor and sorrowful of Christ's flock. In **1209** Innocent III. constituted them into a new order, not of monks but of Friars (*Fratres* or brethren). The special title of the new order, which after ages have known by the name of Franciscans, was that of Minorites (*Fratres Minores*), or the lesser brethren, because Francis in his humility declared them to be less than the least of Christ's servants. Like Francis, they were to be mendicants, begging their food from day to day. Having nothing themselves, they would be the better able to touch the hearts of those who had nothing. Yet it was not so much the humility of Francis as his loving heart which distinguished him amongst men. Not only all human beings but all created things were dear to him. Once he is said to have preached to birds. He called the sun and the wind his brethren, the moon and the water his sisters. When he died the last feeble words which he breathed were, " Welcome, sister Death ! "

6. **St. Dominic.**—Another order arose about the same time in

Spain. Dominic, a Spaniard, was appalled, not by the misery, but by the ignorance of mankind. The order which he instituted was to be called that of the Friars Preachers, though they have in later times usually been known as Dominicans. Like the Franciscans they were to be Friars, or brothers, because all teaching is vain, as much as all charitable acts are vain, unless brotherly kindness be at the root. Like the Franciscans they were to be mendicants, because so only could the world be convinced that they sought not their own good, but to win souls to Christ.

7. **The Coming of the Friars. 1220—1224.**—In **1220** the first Dominicans arrived in England. Four years later, in **1224**, the first Franciscans followed them. Of the work of the early Dominicans in England little is known. They preached and taught, appealing to those whose intelligence was keen enough to appreciate the value of argument. The Franciscans had a different work before them. The misery of the dwellers on the outskirts of English towns was appalling. The townsmen had made provision for keeping good order amongst all who shared in the liberties,[1] or, as we should say, in the privileges of the town ; but they made no provision for good order amongst the crowds who flocked to the town to pick up a scanty living as best they might. These poor wretches had to dwell in miserable hovels outside the walls by the side of fetid ditches into which the filth of the town was poured. Disease and starvation thinned their numbers. No man cared for their bodies or their souls. The priests who served in the churches within the town passed them by, nor had they any place in the charities with which the brethren of the gilds assuaged the misfortunes of their own members. It was amongst these that the Franciscans lived and laboured, sharing in their misery and their diseases, counting their lives well spent if they could bring comfort to a single human soul.

8. **Monks and Friars.**—The work of the friars was a new phase in the history of the Church. The monks had made it their object to save their own souls ; the friars made it their object to save the bodies and souls of others. The friars, like the monks, taught by the example of self-denial ; but the friars added active well-doing to the passive virtue of restraint. Such examples could not fail to be attended with consequences of which those who set

---

[1] A phrase which may serve to keep in mind the medieval meaning of '*libertas*' is to be found in the statement that a certain monastery kept up a pair of stocks '*pro libertate servandâ*'—that is to say, to keep up its franchise of putting offenders into the stocks.

them never dreamed, all the more because the two new orders worked harmoniously towards a common end. The Dominicans quickened the brain whilst the Franciscans touched the heart, and the whole nation was the better in consequence.

9. **The King's Marriage. 1236.**—In 1236 Henry married Eleanor, the daughter of the Count of Provence. The immediate consequence was the arrival of her four uncles with a stream of Provençals in their train. Amongst these uncles William, Bishop-elect of Valence, took the lead. Henry submitted his weak mind entirely to him, and distributed rank and wealth to the Provençals

Longthorpe Manor House, Northampton;
built about 1235. Some of the larger windows are later.

with as much profusion as he had distributed them to the Poitevins in the days of Peter des Roches. The barons, led now by the king's brother, Richard of Cornwall, remonstrated when they met in the Great Council, which was gradually acquiring the right of granting fresh taxes, though all reference to that right was dropped out of all editions of the Great Charter issued in the reign of Henry. For some time they granted the money which Henry continually asked for, coupling, however, with their grant the demand that Henry should confirm the Charter. The king never refused to confirm it. He had no difficulty in making promises, but he never troubled himself to keep those which he had made.

10. **The Early Career of Simon de Montfort. 1231—1243.** —
Strangely enough, Simon de Montfort, the man who was to be the
chief opponent of Henry and his foreign favourites, was himself a
foreigner. He was sprung from a family established in Normandy,
and his father, the elder Simon de Montfort, had been the leader of a
body of Crusaders from the north of France, who had poured over
the south to crush a vast body of heretics, known by the name of
Albigeois, from Albi, a town in which they swarmed. The elder
Simon had been strict in his orthodoxy and unsparing in his cruelty
to all who were unorthodox. From him the younger Simon inherited
his unswerving religious zeal and his constancy of purpose. There
was the same stern resolution in both, but in the younger man these
qualities were coupled with a statesmanlike instinct, which was want-

A ship in the reign of Henry III.

ing to the father. Norman as he was, he had a claim to the earldom of Leicester through his grandmother, and in **1231** this claim
was acknowledged by Henry. For some time Simon continued to
live abroad, but in **1236** he returned to England to be present at
the king's marriage. He was at once taken into favour, and in **1238**
married the king's sister, Eleanor. His marriage was received by
the barons and the people with a burst of indignation. It was
one more instance, it was said, of Henry's preference for foreigners
over his own countrymen. In **1239** Henry turned upon his brother-
in-law, brought heavy charges against him, and drove him from his
court. In **1240** Simon was outwardly reconciled to Henry, but he
was never again able to repose confidence in one so fickle. In
1242 Henry resolved to undertake an expedition to France to

recover Poitou, which had been gradually slipping out of his hands. At a Great Council held before he sailed, the barons, who had no sympathy with any attempt to recover lost possessions in France, not only rated him soundly for his folly, but, for the first time, absolutely refused to make him a grant of money. Simon told him to his face that the Frenchman was no lamb to be easily subdued. Simon's words proved true. Henry sailed for France, but in 1243 he surrendered all claims to Poitou, and returned discomfited. If he did not bring home victory he brought with him a new crowd of Poitevins, who were connected with his mother's second husband. All of them expected to receive advancement in England, and they seldom expected it in vain.

11. **Papal Exactions. 1237—1243.**—Disgusted as were the English landowners by the preference shown by the king to foreigners, the English clergy were no less disgusted by the exactions of the Pope. The claim of Innocent III. to regulate the proceedings of kings had been handed down to his successors and made them jealous of any ruler too powerful to be controlled. The Emperor Frederick II. had not only succeeded to the government of Germany, and to some influence over the north of Italy, but had inherited Naples and Sicily from his mother. The Pope thus found himself, as it were, between two fires. There was constant bickering between Frederick and Gregory IX., a fiery old man who became Pope in 1227, and in 1238 Gregory excommunicated Frederick, and called on all Europe to assist him against the man whom he stigmatised as the enemy of God and the Church. As the king of England was his vassal in consequence of John's surrender, he looked to him for aid more than to others, especially as England, enjoying internal peace more than other nations, was regarded as especially wealthy. In 1237, the year before Frederick's excommunication, Gregory sent Cardinal Otho as his legate to demand money from the English clergy. The clergy found a leader in Robert Grossetête, Bishop of Lincoln, a wise and practical reformer of clerical disorders ; but though they grumbled, they could get no protection from the king, and were forced to pay. Otho left England in 1241, carrying immense sums of money with him, and the promise of the king to present three hundred Italian priests to English benefices before he presented a single Englishman. In 1243 Gregory IX. was succeeded by Innocent IV., who was even more grasping than his predecessor.

12. **A Weak Parliamentary Opposition. 1244.**—Against these evils the Great Council strove in vain to make head. It was now

beginning to be known as Parliament, though no alteration was yet made in its composition.   In 1244 clergy and barons joined in remonstrating with the king, and some of them even talked about restraining his power by the establishment of a Justiciar and Chancellor, together with four councillors, all six to be elected by the whole of the baronage.   Without the consent of the Chancellor thus chosen no administrative act could be done.   The scheme was a distinct advance upon that of the barons who, in 1215, forced the Great Charter upon John.   The barons had then proposed to leave the appointment of executive officials to the king, and to appoint a committee of twenty-five, who were to have nothing to do with the government of the country, but were to compel the king by force to keep the promises which he had made.   In 1244 they proposed to appoint the executive officials themselves.   It was the beginning of a series of changes which ultimately led to that with which we are now familiar, the appointment of ministers responsible to Parliament.   It was too great an innovation to be accepted at once, especially as it was demanded by the barons alone.   The clergy, who were still afraid of the disorders which might ensue if power were lodged in the hands of the barons, refused to support it, and for a time it fell to the ground.   At the same time Richard of Cornwall abandoned the baronial party.   He had lately married the queen's sister, which may have drawn him over to the king ; but it is also probable that his own position as the king's brother made him unwilling to consent to a scheme which would practically transfer the government from the king to the barons.   On the other hand Earl Simon was found on the side of the barons.   He held his earldom by inheritance from his English grandmother, and the barons were willing to forgive his descent from a foreign grandfather when they found him prepared to share their policy.

13. **Growing Discontent.   1244—1254.**—The clergy had to learn by bitter experience that it was only by a close alliance with the barons that they could preserve themselves from wrong.   In 1244 a new envoy from the Pope, Master Martin, travelled over England wringing money from the clergy.   Though he was driven out of the country in 1245, the Papal exactions did not cease.   The Pope, moreover, continued to present his own nominees to English benefices, and in 1252 Grossetête complained that these nominees drew three times as much income from England as flowed into the royal exchequer.   For a time even Henry made complaints, but in 1254 Innocent IV. won him over to his side.   Frederick II. had died in 1250, and his illegitimate son, Manfred, a tried warrior and

an able ruler, had succeeded him as king of Sicily and Naples. Innocent could not bear that that crown should be worn by the son of the man whom he had hated bitterly, and offered it to Edmund, the second son of Henry III. Henry lept at the offer, hoping that England would bear the expense of the undertaking. England was, however, in no mood to comply. Henry had been squandering money for years. He had recently employed Earl Simon in Gascony, where Simon had put down the resistance of the nobles with a heavy hand. The Gascons complained to Henry, and Henry quarrelled with Simon more bitterly than before. In 1254 Henry crossed the sea to restore order in person. To meet his expenses he borrowed a vast sum of money, and this loan, which he expected England to meet, was the only result of the expedition.

14. **The Knights of the Shire in Parliament. 1254.**—During the king's absence the queen and Earl Richard, who were left as regents, and who had to collect money as best they might, gathered a Great Council, to which, for the first time, representative knights, four from each shire, were summoned. They were merely called on to report what amount of aid

A bed in the reign of Henry III.

their constituents were willing to give, and the regents were doubtless little aware of the importance of the step which they were taking. It was only, to all appearances, an adaptation of the summons calling on the united jury to meet at St. Albans to assess the damages of the clergy in the reign of John. It might seem as if the regents had only summoned a united jury to give evidence of their constituents' readiness to grant certain sums of money. In reality the new scheme was sure to take root, because it held out a hope of getting rid of a constitutional difficulty which had hitherto proved insoluble —the difficulty, that is to say, of weakening the king's power to do evil without establishing baronial anarchy in its place. It was certain that the representatives of the free-holders in the counties would not use their influence for the destruction of order.

15. **Fresh Exactions. 1254—1257.**—At the end of 1254 Henry returned to England. In 1255 a new Pope, Alexander IV., confirmed

his predecessor's grant of the kingdom of Sicily to Edmund, on condition that Henry should give a large sum of money for the expenses of a war against Manfred. To make it easy for Henry to find the money, Alexander gave him a tenth of the revenues of the English clergy, on the plea that the clergy had always borne their share of the expenses of a crusade, and that to fight for the Pope against Manfred was equivalent to a crusade. Immense sums were wrung from the clergy, who were powerless to resist Pope and king combined. Their indignation was the greater, not only because they knew that religion was not at stake in the Pope's effort to secure his political power in Italy, but also because the Papal

Barn of thirteenth-century date at Raunds, Northamptonshire.

court was known to be hopelessly corrupt, it being a matter of common talk that all things were for sale at Rome. The clergy indeed were less than ever in a condition to resist the king without support. Grossetête was dead, and the Archbishop of Canterbury, the queen's uncle, Boniface of Savoy, whose duty it was to maintain the rights of the Church, was a man who cared nothing for England except on account of the money he drew from it. Other bishoprics as well were held by foreigners. The result of the weakness of the clergy was that they were now ready to unite with the barons, whom they had deserted in 1244 (see p. 195). Henry's misgovernment, in fact, had roused all classes against him, as the townsmen and the smaller landowners had been even worse treated than the greater

barons.   In **1257** one obstacle to reform was removed.   Richard of
Cornwall, the king's brother, who was formidable through his wealth
and the numbers of his vassals, had for some time taken part against
them.   In **1257** he was chosen king of the Romans by the German
electors, an election which would make him Emperor as soon as he
had been crowned by the Pope.   He at once left England to seek his
fortunes in Germany, where he was well received as long as he had
money to reward his followers, but was deserted as soon as his
purse was empty.

   16. **The Provisions of Oxford.   1258.**—The crisis in England
came in **1258**, whilst Richard was still abroad.   Though thousands
were dying of starvation in consequence of a bad harvest, Henry
demanded for the Pope the monstrous sum of one-third of the revenue
of all England.   Then the storm burst.   At a Parliament at Westminster the barons appeared in arms and demanded, first, the
expulsion of all foreigners, and, secondly, the appointment of a
committee of twenty-four—twelve from the king's party and twelve
from that of the barons—to reform the realm.   The king unwillingly consented, and the committee was appointed.   Later in the
year Parliament met again at Oxford to receive the report of the
new committee.   The Mad Parliament, as it was afterwards called
in derision, was resolved to make good its claims.   The scheme of
reinforcing Parliament by the election of knights of the shire had indeed been suffered to fall into disuse since its introduction in **1254**, yet
every tenant-in-chief had of old the right of attending, and though
the lesser tenants-in-chief had hitherto seldom or never exercised
that right, they now trooped in arms to Oxford to support the barons.
To this unwonted gathering the committee produced a set of proposals which have gone by the name of the Provisions of Oxford.
There was to be a council of fifteen, without the advice of which
the king could do no act, and in this council the baronial party had
a majority.   The offices of state were filled in accordance with the
wishes of the twenty-four, and the barons thus entered into possession of the authority which had hitherto been the king's.   The
danger of the king's tyranny was averted, but it remained to be seen
whether a greater tyranny would not be erected in its stead.   One
clause of the Provisions of Oxford was not reassuring.   The old
Parliaments, which every tenant-in-chief had at least the customary
right of attending, were no longer to exist.   Their place was to be
taken by a body of twelve, to be chosen by the barons, which was to
meet three times a year to discuss public affairs with the council
of fifteen.

17. **The Expulsion of the Foreigners. 1258.**—The first difficulty of the new government was to compel the foreigners to surrender their castles. William de Valence, the king's half-brother, headed the resistance of the foreigners. The barons swore that no danger should keep them back till they had cleared the land of foreigners and had obtained the good laws which they needed. Earl Simon set the example by surrendering his own castles at Kenilworth and Odiham. The national feeling was with Simon and the barons, and at last the foreigners were driven across the sea. For a time all went well. The committee of twenty-four continued its work and produced a further series of reforms. All persons in authority were called on to swear to be faithful to the Provisions of Oxford, and the king and his eldest son, Edward, complied with the demand.

18. **Edward and the Barons. 1259.**—Early in 1259 Richard came back to England, and gave satisfaction by swearing to the Provisions. Before long signs of danger appeared. The placing complete authority in the hands of the barons was not likely to be long popular, and Earl Simon was known to be in favour of a wider and more popular scheme. Hugh Bigod, who had been named Justiciar by the barons, gave offence by the way in which he exercised his office. Simon was hated by the king, and he knew that many of the barons did not love him. The sub-tenants—the Knights Bachelors of England as they called themselves—doubting his power to protect them, complained, not to Simon, but to Edward, the eldest son of the King, that the barons had obtained the redress of their own grievances, but had done nothing for the rest of the community. Edward was now a young man of twenty, hot-tempered and impatient of control, but keen-sighted enough to know, what his father had never known, that the royal power would be increased if it could establish itself in the affections of the classes whose interests were antagonistic to those of the barons. He therefore declared that he had sworn to the Provisions, and would keep his oath ; but that if the barons did not fulfil their own promises, he would join the community in compelling them to do so. The warning was effectual, and the barons issued orders for the redress of the grievances of those who had found so high a patron.

19. **The Breach amongst the Barons. 1259—1261.** —Simon had no wish to be involved in a purely baronial policy. He had already fallen out with Richard de Clare, Earl of Gloucester, the leader of the barons who had resisted the full execution of the promises made at Oxford in the interest of the people at large.

"With such fickle and faithless men," said Simon to him, "I care not to have ought to do. The things we are treating of now we have sworn to carry out. And thou, Sir Earl, the higher thou art the more art thou bound to keep such statutes as are wholesome for the land." The king fomented the rising quarrel, and in 1261 announced that the Pope had declared the Provisions to be null and void, and had released him from his oath to observe them.

20. **Royalist Reaction and Civil War. 1261.**—Henry now ruled again in his own fashion. Even the Earl of Gloucester discovered that if the king was to be resisted it must be by an appeal to a body of men more numerous than the barons alone. He joined Simon in inviting a Parliament to meet, at which three knights should appear for each county, thus throwing over the unfortunate narrowing of Parliament to a baronial committee of twelve, which had been the worst blot on the Provisions of Oxford. In the summer of 1262 the Earl of Gloucester died, and was succeeded by his son, Earl Gilbert, one of Simon's warmest personal admirers. In 1263 Simon, now the acknowledged head of the barons and of the nation, finding that the king could not be brought to keep the Provisions, took arms against him. He was a master in the art of war, and gained one fortified post after another. Henry, being, as usual, short of money, called on the Londoners for a loan. On their refusal Edward seized a sum of money which belonged to them, and so exasperated them that, on the queen's passing under London Bridge, the citizens reviled her and pelted her with stones. The war was carried on with doubtful results, and by the end of the year both parties agreed to submit to the arbitration of the king of France.

21. **The Mise of Amiens. 1264.**—The king of France Louis IX., afterwards known as St. Louis, was the justest and most unselfish of men. In 1259 he had surrendered to Henry a considerable amount of territory in France, which Henry had been unable to re-conquer for himself ; and was well satisfied to obtain from Henry in return a formal renunciation of the remainder of the lands which Philip II. had taken from John. Yet, well-intentioned as Louis was, he had no knowledge of England, and in France, where the feudal nobility was still excessively tyrannical, justice was only to be obtained by the maintenance of a strong royal power. He therefore thought that what was good for France was also good for England, and in the beginning of 1264 he relieved Henry from all the restrictions which his subjects had sought to place upon

him. The decision thus taken was known as the Mise, or settlement, of Amiens, from the place at which it was issued.

22. The Battle of Lewes. 1264.—The Mise of Amiens required an unconditional surrender of England to the king. The Londoners and the trading towns were the first to reject it. Simon put himself at the head of a united army of barons and citizens. In the early morning of May 14 he caught the king's army half asleep at Lewes. Edward charged at the Londoners, against whom he bore a grudge since they had ill-treated his mother, and cleared them off the field with enormous slaughter. When he returned the battle was lost. Henry himself was captured, and Richard, king of the Romans, was found hiding in a windmill. Edward, in spite of his success, had to give himself up as a prisoner.

A fight between armed and mounted knights of the time of Henry III.

23. Earl Simon's Government. 1264—1265.—Simon followed up his victory by an agreement called the Mise of Lewes, according to which all matters of dispute were again to be referred to arbitration. In the meantime there were to be three Electors, Earl Simon himself, the Earl of Gloucester, and the Bishop of Chichester. These were to elect nine councillors, who were to name the ministers of state. To keep these councillors within bounds a Parliament was called, in which with the barons, bishops, and abbots there sat not only chosen knights for each shire, but also for the first time two representatives of certain towns. This Parliament met in **1265**. It was not, indeed, a full parliament, as only Simon's partisans amongst the barons were summoned,

but it was the fullest representation of England as a whole which
had yet met, and not a merely baronial committee like that proposed in 1258. The views of Simon were clearly indicated in an
argumentative Latin poem written after the battle of Lewes by one
of his supporters. In this poem the king's claim to do as he likes
with his own is met by a demand that he shall rule according to
law. Such a demand was made by others than the poet. " The
king," a great lawyer of the day had said, " is not subject to any
man, but to God and the law." The difficulty still remained of

Seal of Robert Fitzwalter, showing a mounted knight in complete mail armour.
Date, about 1265.

ascertaining what the law was. The poet did not, indeed,
anticipate modern theories, and hold that the law was what the
representatives of the people made it to be ; but he held that the
law consisted in the old customs, and that the people themselves
must be appealed to as the witnesses of what those old customs
were. " Therefore," he wrote, " let the community of the kingdom
advise, and let it be known what the generality thinks, to whom their
own laws are best known. Nor are all those of the country so ignorant that they do not know better than strangers the customs of
their own kingdom which have been handed down to them by

their ancestors." [1]   The poet, in short, regarded the Parliament as a national jury, whose duty it was to give evidence on the laws and customs of the nation, in the same way that a local jury gave evidence on local matters.

24. The Battle of Evesham. 1265.—Simon's constitution was premature.   Men wanted a patriotic king who could lead the nation instead of one who, like Henry, used it for his own ends.   The new rulers were sure to quarrel with one another.   If Simon was still Simon the Righteous, his sons acted tyrannically.   The barons began again to distrust Simon himself, and the young Earl of Gloucester, like his father before him, put himself at the head of the dissatisfied barons, and went over to the king.   Edward escaped from confinement, by urging his keepers to ride races with one another, and then galloping off when their horses were too tired to follow him.   Edward and Gloucester combined forces, and, falling on Earl Simon at Evesham, defeated him utterly.   Simon was slain in the fight and his body barbarously mutilated ; but his memory was treasured, and he was counted as a saint by the people for whom he had worked.   Verses have been preserved in which he is compared to

[1] "Igitur communitas regni consulatur ;
　　Et quid universitas sentiat, sciatur,
　　Cui leges propriæ maxime sunt notæ.
　　Nec cuncti provinciæ sic sunt idiotæ,
　　Quin sciant plus cæteris regni sui
　　　　mores,
　　Quos relinquunt posteris hii qui sunt
　　　　priores."

Effigy of a knight at Gosperton, showing armour worn from about 1250 to 1300. Date, about 1270

Archbishop Thomas, who had given himself as a sacrifice for the Church, as Simon had given himself as a sacrifice for the nation.

25. The Last Years of Henry III. 1265—1272.—The storm which had been raised was some time in calming down. Some of Earl Simon's followers continued to hold out against the king. When at last they submitted, they were treated leniently, and in **1267**, at a Parliament at Marlborough, a statute was enacted embodying most of the demands for the redress of grievances made by the earlier reformers. The kingdom settled down in peace, be-

Building operations in the reign of Henry III., with the king giving directions to the architect

cause Henry now allowed Edward to be the real head of the government. Edward, in short, carried on Earl Simon's work in ruling justly, with the advantage of being raised above jealousies by his position as heir to the throne. In **1270** England was so peaceful that Edward could embark on a crusade. At Acre he very nearly fell a victim to a fanatic belonging to a body which counted assassination a religious duty. His wife, Eleanor of Castile, who was tenderly attached to him, had to be led out of his tent, lest her bitter grief should distract him during an operation which the surgeons held to be necessary. In **1272** Henry III. died, and

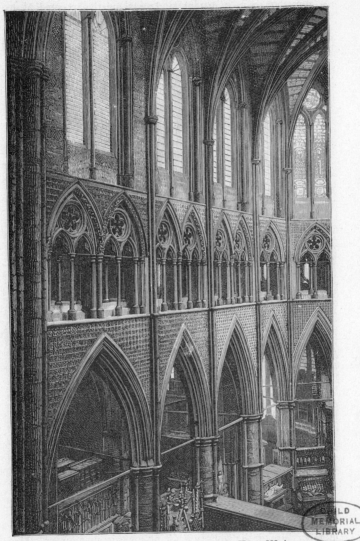

East end of Westminster Abbey Church : begun by Henry III. in 1245.

his son, though in a distant land, was quietly accepted as his successor.

Nave of Salisbury Cathedral Church, looking west.   Date, between 1240 and 1250.

26. General Progress of the Country.—In spite of the turmoils of Henry's reign the country made progress in many ways.   Men busied themselves with replacing the old round-arched churches by

large and more beautiful ones, in that Early English style of
which Lincoln Cathedral was the first example on a large scale.
In **1220** it was followed by Beverley Minster (see p. 189). The nave
of Salisbury Cathedral was begun in **1240** (see p. 206), and a new
Westminster Abbey grew piecemeal under Henry's own supervision
during the greater part of the reign (see p. 205). Mental activity
accompanied material activity. At Oxford there were reckoned 15,000
scholars. Most remarkable was the new departure taken by Walter
de Merton, Henry's Chancellor. Hitherto each scholar had shifted
for himself, lived where he could, and been subjected to little or no
discipline. In founding Merton College, the first college which
existed in the University, Merton proposed not only to erect a

A king and labourers in the reign of Henry III.

building in which the lads who studied might be boarded and
placed under supervision, but to train them with a view to learning
for its own sake, and not to prepare them for the priesthood. The
eagerness to learn things difficult was accompanied by a desire to
increase popular knowledge. For the first time since the Chronicle
came to an end, which was soon after the accession of Henry II., a
book—Layamon's *Brut*—appeared in the reign of John in the
English language, and one at least of the songs which witness to
the interest of the people in the great struggle with Henry III.
was also written in the same language. Yet the great achievement
of the fifty-six years of Henry's reign was—to use the language
of the smith who refused to put fetters on the limbs of Hubert de
Burgh (see p. 188)—the giving of England back to the English

In 1216 it was possible for Englishmen to prefer a French-born Louis as their king to an Angevin John. In 1272 England was indeed divided by class prejudices and conflicting interests, but it was nationally one. The greatest grievance suffered from Henry III. was his preference of foreigners over his own countrymen. In resistance to foreigners Englishmen had been welded together into a nation, and in their new king Edward they found a leader who would not only prove a wise and thoughtful ruler, but who was every inch an Englishman.

Genealogy of John's Sons and Grandsons.

JOHN, 1199–1216

HENRY III. = Eleanor of   Richard,   Eleanor = Simon de Mont-
1216-1272   Provence   Earl of Cornwall   fort
             and King of the Romans

EDWARD I.   Edmund, titular King of Sicily
1272-1307

CHAPTER XIV

EDWARD I. AND EDWARD II.

EDWARD I., 1272—1307.   EDWARD II., 1307—1327

LEADING DATES

Accession of Edward I.	1272
Death of Alexander III.	1285
The Award of Norham	1292
The Model Parliament	1295
The First Conquest of Scotland	1296
Confirmatio Cartarum	1297
Completion of the Second Conquest of Scotland	1304
The Incorporation of Scotland with England	1305
The Third Conquest of Scotland	1306
Accession of Edward II.	1307
Execution of Gaveston	1312
Battle of Bannockburn	1314
Execution of Lancaster	1322
Deposition of Edward II.	1327

1. **The First Years of Edward I.** 1272—1279.—Edward I., though he inherited the crown in 1272, did not return to England till 1274, being able to move in a leisurely fashion across Europe without fear of disturbances at home. He fully accepted those articles of John's

Great Charter which had been set aside at the beginning of the reign of Henry III., and which required that the king should only take scutages and aids with the consent of the Great Council or Parliament. The further requirement of the barons that they should name the ministers of the crown, was allowed to fall asleep. Edward was a capable ruler, and knew how to appoint better ministers than the barons were likely to choose for him.

Great Seal of Edward I.

It was Edward's peculiar merit that he stood forward not only as a ruler but as a legislator. He succeeded in passing one law after another, because he thoroughly understood that useful legislation is only possible when the legislator on the one hand has an intelligent perception of the remedies needed to meet existing evils, and on the other hand is willing to content himself with such remedies as those who are to be benefited by them are

P

ready to accept. The first condition was fulfilled by Edward's own skill as a lawyer, and by the skill of the great lawyers whom he employed. The second condition was fulfilled by his determination to authorise no new legislation without the counsel and consent of those who were most affected by it. He did not, indeed, till late in his reign call a whole Parliament together, as Earl Simon had done. But he called the barons together in any matter which affected the barons, and he called the representatives of the townsmen together in any matter which affected the townsmen, and so on with the other classes.

2. **Edward I. and Wales. 1276 — 1284.** — Outside England Edward's first difficulty was with the Welsh, who, though their Princes had long been regarded by the English Kings as vassals, had practically maintained their independence in the mountainous region of North Wales of which Snowdon is the centre. Between them and the English Lords Marchers, who had been established to keep order in the marches, or border-land, there was nothing but hostility. The Welshmen made forays and plundered the English lands, and the English retorted by slaughtering Welshmen whenever they could come up with them amongst the hills. Naturally the Welsh took the side of any enemy of the English kings with whom it was possible to ally themselves. Llewelyn, Prince of Wales, had joined Earl Simon against Henry III., and had only done homage to Henry after Simon had been defeated. After Henry's death he refused homage to Edward till **1276**. In **1282** he and his brother David renewed the war, and Edward, determined to put an end to the independence of such troublesome neighbours, marched against them. Before the end of the year Llewelyn was slain, and David was captured in **1283**, and executed in **1284**. Wales then came fully under the dominion of the English kings. Edward's second son, afterwards King Edward II., was born at Carnarvon in **1284**, and soon afterwards, having become heir to the crown, upon the death of his elder brother, was presented to the Welsh as Prince of Wales, a title from that day usually bestowed upon the king's eldest son. At the same time, though Edward built strong castles at Conway and Carnarvon to hold the Welsh in awe, he made submission easier by enacting suitable laws for them, under the name of the Statute of Wales, and by establishing a separate body of local officials to govern them, as well as by confirming them in the possession of their lands and goods.

3. **Customs Duties. 1275.** — Though Edward I. was by no means extravagant, he found it impossible to meet the expenses of govern-

ment without an increase of taxation. In **1275** he obtained the consent of Parliament to the increase of the duties on exports and imports which had hitherto been levied without Parliamentary sanction. He was now to receive by a Parliamentary grant a fixed export duty of 6*s*. 8*d*. on every sack of wool sent out of the country, and of a corresponding duty on wool-fells and leather. Under ordinary circumstances it is useless for any government to attempt to gain a revenue by export duty, because such a duty only raises the price abroad of the products of its own country, and foreigners will therefore prefer to buy the articles which they need from some country which does not levy export duties, and where, therefore, the articles are to be had more cheaply. England, however, was, in Edward's time, and for many years afterwards, an exception to the rule. On the Continent men could not produce much wool or leather for sale, because private wars were constantly occurring, and the fighting men were in the habit of driving off the sheep and the cattle. In England

Group of armed knights, and a king in ordinary dress.
Date, *temp*. Edward I.

there were no private wars, and under the king's protection sheep and cattle could be bred in safety. There were now growing up manufactures of cloth in the fortified towns of Flanders, and the manufacturers there were obliged to come to England for the greater part of the wool which they used. They could not help paying not only the price of the wool, but the king's export duty as well, because if they refused they could not get sufficient wool in any other country.

4. **Edward's Judicial Reforms. 1274—1290.**—Every king of England since the Norman Conquest had exercised authority in a twofold capacity. On one hand he was the head of the nation, on the other hand he was the feudal lord of his vassals. Edward laid more stress than any former king upon his national headship. Early in his reign he organised the courts of law, completing the division of the *Curia Regis* into the three courts which existed till recent times : the Court of King's Bench, to deal with criminal offences reserved for the king's judgment, and with suits in which he was himself concerned ; the Court of Exchequer, to deal with all matters touching the king's revenue ; and the Court of Common Pleas, to deal with suits between subject and subject. Edward took care that the justice administered in these courts should as far as possible be real justice, and in **1289** he dismissed two Chief Justices and many other officials for corruption. In **1285** he improved the Assize of Arms of Henry II. (see p. 154), so as to be more sure of securing a national support for his government in time of danger.

5. **Edward's Legislation. 1279—1290.**—It was in accordance with the national feeling that Edward, in **1290**, banished from England the Jews, whose presence was most profitable to himself, but who were regarded as cruel tyrants by their debtors. On the other hand, Edward took care to assert his rights as a feudal lord. In **1279**, by the statute *De religiosis*, commonly known as the Statute of Mortmain, he forbade the gift of land to the clergy, because in their hands land was no longer liable to the feudal dues. In **1290**, by another statute, *Quia emptores*, he forbade all new sub-infeudation. If from henceforth a vassal wished to part with his land, the new tenant was to hold it, not under the vassal who gave it up, but under that vassal's lord, whether the lord was the king or anyone else. The object of this law was to increase the number of tenants-in-chief, and thus to bring a larger number of land-owners into direct relations with the king.

6. **Edward as a National and as a Feudal Ruler.**—In his government of England Edward had sought chiefly to strengthen his position as the national king of the whole people, and to depress legally and without violence the power of the feudal nobility. He was, however, ambitious, with the ambition of a man conscious of great and beneficent aims, and he was quite ready to enforce even unduly his personal claims to feudal obedience whenever it served his purpose to do so. His favourite motto, ' Keep troth ' (*Pactum serva*), revealed his sense of the inviolability of a personal engagement given or received, but his legal mind often led him into

construing in his own favour engagements in which only the letter
of the law was on his side, whilst its spirit was against him. It
was chiefly in his relations with foreign peoples that he fell into

Nave of Lichfield Cathedral, looking east.   Built about 1280.

this error, as it was here that he was most strongly tempted to lay stress upon the feudal tie which made for him, and to ignore the importance of a national resistance which made against him. In dealing with Wales, for instance, he sent David to a cruel death, because he had broken the feudal tie which bound him to the king of England, feeling no sympathy with him as standing up for the independence of his own people.

7. **The Scottish Succession. 1285—1290.**—In the earlier part of Edward's reign Alexander III. was king of Scotland. Alexander's ancestors, indeed, had done homage to Edward's ancestors, but in **1189** William the Lion had purchased from Richard I. the abandonment of all the claim to homage for the crown of Scotland which Henry II. had acquired by the treaty of Falaise (see pp. 154, 159). William's successors, however, held lands in England, and had done homage for them to the English kings. Edward would gladly have restored the old practice of homage for Scotland itself, but to this Alexander had never given way. To Edward there was something alluring in the prospect of being lord of the whole island, as it would not only strengthen his own personal position, but would bring two nations into peaceful union. Between the southern part of Scotland, indeed, and the northern part of England there was no great dissimilarity. On both sides of the border the bulk of the population was of the same Anglian stock, whilst, in consequence of the welcome offered by the Scottish kings to persons of Norman descent, the nobility was as completely Norman in Scotland as it was in England, many of the nobles indeed possessing lands on both sides of the border. A prospect of effecting a union by peaceful means offered itself to Edward in **1285**, when Alexander III. was killed by a fall from his horse near Kinghorn. Alexander's only descendant was Margaret, a child of his daughter and of King Eric of Norway. In **1290** it was agreed that she should marry the Prince of Wales, but that the two kingdoms should remain absolutely independent of one another. Unfortunately, the Maid of Norway, as the child was called, died on her way to Scotland, and this plan for establishing friendly relations between the two countries came to naught. If it had succeeded three centuries of war and misery might possibly have been avoided.

8. **Death of Eleanor of Castile. 1290.**—Another death, which happened in the same year, brought sorrow into Edward's domestic life. His wife Eleanor died in November. The corpse was brought for burial from Lincoln to Westminster, and the

bereaved husband ordered the erection of a memorial cross at each place where the body rested.

9. **The Award of Norham. 1291—1292** —Edward, sorrowing as he was, was unable to neglect the affairs of State. On the death of the Maid of Norway there was a large number of claimants to the Scottish crown. The hereditary principle, which had long before been adopted in regard to the succession to landed property, was gradually being adopted in most kingdoms in regard to the succession to the crown There were still, however, differences of opinion as to the manner in which hereditary succession ought to be reckoned, and there were now many claimants, of whom at least three could make out a plausible case. David, Earl of Huntingdon, a brother of William the Lion, had left three daughters. The grandson of the eldest daughter was John Balliol ; the son of the second was Robert Bruce ; the grandson of the third was John Hastings. Balliol maintained that he ought to succeed as being descended from the eldest : Bruce urged that the son of a younger daughter was nearer to the common ancestor, David, than the grandson of the elder : whilst Hastings asked that Scotland should be divided

Effigy of Eleanor of Castile, queen of Edward I., in Westminster Abbey.

into three parts—according to a custom which prevailed in feudal estates in which the holder left only daughters—amongst the representatives of David's three daughters.[1] Every one of these three claimants was an English baron, and Bruce held large estates in both countries. The only escape from a desolating civil war seemed to be to appeal to Edward's arbitration, and in 1291 Edward summoned the Scots to meet him at Norham. He then demanded as the price of his arbitration the acknowledgment of his position as lord paramount of Scotland, in virtue of which the Scottish king, when he had once been chosen, was to do homage to himself as king of England. Edward, who might fairly have held that, in spite of the abandonment of the treaty of Falaise by Richard, he had a right to the old vague overlordship of earlier kings, appears to have thought it right to take the opportunity of Scotland's weakness to renew the stricter relationship of homage which had been given up by Richard. At all events, the Scottish nobles and clergy accepted his demand, though the commonalty made some objection, the nature of which has not been recorded. Edward then investigated carefully the points at issue, and in 1292 decided in favour of Balliol. If he had been actuated by selfish motives he would certainly have adopted the suggestion of Hastings that Scotland ought to be divided into three kingdoms.

10. **Disputes with Scotland and France. 1293-1295.**—The new king of Scotland did homage to Edward for his whole kingdom. If Edward could have contented himself with enforcing the ordinary obligations of feudal superiority all might have gone well. Unfortunately for all parties, he attempted to stretch them by insisting in 1293 that appeals from the courts of the king of Scotland should lie

[1] Genealogy of the claimants of the Scottish throne :—

DAVID I.
1124 1153

Henry

MALCOLM IV. 1153-1165	WILLIAM THE LION 1165-1214		David, Earl of Huntingdon	
	ALEXANDER II. 1214 1249	Margaret *m.* Alan, Lord of Galloway	Isabella *m.* Robert Bruce	Ada *m.* Henry Hastings
	ALEXANDER III. 1249-1285	Devorguilla *m.* John Balliol	Robert Bruce the Claimant	Henry Hastings
	Margaret *m.* Eric, king of Norway	Margaret *m.* John, the Black Comyn	JOHN BALLIOL 1292 1296	Robert Bruce	John Hastings, the Claimant
	Margaret, The Maid of Norway	John, the Red Comyn	Edward Balliol	ROBERT BRUCE 1306 1329	

Cross erected near Northampton by Edward I. in memory of Queen Eleanor
built between 1291 and 1294.

to the courts of the king of England. Suitors found that their rights
could not be ascertained till they had undertaken a long and costly
journey to Westminster. A national feeling of resistance was
roused amongst the Scots, and though Edward pressed his claims
courteously, he continued to press them. A temper grew up in
Scotland which might be dangerous to him if Scotland could find
an ally, and an ally was not long in presenting himself. Philip IV.
now king of France, was as wily and unscrupulous as Philip II.
had been in the days of John. Edward was his vassal in Guienne
and Gascony, and Philip knew how to turn the feudal relationship to account in France as well as Edward knew how to turn it
to account in Scotland. The Cinque Ports[1] along the south-eastern
shore of England swarmed with hardy and practised mariners,
and there had often been sea-fights between French and English
sailors quite independently of the two kings. In **1293** there
was a great battle in which the French were worsted. Though
Edward was ready to punish the offenders, Philip summoned him
to appear as a vassal before his lord's court at Paris. In **1294**,
however, an agreement was made between the two kings.
Edward was for mere form's sake to surrender his French fortresses
to Philip in token of submission, and Philip was then to return
them. Philip, having thus got the fortresses into his hands, refused
to return them. In **1295** a league was made between France and
Scotland, which lasted for more than three hundred years. Its
permanence was owing to the fact that it was a league between
nations more than a league between kings.

11. **The Model Parliament. 1295.**—Edward, attacked on two
sides, threw himself for support on the English nation. Towards
the end of **1295** he summoned a Parliament which was in most respects
the model for all succeeding Parliaments. It was attended not only
by bishops, abbots, earls, and barons, by two knights from every
shire, and two burgesses from every borough, but also by representatives of the chapters of cathedrals and of the parochial clergy. It cannot be said with any approach to certainty, whether the Parliament
thus collected met in one House or not. As, however, the barons
and knights offered an eleventh of the value of their movable goods,
the clergy a tenth, and the burgesses a seventh, it is not unlikely
that there was a separation into what in modern times would be
called three Houses, at least for purposes of taxation. At all events,

---

[1] Sandwich, Dover, Hythe, Romney, Hastings; to which were added
Winchelsea and Rye as 'ancient towns,' besides several 'limbs' or dependencies.

the representatives of the clergy subsequently refused to sit in Parliament, preferring to vote money to the Crown in their own convocations.

12. **The first Conquest of Scotland. 1296.**—In 1296 Edward turned first upon Scotland. After he crossed the border Balliol sent to him renouncing his homage. "Has the felon fool done such folly?" said Edward. "If he will not come to us, we will go to him." He won a decisive victory over the Scots at Dunbar. Balliol surrendered his crown, and was carried off, never to reappear in Scotland. Edward set up no more vassal kings. He declared himself to be the immediate king of Scotland, Balliol having forfeited the crown by treason. The Scottish nobles did homage to him. On his return to England he left behind him the Earl of Surrey and Sir Hugh Cressingham as guardians of the kingdom, and he carried off from Scone the stone of destiny on which the Scottish kings had been crowned, and concerning which there had been an old prophecy to the effect that wherever that stone was Scottish kings should rule. The stone was placed, where it still remains, under the coronation-chair of the English kings in Westminster Abbey, and there were those long afterwards who deemed the prophecy fulfilled when the Scottish King

Sir John d'Abernoun, died 1277 : from his brass at Stoke Dabernon : showing armour worn from about 1250 to 1300.

James VI. came to take his seat on that chair as James I. of England.

13. **The Resistance of Archbishop Winchelsey. 1296—1297.** —The dispute with France and the conquest of Scotland cost much money, and Edward, finding his ordinary revenue insufficient, had been driven to increase it by unusual means. He gathered assemblies of the merchants, and persuaded them without the leave of Parliament to increase the export duties, and he also induced the clergy in the same way to grant him large sums. The clergy were the first to resist. In **1296** Boniface VIII., a Pope who pushed to the extreme the Papal claims to the independence of the Church, issued the Bull, *Clericis laicos*, in which he declared that the clergy were not to pay taxes without the Pope's consent ; and when at the end of the year Edward called on his Parliament to grant him fresh sums, Winchelsey, the Archbishop of Canterbury, refused, on the ground of this Bull, to allow a penny to be levied from the clergy. Edward, instead of arguing with him, directed the chief justice of the King's Bench to announce that, as the clergy would pay no taxes, they would no longer be protected by the king. The clergy now found themselves in evil case. Anyone who pleased could rob them or beat them, and no redress was to be had. They soon therefore evaded their obligation to obey the Bull, and paid their taxes, under the pretence that they were making presents to the king, on which Edward again opened his courts to them. In the days of Henry I. or Henry II. it would not have been possible to treat the clergy in this fashion. The fact was, that the mass of the people now looked to the king instead of to the Church for protection, and therefore respected the clergy less than they had done in earlier days.

14. **The ' Confirmatio Cartarum.' 1297.**—In **1297** Edward, having subdued the Scots in the preceding year, resolved to conduct one army to Flanders, and to send another to Gascony to maintain his rights against Philip IV. He therefore called on his barons to take part in these enterprises. Amongst those ordered to go to Gascony were Roger Bigod, Earl of Norfolk, and Humfrey Bohun, Earl of Hereford. They declared that they were only bound to follow the king himself, and that as Edward was not going in person to Gascony they would not go. " By God, Sir Earl," said the king to one of them, " you shall either. go or hang." " By God," was the reply, " I will neither go nor hang." The two earls soon found support. The barons were sore because Edward's reforms had diminished their authority. The clergy were sore because of their recent treatment. The merchants were sore because of the exac-

tions to which they had been subjected. Archbishop Winchelsey bound the malcontents together by asking Edward to confirm *Magna Carta* and other charters granted by his predecessors, and by adding other articles now proposed for the first time, so as to preclude him from demanding taxes not granted by Parliament. Edward found that the new articles restricted his action more than it had been restricted by the older charters. He was deeply vexed, as he thought that he deserved to be trusted, and that, though he had exacted illegal payments, he had only done so out of necessity. He saw, however, that he must yield, but he could not bring himself to yield in person, and he therefore crossed the sea to Flanders, leaving the Prince of Wales to make the required concession. On October 10, **1297**, the *Confirmatio Cartarum*, as it was called, was issued in the king's name. It differed from *Magna Carta* in this, that whereas John had only engaged not to exact feudal revenue from his vassals without consent of Parliament, Edward I. also engaged not to exact customs duties without a Parliamentary grant. From that time no general revenue could be taken from the whole realm without a breach of the law, though the king still continued for some time to raise tallages, or special payments, from the tenants of his own demesne lands.

See p. 243

15. **Wallace's Rising. 1297—1304.**—Whilst Edward was contending with his own people his officers had been oppressing the Scots. They had treated Scotland as a conquered land, not as a country joined to England by equal union. Resistance began in **1297**, and a rising was headed by Wallace, a gentleman of moderate fortune in the western lowlands. Wallace's bold and vigorous attacks gained him the confidence of the lesser gentry and the people, though the nobles, mostly of Norman descent, supported the English government, and only joined Wallace when it was dangerous to stand aloof. In the autumn, an English army advancing into Scotland reached the south bank of the Forth near Stirling. Wallace, who showed on that day that he was skilful as well as brave, drew up his army on the north bank at some little distance from the narrow bridge over which the English must come if they were to attack him. When half of them had crossed, he fell upon that half before the troops in the rear could advance to its succour. Wallace's victory was complete, and he then invaded England, ravaging and slaughtering as far as Hexham.

16. **The Second Conquest of Scotland. 1298—1304.**—In **1298** Edward, who had been unsuccessful on the Continent, made a truce with Philip. Returning to England, he marched against Wallace,

and came up with him at Falkirk. The battle which ensued, like William's victory at Senlac (see p. 96), was a triumph of inventive military skill over valour content to rest upon ancient methods. The Scots were hardy footmen, drawn up in three rings, and provided with long spears. Against such a force so armed the cavalry of the feudal array would dash itself in vain. Edward, however, had marked in his Welsh wars the superiority of the long-bow drawn to the ear—not, as in the case of the shorter bows of older times, to the breast of the archer—and sending its cloth-yard shaft with a strength and swiftness hitherto unknown. He now brought with him a large force of bowmen equipped in this fashion. At Falkirk the long-bow was tried for the first time in any considerable battle. The effect was overwhelming : a shower of arrows poured upon a single point in the ring of the spearmen soon cleared a gap. Edward's cavalry dashed in before the enemy had time to close, and the victory was won. Wallace had had scarcely one of the Scottish nobles with him either at Stirling or at Falkirk, and unless all Scotland combined he could hardly be expected to succeed against such a warrior as Edward. Wallace's merit was that he did not despair of his country, and that by his patriotic vigour he prepared the minds of Scotsmen for a happier day. He himself fled to France, but Scotland struggled on without him. Some of the nobles, now that Wallace was no longer present to give them cause of jealousy, took part in the resistance, and only in **1304** did Edward after repeated campaigns complete his second conquest of the country.

17. **The Incorporation of Scotland with England. 1305.**—In **1305** Wallace, who had returned from France, but had taken no great part in the late resistance, was betrayed to the English. His barbarity in his raid on Northumberland in 1297 (see p. 221) had marked him out for vengeance, and he was executed at Tyburn as a traitor to the English king of Scotland, whose right he had never acknowledged. Edward then proceeded to incorporate Scotland with England. Scotland was to be treated very much as Wales had been treated before. There was to be as little harshness as possible. Nobles who had resisted Edward were to keep their estates on payment of fines, the Scottish law was to be observed, and Scots were to be chosen to represent the wishes of their fellow-countrymen in the Parliament at Westminster. On the other hand, the Scottish nobles were to surrender their castles, and the country was to be governed by an English Lieutenant, who, together with his council, had power to amend the laws.

18. **Character of Edward's Dealings with Scotland.**—Edward's

dealings with Scotland, mistaken as they were, were not those of a self-willed tyrant. If it be once admitted that he was really the lord paramount of Scotland, everything that he did may be justified upon feudal principles. First, Balliol forfeited his vassal crown by breaking his obligations as a vassal. Secondly, Edward, through the default of his vassal, took possession of the fief which Balliol had forfeited, and thus became the immediate lord of Balliol's vassals. Thirdly, those vassals rebelled—so at least Edward would have said—against their new lord. Fourthly, they thereby forfeited their estates to him, and he was therefore, according to his own view, in the right in restoring their estates to them—if he restored them at all—under new conditions. Satisfactory as this argument must have seemed to Edward, it was weak in two places. The Scots might attack it at its basis by retorting that Edward had never truly been lord paramount of Scotland at all ; or they might assert that it did not matter whether he was so or not, because the Scottish right to national independence was superior to all feudal claims. It is this latter argument which has the most weight at the present day, and it seems to us strange that Edward, who had done so much to encourage the national growth of England, should have entirely ignored the national growth of Scotland. All that can be said to palliate Edward's mistake is that it was, at first, difficult to perceive that there was a Scottish nationality at all. Changes in the political aspect of affairs grow up unobserved, and it was not till after his death that all classes in Scotland were completely welded together in resistance to an English king. At all events, if he treated the claim of the Scots to national independence with contempt, he at least strove, according to his own notions, to benefit Scots and English alike. He hoped that one nation, justly ruled under one government, would grow up in the place of two divided peoples.

19. **Robert Bruce. 1306.**—It was better even for England that Edward's hopes should fail. Scotland would have been of little worth to its more powerful neighbour if it had been cowed into subjection ; whereas when, after struggling and suffering for her independence, she offered herself freely as the companion and ally of England to share in common duties and common efforts, the gift was priceless. That Scotland was able to shake off the English yoke was mainly the work of Robert Bruce, the grandson of the Robert Bruce who had been one of the claimants of the Scottish crown at Norham. The Bruces, like Balliol, were of Norman descent, and as Balliol's rivals they had attached themselves to Edward. The time was now come when all chances of

Balliol's restoration were at an end, and thoughts of gaining the crown stirred in the mind of the younger Bruce. After Edward's last settlement of Scotland it was plain that there was no longer room for a Scottish vassal king, and Bruce was therefore driven to connect his own aspirations with those of the Scottish nation. He had, however, one powerful rival amongst the nobles. John Comyn —the Red Comyn, as he was called—had been one of the many claimants of the throne who appeared before Edward at Norham, and he still looked with a jealous eye upon all who disputed his title. He was, however, persuaded in 1306 to meet Bruce in the Grey Friars Church at Dumfries. As Bruce pleaded his own right to the crown, Comyn denounced him as a traitor to Edward. Bruce answered by driving his dagger into him. " I doubt," cried Bruce, as he rushed from the church, " that I have slain the Red Comyn." "I will mak sicker " (*make sure*), said Kirkpatrick, who was in attendance upon him, and, going in, completed the murder. Bruce made for Scone and was crowned king of Scotland in the presence of many of the chief nobility.

20. **Edward's Third Conquest of Scotland and Death. 1306— 1307.**—Edward, to whom Bruce was but a rebel and a murderer, followed hard on his heels, and routed his forces at Methven. Scotland was for a third time conquered, and Bruce's supporters were carried off to English prisons, and their lands divided amongst English noblemen. The Countess of Buchan, who had taken a prominent part in Bruce's coronation, was placed in an iron cage, which was hung high up on the outer wall of the castle of Berwick. Bruce almost alone escaped. He knew now that he had the greater part of the nobility as well as the people at his side, and even in his lonely wanderings and hairbreadth escapes he was, what neither Balliol nor Wallace had been, the true head of the Scottish nation. Before the end of **1306** he reappeared in Carrick, where his own possessions lay, and where the whole population was on his side. He inflicted heavy losses on the English garrisons, and in **1307** Edward once more set out for Scotland ; but he was now old and worn out, and he died at Burgh on Sands, a few miles on the English side of the border.

21. **Edward II. and Piers Gaveston. 1307—1312.**—The new king, Edward II., was as different as possible from his father. He was not wicked, like William II. and John, but he detested the trouble of public business, and thought that the only advantage of being a king was that he would have leisure to amuse himself. During his father's life he devoted himself to Piers Gaveston, a

Gascon, who encouraged
him in his pleasures and
taught him to mistrust his
father. Edward I. banished
Gaveston ; Edward II., immediately on his accession,
not only recalled him, but
made him regent when he
himself crossed to France to
be married to Isabella, the
daughter of Philip IV. The
barons, who were already inclined to win back some of
the authority of which Edward I. had deprived them,
were very angry at the place
taken over their heads by an
upstart favourite, especially
as Gaveston was ill-bred
enough to make jests at their
expense. The barons found
a leader in Thomas, Earl of
Lancaster, the son of that
Edmund, the brother of Edward I., who had received the
title of king of Sicily from the
Pope (see p. 197). Thomas
of Lancaster had very large
estates. He was an ambitious
man, who tried to play the
part which had been played
by Earl Simon without any
of Simon's qualifications for
the position. In 1308 the
king yielded to the barons so
far as to send Gaveston out
of the country to Ireland as
his Lieutenant. In 1309 he
recalled him. The barons
were exasperated, and in the
Parliament of 1310 they
brought forward a plan for

Edward II. ; from his monument in
Gloucester Cathedral.

taking the king's government out of his hands, very much after the fashion of the Provisions of Oxford. Twenty-one barons were appointed Lords Ordainers, to draw up ordinances for the government of the country. In 1311 they produced the ordinances. Gaveston was to be banished for life. The king was to appoint officers only with the consent of the barons, without which he was not to go to war nor leave the kingdom. The ordinances may have been justified in so far as they restrained the authority of a king so incapable as Edward II. Constitutionally their acceptance was a retrograde step, as, like the Provisions of Oxford, they placed power in the hands of the barons, passing over Parliament as a whole. Edward agreed to the ordinances, but refused to surrender Gaveston. The barons took arms to enforce their will, and in 1312, having captured Gaveston, they beheaded him near Warwick without the semblance of a trial.

22. **Success of Robert Bruce.** 1307—1314.—Whilst Edward and the barons were disputing Bruce gained ground rapidly. In 1313 Stirling was the only fortress of importance in Scotland still garrisoned by the English, and the English garrison bound itself to surrender on June 24, 1314, if it had not been previously relieved. Even Edward II. was stirred by this doleful news, and in 1314 he put himself at the head of an army to relieve Stirling. Lancaster, however, and all whom he could influence refused to follow him, on the ground that the king had not, in accordance with the ordinances, received permission from the barons to go to war. On June 24 Edward reached Bannockburn, within sight of Stirling. Like his father, he brought with him English archers as well as English horsemen, but he foolishly sent his archers far in advance of his horsemen, where they would be entirely unprotected. Bruce, on the other hand, not only had a small body of horse, which rode down the archers, but he strengthened the defensive position of his spearmen by digging pits in front of his line and covering them with turf. Into these pits the foremost horses of the English cavalry plunged. Edward's whole array was soon one mass of confusion, and before it could recover itself a body of gillies, or camp-followers, appearing over a hill was taken for a fresh Scottish army. The vast English host turned and fled. Stirling at once surrendered, and all Scotland was lost to Edward. Materially, both England and Scotland suffered grievously from the result of the battle of Bannockburn. English invasions of southern Scotland and Scottish invasions of northern England spread desolation far and wide, stifling the germs of nascent civilisation. Morally, both nations were in the

end the gainers. The hardihood and self-reliance of the Scottish character is distinctly to be traced to those years of struggle against

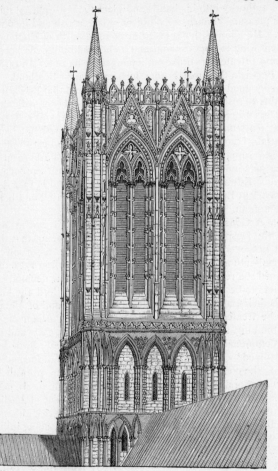

Lincoln Cathedral—the central tower ; built about 1310.

a powerful neighbour. England, too, was the better for being balked of its prey. No nation can suppress the liberty of another without endangering its own.

23. **Lancaster's Government. 1314—1322.**—Edward was thrown by his defeat entirely under the power of Lancaster, who took the whole authority into his hands and placed and displaced ministers at his pleasure. Lancaster, however, was a selfish and incompetent ruler. He allowed the Scots to ravage the north of England without venturing to oppose them, and as he could not even keep order at home, private wars broke out amongst the barons. In 1318 Bruce took Berwick, the great border fortress against Scotland. It was rather by good luck than by good management that Edward was at last able to resist Lancaster. Edward could not exist without a personal favourite, and he found one in Hugh le Despenser. Despenser was at least an Englishman, which Gaveston had not been, and his father, Hugh le Despenser the elder, did his best to raise up a party to support the king. In 1321, however, Parliament, under Lancaster's influence, declared against them and sentenced them to exile. Edward took arms for his favourites, and in 1322 defeated Lancaster at Boroughbridge, and then had him tried and beheaded at Pontefract.

24. **A Constitutional Settlement. 1322.**—Favourites as they were, the Despensers had at least the merit of seeing that the king could not overpower the barons by the mere assertion of his personal authority. At a Parliament held at York in 1322, the king obtained the revocation of the ordinances, and a declaration that 'matters to be established for the estate of our lord the king and of his heirs, and for the estate of the realm and of the people, shall be treated, accorded, and established in Parliaments by our lord the king, and by the consent of the prelates, earls and barons, and commonalty of the realm, according as hath been hitherto accustomed.' Edward I. had in 1295 gathered a full Parliament, including the commons. But there was no law to prevent him or his successors excluding the commons on some future occasion. Edward II. by this declaration, issued with consent of Parliament, confirmed his father's practice by a legislative act. Unless the law were broken or repealed, no future statute could come into existence without the consent of the commons.

25. **The Rule of the Despensers. 1322—1326.**—For some years after the execution of Lancaster, Edward, or rather the Despensers, retained power, but it was power which did not work for good. In 1323 Edward made a truce with Scotland, but the cessation of foreign war did not bring with it a cessation of troubles at home. Edward was entirely unable to control his favourites. The elder Despenser was covetous and the younger

Despenser haughty, and they both made enemies for themselves and the king. Queen Isabella was alienated from her husband, partly by his exclusive devotion to the Despensers and partly by the contempt which an active woman is apt to feel for a husband without a will of his own. In **1325** she went to France, and was soon followed by her eldest son, named Edward after his father. From that moment she conspired against her husband. In **1326** she landed, accompanied by her paramour, Robert Mortimer, and bringing with her foreign troops. The barons rose in her favour. London joined them, and all resistance was speedily beaten down. The elder Despenser was hanged by the queen at Bristol. The younger was hanged, after a form of trial, at Hereford.

26. **The Deposition and Murder of Edward II. 1327.**—Early in **1327** a Parliament met at Westminster. It was filled with the king's enemies, and under pressure from the queen and Mortimer Edward II. was compelled to sign a declaration of his own wrong-doing and incompetency, after which he formally resigned the crown. He was allowed to live for eight months, at the end of which he was brutally murdered in Berkeley Castle. The deposition of Edward II.—for his enforced resignation was practically nothing less than that—was the work of a faithless wife and of unscrupulous partisans, but at least they clothed their vengeance in the forms of Parliamentary action. It was by the action of Parliament in loosing the feudal ties by which vassals were bound to an

Sir John de Creke; from his brass at Westley Waterless, Cambridgeshire: showing armour worn between 1300 and 1335 or 1340. Date, about 1325.

unworthy king, that it rose to the full position of being the representative of the nation, and at the same time virtually proclaimed that

Howden Church, Yorkshire—the west front ; built about 1310-1320.
The tower was built between 1390 and 1407.

the wants of the nation must be satisfied at the expense of the
feudal claims of the king. The national headship of the king would

from henceforward be the distinguishing feature of his office, whilst his feudal right to personal service would grow less and less important every year.

CHAPTER XV

FROM THE ACCESSION OF EDWARD III. TO THE TREATY OF BRETIGNI

1327—1360

LEADING DATES

Reign of Edward III., 1327—1377

Accession of Edward III.	1327
Beginning of the War with France	1337
Battle of Crecy	1346
The Black Death	1348
Battle of Poitiers	1356
Treaty of Bretigni	1360

1. **Mortimer's Government. 1327—1330.**—Edward III. was only fourteen at his accession. For three years power was in the hands of his mother's paramour, Mortimer. Robert Bruce, though old and smitten with leprosy, was still anxious to wring from England an acknowledgment of Scottish independence, and, in spite of the existing truce, sent an army to ravage the northern counties of England. Edward led in person against it an English force far superior in numbers and equipment; but the English soldier needed many things, whilst the Scot contented himself with a little oatmeal carried on the back of his hardy pony. If he grew tired of that he had but to seize an English sheep or cow and to boil the flesh in the hide. Such an army was difficult to come up with. Fighting there was none, except once when the Scots broke into the English camp at night and almost succeeded in carrying off the young king. Mortimer was at his wits' end, and in **1328** agreed to a treaty acknowledging the complete independence of Scotland. It was a wise thing to do, but no nation likes to acknowledge failure, and Mortimer became widely unpopular. He succeeded indeed in breaking up a conspiracy against himself, and in **1330** even executed Edmund, Earl of Kent, a brother of Edward II. The discontented barons found another leader in the king, who, young as he was, had been married at fifteen to Philippa of Hainault. Though

he was already a father, he was still treated by Mortimer as a child, and was virtually kept a prisoner. At Nottingham he introduced a body of Mortimer's enemies into the castle through a secret passage in the rock on which it stood. His mother pleaded in vain for her favourite : " Fair son, have pity on the gentle Mortimer." Mortimer was hanged, and Queen Isabella was never again allowed to take part in public affairs.

2. **The French Succession. 1328—1331.**—Isabella's three brothers, Louis X., Philip V., and Charles IV., had successively reigned in France. Louis X. died in **1316**, leaving behind him a daughter and a posthumous son, who died a week after his birth. Then Philip V. seized the crown, his lawyers asserting that, according to the Salic law, ' no part of the heritage of Salic land can fall to a woman,' and that therefore no woman could rule in France. As a matter of fact this was a mere quibble of the lawyers. The Salic law had been the law of the Salian Franks in the fifth century, and had to do with the inheritance of estates, not with the inheritance of the throne of France, which was not at that time in existence. The quibble, however, was used on the right side. What Frenchmen wanted was that France should remain an independent nation, which it was not likely to do under a queen who might marry the king of another country. The rule thus laid down was permanently adopted in France. When Philip V. died in **1322** the throne passed, not to his daughter, but to his brother, Charles IV., and when Charles died in **1328**, to his cousin, Philip of Valois, who reigned as Philip VI. At that time England was still under the control of Mortimer and Isabella, and though Isabella, being the sister of Charles IV., thought of claiming the crown, not for herself, but for her son, Mortimer did not press the claim. In **1329** he sent Edward to do homage to Philip VI. for his French possessions, but Edward only did it with certain reservations, and in **1330** preparations for war were made in England. In **1331**, after Mortimer's fall, when Edward was his own master, he again visited France, and a treaty was concluded between the two kings in which he abandoned the reservations on his homage.

3. **Troubles in Scotland. 1329—1336.**— On his return, Edward looked in another direction. In **1329** Robert Bruce died, leaving his crown to his son, David II., a child five years old. Certain English noblemen had in the late treaty (see p. 231) been promised restoration of the estates of their ancestors in Scotland, and in **1332** some of them, finding the promise unfulfilled, offered English forces to John Balliol's son, Edward, to help him to the Scottish crown.

Effigies of Edward III. and Queen Philippa; from their tombs in Westminster Abbey.

Aided by his English allies, Edward Balliol landed in Scotland, defeated the Scottish army at Dupplin, and was crowned king. Before the end of the year he was surprised at Annan, and fled to England to appeal to Edward for help.　Though Edward had all the love of enterprise of his grandfather, Edward I., yet there was a marked contrast between the deliberate calculation of Edward I. and the almost accidental way in which Edward III. involved himself in an attempt to regain the lordship of Scotland.　In **1333** he laid siege to Berwick, then in the hands of the Scots.　The Scots advanced into England, and their spearmen crossed a marsh to attack the English array of knights and archers posted on the slope of Halidon Hill.　The arrows poured like rain on their struggling columns.　The Scots were thrown into confusion, and their whole army was almost destroyed.　Berwick was regained, and Bannockburn, it seemed, was avenged.　Edward not only set up Balliol as his vassal, but compelled him to yield all Scotland south of the Forth to be annexed to England.　Such a settlement could not last.　Balliol was as weak as his father had been, and the Scots, recovering courage, drove him out in **1334**.　Edward invaded Scotland again and again.　As long as he was in the country he was strong enough to keep his puppet on the throne, but whenever he returned to England David Bruce's supporters regained strength.　The struggle promised to be lengthy unless help came to the Scots.

4. **Dispute with France.**　**1336**—**1337**.—Philip VI., like Philip IV. in the days of Edward I. (see p. 218), had his own reasons for not allowing the Scots to be crushed.　He pursued the settled policy of his predecessors in attempting to bring the great fiefs into his power, and especially that part of Aquitaine which was still held by the most powerful of his vassals, the king of England. Whilst Edward was doing his best to bring Scotland into subjection by open war, Philip was doing his best to disturb Edward in his hold upon Aquitaine by secret intrigues and legal chicanery. Ill-feeling increased on both sides.　Philip welcomed David Bruce and gave him protection in France, and in **1336** French sailors attacked English shipping and landed plunderers in the Isle of Wight.　In **1337** Edward determined to resist, and the long war roughly known as the Hundred Years' War began.　It was in reality waged to discover by an appeal to arms whether the whole of Aquitaine was to be incorporated with France and whether Scotland was to be incorporated with England.　That which gave it its peculiar bitterness was, however not so much the claims

of the kings, as the passions of their subjects. The national antagonism aroused by the plunderings of French sea-rovers would be invigorated by the plunderings of Englishmen in the fields of France.

5. **Edward's Allies. 1337—1338.**—To Edward it was merely a question of defending, first England, and then Aquitaine, against aggression. He won over, with large offers of money, the alliance of the princes of the Empire whose lands lay round the French frontier to the north and east, and even gained the support of the Emperor Lewis the Bavarian. His relations with Flanders were even more important. In Flanders there had sprung up great manufacturing towns, such as Ghent, Bruges, and Ypres, which worked up into cloth the wool which was the produce of English sheep. These wealthy towns claimed political independence, and thus came into collision with their feudal lord, the Count of Flanders. Early in the reign of Philip VI., the Count, who held the greater part of his lands from the king of France, had appealed to Philip for support, and Philip, who, unlike his wiser predecessors, despised the strength which he might gain from the goodwill of citizens in a struggle against their lords, took the part of the Count, and for a time crushed the citizens at the battle of Cassel. After a while the cities recovered themselves, and formed an alliance under the leadership of Jacob van Arteveldt, a Flemish nobleman, who had ingratiated himself with them by enrolling himself amongst the brewers of Ghent, and who was now successful in urging his countrymen to enter into friendship with Edward.

6. **Chivalry and War.**—In the long run Edward's cause would be found a losing one, but there were circumstances which made it prevail for a time. In France there was a broad distinction between gentlemen on the one side and citizens and peasants on the other. The gentlemen despised all who were not of their own class. In earlier days there had sprung up a view of life known as chivalry, which taught that the knight was bound to observe the laws of honour, to fight fairly, to treat with courtesy a defeated enemy, and to protect women and all who were unable to help themselves. Ennobling as the idea was, it had been narrowed by the refusal of the gentlemen to extend the rules of chivalry beyond their own order, and they were, therefore, ready to exercise cruelty upon those who were not gentlemen, whilst proffering the most high-flown compliments to those who were. In France, too, this broad distinction of ranks told upon the military strength of the crown. The fighting force of the French king was

his feudal array of armour-protected cavalry, composed entirely of gentlemen, and aiming at deciding battles in the old fashion by the rush of horsemen.   If foot soldiers were brought at all into the field they were, for the most part, ill armed and ill trained peasants, exposed to be helplessly slaughtered by the horsemen.

7. **Commerce and War.**—In England, on the other hand, the various orders of society had been welded together into a united people.   The king and his vassals indeed still talked the language of chivalry, but they were wise enough to seek strength elsewhere. War had become in England the affair of the nation, and no longer

A knight—Sir Geoffrey Luttrell, who died 1345—receiving his helm and pennon from his wife.   Another lady holds his shield.

the affair of a class.   It must be waged with efficient archers as well as with efficient horsemen, the archers being drawn from the class of yeomen or free landed proprietors of small plots of land, which was entirely wanting in France.   Such an army needed pay, and the large sums required for the purpose could only be extracted from a nation which, like the English, had grown comparatively rich because it was at peace within its own borders.   Edward was compelled, if he wanted to fight, to encourage trade, though it is only fair to remember that he showed himself ready to encourage trade without any such ulterior object. He brought Flemish weavers into England, and did his best to improve the feeble woollen manufacture of the Eastern counties.

His great resource, however, for purposes of taxation, was the export of wool to the Flemish manufacturing towns. Sometimes he persuaded Parliament to raise the duties upon exported wool; sometimes he raised them, by an evasion of the law, after making a private compact with the merchants without consulting Parliament at all; sometimes he turned merchant himself and bought wool cheaply in England to sell it dear in Flanders. It was said of a great minister of later times that he made trade flourish by means of war.[1] It might be said with greater truth of Edward III. that he made war flourish by means of trade.

8. **Attacks on the North of France. 1338—1340.**—Great as was Edward's advantage in having a united nation at his back, it hardly seemed in the first years of the war as though he knew how to use it. Though he had declared war against Philip in **1337**, he did not begin hostilities till the following year. In **1338**, after landing at Antwerp, he obtained from the Emperor Lewis the title of Imperial Vicar, which gave him a right to the military services of the vassals of the Empire. Crowds of German and Low Country lords pressed into his ranks, but they all wanted high

[1] See the inscription on the monument to the elder Pitt in the Guildhall, in the City of London.

William of Hatfield, second son of Edward III.; from his tomb in York Minster: showing rich costume worn by the youth of the upper classes about 1340. The embroidery on the tunic has been partly worn off on the effigy.

York Minster :—The nave, looking west, built during the first half of the fourteenth
century.   The west window was completed and glazed in 1338.

pay, and his resources, great as they were, were soon exhausted, and he had to pawn his crowns to satisfy their needs. These lords proved as useless as they were expensive. In 1339 Edward crossed the French frontier, but he could not induce Philip to fight, and being deserted by his German allies, he was obliged to return to England. He then attempted to fall back on the support of the Flemings, but was told by them that unless he formally took the title of king of France, which he had only occasionally done before, they could not fight for him, as the king of France, whoever he might

be, was their superior lord, and as such had a claim to their services. After some hesitation, in the beginning of 1340, Edward satisfied their scruples by reviving the claim which he had formerly abandoned, declaring himself to be, in right of his mother, the lawful king of France ; and quartering the French arms with his own. A third territorial question was thus added to the other two. Practically Edward's answer to Philip's effort to absorb all Aquitaine in France was a counterdemand that all France should be absorbed in England.

Royal arms of Edward III., adopted in 1340 and used till about 1405.
From the tomb of Edward III.

9. **Battle of Sluys. 1340.**—Edward had not yet learnt to place confidence in those English archers who had served him so well at Halidon Hill. In 1340, however, he found himself engaged in a conflict which should have taught him where his true strength lay. The French navy held the Channel, and had burnt Southampton. The fleet of the Cinque Ports was no longer sufficient to cope with the enemy. Edward proudly announced that he, like his progenitors, was the lord of the English sea on every side, and called out every vessel upon which he could lay hands. The result was a naval victory at Sluys, in which well-nigh the whole French fleet was absolutely destroyed. It was by the English archers that

the day was won. So complete was the victory that no one dared to tell the ill news to Philip, till his jester called out to him, "What cowards those English are!" "Because," he explained, "they did not dare to leap into the sea as our brave Frenchmen did."

10. **Attacks on the West of France. 1341—1345.**—If Edward was to obtain still greater success, he had but to fight with a national force behind him on land as he had fought at sea; but he was slow to learn the lesson. Personally he was as chivalrous as Philip, and thought that far more could be done by the charge of knights on horseback than by the cloth-yard shafts of the English bowmen. For six more years he frittered away his strength. There was a disputed succession in Brittany, and one of the claimants, John of Montfort, ranged himself on the side of the English. There was fighting in Brittany and fighting on the borders of Edward's lands in Aquitaine, but up to the end of 1345 there was no decisive result on either side. In Scotland, too, things had been going so badly for Edward that in 1341 David Bruce had been able to return, and was now again ruling over his own people.

11. **The Campaign of Creçy. 1346.**—Surprising as Edward's neglect to force on a battle in France appears to us, it must be remembered that in those days it was far more difficult to bring on an engagement than it is in the present day. Fortified towns and castles were then almost impregnable, except when they were starved out; and it was therefore seldom necessary for a commander—on other grounds unwilling to fight—to risk a battle in order to save an important post from capture. Edward, however, does not appear to have thought that there was anything to be gained by fighting. In 1346 he led a large English army into Normandy, taking with him his eldest son, afterwards known as the Black Prince, at that time a lad of sixteen. It had been from Normandy and Calais that the fleets had put out by which the coasts of England had been ravaged, and Edward now deliberately ravaged Normandy. He then marched on, apparently intending to take refuge in Flanders. As the French had broken the bridges over the Seine, he was driven to ascend the bank of the river almost to Paris before he could cross. His burnings and his ravages continued till Philip, stung to anger, pursued him with an army more than twice as numerous as his own. Edward had the Somme to cross on his way, and the bridges over that river had been broken by the French, as those over the Seine had been broken; and but for the opportune discovery of a ford at Blanche Tache Edward would have been

obliged to fight with an impassable river at his back. When he was once over the Somme he refused—not from any considerations of generalship, but from a point of honour—to continue his retreat further. He halted on a gentle slope near the village of Creçy facing eastwards, as Philip's force had swept round to avoid difficulties in the ground, and was approaching from that direction.

12. **The Tactics of Creçy. 1346.**—Great as was Edward's advantage in possessing an army so diverse in its composition as that which he commanded, it would have availed him little if he had not known how to order that army for battle. At once it appeared that his skill as a tactician was as great as his weakness as a strategist. His experience at Halidon Hill (see p. 234) had taught him that the archers could turn the tide of battle against any direct attack, however violent. He knew, too, from the tradition of Bannockburn (see p. 226), that archers could readily be

Shooting at the butts with the long-bow.

crushed by a cavalry charge on the flank; and he was well aware that his own horsemen were in too small numbers to hold out against the vast host of the French cavalry. He therefore drew up his line of archers between the two villages of Creçy and Vadicourt, though his force was not large enough to extend from one to the other. He then ordered the bulk of his horsemen to dismount and to place themselves with levelled spears in bodies at intervals in the line of archers. The innovation was thoroughly reasonable, as spearmen on foot would be able to check the fiercest charge of horse, if only the horse could be exposed to a shower of arrows. The English army was drawn up in three corps, two of them in the front line. The Black Prince was in command of one of the two bodies in front, whilst the king himself took charge of the third corps, which acted as a reserve in the rear.

R

13. **The Battle of Creçy. August 26, 1346.**—When Philip drew nigh in the evening his host was weary and hungry. He ordered his knights to halt, but each one was thinking, not of obeying orders, but of securing a place in the front, where he might personally distinguish himself. Those in the rear pushed on, and in a few minutes the whole of the French cavalry became a disorganised mob. Then Philip ordered 15,000 Genoese crossbowmen to advance against the enemy. At the best a crossbow was inferior to the English long-bow, as it was weaker in its action and consumed more time between each shot. To make matters worse, a heavy shower of rain had wetted the strings of the unlucky Genoese, rendering their weapons useless. The English had covers for their bows, and had kept them dry. The thick shower of their arrows drove the Genoese back. Philip took their retreat for cowardice. "Kill me those scoundrels!" he cried, and the French knights rode in amongst them, slaughtering them at every stride. Then the French horsemen charged the English lines. Some one amongst the Black Prince's retinue took alarm, and hurried to the king to conjure him to advance to the son's assistance. Edward knew better. "Is he dead?" he asked, "or so wounded that he cannot help himself?" "No, sire, please God," was the reply, "but he is in a hard passage of arms, and he much needs your help." "Return," answered the king, "to those that sent you, and tell them not to send to me again so long as my son lives; I command them to let the boy win his spurs." The French were driven off with terrible slaughter, and the victory was won. It was a victory of foot soldiers over horse soldiers—of a nation in which all ranks joined heartily together over one in which all ranks except that of the gentry were despised. Edward III. had contributed a high spirit and a keen sense of honour, but it was to the influence of Edward I.—to his wide and far-reaching statesmanship, and his innovating military genius—that the victory of Creçy was really due.

14. **Battle of Nevill's Cross, and the Siege of Calais. 1346–1347.**—Whilst Edward was fighting in France, the Scots invaded England, but they were defeated at Nevill's Cross, and their king, David Bruce (David II.), taken prisoner. Edward, when the news reached him, had laid siege to Calais. In this siege cannon,[1] which had been used in earlier sieges of the war, were employed, but they were too badly made and loaded with too little gunpowder to do much damage.

---

1 It has been said that they were used at Creçy, but this is uncertain.

In **1347** Calais was starved into surrender, and Edward, who regarded the town as a nest of pirates, ordered six of the principal burgesses to come out with ropes round their necks, as a sign that they were to be put to death. It was only at Queen Philippa's intercession that he spared their lives, but he drove every Frenchman out of Calais, and peopled it with his own subjects. A truce with Philip was agreed on, and Edward returned to England.

15. **Constitutional Progress. 1337—1347.** —Edward III. had begun his reign as a constitutional ruler, and on the whole he had no reason to regret it. In his wars with France and Scotland he had the popular feeling with him, and he showed his reliance on it when, in **1340**, he consented to the abolition of his claim to impose tallage on his demesne lands (see p. 221)—the sole fragment of unparliamentary taxation legally retained by the king after the *Confirmatio Cartarum.* In **1341** the two

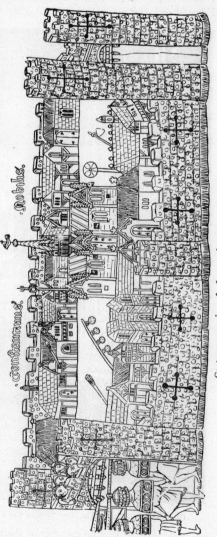

Contemporary view of a fourteenth-century walled town.

Houses of Parliament finally separated from one another, and when Edward picked a quarrel with Archbishop Stratford, the Lords suc-

Gloucester Cathedral. The choir, looking east : built between 1340 and 1350.

cessfully insisted that no member of their House could be tried excepting by his peers. The Commons, on the other hand, were striving

—not always successfully—to maintain their hold upon taxation. In **1341** they made Edward a large money grant on condition of his yielding to their demands, and Edward (whose constitutional intentions were seldom proof against his wish to retain the power of the purse) shamelessly broke his engagement after receiving the money. On other occasions the Commons were more successful ; yet, after all, the composition of their House was of more importance than

The upper chamber or solar at Sutton Courtenay manor-house.
Date, about 1350.

any special victory they might gain. In it the county members— or knights of the shire—sat side by side with the burgesses of the towns. In no other country in Europe would this have been possible. The knights of the shire were gentlemen, who on the Continent were reckoned amongst the nobility, and despised townsmen far too much to sit in the same House with them. In England there was the same amalgamation of classes in Parliament as on the battle-field. When once gentlemen and burgesses formed part of the same assembly, they would come to have common interests; and, in any struggle in which the merchants were engaged, it would be a great gain to them that a class of men trained to arms would be inclined to take their part.

16. **Edward's Triumph. 1347.**—Edward's return after the surrender of Calais was followed by an outburst of luxury. As the sea-rovers of Normandy and Calais had formerly plundered Eng-

Interior of the Hall at Penshurst, Kent: showing the screen with minstrels' gallery over it, and the brazier for fire in the middle: built about 1340.

lishmen, English landsmen now plundered Normandy and Calais. " There was no woman who had not gotten garments, furs, featherbeds, and utensils from the spoils." Edward surrounded himself with feasting and jollity. About this time he instituted the Order of the Garter, and his tournaments were thronged with gay knights and gayer ladies in gorgeous attires. The very priests caught the example, and decked themselves in unclerical garments. Even architecture lent itself to the prevailing taste for magnificence. The beautiful Decorated style which had come into use towards the

end of the reign of Edward I.—and which may be seen [1] in the central
tower of Lincoln Cathedral (see p. 227), in the west front of Howden
Church (see p. 230), and in the nave of York Minster (see p. 238)—

A small house or cottage at Meare, Somerset.   Built about 1350.

Norborough Hill, Northamptonshire.   A manor-house built about 1350.
The dormer windows and addition to the left are of much later date.

was, in the reign of Edward III., superseded by the Perpendicular
style, in which beauty of form was abandoned for the sake of breadth,
as in the choir of Gloucester and the nave of Winchester (see pp. 244,

[1] Lichfield Cathedral (p. 213) is transitional.

276).   Roofs become wide, as in the Hall of Penshurst (see p. 246),
and consequently halls were larger and better adapted to crowded
gatherings than those at Meare and Norborough (p. 247).

17. **The Black Death.   1348.**—In the midst of this luxurious
society arrived, in 1348, a terrible plague which had been sweeping
over Asia and Europe, and which in modern times has been styled
the Black Death.   No plague known to history was so destructive of life.   Half of the population certainly perished, and some
think that the number of those who died must be reckoned at
two-thirds.

18. **The Statute of Labourers.   1349.**—This enormous destruction of life could not fail to have important results on the economic

Ploughing.

condition of the country.   The process of substituting money rents
for labour service, which had begun some generations before
(see p. 168), had become very general at the accession of Edward
III. so that the demesne land which the lord kept in his own

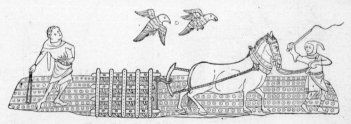

Harrowing.   A boy slinging stones at the birds.

hands was on most estates cultivated by hired labour.   Now, when
at least half of the labourers had disappeared, those who remained,
having less competition to fear, demanded higher wages, whilst at
the same time the price of the produce of the soil was the same or
less than it had been before.   The question affected not merely

the great lords but the smaller gentry as well. The House of Commons, which was filled with the smaller gentry and the well-to-do townsmen—who were also employers of labour—was therefore as eager as the House of Lords to keep down wages. In **1349**

Breaking the clods with mallets

Cutting weeds.

Reaping.

the Statute of Labourers was passed, fixing a scale of wages at the rates which had been paid before the Black Death, and ordering punishments to be inflicted on those who demanded more. It is not necessary to suppose that the legislators had any

tyrannical intentions. For ages all matters relating to agriculture had been fixed by custom ; and the labourers were outrage-
ously violating custom. Custom, however, here found itself in

Stacking corn.

opposition to the forces of nature, and though the statute was often
renewed, with increasing penalties, it was difficult to secure obedience to it in the teeth of the opposition of the labourers. The

Threshing corn with the flail.

chief result of the statute was that it introduced an element of discord
between two classes of society.

19. **The Statute of Treasons. 1352.**—In **1352** was passed the
Statute of Treasons, by which the offences amounting to treason
were defined, the chief of them being levying war against the

king. As no one but a great nobleman was strong enough even to think of levying war against the king, this statute may be regarded as a concession to the wealthier landowners rather than to the people at large.

20. **The Black Prince in the South of France. 1355.**—In 1350 Philip VI. of France died, and was succeeded by his son John. The truce (see p. 243) was prolonged, and it was not till 1355 that war was renewed. Edward himself was recalled to England by fresh troubles in Scotland, but the Black Prince landed at Bordeaux and marched through the south of France, plundering as he went. Neither father nor son seems to have had any idea of gaining their ends except by driving the French by ill-treatment into submission. "You must know," wrote a contemporary in describing the condition of southern Languedoc, "that this was, before, one of the fat countries of the world, the people good and simple, who did not know what war was, and no war had ever been waged against them before the Prince of Wales came. The English and Gascons found the country full and gay, the rooms furnished with carpets and draperies, the caskets and chests full of beautiful jewels ; but nothing was safe from these robbers." The Prince returned to Bordeaux laden with spoils.

21. **The Battle of Poitiers. 1356.**—In 1356 the Black Prince swept over central France in another similar plundering expedition. He was on his way back with his plunder to Bordeaux with no more than 8,000 men to guard it when he learnt as he passed near Poitiers that King John was close to him with 50,000. He drew up his little force on a rising ground amidst thick vineyards, with a hedge in front of him behind which he could shelter his archers. As at Crécy, the greater part of the English horsemen were dismounted, and John, thinking that therein lay their secret of success, ordered most of his horsemen to dismount as well, not having discovered that though spearmen on foot could present a formidable resistance to a cavalry charge, they were entirely useless in attacking a strong position held by archers. Then he sent forward 300 knights who retained their horses, bidding a strong body of dismounted horsemen to support them. The horsemen, followed by the footmen, charged at a gap in the hedge, but the hedge on either side was lined with English bowmen, and men and horses were struck down. Those who survived fled and scattered their countrymen behind. Seeing the disorder, the Black Prince ordered the few knights whom he had kept on horseback to sweep round and to fall upon the confused crowd in the flank. The

archers advanced to second them, and, gallantly as the French fought, their unhorsed knights could accomplish nothing against the combined efforts of horse and foot. King John was taken prisoner and the battle was at an end.

22. **The Courtesy of the Black Prince.**—The Black Prince had been cruel to townsmen and peasants, but he was a model of chivalry, and knew how to deal with a captive king. At supper he stood behind John's chair and waited on him, praising his bravery. "All on our side," he said, "who have seen you and your knights, are agreed about this, and give you the prize and the chaplet if you will wear it." After the astounding victory of Poitiers, the Black Prince, instead of marching upon Paris, went back to Bordeaux. In 1357 he made a truce for two years and returned to England with his royal captive.

23. **Misery of France. 1356—1359.**—In 1356, the year in which the Black Prince fought at Poitiers, his father ravaged Scotland. Edward, however, gained nothing by this fresh attempt at conquest. In his retreat he suffered heavy loss, and in 1357, changing his plan, he replaced David Bruce (see p. 242) on the throne, and strove to win the support of the Scots instead of exasperating them by violence. In the meanwhile the two years' truce brought no good to France. The nobles wrung from the peasants the sums needed to redeem their relatives, who were prisoners in England, and the disbanded soldiers, French and English, formed themselves into free companies and plundered as mercilessly as the Black Prince had done in time of war. Worn down with oppression, the French peasants broke into a rebellion known as the Jacquerie, from the nickname of Jacques-Bonhomme, which the gentry gave to them. After committing unheard-of cruelties the peasants were repressed and slaughtered. An attempt of the States-General—a sort of French Parliament which occasionally met—to improve the government failed. Peace with England was talked of, but Edward's terms were too hard to be accepted, and in 1359 war began again.

24. **Edward's Last Invasion. 1359—1360.**—So miserably devastated was France that Edward, when he invaded the country in 1359, had to take with him not only men and munitions of war, but large stores of provisions. He met no enemy in the field, but the land had been so wasted that his men suffered much from want of food, in spite of the supplies which they had taken with them. "I could not believe," wrote an Italian who revisited France after an absence of some years, "that this was the same

kingdom which I had once seen so rich and flourishing. Nothing presented itself to my eyes but a fearful solitude, an extreme poverty, land uncultivated, houses in ruins. Even the neighbour-hood of Paris manifested everywhere marks of destruction and conflagration. The streets were deserted ; the roads overgrown with weeds ; the whole a vast solitude." In the spring of 1360 Edward moved on towards the banks of the Loire, hoping to find sustenance there. Near Chartres he was overtaken by a terrible storm of hail and thunder, and in the roar of the thunder he thought

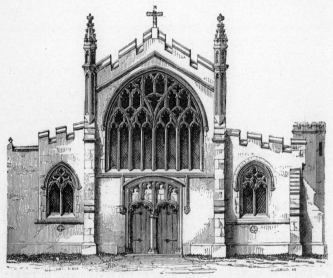

West front of Edington Church, Wilts : built about 1360.
An example of the transition from the Decorated style to the Perpendicular.

that he heard the voice of God reproving him for the misery which he had caused. He abated his demands and signed the treaty of Bretigni.

25. **The Treaty of Bretigni. 1360.**—By the treaty of Bretigni John was to be ransomed for an enormous sum ; Edward was to surrender his claim to the crown of France and to the provinces north of Aquitaine, receiving in return the whole of the duchy of Aquitaine together with the districts round Calais and Ponthieu, all of them to be held in full sovereignty, without any feudal obliga-

tion to the king of France. Probably it cost Edward little to abandon his claim to the French crown, which had only been an after-thought ; and it was a clear gain to get rid of those feudal entanglements which had so frequently been used as a pretext of aggression against the English kings. It was hardly likely, however, that England would long be able to keep a country like Aquitaine, which was geographically part of France and in which French sympathies were constantly on the increase. " We will obey the English with our lips," said the men of Rochelle, when their town was surrendered, " but our hearts shall never be moved towards them."

CHAPTER XVI

REIGN OF EDWARD III. AFTER THE TREATY OF BRETIGNI

1360—1377

LEADING DATES

Reign of Edward III., 1327-1377.

Battle of Navarrete	1367
Renewal of war with France	1369
Truce with France	1375
The Good Parliament	1376
Death of Edward III.	1377

1. **The First Years of Peace. 1360—1364.**—To hold his new provinces the better, Edward sent the Black Prince to govern them in 1363 with the title of Duke of Aquitaine. King John had been liberated soon after the making of the peace, and had been allowed to return to France on payment of part of his ransom, and on giving hostages for the payment of the remainder. In 1363 one of the hostages, his son, the Duke of Anjou, broke his parole and fled, on which John, shocked at such perfidy, returned to England to make excuses for him, and died there in 1364. If honour, he said, were not to be found elsewhere, it ought to be found in the breasts of kings.

2. **The Spanish Troubles. 1364—1368.**—John's eldest son and successor, Charles V., known as the Wise, or the Prudent, was less chivalrous, but more cautious than his father, and soon found an opportunity of stirring up trouble for the Black Prince without exposing his own lands to danger. Pedro the Cruel, king of Castile, who had for some time been the ally of England, had murdered

his wife, tyrannised over his nobles, and contracted an alliance with the Mohammedans of Granada. The Pope having excommunicated him, his own illegitimate brother, Henry of Trastamara, claimed the crown, and sought aid of the king of France. Charles V. sent Bertrand du Guesclin, a rising young commander, to his help. Du Guesclin's army was made up of men of the Free Companies (see p. 252), which still continued to plunder France on their own account after the Peace of Bretigni. In this way Charles got rid of a scourge of his own country at the same time that he attacked an ally of the English. In **1366** Du Guesclin entered Spain. The tyrannical Pedro took refuge at Bayonne, where he begged the Black Prince to help him. The Gascon nobles pleaded with the Prince to reject the monster, but the Prince was not to be held back. "It is not a right thing or reasonable," he said, when they

A gold noble of Edward III., struck between A.D. 1360 and 1369.

urged him to keep aloof from the unjust undertaking to which he invited them, "that a bastard should hold a kingdom, and thrust out of it, and of his heritage, a brother and heir of the land by legal marriage. All kings and sons of kings should never agree nor consent to it, for it is a great blow at the royal state." In **1367** the Black Prince entered Spain, and with the help of his English archers thoroughly defeated Henry at Navarrete. Then vengeance overtook him on the side on which he had sinned. Pedro was as false as he was cruel, and refused to pay the sums which he had engaged to furnish to the Prince's troops. Sickness broke out in the English ranks, and the Black Prince returned to Bordeaux with only a fifth part of his army, and with his own health irretrievably shattered. In **1368** Henry made his way back to Spain, defeated and slew Pedro, and undid the whole work of the Black Prince to the south of the Pyrenees.

Effigy of Edward the Black Prince, from his tomb at Canterbury : showing the type of armour worn from 1335 to 1400.

3. **The Taxation of Aquitaine. 1368—1369.**—Worse than this was in store for the Black Prince. As his soldiers clamoured for their wages, he levied a hearth tax to supply their needs. The Aquitanian Parliament declared against the tax, and appealed to the king of France to do them right. In **1369** Charles, who knew that the men of Aquitaine would be on his side, summoned the Black Prince to Paris to defend his conduct, on the pretext that, as there had been some informality in the treaty of Bretigni, he was himself still the feudal superior of the Duke of Aquitaine. " Willingly," replied the Black Prince when he received the summons, " we will go to the court of Paris, as the king of France orders it ; but it shall be with helmet on head and sixty thousand men with us."

4. **The Renewed War. 1369—1375.**—Edward, by the advice of Parliament, resumed the title of King of France, and war broke out afresh in **1369**. The result of the first war had been owing to the blunders of the French in attacking the English archers with the feudal cavalry. Charles V. and his commander, Du Guesclin, resolved to fight no battles. Their troops hung about the

English march, cut off stragglers, and captured exposed towns. The English marched hither and thither, plundering and burning, but their armies, powerful as they were when attacked in a defensive position, could not succeed in forcing a battle, and were worn out without accomplishing anything worthy of their fame. The Black Prince, soured by failure and ill-health, having succeeded in **1370** in recapturing Limoges, ordered his men to spare no one in the town. " It was great pity," wrote the chronicler Froissart, " for men, women, and children threw themselves on their knees before the Prince, crying ' Mercy ! mercy ! gentle Sire !'"   The Prince, who had waited at table behind a captive king, hardened his heart. More than three thousand—men, women and children—were butchered on that day.   Yet the spirit of chivalry was strong within him, and he spared three gentlemen who fought bravely merely in order to sell their lives dearly.   In **1371** the Black Prince was back in England.   His eldest surviving brother, John of Gaunt— or Ghent—Duke of Lancaster, continued the war in France.   In **1372** the English lost town after town.   In **1373** John of Gaunt set out from Calais.   He could plunder, but he could not make the enemy fight.   " Let them go," wrote Charles V. to his com- manders ; " by burning they will not become masters of your heritage.   Though storms rage over a land, they disperse of them- selves.   So will it be with these English."   When the English reached the hilly centre of France food failed them.   The winter came, and horses and men died of cold and want.   A rabble of half-starved fugitives was all that reached Bordeaux after a march of six hundred miles.   Aquitaine, where the inhabitants were for the most part hostile to the English, and did everything in their power to assist the French, was before long all but wholly lost, and in **1375** a truce was made which put an end to hostilities for a time, leaving only Calais, Cherbourg, Brest, Bayonne, and Bordeaux in the hands of the English.

5. **Anti-Papal Legislation. 1351—1366.**—The antagonism be- tween England and France necessarily led to an antagonism between England and the Papacy.   Since **1305** the Popes had fixed their abode at Avignon, and though Avignon was not yet incorporated with France, it was near enough to be under the control of the king of France.   During the time of this exile from Rome, known to ardent churchmen as the Babylonian captivity of the Church, the Popes were regarded in England as the tools of the French enemy.   The Papal court, too, became distinguished for luxury and vice, and its vast expenditure called for supplies which England was increasingly

S

loth to furnish. By a system of provisions, as they were called, the Pope provided—or appointed beforehand—his nominees to English benefices, and expected that his nominees would be allowed to hold the benefices to the exclusion of those of the patrons. In **1351** the Statute of Provisors [1] attempted to put an end to the system, but it was not immediately successful, and had to be re-enacted in later years. In **1353** a Statute of *Præmunire* [2] was passed, in which, though the Pope's name was not mentioned, an attempt was made to stop suits being carried before foreign courts—in other words, before the Papal court at Avignon. Another claim of the Popes was to the 1,000 marks payable annually as a symbol of John's vassal-age, a claim most distasteful to Englishmen as a sign of national humiliation. Since **1333**, the year in which Edward took the government into his own hands, the payment had not been made, and in **1366** Parliament utterly rejected a claim made by the Pope for its revival.

6. **Predominance of the English Language.**—The national spirit which revealed itself in an armed struggle with the French and in a legal struggle with the Papacy showed itself in the increasing predominance of the English language. In **1362** it supplanted French in the law courts, and in the same year Parliament was opened with an English speech. French was still the language of the court, but it was becoming a foreign speech, pronounced very differently from the ' French of Paris.'

7. **Piers the Plowman. 1362.**—Cruel as had been the direct results of the English victories in France, they had indirectly contributed to the overthrow of that feudalism which weighed heavily upon France and upon all Continental Europe. The success of the English had been the success of a nation strong in the union of classes. The cessation of the war drove the thoughts of Englishmen back upon themselves. The old spiritual channels had been, to a great extent, choked up. Bishops were busy with the king's affairs ; monks had long ceased to be specially an example to the world ; and even the friars had fallen from their first estate, and had found out that, though they might personally possess nothing, their order might be wealthy. The men who won victories in France came home to spend their booty in show and luxury. Yet, for all the splendour around, there was a general feeling that the times were out of joint, and this feeling was strengthened by a fresh in-

[1] Provisors are the persons provided or appointed to a benefice.

[2] So called from the first words of the writs appointed to be issued under it, *Præmunire facias* ; the first of these two words being a corruption of *Præmoneri*.

road of the Black Death in **1361**.   To the prevalent yearning for a
better life, a voice was given by William Langland, whose *Vision
of Piers the Plowman* appeared in its first shape in **1362**.   In the
opening of his poem he shows to his readers the supremacy of the
Maiden Meed—bribery—over all sorts and conditions of men, lay
and clerical.   Then he turns to the purification of this wicked world.
They who wish to eschew evil and to do good inquire their way
to Truth—the eternal God—and find their only guide in ' Piers the
Plowman.'   The simple men of the plough, who do honest work
and live upright lives, know how to find the way to Truth.   That
way lies not through the inventions of the official Church, the
pardons and indulgences set up for sale.   " They who have done
good shall go into eternal life, but they who have done evil into
eternal fire."   Langland's teaching, in short, is the same as that
of the great Italian poet, Dante, who, earlier in the century, had
cried aloud for the return of justice and true religion.   He stands
apart from Dante and from all others of his time in looking for
help to the despised peasant.   No doubt his peasant was idealised, as no one knew better than himself; but it was honesty of
work in the place of dishonest idleness which he venerated.   It
was the glory of England to have produced such a thought far more
than to have produced the men who, heavy with the plunder of unhappy peasants, stood boldly to their arms at Creçy and Poitiers.
He is as yet hardly prepared to say what is the righteousness which
leads to eternal life.   It is not till he issues a second edition in **1377**
that he can answer.   To do well, he now tells us, is to act right-
eously to all in the fear of God.   To do better is to walk in the
way of love : " Behold how good a thing it is for brethren to dwell
in unity."   To do best is to live in fellowship with Christ and the
Church, and in all humility to bring forth the fruits of the Divine
communion.

8. **The Anti-Clerical Party. 1371.**—Langland wished to improve,
not to overthrow, existing institutions, but for all that his work was
profoundly revolutionary.   They who call on those who have left
their first love to return to it are seldom obeyed, but their voice is
often welcomed by the corrupt and self-seeking crowd which is eager,
after the fashion of birds of prey, to tear the carcase from which
life has departed.   A large party was formed in England, especially
amongst the greater barons, which was anxious to strip the clergy
of their wealth and power, without any thought for the better fulfil-
ment of their spiritual functions.   In the Parliament of **1371** bishops
were declared unfit to hold offices of state.   Amongst others who

were dismissed was William of Wykeham, the Bishop of Winchester. He was a great architect and administrator, and having been deprived of the Chancellorship used his wealth to found at Winchester the first great public school in England. By this time a Chancellor was no longer what he had been in earlier days (see p. 127), a secretary to the king. He was now beginning to exercise equitable jurisdiction—that is to say, the right of deciding suits according to equity, in cases in which the strict artificial rules of the ordinary courts stood in the way of justice.

William of Wykeham, Bishop of Winchester, 1367-1404 : from his tomb at Winchester.

9. **The Duke of Lancaster. 1374 —1376.**—In 1374, as soon as the Duke of Lancaster returned from his disastrous campaign (see p. 257), he put himself at the head of the baronial and anti-clerical party. He was selfish and unprincipled, but he had enormous wealth, having secured the vast estates of the Lancaster family by his marriage with Blanche, the granddaughter of the brother of Thomas of Lancaster, the opponent of Edward II. Rich as he was he wished to be richer, and he saw his opportunity in an attack upon the higher clergy, which might end in depriving them not only of political power, but of much of their ecclesiastical property as well. His accession to the baronial party was of the greater importance because he was now practically the first man in the state. The king was suffering from softening of the brain, and had fallen under the influence of a greedy and unscrupulous mistress, Alice Perrers, whilst the Black Prince was disqualified by illness from taking part in the management of affairs. A bargain was struck between the Duke and Alice Perrers, who was able to obtain the consent of the helpless king to anything she pleased. She even sat on the bench with the judges, intimidating them into deciding in favour of the suitors who had bribed her most highly. It seemed as if Langland's

Meed (see p. 259) had appeared in person. The king's patronage was shared between her and Lancaster.

10. **John Wycliffe. 1366—1376.**—If Lancaster's character had been higher, he might have secured a widespread popularity, as the feeling of the age was adverse to the continuance of a wealthy clergy. Even as things were, he had on his side John Wycliffe, the most able reasoner and devoted reformer of his age, who, like others before and after him, imagined that a high spiritual enterprise could be achieved with the help of low and worldly politicians. Wycliffe had distinguished himself at Oxford, and had attracted Lancaster's notice by the ability of his argument against the Pope's claim to levy John's tribute (see p. 258). In 1374 he had been sent to Bruges to argue with the representatives of the Pope on the question of the provisions, and by 1376 had either issued, or was preparing to issue, his work *On Civil Lordship*, in which, by a curious adaptation of feudal ideas, he declared that all men held their possessions direct from God, as a vassal held his estate from his lord ; and that as a vassal was bound to pay certain military services, failing which he lost his estate, so everyone who fell into mortal sin failed to pay his service to God, and forfeited his right to his worldly possessions. In this way dominion, as he said, was founded on grace—that is to say, the continuance of man's right to his possessions depended on his remaining in a state of grace. It is true that Wycliffe qualified his argument by alleging that he was only announcing theoretical truth, and that no man had a right to rob another of his holding because he believed him to be living in sin. It is evident, however, that men like Lancaster would take no heed of this distinction, and would welcome Wycliffe as an ally in the work of despoiling the clergy for their own purposes.

11. **Lancaster and the Black Prince. 1376.**—Ordinary citizens, who cared nothing for theories which they did not understand, were roused against Lancaster by the unblushing baseness of his rule. Nor was this all. The anti-clerical party was also a baronial party, and ever since the Knights Bachelors of England had turned to the future Edward I. to defend them against the barons who made the Provisions of Oxford (see p. 199), the country gentry and townsmen had learnt the lesson that they would be the first to suffer from the unchecked rule of the baronage. They now had the House of Commons to represent their wishes, but as yet the House of Commons was too weak to stand alone. At last it was rumoured that when the Black Prince died his young son Richard was to be set aside, and that Lancaster was to claim the inheritance of the

crown, as an earlier John had claimed it in the place of the youthful Arthur. The Black Prince awoke from his lethargy, and stood forward as the leader of the Commons.

12. **The Good Parliament. 1376.**—A Parliament, known as the Good Parliament, met in **1376**, and, strong through the Black Prince's support, the Commons refused to grant supply till an account of the receipts and expenditure had been laid before them. "What," cried Lancaster, "do these base and ignoble knights attempt? Do they think they be the kings and princes of the land? I think they know not what power I am of. I will therefore, early in the morning, appear unto them so glorious, and will show such power among them, and with such vigour I will terrify them that neither they nor theirs shall dare henceforth to provoke me to wrath." Lancaster soon found that his brother was stronger than he. The Commons obtained a new Council, in which Wykeham was included and from which Lancaster was shut out. They then proceeded to accuse before the House of Lords Richard Lyons and Lord Latimer of embezzling the king's revenue. Lyons, accustomed to the past ways of the court, packed 1,000*l.* in a barrel and sent it to the Black Prince. The Black Prince returned the barrel and the money, and the Lords condemned Lyons to imprisonment. Latimer was also sentenced to imprisonment, but he was allowed to give bail and regained his liberty. These two cases are the first instances of the exercise of the right of impeachment – that is to say, of the accusation of political offenders by the Commons before the Lords. Alice Perrers was next driven from court.

13. **The Last Year of Edward III. 1376—1377.** Whilst Parliament was still sitting the Black Prince, worn out by his exertions, died. His son, young Richard, was at once recognised as heir to the throne. Lancaster, however, regained his influence over his doting father. Alice Perrers and Lord Latimer found their way back to court. The Speaker of the House of Commons was thrown into prison. Frivolous charges were brought against Wykeham, who was deprived of his temporalities and banished from the court. In **1377** a new Parliament, elected under Lancaster's influence, reversed all the proceedings of the Good Parliament, and showed how little sympathy the baronial party had with the people by imposing a poll tax of 4*d.* a head on all except beggars, thus making the payment of a labourer and a duke equal. The bishops, unable to strike at Lancaster, struck at Wycliffe, as his creature. Wycliffe was summoned to appear before an ecclesias-

tical court at St. Paul's, presided over by Courtenay, the Bishop of London. He came supported by Lancaster and a troop of Lancaster's followers. Hot words were exchanged between them and

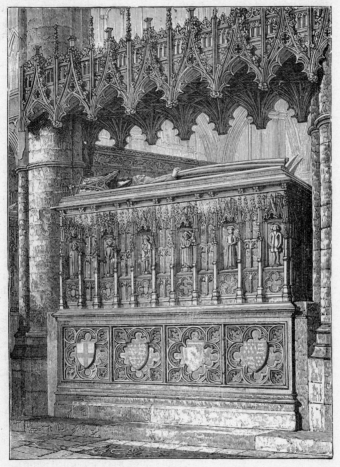

Tomb of Edward III. in Westminster Abbey.

the Bishop. The London crowd took their Bishop's part and the Duke was compelled to flee for his life. In the summer of 1377

Edward III. died, deserted by everyone, Alice Perrers making off, after robbing him of his finger-rings.

14. **Ireland from the Reign of John to that of Edward II.**— When England was gradually losing its hold on France, what hold it had had on Ireland was gradually slipping away. Henry II. had been quite unable to effect in Ireland the kind of conquest which William the Conqueror had effected in England. William had succeeded because he had been able to secure order by placing himself at the head of the conquered nation. In Ireland, in the first place, the king was a perpetual absentee ; and, in the second place, there was no Irish national organisation at the head of which he could have placed himself, even if he had from time to time visited the island. There were separate tribes, each one attached to its own chief and to its own laws and customs. They were unable to drive out their feudal conquerors ; but in the outlying parts of the country, they were able to absorb them, just as the English in their own country absorbed their Norman con-

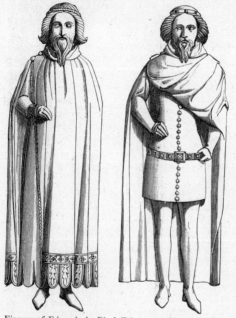

Figures of Edward, the Black Prince, and Lionel, Duke of Clarence, from the tomb of Edward III.; illustrating the ordinary costume of gentlemen at the end of the fourteenth century.

querors. The difference was that in England the conquerors were absorbed into a nation : in Ireland they were absorbed into the several tribes. The few who retained the English laws and habits were, for the most part, confined to the part of Ireland in the neighbourhood of Dublin, which was specially accessible to English influences. In **1315** Edward Bruce, the brother of Robert Bruce, invaded Ireland, and, though he was ultimately defeated and slain, he did enough to shatter the power of the English nobility ; and it was mainly in consequence of his partial success that the authority of the English government was, for some time to come, limited to a certain district round Dublin, known about a century later as the English Pale, the extent of which varied from time to time.

15. **The Statute of Kilkenny. 1367.**—As long as the French wars lasted the attention of the English Government was diverted from Ireland. In 1361, however, the year after the Treaty of Bretigni, the king's son, Lionel Duke of Clarence, was sent to extend English rule. In 1367 he gathered a Parliament of the English colonists. This Parliament passed the Statute of Kilkenny, by which the relations between the two races were defined. Within the Pale English laws and customs were to prevail, and even Irishmen living there were to be debarred from the use of their own language. Beyond the Pale the Irish were to be left to themselves, communication between the two peoples being cut off as much as possible. The idea of conquering Ireland was abandoned, and the idea of maintaining a colony on a definite part of Irish soil was substituted for it. The Statute of Kilkenny was, in short, a counterpart of the Treaty of Bretigni. In both cases Edward III. preferred the full maintenance of his authority over a part of a country to its assertion over the whole.

16. **Weakness of the English Colony. 1367—1377.**—It takes two to make a bargain, and the Irish were not to be prevented from encroaching on the English because the English had resolved no longer to encroach upon them. The renewal of the war with France in 1369 made it impossible to send help from England, and during the latter part of the reign of Edward III. the Irish pillaged freely within the English territory, constantly winning ground from their antagonists.

Genealogy of the more important Sons of Edward III.

EDWARD III.
d. 1377

| Edward, the Black Prince, d. 1376 | Lionel, Duke of Clarence, d. 1368 | John of Gaunt, Duke of Lancaster, d. 1399 | Edmund, Duke of York, d. 14^2 | Thomas, Duke of Gloucester, d. 1397 |

Richard II.
d 1399

CHAPTER XVII

RICHARD II. AND THE SOCIAL REVOLUTION

1377—1381

LEADING DATES

Reign of Richard II., 1377-1399

Accession of Richard II 1377
The peasants' revolt 1381

1. **The First Years of Richard II. 1377—1378.**—"Woe to the land," quoted Langland from Ecclesiastes, in the second edition of *Piers the Plowman*, "when the king is a child." Richard was but ten years of age when he was raised to the throne. The French plundered the coast, and the Scots plundered the Borders. In the presence of such dangers Lancaster and Wykeham forgot their differences, and as Lancaster was too generally distrusted to allow of his acting as regent, the council governed in the name of the young king. Lancaster, however, took the lead, and renewed the war with France with but little result beyond so great a waste of money as to stir up Parliament to claim a control over the expenditure of the Crown.

2. **Wycliffe and the Great Schism. 1378—1381.**—In 1378 began the Great Schism. For nearly half a century from that date there were two Popes, one at Avignon and one at Rome. Wycliffe had been gradually losing his reverence for a single Pope, and he had none left for two. He was now busy with a translation of the Bible into English, and sent forth a band of "poor priests," to preach the simple gospel which he found in it. He was thus brought into collision with the pretensions of the priesthood, and was thereby led to question the doctrines on which their authority was based. In 1381 he declared his disbelief in the doctrine of transubstantiation, and thereby denied to priests that power "of making the body of Christ," which was held to mark them off from their fellowmen. In any case, so momentous an announcement would have cost Wycliffe the hearts of large numbers of his supporters. It was the more fatal to his influence as it was coincident with social disorders, the blame for which was certain, rightly or wrongly, to be laid at his door.

3. **The Poll-taxes. 1379—1381.**—The disastrous war with France made fresh taxation unavoidable. In 1379 a poll-tax was

Richard II. and his first queen, Anne of Bohemia; from the gilt-latten effigies on their tomb in Westminster Abbey, made by Nicholas Broker and Godfrey Prest, coppersmiths of London, in 1395.

imposed by Parliament on a graduated scale, reaching from the 6*l.* 13*s.* 4*d.* required of a duke, to the groat or 4*d.*, representing in those days at least the value of 4*s.* at the present day, required of the poorest peasant. A second poll-tax in **1380** exacted no less than three groats from every peasant, and from every one of his unmarried children above the age of fifteen. In **1381** a tiler of Dartford in Kent struck dead a collector who attempted to investigate his daughter's age in an indecent fashion. His neighbours took arms to protect him. In an incredibly short time the peasants of the east and south of England rose in insurrection.

4. **The Peasants' Grievances.**—The peasants had other grievances besides the weight of taxation thrown on them by a Parliament in which they had no representatives. The landlords, finding it impossible to compel the acceptance of the low wages provided for by the Statute of Labourers (see p. 248), had attempted to help themselves in another way. Before the Black Death the bodily service of villeins had been frequently commuted into a payment of money which had been its fair equivalent, but which, since the rise of wages consequent upon the Black Death, could not command anything like the amount of labour surrendered. The landlords in many places now declared the bargain to have been unfair, and compelled the villeins to render once more the old bodily service. The discontent which prevailed everywhere was fanned not merely by the attacks made by Wycliffe's poor priests upon the idle and inefficient clergy, but by itinerant preachers unconnected with Wycliffe, who denounced the propertied classes in general. One of these, John Ball, a notorious assailant of the gentry, had been thrown into prison. His favourite question was—

> When Adam delved and Eve span
> Who was then a gentleman?

5. **The Peasants' Revolt. 1381.**—From one end of England to another the revolt spread. The parks of the gentry were broken into, the deer killed, the fish-ponds emptied. The court-rolls which testified to the villeins' services were burnt, and lawyers and all others connected with the courts were put to death without mercy. From Kent and Essex 100,000 enraged peasants, headed by Wat Tyler and Jack Straw, released John Ball from gaol and poured along the roads to London. They hoped to place the young Richard at their head against their enemies the gentry. The boy was spirited enough, and in spite of his mother's entreaties insisted on leaving the Tower, and being rowed across the Thames to meet the insurgents on the Surrey shore. Those who were with him, however, refused to allow him to land. The peasants had sympathisers

in London itself, who allowed them to break into the city. Lancaster's palace of the Savoy and the houses of lawyers and officials were sacked and burnt. All the lawyers who could be found were murdered, and others who were not lawyers shared their fate. The mob broke into the Tower, and beheaded Simon of Sudbury, Archbishop of Canterbury, who had, as Chancellor, proposed the obnoxious taxes to Parliament.

6. **The Suppression of the Revolt.** --The boy-king met the mob at Mile-End, and promised to abolish villeinage in England. Charters of manumission were drawn out and sealed, and a great part of the insurgents returned contentedly home. About 30,000, however, remained behind. When Richard came amongst them at Smithfield, Wat Tyler threatened him, and Walworth, the Mayor of London, slew Wat Tyler with his dagger. A shout for vengeance was raised. With astonishing presence of mind Richard rode forward. " I am your king," he said; " I will be your leader." His boldness inspired the insurgents with confidence, and caused them to desist from their threats and to return to their homes. In the country the gentry, encouraged by the failure of the insurgents in London, recovered their courage. The insurrection was everywhere vigorously suppressed. Richard ordered the payment of all services due, and revoked the charters he had granted. The judges on their circuits hanged the ringleaders without mercy. When Parliament met it directed that the charters of manumission should be cancelled. Lords and Commons alike stood up for the rich against the poor, and the boy-king was powerless to resist them, and it is possible that he did not wish to do so.

7. **Results of the Peasants' Revolt.**—The revolt of the peasants strengthened the conservative spirit in the country. The villeinage into which the peasants had been thrust back could not, indeed, endure long, because service unwillingly rendered is too expensive to be maintained. Men were, however, no longer in a mood to listen to reformers. Great noblemen, whose right to the services of their villeins had been denied, now made common cause with the great churchmen. The propertied classes, lay and clerical, instinctively saw that they must hang together. Wycliffe's attack on transubstantiation finding little response, he was obliged to retire to his parsonage at Lutterworth, where he laboured with his pen till his death in **1384**. His followers, known by the nickname of Lollards,[1]

[1] The name is said to have been derived from a low German word, *lollen*, to sing, from their habit of singing, but their clerical opponents derived it from

were, however, for some time still popular amongst the poorer classes.

8. **Chaucer's 'Canterbury Tales.'**—A combination between the great nobles and the higher clergy might, at the end of the fourteenth century, meet with temporary success ; but English society was too diversified, and each separate portion of it was too closely linked to the other to make it possible for the higher classes to tyrannise over the others for any long time. What that society was like is best seen in Chaucer's *Canterbury Tales.* Chaucer was in many ways the exact opposite of Langland, and was the precursor of modern literature as Wycliffe was the precursor of modern religion. He was an inimitable story-teller, with an eye which nothing could escape. He was ready to take men as he found them, having no yearning for the purification of a sinful world. Heroic examples of manly constancy and of womanly purity and devotion, are mingled in his pages with coarse and ribald tales ; still, coarse and ribald as some of his narratives are, Chaucer never attempts to make vice attractive. He takes it rather as a matter of course, calling, not for reproof, but for laughter, whenever those who are doing evil place themselves in ridiculous situations.

Portrait of Geoffrey Chaucer.

9. **The Prologue of the 'Canterbury Tales.'**—Whilst, however, there is not one of the *Canterbury Tales* which fails to bring vividly before the reader one aspect or another of the life of Chaucer's day, it is in the prologue that is especially found evidence of the close connection which existed between different ranks of society. Men and women of various classes are there represented as riding

the Latin *lolium* (tares), as if they were the tares in the midst of the wheat which remained constant to the Church.

together on a pilgrimage to the shrine of St. Thomas of Canterbury, and beguiling the way by telling stories to one another. No baron, indeed, takes part in the pilgrimage, and the villein class is represented by the reeve, who was himself a person in authority, the mere cultivator of the soil being excluded. Yet, within these limits, the whole circle of society is admirably represented. The knight, just returned from deeds of chivalry, is on the best of terms with the rough-spoken miller and the reeve, whilst the hard-working parson, who would gladly learn and gladly teach, and who followed in his own life those precepts which he commended to his parishioners, has no irreconcilable quarrel with the begging friar or with the official of the ecclesiastical courts, whose only object is to make a gain of godliness.

A gentleman riding out with his hawk: from the Luttrell Psalter.

10. **Chaucer and the Clergy.**
—In his representation of the clergy, Chaucer shows that, like Langland, he had no reverence for the merely official clergy. His "poor parson of a town," indeed, is a model for all helpers and teachers. The parson is regardless of his own comfort, ever ready to toil with mind and body for his parishioners, and, above all, resolved to set them an example, knowing

> That if gold ruste, what schulde yren doo?
> For if a prest be foul, on whom we truste,
> No wondur is a lewid man to ruste.[1]

The final character given to him is :—

> A bettre preest I trowe ther nowher non is.
> He waytud after no pompe ne reverence,
> Ne maked him a spiced conscience ; [2]
> But Cristes lore, and his apostles twelve,
> He taught, and ferst he folwed[3] it himselve.

The majority amongst Chaucer's clergy are, however, of a very different kind. There is the parish clerk, who, when he is waving

---

[1] *i.e.*, if a priest, who is like gold, allow himself to rust, or fall into sloth or sin, how can he expect the 'lewid man' or layman, who is as iron to him, to be free from these faults ?

[2] A nice conscience ; to see offence where there is none.   [3] Followed.

the censer in church thinks more of the pretty women there than of his duty; the monk who loves hunting, and hates work and reading; the friar who is ready to grant absolution to any one who will give money to the friars; who has a word and a jest for every man, and presents of knives and pins for the women; who takes a farthing where he cannot get a penny, but turns aside from those who have not even a farthing to give; the pardoner, who has for sale sham relics—a piece of the sail of the ship which carried St. Peter on the sea of Galilee, and a glass of pigs' bones, which he was ready to sell as bones of saints, if he could thereby extract something even from the poorest widow. He would not, he said, work with his hands like the apostles. He wanted to have

Carrying corn—a cart going uphill: from the Luttrell Psalter.

money, wool, cheese, and wheat at other people's expense. Though Wycliffe had failed to reform the Church there was evidently much room for a reformer.

11. **Roads and Bridges.**—Such men as these latter did not go on pilgrimages through pure religious zeal. Villeins, indeed, were "bound to the soil," and lived and died on land which they tilled; but the classes above them moved about freely, and took pleasure in a pilgrimage, as a modern Englishman takes pleasure in a railway excursion. It was considered to be a pious work to make or repair roads and bridges, and the existence of many bridges especially was owing to the clergy. The most famous bridge in England, London Bridge, had been begun in the place of an old wooden one in 1176—in the reign of Henry II.—by a

priest, Peter Colechurch, who obtained gifts for the purpose from notable people of all kinds. It was completed in 1209, houses being built upon it in order that their rents might pay for keeping it in good condition. Local taxes were sometimes levied to maintain the roads and bridges, and in default of these, it was held to be the duty of the owners of land to keep the communications open.

12. **Modes of Conveyance.**—In spite of these precautions, roads were often neglected, so that those who were not obliged to go on foot travelled almost entirely on horseback, women almost always riding astride like men. It was only at the end of the fourteenth century that a few ladies rode sideways. Kings and queens and exceedingly great people occasionally used lumbering but gorgeously ornamented carriages; but this was to enable them to appear in splendour, as this way of travelling must, at least in fine weather, have been far less agreeable than the ordinary ride. The only other wheeled ve-

State carriage of the fourteenth century; from the Luttrell Psalter.

T

hicles in existence were the peasants' carts on two wheels, roughly made in the form of a square box either of boards or of a lighter framework. It was one of the grievances of the peasants that when the king moved from one manor to another his purveyors seized their carts to carry his property, and that though the purveyors were bound by frequently repeated statutes to pay for their hire, these statutes were often broken, and the carts sent back without payment for their use. The same purveyors often took corn and other agricultural produce, for which they paid little or nothing.

13. **Hospitality and Inns.**—When the king arrived in the evening at a town his numerous attendants were billeted upon the townsmen, without asking leave. Monasteries were always ready to offer hospitality to himself or to any great person, and even to provide rougher fare for the poorest stranger in a special guest-house provided for the purpose. In castles, the owner was usually glad to see a stranger of his own rank. The halls were still furnished with movable tables, as in the days before the Conquest (see p. 76), and at night mattresses were placed for persons of inferior rank on the floor, which was strewn with rushes ; whilst a stranger of high rank had usually a bed in the solar (see p. 245) with the lord of the castle. Travellers of the middle class were not thought good enough to be welcomed in monasteries and castles, and were not poor enough to be received out of charity ; and for them inns were provided. These inns provided beds, of which there were several in each room, and the guests then bought their provisions and fuel from the host, instead of being charged for their meals as is now the custom. From a manual of French conversation, written at the end of the fourteenth century for the use of Englishmen, it appears that cleanliness was not always to be found in these inns. " William," one traveller is supposed to say to another, " undress and wash your legs, and rub them well for the love of the fleas, that they may not leap on your legs ; for there is a peck of them lying in the dust under the rushes. . . Hi ! the fleas bite me so, and do me great harm, for I have scratched my shoulders till the blood flows."

14. **Alehouses.**—By the roadside were alehouses for temporary refreshment, known by a bunch of twigs at the end of a pole, from which arose the saying that " Good wine needs no bush." The ale of the day was made without hops, which were still unknown in England, and ale would therefore only keep good for about five days.

15. **Wanderers.**—Besides the better class of travellers the

roads were frequented by wanderers of all kinds, quack doctors, minstrels, jugglers, beggars, and such like. Life in the country was dull, and even great lords took pleasure in amusements which are now only to be heard of at country fairs. Any one who could play or sing was always welcome, and the verses sung were often exceedingly coarse. A tumbler who could stand on his head or balance a heavy article at the end of a stick balanced on his chin, or the leader of a performing bear, was seldom turned away from the door, whilst the pedlar went from place to place, supplying the wants which are now satisfied in the shop of the village or the neighbouring town.

Bear-baiting : from the Luttrell Psalter.

16. **Robbers and Criminals.**—The roads, indeed, were not always safe. Outlaws who had escaped from the punishment due to their crimes took refuge in the broad tracts of forest land which occupied much of the soil which has since been cultivated, shot the king's deer, and robbed merchants and wealthy travellers, leaving the poor untouched, like the legendary Robin Hood of an earlier date. Such robbers were highly esteemed by the poor, as the law from which they suffered was cruelly harsh, hanging being the penalty for thefts amounting to a shilling. Villeins who fled from service could be reclaimed by their masters, unless they could succeed in passing a year in a town, and consequently were often found amongst vagabonds who had to live as best they might, often enough by committing fresh crimes. Prisons, in which even persons guilty of no more than harmless vagabondage were

West end of the nave of Winchester Cathedral: begun by Bishop Edington (who built the great window) between 1360 and 1366: carried on by Bishop William of Wykeham from 1394 to 1416, and finally completed after his death.

confined, reeked with disease, and those who were, as wanderers or drunkards, put in the stocks, had, if an unpleasant, at least a less dangerous experience than the prisoner. One means of escape, indeed, was available to some, at least, of these unfortunates. They could take refuge in the sanctuaries to be found in churches, from which no officer of the law could take them, and, though the Church preserved some guilty ones from just punishment, she also saved many who were either innocent or who were exposed to punishments far too severe for their slight offences.

17. **Justices of the Peace.**—Even harshness is less dangerous than anarchy, and from time to time measures were taken to provide against anarchy. Before the Conquest order had been kept by making either the kindred or the township liable to produce offenders, and this system was maintained by the Norman kings. In the time of Richard I. all men were required to swear to keep the peace, to avoid crime, and to join in the hue and cry in pursuit of criminals. In the time of Henry III. persons called guardians of the peace were occasionally appointed to see that order was kept, and at the accession of Edward III. these officials were established for a time by Act of Parliament as conservators of the peace. In **1360**, the year of the Treaty of Bretigni, they were permanently continued, and the name of Justices of the Peace was given to them. They were to keep the peace in each county, and their number was to be made up of a lord, three or four gentlemen, and a lawyer, who was in those days always a cleric.[1] They were to seize and imprison, and even to try persons accused of crime. The king named these justices, but he had to name all of them except the lawyer from amongst the local landowners. In every way, in the fourteenth century, the chief local landowners were becoming prominent. The kings attempted to govern with their help, both in Parliament and in the counties.

---

[1] Many clerics took one of the minor orders so as to secure the immunities of the clergy, without any intention of being ordained a deacon or a priest.

CHAPTER XVIII

RICHARD II. AND THE POLITICAL REVOLUTION

1382—1399

LEADING DATES

Reign of Richard II., 1377—1399

The impeachment of Suffolk	1386
The Merciless Parliament	1388
Richard begins his constitutional government	1389
Richard's coup-d'état	1397
Deposition of Richard	1399

1. **Progress of the War with France. 1382—1386.**—In 1382 Richard at the early age of fifteen was married to Anne of Bohemia. Though he was a young husband he was at all events old enough to be accused of disasters which he could not avoid. Not only was the war with France not prospering, but English influence was declining in Flanders. In 1382 Philip van Arteveldt, who like his father Jacob (see p. 235) headed the resistance of Ghent against the Count of Flanders, was defeated and slain at Roosebeke by Charles VI., the young king of France. In 1383 an English expedition led by Henry Spencer, Bishop of Norwich, under the pretext of a crusade against the French as the followers of the Pope of Avignon, ended in complete failure, and Flanders, the great purchaser of English wool, fell under the control of France. In 1385 Richard, indeed, invaded Scotland, ravaged the country and burnt Edinburgh, though without producing any permanent result. In 1386 a French fleet and army was gathered at Sluys, and an invasion of England was threatened.

2. **Richard's growing Unpopularity. 1385—1386.**—When the king returned from Scotland in 1385 he made a large creation of peers. He raised his two younger uncles to the Dukedoms of York and Gloucester ; his Chancellor, Michael de la Pole, to the earldom of Suffolk, and his favourite, Robert de Vere, Earl of Oxford, to the marquisate of Dublin, making him not long afterwards Duke of Ireland. Suffolk was an able and apparently an honest administrator, who upheld the king's prerogative against the encroachments of Parliament. Oxford was a gay and heedless companion of

Richard's pleasures, who encouraged him in unnecessary expense, and thereby provoked to resistance those who might have put up with an extension of the royal authority. That resistance, however, was to a great extent due to causes not of Richard's own making. Though the French in 1386 abandoned their attempt at invasion, the preparations to resist them had been costly, and Englishmen were in an unreasonable mood. Things, they said, had not gone so in the days of Edward III. A cry for reform and retrenchment, for more victories and less expense, was loudly raised.

3. **The Impeachment of Suffolk and the Commission of Regency. 1386.**—The discontented found a leader in Gloucester, the youngest of the king's uncles. Wealthy, turbulent, and ambitious, he put himself at the head of all who had a grievance against the king. Lancaster had just sailed for Spain to prosecute a claim in right of his second wife to the throne of Castile, and as York was without ambition, Gloucester had it all his own way. Under his guidance a Parliament demanded the dismissal of Richard's ministers, and, on his refusal, impeached Suffolk. Suffolk, though probably innocent of the charges brought against him, was condemned and driven from power, and Commissioners of regency were appointed for a year to regulate the realm and the king's household, as the Lords Ordainers had done in the days of Edward II. (see p. 226).

4. **The Lords Appellant and the Merciless Parliament. 1387—1388.**—In one way the Commissioners of regency satisfied the desire of Englishmen. In 1387 they sent the Earl of Arundel to sea, and Arundel won a splendid victory over a combined fleet of French, Flemings, and Spaniards. Richard, on the other hand, fearing that they would prolong their power when their year of office was ended, consulted upon the legality of the commission with the judges in the presence of Suffolk and others of his principal supporters, amongst whom was the Duke of Ireland. With one voice the judges declared that Parliament might not put the king in tutelage. Richard then made preparations to prevent by force the renewal of the commission, and to punish as traitors those who had originated it. His intention got abroad, and five lords, the Duke of Gloucester, the Earls of Arundel, Nottingham, Warwick, and Derby, the latter being the son of the absent Lancaster, appeared at the head of an overwhelming force against him. The five lords appellant, as they were called, appealed, or accused of treason five of Richard's councillors before a Parliament which met at Westminster in 1388, by flinging down

their gloves as a token that they were ready to prove the truth of their charge in single combat. The Duke of Ireland, attempting resistance, was defeated by Derby at Radcot Bridge, and finally escaped to Ireland. The Parliament, called by its admirers the Wonderful, and by its opponents the Merciless Parliament, was entirely subservient to the lords appellant, who, instead of meeting their antagonists in single combat, accused them before the House of Lords. The Duke of Ireland, Suffolk, Chief Justice Tresilian, and Brember, who had been Mayor of London, were condemned to be hanged. The two first-named had escaped to the Continent, but the others were put to death. The fifth councillor, the Archbishop of York, escaped with virtual deprivation by the Pope. Four other knights, amongst them Sir Simon Burley, a veteran soldier and trusted companion of the Black Prince, were also put to death. Richard was allowed nominally to retain the crown, but in reality he was subjected to a council in which Gloucester and his adherents were supreme.

5. **Richard's Restoration to Power. 1389.**—Richard's entire submission turned the scale in his favour. England had been dissatisfied with him, but it had never loved the rule of the great feudal lords. Gloucester's council was no more popular than had been the Committees named in the Provisions of Oxford in the reign of Henry III., or the Lords Ordainers in the reign of Edward II., and it fell more easily than any government, before or afterwards. Suddenly, on May 3, **1389**, Richard asked his uncle in full council how old he was. "Your highness," replied Gloucester, "is in your twenty-second year." "Then," said Richard, "I must be old enough to manage my own affairs, as every heir is at liberty to do when he is twenty-one." No attempt having been made to confute this argument, Richard dismissed the council, and ruled once more in person.

6. **Richard's Constitutional Government. 1389—1396.**—This sudden blow was followed by seven years of constitutional government. It seemed as if Richard had solved the problem of the relations between Crown and Parliament, which had perplexed so many generations of Englishmen. In **1389** he appointed ministers at his own pleasure, but when Parliament met in **1390** he commanded them to lay down their offices in order that no one should be deterred from bringing charges against them ; and it was only upon finding that no one had any complaint to bring against them that he restored them to their posts. Nor did he show any signs of irritation against those by whom he had been outraged. Not only did he forbear to recall Suffolk and his other exiled

favourites, but after a little time he admitted Gloucester and his supporters to sit in council alongside of his own adherents.

7. **Livery and Maintenance. 1390.**—During the fourteenth century the importance of the House of Commons had been steadily growing, and the king on the one hand and the great nobles on the other had been sorely tempted to influence the elections unduly. The means of doing so had come with a change in civil relationships, the natural result of that change in military relationships which had given a new character to the wars of Edward III. (see p. 236). Just as the king now fought with paid soldiers of every rank instead of fighting with vassals bound by feudal tenure, so the great nobles surrounded themselves with retainers instead of vassals. The vassal had been on terms of social equality with his lord, and was bound to follow him on fixed terms. The retainer was an inferior, who was taken into service and professed himself ready to fight for his lord at all times and in all causes. In return his lord kept open house for his retainers, supplied them with coats, known as liveries, marked with his badge, and undertook to maintain them against all men, either by open force or by supporting them in their quarrels in the law courts ; and this maintenance, as it was called, was seldom limited to the mere payment of expenses. The lord, by the help of his retainers, could bully witnesses and jurors, and wrest justice to the profit of the wrongdoer. As yet, indeed, the practice had not attained the proportions which it afterwards assumed, but it was sufficiently developed to draw down upon it in **1390** a statute prohibiting maintenance and the granting of liveries. Such a statute was not merely issued in defence of private persons against intimidation ; it also helped to protect the Crown against the violence of the great lords. The growth of the power of the House of Commons was a good thing as long as the House of Commons represented the wishes of the community. It would be a bad thing if it merely represented knots of armed retainers who either voted in their own names according to the orders of their lords, or who frightened away those who came to vote for candidates whom their lords opposed.

8. **Richard's Domestic Policy. 1390—1391.**—It was therefore well for the community that there should be a strong and wise king capable of making head against the ambition of the lords. For some years Richard showed himself wise. Not only did he seek, by opening the council to his opponents, to win over the lords to take part in the peaceable government of the country instead of disturbing it, but he forwarded legislation which carried out the general

wishes of the country. The Statute of Provisors (see p. 258) was re-enacted and strengthened in **1390**, the Statute of Mortmain (see p. 212) in **1391**, and the Statute of Præmunire (see p. 258) in **1393**.

9. **Richard's Foreign Policy. 1389—1396.**—Richard's foreign policy was based upon a French alliance. In **1389** he made a truce with France for three years. Negotiations for a permanent peace were frustrated because the French would make no peace unless Calais were surrendered to them, and English feeling was against the surrender of the claims sanctioned by the Treaty of Bretigni. The truce was, however, prolonged from time to time, and in **1396**, when Richard, who was by that time a widower, married Isabella, the daughter of Charles VI., a child of eight, it was prolonged for twenty-eight years. Wise as this policy was, it was distasteful to Englishmen, and their dissatisfaction rose when they learnt that Richard had surrendered Brest and Cherbourg to the French. It was true that these places had been pledged to him for money, and that he had only given them up as he was bound to do when the money was paid, but his subjects drew no fine distinctions, and fancied that he was equally ready to surrender Calais and Bordeaux.

10. **Richard's Coup d'Etat. 1397.**—Richard knew that Gloucester was ready to avail himself of any widespread dissatisfaction, and that he had recently been allying himself with Lancaster against him. To please Lancaster, who had married his mistress, Catherine Swynford, as his third wife, Richard had legitimatised the Beauforts, his children by her, for all purposes except the succession of the crown, thus giving personal offence to Gloucester. Lancaster's son Derby, and Nottingham, another of the lords appellant (see p. 279), were now favourable to the king, and when rumours reached Richard that Gloucester was plotting against him, he resolved to anticipate the blow. He arrested the three of the lords appellant whom he still distrusted, Gloucester, Warwick, and Arundel, and charged them before Parliament, not with recent malpractices, of which he had probably no sufficient proof, but with the slaughter of his ministers in the days of the Merciless Parliament. Warwick was banished to the Isle of Man, Arundel was executed, and Gloucester imprisoned at Calais, where he was secretly murdered, as was generally believed by the order of the king. Archbishop Arundel, brother of the Earl of Arundel, was also banished. In such contradiction was this sudden outburst of violence to the prudence of Richard's recent conduct, that it has sometimes been supposed that, he had been dissimulating all the time. It is more probable that, without being actually insane, his mind had to some extent given way. He was

always excitable, and in his better days his alertness of mind carried him forward to swift decisions, as when he met the mob at Smithfield, and when he vindicated his authority from the restraint of his uncle. Signs had not been wanting that his native energy was no longer balanced by the restraints of prudence. In 1394 he had actually struck Arundel in Westminster Abbey. In 1397 there was much to goad him to hasty and ill-considered action. The year before complaints had been raised against the extravagance of his household. The peace which he had given to his country was made the subject of bitter reproach against him, and he seems to have believed that Gloucester was plotting to bring him back into the servitude to which he had been subjected by the Commissioners of regency.

11. **The Parliament of Shrewsbury. 1398.**—Whether Richard was mad or not, he at all events acted like a madman. In 1398 he summoned a packed Parliament to Shrewsbury, which declared all the acts of the Merciless Parliament to be null and void, and announced that no restraint could legally be put on the king. It then delegated all parliamentary power to a committee of twelve lords and six commoners chosen from the king's friends. Richard was thus made an absolute ruler unbound by the necessity of gathering a Parliament again. He had freed himself not merely from turbulent lords but also from all constitutional restraints.

12. **The Banishment of Hereford and Norfolk. 1398.**—Richard had shown favour to the two lords appellant who had taken his side. Derby became Duke of Hereford, and Nottingham Duke of Norfolk. Before long Hereford came to the king with a strange tale. Norfolk, he said, had complained to him that the king still distrusted them, and had suggested that they should guard themselves against him. Norfolk denied the truth of the story, and Richard ordered the two to prove their truthfulness by a single combat at Coventry. When the pair met in the lists in full armour Richard stopped the fight, and to preserve peace, as he said, banished Norfolk for life and Hereford for ten years, a term which was soon reduced to six. There was something of the unwise cunning of a madman in the proceeding.

13. **Richard's Despotism. 1398—1399.**—Richard, freed from all control, was now, in every sense of the word, despotic. He extorted money without a semblance of right, and even compelled men to put their seals to blank promises to pay, which he could fill up with any sum he pleased. He too, like the lords, gathered round him a vast horde of retainers, who wore his badge and ill-

treated his subjects at their pleasure. He threatened the Percies, the Earl of Northumberland and his son, Harry Hotspur, with exile, and sent them off discontented to their vast possessions in the North. Early in 1399 the Duke of Lancaster died. His son, the banished Hereford, was now Duke of Lancaster. Richard, however, seized the lands which ought to have descended to him from his father. Every man who had property to lose felt that Lancaster's cause was his own. Richard at this inopportune moment took occasion to sail to Ireland. He had been there once

Meeting of Henry of Lancaster and Richard II. at Flint : from Harl. MS. 1319.

before in 1394 in the vain hope of protecting the English colonists (see p. 265). His first expedition had been a miserable failure : his second expedition was cut short by bad news from England.

14. **Henry of Lancaster in England. 1399.**—Lancaster, with a small force, landed at Ravenspur, in Yorkshire, a harbour which has now disappeared in the sea. At first he gave out that he had come merely to demand his own inheritance. Then he alleged that he had come to redress the wrongs of the realm. Northumberland brought the Percies to his help. Armed men flocked to his support

in crowds. The Duke of York, who had been left behind by Richard as regent, accepted this statement and joined him with all his forces. When Richard heard what had happened, he sent the Earl of Salisbury from Ireland to Wales to summon the Welshmen to his aid. The Welshmen rallied to Salisbury, but the king was long in following, and when Richard landed they had all dispersed. Richard found himself almost alone in Conway Castle, whilst Lancaster had a whole kingdom at his back.

15. **The Deposition of Richard and the Enthronement of Henry IV. 1399.**—By lying promises Lancaster induced Richard

Henry of Lancaster claiming the throne : from Harl. MS. 1319.

to place himself in his power at Flint. " My lord," said Lancaster to him, " I have now come before you have sent for me. The reason is that your people commonly say you have ruled them very rigorously for twenty or two and twenty years ; but, if it please God, I will help you to govern better." The pretence of helping the king to govern was soon abandoned. Richard was carried to London and thrown into the Tower. He consented, probably not till after he had been threatened with the fate of Edward II., to sign his abdication. On the following morning the act of abdication was read in Parliament. The throne was empty.

Then Lancaster stepped forward. " In the name," he said, " of the Father, Son, and Holy Ghost, I, Henry of Lancaster, challenge this realm of England, and the crown with all its members and appurtenances, as I am descended by right line of the blood coming from the good lord King Henry the Third,[1] and through that right God of his grace hath sent me, with help of my kin and of my friends, to recover it, the which realm was in point to be undone for default of governance and undoing of the good laws." The assent of Parliament was given, and Lancaster took his seat in Richard's throne as King Henry IV.

16. **Nature of the Claim of Henry IV.**—The claim which Henry put forward would certainly not bear investigation. It laid stress on right of descent, and it has since been thought that Henry intended to refer to a popular belief that his ancestor Edmund, the second son of Henry III., was in reality the eldest son, but had been set aside in favour of his younger brother, Edward I., on account of a supposed physical deformity from which he was known as Edmund Crouchback. As a matter of fact the whole story was a fable, and the name Crouchback had been given to Edmund not because his back was crooked, but because he had worn a cross on his back as a crusader (see p. 197). That Henry

[1] Genealogy of the claimants of the throne in 1399 :—

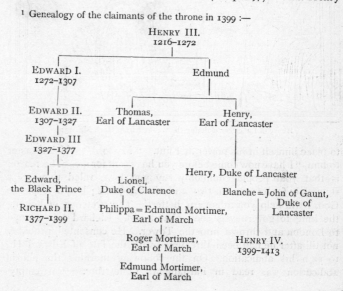

HENRY III.
1216–1272

EDWARD I.
1272–1307

Edmund

EDWARD II.
1307–1327

Thomas,
Earl of Lancaster

Henry,
Earl of Lancaster

EDWARD III
1327–1377

Edward,
the Black Prince

Lionel,
Duke of Clarence

Henry, Duke of Lancaster

RICHARD II.
1377–1399

Philippa = Edmund Mortimer,
Earl of March

Blanche = John of Gaunt,
Duke of
Lancaster

Roger Mortimer,
Earl of March

HENRY IV.
1399–1413

Edmund Mortimer,
Earl of March

should have thought it necessary to allude to this story, if such was really his meaning, shows the hold which the idea of hereditary succession had taken on the minds of Englishmen. In no other way could he claim hereditary right as a descendant of Henry III. Richard had selected as his heir Roger Mortimer, the son of the daughter of Lionel, Duke of Clarence, the next son of Edward III., after the Black Prince, who lived to be old enough to have children. Roger Mortimer, indeed, had recently been killed in Ireland, but he had left a boy, Edmund Mortimer, who, on hereditary principles, was heir to the kingdom, unless the doctrine announced by Edward III. that a claim to the crown descended through females was to be set aside. In fact the real importance of the change of kings lay not in what Henry said, but in what he avoided saying. It was a reversion to the old right of election, and to the precedent set in the deposition of Edward II. Henry tacitly announced that in critical times, when the wearer of the crown was hopelessly incompetent, the nation, represented by Parliament, might step in and change the order of succession. The question at issue was not merely a personal one between Richard and Henry. It was

Effigy of a knight at Clehonger, showing development of plate armour. Date, about 1400.

a question between hereditary succession leading to despotism on the one side, and to parliamentary choice, perhaps to anarchy, on the other. That there were dangers attending the latter solution of the constitutional problem would not be long in appearing.

Books recommended for further study of Part III.

GREEN, J. R.   History of the English People.   Vol. i. pp. 189–520.

STUBBS, W. (Bishop of Oxford).   Constitutional History of England.   Vol. i. chap. xii. sections 151–155 ; vol. ii. chaps. ix. and x.

———   ———   The Early Plantagenets, 129–276.

NORGATE, Miss K.   England under the Angevin Kings.   Vol. ii. p. 390.

MICHELET, J.   History of France (Middle Ages).   Translated by G. H. Smith.

LONGMAN, W.   The History of the Life and Times of Edward III.

GAIRDNER, James.   The Houses of Lancaster and York, pp. 1–64.

ROGERS, James E. Thorold.   A History of Agriculture and Prices in England. Vols. i. and ii.

CUNNINGHAM, W.   Growth of English Industry and Commerce in the Early and Middle Ages, pp. 172–365.

WAKEMAN, H. O. and HASSALL, A. (Editors).   Essays Introductory to the Study of English Constitutional History.

ASHLEY, W. J.   An Introduction to English Economic History and Theory. Vol. i.

JUSSERAND, J. J.   English Wayfaring Life in the Middle Ages.   Translated by Lucy Toulmin Smith (Miss).

BROWNE, M.   Chaucer's England.

JESSOPP, A., Dr.   The Coming of the Friars, and other Historic Essays.

OMAN, C. W. C.   The Art of War in the Middle Ages.

PART IV

LANCASTER, YORK, AND TUDOR. 1399—1509

CHAPTER XIX

HENRY IV. AND HENRY V.

HENRY IV., 1399—1413. HENRY V., 1413—1422

LEADING DATES

Accession of Henry IV.	1399
Statute for the burning of heretics	1401
Battle of Shrewsbury	1403
Fight at Bramham Moor	1408
Succession of Henry V.	1413
Battle of Agincourt	1415
Treaty of Troyes	1420
Death of Henry V.	1422

1. **Henry's First Difficulties.** 1399—1400.—Henry IV. fully understood that his only chance of maintaining himself on the throne was to rule with due consideration for the wishes of Parliament. His main difficulty, like that of his predecessor, was that the great lords preferred to hold their own against him individually with the help of their armies of retainers, instead of exercising political power in Parliament. In his first Parliament an angry brawl arose. The lords who in the last reign had taken the side of Gloucester flung their gloves on the floor of the House as a challenge to those who had supported Richard when he compassed Gloucester's death ; and though Henry succeeded in keeping the peace for the time, a rebellion broke out early in 1400 in the name of Richard. Henry, like the kings before him, found his support against the turbulent nobles in the townsmen and the yeomen, and he was thus able to suppress the rebellion. Some of the noblemen who were caught by the excited defenders of the throne were butchered without mercy and without law.

U

Henry IV. and his queen, Joan of Navarre: from their tomb in Canterbury
Cathedral.

2. Death of Richard II. 1400.—A few weeks after the suppression of this conspiracy it was rumoured that Richard had died in prison at Pontefract. According to Henry's account of the matter he had voluntarily starved himself to death. Few, however, doubted that he had been put to death by Henry's orders. To prove the untruth of this story, Henry had the body brought to St. Paul's, where he showed to the people only the face of the corpse, as if this could be any evidence whatever. After Richard's death, if hereditary succession had been regarded, the person having a claim to the crown in preference to Henry was the young Edmund Mortimer, Earl of March, the descendant of Lionel, Duke of Clarence (see p. 287). Henry therefore took care to keep the boy under custody during the whole of his reign.

3. Henry IV. and the Church.—Besides seeking the support of the commonalty, Henry sought the support of the Church. Since the rise of the friars at the beginning of the thirteenth cen-

Royal arms as borne by Henry IV. after about 1408, and by successive sovereigns down to 1603.

tury (see p. 191) the Church had produced no new orders of monks or friars. In the thirteenth and fourteenth she produced the schoolmen, a succession of great thinkers who systematised her moral and religious teaching. Imagining that she had no more to learn, she now attempted to strengthen herself by persecuting those who disbelieved her teaching, and after the suppression of the revolt of the peasants, made common cause with the landlords, who feared pecuniary loss from the emancipation of the villeins. This conservative alliance against social and religious change was the more easily made because many of the bishops were now members of noble families, instead of springing, as had usually been the case in the better days of the mediæval Church, from poor or middle-class parentage. In the reign of Richard II. a Courtenay, a kinsman of the Earl of Devonshire, had become first Bishop of London (see p. 263), and then Archbishop of Canterbury. He was succeeded in his arch-bishopric by an Arundel, brother of the Earl of Arundel who had been executed by Richard, and Archbishop Arundel was in the days of Henry IV. the spokesman of the clergy.

Thomas Cranley, Archbishop of Dublin, 1397-1417 : from his brass at New College, Oxford. Showing the archiepiscopal mass-vestments and the cross and pall. Date, about 1400.

4. **The Statute for the Burning of Heretics. 1401.**—In 1401 the clergy cried aloud for new powers. The ecclesiastical courts could condemn men as heretics, but had no power to burn them. Bishops and abbots formed the majority of the House of Lords, and though the Commons had not lost that craving for the wealth of the Church which had distinguished John of Gaunt's party, they had no sympathy with heresy. Accordingly the statute for the burning of heretics (*De hæretico comburendo*), the first English law for the suppression of religious opinion, was passed with the ready consent of the king and both Houses. The first victim was William Sawtre, a priest who held, amongst other things, "that after the words of consecration in the Eucharist the bread remains bread, and nothing more." He was burnt by a special order from the king and council even before the new law had been enacted.

5. **Henry IV. and Owen Glendower. 1400—1402.**—If Henry found it difficult to maintain order in England, he found it still more difficult to keep the peace on the

borders of Wales. In **1400** an English nobleman, Lord Grey of Ruthyn, seized on an estate belonging to Owen Glendower, a powerful Welsh gentleman. Owen Glendower called the Welsh to arms, ravaged Lord Grey's lands, and proclaimed himself Prince of Wales. For some years Wales was practically independent. English townsmen and yeomen were ready to support Henry against any sudden attempt of the nobility to crush him with their retainers, but they were unwilling to bear the burden of taxation needed for the steady performance of a national task. In the meanwhile Henry was constantly exposed to secret plots. In **1401** he found an iron with four spikes in his bed. In the autumn of **1402** he led an expedition into Wales, but storms of rain and snow forced him back. His English followers attributed the disaster to the evil spirits which, as they fully believed, were at the command of the wizard Glendower.

6. **The Rebellion of the Percies. 1402—1404.**—The Scots were not forgetful of the advantages to be derived from the divisions of England. They had amongst them some one—whoever he may have been—whom they gave out to be King Richard, and when Henry marched against Wales in **1402** they invaded England. They were met by the Percies and defeated at Homildon Hill. The Percies had still something of the enormous power of the feudal barons of the eleventh century. Their family estates stretched over a great part of Northumberland, and as they were expected to shield England against Scottish invasions they were obliged to keep up a military retinue which might be employed against the king as well as in his service. It was mainly through their aid that Henry had seated himself on the throne. Their chief, the Earl of Northumberland, and his brother, the Earl of Worcester, were aged men, but Northumberland's son, Henry Percy—Harry Hotspur as he was usually called—was of a fiery temper, and disinclined to submit to insult. Hotspur's wife was a Mortimer, and her brother, Sir Edmund Mortimer, the uncle of the young Earl of March, had been taken prisoner by Glendower. It was noticed that Henry, who had ransomed other prisoners, took no steps to ransom Mortimer, and it was believed that he was in no hurry to set free one whose hereditary claim to the crown, like that of the Earl of March, came before his own. Other causes contributed to irritate the Percies, and in **1403**, bringing with them as allies the Scottish prisoners whom they had taken at Homildon Hill, they marched southwards against Henry. Southern England might not be ready adequately to support Henry in an invasion of Wales, but it was in no mood to allow him to be dethroned by the Percies. It rallied to

his side, and enabled him signally to defeat the Percies at Shrewsbury. Hotspur was killed in the fight, and his uncle, the Earl of Worcester, being captured, was beheaded without delay. Northum-

The battle of Shrewsbury: from the "Life of Richard Beauchamp, Earl of Warwick;" drawn by John Rous about 1485.

berland, who was not present at the battle, was committed to prison in **1404**, but was pardoned on promise of submission.

7. **The Commons and the Church.** **1404.**—After such a deliverance the Commons could not but grant some supplies. In the autumn of **1404**, however, they pleaded for the confiscation of the revenues of the higher clergy, which were sufficient, as they alleged, to support 15 earls, 1,500 knights, 6,200 esquires, and 100 hospitals as well. The king refused to listen to the proposal, and money was voted in the ordinary way. It was the first deliberate attempt to meet the growing expenditure of the Crown by the confiscation of ecclesiastical revenue.

8. **The Capture of the Scottish Prince. 1405.**—Early in 1405 Henry was threatened with a fresh attack. Charles VI. of France was now a confirmed lunatic, and his authority had mainly fallen into the hands of his brother Louis, Duke of Orleans, a profligate and unscrupulous man who was regarded by the feudal nobility of France as their leader. The Duke of Orleans refused to consider himself bound to Henry by the truce which had been made with Richard, and, forming an alliance with Owen Glendower, prepared to send a fleet to his aid. When there was war between England and France the Scots seldom remained quiet, but this time Henry was freed from that danger by an unexpected occurrence. The reigning King of Scotland was Robert III., whose father, Robert II., had been the first king of the House of Stuart, and had ascended the throne after the death of David Bruce, as being the son of his sister Margaret.[1] Robert III., weakly in mind and body, had committed to the custody of his brother, the Duke of Albany, his eldest son, the Duke of Rothesay, who had gained an evil name by his scandalous debauchery. Rothesay died in the prison in which his uncle had confined him, and popular rumour alleged that Albany had murdered him to clear the way to the throne. Robert now sent young James, his only surviving son, to be educated in France in order to save him from Albany's machinations. On his way the prince was captured by an English ship, and delivered to Henry, who kept him under guard as a hostage for the peaceful behaviour of his countrymen. The prince, he said, should have been sent to him to be educated, as he could talk French as well as the king of France. When Robert died soon afterwards the

[1] Genealogy of the kings of Scotland from Robert Bruce to James I. :—

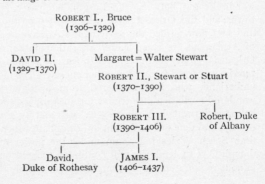

ROBERT I., Bruce
(1306–1329)

DAVID II.   Margaret = Walter Stewart
(1329–1370)

ROBERT II., Stewart or Stuart
(1370–1390)

ROBERT III.   Robert, Duke
(1390–1406)   of Albany

David,   JAMES I.
Duke of Rothesay   (1406–1437)

captive became King James I. ; but he was not allowed to return home, and Albany ruled Scotland as regent in his name.

9. **The Execution of Archbishop Scrope. 1405.**—The capture of such a hostage as James was the more valuable to Henry as at that very moment there was a fresh rising in the North, in which Scrope, the Archbishop of York, took a leading part. The insurgents were soon dispersed, and both Archbishop Scrope and Mowbray, the Earl Marshal, were captured. Henry had them both beheaded, though neither were tried by their peers, and ecclesiastics were not punishable by a secular court. Knowing that the insurrection had been contrived by Northumberland, Henry gave himself no rest till he had demolished the fortifications of his castles of Alnwick, Warkworth, and Prudhoe. Northumberland himself escaped to Scotland.

10. **France, Wales, and the North. 1405—1408.**—In **1405**, whilst Henry was in the North, a French fleet landed a force in Wales and seized Carmarthen. In **1406** the Duke of Orleans attacked the possessions still held by the English in Guienne, but though he plundered the country he could do no more. Once again fortune relieved Henry of a dangerous enemy. The Duke of Orleans had a rival in his cousin John the Fearless, Duke of Burgundy, who, in addition to his own duchy and county of Burgundy, was ruler of Flanders through his mother. His wise and firm government attached the manufacturing towns of Flanders to him, and the example of his government in Flanders won him favour in Paris and other French towns, especially in the north of France. He was, however, personally brutal and unscrupulous, and having entered into a competition for power with the Duke of Orleans, he had him murdered in **1407** in the streets of Paris. At once a civil war broke out between the Burgundian party, supported by the towns, and the Orleans party, which rested on the feudal nobility, and was now termed the party of the Armagnacs, from the Count of Armagnac, its chief leader after the murder of the Duke of Orleans. Henry had no longer to fear invasion from France. In **1408** he was freed from yet another enemy. The old Earl of Northumberland, who had wandered from Scotland to Wales, now wandered north again to try his fortunes in his own country. As he passed through Yorkshire he was met by the sheriff of the county, and defeated and slain on Bramham Moor. At the same time South Wales fell again under the power of the king, and though Owen Glendower still continued to hold out in the mountainous region round Snowdon, his power rapidly declined.

11. **Henry, Prince of Wales.** 1409—1410.—No one had been more helpful to the king in these wars than his son, Henry, Prince of Wales. He had fought at Shrewsbury and in Wales, and had learnt to command as well as to fight. Young as he was—in 1409

Fight in the lists with poleaxes between Richard Beauchamp, Earl of Warwick, and Sir Pandolf Malatesta, at Verona, *temp.* Henry IV.: from the "Life of Richard, Earl of Warwick;" drawn by John Rous about 1485.

he was but twenty-two—he was already seen to be a man born to have the mastery. He took his place in his father's council as well as in his armies in the field. He was skilful, resolute, always knowing his own mind, prompt to act as each occasion arose. He was, moreover, unfeignedly religious. It seemed as if a king as great as Edward I. was about to ascend the throne. Yet between the character of Edward I. and the character of Prince Henry there was a great difference. Edward I. worked for the future as well as

for the present. His constructive legislation served his country for generations after his death. Even his mistaken attempt to unite England and Scotland was, to some extent at least, an anticipation of that which was done by the Act of Union four hundred years after his death. The young Henry had no such power of building for the future. He worked for the present alone, and his work crumbled away almost as soon as he was in his grave. His ideas were the ordinary ideas of his age, and he never originated any of his own. In **1410**, when a heretic, Badby, was led to be burnt, the Prince in vain urged him to recant. As the flames blazed up, the poor wretch, stung by the torment, cried for mercy. The Prince bade the executioners drag away the blazing faggots, and offered Badby support for his lifetime if he would abandon his heresy. Badby refused, and the Prince sternly ordered the executioners to push the faggots back and to finish their cruel work. In that very year the House of Commons, which was again urging the king to confiscate the revenues of the clergy, even urged him also to soften the laws against the Lollards. The king

Costume of a judge, about 1400: from the brass of Sir John Cassy, Chief Baron of the Exchequer, at Deerhurst, Gloucestershire.

refused, and he had no opposition to fear from the Prince of Wales.

12. **The Last Years of Henry IV.**

1411—1413.—It was not long before a bitter quarrel broke out between Henry IV. and his son, which lasted till the death of the old man. In later times stories were told how Prince Henry gave himself up to the society of low and debauched companions, how he amused himself by robbing the

receivers of his own rents, and how, having struck Chief Justice
Gascoigne for sitting in judgment on one of his unruly followers,
he was sent to prison for contempt of court.   There is no real
evidence in support of these stories ; but there is good reason to
believe that, though they were certainly exaggerated, they were
not altogether without foundation.   Since **1410** the Prince kept
house in the heart of London, and, as a young and active man suddenly called from service in the field to live in the midst of the
temptations of a city, he may very well have developed a taste for
boisterous amusements, even if he did not fall into grosser forms of
dissipation.   It is certain that during this period of his life he ran
deeply into debt, and was no longer on good terms with his father.
Yet even the story about the Chief Justice goes on to say that the
Prince took his punishment meekly and offered no resistance, and
that his father thanked God that he had so upright a judge and so
obedient a son.   Political disagreement probably widened the breach
between the King and the Prince.   Henry IV. had grown accustomed
to live from hand to mouth, and had maintained himself on the
throne rather because Englishmen needed a king than because
he was himself a great ruler.   In his foreign policy he was swayed
by the interests of the moment.   In **1411** he helped the Burgundians
against the Armagnacs.   In **1412** he helped the Armagnacs against
the Burgundians.   Prince Henry already aimed at a steady alliance with the Burgundians, with a view to a policy more thorough-
going than that of keeping a balance between the French parties.
The king, too, was subject to epileptic attacks, and to a cutaneous
disorder which his ill-willers branded by the name of leprosy.
It has even been said that in **1412** the Prince urged his father to
abdicate in his favour.   If so, he had not long to wait for the crown.
In **1413** Henry IV. died, and Henry V. sat upon his throne.

13. **Henry V. and the Lollards.   1413—1414.**—Henry V. was
steadied by the duties which now devolved upon him.   He indeed
dismissed from the chancellorship Archbishop Arundel, who had
supported his father against himself, and gave it to his half-uncle,
Henry Beaufort, Bishop of Winchester, one of the legitimated sons
of John of Gaunt and Catherine Swynford (see p. 282), but he allowed
no plans of vengeance to take possession of his mind.   His first
thought was to show that he had confidence in his own title to
the crown.   He liberated the Earl of March, and transferred the
body of Richard II. to a splendid tomb at Westminster, as if he
had nothing to fear from any competitor.   If there was one thing
on which, as far as England was concerned, his heart was set, it

was on strengthening the religion of his ancestors. He founded three friaries and he set himself to crush the Lollards. Sir John Oldcastle, who bore the title of Lord Cobham in right of his wife, was looked up to by the Lollards as their chief supporter. Oldcastle was brought before Archbishop Arundel. Both judge and accused played their several parts with dignity. Arundel without angry reviling asserted the necessity of accepting the teaching of the Church. Oldcastle with modest firmness maintained the falsity of many of its doctrines. In the end he was excommunicated, but

Henry V. : from an original painting belonging to the Society of Antiquaries.

before any further action could be taken he escaped, and was nowhere to be found. His followers were so exasperated as to form a plot against the king's life. Early in **1414** Henry fell upon a crowd of them in St. Giles's Fields. Most escaped, but of those who were taken the greater part were hanged or burnt. The result was a statute giving fresh powers to the king for the punishment of the Lollards. Every book written by them was to be confiscated. Three years later (**1417**) Oldcastle was seized and burnt. He was the last of the Lollards to play an historical part. The Lollards continued to exist in secret, especially in the towns, but there was never again any one amongst them who combined religious fervour with cultivated intelligence.

14. **Henry's Claim to the Throne of France. 1414.**—Henry V. was resolved to uphold the old foreign policy of the days of Edward III. as well as the old religion. In **1414**, whilst he amused the French court by offers of friendship, he was in reality preparing to demand the crown of France as the right of the king of England, leaving out of sight the consideration that if the claim of

Edward III. had been worth anything at all, it would have descended to the Earl of March and not to himself. Everything seemed to combine to make easy an attack on France. Burgundians and Armagnacs were engaged in a death-struggle. In 1413 a riotous Burgundian mob had made itself master of Paris and the Government. Then the Armagnacs had got the upper hand, and the Duke of Burgundy was driven back to his own dominions. Henry now made an alliance with the Duke of Burgundy against the ruling powers, and prepared to invade the distracted land. Thus far he proceeded in imitation of Edward III., who had attacked Philip VI. in alliance with the Flemings. With Edward III., however, the claim to the French crown had always been a secondary consideration. He went to war because French sailors plundered English ports and the French king assisted the Scots. Henry had no such reason to urge. He went to war because he was young and warlike, because the enterprise was easy, and because foreign conquest would unite all Englishmen round his throne. When once the war was begun he was certain to carry it on in a different spirit from that of Edward III. Edward had gone to weaken the plunderers by plundering in return, and to fight battles only when they happened to come in his way. Henry went with the distinct resolution to conquer France and to place the French crown on his own head. Every step which he took was calculated with skill for the attainment of this end. Of immediate, perhaps of lifelong, success Henry was as nearly certain as it was possible to be. Yet, if he had remembered what had been the end of campaigns adorned by the brilliant victories of Creçy and Poitiers, he might have known that all that he could do would end in ultimate failure, and that the day must come when divided France would unite to cast out, if not himself, at least his heirs. It was significant that when his Chancellor, Beaufort, announced to Parliament the king's intention, he took for his text, after the manner of political speakers in those days, ' Let us work while it is called to-day.' Henry was not inclined, as Edward I. had been, to take thought for a distant morrow.

15. **The Invasion of France.** 1415.—In 1415 Henry openly made his claim and gathered his army at Southampton. He there detected a conspiracy to place the Earl of March on the throne, which had been formed by Lord Scrope and Sir Thomas Grey, in combination with March's brother-in-law, the Earl of Cambridge, a son of the Duke of York (see genealogy at p. 327), the son of Edward III. All three were executed, and then Henry sailed

for France. He landed at the mouth of the Seine and besieged Harfleur. Harfleur fell after an heroic defence, and the Seine valley lay open to Henry.[1]   Over two-thirds of his army, however, had perished from dysentery and fever, and with no more, even at the highest calculation, than 15,000 men, he was unable to take advantage of the opportunity to march upon Paris.   His brother the Duke of Clarence, urged him to return to England, but Henry knew that if he went back with baffled hopes his throne would hardly stand the shock.   He resolved to march to Calais.   It might be that he would find a Creçy on the way.

16. **The March to Agincourt.   1415.**—Not a Frenchman could be found who would take seriously Henry's claim to be the true king of France.   When he reached the Somme he found the bridges over the river broken, and he was only able to cross it by ascending it almost to its source.   Then, bending to the left, he pushed on towards Calais.   His own army was by this time scarcely more than 10,000 strong, and he soon learnt that a mighty French host of at least 50,000 men blocked the way at Agincourt.   Though his little band was worn with hunger, he joyfully prepared for battle.   He knew that the Duke of Burgundy had kept aloof, and that the Armagnac army opposed to him was a feudal host of the same character as that which had been defeated at Creçy.   There were no recognised commanders, no subordination, no notion of the superior military power of the English archers.

17. **The Battle of Agincourt, October 25, 1415.**—In the early morning, mass was said in the English army, and Henry's scanty followers prayed earnestly that their king's right, as they believed it to be, might be shown on that day.   Henry's own prayers were long and fervid.   He was told that it was the hour of prime, the first hour of prayer.   " Now," he said, " is good time, for all England prayeth for us, and, therefore, be of good cheer."   He then went forth to marshal his army.   To a knight who wished that every brave Englishman now at home were there, he replied that he would not have one man more.   Few as they were, they were in the hands of God, who could give them the victory.   Henry's tactics were those of Creçy.   He drew up his archers between thick woods which defended their flanks, and with sharp stakes planted in the ground to defend them in front, placing his dismounted horsemen at intervals between the bodies of archers.   The French, however, showed no signs of attacking, and Henry, knowing that unless he cut his way through his soldiers would starve, threw

---

[1] Havre de Grâce was not yet in existence.

tactics to the winds and ordered his archers to advance. He had judged wisely. The French horsemen were on ploughed ground soaked with rain, and when at last they charged, the legs of their horses stuck fast in the clinging mud. The English arrows played thickly on them. Immovable and helpless, they were slaughtered as they stood. In vain their dismounted horsemen pushed forward in three columns upon the English knights. Their charge was vigorously resisted, and the archers, overlapping each column, drew forth the heavy leaden mallets which each man carried, and fell upon the helpless rout with blows which crashed through the iron headpieces of the Frenchmen. Such as could escape fled hastily to the rear, throwing into wild confusion the masses of their country-men who had not as yet been engaged. The battle was won, but unfortunately the victory was stained by a cruel deed. Some French plunderers had got into the rear to seize upon the baggage, and Henry, believing that a fresh enemy was upon him, gave orders, which were promptly carried out, to slay the prisoners. The loss of the French was enormous, and fell heavily on their nobility, always eager to be foremost in fight. Amongst the prisoners who were spared was the young Duke of Orleans.

18. **Henry's Diplomacy. 1416—1417.**—If Henry had not yet secured the crown of France, he had at least made sure of the crown of England. When he landed at Dover he was borne to land on the shoulders of the multitude. He entered London amidst wild enthusiasm. There was no fear of any fresh conspiracy to place the Earl of March on the throne. In 1416 he sent his brother, the Duke of Bedford, to secure Harfleur against a French attack, whilst he himself was diplomatically active in an attempt to win over to his side the Duke of Burgundy and Sigismund, King of the Romans, who actually visited him in England. Sigismund promised much, but had little power to fulfil his promises, whilst the Duke shifted backwards and forwards, looking out for his own advantage and giving no real help to either side. In 1417 the quarrels in France reached a head. The Count of Armagnac, getting into his possession the Dauphin Charles, a boy of fourteen, established a reign of terror in Paris, and the Duke of Burgundy, summoned by the frightened citizens to their help, levied war against the Armagnacs and marched to Paris.

19. **Henry's Conquest of Normandy. 1417 — 1419.** — Henry seized the opportunity and landed in Normandy. Caen was taken by storm, and in a few weeks all Normandy except Rouen had submitted to Henry. There had been a terrible butchery when

Caen was stormed, but when once submission was secured Henry took care that justice and order should be enforced, and that his soldiers should abstain from plunder and outrage. In Paris affairs were growing worse. The citizens rose against the Armagnacs and imprisoned all of them on whom they could lay hands. Then the mob burst into the prisons and massacred the prisoners, the Count of Armagnac himself being one of the number. Henry's army in the meanwhile closed round Rouen. The magistrates, to prolong the defence, thrust out the poorer inhabitants. Henry, who knew not pity when there was a practical object to be gained, thrust them back. During five months the poor wretches wandered about half starved, dying off day by day. On Christmas Day, in honour of Christ's nativity, Henry sent some food to the few who were left. Famine did its work within as well as without the walls, and on January 19, **1419**, Rouen, the old ducal capital of the Norman kings, surrendered to Henry.

20. **The Murder of the Duke of Burgundy and the Treaty of Troyes. 1419 — 1420.** — In the summer of **1419** English troops swept the country even up to the walls of Paris. Henry, however, gained more by the follies and crimes of his enemies than by his own skill. Terrified at the prospect of losing all, Burgundians

Effigy of William Phelip, Lord Baraolf (died 1441), with the Garter and Lancastrian collar of SS. : from his tomb at Dennington, Suffolk. The type of armour here shown prevailed from about 1415 to 1435

and Armagnacs seemed for a moment to forget their quarrel and to be ready to join together in defence of their common country; but the hatred in their hearts could not be rooted out. At a conference between the Duke of Burgundy and the Dauphin on the bridge of

Marriage of Henry V. and Catherine of France: from the 'Life of Richard Beauchamp, Earl of Warwick,' drawn by John Rous about 1485.

Montereau, angry words sprang easily to the lips of both. The Duke put his hand on the pommel of his sword, and some of the Dauphin's attendants, believing their master's life in danger, fell on the Duke and slew him. After this an agreement between the

X

factions was no longer possible. The new Duke of Burgundy, Philip the Good, at once joined the English against the Dauphin, whom he regarded as an accomplice of his father's murderers. Even Queen Isabella, the mother of the Dauphin, shared in the outcry against her own son, and in **1420** was signed the Treaty of Troyes, by which the Dauphin was disinherited in favour of Henry, who was to be king of France on the death of Charles VI. In accordance with its terms, Henry married Charles's daughter Catherine, and ruled France as regent till the time came when he was to rule it as king.

21. **The Close of the Reign of Henry V. 1420 - 1422.**—The Treaty of Troyes was very similar in its stipulations to that which Henry II. had made with Stephen at Wallingford (see p. 137). The result was, as might have been expected, totally different. Henry II. had the English nation behind his back. Henry V. presumed to rule over a foreign nation, the leaders of which had only accepted him in a momentary fit of passion. He never got the whole of France into his power. He held Paris and the North, whilst the Duke of Burgundy held the East. South of the Loire the Armagnacs were strong, and that part of France stood by the Dauphin, though even here the English possessed a strip of land along the sea-coast in Guienne and Gascony, and at one time drew over some of the lords to admit Henry's feudal supremacy. In **1420** Henry fancied it safe for him to return to England, but, in his absence, in the spring of **1421** his brother, the Duke of Clarence, was defeated and slain at Baugé by a force of Frenchmen and of Scottish auxiliaries. Clarence had forgotten that English victories had been due to English archery. He had plunged into the fight with his horsemen, and had paid the penalty for his rashness with his life. Henry hurried to the rescue of his followers, and drove the French over the Loire ; though Orleans, on the north bank of that river, remained unconquered. Instead of laying siege to it Henry turned sharply round northwards to besiege Meaux, the garrison of which was plundering the country round Paris in the name of the Dauphin, and seemed likely to shake the fidelity to Henry even of Paris itself. Meaux held out for many months. When at last it fell, in **1422**, Henry was already suffering from a disease which carried him off before the end of the year at the age of thirty-five. Henry V. had given his life to the restoration of the authority of the Church in England, and to the establishment of his dynasty at home by means of the glory of foreign conquest. What man could do he did, but he could not achieve the impossible.

CHAPTER XX

HENRY VI. AND THE LOSS OF FRANCE. 1422—1451

LEADING DATES
Reign of Henry VI., 1422-1461

The accession of Henry VI. 1422
The relief of Orleans 1429
End of the alliance with the Duke of Burgundy . . . 1435
Marriage of Henry VI. with Margaret of Anjou. . . 1445
Murder of the Duke of Suffolk and Jack Cade's rebellion . 1450
Loss of the last French possessions except Calais . . 1451

1. **Bedford and Gloucester. 1422.**—In England Henry V. was succeeded in 1422 by his son, Henry VI., a child of nine months. In the same year, in consequence of the death of Charles VI., the infant was acknowledged as king of France in the north and east of that country. The Dauphin, holding the lands south of the Loire, and some territory even to the north of it, claimed to reign over the whole of France by hereditary right as Charles VII. Henry V. had appointed his eldest surviving brother, John, Duke of Bedford, regent in France, and his youngest brother, Humphrey, Duke of Gloucester, regent in England.   In England there were no longer any parties banded against the Crown, and the title of the Earl of March had not a single supporter ; but both the Privy Council and the Parliament agreed that the late king could not dispose of the regency by will.   Holding that Bedford as the elder brother had the better claim, they nevertheless, in consequence of his absence in France, appointed Gloucester Protector, with the proviso that he should give up his authority to Bedford if the latter were to return to England.   They also imposed limitations upon the authority of the Protector, requiring him to act by the advice of the Council.

2. **Bedford's Success in France.   1423—1424.**—The English nation was bent upon maintaining its supremacy in France.   Bedford was a good warrior and an able statesman.   In 1423 he prudently married the sister of Philip of Burgundy, hoping thereby to secure permanently the all-important fidelity of the Duke.   His next step was to place difficulties in the way of the Scottish auxiliaries who poured into France to the help of Charles.   Through his influence the captive James I. (see p. 295) was liberated and sent home to Scotland, on the understanding that he would prevent

his subjects from aiding the enemies of England. Bedford needed all the support he could find, as the French had lately been gaining ground. In 1424, however, Bedford defeated them at Verneuil. In England it was believed that Verneuil was a second Agincourt, and that the French resistance would soon be at an end.

3. Gloucester's Invasion of Hainault. 1424.—Bedford's progress in France was checked by the folly of his brother Gloucester, who was as unwise and capricious as he was greedy of power. Gloucester had lately married Jacqueline, the heiress of Holland

and Hainault, though her husband, the Duke of Brabant, was still living, on the plea that her first marriage was null on the ground of nearness of kin. In 1424 Gloucester overran Hainault, which was under the government of the Duke of Brabant, thereby giving offence to the Duke of Burgundy, who was a cousin and ally of the Duke of Brabant, and who had no wish to see the English holding a territory so near to his own county of Flanders.

Henry VI. : from an original picture in the National Portrait Gallery.

The Duke of Brabant recovered Hainault and captured Jacqueline, who had already been abandoned by Gloucester. A coolness arose between the Duke of Burgundy and the English which was never completely removed.

4. Gloucester and Beaufort. 1425—1428.—In England as well as on the Continent Gloucester's self-willed restlessness roused enemies, the most powerful of them being his uncle, the Chancellor, Henry Beaufort, Bishop of Winchester (see pp. 301, 335), a wealthy and ambitious prelate not without those statesmanlike qualities which were sadly lacking to Gloucester. If Beaufort ruled the Council, Gloucester had the art of making himself popular with the multitude, whose sympathies were not likely to be given to a bishop of the type of Beaufort, who practised no austerities and who had nothing in him to appeal to the popular imagination. So bitter was the feud between Gloucester and Beaufort that in 1426 Bedford was obliged to visit England to keep the peace between them. Before he returned to France he persuaded Beaufort to surrender the chancellorship to Kemp, the Bishop of London, and to leave England for a time. Moreover, in 1427 he himself swore that as long as the king was under age the Council and not the Protector was to govern. When Gloucester was asked to take the same oath, he signed it, but refused to swear. In 1428, after Bedford had returned to France, Beaufort came back, bringing with him from Rome the title of Cardinal, and authority to raise soldiers for a crusade against heretics in Bohemia. A storm was at once raised against him. A Cardinal, it was said, was a servant of the Roman See, and as no man could serve two masters, he ought not to hold an English bishopric or to sit in the English Council, far less to send to Bohemia English troops which were needed in France. Gloucester fancied that the opportunity of overthrowing his rival had come. Beaufort, however, was too prudent to press his claims. He absented himself from the Council and allowed the men whom he had raised for Bohemia to be sent to France instead. Before the end of the year the outcry against him died away, and, Cardinal as he was, he resumed his old place in the Council.

5. **The Siege of Orleans. 1428—1429.**—The time had arrived when the presence of every English soldier was needed in France. Bedford had made himself master of almost the whole country north of the Loire except Orleans. If he could gain that city it would be easy for him to overpower Charles, who kept court at Chinon. In 1428, therefore, he laid siege to Orleans. The city, however, defended itself gallantly, though all that the French outside could hope to do was to cut off the supplies of the besiegers. In February 1429 they attempted to intercept a convoy of herrings coming from Paris for the English troops, but were beaten off in what was jocosely styled the Battle of the Herrings, and it seemed as though Orleans, and with it France itself, were doomed. Frenchmen were indeed weary of the foreign yoke and of the arrogant insolence of the rough island soldiers. Yet in France all military and civil organisation had hitherto come from the kings, and unfortunately for his subjects Charles was easy-tempered and entirely incapable either of carrying on war successfully or of inspiring that enthusiasm without which the most careful organisation is as the twining of ropes of sand. It would need a miracle to inspire Frenchmen with the belief that it was possible for them to defeat

the victors of Agincourt and Verneuil, and yet without such a miracle irretrievable ruin was at hand.

6. **Jeanne Darc and the Relief of Orleans. 1429.**—The miracle was wrought by a young maiden of seventeen, Jeanne Darc, the daughter of a peasant of Domremi, in the duchy of Bar. Her home was at a distance from the actual scenes of war, but whilst she was still little more than a child, tales of horror, reaching her from afar, had filled her with 'pity for the realm of France' and for its young king, whom she idealised into the pattern of every virtue. As she brooded over the thought of possible deliverance, her warm imagination summoned up before her bright and saintly forms, St. Michael, St. Catherine, and St. Margaret, who bade her, the chosen of God, to go forth and save the king, and conduct him to Reims to be crowned and anointed with the holy oil from the vessel which, as men believed, had been brought down from heaven in days of old. At last in 1428 her native hamlet was burnt down by a Burgundian band. Then the voices of the saints bade her go to Vaucouleurs, where she would find a knight, Robert de Baudricourt, who would conduct her to Charles. Months passed before Baudricourt would do aught but scorn her message, and it was not till February 1429, when the news from Orleans was most depressing, that he consented to take her in his train. She found Charles at Chinon, and, as the story goes, convinced him of her Divine mission by recognising him in disguise in the midst of his courtiers. Soldiers and theologians alike distrusted her, but her native good sense, her simple and earnest faith, and above all her purity of heart and life disarmed all opposition, and she was sent forth to lead an army to the relief of Orleans. She rode on horseback clothed in armour as a man, with a sword which she had taken from behind the altar of St. Catherine by her side, and a consecrated banner in her hand. She brought with her hope of victory, enthusiasm built on confidence in Divine protection, and wide-reaching patriotism. 'Pity for the realm of France' inspired her, and even the rough soldiers who followed her forsook for a time their debaucheries that they might be fit to follow God's holy maid. Such an army was invincible ; but whilst to the French the maid was an instrument of the mercy of God, to the English she was an emissary of hell and the forerunner of defeat. On May 7 she led the storm of one of the English fortified posts by which the town was hemmed in. After a sharp attack she planted her standard on the wall. The English garrison was slain to a man. The line of the besiegers was broken through, and Orleans was saved. On the 12th the English army was in full retreat.

7. **The Coronation of Charles VII. and the Capture of the Maid. 1429—1430.**—The Maid followed up her victory. She had at her side brave and skilful warriors, such as La Hire and the Bastard of Orleans, the illegitimate son of the murdered Louis of Orleans, and with their help she pressed the English hard, driving them northwards and defeating them at Patay. She insisted on

Fotheringhay Church, Northamptonshire. The contract for building it, between Edward Duke of York, and William Horwod, freemason, is dated September 24, 1434.

conducting Charles to Reims, and he, indolently resisting at first, was carried away by her persistent urgency. Hostile towns opened their gates to her on the way, and on July 17 she saw with chastened joy the man whom she had saved from destruction crowned in the great cathedral of Reims. For her part, she was eager to push on the war, but Charles was slothful, and in a hurry to be back to the pleasures of his court. When she led the troops to the attack of Paris, she was ordered back by the king, and the army sent into winter quarters. In the spring of 1430 the Maid was allowed again to attack the English, but she had no longer the support which she had once had. Many of the French soldiers were meanly jealous of her, and were vexed when they were told that they owed their victories to a woman. On the other side the Duke of Burgundy was frightened by the French successes into giving real aid to Bedford, and on May 23, in a skirmish before Compiegne, her countrymen doing nothing to save or to rescue her, the Maid was taken by Burgundian soldiers. Before the end of the year her captors sold her to the English, who firmly believed her to be a witch.

8. **The Martyrdom at Rouen.** 1431.—The English had no difficulty in finding an ecclesiastical court to judge their prisoner. Even the French clergy detested the Maid as having appealed to supernatural voices which had not been recognised by the Church; and in spite of an intelligent and noble defence she was condemned to be burnt. At the stake she behaved with heroic simplicity. When the flames curled round her she called upon the saints who had befriended her. Her last utterance was a cry of "Jesus!" An Englishman who had come to triumph hung his head for shame. "We are lost," he said; "we have burnt a saint!"

9. **The Last Years of the Duke of Bedford.** 1431—1435.—The English gained nothing by their unworthy vengeance. Though the personal presence of the Maid was no longer there to encourage her countrymen, they had learnt from her to cherish that 'pity for the realm of France' which had glowed so brightly in her own bosom. It was in vain that towards the end of 1431 Bedford carried the young Henry, now a boy of ten years, who had already been crowned in England the year before, to be crowned at Nôtre Dame, the cathedral of Paris. The Parisians were disgusted by the troop of foreigners which accompanied him, and their confidence was shaken when Bedford sent the king back to England as not venturing to trust him amongst his French subjects. In 1432 the armies of Charles VII. stole forwards step by step, and Bedford, who had no money to pay his troops, could do nothing to resist them. The English Parliament, which had cheerfully voted supplies as long as there seemed a prospect of conquering France, hung back from granting them when victories were no longer won. In 1433 Bedford was again forced to return to England to oppose the intrigues of Gloucester, who, though he had lost the title of Protector when the young king was crowned, had thrown the government

into confusion by his intrigues. When Bedford went back to France in 1434 he found the tide running strongly against him. Little more than Paris and Normandy were held by the English, and the Duke of Burgundy was inclining more and more towards the French. In 1435 a congress was held at Arras, under the Duke of Burgundy's presidency, in the hope that peace might be made. The congress, however, failed to accomplish anything, and soon after the English ambassadors were withdrawn Bedford died at Rouen. If so wise a statesman and so skilful a warrior had failed to hold down France, no other Englishman was likely to achieve the task.

10. **The Defection of Burgundy. 1435.**—After Bedford's death the Duke of Burgundy renounced his alliance with the English and entered into a league with Charles VII. In 1430, by the death of the Duke of Brabant, he inherited Brabant, and in 1436 he inherited from the faithless Jacqueline Hainault, Holland, Zealand, and Friesland (see p. 308). He thus, being already Count of Flanders, became ruler over well-nigh the whole of the Netherlands in addition to his own territories in Burgundy. The vassal of the king of France was now a European potentate. England had therefore to count on the enmity of a ruler whose power of injuring her was indeed serious.

11. **The Duke of York in France. 1436—1437.**— Bedford's successor was the young Richard, Duke of York, whose father was that Earl of Cambridge who had been executed at Southampton (see p. 301); whilst his mother was Anne Mortimer, the sister of the Earl of March. As the Earl of March had died in 1425, the Duke of York was now, through his mother, the heir of Lionel, Duke of Clarence, and thus, if hereditary right was to be regarded, heir to the throne. That a man with such claims should have been entrusted with such an office shows how firmly the victories of Henry V. had established the House of Lancaster in England. Disputes in the English Council, however, delayed his departure, and in April 1436, before he could arrive in France, Paris was lost, whilst the Duke of Burgundy besieged Calais. England, stung by the defection of Burgundy, made an unusual effort. One army drove the Burgundians away from before Calais, whilst another under the Duke of York himself regained several fortresses in Normandy, and in 1437 Lord Talbot drove the Burgundians behind the Somme.

12. **The English Lose Ground. 1437—1443.**—Gallant as the Duke of York was, he was soon recalled, and in 1437 was succeeded by Richard Beauchamp, Earl of Warwick. Warwick, however,

failed to do more than to hold what his predecessor had gained, and he died in **1439**. Both in England and France the suffering was terrible, and England would find neither men nor money to support a falling cause. In **1439** a peace conference was held at Calais, but the English continued arrogantly to claim the crown of France, and peace was not to be had. In **1440** York was sent back, and fighting went on till **1443**, in which the English lost ground both in Normandy and in Guienne.

13. **Continued Rivalry of Beaufort and Gloucester. 1439—1441.** —The chief advocate in England of the attempt to make peace at Calais in **1439** had been Cardinal Beaufort, whose immense wealth gave him authority over a Council which was always at its wits' end for money. Beaufort was wise enough to see that the attempt to reconquer the lost territory, or even to hold Normandy, was hopeless. Such a view, however, was not likely to

Gilt-latten effigy (front view) of Richard Beauchamp, Earl of Warwick, died 1439 : from his tomb at Warwick.   Made by William Austen, of London, founder, 1453.

be popular. Nations, like men, often refuse openly to acknowledge failure long after they cease to take adequate means to avert it. Of the popular feeling Gloucester made himself the mouthpiece, and it was by his influence that exorbitant pretensions had been put forward at Calais. In **1440** he accused Beaufort of using his authority for his own private interests, and though Beaufort gave over to the public service a large sum of money which he received as the ransom of the Duke of Orleans from a captivity which had lasted twenty-four years (see p. 303), Gloucester virulently charged him with an unpatriotic concession to the enemy. Gloucester's domestic relations, on the other hand, offered an easy object of attack. When he deserted Jacqueline he took a mistress, Eleanor Cobham, and subsequently married her, which he was able to do without difficulty, as his union with Jacqueline was, in the eyes

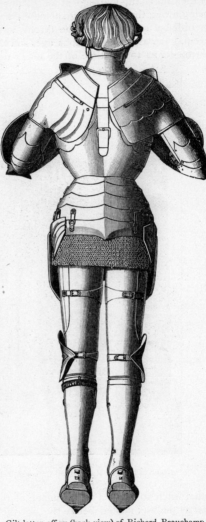

Gilt-latten effigy (back view) of Richard Beauchamp, Earl of Warwick, died 1439 : from his tomb at Warwick.   Made by William Austen, of London, founder, 1453.

of the Church, no marriage at all.   The new Duchess of Gloucester being aware that if the king should die her husband would be next in order of succession to the throne, was anxious to hasten that event.   It was a superstitious age, and the Duchess consulted an astrologer as to the time of the king's death, and employed a re-

Tattershall Castle, Lincolnshire :
built of brick by Ralph, Lord Cromwell, between 1433 and 1455.

puted witch to make a waxen image of the king under the belief that as the wax melted before the fire the king's life would waste away.   In 1441 these proceedings were detected.   The astrologer was hanged, the witch was burnt, whilst the Duchess escaped with doing public penance and with imprisonment for life.   Gloucester could not save her, but he did not lose his place in the Council, where he continued to advocate a war policy, though with less success than before.

14. **Beaufort and Somerset. 1442– 1443.**—In 1442 Henry was in his twenty-first year. Unfeignedly religious and anxious to be at peace with all men, his character was far too weak and gentle to fit him for governing in those rough times. He had attached himself to Beaufort because Beaufort's policy was pacific, and because Gloucester's life was scandalous. Beaufort's position was secured at court, but the situation was not one in which a pacific statesman could hope for success. The French would not consent to make peace till all that they had lost had been recovered ; yet, hardly bested as the English in France were, it was impossible in the teeth of English public opinion for any statesman, however pacific, to abandon lands still commanded by English garrisons. Every year, however, brought the problem nearer to the inevitable solution. In 1442 the French attacked the strip of land which was all that the English now held in Guienne and Gascony, and with the exception of Bordeaux and Bayonne captured almost every fortified town. The command in France was given to Cardinal Beaufort's nephew, John Beaufort, Duke of Somerset. Somerset, who was thoroughly incompetent, did not even leave England till the autumn of 1443, and when he arrived in France accomplished nothing worthy of his office.

15. **The Angevin Marriage Treaty. 1444—1445.**—Henry now fell under the influence of William de la Pole, Earl of Suffolk, a descendant of the favourite of Richard II. Suffolk had fought bravely in France, and had learnt by sad experience the hopelessness of the English cause. In 1444, with the consent of the king and the Parliament, he negotiated at Tours a truce for ten months. In order to make it more lasting there was to be a marriage between Henry and Margaret of Anjou. Her father, René, the Duke of Anjou, was titular king of Jerusalem and Sicily, in neither of which did he possess a foot of ground, whilst his duchy of Anjou was almost valueless to him in consequence of the forays of the English, who still held posts in Maine. Charles had the more readily consented to the truce, because it was understood that the surrender of Maine would be a condition of the marriage. In 1445 Suffolk led Margaret to England, where her marriage to Henry was solemnised. A French queen who brought with her no portion except a truce bought by the surrender of territory could hardly fail to be unpopular in England.

16. Deaths of Gloucester and Beaufort. 1447.—The truce was renewed from time to time, and Suffolk's authority seemed firmly established. In 1447 Gloucester was charged with high treason in a Parliament held at Bury St. Edmunds, but before he had time to answer he was found dead in his bed. His death may, with strong probability, be ascribed to natural causes, but it was widely believed that he had been murdered and that Suffolk was the

Part of Wingfield manor-house, Derbyshire: built by Ralph, Lord Cromwell, about 1440.

murderer. A few weeks later Gloucester's old rival, Cardinal Beaufort, the last real statesman who supported the throne of Henry VI., followed him to the grave, and Suffolk was left alone to bear the responsibility of government and the disgrace of failure.

17. The Loss of the French Provinces. 1448—1449.—Suffolk had undertaken more than he was able to fulfil. Somerset had died in 1444, and Suffolk being jealous of all authority but his own,

he sent York to govern Ireland. He could not secure the fulfil-
ment of the conditions which he had made with the king of France.

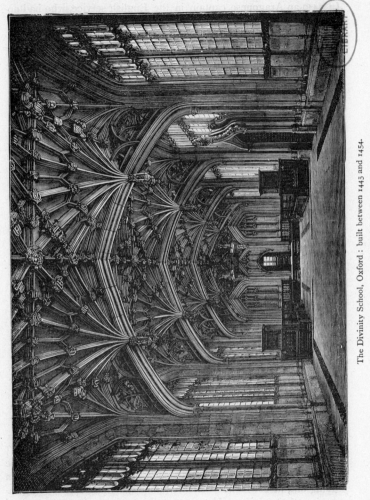

The Divinity School, Oxford : built between 1445 and 1454.

The English commanders refused to evacuate Maine, and in **1448**
a French army entered the province and drove out the English.

Edmund, the new Duke of Somerset, was sent to take the command in Normandy, which had formerly been held by his brother. In **1449** an Aragonese captain in the English service, who had no pay for his troops, having seized Fougères, a place on the frontier of Brittany, for the sake of the booty to be gained, Charles made the attack an excuse for the renewal of the war. So destitute was the condition in which the English forces were left that neither Somerset nor the warlike Talbot (see p. 313), who had recently been created Earl of Shrewsbury, was able to resist him. Rouen fell in **1450**, and in **1450** the whole of Normandy was lost. In **1451** the French attacked Bordeaux and Bayonne, two port-towns which, in consequence of their close commercial intercourse with England, had no wish to transfer their allegiance to Charles. England, however, sent them no succour, and before the end of the year they were forced to capitulate. The relics of Guienne and Gascony thus passed into the hands of the French, and of all the possessions which the kings of England had once held on the Continent Calais alone remained.

CHAPTER XXI

THE LATER YEARS OF HENRY VI. 1450—1461

LEADING DATES

Reign of Henry VI., 1422—1461

Murder of the Duke of Suffolk and Jack Cade's rebellion .	1450
First Protectorate of the Duke of York	1453
First Battle of St. Albans and second Protectorate of the Duke of York	1455
Battle of Blore Heath and the discomfiture of the Yorkists	1459
After a Yorkist victory at Northampton the Duke of York is declared heir to the crown, but is defeated and slain at Wakefield	1460
Battles of Mortimer's Cross, St. Albans, and Towton .	1461
Coronation of Edward IV.	1461

1. The Growth of Inclosures.—Since the insurrection of the peasants in **1381** (see p. 268) villeinage had to a great extent been dying out, in consequence of the difficulty felt by the lords in enforcing their claims. Yet the condition of the classes connected with the land was by no means prosperous. The lords of manors indeed abandoned the old system of cultivating their own lands

by the labour of villeins, or by labourers hired with money paid by
villeins in commutation for bodily service. They began to let out
their land to tenants who paid rent for it ; but even the new system
did not bring in anything like the old profit. The soil had been
exhausted for want of a proper system of manuring, and arable
land scarcely repaid the expenses of its cultivation. For this evil
a remedy was found in the inclosure of lands for pasturage. This
change, which in itself was beneficial by increasing the produc
tiveness of the country, and by giving rest to the exhausted soil,
became oppressive because all the benefit went to the lords of the
manors, whilst the tenants of the manors were left to struggle on as
best they might. Not only had they no share in the increase of
wealth which was brought about by the inclosure of what had
formerly been the common land of the manors, but the poorer
amongst them had less employment than before, as it required fewer
men to look after sheep than to grow corn.

2. **Increasing Power of the Nobility.**—The disproportionate
increase of the wealth of the landowners threw into their hands a
disproportionate amount of power. The great landowner especially
was able to gather bands of retainers and to spread terror around
him. The evil of liveries and maintenance, which had become
prominent in the reign of Richard II. (see p. 281), had increased
since his deposition. It was an evil which the kings were powerless to control. Again and again complaints were raised of 'want
of governance.' Henry V. had abated the mischief for a time by
employing the unruly elements in his wars in France, but it was a
remedy which, when defeat succeeded victory, only increased the
disease which it was meant to cure. When France was lost bands
of unruly men accustomed to deeds of violence poured back into
England, where they became retainers of the great landowners, who
with their help set king and laws at defiance.

3. **Case of Lord Molynes and John Paston.**—The difficulty of
obtaining justice may be illustrated by a case which occurred in
Norfolk. The manor of Gresham belonged to John Paston, a
gentleman of moderate fortune. It was coveted by Lord Molynes,
who had no legal claim to it whatever. Lord Molynes, however,
took possession of it in **1448** with the strong hand. If such a thing
had happened at present Paston would have gone to law ; but to
go to law implies the submitting of a case to a jury, and in those
days a jury was not to be trusted to do justice. In the first place
it was selected by the sheriff, and the sheriff took care to choose
such men as would give a verdict pleasing to the great men whom

Y

he wished to serve, and in the second place, supposing that the sheriff did not do this, a juryman who offended great men by giving a verdict according to his conscience, but contrary to their desire, ran the risk of being knocked on the head before he reached home. Paston accordingly, instead of going to law, begged Lord Molynes to behave more reasonably. Finding his entreaties of no avail, he took possession of a house on the manor. Lord Molynes merely waited till Paston was away from home, and then sent a thousand men, who drove out Paston's wife and pillaged and wrecked the house. Paston ultimately recovered the manor, but redress for the injury done him was not to be had.

4. **Suffolk's Impeachment and Murder. 1450.**—A government which was too weak to redress injuries was certain to be unpopular. The loss of the French possessions made it still more unpopular. The brunt of the public displeasure fell on Suffolk, who had just been made a duke, and who, through the queen's favour, was all-powerful at court. It was believed that he had sold himself to France, and it was known that whilst the country was impoverished large grants had been made to court favourites. An outcry was raised that the king 'should live of his own,' and ask for no more grants from his people. In 1450 Suffolk was impeached. Though the charge brought against him was a tissue of falsehoods, Henry did not dare to shield him entirely, and ordered him into banishment for five years. Suffolk, indeed, embarked for the Continent, but a large ship ranged up alongside of the vessel in which he was. Having been dragged on board amidst cries of "Welcome, traitor!" he was, two days afterwards, transferred to a boat, where his head was chopped off with six strokes of a rusty sword. His body was flung on the beach at Dover.

5. **Jack Cade's Rebellion. 1450.**—Suffolk's supporters remained in office after his death. The men of Kent rose against them, and found a leader in an Irish adventurer, Jack Cade, who called himself Mortimer, and gave out that he was an illegitimate son of the late Earl of March. He established himself on Black-heath at the head of 30,000 men, asking that the burdens of the people should be diminished, the Crown estates recovered, and the Duke of York recalled from Ireland to take the place of the present councillors. Jack Cade's rebellion, in short, unlike that of Wat Tyler, was a political, not a social movement. In demanding that the government should be placed in the hands of the Duke of York, Jack Cade virtually asked that the Duke should step into the place, not of the Council, but of the King—that is to say, that a ruler who

could govern should be substituted for one who could not, and in whose name the great families plundered England. It was this demand which opened the long struggle which was soon to devastate the country. At first it seemed as if Jack Cade would carry all before him. London, which had the most to gain by the establishment of a strong government, opened its gates to him. When, however, he was tested by success, he was found wanting. Striking with his sword the old Roman milestone known as London Stone, he cried out, "Now is Mortimer lord of this city." His followers gave themselves up to wild excesses. They beheaded Lord Say and his son-in-law, the Sheriff of Kent, and carried about their heads on pikes. They plundered houses and shops. The citizens who had invited them to enter now turned against them. After a fight on London Bridge the insurgents agreed to go home on the promise of a pardon. Jack Cade himself, attempting to gather fresh forces, was chased into Sussex and slain.

6. **Rivalry of York and Somerset. 1450—1453.**—In the summer of **1450**, Richard, Duke of York, the real leader of the opposition, came back from Ireland. He found that Somerset, who had just returned from Normandy after the final loss of that province (see p. 320), had succeeded Suffolk in the king's confidence. Somerset, however, was not merely the favourite of Henry and the queen. The bulk of the nobility was on his side, whilst York was supported by the force of popular discontent and by such of the nobility as cherished a personal grudge against Somerset and his friends. In **1451** the loss of Guienne and Gascony increased the weight of Somerset's unpopularity. In **1452** both parties took arms ; but, this time, civil war was averted by a promise from the king that York should be admitted to the Council, and that Somerset should be placed in confinement till he answered the charges against him. On this York dismissed his army. Henry, however, was not allowed to keep his promise, and Somerset remained in power, whilst York was glad to be allowed to retire unhurt. Somerset attempted to recover his credit by fresh victories in France, and sent the old Earl of Shrewsbury to Bordeaux to reconquer Gascony. Shrewsbury was successful for a while, but in **1453** he was defeated and slain at Castillon, and the whole enterprise came to nothing.

7. **The First Protectorate of the Duke of York. 1453—1454.**— Henry's mind had never been strong, and in **1453** it entirely gave way. His insanity was probably inherited from his maternal grandfather, Charles VI. The queen bore him a son, named Edward, but though the infant was brought to his father, Henry gave no sign

of recognising his presence. It was necessary to place the government in other hands, and in **1454** the Duke of York was named Protector by the House of Lords, which, as the majority of its members were at that time ecclesiastics, did not always re-echo the sentiments of the great families. If only the king had remained permanently insane York might have established an orderly government. Henry, however, soon recovered as much sense as he ever had, and York's protectorate came to an end.

8. The First Battle of St. Albans and the Duke of York's Second Protectorate.—The restoration of Henry was in reality the restoration of Somerset. In **1455** York, fearing destruction, took arms against his rival. A battle was fought at St. Albans, in which Somerset was defeated and slain. This was the first battle in the wars known as the Wars of the Roses, because a red rose was the badge of the House of Lancaster, to which Henry belonged, and a white rose the badge of the House of York. After the victory York accompanied the king to London. Though the bulk of the nobility was against him, he had on his side the powerful family of the Nevills, as he had married Cicely Nevill, the sister of the head of that family, the Earl of Salisbury. Still more powerful was Salisbury's eldest son, who had married the heiress of the Beauchamps, Earls of Warwick, and who held the earldom of Warwick in right of his wife.[1] In June **1455** the king was again insane, and York was for the second time named Protector. This Protectorate, however, did not last long, as early in **1456** the king recovered his senses, and York had to resign his post.

[1] Genealogy of the Nevills :—

9. **Discomfiture of the Yorkists. 1456—1459.**—For two years
Henry exercised such authority as he was capable of exercising.
In 1458 he tried his hand at effecting a reconciliation.   The chiefs

A sea-fight : from the ' Life of Richard Beauchamp, Earl of Warwick : '
drawn by John Rous about 1485.

Effigy of Sir Robert Harcourt, K.G. (died 1471): from his tomb at Stanton Harcourt, Oxon: showing armour worn from about 1445 to 1480.

of the two parties walked hand in hand in procession to St. Paul's, York himself leading the queen. The Yorkists founded masses for the repose of the souls of their enemies slain at St. Albans, and paid money to their widows. It seemed as if the old practice of the weregild (see p. 32) had been unexpectedly revived. The spirit which had made weregild possible was, however, no longer to be found. Warwick retired to Calais, of which he was governor, and sent out vessels to plunder the merchant ships of all nations. When he was summoned to Westminster to give account of his actions, a quarrel broke out there between his servants and those of the king. Believing his own life to be in danger, he made his way back to Calais. The Yorkists spent the winter in preparing for war. In the summer of **1459** Lord Audley, sent by the queen to seize the Earl of Salisbury, was defeated by him at Blore Heath, in Staffordshire. Later in the year the two parties with their whole forces prepared for a battle near Ludlow, but the Yorkists found themselves no match for their enemies, and, without fighting, York, with his second son, the Earl of Rutland, took refuge in Ireland. His eldest son Edward, Earl of March, with Salisbury and Warwick, made his way to Calais.

10. **The Battle of Northampton and the Duke of York's Claim to the Throne. 1460.**—In **1460** the Yorkist Earls of Salisbury, Warwick, and March were once more in England. They defeated the royal army at

Northampton and captured the king. York returned from Ireland, and, as soon as Parliament met, took an unexpected step. If hereditary descent was to count for anything, his claim to the throne was superior to that of Henry himself, as he was the heir of Edward III. through his mother Anne, the sister of the last Earl of March.[1] The Duke of York now placed his hand on the throne, claiming it in right of birth. The Lords decided that Henry, to whom they had sworn oaths of fealty, should retain the crown, but that York should succeed him, to the exclusion of Henry's son, Edward, Prince of Wales.

11. **The Battle of Wakefield. 1460.**—The struggle, which had at first been one between two unequal sections of the nobility, each nominally acknowledging Henry VI. as their king, thus came to be one between the Houses of Lancaster and York. The queen, savage at the wrong done to her son, refused to accept the compromise. Withdrawing to the North, she summoned to her aid the Earl of Northumberland and the Lancastrian lords. The North was always exposed to Scottish invasions, and the constant danger kept the inhabitants ready for war, and strengthened the authority of the great lords who led them. For the same reason the people of the North were ruder and less civilised than their fellow-countrymen in the South. Plunder and outrage did not come amiss to men who were frequently subjected to plunder and outrage. An army composed of 18,000 of these rough warriors placed

[1] Genealogy of the Houses of Lancaster and York :—

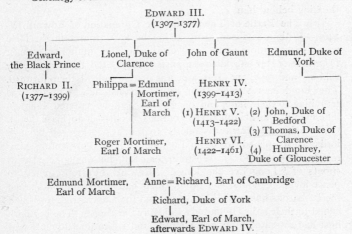

itself at the queen's disposal. With these she routed her enemies at Wakefield. York himself was slain. His son, Rutland, was stabbed to death by Lord Clifford, whose father had been slain at St. Albans. Salisbury was subsequently beheaded by the populace at Pontefract. By command of Margaret, York's head was cut off, and, adorned in mockery with a paper crown, was fixed with those of Salisbury and Rutland above one of the gates of York.

12. **The Battle of Mortimer's Cross and the Second Battle of St. Albans. 1461.**—The battle of Wakefield differed in character from the earlier battles of the war. They had been but conflicts between bands of noblemen and their armed retainers, in which the general population took little part, whilst the ordinary business of the country went on much as usual. At Wakefield not only were cruel passions developed, but a new danger appeared. When Margaret attempted to gain her ends with the help of her rude northern followers, she roused against her the fears of the wealthier and more prosperous South. The South found a leader in York's son, Edward. Though only in his nineteenth year, Edward showed that he had the qualities of a commander. Rapid in his movements, he fell upon some Lancastrian forces and defeated them on February 2, **1461**, at Mortimer's Cross. In the meanwhile Margaret was marching with her northern host upon London, plundering and destroying as she went. Warwick, carrying the king with him, met her on the way, but in the second battle of St. Albans—fought on February 17—was driven back, leaving the king behind him.

13. **The Battle of Towton and the Coronation of Edward IV. 1461.**—With a civilised army at her back, Margaret might have won her way into London, and established her authority, at least for a time. Her unbridled supporters celebrated their victory by robbery and rape, and Margaret was unable to lead them forward. The Londoners steeled their hearts against her. Edward was marching to their help, and on February 25 he entered London. The men of the neighbouring counties flocked in to his support. On March 2 the crown was offered to him at Clerkenwell by such lords as happened to be in London. On his presenting himself to the multitude in Westminster Hall, he was greeted with shouts of " Long live the king ! " Edward IV. represented to peace-loving England the order which had to be upheld against the barbarous host which Margaret and the Lancastrian lords had called to their aid. He had yet to justify the choice. The northern host had retreated to its own country, and Edward swiftly followed

it up. His advanced guard was surprised and driven back at Ferry Bridge ; but his main army pressed on, and on March 29 gained a decisive victory at Towton. The slaughter of the defeated side was enormous. Margaret escaped with Henry to Scotland, and Edward, returning southwards, was crowned at Westminster on June 29.

CHAPTER XXII

THE YORKIST KINGS

EDWARD IV., **1461—1483.** EDWARD V., **1483.** RICHARD III., **1483—1485.**

LEADING DATES

Coronation of Edward IV.	1461
Restoration of Henry VI.	1470
Edward IV. recovers the crown—Battles of Barnet and Tewkesbury	1471
Edward V.	1483
Richard III. deposes Edward V.	1483
Richard III. killed at Bosworth	1485

1. **Edward IV. and the House of Commons. 1461.**—On June 29, **1461,** Edward IV. was crowned, and created his two brothers, George and Richard, Dukes of Clarence and Gloucester. His first Parliament declared the three Lancastrian kings to have been usurpers, and Henry VI., his wife, his son, and his chief supporters, to be traitors. At the end of the session Edward thanked the Commons for their support, and assured them of his resolution to protect them at the hazard of his own life. It was the first time that a king had addressed the Commons, and his doing so was a sign that a new era had begun, in which the wishes of the middle class in town and country were to prevail over those of the great nobles. It did not follow that the House of Commons would take the control of the government into its own hands, as it does at the present day. For a long time the election of the members had been carried out under pressure from the local nobility. If the great men in a county resolved that certain persons should be returned as members, those who came to the place of election in support of others would be driven off, and perhaps beaten or wounded. Consequently each House of Commons had hitherto represented the dominant party, Lancastrian or Yorkist, as the case might be.

Before there could be a House of Commons capable of governing, the interference of the nobles with elections would have to be brought to an end, and it was only by a strong king that their power could be overthrown. The strengthening of the kingship was the only road to future constitutional progress.

2. **Loss of the Mediæval Ideals.**—Before the end of the 15th century the English people had lost all the ideals of the middle ages. The attempt of Henry V. to revive the old ecclesiastical feeling had broken down through the race for material power opened by his French wars, and through the savagery of the wars of the Roses. The new religious feeling of Wycliffe and the nobler Lollards had perished with Sir John Oldcastle from the same causes. Neither the Church nor the opponents of the Church had any longer a sway over men's hearts. The clergy continued to perform their part in the services of the Church not indeed without belief, but without the spiritual fervour which influences the lives of men. The chivalry of

Edward IV. : from an original painting belonging to the Society of Antiquaries.

the middle ages was as dead as its religion. Men spoke of women as coarsely as they spoke of their cattle. Human nature indeed could not be entirely crushed. John Paston's wife (see p. 321), for instance, was quaintly affectionate. "I would," she once wrote to her husband, "ye were at home, if it were for your ease . . . now liever than a gown, though it were of scarlet." But the system of wardship (see p. 116) made marriages a matter of bargain and sale. "For very need," wrote a certain Stephen Scrope, "I was fain to sell a little daughter I have for much less than I should." When Scrope was old he wished to marry Paston's young sister, and the girl was willing to take him if she were sure that his land was not burdened with debt. She would be glad enough to escape from home. Her mother kept her in close confinement and beat her once or twice every week, and sometimes twice a day, so that her head was broken in two or three places. This low and material view of domestic life had led to an equally low and material view of political life, and the cruelty which stained the wars of the Roses was but the outcome of a state of society in which no man cared much for anything except his own greatness and enjoyment. The ideal which shaped itself in the minds of the men of the middle class was a king acting as a kind of chief constable, who, by keeping great men in order, would allow their inferiors to make money in peace.

3. **Fresh Efforts of the Lancastrians. 1462—1465.**—Edward IV. only very partially responded to this demand. He was swift in action when a crisis came, and was cruel in his revenge, but he was lustful and indolent when the crisis was passed, and he had no statesmanlike abilities to lay the foundations of a powerful government. The wars were not ended by his victory at Towton. In **1462** Queen Margaret reappeared in the North, and it was not till **1464** that Warwick's brother, Lord Montague, thoroughly defeated her forces at Hedgeley Moor and Hexham ; for which victories he was rewarded by Edward with the earldom of Northumberland, which had been forfeited by the Lancastrian head of the House of Percy. Montague's victory was marked by the usual butcheries ; the Duke of Somerset, a son of the duke who had been slain at St. Albans, being amongst those who perished on the scaffold. In **1465** Henry himself was taken prisoner and lodged in the Tower.

4. **Edward's Marriage. 1464.**—Whilst these battles were being fought Edward was lingering in the South courting the young widow of Sir John Grey, usually known by her maiden name as Elizabeth Woodville. His marriage to her gave offence to his noble supporters, who disdained to acknowledge a queen of birth so undistinguished ; and their ill-will was increased when they found that Edward distributed amongst his wife's kindred estates and preferments which they had hoped to gain for themselves. The queen's father became Earl Rivers and Lord Constable, and her brothers and sisters were enriched by marriages with noble wards of the Crown. One of her brothers, a youth of twenty, was married to the old Duchess of Norfolk, who was over eighty.

5. Estrangement of Warwick. 1465—1468.—No doubt there was as much of policy as of affection in the slight shown by Edward to the Yorkist nobility. Warwick—the King-maker, as he was called—had special cause for ill-humour. He had expected to be a King-ruler as well as a King-maker, and he took grave offence when he found Edward slipping away from his control. It seemed as if Edward had the settled purpose of raising up a new nobility to counterbalance the old. In **1467** Warwick's brother, the Archbishop of York, was deprived of the chancellorship. In foreign politics, too, Edward and Warwick disagreed. Warwick had taken up the old policy of the Beauforts, and was anxious for an alliance with the astute Louis XI., who had in **1461** succeeded his father, Charles VII., as king of France. Edward, perhaps with some thought passing through his head of establishing his throne by following in the steps of Henry V., declared for an alliance with Burgundy. In **1467** Warwick was allowed to go to France as an ambassador, whilst Edward was entertaining Burgundian ambassadors in England. In the same year Charles the Rash succeeded his father, Philip the Good (see p. 306), as Duke of Burgundy, and in **1468** married Edward's sister, Margaret. The Duke of Burgundy, the rival of the king of France, was the lord of the seventeen provinces of the Netherlands, and his friendship brought with it that peaceful intercourse with the manufacturing towns of Flanders which it was always the object of English policy to secure.

6. Warwick's Alliance with Clarence. 1469—1470.—Warwick, disgusted with Edward, found an ally in Edward's brother, Clarence, who, like Warwick, was jealous of the Woodvilles. Warwick had no son, and his two daughters, Isabel and Anne, would one day share his vast estates between them. Warwick gave Isabel in marriage to Clarence, and encouraged him to think that it might be possible to seat him—in days when everything seemed possible to the strong—on Edward's throne. Edward had by this time lost much of his popularity. His extravagant and luxurious life made men doubt whether anything had been gained by substituting him for Henry, and in **1469** and **1470** there were risings fomented by Warwick. In the latter year Edward, with the help of his cannon, the importance of which in battles was now great, struck such a panic into his enemies at a battle near Stamford that the place of action came to be known as Losecoat Field, from the haste with which the fugitives stripped themselves of their armour to make their flight the easier. Warwick

and Clarence fled across the sea.   Warwick was governor of Calais,
but his own officer there refused to admit him, and he was forced
to take refuge in France.

7. **The Restoration of Henry VI.   1470.**—Warwick knew that
he had no chance of recovering power without the support of the
Lancastrian party, and, disagreeable as it was to him, he allowed
Louis XI. to reconcile him to Queen Margaret, the wife of that
Henry VI., of whom he had been the bitterest enemy.   Louis, who

A fifteenth-century ship: from Harl. MS. 2278.

dreaded Edward's alliance with the Duke of Burgundy, did everything to support Edward's foes, and sent Warwick off to England,
where he was subsequently to be joined by the queen.   Edward,
who was in his most careless mood, was foolish enough to trust
Warwick's brother, Montague, from whom he had taken away,
not only his new earldom of Northumberland to restore it to the
head of the Percies (see p. 331), but all the lands connected with
it, and had thought to compensate him with the mere marquisate

of Montague, unaccompanied by any estate wherewith to support
the dignity of his rank.   Montague turned against him, and
Edward, fearing for his life, fled to Holland.   Warwick became
master of England, and this time the King-maker drew Henry
from the Tower and placed him once more on the throne, imbecile
as he now was.

8. **Edward IV. recovers the Throne.   1471.**—In the spring
of **1471** Edward was back in England, landing at Ravenspur,
where Henry IV. had landed in **1399.**   Like Henry IV., he lyingly
declared that he had come merely to claim his duchy and estates.
Like Henry IV., too, he found a supporter in an Earl of
Northumberland, who was this time the Percy who, Lancastrian
as he was, had been restored by Edward to his earldom at the
expense of Montague.   Clarence, too—false, fleeting, perjured
Clarence, as Shakspere truly calls him—had offered to betray
Warwick.   Edward gathered a sufficient force to march unassailed
to London, where he was enthusiastically received.   Taking with
him the unfortunate Henry he won a complete victory at Barnet.
The battle was fought in a dense fog, and was decided by a panic
caused amongst Warwick's men through the firing of one of their
divisions into another.   Warwick and Montague were among the
slain.   By this time Margaret had landed with a fresh army at
Weymouth.   Edward caught her and her army at Tewkesbury,
where he inflicted on her a crushing defeat.   Her son, Edward
Prince of Wales, was either slain in the battle, or more probably
murdered after the fight was over ; and the Duke of Somerset, the
brother of the duke who had been executed after the battle
of Hexham (see p. 331), the last male heir of the House of
Beaufort, as well as others, who had taken refuge in the abbey, were
afterwards put to death, though Edward had solemnly promised
them their lives.   On the night after Edward's return to London
Henry VI. ended his life in the Tower.   There can be no reasonable doubt that he was murdered, and that, too, by Edward's
directions.

9. **Edward IV. prepares for War with France.   1471—1474.**—
Edward IV. was now all powerful.   He had no competitor to fear.
No descendant of Henry IV. remained alive.   Of the Beauforts, the
descendants of John of Gaunt by Catherine Swynford (see p. 282),
the male line had perished, and the only representative was young
Henry, Earl of Richmond, whose mother, the Lady Margaret,
was the daughter of the first Duke of Somerset, and the cousin of
the two dukes who had been executed after the battles of Hexham

and Tewkesbury.[1] His father, Edmund Tudor, Earl of Richmond, who died before his birth, was the son of a Welsh gentleman of no great mark, who had had the luck to marry Catherine of France, the widow of Henry V. The young Richmond was, however, an exile, and, as he was only fourteen years of age when Edward was restored, no serious danger was as yet to be apprehended from that side. Moreover, the slaughter amongst both the Yorkist and the Lancastrian nobility had, for the time, put an end to all danger of a rising. Edward was, therefore, at liberty to carry out his own foreign policy. He obtained grants from Parliament to enable him, in alliance with Charles of Burgundy, to make war against Louis XI. The grants were insufficient, and he supplemented them by a newly invented system of benevolences, which were nominally free gifts made to him by the well-to-do, but which were in reality exactions, because those from whom they were required dared not refuse to pay. The system raised little general ill will, partly because the small owners of property who were relieved from taxation were not touched by the benevolences, and partly because the end which Edward had put to the civil war made his government welcome. In some cases his personal charm counted for something. One old lady whom he asked for ten pounds

[1] Genealogy of the Beauforts and the Tudors :—

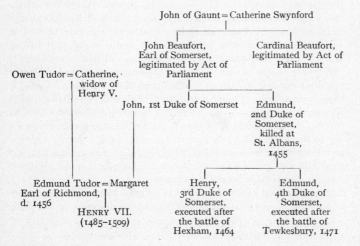

replied that for the sake of his handsome face she would give him twenty. He kissed her and she at once made it forty.

10. **The Invasion of France. 1475.**—In **1475** Edward invaded France. If he could have secured the steady support of the Duke of Burgundy he might have accomplished something, but the Duke's dominions were too scattered to enable him to have a settled policy. He was sometimes led to attack the king of France, because he had interests as a French vassal ; whilst at other times he threw all his strength into projects for encroachments in Germany, because he had also interests as a vassal of the Emperor. When Edward landed Charles was anxious to carry on war in Germany, and would give no help to Edward in France. Louis XI., who preferred a victory of diplomacy to one of force, wheedled Edward into a seven years' truce by a grant of 75,000 crowns, together with a yearly pension of 50,000, and by a promise to marry the Dauphin Charles to Elizabeth, the eldest daughter of the king of England. Louis also made presents to Edward's chief followers, and was delighted when the English army turned its back on France. In consequence of this understanding Queen Margaret recovered her liberty.

11. **Fall and Death of Clarence. 1476—1478.**—Soon after Edward's return he became suspicious of his brother Clarence, who took upon himself to interfere with the course of justice. In **1477** the Duke of Burgundy, Charles the Rash, was slain at Nancy by the Swiss, leaving only a daughter, Mary. Ducal Burgundy was at once seized by Louis, as forfeited for want of male heirs, but Franche Comté, or the county of Burgundy, was a part of the Empire, and therefore beyond his reach ; and this latter district, together with the provinces of the Netherlands, formed a dower splendid enough to attract suitors for Mary's hand. Amongst these was Clarence,[1] now a widower. Edward, who had no wish to see his brother an independent sovereign, forbade him to proceed with his wooing. Other actions of Clarence were displeasing to the king, and when Parliament met, **1478,** Edward with his own mouth accused his brother of treason. Clarence was condemned to death, and perished secretly in the Tower, being, according to rumour, drowned in a butt of malmsey.

12. **The Last Years of Edward IV. 1478—1483.**—The remainder of Edward's life was spent in quiet, as far as domestic affairs were

[1] Mary was the child of an earlier wife of Charles the Bold than Margaret the sister of Edward IV, and Clarence, and the latter was therefore not related to her.

concerned.   In foreign affairs he met with a grave disappointment.
Mary of Burgundy had found a husband in Maximilian, archduke
of Austria, the son of the Emperor Frederick III.   In **1482** she
died, leaving two children, Philip and Margaret.   The men of
Ghent set Maximilian at naught, and, combining with Louis, forced
Maximilian in the treaty of Arras to promise the hand of Margaret
to the Dauphin, and the cession of some Netherlandish territory
to France.   Edward died on April 9, **1483**, and it has been said
that the treaty of Arras, which extended French influence in the
Netherlands, brought about his death.   It is more reasonable
to attribute it to the dissoluteness of his life.

13. **Edward V. and the Duke of Gloucester.   1483.**—Edward IV.
left two sons.   The elder, a boy of twelve, was now Edward V., and
his younger brother, Richard, was Duke of York.[1]   The only grown-
up man of the family was the youngest brother of Edward IV.,
Richard, Duke of Gloucester.   Gloucester had shown himself during
his brother's reign to be possessed of the qualities which fit a man
to fulfil the duties of a high position.   He was not only a good
soldier and an able commander, but, unlike his brother Clarence,
was entirely faithful to Edward, though he showed his independence by refusing to take part in Edward's treaty with Louis of
France.   He had a rare power of winning popular sympathy, and
was most liked in Yorkshire, where he was best known.   He had,
however, grown up in a cruel and unscrupulous age, and had no
more hesitation in clearing his way by slaughter than had Edward
IV. or Margaret of Anjou.   Though absolute proof is wanting, there
is strong reason to believe that he took part in cutting down Prince
Edward after the battle of Tewkesbury, and that he executed his

[1] Genealogy of the Yorkist Kings :—

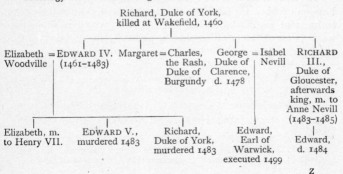

```
                     Richard, Duke of York,
                     killed at Wakefield, 1460
                              |
     ┌──────────┬────────────┼──────────────┬──────────────┐
Elizabeth = EDWARD IV.  Margaret = Charles,  George = Isabel   RICHARD
Woodville | (1461-1483)      the Rash, Duke of | Nevill    III.,
          |                  Duke of  Clarence,|           Duke of
          |                  Burgundy d. 1478  |           Gloucester,
          |                                    |           afterwards
          |                                    |           king, m. to
          |                                    |           Anne Nevill
          |                                    |           (1483-1485)
   ┌──────┼──────────┬─────────────┬──────────┘
Elizabeth, m.   EDWARD V.,    Richard,        Edward,
to Henry VII.   murdered 1483  Duke of York,  Earl of        Edward,
                              murdered 1483   Warwick,       d. 1484
                                             executed 1499
```

brother's orders in providing for the murder of Henry VI. in the Tower. He made no remonstrance against, though he took no part in, the death of Clarence, with whom he was on bad terms, because Clarence claimed the whole of the estates of the King-maker, whose eldest daughter Isabel he had married ; whereas Gloucester, having married the younger daughter Anne, the widow of the slaughtered son of Henry VI. put in a claim to half. Gloucester was now to be tried as he had never been tried before, his brother having appointed him by will to be the guardian of his young nephew and of the kingdom. If the authority thus conferred upon him met with general acceptance, he would probably make an excellent ruler. If it were questioned he would strike out, and show no mercy. In those hard days every man of high position must be either hammer or anvil, and Richard was resolved that he would not be the anvil.

14. **Fall of the Queen's Relations. 1483.**—The young king was at Ludlow, and rode up towards London, guarded by Earl Rivers, his uncle on his mother's side, and by his half-brother, Sir Richard Grey. Another half-brother, the Marquis of Dorset, was lieutenant of the Tower.[1] Gloucester had strong reasons for believing that the Greys intended to keep the young king in their hands and, having him crowned at once, so as to put an end to his own guardianship, to make themselves masters of the kingdom. He therefore struck the first blow. Accompanied by his friend and supporter, the Duke of Buckingham, he overtook the cavalcade, and sent Rivers and Grey prisoners to Pontefract. The queen-mother at once took refuge in the sanctuary at Westminster, whence no one could remove her without violating the privileges of the Church.

15. **Execution of Lord Hastings.**—The young king arrived in London on May 4. The Council acknowledged Gloucester as Protector, and removed Edward to the Tower, which in those days was a place of safety rather than a prison. Dorset, however, had equipped a fleet, and Gloucester was afraid lest a fresh attempt

---

[1] Genealogy of the Woodvilles and Greys :—

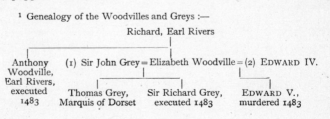

Richard, Earl Rivers

Anthony Woodville, Earl Rivers, executed 1483	(1) Sir John Grey = Elizabeth Woodville = (2) EDWARD IV.	
	Thomas Grey, Marquis of Dorset	Sir Richard Grey, executed 1483	EDWARD V., murdered 1483

might be made by the queen's party to overthrow him.   His
fears were increased because Lord Hastings, the leading member

Large ship and boat of the fifteenth century. The mainsail of the ship has the Beauchamp
arms, and the streamer the bear and ragged staff. From the 'Life of Richard Beauchamp, Earl of Warwick,' by John Rous; drawn about 1485.

of the Council, who had taken his part against the Woodvilles,
now turned against him and began to intrigue with the queen's

supporters. Coming into the council chamber on June 13, he laid bare his left arm, which had been withered from his birth, and declared that the mischief was the effect of witchcraft, and that the witches were the queen and Jane Shore, who had been one of the many mistresses of Edward IV., and was now the mistress of Hastings. Hastings admitted that the queen and Jane Shore were worthy of punishment if they were guilty. "What!" cried Gloucester, "dost thou serve me with ifs and with ands? I tell thee they have done it, and that I will make good on thy body, traitor." Gloucester struck his fist on the table. Armed men rushed in, dragged Hastings out, and cut off his head on a log of wood. Jane Shore was compelled to do public penance in a white sheet. Of the causes of Hastings' desertion of Gloucester it is impossible to speak with certainty. It is a probable conjecture that he had discovered that Gloucester entertained the thought of making himself more than Protector. Young Edward's coronation would make the boy capable, formally at least, of exercising royal power, and as it was known that the boy loved his mother's relations, it was almost certain that he would place the Woodvilles in power. Now that Gloucester had imprisoned Rivers and Grey, it was certain that the first thing done by the Woodvilles, if they got a chance, would be to send Gloucester to the scaffold, and Gloucester was not the man patiently to allow himself to be crushed. It is ridiculous to speak of Gloucester as an accomplished dissembler. The story of witchcraft served its purpose, but it was the stupid lie of a man who had not hitherto been accustomed to lying.

16. **Deposition of Edward V. 1483.**—The execution of Hastings was promptly followed by the execution of Rivers and Grey. Dorset saved himself by escaping beyond sea. By threats Gloucester got the Duke of York into his hands, and lodged him with his brother in the Tower. He was now in a temper which would stop at no atrocity. He put up a Dr. Shaw to preach a sermon against Edward's claim to the throne. In those days if a man and woman made a contract of marriage neither of the contracting parties could marry another, though no actual marriage had taken place. Shaw declared that Edward IV. had promised marriage to one of his mistresses before he met Elizabeth Woodville, and that therefore, his marriage with Elizabeth being invalid, all his children by her were illegitimate, and Gloucester was the true heir to the throne. Further, Shaw declared that Gloucester was the only legitimate son of the Duke of York, both Edward IV.

and Clarence being the sons of their mother by some other man.
That Richard should have authorised so base an attack upon his
mother's honour shows the depth of infamy to which he had now
sunk. At first it seemed as if he had lowered himself to no purpose.
The hearers of the sermon, instead of shouting, " God save King
Richard ! " held their peace. At a meeting in the City the Duke of
Buckingham told the same story as had been told by Shaw, and there
the servants of the two dukes shouted for ' King Richard,' and their
voice was taken as the voice of the City.   On June 25 Parliament

declared Gloucester to
be the lawful heir, and
on July 6 he was crowned
as Richard III. The
Woodvilles were not
popular, and the blood-
shed with which Richard
had maintained himself
against them was readily
condoned.

17. **Buckingham's
Rebellion. 1483.**—Rich-
ard's enemies were
chiefly to be found
amongst the nobility.
No nobleman could feel
his life secure if he
crossed Richard's path.
The first to revolt was
Buckingham, who had
played the part of a king-
maker, and who was dis-
appointed because Rich-
ard did not reward him
by conceding his claim
to estates so vast that if
he possessed them he

Richard III. : from an original painting belonging
to the Society of Antiquaries.

would have been master of England.   Buckingham, who was descended from Edward III. through his youngest son, the Duke of
Gloucester, at first thought of challenging a right to the throne for
himself, but afterwards determined to support the claim of the
Earl of Richmond, the Tudor heir of the House of Lancaster
(see p. 334). He was skilfully led from one step to another by John

Morton, Bishop of Ely, one of the ablest statesmen of the day. Richmond was to sail from Brittany, where he was in exile, and Buckingham was to raise forces in Wales, where the Welsh Tudors were popular, whilst other counties were to rise simultaneously. The rebellion came to nothing. Heavy rains caused a flood of the Severn, and Buckingham, in Shropshire, was cut off from his army in Wales. Buckingham was betrayed to Richard, and on November 2 was beheaded at Salisbury.

18. **Murder of the Princes. 1483.**—At some time in the summer or autumn the princes in the Tower ceased to live. There had been movements in their favour in some counties, and there can be no reasonable doubt that Richard had them secretly killed. It was only by degrees that the truth leaked out. Wherever it was believed it roused indignation. Murders there had been in plenty, but the murdered as yet had been grown men. To butcher children was reserved for Richard alone.

19. **Richard's Government. 1484—1485.**—As long as the last tale of murder was still regarded as doubtful, Richard retained his popularity. In a Parliament which met in January 1484 he enacted good laws, amongst which was one declaring benevolences illegal. In the summer he was welcomed as he moved about, yet he knew that danger threatened. Richmond was preparing invasion and the hollow friendship of the English nobility was not to be trusted. In vain Richard scattered gifts in profusion amongst them. They took the gifts and hoped for deliverance. The popular good-will grew cooler, and in the winter Richard, needing money, and not venturing to summon another Parliament, raised a forced loan. A loan not being a gift, he did not technically break the statute against benevolences though practically he set it at naught. Domestic misfortunes came to add to Richard's political troubles. His only son, Edward, died in 1484. His wife, Anne, died in 1485. Richard was now eager, if he had not been eager before, to marry his niece, Elizabeth of York, the daughter of Edward IV. This monstrous proposal was scouted by his own supporters, and he had reluctantly to abandon the scheme. If there could be queens in England, Elizabeth was on hereditary principles the heiress of the throne, unless, indeed, Richard's argument against her mother's marriage (see p. 340) was to be accepted. Richmond was naturally as anxious as Richard could be to win her hand, and his promise to marry her was the condition on which he obtained the support of those Yorkists who were Richard's enemies.

20. **Richard Defeated and Slain at Bosworth. 1485.**—In June **1485** Richmond landed at Milford Haven. As he marched on he was joined by considerable numbers, but on August 22 he found Richard waiting for him near Bosworth, with a host far larger than his own. Richard, however, could not count on the fidelity of his own commanders. Lord Stanley, who had married Richmond's widowed mother, the Lady Margaret (see p. 334), together with his brother, Sir William Stanley, were secretly in accord with Richmond, though they had placed themselves on Richard's side. When the battle began Stanley openly joined Richmond, whilst the Earl of Northumberland who was also nominally on Richard's side withdrew his forces and stood aloof. Knowing that defeat was certain, Richard, with the crown on his head, rushed into the thick of the fight and met a soldier's death. After the battle the fallen crown was discovered on a bush, and placed by Stanley, amidst shouts of ' King Henry ! ' on Richmond's head.

CHAPTER XXIII

HENRY VII. 1485–1509

LEADING DATES

Accession of Henry VII.	1485
The Battle of Stoke	1487
Poynings' Acts	1494
Capture of Perkin Warbeck	1497
Alliance with Scotland	1503
Death of Henry VII.	1509

1. **The First Measures of Henry VII. 1485—1486.**—Henry VII. owed his success not to a general uprising against Richard, but to a combination of the nobles who had hitherto taken opposite sides. To secure this combination he had promised to marry Elizabeth, the heiress of the Yorkist family. Lest an attempt should be made to challenge her title, Henry imprisoned in the Tower the Earl of Warwick, the son of Clarence, who might possibly maintain that a female was incapable of inheriting. He was indeed unwilling to have it thought that he derived his title from a wife, and when Parliament met on November 7 he obtained from it a recognition of

his own right to the throne, though it would have puzzled the most acute controversialist to discover in what that right consisted. Parliament, therefore, contented itself with declaring that the

Henry VII. : from an original picture in the National Portrait Gallery.

inheritance of the crown was to 'be, rest, and abide in King Henry VII. and his heirs,' without giving any reasons why it was to be so.[1]   As far as the House of Lords was concerned the atten-

---

[1] Abbreviated genealogy of Henry VII. and his competitors :—

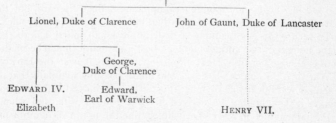

dance when this declaration was made was scanty. Only twenty-nine lay peers were present, not because many of the great houses had become extinct, but because some of the principal Yorkist peers had been attainted, and others had been left without a summons. In the quieter times which followed this slur upon them was removed, and the House of Lords was again filled. On January 18, **1486**, Henry married Elizabeth. This marriage and the blending of the white and red rose in the Tudor badge was Henry's way of announcing that he intended to be the king of both parties.

Elizabeth of York, queen of Henry VII. : from an original
picture in the National Portrait Gallery.

2. Maintenance and Livery.—Henry could not maintain himself on the throne merely by the support of the nobility. The middle classes, as in the days of Edward IV., called out for a strong king, and were ready to overlook violence and cruelty if only order could be secured. Henry was shrewd enough to know that their aid was indispensable, and, Lancastrian as he was, he adopted the policy of the Yorkist kings. Economical and patient, he might succeed where Edward IV. had partially failed. He had no injuries to avenge, no cruelties to repay. He clearly saw that both the throne and the lives and properties of the middle classes were rendered insecure by maintenance and livery—the support given by the great landowners to their retainers, and the granting of badges by which the retainers might recognise one another, and thus become as it were a uniformed army ready to serve their lords in the field.   Against these abuses Richard II. had directed a statute, (see p. 281) and that statute had been confirmed by Edward IV. These laws had, however, been inoperative ; and Henry, in his first Parliament, did not venture to do more than to make the peers swear to abandon their evil courses.

3. **Lovel's Rising.   1486.**—In **1486** Lord Lovel, who had been one of Richard's ministers, rose in arms and seized Worcester. Henry found warm support even in Yorkshire, where Richard had been more popular than elsewhere.   At short warning a 'marvellous great number of esquires, gentlemen, and yeomen' gathered round him, and the rebellion was easily put down.

Lovel escaped to Flanders, where he found a protector in Margaret, the dowager Duchess of Burgundy, the sister of Edward IV. and Richard III. Before long a new attack upon Henry was developed.   For the first time an English king had to ward off danger from Ireland.

4. **Lancaster and York in Ireland. 1399—1485.**—Since the expedition of Richard II. no king had visited Ireland, and the English colonists were left to defend themselves against the Celtic

Tudor rose (white and red): from the gates of the Chapel of Henry VII.

tribes as best they might.   In **1449** Richard, Duke of York, who had not at that time entered on his rivalry with Henry VI., was sent to Dublin as Lord Lieutenant (see p. 319) where he remained till **1450**, and gained friends amongst both races by his conciliatory firmness.   In **1459**, after the break-up of his party at Ludlow (see p. 326), he appeared in Ireland in the character of a fugitive seeking for allies.   Between him and the English colony a bargain was soon struck.   They gave him troops which fought gallantly for him at Wakefield, and he, claiming to be Lord Lieutenant, assented to an act in which they asserted the complete legislative independence of the Parliament of the colony.   The colony, therefore, became distinctly Yorkist.   Its leader was the Earl of Kildare, the chief of the eastern Fitzgeralds or Geraldines, the Earl of Desmond being the chief of the Geraldines of the West.   Between them was the Earl of Ormond, the chief of the Butlers, the hereditary foe of the

Geraldines, who, probably merely because his rivals were Yorkist, had attached himself to the Lancastrian party. All three were of English descent, but all three exercised the tribal authority of an Irish chief, and were practically independent of English control. Ormond fought at Towton on the Lancastrian side, and was executed after the battle. Family quarrels broke out amongst his kindred, and for the time Kildare was supreme in the English Pale (see p. 265).

5. **Insurrection of Lambert Simnel. 1487.**—Kildare and the colonists had every reason to distrust Henry, but to oppose him they needed a pretender. They found one in the son of an Oxford tradesman, a boy of ten, named Lambert Simnel, who had been persuaded to give himself out as the Earl of Warwick, who, as it was said, had escaped from the Tower. In **1487** Simnel landed in Ireland, where he was soon joined by Lord Lovel from Flanders, and by the Earl of Lincoln, of the family of Pole or De la Pole,[1] whose mother, Elizabeth, was the eldest sister of Edward IV., and who had been named by Richard III. as his heir after the death of his son (see p. 342). Lincoln and Lovel, after crowning Simnel at Dublin, crossed to Lancashire, taking with them the pretender, and 2,000 trained German soldiers under Martin Schwarz ; as well as an Irish force furnished by Kildare. Scarcely an Englishman would join them, and on June 16 they were utterly defeated by Henry at Stoke, a village between Nottingham and Newark. Lincoln and Schwarz were slain. Lovel was either drowned in the Trent or, according to legend, was hidden in an underground vault, where he was at last starved to death through the neglect of the man whose duty it was to provide him with food. Simnel

---

[1] Genealogy of the De la Poles and Poles :—

Richard, Duke of York

Elizabeth = John de la Pole, Duke of Suffolk

George, Duke of Clarence, died 1477

John de la Pole, Earl of Lincoln, killed at Stoke, 1487

Edmund de la Pole, Earl of Suffolk, beheaded 1513

Sir Richard de la Pole, killed at Pavia, 1525

Margaret, Countess of Salisbury = Sir Richard Pole

Henry, Lord Montague, beheaded 1538

Reginald Pole, Cardinal and Archbishop of Canterbury, died 1558

was pardoned, and employed by Henry as a turnspit in his kitchen.

6. The Court of Star Chamber. 1487.—Nothing could serve Henry better than this abortive rising. At Bosworth he had been the leader of one party against the other. At Stoke he was the leader of the nation against Irishmen and Germans. He felt himself strong enough in his second Parliament to secure the passing of an act to ensure the execution of the engagements to which the lords had sworn two years before (see p. 345). A court was to be erected, consisting of certain specified members of the Privy Council and of two judges, empowered to punish with fine and imprisonment all who were guilty of interfering with justice by force or intrigue. The new court, reviving, to some extent, the disused criminal authority of the king's Council, sat in the Star Chamber [1] at Westminster. The results of its establishment were excellent. Wealthy landowners, the terror of their neighbours, who had bribed or bullied juries at their pleasure, and had sent their retainers to inflict punishment on those who had displeased them, were brought to Westminster to be tried before a court in which neither fear nor favour could avail them. It was the greatest merit of the new court that it was not dependent on a jury, because in those days juries were unable or unwilling to give verdicts according to their conscience.

7. Henry VII. and Brittany. 1488—1492.—Henry VII. was a lover of peace by calculation, and would gladly have let France alone if it had been possible to do so. France, however, was no longer the divided power which it had been in the days of Henry V. When Louis XI. died in 1483, he left to his young son, Charles VIII., a territory the whole of which, with the exception of Brittany, was directly governed by the king. Charles's sister, Anne of Beaujeu, who governed in his name, made it the object of her policy to secure Brittany. She waged war successfully against its duke, Francis II., and after he died, in 1488, she continued to wage war against his daughter, the Duchess Anne. In England there was a strong feeling against allowing the Duchess to be overwhelmed. At the beginning of 1489 Henry, having received from Parliament large supplies, sent 6,000 Englishmen to Anne's assistance. Maximilian—whose hold on the Netherlands, where he ruled in the name of his young son, Philip (see p. 337), was always slight—proposed marriage to the

---

[1] So called either because the roof was decorated with stars or because it was the room in which had formerly been kept Jewish bonds or 'starres.'

young duchess, and in **1490** was wedded to her by proxy. He was a restless adventurer, always aiming at more than he had the means of accomplishing. Though he could not find time to go at once to Brittany to made good his claim, yet in **1491** he called on Henry to assist him in asserting it.

8. **Cardinal Morton's Fork. 1491.**—Henry, who knew how un-popular a general taxation was, fell back on the system of benevo-lences (see p. 335), excusing his conduct on the plea that the statute of Richard III. abolishing benevolences (see p. 342) was invalid, because Richard himself was a usurper. In gathering the benevolence the Chancellor, Cardinal Morton, who had been helpful to Henry in the days of his exile (see p. 341), invented a new mode of putting pressure on the wealthy, which became known as Cardinal Morton's fork. If he addressed himself to one who lived in good style, he told him that his mode of living showed that he could afford to give money to the king. If he had to do with one who appeared to be economical, he told him that he must have saved and could therefore afford to give money to the king. Before Henry could put the money thus gained to much use, Anne, pressed hard by the French, repudiated her formal marriage with Maximilian, who had never taken the trouble to visit her, and gave her hand to Charles VIII., who on his part refused to carry out his contract to marry Maximilian's daughter Margaret (see p. 337). From that time Brittany, the last of the great fiefs to maintain its independence, passed under the power of the king of France. Feudality was everywhere breaking down, and in France, as in England, a strong monarchy was being erected on its ruins.

9. **The Invasion of France. 1492.**—Maximilian's alliance had proved but a broken reed, but there was now arising a formid-able power in the south of Europe, which might possibly give valu-able support to the enemies of France. The peninsula to the south of the Pyrenees had hitherto been divided amongst various states, but in **1469** a marriage between Ferdinand, king of Aragon, and Isabella, the heiress of Castile, united the greater part under one dominion. Ferdinand and Isabella were, for the present, fully occupied with the conquest of Granada, the last remnant of the possessions of the Moors in Spain, and that city did not surrender till early in **1492**. In the meanwhile all England was indignant with the king of France on account of his marriage with the heiress of Brittany. Money was voted and men were raised, and on October 2, **1492**, Henry crossed to Calais to invade France. He

was, however, cool enough to discover that both Ferdinand and Maximilian wanted to play their own game at his expense, and as Anne of Beaujeu was ready to meet him half-way, he concluded a treaty with the French king on November 3 at Etaples, receiving large sums of money for abandoning a war in which he had nothing to gain. In 1493 the Spaniards followed Henry's example, and made a peace with France to their own advantage.[1]

10. **Perkin Warbeck.** 1491—1494.—Henry's prudent relinquishment of a war of conquest was not likely to bring him popularity in England, and his enemies were now on the watch for another pretender to support against him. Such a pretender was found in Perkin Warbeck, a Fleming of Tournay, who had landed at Cork in the end of 1491 or the beginning of 1492, and who had been pressed by the townsmen to give himself some name which would attach him to the Yorkist family. He allowed them to call him Richard, Duke of York, the younger of the princes who had been murdered in the Tower. He received support from Desmond, and probably from Kildare, upon which Henry deprived Kildare of the office of Lord Deputy. Perkin crossed to France, and ultimately made his way to Flanders, where he was supported by Margaret of Burgundy. In 1493 Henry demanded his surrender, and on receiving a refusal broke off commercial intercourse between England and Flanders. The interruption of trade did more harm to England than to Flanders, and gave hopes to the Yorkist party that it might give rise to ill-will between the nation and the king. For some time, however, no one gave assistance to Perkin, and in 1494 Charles VIII. crossed the Alps to invade Italy, and drew the attention of the Continental powers away from the affairs of England.

11. **Poynings' Acts.** 1494.—Henry seized the opportunity to

[1] Genealogy of the Houses of Spain and Burgundy :—

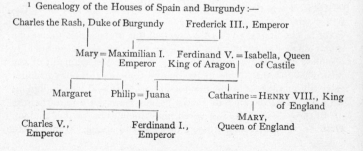

bring into obedience the English colony in Ireland. He sent over as Lord Deputy Sir Edward Poynings, a resolute and able man. At a Parliament held by him at Drogheda two acts were passed. By the one it was enacted that all English laws in force at that time should be obeyed in Ireland ; by the other, known for many generations afterwards as Poynings' Law, no bill was to be laid before the Irish Parliament which had not been previously approved by the king and his Council in England. At the same time the greater part of the Statute of Kilkenny (see p. 265) was re-enacted ; and restricted the authority of the Government at Dublin to the English Pale.

12. **Perkin's First Attempt on England. 1495.**—Henry's firm government in England had given offence even to men who were not Yorkists. Early in **1495** he discovered that Sir William Stanley, who had helped him to victory at Bosworth, had turned against him. Stanley, who was probably involved in a design for sending Perkin to invade England, was tried and executed. In the summer of **1495** Perkin actually arrived off Deal. Being no warrior, he sent a party of his followers on shore, though he remained himself on shipboard to see what would happen. The countrymen fell upon the invaders, who were all slain or captured. Then Perkin sailed to Ireland, was repulsed at Waterford, and ultimately took refuge in Scotland, where King James IV., anxious to distinguish himself in a war with England, acknowledged him as the Duke of York, and found him a wife of noble birth, Lady Catherine Gordon. It was probably in order to rally even the most timid around him, in face of such a danger, that Henry obtained the consent of Parliament to an act declaring that no one supporting a king in actual possession of the crown could be subjected to the penalty of treason in the event of that king's dethronement.

13. **The Intercursus Magnus. 1496.**—The danger of a Scottish invasion made Henry anxious to be on good terms with his neighbours. Maximilian had become Emperor in **1493** upon his father's death. In the Netherlands, however, his influence had declined, as his son, the young Archduke Philip, was now growing up, and claimed actually to rule the country which he had inherited from his mother, Mary of Burgundy (see p. 337), his father having merely the right of administering the government of it till he himself came of age. It was therefore with Philip, and not with Maximilian, that Henry concluded, in **1496**, a treaty known as the *Intercursus Magnus*, for the encouragement of trade between England and the Netherlands, each

party engaging at the same time to give no shelter to each other's rebels.

14. Kildare Restored to the Deputyship. 1496.—In Ireland also Henry was careful to avert danger. The government of Poynings had not been entirely successful, and the Geraldines had taken good care to show that they could be troublesome in spite of the establishment of English government. The Earl of Kildare was at the time in England, and a story is told of some one who, having brought a long string of charges against him, wound up by saying that all Ireland could not govern the Earl, whereupon the king replied that then the Earl should govern all Ireland. The story is untrue, but it well represents the real situation. In 1496 Henry sent Kildare back as Lord Deputy. A bargain seems to have been struck between them. Henry abandoned his attempt to govern Ireland from England, and Kildare was allowed to use the king's name in any enterprise upon which his heart was set, provided that he did not support any more pretenders to the English throne.

15. Perkin's Overthrow. 1496—1497.—In the autumn of 1496 James IV. made an attack on England in Perkin's name, but it was no more than a plundering foray. Henry, however, early in 1497, obtained from Parliament a grant of money, to enable him to resist any attempt to repeat it. This grant had unexpected consequences. The Cornishmen, refusing payment, marched up to Blackheath, where on June 18 they were overpowered by the king's troops. James IV., thinking it time to be quit of Perkin, sent him off by sea. In July Perkin arrived at Cork, but there was no shelter for him there now that Kildare was Lord Deputy, and in September he made his way to Cornwall. Followed by 6,000 Cornishmen he reached Taunton, but the news of the defeat of the Cornish at Blackheath depressed him, and the poor coward ran away from his army and took sanctuary in Beaulieu Abbey. He was brought to London, where he publicly acknowledged himself to be an impostor. Henry was too humane to do more than place him in confinement.

16. European Changes. 1494—1499.—In 1494 Charles VIII. had passed through Italy as a conqueror to make good his claims to the kingdom of Naples. In 1495 he had returned to France, and in 1496 the French army left behind had been entirely destroyed. Yet the danger of a renewed attack from France made the other Continental powers anxious to unite, and in 1496 the Archduke Philip married Juana, the eldest daughter of Ferdinand

Tower of St. Mary's Church, Taunton : built about 1500.

A A

and Isabella, whilst his sister was sent to Spain to be married to their only son, Juan. In **1497** the death of the young prince led to consequences unexpected when the two marriages were arranged. Philip, who held Franche Comté and the Netherlands, and who was through his father Maximilian heir to the German dominions of the House of Austria, would now, that his wife had become the heiress of Spain, be able to transmit to his descendants the whole of the Spanish monarchy as well. That monarchy was no longer confined to Europe. Portugal at the end of the fourteenth century had led the way in maritime adventure, and Portuguese navigators discovered a way to India round the Cape of Good Hope. Spain was anxious to do as much, and in **1492** Columbus had discovered the West Indies, and the kings of Spain became masters of the untold wealth produced by the gold and silver mines of the New World. It was impossible but that the huge power thus brought into existence would one day arouse the jealousy of Europe. For the present, however, the danger was less than it would be after the deaths of Ferdinand and Isabella, as the actual combination of their territories with those which Philip was to inherit from Maximilian had not been effected. In **1499** France gave a fresh shock to her neighbours. Charles VIII. had died the year before, and his successor, Louis XII., invaded Italy and subdued the duchy of Milan, to which he had set up a claim. Naturally the powers jealous of France sought to have Henry on their side. There had been for some time a negotiation for a marriage between Henry's eldest son, Arthur, Prince of Wales, and Catherine of Aragon, the youngest daughter of Ferdinand and Isabella, but hitherto nothing had been concluded.

17. **Execution of the Earl of Warwick. 1499.**—Perkin had long been eager to free himself from prison. In **1498** he was caught attempting to escape, but Henry contented himself with putting him in the stocks. He was then removed to the Tower, where he persuaded the unhappy Earl of Warwick (see p. 343) to join him in flight. It is almost certain that Warwick was guilty of no more, but Henry, soured by the repeated attempts to dethrone him, resolved to remove him from his path. On trumped-up evidence Warwick was convicted and executed, and Perkin shared his fate.

18. **Prince Arthur's Marriage and Death. 1501—1502.**— Warwick's death was the one judicial murder of Henry's reign. To the Spaniards it appeared to be a prudent action which had cleared away the last of Henry's serious competitors. The negotia-

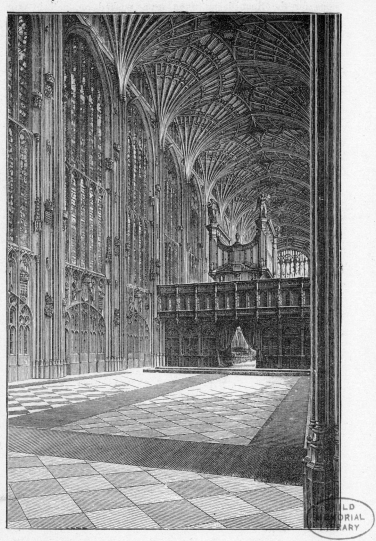

King's College Chapel, Cambridge (looking east).   Begun by Henry VI. in 1441 ;
completed by Henry VII.   The screen built between 1531 and 1535.

tions for the Spanish marriage were pushed on, and in 1501 Catherine, a bride of fifteen, gave her hand to Arthur, a bridegroom of fourteen. In 1502 the prince died, and the attempt to bind England and Spain together seemed to have come to an end.

19. **The Scottish Marriage. 1503.**—Another marriage treaty proved ultimately to be of far greater importance. Henry was sufficiently above the prejudices of his time to be anxious to be on good terms with Scotland. For some time a negotiation had been in progress for a marriage between James IV. and Henry's daughter, Margaret. The marriage took place in 1503. To the counsellors who urged that in the case of failure of Henry's heirs in the male line England would become subject to Scotland Henry shrewdly replied that there was no fear of that, as 'the greater would draw the less.'

20. **Maritime Enterprise.**—Henry's chief merit was that he had re-established order. Commercial prosperity followed, though the commerce was as yet on a small scale. It is probable that the population of England was no more than 2,500,000. London contained but 130,000 inhabitants, whilst Paris contained 400,000. There was no royal navy, as there was no royal army, but merchant vessels were armed to protect themselves. The company of Merchant Adventurers made voyages to the Baltic, and the men of Bristol sent out fleets to the Iceland fishery. Henry did what he could to encourage maritime enterprise. He had offered to take Columbus into his service before the great navigator closed with Spain, and in 1497 he sent the Venetian, John Cabot, and his sons across the Atlantic, where they landed in Labrador before any Spaniards had set foot on the American continent. England however, was as yet too poor to push these discoveries farther, and the lands beyond the sea were for the present left to Spain.

21. **Growth of the Royal Power.**—The improvement in the general well-being of the country had been rendered possible by the extension of the royal power, and the price paid for order was the falling into abeyance of the constitutional authority of Parliaments. The loss indeed was greater in appearance than in reality. In the fifteenth century the election of members of the House of Commons depended more upon the will of the great lords than upon the political sentiments of the community. In the first half of the sixteenth century they depended on the will of the king. The peculiarity of the Tudor rule was that its growing despotism was

exercised without the support of the army.   It rested on the good-will of the middle classes.   Treading cautiously in the steps of Edward IV., Henry VII. recognised that in order to have a full treasury it was less dangerous to exact payments illegally from the few than to exact them legally from the many.   Hence his recourse in times of trouble to benevolences.   Hence, too, the eagerness with which he gathered in fines.   The Cornish rebels were fined indi-vidually.   The great lords who persisted in keeping retainers were fined.   On one occasion the king visited the Earl of Oxford, and found, when he went away, a band of retainers drawn up to do him honour.   " My lord," he said, " I thank you for your entertainment, but my attorney must speak with you."   If there was a man in England who had deserved well of Henry it was Oxford, but Oxford had to pay 15,000*l.*, a sum worth perhaps 180,000*l.* at the present day, to atone for his offence.   No services rendered to Henry were to excuse from obedience to the law.

22. **Empson and Dudley.**—As Henry grew older the gathering of money became a passion.   His chief instruments were Empson and Dudley, who under pretence of enforcing the law established the worst of tyrannies.   Even false charges were brought for the sake of extracting money.   At the end of his reign Henry had accumulated a hoard of 1,800,000*l.*, mainly gathered by injustice and oppression.   The despotism of one man was no doubt better than the despotism of many, but the price paid for the change was a heavy one.

23. **Henry and his Daughter-in-law.   1502—1505.**—On the death of Prince Arthur in **1502**, Ferdinand and Isabella proposed that their daughter Catharine should marry her brother-in-law, Henry, the only surviving son of the king of England, though the boy was six years younger than herself.   They had already paid half their daughter's marriage portion, and they believed, probably with truth, that they had little chance of recovering it from Henry VII., and that it would therefore be more economical to re-marry their daughter where they would get off with no more expense than the payment of the other half.   Henry on the other hand feared lest the repayment of the first half might be demanded of him, and consequently welcomed the proposal.   In **1503** a dispensation for the marriage was obtained from Pope Julius II., but in **1505**, when the time for the betrothal arrived, the young Henry protested, no doubt at his father's instigation, that he would proceed no farther.

24. **The Last Years of Henry VII.   1505—1509.**—Circum-

stances were changed by the death of Isabella in **1504**, when her son-in-law, the Archduke Philip, claimed to be sovereign of Castile in right of his wife Juana. Philip, sailing from the Netherlands to Spain in **1506**, was driven into Weymouth by a storm, and Henry seized the opportunity of wringing from him commercial concessions as well as the surrender of Edmund de la Pole, a brother of the Earl of Lincoln who perished at Stoke, and a nephew of Edward IV.   Henry was himself now a widower on the look-out for a rich wife, and Philip promised him the hand of his sister, Margaret, who had formerly been betrothed to Charles VIII. (see p. 337).   Once more, however, the conditions of the game changed. Philip died a few months after his arrival in Spain, leaving a mad widow, and as Ferdinand then regained his authority Catharine's marriage was again discussed. Other schemes were also proposed, amongst them one for marrying Catharine, not to the young prince, but to her old father-in-law, the king. In **1509**, before any of these plans could take effect, Henry VII. died.   He deserves to be reckoned amongst the kings who have accomplished much for England. If he was not chivalrous or imaginative, neither was the age in which he lived. His contemporaries needed a chief constable to keep order, and he gave them what they needed.

25. **Architectural Changes and the Printing Press.**—Architecture, which in England, as upon the Continent, had been the one great art of the Middle Ages, was already, though still instinct with beauty, giving signs in its over-elaboration of approaching decadence. To the tower of Fotheringhay Church (see p. 311) had succeeded the tower of St. Mary's, Taunton. To the roof of the nave of Winchester Cathedral (see p. 276) had succeeded the roof of the Divinity School at Oxford (see p. 319), and of the chapel of King's College, Cambridge (see p. 355).   Art in this direction could go no farther. The new conditions in which the following age was to move were indicated by the discovery of America and the invention of printing. New objects of knowledge presented themselves, and a new mode of spreading knowledge was at hand. In the reign of Edward IV., Caxton, the earliest English printer, set up his press at Westminster, and the king and his nobles came to gaze at it as at some new toy, little knowing how profoundly it was to modify their methods of government. Henry VII. had enough to do without troubling himself with such matters. It was his part to close an epoch of English history, not to open a fresh one.

Books recommended for further study of Part IV.

GREEN, J. R.   History of the English People. Vol. i. p. 521–Vol. ii. p. 77.

STUBBS, W. (Bishop of Oxford).   Constitutional History of England, Vol. ii. from p. 441, and Vol. iii.

HALLAM, H.   Constitutional History of England, Vol. i. pp. 1–15.

ROGERS, J. E. THOROLD.   History of Agriculture and Prices. Vols. iii. and iv.

CUNNINGHAM, W.   The Growth of English Industry and Commerce. Vol. i. pp. 335–449.

WYLIE, J. H.   History of England under Henry IV.

GAIRDNER, JAMES.   Lancaster and York.

————————   Richard III.

————————   Henry VII.

RAMSAY, SIR JAMES.   Lancaster and York.

PART V

THE RENASCENCE AND THE REFORMATION
1509—1603

CHAPTER XXIV

HENRY VIII. AND WOLSEY. 1509—1527

LEADING DATES

Reign of Henry VIII., 1509-1547

Accession of Henry VIII.	1509
Henry's first war with France	1512
Peace with France	1514
Charles V. elected Emperor	1519
Henry's second French war	1522
Francis I. taken captive at Pavia	1525
The sack of Rome and the alliance between England and France	1527

1. **The New King. 1509.**—Henry VIII. inherited the handsome face, the winning presence, and the love of pleasure which distinguished his mother's father, Edward IV., as well as the strong will of his own father, Henry VII. He could ride better than his grooms, and shoot better than the archers of his guard. Yet, though he had a ready smile and a ready jest for everyone, he knew how to preserve his dignity. Though he seemed to live for amusement alone, and allowed others to toil at the business of administration, he took care to keep his ministers under control. He was no mean judge of character, and the saying which rooted itself amongst his subjects, that 'King Henry knew a man when he saw him,' points to one of the chief secrets of his success. He was well aware that the great nobles were his only possible rivals, and that his main support was to be found in the country gentry and the townsmen. Partly because of his youth, and partly because the result of the

II.   B B political struggle had already been determined when he came to the throne, he thought less than his father had done of the importance

Henry VIII. : from a painting by Holbein about 1536, belonging to Earl Spencer.

of possessing stored up wealth by which armies might be equipped and maintained, and more of securing that popularity which at

least for the purposes of internal government, made armies unnecessary. The first act of the new reign was to send Empson
and Dudley to the Tower, and it was significant of Henry's policy
that they were tried and executed, not on a charge of having extorted money illegally from subjects, but on a trumped up charge
of conspiracy against the king. It was for the king to see that
offences were not committed against the people, but the people
must be taught that the most serious crimes were those committed
against the king. Henry's next act was to marry Catherine. Though
he was but nineteen, whilst his bride was twenty-five, the marriage
was for many years a happy one.

2. **Continental Troubles. 1508—1511.**—For some time Henry
lived as though his only object in life was to squander his father's
treasure in festivities. Before long, however, he bethought himself
of aiming at distinction in war as well as in sport. Since Louis XII.
had been king of France (see p. 354) there had been constant wars
in Italy, where Louis was striving for the mastery with Ferdinand
of Aragon. In 1508 the two rivals, Ferdinand and Louis, abandoning their hostility for a time, joined the Emperor Maximilian (see pp.
337, 348) and Pope Julius II. in the League of Cambrai, the object
of which was to despoil the Republic of Venice. In 1511 Ferdinand
allied himself with Julius II. and Venice in the Holy League, the
object of which was to drive the French out of Italy. After a while
the new league was joined by Maximilian, and every member of it
was anxious that Henry should join it too.

3. **The Rise of Wolsey. 1512.**—England had nothing to gain
by an attack on France, but Henry was young, and the English
nation was, in a certain sense, also young. It was conscious of
the strength brought to it by restored order, and was quite
ready to use this strength in an attack on its neighbours. In the
new court it was ignorantly thought that there was no reason why
Henry VIII. should not take up that work of conquering France
which had fallen to pieces in the feeble hands of Henry VI. To
carry on his new policy Henry needed a new minister. The best
of the old ones were Fox, the Bishop of Winchester, and Thomas
Howard, Earl of Surrey, who, great nobleman as he was, had
been contented to merge his greatness in the greatness of the king.
The whole military organisation of the country, however, had to
be created afresh, and neither Fox nor Surrey was equal to such
a task. The work was assigned to Thomas Wolsey, the king's
almoner, who, though not, as his enemies said, the son of a butcher,
was of no exalted origin. Wolsey's genius for administration at

once manifested itself. He was equally at home in sketching out a plan of campaign, in diplomatic contests with the wariest and most experienced statesmen, and in providing for the minutest details of military preparation.

4. **The War with France. 1512—1513.**—It was not Wolsey's fault that his first enterprise ended in failure. A force sent to attack France on the Spanish side failed, not because it was ill-equipped, but because the soldiers mutinied, and Ferdinand, who had promised to support it, abandoned it to its fate. In **1513** Henry himself landed at Calais, and, with the Emperor Maximilian serving under him, defeated the French at Guinegatte in an engagement known, from the rapidity of the flight of the French, as the Battle of the Spurs. Before the end of the autumn he had taken Terouenne and Tournai. War with France, as usual, led to a war with Scotland. James IV., during Henry's absence, invaded Northumberland, but his army was destroyed by the Earl of Surrey at Flodden, where he himself was slain.

5. **Peace with France. 1514.**—Henry soon found that his allies were thinking exclusively of their own interests. In **1512** the French were driven out of Italy, and Ferdinand made himself master of Navarre. In **1513** the warlike Pope, Julius II., died, and a fresh attempt of Louis to gain ground in Italy was decisively foiled. Henry's allies had got what they wanted, and in **1514** Henry discovered that to conquer France was beyond his power. Louis was ready to come to terms. He was now a widower. Old in constitution, though not in years, he was foolish enough to want a young wife. Henry was ready to gratify him with the hand of his younger sister Mary. The poor girl had fallen in love with Henry's favourite, Charles Brandon, Duke of Suffolk, a man of sturdy limbs and weak brain, and pleaded hard against the marriage. Love counted for little in those days, and all that she could obtain from her brother was a promise that if she married this time to please him, she should marry next time to please herself. Louis soon relieved her by dying on January 1, **1515**, after a few weeks of wedlock, and his widow took care, by marrying Suffolk before she left France, to make sure that her brother should keep his promise.

6. **Wolsey's Policy of Peace. 1514—1518.**—In **1514** the king made Wolsey Archbishop of York. In **1515** the Pope made him a Cardinal. Before the end of the year he was Henry's Chancellor. The whole of the business of the government passed through his hands. The magnificence of his state was extraordinary. To all observers he seemed to be more a king than the king himself. Behind him

was Henry, trusting him with all his power, but self-willed and un-controllable, quite ready to sacrifice his dearest friend to satisfy his least desire. As yet the only conflict in Henry's mind was the conflict about peace or war with France. Henry's love of display and renown had led him to wish to rival the exploits of Edward III.

Cardinal Wolsey : from an original picture belonging to the
Hon. Sir Spencer Ponsonby-Fane, K.C.B.

and Henry V. Wolsey preferred the old policy of Richard II. and Henry VI., but he knew that he could only make it palatable to the king and the nation by connecting the idea of peace with the idea of national greatness. He aspired to be the peace-maker of Europe, and to make England's interest in peace the law of the world.   In **1515** the new king of France, Francis I., needed peace with England because he was in pursuit of glory in Italy, where he won a brilliant victory at Marignano.   In **1516** Ferdinand's death gave Spain to his grandson, Charles, the son of Philip and Juana (see p. 358), and from that time Francis and Charles stood forth as the rivals for supremacy on the Continent.   Wolsey tried his best to maintain a balance between the two, and it was owing to his ability that England, thinly populated and without a standing army, was eagerly courted by the rulers of states far more powerful than herself. In **1518** a league was struck between England and France, in which Pope Leo X., the Emperor Maximilian, and Charles, king of Spain, agreed to join, thus converting it into a league of universal peace. Yet Wolsey was no cosmopolitan philanthropist.   He believed that England would be more influential in peace than she could be in war.

7. **Wolsey and the Renascence.**—In scheming for the elevation of his own country by peace instead of by conquest, Wolsey reflected the higher aspirations of his time.   No sooner had internal order been secured, than the best men began to crave for some object to which they could devote themselves, larger and nobler than that of their own preservation.   Wolsey gave them the contemplation of the political importance of England on the Continent.   The noblest minds, however, would not be content with this, and an outburst of intellectual vigour told that the times of internal strife had passed away.   This intellectual movement was not of native growth.   The Renascence, or new birth of letters, sprung up in Italy in the four-teenth century, and received a further impulse through the taking of Constantinople by the Turks in **1453**, when the dispersal of Greek teachers from the East revived the study of the Greek language.   It was not merely because new teachers landed in Italy that the literature of the ancient world was studied with avidity.   Men were weary of the mediæval system, and craved for other ideals than those of the devotees of the Church.   Whilst they learnt to admire the works of the Greek and Latin authors as models of literary form, they caught something of the spirit of the ancient world.   They ceased to look on man as living only for God and a future world, and regarded him as devoting himself to the service of his fellow-men, or even—in lower minds the temptation lay perilously near— as living for himself alone.   Great artists and poets arose who gave expression to the new feeling of admiration for human action and human beauty, whilst the prevailing revolt against the religion of the middle ages gave rise to a spirit of criticism which refused belief to popular legends.

8. **The Renascence in England.**—The spirit of the Renascence was slow in reaching England. In the days of Richard II. Chaucer visited Italy, and Italian influence is to be traced in his Canterbury Tales. In the days of Henry VI. the selfish politician, Humphrey, Duke of Gloucester, purchased books, and gave to Oxford a collection which was the foundation of what was afterwards known as the Bodleian Library. Even in the Wars of the Roses the brutal John Tiptoft, Earl of Worcester, and the gentle Earl Rivers, the brother of Elizabeth Woodville, were known as patrons of letters. The invention of printing brought literature within reach of those to whom it had hitherto been strange. Edward IV. patronised Caxton, the first English printer. In the peaceful reign of Henry VII. the seed thus sown sprang into a crop. There was, however, a great difference between the followers of the new learning in England and in Italy. In Italy, for the most part, scholars mocked at Christianity, or treated it with tacit contempt. In England there was no such breach with the religion of the past. Those who studied in England sought to permeate their old faith with the new thoughts.

9. **The Oxford Reformers.**—Especially was this the case with a group of Oxford Reformers, Grocyn, Linacre, and Colet, who were fighting hard to introduce the study of Greek into the University. Among these Colet specially addicted himself to the explanation of the epistles of St. Paul, insisting on following their plain meaning instead of the mystical interpretations then in vogue. In 1510 he founded St. Paul's School, that boys might be there taught without being subjected to the brutal flogging which was in those days the lot even of the most diligent of schoolboys. The most remarkable member of this group of scholars was Thomas More. Young More, who had hoped much from the accession of Henry VIII., had been disappointed to find him engaging in a war with France instead of cultivating the arts of peace. He meditated deeply over the miseries of his fellow-men, and longed for a time when governments would think it to be their highest duty to labour for those who are too weak to help themselves.

10. **'The Utopia.'** 1515—1516.—In 1515 and 1516 More produced a book which he called *Utopia*, or Nowhere, intending it to serve as a satire on the defects of the government of England, by praising the results of a very different government in his imaginary country. The Utopians, he declared, fought against invaders of their own land or the land of their allies, or to deliver other peoples from tyranny, but they made no wars of aggression. In peace no

one was allowed either to be idle or overworked. Everyone must work six hours a day, and then he might listen to lectures for the improvement of his mind. As for the religion of Utopia, no one was to be persecuted for his religious opinions, as long as he treated respectfully those who differed from him. If, however, he used scornful and angry words towards them, he was to be banished, not as a despiser of the established religion, but as a stirrer up of dissension. Men of all varieties of opinion met together in a common temple, the worship in which was so arranged that all could take part in it. Amongst their priests were women as well as men. More practical was the author's attack on the special abuses of the times. England swarmed with vagrants, who easily passed into robbers, or even murderers. The author of *Utopia* traced the evil to its roots. Soldiers, he said, were discharged on their return home, and, being used to roving and dissolute habits, naturally took to vagrancy. Robbery was their only resource, and the law tempted a robber to murder. Hanging was the penalty both for robbing and murder, and the robber, therefore, knowing that he would be hanged if he were detected, usually killed the victim whom he had plundered in order to silence evidence against himself; and More consequently argued that the best way of checking murder would be to abolish the penalty of death for robbery. Another great complaint of More's was against the ever-growing increase of inclosures for pasturage. "Sheep," he said, "be become so great devourers and so wild that they eat up and swallow down the very men themselves. They consume, destroy, and devour whole fields, houses, and cities." More saw the evil, but he did not see that the best remedy lay in the establishment of manufactures, to give employment in towns to those who lost it in the country. He wished to enforce by law the reversion of all the new pasturage into arable land.

11. **More and Henry VIII.**—Henry VIII. was intolerant of those who resisted his will, but he was strangely tolerant of those who privately contradicted his opinions. He took pleasure in the society of intelligent and witty men, and he urged More to take office under him. More refused for a long time, but in **1518**—the year of the league of universal peace—believing that Henry was now a convert to his ideas, he consented, and became Sir Thomas More and a Privy Councillor. Henry was so pleased with his conversation that he tried to keep him always with him, and it was only by occasionally pretending to be dull that More obtained leave to visit his home.

12. **The Contest for the Empire. 1519.**—In January **1519** the Emperor Maximilian died.   His grandson Charles was now possessed of more extensive lands than any other European sovereign.   He ruled in Spain, in Austria, in Naples and Sicily, in the Netherlands, and in the County of Burgundy, usually known as Franche Comté.   Between him and Francis I. a struggle was inevitable.   The chances were apparently, on the whole, on the side of Charles.   His dominions, indeed, were scattered, and devoid of the strength given by national feeling, whilst the smaller dominions of Francis were compact and united by a strong national bond.   In character, however, Charles had the superiority.   He was cool and wary, whilst Francis was impetuous and uncalculating. Both sovereigns were now candidates for the Empire.   The seven electors who had it in their gift were open to bribery.   Charles bribed highest, and being chosen became the Emperor Charles V.

13. **The Field of the Cloth of Gold. 1520.**—Wolsey tried hard to keep the peace.   In **1520** Henry met Francis on the border of the territory of Calais, and the magnificence of the display on both sides gave to the scene the name of the Field of the Cloth of Gold. In the same year Henry had interviews with Charles.   Peace was for a time maintained, because both Charles and Francis were still too much occupied at home to quarrel, but it could hardly be maintained long.

14. **The Execution of the Duke of Buckingham. 1521.**—Henry was entirely master in England.   In **1521** the Duke of Buckingham, son of the Buckingham who had been beheaded by Richard III., was tried and executed as a traitor.   His fault was that he had great wealth, and that, being descended from the Duke of Gloucester, the youngest son of Edward III., he had not only cherished some idea of claiming the throne after Henry's death, but had chattered about his prospects.   In former days justice was not to be had by those who offended the great lords.   Now, one despot had stepped into the place of many, and justice was not to be had by those who offended the king.   The legal forms of trial were now as before observed.   Buckingham was indeed tried before the court of the Lord High Steward, which consisted of a select number of peers, and which had jurisdiction over peers when Parliament was not sitting. These, however, were no more than forms.   It was probably a mingled feeling of gratitude and fear which made peers as well as ordinary juries ready to take Henry's word for the guilt of any offender.

15. **Another French War. 1522—1523.**—The diplomacy of

The embarkation of Henry VIII. from Dover, 1520 : from the original painting at Hampton Court.

those days was a mere tissue of trickery and lies. Behind the falsehood, however, Wolsey had a purpose of his own, the maintenance of peace on the Continent. Yet, in 1521 war broke out between Charles and Francis, both of whom laid claim to the Duchy of Milan, and it was evident that Wolsey would be unable to keep England out of the struggle. If there was to be fighting Henry preferred to fight France rather than to fight Charles.

In 1522, in conjunction with Charles, he invaded France. There was burning and ravaging enough, but nothing of importance was done. Nevertheless in 1523 Henry was in high spirits. A great French noble, the Duke of Bourbon, provoked by ill-treatment, revolted against Francis, and Henry and Charles fancied that he would open a way to them into the heart of France. If Henry was to be crowned a: Paris, which was the object on which he was bent, he must have a supply of money from his subjects. Though no Parliament had been summoned for nearly eight years, one was summoned now, of which More was the Speaker. Wolsey asked for an enormous grant of 800,000*l.*, nearly equal to 12,000,000*l.* at the present day. Finding that the Commons hesitated, he swept into the House in state to argue with them. Expecting

Cup and Cover, 1523, at Barber Surgeons' Hall, London.

a reply, and finding silence, he turned to More, who told him that it was against the privilege of the House to call on it for an immediate answer. He had to depart unsatisfied, and after some days the House granted a considerable sum, but far less than that which had been demanded. Wolsey was now in a position of danger. His own policy was pacific, but his master's policy was warlike, and he had been obliged to make himself the unquestioning mouth-

piece of his master in demanding supplies for war.   He had long
been hated by the nobles for thrusting them aside.   He was now
beginning to be hated by the people as the supposed author of an
expensive war, which he would have done his best to prevent.
He had not even the advantage of seeing his master win laurels in
the field.   The national spirit of France was roused, and the combined attack of Henry and Charles proved as great a failure in **1523**
as in **1522**.   The year **1524** was spent by Wolsey in diplomatic
intrigue.

16. **The Amicable Loan.   1525.**—Early in **1525** Europe was
startled by the news that Francis had been signally defeated by
the Imperialists at Pavia, and had been carried prisoner to Spain.
Wolsey knew that Charles's influence was now likely to predomi-
nate in Europe, and that unless England was to be overshadowed
by it, Henry's alliance must be transferred to Francis.   Henry,
however, saw in the imprisonment of Francis only a fine opportunity for conquering France.   Wolsey had again to carry out his
master's wishes as though they were his own.   Raking up old precedents, he suggested that the people should be asked for what was
called an Amicable Loan, on the plea that Henry was about to invade France in person.   He obtained the consent of the citizens
of London by telling them that, if they did not pay, it might 'fortune
to cost some their heads.'   All over England Wolsey was cursed as
the originator of the loan.   There were even signs that a rebellion
was imminent.   In Norfolk when the Duke of Norfolk demanded
payment there was a general resistance.   On his demanding the
name of the captain of the multitude which refused to pay, a man
told him that their captain's 'name was Poverty,' and 'he and his
cousin Necessity' had brought them to this.   Wolsey, seeing that
it was impossible to collect the money, took all the unpopularity of
advising the loan upon himself.   'Because,' he wrote, 'every man
layeth the burden from him, I am content to take it on me, and to
endure the fame and noise of the people, for my good-will towards
the king . . . but the eternal God knoweth all.'   Henry had no
such nobility of character as to refuse to accept the sacrifice.   He
liked to make his ministers scapegoats, to heap on their heads the
indignation of the people that he might himself retain his popularity.   For three centuries and a half it was fully believed that the
Amicable Loan had originated with Wolsey.

17. **Closing Years of Wolsey's Greatness.   1525—1527.**—All
idea of continuing the war being now abandoned, Wolsey cautiously
negotiated for an alliance with France, and in the autumn of **1525**

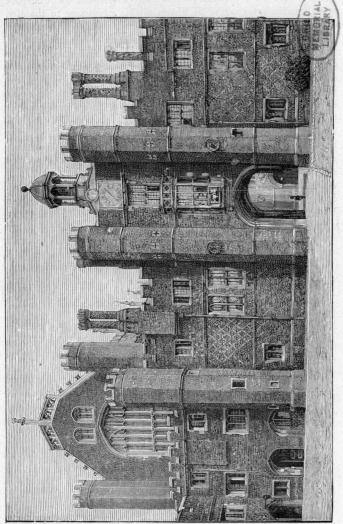

Hampton Court; built by Cardinal Wolsey, finished in 1526.

peace was signed between France and England. In February
1526 Charles set Francis at liberty on his promising to abandon
to him large tracts of French territory. As soon as he was out of
Spain Francis declared that, without the consent of his subjects,
such promises were not binding on him. An Italian league, jealous
of Charles's power, gathered round the Pope, Clement VII., to
oppose him. In May **1527** the exiled Duke of Bourbon, who was
now one of Charles's generals, took Rome by assault. He was
himself slain as he mounted the wall, but his followers took prisoner
the Pope, and sacked Rome with horrible barbarity. Wolsey was
too worldly-minded to be shocked at the Pope's misfortunes ; but
he had much to fear from the enormous extension of the Emperor's
power. For some weeks he had been negotiating a close alliance
with France on the basis of a marriage between Henry's only surviving child, Mary, and the worn-out voluptuary Francis. Suddenly the scheme was changed to a proposal for a marriage between
Mary, who was ten years old, and the second son of Francis, who
was but six. The bargain was concluded, and for a time there
was some thought of carrying it out. At all events when the news
of the sack of Rome arrived, England and France were already in
close alliance. Wolsey's position was, to all outward appearance,
secure.

CHAPTER XXV

THE BREACH WITH THE PAPACY. 1527—1534

LEADING DATES

Reign of Henry VIII., 1509-1547

Henry seeks for a divorce .	1527
His suit before a Legatine Court	1529
Fall of Wolsey .	1529
The clergy acknowledge Henry to be Supreme Head of the Church of England	1531
The first Act of Annates .	1532
The king's marriage to Anne Boleyn and the Act of Appeals .	1533
Cranmer's sentence of divorce	1533
The final separation from Rome	1534

1. The Papacy and the Renascence.—The Renascence alone
could not make the world better, and in many respects it made it
worse. The respect which it paid to humanity, which was its

leading characteristic, allied itself in More with a reverence for God, which led him to strive to mellow the religious teaching of the Middle Ages, by fitting it for the needs of the existing world. Too many threw off all religious restraints, and made it their first thought to seek their own enjoyment, or the triumphs of their own intellectual skill. Sensual delights were pursued with less brutal directness, but became more seductive and more truly debasing by the splendour and gracefulness of the life of which they formed a part. In Italy the Popes swam with the current. Alexander VI. (**1492—1503**) gave himself up to the most degrading vices. Julius II. (**1503—1513**) was a passionate warrior struggling for the extension of his temporal possessions. Leo X. (**1513—1521**) was a polished lover of art, perfectly indifferent to religious duty. " Let us enjoy the Papacy," he said when he was elected, " since God has given it to us." Amidst the lust of the flesh, the lust of the eyes, and the pride of life, the Popes became as other Italian princes, no better and no worse. Spiritual guidance was no longer to be expected of them.

2. **Wolsey and the Papacy.**—By Wolsey and his master the Papacy was respected as a venerable and useful institution, the centre of a religious organisation which they believed to be of divine origin, though when it came in conflict with their own projects they were quite ready to thwart it. In **1521** Leo X. died, and Wolsey, having some hopes of being himself elected, asked Charles V. to send troops to compel the cardinals to choose him, promising to pay the expenses of the armament. Charles, though, in the previous year, he had offered to support Wolsey's candidature at the next vacancy, now deserted him, and the new Pope was Adrian VI., who in 1523 was succeeded by Clement VII. (see p. 374).

3. **Wolsey's Legatine Powers.**—It is unlikely that Wolsey was much disappointed. His chief sphere of action was England, where since **1518** he had held unwonted authority, as in that year he had been appointed Legate *a latere*[1] by Leo X. at Henry's request, and the powers of a Legate *a latere* were superior even to those of Warham, the Archbishop of Canterbury. Wolsey was therefore clothed with all the authority of king and Pope combined. His own life was, indeed, like those of many churchmen in his day, very far from the ideal of Christianity; but for all that he had that respect for religious order which often lingers in the hearts of men who break away from the

[1] *i.e.* a Legate sent from the Pope's side, and therefore having power to speak almost with full Papal authority.

precepts of religion, and he was too great a statesman to be blind
to the danger impending over the Church. The old order was
changing, and Wolsey was as anxious as More, though from more

Portrait of William Warham, Archbishop of Canterbury, 1503–1532, showing the ordinary
episcopal dress, with the mitre and archiepiscopal cross : from a painting belonging
to Viscount Dillon, dated 1527.

worldly motives, that the change should be effected without
violence. He knew that the Church was wealthy, and that wealth
tempted plunderers, and he also knew that, with some bright ex-

ceptions, the clergy were ignorant, and even when not absolutely dissolute were remiss and easy-going in their lives. He was, therefore, anxious to make them more worthy of respect, and, with the consent of king and Pope, he began in 1524 to dissolve several small monasteries, and to apply their revenues to two great colleges, the one founded by him at Oxford and the other at Ipswich. He hoped that without any change of doctrine or organisation the Church would gradually be purified by improved education, and would thus once more command the respect of the laity.

4. **Henry VIII. and the Clergy.**—With Wolsey's object Henry, being himself well educated and well read, fully sympathised. For many years there had been a tacit understanding between the king and the Pope, and now that both the king and the Pope supported Wolsey's action there seemed to be less danger than ever of any disturbance of the friendly relations between Church and State. Yet though Henry was on good terms with the Pope, he had made up his mind that whenever there was a conflict of jurisdiction in ecclesiastical matters his own will, and not that of the clergy, was to be predominant. As early as in 1515, when a question of this kind was moved, Wolsey asked on behalf of the clergy that it might be referred to the Pope. "We," said Henry proudly, " are by God's grace king of England, and have no superior but God ; we will maintain the rights of the crown like our predecessors ; your decrees you break and interpret at your pleasure, but we will not consent to your interpretation of them any more than our predecessors have done." Henry VIII., in short, took up the position which Henry II. had assumed towards the clergy of his day, and he was far more powerful to give effect to his views than Henry II. had ever been. Such an act of self-assertion would probably have caused a breach with the great Popes of the middle ages, such as Gregory VII. or Innocent III. Leo X. was far too much a man of the world to trouble himself about such matters.

5. **German Lutheranism.**—Before many years had passed the beginnings of a great religious revolution which appeared in Germany served to bind Henry and Leo more closely together. Martin Luther, a Saxon friar, had been disgusted by the proceedings of a hawker of indulgences, who extracted small sums from the ignorant by the sale of the remission of the pains of purgatory. What gave world-wide importance to Luther's resistance was that he was not only an eloquent preacher of morality, but the convinced maintainer of a doctrine which, though not a new one, had long been laid aside. He preached justification by faith, and the

II.

Tower of Fountains Abbey church ; built by Abbot Huby.
1494–1526.

acceptance of his teaching implied even more than the acceptance of a new doctrine. For centuries it had been understood that each Christian held intercourse with God through the sacraments and ordinances of the Church. His individuality was, as it were, swallowed up in the vast community to which he belonged. Luther taught each of his hearers that the important thing was his faith, that is to say his immediate personal relation with God, and that the intervention of human beings might, indeed, be helpful to him, but could be no more. Such a doctrine touched all human activity. The man who in religion counted his own individual faith as the one thing necessary was likely to count his own individual convictions in social or political matters as worth more to him than his obedience to the authority of any government. In Luther's teaching was to be found the spirit of political as well as of religious liberty. This side of it, however, was not likely to reveal itself at once. After a time Luther shook off entirely the claims of the Papacy upon his obedience, but he magnified the duty of obeying the princes who gave him their support in his struggle with the Pope.

6. Henry's Controversy with Luther.—Luther, when once he was engaged in controversy with the Papacy, assailed other doctrines than those relating to justification. In **1521** Henry, vain of his theological learning, wrote a book against him in defence of the seven sacraments. Luther, despising a royal antagonist, replied with scurrilous invective. Pope Leo was delighted to have found so influential a champion, and conferred on Henry the title of Defender of the Faith. If Henry had not been moved by stronger motives than controversial vanity he might have remained the Pope's ally till the end of his life.

7. Queen Catharine and Anne Boleyn.—It was a great disappointment to Henry that he had no surviving male children. England had never been ruled by a queen, and it was uncertain whether Henry's daughter, Mary, would be allowed to reign. Henry had already begun to ask himself whether he might not get rid of his wife, on the plea that a marriage with his brother's wife was unlawful, and this consideration had the greater weight with him because Catharine was five years older than himself and was growing distasteful to him. When in **1521**, in his book against Luther, he assigned a divine origin to the Papacy, he told More of a secret reason for this exaltation of the Pope's power, and it is possible that this reason was his desire to obtain from the Pope a divorce under the pretext that it would secure a peaceful succes-

sion.   At all events his scruples regarding his marriage with
Catharine were quickened in **1522** by the appearance at court of
Anne Boleyn, a sprightly black-eyed flirt in her sixteenth year,
who took his fancy as she grew into womanhood.   Flirt as she
was, she knew her power, and refused to give herself to him except

Catharine of Aragon : from a painting in the National Portrait Gallery.

in marriage.   The king, on his part, being anxious for a legitimate
son, set his heart on a divorce which would enable him to marry
Anne.   Wolsey, knowing the obstacles in the way, urged him to
abandon the project ; but it was never possible to turn Henry from
his course, and Wolsey set himself, in this as in all things else, to

The Gatehouse of Coughton Court, Warwickshire; built about 1530.

carry out his master's wishes, though he did so very reluctantly. Moral scruples had little weight with Wolsey, but in **1525**, when he learnt the king's design, there were strong political reasons against its execution, as England was in alliance with Catharine's nephew, the Emperor, Charles V., and a divorce would be certain to endanger the alliance.

8. **Henry's Demand for a Divorce. 1527—1528.**—Two years later, in **1527**, as Henry was veering round towards a French alliance (see p. 374), he had no longer much reason to consider the feelings of the Emperor. On the other hand, the strong position which Charles occupied in Italy after the sack of Rome made it improbable that Clement VII. who was then Pope, and who thought more of his political than of his ecclesiastical position, would do anything to thwart the Emperor. An attempt made by Henry in **1527** to draw Clement to consent to the divorce failed, and in **1528** Wolsey sent to Rome his secretary, Stephen Gardiner, an adroit man of business, to induce Clement to appoint legates to decide the question in Henry's favour. Clement, anxious to please all parties, appointed Wolsey and another cardinal, Campeggio, as his legates, but took care to add that nothing done by them should be valid until it had received his own approval.

9. **The Legatine Court. 1529.**—The court of the two legates was opened at Blackfriars in **1529**. Before proceeding to business they tried hard to induce either Henry to abstain from asking for a divorce or Catharine to abstain from resisting his demand. In such a matter Catharine was as firm as the self-willed Henry. Even if she could consent to leave the throne, she could not, if she retained any sense of womanly dignity, acknowledge that she had never been a wife to Henry, or suffer her daughter to be branded with illegitimacy. When king and queen were at last cited to appear Catharine knelt before her husband. She had, she said been his true and obedient wife for twenty years, and had done nothing to deserve being put to open shame. As it was, she appealed to Rome. The queen's cause was popular with the masses, who went straight to the mark, and saw in the whole affair a mere attempt to give a legal covering to Henry's lust. The legates refused to consider the queen's appeal, but when they came to hear arguments on the merits of the case they were somewhat startled by the appearance of the aged Fisher, Bishop of Rochester, one of the holiest and most learned prelates of the day, who now came voluntarily, though he knew that Henry's wrath was deadly, to support the cause of Catharine. Campeggio took advantage of

the strong feeling which was growing against the king to interpose
delays which he knew to be well-pleasing to Clement, and before
these delays were at an end Clement annulled all the proceedings
in England and revoked the cause to Rome. Most probably he
was alarmed at the threats of the Emperor, but he had also reasons
of his own for the course which he took. Henry did not ask for
a divorce on any of the usual grounds, but for a declaration that
his marriage had been null from the beginning. As, however, his
marriage had been solemnised with a Papal dispensation, Clement
was asked to set aside the dispensation of one of his predecessors,
a proceeding to which no Pope with any respect for his office
could reasonably be expected to consent.

10. **The Fall of Wolsey. 1529—1530.**—Henry was very angry
and made Wolsey his victim. Wolsey's active endeavours to procure the divorce counted as nothing. It was enough that he had
failed. He was no longer needed to conduct foreign affairs, as
Henry cared now only for the divorce, and raised no objection
when Charles and Francis made peace at Cambrai without consulting his interests. The old nobility, headed by the Duke of
Norfolk, who as Earl of Surrey had been the victor of Flodden,
had long hated Wolsey bitterly, and the profligate courtiers, together with the friends and relatives of Anne, hated him no less
bitterly now. Before the end of the year proceedings under the
Statute of Præmunire (see pp. 258, 382) were taken against him on
the ground that he had usurped legatine powers. It was notorious
that he had exercised them at the king's wish, and he could have
produced evidence to show that this had been the case. In those
days, however, it was held to be a subject's duty not to contest the
king's will, and Wolsey contented himself with an abject supplica-
tion for forgiveness. He was driven from his offices, and all his
goods and estates seized. The college which he had founded at
Ipswich was sold for the king's use, and his college at Oxford, then
known as Cardinal College, was also seized, though it was afterwards refounded under the name of Christchurch by the robber
king. Wolsey was reduced to extreme poverty. In **1530** he was
allowed to return to the possession of the archbishopric of York ;
but he imprudently opened communications with the French
ambassador, and harmless as they were, they gave a handle to his
enemies. Henry ordered him to be charged with treason. The
sufferings of his mind affected his body, and on his way to London
he knew that he was a dying man. " Father Abbot," he said, in
taking shelter in Leicester Abbey, " I am come hither to leave my

bones among you." "If I had served my God," he acknowledged
as he was passing away, "as diligently as I have done my king,
He would not have given me over in my grey hairs."

Hall of Christchurch, Oxford; built by Cardinal Wolsey, and finished in 1529.

11. **The House of Commons and the Clergy. 1529.**—No king ever felt the importance of popularity like Henry, and the compassion which had been freely given to Catharine by the crowd, on her appearance in the Legatine Court, made it necessary for him to find support elsewhere. It had been Wolsey's policy to summon Parliament as seldom as possible. It was to be Henry's policy to summon it as frequently as possible. He no longer feared the House of Lords, and either he or Wolsey's late servant, Thomas Cromwell, an able and unscrupulous man, who rose rapidly in Henry's favour, perceived the use which might be made of the House of Commons. By his influence the king could carry the elections as he pleased, and when Parliament met in 1529 it contained a packed House of Commons ready to do the king's bidding. The members were either lawyers or country gentlemen, the main supports of the Tudor monarchy, and Henry strengthened his hold upon them by letting them loose on the special abuses which had grown up in the ecclesiastical courts. Lawyers and country gentlemen were very much what they had been in the fifteenth century, without large political ideas or fine spiritual perceptions ; but now that they were relieved of the oppression of the great nobles they turned upon the clergy, who claimed fees and dues which they disliked paying, and who used the powers of the ecclesiastical tribunals to exact heavy payments for moral and spiritual offences.

12. **The Universities Consulted. 1530.**—Henry had as yet no thought of breaking with the Pope. He wanted to put pressure on him to make him do what he had come to regard as right. In 1530 he sent to the universities of Europe to ask their opinion on the question whether a marriage with a brother's widow was contrary to the law of God. The whole inquiry was a farce. Wherever Henry or his allies could bribe or bully the learned doctors, an answer was usually given in the affirmative. Wherever the Emperor could bribe or bully, then the answer was usually given in the negative. That the experiment should have been tried, however, was a proof of the strength of the spirit of the Renascence. A questions of morals which the Pope hesitated to decide was submitted to the learning of the learned.

13. **The Clergy under a Præmunire. 1530—1531.**—Towards the end of 1530 Henry charged the whole clergy of England with a breach of the Statute of Præmunire by their submission to Wolsey's legatine authority. A more monstrous charge was never brought, as when that authority was exercised not a priest in England dared to offend the king by resisting it. When the Convocation of Canter-

bury met in 1531, it offered to buy the pardon of the clergy by a grant of 100,000*l*., to which was afterwards added 18,000*l*. by the Convocation of York. Henry refused to issue the pardon unless the clergy would acknowledge him to be supreme head of the Church of England.

14. **The King's Supreme Headship acknowledged by the Clergy. 1531.**—The title demanded by Henry was conceded by the clergy, with the qualification that he was Supreme Head of the English Church and clergy so far as was allowed by the law of Christ. The title thus given was vague, and did not bar the acknowledgment of the Papal authority as it had been before exercised, but its interpretation would depend on the will of the stronger of the two parties. As far as the Pope was concerned, Henry's claim was no direct invasion of his rights. The Pope had exercised authority and jurisdiction in England, but he had never declared himself to be Supreme Head of the Church either in England or anywhere else. Henry indeed alleged that he asked for nothing new. He merely wanted to be known as the supreme authority in the relations between the clergy and the laity. Nevertheless it was a threat to the Pope, who might well fear lest the clergy, after giving way to the assumption of a title which implied authority over themselves, might give way to the widening of that same authority over matters on which the Pope's claims had hitherto been undoubted.

15. **The Submission of the Clergy. 1532.**—Everything done by Henry at this crisis was done with a view to the securing of his purposed divorce. In the Parliament which sat in 1532 the Commons were again let loose upon the clergy, and Henry, taking their side, forced Convocation [1] to sign a document known as the submission of the clergy. In this the clergy engaged in the first place neither to meet in Convocation nor to enact or execute new canons without the king's authority, and, secondly, to submit all past ecclesiastical legislation to examination with a view to the removal of everything prejudicial to the royal prerogative. The second article was never carried into effect, as the first was enough for Henry. He was now secure against any attempt of the clergy in Convocation to protest against any step that he might take about the divorce, and he was none the less pleased because he

---

[1] There were two Convocations, of the two provinces of Canterbury and York, but the former was so much more important that it is usually spoken of simply as Convocation.

had incidentally settled the question of the relations between the clerical legislature and the Crown.

16. **Sir Thomas More and the Protestants. 1529—1532.**—The submission of the clergy cost Henry the services of the best and

Sir Thomas More, wearing the collar of SS : from an original portrait painted by Holbein in 1527, belonging to Edward Huth, Esq.

wisest of his statesmen. Sir Thomas More had been appointed Chancellor on Wolsey's fall in **1529**. When More wrote the *Utopia*, Luther had not yet broken away from the Papacy, and the tolerant principles of the author of that book had not been put to the test. Even in the *Utopia* More had confined his tolerance to those who argued in opposition to the received religion without anger or spite, and when he came to be in office he learnt by practical experience that opposition is seldom carried on in the spirit of meekness. Protestantism, as the Lutheran tenets began to be called in 1529, spread into England, though as yet it gained a hold only on a few scattered individuals. Here and there thoughtful men, dissatisfied with the teaching given to them and with the lives of many of their teachers, embraced the Lutheran doctrine of justification by faith. Even the best of them could hardly be expected to treat with philosophic calm the doctrines which they had forsaken ; whilst some of their converts took a pleasure in reviling the clergy and the common creed of the vast majority of Englishmen. With many again the doctrine of justification by faith slipped into the condemnation of the merit of good works, and even into a light estimation of good works themselves. For this bitterness of speech and mind More had no tolerance, and while he pursued his antagonists with argument and ridicule, he also used his authority to support the clergy in putting down what they termed heresy by the process of burning the obstinate heretic.

17. **Resignation of Sir Thomas More. 1532.**—More had no ground for fearing that the increase of the king's authority over the clergy would at once encourage revolt against the Church. Henry was a representative Englishman, and neither he nor the House of Commons had the least sympathy with heresy. They wanted to believe and act as their fathers had done. More, however, was sufficiently prescient to foresee that a lay authority could not for ever maintain this attitude. Laymen were certain to be moved by the current of thought which prevailed in their age, and it was only, he believed, the great Papal organisation which could keep them steady. Though Henry had not yet directly attacked that organisation, he might be expected to attack it soon, and, in 1532, More retired from all connection with Henry's government rather than take part in that attack.

18. **The First Act of Annates. 1532.**—Having secured himself, as it were, in the rear by the submission of the clergy, Henry proceeded to deal with the Pope. He still wished if possible to win him to his side, and before the end of 1532 he obtained from Parliament an Act of Annates. Annates were the first-fruits or first year's income of ecclesiastical benefices, and by this Act the first-fruits of bishoprics, which had hitherto been paid to the Pope, were to be kept back. The Act was not, however, to come into force till the king had ratified it, and Henry refused for a time to ratify

it hoping to reduce Clement to submission by suspending over his head a threat upon his purse.

19. **The King's Marriage and the Act of Appeals. 1533.**— Henry, however, found that Clement was not to be moved, and his patience coming at last to an end, he was secretly married to Anne Boleyn on January 25, **1533**. Now that he had reluctantly given up hope of obtaining a favourable decision from the Pope, he resolved to put an end to the Papal jurisdiction in England. Otherwise if he obtained a sentence in an English ecclesiastical court declaring his marriage with Catharine to be null from the beginning, his injured wife might appeal to the superior court of the Pope. He accordingly obtained from Parliament the Act of Appeals, declaring that the king held the supreme authority in England, and that as under him all temporal matters were to be decided by temporal judges, and all spiritual matters by spiritual judges, no appeals should hereafter be suffered to any authority outside the realm. Henry was capable of any meanness to serve his ends, but he also knew how to gain more than his immediate ends by connecting them with a large national policy. He almost made men forget the low design which prompted the Act of Appeals by fixing their eyes on the great object of national independence.

20. **Archbishop Cranmer and the Court at Dunstable. 1533.**— Henry found a convenient instrument for his personal as well as for his national policy in Thomas Cranmer, whom he appointed Archbishop of Canterbury in the spring of **1533**. Cranmer was intellectually acute, and took a worthy part in the further development of the English Church ; but he was morally weak, and inclined to carry out orders whatever they might be, especially if they came from a king as strong-willed as Henry. He had already thrown himself as an active agent into the cause of Henry's divorce, and he was now prepared as archbishop to give effect to his arguments. In March Convocation was half persuaded, half driven to declare Catharine's marriage to be void, and in May Cranmer, sitting at Dunstable in his archiepiscopal court, pronounced sentence against her. In accordance with the Act of Appeals the sentence was final, but both Henry and Cranmer feared lest Catharine should send her counsel to make an appeal to Rome, and they were therefore mean enough to conceal from her the day on which sentence was to be given. The temporal benefits which the Pope derived from England were now to come to an end as well as his spiritual jurisdiction, and in July the king ratified the Act of Annates.

21. **Frith and Latimer. 1533.**—When a man of special intellectual acquirements like Cranmer could descend to the trick which he had played at Dunstable, it was time that some one should be found who, in the stedfastness of his faith, would refuse to truckle to the king, and would maintain the rights of individual conscience as well as those of national independence. The teaching of Zwingli, a Swiss reformer, who held that the bread and wine in the Sacrament of the Lord's Supper was a mere sign of the Body and Blood of the Redeemer, was beginning to influence the English Protestants, and its reception was one more reason for the mass of Englishmen to send to prison or the stake those who maintained what was, in their eyes, so monstrous a heresy. Amongst the noblest of the persecuted was John Frith, who, whilst he stoutly held to the belief that the doctrine of transubstantiation was untrue, begged that men should be left 'to think thereon as God shall instil in any man's mind, and that neither part condemn other for this matter, but receive each other in brotherly love, reserving each other's infirmity to God.' Frith was in advance of his time as the advocate of religious liberty as well as of a special creed, and he was burnt alive. Henry meant it to be understood that his supreme headship made it easier, and not harder, to suppress heresy. He might have succeeded if he had had merely to deal with a few heroes like Frith. That which was beyond his control was the sapping process of the spirit of the Renascence, leading his bishops, and even himself, to examine and explain received doctrines, and thus to transform them without knowing what they were doing. Hugh Latimer, for instance, a favourite chaplain of the king, was, indeed, a preacher of righteousness, testing all things rather by their moral worth than by their conformity to an intellectual standard. The received doctrines about Purgatory, the worship of the saints, and pilgrimages to their images seemed to him to be immoral ; but as yet he wished to purify opinion, not to change it altogether, and in this he had the support of the king, who, in 1535, made him Bishop of Worcester.

22. **Completion of the Breach with Rome. 1533—1534.**— Before 1533 was over Henry appealed from the Pope to a General Council. Clement not only paid no heed to his appeal, but gave sentence in favour of Catharine. When Parliament met in 1534, therefore, Henry was obliged to strengthen his position of hostility to the Pope. He procured from it three Acts. The first of these was a second Act of Annates, which conferred on him absolutely not only the first-fruits of bishoprics which had been the subject of

the conditional Act of Annates in 1532 (see p. 388), but also the first-fruits of all the beneficed clergy, as well as a tenth of each year's income of both bishops and beneficed clergy, all of which payments had been hitherto made to the Pope. Incidentally this Act also regulated the appointment of bishops, by ordering that the king should issue a *congé d'élire* to the chapter of the vacant see, together with a letter missive compelling the choice of his nominee. The second was an Act concerning Peter's pence, abolishing all minor payments to the Pope, and cutting away all interference of the Pope by transferring his right to issue licences and dispensations to the Archbishop of Canterbury. The third confirmed the submission of the clergy and enacted that appeals from the courts of the Archbishop should be heard by commissioners appointed by the King, and known as the delegates of Appeals. It was by these Acts that the separation between the Churches of England and Rome was finally effected. They merely completed the work which had been done by the great Act of Appeals in 1533. The Church of England had indeed always been a national Church with its own ecclesiastical assemblies, and with ties to the Crown which were stretched more tightly or more loosely at various times. It had, however, maintained its connection with the Continental Churches by its subordination to the Pope, and this subordination had been made real by the subjection of its courts to appeals to Rome, and by the necessity of recurring to Rome for permission to do certain things prohibited by English ecclesiastical law. All this was now at an end. The old supremacy of the king was sharpened and defined. The jurisdiction of the Pope was abolished. Nominally the English ecclesiastical authorities became more independent ; more capable of doing what seemed to them to be best for the Church of the nation. Such at least was the state of the law. In practice the English ecclesiastical authorities were entirely at Henry's bidding. In theory and in sentiment the Church of England was still a branch of the Catholic Church, one in doctrine and in discipline with the Continental Churches. Practically it was now, in a far more unqualified sense than before, a national Church, ready to drift from its moorings and to accept new counsels whenever the tide of opinion should break strongly upon it.

CHAPTER XXVI

THE ROYAL SUPREMACY. 1534—1547

LEADING DATES

Reign of Henry VIII., 1509-1547

The Acts of Succession and Supremacy	1534
Execution of Fisher and More.	1535
Dissolution of the smaller monasteries and the Pilgrimage of Grace	1536
Destruction of relics and images	1538
The Six Articles and the Act granting to the king the greater monasteries	1539
Fall of Cromwell.	1540
Henry VIII. king of Ireland	1541
Solway Moss	1542
Death of Henry VIII.	1547

1. **The Act of Succession. 1534.**—In September **1533** Anne had given birth to a daughter, who was afterwards Queen Elizabeth. In **1534** Parliament passed an Act of Succession. Not only did it declare Anne's marriage to be lawful and Catharine's unlawful, and consequently Elizabeth and not Mary to be heir to the crown, but it required all subjects to take an oath acknowledging their approval of the contents of the Act. More and Fisher professed themselves ready to swear to any succession which might be authorised by Act of Parliament ; but they would not swear to the illegality of Catharine's marriage. It was on this point that Henry was most sensitive, as he knew public opinion to be against him, and he threw both More and Fisher into the Tower. In the year before the language held in the pulpit on the subject of Henry's marriage with Anne in his wife's lifetime had been so strong that Cranmer had forbidden all preaching on the subject of the king's laws or the succession to the throne. Of the clergy, the friars were still the most resolute. Henry now sent commissioners to visit the friaries, and those in which the oath was refused were summarily suppressed.

2. **The Acts of Treason and Supremacy. 1534.**—In **1534** Parliament also passed a new Act of Treasons which made it high treason to wish or practise harm to the king, the queen, and their heirs, to use words denying their titles, or to call the king a 'heretic, schismatic, tyrant, infidel, or usurper of the crown.' Later in the same

year, but in a fresh session, Parliament passed the Act of Supremacy, which confirmed the title of Supreme Head on earth of the Church of England, a title very similar to that to which the king had obtained the qualified assent of the clergy in 1531 (see p. 386). From that time anyone who denied the king to be the Supreme Head of the Church of England was liable to a traitor's death.

3.—**The Monks of the Charterhouse. 1534.**—It can hardly be doubted that Henry's chief adviser in these tyrannical measures was the able and unscrupulous Cromwell. It was Cromwell's plan to exalt the royal authority into a despotism by means of a subservient Parliament. He was already Henry's secretary ; and in 1535 was appointed the king's Vicar-General in ecclesiastical matters. He was quite ready to push the Acts of Parliament which had recently been passed to their extreme consequences. His first object was to get rid of the Friars Observant, who had shown themselves most hostile to what they called in plainness of speech the king's adultery. All

John Fisher, Bishop of Rochester, 1504–1535 ; from a drawing by Holbein in the Royal Library, Windsor Castle.

their houses were suppressed, and some of the inmates put to death. Then Cromwell fell on the London Charterhouse,[1] the inmates of which had been imprisoned in the year before simply for a refusal to take the oath of the Act of Succession, though they had not uttered a word against the king's proceedings. They could now be put to death under the new Treason Act, for denying the king's supremacy, and many of them were accordingly executed after the usual barbarous fashion, whilst others perished of starvation or of diseases contracted in the filthy prisons in which they were confined.

---

[1] The Charterhouse here means the house of the Carthusians.

'I profess," said the Prior, Houghton, "that it is not out of obstinate malice or a mind of rebellion that I do disobey the king, but only for the fear of God, that I offend not the Supreme Majesty; because our Holy Mother the Church hath decreed and appointed otherwise than the king and Parliament hath ordained." Houghton and his fellows were as truly martyrs as Frith had been. They at least had sown no seeds of rebellion, and they died because a tyrannical king insisted on ruling over consciences as well as over bodily acts.

4. **Execution of Fisher and More.** 1535.—Fisher and More were the next to suffer on the same charge, though their sentences were commuted to death by beheading. More preserved his wit to the last. "I pray you," he said as he mounted the scaffold, "see me safe up, and for my coming down I will shift for myself." After he had knelt to place his head on the block, he raised it again to move his beard aside. "Pity," he muttered, "that should be cut that has not committed treason."

5. **The Dissolution of the Smaller Monasteries.** 1536.—Money never came amiss to Henry, and Cromwell now rooted himself firmly in his master's favour by pointing out to him fresh booty. The English monasteries were rich and weak, and it was easy to trump up or exaggerate charges against them. Cromwell sent commissioners to inquire into their moral state (1535), and the commissioners, who were as unscrupulous as himself, rushed round the monasteries in such a hurry that they had no time to make any real inquiry, but nevertheless returned with a number of scandalous tales. These tales referred to some of the larger monasteries as well as the smaller, but, when Parliament met in 1536, Henry contented himself with asking that monasteries having property worth less than 200*l*. a year should be dissolved, and their estates given to himself, on the ground that whilst the smaller ones were dens of vice the larger ones were examples of virtue. Parliament granted his request, and the work of spoliation began. There can be no doubt that vice did exist in the monasteries, though there was not so much of it as the commissioners asserted. It would have been indeed strange if innocence had been preserved in communities living in enforced celibacy, with no stress of work to occupy their thoughts, and with the high ideals of their profession neglected or cast aside. On the other hand, the monks were easy landlords, were hospitable to the stranger and kindly to the poor, whilst neither the king himself nor those to whom he gave or sold the lands which he acquired cared for more than to make money. The real weakness of the monks lay in their failure to conciliate the more active minds of the

age, or to meet its moral needs. The attack upon the vast edifice of Henry's despotism in Church and State could only be carried on successfully by the combined effort of men like the scholars of the Renascence, whose thoughts were unfettered, and of those who, like the Protestants, were full of aggressive vigour, and who substituted for the duty of obedience the duty of following their own convictions.

6. **The Execution of Anne Boleyn. 1536.**—Before the end of 1536 there was a new queen. Henry became tired of Anne, as he had been tired of Catharine, and on a series of monstrous charges, so monstrous as to be hardly credible, he had her tried and executed. Her unpardonable crime was probably that her only living child was a daughter, and not a son. Ten days after Anne's death Henry married a third wife, Jane Seymour. As Catharine was now dead, there could be no doubt of the legitimacy of Jane's offspring, but to make assurance doubly sure, a new Parliament passed an Act

Edward Seymour, Earl of Hertford, brother of Jane Seymour, afterwards Duke of Somerset, known as 'the Protector,' at the age of 28 (1535), 1507–1552: from a painting at Sudeley Castle.

settling the succession on Jane's children, and declaring both Mary and Elizabeth illegitimate.

7. **The Ten Articles. 1536.**—It is probable that when Henry took the title of Supreme Head he intended to maintain the doctrines and practices of the Church exactly as he found them. In 1536 the clergy were crying out not merely against attacks on their faith, but against the ribaldry with which these attacks were often conducted. One assailant, for instance, declared the oil used in extreme unction to be no more than the Bishop of Rome's grease or butter, and

another that it was of no more use to invoke a saint than it was to whirl a stone against the wind. Many of the clergy would have been well pleased with mere repression. Henry, however, and the bishops whom he most trusted wished repression to be accompanied with reasonable explanations of the doctrines and practices enforced. The result was seen in the Ten Articles which were drawn up by Convocation, and sent abroad with the authority of the king. There was to be uniformity, to be obtained by the circulation of a written document, in which the old doctrines were stripped of much that had given offence, and their acceptance made easy for educated men. Of the seven sacraments, three only, Baptism, Penance, and the Sacrament of the Altar, were explained, whilst the other four —those of Marriage, Orders, Confirmation, and Extreme Unction— were passed over in silence. On the whole the Ten Articles in some points showed a distinct advance in the direction of Lutheranism, though there was also to be discerned in them an equally distinct effort to explain rather than to reject the creed of the mediæval Church.

8. **The Translation of the Bible authorised. 1536.**—The same tendency to appeal to educated intelligence showed itself in the sanction given by the king and Cromwell in 1536 to a translation of the Bible which had been completed in 1535 by Miles Coverdale, whose version of the New Testament was founded on an earlier one by Tyndale. It is probable that Henry, in authorising the circulation of this version, thought of the support which he might derive from the silence of the Bible on the Papal claims. The circulation of the Bible was, however, likely to work in a direction very different from that of the Ten Articles. The Ten Articles were intended to promote unity of belief. The Bible, once placed in the hands of everyone who could read, was likely to promote diversity. It would be the storehouse in which Lutherans, Zwinglians, and every divergent sect would find weapons to support their own special ideas. It would help on the growth of those individual opinions which were springing up side by side with the steady forward progress of the clergy of the Renascence. The men who attempted to make the old creed intellectually acceptable and the men who proclaimed a new one, under the belief that they were recurring to one still older, were together laying the foundations of English Protestantism.

9. **The Pilgrimage of Grace. 1536—1537.**—Slight as these changes were, they were sufficient to rouse suspicion that further change was impending. The masses who could neither read nor write were stirred by the greed and violence with which the disso-

lution of the smaller monasteries was carried on, and by the cessation of the kindly relief which these monasteries had afforded to the wants of the poor. A rumour spread that when Cromwell had despoiled the monasteries he would proceed to despoil the parish churches. In the autumn of 1536 there was a rising in Lincolnshire, which was easily suppressed, but was followed by a more formidable rising in Yorkshire. The insurgents, headed by Robert Aske, called it the Pilgrimage of Grace, and bore a banner embroidered with the five wounds of Christ. They asked among other things for the restoration of the monasteries, the punishment of Cromwell and his chief supporters, the deprivation of the reforming bishops, the extirpation of heresy, and the restoration of the Papal authority in a modified form. Their force grew so large that the Duke of Norfolk, who was sent to disperse it, did not venture to make the attempt, and the king found himself obliged to issue a general pardon and to promise that a Parliament should meet in the North for the redress of grievances. On this the insurgents returned home. Early in 1537 Henry, who had no intention of keeping his word, took advantage of some new troubles in the North to declare that his engagement was no longer binding, and seized and executed, not merely the leaders, but many of the lesser supporters of the insurrection. Of the Parliament in the North nothing more was heard, but a Council of the North was established to keep the people of those parts in order, and to execute justice in the king's name.

10. **Birth of a Prince.** 1537.—In 1537 Jane Seymour gave birth to a boy, who was afterwards Edward VI. Henry had at last a male heir of undoubted legitimacy, but in a few days his wife died.

11. **The Beginning of the Attack on the Greater Monasteries.** 1537—1538.—The failure of the Pilgrimage of Grace brought in fresh booty to Henry. Abbots and priors who had taken part in it, or were accused of doing so, were hanged, and their monasteries confiscated. Where nothing could be proved against the greater monasteries, which had been declared by Parliament to be free from vice, their heads were terrified into an appearance of voluntary submission. Cromwell had his spies and informers everywhere, and it was as easy for them to lie as to speak the truth. In 1537 and 1538 many abbots bowed before the storm, and, confessing that they and their monks had been guilty of the most degrading sins, asked to be allowed to surrender their monasteries to the king. Cromwell's commissioners then took possession, sold the bells, the lead on the roof, and every article which had its price, and left the walls to serve as a quarry for the neighbourhood.

The lands went to the king. It not unfrequently happened that Henry promoted to ecclesiastical benefices those monks who had been most ready to confess themselves sinners beyond other men. There is no doubt that the confessions were prepared beforehand to deceive contemporaries, and there is therefore no reason why they should deceive posterity.

12. **Destruction of Relics and Images. 1538.**—The attack on the monasteries was accompanied by an attack on relics and such images as attracted more than ordinary reverence. The explanation of the zeal with which they were hunted down is in many cases to be found in the gold and jewels with which they were adorned. Some of them were credited with miraculous powers. The figure of the Saviour on the rood at Boxley, in Kent, moved its head and eyes. A phial at Hales, in Worcestershire, contained a substance which had been brought from Germany in the thirteenth century, and was said to be the blood of the Saviour. Pilgrims thronged in numbers to adore, and their offerings brought in no small profit to the monks who owned such treasures. What was fondly believed by the common people was derided by critical spirits, and Henry was well pleased to destroy all reverence for anything which brought credit to the monks. The rood of Boxley was exhibited in London, where the Bishop of Rochester pulled the wires which caused its motions, and the blood in the phial of Hales was declared to be no more than a coloured gum. An ancient wooden figure, worshipped in Wales under the name of Darvel Gathern, served to make a fire which burned Friar Forest, who maintained that in spiritual things obedience was due to the Pope and not to the king. Instead of hanging him under the Treason Act (see p. 392) Henry had him burnt as a heretic. It was the first and only time when the denial of the royal supremacy was held to be heresy. When war was made against superstition, the shrine of St. Thomas of Canterbury could hardly be allowed to escape. Thomas was a saint who had bearded a king, and his shrine, which had attracted such crowds of pilgrims that the marks which they left as they shuffled forward on their knees towards it are still to be seen on the stone floor, was smashed, and the bones of the saint burnt. Shrines were usually covered with gold and jewels, and all shrines shared the fate of that of St. Thomas.[1] The images in parish churches,

---

[1] Shrines were receptacles above ground of the bodies of saints. That of Edward the Confessor at Westminster was rebuilt by queen Mary, and that of St. Alban at St. Albans in recent times. These two are the only shrines now to be seen in England.

not being attractive to the covetous, and being valued by the people for ordinary purposes of devotion, were still left untouched.

13. **The Trial of Lambert. 1538.**—Henry's violence against monasticism and superstition made him extremely anxious to show his orthodoxy. The opinion held by Zwingli, the reformer of Zürich, that the Body and Blood of Christ were in no way present in the sacrament of the Lord's Supper was now spreading in England, and those who held it were known as Sacramentaries. One of these, John Lambert, was tried before Henry himself. Henry told Lambert scornfully that the words of Christ, ' This is My Body,' settled the whole question, and Lambert was condemned and burnt.

14. **The Marquis of Exeter and the Poles. 1538.**—Amongst the descendants of the Duke of Clarence was Reginald Pole.[1] He had been scandalised by the divorce, had left England, had been made a Cardinal in 1536, and had poured out a torrent of invective against the wickedness of Henry. In the end of 1538 Henry, having been informed that some of Pole's kinsfolk had been muttering dissatisfaction, sent them to execution together with his own cousin, the Marquis of Exeter, the son of his mother's sister.

15. **The Six Articles. 1539.**—Cruel and unscrupulous as Henry was, he was in many respects a representative Englishman, sympathising with the popular disgust at the spread of ideas hitherto unheard of. In a new Parliament which met in 1539 he obtained the willing consent of both Houses to the statute of the Six Articles. This statute declared in favour of : (1) the real presence of ' the natural Body and Blood of Christ ' in the Lord's Supper ; (2) the sufficiency of communion in one kind ; (3) clerical celibacy ; (4) the perpetual obligation of vows of chastity ; (5) private masses ; and (6) auricular confession. Whoever spoke against the first was to be burnt ; whoever spoke against the other five was to suffer imprisonment and loss of goods for the first offence, and to be hanged

---

[1] Genealogy of the de la Poles and Poles :—

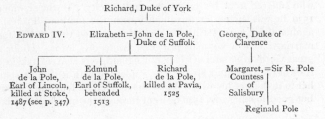

for the second. By those who suffered from the Act it was known
as 'The Whip with Six Strings.' Cranmer, who was a married
archbishop, was forced to dismiss his wife. Bishops Latimer and
Shaxton, whose opinions had gradually advanced beyond the line
at which Henry's orthodoxy ended, were driven from their sees ;
but the number of those put to death under the new Act was not
great.

16. **Completion of the Suppression of the Monasteries. 1539
—1540.**—So completely was the statute of the Six Articles in accordance with public opinion, that Henry had no difficulty in obtaining
the consent of Parliament to an Act giving to his proclamations
the force of law, and to another Act securing to him the whole of
the monasteries whether they had been already suppressed or not.
Before the end of **1540** not a single monastery was left. Three
abbots, those of Glastonbury, Colchester, and Reading, had been
hanged the year before after the mere semblance of a trial. The
disappearance of the abbots from the House of Lords made the
lay peers, for the first time, more numerous than the ecclesiastical
members of the House. The lay peers, on the other hand, were
reinforced by new creations from amongst Henry's favourites,
whom he had enriched by grants of abbey lands. The new peers
and the more numerous country gentlemen who had shared in the
spoil were interested in maintaining the independence of the
English Church, lest the Pope, if his jurisdiction were restored,
should insist on their disgorging their prey. Of that which fell into
the hands of the king, a small portion was spent on the foundation
of five new bishoprics, whilst part of the rest was employed on
shipbuilding and the erection of fortifications on the coast, part in
meeting the general expenditure of the Crown.

17. **Anne of Cleves and the Fall of Cromwell. 1539—1540.**—
In all that had been done Cromwell had been the leading spirit.
It had been his plan to erect an absolute despotism, and thereby
to secure his own high position and to enrich himself as well as his
master. He was naturally hated by the old nobility and by all
who suffered from his extortions and cruelty. In the summer of
1539 he was eager for an alliance with the German Protestants
against the Emperor Charles V., and suggested to Henry a fourth
marriage with a German princess, Anne of Cleves. Holbein, a
great German painter settled in England, was sent to take a portrait of the lady, and Henry was so pleased with it that he sent for
her to make her his wife. When she arrived he found her anything
but good-looking. In **1540** he went through the marriage ceremony

with her, but he divorced her shortly afterwards.   Fortunately for herself, Anne made no objection, and was allowed to live in England on a good allowance till her death.   For a time Cromwell seemed to be as high as ever in Henry's good opinion, and was created Earl of Essex.   Henry, however, was inwardly annoyed, and he had always the habit of dropping ministers as soon as their unpopularity brought discredit on himself.   Cromwell was charged with treason by the Duke of Norfolk.   A Bill of attainder [1] was rapidly passed, and Cromwell was sent to the scaffold without being even heard in his own defence.

18. **Catherine Howard and Catherine Parr.   1540—1543.**—In **1540** Henry married a fifth wife, Catherine Howard.   Norfolk, who was her uncle, gained the upper hand at court, and was supported by Gardiner (see p. 382), now Bishop of Winchester, who was strongly opposed to all further ecclesiastical innovations.   Those who denied the king's supremacy were sent to the gallows, those who denied the doctrine of transubstantiation to the stake.   In **1541** the old Countess of Salisbury, the mother of Cardinal Pole, and the daughter of the brother of Edward IV., was executed in the belief that she had favoured an abortive conspiracy.   Before the end of **1540** Henry discovered that his young wife had, before her marriage, been guilty of incontinency, and in **1542** she was beheaded.   In **1543** Henry married a sixth wife, Catherine Parr, who actually survived him.

19. **Ireland.   1534.**—Henry's masterful rule had made him many enemies abroad as well as at home, and he was therefore constantly exposed to the risk of an attack from the Continent. In the face of such danger he could no longer allow Ireland to remain as disorganised as it had been in his father's reign and in the early years of his own, lest Ireland should become the stepping-stone to an invasion of England.   In Ireland the Celtic chiefs maintained their independence, carrying on destructive wars with one another, both they and their followers being inspired

---

[1] A Bill of attainder was brought into one or other of the Houses of Parliament, and became law, like any other Act of Parliament, after it had passed both Houses and received the Royal assent.   Its object was condemnation to death, and, as the legislative powers of Parliament were unlimited, it need not be supported by the production of evidence, unless Parliament chose to ask for it.   Henry VIII. preferred this mode of getting rid of ministers with whom he was dissatisfied to the old way of impeachment ; as in an impeachment (see p. 262) there was at least the semblance of a judicial proceeding, the Commons appearing as accusers, and the Lords as judges.

with a high spirit of tribal patriotism, but without the slightest idea of national union. The Anglo-Norman lords ruling a Celtic population were quite as quarrelsome and even more oppressive than the Celtic chiefs, whilst the inhabitants of the English Pale (see p. 265), ruled over by what was only in name a civilised government, were subjected alike to the oppressive exactions of the authorities at Dublin and to the plundering of the so-called 'Irish enemies,' from whom these authorities were unable to protect them. The most powerful of the Anglo-Norman lords was still the Earl of Kildare (see p. 347), who, whenever he bore the title of Lord Deputy, unblushingly used the king's name in wreaking vengeance on his private enemies.

20. **The Geraldine Rebellion. 1534—1535.**—In 1534 Henry summoned Kildare to England and threw him into the Tower. On a rumour of Kildare's death his son, Lord Thomas Fitzgerald—Silken Thomas, as he was called in Ireland—rose against the king. The Geraldines, as the Fitzgeralds were sometimes called, had often frightened kings by rebelling, but this time they failed in their object. In 1535 the Lord Deputy Skeffington brought heavy guns and battered down the walls of the great Geraldine castle at Maynooth. One by one all the males of Kildare's family, with the exception of two boys, were captured and put to death.

21. **Lord Leonard Grey. 1536—1539.**—Lord Leonard Grey became Lord Deputy in 1536. The Irish Parliament which met in that year was still only a Parliament of the English Pale, but its acts showed that Henry intended, if possible, to rule all Ireland. On the one hand the royal supremacy was declared. On the other hand an Act was passed which showed how little was, in those days, understood of the difficulties standing in the way of the assimilation of two peoples at different stages of civilisation. The native Irish were ordered to be exactly as the English. They were to use the English language, to adopt the English dress, and to cut their hair after the English fashion. It was to be in the Church as it was to be in the State. No one was to receive any ecclesiastical preferment who did not speak English. Such laws naturally could not be put in force, but they served as indications of the spirit of the Government. Even more obnoxious was the conduct of the Archbishop of Dublin, George Browne, a mere creature of Henry and Cromwell. The assertion of the royal supremacy, indeed, if it had stood alone, would have made little difference in the church-life of Ireland. Browne, however, persisted, in obedience to orders from England, in destroying relics and images which

were regarded by the whole population with the deepest reverence. The doubting spirit of the Renascence found no echo in Ireland, because that country was far behind England in education and

King Henry VIII.: from a picture belonging to the Earl of Warwick.

culture. It would have been of less consequence if these unwise proceedings had been confined to the English Pale. Lord Leonard Grey was, however, a stern warrior, and carried his arms successfully amongst the Irish tribes. When he left Ireland in 1539 a large part of the Celtic population had been compelled to submit to Henry, and that population was even less prepared than were the inhabitants of the Pale for violent alterations of religious ceremonial.

22. **Henry VIII. King of Ireland. 1541.**—In 1541 a Parliament at Dublin acknowledged Henry to be king of Ireland. Hitherto he had been but Lord of Ireland. As that title had been granted by Pope Adrian IV. to Henry II. (see p. 152), Henry VIII. wished to have a new one which should mark his complete independence of Rome. This Parliament was the first attended by the native chiefs, and the assumption of the new title therefore indicated a new stage in Irish history. Unfortunately Henry bent himself to conciliate the chiefs rather than their tribes. He gave to the chiefs English titles—the O'Neill, for instance, becoming Earl of Tyrone, and O'Brien, Earl of Thomond—whilst he hoped to win their support by dissolving the monasteries, and by giving them a share in the plunder. All this Henry did in the hope that the chiefs would use their influence to spread English habits and English law amongst a people who were attached to their own ways. For the time he gained what he wanted. As long as the plunder of the abbeys was to be had the chiefs kept quiet. When that had been absorbed both chiefs and people would revolt against a Government which wanted to bring about, in a few years, a complete change in their mode of life. It is indeed useless to regret that Henry did not content himself with forcing the tribes to keep peace with one another, whilst allowing them gradually to grow in civilisation in their own fashion. There are often things which it would be well to do, but which no government can do. In the first place Henry had not money enough to enforce peace, the whole revenue of Ireland at that time being no more than 5,000*l.* a year. In the second place he was roused to futile efforts to convert Irishmen into Englishmen because he was in constant dread of the intervention in Ireland of his Continental enemies.

23. **Solway Moss. 1542.**—Henry was probably the more distrustful of a possibly independent Ireland because an actually independent Scotland gave him so much trouble. In Scotland there had been no Wars of the Roses, and the warlike nobility still resembled petty kings in their own districts. James V., the son of

Henry's sister Margaret, strove to depress the nobles by allying himself with the Church and the Commons. Scotland was always ready to come to blows with England, and the clergy urged James to break with a king of England who had broken with the Pope. From 1532 to 1534 there had been actual war between the kingdoms. Even after peace was restored James's attitude was constantly menacing. In 1542 war broke out again, and the Duke of Norfolk crossed the Tweed and wasted the border counties of Scotland. Then James launched an army across the Border into Cumberland. His distrust of the nobles, however, made him place at the head of it a mere court favourite, Oliver Sinclair. The Scottish army was harassed by the horsemen of the English border, and as night was drawing on was suddenly assailed by a small English party. Having no confidence in Sinclair, the whole multitude fled in a panic, to be slain or captured in Solway Moss. James's health

Angel of Henry VIII. 1543.

broke down under the evil tidings. As he lay sick news was brought to him that his wife had given birth to a child. Hearing that the child was a girl, and remembering how the heiress of the Bruces had brought the crown to the House of Stuart (see p. 295), he was saddened by the thought that the Stuart name also would come to an end. "It came with a lass," he murmured, "and it will go with a lass." In a few days he died, and his infant daughter, the Queen of Scots, received the name of Mary.[1]

24. **War with Scotland and France. 1542—1546.**—Henry, anxious to disarm Scottish hostility, proposed a marriage between his son Edward and the young queen. The proposal was rejected, and an alliance formed between Scotland and France. In 1544 Henry, having formed an alliance with Charles V., who was now at war with France, invaded France and took Boulogne after a

---

[1] James's foreboding was not realised, because Mary married a Stuart.

long siege—thus enlarging the English possessions in the neighbourhood of Calais—whilst Charles concluded a peace with

Part of the encampment at Marquison, 1544, showing military equipment in the time of Henry VIII.: from an engraving made by Vertue for the Society of Antiquaries from the now destroyed painting at Cowdray House.

Francis at Crêpy and left his ally in the lurch. In the same year Henry sent Lord Hertford, Jane Seymour's brother, to invade

Part of the siege of Boulogne by Henry VIII., 1544, showing military operations: from an engraving made by Vertue for the Society of Antiquaries from the now destroyed painting at Cowdray House.

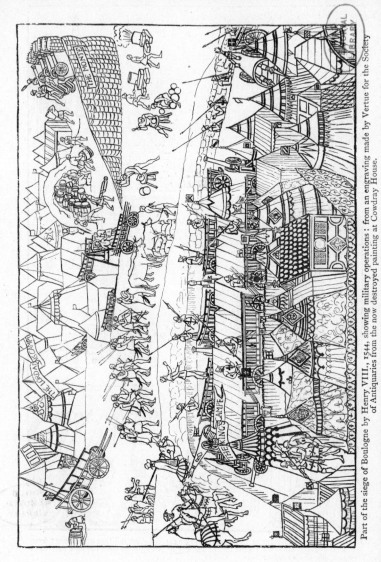

Part of the siege of Boulogne by Henry VIII., 1544, showing military operations; from an engraving made by Vertue for the Society of Antiquaries from the now destroyed painting at Cowdray House.

Scotland. Hertford burnt every house and cottage between Berwick and Edinburgh, took Edinburgh itself, and burnt the town. In **1546** peace was made between England and France, in which Scotland was included. The war had been expensive, and in **1544** Parliament had come to Henry's help by enacting that he need not repay a loan which he had gathered, yet even then Henry had had recourse to the desperate remedy of debasing the coinage.

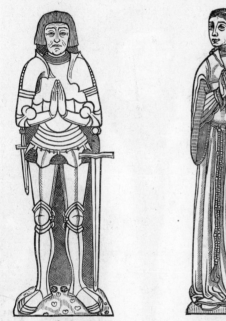

Armour as worn in the reign of Henry VIII.: from the brass of John Lymsey, 1545, in Hackney Church.

Margaret, wife of John Lymsey: from her brass in Hackney Church, showing the costume of a lady *circa* 1545.

25. **The Litany and the Primer. 1544—1545.**—In **1544**, when Henry was besieging Boulogne, Cranmer ordered prayers to be offered for his success. In the true spirit of the Renascence he wished these prayers to be intelligible, and directed that they should be in English. In the same year he composed the English Litany, intended to be recited by priests and people going in procession. This Litany was the foundation-stone of the future Book

II.   E E of Common Prayer. It was issued in **1544** together with a Primer, or book of private prayer, also in English. In the public services the Creed, the Lord's Prayer, and the Ten Commandments were to be in English, the remainder being left in Latin as before.

26. **The Last Days of Henry VIII.** 1545–1547.—When once

Thomas Howard third Duke of Norfolk, 1473(?)–1554 :
from the picture by Holbein at Windsor Castle.

inquiring intelligence is let loose on an antiquated system, it is hard to say where the desire of making alterations will stop, and there are reasons to believe that Henry was contemplating further changes. There were two parties at court, the one anxious to resist further change, headed, amongst the temporal lords, by the Duke of

Norfolk and his son, the Earl of Surrey, and amongst the bishops by Gardiner ; the other, desiring doctrinal innovations, especially if money was to be got by them, headed by the Earl of Hertford. In 1545 an Act had been passed for the dissolution of chantries, hospitals, and free chapels. The chantries had been founded for the maintenance of priests to say mass for the souls of the founders, and it was convenient for those who sought to divert this maintenance to their own use to believe that it was wrong to pray for the dead.   In the end of 1546 Henry was taken ill, and, feeling himself to be dying, ordered the arrest of Norfolk and Surrey on charges of treason.   It is probable that Henry turned against Norfolk and Surrey because he thought Hertford, as the uncle of the young Prince of Wales, more likely to be faithful to the future king.   On January 27, 1547, Surrey was executed.   His father was to have suffered on the 28th.   Before he reached the scaffold, Henry died, and he was conducted back to prison.   Henry, before his death, had done something to provide against the danger of a disputed succession.   An Act of Parliament, passed in 1544, had given back to Mary and Elizabeth the places in the line of inheritance to which they would have been entitled if no doubt had ever been cast on the legitimacy of their birth,[1] and had authorised Henry to provide by will for the future occupancy of the throne in case of the failure of his own descendants.   In accordance with this Act he left the crown, in case of such failure, to the descendants of his younger sister Mary, leaving out those of his elder sister Margaret, with whose son, James V., he had had so much reason to be displeased.

---

[1] Genealogy of the children of Henry VIII. :—

(1) Catharine =	HENRY VIII. =	(2) Anne	= (3) Jane Seymour	= (4) Anne of
of Aragon		Boleyn		Cleves
				= (5) Catherine
MARY	ELIZABETH	EDWARD VI.		Howard
(1553–1558)	(1558–1603)	(1547–1553)		= (6) Catherine
				Parr

CHAPTER XXVII

EDWARD VI. AND MARY

EDWARD VI., 1547—1553. MARY, 1553—1558.

LEADING DATES

Somerset's Protectorate	1547
First Prayer Book of Edward VI.	1549
Fall of Somerset	1549
Second Prayer Book of Edward VI.	1552
Death of Edward VI. and accession of Mary	1553
Mary's marriage with Philip	1554
Submission to Rome and re-enactment of the heresy laws	1554
Beginning of the persecution	1555
War with France	1557
Loss of Calais and death of Mary	1558

1. **Somerset becomes Protector. 1547.**—The new king, Edward VI., was but a boy, and Henry had directed that England should be governed during his son's minority by a body composed of the executors of his will and other councillors, in which neither the partisans of change nor the partisans of the existing order should be strong enough to have their own way. The leading innovators, pretending to be anxious to carry out his wishes, asserted that he had been heard to express a desire that they should be made peers or advanced in the peerage, and should receive large estates out of the abbey lands. After gaining their object, they set aside Henry's real plan for the government of the realm, and declared Hertford (who now became Duke of Somerset) to be Protector. A council was formed, from which Gardiner and the Lord Chancellor Wriothesley were excluded as likely to take part against them.

2. **The Scotch War. 1547—1548.**—Somerset was as greedy of Church property as the greediest, but he was covetous also of popularity, and had none of that moderating influence which Henry, with all his faults, possessed. He had always too many irons in the fire, and had no sense of the line which divides the possible from the impossible. His first thought was to intervene in Scotland. For some time past Protestant missionaries had been attempting to convert the Scottish people, but most of them had been caught and burnt. Cardinal Beaton, the Archbishop of St.

Andrews, had lately burnt George Wishart, a noted Protestant. In 1546 the Cardinal was murdered in revenge by a party of Protestants, who seized on the castle of St. Andrews.   A French fleet, however, recaptured the castle, and Somerset, who had sent no help to the Protestants in St. Andrews, marched into Scotland in the hope of putting an end to all future troubles between the kingdoms by marrying the young Queen of Scots to Edward.   He carried with him a body of foreign mercenaries armed with the improved weapons of Continental warfare, and with their help he defeated and slaughtered the Scotch army at Pinkie Cleugh, burnt Holyrood and Leith, and carried destruction far and wide.   Such rough wooing exasperated the Scots, and in 1548 they formed a close alliance with Henry II., who had succeeded Francis I. as king of France, and sent their young queen across the sea, where she was married to Henry's eldest son, the Dauphin Francis. Somerset had gained nothing by his violence.

3. **Cranmer's Position in the Church of England. 1547.**— Somerset's ecclesiastical reforms were as rash as his political enterprises.   Cranmer had none of that moral strength which would have made some men spurn an alliance with the unscrupulous politicians of the time.   He was a learned student, and through long study had adopted the principle that where Scripture was hard to understand it was to be interpreted by the consent of the writers of the first ages of Christianity.   As he had also convinced himself that the writers of the first six centuries had known nothing of the doctrine of transubstantiation, he was now prepared to reject it—though he had formerly not only believed it, but had taken part in burning men who denied it.   It is quite possible that if Henry had been still alive Cranmer would have been too much overawed to announce that he had changed his opinion.   His exact shade of belief at this time is of less importance than the method by which he reached it.   In accepting the doctrines and practices of the existing Church till they were tested and found wanting by a combination of human reason and historical study of the scriptures, interpreted in doubtful points by the teaching of the writers of the early Church, Cranmer more than any one else preserved the continuity of the Church of England, and laid down the lines on which it was afterwards to develop itself.   There was, therefore, a great gulf between Cranmer and the advanced Protestants, who, however much they might differ from one another, agreed in drawing inferences from the Scripture itself, without troubling themselves whether these inferences conformed in any way to the

earlier teaching. This gulf was constantly widening as time went on, and eventually split English Protestantism into fractions.

4. **Ecclesiastical Reforms. 1547—1548.**—In 1547 a fresh blow was struck at the devotions of the people. In the churches—by the order of the Government—there was much smashing of images and of painted glass bright with the figures of saints and angels.

Thomas Cranmer, Archbishop of Canterbury, 1533–1556: from a painting dated 1547, at Jesus College, Cambridge.

Gardiner, who protested that the Government had no authority to alter religion till the king was of age, was sent to prison as the easiest mode of confuting him. As Parliaments were usually packed in those days, it does not follow that the nation was eager for changes because Parliament ordered them. There was, however, no difficulty in filling the benches of the House of Commons with men who profited by the plunder of the Church, and when

Parliament met, it showed itself innovating enough. It repealed all the statutes giving special powers to Henry VIII. and all laws against heresy. It also passed an Act vesting in the reigning king the whole of the chantries and other like foundations which Henry had been permitted to take, but which he had left untouched. Cranmer, indeed, would have been glad if the money had been devoted to the relief of the poorer clergy, but the grasping spirit of the laymen was too strong for him. So violent was the race for wealth that the Act decreed the confiscation even of the endowments of lay corporations, such as trading companies and guilds, on the excuse that part of their funds was applied to religious purposes. It was soon, however, found that an attempt to enforce this part of the Act would cause resistance, and it was therefore abandoned. In 1548 the Government issued orders abolishing a great variety of Church practices, and, in consequence of the opposition offered by the clergy to these sudden measures ordered that no sermons should be preached except by a few licensed preachers.

5. **The First Prayer Book of Edward VI.   1549.**—In 1549 Parliament authorised the issue of a Prayer Book in English, now known as the First Prayer Book of Edward VI. The same Parliament also passed an Act permitting the marriage of the clergy.

6. **The Insurrection in the West.   1549.**—Somerset's own brother, Lord Seymour of Sudley, was sent to the block by this Parliament. He had spoken rashly against the Protector's government, but it has been thought by some that his main fault was his strong language against the rapacity with which Church property was being divided amongst the rich. That rapacity was now reaching its height. The Protector had set an evil example in order to raise the palace which, though it has since been rebuilt, still bears the name of Somerset House. He had not only seized on a vast amount of ecclesiastical property, but had pulled down a parish church and had carted off the bones of the dead from their graves. The Reformers themselves, men of the study as most of them were, had gone much farther than the mass of the people were prepared to follow. In 1549 an insurrection burst out in Devon and Cornwall for the restoration of the old religion, which was only suppressed with difficulty.

7. **Ket's Rebellion.   1549.**—Another rising took place in Norfolk, headed by Ket, a tanner. Ket's rebellion was directed not so much against ecclesiastical reforms, as against civil oppression. The gentry, who had been enriching themselves at the expense of

the clergy, had also been enriching themselves at the expense of the poor. The inclosures against which More had testified were multiplied, and the poor man's claims were treated with contempt. Ket gathered his followers under a tree, which he called the Oak of Reformation, on Mousehold Hill, outside Norwich, and sent them to pull down the palings of the inclosures. The Earl of Warwick —the son of that Dudley who, together with Empson, had been the object of popular hatred in the reign of Henry VII. (see p. 357) —dispersed the insurgents with great slaughter ; but it was noted that both here and in the West the Government was driven to use the bands of German and Italian mercenaries which Somerset had gathered for the war in Scotland. It was the first time since the days of John (see p. 182) that foreign troops had been used to crush an English rising.

8. **The Fall of Somerset. 1549.**—Somerset no longer pleased any single party. His invasion of Scotland had led to a war with France, and to carry on that war he had found it necessary to debase the coinage still further than it had been debased by Henry VIII. All the disturbance of trade, as well as the disturbance of religion, was laid to his door. At the same time he was too soft-hearted to satisfy his colleagues in the Council, and had shown himself favourable to the outcry against inclosures. Accordingly, before the end of 1549 his colleagues rose against him, and thrust him into the Tower. The Protectorate was abolished. Hence-forth the Council was to govern, but the leading man in the Council was Warwick.

9. **Warwick and the Advanced Reformers. 1549.**—Religion was a matter to which Warwick was supremely indifferent. It was an open question when he rose to power whether he would protect the men of the old religion or the advanced reformers. He chose to protect the advanced reformers. Even before Somerset's fall Cranmer had been pushing his inquiries still farther, and was trying to find some common ground with Zwinglian (see p. 399) and other reformers, who went far beyond Luther. Foreign preachers, such as Bucer and Peter Martyr, were introduced to teach religion to the English, as foreign soldiers had been introduced to teach them obedience. Bishops were now ap-pointed by the king's letters-patent, without any form of election. Gardiner and Bonner, refusing to accept the new state of things, were deprived of their sees of Winchester and London, and Ponet and Ridley set in their places. Ridley's moral character was as distinguished as Ponet's was contemptible. Hooper was

made Bishop of Gloucester. For some time he hung back, refusing to wear the episcopal vestments as being a mark of Antichrist, but at last he allowed himself to be consecrated in them, though he cast them off as soon as the ceremony was over.

10. **Latimer's Sermons. 1548—1550.**—Latimer had refused to return to the bishopric from which he had been thrust by Henry VIII., but he lashed from the pulpit the vices of the age, speaking

Nicholas Ridley, Bishop of London, 1550–1553 : from the
National Portrait Gallery.

plainly in the presence of the court of its greed and oppression. It was not enough, he said, for sinners to repent : let them make restitution of their ill-gotten gains. In **1550** the courtiers became tired of his reproofs, and he was no longer allowed to preach before the king.

11. **Warwick and Somerset. 1550—1552.**—In **1550** Warwick was compelled to make a peace with France, and gave up Boulogne as its price. In **1551** he was very nearly drawn into war with the Emperor on account of his refusal to allow mass to be celebrated

in the household of the king's sister, Mary. Finally, however, he gave way, and peace was maintained. There was a fresh issue of base money, and a sharp rise of prices in consequence. Now that there were no monasteries left to plunder, bishoprics were stripped of their revenues, or compelled to surrender their lands. Hooper was given the ecclesiastical charge of the see of Worcester in addition to that of Gloucester, but he was driven to surrender all the income of the bishopric of Gloucester. The see of Durham was not filled up, and before the end of the reign it was suppressed by Act of Parliament, and ceased to have a legal existence till it was restored by Edward's successor. So unpopular did Warwick become that Somerset began to talk as though he might supplant his supplanter. His rash words were carried to the young king, who had for some time shown an interest in public affairs, and who now took the part of Warwick, whom he created Duke of Northumberland, against his own uncle. Somerset was arrested, and in 1552 was tried and beheaded.

12. **The Second Prayer Book of Edward VI. 1552.**—In 1552 Parliament authorised the issue of a revised Prayer Book, known as the Second Prayer Book of Edward VI. The first book had been framed by the modification of the old worship under the influence of Lutheranism. The second book was composed under the influence of the Swiss Reformers. The tendency of the two books may be gathered from the words ordered to be employed in the administration of the bread in the Communion. In the first Prayer Book they had been : "The Body of our Lord Jesus Christ, which was given for thee, preserve thy body and soul unto ever-lasting life." In the second they were : "Take and eat this in remembrance that Christ died for thee, and feed on Him in thy heart by faith with thanksgiving." There were some who urged that the Communion should no longer be received kneeling. It was significant that their leaders were foreigners—John Alasco, a Pole, and John Knox, a Scot, who was hereafter to be the father of a Scottish reformation more drastic than that of England. Cranmer withstood them successfully. The dispute marked the point beyond which the spirit of the Renascence refused to go. In the midst of his innovations Cranmer preserved not only a reverent spirit, but an admiration for the devotional style of the prayers of the medieval Church, which he therefore maintained even in the midst of the great changes made, mainly at least by himself, in the second Prayer Book. Happily, amidst these disputations, there was one point on which both parties could combine—namely,

on the encouragement of education. The reign of Edward VI. is marked by the foundation of grammar-schools—too scantily carried out, but yet in such a measure as to mark the tendencies of an age which was beginning to replace the mainly ecclesiastic education of the monasteries by the more secular education of modern times.

13. **The Forty-two Articles. 1553.**—Edward was now a pre-

King Edward VI. : from a picture belonging to H. Hucks Gibbs, Esq.

cocious youth, taught by much adulation to be confident in his own powers. He had learnt to regard all defection from Protestant orthodoxy as a crime. The statute which repealed the heresy laws did not altogether stop the burning of heretics, as the lawyers discovered that heresy was punishable by the common law. In 1550 Joan Bocher was burnt for denying the Incarnation, and in 1551 Van Parris, a Fleming, was burnt on the same charge. The persecution however, was much more restricted than in the preceding reign. Few persons were punished, and that only for opinions of an abnormal character. In 1553 forty-two articles of faith, afterwards, in the reign of Elizabeth, converted into thirty-nine, were set forth as a standard of the Church's belief by the authority of the king. So completely did the reforming clergy recognise their entire dependence on the king, that by a slip of the pen Hooper once wrote of 'the king's majesty's diocese of Worcester and Gloucester.'

14. **Northumberland's Conspiracy. 1553.**—A religious system built up solely on the will of the king, was hardly likely to survive him. By this time it was known that Edward was smitten with consumption, and could not live. Northumberland cared little for religion, but he cared much for himself. He knew that Mary was, by Henry's will sanctioned by Act of Parliament, the heiress of the throne, and that if Mary became queen he was hardly likely to escape the scaffold. He was daring as well as unscrupulous, and he persuaded Edward to leave the crown by will to Lady Jane Grey, the granddaughter of Mary, Duchess of Suffolk, the younger sister of Henry VIII. He secured (as he hoped) Lady Jane's devotion by marrying her to his own son, Lord Guilford Dudley. As Lady Jane was a convinced Protestant, Edward at once consented. His father, he thought, had left the crown by will in the case of the failure of his own heirs (see p. 411), and why should not he? He had been taught to think so highly of the kingship that he did not remember that his father had been authorised by Act of Parliament to will away the crown in the case of his children's death without heirs, whereas no such authority had been given by Parliament to himself. He forced—by commands and entreaties—the councillors and the judges to sign the will. Cranmer was the last to sign, and was only moved to do so by the sad aspect of his suffering pupil. Then Edward died, assured that he had provided best for the Church and nation.

15. **Lady Jane Grey. 1553.**—On July 10 Lady Jane Grey, a pure-minded, intelligent girl of sixteen, was proclaimed queen in London. She was a fervent Protestant, and there were many Protestants in London. Yet, so hated was Northumberland, that even Protestants would have nothing to say to one who had been advanced by him. Lady Jane passed through the streets amidst a dead silence. All England thought as London. In a few days Mary was at the head of 30,000 men. Northumberland led against her what troops he could gather, but his own soldiers threw their caps in the air and shouted for Queen Mary. On the 19th Mary

was proclaimed queen in London, and the unfortunate Jane passed from a throne to a prison.[1]

16. **Mary restores the Mass.** 1553.—Mary, strong in her popularity, was inclined to be merciful. Amongst those who had combined against her only Northumberland and two others were executed—the miserable Northumberland declaring that he died in the old faith. Mary made Gardiner her Chancellor. Some of the leading Protestants were arrested, and many fled to the Continent. The bishops who had been deprived in Edward's reign were reinstated, and the mass was everywhere restored. The queen allowed herself to be called Supreme Head of the Church, and at first it seemed as though she would be content to restore the religious system of the last year of Henry's reign, and to maintain the ecclesiastical independence of the country.

17. **Mary's First Parliament.** 1553.—By taking this course Mary would probably have contented the great majority of her subjects, who were tired of the villainies which had been cloaked under the name of Protestantism, and who were still warmly attached to the religion of their fathers. She was, however, anxious to restore the authority of the Pope, and also to marry Philip, the eldest son of her cousin, the Emperor Charles V. It was natural that it should be so. Her mother's life and her own youth had been made wretched, not by Protestants, but by those who, without being Protestants, had wrought the separation from Rome in the days of Henry, at a time when only the Pope's adherents had maintained the legitimacy of her own birth and of her mother's marriage. In subsequent times of trouble Charles V. had sympathised with

[1] Genealogy of the Greys:—

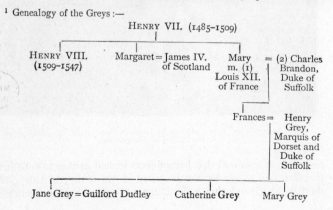

HENRY VII. (1485–1509)

HENRY VIII. (1509–1547)   Margaret = James IV. of Scotland   Mary m. (1) Louis XII. of France   = (2) Charles Brandon, Duke of Suffolk

Frances = Henry Grey, Marquis of Dorset and Duke of Suffolk

Jane Grey = Guilford Dudley   Catherine Grey   Mary Grey

her, and it was by his intervention that she had been allowed to continue her mass in her brother's reign. Mary also wished to restore to the Church its lands. On the other hand, when Parlia-

Queen Mary Tudor: from a painting by Lucas de Heere, dated 1554, belonging to the Society of Antiquaries.

ment met it appeared that her subjects wished neither to submit to Rome, nor to surrender the property of which they had deprived the Church, though they were delighted to restore the worship and practices which had prevailed before the death of Henry VIII. Parliament, therefore, authorised the re-establishment of the mass, and repealed the Act allowing the clergy to marry, but it presented a petition against a foreign marriage. Although the hatred of Spain which grew up a few years later was not yet felt, Englishmen did not wish their country to become a dependent province on any foreign monarchy whatever. Mary dissolved Parliament rather than take its advice.

18. **Wyatt's Rebellion. 1554.**—The result was an insurrection, the aim of which was to place Mary's half-sister, Elizabeth, on the throne. Lady Jane's father, the Duke of Suffolk, was to raise the Midlands and Sir Thomas Wyatt to raise Kent. Suffolk failed, but Wyatt, with a large following, crossed the Thames at Kingston, and pushed on towards the City. His men, however, were for the most part cut off in an engagement near Hyde Park corner, and it was with only three hundred followers that he reached Ludgate— to find the gate closed against him. 'I have kept touch,' he said, and suffered himself to be led away a prisoner. Mary was no longer merciful. Not only Suffolk and Wyatt, but the innocent Lady Jane and her young husband, Guilford Dudley, were sent to the block. Elizabeth herself was committed to the Tower. She fully believed that she was to die, and sat herself down on a wet stone, refusing for some time to enter. In many ways she had shown that she bore no goodwill to her sister or her sister's plans, but she had been far too prudent to commit to writing any words expressing sympathy with Wyatt. Being far too popular to be safely put to death on any testimony which was not convincing, Elizabeth was before long removed from the Tower and placed at Woodstock, under the charge of Sir Henry Bedingfield, but was after a few months allowed to retire to Hatfield.

19. **The Queen's Marriage.**—A Parliament which met in April 1554 gave its consent to Mary's marriage, but it would not pass Bills to restore the old statutes for the persecution of heretics. Though it was now settled that the queen was to marry Philip, yet never was a wooer so laggard. For some weeks he would not even write to his betrothed. The fact was that she was twelve years older than himself, and was neither healthy nor good-looking. Philip, however, loved the English crown better than he loved its wearer, and in July he crossed the sea and was married at Winchester to the queen of England. Philip received the title of king, and the names of Philip and Mary appeared together in all official documents and their heads on the coins.

20. The Submission to Rome. 1554.—After the marriage a new Parliament was called, more subservient than the last. In most things it complied with Mary's wishes. It re-enacted the statutes for the burning of heretics and agreed to the reconciliation of the Church of England to the see of Rome, but it would not surrender the abbey lands. Only after their possession had been confirmed did it give its consent to the acknowledgment of the Pope's authority. Then Cardinal Pole (see p. 399), who had been sent to England as the Pope's legate, was allowed to receive the submission of England. The queen, the king, and both Houses knelt before him, confessed their sin of breaking away from the Roman see, and received absolution from his mouth. To Mary the moment was one of inexpressible joy. She had grieved over the separation from Rome as a sin burdening her own conscience, and she believed with all her heart that the one path to happiness, temporal and eternal, for herself and her realm, was to root out heresy, in the only way in which it seemed possible, by rooting out the heretics.

21. The Beginning of the Persecution. 1555.—It was not only Mary who thought it meet that heretics should be burnt. John Rogers, who was the first to suffer, had in the days of Edward pleaded for the death of Joan Bocher (see p. 419). He was followed to the stake by Bishop Hooper, who was carried to Gloucester, that he might die at the one of his two sees which he had stripped of its property to enrich the Crown (see p. 418). He and many another died bravely for their faith, as More and Forest had died for theirs (see pp. 394, 398). Rowland Taylor, for instance (a Suffolk clergyman), was condemned in London to be burnt, and sent to his own county to die. As he left his prison in the dark of the early morning he found his wife and children waiting for him in the street. He was allowed to stop for a moment, and knelt down on the stones, repeating the Lord's Prayer with his family. "Farewell, my dear wife," he said, as soon as he had risen from his knees; "be of good comfort, for I am quiet in my conscience. God shall stir up a father for my children." "Thanked be God," he exclaimed when he at last reached the village where his voice had once been heard in the pulpit, and where now the stake rose up amidst the faggots which were to consume him, "I am even at home!" After he had been tied to the stake a wretch threw a faggot at his face. "O friend," he said gently, "I have harm enough: what needed that?" The flames blazed up around his suffering body, and Rowland Taylor entered into his rest.

Ridley and Latimer were burnt at Oxford, in the town ditch, in front of Balliol College. "Be of good comfort, Master Ridley, and play the man," cried Latimer, when the fire was lighted at his feet. "We shall this day light such a candle, by God's grace, in England, as I trust shall never be put out."

22. **Death of Cranmer.** **1556.**—Cranmer would have accompanied Ridley and Latimer to the stake, but as he alone of the

Hugh Latimer, Bishop of Worcester, 1535-39, burnt 1555: from the National Portrait Gallery.

three had been consecrated a bishop in the days when the Pope's authority was accepted in England, it was thought right to await the Pope's authority for the execution of his sentence. In 1556 that authority arrived. Cranmer's heart was as weak as his head was strong, and he six times recanted, hoping to save his life. Mary specially detested him, as having sat in judgment on her mother (see p. 389), and she was resolved that he should die. Finding his recantation useless, he recovered his better mind, and renounced his recantation.

" I have written," he said, "many things untrue ; and forasmuch as my hand offended in writing contrary to my heart, my hand therefore shall be the first burnt." He was hurried to the stake, and when the flames leapt up around him held his right hand steadily in the midst of them, that it might be 'the first burnt.'

23. **Continuance of the Persecution. 1556—1558.**—Immediately after Cranmer's death Pole became Archbishop of Canterbury. The persecution lasted for two years more. The number of those who suffered has been reckoned at 277. Almost all of these were burnt in the eastern and south-eastern parts of England. It was there that the Protestants were the thickest. New opinions always flourish more in towns than in the country, and on this side of England were those trading towns, from which communication with the Protestants of the Continent was most easy. Sympathy with the sufferers made these parts of the kingdom more strongly Protestant than they had been before.

24. **The Queen's Disappointment. 1555—1556.**—Mary was a sorrowful woman. Not only did Protestantism flourish all the more for the means which she took to suppress it, but her own domestic life was clouded. She had longed for an heir to carry on the work which she believed to be the work of God, and she had even imagined herself to be with child. It was long before she abandoned hope, and she then learnt also that her husband—to whom she was passionately attached—did not love her, and had never loved anything in England but her crown. In 1555 Philip left her. He had indeed cause to go abroad. His father, Charles V., was broken in health, and, his schemes for making himself master of Germany having ended in failure, he had resolved to abdicate. Charles was obliged to leave his Austrian possessions to his brother Ferdinand ; and the German electors, who detested Philip and his Spanish ways, insisted on having Ferdinand as Emperor. Charles could, however, leave his western possessions to his son, and in 1556 he completed the surrender of them. Mary's husband then became Philip II. of Spain, ruling also over large territories in Italy, over Franche Comté, and the whole of the Netherlands, as well as over vast tracts in America, rich in mines of silver and gold, which had been appropriated by the hardihood, the cruelty, and the greed of Spanish adventurers. No prince in Europe had at his command so warlike an army, so powerful a fleet, and such an abounding revenue as Philip had at his disposal. Philip's increase of power produced a strong increase of the anti-Spanish feeling in England, and conspiracies were formed against Mary,

who was believed to be ready to welcome a Spanish invading army.

25. **War with France and the Loss of Calais. 1557—1558.—** In 1557 Philip was at war with France, and, to please a husband who loved her not, Mary declared war against Philip's enemy. She sent an English army to her husband's support, but though Philip gained a crushing victory over the French at St. Quentin, the English troops gained no credit, as they did not arrive in time to take part in the battle. In the winter, Francis, Duke of Guise, an able French warrior, threatened Calais. Mary, who, after wringing a forced loan from her subjects in the summer, had spent it all, had little power to help the governor, Lord Wentworth, and persuaded herself that the place was in no danger. Guise, however, laid siege to the town. The walls were in disrepair and the garrison too small for defence. On January 6, 1558, Guise stormed Calais, and when, a few days afterwards, he also stormed the outlying post of Guisnes, the last port held by the English in France fell back into the hands of the French. Calais was now again a French town, after having been in the hands of strangers for 211 years.

26. **Death of Mary. 1558.—** The loss of Calais was no real misfortune to England, but it was felt as a deep mortification both by the queen and by her people. The people distrusted Mary too much to support her in the prosecution of the war. They were afraid of making Philip more powerful. Mary, hoping that Heaven might yet be gracious to her, pushed on the persecution, and sent Protestants in large numbers to the stake. Philip had visited her the year before, in order to persuade her to join him against France, and she again fancied herself to be with child. Her husband had once more deserted her, and she now knew that she was suffering—without hope—from dropsy. On November 17 she died, sad and lonely, wondering why all that she had done, as she believed on God's behalf, had been followed by failure on every side—by the desertion of her husband and the hatred of her subjects. Happily for himself, Pole too died two days afterwards.[1]

---

[1] The 19th is the date of Machyn's contemporary diary ; but other authorities make it the 17th or 18th.

CHAPTER XXVIII

THE ELIZABETHAN SETTLEMENT IN CHURCH AND STATE

1558—1570

LEADING DATES

Reign of Elizabeth, 1558—1603

Accession of Elizabeth	1558
The Acts of Supremacy and Uniformity	1559
The Treaty of Edinburgh	1560
Mary Stuart lands in Scotland	1561
End of the Council of Trent	1563
Marriage of Mary and Darnley	1565
Murder of Darnley	1567
Escape of Mary into England	1568
The rising in the North	1569
Papal excommunication of Elizabeth	1570

1. **Elizabeth's Difficulties. 1558.**—Elizabeth, when she received the news of her sister's death, was sitting under an oak in Hatfield Park (see p. 423). "This," she exclaimed, "is the Lord's doing, and it is marvellous in our eyes." Her life's work was to throw down all that Mary had attempted to build up, and to build up all that Mary had thrown down. It was no easy task that she had undertaken. The great majority of her subjects would have been well pleased with a return to the system of Henry VIII.—that is to say, with the retention of the mass, together with its accompanying system of doctrine, under the protection of the royal supremacy, in complete disregard of the threats or warnings of the Pope. Elizabeth was shrewd enough to see that this could not be. On the one hand, the Protestants, few as they were, were too active and intelligent to be suppressed, and, if Mary's burnings had been unavailing, it was not likely that milder measures would succeed. On the other hand, the experience of the reign of Edward VI. had shown that immutability in doctrine and practice could only be secured by dependence upon the immutable Papacy, and Elizabeth had made up her mind that she would depend on no one but herself. She would no more place herself under the Pope than she would place herself under a husband. She cared nothing for theology, though her inclinations drew her to a more elaborate ritual than that which the Protestants had to offer. She was, however,

intensely national, and was resolved to govern so that England might be great and flourishing, especially as her own greatness would depend upon her success. For this end she must establish national unity in the Church, a unity which, as she was well aware, could only be attained if large advances were made in the direction of Protestantism. There must be as little persecution as possible, but extreme opinions must be silenced, because there was a danger lest those who came under their influence would stir up civil war in order to make their own beliefs predominant. The first object of Elizabeth's government was internal peace.

2. **The Act of Uniformity and Supremacy. 1559.**—Elizabeth marked her intentions by choosing for her secretary Sir William Cecil, a cautious supporter of Protestantism, the best and most faithful of her advisers. As Convocation refused to hear of any change in the Church services, she appointed a commission composed of divines of Protestant tendencies, who recommended the adoption, with certain alterations,[1] of the second Prayer Book of Edward VI. Elizabeth's first Parliament, which met in 1559, passed an Act of Uniformity forbidding the use of any form of public prayer other than that of the new Prayer Book. The same Parliament also passed a new Act of Supremacy, in which the title of Supreme Head of the Church was abandoned, but all the ancient jurisdiction of the Crown over ecclesiastical persons was claimed. This Act imposed an oath in which the queen was acknowledged to be the Supreme Governor of the Realm ' as well in all spiritual or ecclesiastical things as temporal ' ; but this oath, unlike that imposed by Henry VIII., was only to be taken by persons holding office or taking a university degree, whilst a refusal to swear was only followed by loss of office or degree. The maintenance of the authority of any foreign prince or prelate was to be followed by penalties increased upon a repetition of the offence, and reaching to a traitor's death on the third occasion.

3. **The new Bishops and the Ceremonies. 1559—1564.**—All the bishops except one refusing to accept the new order of things, new ones were substituted for them, the old system of election by the chapters on a royal *congé d'élire* being restored (see pp. 391, 415). Matthew Parker, a moderate man after Elizabeth's own heart, became Archbishop of Canterbury. Very few of the old clergy who had said mass in Mary's reign refused to use the new Prayer

---

[1] The most noteworthy of these alterations was the amalgamation of the forms used respectively in the two Prayer Books of Edward VI. at the administration of the Communion (see p. 418).

Book, and as Elizabeth prudently winked at cases in which persons of importance had mass said before them in private, she was able to hope that, by leaving things to take their course, a new generation would grow up which would be too strong for the lovers of the old ways. The main difficulty of the bishops was with the Protestants. Many of those who had been in exile had returned with a strengthened belief that it was absolutely unchristian to adopt any vestments or other ceremonies which had been used in the Papal Church, and which they, therefore, contumeliously described as rags of Antichrist. A large number even of the bishops sympathised with them, and opposed them only on the ground that, though it would have been better if surplices and square caps had been prohibited, still, as such matters were indifferent, the queen ought to be obeyed in all things indifferent. To Elizabeth refusal to wear the surplice was not only an act of insubordination, but likely to give offence to lukewarm supporters of the Church system which she had established, and had, therefore, a tendency to set the nation by the ears. In Parker she found a tower of strength. He was in every sense the successor of Cranmer, with all Cranmer's strength but with none of Cranmer's weakness. He fully grasped the principle that the Church of England was to test its doctrines and practices by those of the Church of the first six hundred years of Christianity, and he, therefore, claimed for it catholicity, which he denied to the Church of Rome; whilst he had all Cranmer's feeling for the maintenance of external rites which did not directly imply the existence of beliefs repudiated by the Church of England.

4. **Calvinism.**—The returning exiles had brought home ideas even more distasteful to Elizabeth than the rejection of ceremonies. The weak point of the Lutherans in Germany, and of the reformers in England, had been their dependence upon the State. This dependence made them share the blame which fell upon rulers who, like Henry VIII., were bent on satisfying their passions, or, like Northumberland, on appropriating the goods of others. Even Elizabeth thought first of what was convenient for her government, and secondly, if she thought at all, of the quest after truth and purity. In Geneva the exiles had found a system in full working order which appeared to satisfy the cravings of their minds. It had been founded by a Frenchman, John Calvin, who in 1536 had published *The Institution of the Christian Religion*, in which he treated his subject with a logical coherence which impressed itself on all Protestants who were in need of a definite creed. He had soon after-

wards been summoned to Geneva, to take charge of the congregation there, and had made it what was extensively believed to be, a
model Church. With Calvin everything was rigid and defined, and
he organised as severely as he taught. He established a discipline
which was even more efficacious than his doctrine. His Church
proclaimed itself, as the Popes had proclaimed themselves, to be
independent of the State, and proposed to uphold truth and right irrespective of the fancies and prejudices of kings. Bishops there were to
be none, and the ministers were to be elected by the congregation.
The congregation was also to elect lay-elders, whose duty it was to
enforce morality of the strictest kind ; card-playing, singing profane
songs, and following after amusements on the Sunday—or Sabbath
as it was called in Geneva—being visited with excommunication.
The magistrates were expected to inflict temporal penalties upon
the offender. This Presbyterian system, as it was called, spread
to other countries, especially to countries like France, where the
Protestant congregations were persecuted by the Government. In
France a final step was taken in the Presbyterian organisation.
The scattered congregations elected representatives to meet in
synods or assemblies, and the French Government, in this way,
found itself confronted by an ecclesiastical representative republic.

5. **Peace with France. 1559.**—It was this Calvinistic system
which was admired by many of the exiles returning to England,
but which Elizabeth detested as challenging her own authority.
Her only chance of resisting with success lay in her power of
appealing to the national instinct, and of drawing men to think
more of unity and peace at home than of that search after truth
which inevitably divides, because all human conceptions of truth
are necessarily imperfect, and are differently held by different
minds. To do this she must be able to show that she could maintain her independence of foreign powers. Though her heart was
set on the recovery of Calais, she was obliged in 1559 to make
peace with France, obtaining only a vague promise that it might
be restored at a future time. Shortly afterwards peace was made
between France and Spain at Câteau Cambresis. Elizabeth was
aware that, though neither Philip II. of Spain nor Henry II. loved
her, neither of them would allow the other to interfere to her detri-
ment. She was therefore able to play them off one against the
other. Her diplomacy was the diplomacy of her time. Elizabeth
like her contemporaries, lied whenever it suited her to lie, and made
promises which she never intended to perform. In this spirit she
treated the subject of her marriage. She at once rejected Philip,

who, though he was her brother-in-law, proposed to marry her immediately after her accession, but when he suggested other candidates for her hand, she listened without giving a decided answer. It was convenient not to quarrel with Philip, but it would be ruinous to accept a husband at his choice.

6. **The Reformation in Scotland. 1559.**—Philip was formidable to Elizabeth because he might place himself at the head of the English Catholics. Henry was formidable because the old alliance between France and Scotland, confirmed by the recent marriage of the Dauphin with Mary Stuart, made it easy for him to send French troops by way of Scotland into England. Early in Elizabeth's reign, however, events occurred in Scotland which threatened to sever the links between that country and France. The Regent, Mary of Guise—mother of the absent queen and sister of the Duke of Guise, the French conqueror of Calais, and leader of the French Catholics—was hostile to the Protestants not only by conviction, but because there had long been a close alliance between the bishops and the Scottish kings in their struggle with the turbulent nobles. The wealth of the bishops, however, great according to the standard of so poor a country, tempted the avarice of the nobles, and their profligacy, openly displayed, offended all who cared for morality. In 1559 a combination was formed amongst a large number of the nobles, known as the Lords of the Congregation, to assail the bishops. John Knox, the bravest and sternest of Calvinists, urged them on. The Regent was powerless before them. The mass was suppressed, images destroyed, and monasteries pulled down. Before long, however, the flood seemed about to subside as rapidly as it rose. The forces of the lords consisted of untrained peasants, who could not keep the field when the labours of agriculture called them home, and rapidly melted away. Then the Lords of the Congregation, fearing disaster, called on Elizabeth for help.

7. **The Claims of Mary Stuart. 1559.**—Elizabeth was decided enough when she could see her way clearly. When she did not she was timid and hesitating, giving contradictory orders and making contradictory promises. She detested Calvinism, and regarded rebellion as of evil example. She especially abhorred Knox, because in her sister's reign he had written a book against *The Monstrous Regimen of Women*, disbelieving his asserti n that she was herself an exception to the rule that no woman was fit to govern. It is therefore almost certain that she would have done nothing for the Lords of the Congregation if France had done

nothing for the Regent. Henry II., however, was killed by an accidental lance-thrust which pierced his eye in a tournament, and on the accession of his son as Francis II., Mary Stuart, now queen of France, assumed the arms and style of queen of England.[1] The life-long quarrel between Elizabeth and Mary could hardly be staved off. Not only did they differ in religion, but there was also between them an irreconcilable political antagonism closely connected with their difference in religion. If the Papal authority was all that Mary believed it to be, Elizabeth was a bastard and a usurper. If the national Church of England had a right to independent existence, and the national Parliament of England to independent authority, Mary's challenge of Elizabeth's title was an unjustifiable attack on a sovereignty acknowledged by the constitutional authorities of the English nation.

8. **The Treaty of Edinburgh. 1560.**—In spite of Cecil's urgency Elizabeth was slow to assist the Scottish rebels. For some months Mary of Guise had been gathering French troops to her support, and she at last had a foreign army at her command powerful enough to make her mistress of Scotland, and to form the nucleus of a larger force which might afterwards be sufficiently powerful to make her mistress of England. This was more than Elizabeth could bear, and in January 1560 she sent her fleet with troops to the help of the Lords of the Congregation. The French retreated into Leith, where they were besieged by the allied forces. In June the Regent died, and in July Leith surrendered. By a treaty signed at Edinburgh the French agreed to leave Scotland, and to acknowledge Elizabeth's title to the English crown. In December Francis II. died, and as his brother, who succeeded him as Charles IX., was too young to govern, his mother, Catherine de Medicis, acted as regent. Catherine was jealous of the Duke of Guise, and also of his niece, Mary Stuart, the widow of her eldest

---

[1] Genealogy of the last Valois kings of France :—

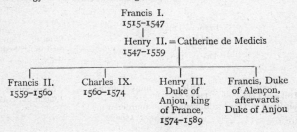

Francis I.
1515–1547

Henry II. = Catherine de Medicis
1547–1559

| Francis II. | Charles IX. | Henry III. | Francis, Duke |
| 1559–1560 | 1560–1574 | Duke of Anjou, king of France, 1574–1589 | of Alençon, afterwards Duke of Anjou |

son.[1] Mary, finding no longer a home in France, was driven for refuge to her own unruly realm of Scotland.

9. **Scottish Presbyterianism. 1561.**—The Scots had not failed to profit by the cessation of authority following on the death of Mary of Guise. They disclaimed the authority of the Pope and made it punishable to attend mass, the penalty for the third offence being death. The English Reformation had been the work of the king and of the clergy of the Renascence, and had, therefore, been carried on under the form of law. The Scottish Reformation had been the revolutionary work of the nobility and of the Calvinistic clergy. In England the power of the State had been strengthened. In Scotland it was weakened. Almost from the beginning the nobles who had taken part in the revolution showed signs of disagreement. A few of them were earnest Protestants, but there were more who cared only for political or personal ends. " I have lived many years," said the aged Lord Lindsay; "now that it hath pleased God to let me see this day . . . I will say with Simeon, ' Now lettest Thou thy servant depart in peace.' " Hey then ! " said Maitland of Lethington sarcastically, when he heard that the clergy claimed to govern the Church and own its property in the place of the bishops, " we may all bear the barrow now to build the house of the Lord." Knox organised the Church on a democratic and Presbyterian basis with Church Courts composed of the minister and lay elders in every parish, with representative Presbyteries in every group of parishes, and with a representative General Assembly for all Scotland. Like a prophet of old, Knox bitterly denounced those who laid a finger on the Church's discipline. The nobles let him do as he would as far as religion was concerned, but they insisted on retaining nominal bishops, not

---

[1] Genealogy of the Guises :—

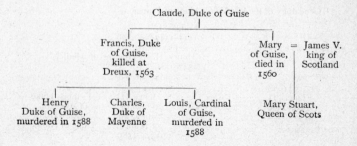

Claude, Duke of Guise

Francis, Duke of Guise, killed at Dreux, 1563

Mary of Guise, died in 1560 = James V. king of Scotland

Henry Duke of Guise, murdered in 1588

Charles, Duke of Mayenne

Louis, Cardinal of Guise, murdered in 1588

Mary Stuart, Queen of Scots

to rule the Church, but to hold the Church lands and pass the rents over to themselves.

10. **Mary and Elizabeth. 1561.**—In August 1561 Mary landed in Scotland, having come by sea because Elizabeth refused to allow her to pass through England unless she would renounce her claim to the English crown. Mary would perhaps have yielded if Elizabeth would have named her as her successor. Elizabeth would do nothing of the kind. She had a special dislike to fixing on any one as her successor. About this time she threw into prison Lady Catherine Grey for committing the offence of marrying without her leave. Lady Catherine was the next sister of Lady Jane Grey, and therefore Elizabeth's heir if the will of Henry VIII. in favour of the Suffolk line (see p. 410) was to be held binding. Elizabeth no doubt had a political object in showing no favour to either of her expectant heirs. By encouraging Catherine's hopes

A ' milled ' half-sovereign of Elizabeth, 1562–1568.

she would drive her Catholic subjects to desperation. By encouraging Mary's she would drive her Protestant subjects to desperation. Yet there was also strong personal feeling to account for her conduct. She was resolved never to marry, however much her resolution might cost her. Yet she too was a very woman, hungry for manly companionship and care, and, though a politician to the core, was saddened and soured by the suppression of her womanly nature. To give herself a husband was to give herself a master, yet she dallied with the offers made to her, surely not from political craft alone. The thought of marriage, abhorrent to her brain, was pleasant to her heart, and she could not lightly speak the positive word of rejection. Even now, in the vain thought that she might rule a subject, even if she became his wife, she was toying with Lord Robert Dudley, the handsome and worthless son of the base Northumberland. So far did she carry her flirtations that tales against her fair fame were spread abroad, but marry him she never did. Her treatment of the Lady Catherine was doubtless caused far less by her fear of the claims of the Suffolk line than by her reluctance to think of one so near to her as a happy wife, and as years grew upon her she bore hardly on those around her who refused to live in that state of maidenhood which she had inflicted on herself.

11. **The French War. 1562—1564.**—Elizabeth and Mary were not merely personal rivals. The deadly struggle on which they had entered was a European one, and the success or failure of the Catholic or the Protestant cause in some Continental country might determine the future history of Britain. In **1562** a civil war broke out between the French Protestants—or Huguenots,[1] as they were usually called in France—and their Catholic fellow-subjects. The leaders of the Huguenots obtained Elizabeth's aid by offering her Havre, which she hoped to exchange for Calais. The Huguenots were, however, defeated at the battle of Dreux, though Guise, who commanded the Catholics, was in the moment of victory shot dead by an assassin. In **1563** peace was patched up for a time between the French parties, but Elizabeth refused to surrender Havre, till a plague broke out amongst the English garrison, and drove the scanty remnants of it back to England. In **1564** Elizabeth was forced to make peace without recovering Calais. The war thus ended was the only one in which she ever took part except when absolutely no alternative was left to her.

12. **End of the Council of Trent. 1563.**—If Rome was to be victorious she must use other than carnal weapons. The main cause of the growth of Protestantism had been the revolt of honest minds against the profligacy of the Popes and the clergy. The Popes had after a long time learnt the lesson, and were now as austerely moral as Calvin himself. They had of late busied themselves with bringing the doctrines of the Church into a coherent whole, in order that they might be referred to with as much certainty as the *Institution* of Calvin was referred to by the Calvinist. This work was accomplished by an ecclesiastical council sitting at Trent, and composed mainly of Spanish and Italian prelates. The Council, having completed its task, broke up in **1563**.

13. **The Jesuits.**—The main instruments of the Popes to win back those who had broken loose from their authority were the

---

[1] Probably from *Eidgenossen*, the name of the Swiss Confederates, because the first Protestants who appeared at Geneva came from Switzerland, and no French-speaking mouth could pronounce such a word as ' Eidgenossen.'

members of the Society of Jesus, usually known as Jesuits. The society was founded in **1540** by Ignatius Loyola, a Spanish knight who, having been incapacitated by a wound for a military career, had devoted himself to the chivalry of religion. The members of the society which he instituted were not, like the monks, to devote themselves to setting an example of ascetic self-denial, nor, like the friars, to combine asceticism with preaching or well-doing. Each Jesuit was to give himself up to winning souls to the Church, whether from heathenism or from heresy. With this end, the old soldier who established the society placed it under more than military discipline. The first virtue of the Jesuit was obedience. He was to be in the hands of his superior as a stick in the hand of a man. He was to do as he was bidden, unless he was convinced that he was bidden to commit sin. What was hardest, perhaps, of all was that he was not allowed to judge his own character in choosing his work. He might think that he was admirably qualified to be a missionary in China, but if his superior ordered him to teach boys in a school, a schoolmaster he must become. He might believe himself to be a great scholar and fitted by nature to impart his knowledge to the young, but if his superior ordered him to go as a missionary to China, to China he must go. Discipline voluntarily accepted is a great power in the world, and this power the Jesuits possessed.

14. **The Danger from Scotland. 1561—1565.**—Whilst the opposing forces of Calvinism and the reformed Papacy were laying the foundations of a struggle which would split western Europe in twain, Elizabeth was hampered in her efforts to avert a disruption of her own realm by the necessity of watching the proceedings of the Queen of Scots. If in Elizabeth the politician predominated over the woman, in Mary the woman predominated over the politician. She was keen of sight, strong in feeling, and capable of forming far-reaching schemes, till the gust of passion swept over her and ruined her plans and herself together. After her arrival in Scotland she not only acknowledged the new Calvinistic establishment, but put down with a strong hand the Earl of Huntly, who attempted to resist it, whilst on the other hand she insisted, in defiance of Knox, on the retention of the mass in her own chapel. It is possible that there was in all this a settled design to await some favourable opportunity, as she knew that there were many in Scotland who cherished the old faith. It is possible, on the other hand, that she thought for a time of making the best of her uneasy position, and preferred to be met

with smiles rather than with frowns. Knox, however, took care that there should be frowns enough. There was no tolerant thought in that stern heart of his, and he knew well that Mary would in the end be found to be fighting for her creed and her party. Her dancing and light gaiety he held to be profane. The mass, he said, was idolatry, and according to Scripture the idolater must die. There was in Scotland as yet no broad middle class on which Mary could rely, and, feeling herself insulted both as a queen and as a woman, she took up Knox's challenge. She had but the weapons of craft with which to fight, but she used them admirably, and before long, with her winning grace, she had the greater number of the nobility at her feet.

15. **The Darnley Marriage. 1565.**—The sense of mental superiority could not satisfy a woman such as Mary. Her life was a lonely one, and it was soon known that she was on the look-out for a husband. The choice of a husband by the ruler of Scotland could not be indifferent to Elizabeth, and in 1564 Elizabeth offered to Mary her own favourite Dudley, whom she created Earl of Leicester. Very likely Elizabeth imagined that Leicester would be as pleasing to Mary as he was to herself. Mary could only regard the proposal as an insult. In 1565 she married her second cousin, Henry Stuart, Lord Darnley.[1] Elizabeth was alarmed, taking the marriage as a sign that Mary intended to defy her in everything, and urged the Scottish malcontents, at whose head was Mary's illegitimate brother, the Earl of Murray, to rebel. Mary chased them into England, where Elizabeth protested loudly and falsely that she knew nothing of their conspiracy.

16. **The Murder of Rizzio. 1566.**—Mary had taken a coarse-minded fool for her husband, and had to suffer from him all the tyranny which a heartless man has it in his power to inflict on a woman. Her heart craved for affection, and Darnley, who plunged

[1] Genealogy of Mary and Darnley :—

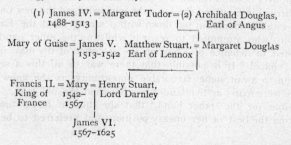

without scruple into the most degrading vice, believed, or affected to believe, that his wife had sacrificed her honour to David Rizzio, a cultivated Italian who acted as her secretary, and carried on her correspondence with the Continental powers. A league for the murder of Rizzio—such things were common in Scotland—was formed between Darnley and the Protestant lords. On March 9, 1566, they burst into Mary's supper-room at Holyrood. Rizzio clung to his patroness's robe, but was dragged off and slain. Murray with his fellow-conspirators came back to Scotland. Mary, however, with loving looks and words, won over the husband whom she despised, broke up the confederacy, and drove most of the confederates out of the country.

17. **The Murder of Darnley. 1567.**—On June 19, 1566, Mary gave birth to a son, afterwards James VI. of Scotland, and James I. of England. His birth gave strength to the party in England which was anxious to have Mary named heiress of the crown. Whatever little chance there was of Elizabeth's consent being won was wrecked through a catastrophe in which Mary became involved. Mary despised her miserable husband as thoroughly as he deserved. He at least, weak as water, could give her no help in her struggle with the nobles. Her passionate heart found in the Earl of Bothwell one who seemed likely to give her all that she needed—a strong will in a strong body, and a brutal directness which might form a complement to her own intellectual keenness. Mary and Bothwell were both married, but Bothwell at least was not to be deterred by such an obstacle as this. The evidence on Mary's conduct is conflicting, and modern enquirers have not succeeded in coming to an agreement about it. It is possible that she did not actually give her assent to the evil deed which set her free ; but it can hardly be doubted that she at least willingly closed her eyes to the preparations made for her husband's murder. Whatever the truth as to her own complicity may be, it is certain that on February 10, 1567, Darnley was blown up by gunpowder at Kirk o' Field, a lonely house near Edinburgh, and slain by Bothwell, or by Bothwell's orders, as he was attempting to escape. Bothwell then obtained a divorce from his own wife, carried Mary off—not, as was firmly believed at the time, against her will—and married her.

18. **The Deposition and Flight of Mary. 1567—1568.**—Mary, in gaining a husband, had lost Scotland. Her subjects rose against her as an adulteress and a murderess. At Carberry Hill, on June 15, 1567, her own followers refused to defend her, and she was forced to surrender, whilst Bothwell fled to Denmark, remaining

Silver-gilt standing cup made in London in 1569-70, and given to Corpus Christi College, Cambridge, by Archbishop Parker.

in exile for the rest of his life. Mary was imprisoned in a castle on an island in Loch Leven, and on July 24 she was forced to abdicate in favour of her son. Murray acted as regent in the infant's name. On May 2, **1568**, Mary effected her escape, and rallied to her side the family of the Hamiltons, which was all-powerful in Clydesdale. On May 13 she was defeated by Murray at Langside, near Glasgow. Riding hard for the Solway Firth, she threw herself into a boat, and found herself safe in Cumberland. She at once appealed to Elizabeth, asking not for protection only, but for an English army to replace her on the throne of Scotland.

19. **Mary's Case before English Commissioners. 1568—1569.** Elizabeth could hardly replace her rival in power, and was still less inclined to set her at liberty, lest she should go to France, and bring with her to Scotland another French army. After innumerable changes of mind Elizabeth appointed a body of commissioners to consider the case against Mary. Before them Murray produced certain letters contained in a casket, and taken after Bothwell's flight. The casket letters, as they are called, were alleged to be in Mary's handwriting, and, if genuine, place out of doubt her guilty passion for Bothwell, and her connivance in her husband's

murder. They were acknowledged by the commissioners, with the concurrence of certain English lords who were politically partisans of Mary, to be in her hand. Mary—either, as her adversaries allege, because she knew that she was guilty, or as her supporters allege, because she was afraid that she could not obtain justice—withdrew her advocates, and pleaded with Elizabeth for a personal interview. This Elizabeth refused to grant, but on the other hand she denied the right of the Scots to depose their queen. Mary remained virtually a prisoner in England. She was an interesting prisoner, and in spite of all her faults there were many who saw in her claim to the English crown the easiest means of re-establishing the old Church and the old nobility.

20. **The Rising in the North.** 1569.—The old Church and the old nobility were strongest in the North, where the Pilgrimage of Grace had broken out in 1536 (see p. 397). The northern lords, the Earls of Northumberland and Westmorland, longed to free Mary, to proclaim her queen of England, and to depose Elizabeth. They were, however, prepared to content themselves with driving Cecil from power, with forcing Elizabeth to acknowledge Mary as her heir, and to withdraw her support from Protestantism. Mary, according to this latter plan, was to marry the Duke of Norfolk, the son of that Earl of Surrey who had been executed in the last days of Henry VIII. (see p. 411). On October 18 Elizabeth, suspecting that Norfolk was entangling himself with the Queen of Scots, sent him to the Tower. Northumberland and Westmorland hesitated what course to pursue, but a message from the Queen requiring their presence at Court decided them, and they rose in insurrection. On November 14, with the northern gentry and yeomanry at their heels, they entered Durham Cathedral, tore in pieces the English Bible and Prayer Book, and knelt in fervour of devotion whilst mass was said for the last time in any one of the old cathedrals of England. Elizabeth sent an army against the earls. Both of them were timorous and unwarlike, and they fled to Scotland before the year was ended, leaving their followers to the vengeance of Elizabeth. Little mercy was shown to the insurgents, and cruel executions followed this unwise attempt to check the progress of the Reformation.

21. **The Papal Excommunication.** 1570.—Elizabeth, it seemed for all her triumph over the earls, had a hard struggle still before her. In January 1570 the regent Murray was assassinated by Hamilton of Bothwellhaugh, and Mary's friends began again to raise their heads in Scotland. In April Pope Pius V. excommunicated Elizabeth and absolved her subjects from their allegiance.

II.　　　　　　　　　　　　　　　　　　　　　　　G G

In May, a fanatic named Felton affixed the Pope's bull of excommunication to the door of the Bishop of London's house. Felton was eventually seized and executed, but his deed was a challenge which Elizabeth would be compelled to take up. Hitherto she had trusted to time to bring her subjects into one way of thinking, knowing that the younger generation was likely to be on her side. She had taken care to deal as lightly as possible with those who shrank from abandoning the religion of their childhood, and she had recently announced that they were free to believe what they would if only they would accept her supremacy. The Pope had now made it clear that he would not sanction this compromise. Englishmen must choose between him and their queen. On the side of the Pope it might be argued with truth that with Elizabeth on the throne it would be impossible to maintain the Roman Catholic faith and organisation. On the side of the queen it might be argued that if the Papal claims were admitted it would be impossible to maintain the authority of the national government. A deadly conflict was imminent, in which the liberty of individuals would suffer whichever side gained the upper hand. Nations, like persons, cannot attend to more than one important matter at a time, and the great question at issue in Elizabeth's reign was whether the nation was to be independent of all foreign powers in ecclesiastical as well as in civil affairs.

CHAPTER XXIX

ELIZABETH AND THE EUROPEAN CONFLICT. 1570—1587

LEADING DATES

Reign of Elizabeth, 1558—1603

The Execution of the Duke of Norfolk . . .	1572
The foundation of the Dutch Republic . . .	1572
The arrival of the Jesuits	1580
The Association	1584
Babington's Plot	1586
Execution of Mary Stuart	1587

1. **The Continental Powers. 1566—1570.**—If the Catholic powers of the Continent had been able to assist the English Catholics Elizabeth would hardly have suppressed the rising in the North. It happened, however, that neither in the Spanish Nether-

lands nor in France were the governments in a position to quarrel with her. In the Netherlands Philip, who burnt and slaughtered Protestants without mercy, was in 1566 opposed by the nobility, and in 1568 he sent the Duke of Alva, a relentless soldier, to Brussels with a Spanish army to establish the absolute authority of the king and the absolute authority of the Papacy. In 1569 Alva believed himself to have accomplished his task by wholesale executions, and by the destruction of the constitutional privileges of the Netherlanders. His rule was a grinding tyranny, rousing both Catholics and Protestants to cry out for the preservation of their customs and liberties from the intruding Spanish army. Alva had therefore no men to spare to send to aid the English Catholics. In France the civil war had broken out afresh in 1568, and in 1569 the Catholics headed by Henry, Duke of Guise, the son of the murdered Duke Francis (see p. 436), and by Henry, Duke of Anjou, the brother of the young king, Charles IX., won victories at Jarnac and Moncontour. Charles and his mother took alarm lest the Catholics should become too powerful for the royal authority, and in 1570 a peace was signed once more, the French king refusing to be the instrument of persecution and being very much afraid of the establishment of a Catholic government in England which might give support to the Catholics of France. Accordingly in 1570, France would not interfere in England if she could, whilst Spain could not interfere if she would.

2. **The Anjou Marriage Treaty and the Ridolfi Plot. 1570— 1571.**—For all that, Elizabeth's danger was great. In 1570 she had done her best to embroil parties in Scotland lest they should join against herself. The bulk of the nobility in that country had thrown themselves on the side of Mary, and were fighting against the new regent, Lennox, having taken alarm at the growth of the popular Church organisation of Knox and the Presbyterians, who sheltered themselves under the title of the little James VI. At home Elizabeth expected a fresh outbreak, and could not be certain that Alva would be unable to support it when it occurred. Cecil accordingly pleaded hard with her to marry the frivolous Duke of Anjou. He thought that unless she married and had children, her subjects would turn from her to Mary, who, having already a son, would give them an assured succession. If she was to marry, an alliance with the tolerant Government of France was better than any other. Elizabeth indeed consented to open negotiations for the marriage, though it was most unlikely that she would ever really make up her mind to it. The English Catholics, in conse-

quence, flung themselves into the arms of the king of Spain, and in March **1571**, Ridolfi, a Florentine banker residing in England, who carried on their correspondence with Alva, crossed to the Netherlands to inform him that the great majority of the lay peers had invited him to send 6,000 Spanish soldiers to dethrone Elizabeth and to put Mary in her place. Norfolk, who had been released from the Tower (see p. 441), was then to become the husband of Mary, and it was hoped that there would spring from the marriage a long line of Catholic sovereigns ready to support the Papal Church.

3. **Elizabeth and the Puritans.**—Elizabeth's temporising policy had naturally strengthened the Calvinism of the Calvinistic clergy. In every generation there are some who ask not what is expedient but what is true, and the very fact that they aim at truth, in defiance of all earthly considerations, not merely assures them influence, but diffuses around them a life and vigour which would be entirely wanting if all men were content to support that which is politically or socially convenient. Such were the best of the English Puritans, so called because, though they did not insist upon the abolition of Episcopacy or the establishment of the Calvinistic discipline (see p. 431), they contended for what they called purity of worship, which meant the rejection of such rites and vestments as reminded them of what they termed the idolatry of the Roman Church. Elizabeth and Parker had from time to time interfered, and some of the Puritan leaders had been deprived of their benefices for refusing to wear the cap and surplice.

4. **Elizabeth and Parliament. 1566.**—From **1566** to **1571** Elizabeth abstained from summoning a Parliament, having been far more economical than any one of the last three sovereigns. Early in her reign she had restored the currency, and after the session of **1566** had actually returned to her subjects a subsidy which had been voted to her and which had been already collected. Her reason for avoiding Parliaments was political. Neither of the Houses was likely to favour her ecclesiastical policy. The House of Lords wanted her to go backwards—to declare Mary her successor and to restore the mass. The House of Commons wanted her to go forwards—to marry, and have children of her own, and to alter the Prayer Book in a Puritan direction. In **1566**, if the House of Commons had really represented the average opinion of the nation, she would have been obliged to yield. That

---

[1] A subsidy was a tax on lands and goods voted by Parliament to the Crown, resembling in many respects the modern income-tax.

it did not was partly owing to the imposition in **1562** of the oath of supremacy upon its members, by which all who favoured the Pope's authority were excluded from its benches, but still more on account of the difficulty of packing a Parliament so as to suit the queen's moderate ideas. Those who admired the existing Church system were but few. The majority of the nation, even if those who refused to accept the Royal supremacy were left out of account, was undoubtedly sufficiently attached to the old state of things to be favourable at least to Mary's claim to be acknowledged as heir to the throne. To Elizabeth it was of the first importance that the influence of the Crown should be used to reduce the numbers of such men in the House of Commons. If, however, they were kept out, there was nothing to be done but to favour the election of Puritans, or at least of those who had a leaning towards Puritanism. The queen, therefore, having to make her choice between those who objected to her proceedings as too Protestant and those who objected to them as not Protestant enough, not unnaturally preferred the latter.

5. A Puritan Parliament. 1571.—In **1571** Elizabeth had to deal with a Puritan House of Commons. The House granted supplies, and wanted to impose new penalties on the Roman Catholics and to suppress ecclesiastical abuses. One of the members named Strickland, having proposed to ask leave to amend the Prayer Book, the Queen ordered him to absent himself from the House. The House was proceeding to remonstrate when Elizabeth, too prudent to allow a quarrel to spring up, gave him permission to return. She had her way, however, and the Prayer Book remained untouched. She was herself a better representative of the nation than the House of Commons, but as yet she represented it only as standing between two hostile parties ; though she hoped that the time would come when she would have a strong middle party of her own.

6. The Duke of Norfolk's Plot and Execution. 1571—1572. For the present Elizabeth's chief enemies were the conspirators who were aiming at placing Mary on her throne. In April **1571** Ridolfi reached the Netherlands, and urged Alva to send a Spanish army to England. Alva was cautious, and thought the attempt dangerous unless Elizabeth had first been killed or captured. Philip was consulted, gave his approval to the murder, but afterwards drew back, though he ordered Alva to proceed with the invasion. In the meanwhile Cecil, who had just been made Lord Burghley, came upon traces of the plot. Norfolk was arrested, and before the end of the year everything was known. Though the proposal of a marriage between Elizabeth and the Duke of Anjou had lately broken down, she now, in her anxiety to find support in France against Spain, entered into a negotiation to marry Anjou's brother, the Duke of Alençon, a vicious lad twenty-one years younger than herself. Then she was free to act. She drove the Spanish ambassador out of England, and Norfolk was tried and convicted of treason. A fresh Parliament meeting in 1572 urged the queen to consent to the execution of Mary. Elizabeth refused, but she sent Norfolk to the block.

7. **The Admonition to Parliament. 1572.**—The rising in the North and the invitation to bring a Spanish army into England could not but fan the zeal of the Puritans. At the beginning of the reign they had contented themselves with calling for the abolition of certain ceremonies. A more decided party now added a demand for the abolition of episcopacy and the establishment of Presbyterianism and of the complete Calvinistic discipline. The leader of this party was Thomas Cartwright, a theological professor at Cambridge, the university which had produced the greater number of the reformers, as it now produced the greater number of Puritans. In 1570, Cartwright was expelled from his Professorship. He sympathised with *An Admonition to Parliament* written in 1572 by two of his disciples, and himself wrote *A Second Admonition to Parliament*, to second their views. Cartwright was far from claiming for the Puritans the position of a sect to be tolerated. He had no thought of establishing religious liberty in his mind. He declared the Presbyterian Church to be the only divinely appointed one, and asked that all Englishmen should be forced to submit to its ordinances. The civil magistrate was to have no control over its ministers. All active religious feeling being enlisted either on the Papal or the Puritanical side, Elizabeth's reformed, but not Puritan, Church seemed likely to be crushed between two forces. It was saved by the existence of a large body of men who cared for other things more than for religious disputes, and who were ready to defend the Queen as ruler of the nation without any special regard for the ecclesiastical system which she maintained.

8. **Mariners and Pirates.**—Of all Elizabeth's subjects there were none who stood their country in such good stead in the impending conflict with Spain and the Papacy as the mariners. Hardy and reckless, they cared little for theological distinctions or for forms of Church government, their first instinct being to fill their own purses either by honest trade if it might be, or by piracy if that seemed

likely to be more profitable. Even before Elizabeth's accession, the Channel and the seas beyond it swarmed with English pirates. Though the pirates cared nothing for the nationality of the vessels which they plundered, it was inevitable that the greatest loss should fall on Spain. Spain was the first maritime power in the world, and her galleons as they passed up to Antwerp to exchange the silks and spices of the East for the commodities of Europe, fell an easy prey to the swift and well-armed cruisers which put out from English harbours. The Spaniards retaliated by seizing English sailors wherever they could lay their hands upon them, sometimes hanging them out of hand, sometimes destroying them with starvation and misery in fetid dungeons, sometimes handing them over to the Inquisition—a court the function of which was the suppression of heresy—in other words, to the torture-room or the stake.

9. **Westward Ho!**—Every year the hatred between the mariners of Spain and England grew more bitter, and it was not long before English sailors angered the king of Spain by crossing the Atlantic to trade or plunder in the West Indies, where both the islands and the mainland of Mexico and South America were full of Spanish settlements. In those days a country which sent out colonies claimed the sole right of trading with them; besides which the king of Spain claimed a right of refusing to foreigners an entrance into his American dominions because, towards the end of the fifteenth century, Pope Alexander VI. being called on to mediate between Spain and Portugal, had drawn a line on the map to the east of which was to be the Portuguese colony of Brazil, whilst all the rest of America to the west of it was to be Spanish. From this the Spaniards reasoned that all America except Brazil was theirs by the gift of the Pope—which in their eyes was equivalent to the gift of God. English sailors refusing to recognise this pretension, sailed to the Spanish settlements to trade, and attacked the Spanish officials who tried to prevent them. The Spanish settlers were eager to get negro slaves to cultivate their plantations, and Englishmen were equally eager to kidnap negroes in Africa and to sell them in the West Indies. A curious combination of the love of gain and of Protestantism sprang up amongst the sailors, who had no idea that to sell black men was in any way wrong. One engaged in this villanous work explained how he had been saved from the perils of the sea by 'Almighty God, who never suffers his elect to perish!' There was money enough to be got, and sometimes there would be hard fighting and the gain or loss of all.

10. **Francis Drake's Voyage to Panama. 1572.**—The noblest of these mariners was Francis Drake. Sickened by one experience

FRANCISCVS DRAECK NOBILISSIMVS EQVES ANGLIÆ AN ÆT SVE 43

Sir Francis Drake, in his 43rd year : from the engraving by Elstracke.

of the slave trade, and refusing to take any further part in it, he flew at the wealth of the Spanish Government. In 1572 he sailed for Nombre de Dios, on the Atlantic side of the isthmus of

Panama. Thither were brought once a year gold and silver from the mines of Peru. In the governor's house Drake found a pile of silver bars. " I have now," he said to his men, " brought you to the mouth of the treasury of the world." He himself was wounded, and his followers, having little spirit to fight without their leader, were beaten off. " I am resolved," he said somewhat later to a Spaniard, " by the help of God, to reap some of the golden harvest which you have got out of the earth and sent to Spain to trouble the earth." It was his firm conviction that he was serving God in robbing the king of Spain. Before he returned some Indians showed him from a tree on the isthmus the waters of the Pacific, which no civilised people except the Spaniards had ever navigated. Drake threw himself on his knees, praying to God to give him life and to allow him to sail an English vessel on those seas.

11. **The Seizure of Brill, and the Massacre of St. Bartholomew. 1572.**—Exiles from the Netherlands took refuge on the sea from Alva's tyranny, and plundered Spanish vessels as Englishmen had done before. In 1572 a party of these seized Brill and laid the foundations of the Dutch Republic. They called on Charles IX. of France to help them, and he (being under the influence of Coligny, the leader of the Huguenots) was eager to make war on Spain on their behalf. Charles's mother, Catherine de Medicis, was, however, alarmed lest the Huguenots should grow too powerful, and frightened her son with a tale that they were conspiring against him. He was an excitable youth, and turned savagely on the Huguenots, encouraging a fearful butchery of them, which is known as the Massacre of St. Bartholomew, because it took place on August 24, which was St. Bartholomew's day. Coligny himself was among the victims.

12. **The Growth of the Dutch Republic. 1572—1578.**—By this time the provinces of Holland and Zeeland had risen against Spain. They placed at their head the Prince of Orange with the title of Stadtholder or Lieutenant, as if he had been still the lieutenant of the king of Spain whom he resisted. The rebels had but a scanty force wherewith to defend themselves against the vast armies of Spain. Alva took town after town, sacked them, and butchered man, woman and child within. In 1574 Leyden was saved from his attack. Holland is below the sea-level, and the Dutch cut the dykes which kept off the sea, and when the tide rushed in, sent flat-bottomed vessels over what had once been land, and rescued the town from the besiegers. Alva, disgusted at his failure, returned to Spain. In 1576 his successor Requesens died. Spain, with all the wealth

of the Indies pouring into it, was impoverished by the vastness of the work which Philip had undertaken in trying to maintain the power of the Roman Catholic Church in all western Europe. The expenses of the war in the Netherlands exhausted his treasury, and on the death of Requesens, the Spanish army mutinied, plundered even that part of the country which was friendly to Spain, and sacked Antwerp with barbarous cruelty. Then the whole of the seventeen provinces of the Netherlands drove out the Spaniards, and bound themselves by the Pacification of Ghent into a confederate Republic. In 1578 Alexander, duke of Parma, arrived as the Spanish governor. He was a great warrior and statesman, and he won over the Catholic provinces of the southern Netherlands to his side. By the Union of Utrecht the Prince of Orange formed a new confederate republic of the seven northern provinces, which were mainly Protestant.

13. **Quiet Times in England.** **1572—1577.**—The Spaniards were no longer able to interfere in England. Elizabeth was equally safe from the side of France. In 1574 Charles IX. died, and was succeeded by Elizabeth's old suitor Anjou as Henry III. There were fresh civil wars which gave him enough to do at home. In 1573 Elizabeth sent aid to the party of the young king in Scotland, and suppressed the last remnants of Mary's party there. In England she pursued her old policy. Men might think what they would, but they must not discuss their opinions openly. There must be as little preaching as possible, and when the clergy began to hold meetings called prophesyings for discussion on the Scriptures, she ordered Grindal, who had succeeded Parker as Archbishop of Canterbury, to suppress them, and on his refusal in 1577 suspended him from his office, and put down the prophesyings herself.

14. **Drake's Voyage.** **1577—1580.**—Elizabeth had no sympathy with the heroic Netherlanders, who fought for liberty and conscience, but she had sympathy with the mariners who by fair means or foul brought treasure into the realm. In 1577 Drake sailed for that Pacific which he had long been eager to enter. Passing through the Straits of Magellan, he found himself alone on the unknown ocean with the 'Pelican,' a little ship of 100 tons. He ranged up the coast of South America, seizing treasure where he landed, but never doing any cruel deed. The Spaniards, not thinking it possible that an English ship could be there, took the 'Pelican' for one of their own vessels, and were easily caught. At Tarapaca, for instance, Drake found a Spaniard asleep with bars of silver by his side. At another landing place he found eight llamas laden with

silver. So he went on, till he took a great vessel with jewels in plenty, thirteen chests of silver coin, eighty pounds' weight of gold, and twenty-six tons of silver. With all this he sailed home by way of the Cape of Good Hope, arriving in England in 1580, being the first commander who had circumnavigated the globe.[1] The king of Spain was furious, and demanded back the wealth of which his subjects had been robbed. Elizabeth gave him good words, but not a penny of money or money's worth.

15. **Ireland and the Reformation. 1547.**—Since the death of Henry VIII. the management of Ireland had been increasingly difficult. An attempt had been made in the reign of Edward VI. to establish the reformed religion. All that was then done had been overthrown by Mary, and what Mary did was in turn overthrown by Elizabeth. As yet, however, the orders of the English Government to make religious changes in Ireland were of comparatively little importance. The power of the Government did not reach far, and even in the districts to which it extended there was none of that mental preparation for the reception of the new doctrines which was to be found in England. The Reformation was accepted by very few, except by English officials, who were ready to accept anything to please the Government. Those who clung to the old ways, however, were not at all zealous for their faith, and there was as yet no likelihood that any religious insurrection like the Pilgrimage of Grace or the rising in the North would be heard of in Ireland. The lives of the Celtic chiefs and the Anglo-Norman lords were passed in bloodshedding and looseness of life, which made them very unfit to be champions of any religion whatever.

Armour as worn during the reign of Elizabeth : from the brass of Francis Clopton, 1577, at Long Melford, Suffolk.

16. **Ireland under Edward VI. and Mary. 1547—1558.**—The real difficulty of the English Government in Ireland lay in its relations with the Irish tribes, whether under Celtic chiefs or Anglo-Norman lords. At the end of the reign of Edward VI. an attempt had been made to revert to the better part of the policy of Henry

[1] Magellan died on the way, though his ship completed the voyage round the world.

VlII., and the heads of the tribes were entrusted by the government with powers to keep order in the hope that they would gradually settle down into civilisation and obedience. Such a policy required almost infinite patience on the part of the Government, and the Earl of Sussex, who was Lord Deputy under Mary, began again the old mischief of making warlike attacks upon the Irish which he had not force or money enough to render effectual. It was Mary and not a Protestant sovereign who first sent English colonists to occupy the lands of the turbulent Irish in King's County and Queen's County—then much smaller than at present. A war of extermination at once began. The natives massacred the intruders and the intruders massacred the natives, till—far on in Elizabeth's reign—the natives had been all slaughtered or expelled. There was thus introduced into the heart of Ireland a body of Englishmen who, no doubt, were far more advanced in the arts of life than the Irish around them, but who treated the Irish with utter contempt, and put them to death without mercy.

17. **Elizabeth and Ireland. 1558—1578.**—From the time of the settlement of King's and Queen's Counties all chance of a peaceable arrangement was at an end. Elizabeth had not money enough to pay an army capable of subduing Ireland, nor had the Irish tribes sufficient trust in one another to unite in national resistance. There was, in fact, no Irish nation. Even Shan O'Neill, the most formidable Irish opponent of the English Government, who was predominant in the North during the early part of Elizabeth's reign, failed because he tried to reduce the other Ulster chiefs to subjection to himself, and in 1567 was overthrown by the O'Donnells, and not by an English army. When the English officials gained power, they were apt to treat the Irish as if they were vermin to be destroyed. New attempts at colonisation were made, but the Irish drove out the colonists, and Ireland was in a more chaotic state than if it had been left to its own disorder.

18. **The Landing at Smerwick, and the Desmond Rising. 1579—1583.**—Elizabeth's servants were the more anxious to subdue Ireland by the process of exterminating Irishmen, because they believed that the Irish would welcome Spaniards if they came to establish a government in Ireland hostile to Elizabeth. On the other hand, the English Catholics, and especially the English Catholic clergy in exile on the Continent, fancied, wrongly, that the Irish were fighting for the papacy, and not for tribal independence, or, rather, for bare life, which tribal independence alone secured. In 1579 Sir James Fitzmaurice landed with a few men at Dingle,

under the authority of the Pope, but was soon defeated and slain. In 1580 a large number of Spaniards and Italians landed at Smerwick, but was overpowered and slaughtered by Lord Grey, the Lord Deputy. Then the Earl of Desmond, the head of a branch of the family of Fitzgerald, all-powerful in Munster, rose. The insurrection was put down, and Desmond himself slain, in 1583. It is said that in 1582 no less than 30,000 perished—mostly of starvation—in a single year. It is an English witness who tells us of the poor wretches who survived, that ' out of every corner of the woods and glens they came creeping forth upon their hands, for their legs could not bear them ; they spoke like ghosts crying out of their graves ; they did eat the dead carrions, happy where they could find them.'

19. **The Jesuits in England. 1580.**—In England the landing of a papal force at Smerwick produced the greater alarm because Parma (see p. 450) had been gaining ground in the Netherlands, and the time might soon come when a Spanish army would be available for the invasion of England. For the present what the Government feared was any interruption to the process by which the new religion was replacing the old. In 1571 there had been an act of Parliament in answer to the Papal Bull of Deposition (see p. 442), declaring all who brought Bulls into the country, and all who were themselves reconciled to the see of Rome, or who reconciled others to be traitors, but for a long time no use was made by Elizabeth of these powers. The Catholic exiles, however, had witnessed with sorrow the gradual decay of their religion in England, and in 1568 William Allen, one of their number, had founded a college at Douai (removed in 1578 to Reims) as a seminary for missionaries to England. It was not long before seminary priests, as the missionaries were called, began to land in England to revive the zeal of their countrymen, but it was not till 1577 that one of them, Cuthbert Mayne, was executed, technically for bringing in a copy of a Bull of a trivial character, but really for maintaining that Catholics would be justified in rising to assist a foreign force sent to reduce England to obedience to the Papacy. There were, in fact, two rival powers inconsistent with one another. If the Papal power was to prevail, the Queen's authority must be got rid of. If the Queen's power was to prevail, the Pope's authority must be got rid of. In 1580 two Jesuits, Campion and Parsons, landed. They brought with them an explanation of the Bull of Deposition, which practically meant that no one need act on it till it was convenient to do so. They went about making converts and strengthening the lukewarm in the resolution to stand by their faith.

20. **The Recusancy Laws. 1581.**—Elizabeth in her dread of religious strife had done her best to silence religious discussion and even religious teaching. Men in an age of religious controversy are eager to believe something. All the more vigorous of the Protestants were at this time Puritans, and now the more vigorous of those who could not be Puritans welcomed the Jesuits with joy. There were never many Jesuits in England, but for a time they gave life and vigour to the seminary priests who were not Jesuits. In **1581** Parliament, seeing nothing in what had happened but a conspiracy against the Crown, passed the first of the acts which became known as the Recusancy laws. In addition to the penalties on reconciliation to Rome and the introduction of Bulls, fines and imprisonment were to be inflicted for hearing or saying mass, and fines upon lay recusants—that is to say, persons who refused to go to church. Catholics were from this time frequently subjected to torture to drive them to give information which would lead to the apprehension of the priests. Campion was arrested and executed after cruel torture ; Parsons escaped. If the Government and the Parliament did not see the whole of the causes of the Jesuit revival, they were not wrong in seeing that there was political danger. Campion was an enthusiast. Parsons was a cool-headed intriguer, and he continued from the Continent to direct the threads of a conspiracy which aimed at Elizabeth's life.

21. **Growing Danger of Elizabeth. 1580—1584.**—Elizabeth was seldom startled, but her ministers were the more frightened because the power of Spain was growing. In **1580** Philip took possession of Portugal and the Portuguese colonies, whilst in the Netherlands Parma was steadily gaining ground. Elizabeth had long been nursing the idea of the Alençon marriage (see p. 446), and in **1581** it seemed as if she was in earnest about it. She entertained the Duke at Greenwich, gave him a kiss and a ring, then changing her mind sent him off to the Netherlands, where he hoped to be appointed by the Dutch to the sovereignty of the independent states. In the spring of **1582** a fanatic, Jaureguy, tried to murder the Prince of Orange at Philip's instigation. Through the summer of that year Parsons and Allen were plotting with Philip and the Duke of Guise, for the assassination of Elizabeth, on the understanding that as soon as Elizabeth had been killed, Guise was to send or lead an army to invade England. They hoped that such an army would receive assistance from Scotland, where the young James had become the tool of a Catholic intriguer whom he made

Duke of Lennox.   Philip, however, was too dilatory to succeed.   In
August James was seized by some Protestant Lords, and Lennox

Hall of Burghley House, Northamptonshire, built about 1580; from Drummond's
Histories of Noble British Families, vol. i.

was soon driven from the country.   In **1583** there was a renewal of
the danger.   The foolish Alençon, wishing to carve out a principality for himself, made a violent attack on Antwerp and other

Flemish towns which had allied themselves with him, and was consequently driven from the country; whilst Parma, taking advantage of this split amongst his enemies, conquered most of the towns—Antwerp, however, being still able to resist. He now held part of the coast line, and a Spanish invasion of England from the Netherlands once more became feasible. In November 1583 a certain Francis Throgmorton, having been arrested and racked, made known to Elizabeth the whole story of the intended invasion of the army of Guise. In January 1584 she sent the Spanish ambassador, Mendoza, out of England. On June 29 Balthazar Gerard assassinated the Prince of Orange.

22. **The Association. 1584—1585.**—Those who had planned the murder of the Prince of Orange were planning the murder of Elizabeth. In their eyes she was a usurper, who by main force held her subjects from all hope of salvation by keeping them in ignorance of the teaching of the true Church, and they accordingly drew the inference that it was lawful to murder her and to place Mary on her throne. They did not see that they had to do with a nation and not with a queen alone, and that, whether the nation was as yet Protestant or not, it was heart and soul with Elizabeth against assassins and invaders. In November 1584, at the instigation of the Council, the mass of Englishmen—irrespective of creed—bound themselves in an association not only to defend the Queen, but, in case of her murder, to put to death the person for whose sake the crime had been committed—or, in other words, to send Mary to the grave instead of to the throne. In 1585 this association, with considerable modifications, was confirmed by Parliament. At the same time an act was passed banishing all Jesuits and seminary priests, and directing that they should be put to death if they returned.

23. **Growth of Philip's Power. 1584—1585.**—In the meantime Philip's power was still growing. The wretched Alençon died in 1584, and a far distant cousin of the childless Henry III., Henry king of Navarre, who was a Huguenot, became heir to the French throne. Guise and the ardent Catholics formed themselves into a league to exclude Huguenots from the succession, and placed themselves under the direction of the king of Spain. A civil war broke out once more in 1585, and if the league should win (as at first seemed likely) Philip would be able to dispose of the resources of France in addition to his own. As Guise had now enough to do at home, Philip took the invasion of England into his own hands. He had first to extend his power in the Netherlands. In August the great port of Antwerp surrendered to Parma. The Dutch had

offered to make Elizabeth their sovereign, and, though she had prudently refused, she sent an army to their aid, but neutralised the gift by placing the wretched Leicester at its head, and by giving him not a penny wherewith to pay his men. In 1586, after an attempt (after Alençon's fashion) to seize the government for himself, Leicester returned to England, having accomplished nothing. What Elizabeth did not do was done by a crowd of young Englishmen who pressed over to the Netherlands to fight as volunteers for Dutch freedom. The best known of these was Sir Philip Sidney, whose head and heart alike seemed to qualify him for a foremost place amongst the new generation of Englishmen. Unhappily he was slain in battle near Zutphen. As he lay dying he handed a cup of water untasted to another wounded man. 'Thy necessity,' he said to him, 'is greater than mine.' Parma took Zutphen, and the territory of the Dutch Republic—the bulwark of England—was the smaller by its loss. By sea England more than held her own, and in 1586 Drake returned from a voyage to the West Indies laden with spoils.

24. **Babington's Plot, and the Trial of Mary Stuart. 1586.**— The Spanish invasion being still delayed, a new plot for murdering Elizabeth was formed. A number of young Catholics (of whom Anthony Babington was the most prominent) had been allowed to remain at Court by Elizabeth, who was perfectly fearless. Acting under the instructions of a Jesuit named Ballard, they now sought basely to take advantage of their easy access to her person to assassinate her. They were detected and executed, and Walsingham, the Secretary of State who conducted the detective department of the government, discovered, or said that he had discovered, evidence of Mary Stuart's approving knowledge of the conspiracy. Elizabeth's servants felt that there was but one way of saving the life of the queen, and that was by taking the life of her whose existence made it worth while to assassinate Elizabeth. Mary was brought to trial and condemned to death on a charge of complicity in Babington's plot. When Parliament met it petitioned Elizabeth to execute the sentence. Elizabeth could not make up her mind. She knew that Mary's execution would save herself and the country from enormous danger, but she shrank from ordering the deed to be done. She signed the warrant for Mary's death, and then asked Mary's gaoler Paulet to save her from responsibility by murdering his prisoner. On Paulet's refusal she continued her vacillations, till the Council authorised Davison, Walsingham's colleague in the Secretaryship, to send off the warrant without further orders.

25. **Execution of Mary Stuart. 1587.**—On February 8, **1587**, Mary Stuart was beheaded at Fotheringhay. Elizabeth carried out to the last the part which she had assumed, threw the blame on Davison, dismissed him from her service, and fined him heavily. After Mary's death the attack on England would have to be conducted in open day. It would be no advantage to Philip and the Pope that Elizabeth should be murdered if her place was to be taken, not by Mary, but by Mary's Protestant son, James of Scotland.

CHAPTER XXX

ELIZABETH'S YEARS OF TRIUMPH. 1587—1603

LEADING DATES

Reign of Elizabeth, 1558—1603

Drake singes the King of Spain's beard	1587
The defeat of the Armada	1588
The rising of O'Neill	1594
The taking of Cadiz	1596
Essex arrives in Ireland	1599
Mountjoy arrives in Ireland	1600
The Monopolies withdrawn	1601
Conquest of Ireland, and death of Elizabeth	1603

1. **The Singeing of the King of Spain's Beard. 1587.**—After Mary's execution Philip claimed the crown of England for himself or his daughter the Infanta Isabella, on the plea that he was descended from a daughter of John of Gaunt, and prepared a great fleet in the Spanish and Portuguese harbours for the invasion of England. In attempting to overthrow Elizabeth he was eager not merely to suppress English Protestantism, but to put an end to English smuggling and piracy in Spanish America, and to stop the assistance given by Englishmen to the Netherlanders who had rebelled against him. Before his fleet was ready to sail Drake appeared off his coast, running into his ports, burning his store-ships, and thus making an invasion impossible for that year (**1587**). Drake, as he said on his return, had singed the king of Spain's beard.

2. **The Approach of the Armada. 1588.**—The Invincible Armada,[1] as some foolish Spaniards called Philip's great fleet, set

---

[1] 'Armada' was the Spanish name for any armed fleet

out at last in **1588**.   It was to sail up the Channel to Flanders, and to transport Parma and his army to England.   Parma's soldiers were the best disciplined veterans in Europe, while Elizabeth's were raw militia, who had never seen a shot fired in actual war. If, therefore, Parma succeeded in landing, it would probably go

Sir Martin Frobisher, died 1594 : from a picture belonging to the Earl of Carlisle.

hard with England.   It was, therefore, in England's interest to fight the Armada at sea rather than on land.

3. **The Equipment of the Armada.   1588.**—Even at sea the odds were in appearance against the English.   The Spanish ships were not indeed so much larger than the largest English vessels as has often been said, but they were somewhat larger, and they were

built so as to rise much higher out of the water, and to carry a greater number of men. In fact, the superiority was all on the English side. In great military or naval struggles the superiority of the victor is usually a superiority of intelligence, which shows itself in the preparation of weapons as much as in conduct in action. The Spanish ships were prepared for a mode of warfare which had hitherto been customary. In such ships the soldiers were more numerous than the sailors, and the decks were raised high above the water, in order that the soldiers might command with their muskets the decks of smaller vessels at close quarters. The Spaniards, trusting to this method of fighting, had not troubled themselves to improve their marine artillery. The cannon of their largest ships were few, and the shot which they were capable of firing was light. Philip's system of requiring absolute submission in Church and State had resulted in an uninventive frame of mind in those who carried out his orders. He had himself shown how little he cared for ability in his selection of an admiral for his fleet. That post having become vacant by the death of the best seaman in Spain, Philip ordered the Duke of Medina Sidonia to take his place. The Duke answered—with perfect truth—that he knew nothing about the sea and nothing about war ; but Philip, in spite of his candour, bade him go, and go he did.

4. **The Equipment of the English Fleet. 1588.**—Very different was the equipment of the English fleet. Composed partly of the queen's ships, but mainly of volunteers from every port, it was commanded by Lord Howard of Effingham, a Catholic by conviction. The very presence of such a man was a token of a patriotic fervour of which Philip and the Jesuits had taken no account, but which made the great majority of Catholics draw their swords for their queen and country. With him were old sailors like Frobisher, who had made his way through the ice of Arctic seas, or like Drake, who had beaten Spaniards till they knew their own superiority. That superiority was based not merely on greater skill as sailors, but on the possession of better ships. English ship-builders had adopted an improved style of naval architecture, having constructed vessels which would sail faster and be more easily handled than those of the older fashion, and—what was of still greater importance—had built them so as to carry more and heavier cannon. Hence, the English fleet, on board of which the number of sailors exceeded that of the soldiers, was in reality—if only it could avoid fighting at close quarters—far superior to that of the enemy.

The Spanish Armada. Fight between the English and Spanish fleets off the Isle of Wight, July 25, 1588 : from tapestry formerly in the House of Lords.

5. **The Defeat of the Armada. 1588.**—When the Armada was sighted at the mouth of the Channel, the English commander was playing bowls with his captains on Plymouth Hoe. Drake refused to break off his amusement, saying that there was time to finish the game and to beat the Spaniards too. The wind was blowing strongly from the south-west, and he recommended Lord Howard to let the Spaniards pass, that the English fleet might follow them up with the wind behind it. When once they had gone by they were at the mercy of their English pursuers, who kept out of their way whenever the Spaniards turned in pursuit. The superiority of the English gunnery soon told, and, after losing ships in the voyage up the Channel, the Armada put into Calais. The English captains sent in fire-ships and drove the Spaniards out. Then came a fight off Gravelines—if fight it could be called—in which the helpless mass of the Armada was riddled with English shot. The wind rose into a storm, and pursuers and pursued were driven on past the coast of Flanders, where Parma's soldiers were blockaded by a Dutch fleet. Parma had hoped that the Armada when it came would set him free, and convoy him across to England. As he saw the tall ships of Spain hurrying past before the enemy and the storm, he learnt that the enterprise on which he had set his heart could never be carried out.

6. **The Destruction of the Armada. 1588.**—The Spanish fleet was driven northwards without hope of return, and narrowly escaped wreck on the flats of Holland. "There was never anything pleased me better," wrote Drake, as he followed hard, "than seeing the enemy flying with a southerly wind to the northwards. . . . With the grace of God, if we live, I doubt not, ere it be long, so to handle the matter with the Duke of Sidonia as he shall wish himself at St. Mary Port[1] amongst his orange trees." Before long even Drake had had enough. Elizabeth, having with her usual economy kept the ships short of powder, they were forced to come back. The Spaniards had been too roughly handled to return home by the way they came. Round the north of Scotland and the west of Ireland they went, strewing the coast with wrecks. About 120 of their ships had entered the Channel, but only 54 returned. "I sent you," said Philip to his admiral, "to fight against men, and not with the winds." Elizabeth, too, credited the storms with her success. She struck a medal with the inscription, "God blew with his wind and they were scattered." The winds had done their

---

[1] A place near Cadiz where the Duke's residence was.

Sir Walter Raleigh (1552–1618) and his eldest son Walter, at the age of eight : from a picture, dated 1602, belonging to Sir J. F. Lennard, Bart.

part, but the victory was mainly due to the seamanship of English mariners and the skill of English shipwrights.

7. **Philip II. and France.   1588—1593.**—Philip's hopes of controlling France were before long baffled as completely as his hopes of controlling England.   In 1588 Guise, the partisan of Spain, was murdered at Blois by the order of the king in his very presence. In 1589 Henry III. was murdered in revenge by a fanatic, and the Huguenot king of Navarre claimed the crown as Henry IV.   The League declared that no Huguenot should reign in France.   A struggle ensued, and twice when Henry seemed to be gaining the upper hand Philip sent Parma to aid the League.   The feeling of the French people was against a Huguenot king, but it was also against Spanish interference.   When in 1593 Henry IV. declared himself a Catholic, Paris cheerfully submitted to him, and its example was speedily followed by the rest of France.   Elizabeth saw in Henry IV. a king whose position as a national sovereign resisting Spanish interference much resembled her own, and in 1589 and again in 1591 she sent him men and money.   A close alliance against Spain sprang up between France and England.

8. **Maritime Enterprises.   1589—1596.**—It was chiefly at sea, however, that Englishmen revenged themselves for the attack of the Armada.   In 1592 Drake and Sir John Norris sacked Corunna but failed to take Lisbon.   Other less notable sailors plundered and destroyed in the West Indies.   In 1595 Drake died at sea. In the same year Sir Walter Raleigh, who was alike distinguished as a courtier, a soldier, and a sailor, sailed up the Orinoco in search of wealth.   In 1596 Raleigh, together with Lord Howard of Effingham and the young Earl of Essex, who was in high favour with the Queen, took and sacked Cadiz.   Essex was generous and impetuous, but intensely vain, and the victory was followed by a squabble between the commanders as to their respective merits.

9. **Increasing Prosperity.**—It was not so much the victories as the energy which made the victories possible that diffused wealth and prosperity over England.   Trade grew together with piracy and war.   Manufactures increased, and the manufacturers growing in numbers needed to be fed.   Landed proprietors, in consequence, found it profitable to grow corn instead of turning their arable lands into pasture, as they had done at the beginning of the century. The complaints about inclosures (see pp. 368, 415) died away.   The results of wealth appeared in the show and splendour of the court, where men decked themselves in gorgeous attire, but still more in the gradual rise of the general standard of comfort.

10. **Buildings.**—Even in Mary's days the good food of English-men had been the wonder of foreigners. "These English," said a Spaniard, "have their houses of sticks and dirt, but they fare commonly as well as the king." In Elizabeth's time the houses were improved. Many windows, which had, except in the houses of the great, been guarded with horn or lattice, were now glazed, and even in the mansions of the nobility large windows stood in striking contrast with the narrow openings of the buildings of the middle ages. Glass was welcome, because men no longer lived—as they had lived in the days when internal wars were frequent —in fortified castles, where, for the sake of defence, the openings were narrow and infrequent. Elizabethan manor-houses, as they are now termed, sometimes built in the shape of the letter E, in honour, as is sometimes supposed, of the Queen's name, rose all over the

A mounted soldier at the end of the sixteenth century: from a broadside printed in 1596.

country to take the place of the old castles. They had chimneys to carry off the smoke, which, in former days, had, in all but the largest houses, been allowed to escape through a hole in the roof. See pp. 466, 467, 469–471.

11. **Furniture.**—The furniture within the houses underwent a change as great as the houses themselves. When Elizabeth came to the throne people of the middle class were content to lie on a straw pallet, with a log of wood, or at the best a bag of chaff, under their heads. It was a common saying that pillows were fit only

Wollaton Hall, Nottinghamshire; built by Thorpe for Sir Francis Willoughby about 1580–1588.

Hardwick Hall, Derbyshire ; built by Elizabeth, Countess of Shrewsbury, about 1597.

for sick women. Before many years had passed comfortable bedding had been introduced. Pewter platters and tin spoons replaced wooden ones. Along with these improvements was noticed a universal chase after wealth, and farmers complained that landlords not only exacted higher rents, but themselves engaged in the sale of the produce of their lands.

12. Growing Strength of the House of Commons.—This increase of general prosperity could not but strengthen the House of Commons. It was mainly composed of country gentlemen, and it had been the policy of the Tudors to rely upon that class as a counterpoise to the old nobility. Many of the country gentlemen were employed as Justices of the Peace, and Elizabeth had gladly increased their powers. When, therefore, they came to fulfil their duties as members of Parliament, they were not mere talkers unacquainted with business, but practical men, who had been used to deal with their own local affairs before being called on to discuss the affairs of the country. Various causes made their opinions more important as the reign went on. In the first place, the national uprising against Spain drew with it a rapid increase of Protestantism in the younger generation, and, for this reason, the House of Commons, which, at the beginning of the reign, represented only a Protestant minority in the nation itself (see p. 428), at the end of the reign represented a Protestant majority, and gained strength in consequence. In the second place, Puritanism tended to develope independence of character, whilst the queen was not only unable to overawe the Puritan members of the House, but, unlike her father, had no means of keeping the more worldly-minded in submission by the distribution of abbey lands.

13. Archbishop Whitgift and the Court of High Commission. 1583.—The Jesuit attack in 1580 and 1581 strengthened the queen's resolution to put an end to the divisions which weakened the English Church, as she was still afraid lest Puritanism, if unchecked, might give offence to her more moderately-minded subjects and drive them into the arms of the Papacy. In 1583, on Grindal's death, she appointed to the Archbishopric of Canterbury Whitgift, who had taken a leading part in opposing Cartwright (see p. 446). Whitgift held that as questions about vestments and ceremonies were unimportant, the queen's pleasure in such matters ought to be the rule of the Church. He was, however, a strict disciplinarian, and he was as anxious as the queen to force into conformity those clergy who broke the unity of the Church for the sake of what he regarded as mere crotchets of their own, especially

E-shaped house, Beaudesert, Staffordshire; built by Thomas, Lord Paget, about 1601.

as some of them were violent assailants of the established order. In virtue of a clause in the Act of Supremacy the queen erected a Court of High Commission. Though many laymen were members of the new Court, they seldom attended its sittings, and it was therefore practically managed by bishops and ecclesiastical lawyers. Its business was to enforce conformity on the clergy, and under Whitgift it acted most energetically, driving from their livings and committing to prison clergymen who refused to conform.

14. **The House of Commons and Puritanism. 1584.**—The severity of the High Commission roused some of the Puritan clergy to attempt—in private meetings—to bring into existence something of the system of Presbyterianism, but the attempt was soon abandoned. Few amongst the Protestant laity had any liking for Presbyterianism, which they regarded as oppressive and intolerant, and it had no deep roots even amongst the Puritan clergy. If many members of the House of Commons were attracted to Puritanism, as opposed to Presbyterianism, it was partly because at the time of a national struggle against Rome, they preferred those amongst the clergy whose views were most antagonistic to those of Rome ; but still more because they admired the Puritans as defenders of morality. Not only were the Church courts oppressive and meddlesome, but plain men were disgusted at a system in which ignorant and lazy ministers who conformed to the Prayer Book were left untouched, whilst able and energetic preachers who refused to adopt its ceremonies were silenced.

15. **The Separatists.**—The desire for a higher standard of morality, which made so many support the Puritan demand for a further reformation of the Church, drove others to denounce the Church as apostate. Robert Browne, a clergyman, was the first to declare in favour of a system which was neither Episcopal nor Presbyterian. He held it to be the duty of all true Christians to separate themselves from the Church, and to form congregations apart, to which only those whose religion and morality were beyond question should be admitted. These separatists, as they called themselves, were known as Brownists in common speech. Unfortunately their zeal made them uncharitably contemptuous of those who were less zealous than themselves, and it was from amongst them that there came forth—beginning in 1588—a series of virulent and libellous attacks on the bishops, known as the Marprelate Tracts, printed anonymously at a secret press. Browne and his followers advocated complete religious liberty—denying the right of the State to interfere with the conscience. The doctrine

Ingestre Hall, Staffordshire ; built about 1601.

was too advanced for general acceptance, and the violence of the Marprelate Tracts gave offence even to the Puritans. Englishmen might differ as to what sort of church the national church should be, but almost all were as yet agreed that there ought to be one national church and not a number of disconnected sects. In **1593** an act of Parliament was passed imposing punishment on those who attended conventicles or private religious assemblies, and in the course of the year three of the leading separatists—Barrow, Greenwood, and Penry—were hanged, on charges of sedition.

16. **Whitgift and Hooker.**—The Church of England would certainly not have sustained itself against the Puritans unless it had found a champion of a higher order than Whitgift. Whitgift maintained its organisation, but he did no more. Cranmer, at the beginning of the Reformation, had declared the Bible as interpreted by the writers of the first six centuries to be the test of doctrine, but this assertion had been met during the greater part of Elizabeth's reign, on the one hand by the Catholics, who asserted that the Church of the first six centuries differed much from the Church of England of their day, and on the other hand by the Puritans, who asserted that the testimony of the first six centuries was irrelevant, and that the Bible alone was to be consulted. Whitgift had called both parties to obedience, on the ground that they ought to submit to the queen in indifferent matters. Hooker in the opening of his *Ecclesiastical Polity* called the Puritans to peace. " This unhappy controversy," he declared, " about the received ceremonies and discipline of the Church of England, which hath so long time withdrawn so many of her ministers from their principal work and employed their studies in contentious oppositions, hath, by the unnatural growth and dangerous fruits thereof, made known to the world that it never received blessing from the Father of peace." Hooker's teaching was distinguished by the importance which he assigned to 'law,' as against the blind acceptance of Papal decisions on the one side and against the Puritan reverence for the letter of the scriptures on the other. The Puritans were wrong, as he taught, not because they disobeyed the queen, but because they did not recognise that God revealed Himself in the natural laws of the world as well as in the letter of Scripture. " Of law," he wrote, " there can be no less acknowledged than that her seat is the bosom of God, her voice the harmony of the world : all things in heaven and earth do her homage—the very least as feeling her care, and the greatest as not exempted from her power : both angels and men and creatures of what condition

soever—though each in different sort and manner, yet all with universal consent—admiring her as the mother of their peace and joy." It was therefore unnecessary, according to Hooker's teaching, to defend certain usages on the ground of their sanction by tradition or by Papal authority, as it was unreasonable to attack them on the ground that they were not mentioned in Scripture. It was sufficient that they were fitting expressions of the feelings of reverence which had been implanted by God in human nature itself.

Coaches in the reign of Elizabeth : from *Archæologia*

17. **Spenser, Shakspere, and Bacon.**—With the stately periods of Hooker English prose entered on a new stage. For the first time it sought to charm and to invigorate, as well as to inform the world. In Spenser and Shakspere are to be discerned the same influences as those which made Hooker great. They, too, are filled with reverence for the reign of law. Spenser, in his *Faerie Queen*, set forth the greatness of man in following the laws which

rule the moral world—the laws of purity and temperance and justice; whilst Shakspere, in the plays which he now began to pour forth, taught them to recognise the penalties which follow hard on him who disregards not only the moral but also the physical laws of the world in which he lives, and to appraise the worth of

William Shakspere : from the bust on his tomb at Stratford-on-Avon.

man by what he is and not by the dogmas which he accepts. That nothing might be wanting to point out the ways in which future generations were to walk, young Francis Bacon began to dream of a larger science than had hitherto been possible—a science based on a reverent inquiry into the laws of nature.

18. **Condition of the Catholics. 1588—1603.**—Bacon cared for many matters, and one of his earliest recommendations to Elizabeth had been to make a distinction between the Catholics who would take an oath to defend her against all enemies and those who would not. The patriotism with which many Catholics had taken her side when the Armada appeared ought to have procured the acceptance of this proposal. It is seldom, however, that either men or nations change their ways till long after the time when they ought to change them. Spain and the Pope still threatened, and all Catholics were still treated as allies of Spain and the Pope, and the laws against them were made even more severe during the remainder of the reign.

19. **Irish Difficulties. 1583—1594.**—The dread of a renewal of a Spanish invasion was productive of even greater mischief in Ireland than in England. After the suppression of the Desmond insurrection, an attempt was made to colonise the desolate lands of Munster (see p. 453) with English. The attempt failed, chiefly because—though courtiers willingly accepted large grants of lands— English farmers refused to go to Ireland in sufficient numbers to till the soil. On the other hand, Irishmen enough reappeared to claim their old lands, to rob, and sometimes murder, the few settlers who came from England. The settlers retaliated by acts of violence. All over Ireland the soldiers, left without pay, spoiled and maltreated the unfortunate inhabitants. The Irish, exasperated by their cruelty, longed for someone to take up their cause, and in **1594** a rising in Ulster was headed by Hugh O'Neill, known in England as the Earl of Tyrone. How bitter the Irish feeling was against England is shown by the fact that the other Ulster chiefs, who usually quarrelled with one another, now placed themselves under O'Neill.

20. **O'Neill and the Earl of Essex. 1595—1600.**—In 1595 O'Neill applied to the king of Spain for help ; but Spain was weaker now than in former years, and though Philip promised help, he died in **1598** without fulfilling his engagement, being succeeded by his son, Philip III. In the same year O'Neill utterly defeated an English army under Bagenal on the Blackwater. All Celtic Ireland rose in his support, and in **1599** Elizabeth sent her favourite, Essex, to conquer Ireland in good earnest, lest it should fall into the hands of the king of Spain. Essex, through mismanagement, failed entirely, and after a great part of his army had melted away he came back to England without leave. On his arrival, knowing Elizabeth's fondness for him, he hoped to surprise her into forgive-

ness of his disobedience, and rushed into Elizabeth's presence in his muddy and travel-stained clothes.

21. Essex's Imprisonment and Execution. 1599—1601.—The queen, who was not accustomed to allow even her favourites to run away from their posts without permission, ordered him into confinement. In 1600, indeed, she restored him to liberty, but forbade him to come to court. Essex could not brook the dis-

Robert Devereux, second Earl of Essex, K.G., 1567-1601 : from a painting by Van Somer, dated 1599, belonging to the Earl of Essex.

grace, especially as the queen made him suffer in his pocket for his misconduct. As she had little money to give away, Elizabeth was in the habit of rewarding her courtiers by grants of monopoly— that is to say, of the sole right of selling certain articles, thus enabling them to make a profit by asking a higher price than they could have got if they had been subjected to competition. To Essex she had given a monopoly of sweet wines for a term of years, and now that the term was at an end she refused to renew the grant. Early in **1601** Essex—professing not to want to injure the queen, but merely to force her to change her ministers—rode

Queen Elizabeth, 1558–1603 : from a painting belonging to the University of Cambridge.

at the head of a few followers into the City, calling on the citizens to rise in his favour. He was promptly arrested, and in the course of the enquiries made into his conduct it was discovered that when he was in Ireland he had entered into treasonable negotiations with James VI. At his trial, Bacon, who had been most kindly treated by Essex, shocked at the disclosure of these traitorous proceedings, turned against him, and, as a lawyer, argued strongly that he had been guilty   The Earl was convicted and executed.

22. **Mountjoy's Conquest of Ireland.   1600—1603.**—In 1600, after Essex had deserted Ireland, Lord Mountjoy was sent to take his place. He completed the conquest systematically, building forts as places of retreat for his soldiers whenever they were attacked by overwhelming numbers, and from which he could send out flying columns to devastate the country after the enemy had retreated. In 1601 a Spanish fleet and a small Spanish army at last arrived to the help of the Irish, and seized Kinsale. The English forces hemmed them in, defeated the Irish army which came to their support, and compelled the Spaniards to withdraw. The horrid work of conquering Ireland by starvation was carried to the end. "No spectacle," wrote Mountjoy's English secretary, "was more frequent in the ditches of the towns, and especially in wasted countries, than to see multitudes of these poor people dead, with their mouths all coloured green by eating nettles, docks, and all things they could rend up above ground." In one place a band of women enticed little children to come among them, and murdered them for food. At last, in 1603, O'Neill submitted. Ireland had been conquered by England as it had never been conquered before.

23. **Parliament and the Monopolies.   1601.**—The conquest of Ireland was expensive and in 1601 Elizabeth summoned Parliament to ask for supplies. The House of Commons voted the money cheerfully, but raised an outcry against the monopolies. Elizabeth knew when to give way, and she announced her intention of cancelling all monopolies which could be shown to be burdensome. "I have more cause to thank you all than you me," she said to the Commons when they waited on her to express their gratitude; "for had I not received a knowledge from you, I might have fallen into the lap of an error, only for lack of true information. I have ever used to set the last judgment-day before mine eyes, and so to rule as I shall be judged to answer before a higher Judge—to whose judgment-seat I do appeal, that never thought was cherished in my heart that tended not to my people's good. Though you have had, and may have, many princes, more mighty and wise, sitting in this seat, yet you never had, or ever shall have, any that will be more careful and loving."

24. **The Last Days of Elizabeth. 1601—1603.**—These were the last words spoken by Elizabeth to her people. She had many faults, but she cared for England, and, more than any one else, she had made England united and prosperous. She had found it distracted, but by her moderation she had staved off civil war, till the country had rallied round the throne. No doubt those who worked most hard towards this great end were men like Burghley

William Cecil, Lord Burghley, K.G., 1520–1598 : from a painting
in the Bodleian Library, Oxford.

and Walsingham in the State, and men like Drake and Raleigh at sea ; but it was Elizabeth who, being what she was, had given to each his opportunity. If either Edward VI. or Mary had been in her place, such men would have found no sphere in which their work could have been done, and, instead of telling of 'the spacious times of great Elizabeth,' the historian would have had to narrate the progress of civil strife and of the mutual conflict of ever-narrowing creeds. The last days of the great queen were gloomy, as far as she was personally concerned. Burghley, the wisest of her ministers, died in **1598**. In his last days he had urged the queen to bring to an end the war with Spain, which no longer served any useful purpose ; and when Essex pleaded for its continuance, the aged statesman opened the Bible at the text, " Bloody and deceitful men shall not live out half their days." In **1603** Elizabeth herself died at the age of sixty-nine. According to law, the heir to the crown was William Seymour, who, being the son of the Earl of Hertford and Lady Catherine Grey, inherited the claims of the Suffolk line (see pp. 411, 435). There were, however, doubts about his legitimacy, as, though his parents had been married in due form, the ceremony had taken place in private, and it was believed by many that it had never taken place at all. Elizabeth had always refused to allow her heir to be designated ; but as death approached she indicated her preference for James, as having claim to the inheritance by descent from her own eldest aunt, Margaret (see p. 411). " My seat," she said, " hath been the seat of kings, and I will have no rascal to succeed me." " And who," she added, " should that be but our cousin of Scotland ? "

Books recommended for further study of Part IV.

BREWER, J. S.   The Reign of Henry VIII. from his Accession to the Death of Wolsey.

DIXON, CANON R. W.   History of the Church of England from the Abolition of the Roman Jurisdiction.

FROUDE, J. A.   History of England from the Fall of Wolsey to the Death of Elizabeth.   Vols. v.–xii.

MOTLEY, J. L.   The Rise of the Dutch Republic.

————————   The History of the United Netherlands.

MULLINGER, J. B.   History of the University of Cambridge.   Vol. ii.

STRYPE, J.   Annals of the Reformation.

—————   Life and Acts of Aylmer.

—————   ,,   ,,   Grindal.

—————   ,,   ,,   Whitgift.

NICOLAS, Sir W. H.   Life of Sir C. Hatton.

———————————   ,,   W. Davison.

SPEDDING, J.   Letters and Life of Francis Bacon.   Vol. i.–iii. p. 58.

EDWARDS, E.   The Life of Sir W. Raleigh.

PART VI

THE PURITAN REVOLUTION. 1603—1660

CHAPTER XXXI

JAMES I. 1603—1625

LEADING DATES

Accession of James I. 1603
The Hampton Court Conference 1604
Gunpowder Plot 1605
Foundation of Virginia 1607
The Great Contract 1610
Beginning of the Thirty Years' War 1618
Foundation of New England 1620
Condemnation of the Monopolies and fall of Bacon . . 1621
Prince Charles's visit to Madrid 1623
Breach with Spain 1624
Death of James I. 1625

1. **The Peace with Spain.** 1603—1604.—At the end of Elizabeth's reign there had been much talk of various claimants to the throne, but when she died no one thought seriously of any one but James. The new king at once put an end to the war with Spain, though no actual treaty of peace was signed till 1604. James gave his confidence to Sir Robert Cecil, Lord Burghley's second son, whom he continued in the office of Secretary of State, which had been conferred on him by Elizabeth. The leader of the war-party was Raleigh, who was first dismissed from his offices and afterwards accused of treason, on the charge of having invited the Spaniards to invade England. It is most unlikely that the charge was true, but as Raleigh was angry at his dismissal, he may have spoken rashly. He was condemned to death, but James commuted the sentence to imprisonment.

2. **The Hampton Court Conference.** 1604.—The most important question which James had to decide on his accession was

that of religious toleration. Many of the Puritan clergy signed a petition to him known as the Millenary Petition, because it was intended to be signed by a thousand ministers. A conference was held on January 14, **1604**, in the king's presence at Hampton Court, in which some of the bishops took part, as well as a deputation of Puritan ministers who were permitted to argue in favour of the demands put forward in the petition. The Puritan Clergy had by this time abandoned Cartwright's Presbyterian ideas (see p. 446) and merely asked that those who thought it wrong to wear surplices and to use certain other ceremonies might be excused from doing so, without breaking away from the national church. James listened quietly to them, till one of them used the word Presbytery. He at once flew into a passion. "A Scottish Presbytery," he said, "agreeth as well with a monarchy as God with the devil. Then Jack and Tom and Will and Dick shall meet, and at their pleasures censure me and my council. . . . Until you find that I grow lazy —let that alone." James ordered them to conform or to leave the ministry. He adopted the motto, "No bishop, no king!" Like Elizabeth, he used the bishops to keep the clergy from gaining power independent of the Crown. The bishops were delighted, and one of them said that 'his Majesty spoke by the inspiration of God.'

Royal Arms borne by James I. and succeeding Stuart sovereigns.

3. **James and the House of Commons.**—In **1604** Parliament met. The members of the House of Commons had no more wish than James to overthrow the bishops, but they thought that able and pious ministers should be allowed to preach even if they would not wear surplices, and they were dissatisfied with the king's decision at Hampton Court. On the other hand, James was anxious to obtain their consent to a union with Scotland, which the Commons disliked, partly because the king had brought many Scotsmen with him, and had supplied them with English lands and money. Financial difficulties also arose, and the session ended in a quarrel between the king and the House of Commons. Before the year was over he had deprived of their livings many of the clergy who refused to conform.

4. Gunpowder Plot. 1604—1605.—Not only the Puritans, but the Catholics as well, had appealed to James for toleration. In the first year of his reign he remitted the recusancy fines (see p. 454). As might be expected, the number of recusants increased, probably because many who had attended church to avoid paying fines stayed away as soon as the fines ceased to be required. James took alarm, and in February 1604 banished the priests from London. On this, a Catholic named Robert Catesby proposed to a few of his friends a plot to blow up king, Lords, and Commons with gunpowder at the opening of Parliament. The king had two sons, Henry and Charles, and a little daughter, Elizabeth. Catesby, expecting that the two princes would be destroyed with their father, intended to make Elizabeth queen, and to take care that she was brought up as a Roman Catholic. Guy Fawkes, a cool soldier, was sent for from Flanders to manage the scheme. The plotters took a house next to the House of Lords, and began to dig through the wall to enable them to carry the powder into the basement. The wall, however, was nine feet thick, and they, being little used to mason's work, made but little way. In the spring of 1605 James increased the exasperation of the plotters by re-imposing the recusancy fines on the Catholic laity. Soon afterwards their task was made more easy by the discovery that a coal-cellar reaching under the floor of the House of Lords was to be let. One of their number hired the cellar, and introduced into it barrels of powder, covering them with coals and billets of wood. Parliament was to be opened for its second session on November 5, and in the preceding evening Fawkes went to the cellar with a lantern, ready to fire the train in the morning. One of the plotters, however, had betrayed the secret. Fawkes was seized, and his companions were pursued. All the conspirators who were taken alive were executed, and the persecution of the Catholics grew hotter than before.

5. The Post-nati. 1606—1607.—When another session opened in 1606 James repeated his efforts to induce the Commons to do something for the union with Scotland. He wanted them to establish free trade between the countries, and to naturalise his Scottish subjects in England. Finding that he could obtain neither of his wishes from Parliament, he obtained from the judges a decision that all his Scottish subjects born after his accession in England—the *Post-nati*, as they were called—were legally naturalised, and were thus capable of holding land in England. He had to give up all hope of obtaining freedom of trade.

6. Irish Difficulties. 1603—1610.—James was the first English sovereign who was the master of the whole of Ireland. He tried to win the affection of the tribes by giving them the protection of English law against the exactions of their chiefs. Naturally, the chiefs resented the change, while the tribesmen distrusted the interference of Englishmen from whom they had suffered so much. In 1607 the chiefs of the Ulster tribes of O'Neill and O'Donnell—known in England as the Earls of Tyrone and Tyrconnell—seeing resistance hopeless, fled to Spain. James ignored the Irish doctrine that the land belonged to the tribe, and confiscated six counties as if they had been the property of the chiefs, according to the feudal principles of English law. He then poured in English and Scottish colonists, leaving to the natives only the leavings to live on.

7. **Bate's Case and the New Impositions. 1606—1608.**—The state of James's finances was almost hopeless. Elizabeth, stingy as she was, had scarcely succeeded in making both ends meet, and James, who had the expense of providing for a family, from which Elizabeth had been free, would hardly have been able to meet his expenditure even if he had been economical. He was, however, far from economical, and had given away lands and money to his Scottish favourites. There was, therefore, a large deficit, and James wanted all the money he could get. In 1606 a merchant named Bate challenged his right to levy an imposition on currants, which had already been levied by Elizabeth. The Court of Exchequer, however, decided that the king had the right of levying impositions—that is to say, duties raised by the sole authority of the king—without a grant from Parliament—holding that the *Confirmatio Cartarum* (see p. 221), to which Bate's counsel appealed, only restricted that right in a very few cases. Whether the argument of the judges was right or wrong, they were the constitutional exponents of the law, and when Cecil (who had been James's chief minister from the beginning of the reign, and was created Earl of Salisbury in 1605) was made Lord Treasurer as well as Secretary in 1608, he at once levied new impositions to the amount of about 70,000*l*. a year, on the plea that more money was needed in consequence of the troubles in Ireland.

8. **The Great Contract. 1610—1611.**—Even the new impositions did not fill up the deficit, and Parliament was summoned in 1610 to meet the difficulty. It entered into a bargain—the Great Contract, as it was called—by which, on receiving 200,000*l*. a year, James was to abandon certain antiquated feudal dues, such as those of wardship and marriage (see p. 116). An agreement was also come to on the impositions. James voluntarily remitted the

North-west view of Hatfield House, Herts ; built for Robert Cecil, first Earl of Salisbury, between 1605 and 1611.

most burdensome to the amount of 20,000*l.* a year, and the House of Commons agreed to grant him the remainder on his passing an Act declaring illegal all further levy of impositions without a Parliamentary grant. Unfortunately, before the details of the Great Contract were finally settled, fresh disputes arose, and early in 1611, James dissolved his first Parliament in anger without settling anything either about the feudal dues or about the impositions.

9. **Bacon and Somerset. 1612—1613.**—In 1612 Salisbury died, and Bacon, always ready with good advice, recommended James to abandon Salisbury's policy of bargaining with the Commons. Bacon was a warm supporter of monarchy, because he was anxious for reforms, and he believed that reforms were more likely to come from the king and his Council than from a House of Commons —which was mainly composed of country gentlemen, with little knowledge of affairs of State. Bacon, however, knew what were the conditions under which alone a monarchical system could be maintained, and reminded James that king and Parliament were members of one body, with common interests, and that he could only expect the Commons to grant supplies if he stepped forward as their leader by setting forth a policy which would commend itself to them. James had no idea of leading, and, instead of taking Bacon's advice, resolved to do as long as he could without a Parliament. A few years before he had taken a fancy to a handsome young Scot named Robert Carr, thinking that Carr would be not only a boon companion, but also an instrument to carry out his orders, and relieve him from the trouble of dispensing patronage. He enriched Carr in various ways, especially by giving him the estate of Sherborne, which he took from Raleigh on the ground of a flaw in the title—though he made Raleigh some compensation for his loss. In 1613 he married Carr to Lady Essex, who had been divorced from her husband under very disgraceful circumstances, and created him Earl of Somerset. Somerset was brought by this marriage into connection with the family of the Howards—his wife's father, the Earl of Suffolk, being a Howard. As the Howards were for the most part Roman Catholics at heart, if not openly, Somerset's influence was henceforth used in opposition to the Protestant aims which had found favour in the House of Commons.

10. **The Addled Parliament. 1614.**—In spite of Somerset and the Howards, James's want of money drove him, in 1614, to call another Parliament. Instead of following Bacon's advice that he

should win popularity by useful legislative projects, he tried first to secure its submission by encouraging persons who were known as the Undertakers because they undertook that candidates who supported the king's interests should be returned. When this failed, he again tried, as he had tried under Salisbury's influence

Thomas Howard, Earl of Suffolk : from a painting belonging to T. A. Hope, Esq.

in 1610, to enter into a bargain with the Commons. The Commons, however, replied by asking him to abandon the impositions and to restore the nonconforming clergy ejected in 1604 (see p. 482). On this James dissolved Parliament. As it granted no supplies, and passed no act, it became known as the Addled Parliament.

11. **The Spanish Alliance. 1614—1617.**—James was always anxious to be the peacemaker of Europe, being wise enough to see that the religious wars which had long been devastating the Continent might be brought to an end if only the contending parties would be more tolerant. It was partly in the hope of gaining influence to enable him to carry out his pacificatory policy that he aimed, early in his reign, at marrying his children into influential families on the Continent. In **1613** he gave his daughter Elizabeth to Frederick V., Elector Palatine, who was the leader of the German Calvinists, and he had long before projected a marriage between his eldest son, Prince Henry, and a Spanish Infanta. Prince Henry, however, died in **1612**, and, though James's only surviving son, Charles, was still young, there had been a talk of marrying him to a French princess. The breaking-up of the Parliament of **1614** left James in great want of money ; and, as he had reason to believe that Spain would give a much larger portion than would be given with a French princess, he became keenly eager to marry his son to the Infanta Maria, the daughter of Philip III. of Spain. Negotiations with this object were not formally opened till **1617**, and in **1618** James learnt that the marriage could not take place unless he engaged to give religious liberty to the English Roman Catholics. He then offered to write a letter to the king of Spain, promising to relieve the Roman Catholics as long as they gave no offence, but Philip insisted on a more binding and permanent engagement, and, on James's refusal to do more than he had offered to do, Gondomar, the very able Spanish ambassador who had hitherto kept James in good humour, was withdrawn from England, and the negotiation was, for the time, allowed to drop.

12. **The rise of Buckingham. 1615—1618.**—In **1615** Somerset and his wife were accused of poisoning Sir Thomas Overbury. There can be no doubt that the Countess was guilty, but it is less certain what Somerset's own part in the matter was. In **1616** they were both found guilty, and, though James spared their lives, he never saw either of them again. He had already found a new favourite in George Villiers, a handsome youth who could dance and ride gracefully, and could entertain the king with lively conversation. The opponents of the Spanish alliance had supported Villiers against Somerset, but they soon found that Villiers was ready to throw himself on the side of Spain as soon as he found that it would please the king. James gave him large estates, and rapidly advanced him in the peerage, till, in **1618**, he created him Marquis of Buckingham. He also made him Lord Admiral in the

hope that he would improve the navy, and allowed all the patronage of England to pass through his hands. Statesmen and lawyers had to bow down to Buckingham if they wished to rise. No wonder the young man felt as if the nation was at his feet, and gave himself airs which disgusted all who wished to preserve independence of character.

13. **The Voyage and Execution of Raleigh. 1617—1618.**—In 1617 Raleigh, having been liberated through Buckingham's influence, sailed for the Orinoco in search of a gold-mine, of which he had heard in an earlier voyage in Elizabeth's reign (see p. 464). He engaged, before he sailed, not to touch the land of the king of Spain, and James let him know that, if he broke his promise, he would lose his head. It was, indeed, difficult to say where the lands of the king of Spain began or ended, but James left the burden of proving this on Raleigh ; whilst Raleigh, imagining that if only he could find gold he would not be held to his promise, sent his men up the river, without distinct orders to avoid fighting. They attacked and burnt a Spanish village, but never reached the mine. Heart-broken at their failure, Raleigh proposed to lie in wait for the Spanish treasure-ships, and, on the refusal of his captains to follow him in piracy, returned to England with nothing in his hands. James sent him to the scaffold for a fault which he should never have been given the chance of committing. Raleigh was the last of the Elizabethan heroes—a many-sided man : soldier, sailor, statesman, historian, and poet. He was as firmly convinced as Drake had been that there was no peace in American waters, and that to rob and plunder Spaniards in time of peace was in itself a virtue. James's unwise attempt to form a close alliance with Spain made Raleigh a popular hero.

14. **Colonisation of Virginia and New England. 1607—1620.**— Gradually Englishmen learned to prefer peaceable commerce and colonisation to piratical enterprises. In 1585 Raleigh had sent out colonists to a region in North America to which he gave the name of Virginia, in honour of Elizabeth, but the colonists either returned to England or were destroyed by the Indians. In 1607 a fresh attempt was made, and, after passing through terrible hardships, the Colony of Virginia grew into a tobacco-planting, well-to-do community. In 1608 a congregation of Separatists emigrated from England to Holland, and, after a while, settled at Leyden, where, anxious to escape from the temptations of the world, many of them resolved to emigrate to America, where they might lead an ideally religious life. In 1620 the emigrants, a hundred in all, 'lifting up

their eyes to heaven, their dearest country,' crossed the Atlantic in the 'Mayflower,' and found a new home which they named Plymouth. These first emigrants, the Pilgrim Fathers, as their descendants fondly called them, lost half their number by cold and disease in the first winter, but the remainder held on to form a nucleus for the Puritan New England of the future.

15. **The Beginning of the Thirty Years' War. 1618—1620.**— As yet, however, these small beginnings of a colonial empire attracted little attention in England. Men's thoughts ran far more on a great war—the Thirty Years' War—which, in 1618, began to desolate Germany. In that year a revolution took place in Bohemia, where the Protestant nobility rose against their king, Matthias, a Catholic, who was at the same time Emperor, and, in 1619, after the death of Matthias, they deposed his successor, Ferdinand, and chose Frederick, the Elector Palatine, James's Calvinist son-in-law, as king in his place. Almost at the same time Ferdinand became by election the Emperor Ferdinand II. James was urged to interfere on behalf of Frederick, but he could not make up his mind that the cause of his son-in-law was righteous, and he therefore left him to his fate. Frederick's cause was, however, popular in England, and in 1620, when there were rumours that a Spanish force was about to occupy the Palatinate in order to compel Frederick to abandon Bohemia, James—drawing a distinction between helping his son-in-law to keep his own and supporting him in taking the land of another—went so far as to allow English volunteers, under Sir Horace Vere, to garrison the fortresses of the Palatinate. In the summer of that year, a Spanish army, under Spinola, actually occupied the Western Palatinate, and James, angry at the news, summoned Parliament in order to obtain a vote of supplies for war. Before Parliament could meet, Frederick had been crushingly defeated on the White Hill, near Prague, and driven out of Bohemia.

16. **The Meeting of James's Third Parliament. 1621.**—Parliament, when it met in 1621, was the more distrustful of James, as Gondomar had returned to England in 1620 and had revived the Spanish marriage treaty. When the Houses met, they were disappointed to find that James did not propose to go to war at once. James fancied that, because he himself wished to act justly and fairly, every one of the other Princes would be regardless of his own interests, and, although he had already sent several ambassadors to settle matters without producing any results, he now proposed to send more ambassadors, and only to fight if negotia-

tion failed. On learning this, the House of Commons only voted
him a small supply, not being willing to grant war-taxes unless it

King James I.: from a painting by P. van Somer, dated 1621, in the
National Portrait Gallery.

was sure that there was to be a war.   Probably James was right in not engaging England in hostilities, as ambition had as much to do with Frederick's proceedings as religion, and as, if James had helped his German allies, he could have exercised no control over them ; but he had too little decision or real knowledge of the situation to inspire confidence either at home or abroad ; and the Commons, as soon as they had granted a supply, began to criticise his government in domestic matters.

17. **The Royal Prerogative.   1616—1621.**—Elizabeth had been high-handed enough, but she had talked little of the rights which she claimed, and had set herself to gain the affection of her subjects. James, on the other hand, liked to talk of his rights, whilst he took

no trouble to make himself popular.   It was his business, he held, to see that the judges did not break the law under pretence of administering it.   "This," he said in **1616**, " is a thing regal and proper to a king, to keep every court within its true bounds."   More startling was the language which followed. "As for the absolute prerogative of the Crown," he declared, " that is no subject for the tongue of a lawyer, nor is it lawful to be disputed.   It is atheism and blasphemy to dispute what God can do : good Christians content themselves with His will revealed in His word ; so it is presumption and high contempt in a subject to dispute what a king

Civil costume about 1620 : from a contemporary broadside.

can do, or say that a king cannot do this or that ; but rest in that which is the king's will revealed in his law."   What James meant was that there must be in every state a power above the law to provide for emergencies as they arise, and to keep the authorities— judicial and administrative—from jostling with one another.   At present this power belongs to Parliament.   When Elizabeth handed on the government to James, it belonged to the Crown.   What James did not understand was that, in the long run, no one—either king or Parliament—will be allowed to exercise powers which are unwisely used.   Such an idea probably never entered into James's mind, because he was convinced that he was himself not only the best but the wisest of men, whereas he was in reality—as Henry IV. of France had said of him—' the wisest fool in Christendom.'

18. **Financial Reform.   1619.**—James not only thought too

The Banqueting Hall of the Palace of Whitehall (from the north-east) ; built from the designs of Inigo Jones, 1619–1621.

highly of his own powers of government, but was also too careless to check the misdeeds of his favourites. For some time his want of money led him to have recourse to strange expedients. In 1611 he founded the order of baronets, making each of those created pay him 1,080*l.* a year for three years to enable him to support soldiers for the defence of Ulster. After the first few years, however, the money, though regularly required of new baronets, was invariably repaid to them. More disgraceful was the sale of peerages, of which there were examples in 1618. In 1619, however, through the exertions of Lionel Cranfield, a city merchant recommended to James by Buckingham, financial order was comparatively restored, and in quiet times the expenditure no longer much exceeded the revenue.

19. **Favouritism and Corruption.**—Though James did not obtain much money in irregular ways, he did not keep a watchful eye on his favourites and ministers. The salaries of Ministers were low, and were in part themselves made up by the presents of suitors. Candidates for office, who looked forward to being enriched by the gifts of others, knew that they must pay dearly for the goodwill of the favourites through whom they gained promotion. In 1620 Chief Justice Montague was appointed Lord Treasurer. "Take care, my lord," said Bacon to him, when he started for Newmarket to receive from the king the staff which was the symbol of his office, "wood is dearer at Newmarket than in any other place in England." Montague, in fact, had to pay 20,000*l.* for his place. Others, who were bachelors or widowers, received promotion on condition of marrying one of the many penniless young ladies of Buckingham's kindred.

20. **The Monopolies Condemned. 1621.**—The Commons, therefore, in looking for abuses, had no lack of subjects on which to complain. They lighted upon monopolies. James, soon after his accession, had abolished most of those left by Elizabeth, but the number had been increased partly through a wish to encourage home manufactures, and partly from a desire to regulate commerce. One set of persons, for example, had the sole right of making glass, because they bound themselves to heat their furnaces with coal instead of wood, and thus spared the trees needed for shipbuilding. Others had the sole right of making gold and silver thread, because they engaged to import all the precious metals they wanted, it being thought, in those days, that the precious metals alone constituted wealth, and that England would therefore be impoverished if English gold and silver were wasted on personal adornment. There is no doubt that courtiers received payments

from persons interested in these grants, but the amount of such payments was grossly exaggerated, and the Commons imagined that these and similar grievances owed their existence merely to the desire to fill the pockets of Buckingham and his favourites. There was, therefore, a loud outcry in Parliament. One of the main promoters of these schemes, Sir Giles Mompesson, fled the kingdom. Others were punished, and the monopolies recalled by

Francis Bacon, Viscount St. Alban, Lord Chancellor: from the
National Portrait Gallery.

the king, though as yet no act was passed declaring them to be illegal.

21. **The Fall of Bacon. 1621.**—After this the Commons turned upon Bacon. He was now Lord Chancellor, and had lived to find that his good advice was never followed. He had, nevertheless, been an active and upright judge. The Commons, however, distrusted him as having supported grants of monopolies, and,

when charges of bribery were brought against him, sent them up to the Lords for enquiry. At first Bacon thought a political trick was being played against him. He soon discovered that he had thoughtlessly taken gifts even before judgment had been given, though if they had been taken after judgment, he would—according to the custom of the time—have been considered innocent. His own opinion of the case was probably the true one. His sentence, he said, was ' just, and for reformation's sake fit.' Yet he was ' the justest Chancellor' that had been since his father's time, his father, Sir Nicholas Bacon, having creditably occupied under Elizabeth the post which he himself filled under James. He was stripped of office, fined, and imprisoned. His imprisonment, however, was extremely brief, and his fine was ultimately remitted. Though his trial was not exactly like that of the old impeachments, it was practically the revival of the system of impeachments which had been disused since the days of Henry VI. It was a sign that the power of Parliament was increasing and that of the king growing less.

22. Digby's Mission, and the Dissolution of Parliament. 1621.—The king announced to Parliament that he was about to send an ambassador to Vienna to induce the Emperor Ferdinand to be content with the re-conquest of Bohemia, and to leave Frederick undisturbed in the Palatinate. Parliament was therefore adjourned, in order to give time for the result of this embassy to be known ; and the Commons, at their last sitting, declared—with wild enthusiasm —that, if the embassy failed, they would support Frederick with their lives and fortunes. When Lord Digby, who was the chosen ambassador, returned, he had done no good. Ferdinand was too anxious to push his success further, and Frederick was too anxious to make good his losses for any negotiation to be successful. The Imperialists invaded the Palatinate, and in the winter James called on Parliament—which had by that time re-assembled after the adjournment—for money sufficient to defend the Palatinate till he had made one more diplomatic effort. The Commons, believing that the king's alliance with Spain was the root of all evil, petitioned him to marry his son to a Protestant lady, and plainly showed their wish to see him at war with Spain. James replied that the Commons had no right to discuss matters on which he had not consulted them. They drew up a protestation asserting their right to discuss all matters of public concernment. James tore it out of their journal-book, and dissolved Parliament, though it had not yet granted him a penny.

23. **The Loss of the Palatinate. 1622.**—In 1614, James, being in want of money, had had recourse to a benevolence—the lawyers having advised him that, though the Act of Richard III. (see p. 342) made it illegal for him to compel its payment, there was no law against his asking his subjects to pay it voluntarily. . He took the same course in 1622, and got enough to support the garrisons in the Palatinate for a few months, as many who did not like to give the money feared to provoke the king's displeasure by a refusal. Before the end of the year, however, the whole Palatinate, with the exception of one fortress, had been lost.

24. **Charles's Journey to Madrid. 1623.**—It was now time to try if the Spanish alliance was worth anything. Early in 1623, Prince Charles, accompanied by Buckingham, started for Madrid to woo the Infanta in person. The young men imagined that the king of Spain would be so pleased with this unusual compliment, that he would use his influence—and, if necessary, his troops—to obtain the restitution of the Palatinate to Charles's brother-in-law, the Elector Frederick. The Infanta's brother, Philip IV., was now king of Spain, and he had lately been informed by his sister that she was resolved not to marry a heretic. Her confessor had urged her to refuse. "What a comfortable bedfellow you will have !" he said to her : "he who lies by your side, and will be the father of

Costume of a lawyer : from a broadside, dated 1623.

your children, is certain to go to hell." Philip and his prime minister Olivares feared lest, if they announced this refusal, it would lead to a war with England. They first tried to convert the prince to their religion, and when that failed, secretly invited the Pope to refuse to grant a dispensation for the marriage. The Pope, however, fearing that, if he caused a breach, James and Charles would punish him by increasing the persecution of the English Catholics, informed Philip that he should have the dispensation for his sister, on condition not only that James and Charles should swear to grant religious liberty to the Catholics in England, but that he should himself swear that James and Charles would keep their word.

25. The Prince's Return. 1623.—Philip referred the point

The Upper House of Convocation: from a broadside, dated 1623.

whether he could conscientiously take the oath to a committee of theologians. In the meantime, Charles attempted to pay court to the Infanta. Spanish etiquette was, however, strict, and he was not allowed to speak to her, except in public and on rare occasions.

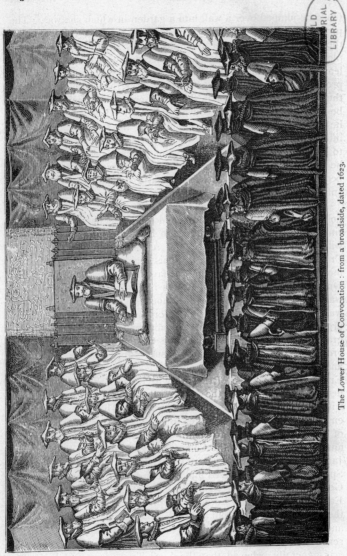

The Lower House of Convocation : from a broadside, dated 1623.

Once he jumped over a wall into a garden in which she was. The poor girl shrieked and fled. At last Charles was informed that the theologians had come to a decision. He might marry if he pleased, but, the moment that the ceremony was over, he was to leave for England. If, at the end of six months, he had not only promised religious liberty to the Catholics, but had actually put them in the enjoyment of it, then, and only then, his wife should be sent after him. Charles was indignant—the more so because he learnt that there was little chance that the king of Spain would interfere to restore the Protestant Frederick by force—and returned to England eager for war with Spain. Never before or after was he so popular as when he landed at Portsmouth—not so much because he had come back, as because he had not brought the Infanta with him.

26. **The Last Parliament of James I. 1624.**—James's foreign policy had now hopelessly broken down. He had expected that simply because it seemed to him to be just, Philip would quarrel with the Emperor for the sake of restoring the Palatinate to a Protestant. When he found that this could not be, he had nothing more to propose. His son and his favourite, who had been created Duke of Buckingham whilst he was in Spain, urged him to go to war, and early in **1624** James summoned a new Parliament, which was entirely out of his control. For the time Buckingham, who urged on the war, was the most popular man in England. A large grant of supply was given, but the Commons distrusting James, ordered the money to be paid to treasurers appointed by themselves, and to be spent only upon four objects—the repairing of forts in England, the increase of the army in Ireland, the fitting-out of a fleet, and the support of the Dutch Republic, which was still at war with Spain, and of other allies of the king. The king, on his part, engaged to invite friendly states to join him in war for the recovery of the Palatinate, and to summon Parliament in the autumn to announce the result. The Commons were the less anxious to trust James with money as they were in favour of a maritime war against Spain, whilst they believed him to be in favour of a military war in Germany. They had reason to think that Cranfield, who was now Earl of Middlesex and Lord Treasurer, had used his influence with the king to keep him from a breach with Spain ; and, with Charles and Buckingham hounding them on, they now impeached Middlesex on charges of malversation, and drove him from office. It was generally believed that the Lord Treasurer owed his fall to his dislike of a war which would be ruinous to the finances

which it was his business to guard. The old king could not resist, but he told his son that, in supporting an impeachment, he was preparing a rod for himself. Before the end of the session the king agreed to an act abolishing monopolies, except in the case of new inventions.

27. **The French Alliance.**—Even before Parliament was prorogued, a negotiation was opened for a marriage between Charles and Henrietta Maria, the sister of Louis XIII., king of France. Both James and Charles had promised Parliament that, if the future queen were a Roman Catholic, no religious liberty should be granted to the English Catholics by the marriage treaty. Both James and Charles gave way when they found that Louis insisted on this concession, and promised religious liberty to the Catholics. Consequently, they did not venture to summon Parliament till the marriage was over and it was too late to complain. Yet Buckingham, who was more firmly rooted in Charles's favour than he had ever been in that of his father, had promised money in all directions. Before the end of the year he had engaged to find large sums for the Dutch Republic to fight Spain, 30,000*l*. a month for Christian IV., king of Denmark, to make war in Germany against the Emperor, 20,000*l*. a month for Count Mansfeld, a German adventurer, to advance to the Palatinate, and anything that might be needed for a fleet to attack the Spanish ports. James, in short, was for a war by land, the Commons for a war by sea, and Buckingham for both.

28. **Mansfeld's Expedition, and the Death of James I. 1624–1625.**—Before the end of **1624**, twelve thousand Englishmen were gathered at Dover to go with Mansfeld to the Palatinate. The king of France, who had promised to help them, refused to allow them to land in his dominions. It was accordingly resolved that they should pass through Holland. James, however, had nothing to give them, and they were consequently sent across the sea without money and without provisions. On their arrival in Holland they were put on board open boats to make their way up the Rhine. Frost set in, and the boats were unable to stir. In a few weeks three-fourths of the men were dead or dying. It was Buckingham's first experience of making war without money and without Parliamentary support. Before anything further could be done, James was attacked by a fever, and, on March 27, **1625**, he died. Though his reign did not witness a revolution, it witnessed that loosening of the bonds of sympathy between the ruler and the ruled which is often the precursor of revolution.

CHAPTER XXXII

THE GROWTH OF THE PERSONAL GOVERNMENT OF CHARLES I.
1625—1634

LEADING DATES

The Reign of Charles I., 1625-1649

Charles's first Parliament and the expedition to Cadiz . 1625
Charles's second Parliament and the impeachment of
    Buckingham 1626
The expedition to Ré 1627
Charles's third Parliament and the Petition of Right . 1628
Dissolution of Charles's third Parliament 1629
Laud, Archbishop of Canterbury 1633
Prynne's sentence executed 1634

1. **Charles I. and Buckingham. 1625.**—The new king, Charles I., was more dignified than his father, and was conscientiously desirous of governing well. He was, unfortunately, extremely unwise, being both obstinate in persisting in any line of conduct which he had himself chosen, and ready to give way to the advice of others in matters of detail. Buckingham, who sympathised with him in his plans, and who was never at a loss when called on to express an opinion on any subject whatever, had now made himself completely master of the young king, and was, in reality, the governor of England far more than Charles himself. On May 1 Charles was married by proxy to Henrietta Maria, and Buckingham fetched home the bride.

2. **Charles's First Parliament. 1625.**—Charles was eager to meet his first Parliament, because he thought that it would grant him enormous sums of money to carry on the war with Spain, on which he had set his heart. He forgot that its members would be disgusted at the mismanagement of Mansfeld's expedition, and at the favour shown by himself to the Catholics in consequence of his marriage. When Parliament met on June 18, the House of Commons voted a small sum of 140,000*l.*, and asked him to put in execution the recusancy laws. Charles adjourned Parliament to Oxford, as the plague was raging in London, in order that he might urge it to vote him a larger sum. It met at Oxford on August 1, but the Commons refused to vote more money, unless counsellors in whom they could confide—in other words, counsellors other than

Buckingham—had the spending of it. Charles seeing that, if the Commons could force him to accept ministers against his wish, they would soon control himself, dissolved the Parliament. On everything else he was ready to give way—making no objection to the renewal of the persecution of the Catholics, whom a few months ago he had solemnly promised in his marriage treaty to protect. Though the question now raised was whether England was to be ruled by the king or by the House of Commons, it would be a mistake to think that the Commons were consciously aiming at sovereignty. They saw that there was mismanagement, and all that they wanted was to stop it.

3. **The Expedition to Cadiz. 1625.**—Charles thought that, if he could gain a great victory, there would be no further talk about mismanagement. Scraping together what money he could, he sent a great fleet and army, under the command of Sir Edward Cecil, to take Cadiz, the harbour of which was the port at which the Spanish treasure ships arrived from America once a year, laden with silver and gold from the mines of America. The greater part of Cecil's fleet was made up of merchant-vessels pressed by force into the king's service. Neither soldiers nor sailors had any heart in the matter. The masters of the merchant vessels did all they could to keep themselves out of danger. The soldiers after landing outside the town got drunk in a body, and would have been slaughtered if any Spaniards had been near. Cecil failed to take Cadiz, and after he left it, the Spanish treasure-ships from America, which he hoped to capture, got safely into Cadiz harbour, whilst he was looking for them in another part of the sea. The great expedition sent by Buckingham to Cadiz was as complete a failure as that which he had sent out the year before under Mansfeld. Whilst Cecil was employed in Spain Buckingham himself went to the Hague to form a continental alliance for the recovery of the Palatinate, hoping especially to secure the services of Christian IV., king of Denmark. Finding Christian quite ready to fight, Buckingham tried to pawn the king's jewels at Amsterdam in order to supply him with 30,000*l.* a month, which he had promised to him. No one would lend money on the jewels, and Buckingham came back, hoping that a second Parliament would be more compliant than the first.

4. **Charles's Second Parliament. 1626.**—The new Parliament met on February 6, 1626. Charles, in order to secure himself against what he believed to be the attacks of interested and ambitious men, had hit on the clever expedient of making sheriffs

of the leaders of the Opposition, so as to secure their detention in their own counties. The Opposition, however, found a leader in Sir John Eliot, who, though he had formerly been a friend of Buckingham, was now shocked at the misconduct of the favourite and regarded him as a selfish and unprincipled adventurer. Eliot was not only a natural orator, but one of the most pure-minded of

King Charles I. : from a painting by Van Dyck.

patriots, though the vehemence of his temperament often carried him to impute more evil to men of whom he thought badly than they were really guilty of. At present, he was roused to indignation against Buckingham, not only on account of the recent failures, but because, in the preceding summer, he had lent some English ships to the French, who wanted to use them for suppressing the Huguenots of Rochelle, then in rebellion against their king, Louis XIII. Before long the Commons, under Eliot's guidance, impeached Buckingham of all kinds of crime, making against him charges of some of which he was quite innocent, whilst others were much exaggerated. The fact that the only way to get rid of an unpopular minister was to accuse him of crime, made those who would otherwise have been content with his dismissal ready to believe in his guilt. Charles's vexation reached its height when he heard that Eliot had branded Buckingham as Sejanus. "If he is

Queen Henrietta Maria, wife of Charles I. : from a painting by Van Dyck.

Sejanus," he said, "I must be Tiberius." Rather than abandon his minister, he dissolved Parliament, before it had voted him a sixpence.

5. **The Forced Loan. 1626.**—If the war was to go on, money must in some way or other be had. Charles asked his subjects to bestow on him a free gift for the purpose. Scarcely any one gave him anything. Then came news that the king of Denmark, to whom the promised 30,000*l.* a month had not been paid (see

p. 501, 503), had been signally defeated at Lutter, so that the recovery of the Palatinate was further off than ever. Some clever person suggested to Charles that, though the Statute of Benevolences (see p. 342) prohibited him from making his subjects give him money, no law forbade him to make them lend, even though there was no chance that he would ever be able to repay what he borrowed. He at once gave orders for the collection of a forced loan. Before this was gathered in, troubles arose with France. Louis XIII. was preparing to besiege Rochelle, and Charles believed himself to be in honour bound to defend it because Louis had at one time promised him that he would admit his Huguenot subjects to terms. Besides, he had offended Louis by sending out of the country the queen's French attendants, thinking, probably with truth, that they encouraged her to resent his breach of promise about the English Catholics (see p. 501).

6. **The Expedition to Ré.** 1627.—In 1627 war broke out between France and England. Payment of the forced loan was urged in order to supply the means. Chief Justice Crewe, refusing to acknowledge its legality, was dismissed. Poor men were forced to serve as soldiers ; rich men were sent to prison. By such means a considerable sum was got together. A small force was sent to help the king of Denmark, and a fleet of a hundred sail, carrying soldiers on board, was sent to relieve Rochelle, under the command of Buckingham himself. On July 12 Buckingham landed on the Isle of Ré, which would form a good base of operations for the relief of Rochelle. He laid siege to the fort of St. Martin's on the island, and had almost starved it into surrender, when, on September 27, a relieving force of French boats dashed through the English blockading fleet, and re-victualled the place. Buckingham, whose own numbers had dwindled away, called for reinforcements from England. Charles did what he could, but Englishmen would lend no money to succour the hated Buckingham ; and, before reinforcements could arrive, a French army landed on the Isle of Ré, and drove Buckingham back to his ships. Out of 6,800 soldiers, less than 3,000—worn by hunger and sickness —returned to England.

7. **The Five Knights' Case.** 1627.—Buckingham was more unpopular than ever. " Since England was England," we find in a letter of the time, " it received not so dishonourable a blow." Attention was, however, chiefly turned to domestic grievances. Soldiers had been billeted on householders without their consent, and martial law had been exercised over civilians as well as

soldiers.   Moreover, the forced loan had been exacted, and some of those who refused to pay had been imprisoned by the mere order of the king and the Privy Council.   Against this last injury, five knights, who had been imprisoned, appealed to the Court of King's Bench.   A writ of *habeas corpus* was issued—that is to say, an order was given to the gaoler to produce the prisoners before the Court, together with a return showing the cause of committal.   All that the gaoler could show was that the prisoners had been committed by order of the king, signified by the Privy Council.   The lawyers employed by the five knights argued that every prisoner

Tents and military equipment in the early part of the reign of Charles I.: from the monument of Sir Charles Montague (died in 1625) in the church of Barking, Essex.

had a right to be tried or liberated on bail ; that, unless cause was shown—that is to say, unless a charge was brought against him— there was nothing on which he could be tried ; and that, therefore, these prisoners ought to be bailed.   The lawyers for the Crown argued that when the safety of the state was concerned, the king had always been allowed to imprison without showing cause, and that his discretion must be trusted not to imprison any one excepting in cases of necessity.   The judges did not decide this point, but sent the five knights back to prison.   In a few days, all the prisoners were set free, and Charles summoned a third Parliament, hoping that it would vote money for a fresh expedition to relieve Rochelle.

8. **Wentworth and Eliot in the Third Parliament of Charles I. 1628.**—Charles's third Parliament met on March 17, **1628.** The leadership was at once taken by Sir Thomas Wentworth, who, as well as Eliot, had been imprisoned for refusing to pay the loan. Though the two men now worked together, they were, in most points, opposed to one another. Eliot had been a warm advocate of the war with Spain, till he found it useless to carry on the war under Buckingham's guidance. Wentworth disliked all wars, and especially a war with Spain. Eliot believed in the wisdom of the House of Commons, and thought that, if the king always took its advice, he was sure to be in the right. Wentworth thought that the House of Commons often blundered, and that the king was more likely to be in the right if he took advice from wise counsellors. Wentworth, however, believed that in this case Charles had unfortunately preferred to take the advice of foolish counsellors, and though not sharing the opinions of Eliot and his friends, threw himself into the struggle in which the House of Commons was trying to stop Buckingham in his rash course. From time to time Wentworth contrived to show that he was no enemy of the king, or of a strong government such as that which had existed in the reign of Elizabeth. He was, however, an ardent and impetuous speaker, and threw himself into any cause which he defended with more violence than he could, in calmer moments, have justified to himself. He saw clearly that the late aggressions on the liberty of the subject weakened, instead of strengthening, the Crown ; and he now proposed a bill which should declare them illegal in the future. Charles refused to accept the bill, and Wentworth, unwilling to take a prominent part in a struggle with the king himself, retired into the background for the remainder of the session.

9. **The Petition of Right. 1628.**—Instead of Wentworth's bill, Eliot and the lawyers—Coke and Selden being prominent amongst them—brought forward a Petition of Right, not merely providing for the future, but also declaring that right had actually been violated in the past. Charles was willing to promise everything else asked of him, but he resisted the attempt to force him to promise never to imprison without showing cause, and thus to strip himself of the power of punishing offences directed against the safety of the State. The Commons, who held that he had directed his powers against men who were patriots, proved inexorable. Charles

needed money for another fleet which he was preparing for the relief of Rochelle, which was straitly besieged by the French king. He tried hard to get over the difficulty by an evasive answer, but at last, on June 7, he gave way, and the Petition of Right became the law of the land. After that, so far as the

George Villiers, first Duke of Buckingham, 1592–1628: from the National Portrait Gallery.

law went, there was to be no more martial law or enforced billeting, no forced loans or taxes imposed without a Parliamentary grant, or imprisonment without cause shown.

10. **Tonnage and Poundage. 1628.**—Before the end of the session a fresh question was raised. For many reigns Parliament had voted to each king for life, at the beginning of his reign, certain

customs duties known as Tonnage and Poundage. In addition to these James had added the impositions (see p. 484) without a Parliamentary grant. In the first Parliament of Charles, the Commons, probably wishing to settle the question of impositions before permanently granting Tonnage and Poundage, had passed a bill granting the latter for a single year ; but that Parliament had been dissolved before the bill had passed the Lords. The second Parliament was dissolved before the Commons had even discussed the subject, and the third Parliament now sitting had found no time to attend to it till after the Petition of Right had been granted. Now that the session was drawing to a close the Commons again proposed to grant Tonnage and Poundage for a year only. Charles, who had been levying the duties ever since his accession, refused to accept a grant on these terms, and the Commons then asserted that the clause of the Petition of Right forbidding him to levy taxes without a vote of Parliament made his raising of Tonnage and Poundage illegal. It was a nice legal point whether customs were properly called taxes, and Charles answered that he did not think that in demanding the petition they had meant to ask him to yield his right to Tonnage and Poundage, and that he was sure he had not meant to do so. The Commons then attacked Buckingham, and on June 26 Charles prorogued Parliament.

11. **Buckingham's Murder. 1628.**—In return for the Petition of Right Charles had received a grant of money large enough to enable him to send out his fleet. In August Buckingham went to Portsmouth to take the command. He was followed by John Felton, an officer to whom he had refused employment, and who had not been paid for his former services. Language used by the House of Commons in their recent attack on Buckingham persuaded Felton that he would render service to God and man by slaying the enemy of both. On August 23 he stabbed the Duke as he came out from breakfast, crying, 'God have mercy on thy soul !' Buckingham fell dead on the spot. The fleet went out under the command of the Earl of Lindsey to relieve Rochelle, but it failed utterly. There was no heart in the sailors or resolution in the commanders. Rochelle surrendered to the King of France, and Charles was left to bear the weight of the unpopularity of his late favourite.

12. **The Question of Sovereignty. 1628.**—Charles was anxious to come to terms with his Parliament on the question of Tonnage and Poundage, and would probably have consented to accept the compromise proposed in **1610** (see p. 486). Neither party, indeed, could afford to surrender completely to the other. The customs

duties were already more than a third of the revenue, and, if Charles could levy what he pleased, he might so increase his income as to have no further need of parliaments ; whereas, if the Commons refused to make the grant, the king would soon be in a state of bankruptcy. The financial question, in short, involved the further question whether Charles or the Parliament was to have the sovereignty. Dangerous as it would be for both parties to enter upon a quarrel which led up to such issues, it was the more difficult to avoid it because the king and the Commons were already at variance on another subject of pre-eminent importance.

13. **Protestantism of the House of Commons. 1625—1628.—** That subject was the subject of religion. The country gentlémen, who almost entirely filled the benches of the House of Commons, were not Puritan in the sense in which Cartwright had been Puritan in Elizabeth's reign (see p. 446). They did not wish to abolish epis-copacy or the Prayer Book ; but they were strongly Protestant, and their Protestantism had been strengthened by a sense of danger from the engagements in favour of the English Catholics into which James and Charles had entered. Lately, too, the power of the Catholic States on the Continent had been growing. In 1626 the King of Denmark had been defeated at Lutter. In 1628 the French Huguenots had been defeated at Rochelle. It was probably in consequence of these events that there was in England a revival of that attachment to Calvinistic doctrines which had accompanied the Elizabethan struggle against Spain and the Pope.

14. **Religious Differences. 1625—1628.—** On the other hand, a small but growing number amongst the clergy were breaking away from the dogmas of Calvinism, and especially from its stern doctrine on the subject of predestination. The House of Commons claimed to represent the nation, and it upheld the unity of the national belief as strongly as it had been upheld by Henry VIII. In 1625 the House summoned to its bar Richard Montague, who had challenged the received Calvinist opinions on the ground that they were not the doctrines of the Church of England. In 1626 it impeached him. Naturally, Montague and those who agreed with him warmly supported the royal power, and in 1627 urged the duty of paying the forced loan. Another clergyman, Roger Manwaring, preached sermons in which Parliaments were treated with con-tempt, and the Commons retaliated by impeaching the preacher. Charles would have acted in a spirit in advance of his times, and certainly in advance of his opponents, if he had merely upheld the right of the minority to liberty of speech. Instead of contenting

himself with this he made Montague Bishop of Chichester and gave Manwaring a good living.

15. **The King's Declaration. 1628.**—With the intention of smoothing matters down, Charles issued a declaration prefixed to the Articles, which would, as he hoped, make for peace. No one was in future to speak in public on the controverted points. Charles probably believed himself to be acting fairly, whilst, in reality, his compromise was most unfair. The Calvinists, who believed their views about predestination to be of the utmost importance to the souls of Christians, were hardly treated by the order to hold their tongues on the subject. Their opponents did not care about the doctrine at all, and would be only too glad if nothing more was heard of it. Charles, however, was but following in Elizabeth's steps in imposing silence and calling it peace. But the times were different. There was no longer a Catholic claimant of the throne or a foreign enemy at the gates to cause moderate men to support the government, even in its errors.

16. **The Second Session of the Third Parliament of Charles I. 1629.**—The Houses met for a second session on January 20, **1629.** The Commons attacked the clergy on a side on which they were especially vulnerable. Some of those who had challenged the Calvinistic doctrines had revived certain ceremonial forms which had generally fallen into disuse. In Durham Cathedral especially, parts of the service had been sung which had not been sung before, and the Communion table, which had hitherto stood at the north door and had been moved to the middle of the choir when needed, had been permanently fixed at the east end of the chancel. The Commons were indignant at what they styled Popish practices, and summoned the offenders before them. Then they turned to Tonnage and Poundage. Eliot, instead of confronting the difficulty directly, attempted to make it a question of privilege. The goods of a member of the House, named Rolle, had been seized for non-payment of Tonnage and Poundage, and Eliot wished to summon the Custom House officers to the bar, not for seizing the goods of an Englishman, but for a breach of privilege in seizing the goods of a member of Parliament. Pym, who occupied a prominent position amongst the popular party, urged the House to take broader ground : " The liberties of this House," he said, " are inferior to the liberties of this kingdom. To determine the privileges of this House is but a mean matter, and the main end is to establish possession of the subjects." [1] Eliot carried the

---

[1] *i.e.* to establish the right of the subjects to possess their property.

House with him, but Charles supported his officers, and refused to allow them to appear at the bar of the House. Once more the question of sovereignty was raised. The House was adjourned by the king's order in the hope that a compromise might be discovered.

17. **Breach between the King and the Commons. 1629.**—No compromise could be found, and on March 2 a fresh order for adjournment was given. When Finch, the Speaker, rose to announce it, two strong young members, Holles and Valentine, pushed him back into his chair whilst Eliot read three resolutions to the effect that whoever brought in innovations in religion, or introduced opinions differing from those of the true and orthodox church ; whoever advised the levy of Tonnage and Poundage without a grant by Parliament ; and whoever voluntarily paid those duties, was an enemy to the kingdom and a betrayer of its liberties. A wild tumult arose. A rush was made to free the Speaker, and another rush to hold him down. One member, at least, laid his hand on his sword. The doors were locked, and, amidst the hubbub, Holles repeated the resolutions, which were accepted with shouts of ' Aye, aye.' Then the doors were opened, and the members poured out. The king at once dissolved Parliament, and for eleven years no Parliament met again in England.

18. **The Constitutional Dispute. 1629.**—The constitutional system of the Tudor monarchy had practically broken down. The nation had, in the sixteenth century, entered upon a struggle for national independence. Henry VIII. and Elizabeth had headed it in that struggle, and the House of Commons had but represented the nation in accepting Henry VIII. and Elizabeth as supreme rulers. The House of Commons now refused to admit that Charles was its supreme ruler, because he could neither head the nation, nor understand either its wants or its true needs. Yet the House had not as yet shown its capacity for taking his place. It had criticised his methods of government effectively, but had displayed its own intolerance and disregard for individual liberty. Yet, till it could learn to respect individual liberty, it would not be likely to gain the sovereignty at which it aimed. A king becomes powerful when men want a strong government to put down enemies abroad or petty tyrants at home. A Parliament becomes powerful when men want to discuss political questions, and political discussion cannot thrive when voices disagreeable to the majority are silenced. The House of Commons had thought more of opposing the king than of laying a wide basis for its own power, and now it was, for a time at least, silenced.

19. **The Victory of Personal Government.** 1629—1632.— Charles was now to show whether he could do better than the Commons. He had gained one great convert soon after the end of the first session of the last Parliament. Wentworth, satisfied, it is to be supposed, with the Petition of Right, and dissatisfied with the claim to sovereignty put forward by the Commons, came over to his side and was made first a baron and then a viscount, after which before the end of 1628 he was made President of the Council of the North (see p. 397). Wentworth was no Puritan, and the claim of the Commons, in the second session, to meddle with religion no doubt strengthened him in his conviction that he had chosen the right side. Before the end of 1629 he became a Privy Councillor. The most influential member of Charles's Council, however, was Weston, the Lord Treasurer. Peace was made with France in 1629, and with Spain in 1630. To bring the finances into order, the king insisted on collecting the customs without a Parliamentary grant, and Chambers, a merchant who refused to pay, was summoned before the Council, and then fined 2,000*l.* and imprisoned for saying that merchants were more wrung in England than they were in Turkey. The leading members who had been concerned in the disturbance at the last meeting of Parliament were imprisoned, and three of them, Eliot, Holles, and Valentine, were charged before the King's Bench with riot and sedition. They declined to plead, on the ground that the judges had no jurisdiction over things done in Parliament. The judges held that riot and sedition must be punished somewhere, and that as Parliament was not always sitting it must be punished by themselves. As the accused still refused to plead they were fined and imprisoned. Eliot died of consumption in the Tower in 1632. Charles had refused to allow him to go into the country to recover his health, and after his death he refused to allow his children to dispose of his body. Eliot was the martyr, not of individual liberty, but of Parliamentary supremacy. Charles hated him because he regarded him as the factious accuser of Buckingham.

20. **Star Chamber Sentences.** 1630—1633.—The first years of unparliamentary government were, on the whole, years of peace and quiet. The Star Chamber, which under Henry VII. had put down the old nobility, was now ready to put down the opponents of the king. Its numbers had grown with its work, and all of the Privy Councillors were now members of it, the only other members being two judges. It was therefore a mere instrument in the king's hands. In 1630 Alexander Leighton was flogged and

mutilated by order of the Star Chamber for having written a virulent libel against the bishops ; in which he blamed them for all existing mischiefs, including the extravagance of the dress of the ladies, and ended by advising that they should be smitten under the fifth rib. In **1633** the same court fined Henry Sherfield for breaking a church window which he held to be superstitious. The bulk of Englishmen were not touched by these sentences, and there was more indigna-

Sir Edward and Lady Filmer : from their brass at East Sutton, Kent, showing armour and dress worn about 1630.

tion when, in order to pay off debts contracted in time of war, Charles ordered the enforcement of fines upon all men holding by military tenure lands worth 40*l.* a year who had neglected to be knighted. The Court of Exchequer held that the fines were legal ; but the whole system of military tenure was obsolete, and those who suffered regarded themselves as wronged through a mere technicality.

21. **Laud's Intellectual Position. 1629—1633.**—For all matters relating to the Church Charles's principal adviser was William Laud, now Bishop of London. As far as doctrine was concerned Laud carried on the teaching of Cranmer and Hooker. He held that the basis of belief was the Bible, but that the Bible was to be interpreted by the tradition of the early church, and that all doubtful points were to be subjected, not to heated arguments in the pulpits, but to sober discussion by learned men. His mind, in short, like those of the earlier English reformers, combined the Protestant reliance on the Scriptures with reverence for ancient tradition and with the critical spirit of the Renascence. Laud's difficulty lay, as theirs had lain, in the impossibility of gaining over any large number of his fellow-countrymen. Intelligent criticism and intelligent study were only for the few. Laud, as he himself plaintively declared, was in danger of being crushed between the upper and lower mill-stones of Puritanism and the Papacy.

22. **Laud as the Upholder of Uniformity.**—In all this there was nothing peculiar to Laud. What was peculiar to him was his perception that intellectual religion could not maintain itself by intellect alone. Hooker's appeals to Church history and to the supremacy of reason had rolled over the heads of men who knew nothing about Church history, and who did not reason. Laud fell back upon the influence of ceremonial. "I laboured nothing more," he afterwards said, "than that the external public worship of God—too much slighted in most parts of the kingdom—might be preserved, and that with as much decency and uniformity as might be ; being still of opinion that unity cannot long continue in the Church when uniformity is shut out of the Church door." He, like Eliot and the Parliamentarians, was convinced that there could be but one Church in the nation. As they sought to retain their hold on it by the enforcement of uniformity of doctrine, Laud sought to retain his hold on it by enforcing uniformity of worship. To do this he attempted to put in force the existing law of the Church as opposed to the existing practice. What he urged men to do he believed to be wholly right. He himself clung with all his heart to the doctrine of the divine right of episcopacy, of the efficacy of the Sacraments, and to the sobering influence of appointed prayers and appointed ceremonies. What he lacked was broad human sympathy and respect for the endeavour of each earnest man to grow towards perfection in the way which seems to him to be best. Men were to obey for their own good, and to hold their tongues. The king was the supreme governor, and with his authority, as exercised

in the Courts of Star Chamber and High Commission, Laud hoped
to rescue England from Pope and Puritan.

23. **The Beginning of Laud's Archbishopric. 1633—1634.—**
In 1633 Laud became Archbishop of Canterbury. He at once made
his hand felt in every direction. By his advice, in consequence of
an attempt of the judges to put an end to Sunday amusements,
Charles republished the *Declaration of Sports* which had been

Archbishop Laud : from a copy in the National Portrait Gallery
by Henry Stone, from the Van Dyck at Lambeth.

issued by his father, authorising such amusements under certain
restrictions. Where, however, James had contented himself with
giving orders, Charles insisted on having the Declaration read in
church by all the clergy, and roused the resistance of those who
regarded Sunday amusements as a breach of the Sabbath. Laud
was also anxious to see the Communion table standing everywhere
at the east end of the church. No doubt his anxiety came in part

from his reverence of the holy sacrament for which it was set apart, but it also arose from his dislike to the base purposes for which it

Silver-gilt tankard made at London in 1634–35, now belonging to the Corporation of Bristol.

was often made to serve.   Men often put their hats on it, or used it as a writing table.   The canons, or laws of the Church, indeed, directed that the position of the table should, when not in use, be at the east end, though at the time of Communion it was to be placed in that part of the church or chancel from which the minister could best be heard.   A case was brought before the king and the Privy Council in **1633**, and it was then decided that the bishop or other proper authority should settle what was the position from which the minister could best be heard.   Of course the bishops settled that that place was the east end of the chancel.

24. **Laud and Prynne. 1633—1634.**—Amongst the most virulent opponents of Laud was William Prynne, a lawyer whose extensive study of theology had not tended to smooth away the asperities of his temper.   He was, moreover, a voluminous writer, and had written books against drinking healths and against the wearing of long hair by men, in which these follies had been treated as equally blameworthy with the grossest sins.   Struck by the immorality of the existing drama, he attacked it in a heavy work called *Histrio-mastix*, or The scourge of stage players, in which he held the frequenting of theatres to be the cause of every crime under the sun.   He pointed out that all the Roman emperors who had patronised the drama had come to a bad end, and this was held by the courtiers to be a reflection on Charles, who patronised the drama.   He inserted in the index a vile charge against all actresses, and this was held to be an insult to the queen, who was at the time taking part in the rehearsal of a theatrical representation.   Accordingly in **1633** Prynne was sentenced by the Star Chamber to lose his ears in the pillory, to a heavy fine, and to imprisonment during the king's pleasure.   In **1634** the sentence was carried out. Prynne's case, however, awakened no general sympathy, and the king does not appear to have as yet become widely unpopular. The young lawyers came to Whitehall to give a masque or dramatic representation in presence of the king and queen, in order to show their detestation of Prynne's conduct, whilst John Milton, the strictest and most pure-minded of poets, wrote a masque, *Comus*, to show how little sympathy he had with Prynne's sweeping denunciations.   Yet, though Milton opposed Prynne's exaggeration, his own poetry was a protest against Laud's attempt to reach the mind through the senses.   Milton held to the higher part of the Puritan teaching, that the soul is to lead the body, and not the body the soul.   " So dear," he wrote in *Comus*,

> to Heaven is saintly chastity,
> That, when a soul is found sincerely so,
> A thousand liveried angels lackey her,
> Driving far off each thing of sin and guilt

> And, in clear dream and solemn vision,
> Tell her of things that no gross ear can hear,
> Till oft converse with heavenly habitants
> Begin to cast a beam on the outward shape,
> The unpolluted temple of the mind,
> And turns it by degrees to the soul's essence,
> Till all be made immortal.

CHAPTER XXXIII

THE OVERTHROW OF THE PERSONAL GOVERNMENT OF CHARLES I. **1634—1641**

LEADING DATES

The Reign of Charles I., 1625—1649

The Metropolitical Visitation	1634
First Ship-money Writ (to the port-towns) . .	1634
Second Ship-money Writ (to all the counties) .	1635
Prynne, Burton, and Bastwick in the pillory . .	1637
Riot in Edinburgh	1637
Scottish National Covenant	1638
Judgment in Hampden's Case	1637–1638
First Bishops' War	1639
Short Parliament	1640
Second Bishops' War	1640
Meeting of the Long Parliament	1640
Execution of Strafford, and Constitutional Reforms	1641

1. The Metropolitical Visitation. 1634—1637.—The antagonism which Laud had begun to rouse in the first months of his arch-bishopric became far more widely spread in the three years beginning in **1634** and ending in **1637**, in consequence of a Metropolitical Visitation—that is to say, a visitation which he conducted by the Metropolitan or Archbishop—either in person or by deputy—to enquire into the condition of the clergy and churches of the Province of Canterbury ; a similar visitation being held in the Province of York by the authority of the Archbishop of York. Every clergyman who refused to conform to the Prayer Book, who resisted the removal of the Communion table to the east end of the chancel, or who objected to bow when the sacred name of Jesus was pronounced, was called in question, and if obstinate, was brought before the High Commission and suspended from the exercise of his functions or deprived of his living. Laud wanted to reach unity through uniformity, and made the canons of the Church his standard of uniformity. Even moderate men suspected that he sought to subject England again to the Pope. The queen, too, entertained a Papal agent at her Court, and a few successful conversions, brought about by Con, who at one time resided with her in that capacity, frightened the country into the belief that a plot existed to overthrow Protestantism. Some of Laud's clerical supporters favoured this idea, by talking about such topics as altars and the invocation of the saints, which had hitherto been held to have no place in Protestant teaching. The result was that moderate Protestants now joined the Puritans in opposing Laud.

2. **Prynne, Bastwick, and Burton. 1637.**—Laud had little hope of being able to abate the storm. One of his best qualities was that he was no respecter of persons, and he had roused animosity in the upper classes by punishing gentlemen guilty of immorality or of breaches of church discipline as freely as he punished more lowly offenders. In 1637 he characteristically attempted to defend himself from the charge of being a Papist and an innovator in religion by bringing three of his most virulent assailants—Prynne, Bastwick, and Burton—before the Star Chamber. The trial afforded him the opportunity of making a speech in his own defence, to which nobody paid the least attention. As a matter of course the accused were heavily punished, being sentenced to lose their ears in the pillory, to pay a fine of 5,000*l*., and to imprisonment for life. It was not now as it had been in 1634, when Prynne stood alone in the pillory, no man regarding him. The three victims had a triumphal reception on their way to the pillory. Flowers and sweet herbs were strewed in their path. The crowd applauded them whilst they suffered. On their way to their several prisons in distant parts of the country men flocked to greet them as martyrs.

3. **Financial Pressure. 1635—1637.**—Revolutions are never successful without the guidance of men devoted to ideas; but on the other hand they are not caused only by grievances felt by religious or high-minded people. To stir large masses of men to resistance, their pockets must be touched as well as their souls. In 1635 Weston, who had been created Earl of Portland, died, and a body of Commissioners of the Treasury, who succeeded him, laid additional impositions on commerce and established corporations for exercising various manufactures under the protection of monopolies. This proceeding was according to the letter of the law, as corporations had been

exempted from the act in restraint of monopolies which had been passed in 1624 (see p. 501). So, too, was a claim put forward by Charles in 1637 to levy fines from those who had encroached on the old boundaries of the forests. It is true that, in the teeth of the opposition roused, Charles exacted but a small part of the fines imposed, but he incurred almost as much obloquy as if he had taken the whole of the money.

4. **Ship-money. 1634—1637.**—More important was Charles's effort to provide himself with a fleet. As the Dutch navy was powerful, and the French navy was rapidly growing in strength, Charles, not unnaturally, thought that England ought to be able to meet their combined forces at sea. In 1634, by the advice of Attorney-General Noy, he issued writs to the port towns, to furnish him with ships. He took care to ask for ships larger than any port —except London—had got, and then offered to supply ships of his own, on condition that the port towns should equip and man them. In 1635—Noy having died in the meantime—Charles asked for ships not merely from the ports, but from the inland as well as from the maritime counties. Again London alone provided ships ; in all the rest of England money had to be found to pay for the equipment and manning of ships belonging to the king. In this way Charles got a strong navy which he manned with sailors in the habit of managing ships of war, and entirely at his own orders. The experience of the Cadiz voyage had shown him that merchant-sailors, such as those who had done good service against the Armada, were not to be trusted to fight in enterprises in which they took no interest, and it is from the ship-money fleet that the separation of the naval and mercantile marine dates. Necessarily, however, Englishmen began to complain, not that they had a navy, but that the money needed for the navy was taken from them without a Parliamentary grant. Year after year ship-money was levied, and the murmurs against it increased. In February, 1637, Charles consulted the judges, and ten out of the twelve judges declared that the king had a right to do what was necessary for the defence of the realm in time of danger, and that the king was the sole judge of the existence of danger.

5. **Hampden's Case. 1637—1638.**—It was admitted that, in accordance with the Petition of Right, Charles could not levy a tax without a Parliamentary grant. Charles, however, held that ship-money was not a tax, but money paid in commutation of the duty of all Englishmen to defend their country. Common sense held that, whether ship-money was a tax or not, it had been

levied without consulting Parliament, simply because the king shrank from consulting Parliament ; or, in other words, because he was afraid that Parliament would ask him to put an end to Laud's system of managing the Church. Charles was ready, as he said, to allow to Parliament liberty of counsel, but not of control. The sense of irritation was now so great that the nation wanted to control the Government, and knew that it would never be able to do so if Charles could, by a subterfuge, take what money he needed without summoning Parliament. Of this feeling John Hampden, a Buckinghamshire squire, became the mouthpiece. He refused to pay 20s. levied on his estate for ship-money. His case was argued before the twelve judges sitting in the Exchequer Chamber. In 1638 two pronounced distinctly in his favour, three supported him on technical grounds, and seven pronounced for the king. Charles continued to levy ship-money, but the arguments of Hampden's lawyers were circulated in the country, and the judgment of the majority on the Bench was ascribed to cowardice or obsequiousness. Their decision ranged against the king all who cared about preserving their property, as the Metropolitical visitation had ranged against him all who cared for religion in a distinctly Protestant form. Yet, even now, the Tudor monarchy had done its work too thoroughly, and had filled the minds of men too completely with the belief that armed resistance to a king was unjustifiable, to make Englishmen ripe for rebellion. They preferred to wait till some opportunity should arrive which would enable them to express their disgust in a constitutional way.

6. **Scottish Episcopacy. 1572—1612.**—The social condition of Scotland was very different from that of England. The nobles there had never been crushed as they had been in England, and they had tried to make the reformation conduce to their own profit. In 1572 they obtained the appointment of what were known as Tulchan bishops, who, performing no episcopal function, received the revenues of their sees and then handed them over to certain nobles.[1] The Presbyterian clergy, however, represented the popular element in the nation—and that element, though it had hitherto been weak, was growing strong through the discipline which it received in consequence of the leading share assigned to the middle and lower classes in the Church Courts (see p. 434). The disagreement between these classes and the nobles gave to James the part of arbitrator, and thus conferred on him a power which no Scottish

---

[1] A Tulchan was a stuffed calf's skin set by a cow to induce her to give her milk freely.

king had had before.   After much vacillation, he consented, in **1592**, to an act fully re-establishing the Presbyterian system.   It was not long before he repented.   The Presbyterian clergy attacked his actions from the pulpit, and one of them, Andrew Melville, plucking him by the sleeve, called him 'God's silly vassal.' The nobles, too, were angry because the clergy assailed their vices, and tried to subject them to the discipline of the Church. Though their ancestors had, at almost all times, been the adversaries of the kings, they now made common cause with James. Gradually episcopacy was restored.   Bishops were re-appointed in **1599**. Step by step episcopal authority was regained for them.   In **1610** three of their number were consecrated in England, and in **1612** the Scottish Parliament ratified all that had been done.

7. **The Scottish Bishops and Clergy. 1612—1637.**—In England bishops had a party (lay and clerical) behind them.   In Scotland they were mere instruments of the king and the nobles to keep the clergy quiet.   In **1618**, James, supported by the bishops and the nobles, forced upon a general assembly the acceptance of the Five Articles of Perth, the most important of which was a direction that the Communion should be received in a kneeling posture. Yet, in spite of all that James had done, the local popular Church courts still existed, and the worship of the Church remained still distinctly Calvinistic and Puritan.   Charles was more eager than his father to alter the worship of the Scottish Church, and, in **1637**, at his command, certain Scottish bishops—often referring for advice to Laud—completed a new Prayer Book, not unlike that in use in England, but differing from it, for the most part, in a sense adverse to Puritanism.   The clergy declared against it, and this time the clergy had on their side the nobles, who not only feared lest Charles should take from them the Church lands appropriated by their fathers, but were also irritated at the promotion of some bishops to high offices which they claimed for themselves.

8. **The Riot at Edinburgh and the Covenant. 1637—1638.**— On July 23, **1637**, an attempt was made to read the new service in St. Giles's, at Edinburgh.   The women present burst into a riot, and one of them threw her stool at the head of the officiating minister, fortunately missing him.   All Scotland took part with the rioters.   The new Prayer Book was hated, not only because it was said to be Popish, but also because it was English.   In November four committees, known as the Tables, practically assumed the government of Scotland.   In February, **1638**, all good Scots were signing a National Covenant.   Nothing was said in it

about episcopacy, but those who signed it bound themselves to labour, by all means lawful, to recover the purity and liberty of the Gospel, as it was established and professed before the recent innovations.

9. The Assembly of Glasgow, and the Abolition of Episcopacy. 1638.—The greater part of 1638 was passed by Charles in an endeavour to come to an understanding with the Scots. On September 2 he revoked the Prayer Book, and offered to limit the powers of the bishops. On November 21 a general assembly met at Glasgow, in which ninety-six lay members—for the most part noblemen—sat with 144 clergymen, and which may therefore be regarded as a sort of Ecclesiastical Parliament in which the clergy predominated as the nobles predominated in the single house which made up the real Parliament. The Assembly claimed to judge the bishops, on which the king's commissioner, the Marquis of Hamilton, dissolved the Assembly rather than admit its claim. The Assembly, however, on the ground that it possessed a Divine right to settle all affairs relating to the Church independently of the King, sat on, as if nothing had happened, deposed the bishops, and re-established the Presbyterian system.

10. The First Bishops' War. 1639.—In refusing to obey the order for dissolution, the Scottish General Assembly had practically made itself independent of the king, and Charles was driven—unless he cared to allow the establishment of a precedent, which might some day be quoted against him in England—to make war upon the Scots. Yet he dared not summon the English Parliament, lest it should follow their example, and he had to set forth on what came to be known as the First Bishops' War—because it was waged in the cause of the bishops—with no more money than he could get from a voluntary contribution, not much exceeding 50,000*l.* Soon after he reached Berwick with his army, he found that the Scots had, on Dunse Law,[1] an army almost equal to his own in numbers, commanded by Alexander Leslie, an old soldier who had fought in the German wars, and mainly composed of veterans, who had seen much service on the Continent, whilst his own men were raw recruits. His money soon came to an end, and it was then found impossible to keep the army together. The war was one in which there was no fighting, and in which only one man was killed, and he by an accident. On June 24 Charles signed the Treaty of Berwick. Both sides passed over in silence the deeds of the Glasgow Assembly, but a promise was given that all affairs civil

[1] 'Law,' in the Lowlands of Scotland, means a solitary hill.

and ecclesiastical should be settled in an assembly and Parliament. Assembly and Parliament met at Edinburgh, and declared in favour of the abolition of episcopacy ; but Charles, who could not, even now, make up his mind to submit, ordered the adjournment of the Parliament, and prepared for a new attack on Scotland.

11. **Wentworth in Ireland.** **1633—1639.**—In preparing for a new war, Charles had Wentworth by his side. Wentworth, who was by far the ablest of his advisers, after ruling the north of England (see p. 514) in a high-handed fashion, had, in **1632**, been appointed Lord Deputy of Ireland. In **1634** he summoned an Irish Parliament, taking care that the English Protestant settlers and the Irish Catholics should be so evenly balanced that he could do what he would with it. He carried through it admirable laws and a vote of money which enabled him to be independent of Parliament for some time to come. As far as its material interests were concerned, Ireland had never been so prosperous. Trade grew, and the flax industry of the North sprang into existence under Wentworth's protection. Churches which had lain in ruins since the deso-

Soldier armed with a pike : from a broadside, printed *circa* 1630.

Soldier with musket and crutch : from a broadside printed about 1630.

lating wars of Elizabeth's reign were rebuilt, and able and active ministers were invited from England. The Earl of Cork, who had illegally seized Church property to his own use, was heavily fined, and Lord Mountnorris, a self-seeking official, who refused to resign his office, was brought before a court-martial and condemned to death ; though Wentworth let him know that his life was in no danger, and that all that was wanted of him was the resignation of an office which he was unfitted to fill. Wentworth required all the officers of the Crown to live up to the motto of 'Thorough,' which he had adopted for himself, by which he meant a 'thorough' devotion to the service of the king and the State, without regard for private interests.

12. **The Proposed Plantation of Connaught.**—Wentworth gave great offence to the English officials and settlers by the harsh and overbearing way in which he kept them in order. His conduct to the Celtic population was less violent than that of some other lord deputies, but he had no more idea than his predecessors of leaving the Irish permanently to their own customs and religion. He believed that, both for their own good and for the safety of the English Crown, they must be made as like Englishmen as possible, and that, to effect this, it would be necessary to settle more Englishmen in Ireland to overawe them. Accordingly, in 1635, he visited Connaught, where he raked up an old claim of the king's to the whole land of the province, though Charles had promised not to put forward any such claim at all. In every county of Connaught except Galway, a jury was found to give a verdict in favour of the king's claim. The jury in County Galway refused to do his bidding, and Wentworth had the jurymen fined, and the land of the county seized by the order of the Irish Court of Exchequer, which pronounced judgment without a jury. He then invited English settlers to Connaught ; but he found that few English settlers would go to such a distance from their homes. Perhaps many refused to come because they distrusted Wentworth. Yet, for the moment, his government appeared successful. In 1639 he visited England, and Charles, who needed an able counsellor, made him Earl of Strafford, and from that time took him for his chief adviser.

13. **The Short Parliament. 1640.**—Strafford's advice was that Charles should summon an English Parliament, whilst he himself held a Parliament in Dublin, which might show an example of loyalty. The Irish Parliament did all that was expected of it, the Catholic members being especially forward in voting supplies in

the hope that, if they helped Charles to conquer the Scots, he would allow freedom of religion in Ireland. In England, Parliament met on April 13. Pym at once laid before the Commons a statement of the grievances of the nation, after which the House resolved to ask for redress of these grievances before granting supply. Charles offered to abandon ship-money if the Commons would give him twelve subsidies equal to about 960,000*l.* The Commons hesitated about granting so much, and wished the king to yield on other points as well as upon ship-money. In the end they prepared to advise Charles to abandon the war with Scotland altogether, and, to avoid this, he dissolved Parliament on May 5. As it had sat for scarcely more than three weeks, it is known as the Short Parliament.

14. **The Second Bishops' War. 1640.**—In spite of the failure of the Parliament, Charles gathered an army by pressing men from all parts of England, and found money to pay them for a time by buying a large quantity of pepper on credit and selling it at once for less than it was worth. The soldiers, as they marched northwards, broke into the churches, burnt the Communion rails, and removed the Communion tables to the middle of the building. There was no wish amongst Englishmen to see the Scots beaten. The Scots, knowing this, crossed the Tweed, and, on August 28, routed a part of the English army at Newburn on the Tyne. Even Strafford did not venture to advise a prolongation of the war. Negotiations were opened at Ripon, and Northumberland and Durham were left in the hands of the Scots as a pledge for the payment of 850*l.* a day for the maintenance of their army, till a permanent treaty could be arranged. Charles, whose money was already exhausted, summoned a Great Council, consisting of Peers alone, to meet at York. All that the Great Council could do was to advise him to summon another Parliament, and that advice he was obliged to take.

15. **The Meeting of the Long Parliament. 1640.**—On November 3, **1640**, the new Parliament, which was to be known as the Long Parliament, met. Pym once more took the lead, and proposed the impeachment of Strafford, as the king's chief adviser in the attempt to carry on war in defiance of Parliament. Strafford had also collected an Irish army for an attack on Scotland, and it was strongly believed that he had advised the king to use that army to reduce England as well as Scotland under arbitrary government. The mere suspicion that he had threatened to bring an Irish army into England roused more than ordinary indignation, as, in those days, Irishmen were both detested and despised in England.

Strafford was therefore impeached, and sent to the Tower. Laud was also imprisoned in the Tower, whilst other officials escaped to the Continent to avoid a similar fate. The Houses then proceeded to pass a Triennial Bill, directing that Parliament should meet every three years, even if the king did not summon it, and to this, with some hesitation, Charles assented. He could not, in fact, refuse anything which Parliament asked, because, if he had done so, Parliament would give him no money to satisfy the Scots, and if the Scots were not satisfied, they would recommence the war.

16. **The Impeachment of Strafford. 1641.**—On March 22, **1641**, Strafford's trial was opened in Westminster Hall. All his overbearing actions were set forth at length, but, after all had been said, a doubt remained whether they constituted high treason, that crime having been strictly defined by a statute of Edward III. (see p. 250). Young Sir Henry Vane, son of one of the Secretaries of State, found amongst his father's papers a note of a speech delivered by Strafford in a Committee of the Privy Council just after the breaking up of the Short Parliament, in which he had spoken of the king as loose and absolved from all rules of government. "You have an army in Ireland," Strafford was reported to have said, "you may employ here to reduce this kingdom, for I am confident as anything under heaven, Scotland shall not hold out five months." The Commons were convinced that 'this kingdom' meant England and not Scotland ; but there were signs that the lords would be likely to differ from them, and the Commons accordingly abandoned the impeachment in which the lords sat as judges, and introduced a Bill of Attainder (see p. 401, note), to which, after the Commons had accepted it, the lords would have to give their consent if it was to become law, as in the case of any ordinary Bill.

17. **Strafford's Attainder and Execution.**—Pym would have preferred to go on with the impeachment, because he believed that Strafford was really guilty of high treason. He held that treason was not an offence against the king's private person, but against the king as a constitutional ruler, and that Strafford had actually diminished the king's authority by attempting to make him an absolute ruler, and thereby to weaken Charles's hold upon the goodwill of the people. This argument, however, did not break down the scruples of the Peers, and if Charles had kept quiet, he would have had them at least on his side. Neither he nor the queen could keep quiet. Before the end of **1640** she had urged the

Pope to send her money and soldiers, and now she had a plan for bringing the defeated English army from Yorkshire to Westminster to overpower Parliament. Then came an attempt of Charles to get possession of the Tower, that he might liberate Strafford by force. Pym, who had learnt the secret of the queen's army-plot, disclosed it, and the peers, frightened at their danger, passed the Bill of Attainder. A mob gathered round Whitehall and howled for the execution of the sentence. Charles, fearing lest the mob should take vengeance on his wife, weakly signed a commission appointing commissioners to give the royal assent to the Bill, though he had promised Strafford that not a hair of his head should be touched. With the words, " Put not your trust in princes " on his lips, the great royalist statesman prepared for the scaffold. On May 12 he was beheaded, rather because men feared his ability than because his offences were legally punishable with death.

18. **Constitutional Reforms. 1641.**—Englishmen would not have feared Strafford if they could have been sure that the king could be trusted to govern according to law, without employing force to settle matters in his own way. Yet, though the army-plot had made it difficult to feel confidence in Charles, Parliament was at first content to rely on constitutional reforms. On the day on which Charles assented to the bill for Strafford's execution he assented to another bill declaring that the existing Parliament should not be dissolved without its own consent, a stipulation which made the House of Commons legally irresponsible either to the king or to its constituents, and which could only be justified by the danger of an attack by an armed force at the bidding of the king. Acts were passed abolishing the Courts of Star Chamber and the High Commission, declaring ship-money to be illegal, limiting the king's claims on forests, prohibiting fines for not taking up knighthood, and preventing the king from levying Tonnage and Poundage or impositions without a Parliamentary grant. Taking these acts as a whole, they stripped the Crown of the extraordinary powers which it had acquired in Tudor times, and made it impossible for Charles, legally, to obtain money to carry on the government without the goodwill of Parliament, or to punish offenders without the goodwill of juries. All that was needed in the way of constitutional reform was thus accomplished. As far as law could do it, the system of personal government which Charles had in part inherited from his predecessors and in part had built up for himself, was brought to an end.

CHAPTER XXXIV

THE FORMATION OF PARLIAMENTARY PARTIES AND THE FIRST YEARS OF THE CIVIL WAR. 1641—1644

LEADING DATES
Reign of Charles I., 1625—1649

The Debate on the Grand Remonstrance	Nov. 23, 1641
The Attempt on the Five Members	Jan. 4, 1642
The Battle of Edgehill	Oct. 23, 1642
The Fairfaxes defeated at Adwalton Moor	June 30, 1643
Waller's Defeat at Roundway Down	July 13, 1643
The Raising of the Siege of Gloucester	Sept. 5, 1643
The First Battle of Newbury	Sept. 20, 1643
The Solemn League and Covenant taken by the Houses	Sept. 25, 1643
The Scottish Army crosses the Tweed	Jan. 19, 1644
The Battle of Marston Moor	July 2, 1644
Capitulation of Essex's Infantry at Lostwithiel	Sept. 2, 1644
The Second Battle of Newbury	Oct. 27, 1644

1. **The King's Visit to Scotland. 1641.**—If Charles could have inspired his subjects with the belief that he had no intention of overthrowing the new arrangements by force, there would have been little more trouble. Unfortunately, this was not the case. In August, indeed, the Houses succeeded in disbanding the English army in Yorkshire, and in dismissing the Scottish army across the Tweed ; but, in the same month, Charles set out for Scotland, ostensibly to give his assent in person to the Acts abolishing episcopacy in that country, but in reality to persuade the Scots to lend him an army to coerce the English Parliament. Pym and Hampden suspecting this, though they could not prove it, felt it necessary to be on their guard.

2. **Parties formed on Church Questions. 1641.**—There would, however, have been little danger from Charles if political questions alone had been at stake. Parliament had been unanimous in abolishing his personal government, and no one was likely to help him to restore it by force. In ecclesiastical questions, however, differences arose early. All, indeed, wished to do away with the practices introduced by Laud, but there was a party, which though willing to introduce reforms into the Church, and to subject it to Parliament, objected to the introduction of the Presbyterian system,

lest presbyters should prove as tyrannical as bishops. Of this party, the leading members were Hyde, a politician who surveyed State affairs with the eyes of a lawyer, and the amiable Lord Falkland, a scholar and an enthusiast for religious toleration. On the other hand, there was a party which believed that the abolition of episcopacy was the only possible remedy for ecclesiastical tyranny. If Charles had openly supported the first party, it might, perhaps, have been in a majority ; but as he did nothing of the sort, an impression gained ground that if bishops were not entirely abolished, they would sooner or later be restored by the king to their full authority, in spite of any limitations which Parliament might put upon them. Moreover, the lords, by throwing out a bill for removing the bishops from their House, exasperated even those members who were still hesitating. A majority in the Commons supported a bill, known as the Root and Branch Bill, for the abolition of episcopacy and for the transference of their jurisdiction to committees of laymen in each diocese. Though this bill was not passed, its existence was sure to intensify the dislike of the king to those who had brought it in.

3. **Irish Parties. 1641.**—Before the king returned from Scotland, news arrived from Ireland which increased the difficulty of maintaining a good understanding with Charles. Besides the English officials, there were two parties in Ireland discontented with Strafford's rule. Of these one was that of the Catholic lords, mostly of English extraction, who wanted toleration for their religion and a large part in the management of the country. The other was that of the native Celts, who were anxious to regain the lands of which they had been robbed and to live again under their old customs. Both parties were terrified at the danger of increased persecution by the Puritan Parliament at Westminster, especially as the government at Dublin was in the hands of two lords justices, of whom the more active, Sir William Parsons, advocated repressive measures against the Catholics, and the introduction of fresh colonists from England to oust the Irish more completely from the land. In the spring of **1641** the Catholic lords had emissaries at Charles's court offering to send an army to his help in England, if he would allow them to seize Dublin and to overthrow the Government carried on there in his name.

4. **The Irish Insurrection. 1641.**—Nothing was settled when Charles left England, and in October the native Irish, impatient of delay, attempted to seize Dublin for themselves. The plot was, however, detected, and they turned savagely on the English and

Scottish colony in Ulster. Murders, and atrocities worse than ordinary murder, were committed in the North of Ireland. At Portadown the victims were driven into a river and drowned. Women were stripped naked and turned into the wintry air to die of cold and starvation, and children were slaughtered as ruthlessly as full-grown men. The lowest estimate of the destruction which reached England raised the number of victims to 30,000, and, though this was doubtless an immensely exaggerated reckoning, the actual number of victims must have reached to some thousands. In England a bitter cry for vengeance went up, and with that cry was mingled distrust of the king. It was felt to be necessary to send an army into Ireland, and, if the army was to go under the king's orders, there was nothing to prevent him using it—after Ireland had been subdued—against the English Parliament.

5. **The Grand Remonstrance. 1641.**—The perception of this danger led the Commons to draw up a statement of their case, known as the Grand Remonstrance. They began with a long indictment of all Charles's errors from the beginning of his reign, and, though the statements were undoubtedly exaggerated, they were adopted by the whole House. When, however, it came to the proposal of remedies, there was a great division amongst the members. The party led by Pym and Hampden, by which the Remonstrance had been drawn up, asked for the appointment of ministers responsible to Parliament, and for the reference of Church matters to an Assembly of divines nominated by Parliament. The party led by Hyde and Falkland saw that the granting of these demands would be tantamount to the erection of the sovereignty of Parliament in Church and State ; and, as they feared that this in turn would lead to the establishment of Presbyterian despotism, they preferred to imagine that it was still possible to make Charles a constitutional sovereign. On November 23 there was a stormy debate, and the division was not taken till after midnight. A small majority of eleven declared against the king. The majority then proposed to print the Remonstrance for the purpose of circulating it among the people. The minority protested, and, as a protest was unprecedented in the House of Commons, a wild uproar ensued. Members snatched at their swords, and it needed all Hampden's persuasive pleadings to quiet the tumult.

6. **The King's Return. 1641.**—Charles had at last got a party on his side. When, on November 25, he returned to London, he announced that he intended to govern according to the laws, and

would maintain the 'Protestant religion as it had been established in the times of Elizabeth and his father.' He was at once greeted with enthusiasm in the streets, and felt himself strong enough to refuse to comply with the request of the Remonstrance. If only he could have kept quiet, he would probably, before long, have had a majority, even in the House of Commons, on his side. It was, however, difficult for Charles to be patient. He was kept short of money by the Commons, and he had not the art of conciliating opponents. On December 23 he appointed Lunsford, a debauched ruffian, Lieutenant of the Tower, and the opponents of the Court naturally saw in this unwarrantable proceeding a determination to use force against themselves. On December 26 they obtained Lunsford's dismissal, but on the following day they heard that the rebellion in Ireland was spreading, and the increased necessity of providing an army for Ireland impressed on them once more the danger of placing under the orders of the king forces which he might use against themselves.

7. The Impeachment of the Bishops. 1641.—In order to make sure that the House of Lords would be on their side in the time of danger which was approaching, the Commons and their supporters called out for the exclusion of the bishops and the Roman Catholic peers from their seats in Parliament. A mob gathered at Westminster, shouting, No bishops! No Popish lords! The king gathered a number of disbanded officers at Whitehall for his protection, and these officers sallied forth beating and chasing the mob Another day Williams, Archbishop of York, having been hustled by the crowd, he and eleven other bishops sent to the Lords a protest that anything done by the House of Lords in their absence would be null and void. The Peers, who had hitherto supported the king, were offended, and, for a time, made common cause with the other House against him ; whilst the Commons impeached as traitors the twelve bishops who had signed the protest, wanting, not to punish them, but merely to get rid of their votes.

8. The Impeachment of the Five Members. 1642.—Charles, on his part, was exasperated, and fancied that he could strike a blow which his opponents would be unable to parry. He knew that the most active of the leaders of the opposition, Lord Kimbolton in the House of Lords, and Pym, Hampden, Hazlerigg, Holles, and Strode in the Commons, had negotiated with the Scots before they invaded England in 1640, and he believed that they had actually invited them to enter the kingdom in arms. If this was true, they had legally been guilty of treason, and on January 3,

1642, Charles ordered the Attorney-General to impeach them as traitors. Doubts were afterwards raised whether the king had a right to impeach, but Charles does not seem to have doubted at the time that he was acting according to law.

9. **The Attempt on the Five Members. 1642.**—As the Commons showed signs of an intention to shelter these five members from arrest, Charles resolved to seize them himself. On the 4th of January, followed by about 500 armed men, he betook himself to the House of Commons. Leaving his followers outside, he told the House that he had come to arrest five traitors. As they had already left the House and were on their way to the city, he looked round for them in vain, and asked Lenthall, the Speaker, where they were. " May it please your Majesty," answered Lenthall, kneeling before him, " I have neither eyes to see nor tongue to speak in this place, but as this House is pleased to direct me." Charles eagerly looked round for his enemies. " The birds are flown," he exclaimed, when he failed to descry them. He had missed his prey, and, as he moved away, shouts of " Privilege ! privilege ! " were raised from the benches on either side.

10. **The Commons in the City. 1642.**—The Commons, believing that the king wanted, not to try a legal question, but to intimidate the House by the removal of its leaders, took refuge in the City. The City, which had welcomed Charles in November, when it was thought that he was come to maintain order according to law, now declared for the Commons. On January 10 Lord Kimbolton and the five members were brought back in triumph to Westminster by the citizens. Charles had already left Whitehall, never to return till the day on which he was brought back to be tried for his life.

11. **The Struggle for the Militia. 1642.**—There was little doubt that if Charles could find enough support, the questions at issue would have to be decided by arms. To gain time, he consented to a Bill excluding the bishops from their seats in the House of Lords, and he then sent the queen abroad to pawn or sell the Crown jewels and to buy arms and gunpowder with the money. He turned his own course to the north. A struggle arose between him and the Houses as to the command of the militia. There was no standing army in England, but the men of military age were mustered every year in each county, the fittest of them being selected to be drilled for a short time, at the expiration of which they were sent home to pursue their ordinary avocations. These drilled men were liable to be called out to defend their

county against riots or invasion, and when they were together were formed into regiments called trained bands. All the trained bands in the country were spoken of as the militia. The Houses asked Charles to place the militia under officers of their choosing. " Not for an hour," replied Charles ; " it is a thing with which I would not trust my wife and children." The feeling on both sides grew more bitter ; Charles, after taking up his quarters at York, rode to Hull, where there was a magazine of arms of which he wished to possess himself. Sir John Hotham, the Parliamentary commander, shut the gates in his face. Both Charles and the Parliament began to gather troops. The Parliament appointed the Earl of Essex, the son of Elizabeth's favourite, a steady, honourable man, without a spark of genius, as their general. On August 22, **1642**, Charles set up his standard at Nottingham as a sign of war.

12. **Edgehill and Turnham Green. 1642.**—The richest part of England—the south-east—took, on the whole, the side of the Parliament ; the poorer and more rugged north-west took, on the whole, the side of the king. The greater part of the gentry were cavaliers or partisans of the king ; the greater part of the middle class in the towns were partisans of the Parliament, often called Roundheads in derision, because some of the Puritans cropped their hair short. After a successful skirmish at Powick Bridge Charles pushed on towards London, hoping to end the war at a blow. On October 23 the first battle was fought at Edgehill. The king's nephew, Prince Rupert, son of Elizabeth and the Elector Palatine, commanded his cavalry. With a vigorous charge he drove before him the Parliamentary horse in headlong flight ; but he did not pull up in time, and when he returned from the pursuit he found that the royalist infantry had been severely handled, and that it was too late to complete the victory which he had hoped to win. The fruits of victory, however, fell to the king. The cautious Essex drew back and Charles pushed on for London, reaching Brentford on November 12. That he did not enter London as a conqueror was owing to the resistance of the London trained bands, the citizen-soldiery of the capital. On the 13th they barred Charles's way at Turnham Green. The king hesitated to attack, and drew back to Oxford. He was never to have such another chance again.

13. **The King's Plan of Campaign. 1643.**— Charles's hopes of succeeding better in **1643** were based on a plan for overwhelming London with superior force. He made Oxford the headquarters of his own army, and he had a second army under Sir Ralph

II.   N N

Hopton in Cornwall, and a third army under the Earl of Newcastle in Yorkshire. His scheme was, that whilst he himself attacked London in front, Hopton should advance through the southern counties into Kent, and Newcastle through the eastern counties into Essex. Hopton and Newcastle would then be able to seize the banks on either side of the Thames below London, and thus to interrupt the commerce of the city, without which it would be impossible for it to hold out long.

14. **Royalist Successes. 1643.**—The weak point in Charles's plan was that his three armies were far apart, and that the Earl of Essex, now stationed in London, might fall upon his main army before Newcastle and Hopton could come to its aid. Towards the end of April, Essex besieged and took Reading, but his troops melted away from disease, and he did not advance against Oxford till June, when his cautious leadership was not likely to effect anything decisive. In the meanwhile the king's party was gaining the upper hand elsewhere. On May 16 Hopton completely defeated the Parliamentarians at Stratton in Cornwall, and was then ready to march eastwards. On June 18 Hampden received a mortal wound in a skirmish at Chalgrove Field. On July 5 Hopton got the better of one of the most energetic of the Parliamentary generals, Sir William Waller, on Lansdown, near Bath, and on July 13 his army thoroughly overthrew the same commander at Roundway Down, near Devizes. On July 26 Bristol was stormed by Rupert. Hopton now hoped to be able to push on towards Kent without difficulty. In the north, too, the king's cause was prospering. On June 30, Newcastle defeated the Parliamentarians, Lord Fairfax and his son, Sir Thomas Fairfax, at Adwalton Moor, close to Bradford. He, too, hoped to be able to push on southwards. It seemed as if the king's plan would be carried out before the end of the summer, and that London would be starved into surrender.

15. **The Siege of Gloucester. 1643.**—Charles, however, failed to accomplish his design, mainly because the armies of Hopton and Newcastle were formed for the most part of recruits, levied respectively in the west and in the north of England, who cared more for the safety of their own property and families than for the king's cause. In the west, Plymouth, and in the north, Hull, were still garrisoned by the Parliament. Hopton's men were, therefore, unwilling to go far from their homes in Cornwall as long as their fields were liable to be ravaged by the garrison of Plymouth, and in the same way, Newcastle's men would not go far from Yorkshire as long as their fields were liable to be ravaged by the

garrison of Hull. The Welshmen, also, who served in the king's own army found their homes endangered by a Parliamentary garrison at Gloucester, and were equally unwilling to push forward. Charles had, therefore, to take Plymouth, Hull, and Gloucester, if he could, before he could attack London. In August he laid siege in person to Gloucester. The London citizens at once perceived that, if Gloucester fell, their own safety would be in peril, and amidst the greatest enthusiasm the London trained bands marched out to its relief. On September 5 the king raised the siege on their approach.

16. **The First Battle of Newbury. 1643.**—Charles did not, however, give up the game. Hurrying to Newbury, and reaching it before Essex could arrive there on his way back to London, he blocked the way of the Parliamentary army. Essex, whose provisions were running short, must force a passage or surrender. On September 20 a furious battle was fought outside Newbury, but when the evening came, though Essex had gained ground, the royal army still lay across the London road. It had, however, suffered heavy losses, and its ammunition being almost exhausted, Charles marched away in the night, leaving the way open for Essex to continue his retreat to London. In this battle Falkland was slain. He had sided with the king, not because he shared the passions of the more violent Royalists, but because he feared the intolerance of the Puritans. Charles's determination to conquer or perish rather than to admit of a compromise had saddened his mind, and he went about murmuring, 'Peace! peace!' He was weary of the times, he said, on the morning of the battle, but he would 'be out of it ere night.' He threw himself into the thick of the fight and soon found the death which he sought.

17. **The Eastern Association. 1643.**—Whilst in the south the resistance of Gloucester had weakened the king's power of attack, a formidable barrier was being raised against Newcastle's advance in the east. Early in the war, certain counties in different parts of the country had associated themselves together for mutual defence, and of these combinations the strongest was the Eastern Association, comprising the counties of Norfolk, Suffolk, Essex, Cambridge and Hertford. These five counties raised forces in common and paid them out of a common purse.

18. **Oliver Cromwell. 1642—1643.**—The strength which the Eastern Association soon developed was owing to its placing itself under the leadership of Oliver Cromwell, a member of Parliament, who had taken arms when the civil war began, and who soon distinguished himself by his practical sagacity. "Your

troops," he said to Hampden after the flight of the Parliamentary cavalry at Edgehill, " are, most of them, old decayed serving men and tapsters, and such kind of fellows, and their troops are gentlemen's sons, younger sons, and persons of quality ; do you think that the spirits of such base and mean fellows will ever be able to encounter gentlemen that have honour and courage and resolution in them ? You must get men of a spirit, and take it not ill what I say—I know you will not—of a spirit that is likely to go on as far as gentlemen will go ; or else you will be beaten still." It was this idea which Cromwell, having been appointed a colonel, put in execution in the Eastern Association. He took for his soldiers sternly Puritan men, who had their hearts in the cause ; but he was not content with religious zeal alone. Every one who served under him must undergo the severest discipline. After a few months he had a cavalry regiment under his orders so fiery and at the same time so well under restraint that no body of horse on either side could compare with it.

19. **The Assembly of Divines. 1643.**—Whilst the armies were fighting with varying success, Pym, with undaunted courage, was holding the House of Commons to its task of resistance. After the Royalist successes in June and July, the great peril of the Parliamentary cause made him resolve to ask the Scots for help. The Scots, thinking that if Charles overthrew the English Parliament he would next fall upon them, were ready to send an army to fight against the king, but only on the condition that the Church of England should become Presbyterian like their own. Already some steps had been taken in this direction, and on July 1 a Puritan Assembly of divines met at Westminster to propose ecclesiastical alterations, which were to be submitted to Parliament for its approval.

20. **The Solemn League and Covenant. 1643.**—In August, commissioners from the English Parliament, of whom the principal was Sir Henry Vane, arrived in Edinburgh to negotiate for an alliance. The result was a treaty between the two nations, styled the Solemn League and Covenant—usually known in England simply as the Covenant, but altogether different from the National Covenant, signed by the Scots only in 1638 (see p. 525). The Scots wished the English to bind themselves to ' the reformation of religion in the Church of England according to the example of the best reformed churches ' ; in other words, according to the Presbyterian system. Vane, however, who was eager for religious liberty, insisted on slipping in the words, ' and according to the Word of God.' The Scots could not possibly refuse to accept

the addition, though, by so doing, they left it free to every Englishman to assert that any part of the Presbyterian system which he disliked was not 'according to the Word of God.' The Covenant, thus amended, was carried to England, and on September 25, five days after the battle of Newbury, was sworn to by the members of the two Houses, and was soon afterwards ordered to be sworn to by every Englishman. Money was then sent to Scotland, and a Scottish army prepared to enter England before the opening of the next campaign.

21. **The Irish War. 1641—1643.**—Whilst Parliament looked for help to Scotland, Charles looked to Ireland. The insurrection in the north of Ireland in October, **1641** (see p. 533) had been the affair of the Celtic natives ; but in December they were joined by the Catholic lords and gentry of Norman or English descent. For the first time in Ireland there was a contest between Catholic and Protestant, instead of a contest between Celts on one side, and those who were not Celts on the other. The allies were not likely to be very harmonious, as the Celts wished to return to their old tribal institutions, and the Catholic lords wished to be predominant in Parliament in agreement with the king. For the present, however, they were united by the fear that the Puritan Parliament in England and the Puritan Government in Dublin (see p. 533) would attempt to destroy them and their religion together. The outbreak of the Civil War in England, in **1642**, made it impossible for either king or Parliament to send sufficient troops to overpower them. In May they had chosen a Supreme Council to govern revolted Ireland, and in October a General Assembly of the Confederate Catholics, as they styled themselves, was held at Kilkenny. The Assembly petitioned Charles for the redress of grievances, and in January, **1643**, Charles opened negotiations with them, hoping to obtain an Irish army with which he might carry on war in England. In March they offered him 10,000 men if he would consent to allow a Parliament mainly composed of Catholics to meet at Dublin and to propose bills for his approval. Charles, who liked neither to make this concession nor to relinquish the hope of Irish aid, directed a cessation of arms in Ireland, in the hope that an agreement of some kind might ultimately be come to. In accordance with this cessation, which was signed on September 15, the coast-line from Belfast to Dublin, and a patch of land round Cork, was in the possession of the English forces, whilst a body of Scots, under Monro, held Carrickfergus, but all the rest of Ireland was in the hands of the Confederates.

22. **Winceby and Arundel. 1643—1644.**—As yet Charles had to depend on his English forces alone. In the beginning of September, Newcastle, lately created a Marquis, laid siege to Hull. If Hull fell, he would be able to sweep down on the Eastern Association. The Earl of Manchester- –known as Lord Kimbolton at the time of the attempt on the five members—had been appointed general of the army of that Association, with Cromwell as his lieutenant-general. On October 11 Cromwell defeated a body of Royalist horse at Winceby. On the 12th, Newcastle raised the siege of Hull. All danger of Newcastle's marching southwards was thus brought to an end. In the South, Hopton succeeded in reaching Sussex, and, in December, took Arundel Castle; but the place was retaken by Sir William Waller on January 6, **1644**. Here, too, the Royalist attack received a check, and there was no longer any likelihood that the king's forces would be able to starve out London by establishing themselves on the banks of the Thames.

23. **The Committee of Both Kingdoms. 1644.**—Pym, whose statesmanship had brought about the alliance with the Scots, died on December 8, **1643**. On January 19 the Scots crossed the Tweed again under the command of Alexander Leslie (see p. 526), who had been created Earl of Leven when Charles visited Edinburgh in **1641**. On the 25th, Sir Thomas Fairfax defeated, at Nantwich, a force of English soldiers who had been freed from service in Ireland by the cessation of arms, and had been sent by Ormond, who had recently been named by Charles Lord Lieutenant of Ireland, to support the royalist cause in England. Pym's death, and the necessity of carrying on joint operations with the Scots, called for the appointment of some definite authority at Westminster, and, on February 16, a Committee of Both Kingdoms, composed of members of one or other of the two Houses, and also of Scottish Commissioners sent to England by the Parliament of Scotland, was named to control the operations of the armies of the two nations.

24. **The Campaign of Marston Moor. 1644.**—The spring campaign opened successfully for Parliament. In March, indeed, Rupert relieved Newark, which was hardly pressed by a Parliamentary force; but in April Waller defeated Hopton at Cheriton, near Alresford, whilst in the North, Sir Thomas Fairfax, together with his father, Lord Fairfax, seized upon Selby, and joined the Scots in besieging York, into which Newcastle had been driven. In May, Manchester stormed Lincoln, and he too joined the forces before York. At the king's headquarters there was deep alarm.

Essex and Waller were approaching to attack Oxford, but Charles slipping out of the city before it was surrounded despatched Rupert to the relief of York. At Rupert's approach the besiegers retreated. On July 2 Rupert and Newcastle fought a desperate battle on Marston Moor, though they were decidedly outnumbered by their opponents. The whole of the right wing of the Parliamentarians, and part of the centre, fled before the Royalist attack ; but on their left, Cromwell restored the fight, and drove Rupert in flight before him. Cromwell did not, however, as Rupert had done at Edgehill, waste his energies in the pursuit of the fugitives. Promptly drawing up, he faced round, and hurled his squadrons upon the hitherto victorious Royalists in the other parts of the field. The result was decisive. " It had all the evidence," wrote Cromwell, " of an absolute victory, obtained by the Lord's blessing upon the godly party principally. We never charged but we routed the enemy. God made them as stubble to our swords." All the north of England, except a few fortresses, fell into the hands of Parliament and the Scots.

25. **Presbyterians and Independents. 1644.**—Cromwell spoke of Marston Moor as a victory of the 'godly party.' The Westminster Assembly of Divines had declared strongly in favour of Presbyterianism, but there were a few of its members—only five at first, known as the five Dissenting Brethren—who stood up for the principles of the Separatists (see p. 470) wishing to see each congregation independent of any general ecclesiastical organisation. From holding these opinions they were beginning to be known as Independents. These men now attracted to themselves a considerable number of the stronger-minded Puritans, such as Cromwell and Vane, of whom many, though they had no special attachment to the teaching of the Independent divines, upheld the idea of toleration, whilst others gave their adherence to one or other of the numerous sects which had recently sprung into existence. Cromwell, especially, was drawn in the direction of toleration by his practical experience as a soldier. It was intolerable to him to be forbidden to promote a good officer on the ground that he was not a Presbyterian. On one occasion he was asked to discard a certain officer because he was an Anabaptist. " Admit he be," he had replied ; " shall that render him incapable to serve the public ? Take heed of being too sharp, or too easily sharpened by others, against those to whom you can object little but that they square not with you in every opinion concerning matters of religion." He had accordingly filled his own regiments with men of every variety of Puritan opinion, choosing for promotion the best soldier, and not

the adherent of any special Church system.   These he styled ' the godly party,' and it was by the soldiers of ' the godly party,' so understood, that Marston Moor had been won.

26. **Essex's Surrender at Lostwithiel.   1644.**—Essex was the hope of the Presbyterians who despised the sects and hated toleration.   Being jealous of Waller, he left him to take Oxford alone, if he could, and marched off to the West, to accomplish what he imagined to be the easier task of wresting the western counties from the king.   Charles turned upon Waller, and fought an indecisive action with him at Cropredy Bridge, after which Waller's army, being composed of local levies with no heart for permanent soldiering, melted away.   Charles then marched in pursuit of Essex, and surrounded him at Lostwithiel, in Cornwall. Essex's provisions fell short ; and on September 2, though his horse cut their way out, and he himself escaped in a boat, the whole of his infantry capitulated.

27. **The Second Battle of Newbury.   1644.**—London was thus laid bare, and Parliament hastily summoned Manchester and the army of the Eastern Association to its aid.   Manchester, being good-natured and constitutionally indolent, longed for some compromise with Charles which might bring about peace.   Cromwell, on the other hand, perceived that no compromise was possible with Charles as long as he was at the head of an army in the field. A second battle of Newbury was fought, on October 27, with doubtful results : Manchester showed little energy, and the king was allowed to escape in the night.   Cromwell, to whom his sluggishness seemed nothing less than treason to the cause, attacked Manchester in Parliament, not from personal ill-will, but from a desire to remove an inefficient general from his command in the army.   Two parties were thus arrayed against one another : on the one side the Presbyterians, who wanted to suppress the sects and, if possible, to make peace ; and on the other side the Independents, who wanted toleration, and to carry on the war efficiently till a decisive victory had been gained.

CHAPTER XXXV

THE NEW MODEL ARMY. 1644—1649

LEADING DATES

Reign of Charles I., 1625—1649

Battle of Naseby . . . . . . June 14, 1645
Glamorgan's Treaty . . . . . . Aug. 25, 1645
Charles in the hands of the Scots . . . . May 5, 1646
Charles surrendered by the Scots . . . . Jan. 30, 1647
Charles carried off from Holmby . . . . June 5, 1647
The Army in Military Possession of London . Aug. 7, 1647
Charles's Flight from Hampton Court . . . Nov. 11, 1647
The Second Civil War . . . . . April to Aug., 1648
Pride's Purge . . . . Dec. 6, 1648
Execution of Charles . . . . . . Jan. 30, 1649

I. **The Self-denying Ordinance and the New Model. 1645.**—
Cromwell dropped his attack on Manchester as soon as he found
that he could attain his end in another way. A proposal was made
for the passing of a Self-denying Ordinance,[1] which was to exclude
all members of either House from commands in the army. The
Lords, knowing that members of their House would be chiefly affected
by it, threw it out, and the Commons then proceeded to form a
New Model Army—that is to say, an army newly organised, its
officers and soldiers being chosen solely with a view to military
efficiency. Its general was to be Sir Thomas Fairfax, whilst the
lieutenant-general was not named; but there can be little doubt
that the post was intended for Cromwell. After the Lords had
agreed to the New Model, they accepted the Self-denying Ordinance
in an altered form, as, though all the existing officers were directed
to resign their posts, nothing was said against their re-appointment.
Essex, Manchester, and Waller resigned, but when the time came
for Cromwell to follow their example, he and two or three others
were appointed to commands in the new army. Cromwell became
Lieutenant-General, with the command of the cavalry. The New
Model was composed partly of pressed men, and was by no means,

[1] An ordinance was at this time in all respects similar to an Act of Parliament, except that it did not receive the Royal assent. In the middle ages an ordinance was exactly the reverse, being issued by the King without Parliamentary approval.

as has been often said, of a sternly religious character throughout; but a large number of decided Puritans had been drafted into it, especially from the army of the Eastern Association; and the majority of the officers were Independents, some of them of a strongly Sectarian type. The New Model Army had the advantage of receiving regular pay, which had not been the case before; so that the soldiers, whether Puritans or not, were now likely to stick to their colours.

2. **Milton's 'Areopagitica.'** 1644.—By Cromwell, who in consequence of his tolerance was the idol of the Sectarians in the army, religious liberty had first been valued because it gave him the service of men of all kinds of opinions. On November 24, 1644, Milton, some of whose books had been condemned by the licensers of the press appointed by Parliament, issued *Areopagitica*, in which he advocated the liberty of the press on the ground that excellence can only be reached by those who have free choice between good and evil. "He that can apprehend," he wrote, "and consider vice with all her baits and seeming pleasures, and yet abstain—he is the true warfaring Christian. I cannot praise a fugitive and cloistered virtue, unexercised and unbreathed, that never sallies out and seeks her adversary, but slinks out of the race, when that immortal garland is to be run for, not without dust and heat." Liberty was good for religion as much as it was for literature. "These are the men," he continued, "cried out against for schismatics and sectaries, as if, while the temple of the Lord was building, there should be a sort of irrational men who could not consider there must be many schisms and many dissections made in the quarry and in the timber ere the house of God can be built." The perfection of the building consisted "in this—that out of many moderate varieties and brotherly dissimilitudes that are not vastly disproportional, arises the goodly and the graceful symmetry that commends the whole pile and structure."

3. **The Execution of Laud.** 1645.—In Parliament, at least, there was one direction in which neither Presbyterian nor Independent was inclined to be tolerant. They had all suffered under Laud, and Laud's impeachment was allowed to go on. The House of Lords pronounced sentence against him, and on January 10, 1645, he was beheaded. The Presbyterians had the majority in the House of Commons, and they were busy in enforcing their system, as far as Parliamentary resolutions would go. The Independents had to wait for better times.

4. **Montrose and Argyle.** 1644.—For the present, however,

the two parties could not afford to quarrel, as a powerful diversion in the king's favour was now threatening them from Scotland. The Marquis of Montrose, who, in the Bishops' Wars, had taken part with the Covenanters, had grown weary of the interference of the Scottish Presbyterian clergy with politics, and still more weary of the supremacy in Scotland of the Marquis of Argyle, who had all the organisation of the Presbyterian Church at his disposal. Montrose saw that, though Argyle was too strong for him in the Lowlands, it was possible to assail him with effect in the Highlands, where he had made many enemies. In the Lowlands Argyle was regarded as a Scottish nobleman. In the Highlands he was the chief of the clan of the Campbells, which had often unscrupulously extended its borders at the expense of its neighbours, especially at the expense of the various clans of the Macdonalds. Montrose therefore hoped that if he threw himself into the Highlands, he might make use of the enmity of these clans against the Campbells to crush Argyle and to exalt the king.

5. **Montrose in the Highlands. 1644—1645.**—In 1644, shortly after the battle of Marston Moor, Montrose made his way to the Highlands with only two followers. He was the first to discover the capacity of the Highlanders for war. With their help, and with the help of a trained Irish contingent, mostly composed of the descendants of Highlanders who had emigrated to Ireland, he beat the Scottish forces at Tippermuir and Aberdeen, and then, crossing the mountains, amidst the snows of winter, harried the lands of the Campbells. On February 2, 1645, he defeated Argyle's clansmen at Inverlochy, whilst Argyle himself—who was no warrior—watched their destruction from a boat. Wherever Montrose went the heavy Lowland troops toiled after him in vain. On May 9 he overthrew another army under Baillie at Auldearn. Leven's Scottish army in Yorkshire had enough to do to bar the way against Montrose in case of his issuing from the mountains and attempting to join forces with Charles in England. With any other troops Montrose would probably have made the attempt already ; but his Highlanders were accustomed to return home to deposit their booty in their own glens as soon as a battle had been won, and, therefore, victorious as he had been, he was unable to leave the Highlands.

6. **The New Model Army in the Field. 1645.**—The New Model army started on its career in April. Cromwell, with his highly-trained horse, swept round Oxford, cutting off Charles's supplies ; whilst Fairfax was sent by the Committee of Both Kingdoms (see p. 542)

to the relief of Taunton, which had been gallantly holding out under Robert Blake. A detachment of Fairfax's force sufficed to set Taunton free. His main force was stupidly sent by the Committee to besiege Oxford, though the king was marching northwards, and might fall upon Leven's Scots as soon as he reached them. On May 31, however, Charles turned sharply round, and stormed Leicester. The popular outcry in London compelled the Committee to allow their commander-in-chief to act on his own discretion ; and Fairfax, abandoning the siege of Oxford, marched straight in pursuit of the Royal army.

7. **The Battle of Naseby. 1645.**—On June 14 Fairfax overtook the king at Naseby. In the battle which followed, the Parliamentary army was much superior in numbers, but it was largely composed of raw recruits (see p. 545), and its left wing of cavalry— under Cromwell's son-in-law, Ireton—was routed by the king's right, under Rupert. As he had done at Edgehill, Rupert galloped hard in pursuit, without looking back. The Parliamentary infantry in the centre was by this time pressed hard, but Cromwell, on the right, at the head of a large body of cavalry, scattered the enemy's horse before him. Then, as at Marston Moor, he halted to see how the battle went elsewhere. Sending a detachment to pursue the defeated Royalists, he hurled the rest of his horse on the king's foot, who were slowly gaining ground in the centre. In those days, when half of every body of infantry fought with pikes, and the other half with inefficient muskets, it was seldom that foot-soldiers could withstand a cavalry charge in the open, and the whole of Charles's infantry, after a short resistance, surrendered on the spot. Rupert returned only in time to see that defeat was certain. The king, with what horse he could gather round him, made off as fast as he could. The stake played for at Naseby was the crown of England, and Charles had lost it.

8. **The Results of Naseby. 1645.**—Disastrous as Charles's defeat had been, he contrived to struggle on for some months. The worst thing that befel him after the battle was the seizure of his cabinet containing his correspondence, which revealed his constant intrigues to bring alien armies—French, Lorrainers, and Irish —into England. It was, therefore, in a more determined spirit than ever that Parliament carried on the war. After retaking Leicester, on June 18, Fairfax marched on to the West, where the king's eldest son, Charles, Prince of Wales, had been since the summer of **1644**, and where debauched and reckless Goring was at the head of a Royalist army. On July 10 Fairfax routed him at Langport, and on

July 23 took Bridgwater. Then, leaving forces to coop up Goring's remaining troops, Fairfax turned eastward, took Sherborne on August 2, whilst the Scots, who after Naseby had marched southwards, were besieging Hereford. On September 1, however, the king relieved Hereford, and fancied he might still retrieve his fortunes. On September 10, he received a severe blow. Fairfax stormed the outer defences of Bristol, and Rupert, who commanded the garrison, at once capitulated. There can be little doubt that he had no other choice ; but Charles would hear no excuse, and dismissed him from his service.

9. **Charles's Wanderings. 1645.**—Charles's hopes were always springing up anew, and now that Rupert had failed him, he looked to Montrose for deliverance. Montrose, on July 4, had won another victory at Alford, and, on August 14, a still more crushing victory at Kilsyth, after which he had entered Glasgow, and received the submission of the Lowlands. Charles marched northward to meet him, but on the way was met and defeated by the Parliamentary general, Poyntz, on Rowton Heath. Almost immediately afterwards he heard the disastrous news that David Leslie, an able officer who had won renown in the German wars, and had fought well at Marston Moor, had been despatched from the Scottish army in England, had fallen upon Montrose at Philiphaugh, at a time when he had but a scanty following with him, and had utterly defeated him. After this Cromwell reduced the South, capturing Winchester and Basing House, whilst Fairfax betook himself to the siege of Exeter. In October, Charles, misled by a rumour that Montrose had recovered himself, made one more attempt to join him ; but he was headed by the enemy, and compelled to retreat to Oxford, where, with all his followers ardently pleading for peace, he still maintained that his conscience would not allow him to accept any terms from rebels, or to surrender the Church of England into their hands.

10. **Glamorgan in Ireland. 1645—1646.**—Not one of Charles's intrigues with foreign powers did him so much harm as his continued efforts to bring over an Irish army to fight his battles in England. In 1645 he despatched the Roman Catholic Earl of Glamorgan to Ireland, giving him almost unlimited powers to raise money and men, and to make treaties with this object, but instructing him to follow the advice of Ormond. When Glamorgan arrived in Ireland, in August, he found that the Confederate Catholics were resolved to demand that all the churches in Ireland, except the few still in the hands of the English, should be

given permanently to the Catholics, and that permission should be granted to their clergy to exercise jurisdiction in matters spiritual and ecclesiastical. Though Glamorgan knew that Charles had never approved of these concessions, he signed a treaty, on August 25, 1645, in which he granted all that was asked, in consideration of an engagement by the Confederates to place him at the head of 10,000 Irishmen destined for England. Before anything had been done, a Papal Nuncio, Rinuccini, landed in Ireland and required fresh concessions, to which Glamorgan readily assented. On January 16, 1646, however, before Glamorgan's army was ready to start, the treaty which he had made in August became known

A gentleman.   A gentlewoman.

Ordinary civil costume *temp.* Charles I. : from Speed's map of 'The Kingdom of England,' 1646.

at Westminster ; and, though Charles promptly disavowed having authorised its signature, there remained a grave suspicion that he was not as innocent as he pretended to be.

11. **The King's Flight to the Scots. 1646.**—In the beginning of 1646 the Civil War virtually came to an end. On March 14, Charles's army in the West surrendered to Fairfax in Cornwall, and in the same month the last force which held the field for him was overthrown at Stow-on the-Wold. Many fortresses still held out, but, as there was no chance of relief, their capture was only a question of time ; and though the last of them—Harlech Castle— did not surrender till 1647, there was absolutely no doubt what the result would be. Charles, now again at Oxford, had but to choose

to whom he would surrender. He chose to give himself up to the Scots, whose army was at the time besieging Newark. He seems to have calculated that they would replace him on the throne without insisting on very rigorous conditions, thinking that they would rather restore him to power than allow the English army, formidable as it was, to have undisputed authority in England, and possibly to crush the independence of Scotland. The Scots, on the other hand, seem to have thought that, when Charles was once in their power, he must, for his safety's sake, agree to establish Presbyterianism in England, by which means the party which would of necessity lean for support on themselves would have

A citizen.

A citizen's wife.

Ordinary civil costume *temp.* Charles I. : from Speed's map of 'The Kingdom of England, 1646.

the mastery in England. On May 5, **1646**, Charles rode in to the quarters of the Scottish army at Southwell, a few miles from Newark.

12. **Charles at Newcastle. 1646.**—Newark at once surrendered, and Charles was conveyed to Newcastle, where, as he refused to consent to the establishment of Presbyterianism in England, he was practically treated as a prisoner. At the end of **1645** and the beginning of **1646** there had been fresh elections to fill up seats in the House of Commons left vacant by Royalists expelled for taking the king's part ; but, though many Independent officers were chosen, there was still a decidedly Presbyterian majority. On July 14 propositions for peace were delivered to Charles on

behalf of Parliament and the Scots. He was to surrender his power over the militia for twenty years, to take the Covenant, and to support Presbyterianism in the Church. Charles, in his correspondence with his wife, showed himself more ready to abandon the militia than to abandon episcopacy; whilst she, being a Roman Catholic, and not caring for bishops whom she counted as heretics, advised him at all hazards to cling to the command of the militia. Charles hoped everything from mere procrastination. "All my endeavours," he wrote to the queen, "must be the delaying of my answer till there be considerable parties visibly formed"—in other words, till Presbyterians and Independents were ready to

A countryman.　　　　　　A countrywoman.

Ordinary civil costume *temp.* Charles I. : from Speed's map of ' The Kingdom of England,' 1646.

come to blows, and, therefore, to take him at his own price. In order to hasten that day, he made in October a proposal of his own, in which he promised, in case of his being restored to power, to establish Presbyterianism for three years, during which time the future settlement of the Church might be publicly discussed. He, however, took care to make no provision for the very probable event of the discussion leaving parties as opposed to one another as they had been before the discussion was opened, and it was obvious that, as he had never given the royal assent to any Act for the abolition of episcopacy, the whole episcopal system would legally occupy the field when the three years came to an end. The Presbyterians would thus find themselves checkmated by an unworthy trick.

13. **The Removal of the King to Holmby. 1647.**—The Scots, discontented with the king's refusal to accept their terms, began to open their ears to an offer by the English Parliament to pay them the money owing to them for their assistance, on the open understanding that they would leave England, and the tacit understanding that they would leave the king behind them. Once more they implored Charles to support Presbyterianism, assuring him that, if he would, they would fight for him to a man. On his refusal, they accepted the English offer, took their money, and on January 30, **1647**, marched away to their own country, leaving Charles in the hands of Commissioners of the English Parliament, who conveyed him to Holmby House, in Northamptonshire.

14. **Dispute between the Presbyterians and the Army. 1647.**— The leading Presbyterians, of whom the most prominent was Holles (see p. 535), were so anxious to come to terms with the king, that before the end of January they accepted Charles's illusory proposal of a three years' Presbyterianism (see p. 552), offering to allow him to come to London or its neighbourhood in order to carry on negotiations. The fact was, that they were now more afraid of the army than of the king, believing it to be ready to declare not merely for toleration of the sects, but also for a more democratic form of government than suited many of the noblemen and gentlemen who sat on the benches of the Lords and Commons. In March the Commons voted that only a small body of cavalry should be kept up in England, and no infantry at all, except a small force needed to garrison the fortresses, and also that when the infantry regiments were broken up the disbanded soldiers should be asked to volunteer for service in Ireland. Of the cavalry in England Fairfax was to be general, but no officer under him was to hold a higher rank than that of colonel, a rule which would enable Cromwell's opponents in Parliament to oust him from his position in the army. So strong was the feeling in the nation for peace, and for the diminution of the heavy burden of taxation which the maintenance of the army required, that the Presbyterians would probably have gained their object had they acted with reasonable prudence, as a large number of soldiers had no sympathy with the religious enthusiasts in the ranks. There were, however, considerable arrears of pay owing to the men, and had they been paid in ready money, and an ordinance passed indemnifying them for acts done in war-time, most, if not all, would, in all probability, either have gone home or have enlisted for Ireland. Instead of doing this, Parliament only voted a small part of the arrears, and

fiercely denounced the army for daring to prepare a petition
to Fairfax asking for his support in demanding full pay and
indemnity. In a few weeks Parliament and army were angrily
distrustful of one another, and the soldiers, organising themselves,
chose representatives, who were called Agitators [1] or agents, to
consult on things relating to their present position.

15. **Cromwell and the Army. 1647.**—Cromwell's position
during these weeks was a delicate one. He sympathised not only
with the demands of the soldiers for full pay, but also with the
demand of the religious enthusiasts for toleration. Yet he had
a strong sense of the evil certain to ensue from allowing an army
to overthrow the civil institutions of the country,[2] and both as a
member of the House of Commons and as an officer he did his
best to avert so dire a catastrophe. In March he had even proposed to leave England and take service in Germany under the
Elector Palatine, the son of Frederick and Elizabeth (see p. 488).
As this plan fell through, he was sent down, in May, with other
commissioners, to attempt to effect a reconciliation between the
army and the Parliament. In this he nearly succeeded; but a
few days after his return to Westminster Parliament decided to
disband the army at once, without those concessions which, in
consequence of Cromwell's report, it at first seemed prepared to
make. The soldiers, finding that only a small portion of their
arrears was to be paid, refused to disband, and before the end of
May everything was in confusion.

16. **The Abduction of the King. 1647.**—The fact was that
the Presbyterian leaders fancied themselves masters of the situation. Receiving a favourable answer from the king to the proposals made by them in January (see p. 553), they entered into
a negotiation with the French ambassador and the Scottish commissioners to bring about a Scottish invasion of England on the
king's behalf, and this invasion was to be supported by a Presbyterian and Royalist rising in England. In the meanwhile Charles
was to be conveyed away from Holmby to preserve him from the

---

[1] The name 'Adjutator,' often given to these men, is undoubtedly a mere
blunder. The use of the verb 'to agitate' in the sense of 'to act,' and of the
noun 'agitator,' in the sense of an agent, is now obsolete.

[2] Cromwell did not hold that, in fighting against the king, he had himself
been assailing the civil institutions of the country. In his eyes, as in the eyes
of all others on his side, the king was the aggressor, attacking those institutions,
and war against him was therefore defensive, being waged to save the most
important part of them from destruction.

army. This design was betrayed to Cromwell, and, in consequence, he secretly gave instructions to a certain Cornet Joyce to take a body of cavalry to hinder the Scots and Presbyterians from carrying off the king, but only, as it seems, to remove him from Holmby if force was likely to be used on the other side. On June 3, Joyce, with a picked body of horse, appeared at Holmby. On the 4th he received news which led him to think that a Presbyterian body of troops was approaching with the intention of taking possession of the king's person. Late in the evening, therefore, imagining that the danger foreseen as possible in Cromwell's instructions had really arrived, he invited the king to leave Holmby the next morning. When the morning came Charles, stepping out on the lawn, asked Joyce for a sight of the commission which authorised him to give such unexpected orders. "There is my commission," answered Joyce, pointing to his soldiers. There was no resisting such an argument, and Charles was safely conducted to Newmarket.

17. **The Exclusion of the Eleven Members.** **1647.**—Parliament, dissatisfied with this daring act, began to levy troops in London, and reorganised the London trained bands, excluding all Independents from their ranks. The army declared that eleven members of the House of Commons—the leaders of the Presbyterian party—were making arrangements for a new war, and sent in charges against them. The eleven members, finding themselves helpless, asked leave of absence. The City of London was as Presbyterian as Parliament. A mob burst into the House, and, under stress of violence, the Independent members, together with the Speakers of the two Houses, left Westminster and sought protection with the army. The Presbyterians kept their seats, and voted to resist the army by force. The army took advantage of the tumult to appear on the scene as the vindicators of the liberties of Parliament and, marching upon London, passed through the City on August 7, leaving sufficient forces behind to occupy Westminster and the Tower. The eleven Presbyterian members sought refuge on the Continent.

18. **The Heads of the Proposals.** **1647.**—In the meanwhile Cromwell was doing his best to come to an understanding with Charles. A constitutional scheme, to which was given the name of *The Heads of the Proposals*, was drawn up by Ireton and presented in the name of the army to the king. It provided for a constant succession of biennial Parliaments with special powers over the appointment of officials, and it proposed to settle the religious difficulty by giving complete religious liberty to all except

Roman Catholics. Those who chose to do so might submit to the jurisdiction of bishops, and those who chose to do so might submit to the jurisdiction of a presbytery ; but no civil penalties were to be inflicted on those who objected either to Episcopacy or to Presbyterianism or to both.

19. **The King's Flight to the Isle of Wight. 1647.**—No proposals so wise and comprehensive had yet been made, but neither Charles nor the Parliament was inclined to accept them. Many of the Agitators, finding that there was still a Presbyterian majority in Parliament, talked of using force once more and of purging the Houses of all the members who had sat in them whilst the legitimate Speakers were absent. In the meanwhile the king grew more hostile to Cromwell every day, and entered secretly into a fresh negotiation with the Scottish commissioners who formed part of the Committee of both Kingdoms, asking them for the help of a Scottish army. The more advanced Agitators proposed a still more democratic constitution than *The Heads of the Proposals*, under the name of *The Agreement of the People*, and attempted to force it upon their officers by threats of a mutiny. At the same time, they and some of the officers talked of bringing the king to justice for the bloodshed which he had caused. Charles, becoming aware of his danger, fled on November 11 to the Isle of Wight, thinking that it would be easy to escape whenever he wished. He was, however, detained in Carisbrooke Castle, where he was treated very much as a prisoner.

20. **The Scottish Engagement, and the Vote of No Addresses. 1647—1648.**—Cromwell put down the mutiny in the army, but he learnt that the king was intriguing with the Scots, and at last abandoned all hope of settling the kingdom with Charles's help. On December 26, **1647**, Charles entered into an *Engagement* with the Scottish commissioners. On the condition of having toleration for his own worship, according to the Prayer Book, he agreed to establish Presbyterianism in England for three years, and to suppress all heresy. The Scottish army was then to advance into England to secure the king's restoration to power in accordance with the wishes of a free Parliament, to be chosen after the existing one had been dissolved. The English Parliament, indeed, had no knowledge of this engagement, but finding that Charles refused to accept their terms, they replied, on January 17, **1648**, by a Vote of No Addresses, declaring that they would make no more proposals to the king.

21. **The Second Civil War. 1648.**—The majority of English-

men were, on the contrary, ready to take Charles at his word. Men were weary of being controlled by the army, and still more of paying the taxes needed for the support of the army. There were risings in Wales and Kent, and a Scottish army prepared to cross the borders under the Duke of Hamilton. The English army had, however, made up its mind that Charles should not be restored. Fairfax put down the rising in Kent after a sharp fight at Maidstone, and drove some of the fugitives across the Thames into Essex, where being outnumbered they took refuge in Colchester. Fairfax, following them up, laid siege to Colchester, though the Londoners threatened to rise in his rear, and a great part of the fleet deserted to the Prince of Wales, who came from France to take the command. In the meanwhile Cromwell suppressed the insurrection in Wales, and then marched northwards. On August 17, with less than 9,000 men, he fell upon the 24,000 who followed Hamilton, and, after three days' fighting, routed them utterly. On August 28 Colchester surrendered to Fairfax.

22. **Pride's Purge. 1648.**—The army had lost all patience with the king, and it had also lost all patience with Parliament. Whilst Fairfax and Cromwell were fighting, the Houses passed an ordinance for the suppression of heresy, and opened the negotiations with the king which bear the name of the Treaty [1] of Newport. The king only played with the negotiations, trying to spin out the time till he could make his escape, in order that he might, with safety to his own person, obtain help from Ireland or the Continent. The army was tired of such delusions, seeing clearly that there could be no settled government in England as long as Charles could play fast-and-loose with all parties, and it demanded that he should be brought to justice. By military authority he was removed on December 1 from Carisbrooke to the desolate Hurst Castle, where no help could reach him. On December 5 the House of Commons declared for a reconciliation with the king. On the 6th a body of soldiers, under the command of Colonel Pride, forced it to serve the purposes of the army by forcibly expelling all members who took the side of the king. This act of violence is commonly known as Pride's Purge.

23. **The High Court of Justice. 1649.**—On January 1, **1649**, the purged House proposed to appoint a High Court of Justice to try Charles, but the Lords refused to take part in the act. On the 4th the Commons declared that the people were, under God, the source

---

[1] A treaty then meant a negotiation, not, as now, the document which results from a successful negotiation.

View of the west side of the Banqueting House, Whitehall : from an engraving by Terasson, dated 1713. It is probable that Charles came out through the middle window of the Hall itself.

of all just power, and that the House of Commons, being chosen by the people, formed the supreme power in England, having no need of either king or House of Lords.   Never was constitutional pedantry carried further than when this declaration was issued by a mere fragment of a House which, even if all its members had been present, could only claim to have represented the people some years before.   On January 9 a special High Court of Justice was constituted by the mutilated House of Commons alone, for the trial of the king.   On January 19 Charles was brought up to Westminster. Only the sternest opponents of Charles would consent to sit on the Court which tried him.   Of 135 members named, only 67

Execution of King Charles I., January 30, 1649 : from a contemporary broadside.

were present when the trial began.   Fairfax was amongst those appointed, but he absented himself, and when his name was called, his wife cried out, " He is not here, and will never be ; you do wrong to name him."

24. **The King's Trial and Execution. 1649.**—Charles's accusers had on their side the discredit which always comes to those who, using force, try to give it the appearance of legality.   Charles had all the credit of standing up for the law, which, in his earlier life, he had employed to establish absolutism.   He refused to plead before the Court, on the ground that it had no jurisdiction over a king.   His assailants fell back on the merest technicalities.

Instead of charging him with the intrigues to bring foreign armies into England, of which he had been really guilty, they accused him of high treason against the nation, because, forsooth, he had appeared in arms against his subjects in the first Civil War. The Court, as might have been expected, passed sentence against him, and, on January 30, he was beheaded on a scaffold in front of his own palace at Whitehall.

25. **Results of Charles's Execution. 1649.**—With the king's execution all that could be permanently effected by his opponents had been accomplished. When the Long Parliament met, in November **1640**, all Englishmen had combined to bring Charles to submit to Parliamentary control. After the summer of **1641** a considerable part of the nation, coming to the conclusion that Charles was ready to use force rather than to submit, took arms against him to compel him to give way. Towards the end of **1647** a minority of Englishmen, including the army, came to the conclusion that it was necessary to deprive Charles of all real power, if the country was not to be exposed to constantly recurring danger whenever he saw fit to re-assert his claims to the authority which he had lost. In **1648** a yet smaller minority came to the conclusion that security could only be obtained if he were deprived of life. In depriving the king of life all had been done which force could do. The army could guard a scaffold, but it could not reconstruct society. The vast majority of that part of the nation which cared about politics at all disliked being ruled by an army even more than it had formerly disliked being ruled by Charles, and refused its support to the new institutions which, under the patronage of the army, were being erected in the name of the people.

CHAPTER XXXVI

THE COMMONWEALTH AND PROTECTORATE. 1649—1660

LEADING DATES

The Establishment of the Commonwealth 1649
Cromwell in Ireland 1649
Battle of Dunbar . . . . Sept. 3, 1650
Battle of Worcester . . . . Sept. 3, 1651
The Long Parliament dissolved by Cromwell . . April 20, 1653
The so-called Barebones Parliament . . July 4 to Dec. 11, 1653
Establishment of the Protectorate . . . . . Dec. 16, 1653
The First Protectorate Parliament . Sept. 3, 1654, to Jan. 22, 1655
Treaty of Alliance with France . . . . . . Oct. 24, 1655
The Second Protectorate Parliament . Sept. 17, 1656, to Feb. 4, 1658
Death of Oliver Cromwell . . . . Sept. 3, 1658
Richard Cromwell's Protectorate . Sept. 3, 1658, to April 22, 1659
The Long Parliament Restored . . . . May 7 to Oct. 13, 1659
Military Government . . . . . . Oct. 13 to Dec. 26, 1659
The Long Parliament a Second Time } Dec. 26, 1659, to March 16, 1660
   Restored . . . . . . }
The Declaration of Breda . . . . April 4, 1660
Meeting of the Convention Parliament . . . April 14, 1660
Resolution that the Government is by King, Lords, } May 1, 1660
   and Commons . . . . }

1. **Establishment of the Commonwealth. 1649.**—It was not to be expected that the men in Parliament or in the army by whom great hopes of improvement were entertained should discover that they had done all that it was possible for them to do. They believed it to be still in their power to regenerate England. The House of Commons declared England to be a Commonwealth, 'without a king or House of Lords,' and, taking the name of Parliament for itself, appointed forty-one persons to be a Council of State, charged with the executive government, and renewed annually. Most members of the Council of State were also members of Parliament ; and, as the attendance in Parliament seldom exceeded fifty, the Councillors of State (if they agreed together) were able to command a majority in Parliament, and thus to control its decisions. Such an arrangement was a mere burlesque on Parliamentary institutions, and could hardly have existed for a week if it had not been supported by the ever-victorious army. In the army, indeed, it had its opponents, who, under the name of Levellers, called out for a more truly democratic government ;

but they had no man of influence to lead them. Cromwell had too much common sense not to perceive the difficulty of establishing a democracy in a country in which that form of government had but few admirers, and he suppressed the Levellers with a strong hand. In quiet times, Cromwell would doubtless have made some attempt to place the constitution of the Commonwealth on a more satisfactory basis, but for the present it needed to be defended rather than improved.

2. **Parties in Ireland. 1647—1649.**—In Ireland the conjunction formed at the end of **1641** between the Catholic lords and the native Irish broke down in **1647**. Rinuccini, the Papal Nuncio (see p. 550), discovered that Ireland could only be organised to resist English Puritanism under the authority of the Papal clergy, as there was not sufficient union amongst the Irish themselves to admit the existence of lay national institutions. He was unable to carry his idea into effect. Ormond, the king's Lord-lieutenant, who was himself a Protestant, left Ireland, and handed over Dublin to the Parliamentary troops under Michael Jones, rather than see it in the hands of Rinuccini and the Celts. Even the Catholic lords objected to become the servants of a clerical State, and Rinuccini, baffled on every side, was obliged to return to Italy. In September, **1648,** Ormond returned to Ireland, where he soon afterwards entered into a close alliance with the Catholic lords, who were to receive religious toleration, and in return to defend the king. After the king's execution, Charles II. was proclaimed in Ireland. Ormond, having now an army in which Irish Catholics and English Royalist Protestants were combined, hoped to be able to overthrow the Commonwealth both in Ireland and in England.

3. **Cromwell in Ireland. 1649—1650.**—To Cromwell such a situation was intolerable. His Puritan zeal led him to regard with loathing Ormond's league with the Catholics, and he was too thorough an Englishman not to resolve that, if there was to be a struggle, England must conquer Ireland, and not Ireland England. On August 15 he landed at Dublin. On September 11 he stormed Drogheda, where he put 2,000 men to the sword, a slaughter which was in strict accordance with the laws of war of that day, which left garrisons refusing, as that of Drogheda had done, to surrender an indefensible post, when summoned to do so, to the mercy or cruelty of the enemy. Cromwell had a half-suspicion that some farther excuse was needed. "I am persuaded," he wrote, "that this is a righteous judgment of God upon those barbarous wretches who have imbrued their hands in so much innocent blood; and that it

will tend to prevent the effusion of blood for the future—which are the satisfactory grounds to such actions, which otherwise cannot but work remorse and regret." At Wexford, where the garrison continued to defend itself after the walls had been scaled, there was another slaughter. Town after town surrendered. In the spring of 1650 Cromwell left Ireland. The conquest was prosecuted by his successors, Ireton and Ludlow, with savage effectiveness ; and when at last, in 1652, the war came to an end, a great part of three out of the four provinces of Ireland was confiscated for the benefit of the conquering race. The Catholic landowners of Ireland who had borne arms against the Parliament were driven into the wilds of Connaught, to find there what sustenance they could.

4. **Montrose and Charles II. in Scotland. 1650.**—In 1650 Cromwell's services were needed in Scotland. In the spring, Montrose reappeared in the Highlands, but was betrayed, carried to Edinburgh, and executed as a traitor. On June 24 Charles II. landed in Scotland, and, on his engaging to be a. Presbyterian king, found the whole nation ready to support him. Fairfax declined to lead the English army against Charles, on the plea that the Scots had a right to choose their own form of government. Cromwell had no such scruples, knowing that, if Charles were once established in Scotland, the next thing would be that the Scots would try to impose their form of government on England. Cromwell, being appointed General in the room of Fairfax, marched into Scotland, and attempted to take Edinburgh ; but he was out-manœuvred by David Leslie (see p. 549), who was now the Scottish commander, and, to save his men from starvation, had to retreat to Dunbar.

5. **Dunbar and Worcester. 1650—1651.**—Cromwell's position at Dunbar was forlorn enough. The Scots seized the passage by which alone he could retreat to England by land, whilst the mass of their host was posted inaccessibly on the top of a long hill in front of him. If he sailed home, his flight would probably be the signal for a rising of all the Cavaliers and Presbyterians in England. The Scots, however, relieved him of his difficulties. They were weary of waiting, and, on the evening of September 2, they descended the hill. Early on the morning of the 3rd, Cromwell, crying " Let God arise ; let His enemies be scattered," charged into their right wing before the whole army had time to draw up in line of battle, and dashed them into utter ruin. Edinburgh surrendered to him, but there was still a large Scottish army on foot, and, in August 1651, its leaders, taking Charles with them,

pushed on into England, where they hoped to raise an insurrection before Cromwell could overtake them.   On they marched, with Cromwell following hard upon their heels.   Fear kept those who sympathised with Charles from rising, and, at Worcester, on September 3—the anniversary of the battle of Dunbar—Cromwell absolutely destroyed the Scottish army.   Those who were not slain were taken prisoners, and many of the prisoners sent as slaves to Barbadoes.   "The dimensions of this mercy," wrote Cromwell, "are above my thoughts.   It is, for aught I know, a crowning mercy."   He spoke truly.   Never again was he called on to draw

A coach of the middle of the seventeenth century : from an engraving by John Dunstall.

sword in England.   Charles succeeded in making his escape to France, on one occasion concealing himself amidst the thick leafage of an oak, whilst his pursuers rode unwittingly below.

6. **The Navigation Act.   1651.**—Ever since the days of James I. there had existed a commercial rivalry between England and the Dutch Republic, and disputes relating to trade constantly arose. Latterly these disputes had been growing more acute.   Early in **1648** Spain came to terms with the Dutch by acknowledging their independence, and, later in the same year, the Thirty Years' War in Germany was brought to an end by the Peace of Westphalia,

though war between France and Spain still continued. Henceforth religion was no longer made the pretext for war on the Continent ; and States contended with one another because they wished either to annex territory, or to settle some trade dispute in their own favour. In **1650** the Stadholder, William II.—the son-in-law of Charles I.—died, and the office which he held was abolished, the government of the Dutch Republic falling completely under the control of the merchants of the Province of Holland, in which were situated the great commercial ports of Amsterdam and Rotterdam. The Dutch had got into their hands the carrying trade of Europe. In **1651** the English Parliament passed the Navigation Act, to put an end to this state of things. English vessels alone were to be allowed to import goods into England, except in the case of vessels belonging to the country in which the goods which they carried were produced.

7. **The Dutch War. 1652—1653.**—War with the Dutch soon followed. Vane, the leading man in the Committee of the Council of State which managed the navy, had put the fleet into excellent condition. Its command was given to Blake, who had been noted as a soldier by the defence of Taunton (see p. 547) in the Civil War, but who never went to sea till **1649**, when he was over fifty. Yet Blake soon found himself at home on board ship, and won the confidence of officers and men. Battle after battle was fought between the English and Dutch fleets. The sturdy antagonists were well matched, though the English ships were larger and more powerfully armed. In November **1652**, Tromp (the Dutch Admiral) got the better of Blake, but in February **1653** there was another battle, in which Blake got the upper hand ; but it was no crushing victory, like Dunbar and Worcester. In the summer of **1653** the English gained two more victories, but though they attempted to blockade the Dutch ports, they were obliged to give up the attempt.

8. **Unpopularity of the Parliament. 1652—1653.**—At home, the truncated Parliament was becoming increasingly unpopular. Ever since the end of the first Civil War, Parliament had supplied itself with money by forcing Royalists to compound—that is to say, to pay down a sum of money, without which they were not allowed to enjoy their estates ; and these compositions, as they were called, were still exacted from men who had joined in the second Civil War, or had favoured the invasion by Charles II. The system, harsh in itself, was not fairly carried out. Members of Parliament took bribes, and let the briber off more easily than they

did others who neglected to give them money. Those who were not Royalists had grievances of their own. Many of the members used their power in their own interest, disregarding justice, and promoting their sons and nephews in the public service.

9. **Vane's Reform Bill. 1653.**—For a long time Cromwell and the officers had been urging Parliament to dissolve itself and to provide for the election of a new Parliament, which would be more truly representative.   Vane had, indeed, brought in a Reform Bill, providing for a redistribution of seats, depriving small hamlets of the franchise, and conferring it upon populous towns and counties ; but the discussion dragged on, and the army was growing impatient.   Yet, impatient as the army was, officers and politicians alike recognised that a freely-elected Parliament would probably overthrow the Commonwealth and recall the king.   Cromwell suggested that a committee of officers and politicians should be formed to consult on securities to be taken against such a catastrophe.   The securities which pleased the members of Parliament were, that all members then sitting should continue to sit in the next Parliament, without fresh election, and should be formed into a committee having power to reject any new member whom they considered it desirable to exclude.

10. **Dissolution of the Long Parliament by Cromwell. 1653.**—Cromwell, who disliked this plan, was assured, on April 19, by one of the leading members of Parliament that nothing would be done in a hurry.   On the next day, April 20, he heard that the House was passing its bill in the form which he disliked.   Going to the House, when the last vote on the bill was about to be taken he rose to speak.   Parliament, he said, had done well in its care for the public good, but it had been stained with 'injustice, delays of justice, self-interest.'   Being interrupted by a member, he blazed up into anger.   "Come, come ! " he cried ;   "we have had enough of this.   I will put an end to this.   It is not fit you should sit here any longer."   He called in his soldiers, and bade them clear the House, following the members with words of obloquy as they passed out.   "What shall we do with this bauble?" he asked, taking up the mace.   "Take it away."   "It is you," he said to such of the members as still lingered, "that have forced me to do this.   I have sought the Lord night and day, that He would rather slay me than put me upon the doing of this work."

11. **The so-called Barebone's Parliament. 1653.**—Cromwell and the officers shrank from summoning an elected Parliament. They gathered an assembly of their own nominees, to which men

gave, in derision, the title of the Barebone's Parliament, because a certain Praise-God Barebone sat in it. In a speech at its opening, on July 4, Cromwell told them that England ought to be governed by godly men, and that they had been selected to govern it because they were godly. Unfortunately, many of these godly men were crotchety and impracticable. A large number of them wanted to abolish the Court of Chancery without providing a substitute,

Oliver Cromwell: from the painting by Samuel Cooper
at Sidney Sussex College, Cambridge.

and a majority resolved to abolish tithes without providing any other means for the support of the clergy. At the same time, enthusiasts outside Parliament—the Fifth Monarchy men, as they were called—declared that the time had arrived for the reign of the saints, and that they were themselves the saints. All who had anything to lose were terrified, and turned to Cromwell for support, as it was known that no man in England had stronger common sense, or was less likely to be carried away by such dreamers. In the Parliament itself there was a strong minority which thought it desirable that, if tithes were abolished, support should be provided for the clergy in some other way. These men, on December 11, got up early in the morning, and, before their opponents knew what they were about, declared Parliament to be dissolved, and placed supreme authority in the hands of Cromwell.

12. **The Protectorate, and the Instrument of Government. 1653.**—On December 16 a constitutional document, known as *The Instrument of Government*, was drawn up by Cromwell's leading supporters, and accepted by himself. Cromwell was to be styled Lord Protector, a title equivalent to that of Regent, of which the last instance had been that of the Protector Somerset (see p. 412). The Protector was to enter, to some extent, upon the duties which had formerly devolved on the king. There was to be a Parliament consisting of a single House, which was to meet once in three years, from which all who had taken the king's part were excluded, as they also were from voting at elections. The constituencies were to be almost identical with the reformed ones established by Vane's Reform Bill (see p. 566). The Protector was to appoint the executive officials, and to have a fixed revenue sufficient to pay the army and navy and the ordinary expenses of Government; but if he wanted more for extraordinary purposes he could only obtain it by means of a Parliamentary grant. New laws were to be made by Parliament alone, the Protector having no veto upon them, though he was to have an opportunity of criticising them, if he wished to urge Parliament to change its purpose. The main lines of the constitution were, however, laid down in the Instrument itself, and Parliament had no power given it to make laws contrary to the Instrument. In the executive government the Protector was restrained, not by Parliament, but by a Council of State, the members of which he could not dismiss as the king had dismissed his Privy Councillors. The first members were nominated in the Instrument, and were appointed for life; but when vacancies occurred, Parliament was to give in six names, of which the Council was to select two, leaving to the Protector only the final choice of one out of two. Without the consent of this entirely independent Council, the Protector could take no step of importance.

13. **Character of the Instrument of Government.**—The Instrument of Government allowed less Parliamentary control than had been given to the Long Parliament after the passing of the Tri-

ennial Act and the Tonnage and Poundage Act (see pp. 530, 531) : as, though Parliament could now pass laws without any check corresponding to the necessity of submitting them to the royal assent, it could not pass laws on the constitutional points which the Instrument of Government professed to have settled for ever. Neither—except when there was an extraordinary demand for money—could it stop the supplies, so as to bring the executive under its power. It was, rather, the intention of the framers of the Instrument to prevent that Parliamentary absolutism which had proved so hurtful in the later years of the Long Parliament. On the other hand, they gave to the Council of State a real control over the Protector ; and it is this which shows that they were intent on averting absolutism in the Protector, as well as absolutism in Parliament, though the means taken by them to effect their end was different from anything adopted by the nation in later years.

14. **Oliver's Government. 1653—1654.**—Before meeting Parliament, Oliver had some months in which he could show the quality of the new Government. On April 5, 1654, he brought the war with the Dutch to a close, and subsequently concluded treaties with other European powers. On July 10 he had Dom Pantaleon Sa, the brother of the Portuguese ambassador, beheaded for a murder. He had more than enough domestic difficulties to contend with. The Fifth-Monarchy men, and other religious enthusiasts, attacked him for treachery to republicanism, whilst Charles II. offered rewards to his followers for the murder of the usurper. Some of the republicans were imprisoned, and Gerard and Vowel, who tried to murder Oliver, were executed. In the meanwhile, the Protector and Council moved forward in the path of conservative reform. The Instrument allowed them to issue ordinances, which would be valid till Parliament could examine them ; and, amongst others which he sent forth, was one to reform the Court of Chancery, and another to establish a Commission of Triers, to reject all ministers presented to livings, if it considered them to be unfit, and another Commission of Ejectors, to turn out those who, being in possession, were deemed unworthy. Oliver would have nothing to say to the Voluntary system. Tithes were to be retained, and religious worship was to be established ; but there was to be no inquiry whether the ministers were Presbyterians, Independents, or anything else, provided they were Puritans. There was to be complete toleration of other Puritan congregations not belonging to the established churches ; whilst the Episcopalians, though not

legally tolerated, were as yet frequently allowed to meet privately without notice being taken of them. Other ordinances decreed a complete Union with Scotland and Ireland, both countries being ordered to return members to the Parliament at Westminster. As far as the real Irish were concerned, this Union was entirely illusory, as all Roman Catholics were excluded from the franchise.

15. **The First Protectorate Parliament. 1654—1655.**—On September 3, **1654**, the First Protectorate Parliament met. Its first act was to question the authority of private persons to frame a constitution for the State, and it then proceeded to draw up a new constitution, altering the balance in favour of Parliament, and expressly declaring that the constitution was liable to revision whenever the Protector and Parliament agreed to change it. Oliver and the Parliament thus found themselves at issue on a point on which compromise was impossible. Parliament, as representing the nation, claimed the right of drawing up the constitution under which the nation was to live. Oliver claimed the right of fixing limits on Parliamentary absolutism ; for though, in the suggested constitution, Parliament only proposed to make change possible with the consent of the Protector, it had taken care to make the Council of State responsible to Parliament, thereby rendering it very difficult for the Protector to refuse his consent to anything on which Parliament insisted. The only real solution of the difficulty lay in a frank acknowledgment that the nation must be allowed to have its way for evil or for good. This was, however, precisely what Oliver could not bring himself to acknowledge. He suspected—doubtless with truth—that, if the nation were freely consulted, it would sweep away not only the Protectorate, but Puritanism itself. He therefore required the members of Parliament to sign a paper acknowledging the government as established in a single person and in Parliament, and turned out of the House those who refused to sign it. On January 22, finding that those who remained persisted in completing their new constitution, he dissolved Parliament.

16. **The Major-Generals. 1655.**—The Instrument of Government authorised the Protector to levy sufficient taxes without consent of Parliament to enable him to meet the expenditure in quiet times, and after the dissolution Oliver availed himself of this authorisation. Many people, however, refused to pay, on the ground that the Instrument, unless recognised by Parliament, was not binding ; and, as some of the judges agreed with them, Oliver could only enforce payment by turning out those judges who

opposed him, and putting others in their places. Moreover, the Government was embarrassed by attempts to overthrow it. There were preparations for resistance by the republicans in the army—suppressed, indeed, before they came to a head, by the arrest and imprisonment of the leaders—and there was an actual Royalist outburst, with wide ramifications, which was, for the most part, anticipated, but which showed itself openly in the South of England, where a Royalist gentleman named Penruddock rode, into Salisbury, at the head of 200 men, and seized the judges who had come down for the assizes. In the face of such danger, Oliver abandoned all pretence of constitutional government. He divided England into ten military districts, over each of which he set a Major-General, with arbitrary powers for maintaining order, and, by a mere stroke of the pen, ordered a payment of 10 per cent. on the incomes of Royalists which was to be collected by the Major-Generals. Military rule developed itself more strongly than ever before. On November 27 Oliver, in his fear of the Royalists, ordered the suppression of the private worship of those who clung to the Book of Common Prayer ; perceiving rightly that the most dangerous opponents of his system were to be found amongst sincere Episcopalians.

17. **Oliver's Foreign Policy. 1654—1655.**—Partly, perhaps, because he hoped to divert attention from his difficulties at home, partly because he wished his country to be great in war as well as in peace, Oliver had for some time been engaging in naval enterprise. In the early part of his career he had been friendly to Spain, because France intrigued with the Presbyterians and the king. France and Spain were still at war, and when Cromwell became Protector he offered his alliance to Spain, on condition that Spain would help him to reconquer Calais, and would place Dunkirk in his hands as a pledge for the surrender of Calais after it had been taken. He also asked for freedom of commerce in the West Indies, and for more open liberty of religion for the English in the Spanish dominions than had been offered by Spain in its treaty with Charles I. To these demands the Spanish ambassador replied sharply that to ask these two things was to ask his master's two eyes, and plainly refused to admit an English garrison into Dunkirk. Upon this, Cromwell sent out, in the end of 1654, two fleets, one—under Blake—to go to the Mediterranean, to get reparation from the Duke of Tuscany and the pirates of Tunis for wrongs done to English commerce ; and the other—under Penn and Venables—to seize some great Spanish island in the West

Indies. Blake was successful, but Penn and Venables failed in an attempt on San Domingo, though they took possession of Jamaica, which at that time was not thought to be of any great value.

18. **The French Alliance. 1655.**—As Oliver could not get what he wanted from Spain, he offered his alliance to France. Mazarin, the French Minister, met him half-way, and a bargain was struck for the landing of English troops to help the French. Dunkirk was to be taken by the combined forces, and was to be surrendered to Oliver. Freedom of religion was to be accorded to Englishmen in France. Before any treaty had been signed, news arrived that the Duke of Savoy had sent his soldiers to compel his Vaudois subjects to renounce their religion, which was similar to that of the Protestants, though it had been embraced by them long before Luther's Reformation. These soldiers committed terrible outrages amongst the peaceful mountaineers. Those who escaped the sword were carried off as prisoners, or fled to the snowy mountains, where they perished of cold and hunger. Milton's voice was raised to plead for them. "Avenge," he wrote—

> "O Lord, thy slaughtered saints, whose bones
> Lie scattered on the Alpine mountains cold—
> Even men who kept Thy truth, so pure of old,
> When all our fathers worshipped stocks and stones."

Cromwell at once told Mazarin that, if he cared for the English alliance, this persecution must stop. Mazarin put pressure on the Duke of Savoy, and liberty of worship was secured to the Vaudois. Then, on October 24, **1655**, Oliver concluded the alliance with France.

19. **Oliver's Second Parliament, and the Humble Petition and Advice. 1656.**—War is expensive, and, in **1656**, Oliver called a second Parliament, to give him money. He would gladly have received a constitutional support for his Government, yet it was certain that any freely-elected Parliament would try to grasp authority for itself. When Parliament met, on September 17, Cromwell began by excluding about a hundred members who were likely to oppose him. After this, his relations with the House were smoother than they had been in **1654**—especially as news arrived that Stainer, with a part of Blake's ships, had captured the Spanish treasure-fleet on its way from America ; and, before long, thirty-eight waggons, laden with Spanish silver, rolled through the London streets. Parliament voted the money needed, and Oliver, in return, withdrew the Major-Generals. Then there was

discovered a plot to murder the Protector, and Parliament, anxious for security, drew up amendments to the Constitution, known as *The Humble Petition and Advice*. There was to be a second House, to revise the decisions of the existing one, which was again to be called the House of Commons. Members of the Council of State were to be approved by Parliament, and the power of excluding members was to be renounced by the Protector. Oliver was asked to take the title of king, with the right of naming his own successor. He refused the kingship, as the army disliked it, and also, perhaps, because he felt that there would be an incongruity in its assumption by himself. The rest of the terms he accepted, and, on June 26, **1657**, before the end of the session, he was installed as Lord Protector with greater solemnity than before. It was already known that, on April 20, Blake had destroyed a great Spanish fleet at Santa Cruz, in Teneriffe. On his way back, on August 7, he died at sea, and was brought home to be buried in Westminster Abbey.

20. **The Dissolution of the Second Protectorate Parliament. 1658.**—The new arrangements were a concession to the instinctive feeling of the nation that, the nearer it could get back to the old constitution, the safer it would be. On January 20, **1658**, Parliament met for its second session. The House of Commons had to take back the hundred excluded members who were enemies of Oliver, and to lose a large number of Oliver's warmest supporters, who were removed to the other House. The Commons had no longer an Oliverian majority, and, without attacking the Protector himself, they now attacked the other House which he had formed, and which gave itself the airs of the ancient House of Lords. On February 4, in a speech of mingled sadness and irritation, Oliver dissolved his second Parliament. "The Lord," he said, "judge between me and you."

21. **Victory Abroad and Failure at Home. 1657—1658.**—Abroad, Oliver's policy was crowned with success. In **1657**, 6,000 English troops were sent to co-operate with the French army, and the combined forces captured Mardyke. On June 4, **1658**, they defeated the Spanish army in a great battle on the Dunes, and on the 14th Dunkirk surrendered, and was placed in the hands of the English. It has often been doubted whether these successes were worth gaining. France was growing in strength, whilst Spain was declining, and it would not be long before France would become as formidable to England as Spain had been in the days of Elizabeth. Cromwell, however, was not the man to base his

policy on the probabilities of the future. At home and abroad he faced the present, and, since the day on which the king had mounted the scaffold, the difficulties at home had been overwhelming. Though his efforts to restore constitutional order had been stupendous, and his political aims had been noble, yet, in struggling to maintain order amidst chaos, he was attempting that which he, at least, could never do. Men will submit to the clearly expressed will of the nation to which they belong, or to a government ruling in virtue of institutions which they and their ancestors have been in the habit of obeying, but they will not long submit to a successful soldier, even though, like Oliver, he be a statesman as well.

22. **Oliver's Death. 1658.**—Oliver was growing weary of his unending, hopeless struggle. On August 6, **1658,** he lost his favourite daughter, and soon afterwards he sickened. There were times when old doubts stole over his mind : " It is a fearful thing," he repeated, " to fall into the hands of the living God." Such fears did not retain their hold on his brave spirit for long : " I am a conqueror," he cried, "and more than a conqueror, through Christ that strengtheneth me." On August 30 a mighty storm passed over England. The devil, said the Cavaliers, was fetching home the soul of the usurper. Oliver's own soul found utterance in one last prayer of faith : " Lord," he murmured, "though I am a miserable and wretched creature, I am in covenant with Thee through grace ; and I may, I will come to Thee, for Thy people. Thou hast made me, though very unworthy, a mean instrument to do them some good, and Thee service ; and many of them have set too high a value upon me, though others wish, and would be glad of, my death. . . . Pardon such as desire to trample upon the dust of a poor worm, for they are Thy people too ; and pardon the folly of this short prayer, even for Jesus Christ's sake, and give us a good night, if it be Thy pleasure. Amen." For three days more Oliver lingered on. On September 3, the anniversary of Dunbar and Worcester, he passed away to the rest which he had never known on earth.

23. **Richard Cromwell. 1658—1659.**—On his deathbed Oliver named, or was said to have named, his eldest son Richard as his successor. The nation preferred Richard to his father, because he was not a soldier, and was very little of a Puritan. On January 27, **1659,** a new Parliament met, chosen by the old, unreformed constituencies, as they had existed in the time of Charles I.; and not by those reformed ones appointed by the Instrument of Government, though Royalists were still excluded both from voting

at the elections and from sitting in Parliament. In this Parliament a majority supported Richard, hoping that he would consult the wishes of the army less than his father had done. For that very reason the officers of the army turned against him, and asked not only that Fleetwood, Oliver's son-in-law, should be their commander, but that he should be entirely independent of the authority of the Protector. Richard nominated Fleetwood, but insisted upon his acting under the Protector as his Lieutenant-General. Parliament upheld the control of the civil power over the army. On April 22 the soldiers forced Richard to dissolve Parliament. On May 25 Richard abdicated and the Protectorate came to an end.

24. **The Long Parliament Restored. 1659.**—Already on May 7, at the invitation of the soldiers, forty-two members of the so-called Rump—the portion of the Long Parliament which had continued sitting till it was ejected by Cromwell in 1653 (see p. 566)—had installed themselves at Westminster. No hereditary king was ever more tenacious of his rights than they. They told the officers ' that the Parliament expected faithfulness and obedience to the Parliament and Commonwealth,' and, declaring all Oliver's acts to have been illegal, resolved that all who had collected taxes for him must repay the money. The officers, many of whom had, as Major-Generals, gathered taxes by authority from Oliver, were naturally indignant. " I know not," said Lambert—one of the most distinguished of Oliver's officers—" why they should not be at our mercy as well as we at theirs." Before anything could be done, news arrived that Sir George Booth had risen in Cheshire for Charles II. Lambert marched against him, and defeated him at Winnington Bridge. When he returned, the officers made high demands of Parliament, and, when these were rejected, they sent troops, on October 13, to keep the members out of the House. " Do you not know me ? " said the Speaker, Lenthall. " If you had been with us at Winnington Bridge," said a soldier, " we should have known you."

25. **Military Government. 1659.**—The soldiers had come to despise civilians merely because they were civilians. They tried to govern directly, without any civilian authority whatever. The attempt proved an utter failure. It was discovered that taxes were paid less readily than when there had been a civilian Government to exact them. The soldiers quarrelled amongst themselves, and the officers, finding themselves helpless, restored the Rump a second time. On December 26 it resumed its sittings at Westminster.

26. **Monk and the Rump. 1660.**—George Monk, who com-

manded the forces in Scotland, had little inclination to meddle with politics ; but he was a thorough soldier, and being a cool, resolute man, was determined to bear this anarchy no longer. On January 1, **1660**, he crossed the Border with his army, and on January 11 was joined by Fairfax at York, who brought with him all the weight of his unstained name and his high military reputation. On February 3 Monk entered London, evidently wishing to feel his way. On February 6 the City of London, which had no members sitting in the Rump, declared that it would pay no taxes without representation. Monk was ordered by the Rump to suppress the resistance of the City. On the 10th he reached Guildhall. Keeping his ears open, he soon convinced himself that the Rump was detested by all parties, and, on the morning of the 16th, declared for a free Parliament.

27. **End of the Long Parliament. 1660.**—It was easy to coerce the Rump, without the appearance of using violence. On February 26, under pressure from Monk, it called in the Presbyterian members shut out by Pride's Purge (see p. 557). After they had taken their seats, a dissolution, to be followed by new elections, was voted. At last, on March 16, the Long Parliament came, by its own act, to its unhonoured end. The destinies of England were to be placed in the hands of the new Parliament, which was to be freely elected. The Restoration was a foregone conclusion. The predominant wish of Englishmen was to escape from the rule of soldiers, and, as every recent form of civil government had been discredited, it was natural to turn back to that which had flourished for centuries, and which had fallen rather through the personal demerits of the last king than through any inherent vices of the system.

28. **The Declaration of Breda. 1660.**—On April 4 Charles signed a declaration, known as the Declaration of Breda. He offered a general pardon to all except those specially exempted by Parliament, and promised to secure confiscated estates to their new owners in whatever way Parliament should approve. He also offered to consent to a bill for satisfying the arrears of the soldiers, and to another bill for the establishment of 'a liberty for tender consciences.' By the Declaration of Breda, Charles had carefully thrown upon Parliament the burden of proposing the actual terms on which the settlement was to be effected, and at the same time had shaken himself free from his father's policy of claiming to act independently of Parliament. The new Parliament, composed of the two Houses of Lords and Commons, was

known as the Convention Parliament, because, though conforming in every other respect to the old rules of the Constitution, the House of Commons was chosen without the king's writs. It met on April 25. The Declaration of Breda reached it on May 1. After unanimously welcoming the Declaration, Parliament resolved that, 'according to the ancient and fundamental laws of this kingdom, the Government is, and ought to be, by King, Lords, and Commons.' The Puritan Revolution had come to an end.

Books recommended for further study of Part VI.

RANKE, L.   History of England (English Translation).   Vol. i. p. 386—vol. iii. p. 308.

HALLAM, H.   Constitutional History of England.   Chaps. VI.-X.

GARDINER, S. R.   History of England from 1603–1642.

———— ——   History of the Great Civil War.

MASSON.   Life of Milton, and History of his Time.   Vols. i.-v.

FORSTER, J.   Life of Sir John Eliot.

————   The Grand Remonstrance.

————   Arrest of the Five Members.

GUIZOT, F.   Charles I.

————   Cromwell.

————   Richard Cromwell.

HANNAY, D.   Admiral Blake.

PART VII

THE POLITICAL REVOLUTION. 1660—1689

CHAPTER XXXVII

CHARLES II. AND CLARENDON. 1660—1667

LEADING DATES

Reign of Charles II., 1660—1685.

Charles II. lands at Dover	May 25, 1660
Dissolution of the Convention Parliament	Dec. 29, 1660
Meeting of the Cavalier Parliament	May 8, 1661
Corporation Act	1661
Act of Uniformity	1662
Expulsion of the Dissenting Ministers	Aug. 24, 1662
The King declares for Toleration	Dec. 26, 1662
Repeal of the Triennial Act	1664
Conventicle Act	1664
First Dutch War of the Restoration	1665
The Plague	1665
Five Mile Act	1665
Fire of London	1666
Peace of Breda	July 31, 1667
Clarendon's Fall	1667

1. **Return of Charles II.** 1660.—On May 25, 1660, Charles II. landed at Dover, amidst shouting crowds. On his thirtieth birthday, May 29, he entered London, amidst greater and equally enthusiastic crowds. At Blackheath was drawn up the army which had once been commanded by Cromwell. More than anything else, the popular abhorrence of military rule had brought Charles home, whilst the army itself, divided in opinion, and falling under the control of Monk, was powerless to keep him away. When the king reached Whitehall he confirmed Magna Carta, the Petition of Right, and other statutes by which the royal power had at various times been limited.

2. **King and Parliament. 1660.**—Something more than Acts of Parliament was needed to limit the power of the king. It had been found useless to bind Charles I. by Acts of Parliament,

Charles II. : from the portrait by Sir Peter Lely in Christ's Hospital, London.

because he tried again and again to introduce foreign armies into England to set Parliament at naught. Charles II. was, indeed, a man of far greater ability than his father, and was quite as ready as his father to use foreign help to get his way at home.

In the first year after his return he tried to get money both from the Dutch and from the Spaniards in order to make himself independent of Parliament, but his character was very different from his father's, in so far as he always knew—what Charles I. never knew—how much he could do with impunity. Having none of his father's sense of duty, he was always inclined to give way whenever he found it unpleasant to resist. He is reported to have said that he was determined that, whatever else happened, he would not go on his travels again, and he was perfectly aware that if a single foreign regiment were brought by him into England, he would soon find himself again a wanderer on the Continent. The people wished to be governed by the king, but also that the king should govern by the advice of Parliament. The restoration was a restoration of Parliament even more than a restoration of the king.

3. **Formation of the Government. 1660.**—The Privy Council of Charles II. was, at the advice of Monk, who was created Duke of Albemarle in July, composed of Cavaliers and Presbyterians. It was, however, too numerous to direct the course of government, and Charles adopted his father's habit of consulting, on important matters, a few special ministers, who were usually known as the Junto. Albemarle, as he knew little and cared less about politics, soon lost the lead, and the supreme direction of affairs fell to Hyde, the Lord Chancellor. Charles was too indolent and too fond of pleasure to control the government himself, and was easily guided by Hyde, who was thoroughly loyal to him, and an excellent man of business. Hyde stood to the king's other advisers very much in the position of a modern Prime Minister, but he carefully avoided introducing the name, though it was already in vogue in France, and contented himself with the real influence given him by his superior knowledge. In religion and politics he was still what he had been in 1641 (see pp. 533, 534). He was a warm supporter of episcopacy and the Prayer Book. As a lawyer, he applauded the political checks upon the Crown which had been the work of the first months of the Long Parliament, whilst he detested all the revolutionary measures by which, in the autumn of 1641, attempts had been made to establish the supremacy of Parliament over the king.

4. **The Political Ideas of the Convention Parliament. 1660.**— Hyde's position was the stronger because, in politics at least, the Convention Parliament agreed with him. The Cavaliers in it naturally accepted the legislation of the Long Parliament, up to August 1641, when Charles I. left for Scotland (see p. 532), as their

own party had concurred in it. The Presbyterians, on the other hand, who now represented the party which had formerly been led by Pym and Hampden, saw no reason to distrust Charles II. as they had distrusted his father, and were, therefore, ready to abandon the demand for further restrictions on the royal power, on which they had vehemently insisted in the latter part of **1641** and in the earlier part of **1642** (see p. 534). In constitutional matters, therefore, Cavaliers and Presbyterians were fused into one, on the basis of

Edward Hyde, first Earl of Clarendon, 1608-1674 : from an engraving by Loggan.

taking up the relations between the Crown and Parliament as they stood in August **1641**. This view of the situation was favoured by the lawyers, one of whom, Sir Orlando Bridgman, pointed out that, though the king was not responsible, his ministers were ; and, for the time, every one seemed to be satisfied with this way of keeping up the indispensable understanding between king and Parliament. What would happen if a king arose who, like Charles I., deliberately set himself against Parliament, no one cared to inquire.

    5. **Execution of the Political Articles of the Declaration of**

Breda. 1660.—Of the four articles of the Declaration of Breda, three were concerned with politics, and these were adopted by Parliament, with such modifications as it pleased to make. The estates of the king and of the bishops and chapters were taken out of the hands of those who had acquired them, but all private sales were declared valid, though Royalists had often sold their land in order to pay the fines imposed on them by the Long Parliament. An Act of Indemnity was passed, in which, however, there were many exceptions, and, in the end, thirteen regicides, together with Vane, were executed, and the bodies of Cromwell, Ireton, and Bradshaw

A mounted nobleman and his squire : from Ogilby's *Coronation Procession of Charles II.*

dug up and hanged. The bodies of other noted persons, including those of Pym and Blake, which had been buried in Westminster Abbey, were also dug up, and thrown into a pit outside. Many regicides and other partisans of the Commonwealth and Protectorate were punished with imprisonment and loss of goods, whilst others, again, who escaped, remained exiles till their death. Money was raised in order that the army might be paid as had been promised, after which it was disbanded. Feudal dues and purveyance were abolished, and an excise voted to Charles in their place. The whole revenue of the Crown was fixed at 1,200,000*l.*

6. Ecclesiastical Debates. 1660.—On ecclesiastical matters the two parties were less harmonious. The cavaliers wanted to restore episcopacy and the Prayer Book. The Presbyterians were ready to go back in religion, as in politics, to the ideas of August, **1641**, and to establish a modified episcopacy, in which bishops would be surrounded with clerical councillors, whose advice they would be bound to take. To this scheme Charles gave his approval, and it is probable that if nothing else had been in question Parliament would have accepted it. Charles, however, had an object of his own. His life was dissolute, and, being without any religious convictions, he cherished, like some other dissolute men of that time, a secret attachment to the Church of Rome. In order to do that Church a good turn, he now asked for a toleration in which all religions should be included. The proposal to include Roman Catholics in the proposed toleration wrecked the chances of modified episcopacy. Cavaliers and Presbyterians were so much afraid

Dress of the Horse Guards at the Restoration : from Ogilby's *Coronation Procession of Charles II.*

Yeoman of the Guard : from Ogilby's *Coronation Procession of Charles II.*

of the Roman Catholics that when a bill for giving effect to the scheme for uniting episcopacy and Presbyterianism was brought into Parliament, it was rejected through fear lest it should be a prelude to some other tolerationist measure favouring the Roman Catholics.   On December 29, **1660**, the Convention Parliament was dissolved.

7. **Venner's Plot and its Results. 1661.**—No one in the Convention Parliament had had any sympathy with the Independents, and still less with the more fanatical sects which had received toleration when the Independents were in power.   The one thing which the people of England as a body specially detested was the rule of the

Shipping in the Thames, *circa* 1660 : from Pricke's *South Prospect of London.*

Cromwellian army, and the two parties therefore combined to persecute the Independents by whom that army had been supported.   In January, **1661**, a party of fanatics, knowing that they at least had nothing to hope, rose in insurrection in London under one Venner, a cooper.   The rising was easily put down, but it gave an excuse to Charles—who was just then paying off the army—to retain two regiments, one of horse and one of foot, besides a third, which was in garrison at Dunkirk.   There was thus formed the nucleus of an army the numbers of which, before long, amounted to 5,000.   To have an armed force at all was likely to bring suspicion upon Charles, especially as his revenue did not suffice for the payment of 5,000 men without having recourse to means which would cause ill-feeling between himself and Parliament.

8. The Cavalier Parliament, and the Corporation Act. 1661. On May 8, 1661, a new Parliament, sometimes known as the Cavalier Parliament, met. In times of excitement, nations are apt to show favour to the party which has a clear and decided opinion; and, on this occasion, nine-tenths of the new members were Cavaliers. The new Parliament voted that neither House could pretend to the command of the militia, nor could lawfully make war upon the king. Before the end of 1661 it passed the Corporation Act, which was aimed at the Presbyterians as well as at the Independents. All who held office in municipal corporations were to renounce the Covenant, and to take an oath of non-resistance, declaring it to be unlawful to bear arms against the king ; and no one in future was to hold municipal office who had not received the Sacrament according to the rites of the Church of England. This Act did more than exclude from corporations those who objected to submit to its injunctions. In many towns the corporations elected the members of the House of Commons, and hence, by excluding non-conformists from corporations in towns, Parliament indirectly excluded them from many seats in the House of Commons.

9. The Savoy Conference, and the Act of Uniformity. 1661– 1662.—After the dissolution of the Convention Parliament, the old number of bishops was filled up, and, in April 1661, a conference between some bishops and some Presbyterian clergy was held at the Savoy Palace, and has therefore been known as the Savoy Conference. The two parties differed too much to come to terms, and the whole question of the settlement of the Church was left to the Cavalier Parliament. In 1662 Parliament decided it by passing the Act of Uniformity. Every clergyman and every schoolmaster refusing to express, by August 24, his unfeigned consent to everything contained in the Book of Common Prayer, was to be precluded from holding a benefice. On August 24 (St. Bartholomew's day), about 2,000 clergy resigned their cures for conscience' sake, as their opponents had, in the time of Puritan domination, been driven from their cures, rather than take the Covenant.

10. The Dissenters. 1662.—The expulsion of the dissenting clergy, as they were now called, made a great change in the history of English Christianity. The early Puritans wished, not to separate from the national Church, but to mould the national Church after their own fashion. The Independents set the example

II.   Q Q

of separating from the national Church, in order to form communities
outside it.   The Presbyterian clergy who kept up the tradition of
the early Puritans were now driven out of the national Church, and
were placed in very much the same position as the Independents.
Hence, these two bodies, together with the Baptists and the Society
of Friends—popularly known as Quakers—and other sects which
had recently arisen, began to be known by the common name of
Dissenters.   The aim of those who had directed the meeting of the
Savoy Conference had been to bring about comprehension, that is to
say, the continuance within the Church of those who, after its close,
became Dissenters.   Their failure had resulted from the impossibility of finding any formularies which could satisfy both parties ;
and in consequence of this failure the Dissenters now abandoned
all thought of comprehension, and contented themselves with asking
for toleration, that is to say, for permission to worship apart from
the Church, in their own assemblies.

11. **The Parliamentary Presbyterians.   1662.**—The Presbyterian clergy were followed by most of their supporters among
the tradesmen and merchants of the towns.   They were not
followed by the Presbyterians among the gentry.   The party in
Parliament, which had hitherto styled itself Presbyterian, had
originally become so mainly through dislike of the power of
the bishops.   They now consented to accept the Prayer Book, when
they found that the regulation of the Church was to depend on
Acts of Parliament and not either on the bishops or the king.   The
few members of the House of Commons who had hitherto been
known as Presbyterians formed the nucleus of a party of toleration,
asking for a modification of the law against Dissenters, though
refusing to become Dissenters themselves.

12. **Profligacy of the Court.   1662.**—On the other hand, the
members of the Cavalier party had, in 1641, become Royalists because they desired the retention of the doctrine and discipline of the
Church of England, and, in 1662, the Cavaliers were supporters of
the Church even more than they were Royalists.   As soon as Charles
expressed his approval of the Act of Uniformity, and not before,
the House of Commons voted him a chimney tax of two shillings
on every chimney.   If Charles had been an economical man,
instead of an extravagant one, he might possibly have contrived to
live within his income.   He was, however, beyond measure extravagant.   The reaction against Puritanism was not political only.
There were plenty of sober men amongst the English gentry, but
there were also many who had been so galled by the restrictions

of Puritanism that they had thrown off all moral restraint. Riot and debauchery became the fashion, and in this bad fashion Charles's court led the way.

13. **Marriage of Charles II., and Sale of Dunkirk. 1662.—** In 1662 Charles married Catharine of Braganza, a Portuguese Princess. He professed his intention of leading a new life, but he was weak as water, and he soon returned to his evil courses. Politically alone was the marriage of importance. Catharine brought with her the possessions of Tangier, and of Bombay, the first spot on the soil of India acquired by the English Crown. It was also a seal of friendship between Charles and Louis XIV. of France. Louis had made peace with Spain by the Treaty of the Pyrenees in 1659, but he still sympathised with the efforts of Portugal to maintain the independence of which Spain had robbed her in 1580 (see p. 454), and which she had recovered in 1640. Charles's marriage was, therefore, a declaration in favour of France. In November, 1662, after Parliament had dispersed for a vacation, he further showed his attachment to France, by selling Dunkirk to Louis for 200,000*l*. By abandoning Dunkirk, Charles saved an annual cost of 120,000*l*., which he would be able, if he pleased, to spend on an army. It may be doubted whether the possession of Dunkirk was of any real use, but there was a howl of indignation, in consequence of its loss, especially directed against Hyde, who had been created Earl of Clarendon in 1661, and was building a town house on a scale commensurate with his dignity. This house was popularly called Dunkirk House, it being falsely supposed that Clarendon received from Louis bribes which were expended upon it.

14. **The Question of Toleration Raised. 1662—1663.—**Before Parliament met, Charles, on December 26, 1662, issued a declaration in favour of toleration. He asked Parliament to pass an Act enabling him to mitigate the rigour of the Act of Uniformity by exercising that dispensing power 'which he conceived to be inherent in him.' Again and again, in former reigns, the king had dispensed from the penalties imposed by various laws, though there had been times when Parliament had remonstrated in cases where those penalties were imposed to restrain the Roman Catholic religion. When Parliament met again in 1663, the Cavaliers rejected the king's proposal. They would hear nothing of toleration for Dissenters, and still less of toleration for 'Papists.' The fear of a restoration of 'Popery' was the strongest motive of Englishmen of that day, and Charles, who, unlike his father,

always recoiled from strong opposition, even consented to banish all Roman Catholic priests. Yet it was in their interest and not in that of the Dissenters that he had issued his declaration. This affair sowed the first seeds of ill-will between Charles and Clarendon, as the latter had warmly supported the opposition to the Declaration.

15. **The Conventicle Act. 1664.**—Parliament was roused to proceed still farther in its course of intolerance. The Act of Uniformity had turned the Dissenting clergy out of the Church, but had not prevented them from holding meetings for worship. In May **1664** a Conventicle Act was passed, by which any adult attending a conventicle was made liable to an ascending scale of penalties, ending in seven years' transportation, according to the number of times that the offence had been committed. A conventicle was defined as being a religious meeting not in accordance with the practice of the Church of England, at which more than four persons were present in addition to the household.   The sentence of transportation was, indeed, a terrible one, as it implied working like a slave, generally under the burning sun in Barbadoes or some West India colony. The simple-minded Pepys, whose Diary throws light on the social conditions of the time, met some of the worshippers on their way to the inevitable sentence. " They go like lambs," he writes, " without any resistance. I would to God they would conform, or be more wise and not be catched." It was fear which produced the eagerness of English gentlemen to persecute Dissenters. They remembered how they had themselves been kept under by Cromwell's Puritan army, and, knowing that most of Cromwell's soldiers were still in the prime of life, they feared lest, if the Dissenters were allowed to gather head, they might become strong enough to call again to arms that ever-victorious army.

16. **The Repeal of the Triennial Act. 1664.**—In the spring of **1664**, before the passing of the Conventicle Act, the Cavalier Parliament had been alarmed lest it should be thought that it ought to be dissolved in the following May, because it would then have sat three years, in compliance with the Triennial Act. In reality there was nothing in the Triennial Act or in any other Act which rendered Parliament liable to dissolution, as long as the king lived, unless he chose to dissolve it ; but Charles, who did not like the fetters which that Act imposed upon him, took the opportunity to ask Parliament to repeal it. This was promptly done, though in the Act of Repeal was included a clause to the effect that there should, in future, be no intermission of Parliaments for more than

three years.　As the whole of the machinery invented by the Long Parliament for giving effect to such a clause (see p. 530) had vanished, no king could now be compelled to summon Parliament unless he wished to do so.

17　**Growing Hostility between England and the Dutch. 1660—1664.**—It was not fear, but commercial rivalry, which made England hate the Dutch.　In **1660** the Convention Parliament had re-enacted the Navigation Act (see p. 565).　Legislation alone, however, could not prevent the Dutch from driving the English out of the markets of the world, either by superior trading capacity, or by forcibly excluding them from ports in which Dutch influence was supreme.　Besides this, the Dutch refused to surrender Pularoon, a valuable spice-bearing island in the East Indies, though they had engaged to do so by treaty.　If there was anything about which Charles II. was in earnest it was in the spread of English colonies and commerce.　He had also private reasons for bearing ill-will against the Dutch, who by abolishing the office of Stadholder (see p. 565) in **1650,** had deprived the young William of Orange, the son of Charles's sister Mary, of any post in the Republic.　The seven provinces were held together by the necessity of following the counsels of the Province of Holland, by far the most extensive and the wealthiest of the seven, if they were to preserve any unity at all.　The opinion of this Province was the more readily accepted because the provincial states by which it was governed submitted to be led by their pensionary, John de Witt, one of the most vigorous and most prudent statesmen of the age.　A pensionary was only an officer bound to carry out the orders of the States, but the fact that all business passed through his hands made a man of John de Witt's ability, the director of the policy which he was supposed to receive from others.

18.　**Outbreak of the First Dutch War of the Restoration. 1664—1665.**—In **1664** hostilities broke out between England and the Dutch Republic, without any declaration of war.　English fleets captured Dutch vessels on the coast of Africa, seized islands in the West Indies, and took possession of the Dutch settlement in America called by its founders New Amsterdam, but re-named by the English New York, after the king's only surviving brother, the Duke of York, who was Lord High Admiral.　Later in the year, De Ruyter, one of the best of the Dutch admirals, retaliated by seizing most of the English forts on the coast of Guinea, and in **1665** war was openly declared.　Parliament made what was then the enormous grant of 2,500,000*l.*, and on June 3 a battle was fought off Lowestoft in which the English were completely victorious.

19. **The Plague. 1665.**—The rejoicing in England was marred by a terrible calamity. For more than half a century the Plague had appeared in England, at intervals of five years. It now broke out with unusual virulence, especially in London. The streets there were narrow and dirty, and the air was close, because the upper storeys of the houses overhung the lower ones. No medical aid appeared to avail anything against the Plague. On the door of every house in which it appeared was painted a red cross with the words, "The Lord have mercy upon us." Every one rich enough fled into the country and spread the infection. "How fearful," wrote a contemporary, "people were, thirty or forty, if not a hundred miles from London, of anything that they brought from any mercer's or draper's shop ; or of any goods that were brought to them ; or of any persons that came to their houses ! How they would shut their doors against their friends ; and if a man passed over the fields, how one would avoid another ! " The dead were too numerous to be buried in the usual way, and carts went their rounds at night, accompanied by a man ringing a bell and calling out, " Bring out your dead." The corpses were flung into a huge pit without coffins, there being no time to provide them for so many. It was not till winter came that the sickness died away.

20. **The Five Mile Act. 1665.**—In October, Parliament met at Oxford, through fear of the Plague. It offered the king 1,250,000*l.* for the war if he would consent to fresh persecution of the Dissenters. He took the money, and gave his assent to the Five Mile Act. The Conventicle Act had been largely evaded, and, during the Plague, Dissenting ministers had preached in pulpits from which the clergy had fled through fear of. infection. The Five Mile Act was to strike at the ministers ejected on St. Bartholomew's day. Not one of them was allowed to come within five miles of a borough town, or of any place in which he had once held a cure, and was therefore likely to find a congregation, unless he would take the oath of non-resistance, and swear that he would never endeavour to alter the government in Church or State, a condition to which few, if any, of the Dissenters were willing to submit.

21. **Continued Struggle with the Dutch. 1665—1666.** In the autumn of **1665** the ravages of the Plague kept the English fleet in the Thames, and the Dutch held the sea. On land they were

exposed to some peril. Ever since their peace with Spain, in **1648**, they had allowed their military defences to fall into decay, on the supposition that they would have no more enemies who could dispose of any formidable land-force. Now even a petty prince like the Bishop of Münster, hired by Charles, was able, in October, to over-run two of their eastern provinces. The Dutch called upon the king of France, Louis XIV., for help, and he, being bound by treaty to assist them, declared war against England in January

Old St. Paul's, from the east, showing its condition just before the Great Fire
from an engraving by Hollar.

1666. If he had given earnest support to the Dutch the conse-quences would have been serious for England, but though he and other continental allies of the Dutch frightened off the Bishop of Münster from his attack on the Republic, Louis had no wish to help in the destruction of the English navy. What he wanted was to see the Dutch and English fleets destroy one another in order that his own might be mistress of the sea. Through the first four days of June a desperate naval battle was fought between the English and the Dutch, off the North Foreland, at the end of which the

English fleet, under Albemarle and Rupert, was driven to take shelter in the Thames, whilst the Dutch had been so crippled as to be forced to put back to refit. On July 25 and 26 there was another battle off the mouth of the Thames. This time the Dutch had the worst, and in August the English fleet sailed along the islands at the entrance of the Zuyder Zee, destroying 160 merchant ships and burning a town. The struggle had been a terrible one. The sailors of both nations were equally brave, and equally at home in a sea-fight, but the English ships were better built and the English guns were better, whilst the Dutch commanders did not work well together in consequence of personal and political jealousies.

22. The Fire of London. 1666.—In September, **1666**, London suffered a calamity only second to that of the Plague. A fire broke out, and burnt for three days. All the City from the Tower to the Temple, and from the Thames to Smithfield, was absolutely destroyed. Old St. Paul's, the longest cathedral in England, perished in the flames. Great as the suffering caused by the fire was, it was not without its benefits, as the old houses with their overhanging storeys were destroyed by it, and were replaced by new ones built in the modern fashion, so that there was more air in the streets. After this reconstruction of London it was never again visited by the Plague.

23. Designs of Louis XIV. 1665—1667.—Soon after the fire died down Parliament voted 1,800,000*l.* for continuing the war, but the country was exhausted, and it was known that it would be impossible to collect so large a sum. Both king and Parliament were therefore anxious for peace, and there were now reasons which made the Dutch also ready to make peace. In **1665** Philip IV. of Spain died, and was succeeded by his only surviving son, Charles II., as yet a mere child, hopelessly weak in body and mind. Philip also left two daughters, the elder, Maria Theresa, a child of his first wife, being the wife of Louis, whilst the younger, Margaret Theresa, the wife of the Emperor Leopold I., was, with Charles II., the offspring of a second marriage.[1] Both of the daughters had renounced all future claim to the Spanish Crown, but Louis, knowing that the young Charles II. of

---

[1] Genealogy of the surviving children of Philip IV :—

1. Elizabeth of France = Philip IV. = 2. Mary of Austria.

Maria Theresa = Louis XIV.	Margaret Theresa = Leopold I.	Charles II.

Spain was so sickly as to make his early death probable, was prepared to assert his wife's claim whenever that event took place. In the meanwhile he put forward a demand that the greater part of the Spanish Netherlands should be immediately handed over to her, because in those countries there was a law, known as the law of devolution, enacting that the daughter of a first wife should receive a larger share of her father's property than a son of the second. Louis chose to construe a right to succeed to property as though it implied a right to govern. In March, 1667, he made a secret treaty with Charles II. of England, in which, on condition of his engaging not to help the Dutch, he was allowed to do as he pleased in the Spanish Netherlands. In May he began what is known as the War of Devolution, with Spain. Spain had neither money nor means to defend her territory in the Netherlands, and the French armies captured one place after another.

24. **The Dutch in the Medway, and the Peace of Breda. 1667.**—The advance of Louis into the Spanish Netherlands and the establishment of the French armies so near their frontier in the place of the now exhausted forces of Spain greatly alarmed the Dutch. The mere risk of this danger had, even before the war between France and Spain began, inclined them to peace with England, and a conference was opened at Breda to consider the terms. All was quickly agreed on except the question about the right of England to Pularoon (see p. 589), and Charles, imagining that this would be settled in his favour, dismissed his sailors and dismantled his fleet, in order to save money to spend on his own extravagant pleasures. The Dutch fleet at once entered the Thames, sailed up the Medway, burnt three men-of-war, and carried off a fourth. For some days it blockaded the Thames, so that the Londoners could get no coals. Men openly said that such things would not have happened if Oliver had been living. Orders were sent to the English ambassadors at Breda to give up Pularoon, and on July 31 the Treaty of Breda was signed. It was not wholly disastrous. If England lost her last hold on the spice islands of the East, she gained New York and all the territory formerly Dutch in the West, which had broken up the continuity of her colonies in America.

25. **Clarendon and the House of Commons. 1667.**—The events of the last months of the war had produced important effects upon the temper of Parliament. Long before the Dutch appeared in the Medway, the House of Commons had demanded an inquiry into the expenditure of the money granted to the

Crown, suspecting that much of the supply distinctly intended for purposes of war had been diverted to pay for the amusements of the Court. This demand, which opened a new chapter in the history of the financial struggle between the House of Commons and the Crown, brought the Commons into collision with Clarendon. It had been settled by the Long Parliament that the king was to levy no taxes without a grant from Parliament. The Cavalier Parliament, Royalist as it was, was beginning to ask that the king should not spend the proceeds of taxes without the approbation of Parliament. When once this had been secured, Parliament would indubitably become supreme. Against this attempt to obtain the mastery Clarendon struggled. He was a good lawyer and an excellent man of business, but he was not a statesman of genius. He wanted each part of the government to act in harmony with the others; but he could never understand the meaning of the saying that if two men ride on horseback, one must ride in front. He wanted the king and Parliament both to ride in front, both—that is to say —to have their own way in certain directions. His notion of a king was that of one prudently doing his best for his people, always ruling according to law, and irresponsible in everything, even in the expenditure of money. A wasteful, riotous Charles II. was a phenomenon for the control of which his constitutional formulas were not prepared.

26. **The Fall of Clarendon. 1667.**—Though Clarendon was unable to concur in any diminution of the power of the Crown, his eyes were widely open to the profligacy of Charles's life. Again and again he had remonstrated with him, and had refused to pass under the great seal grants in favour of Lady Castlemaine, to whom, amongst his many mistresses, Charles was at this time most completely subjugated. As might have been expected, this abandoned woman irritated her paramour against his upright Chancellor, telling him that he was no king as long as he was ruled by Clarendon. As Parliament continued its attacks, Charles, on August 30, dismissed Clarendon from office. On October 10, the fallen minister was impeached by the House of Commons, on charges the greater part of which were ridiculously untrue. He tried to rouse Charles to support him, reminding him that, after Charles I. allowed Strafford to die, the king's own head had fallen on the scaffold. Charles II., an easy-going but clever politician, probably thought that he could always escape his father's fate by refraining from imitating his father's stiffness. He gave Clarendon a strong hint to withdraw, and on November 29 the minister who

had done more than any other man to establish the restored monarchy, fled to France, never to return alive.

27. **Scotland and Ireland. 1660.**—At the Restoration, the close connection established by Cromwell between England and Scotland was necessarily broken up. Scotland hated English control even when it came in the guise of a union of Parliaments, and the old relation of separate states united only by the Crown was at once resumed. Argyle and his principal followers were executed as traitors. The main profit of the restoration in Scotland, however, fell to the nobility. The clergy was discredited by its divisions, and the noblemen, whose fathers had supported Presbyterianism against Charles I., now supported Charles II. against Presbyterianism. Once more, as in the days of James I., the clergy were muzzled by the restoration of episcopacy and the assertion of the authority of the Crown. In Ireland the main question was how to satisfy alike the recent English immigrants who had received lands from Cromwell and the Irish proprietors who had been deprived of their lands in favour of the intruders. In 1661, at the king's desire, an Act of Settlement was passed, making, in elaborate detail, an attempt to satisfy as many as possible of both parties ; but as men of English descent and Protestant religion filled the Irish House of Commons, the English settlers contrived to maintain, by constitutional authority, much of what they had taken with the strong hand. According to the best evidence now procurable, whereas before 1641 about two-thirds of Irish lands fit for cultivation had been in the hands of Catholics, before the end of the reign of Charles II. two-thirds were in the hands of Protestants.

CHAPTER XXXVIII

CHARLES II. AND THE CABAL. 1667—1674

LEADING DATES

Reign of Charles II., 1660—1685

Treaty of Dover	June 1, 1670
Second Dutch War of the Restoration . .	March 13, 1672
Declaration of Indulgence	March 15, 1672
Test Act	March 29, 1673
Dismissal of Shaftesbury	Nov. 9, 1673
Peace with the Dutch	Feb. 19, 1674

1. **Milton and Bunyan.**—Whilst Clarendon and his allies were fortifying the legal position of the Church of England, the old Puritanism which they attempted to crush found a voice in literature. Milton, who had become blind, in consequence of his intense devotion to the service of the State, as the secretary of Cromwell, at last, after long preparation, gave to the world 'Paradise Lost,' in 1667. The poem was Puritan, not only because its main theme was the maintenance or destruction of the purity of a single human soul, but because it based that purity on obedience to the commands of the great Taskmaster ; whilst, in the solemn cadence of its blank verse there is something to remind the reader of the stern world of duty, in the midst of which the nobler spirits of the Commonwealth and Protectorate had moved. As Milton was the poet of Puritanism, John Bunyan was the prose-poet of Dissent. He had himself fought as a soldier on the side of Parliament in the Civil War, and, having become an earnest Baptist preacher, he continued to preach after the Restoration, and, boldly defying the law, was requited with a long imprisonment. His masterpiece, 'The Pilgrim's Progress,' was probably not written till 1675, but many of his religious writings were published before that date. His force of imagination made him the greatest allegorist the world has seen. His moral aim lay in the preservation of a few choice souls from the perils and temptations of a society wholly given up to evil.

2. **Butler and the Dramatists.**—There was, doubtless, much in

the world round Milton and Bunyan to awake indignation. Samuel Butler was a man of genius, but his 'Hudibras,' which appeared in 1663, shows but poorly by the side of 'Paradise Lost' and 'The

Gul. Faithorne ad Vivum   *Delin. et sculpsit.*

Joannis Miltoni Effigies Ætat: 62.
1670

John Milton in 1670.

Pilgrim's Progress.' This mock-heroic account of a Puritan knight is the work of a strong writer, who can find nothing better to

do with the warriors and disputants who had lately controlled
England than to laugh at them.   The mass of Restoration poetry
was far weaker than 'Hudibras,' whilst its dramatic writers vied
with one another in the expression of licentious thought either
in prose or in the regular heroic couplets which were, at this
time, in vogue.   It was, indeed, impossible to put much human
passion into two neat lines which had to be made to rhyme ; but
at Court love-making had been substituted for passion, and the
theatres, now re-opened, after they had been suppressed by the
Puritans, were meant for the vicious Court and not for the people
at large.

3. **Reason and Science.**—The satire of Butler, and the licen-
tiousness of the dramatists, both sprang from a reaction against
the severe morality of the Puritans ; but it would have been a poor
prospect for the generation following that of Puritan repression
if the age had not produced any positive work of its own.   Its
work was to be found in the increase of respect for human reason.
In the better minds amongst the clergy of the Restoration, the
reasonable character of the Church of England was more than ever
predominant.   A few, such as Wilkins, Bishop of Chester, and
Stillingfleet, Dean of St. Paul's, were even anxious to find some
way of comprehension by which Dissenters might be reconciled
to the Church, whilst others, like Morley and Barrow, attached far
more importance to arguments addressed to the understanding, than
to that uniformity of ceremonial which had been so dear to the mind
of Laud.   Still more important was the spread of devotion to natural
science.   The Royal Society, founded for its promotion in 1660,
brought together men who thought more about air-pumps than
about the mysteries of theology ; and it was mainly the results of
their inquiries which made any renewed triumph of Puritanism
impossible.   In 'The Pilgrim's Progress' the outer world was
treated as a mere embarrassment to the pursuit of spiritual perfection.   By the Fellows of the Royal Society it was treated as
calling for reverent investigation, in order that, in the words of
Bacon, nature might be brought into the service of man by his
obedience to her laws.

4. **Charles II. and Toleration.   1667.**—In the long run the
rise of the scientific spirit would conduce to religious toleration,
because scientific men have no reason to desire the suppression of
any form of religious belief.   The first step taken after the restoration in the direction of religious toleration had come from Charles
(see p. 581), who was actuated partly by a sneaking fondness for the

Roman Catholic Church and partly by dislike of being dictated to by Parliament. He therefore, after Clarendon's fall, gave his confidence mainly to men who, for various reasons, were inclined to support his wishes in this respect.

5. **Buckingham and Arlington. 1667—1669.**—Amongst these men the principal were the Duke of Buckingham and Lord Arlington. Buckingham, the son of the favourite of Charles I.— 'everything by turns and nothing long'—was trying his hand at politics by way of amusement. Arlington, who, like Charles, hardly knew whether he was Catholic or Protestant, was entrusted, as Secretary of State, with the direction of foreign affairs. He was a man of considerable ability, but perfectly unscrupulous in shifting his ground to suit his personal ambition. Both hated Clarendon as sour and austere, and both were ready to support the king in any scheme upon which he might set his heart. The Dissenters confined to prison were liberated, and a Bill prepared to modify the ceremonies of the Church, so as to enable the expelled Presbyterians to re-enter the Church. When, however, Parliament met in February, 1668, it showed its determination to have nothing to do with either toleration or comprehension (see p. 598). It offered the king 300,000*l*., but only under the implied condition that he would abandon his scheme. Charles took the money and dropped his scheme. He prorogued Parliament in May, and did not re-assemble it till October, 1669. Whilst Parliament was not in session Charles sheltered the Dissenters from persecution, and even thought of dissolving Parliament. Albemarle (see p. 580), however, cautiously reminded him that, even if he got a new Parliament in which the Dissenters and their friends were predominant, it would probably cause him trouble by wanting to persecute those who had hitherto persecuted the Dissenters. Accordingly Charles, who hated nothing so much as trouble, not only allowed the old Parliament to meet again, but even issued a proclamation enforcing the penal laws against Dissenters.

6. **The Triple Alliance. 1668.**—In 1668 a triple alliance was formed between England, the Dutch Republic, and Sweden, to put an end to the War of Devolution (see p. 593). Its originators were De Witt, and Sir William Temple, the English ambassador at the Hague. The allies demanded that Louis should content himself with certain strong towns on his northern frontier which he had already conquered from Spain, and should desist from attempting to conquer more. Louis assented, and the Peace of Aix-la-Chapelle was signed on these conditions. In England

there was already a rising feeling against the French, and Charles acquired no little popularity by his supposed firmness. In reality he had betrayed the secrets of the alliance to Louis, and had only shown his teeth to gain good terms for himself from the French king.

7. Charles's Negotiations with France. 1669—1670.—Louis owed the Dutch a deep grudge, and set himself to win Charles to neutrality, if not to active help, in the war which he now purposed to make against them. Charles disliked the Dutch as the commercial rivals of England, and was ready to sell himself to Louis if only the price offered was high enough. Though Charles never suffered religion of any kind to be a check on his conduct, his facile nature yearned after the imposing authority of the Roman Church. In **1669** his brother, James, avowed himself a Catholic, and in the same year Charles, under the strictest secrecy, declared his own conversion to a small circle of men whom he could trust. Before the end of the war he offered Louis support against the Dutch, but asked such enormous concessions in return that Louis refused to agree to them. Charles, before lowering the terms of his bargain with Louis, drove another bargain with his Parliament. In the spring of **1670**, by dropping his demand for toleration, he obtained a grant of 300,000*l.* a year for eight years. In return he gave the royal assent to a second Conventicle Act, even more stringent than the first.

8. The Treaty of Dover. 1670.—Having secured a grant, Charles prorogued Parliament, which he had deceived by giving it to understand that he had abandoned the idea of toleration, and turned to Louis. Louis sent over Charles's youngest sister, Henrietta, Duchess of Orleans, to conclude an alliance, and on June 1, **1670**, a treaty between England and France was secretly signed at Dover. Charles agreed to join Louis in his projected war against the Dutch, by sending an English force of 6,000 men to serve in the French army, and to assist Louis to seize upon the territories of the Spanish monarchy in the event of the death of Charles II. of Spain without male heirs. Charles was also to acknowledge himself a Catholic whenever he thought fit to do so. To support Charles against his subjects in case of their resisting him in the declaration of his conversion, Louis was to give him 154,000*l.* and the aid of 6,000 troops to be employed in England in his defence. Moreover, Charles was to receive 230,000*l.* a year during the proposed war, and thirty French ships were to serve under an English admiral. At the end of the war he was to receive Walcheren,

Sluys and Cadsand from the Dutch Republic, and ultimately, if Louis made good his claims to the Spanish monarchy, he was to gain from Spain, Ostend, Minorca, and various territories in South America.   Charles II. was no more scrupulous than his father had been about using the troops of foreign princes to suppress the opposition of his own subjects, but he was shrewd enough to know—what Charles I. had never known—that foreign princes would not lend him

Temple Bar, London, built by Sir Christopher Wren in 1670.   Taken down in 1878 and since rebuilt at Waltham Cross.

troops unless he gave them something in return.   The breach of the Triple Alliance and the assistance offered by Charles to Louis in the proposed war against the Dutch were considered in France to be a fair equivalent for the payments which Louis had bound himself to make.   It was another question whether Charles could be kept to his engagements.   To secure this as much as possible Louis sent

II.   R R

him over a new French mistress, Louise de Keroualle. Charles soon created her Duchess of Portsmouth, and she fulfilled her duty to her own king by betraying to him all the secrets of her lover.

9. The Cabal. 1670.—After Clarendon's fall Charles had been his own chief minister. The ministers whom he consulted from time to time were known as his Cabal, a word then applied to any body of secret advisers, without carrying with it the opprobrious meaning which it now has. At last the wits discovered that the initials of five ministers who were principally consulted about the time of the Treaty of Dover, Clifford, Arlington, Buckingham, Ashley, and Lauderdale, spelt the word cabal, and writers have since talked about them as forming what has been called the Cabal Ministry, though no such ministry, in the modern sense of the word, ever existed. Not only did they not form a council meeting for purposes of government, but, though they agreed together in favouring toleration, they disagreed on other points. Nor were they usually consulted by Charles in a body. Sometimes he took the advice of persons not of their number; sometimes he took the advice of some of them only, whilst he kept the others entirely in the dark. Thus Clifford, who was a brave and honest Catholic, and Arlington, who would support any measure as long as it was his interest to do so, knew all about the Treaty of Dover, whilst Buckingham, Lauderdale, and Ashley were in complete ignorance of it. Of Buckingham and Arlington enough has been already said (see p. 599). Lauderdale, who had little to do with English affairs, kept himself almost entirely to the task of building up the king's authority in Scotland, where he had already got together an army completely at Charles's disposal. The character of Ashley deserves a longer consideration.

10. Ashley's Policy.—Anthony Ashley Cooper,[1] who had been created Lord Ashley since the Restoration, had changed sides again and again during the late troubles. He was a born party-leader, and had signalised himself as a youth at Exeter College, Oxford, by leading a successful revolt of the freshmen against the older undergraduates, who, according to custom, tried to skin the chins of the freshmen and to force them to drink a nauseous compound prepared for the occasion. Though in party conflict he was quite unscrupulous and despised no means which would enable him to gain his ends, he had the statesmanlike qualities of common sense and moderation. He had deserted Charles I. when he leant upon the Catholics (see p. 541), had supported Cromwell in his struggle

---

[1] Two Christian names were exceedingly rare in the seventeenth century.

with the zealots of the Barebone's Parliament (see p. 566), and had left him when he rejected the constitutional scheme of the first Parliament of the Protectorate (see p. 570). In disgust at the humours of the Rump and the army, he had done everything in his power to hasten the Restoration, and had soon shown hostility to Clarendon and to the persecuting laws of the Cavalier Parliament. In fact, there were two principles to which he was never entirely false, a love of Parliamentary government and a love of toleration, which last was based, not as was that of Oliver, upon sympathy with religious zeal of every kind, but upon dislike of clerical interference. At present he attached himself to Charles, because he knew of Charles's alleged wish to establish toleration, and knew nothing of the conspiracy against Parliament on which Charles had embarked, or of Charles's secret design to favour the Roman Church under cover of a general scheme of toleration.

11. **Buckingham's Sham Treaty. 1671.**—To deceive those who were in ignorance of the secret treaty of the previous year, Buckingham was sent to Paris to negotiate a sham treaty in which all mention of Charles's conversion was omitted, and the whole of the money offered by Louis represented as given solely for the war. Charles particularly enjoyed making a fool of Buckingham, who imagined himself to be exceedingly clever, and he had also the temporary satisfaction of gaining the hearty support of Ashley as well as Buckingham, because Ashley was quite ready to accept Louis' help in a joint enterprise for crushing the commerce of the Dutch, and had no scruples about abandoning the Triple Alliance. Charles was the more ready to begin the war because he had lately succeeded in obtaining from Parliament another 800,000*l.* on the false plea that he wanted the money to enable him to hold head at sea against the French as well as the Dutch. As soon as the money was obtained he prorogued Parliament.

12. **The Stop of the Exchequer. 1672.**—Charles prudently delayed the declaration of his conversion to a more convenient season, but the opening of the war was fixed for the spring of 1672. In spite of the large sums which he drew from Louis and from Parliament, his finances were in hopeless confusion, because of the enormous amount of money which he squandered on his numerous mistresses and his illegitimate children. It is said that the yearly income of the Duchess of Portsmouth was 40,000*l.*, and that in one year she received no less than 136,000*l.* A caricature published in Holland aptly represented him as standing between two women, with empty pockets hanging out. At this time he had in his

exchequer 1,400,000*l.*, lent to him by the goldsmiths who, in those days, acted as bankers. On January 2, 1672, probably at Clifford's suggestion, he refused to repay the principal, and arbitrarily diminished the interest from 12 to 6 per cent.[1]   In consequence of this stop of the exchequer, as it was called, many of the goldsmiths became bankrupt, but Clifford became a peer and Lord High Treasurer.

Anthony Ashley-Cooper, first Earl of Shaftesbury, 1621–1683 :
from the National Portrait Gallery.

13. **The Declaration of Indulgence. 1672.**—On March 15, Charles, though still hesitating to proclaim himself a Catholic, issued a Declaration of Indulgence. Claiming a dispensing power,[2] he

---

[1] In the time of James I. the usual interest was 10 per cent. The Long Parliament paid 8.

[2] The right of pardon allows the king to remit the consequences to a particular person of a sentence passed on him. The right of dispensation allows him to remit beforehand the consequences of a breach of a law either to such persons as are named, or to all persons generally who may commit such a breach.

suspended all penal laws in matters ecclesiastical, affecting either recusants or non-conformists, thus giving complete religious liberty to Roman Catholics as well as to Dissenters. To this measure, wise and statesmanlike in itself, but marred by the motives of its author and by its defiance of the law and of public opinion, Ashley gave his hearty support. He was rewarded with the Earldom of Shaftesbury. He had shortly before been made Lord Chancellor : being the last who held that post without being a lawyer. At that time the decisions of the Court of Chancery were still given in accordance with the view taken by the Chancellor of what seemed fair and equitable, and did not therefore require any elaborate legal knowledge. Even Shaftesbury's bitterest enemies acknowledged that he was scrupulously just.

14. **The Second Dutch War of the Restoration. 1672.**—Both Charles and Louis had resolved to take the Dutch by surprise. On March 13, Admiral Holmes, obeying orders, attacked a rich Dutch merchant fleet sailing up the Channel, before war was declared, but only succeeded in taking two vessels. In the war now begun the discipline of the English navy was worse, and that of the Dutch navy better, than it had been in the former war (see p. 591). On June 7 there was a fierce sea-fight in Southwold Bay, in which the Dutch had slightly the advantage. Louis, on his part, crossed the Rhine, and fell upon the Dutch territory. As a land attack had not been expected, the military preparations were incomplete, and the fortresses out of repair. One place after another capitulated to the French. The young William III., Prince of Orange, Charles's nephew, had been named Captain-General, but his army was too small to encourage him to risk a battle. Then De Witt took a heroic resolution. On June 18 he cut the dykes which protected the low-lying land from the sea which stood at a higher level. In rushed the waters, Louis found his progress stopped. De Witt had the blame of the failure to prevent the invasion ; William, coming after him, had the credit of the resistance. The Republic needed a strong hand to preserve it, and the office of Stadholder was revived and given to William. Shortly afterwards De Witt, together with his brother, was brutally murdered at the Hague. William, who detested De Witt for having so long deprived him of the power which he considered his due, not only took no steps to hinder the assassination, but actually protected the murderers. Disgraceful as his conduct was, he had a temper as heroic as De Witt's. Buckingham came to urge him to submit to Louis' terms. "Do you not see," said the Englishman, "that the

Republic is lost?" " I know one sure means of never seeing it,"
was William's firm reply—" to die on the last dyke." His confidence was justified. Louis could not pierce the girdle of waters
which surrounded the Dutch towns, and, returning to Paris,
brought the campaign to an end.

15. 'Delenda est Carthago.' 1673.—On February 4, 1673.
Charles, having once more spent all his money, again met his
Parliament. Shaftesbury urged the voting of supply for the war
with the Dutch, whom he styled the eternal enemies of England,
quoting the saying of Cato—*Delenda est Carthago*—as though
they were to be destroyed as being to England what Carthage
had been to Rome. So far as the war was concerned, the
House of Commons answered his appeal by offering 1,260,000*l.*,
though they kept back the Bill till they had brought him to
terms.

16. **Withdrawal of the Declaration of Indulgence. 1673.**—
It was at the withdrawal of the Declaration of Indulgence that the
House was aiming. In vain Charles simulated firmness, declaring
himself to be resolved to stick to his declaration. The Commons
bitterly resented his interference with the law. Forty statutes, it was
said, had been violated by the Declaration, and the house passed a
resolution that ' penal statutes in matters ecclesiastical cannot be
suspended but by act of Parliament.' Both sides were anxious to
limit the question to ecclesiastical statutes : Charles, because the
powers over the Church conferred on the Tudor sovereigns were
vague, and therefore more defensible than those exercised by them
in political matters ; the Commons, because they had precedents
of Parliamentary resistance to dispensations granted to recusants,
whereas former kings had usually been allowed without contradiction to suspend the law in commercial matters. Charles tried
to evade the summons of the Commons, but the Lords having
come on March 7 to the same conclusion as the other House, he
gave way on the 8th and recalled his Declaration. As no new
statute was passed on the subject, the legal question remained just
where it was before.

17. **The Test Act. 1673.**—Charles had entered on a struggle
with Parliament and had been defeated. The Royalist Parliament
of 1661 was still Royalist so far as the maintenance of the throne
was concerned, but it had entered on a course of opposition which
had brought it into open collision with the king. From first to
last the chief characteristic of this Parliament was its resolution
to maintain the supremacy of the Church, and it was now obvious

that the Church was in more danger from Roman Catholics than from Dissenters. Though Charles's conversion (see p. 600) was unknown, it was no secret that the Duke of York, the heir to the throne, was a Catholic, and, in spite of the veil thrown over the terms of the Treaty of Dover, the danger of an invasion by French troops in support of the English Catholics was obvious to all. For the first time since the Restoration a Bill was brought in to relieve Protestant Dissenters, and, though this proposal came to nothing, the very fact of its being made showed that a new state of feeling was growing up. Arlington, seeing how things stood, and wishing to oust the Catholic Clifford from the Treasury that he might be his successor, put up a member of the Commons to propose a Bill which soon became law under the name of the Test Act. By it, no one was to hold office who refused to take the test—that is to say, to make a declaration of his disbelief in the doctrine of Transubstantiation and to receive the Sacrament according to the rites of the Church of England. It was only after Charles had given his assent to this Act on March 29 that the proposed grant of 1,260,000*l*. was actually made.

18. **Results of the Test Act. 1673.**—Though most Dissenters were excluded from office by the latter clause of the Test Act, there were some who did not feel their opposition to the Church to be so strong as to preclude them from taking the Sacrament occasionally according to its rites. Every honest Roman Catholic, on the other hand, was at once driven from office. The Duke of York surrendered the Admiralty and Clifford the Treasury. The Test Act was not a persecuting Act in the sense in which the Conventicle Act and the Five Mile Act were persecuting Acts. It inflicted no direct penalty on the mere holding of a special belief, or on the attendance on a special form of worship, but excluded persons holding a certain religious belief from offices the retention of which, according to the prevalent conviction, would be dangerous to the State.

19. **Continuance of the Dutch War. 1673.**—The Treasurership, taken from Clifford, was given, not to Arlington, but to Sir Thomas Osborne, whose sentiments, being strongly in favour of maintaining the predominance of the Church of England, were likely to commend him to the good-will of the Houses. In foreign policy he represented what was fast becoming a general opinion, that, as the main danger to England came from France, it had been a mistake to go to war with the Dutch. This belief was driven home by disasters at sea in the summer of 1673. In May, a com-

bined French and English fleet, under Prince Rupert, fought without advantage against the Dutch. In August Rupert was defeated off the Texel, because the French fleet, which accompanied him, took no part in the action, Louis not wishing to see the English masters of the sea. On this, the English nation turned all its hatred against France.

20. **The Duke of York's Marriage and Shaftesbury's Dismissal. 1673.**—The alarm inspired by the Catholics was increased in the course of **1673** by a marriage which took place in the Royal family. Soon after the Restoration the Duke of York had married Clarendon's daughter, Anne Hyde, and had by her two daughters, Mary and Anne, both of whom were brought up as Protestants, so that, if the Duke outlived his brother, he would, when he himself died, transmit the crown to a Protestant queen. He was now, however, a widower, and took as his second wife a Catholic princess, Mary of Modena. If the new Duchess should bear a son, the boy, who would inevitably be educated as a Catholic, would be the future king of England. When Parliament met in October it was highly indignant, and, as it attacked the king's ministers, it was prorogued after a session of a few days. Charles revenged himself by dismissing a minister whom the Commons had not attacked. Shaftesbury had, earlier in the year, learned the contents of the secret articles of the Treaty of Dover, and had thereby discovered that Charles had made a fool of him as completely as he had made a fool of Buckingham when he sent him to negotiate a sham treaty (see p. 603). Shaftesbury remained true to his policy of toleration, but it was now to be toleration for Dissenters alone. Toleration for Catholics, he now knew, was connected with a scheme for overthrowing English independence with the aid of French soldiers. Accordingly, he supported the Test Act, and, as he continued uncompliant, Charles, on November 9, dismissed him. Shaftesbury at once threw himself into the most violent opposition. Buckingham was dismissed not long afterwards, and the so-called Cabal was thus finally broken up.

21. **Peace with the Dutch. 1674.**—The war with the Dutch was brought to an end by a treaty signed on February 19, **1674**. On the 24th Charles prorogued Parliament, and did not summon it again for more than a year. During the interval, he attempted to win friends all round, without committing himself to any definite policy. On the one hand, he remained on friendly terms with Louis, whilst, on the other hand, he offered the hand of Mary, the eldest child of his brother James, to her cousin, William

of Orange. William's position was far higher than it had been two years before. He was now at the head of an alliance in which the Emperor Leopold, the King of Spain, and the Duke of Lorraine combined with him to restrain the inordinate ambition of Louis. It is true that his generalship was less conspicuous than his diplomacy, and that in the whole course of his life he never succeeded in beating a French army in the field. Yet even in war his indomitable courage and conspicuous coolness stood him in good stead, and he knew better than most commanders how to gather his troops after a defeat and to place them in strong positions in which the enemy did not dare to attack them. The history of Europe during the remainder of his life was the history of a duel between the ambitious and autocratic Louis and the cool-headed William, the first magistrate of a republic in which his action was checked by constitutional restraints on every side, and the head of a coalition of which the members were always prone to take offence and to pursue their individual interests at the sacrifice of the common good. To win England to the alliance was, for William, a most desirable object, but he knew that James might very well have a son by his second marriage, and, knowing that in that case he would reap no political advantage from a marriage with Mary, he for the present refused the offer of her hand.[1]

[1] Genealogy of some of the descendants of Charles I. :—

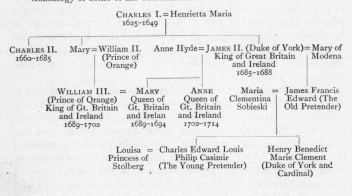

CHARLES I. = Henrietta Maria
1625–1649

CHARLES II.   Mary = William II.   Anne Hyde = JAMES II. (Duke of York) = Mary of
1660–1685   (Prince of   King of Great Britain   Modena
                      Orange)   and Ireland
                                              1685–1688

WILLIAM III.   =   MARY   ANNE   Maria   = James Francis
(Prince of Orange)   Queen of   Queen of   Clementina   Edward (The
King of Gt. Britain Gt. Britain Gt. Britain Sobieski   Old Pretender)
and Ireland   and Irelan and Ireland
1689–1702   1689–1694   1702–1714

Louisa = Charles Edward Louis   Henry Benedict
Princess of   Philip Casimir   Marie Clement
Stolberg   (The Young Pretender)   (Duke of York and
                                        Cardinal)

CHAPTER XXXIX

DANBY'S ADMINISTRATION AND THE THREE SHORT PARLIAMENTS. 1675—1681

LEADING DATES

Reign of Charles II., 1660—1685

Rejection of the Non-Resistance Bill 1675
Marriage of William and Mary . . . . Nov. 15, 1677
The Peace of Nymwegen . . . . . . July 31, 1678
The Popish Plot 1678
Dissolution of the Cavalier Parliament . . . Jan 24, 1679
The First Short Parliament . . March 6—May 27, 1679
The Second Short Parliament . . Oct. 21, 1680—Jan 18, 1681
The Third Short Parliament . . March 21—March 28, 1681

1. **Growing Influence of Danby.** 1675.—Charles's effort to govern in his own way having ended in failure, and, in what he thought to be of more consequence, discomfort to himself, he discovered that he would lead an easier life if he were on good terms with his Parliament than if he quarrelled with it. Being now disposed to throw over whatever troublesome convictions he had imagined himself to have, he gave his confidence to Osborne (see p. 607), whom he had recently created Earl of Danby. Danby revived the domestic policy of Clarendon by maintaining, in accordance with the majority of the Cavalier Parliament, the supremacy of the Church of England over Catholics and Dissenters, and, equally in accordance with the majority of that Parliament, opposed Louis abroad.

2. **Parliamentary Parties.** 1675.—The decision of Charles to support Danby in carrying out a definite policy completed the formation of separate Parliamentary parties. These had, indeed, existed in the Long Parliament under various names, and had reappeared after the Restoration ; but in the Cavalier Parliament the minority in favour of toleration had, at first, been exceedingly small, and, though it had grown larger in the days of the Cabal, it had been distracted by distrust of Charles when he appeared as a patron of toleration. The situation was now clear and the leaders distinctly known. On the one side was Danby and ' No toleration,' on the other side was Shaftesbury and ' Toleration for Dissenters only.' Neither side shrank from base means of acquiring strength.

The ministers who formed the Cabal are said to have been the first who bribed members of the House of Commons, but it was Danby who reduced bribery to a system which was afterwards extended by his successors. Shaftesbury's followers, on the other hand, were quite ready to enter into the pay of Louis, if he would help them to overthrow Danby and would strengthen them against the king.

3. **The Non-Resistance Bill. 1675.**—When Parliament met in April 1675, Danby produced a Bill which was intended to secure his hold on the House of Commons, whatever might be the opinion prevailing in the country. No one was to be allowed to hold office or to sit in Parliament unless he would swear that he believed resistance to the Crown to be in all cases illegal, and that he would never endeavour to alter the government in Church or State. If the Bill had passed, the future liberty of Parliament would have been fettered, and few, if any, who did not approve of the existing Church system could have entered Parliament. The Bill passed the Lords, but while it was still under discussion in the Commons Shaftesbury stirred up so bitter a quarrel between the Houses, that Charles

Ordinary dress of gentlemen in 1675 : from Loggan's *Oxonia Illustrata*.

prorogued Parliament before the Bill could be converted into law.

4. **Charles a Pensionary of France. 1675—1676.**—Parliament, in its distrust of the king, refused him supplies, upon which Charles prorogued it for fifteen months. Louis, who feared lest Parliament should drive Charles into joining the alliance against him, was so pleased to see its sittings interrupted for so long a time that he granted to Charles a pension of 100,000*l.* a year, to make him independent of his subjects. The result was that whilst Charles

allowed Danby to have his own way in domestic affairs, he refused to allow him to detach England from the French alliance. It was not, however, merely his personal interests which drew him to Louis, as he took a real interest in the prosperity of English trade, and was unable to get over his jealousy of the Dutch. In November 1676, he obtained from Louis a treaty by which the French renounced a claim made by them to seize Dutch goods conveyed in English ships, hoping by this to gain the goodwill of Parliament at its next meeting. He could not understand how completely the alarm of his subjects lest their national religion and independence should be assailed by the French had made them forgetful of their commercial jealousy of the Dutch.

5. **Two Foreign Policies. 1677.** — On February 15, 1677, Parliament again met. Shaftesbury and his allies attempted to steal a march on Danby by producing two old statutes of Edward III. which directed that Parliaments should be held every year, founding on it an argument that the existing Parliament, not having met for a year, had legally ceased to exist. The House of Lords sent Shaftesbury and three other peers to the Tower for their pains, and the Commons contemptuously rejected a

Cup presented, 1676, by King Charles II. to the Barber Surgeons' Company.

similar argument put forward in their own House. Danby found himself triumphant. The Commons granted 600,000*l.* for increasing the navy. Danby then carried a Bill through the House of Lords for securing the Protestant religion in the event of a Catholic—James being, of course, intended—coming to the throne, though the Bill did not pass the Commons, apparently from a feeling that its provisions were insufficient. The eyes of Englishmen were, however, principally fixed on the Continent. In the preceding year the French had gained two great naval victories, in one of which De Ruyter had been slain, and in the spring of 1677 Louis carried one place after another in the Spanish Netherlands. Both Houses now asked Charles to join the alliance against France, whereupon Charles indignantly prorogued Parliament. When he was urged by the Dutch ambassador to act upon the wishes of the Houses he threw his handkerchief into the air, with the accompanying words : " I care just that for Parliament."

6. **The Marriage of the Prince of Orange. 1677.**—Louis paid to Charles 1,600,000*l.* for the prorogation which rid France for a time from the danger of a war with England. Charles, however, shrank from a renewal of the struggle with his Parliament on its next meeting, and, though he was resolved not to go to war with France if he could help it, he was ready to help in bringing about a general peace which would relieve him from all further invitation to join the allies. He accordingly welcomed Danby's suggestion that the plan for a marriage between the Prince of Orange and James's daughter Mary should be again taken up, especially as he hoped that it would break down the good understanding which existed between the Prince and Shaftesbury, and would smooth away the hostility of his subjects to his brother's right of succession. William, knowing that the feeling of Englishmen of both parties was in his favour, visited his uncles, and his marriage with Mary took place on November 15, 1677. The marriage, which was to prove of incalculable importance in the future, was of great significance even at the time, as it marked the end of the hostile feeling against the Dutch which, for so many years, had been the dominant note of English foreign politics.

7. **Danby's Position. 1677.**—Though Danby had brought Charles round to support his foreign as well as his domestic policy, his success was more apparent than real. The fact was that his foreign and domestic policies were inconsistent with one another. In the long run it would be found impossible to contend against the French king and the English Catholics supported by him,

Steeple of the Church of St. Mary-le-Bow, London ; built by Sir Christopher Wren between 1671 and 1680.

without calling in the aid of those Protestant Dissenters who were most hostile to Louis. Englishmen attached to the Church were being led by their growing distrust of France to a tenderer feeling towards Dissenters, and the spread of this feeling made in favour of Shaftesbury, who favoured toleration, and not in favour of Danby, who opposed it. For the present, however, Danby could count on the Parliamentary majority which agreed with him, and neither he nor the king wished to risk a dissolution.

8. **The Peace of Nymwegen. 1678.**—When Parliament met in February **1678**, Charles appeared full of determination. He declared that, unless Louis agreed to make peace with the Dutch on reasonable terms, he would go to war with France. The Commons at once resolved to grant him 1,000,000*l.*, and to support an army of 30,000 men and a fleet of 90 ships. Before this resolution was embodied in an Act, without which Charles could not touch the money, the followers of Shaftesbury took alarm. They believed— and, as is now known, not without reason—that Charles intended to use the troops to make himself absolute. They not only pressed him to disband what troops· he had, but they entered into communication with Louis' ambassador, in the hope

that he would support them in forcing Charles to dismiss his troops and to dissolve Parliament, some of them even accepting from him gifts of money. Charles, on his part, vacillated, doubting which was the best policy for him to adopt. At one time he was eager to assist the Dutch, and sent troops to their succour in the hope that a victorious army might afterwards be useful to him in England. At another time he made overtures to Louis with the object of securing his support. In the end, on July 31, Louis and the Dutch made peace at Nymwegen without consulting Charles at all. Louis gained Franche Comté and a large number of fortresses on his northern frontier, which had formerly belonged to Spain. Though he had failed to destroy the Dutch Republic, he had shown himself superior in war to a great continental coalition, and had made France the predominant power in Europe.

9. **The Popish Plot. 1678.**—The part played by the king left the English people gravely dissatisfied with him. They feared lest he should seek to overwhelm their liberties by military force and should bring in French regiments to support his own troops. Their suspicions were heightened by the knowledge that, if Charles died, his brother, an uncompromising Roman Catholic, would succeed him. In August, 1678, a villain appeared to profit by this prevalent distrust. Titus Oates, a liar from his youth up, who had tried various religions and had recently professed himself a Catholic, announced the existence of a great ' Popish plot.' Charles, he said, was to be murdered, and James set upon the throne as the agent of the Jesuits. A French army was to land to support him, and Protestantism was to be absolutely suppressed. It was true that many Catholics were anxious to see James on the throne and had expressed contempt at Charles's conduct in refusing to declare himself one of themselves, but the rest of Oates's story was absolutely false.

10. **Growing Excitement. 1678.**—Oates's depositions were taken before a Middlesex magistrate, Sir Edmond Berry Godfrey. The next morning Godfrey was found murdered in the fields near Primrose Hill. All London was wild with excitement. It was widely believed that ' the Papists' had murdered him to punish him for listening to Oates. It was also held to be an undoubted truth that ' the Papists' were about to set fire to London, and to murder all good Protestants. A joiner named College made his fortune by inventing a pocket flail, tipped with lead, which was called the Protestant flail, and was to be used by sober citizens to brain ' Popish' assassins. When Parliament met on

October 21 Shaftesbury, who had been liberated early in the year, unscrupulously encouraged belief in the supposed plot. Up to that time Catholic peers had kept their seats in the House of Lords, and a few Catholics had surreptitiously sat in the Commons. A new Test Act was now passed by which they were excluded [1] from both Houses, though the Duke of York was exempted by name from its operation. Five Catholic peers were thrown into the Tower, and Coleman, the secretary of the Duchess of York, who had in his custody papers implying that James had a design for forwarding the interests of his religion, was tried and executed.

11. Danby's Impeachment and the Dissolution of the Cavalier Parliament. 1678—1679.—The mark at which Shaftesbury aimed was the overthrow of Danby. Danby had always, as far as his own opinion went, been a warm antagonist of France, but a minister was still, in those days, in reality the servant of the king, and was bound to carry out his master's orders, even when they were against his own conviction. Danby had, therefore, at the time when the Peace of Nymwegen was under discussion, written letters to Ralph Montague, the English ambassador in France, bidding him to ask Louis for a considerable payment to Charles, and, at the same time, explaining that the money was needed to make Charles independent of Parliament. Montague, having subsequently returned to England, brought this letter before the House of Commons. The House at once impeached Danby, under the false impression that he had been really subservient to France all the while. Charles had become attached to Danby, and knew that, if the proceedings against him were carried on, matters would come to light which he had every reason to conceal. To save himself and his minister, on January 24, **1679**, he dissolved the Cavalier Parliament, which had now sat for more than seventeen years.

12. The Meeting of the First Short Parliament. 1679.—When the elections to a new Parliament—the first of three short Parliaments—were completed, Charles found that, with the exception of at most thirty members, the opposition had gained every seat. Bowing to the storm, he sent his brother to Brussels, and expressed his readiness to place himself at the head of the Protestants of the Continent. When, however, Parliament met, on March 6, **1679**, it was found that both Houses were more anxious

---

[1] By the Test Act of 1672 offices only were closed to the Catholics (see p. 607); the oath of supremacy, which had to be taken by every member of the House of Commons, being held sufficient to exclude them from that Assembly. Peers might sit in the House of Lords without taking the oath.

about the fate of Protestantism at home than about that of Protestants abroad. The Commons renewed the impeachment of Danby, upon which Danby produced a free pardon from the king. The Lords decided that a pardon could not be pleaded in bar of an impeachment, but, in the end, proceedings against Danby were dropped on his being deprived of office and committed to the Tower. By the advice of Sir William Temple, Charles tried a new experiment in government.. A new Privy Council was appointed of thirty members, fifteen being ministers of the Crown and fifteen influential lords and commoners, by the advice of which the king was always to be guided. Shaftesbury was appointed President of this Council, but it was soon found to be too large a body to manage affairs which required secrecy, and a small committee was therefore formed out of it for the consideration of all important business.

13. **The Exclusion Bill and the Habeas Corpus Act. 1679.**— Charles, now that he experienced the strength of the opposition, was prepared to give way on every point except one—the maintenance of his brother's right of succession, which the new House of Commons was prepared to attack. He accordingly offered to place the strongest restrictions upon the power of a Catholic king. To the House of Commons, on the other hand, all restrictions appeared insufficient. The members believed seriously that no law would be able to bind a ' Popish ' king. They thought that if he was determined—and it was taken for granted that he would be determined—to overthrow the Protestant religion, he would be able to do so. Lord Russell, the eldest son of the Duke of Bedford— the chief leader of Shaftesbury's party in the House of Commons— was not in the habit of using exaggerated language. Yet even he declared that, if James became king, his subjects must make up their mind to become ' Papists ' or to be burnt. An Exclusion Bill was brought in, excluding the Duke of York from the throne. It was read twice, but not passed, as Charles first prorogued, and then, on May 27, dissolved Parliament. The only Act of importance produced in this Parliament was the *Habeas Corpus Act*, which finally put an end to sundry methods by which the Crown had evaded the rule requiring the issue of writs of *Habeas Corpus*, by which prisoners secured their right to be tried or liberated.

14. **Shaftesbury and the King. 1679.**—New elections were held, with the result that a House of Commons was chosen even more bitterly hostile to the Court than its predecessor. Shaftesbury

was now at the height of his glory. Oates and other informers were adding new lies to those which they had told before, and the continual trials and executions of the Catholics for participation in the supposed Popish Plot kept the excitement in favour of the Exclusion Bill at a fever heat. Shaftesbury's position was very similar to Pym's in 1641. He had on his side the fundamental principle that a nation cannot safely be governed by a ruler whose ideas on the most important question of the day are directly opposed to those of his subjects, and he was right, as the result showed, in holding that, in the seventeenth century, a Catholic king could not satisfactorily govern a Protestant people. After Danby's fall, the king became the real head of the party opposed to Shaftesbury. His ability had always been great, but hitherto he had alienated those who were disposed to be his friends by attempting to establish an absolute government with the help of the king of France and of an army dependent on himself. He now set himself to overthrow Shaftesbury by appealing to a popular sentiment which was quite as strong, and might be stronger, than the dislike of a Catholic successor ; that is to say, to the horror with which anything which threatened a new civil war filled the hearts of his subjects.

15. **Shaftesbury and Halifax. 1679.**—Shaftesbury had already allowed it to be known that he intended, if he carried the Exclusion Bill, to propose that the future king should be the Duke of Monmouth. Monmouth was the eldest of Charles's illegitimate sons, and it was currently, though falsely, believed that Charles had been privately married to his mother, so that he might rightly be regarded as the heir to the Crown. Charles, who knew better than any one else that this story was untrue, stood faithfully by his brother, and, though his constancy made little impression as yet, he had on his side a man whose judgment might usually be taken as an indication of the ultimate decision of public opinion. That man was George Savile, Earl, and afterwards Marquis of Halifax. He had been one of the bitterest enemies of Danby, but he devoted himself to no party. He called himself a Trimmer, as if his business was to trim the boat, and to throw himself against each party in turn as it grew violent in consequence of success. He now supported the king against Shaftesbury, on the ground that it was uncertain whether James would survive his brother, and that, if he did, he was not likely to survive him long ; whereas, the succession of the Duke of Monmouth would not only exclude from the throne the Catholic James, but also his daughters, who were both Protestants.

As Monmouth had no real hereditary right, there was every likelihood that, even if he ascended the throne, his claim would be opposed by partisans of James's eldest daughter, the Princess of Orange, and that a civil war would ensue.

16. **The Divine Right of Kings. 1679.**—The fear of civil war already frightened some, and would in time frighten more, into the acceptance of a doctrine which seems very absurd now—the doctrine of Divine indefeasible hereditary right—that is to say, that the succession as it was established by English law was established by Divine appointment, so that, though indeed subjects might refuse to obey the king, if he ordered them to commit sin, it was their duty to bear uncomplainingly any punishment that he might impose on them, however tyrannical he might be. Such a doctrine was credited, not because those who held it were absolutely silly, but because they were more afraid of rebellion and civil war than they were of the tyranny of kings. For the present, however, such ideas had little hold on the new Parliament, and Charles prorogued it to give time for them to grow.

17. **The Highland Host. 1677—1678.**—Events were in the meanwhile passing in Scotland which helped to impress upon those who were easily frightened the idea that the only security against rebellion lay in a general submission to established institutions in Church and State. For many years Lauderdale had been, with Charles's full support, the absolute ruler of Scotland. He put down with a high hand the opposition of noblemen in Parliament, but he could not put down the religious zeal of the peasants, who, especially in the western Lowlands, combined zeal for Presbyterianism and the Covenant with exasperation against a Government which persecuted them. They held meetings for prayer and preaching on the open hill-sides, and the Government, failing to suppress these Conventicles, as they were called, by process of law, sent into the disaffected districts, in 1677, a body of half-savage Highlanders known as the Highland Host, to reduce them to obedience by plunder and outrage.

18. **Drumclog and Bothwell Bridge. 1679.**—When the Highland Host had done its work it left behind a people whose temper was thoroughly soured. Political hatred of the oppressors mingled with religious zeal. The Covenanters, as those were called who denounced episcopacy as a breach of the Covenant (see p. 525), regarded themselves as God's chosen people and all who supported their persecutors as the children of the devil, against whom it was lawful to draw the sword. To many of the Scottish gentry

s s 2

such talk as this appeared to be contemptible and dangerous fanaticism. Amongst those who strove most heartily against it was an active officer, John Graham of Claverhouse, who, being employed to quiet the country, shot or haled to prison men whom he thought likely to be forward in rebellion. On May 3, **1679**, a band of fanatics murdered, on Magus Moor, near St. Andrews, James Sharp, Archbishop of St. Andrews, who was known to be eager to call for the persecution of the Covenanters, and who was peculiarly hated as having been once a Presbyterian himself. On June 3 Claverhouse was driven back at Drumclog by an armed conventicle which he attempted to suppress. The peasants of the West rose in arms and declared against the king's supremacy over the Church, and against Popery, Prelacy, and the succession of the Duke of York, but on June 22, Monmouth, who had been sent at the head of an army against them, defeated them at Bothwell Bridge, near Hamilton, and entirely suppressed the rebellion. Many of the prisoners were executed after being tortured to extract from them information against their accomplices, and this cruelty was exercised under the orders of the Duke of York, who had been sent to Scotland as Lord High Commissioner.[1]

19. **Petitioners and Abhorrers. 1680.**—Encouraged by his success in Scotland, Charles dismissed Shaftesbury from the presidency of the Council and got rid of his principal supporters. Temple's reformed Council came thereby to an end. When Monmouth returned from Scotland his father refused to see him and sent him away from London. In the beginning of **1680** Shaftesbury's party sent up numerous petitions to ask Charles to allow Parliament to meet, and his opponents sent up petitions expressing abhorrence at such an attempt to force the king's will. For a time the two parties were known as Petitioners and Abhorrers, names which were soon replaced by those of Whigs and Tories. These celebrated names were at first merely nicknames. The courtiers called the Petitioners Whigs—an abbreviation of Whigamore, the name by which the peasants of the west of Scotland were familiarly known, from the cry of 'Whiggam' with which they were accustomed to encourage their horses. The name Whig therefore implied that the petitioners were no better than Covenanting rebels. The Petitioners, on the other hand, called their opponents Tories—the name given to brigands in Ireland, implying that they were no better than Popish thieves.

20. **The Second Short Parliament. 1680—1681.**—Each party

---

[1] Scott's *Old Mortality* is founded on these events.

did all that could be done to court popularity.   Monmouth made a triumphant progress in the west of England.   On the other hand, James, on his return from Scotland, had a good reception even in London, the head-quarters of his opponents.   On June 26, 1680, Shaftesbury appeared at Westminster and indicted James as a recusant.   At last, on October 21, the second Short Parliament met.   The Exclusion Bill was rapidly passed through the Commons.   In the Lords, Halifax carried the House with him by an eloquent and closely-reasoned speech, in which the claims of the Princess of Orange were dwelt on as superior to those of Monmouth, and the Bill was, in consequence, rejected.   On December 29 Lord Stafford, a Catholic peer, was executed on a false charge of a design to murder the king.   When he protested his innocence on the scaffold, shouts were raised of " God bless you, my lord !   We believe you, my lord !"   Charles saw in these shouts an indication that the tide of opinion was turning in his favour, and, on January 18, **1681**, dissolved Parliament.

21. **The Third Short Parliament. 1681.**—Charles summoned a new Parliament to meet at Oxford, where it would not be exposed to any violent interruption by Shaftesbury's ' brisk boys '—as his noisy London supporters were called—who might, it was feared, repeat the exploits of the City mob in **1641** (see p. 535).   The new House of Commons was again predominantly Whig, and it was thought by the Whigs that Oxford had been selected as the place of meeting because the University was eminently Tory, with the deliberate intention of overpowering them by force.   Their alarm increased when they learned that the king was bringing his guards with him.   Accordingly the Whigs armed themselves and their servants in self-defence, and, in this guise, rode into Oxford.   Parliament was opened on March 21, 1681, and Charles then offered to assent to any scheme for stripping his brother of royal authority, if only he were recognised as king.   Shaftesbury replied that the only way of ending the dispute was to declare Monmouth heir to the Crown.   As the Commons supported Shaftesbury, Charles, on March 28, dissolved his third Short Parliament.   So much was he afraid that the Whig members and their servants might lay violent hands on him, that he drove in one coach to Christchurch Hall, where the House of Lords was sitting, and sent his robes by another, in order that it might not be guessed that a dissolution was intended.   He soon found that he could now count on popular support in almost every part of England.   The mass of people judge more by what they see than by what they hear.   The pistols in the hands of the

Whig members when they rode into Oxford had driven into men's heads the belief that they intended to gain their ends by civil war, and, much as the nation disliked the idea of having a ' Popish ' king, it disliked the idea of civil war still more, and rallied round the king.

CHAPTER XL

THE LAST YEARS OF CHARLES II. 1681—1685

LEADING DATES

Reign of Charles II., 1660—1685

Tory Reaction	1681
Flight of Shaftesbury	1682
Forfeiture of the Charter of the City of London . . .	1683
The Rye House Plot	1683
Executions of Russell and Sidney	1683
Death of Charles II.	Feb. 6, 1685

1. **Tory Reaction. 1681.**—The Tory reaction which followed made itself especially felt in the law-courts. Judges and juries who had combined to send to death innocent Catholics, upon the testimony of forsworn informers, now combined to send to death ardent Whigs, upon the testimony of informers equally base. College, the inventor of the Protestant flail (see p. 615), was condemned to death, as having borne arms in Oxford during the last Parliament, and others shared his fate on equally slight grounds. In the City of London, however, it was still impossible to secure a verdict against a Whig. Juries were everywhere nominated by the sheriff of the county, and sheriffs were, in political cases, ready to compose a jury of political partisans. In every part of England except Middlesex, the sheriffs were named by the king, and were, therefore, Tories. The City of London, which was strongly Whig, had the privilege of electing sheriffs for London and Middlesex, and these sheriffs took care that Middlesex juries should be composed of Whigs. Shaftesbury was accused of high treason, but before he could be tried the Grand Jury of Middlesex had to find a true bill against him—that is to say, to declare that there was sufficient evidence against him to call for a trial. On November 24, **1681,** the Grand Jury, composed of his own political partisans, threw out the bill, and he was at once set at liberty.

2. **'Absolom and Achitophel.' 1681.**—A few days before Shaftesbury's release, Dryden, the greatest living master of the heroic couplet, strove to stir up men's minds against the prisoner by his satire of 'Absolom and Achitophel,' in which the part of the tempter Achitophel was assigned to Shaftesbury and the part of the tempted Absolom to Monmouth. Shaftesbury was described as

> For close designs and crooked councils fit ;
> Sagacious, bold, and turbulent of wit ;
> Restless, unfixed in principles and place ;
> In power unpleased, impatient of disgrace ;
> A fiery soul, which worketh out its way,
> Fretted the pigmy body to decay,
> And o'er-informed the tenement of clay.
> A daring pilot in extremity ;
> Pleased with the danger when the waves ran high,
> He sought the storms ; but, for a calm unfit,
> Would steer too nigh the sands to show his wit.

3. **The Scottish Test Act and the Duke of York's Return. 1681—1682.**—The 'daring pilot's' course was nearly run. Before long, on May 27, **1682**, Shaftesbury's most conspicuous enemy, the Duke of York, returned from Scotland. Whilst he was in Scotland he had obtained an Act from the Scottish Parliament, binding on all officials a new test, requiring them to swear to the doctrine of hereditary right and to the maintenance of the episcopal Church. The Earl of Argyle, the son of the Marquis of Argyle, the political leader of the Covenanters against Charles I., having inherited his father's Presbyterianism, not only refused the oath, but gave reasons for refusing. The Crown lawyers declared that his reasons poisoned the minds of the subjects against the king, and he was tried and condemned to death under an old statute against leasing-making— literally, the making of lies—which had been passed about a century before to punish court favourites who sowed dissension between the king and his people by poisoning the mind of the king against his subjects. Argyle, however, escaped to Holland, and on April 20, **1682,** James reached London.

4. **The City Elections. 1682.**—The first thing on which, after James's return, the king's ministers set their heart, was to strike a blow at Shaftesbury. As he lived in his house in Aldersgate Street and took care never to leave the City, it was impossible to bring him to trial as long as the sheriffs of London and Middlesex were Whigs. The Lord Mayor, Moore, was gained by the Court, and, by various unscrupulous contrivances, he secured the appointment

of two Tory sheriffs, and, even before the end of 1682, of a Tory Lord Mayor named Prichard as his own successor. There would no longer be any difficulty in filling the Middlesex jury box with Tories.

5. **Flight and Death of Shaftesbury. 1682—1683.**—Shaftesbury had for some time been keenly alive to the danger impending over him. He had wild followers in the City ready to follow him in acts of violence, and he had proposed to Russell and Monmouth that the king's guards at Whitehall should be attacked, and the king compelled to do his bidding. Russell and Monmouth recoiled from an act of violence which would certainly end in bloodshed. Shaftesbury still hoped to effect his end by the aid of his less scrupulous supporters ; but time slipped away, and on October 19, three days before Prichard's election, he fled to Holland, where he died on January 22, 1683. With all his faults, he had led the way on that path in which the English nation was, before long, to walk, as he had latterly striven for a combination of Parliamentary supremacy with toleration for dissenters and without toleration for Catholics. His personal failure was due to the disquietude caused by his turbulence in the minds of that large part of the community which regards orderly government as a matter of primary necessity.

6. **The Attack on the City. 1682—1683.**—The difficulty which Charles had experienced in bending the city to his will made him anxious to provide against similar resistance in the future. Taking care to effect his objects under, at least, the form of law, he enforced on the electors in the City, who were called in December to choose the Common Council, the oath of supremacy and the proof required by the Corporation Act of having received the Sacrament in the Church. The result was that a Tory majority was returned on the Common Council. Following up this blow in 1683, he called on the City to show cause, by a writ known as '*Quo Warranto*,' before the King's Bench, why its charter should not be forfeited, in consequence of its having imposed irregular tolls and having attacked the king's authority in a petition exhibited in 1680. The King's Bench decided against the City, and the king then offered to restore the charter on certain conditions, of which the principal was, that he was to have a veto on the election of its principal officers. At first the City accepted his terms, but, before the end of the year, it drew back, and the king then named the Lord Mayor and other officers directly, paying no further regard to the municipal self-government under which the City had, for many centuries, conducted its own affairs.

7. **The Remodelling of the Corporations. 1683—1684.** — A

large number of other corporate towns were treated as London had been treated. By a plentiful use of writs of *Quo Warranto*, the judges on circuit obtained the surrender of their charters, after which the king issued new ones in which Tories alone were named as members of the corporations. It was said of Jeffreys, one amongst the judges who was most subservient, that he ' made all charters, like the walls of Jericho, fall down before him.' The object of these proceedings was to make sure of a Tory Parliament when the time came for fresh elections. In a large number of boroughs the corporations chose the members, and in such cases wherever the corporation had been remodelled, there would be a safe Tory seat. At the same time the laws against the Dissenters were strictly executed, and the prisons filled with their ministers.

8. **The Rye House Plot. 1683.**—When injustice is done under legal forms, there are usually some persons who think it allowable to appeal to force. Some of Shaftesbury's more violent followers formed a plot to attack the king and his brother at the Rye House on their return from Newmarket, and either to seize or murder them. The plot failed, as Charles passed the Rye House some days earlier than was expected, and several of the conspirators were taken and executed.

9. **The Whig Combination. 1683.**—The discovery of the Rye House Plot brought to light a dangerous combination amongst the Parliamentary Whigs, in which Monmouth, Russell, Essex, Lord Howard of Escrick, and other notable persons were implicated. They had, indeed, kept themselves free from any intention to offer personal violence to the king, but they had attempted to form an association strong enough to compel him to summon another Parliament, though apparently without coming to a definite conclusion as to the way in which they were to use compulsion. In their own eyes their project was no more than constitutional agitation. In the eyes of the king and of the Crown lawyers it was a preparation for rebellion. Essex committed suicide in prison, whilst Howard of Escrick turned informer against his friends.

10. **Trial and Execution of Lord Russell. 1683.**—Russell was accordingly put on his trial as a traitor. In those days no one on his trial for treason was allowed to be defended by a lawyer, as far as the facts of the case were concerned, but no objection was taken to his having some one near him to take notes of the evidence and to assist his memory. " Your friends," wrote his wife to him shortly before the trial, " believing I can do you some service at your trial, I am extremely willing to try. My

resolution will hold out, pray let yours." Her offer was accepted, and she gave her husband all the help that it was possible to give. The jury, however, brought in a verdict of guilty, and sentence of death followed. In prison Russell was visited by two ministers, Tillotson and Burnet. No clergymen in England were more liberal-minded than these two, yet they urged the prisoner to acknowledge that resistance to the king was in all cases unlawful. Russell maintained that, in extreme cases, subjects might resist. Here lay the root of the political animosity between Whig and Tory. Whether an extreme case had occurred was a matter of opinion. " As for the share I had in the prosecution of the Popish Plot," Russell declared on the scaffold, " I take God to witness that I proceeded in it in the sincerity of my heart, being then really convinced, as I am still, that there was a conspiracy against the king, the nation, and the Protestant religion." It was because the nation at large no longer held this to be true that the Tories were in power.

11. **Execution of Algernon Sidney.   1683.**—Russell's trial was followed by that of Algernon Sidney. Though the real charge against him was that of having conspired against the king, only one, and that a not very credible, witness could be produced as evidence of this; and the prosecuting lawyers then brought forward a treatise, written in his own hand, but neither printed nor circulated in manuscript, in which he had advocated the right of subjects to depose their king. This was held to be equivalent to having a second witness against him, and Sidney was condemned and executed. He was a theoretical Republican, and it was hard to bring up against him a writing which he had never published. Other less important Whigs were also put to death. Monmouth owed his pardon to his father's tenderness, but, as he still continued to bear himself as the head of a party, he was sent into honourable exile in Holland.

12. **Parties at Court.   1684.**—In the spring of **1684** three years had passed without a Parliament, although the statute repealing the Triennial Act (see p. 588) had declared that Parliament ought to be summoned every three years. So sure was Charles of his ground that he liberated Danby without causing a murmur of complaint. At Court there were two parties, one led by Halifax, which urged that, by summoning a Parliament now, Charles would not only comply with the law, but would have a Parliament as loyal as the Cavalier Parliament had been ; the other, led by Lawrence Hyde, the second son of Clarendon,

who had recently been created Earl of Rochester. Rochester, who was the highest of Tories, pointed out that the law prescribed no means by which the king could be compelled to call a Parliament if he did not wish to do so, and that, after all, the Cavalier Parliament, loyal as it was at first, had made itself very disagreeable to the king during the latter years of its existence. All through the year Charles hesitated and left the question undecided. The king of France, who was renewing his aggressions on the Continent under the guise of legal claims, was ready to do all he could to prevent the meeting of an English Parliament, which would, in all probability, declare against him, and by sending money to Charles from time to time, he saved him from the necessity of asking his subjects for support.

13. **Death of Charles II. 1685.**—On February 2, 1685, before anything had been decided, Charles was struck down by an apoplectic stroke. It was soon known that he was dying. Sancroft, the Archbishop of Canterbury, spoke plainly to him : " It is time," he said, " to speak out ; for, sir, you are about to appear before a Judge who is no respecter of persons." The king took no notice, and, after a while, the Duke of York came to his bed-side and asked his brother whether he wished to be reconciled to the Church of Rome. " Yes," murmured the dying man, " with all my heart !' James sent for a priest, directing the bishops and the courtiers to leave the room. Charles was duly reconciled, receiving absolution and the sacraments of the Roman Church. He lingered for some days, and begged pardon of those around him. He had been, he said, an unconscionable time in dying, but he hoped they would excuse it. On February 6 he died.

14. **Constitutional Progress. 1660—1685.**—The twenty-five years of the reign of Charles II. were years of substantial constitutional progress. Charles did not, indeed, acknowledge that Parliament had that right of directing the choice of his ministers which the Long Parliament had upheld against his father in the Grand Remonstrance ; but though he took care that his ministers should be responsible to himself and not to Parliament, he had also taken care, on the whole, to adapt the selection of his ministers to the changing temper of Parliament and the nation. Clarendon, the Cabal, and Danby had all been allowed to disappear from office when Parliament turned against them. The formation of Parliamentary parties, again, was itself a condition of Parliamentary strength. The Cavalier Parliament had been weakened in its later years by the uncertainty of its aims. At one time the king's

reliance upon France and his tendency to rest his government on armed force provoked a majority to vote against him. At another time some concession made by him to their wishes brought

round a majority to his side. In the latter years of Charles's reign this uncertainty was at an end. Charles had thrown his dependence on France and the army into the background, and in a struggle, the successful issue of which would bring no personal advantage to himself, had taken his stand on the intelligible principle of defending his brother's succession. He had consequently rallied round the throne all who thought the maintenance of order to be of supreme importance, whilst all who suspected that the order which Charles maintained was hurtful and oppressive combined against him. This sharp division of parties ultimately

Dress of ladies of quality : from Sandford's *Coronation Procession of James II.*

strengthened the power of Parliament. The intemperance of Charles's adversaries had indeed given him the upper hand for the time, but, if ever the day came when a king made himself unpopular, a Parliament opposed to him would be all the stronger if its majority were of one mind in supporting definite principles under definite leaders. Charles II., in short, did not live to see the establishment of Parliamentary government, but he unwittingly prepared the way for it.

Ordinary attire of women of the lower classes : from Sandford's *Coronation Procession of James II.*

15. **Prosperity of the Country.**—The horror of a renewal of civil war, which was partly the result of sad experience, was also

the result of the growth of the general well-being of the community. The population of England now exceeded 5,000,000. Rents were rising, and commerce was rapidly on the increase. Fresh colonies—amongst them Pennsylvania and Carolina—were founded in America. In England itself the growth of London was an index to the general prosperity. In those days the City was the home of the merchants, who did not then leave the place where their

Coach of the latter half of the seventeenth century : from Loggan's
Oxonia Illustrata.

business was done to spend the evening and night in the suburbs. Living side by side, they clung to one another, and their civic ardour created a strength which weighed heavily in the balance of parties. The opposition of the City to Charles I. had given the victory to Parliament in the civil war, and its dislike of military government had done much to bring about the Restoration. The favour of the City had been the chief support of Shaftesbury, and it was only by

Wagon of the second half of the seventeenth century : from Loggan's *Oxonia Illustrata.*

overthrowing its municipal institutions that Charles II. had succeeded in crippling its power to injure him. In the meantime a new forest of houses was springing up on sites between Lincoln's Inn and what is now known as Soho Square, and round St. James's Church. The Court and the frequent meetings of Parliament attracted to London many families which, a generation earlier, would have lived entirely in the country.

16. **The Coffee Houses.**—Nothing has made a greater change in the material habits of Europeans than the introduction of warm beverages.   Chocolate first made its way into England in the time of the Commonwealth, but it was for some time regarded merely as a medicine, not to be taken by the prudent except under a physician's orders, though those interested in its sale declared that it was suitable for all, and would cure every possible complaint.   Chocolate was soon followed by coffee, and coffee soon became fashionable, not as a medicine, but as a pleasant substitute for beer and wine.   The introduction of tea was somewhat later.

Reaping and harvesting in the second half of the seventeenth century ; Cambridge in the distance : from Loggan's *Cantabrigia Illustrata.*

It was in the reign of Charles II. that coffee-houses arose in London, and became places of resort, answering the purposes of the modern clubs.   They soon acquired political importance, matters of state being often discussed in them, and the opinion of their frequenters carrying weight with those who were directly concerned with Government.   The gathering of men of intellectual prominence to London was a marked feature of the time, and, except at the universities, there was scarcely a preacher or a theological writer of note who was not to be found either in the episcopate or at the head of a London parish.

17. **Condition of London.**—The arrangements for cleanliness did not keep pace in London with the increased magnificence of the dwellings. The centre of Lincoln's Inn Fields, for instance, was a place where rubbish was shot, and where beggars congregated. St. James's Square was just as bad, whilst filthy and discoloured streams poured along the gutters, and carts and carriages splashed mud and worse than mud over the passengers on foot. At the beginning of the reign of Charles II. the streets were left in darkness, and robbers made an easy prey of those who ventured out after dark. Young noblemen and gentlemen when drunk took pleasure in knocking down men and insulting women. These were they of whom Milton was thinking when he declared that

> In luxurious cities, when the noise
> Of riot ascends above their loftiest towers,
> And injury, and outrage : and when night
> Darkens the streets, then wander forth the sons
> Of Belial, flown with insolence and wine.

Something was, however, done before the end of the reign to mitigate the dangers arising from darkness. One man obtained a patent for lighting London, and it was thought a great thing that he placed a lantern in front of one door in every ten in winter only, between six and midnight.

18. **Painting.**—The art of the time, so far as painting was concerned, was entirely in the hands of foreigners. Van Dyck, a Fleming, from Antwerp, had left to the world numerous representations of Charles I. and Henrietta Maria, of Strafford and Laud, and of the ladies and gentlemen who thronged the Court. An Englishman, Samuel Cooper, made posterity acquainted with the features of Cromwell (see p. 567). Charles II. again called in the services of a foreigner, whose real name was Van der Goes, but who called himself Lely, because his father's house on the borders of Germany and the Netherlands was known by the sign of the Lily. Lely painted Court beauties and Court gentlemen. He had far less power than Van Dyck of presenting on canvas the mind which lies behind the features, and in many cases those who sat to him had minds less worthy of being presented than those with which Van Dyck had to do. When Charles II. wished for a painting of the sea and of shipping he had to send for a Dutch painter, Vandevelde ; whilst an Italian, Verrio, decorated his ceilings with subjects taken from heathen mythology.

19. **Architecture.**—In architecture alone English hands were

found to do the work required ; but the style in which they built was not English but Italian. The rows of pillars and round arches, with the meaningless decorations which bespoke an age preferring sumptuousness to beauty, superseded the quaint Elizabethan and early Jacobean houses, which seemed built for comfort rather than for display, such as Ingestre Hall (see p. 471) and Hatfield House (see p. 485). In the reign of James I., Inigo Jones planned the great banqueting hall at Whitehall (see p. 493), and so contemptuous was he of the great architecture of the middle ages, that he fitted on an Italian portico to the west front of the old St. Paul's. This style of building culminated in the work of Sir Christopher Wren. The fire of London gave him an opportunity which he did not throw away. The steeple of St. Mary-le-Bow is an example of his powers of design (see p. 614), but his greatest achievement, the new St. Paul's, was, when Charles II. died, only slowly rising from the ground, and it remained uncompleted till long after Charles II. had been laid in the grave.

Costume of a gentleman : from Sandford's *Coronation Procession of James II.*

20. **Science.**—The foundation of the Royal Society (see p. 598) had borne ample fruit. Halley and Flamsteed were the astronomers of the time till their fame was eclipsed by that of Isaac Newton, who before the end of the reign of Charles II. was already meditating on the views contained in his ‘Principia,’ in which the law of gravitation was set forth, though that work was not written till after the death of that king.

21. **Difficulties of Communication.**—Difficulties of communication served both to encourage town life and to hinder the increase of manufactures at any considerable distance from the sea. The roads were left to each parish to repair, and the parishes usually did as little as possible. In many places a mere quagmire took the

place of the road. Young and active men, and sometimes ladies, travelled on horseback, and goods of no great weight were transmitted on packhorses. The family coach, in which those who were too dignified or too weak to ride made their way from one part of the country to another, was dragged by six horses, and often sank so deeply in the mud as only to be extricated by the loan of additional plough horses from a neighbouring farm, whilst heavy goods were conveyed in lumbering waggons, still more difficult to move even at a moderate speed. For passengers who could not afford to keep a coach the carrier's waggon served as a slow conveyance ; but before the end of the reign of Charles II. there had been introduced a vehicle known as The Flying Coach, which managed to perform a journey at the rate of fifty miles a day in summer and thirty in winter, in districts in which roads were exceptionally good.

22. **The Country Gentry and the Country Clergy.** — These difficulties of communication greatly affected the less wealthy of the country gentry and the country clergy. A country gentleman of large fortune, indeed, would occasionally visit London and appear as a visitor at the house of some relative or friend to whom he was specially attached. The movements, however, even of this class were much restricted, whilst men of moderate estate seldom moved at all. The refinements which at present adorn country life were not then to be found. Books were few, and the man of comparatively slender means found sufficient occupation in the management of his land and in the enjoyment of field sports. His ideas on politics were crude, and, because they were crude, were pertinaciously held. The country clergyman was relatively poorer than the country squire ; and had few means of cultivating his mind or of elevating the religion of his parishioners. The ladies of the houses of even the richest of the landed gentry were scarcely educated at all, and, though there were bright exceptions, any one familiar with the correspondence of the seventeenth century knows that, if he comes across a letter particularly illegible and uninteresting, there is a strong probability that the writer was a woman.

23. **Alliance between the Gentry and the Church.** — A common life passed in the country under much the same conditions naturally drew together the squire and the rector or vicar of his parish. A still stronger bond united them for the most part in a common Toryism. They had both suffered from the same oppression : the squire, or his predecessor, had been heavily fined by a Puritan

II.

T T

Parliament or a Puritan Lord Protector, whilst the incumbent or his predecessor had been expelled from his parsonage and deprived of his livelihood by the same authority. They therefore naturally combined in thinking that the first axiom in politics was to keep Dissenters down, lest they should do again what men like-minded with themselves had done before. Unless some other fear, stronger still, presented itself to them, they would endure almost anything from the king rather than risk the return to power of the Dissenters or of the Whigs, the friends of the Dissenters.

CHAPTER XLI

JAMES II.   1685—1689

LEADING DATES

Accession of James II.	Feb. 6, 1685
Meeting of Parliament	May 19, 1685
Battle of Sedgemoor.	July 6, 1685
Prorogation of Parliament	Nov. 20, 1685
The Judges allow the King's Dispensing Power	June 21, 1686
First Declaration of Indulgence	April 4, 1687
Second Declaration of Indulgence	April 22, 1688
Birth of the Son of James II.	June 10, 1688
Acquittal of the Seven Bishops	June 30, 1688
Landing of William of Orange	Nov. 5, 1688
The Crown accepted by William and Mary	Feb. 13, 1689

1. **The Accession of James II. 1685.**—The character of the new king, James II., resembled that of his father. He had the same unalterable belief that whatever he wished to do was absolutely right; the same incapacity for entering into the feelings or motives of his opponents, and even more than his father's inability to see faults in those who took his side. He was bent on procuring religious liberty for the Catholics, and at first imagined it possible to do this with the help of the clergy and laity of the Church of England. In his first speech to the Privy Council he announced his intention of preserving the established government in Church and State. He had mass, indeed, celebrated with open doors in his chapel at Whitehall, and he continued to levy taxes which had been granted to his brother for life only; yet, as he issued writs for a Parliament, these things did not count much against him.

Unless, indeed, he was to set the law and constitution at defiance he could do no otherwise than summon Parliament, as out of 1,400,000*l.* which formed the revenue of the Crown, 900,000*l.* lapsed on Charles's death. James, however, secured himself against all eventualities by procuring from Louis a promise of financial aid in case of Parliament's proving restive. Before Parliament met, the king's inclinations were manifested by sentences pronounced by

James II.: from the National Portrait Gallery.

judges eager to gain his favour. On the one hand, Titus Oates was subjected to a flogging so severe that it would have killed anyone less hardy than himself. On the other hand, Richard Baxter, the most learned and moderate of Dissenters, was sent to prison after being scolded and insulted by Jeffreys, who, at the end of the late reign, had, through James's influence, been made Chief Justice of the King's Bench.

2. **A Tory Parliament. 1685.**—Parliament met on May 19. The House of Commons was Tory by an enormous majority, partly because the remodelled corporations (see p. 625) returned Tory members, but still more because the feeling of the country ran strongly in James's favour. The Commons granted to him the full revenue which had been enjoyed by his brother, and refused to listen to a few of its members who raised objections to some things which had been recently done. The House had not been long in session when it heard of two invasions, the one in Scotland and the other in England.

3. **Argyle's Landing. 1685.**—In Scotland the upper classes were animated by a savage resolve to keep no terms with the Covenanters, whose fanatical violence alarmed them. The Scottish Parliament, soon after the accession of James, passed a law punishing with death any one attending a conventicle. Argyle, believing, in his exile in Holland, that all honest Scots would be ready to join him against the tyranny of the Government,

Yeomen of the Guard : from Sandford's *Coronation Procession of James II.*

sailed early in May at the head of a small expedition, and arrived in the Firth of Clyde. He had himself no military skill, and his followers, no less ignorant than himself, overruled everything that he proposed. Soon after landing he was captured and carried to Edinburgh, where, as he was already legally condemned to death (see p. 623), he was executed on June 30 without further trial. On the night before his death a member of the Council came to see him in his cell, where he found him in a placid slumber. The visitor rushed off in agony to the house of a friend. "I have been," he said, " in Argyle's prison. I have seen him within an hour of eternity, sleeping as sweetly as ever man did. But as for me—" His voice failed him, and he could say no more.

4. **Monmouth's Landing. 1685.**—In the meanwhile Monmouth, the champion of the Dissenters and extreme Protestants, had, on June 11, landed at Lyme. So popular was he in the west of England that the trained bands could not be trusted to oppose him, and he was left unassailed till regiments of the regular army could be brought against him. The peasants and townsmen of the western counties flocked to join Monmouth, and he entered Taunton at the head of 5,000 men ; but not a single country gentleman gave him his support. Parliament passed against him an Act of Attainder, condemning him to death without further trial, and the king marched in person against him at the head of a disciplined force. Monmouth declared himself to be the legitimate king, and, his name being James, he was popularly known amongst his followers as King Monmouth, in order to prevent confusion. He advanced as far as Philip's Norton : there, hopeless of gaining support amongst the governing classes, he fell back on Bridgwater. The king followed him with 2,500 regular troops, and 1,500 from the Wiltshire trained bands. Monmouth was soldier enough to know that, with his raw recruits, his only chance lay in surprising the enemy. The king's army lay on Sedgemoor, and Monmouth, in the early morning of July 6, attempted to fall on the enemy unawares. Broad ditches filled with water checked his course, and the sun was up before he reached his goal. It was inevitable that he should be beaten ; the only wonder was that his untrained men fought so long as they did. Monmouth himself fled to the New Forest, where he was captured and brought to London. James admitted him to his presence, but refused to pardon him. On July 15 he was executed as an attainted traitor without further trial.

5. **The Bloody Assizes. 1685.**—Large numbers of Monmouth's followers were hanged by the pursuing soldiers without form of law. Many were thrust into prison to await their trial. Jeffreys, the most insolent of the judges, was sent to hold, in the western counties, what will always be known as the Bloody Assizes. It is true that the law which he had to administer was cruel, but Jeffreys gained peculiar obloquy by delighting in its cruelty, and by sneering at its unhappy victims. At Winchester he condemned to death an old lady, Alice Lisle, who was guilty of hiding in her house two fugitives from vengeance. At Dorchester 74 persons

were hanged. In Somersetshire no less than 233 were put to death. Jeffreys overwhelmed his victims with scornful mockery. One of them pleaded that he was a good Protestant : " Protestant ! " cried Jeffreys, " you mean Presbyterian ; I'll hold you a wager of it. I can smell a Presbyterian forty miles." Some one tried to move his compassion in favour of one of the accused. " My lord," he said, " this poor creature is on the parish." " Do not trouble yourselves," was the only answer given, " I will ease the parish of the burden," and he ordered the man to be hanged at once. The whole number of those who perished in the Bloody Assizes was 320, whilst 841 were transported to the West Indies to work as slaves under a broiling sun. James welcomed Jeffreys on his return, and made him Lord Chancellor as a reward for his achievements.

6. The Violation of the Test Act. 1685.—James's success made him believe that he could overpower any opposition. He had already increased his army and had appointed officers who had refused to take the test. On his return to London he resolved to ask Parliament to repeal the Test Act, and dismissed Halifax for refusing to support his proposal. It would probably have been difficult for him to obtain the repeal even of the Recusancy Laws which punished Catholics for acting on their religious belief. It was not only hopeless, but rightly hopeless, for him to ask for a repeal of the Test Act, which, as long as a Catholic king was on the throne, stood in the way of his filling all posts in the army as well as in the state with men who would be ready to assist him in designs against the religion and liberties of Englishmen. If anything could increase the dislike of the nation to the repeal of the Test Act it was the fact that, in that very year, Louis had revoked the Edict of Nantes issued by his ancestor, Henry IV., to protect the French Protestants, and had handed them over to a cruel persecution. It might be fairly argued that what Louis had done, James, if he got the power, might be expected to do hereafter.

7. Breach between Parliament and King. 1685.—When the Houses, which had adjourned when the king went into the West, met again on November 9, James informed them not only that he had appointed officers disqualified by law, but that he was determined not to part with them. The House of Commons, the most loyal House that had ever been chosen, remonstrated with him, and there were signs that the Lords intended to support the remonstrance. On November 20 James prorogued Parliament.

8. The Dispensing Power. 1686.—Like his father, James

liked to think that, when he broke the laws, he was acting legally, and he remembered that the Crown had, in former days, exercised a power of dispensing with the execution of the laws (see p. 604). This power had, indeed, been questioned by the Parliament in 1673 (see p. 606), but there was no statute or legal judgment declaring it to be forbidden by law. James now wanted to get a decision from the judges that he possessed the dispensing power, and when he found that four of the judges disagreed with him, he replaced them by four judges who would decide in his favour. Having thus packed the Bench, he procured the bringing of a collusive action against Sir Edward Hales, who, having been appointed an officer in the army, had, as a Catholic, refused to take the test. Hales produced a dispensation from the king, and, on June 21, 1686, the judges decided that such dispensations freed those who received them from the penalties imposed by any laws whatever.

9. **The Ecclesiastical Commission. 1686.**—James, in virtue of his dispensing power, had already authorised some clergymen of the Church of England, who had turned Roman Catholics, to retain their benefices. Obadiah Walker, the Master of University College, Oxford, became a Roman Catholic, set up a press for the printing of Roman Catholic tracts, and had mass celebrated openly in the college. Yet he was allowed to retain his post. Then the king appointed Massey, an avowed Roman Catholic, to the Deanery of Christchurch, and Parker, a secret Roman Catholic, to the Bishopric of Oxford. Naturally the clergy who retained the principles of the Church of England preached sermons warning their hearers against the errors of the Church of Rome. James ordered them to be silent, and directed Compton, Bishop of London, to suspend Sharp, the Dean of Norwich, for preaching against the Papal doctrines. As Compton refused to obey, James, on July 11, constituted an Ecclesiastical Commission Court, at the head of which was Jeffreys. It is true that the Court of High Commission had been abolished by a statute of the Long Parliament, but James argued that his father's court, having power to punish the laity as well as the clergy, could be abolished by Act of Parliament, whereas, a king being supreme governor of the Church, might provide for the punishment of the clergy alone, in any way that he thought fit, without taking account of Acts of Parliament. The first act of the new court was to suspend Compton for his refusal to suspend Sharp. James therefore had it in his power to stop the mouths of all the religious teachers in the realm.

10. **Scotland and Ireland. 1686—1687.**—In Scotland James

insisted on a Parliamentary repeal of all laws imposing penalties on Roman Catholics. The Scottish Parliament, subservient as it had been to Charles II., having refused to comply with this demand, James dispensed with all these laws by his own authority, thereby making Scottish Episcopalians almost as sullen as Scottish Covenanters. In Ireland James had on his side the whole Catholic Celtic population, which complained of wrongs committed against their religion and property by the English colonists. James determined to redress these wrongs. In February, 1687, he sent over to Ireland as Lord Deputy the Earl of Tyrconnel, whose character was low, and who had been known at Charles's Court as Lying Dick Talbot. He was, however, a Roman Catholic, and would carry out the king's will in Ireland without remorse.

11. **The Fall of the Hydes. 1686—1687.**—To make way for Tyrconnel, the former lord-lieutenant, Clarendon, the eldest son of the late Chancellor, was recalled from Ireland, his fall being preceded by that of his younger brother Rochester (see p. 627). Rochester was devoted to the maintenance of the Royal power ; but James told him that he must change his religion if he wished to keep his office, and on his refusal he was dismissed.

12. **The Declaration of Indulgence. 1687.**—The dismissal of Rochester was the strongest possible evidence that James's own spirit was intolerant. Yet he was driven, by the course which he had taken, into the adoption of the principle of toleration, and no doubt persuaded himself that he accepted toleration on its own merits. At first he had hoped to obtain favours for the Roman Catholics with the goodwill of the Church of England, whilst continuing the persecution of Dissenters. He now knew that this was impossible, and he therefore resolved to make friends of the Dissenters by pronouncing for a general toleration. He first had private interviews with the leading men in both Houses, in the hope that they would, if Parliament were re-assembled, assist in the repeal of all penal laws bearing on religion. These closetings, as they were called,[1] proving ineffectual, he issued, by his own authority, on April 4, 1687, a Declaration of Indulgence, suspending all laws against Roman Catholics and Dissenters alike, and giving permission to both to worship publicly. The result of the Declaration was not all that James desired. Many of the Dissenters, indeed, accepted their freedom joyfully. Most of them, however, dreaded a gift which seemed only intended to elevate the Roman Catholics, and opened their ears to the pleadings of the Churchmen, who now

---

[1] Because the interviews took place in the king's closet, or private room.

assured their old enemies that if they would have a little patience they should, in the next Parliament, have a toleration secured by law. This, argued the Churchmen, would be of far more use to them than one granted by the king, which would avail them nothing whenever the king died and was succeeded by his Protestant daughter, the Princess of Orange.

13. **The Expulsion of the Fellows of Magdalen. 1687.**— Scarcely was the Declaration issued when James showed how little he cared for law or custom. There was a vacancy in the Presidentship of Magdalen College, Oxford, and James commanded the Fellows to choose one Farmer, a man of bad character, and a Roman Catholic. On April 15 the Fellows, as they had the undoubted right to do, chose Hough. In June they were summoned before the Ecclesiastical Commission, which declared Hough's election to be void, and ordered them to choose Parker, who, though at heart a Roman Catholic, was nominally the Protestant Bishop of Oxford (see p. 638). They answered simply that, as Hough had been lawfully elected, they had no right to choose another President in his lifetime. Jeffreys bullied them in vain. James insisted on their accepting Parker, and on acknowledging the legality of the proceedings of the Ecclesiastical Commission. All but two, having refused to submit, were turned out of the College and left to beg their bread. When the Commissioners attempted to install Parker in his office not a blacksmith in Oxford would consent to break open the lock of the President's lodgings. The servants of the Commissioners were at last employed to force the door, and it was in this way that Parker took possession of the residence to which Hough alone had a legal claim. The expelled Fellows were not left to starve, as there was scarcely a gentleman in England who would not have been proud to receive one of them into his house.

14. **An Attempt to pack a Parliament. 1687.**—James was anxious to obtain Parliamentary sanction for his Declaration of Indulgence. He dissolved the existing Parliament, hoping to find a new one more to his taste. As he had packed the Bench of Judges in 1686, he tried to pack a Parliament in 1687. A board of regulators was appointed, with Jeffreys at its head, to remodel the corporations once more, appointing Roman Catholics and Dissenters to sit in them. James expected that these new members would elect tolerationists to the next House of Commons. So strong, however, was public opinion against the king that even the new members chosen expressly to vote for the king's nominees could not be relied

on. The design of calling a new Parliament was therefore abandoned for the time

15. **A Second Declaration of Indulgence. 1688.**—On April 22, 1688, James issued a second Declaration of Indulgence, which he ordered to be read in all the churches. Most of the clergy objecting to read it, seven bishops signed a petition asking that the clergy might be excused. Six of these bishops—Sancroft, the Archbishop of Canterbury, who was the seventh, having been forbidden to appear before the king—presented the petition to James at Whitehall. James was startled when it was placed in

his hands. "This," he said, "is a great surprise to me. I did not expect this from your Church, especially from some of you. This is a standard of rebellion." In vain the bishops protested that they hated the very sound of rebellion. James would not listen to their excuses. "This," he persisted in saying, "is rebellion. This is a standard of rebellion. Did ever a good churchman question the dispensing power before? Have not some of you preached for it and written for it? It is a standard of rebellion. I will have my declaration published." One of the bishops replied that they were bound to fear God as well as to honour the king. James only grew more angry

Dress of a bishop in the second half of the seventeenth century: from Sandford's *Coronation Procession of James II.*

and told them, as he sent them away, that he would keep their petition, with the evident intention of taking legal proceedings against them. "God," he said, as he dismissed them, "has given me the dispensing power, and I will maintain it. I tell you there are still seven thousand of your Church who have not bowed the knee to Baal."

16. **Resistance of the Clergy. 1688.**—When the day came for the reading of the Declaration scarcely a clergyman obeyed the king's order. In one of the London churches Samuel Wesley, father of the John Wesley who was, by his preaching, to move the hearts of the next generation, preached a sermon on the text, "Be it known unto thee, O king, that we will not serve thy gods, nor worship the golden image which thou hast set up." In Westminster Abbey, when the officiating minister, Bishop Sprat, a

courtly prelate, began to read the Declaration, the whole congregation rose in a body and streamed out of the church.

17. **The Trial of the Seven Bishops. 1688.**—James ordered that the seven bishops should be tried, on the plea that their petition was a seditious libel. The trial took place in Westminster Hall on June 29. The first difficulty of the prosecution was to show that the so-called libel had been published—that is to say, had been shown to any one—as no one was present besides the bishops when James received it, and the king could not be put into the witness-box. At last sufficient evidence was tendered by the Earl of Sunderland—a minister who, unlike Rochester, had changed his religion to keep his place—to convince the court that the petition had been delivered to James. The lawyers on both sides then addressed the jury on the question whether the petition was really a libel. The jury retired to deliberate, and at first nine of them were for the bishops and three for the king. Two of the latter gave way, but the other, a certain Arnold, who was the king's brewer, held out. "Whatever I do," he said, "I am sure to be half ruined. If I say *Not Guilty* I shall brew no more for the king, and if I say *Guilty* I shall brew no more for anybody else." He decided that the king's custom was the best worth keeping. To a gentleman named Austen who proposed to argue with him he replied that his mind was already made up. "If you come to that," replied Austen, "look at me. I am the largest and strongest of this twelve ; and before I find such a petition a libel, here I will stay till I am no bigger than a tobacco pipe." The jury were locked up through the night, and when the morning of the 30th came Arnold had given way. A verdict of *Not Guilty* was given in. The crowds in Westminster Hall and in the streets of London burst out into shouts of joy. At Hounslow, where James was reviewing the regiments on which he trusted to break down all popular resistance, the soldiers shouted like the rest. James asked what it all meant. "Nothing," he was told ; "the soldiers are glad that the bishops are acquitted." "Do you call that nothing?" he answered. "So much the worse for them."

18. **Invitation to William of Orange. 1688.**—The acquittal of the Bishops would, but for one circumstance, have strengthened the nation in its resolution patiently to wait till James's death placed his daughter on the throne. On June 10, however, a son had been born to James, and that fact changed the whole situation. The boy would be educated in his father's religion, and England was threatened with a Roman Catholic dynasty in which each

successive ruler would, from his childhood, be brought up in the belief that he might break through all legal restraints whenever he could have the approval of judges appointed by himself and liable to dismissal whenever he pleased. At first the general dislike of this disagreeable fact took the shape of incredulity, and it was almost universally believed, without a shadow of foundation, that the boy was a supposititious child procured from some poor mother and brought in a warming-pan into the queen's chamber. Whether he were supposititious or not, there was no doubt that he would be treated as James's heir. Tories were as much concerned as Whigs at the prospect before them. The doctrine of non-resistance was forgotten, and on June 30, the day of the bishops' acquittal, seven important personages, some being Whigs and some Tories, invited the Prince of Orange to land with an armed force to defend the liberties of England.

19. **Landing of William. 1688.**—William would probably not have accepted the invitation if the constitutional rights of Englishmen had alone been at stake; but he had made it the object of his life to struggle against Louis, and he knew that war was on the point of breaking out between Louis and an alliance in which almost every European prince took part excepting James. He accepted the invitation that he might bring England into that alliance; and made preparations, which could not be hidden from James. James made concessions, abolished the Ecclesiastical Commission, gave back the charters of the City of London and the other corporations, and restored the Fellows of Magdalen. Anxious as William was to come, he was delayed for some time. The army of Louis was on the southern frontier of the Spanish Netherlands, and William could not stir as long as an invasion of his Spanish allies was threatened. Louis, however, offered James the assistance of his fleet to repel the expected Dutch expedition. James replied that he was quite able to take care of himself. Louis lost his temper, withdrew his army from the frontier of the Netherlands, and sent it to begin the war with the allies by burning and ravaging the Palatinate. William put to sea, intending to land in Torbay. On the morning of November 5 it was found that the fleet had passed the haven for which it was bound; and as the wind was blowing it strongly on, there seemed no possibility of returning. William believed that nothing but failure was before him. "You may go to prayers, doctor," he said to Burnet, an English clergyman who accompanied him; "all is over." In a moment the wind changed and bore the fleet back into Torbay, and William

was enabled to land safely at Brixham. Burnet, a warm-hearted but garrulous and inquisitive man, began asking him questions about his plans. If there was one thing that William disliked more than another, it was the interference of clergymen in military matters. He therefore looked Burnet in the face, replying only by another question : " Well, doctor, what do you think of pre-destination now ? " Both he and Burnet were convinced that God had Himself guided them thus far in safety for the deliverance of His people.

20. **William's March upon London. 1688.**—William marched upon London, and, after a while, the gentry of the counties through which he passed poured in to support him. The north and the midlands rose under the Earls of Devonshire and Danby and other lords, Whig and Tory. The doctrine of non-resistance was thrown to the winds. James set out with his troops to combat William. He reached Salisbury, but the officers of his own army and his courtiers deserted him. Amongst those who fled to William was Lord Churchill, afterwards known as the Duke of Marlborough and the greatest soldier of the age. He had received many favours from James, which he now repaid by inciting all those whom he could influence to abandon their king. Amongst these was James's younger daughter Anne, over whom Churchill's wife exercised a most powerful influence, and who now, together with her husband, Prince George of Denmark, fled to William. James, left almost alone, made his way back to London, which he reached on November 27. On the 30th he ordered the pre-paration of writs for the election of a Parliament, and proposed an accommodation with William, who by that time had reached Hungerford. It was agreed that both armies should remain at a distance of forty miles from London in order to enable the new Parliament to meet in safety. James was, in reality, de-termined not to submit. On December 10 he sent his wife and son to France. On the 11th he attempted to follow them, burning the writs and dropping the great seal into the Thames, in the hope that everything might fall into confusion for want of the symbol of legitimate authority. There were riots in London, and the Roman Catholic chapels were sacked and destroyed. There was a general call to William to hasten his march. On the 12th, however, James was stopped near Sheerness by some fishermen and brought back to London. William had no mind to have a second royal martyr on his hands, and did everything to frighten James into another flight. On December 18 James left London

and William arrived at Whitehall. On December 23, with William's connivance, James embarked for France.

21. **A Convention Parliament Summoned. 1688.**—Amongst the crowd which welcomed William was Sergeant Maynard, an old man of ninety. " You must," said William to him, " have survived all the lawyers of your standing." " Yes, sir," replied Maynard, " and, but for your Highness, I should have survived the laws too." He expressed the general sense of almost every Englishman. How to return to a legal system with the least possible disturbance was the problem to be faced. William consulted the House of Lords and an assembly composed of all persons who had sat in any of Charles's Parliaments, together with special representatives of the City. Members of James's one Parliament were not summoned, on the plea that the return to it of members chosen by the remodelled corporations made it no true Parliament. The body thus consulted advised William to call a Convention, which would be a Parliament in everything except that there was no king to summon it.

22. **The Throne declared Vacant. 1689.**—On January 22, **1689,** the Convention met. The House of Commons contained a majority of Whigs, whilst the Tories were in a majority in the Lords. On the 28th the Commons resolved that " king James II., having endeavoured to subvert the constitution of the kingdom by breaking the original contract between king and people, and by the advice of Jesuits and other wicked persons having violated the fundamental laws and having withdrawn himself out of the kingdom, had abdicated the government, and that the throne had thereby become vacant." This lumbering resolution was unanimously adopted. The Whigs were pleased with the clause which made the vacancy of the throne depend on James's misgovernment, and the Tories were pleased with the clause which made it depend on his so-called voluntary abdication. The Tories in the Lords proposed that James should remain nominally king, but that the country should be governed by a regent. Danby, however, and a small knot of Tories supported the Whigs, and the proposal was rejected. Danby had, indeed, a plan of his own. James, he held, had really abdicated, and the crown had therefore passed to the next heir. That heir was not, according to him, the supposititious infant, but the eldest daughter of James, Mary Princess of Orange, who was now in her own right queen of England. It was an ingenious theory, but two circumstances were against its being carried into practice. In the first place, Mary scolded Danby for

daring to set her above her husband. In the second place William made it known that he would neither be regent nor administer the government under his wife. Danby therefore withdrew his motion, and on February 6 the Lords voted, as the Commons had voted before, that James had abdicated and the throne was vacant.

23. **William and Mary to be Joint Sovereigns. 1689.**—A Declaration of Rights was prepared condemning the dispensing power as lately exercised and the other extravagant actions of James II., while both Houses concurred in offering the crown to William and Mary as joint sovereigns. As long as William lived he was to administer the government, Mary only attaining to actual power in the event of her surviving her husband. After the death of both, the crown was to go first to any children which might be born to them, then to Anne and her children, and, lastly, to any children of William by a second wife in case of his surviving Mary and marrying again. As a matter of fact, William had no children by Mary, who died about eight years before him, and he never married again. On February 13 William and Mary accepted the crown on the conditions offered to them.

24. **Character of the Revolution.**—The main characteristic of the revolution thus effected was that it established the supremacy of Parliament by setting up a king and queen who owed their position to a Parliamentary vote. People had been found to believe that James II. was king by a Divine right. Nobody could believe that of William. Parliament, which had set him up, could pull him down, and he would have therefore to conform his government to the will of the nation manifested in Parliament. The political revolution of 1689 succeeded, whilst the Puritan Revolution of 1641 failed, because, in 1641, the political aim of setting the Parliament above the king was complicated by an ecclesiastical dispute which had split Parliament and the nation into two hostile parties. In 1689 there was practically neither a political nor an ecclesiastical dispute. Tories and Whigs combined to support the change, and Churchmen and Dissenters made common cause against the small Roman Catholic minority which had only been dangerous because it had the Crown at its back, and because the Crown had been supported by Louis and his armies. A Revolution thus effected was, no doubt, far less complete than that which had been aimed at by the more advanced assailants of the throne of Charles I. It did not aim at changing more than a small part of the political constitution of the country, nor at changing any part whatever of its social institutions. Its programme, in short, was

one for a single generation, not one, like that of the ' *Heads of the Proposals*' (see p. 555) or the ' *Agreement of the People*' (see p. 556) for several generations. Consequently it did not rouse the antagonism which had been fatal even to the best conceived plans of the Commonwealth and Protectorate. It is much to be regretted that the moral tone of the men who brought about the Revolution of **1689** was lower than that which had brought about the Revolution of **1641**. That this was the case, however, was mainly the fault of the unwise attempt of the Puritans to enforce morality by law. The individual liberty which was encouraged by the later revolution would in due time work for morality as well as for political improvement.

Books recommended for further study of Part VII.

RANKE, L.   English History (English translation).   Vol. iii. p. 310–
            vol. iv. p. 528.
AIRY, O.   The English Restoration and Louis XIV.
CHRISTIE, W. D.   Life of A. A. Cooper, first Earl of Shaftesbury.
MACAULAY, Lord.   History of England from the Accession of
            James II.   Vols. i. and ii.
HALLAM, H.   Constitutional History.   Chapters XI.–XIV.
MAHAN, A. T.   Influence of the Sea-power upon History.   Chapters
            I.–III.

PART -VIII

THE RISE OF CABINET GOVERNMENT

1689—1754

CHAPTER XLII

WILLIAM III. AND MARY II.

WILLIAM III. 1689 - 1702.   MARY II. 1689—1694

LEADING DATES

The Mutiny Act and the Toleration Act	1689
Battle of Killiecrankie	July 27, 1689
Relief of Londonderry	July 30, 1689
Battle of the Boyne	July 1, 1690
Surrender of Limerick	Oct. 3, 1691
Massacre of Glencoe	Feb. 13, 1692
Battle of La Hogue	May 19, 1692
The Formation of the Whig Junto	1693—1694
The Triennial Act	1694
Death of Mary	Dec. 28, 1694

1. **The new Government and the Mutiny Act. 1689.**—It was unlikely that William would long be popular. He was cold and reserved, and he manifestly cared more for the struggle on the Continent than for the strife which never ceased between English parties. Yet he was sagacious enough to know that it was only by managing English affairs with firmness and wisdom that he could hope to carry England with him in his conflict with France ; and he did his work so well that, though few of his new subjects loved him, most of them learned to respect him. As he owed his crown to the support of both parties, he chose his first ministers from both. In March his throne was exposed to some danger. The army was dissatisfied in consequence of the shabby part which

III.   U U

it had played when called on to defend James II., and one regiment mutinied. Only the Dutch troops could be trusted, and it was by them that the mutiny was suppressed. The punishment of mutinous soldiers by courts martial had been forbidden by the Petition of Right (see p. 508). Parliament now passed a Mutiny Act,

William III.

which authorised the maintenance of discipline by such courts for six months only. The Act has been since renewed from year to year, and as, if it dropped, the king would have no lawful means of maintaining discipline, Parliament thus maintains control over the army.

2. **The Toleration Act and the Nonjurors. 1689.**—Still more

important was the Toleration Act, which gave to Dissenters the legal right to worship publicly, on complying with certain formalities. From this toleration Unitarians and Roman Catholics were excluded. The great mass of Protestant Dissenters were well satisfied, and the chief cause of religious strife was thus removed.

Mary II.

An attempt made to carry a Comprehension Bill (see pp. 598, 599), which was intended to attract Dissenters to the Church by altering the Prayer Book, ended in complete failure. All holders of office in Church and State were required to take the oaths of supremacy and allegiance to the new sovereigns. About 400 of the clergy with Archbishop Sancroft and six other bishops refused to swear. Their offices were conferred on others, and they, holding that they and those who continued to acknowledge them were the true Church, founded a body which, under the name of Nonjurors, continued to exist for more than a century.

3. Locke's Letters on Toleration. 1689.—The Toleration Act itself was in the main the fruit of the change which had taken place in the political circumstances of the nation since the Restoration. Men had had reason to be afraid of Roman Catholics, and were no longer afraid of Dissenters. Alongside of this political change, however, had grown up a change of opinion amongst the thinking men who had especial influence in the Whig party. In **1689** the philosopher Locke published his ' Letters on Toleration.' They were much less heroic than Milton's ' Areopagitica ' (see p. 546), and instead of dwelling on the bracing effects of liberty on the human spirit, maintained the view that the State had no business to interfere with religious conviction. A Church, according to Locke, was ' a voluntary society of men joining themselves together of their own accord, in order to the public worshipping of God in such manner as they shall judge acceptable to Him and effectual to the salvation of their souls.' On such voluntary associations the State had no right to impose penalties.

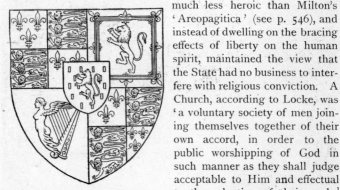

Royal Arms as borne by William III.

4. Establishment of Presbyterianism in Scotland. 1689.—In Scotland and Ireland William had to fight for his crown. In Scotland, before the Parliament met, the Episcopal clergy were ' rabbled,' that is to say, were driven from their parishes with insult and ill-usage by angry crowds. Parliament then declared James to have forfeited the crown and gave it to William and Mary. It also declared Presbyterianism to be the religion of the country.

5. Killiecrankie. 1689.—To many of the nobles the establishment of a clergy which owed them no respect was distasteful, and some, of whom the most conspicuous were the Duke of Gordon and Viscount Dundee, who had till lately been known as Graham of Claverhouse (see p. 620), drew their swords for James. Gordon held out in Edinburgh Castle till June 13. Dundee, following the example of Montrose (see p. 547), a Graham like himself, gathered the Highland clans around him.   On July 27, he drew up his force on the flat ground at the head of the pass of Killiecrankie. William's general, Mackay, toiled up the steep hillside to attack him.   His soldiers had been supplied with bayonets, a new French inven-tion intended to make each soldier a pikeman as well as a musketeer. The invention had not yet been per-fected, and the bayonets had to be fixed in the muzzles of the guns. When Mackay's men reached the top exhausted by the climb and the summer heat, they fired their shots, and then, seeing the Highlanders rushing upon them, fumbled with their bayonets.   Before they could get them fixed the Highlanders, with their flashing broadswords, were upon them.   Dundee had been killed by the first fire, but his men swept the lowland soldiers down the pass, leaping lightly over the rocks and slaying as they went.   The High-landers, caring more for plunder than for James, returned home to deposit their booty in safety.

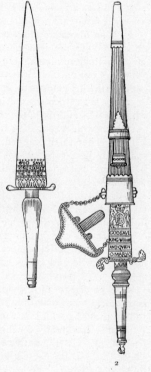

1, Bayonet as made in 1686.
2, Bayonet of the time of William and Mary.

6. **The Pacification of the High-lands.   1691—1692.**—The High-landers were poor, and in **1691** a dis-tribution of 15,000*l.* amongst the chiefs of the clans brought them one by one to submission.   December 31 was announced as the last day on which the oaths acknowledging Wil-liam would be accepted.   By that time all had resolved to give way ; but one of the number, MacIan Glencoe, the head of a small clan, one of the many into which the Macdonalds were divided, took pride in being the last to sub-mit, and made his appearance on the 31st.   Unfortunately he by mistake came to a gentleman who had no authority to accept his oath, and when he reached a person who could accept it, the

appointed day had passed. The Master of Stair,[1] William's chief minister in Scotland, thought this an excellent opportunity to show the Highlanders that the Government could punish as well as reward, and asked William's leave to destroy MacIan's clan, on the plea that they had, like most other Highland clans, been guilty in past time of acts of brigandage and murder. William gave his assent, writing that it would be good to ' extirpate that set of thieves.'

7. **The Massacre of Glencoe. 1692.**—The Master of Stair proceeded to execute, in a peculiarly treacherous manner, the order which he had obtained. He sent into Glencoe a party of soldiers, who gave out on their arrival that they had come as friends. They lived with the clansmen, ate at their tables, joked, and played at cards with them. On the morning of February 13, **1692,** whilst it was still dark, the soldiers surrounded the huts of those very men with whom they had been making merry the evening before. They then dragged many of them out of their beds and murdered them, firing at such as fled. Not a few, indeed, succeeded in making their escape, but the mountains on either side of the glen were lofty and rugged, and most of those who took refuge in them died of cold and hunger amidst the rocks and the snow. When the tale was told at Edinburgh the Scottish Parliament broke out into indignation, and William had to dismiss the Master of Stair from office. It was the first time that the Lowland Scotch had shown compassion for Highlanders. Hitherto they had always treated them as a wild and savage race of plunderers for whom there was no mercy.

8. **The Siege of Londonderry. 1689.**—In Ireland William had to deal with something like national resistance. On March 12 James, bringing with him some French officers, landed at Kinsale. Tyrconnel had ready for him an ill-equipped and ill-disciplined Irish army. To the native Irish James was still the lawful king, whose title was unaffected by anything that an English Parliament could do. To the English and Scottish colonists he was a mere usurper, the enemy of their creed and nation. The northern Protestants, chased from their homes with outrage, took refuge in Enniskillen and Londonderry. In Londonderry the governor, Lundy, prepared to surrender, but when James arrived with his army the inhabitants took the defence into their own hands and closed the gates in his face. The besiegers strictly blockaded

---

[1] In Scotland, the eldest sons of lords and viscounts were known by the title of Master.

the town by land and threw a boom across the river Foyle, so that no food might enter from the sea. The defenders were before long reduced to feed on horse-flesh, and they had not much of that. From the top of the cathedral they could see ships which William had sent to their relief, but the ships lay inactive for weeks. Men who had been well off were glad to feed on the flesh of dogs, and even to gnaw hides in the hope of getting nourishment out of them. At last, on July 30, three of the ships moved up the river. One of them dashed at the boom and broke it, though she was herself driven on shore by the recoil. The tide, however, rose and floated her off. The whole store of food was borne safely to the town, and Londonderry was saved. James and his Irish army marched away. On the day of his retreat an Irish force was defeated at Newtown Butler by the Protestants of Enniskillen.

9. **The Irish Parliament. 1689.**—On May 7, whilst James was before Londonderry, the Irish Parliament met at Dublin. The House of Commons was almost entirely composed of native Irish, and the Parliament passed an Act annulling all the English confiscations since 1641. The lands taken by force in times past were to be restored to the Irish owners or their heirs. Those English, however, who had acquired Irish confiscated lands by purchase were to be compensated, and to find money for this compensation an Act of Attainder was passed against about 2,000 of William's partisans. As most of them were out of harm's way, but little blood was likely to be shed, though a great deal of property would change owners. A considerable part of Irish land having been confiscated by the English authorities during the past forty years, this proceeding did not appear in Ireland to be as outrageous as it would have seemed in a settled country like England.

10. **Schomberg sent to Ireland. 1689.**—Once more England and Ireland were brought into direct antagonism. Not only did Protestant Englishmen sympathise deeply with the wrongs of their countrymen in Ireland, whilst they were unable to perceive that the Irish had suffered any wrongs at all, but they could not fail to see that if James established himself in Ireland, he would next attempt, with French help, to establish himself in England. As it had been in Elizabeth's reign so it was now. Either England must conquer Ireland, or Ireland would be used by a foreign nation to conquer England. Accordingly, in August, Schomberg—who had been a French marshal, but, being a Protestant, had resigned his high position after the Revocation of the Edict of Nantes (see p. 638) rather than renounce his

faith—was sent by William with an English army to Carrickfergus. The weather was bad, and the arrangements of the commissariat were worse, so that disease broke out among the soldiers, and nothing serious was done during the remainder of the year.

11. **The Bill of Rights and the Dissolution of the Convention Parliament. 1689—1690.**—In England, the Convention Parliament had passed a Bill of Rights, embodying the demands of the former Declaration of Rights (see p. 647). Since then it had grown intractable. The Whig majority had forgotten the services rendered by the Tories against James, and, treating them as enemies, was eager to take vengeance on them. When, therefore, a Bill of Indemnity was brought in, the Whigs excepted from it so many of the Tory leaders on the ground that they had supported the harsh acts of the last two kings, that William, who cared for neither party, suddenly prorogued Parliament and then dissolved it.

12. **Settlement of the Revenue. 1690.**—A new Parliament, in which the majority was Tory, met on March 20, **1690,** and by confining to four years their grant of nearly half the revenue of the Crown, put a check upon any attempt of a future king to make himself absolute. Subsequently the grant became annual ; after which no king could avoid summoning Parliament every year, as he could not make himself financially independent of the House of Commons. The supremacy of Parliament was thus, as far as law could do it, practically secured. Finally, an Act of Grace [1] gave an indemnity to all excepting a few persons, to whom no harm was intended as long as they abstained from attacking the Government.

13. **The Conquest of Ireland. 1690—1691.** On June 14, **1690,** William landed at Carrickfergus. On July 1, he defeated James at the battle of the Boyne. Schomberg was killed, and James fled to Kinsale, where he embarked for France. William entered Dublin in triumph, and, marching on through the country, on August 8 laid siege to Limerick. Wet weather set in and caused disease amongst the besiegers, whilst the Irish general, Sarsfield, sweeping round them, destroyed the siege guns on their way to batter the walls. William for the time abandoned the attack and returned to England. In **1691** a Dutch general, Ginkell, was placed in command of the English army. Under him were Mackay, who had been defeated at Killiecrankie, and Ruvigny, a

---

[1] An Act of Grace was similar to an Act of Indemnity, except that it originated with the king, and could only be accepted or rejected, not amended by the Houses.

French Protestant refugee. Thus commanded, William's troops took Athlone on June 30, and on July 12 destroyed the Irish army at Aughrim. Limerick was again besieged, and, on October 3, it capitulated. All officers and soldiers who wished to go to France were allowed to emigrate. To the Irish Catholics were granted such privileges in the exercise of their religion as they had enjoyed in the reign of Charles II., when there had been a connivance at the exercise of the Roman Catholic worship so long as it was not obtrusive. The Irish Parliament, however, representing now the English colony alone, called for persecuting measures, and William had to govern Ireland, if he was to govern Ireland at all, in accordance with its wishes. Limerick became deservedly known amongst the Irish as ' the City of the violated treaty.'

14. **War with France. 1689—1690.**—In the meantime, whilst William was distracted by foes in his own kingdom, Louis had been doing his best to get the better of his enemies. In **1689** the allies were able to make head against him without any decisive result. In **1690** Louis sent his best Admiral, Tourville, to sweep the Channel and invade England whilst William was away in Ireland. Off Beachy Head Tourville was met by a combined English and Dutch fleet. In the battle which followed, the English Admiral, Herbert, who had lately been created Lord Torrington, kept, probably through mere mismanagement, his own ships out of harm's way, whilst he allowed his Dutch allies to expose themselves to danger. Under these circumstances Tourville gained the victory, whilst in the Netherlands the French Marshal, Luxembourg, defeated the allied armies at Fleurus. Though William had been for some time unpopular in England as a foreigner, yet the nation now rallied round him as the enemy of the French. Tourville sailed down the Channel, and asked a fisherman with whom he came up what he thought of King James. "He is a very worthy gentleman, I believe," was the reply, " God bless him." Tourville then asked the fisherman to take service on board his ship. "What ? I," answered the man, " go with the French to fight against the English ? Your honour must excuse me ; I could not do it to save my life." Thousands of Englishmen who were indifferent to the claims of James or William would have nothing to say to James because he had put himself under the protection of the French.

15. **Disgrace of Marlborough. 1691—1692.**—Churchill, who had been created Earl of Marlborough by William, had won distinction as a soldier both in Ireland and in the Netherlands. Both as an

Englishman and as a soldier he was offended at the favour shown to foreigners by William. Dutchmen and Frenchmen were promoted over the heads of English officers. Dutchmen filled the most lucrative posts at court, and were raised to the English peerage. It was, perhaps, natural that William should advance those whom he knew best and trusted most, but in so doing he alienated a great number of Englishmen. Men high in office doubted whether a government thus constituted could last, and, partly because they were personally disgusted, partly because they wished to make themselves safe in any event, entered into communication with James, and promised to support his claims, a promise which they intended to keep or break as might be most convenient to themselves. Marlborough went further than any. In **1691**, he offered to move an address in the House of Lords, asking William to dismiss the foreigners, assuring James that, if William refused, the army and navy would expel him from England ; and he also induced the Princess Anne to put herself in opposition to her sister, the Queen. On this William deprived Marlborough of all his offices.

16. **La Hogue, Steinkirk, and Landen. 1692—1693.**—Amongst those who had offered their services to James was Admiral Russell, a brother of the Lord Russell who had been beheaded (see p. 626). He was an ill-tempered man, and being dissatisfied in consequence of some real or fancied slight, told a Jacobite agent that he was willing to help James to regain the throne. Yet his offer was not without limitation. " Do not think," he added, " that I will let the French triumph over us in our own sea. Understand this, that if I meet them I fight them ; ay, though His Majesty himself should be on board." Russell kept his word as far as the fighting was concerned. When in **1692** a French fleet and army were made ready for the invasion of England, he met the fleet near the Bay of La Hogue and utterly defeated it. His sailors followed up their victory and set on fire the greater number of the French ships, though they lay under the protection of batteries on shore. The French navy, indeed, was not swept from the sea, but the mastery had passed into the hands of the English. No further attempt was made by the French in this war to invade England, and Louis, intent upon victories on shore, took little trouble to maintain his navy. On land Louis still had the superiority. In **1692**, the year of the English victory at La Hogue, his army took Namur, and defeated the allies at Steinkirk with William at their head. In **1693** the French won another victory at Neerwinden, or, according to another name sometimes given to the battle, at Landen.

17. **Beginning of the National Debt. 1692.**—After both these

defeats, William had, in his usual fashion, so rallied his defeated troops, that the French gained little by their victories.   In the end success would come to the side which had most endurance.   Money was as much needed as men, and, in **1692**, Parliament decided on borrowing 1,000,000*l.* for the support of the war.   Kings and Parliaments had often borrowed money before, but in the long run they had failed either to pay interest or to repay the principal, and this loan is understood to be the beginning of the National Debt, because it was the first on which interest was steadily paid.   The last piece of gold, the French king had said, would carry the day, and England with her commerce was likely to provide more gold than France, where trade was throttled by the constant interference of the Government, and deprived of the protection of an efficient navy.

18. **Disorder in the Government. 1693.**—On his return after his defeat at Neerwinden, William found everything in disorder.   The House of Commons was out of temper in consequence of the military failure, and still more because of the corruption prevailing amongst the king's ministers, and the disorder of the administration.   The system of drawing ministers from both parties had led to quarrels, and the House of Commons was at least as inefficient as the Government.   There was no assured majority in it.   If, as often happened, fifty or a hundred Whigs went off one day to amuse themselves at tennis, or to see a new play or a cock-fight, the Tories carried everything before them.   If, on another day, fifty or a hundred Tories chose to disport themselves in the same manner, the Whigs could undo all that had been done by their rivals.   There was, in those times, no fear of the constituencies before the eyes of a member of Parliament.   No division-lists were printed and no speeches reported.   "Nobody," said an active politician, "can know one day what a House of Commons will do the next."

19. **The Whig Junto. 1693-1694.**—Acting upon the advice of Sunderland, who, though in James's reign he had changed his religion to retain his place, was a shrewd observer of mankind, William provided a remedy for these disorders.   Before the end of **1694** he discharged his Tory ministers and filled their posts with Whigs, who had now the sole possession of office.   The four leading Whigs, who were consulted on all important matters and who were popularly known as the Junto, were Lord Somers, the Lord Keeper, a statesmanlike and large-minded lawyer ; Admiral Russell, the First Lord of the Admiralty ; Charles Montague, the Chancellor of the Exchequer, an acute and

able financier ; and Thomas Wharton, afterwards Lord Wharton, Comptroller of the Household, a man of the worst character but an excellent electioneering agent, versed in all the arts which win adherents to a political party. What William hoped from this change of system was that, by having ministers who were of one mind, he would be able to have a House of Commons of one mind. Whig members would think it worth while to attend the House steadily, at personal inconvenience to themselves, not only because they wished to keep their own friends in office, but because those friends, as long as they remained in office, would dispose of plenty of well-paid posts and rewards of various kinds, and were more likely to give them to men who voted steadily for them than to those who did not.

20. **The Junto the Beginning of the Modern Cabinet.**— Nothing was further from William's thoughts than the introduction of a new kind of government. The ministers were still his ministers, and what he expected of them was that they would carry on the war more efficiently. Nevertheless, the formation of the Junto was a great step in advance in the direction of the modern Cabinet system, because it recognised frankly what Charles II. had occasionally recognised tacitly, that the growth of the power of the House of Commons was so great that the king could not govern satisfactorily unless the views of his ministers accorded with those of a majority of the House of Commons. It is evident now that this admission would ultimately lead to government, not by the king, but by a Cabinet supporting itself on an organised party in the House of Commons ; but ideas grow slowly, and there would be much opposition to overcome before such a system could take root with general approbation.

21. **The Bank of England. 1694.**—The increased strength of William's government was not long in showing itself. In 1694 the Bank of England was founded, at the suggestion of William Paterson, a Scotchman who, through the influence of Montague, had become a member of the House of Commons. The growing wealth of the country made it necessary that a place should be found in which money might be more safely deposited than with the goldsmiths (see p. 604), and the new Bank, having received deposits of money, made a loan to the Crown on the security of a Parliamentary promise that interest should be paid till the capital was returned. The Government was thereby put in possession of sufficient resources to enable it to carry on the war successfully. This would not have happened unless moneyed men had been

confident in the stability of William's government and of Parliamentary institutions.

22. The Place Bill. 1694.—Useful as the concentration of power in the hands of the Whig Junto was, it raised alarm lest the ministers should become too strong. The system of winning votes in Parliament by corruption was on the increase, and the favourite device of a minister in need of support was to give to a member of the House of Commons a place revocable at the pleasure of the Crown, and thereby to bind him by self-interest to vote as the minister pleased. This system, bad enough when the ministers were of different parties, became intolerable when they were all of one party, and it now seemed possible that the Whig Junto might keep itself permanently in office by the votes which it purchased. Independent members, indeed, had from time to time introduced a Place Bill, making it illegal for any member of the House of Commons to hold not merely small offices unconnected with politics, but even the great ministerial posts, such as those of a Secretary of State or a Chancellor of the Exchequer ; but the influence of the ministers had been too strong for them, and they were no more successful in 1694 than they had been in former years.

23. The Second Triennial Act. 1694.—Another grievance was actually removed in 1694. As the law then stood a king who had a Parliament to his mind might retain it to his death, even if the feelings of the nation had undergone a complete change, as had been the case in the course of the seventeen and a half years during which Charles II. retained the Cavalier Parliament. By the Triennial Act of 1694 it was enacted that no Parliament should last longer than three years. It was, therefore, quite different from the Triennial Act of 1641 (see p. 530), which enacted that a Parliament should be summoned at least once in three years.

24. Death of Mary. 1694.—Scarcely was the Triennial Act passed when Queen Mary was attacked by the small-pox, and in those days, when vaccination had not yet been discovered, the ravages caused by the small-pox were enormous. The physicians soon assured William that there was no hope. He was stern and self-contained in the presence of most men, but he was warmly affectionate to the few whom he really loved. His grief was now heart-rending : " There is no hope," he said to one of the bishops. " I was the happiest man on earth, and I am the most miserable. She had no fault—none : you knew her well, but you could not know—nobody but myself could know—her goodness." The

Part of Greenwich Hospital.   Built after the design of Sir Christopher Wren.

queen died, but she left a memorial behind her.   Charles II. had begun to build a magnificent palace at Greenwich.   When the news of the Battle of La Hogue reached England, Mary announced her intention of completing the palace as a place of refuge for sailors disabled in the service of their country.   Greenwich Hospital is the lasting monument of the gentle queen.

CHAPTER XLIII

WILLIAM III (*alone*).   1694—1702

LEADING DATES

William III., 1689—1702

The Liberty of the Press	1695
The Assassination Plot	1696
Treaty of Ryswick	1697
The First Partition Treaty	1698
The Second Partition Treaty	1700
Death of Charles II. of Spain	Nov. 1, 1700
The Act of Settlement	1701
Death of James II.	Sept. 6, 1701
The Grand Alliance	Sept. 7, 1701
Death of William III.	March 8, 1702

1. **The Liberty of the Press.   1695.**—Ever since the Restoration, except for a short interval, there had been a series of licensing acts, authorising the Crown to appoint a licenser, without whose leave no book or newspaper could be published.   In 1695 the House of Commons refused to renew the Act, and the press suddenly became free.   The House does not seem to have had any idea of the importance of this step, and established the liberty of the press simply because the licensers had given a good deal of annoyance.   Yet what they did would hardly have been done twenty years before.   The Toleration Act, allowing men to worship as they pleased, and to preach as they pleased, had brought about a state of mind which was certain, before long, to lead to the permission to men to print what they pleased.

2. **The Surrender of Namur.   1695.**—The campaign of 1695, in the Netherlands, was marked by William's first success.   His financial resources were now far greater than those of Louis, and he took Namur, though a French army was in the field to relieve

it. The French had never lost a battle or a fortified town during fifty-two years, but at last their career of victory was checked.

3. The Restoration of the Currency and the Treason-Trials Act. 1696.

At home Charles Montague, with the assistance of Sir Isaac Newton, the great mathematician and astronomer, succeeded in restoring the currency. Coins, up to that time, had been usually struck with smooth edges, and rogues had been in the habit of clipping off thin flakes of gold or silver as they passed through their hands. The result was that sixpences or shillings were seldom worth their full value. There were constant quarrels over every payment. New coins were now issued with milled edges, so that it would be impossible for anyone to clip them without being detected. The act authorising the re-coinage was followed by another, allowing persons accused of treason to have lawyers to plead for them in court; a permission which, up to this time, had been refused.

4. Ministerial Corruption. 1695—1696.

In spite of the success of William's government, there were in existence grave causes of dissatisfaction with the state of affairs. Corruption reigned amongst those whose influence was worth selling. In 1695 the Duke of Leeds—better known by his earlier title of Danby—was found guilty of taking a bribe, and it was well known that even ministers who did not take bribes became wealthy by means of gifts received for their services, as, indeed, ministers had done in former reigns. What was worse still, English ministers had, almost from the beginning of William's reign, endeavoured to make their position sure in the event of a counter-revolution, by professing allegiance to James whilst they remained in the service of William. At one time Marlborough had been guilty of even greater baseness, having sent to James information of an English expedition against Brest, in consequence of which the expedition was driven off with heavy loss, and its commander, Talmash, slain. No wonder William trusted his Dutch servants as he trusted no English ones, and that he sought to reward them by grants which, according to precedents set by earlier Kings, he held himself entitled to make out of the property of the Crown. Bentinck, to whom he was especially attached, he had made Earl of Portland; but when, in 1696, he proposed to give him a large estate in Wales, the Commons remonstrated, and Portland declined the gift.

5. The Assassination Plot. 1696.

From the unpopularity which attached itself to William in consequence of these pro-

ceedings the Jacobites conceived new hopes. Louis offered to
send soldiers to their help if they would first rise in insurrection.

Front of Hampton Court Palace ; built by Sir Christopher Wren for William III.

They, on the other hand, offered to rise if Louis would first send
soldiers. About forty Jacobites agreed in thinking that the shortest
way out of the difficulty was to murder William. They knew that,

III.   X X

when he went out hunting from Hampton Court, he returned by a
narrow lane, and that he usually had with him only twenty-five
guards.   They thought it would be easy work to spring into the
lane and shoot him.   The plot was, however, betrayed, and some

Part of Hampton Court ; built for William III. by Sir Christopher Wren.

of the plotters were executed.   The discovery of this design to
assassinate William made him once more popular.   In imitation
of what had been done when Elizabeth's life was in danger
(see p. 456), the greater part of the Lords and Commons bound
themselves by an association to defend William's government,

and to support the succession of the Princess Anne in the event of his death. The form of this association was circulated in the country, and signed by thousands.

6. The Peace of Ryswick. 1697.—Since the taking of Namur there had been no more fighting. In 1697 a general peace was signed at Ryswick. Louis gave up all the conquests which he had made in the war, and acknowledged William as king. William had, for the first time, the satisfaction of bringing to a close a war from which his great antagonist had gained no advantage. France was impoverished and England was prosperous. As Louis had said, the last gold piece had won (see p. 659). William returned thanks for the peace in the new St. Paul's built by Sir Christopher Wren in place of the old cathedral destroyed in the great fire (see p. 592).

7. Reduction of the Army. 1698—1699.—Scarcely was the war at an end when a controversy broke out between William and the House of Commons. William knew that the larger the armed force which England could maintain, the more chance there was that Louis would keep the peace which he had been forced to sign. The Commons, on the other hand, were anxious to diminish the expenditure, and were specially jealous of the existence of a large standing army which might be used, as it had been used by Cromwell, to establish an absolute government. Many Whigs deserted the ministers and joined the Tories on this point. In January 1698, the army was reduced to 10,000 men. In December it was reduced to 7,000. In March 1699, William was compelled to dismiss his Dutch guards. His irritation was so great that it was with the greatest difficulty that he was held back from abdicating the throne.

8. Signature and Failure of the First Partition Treaty. 1698—1699.—In the meanwhile, William was engaged in a delicate negotiation. It was well known that, whenever Charles II. of Spain died, Louis XIV. would claim the Spanish monarchy for one of his own family in right of his wife, Charles's eldest sister, Maria Theresa, whilst the Emperor Leopold would also claim it for himself or for one of his sons in the right of his mother, Maria, the aunt of Charles, on the ground that she was the only one amongst the sisters and aunts of Charles II. who had not renounced the succession. His own first wife Margaret Theresa, and Louis's wife Maria Theresa, who were both sisters of the King of Spain, as well as Louis's mother Anne, had all, on their respective marriages abandoned their claims. It was unlikely that either France or

Austria would submit without compulsion to see the territories of its rival increased so largely ; and in **1698,** William, hoping to avert a war, signed a secret Partition Treaty with Louis.   According to this treaty the bulk of the Spanish monarchy was to be assigned

West front of St. Paul's Cathedral church ; built by Sir Christopher Wren.

to a young man whose own territories were too small to give umbrage either to France or to Austria if he added to them those of the Spanish monarchy. This young man was the Electoral Prince of Bavaria, the grandson of Leopold by his first wife, Charles's sister Margaret Theresa,[1] whilst small portions of the territory under the Spanish Crown were to be allotted respectively to Louis's eldest son, the Dauphin, and to the Archduke Charles, the younger of Leopold's two sons by a second wife. Unfortunately, the death of the Electoral Prince in February **1699** overset this arrangement and enormously increased the difficulty of satisfying both France and Austria, especially as it was just at this time that Parliament reduced William's army to 7,000 men (see p. 667), thus leading Louis to suppose that he might defy England with impunity.

9. **Break-up of the Whig Junto. 1699.**—In home affairs, too, William was in considerable difficulty. When he had brought together the Whig Junto, he had done so because he found it convenient, not because he thought of binding himself never to keep ministers in office unless they were supported by a majority in the House of Commons. The modern doctrine that for ministers to remain in office after a serious defeat in the House of Commons is injurious both to themselves and to the public service had not yet been heard of, and this lesson, like so many others, had to be learned by experience. Again and again in the debates on the reduction of the army the ministers had been outvoted. The House also found fault with the administration of the Admiralty by Russell, who in **1697** had been created Earl of Orford, and appointed a

---

[1] Genealogy of the claimants of the Spanish monarchy (the names of the claimants are in capitals, and the names of princesses who had renounced their claims in italics) :—

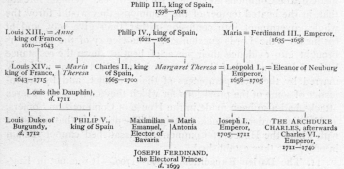

Philip III., king of Spain, 1598—1621

Louis XIII., = *Anne* king of France, 1610—1643

Philip IV., king of Spain, 1621—1665

Maria = Ferdinand III., Emperor, 1635—1658

Louis XIV., = *Maria* king of France, *Theresa* 1643—1715

Charles II., king of Spain, 1665—1700

Margaret Theresa = Leopold I., = Eleanor of Neuburg Emperor, 1658—1705

Louis (the Dauphin), *d.* 1711

Louis Duke of Burgundy, *d.* 1712

PHILIP V., king of Spain

Maximilian = Maria Emanuel, Antonia Elector of Bavaria

JOSEPH FERDINAND, the Electoral Prince. *d.* 1699

Joseph I., Emperor, 1705—1711

THE ARCHDUKE CHARLES, afterwards Charles VI., Emperor, 1711—1740

commission, in defiance of the ministers, to take into consideration certain extensive grants of forfeited estates in Ireland which had been made by William to his favourites. Though William failed to perceive the impossibility of governing satisfactorily with ministers who had against them a joint majority composed of Tories and discontented Whigs, those who were personally affected by its attacks readily perceived the danger into which they were running. In the course of **1699** Orford and Montague resigned their offices. William fell back upon his original system of combining Whigs and Tories. The Whigs, however, still preponderated, especially as Somers, the wisest statesman of the day, remained Lord Chancellor.

10. **The Irish Grants and the Fall of Somers. 1700.**—After the reduction of Ireland large tracts of land had fallen to the Crown, and William had made grants out of them to persons whom he favoured, especially to persons of foreign origin. Amongst these were brave foreign soldiers like Ginkell and Ruvigny (see p. 656), now Earls of Athlone and Galway, as well as mere personal favourites, such as Elizabeth Villiers, who had, many years before, been William's mistress. In **1700**, however, the Commons proposed to annul all William's Irish grants. Besides this the House proposed to grant away some of the estates to favourites of their own, and declared land forfeited which in law had never been forfeited at all. As the Lords resisted the latter parts of this scheme, the Commons invented a plan for coercing them. They tacked their bill, about Irish forfeitures to their grant of supplies for the year; that is to say, made it part of the bill by which the supplies were given to the Crown. As the peers were not allowed to alter a money bill, they must accept or reject the whole, including the provisions made by the Commons about the Irish forfeitures. William foresaw that, in the heated temper of the Commons, they would throw the whole government into confusion rather than give way, and at his instance the Lords succumbed. The victory of the Commons brought into evidence their power of beating down the resistance both of the king and of the House of Lords, but it was a victory marred by the intemperateness of their conduct, and by the injustice of some of the provisions for which they contended. Fierce attacks had also been made in the House of Commons on Somers, and William ordered Somers to resign. The principle that ministers with whom the House of Commons is dissatisfied cannot remain in office was thus established.

11. **The Darien Expedition. 1698—1700.**—It was not in Eng-

land only that William met with resistance. The commerce of Scotland was small, and Scotchmen were excluded from all share in the English trading companies. Paterson, who had been the originator of the Bank of England, urged his countrymen to settle in Darien, as the Isthmus of Panama was then called, where, placed as they would be between two oceans, they would, as he told them, have the trade of the world in their hands. Forgetting not only that Darien was claimed by Spain, but that its climate was exceedingly unhealthy, Scotchmen of all ranks joined eagerly in a company which was to acquire this valuable position. In **1698** and **1699** two expeditions sailed to take possession of the isthmus. By the spring of **1700** most of those who had set out with the highest hopes had perished of disease, whilst the few who remained alive had been expelled by the Spaniards. All Scotland threw the blame of the disaster on William, because he had not embroiled England in war with Spain to defend these unauthorised intruders on her domain.

12. **The Second Partition Treaty. 1700.**—In the spring of **1700**, whilst the weakness and unpopularity of William were being published to the world, he concluded a second partition treaty with Louis. The Archduke Charles was to be king of Spain, of the Spanish Netherlands, and of all the Spanish colonies ; France was to have Guipuscoa, on the Spanish shore of the Bay of Biscay, and all the Spanish possessions in Italy, though Louis declared his intention of abandoning the Duchy of Milan to the Duke of Lorraine in exchange for Lorraine. The proposal of this Treaty came from Louis, who certainly had very little idea of carrying it into effect, whilst the Emperor, who would gain much by it for his son, the Archduke Charles, refused his consent, perhaps thinking that it was of little importance to him to place his son on the throne of Spain, if Italy, which lay so much nearer to his own hereditary dominions, was to be abandoned to the French.

13. **Deaths of the Duke of Gloucester and of the King of Spain. 1700.**—Two deaths, which occurred in **1700**, affected the politics of England and Europe for some time to come. Anne had had several children, all of whom died young, the last of them, the Duke of Gloucester, dying on July 29 in this year. The question of the succession to the throne after Anne's death was thus thrown open. Charles II. of Spain died on November 1. Louis had long been intriguing for his inheritance, and his intrigues had been success-ful. Charles, before he died, left by will the whole of his dominions to Louis's grandson, Philip, hereafter to be known as Philip V., king

of Spain. Louis accepted the inheritance, and threw to the winds the Partition Treaty which he had made with William.

14. **A Tory Ministry. 1700—1701.**—It seemed as if the chief work of William's life had been undone, and that France would domineer over Europe unchecked. In England there was but little desire to engage in a new war, and, before the end of 1700, William was obliged to appoint a Tory ministry. There was a Tory majority in the new Parliament which met on February 6, 1701. The great majority of the Tories had by this time thrown off their belief in the indefeasible Divine right of kings, and acknowledged William without difficulty. Their chief political ideas were the maintenance of peace abroad, and the pre-eminence of the Church of England at home, though they—more or less thoroughly—accepted the Toleration Act. Their main supporters were the country gentlemen and the country clergy, whilst the Whigs, who supported William in his desire for a war with France, and who took under their patronage the Dissenters, were upheld by the great landowners, and by the commercial class in the towns.

15. **The Act of Settlement and the Succession. 1701.**—The first work of the Tory Parliament was the Act of Settlement. By this Act the succession was settled, after Anne's death, on Sophia, Electress of Hanover, and her descendants. She was the daughter of Elizabeth, queen of Bohemia (see pp. 488, 490), and was thus the granddaughter of James I. The principle on which the selection rested was that she was the nearest Protestant heir, all the living descendants of Charles I., except William and Anne, being Roman Catholics.

16. **The Act of Settlement and the Crown. 1701.**—The view that the nation had a right to fix the succession was now accepted by the Tories as fully as by the Whigs ; but the Tories, seeing that William was inclined to trust their opponents more than themselves, now went beyond the Whigs in their desire to restrict the powers of the Crown. By the Tory Act of Settlement the future Hanoverian sovereign was (1) to join in the Communion of the Church of England ; (2) not to declare war without consent of Parliament on behalf of territories possessed by him on the Continent, and (3) not to leave the three kingdoms without consent of Parliament—an article which was repealed in the first year of George I. A stipulation (4) that no pardon under the great seal was to be pleadable in bar of impeachment, was intended to prevent William or his successors from protecting ministers against Parliament, as Charles II. had attempted to do

in Danby's case (see p. 617). A further stipulation was (5) that after Anne's death no man, unless born in England or of English parents abroad, should sit in the Privy Council or in Parliament, or hold office or lands granted him by the Crown. These five articles all sprang from jealousy of a foreign sovereign. A sixth, enacting (6) that the judges should, henceforward, hold their places as long as they behaved well, but might be removed on an address from both Houses of Parliament, was an improvement in the constitution, irrespective of all personal considerations. It has prevented, ever since, the repetition of the scandal caused by James II. when he changed some of the judges for the purpose of getting a judgment in his own favour (see p. 639).

17. **The Act of Settlement and the Ministers. 1701.**—There were two other articles in the Act, of which one (7) declared that, under the future Hanoverian sovereign, all matters proper to the Privy Council should be transacted there, and that all resolutions taken in it should be signed by those councillors who assented to them ; whilst the other (8) embodied the provisions of the rejected Place Bill (see p. 661), to the effect that no òne holding a place or pension from the Crown should sit in the House of Commons. Both these articles were directed, not so much against the Crown as against the growing power of the ministers. At this time, indeed, the prevailing wish of the country squires who made up the bulk of the Tory party was to make the House of Commons effectively, as well as in name, predominant ; and they therefore watched with alarm the growth of the power of the Cabinet, as the informal meetings of the ministers who directed the affairs of the kingdom were now called. As the Cabinet, unlike the old Privy Council, kept no record of its proceedings, the Tories were alarmed lest its members should escape responsibility, and should also, by offering places and pensions to their supporters in the House, contrive to secure a majority in it, even when they had the greater number of independent members against them. The article relating to the Privy Council was, however, repealed early in the next reign, as it was found that no one was willing to give advice if he was liable to be called in question and punished for giving it, so that the system of holding private Cabinet meetings where advice could be given without fear of consequences was not long interrupted. The article for excluding placemen and pensioners, on the other hand, merely overshot the mark, and in the next reign it was so modified that only holders of new places created subsequently to 1705 were excluded from the House, as well as persons who held pensions revocable at the

pleasure of the Crown ; whilst all members accepting old places were to vacate their seats, and to appeal for re-election to a constituency if they thought fit to do so. Subsequent legislation went farther and disqualified persons holding many of the old places from sitting in parliament, with the general result that, whilst the holders of pensions and smaller places are now excluded from the House of Commons, the important ministers of the Crown are allowed to sit there, thereby keeping up that close connection between ministers and Parliament which is so efficacious in promoting a good understanding between them.

18. **The Tory Foreign Policy. 1701.**—In foreign policy the Tories blamed William and the Whigs for concluding the Partition Treaties. France and Spain, they held, would still be mutually jealous of one another, even though Louis sat on the throne of France and his grandson on the throne of Spain, whereas the territory which, according to the second treaty, would have been actually annexed to France, would have given to Louis exorbitant influence in Europe. Accordingly they impeached the leading Whigs, Somers, Portland, Orford, and Montague, who had lately become Lord Halifax. The impeached peers were, however, supported by the House of Lords, and nothing could be done against them. If only Louis had behaved with ordinary prudence, the peace policy of the Tories would have carried the day. He seemed, however, resolved to show that he meant to dispose of the whole of the forces of both monarchies. There was a line of fortified towns, known as the barrier fortresses, raised on the southern frontier of the Spanish Netherlands, to defend them against France, at a time when France and Spain were hostile. As the Spanish Government had lately shown itself incapable of keeping fortresses in repair or of providing them with sufficient garrisons, it had been agreed that half of each garrison should be composed of Dutch soldiers. Early in 1701, Louis, with the assistance of the Spanish half of each garrison, got possession of every one of these fortresses in a single night, turned out the Dutch, and replaced them by French soldiers. For all military purposes the Spanish Netherlands might as well have been under the immediate government of Louis.

19. **The Kentish Petition. 1701.**—To the Dutch the possibility of a French army advancing without hindrance to their frontier was extremely alarming ; while in England there had always been a strong feeling against the occupation by the French of the coast opposite the mouth of the Thames. Louis's interference in the Netherlands therefore did something to rouse a warlike spirit in

England.   In April a petition to the House of Commons was
drawn up by the gentlemen of Kent and presented by five of
their number.   This Kentish Petition asked the Commons to support the king and to ' turn their loyal addresses into Bills of supply.'
The House sent the five who brought the petition to the Tower, on
the plea that the constituencies had done their work when they had
elected their members, and had no right to influence the proceedings of the House when once the elections had been completed.
As the Tories had defended the authority of the House against the
ministers, so they now defended it against the electors.

20. **The Grand Alliance. 1701.**—William saw that the feeling
of the country would soon be on the side of war.   Having obtained
the consent, even of the Tory House of Commons, to defensive
measures, he raised new troops and sent 10,000 men to protect the
Dutch against any attack which Louis might make upon them.   At
the head of this force he placed Marlborough, whom he had again
taken into favour (see p. 658).   In September he advanced a step
farther.   War had already broken out in Italy between France and
Spain on the one side, and the Emperor Leopold, as ruler of the
Austrian dominions, on the other.   Both William and the Dutch
would have been glad of a compromise with Louis, and would have
left Spain to Philip V. if Leopold could have part, at least, of the
Spanish dominions in Italy.   Louis would hear of no compromise,
and on September 7 William signed the Grand Alliance, as it was
called, between England, Austria, and the Dutch Republic ; of
which the objects were to restore to the Dutch the control of the
barrier fortresses, to secure to Leopold the Italian possessions of
Spain, and to provide that the Crowns of France and Spain should
never be united.

21. **Death of James II. 1701.**—The day before this treaty
was signed James II. died in France.   Louis at once acknowledged
as king his son, the child who had been held in England to be
supposititious, and who was afterwards known as the Pretender by
his enemies, and as James III. by his friends.   At once all England
burst into a storm of indignation against Louis, for having dared to
acknowledge as king of England a boy whose title had been rejected
by the English Parliament and nation.   William seized the opportunity and dissolved the Tory Parliament.   A new Parliament was
returned with a small Whig majority.   It passed an Act ordering
all persons holding office to take an oath of abjuration of the
Pretender's title, and raised the army to 40,000 men, granting at
the same time a considerable sum for the navy.

22. **Death of William.** **1702.**—Early in **1702** William was looking forward to taking the command in the war which was beginning. On February 20 his horse stumbled over a mole-hill in Hampton Park. He fell, and broke his collar bone. He lingered for some days, and, on March 8, he died. His work, if not accomplished, was at least in a fair way of being accomplished. His main object in life had been to prevent Louis from domineering in Europe, whilst the maintenance of the constitutional liberties of England had been with him only a secondary object. That he succeeded in what he undertook against Louis was owing, primarily, to the self-sufficiency and obstinacy, first of Louis himself and then of James II. ; but all the blunders of his adversaries would have availed him little if he had not himself been possessed of invincible patience and of the tact which perceives the line which divides the practicable from the impracticable. That he was a Continental statesman with Continental aims stood in the way of his popularity in England. His merit was that, being aware how necessary English support was to him on the Continent, he recognised that his only hope of securing the help of England lay in persistent devotion to her domestic interests and her constitutional liberties ; and that devotion, in spite of some blunders and some weaknesses, he uninterruptedly gave to her during the whole course of his reign.

CHAPTER XLIV

ANNE. 1702—1714

LEADING DATES

Accession of Anne 1702
Battle of Blenheim 1704
Battle of Ramillies 1706
Union with Scotland 1707
Battles of Almanza and Oudenarde 1708
Battle of Malplaquet 1709
The Sacheverell Trial 1710
Battles of Brihuega and Villa Viciosa 1710
Dismissal of Marlborough and Creation of Twelve Peers 1711
Treaty of Utrecht 1713
Death of Anne 1714

1. **Marlborough and the Tories.** **1702.**—Anne was a good-hearted woman of no great ability, warmly attached to the Church of England, and ready to support it in its claims against the

Dissenters.   She therefore preferred the Tories to the Whigs, and filled all the ministerial offices with Tories.   Marlborough, who, through his wife, had boundless influence over the Queen, found it expedient to declare himself a Tory, though he had little sympathy

Queen Anne ; from a portrait by Sir Godfrey Kneller

with the extravagances of the extreme members of that party, and wanted merely to have a firm Government which would support him in his military enterprises.   His chief ally was Lord Godolphin, to whose son one of his daughters was married.   Godolphin was

Lord Treasurer, and, being an excellent financier, was likely to be able to find the money needed for a great war. He was also a fitting man to keep the ministers from quarrelling with one another. He had frequently been in office, and he liked official work better than party strife. " Little Sidney Godolphin," Charles II. had once said of him, " is never in the way, and never out of the way," and this character he retained to the end.

2. **Louis XIV. and Marlborough.   1702.**—As far as the war and foreign affairs were concerned, Marlborough was the true successor of William III.   The difficulties with which he had to contend were, indeed, enormous.   Louis XIV., at the opening of the war, had a fine military position.   His flanks were guarded by the possession of the Spanish Netherlands on the left and of Spain itself on the right, whilst an alliance which he formed with the Elector of Bavaria gave him military command of a tract of land accessible without much difficulty from his own territory. This tract, on the one hand, enabled a French army to make an easy attack on the Austrian dominions beyond the Inn, whilst on the other hand it divided the forces of the allies into two parts, cutting off the Austrian army in Italy, under Prince Eugene, from the English and Dutch armies in the Netherlands, both of which were under the command of Marlborough.   Louis was, moreover, the sole master of all his armies, and could easily secure obedience to his orders.   Marlborough had the more difficult task of securing obedience, not only from the English and Dutch armies, but from the numerous contingents sent by the German princes, most of whom now joined the Grand Alliance.   The most important of these princes was Frederick I., the Elector of Brandenburg, who had been made by the Emperor king of Prussia, in order to induce him to join the allies.   To the difficult task of guiding this hetero-geneous following, Marlborough brought not only a consummate military genius far transcending that of William, but a temper as imperturbable as William's own.

3. **Marlborough's First Campaign in the Netherlands.   1702—1703.**—Marlborough's aim was to break Louis's power in South Germany, but he knew better than to attempt this at once.   The French held the fortresses of the Spanish Netherlands and of the Rhine-country, covering the roads by which the Dutch territory could be assailed with advantage on its eastern and south-eastern sides ; and, as long as this was the case, it was certain that the Dutch would not allow their army to go far from home.   Marl-borough therefore devoted the two campaigns of **1702** and **1703** to

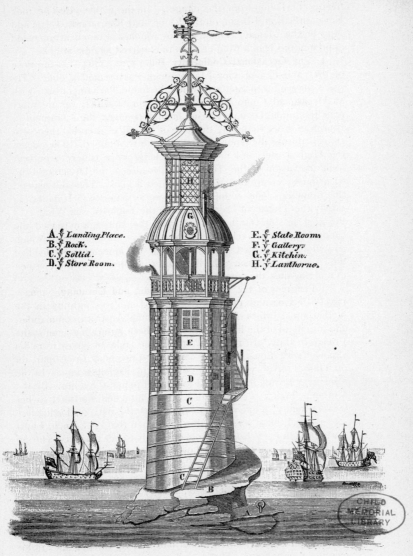

A. ẏ Landing Place.
B. ẏ Rock.
C. ẏ Sollid.
D. ẏ Store Room.

E. ẏ State Room.
F. ẏ Gallery.
G. ẏ Kitchin.
H. ẏ Lanthorne.

The first Eddystone Lighthouse, erected in 1697; destroyed in 1703

freeing the Dutch from this danger. In these two years he took Kaiserswerth and Bonn, on the Rhine, and Roermonde, Liège and Huy on the Meuse. The roads by which a French army could approach the Dutch frontier were thus barred against attack.

4. **The Occasional Conformity Bill. 1702—1703.**—At the close of the campaign of 1702 Marlborough was created a duke. He spent the winter in England, where he found Parliament busy with an Occasional Conformity Bill, the object of which was to inflict penalties upon Dissenters who, having received the sacrament in church in order to qualify themselves for office, attended their own chapels during the tenure of the office thus obtained. The queen, the High Tories, and most of the clergy were eager to prevent such an evasion of the Test Act, especially as the Dissenters who occasionally conformed were Whigs to a man. The Bill passed the Commons, where the Tories were a majority. It failed to satisfy the House of Lords, in which the majority was Whig. In the next session, at the end of 1703, the Bill again passed the Commons, but was rejected by the Lords. Though Marlborough and Godolphin voted for it to please the queen, they disliked the measure, as causing ill-will between parties which they wished to unite against the common enemy.

5. **Progress of the War in Italy, Spain and Germany. 1702—1703.**—In 1702 and 1703, whilst Marlborough was fighting in the Netherlands, Prince Eugene of Savoy, the Austrian commander, and a general of the highest order, had been struggling against the French in Italy. In 1703 he won over the Duke of Savoy from his alliance with Louis, but he could not prevent a great part of the Duke's territory from being overrun by French troops. In the same year Portugal deserted France and joined the allies. By the Methuen Treaty now formed, England attached Portugal to her by community of interests, engaging that the duty on Portuguese wines should be at least one-third less than that on French, whilst Portugal admitted English woollen goods to her market. During the first two years of the war, however, little of military importance took place in any part of the Peninsula. By the end of 1703 the combined forces of the French and Bavarians had gained considerable successes in Germany, and, by the capture of Augsburg, Old Breisach and Landau, had secured the communications between France and Bavaria.

6. **Ministerial Changes. 1703—1704.**—Before Marlborough could assail Louis' position in Germany he had to make sure of his own position at home. The High Tories weakened him not only by

alienating the Dissenters, but by their lukewarmness about the war. Their leaders, the Earls of Rochester and Nottingham, held that the war ought to be mainly carried on at sea and to be purely defensive on land, and had no sympathy with Marlborough in his design of destroying the predominance of Louis in Europe. Early in **1703** Marlborough found an opportunity of getting rid of Rochester. In the spring of **1704** he came into collision with Nottingham. There was a rising of the Protestant subjects of Louis in the Cevennes, usually known as the rising of the Camisards, because they fought with their shirts over their clothes. Marlborough was anxious to assist them, but was thwarted by Nottingham, who held it to be wrong, in any case, to support rebellion. Nottingham was accordingly dismissed, and the vacant places were filled by Harley and St. John. Both of the new ministers called themselves moderate Tories. Harley was an influential member of Parliament, with a talent for intrigue and a love of middle courses. St. John, profligate in his life, was the most brilliant orator and the ablest and most unscrupulous politician of the day. A few Whigs, of no great note, also received places. It was Marlborough's policy to

Steeple of St. Bride's, Fleet Street, London; built by Sir Christopher Wren, 1701–1703.

III.   Y Y

secure the support of a body of ministers who would avoid irritating anyone, and would thus help him in his military designs. An attempt made by the High Tories in the Commons to force the Lords to accept the Occasional Conformity Bill, by tacking it (see p. 670) to a Bill for a land tax, was defeated with the help of Harley and St. John.

7. **The Campaign of Blenheim. 1704.**—The campaign of 1704 was likely to be a critical one. The French and Bavarians intended to push on to Vienna and to compel the Emperor to separate himself from his allies. Marlborough, perceiving that if the French were allowed to carry their project into execution they would become the masters of Europe, anticipated them by marching to the Upper Danube, carrying with him the Dutch army in spite of the reluctance of the Dutch Government. Having effected a junction with the Austrian commander Prince Eugene, and with Louis of Baden who was at the head of the forces of other German states, the combined armies stormed the Schellenberg, a hill over Donauwörth, and then devastated Bavaria. A French army under Marshal Tallard hastened to the aid of the Elector of Bavaria. Marlborough and Eugene, between whom no jealousies ever arose, turned round, and utterly defeated Tallard at Blenheim. It was Marlborough's genius which had foreseen the surprising results of a victory on the Danube. His success marks the end of a period of French military superiority in Europe. The French had won every battle in which they had been engaged since 1643, when they defeated the Spaniards at Rocroi. It was, however, something more than prestige which was lost by France. The whole of the territory of the Duke of Bavaria, the most important German ally of Louis, was at the mercy of the allies, and before the end of the year scarcely a vestige of French authority was left in Germany. Marlborough received a grant of the manor of Woodstock, on which the huge and ungraceful pile which bears the name of Blenheim was built for him at the public expense.

8. **Operations in Spain. 1704—1705.**—In 1704 the Archduke Charles, assuming the name of Charles III. of Spain, landed at Lisbon. The Spaniards regarded him as a foreign intruder, whilst they cherished Philip V. as if he had been their native king. The first foothold which Charles acquired in Spain was at Gibraltar, which surrendered in August to the English admiral, Sir George Rooke. In 1705 the French and Spaniards tried in vain to retake the fortress. The most important success of the allies in 1705 was the capture of Barcelona—an achievement of which the chief merit

Part of Blenheim ; built by Vanbrugh in 1704.

belongs to the English commander, the eccentric Lord Peterborough, whose brilliant conceptions were too often thrown away by his ignorance of that art in which Marlborough excelled, the art of courteously overlooking the defects of others. The importance of Barcelona arose from its being the chief place in Catalonia, a province which clung to its local independence, and which vigorously espoused the cause of Charles, simply because Philip ruled in Castile. Soon afterwards Valencia was overrun by the allies. In other parts of Europe there were no military events of note. In the course of 1705 the Emperor Leopold I. died, and his son Joseph (the elder brother of the Archduke Charles) succeeded him in the empire as well as in his hereditary dominions.

9. **A Whig Parliament. 1705—1706.**—At home the High Tories raised the cry of " The Church in danger " ; but a Whig majority was returned to Parliament, and Marlborough and Godolphin entered into friendly communications with the Whig leaders. One of the results of the understanding arrived at was a compromise on that article in the Act of Settlement which would, after the accession of the House of Hanover, have excluded ministers as well as other placemen from the House of Commons (see p. 673). It was arranged in 1706 that the holding of a pension or of an office created after October 25, 1705, should disqualify, whilst all other offices should be compatible with a seat, provided that the holder, at the time of his appointment, presented himself for a fresh election.

10. **The Campaign of 1706 in the Netherlands and in Italy. 1706.**—In May, 1706, Marlborough won a second great victory at Ramillies, and before long, except that they continued to hold a few isolated fortresses, the French were swept out of the Spanish Netherlands as they had been swept out of Germany in 1704. In September, Eugene came to the succour of the Duke of Savoy, defeated the French who were besieging Turin, and drove their armies out of Italy.

11. **Campaign of 1706 in Spain. 1706.**—In Spain the success of the allies was less unmixed. Barcelona indeed beat off a French besieging army, and the old Huguenot refugee Ruvigny, now known as the Earl of Galway (see p. 670), marched from Portugal and occupied Madrid in June ; but the Portuguese under his command left him in order to plunder, and, before the end of July, he learnt that the French commander, the Duke of Berwick (the illegitimate son of James II. by Marlborough's sister, Arabella Churchill), had received ample reinforcements. As all the country

round was hostile, Galway had nothing for it but to leave Madrid. In August he was joined by the Archduke Charles and Peterborough, though the latter soon afterwards betook himself to Italy on diplomatic service. When Peterborough afterwards returned to Spain, all authority had slipped out of his hands. Galway, unable to maintain himself in Castile, retreated to Valencia. Whilst he had been in the interior, Aragon had declared for Charles, and Alicante had been captured by an English fleet.

12. **The Union with Scotland.** 1702—1707.—Far more important to England than all that was taking place in Spain was the conclusion of the Union with Scotland. In 1702 Commissioners had met to discuss its terms. The Scots had naturally been anxious for freedom of trade and equality of commercial privileges.

As the English were unwilling to grant this, the Scottish Parliament, in 1703, retorted by an Act of Security, providing that the successor to the Scottish crown, after the queen's death, should not be the same person as the successor to the crown of England. In 1704, in consequence of the defiant attitude of Scotland, the queen was forced to give the royal assent to the Act of Security. What the Scots virtually meant by it was, that England must make her choice either to accept Scotland as an equal

Royal Arms as borne by Anne.

partner with full equality of benefits and rights, or must have her as an alienated neighbour with a national sovereign of her own, capable of renewing that ancient league with France which had cost England so dear in earlier times. England retaliated with an enactment that Scotchmen, coming to England, should no longer enjoy the privileges to which they were entitled by the decision of the Judges in the case of the *Postnati* (see p. 483), until the Scottish Parliament had settled the succession in the same way that it was settled in England. Godolphin and his fellow-ministers were, however, too wise to prolong this war of threats. They gave way on free trade and commercial equality, and in 1707 the union of the two nations and the two Parliaments was finally accepted on both sides   Forty-five members of the House of Commons were to be chosen by Scottish constituencies, and the Scottish peers were to elect sixteen of their own number to sit in the House of Lords. Scotland maintained her own Church, her own law, and the control of her own fortresses. She remained a nation in heart, voluntarily merging her legislative authority in that of the neighbouring nation.

13. **The Irish Penal Laws.**—It would have been well both for England and Ireland if the Irish race had been capable of enforcing its claims even to a just and lenient treatment by its masters. Unfortunately the Irish population, beaten in war and deprived of its natural leaders by the emigration of its most vigorous soldiers, was subjected to the Parliament of the British Protestant colony. In spite of the terms made at Limerick (see p. 657), the Parliament at Dublin, after excluding Catholics from its benches, passed laws of which the result was to make wellnigh intolerable the position of the professors of the religion of at least three-fourths of the inhabitants of Ireland. Catholic landowners were impoverished by an enforced partition of their lands amongst their sons, and by the enactment that if a single son turned Protestant the whole of the inheritance was to pass to him. Catholic children, upon the death of their fathers, were entrusted to Protestant guardians, who were directed to bring them up as Protestants. A Catholic priest who converted a Protestant to his faith was to be imprisoned, and one who celebrated a marriage between a Catholic and a Protestant was to be hanged. Oaths were imposed on the priests which no conscientious Catholic could take, and each priest who refused the oath was to be banished, and, if he returned to Ireland, was to forfeit his life. Any persons refusing to give evidence which might lead to the detection of such priests were liable to imprisonment or fine. In addition to these and other similar enactments, the Irishman who was true to his religion had to bear the daily scorn and contumely of men of English or Scottish descent and religion, who looked upon him as a being of an inferior race, and scarcely deigned to admit him even to their presence.

14. **Irish Commerce Crushed.**—Though the Parliament in Dublin was allowed to deal thus with the lives and property of those whom its members would have scorned to speak of as their fellow-countrymen, it had to purchase the support of England by submitting to that English commercial monopoly against which the Scots had successfully rebelled. In the reign of Charles II. landowners in Ireland—for the most part Protestant landowners—

exported cattle to England until the English Parliament absolutely killed this trade by prohibiting the reception at any English port of cattle, sheep, and swine, beef, pork, and mutton, and even of butter and cheese imported from Ireland, lest they should compete with the produce of the English landowner. Debarred from this source of prosperity Ireland made steady progress in woollen manufactures till, in **1699**, the English Parliament forbade the export of woollen goods from Ireland to any country except to England, where they were practically barred out by prohibitive duties, lest their sale should injure the profits of English manufacturers. The ruling race in Ireland was too dependent on the English Parliament to be capable of resisting these enactments.

15. **Gradual Formation of a Whig Ministry. 1705—1708.**— In England power passed gradually into the hands of Whig ministers. In **1705** the Whig Cowper became Lord Chancellor. In **1706** the Earl of Sunderland,[1] Marlborough's son-in-law, became Secretary of State. The queen was strongly averse to Sunderland's promotion, as she looked on the Whigs as enemies of the Church, and Sunderland was the most acrimonious of the Whigs. Moreover, Anne was growing weary of the arrogant temper of the Duchess of Marlborough, and had begun to transfer her confidence to Harley's cousin, Abigail Hill, who became Mrs. Masham in **1707**, a soft-spoken, unpretentious woman, whose companionship was calm and soothing. There was, however, a grave political question at issue as well as a personal one. The Whigs, finding the Tories lukewarm about the war and harsh towards the Dissenters, insisted on the appointment of a compact ministry consisting of Whigs alone. The queen, on the other hand, upheld the doctrine that the choice of ministers depended on herself, and that it was desirable to unite moderate men of both parties in her service. Harley supported her in this view, and, being detected by his colleagues in intriguing against them with the help of Mrs. Masham, was, together with St. John, turned out of office in February, **1708**. By the end of that year the ministry became completely Whig. Marlborough and Godolphin declared themselves to be Whigs, Somers became President of the Council, Wharton Lord-Lieutenant of Ireland.

16. **Progress of Cabinet Government. 1708.**—In one respect the Whig ministry completed in **1708** resembles that which served William III. under the name of the Whig Junto in **1695**. Both were formed of men of one political opinion : both owed their

---

[1] Son of the minister of Charles II. and James II.

influence to the necessity of unity of action in time of war. There was, however, one great difference between the two ministries. The Whig ministry of William III. was formed by the sovereign for his own purposes; whereas the Whig ministry of Anne was

Sarah, Duchess of Marlborough: from a portrait, by Sir G. Kneller, belonging to Earl Spencer, K.G.

formed in defiance of the sovereign. The idea of government by a Cabinet resting on a party majority in Parliament, and forcing its will on the sovereign, originated with the Tory ministers who forced themselves on William III. towards the end of his reign, but it first took definite shape in the Whig ministry of the reign of Anne.

17. **Progress of the War. 1707—1708.**—There had been nothing to dazzle the eyes of Englishmen in the campaign of 1707. An attempt to take Toulon, by a joint attack of Prince Eugene on land and of the English navy under Sir Cloudesley Shovel, had

John Churchill, first Duke of Marlborough : from a portrait belonging to
Earl Spencer, K.G.

failed, and, on the return of the fleet, three English ships were wrecked off the Scilly Isles and the admiral himself drowned. In Spain Galway was defeated at Almanza, and nearer home all the success achieved was that the Pretender, after setting forth to invade Scotland with a French force, thought it prudent to return without landing. The campaign of **1708** was of a different character. The Dutch had made themselves disagreeable in the conquered Spanish Netherlands, and the French general, Vendôme, was therefore welcomed by the inhabitants, and took Ghent and Bruges with little difficulty. Marlborough, however, met him at Oudenarde, utterly defeated him, and, before the end of the year, not only retook the places which had been lost, but, advancing on French territory, took Lille after a prolonged siege. In the same year General Stanhope reduced Minorca, an island of importance from the goodness of its harbour, Port Mahon, which formed an excellent basis for naval operations in the Mediterranean.

18. **The Conference at The Hague and the Battle of Malplaquet. 1709.**—In France the peasants were starving, and Louis, in quest of peace, entered on negotiations at The Hague. The allies insisted upon his abandonment not only of portions of his own territory, but upon the surrender by his grandson of the whole of the Spanish monarchy. To all this he agreed, but when he found that, instead of obtaining peace in return, he was only to have a two months' truce, during which he was to join in expelling his grandson from Spain, he drew back. "If I must wage war," he said, "I would rather wage it against my enemies than against my children." No doubt the allies believed that they could not trust Louis really to abandon Philip unless he actually sent an army against him. They were at fault, partly in being blind to the impossibility of holding Spain in defiance of the Spaniards, partly in neglecting to foresee that the English nation would not long continue to support a war waged for an object which seemed to concern it so little as the possession of the Spanish Peninsula. Finding that nothing more was to be had by negotiation, Louis put forth all his strength. He sent forth a fresh army ill-clothed and half-starved, but resolute to do its utmost for its country's sake. This army was, on September 11, attacked at Malplaquet by the combined forces of Marlborough and Eugene. The allies were again victorious, but they lost 20,000 men, whilst only 12,000 fell on the side of the French.

19. **The Sacheverell Trial. 1710.**—Before another campaign was opened the Whig ministry was tottering to its fall. On November 5, **1709**, a certain Dr. Sacheverell preached in St. Paul's a sermon upholding the doctrine of non-resistance (see p. 611), attacking the Dissenters, reviling toleration, and personally abus-

ing Godolphin. In spite of Somers's advice to leave Sacheverell alone, the Whig ministers decided to impeach him. What the Whigs wanted was an opportunity for solemnly recording their views on the principles of resistance and toleration established at the Revolution, and such an opportunity they obtained during the impeachment, which occupied the first months of 1710. Dissenters, however, who were mainly drawn from the middle classes, were no more liked by the mob than they were by the country gentlemen, and their discredit was shared by their protectors the Whigs. When the queen passed there were shouts raised of " God bless your Majesty and the Church. We hope your Majesty is for Dr. Sacheverell." There were riots in the streets, and Dissenters' chapels were sacked and burnt. In the end the Whig House of Lords pronounced Sacheverell guilty, but did not venture to do more than order his sermons to be burnt and himself prohibited from preaching for the next three years. By this sentence which was a virtual defeat of the Whigs and a triumph of the Tories, Sacheverell gained rather than lost by his condemnation. Wherever he went he was uproariously welcomed, and he was consoled for his enforced silence with a well-endowed living.

20. **The Fall of the Whigs.** 1710.—Anne saw in this outburst a sign that it would now be easy for her to get rid of her ministers. She was the better able to make the attempt, as there were, in the spring of 1710, fresh conferences for peace at Gertruydenberg, in which it was proposed to solve all difficulties by leaving to Philip some part of the Spanish monarchy other than Spain itself. No general agreement, however, could be obtained, and England seemed to be committed to an interminable war. All the blame of its continuance was unjustly thrown on Marlborough. The queen effected cautiously the change which she was bent on making. Harley, who was her chief adviser, recommended her to revert to the system which had prevailed when he had been last in office (see p. 687), and to form a ministry composed of moderate Whigs and Tories of which the direction should fall to herself.

21. **A Tory Parliament and Ministry.** 1710.—Harley's plan óf a combined ministry fell to the ground. A new House of Commons, elected in 1710, being strongly Tory, resolved to secure power, permanently if possible, for the country gentry and the country clergy, and to reduce to impotence the wealthy peers, with the merchants and Dissenters who formed the strength of the Whigs. Harley and St. John were compelled by their supporters to form a purely Tory ministry.

22. **Brihuega and Villa Viciosa. 1710.**—The Tories had no wish to keep up the war except so far as it would serve special English interests, and, in the course of 1710, the danger of being engaged in an endless war in Spain appeared greater than ever. In the summer, indeed, the combined English and Austrian armies defeated the Spaniards at Saragossa, and Charles once more entered Madrid as a conqueror ; but, before the end of the year, one of Louis's best generals, Vendôme, was sent to Spain to lead the French and Spanish armies. On December 9 he compelled Stanhope, the English commander, to surrender at Brihuega, and though a battle which he fought on the 10th with the Austrian Staremberg at Villa Viciosa was indecisive, Staremberg was obliged to retreat to Barcelona, leaving all Spain, except Catalonia, in the hands of Philip.

23. **Overtures to France. 1710—1711.**—Even before this bad news reached England, Harley and St. John, without troubling themselves about the interests of their allies, had opened secret negotiations for peace, on the basis of leaving Spain to Philip, and of acquiring for England separately as many advantages as possible. The Tory party had never had much inclination to defend the interests of Europe as a whole, and, at the end of 1710, it might reasonably be doubted whether the interests of Europe as a whole were to be served by prolonging the struggle to place the Archduke Charles on the throne of Spain. The real objection against the conduct of the new ministers was not that they opened negotiations for peace, but that they negotiated after the fashion of conspirators. Not only did they, in 1711, send secret emissaries, first Gautier and afterwards the poet Prior, to treat privately with Louis, but when, in the September of that year, preliminaries were agreed to as a basis for a private understanding between England and France, they actually communicated a false copy of them to the Dutch. By this time, indeed, there was a fresh reason for making peace. The Emperor Joseph I. had died in April without leaving a son, and was succeeded in his hereditary dominions by his brother, the Archduke Charles. It might fairly be argued that it was at least as dangerous in 1711 to give the whole of the Spanish dominions to the ruler of the Austrian territories, as it had been in 1702 to give them to the grandson of the king of France.

24. **Literature and Politics. 1710.**—In order to defend their policy the Tory ministers had, on their first accession to power, looked about for literary supporters. In the reign of Anne a literature had arisen in prose and verse which may fairly be de-

scribed as prosaic. It had nothing of the high imagination which illuminated the pages of the great Elizabethan writers. It was sensible and intelligent, aiming not at rousing the feelings, but at being plainly understood. Addison, in his writings, for instance, mingled criticism with attractive arguments in favour of a morality of common sense, which he addressed to that numerous class which shrank from the high demands of Milton. Addison, like most other writers of the day, was a Whig, the political views of the Whigs having, at that time, a strong hold upon men of intelligence. Writers like Addison exercised considerable influence over the frequenters of the London coffee-houses, where political affairs were discussed. The support of this class, usually spoken of as 'the Town,' was at that time more worth winning than either before or since. As there were no Parliamentary reports, and no speeches on politics delivered in public, only those who lived near the place in which Parliament met could have any knowledge of the details of political action. They gained this knowledge from the lips of the actors, and were able, by their personal conversation, to influence in turn the conduct of the actors themselves. The services of a persuasive writer who had the ear of 'the Town' was therefore coveted by every body of ministers.

25. **Jonathan Swift.**—The writer won over by the Tory ministers was Jonathan Swift. He was unequalled in satirical power, arising from a combination of lucid expression with a habit of regarding the actions of men as springing from the lowest motives. He was a clergyman, and he wished to be a bishop. At first he attached himself to the Whigs. The Whigs, however, were unwilling, or perhaps unable, to give him what he wanted, his writings being of too unclerical a nature ; and all that they procured for him was a living in Ireland, which he seldom visited. With personal motives were mingled more creditable reasons for disliking the Whigs. He was devoted to the interests of the Church of England, not as a fosterer of spiritual life, but as a bulwark against what he regarded as the extravagance of the Roman Catholics on the one hand, and of the Dissenters on the other. In the beginning of the reign Anne had made over the tenths and first-fruits of the English clergy, annexed to the Crown by Henry VIII. (see p. 390), to a body of commissioners, who were to use them for the increase of the means of the poorer clergy. Swift wanted to see this grant, usually known as Queen Anne's Bounty, extended to Ireland. The Whig ministers had not only refused this, but had shown signs of intending to give the Dissenters

a share of political power. Swift was afraid that, if Parliament and public offices were thrown open to Dissenters, there would be again a government as fanatical as that which popular imagina-

Jonathan Swift, D.D., Dean of St. Patrick's, Dublin; from the
National Portrait Gallery.

tion believed Cromwell's to have been, and it was partly in consequence of this fear that he deserted the Whigs and joined the Tories. His first article in defence of his new allies was written in November **1710**. A year later in November **1711**, shortly after the preliminaries of peace had been signed, appeared *The Conduct of the Allies*. Every action of the Dutch and of the Austrians was traced to mean cupidity, in order that England might be urged to look upon the war as a mere scramble for wealth and power, in which she was entitled to the largest share of the plunder.

26. **The Imperial Election. 1711.**—The English ministers, at least, could not lay claim to any superior morality. In the spring of 1711, although engaged in a secret negotiation with Louis, which led before the end of the year to the signature of preliminaries (see p. 692), they had sent Marlborough to Flanders with loud professions of intending to carry on the war vigorously, and Marlborough, though his wife had just been dismissed from all her posts at Court, set out with the full expectation of striking a decisive blow against the French. In this he failed, mainly for want of proper support from his own Government. On the other hand, the Archduke, now a candidate for the empire, justified Swift's contention by recalling his own troops under Eugene to support his personal claims. In October 1711 he was chosen emperor as Charles VI., after leaving Marlborough with forces quite inadequate to the accomplishment of anything of importance.

27. **The Occasional Conformity Act and the Creation of Peers. 1711.**—When Parliament met on December 7, the Whigs, who at this time had very nearly a majority in the House of Lords, secured one by an unprincipled coalition with Nottingham, one of the strictest of Tories, who was discontented because he was excluded from office. They agreed to vote for the Occasional Conformity Bill (see p. 680), to please him, and he agreed to vote for a warlike policy on the Continent, to please them. The Occasional Conformity Bill therefore became law, whilst the ministerial foreign policy was condemned by the House of Lords. The credit of that House stood high, and, though the ministers had the House of Commons at their back, most of them thought that it would be impossible to defy its censures. Harley, however, who was not easily frightened, persuaded the queen first to dismiss Marlborough from all his offices, and then to create twelve new Tory peers. By this means the ministry secured a majority in that House which had alone opposed them. Apart from the immediate questions of the day, this creation of peers had a wide constitutional significance. Just as the deposition of James II. had made it evident that if king and Parliament pulled different ways it was for the king to give way, so the creation of peers in 1711 made it evident that if the

two Houses pulled different ways, it was for the House of Lords to give way.

28. **The Armistice and the Treaty of Utrecht. 1712—1713.—** In 1712 the Duke of Ormond, a strong Tory, was sent to command in the Netherlands. After operations had commenced, he received a despatch from St. John not only restraining him from fighting, in consequence of an understanding with France, but directing him to conceal these orders from his Dutch allies. If Ormond had obeyed these orders, he would have exposed the Dutch to inevitable defeat ; but he was too much of a gentleman to let his allies attack the enemy in the false belief that they would be assisted by the English, and he therefore saved their army by disclosing his secret instructions. The negotiations with France were now pushed on. Shabby as the conduct of the ministers was, they had now the full confidence of the queen, who in 1711 made Harley Lord High Treasurer and Earl of Oxford, and, in 1712, made St. John Viscount Bolingbroke. In July the French fell upon Eugene and defeated him at Denain, and the Dutch, seeing the difficulty of carrying on war without English support, agreed to make peace on the terms proposed by England. On March 31, 1713, a treaty of peace, in which, for the present, the Emperor declined to share, was signed at Utrecht.

29. **Terms of the Treaty of Utrecht. 1713.—**As far as the continental Powers were concerned the main conditions of the Treaty of Utrecht were that Spain and the Indies should remain under Philip V., and that Sicily was to go to the Duke of Savoy, who was to bear the title of king of Sicily ; whilst Naples, the duchy of Milan, and the Spanish Netherlands were given to Charles VI., though the last-named territory was to be retained by the Dutch till he agreed to sign the Treaty. The Dutch were to be allowed to place garrisons in certain towns of the so-called barrier (see p. 674) on the southern frontier of what had lately been the Spanish Netherlands. England obtained the largest share of the material advantages of the peace, whilst she lost credit by her ill-faith in concealing her abandonment of her allies, and especially in giving up the Catalans to the vengeance of Philip. In Europe she was to keep Gibraltar and Minorca, and obtained from France a promise to destroy the fortifications of Dunkirk. In America she acquired territory round Hudson's Bay, Nova Scotia, Newfoundland, and the French part of St. Christopher's. By an accompanying treaty with Spain, called the Assiento Treaty, she had the sole right of importing negro slaves into the Spanish colonies in America, a traffic which would now be scouted as infamous but

which was then coveted as lucrative, and she also obtained the right of sending yearly to Panama a ship of 600 tons laden with goods for the Spanish colonists.

30. **Effect of the Treaty of Utrecht on International relations.**—The general character of the Treaty of Utrecht is of greater historical importance than its details. It marks the end of a period of European history during which there was often some reality and always some pretence of combining together for common purposes of general interest, and not merely for the particular interests of the several states. Down to the Treaties of Westphalia (see p. 564) in **1648**, Catholics had combined against Protestants and Protestants against Catholics. After that date, States which feared the overbearing insolence of Louis XIV. had combined against France. The Treaty of Utrecht ushered in a period lasting almost to the end of the eighteenth century, when each State stood up for its own interests alone, when no steady combinations could be formed, and when greed for material accessions was most conspicuous because no purpose of seeking the general good existed. Swift threw the blame upon the allies, and the Whigs threw the blame upon the Tories. The truth is that States combine readily through fear, and very seldom through a desire for the common good, and when Louis XIV. ceased to be formidable each State thought exclusively of its own interests.

31. **England as a sea-power. 1713.**—The success of the Tory ministers seemed complete. In reality, the very terms of the Treaty of Utrecht revealed their weakness. In seeking to gain material advantages for England, Oxford and Bolingbroke had been forced to look for them in advantages to trade, and in the increase of colonial dominion by which trade might be encouraged. Thereby they strengthened the trading class, which was the main support of the Whigs, whilst the landed gentry, on whom their own power mainly rested, received no benefit. Not that the Tories could well help doing what they had done. During the two wars which had been waged since the fall of James II. an immense change had been taking place in the relations between England and the other European States, irrespective of the victories of Marlborough in the field. Both France and the States General of the Dutch Netherlands had been forced to wage an exhausting war on their land frontier. The consequence was that the Dutch were no longer able to compete with the English at sea, and that Louis being, after the battle of La Hogue, compelled to limit his efforts either at sea or on land, decided to limit them at sea. The

result was, that though there were no important English naval victories between the battle of La Hogue and the Peace of Utrecht, the English navy at the end of the war was vastly superior to the navies of its only possible rivals, France and the Dutch Republic.

Henry St. John, Viscount Bolingbroke : from a picture by Sir Godfrey Kneller.

England was now the one great sea-power in Europe, not so much through her own increasing strength as through the decay of the maritime vigour of other states.

32. Position of the Tories. 1711—1713.---The increase of maritime power necessarily leading to an increase of the influence of the commercial class, the Tory leaders were filled with alarm about the future, and tried to secure their power by legislation which, as they hoped, might arrest the changes which seemed likely in the future, and to strengthen their party by artificial means against changes of public opinion, much as the men of the Long Parliament and the Protectorate had formerly tried to do. In 1711 the Occasional Conformity Act had gone far to prevent Dissenters from holding office or sitting in Parliament, and earlier in the same year had been passed a Property Qualification Act which enacted that no one who did not hold land worth at least 200*l.* a year should sit in the House of Commons, thus excluding mere traders, who were for the most part Whigs. In 1713 the Tories were confronted with a further difficulty. Anne's health was failing, and the legal heir, the Electress Sophia, and her son, the Elector of Hanover, were both favourable to the Whigs. The Tories began to talk of securing the succession to the Pretender, the son of James II., by force or fraud. If only he had changed his religion and had avowed himself a Protestant, it is almost certain that an effort, possibly successful, would have been made to place him on the throne when Anne died. The Pretender was a man of little capacity, but he was too honest to change his religion for worldly ends, and he flatly refused to do so. The Tories were split into hostile parties by his refusal. Some, the pure Jacobites, clung to him in spite of it; some went over to the Whigs. The bulk of them were too bewildered to know what to do. They were aware that their supporters, the country gentry and the country clergy, would refuse to submit to a Roman Catholic king, and yet they could not voluntarily support the claims of the Electress Sophia and her son, whose succession they feared. To add to the distractions of the party its leaders, Oxford and Bolingbroke, quarrelled with one another.

33. The Last Days and Death of Anne. 1714.—In 1714 Swift suggested that the difficulty would be at an end if his friends would accept the Hanoverian succession, and at the same time so weaken the Whigs by repressive legislation that the new Hanoverian sovereign would be obliged to govern in accordance with the will of the Tories. In pursuance of this plan Bolingbroke carried through Parliament a Schism Act, by which no one was allowed to keep a school without license from the bishop. Oxford, who was always in favour of a middle course, and therefore disliked violent

measures against the Dissenters, was driven from office, and Bolingbroke then hoped to control the Government for some time to come.
Before a successor to Oxford was appointed, whilst the ministers
were without any distinct policy or acknowledged head, and whilst
even Bolingbroke himself had not definitely made up his mind as to

The Choir of St. Paul's Cathedral church, looking west, as finished by Sir Christopher
Wren: from an engraving by Trevit, about 1710.

his future plans, the queen was taken ill. Bolingbroke's enemies,
the Dukes of Somerset and Argyle, made their appearance unexpectedly in the Council, and obtained the consent of the queen
to the appointment of the Duke of Shrewsbury as Treasurer. The
queen died on August 1, and the Elector of Hanover, now heir to

the Crown by the provisions of the Act of Settlement (see p. 672), in consequence of the recent death of his mother, the Electress Sophia, was at once proclaimed by the title of George I.

34. **Politics and Art.**—In art as in politics the end of the reign of Anne completes a change long in progress from the ideal to the convenient. As in affairs of state the material interests of the country gentleman and of the trader took the place of the great causes which called out the enthusiasm of Cavalier and Roundhead in the Civil War, so in art painting became a mode of perpetuating the features of those who were rich enough to pay for having their portraits taken ; and architecture, which had long forgotten the life and beauty of the mediæval churches, was losing even the stateliness which Sir Christopher Wren gave to such buildings as the new St. Paul's (p. 668) and Greenwich Hospital (p. 662). Even Wren could not give much of this high quality to steeples such as those of St. Bride's, Fleet Street (p. 681), because the horizontal lines of an architecture derived from the Greeks through the Romans are unsuited to the soaring motive of a mediæval spire ; nor could his domestic buildings, such as those at Hampton Court (pp. 665, 666), altogether overcome the necessity of making the inmates comfortable at the expense of architectural beauty. His successor, Vanbrugh, in building Blenheim Palace (see p. 683), sought out combinations neither graceful nor dignified in the hope of thereby avoiding that which was merely commonplace ; but on the whole it was the commonplace which was gaining ground, and which ultimately pervaded the domestic buildings raised during the greater part of the eighteenth century.

CHAPTER XLV

TOWNSHEND, SUNDERLAND, AND WALPOLE. 1714—1737

LEADING DATES

Reign of George I., 1714—1727.   Reign of George II., 1727 - 1760

Accession of George I.	August 1, 1714
Mar's Rising	1715
The Septennial Act	1716
The South Sea Bubble	1720
Walpole, First Lord of the Treasury	1721
Accession of George II.	June 12, 1727
The Excise Bill	1733
Death of Queen Caroline	November 20, 1737

1. **George I. and the Whigs. 1714.**—Before George I.[1] arrived in England a thorough change was made by his orders in all the offices of Government. With scarcely an exception all Tories were

[1] Genealogy of the first three Hanoverian kings :—

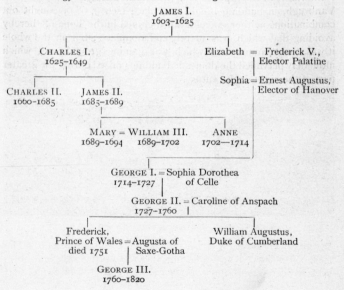

JAMES I.
1603–1625

CHARLES I.
1625–1649

Elizabeth = Frederick V.,
Elector Palatine

CHARLES II.   JAMES II.
1660–1685   1685–1689

Sophia = Ernest Augustus,
Elector of Hanover

MARY = WILLIAM III.   ANNE
1689–1694   1689–1702   1702—1714

GEORGE I. = Sophia Dorothea
1714–1727   of Celle

GEORGE II. = Caroline of Anspach
1727–1760

Frederick,
Prince of Wales = Augusta of
died 1751   Saxe-Gotha

William Augustus,
Duke of Cumberland

GEORGE III.
1760–1820

dismissed, and Whigs appointed in their place. As the new king intended to take a leading part in the Government, he placed the more important offices in the hands of men who had hitherto been

GEORGIUS D:G: Mag: BRITANNIÆ
FRANCIÆ ET HIBERN:*REX*.
FIDEI DEFENSOR

George I. : from an engraving by Vertue.

less prominent than the great Whig leaders of Anne's reign. The most conspicuous of the new ministers was Lord Townshend, who became Secretary of State. When the king arrived he found that his own power was much less than he had expected. He could not speak English, and all communications between himself and his ministers were carried on in bad Latin. He therefore set the example, which all subsequent sovereigns have followed, of abstaining from attending Cabinet meetings, where the discussion took place in a language unintelligible to him. This abstention had important constitutional results. The Cabinet, which for some time had been growing independent of the sovereign, became still more independent, especially as George knew no more of English ways than he knew of the English language, and was obliged to take most of the advice of his ministers on trust. He could not think of replacing them by Tories, because he had been led to look upon all Tories as Jacobites.

2. **The Whigs and the Nation. 1714.** The Whigs, however, needed the support of Parliament more than the support of the king. The great landowners who directed their policy were wealthy and intelligent, and therefore unpopular amongst the country gentry and the country clergy. They aimed at establishing a sort of aristocratic republic with a king nominally at its head, in which fair play should be given to the Dissenters, and the trading classes encouraged. Yet they were clear-sighted enough to perceive that it was impossible to govern without the support of the House of Commons; and it was with the support of the House of Commons that the Tories in the last four years of Anne's reign had maintained themselves in power by appealing to the prejudices of the country gentry and the country clergy. The Whig tenure of power was, therefore, not likely to last long unless they could find some means of crushing opponents who had been, and might easily be again, more popular than themselves.

3. **The Whigs and Parliament. 1715.**—For the moment, indeed, the Whigs had the advantage. In 1715 a new Parliament was chosen, and many Tories who were, after all, not really Jacobites voted for Whig candidates in alarm lest their own leaders should bring back the Pretender, whom they distrusted as a Roman Catholic. The Whigs, therefore, had a majority in the House of Commons, whilst they had already recovered the majority in the House of Lords which they had temporarily lost by the recent creation of the Tory peers (see p. 695). In order to make their success permanent by getting rid of the leaders of the party opposed to them, the Whigs prepared to impeach Oxford, Bolingbroke, and Ormond as traitors, on the ground of the secret agreements which they had made with the French during the

negotiation of the Treaty of Utrecht. Oxford, with his usual coolness, stayed to face the attack, and got off with two years' imprisonment. Bolingbroke and Ormond fled to France, where Bolingbroke entered the service of the Pretender as Secretary of State. Acts of attainder were passed against both. These high-handed proceedings of the Whigs nearly defeated their object. The German king had by this time become unpopular, and Jacobitism increased amongst the Tories, most of whom had submitted to him at his first coming. In all parts of England and Scotland large numbers made ready for a rising against his government. Bolingbroke urged Louis XIV. to support them. Louis, however, died without having given his consent, and the Jacobites of Great Britain had to dispense with foreign aid.

4. **Mar's Rising.** 1715—1716.—Under these circumstances Bolingbroke urged delay, but the Pretender—headstrong and incompetent—ordered the Earl of Mar, his chief supporter in Scotland, to rise against the Government. On September 3 Mar took the field, and, on October 7, a gentleman of Northumberland, named Forster, declared for the Pretender in the north of England. The Whig ministers, unpopular as they were, had the advantage in their position as the actual rulers of the country, and, now that the Tory leaders had been got rid of, they had the advantage in ability. Argyle commanded for the Government in Scotland, and on November 13 he fought a drawn battle with Mar on Sheriffmuir. Though half of each army defeated half of the other, Mar—who throughout the whole campaign showed himself singularly incompetent—allowed Argyle to secure the advantages of a victory. Forster, though supported by men of influence on both sides of the border —Lord Derwentwater from England and Lords Nithsdale and Kenmure from Scotland—showed himself as incompetent as Mar, and surrendered at Preston on the same day as that on which the battle was fought on Sheriffmuir. On December 2 the Pretender himself landed at Peterhead, and on January 6, **1716**, he entered Dundee. He was, however, so dull and unenterprising that his very followers despised him, some even asking whether he could really speak. By this time the Government, having suppressed all attempts at resistance in England, was preparing to send a powerful army into Scotland, and the Pretender prudently took shipping for France, where he soon dismissed Bolingbroke, whose advice was too good to be to his taste. Derwentwater and Kenmure were beheaded on Tower Hill. Nithsdale escaped through the address of his wife, who visited him in prison, and sent him out dressed

in her clothes. Thirty-eight persons of lower rank were put to death, and the estates of many others were forfeited.

5. **The Septennial Act. 1716.**—Successful as the Whigs had been in the field, they did not venture to face the elections to a new Parliament, which, in accordance with the Triennial Act (see p. 661), must be held in the beginning of **1718**. Accordingly they passed a Septennial Act, by which the existing Parliament prolonged its own duration for four years longer than was allowed by the law as it stood at the time when the House of Commons was chosen. This proceeding strained to the uttermost the doctrine that a British Parliament—unlike Parliaments in countries like the

A Coach of the early part of the eighteenth century : from an engraving by Kip.

present United States, in which a written constitution exists—can make any law it pleases, even if it effects the greatest changes in the institutions of the State. Hitherto the king had acted as a restraint upon Parliament by exercising his right of refusing the Royal Assent to Bills. This prerogative, however, which had been exercised for the last time by Anne in **1707**, now dropped out of use, and Parliament thereby became supreme as far as other branches of the Government were concerned. The question of its relations to the constituencies assumed new importance ; and in **1716** at least the Whigs were of opinion that the duration of Parliament should be lengthened in order to make the House of Commons more independent of them. They were afraid lest the supremacy which had been wrested from the Crown should pass into the hands of an ignorant, ill-informed multitude. Yet they were unable—even if they had been willing—to make the House of Commons a permanent oligarchy. As the duration of Parliament could not be indefinitely prolonged without provoking violent opposition, the Whigs had only gained a respite during which they would have to do their best to make themselves more acceptable to the nation than they were when the Septennial Act was passed.

6. England and France. 1716.—One of the chief causes of the fall of the Whigs in Anne's reign had been their advocacy of war : now, however, they stood forward as the advocates of peace. In effecting this change of front they were helped by the disappearance of those of their leaders who had been foremost in the struggle with France. Somers, Halifax, and Wharton died before the end of 1716, and, though Marlborough still lived, he was incapacitated by disease from acting in public. Still more helpful to the Whig party was a change which had taken place in France. The King of France was now a sickly child, Louis XV., the great-grandson of Louis XIV. If he died (as most people expected him to do), there would be two competitors for the throne of France—the one, his uncle, Philip V. of Spain, the grandson of Louis XIV. (who was, indeed, his nearest male relation, but who, in accordance with the Treaty of Utrecht, had renounced all claim to the French throne), and the other, the duke of Orleans, who was now Regent of France,[1] and was the nearest male relation of Louis XV. after Philip V. As it was believed that, in the event of the young king's death, Philip V. would assert his claim in spite of his renunciation, it was to the interest of the Duke of Orleans to be on friendly terms with

[1] Genealogy of the family of Louis XIV. :—

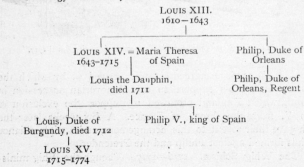

England; whilst it was equally to the interest of England to exclude Philip V. from the French throne, in order to prevent that union between France and Spain which the Whigs had striven to prevent in the late war. It therefore became possible for the Whigs to pursue their aim—the separation between France and Spain—by that peaceful understanding with the French Government which had gained popularity for the Tories in the time of Anne. On

An early form of Steam-pump for mines: from an engraving dated 1717.

November 28, **1716**, an agreement was arrived at by which the Regent promised his support to the Hanoverian succession in England, whilst England promised to support the exclusion of Philip V. from the throne of France. A few weeks later the Dutch gave their assent to this arrangement, and a triple alliance was thus formed against Philip and the Pretender.

7. **The Whig Schism. 1716—1717.**—Though the Whig minis-

ters had their own way in most matters, they found it necessary to comply with the king in some things. He had two ruling motives — anxiety to strengthen the electorate of Hanover, and hatred of his own eldest son George, Prince of Wales. In the interests of Hanover he had, in 1715, purchased the secularised bishoprics of Bremen and Verden from Frederick IV., king of Denmark. Though the Whig ministers had consented to the purchase of these territories, some of them—especially Townshend and his brother-in-law Sir Robert Walpole, who was the ablest of the rising Whigs—had said hard things of the grasping Hanoverian favourites and mistresses, upon whom George squandered English gold. In 1716 the Tzar Peter the Great sent troops into Mecklenburg—the first interference of Russia in Western affairs ; and George, being anxious to keep the Russians at a distance, complained of Townshend for being unwilling to engage England in driving them out. Then, too, the king, who had quarrelled with the Prince of Wales, believed (probably without foundation) that Townshend had shown some favour to the object of his displeasure, on which he took the Secretaryship from him, sending him to Ireland as Lord Lieutenant. In 1717 Charles XII. of Sweden, angry about Bremen and Verden, which he claimed for himself, formed an alliance with Spain—which was once more growing in vigour, under the care of Philip's new Italian minister, Alberoni—and even projected an invasion of Scotland in the interests of the Pretender. The scheme was discovered in England and averted. When Parliament was asked to vote money for a war against Sweden, Walpole spoke but coldly on behalf of the proposal. The king dismissed Townshend, and Walpole resigned. The Whig party being thus split in two, the leaders of the ministry as reconstituted were Sunderland and Stanhope, the latter being the general who had fought in Spain, and who was soon afterwards raised to the peerage as Lord Stanhope.

8. **The Quadruple Alliance. 1718—1720.**—In foreign affairs Sunderland and Stanhope maintained the alliance with France which had been the corner-stone of the policy of their predecessors. In 1717 Alberoni seized Sardinia, which had been given to Austria by the treaty of Utrecht, and sent an army into Sicily to begin the re-conquest of those Italian possessions which Spain had lost by the same treaty. In 1718 was formed a Quadruple Alliance, in which the Emperor joined Great Britain, France, and the Dutch Republic. A Spanish army overran the greater part of Sicily, but the Spanish fleet was destroyed by Admiral Sir George Byng off Cape Passaro. In 1719 Alberoni sent two frigates to land Jacobites in

Scotland.   The expedition failed, and France and England forced Philip to dismiss his minister.   In 1720 Philip agreed to abandon both Sicily and Sardinia.   Sicily was given to Austria, and Sardinia went to the Duke of Savoy, who now bore the title of King of Sardinia, instead of that of King of Sicily ; and soon afterwards the King of Spain removed the obstructions which he had hitherto thrown in the way of the execution of the clause in the Treaty of Utrecht by which the landing of goods at Panama from a single English ship had been permitted (see p. 697).   After this Europe had peace for twelve years.

9. **The Relief of the Dissenters, and the Peerage Bill.   1719.—** The two sections of the Whigs were opposed to one another, rather upon personal than on political grounds.   Walpole was, however, more cautious than Sunderland or Stanhope.   Sunderland and Stanhope, in 1719, obtained the repeal of the Occasional Conformity Act and of the Schism Act, which had been the work of the triumphant Tories in the reign of Anne (see p. 699) ; but when they showed signs of wishing to repeal the Test Act of the reign of Charles II. (see p. 607), thereby not merely offering religious liberty to Dissenters, but also proposing to qualify them for office, Walpole was startled, thinking that the unpopularity of such a measure might prove the ruin of the Whigs.   The main subject of quarrel between the rival statesmen was, however, a Peerage Bill which Sunderland and Stanhope laid before Parliament.   According to this proposal the king was to be allowed to create only six additional peerages (except in the case of a member of the Royal Family), after which he could only make a new peer upon the extinction of an old peerage.   This measure, which passed the House of Lords, was rejected in the Commons, mainly in consequence of Walpole's opposition.   It is hardly to be doubted that its framers looked forward to the possible election of a Tory House of Commons, and wished to hinder a Tory minister from making himself master of the House of Lords by creating a large number of peers, as Harley and St. John had done in 1711 (see p. 695).   According to them, the House of Lords was to be the bulwark of the Whigs against a Tory House of Commons.   It was Walpole's merit that he saw distinctly that this could not be, as the Bill, if it had passed, would have made the House of Lords a narrow oligarchy capable of setting at defiance both the Crown and the House of Commons. It was, moreover, clear to him that the Commons must from henceforth be the chief member of the constitutional organisation.   If the Whigs were to win the battle, they must win it by possessing

a majority in the House of Commons, and not by setting up the artificial barrier of a restricted House of Lords. It is unlikely that Sunderland acknowledged the inferiority of his own statesmanship to that of Walpole, but he had felt his power, and in **1720** admitted both him and Townshend to subordinate offices in the government.

10. **The South Sea Bubble. 1720.**—Few things served the Whigs so well as their adoption of a policy of peace, to which their short war with Spain hardly furnished an exception. With the cessation of the risks due to war trade increased rapidly, and with the increase of trade came a violent increase of speculation. Joint-stock companies, which had hitherto been limited to a few

Group showing costumes and sedan chair, about 1720 : from an engraving by Kip.

great undertakings, were formed in large numbers. Some, being managed by men of experience, met with success ; whilst others, started by swindlers or by persons ignorant of trade, speedily collapsed, and ruined those who had embarked their capital in them. Amongst these latter the most prominent was the South Sea Company, which had been formed by Harley, in **1711**, to carry on such trade with Spanish America as might be rendered possible by the expected treaty with Spain. Trade with the Spanish colonies was allowed by the terms of the Treaty of Utrecht to a single English ship in each year, and the Assiento treaty had also granted to the English the right of importing negroes into them (see p. 696). All classes in England were under the delusion that the wealth of Spanish America was so enormous that this trade would enrich all who took part in it. Consequently the shares of the South Sea Company were eagerly bought. At the same time politicians were growing anxious about the amount of the national debt, and in **1720** a Bill was passed enabling those to whom the nation owed money to take shares in the South Sea Company in the place of their claim upon the nation. Large numbers of all classes accepted this arrangement. Others rushed eagerly to buy shares which were supposed to be of priceless value. Landlords sold their estates, and clergymen and widows brought their savings to invest in the South Sea Company. So great was the demand that in August **1720** shares originally worth 100*l.* were purchased for 1,000*l.* The madness of speculation spread rapidly, and new companies were formed every day for objects unlikely to be remunerative. People actually took shares in one company for making salt-water fresh; in another for transmuting quicksilver into a malleable and fine metal; and in another for importing a number of large jackasses from Spain; whilst one impostor asked the public to take shares in an undertaking the nature of which was in due time to be revealed.

11. **The Bursting of the Bubble. 1720—1721.**—Before long people began to find out that they had paid too highly for the objects of their visionary hopes, and the price of shares rapidly fell. Thousands were reduced to beggary, and the ruined dupes cried out for the punishment of those by whom their hopes had been excited. One peer asked that the directors of the company might be sewn up in sacks and thrown into the Thames. The bitterest indignation, however, was directed against the ministers. Most of them had speculated in the shares, and some of them had made money by actual swindling. In **1721** Aislabie was Chancellor of the Exchequer, and Craggs Secretary of State. Aislabie was sent to the Tower; Craggs died of the small-pox; whilst Craggs' father, the Postmaster-General, took poison. Sunderland was acquitted of dishonourable conduct, but he had been amongst the speculators, and resigned. Stanhope, who had had nothing to do with the speculation, fell into a fit in answering a false accusation, and died.

12. **Walpole called to the Rescue. 1721—1722.**—Amidst the general crash Walpole was called upon to restore order. In April **1721** he became First Lord of the Treasury and Chancellor of the Exchequer. He had a financial ability which was rare in those times, and he made an arrangement which at least left something

to the shareholders, though it gave them far less than they had expected. Walpole's accession to office was the beginning of a ministerial career which lasted twenty-one years. Its immediate result
was of the greatest benefit to the Whigs. The seven years to which
the Septennial Act had extended the duration of the existing Parliament ended in March **1722**. There can hardly be a doubt that
if the elections had taken place a year earlier, they would have

View of the game of Mall : from an engraving by Kip,
about 1720.

resulted in the overthrow of the Whigs. As it was, the country
connected Walpole's name with restored order and financial
probity, and a large Whig majority was accordingly returned.

13. **Corruption under Walpole.**—It was not, however, merely to
the national gratitude that Walpole owed his success at the polls.
When he opposed the Peerage Bill he taught the Whig aristocracy
that it must rely on the House of Commons (see p. 710). Yet it

was hard to see how the House of Commons could represent the people at large, because, for the most part, the people were too ignorant and ill-educated to have any political opinions at all. The electors, if left to themselves, might return a Parliament as Tory as had been the Parliaments which had supported Oxford and Bolingbroke. Therefore the Whigs, even before Walpole secured power, had determined that the electors should not be left to themselves. In many boroughs the right of voting was confined to the corporation ; and as large numbers of these boroughs were mere villages or even hamlets, the members of their corporations were poor men—easily accessible to arguments addressed to their pockets. The wealthiest landowner in the neighbourhood was usually a Whig, who would use his influence and his purse in securing the election of his own nominee. Electors found that, if they voted for the Whig candidate, their lives would be made easy to them, whilst if they voted for the Tory candidate they would be much worse off. In the House of Commons itself the same system of corruption was pursued. What amount of ready money Walpole paid to his supporters has been disputed, and it was certainly much less than has usually been supposed ; but he had in his gift all the offices held under the Crown, a large number of which were sinecures with large pay and no duties. Needy members discovered that if they wanted money they must support Walpole, and ambitious members discovered that if they wanted office they could only obtain it by supporting Walpole. It is therefore not surprising that all the rising talent in the country declared itself Whig.

14. **Walpole and Corruption.**—Yet, evil as this system was, it was rendered tolerable by the knowledge that the only alternative —the return of the Tory party to power, probably bringing with it a restoration of the Stuart dynasty—would have been still more disastrous. The political creed of the Tory squires and of the Tory clergy was founded on religious intolerance and contempt for trade. What they wanted was a king who would keep down dissenters and moneyed men, and accordingly most of the Tories had by this time become Jacobites. The great Whig nobles, on the other hand, were for religious toleration and for weakening the power of the king. The Whigs gained the day, partly because they were more intelligent than their rivals, partly because the predominance even of a corrupt House of Commons—with its free speech and its show of government by argument rather than by arbitrary will—was in itself advantageous as matters then stood.

The interior of St. Martin's-in-the-Fields, London ; built by James Gibbs, 1722–1726.

In all this work they found a fitting leader in Walpole. He was devoted to duty and was single-eyed in devoting himself to the interests of his country ; but his manners and his mind were alike coarse, and he did not shrink from the employment of the lowest means to accomplish his ends. On the other hand it may be said in his favour that he was not vindictive, and that he contented himself with excluding his rivals from power, without even seeking to inflict punishment upon them.

15. '**Quieta non movere.**'—Walpole took for his motto *Quieta non movere* (let sleeping dogs lie). In many periods of English history such a confession would have been disgraceful to a statesman. In Walpole's days it was an honourable one. The work before him was to maintain toleration and constitutional government, and he was aware that he could only hope for success if he

Ploughing with oxen in the eighteenth century.

avoided awakening the ignorant passions which were slumbering around. He remembered the storm of popular rage to which the Whigs had been exposed in the time of the Sacheverell trial (see p. 690), and he was resolved to show no favour to the Dissenters which would provoke another outburst against them. The Dissenters were most eager to obtain a repeal of the Test Act (see p. 606) for themselves, though not for the Catholics. Walpole, who knew the anger which would be excited if he proposed such a measure, always told them that the time was not convenient. At last they asked him to tell them when the time would be convenient. " I will answer you frankly," was his reply, " Never ! " Year after year, however, he passed through Parliament a Bill indemnifying all persons who had held offices in defiance of the Test Act, and thus Dissenters got what they wanted without exciting attention.

16. **The Prime Ministership.**—When any number of men meet

together to transact business, there must be one to take the lead
if their meetings are not to end in confusion. Till the death of
Anne, Cabinets had met in the presence of the sovereign, and
were regarded as his or her advisers. Yet even then their growing
independence was beginning to make it necessary for them to find
a leader or leaders in their own body, and people began to look
first to Marlborough and Godolphin and then to Harley and St. John
as superior to other members of the Cabinet, and even to apply to
one or the other of them loosely the term 'first minister.' After
the accession of George I., when the king ceased to sit in the
Cabinet, it became still more necessary for that body to find a

Mowing grass in the eighteenth century.

leader, and Townshend at first and afterwards Sunderland are
sometimes spoken of by modern writers as Prime Ministers. No
such position was, however, openly assigned to them by contemporaries, and when Walpole entered office in 1721 ministers were
still regarded as equal amongst themselves. It was Walpole's
chief contribution to constitutional progress that he created the
Prime Ministership in his own person, and thereby gave to Cabinet
government that unity which every government must possess
if its action is to be enduring, and which earlier governments
possessed through the presidency of the king. Yet so hateful
was the new idea that Walpole had to disclaim any intention of
making himself Prime Minister ; and the word came into familiar

use by being applied to him tauntingly by his enemies, as the fit name for a minister who wanted to convert all other ministers into his instruments instead of regarding them as his equals.

17. **Walpole and Carteret. 1723—1724.**—Walpole's first trial of strength was with Lord Carteret, one of the Secretaries of State, a man of great ability, who had the advantage of being able to address the king in German, whilst Walpole had to address him in Latin. Walpole founded his policy of peace on an alliance with France, whilst Carteret inherited the tradition of the Whigs of Anne's reign in favour of a continental alliance against France. Between Carteret and Walpole a rivalry soon sprang up, and in **1724** Carteret was forced to resign the Secretaryship, though he remained a member of the Cabinet for some time to come.

18. **Wood's Halfpence. 1724.**—The first instance of Walpole's method of averting popular discontent by avoiding a collision with strong feeling arose when a grant was made to a certain Wood of the right of issuing a copper coinage in Ireland. The coins were good in themselves, but Wood had bought the right of coining them by bribes to the king's German mistresses, and Irishmen naturally concluded that they were to pay the cost. Swift, delighted at the opportunity of scourging his old enemies the Whigs, poured scorn and ridicule upon Wood's Halfpence in 'The Drapier's Letters,' and for the first time in Irish history both races and both creeds were united in resistance to the obnoxious grant. Walpole dreaded a disturbance more than anything else, and the grant was withdrawn.

19. **The Last Years of George I. 1724—1727.**—Walpole's influence deservedly grew from year to year. In spite of great difficulties, he maintained peace abroad. The Duke of Orleans had been dead for some years, and in **1726** Cardinal Fleury—who was as peace-loving as Walpole himself—became Prime Minister to the young king Louis XV., and did everything in his power to prevent war breaking out in Europe. In **1727** George I., as soon as he was able to leave England, crossed the sea to enjoy himself in Hanover. On the way, before he reached Osnabrück, he was struck down by apoplexy in his carriage. His attendants wished to seek help in the nearest village, but were urged on by cries of " Osnabrück ! Osnabrück !" from their half-conscious master. Before the carriage reached Osnabrück George I. was dead.

20. **George II. and Walpole. 1727.**—The new king George II. had the advantage (which his father had not had) of being able to speak English. He was not intelligent, but was straightforward and courageous, and though, like his father, he kept mistresses, he

Church of St. Mary Woolnoth, London; finished in 1727 from the designs of Nicholas Hawksmoor.

was accustomed on all difficult questions to defer to the advice of his wife, Queen Caroline—a woman of sound judgment and of wide intellectual interests. George's first impulse was to choose as his leading minister Sir Spencer Compton, a personal favourite of his own. Compton, however, being ordered to write the speech in which the king was to notify his accession to the Privy Council, was so overpowered by the difficulties of the task that he begged Walpole to write it for him. After this the queen easily persuaded her husband that Compton was not strong enough for the post ; and Walpole, being recalled to office, was soon as much trusted by George II. as he had been by George I.

21. **Breach between Walpole and Townshend. 1730.**—Even after the complete establishment of Parliamentary supremacy the favour of the king was not to be despised ; for, though he could not shake the power of the Whig aristocracy as a whole, yet if one Whig entered upon a rivalry with another, his support would be decisive, at least for a time. Such a rivalry now broke out between Walpole and his brother-in-law, Townshend, who had been Secretary of State since **1721.** The main cause of the quarrel is best described by Walpole himself. " As long," he said, " as the firm was Townshend and Walpole, the utmost harmony prevailed ; but it no sooner became Walpole and Townshend than things went wrong." In other words, the question between them was whether there was to be a Prime Minister or not. Townshend, who was Secretary of State, held to the old doctrine that he was accountable only to the king and Parliament. Walpole held to the new doctrine that he himself—as first Lord of the Treasury— was to direct the policy of the other ministers. It is not by accident that the First Lord of the Treasury has usually been the Prime Minister ; in later years it has been accepted as the general rule. It is his business to find the money expended by the other ministers, and it is therefore only reasonable that decision of a policy which will cost money should rest with him. He should be able to exercise a veto over proposals which lead to an expenditure which, even if it is desirable in itself, may be greater than the country is able or willing to bear. In **1730** Townshend resigned, and being honourably desirous of keeping out of farther disputes with his brother-in-law, remained in private life to the end of his days.

22. **Bolingbroke as Organiser of the Opposition. 1726—1732.**— Already a violent opposition was gathering against Walpole. In **1716** the Pretender, being too stupid to take good advice, had dis-

missed Bolingbroke from his service (see p. 705).   Bolingbroke, by
bribing one of the mistresses of George I., had interested that
king in his favour, and in 1725 his attainder had been reversed.
Walpole, however, had still sufficient influence to procure the main-

Sir Robert Walpole : from the picture by Van Loo in the National Portrait Gallery.

tenance of the clause in the Act of Attainder which excluded him
from the House of Lords.   Bolingbroke, the most eloquent orator
of the day, was thus shut out from the only place in which at that

time it was possible for him to make his eloquence heard. Walpole may well have thought that he had crushed Bolingbroke for ever. He had, however, under-estimated the powers of the Tory leader. Though Bolingbroke could deliver no more orations, he was still master of his pen and of his persuasive tongue, and he set to work to weld together a parliamentary opposition out of the most discordant elements. Those elements were in the main three. There were in the House of Commons about fifty Jacobites, a small number of Tories accepting the House of Hanover, and a gradually-increasing body of Whigs sulky because Walpole did not admit them to a share of power. Of the latter the leader was William Pulteney, an indiscreet politician but an excellent speaker. Between Bolingbroke and Pulteney an alliance was struck, and by the end of 1726 they had combined in publishing *The Craftsman*, a weekly paper in which Walpole was held up to obloquy as erecting a ministerial despotism by the use of corruption.

23. **The Excise Bill. 1733.**—In 1733 Walpole gave a handle to the attacks of his enemies. There was an immense amount of smuggling and of other frauds on the customs revenue. To meet the difficulty Walpole proposed to establish a new system of levying the duties on tobacco, intending, as he gave out, to extend it subsequently to those on wine. According to this new system all tobacco imported was to be brought free of duty into warehouses under Government supervision. The duty would be paid by those who took it out for home consumption, and its sale would only be allowed at shops licensed for the purpose, in the same way that certain houses are licensed for the sale of beer at the present day. As the tax was really paid on an imported article, it would have been more prudent in Walpole if he had continued to call it a customs duty, as an excise was an unpopular form of taxation. He called it, however, an excise, probably because the sale of the tobacco was confined to licensed houses, as the sale of any other excisable article would be. He had, indeed, reason to hope that his plan would prove acceptable. In the first place if it were adopted smuggling would be far more difficult than it had hitherto been, because it would now be more easy to detect the sale of the smuggled article ; and in the second place not only would the public revenue be benefited, but the honest trader would be less liable to be undersold by the smuggler. A third advantage would also be gained. Hitherto goods imported in order to be subsequently exported had had to pay duty, which was only recoverable upon the

Vessels unloading at the Customs House, at the beginning of the eighteenth century.

observance of intricate formalities accompanied by considerable expense. According to Walpole's plan, the tobacco stored in Government warehouses could be exported without any payment at all ; and the export trade of the country would be encouraged by liberating it from unnecessary trammels.

24. The Defeat of the Excise Bill. 1733.—To the arguments which Walpole addressed to the intelligence of his hearers, he took care to add others addressed to their pockets. Almost all the members of the House of Commons were country gentlemen, and Walpole, therefore, reminded them that the revenue would be so increased—at the expense of those who had bought smuggled goods—that he would be able to remit the Land Tax. Walpole's proposals were indeed admirable, but Bolingbroke and Pulteney stirred up popular feeling against them by wild misrepresentations. The masses were persuaded to believe that Walpole wanted to subject them to a general excise, to search their houses at any hour without a warrant, and to raise the price of tobacco. All classes joined in the outcry. The very soldiers were no longer to be depended on. At last Walpole resolved to withdraw the Bill. " I will not," he once said in private conversation, " be the minister to enforce taxes at the expense of blood." It was, in short, wise to convert customs into excise, but it was not expedient. In this regard for expediency lay the sum of Walpole's political wisdom, and it was because he possessed it that the House of Hanover and the constitutional system connected with the House of Hanover rooted themselves in England. If, however, Walpole gave way before the nation, he resolved to be master of the Cabinet, and he summarily dismissed some of his principal colleagues who had been intriguing with the Opposition against him.

25. Disruption of the Opposition. 1734 1735.—Bolingbroke had won the trick, but he could not win the game. The Excise Bill was quickly forgotten, and Walpole's great services were again remembered. In 1734, in a new House of Commons, his supporters were nearly as numerous as before. Bolingbroke was never thoroughly trusted by the discontented Whigs, and in 1735 he retired to France, leaving English politics to shape themselves without his help.

26. The Family Compact. 1733.—Walpole's management of foreign affairs was as dexterous as his management of Parliament. He had hitherto not only kept England from embarking in war, but had contributed his aid to the restoration of peace on the

Continent itself whenever this had been possible. In **1733** a war broke out, usually known as the War of the Polish Succession, but embracing the West of Europe as well. It was noteworthy that in this war France and Spain appeared in close alliance, and that they had signed a secret treaty, known as the Family Compact, which was directed against Austria and England. The two branches of the House of Bourbon were to act together ; and the whole basis of Walpole's foreign policy was thus swept away. At the time when the death of Louis XV. was considered probable (see p. 707), it had been natural that the Duke of Orleans should see in an alliance with England a barrier against the claim likely to be put forward to the French throne by Philip V. ; but all that was altered now. Not only was the Duke of Orleans dead, but Louis XV. had become a husband and a father, and the question of Philip's claim to the succession was therefore no longer important. France had recovered her military strength, and it was believed at the French court that a close alliance with Spain would enable her to dictate terms to Europe. When peace was signed in **1735** at Vienna, Austria ceded Naples and Sicily—with other smaller possessions in Italy—to Charles, the second surviving son of Philip V., whilst Lorraine was given to Stanislaus Leczinski (the father-in-law of Louis XV.), on the understanding that after his death it was to be merged in France. Walpole, who knew of the existence of the Family Compact soon after its signature, had abstained from joining in the war—perhaps thinking that the allies were too well occupied in Europe to meddle with England.

27. **Dissensions in the Royal Family. 1737.**—In **1737** Walpole's position was weakened by two untoward events. A quarrel broke out between George II. and his eldest son Frederick, Prince of Wales ; and the Prince, being turned out of the court, put himself at the head of the Opposition. Not long after this Queen Caroline, Walpole's truest friend, died.

CHAPTER XLVI

WALPOLE, CARTERET, AND THE PELHAMS. 1737—1754

LEADING DATES

Reign of George II., 1727—1760

Jenkins's ear	1738
War with Spain	1739
Resignation of Walpole	Feb. 17, 1742
Resignation of Carteret	Nov. 23, 1744
The Young Pretender's Rising	1745
Battle of Culloden	April 16, 1746
Peace of Aix-la-Chapelle	1748
Death of Henry Pelham	March 6, 1754

1. **The Reign of Common Sense.**—Walpole had been hitherto successful because he had governed on principles of common sense. He had kept the peace and had allowed men to grow rich by leaving them to pursue their own callings without interference. Common sense was, indeed, the chief characteristic of the age. Pope, its leading poet, was conspicuous for felicity of expression and for the ease and neatness with which he dealt with topics relating to man in society. High imagination and the pursuit of ideal beauty had no place in his mind. In matters of religion it was much the same. Those who spoke and wrote on them abandoned the search for eternal verities, contenting themselves with asking where the balance of probability lay, or, at the most, what was the view most suitable to the cultivated reason. To speak of anyone's zeal or enthusiasm was regarded as opprobrious. In social life there was a coarseness which was the natural consequence of the temper of the day. Men drank heavily, and talked openly of their vices.

2. **Smuggling in the West Indies.**—Such a generation turned eagerly to the pursuit of wealth, and chafed at the restrictions which other nations attempted to place on its commerce. It happened that Spain—the weakest of European nations—had the most extended territory open to commercial enterprise. As in the days of Elizabeth (see p. 447), the Spanish Government tried to prevent the English from trading with its American dominions, whilst the Spanish colonists, on the other hand, were anxious to promote a trade by which they were benefited. It was notorious that English merchants did their best to evade the restriction imposed on them

by the Treaty of Utrecht. The one ship of 600 tons which they were allowed by that treaty to send annually to Panama (see p. 697) sailed into the harbour and discharged her goods. As soon as it

George II. : from the portrait by Thomas Hudson in the National Portrait Gallery.

was dark, smaller vessels (which had kept out of sight in the daytime) sailed in and filled it up again, so that the one ship was enabled to put many ship-loads on shore. Besides this, there was an immense amount of smuggling carried on by Englishmen on various parts of the coast of Spanish America. Spanish coast-guards, in return, often seized English vessels which they suspected of smuggling, and sometimes brutally ill-treated their crews. The Spaniards also claimed to have the right of searching English vessels even on the high seas. Besides this, they disputed the English assumption of the right to cut log-wood in the bay of Campeachy, and alleged that the new English colony of Georgia, lately founded in North America, encroached on the boundaries of what was then the Spanish territory of Florida.

3. **Walpole and Spain.**—To Walpole the exceeding energy of the British traders and smugglers was annoying. It was likely to bring on war, and he held war to be the worst of evils. Right or wrong, the smugglers carried on the great movement which has filled the waste places of the world with children of the English race. Walpole entered on negotiations with the Spanish Government, hoping to obtain compensation for wrongs actually inflicted by its agents. Bolingbroke hurried back from France to re-organise the Opposition, at the head of which he now placed the foolish Prince of Wales (see p. 725), who was ready to give his support to any movement against Walpole, simply because Walpole was the favourite minister of his father.

4. **William Pitt. 1738.**—The so-called patriots of the Opposition and the Tories were now joined by a small group of young men called by Walpole the Boys, who were filled with disgust at the corruption around them, and fancied that all that went wrong was the fault of Walpole, and not the fault of the generation in which he lived. Walpole's scorn of the patriots was unmeasured. " All these men have their price," he once said, pointing to the benches on which they were sitting. He could easily make a patriot, he declared on another occasion, by merely refusing an unreasonable request. It was with half-amused contempt that he regarded the Boys. When they were older, he thought, they would discover the necessity of dealing with the world as it was, not as they thought it ought to be. He had found that men could only be governed by offers of money or of money's worth, and so it would ever be. Some, indeed, of the Boys lived to fulfil Walpole's cynical expectation, but there were amongst them a few, especially William Pitt, who maintained in old age the standard of purity

which they had raised in youth. Pitt was a born orator, but as yet his flashing speeches, filled with passionate invective, had little reasoning in them. That which lifted him above the more vehement speakers of that or of any other time was his burning devotion to his country : whether his country was right or wrong he hardly knew or cared. That strength of feeling which the elder generation scouted, broke out in Pitt in the form of enthusiasm —not for any cause sacred to humanity at large, but for the power and greatness of his country. Naturally, he attacked Spain for her claim to the right of search, and for her barbarities to English seamen, whilst he never thought of mentioning the provocation given by the English smugglers.

Coach built for William Herrick, Esq., of Beaumanor, in 1740.

5. **Impending War.** **1738—1739.**—Members of the united opposition had at last a popular cry in their favour. Before the end of **1738** they produced a certain Captain Jenkins, who declared —probably with truth—that his ear had been cut off seven years before on board his own ship by a Spanish coastguard, and who took what he declared to be his ear out of a box to show to a committee of the House of Commons. The Spaniard, he said, had bidden him to take his ear to his king. " I recommended," he explained, when asked what his thoughts had been on the occasion, "my soul to my God, and my cause to my country." The words were repeated from one end of England to the other. " No search !" became the popular cry. In vain Walpole, early in **1739**, announced that Spain had agreed to a treaty indemnifying those English sailors who had suffered actual wrong. The treaty

III.

3 B

made such large counter-demands on England that its concessions
were more nominal than real. The opposition grew in strength,
and before the end of **1739** England went to war with Spain.

6. **The Spanish War and the Resignation of Walpole. 1739
—1742.**—No one now doubts that it would have been better for
Walpole if he had resigned rather than direct a war which he regarded as unjustifiable ; but the principle that a minister should
resign rather than carry out a policy of which he disapproves was
not yet thoroughly established, and Walpole perhaps flattered
himself that he might be able to bring about a peace sooner
than any other minister. He knew that trouble would soon come.
" They may ring the bells now "—as he heard the peals from the
church steeples celebrating the glad tidings that war had been declared—" before long they will be wringing their hands." At first
the war was successful. Admiral Anson sailed round the world,
sacked Paita, a Spanish port in Peru, and captured a rich galleon
which carried on the trade between Acapulco and Manilla. Admiral
Vernon took Porto Bello, on the Atlantic side of the Isthmus of
Panama ; but he failed in an attack on Cartagena, and in another
attack on Santiago. The opposition at home gave all the credit to
the Admiral, and all the blame to Walpole, who was held to have
done little to support a war of which he disapproved, and who
had certainly allowed the navy to deteriorate during the long peace.
In **1741** there were fresh elections, and the energy of the opposition, together with the excited feeling of the country, reduced
Walpole's followers in the new Parliament. In those days election
petitions were decided by a majority of the whole House of Commons, the vote being given strictly on party grounds. Walpole was
beaten on the Chippenham election petition by a majority of one,
and on February 17, **1742**, he resigned, receiving the title of Earl
of Orford. He had done his work. England had, under his rule,
consolidated herself, and had settled down in contented acceptance
of the Hanoverian dynasty and the Parliamentary government
established at the Revolution. It was inexplicable to Walpole that
the first result of the national unity which he had brought about
should be a national determination to go to war in the assertion of
the claims of England.

7. **The New Administration. 1742.**—There was some difficulty
in forming a new ministry. Politicians who had agreed in attacking
Walpole agreed in nothing else, and each thought that his own
claim to office was superior to that of the others. So hopeless
did the task of composing their differences appear, that Pulteney,

who had led the late opposition in the House of Commons, refused
to take office, and consoled himself with being made Earl of Bath.
" Here we are, my Lord !" said the new Earl of Orford to his former
rival, when he met him in the House of Lords—" the two most in-

A sitting in the House of Commons in 1741–42 : from an engraving by Pine.

significant men in England." Orford knew that to leave the House
of Commons was to abandon power. At last the new ministry was
got together, partly from Walpole's enemies and partly from his
friends. Sir Spencer Compton—now made Earl of Wilmington—

became First Lord of the Treasury. He had not talents enough to succeed to the Prime-ministership which Walpole had created. The new administration did what it could to bring Walpole to punishment, but a Committee of the House of Commons failed to substantiate any charge against him.

8. Carteret and Newcastle. 1742.—The ministers were too jealous of each other to admit that anyone could be first amongst them. The two Secretaries of State were the Duke of Newcastle, the head of the Pelham family, and Lord Carteret. Newcastle was ignorant and incompetent, and made himself ridiculous by his fussy attempts to appear energetic. He always, it was said, lost half an hour in the morning and spent the rest of the day in running after it. He had one ruling passion—the love of power, not for the sake of any great policy, but because he enjoyed the distribution of patronage. He was himself incorruptible, but he took pleasure in corrupting others. In the morning his ante-chamber was crowded with place-hunters, and he sometimes rushed out of his bedroom with his face covered with soap-suds to announce to one applicant or another that he was able to gratify him by making his brother a bishop or some poor dependant a tidewaiter. The character of the person appointed was of no moment. One disappointed suitor was heard to mutter, as he left the room: "I was turned out of the navy, I was too debauched to enter the army, and they will not even give me preferment in the Church ! " Carteret, on the other hand, was an able statesman, especially in the department of foreign affairs. He was as energetic as he was able, and as his knowledge of the German language and of German politics quickly gained him the king's favour, he soon became the leading man in the ministry. Practically he inherited Walpole's Prime-ministership, though his authority was by no means so undisputed as Walpole's had been in the later years of his ministry.

9. Beginning of the War of the Austrian Succession. 1740—1742.—When Carteret came into office, Europe was distracted by a fresh war. The Emperor Charles VI. having no son, had persuaded his various hereditary states to accept an arrangement known as the Pragmatic Sanction, according to which they all agreed to transfer their allegiance to his daughter Maria Theresa at his death, and he subsequently obtained from the principal European Governments an acknowledgment of the validity of this document. He died in **1740,** and though Maria Theresa—the Queen of Hungary, as she was called from her principal title—was accepted as ruler by all her father's states, Charles Albert,

Elector of Bavaria, put forth a claim to Bohemia and the Arch-duchy of Austria.   France, anxious to make herself supreme in Germany

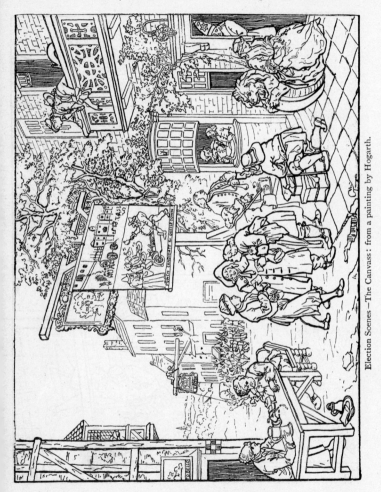

Election Scenes—The Canvass : from a painting by Hogarth.

by the disruption of the dominions of the House of Austria, took up his cause.   Frederick II., who had just succeeded to the throne of Prussia, and to the command of a large, well-disciplined army, seized the opportunity to lay claim to Maria Theresa's province of Silesia, and in 1741 he defeated the Austrians at Mollwitz.   In the same

Election Scenes—The Poll · from a painting by Hogarth.

year a French army crossed the Rhine in support of the Elector of Bavaria, who early in 1742 was chosen emperor under the name of Charles VII.   In the summer of 1742 Maria Theresa signed the

treaty of Breslau, by which she ceded Silesia to Frederick, hoping
to be enabled thereby to cope with her other enemies.

Election Scenes—The Chairing of the Member : from a painting by Hogarth.

10. **Carteret's Diplomacy.** 1742—1744.—The English people
sympathised with Maria Theresa, and George II. warmly supported

her against the French. Carteret's policy was to bring about a
good understanding between Frederick and Maria Theresa, and

Election Scenes—The Election Dinner : from a painting by Hogarth.

to unite all Germany against the French. He very nearly succeeded in his object. In 1743 George II. was in Germany at the
head of an army of Hessians and Hanoverians, combined with

Dutch and Austrian forces. On June 27 he defeated the French at Dettingen on the Main. In July the new Bavarian emperor undertook to desert the French on condition of receiving a subsidy from England ; and if this arrangement had been carried out, all Germany would probably have been united against France. New-castle, however, being jealous of Carteret, and too timid to embark on so far-sighted a combination, refused to sanction the agree-ment, and the German powers were soon once more in strife with one anothe.. In **1744** Frederick and Maria Theresa were again at war, and France—with which, in spite of the battle of Dettingen, only the German Electorate of Hanover, and not England, had as yet been avowedly at war—now declared war against England. Charles Edward, the son of the Pretender—who was known in England as the Young Pretender, and amongst his own friends as the Prince of Wales—was sent with a French fleet to invade England. The fleet was, however, shattered by a storm, and the danger was thus for a time averted.

11. **Carteret and the Family Compact. 1743—1744.**—Carteret's object had been to take up again the policy of the Whigs of Anne's time as opposed to the policy of the time of Walpole. The former had aimed at a general European combination against France, the latter at keeping the peace by a French alliance. Reasons were not wanting for such a change of policy. France was now formidable, not only on account of her renewed military strength, but by reason of her close alliance with Spain (with which Eng-land was still at war), the Family Compact—first signed in **1733** (see p. 725)—having been renewed in **1743**. Carteret, who had a better knowledge of Continental affairs—and especially of German affairs—than any man of his day, thought it wise to oppose so dangerous a combination. There were, however, many difficulties in his way, even as far as the Continent was concerned. The German powers were too intent on their own quarrels to be easily brought to care for common interests, and, as far as England was concerned, Carteret could not reasonably expect support. England had roused herself sufficiently to care for the welfare of her trade and the protection of her smugglers, but she was far more of a maritime than of a Continental power ; and, whilst the effects of the Family Compact—not a syllable of which had yet been made public—were seen in a close alliance between France and Spain on the Continent, no such effects had as yet been seen at sea. When Spain was attacked by England in **1739** France had given no help to her ally. As Carteret was more

remiss even than Walpole in carrying on the maritime war against Spain, people unfairly thought that all his continental schemes were merely the fruit of his subservience to the king's predilection for anything that would profit the Hanoverian electorate. Pitt, who afterwards took up much of Carteret's policy, thundered against him with passionate invective as the base minister who was selling the interests of England for the profit of Hanover.

12. **Carteret's Fall. 1744.**—Other causes contributed to weaken Carteret. He had no voice in the military arrangements, and the armies were put under worn-out or incompetent officers. His greatest weakness, however, arose from his never having sat in

Grenadier of the First Regiment
of Footguards, 1745.

Uniform of the Footguards,
1745.

the House of Commons, and his consequent inability to under-stand its ways. " I want," he said to a young politician, " to instil a noble ambition into you ; to make you knock the heads of the kings of Europe together, and jumble out something that may be of service to this country." " What is it to me," he said on an-other occasion, " who is made a judge or who is a bishop? It is my business to make kings and emperors, and to maintain the balance of Europe." " Then," was the obvious reply, " those who want to be bishops and judges will apply to those who submit to make it their business." Newcastle, at least, stuck to the work of making judges and bishops, and thereby gained the House of Commons to his side. He insisted on Carteret's dismissal, and on November 23, 1744, Carteret—who had just become, by his mother's death, Earl Granville—was driven, in spite of the king's warm support, to resign office.

13. **The Broad-bottomed Administration. 1744.**—Henry Pelham, Newcastle's brother, who had for some time been First Lord of the Treasury, now became virtually Prime Minister. He was a good man of business, and anxious to return to Walpole's policy of peace. His administration was distinguished as the Broad-bottomed Administration, because everyone whose influence or talents rendered him at all dangerous was at once given a place in it. The consequence was that, for the only time since party-government began, there was no Opposition in the House of Commons. For the present, indeed, the king refused to admit Pitt to office, but Pitt knew that the ministers were friendly to him, and abstained from attacking them. When once, however, the Pelhams had turned out Granville, they forgot their professions, and squandered English money on Hanoverian troops and German princes, without any of Carteret's genius to enable them to use their allies for any good purpose whatever. A large British force, indeed, joined the allies to defend the Netherlands against a French army at that time under a great general, Marshal Saxe ; and on May 1, 1745, a battle was fought at Fontenoy. The British column, headed by the king's second son, the Duke of Cumberland, pressed steadily on into the heart of the French line, and, driving everything before it, all but won the day. The Dutch, however, failed to second it, and the French guard, falling upon the isolated column, drove it back. The British army had maintained its honourable traditions, but the French gained the battle ; and the frontier towns of the Austrian Netherlands fell at once into their hands.

14. **The Young Pretender in Scotland. 1745.**—The French victory at Fontenoy encouraged Charles Edward to try his fortunes in Scotland. On July 25, 1745, he landed in Moidart, in the West Highlands, with only seven friends, known afterwards as the "seven men of Moidart." The few Highland chiefs who came to meet him shook their heads at his rash enterprise ; but his gallant bearing and persuasive words soon swept away their scruples, and they bade their clans follow a prince who had thrown himself on the generosity of the Highlanders. On August 19 Charles Edward raised the Royal Standard in Glenfinnan, and was soon at the head of 1,600 men. It was a small force with

which to overrun Scotland, but the Prince had the best of allies in the incapacity of the British commander, Sir John Cope. Military commands were at that time bestowed on men whose friends had influence enough to secure votes to the government in Parliament ; and inquiry was seldom made, when an officer was selected for promotion, whether he was in any way fit for the post. Cope inexplicably withdrew to Inverness, and Charles Edward marched straight upon Edinburgh. In Scotland the traders, having gained much by the Union, were Hanoverians to a man ; [1] but a large part of the population of Edinburgh regretted the loss of the advantages which the town had possessed as a capital, and there was, moreover, a widespread dissatisfaction with the Hanoverian government, because it had imposed an excise on whisky. In Edinburgh, therefore, Charles Edward was welcomed. Before long Cope returned by sea from Inverness to Dunbar, at the head of his little army of 2,200 men. On the morning of September 21, as day was breaking, Charles Edward, now at the head of 2,500 Highlanders, fell upon him at Preston Pans. With a yell and a rush, the Highlanders broke up the English ranks. Cope himself was amongst the foremost in the flight.

15. **The March to Derby. 1745.**—Many of the Highlanders returned to their glens with their booty, but reinforcements streamed in, and Charles Edward, now at the head of 6,000 men, crossed the Border, hoping to rouse England in his support. England was strangely apathetic. Walpole and the Whigs had weaned Englishmen of Jacobitism, but they had never appealed to any popular sentiment, and though few joined Charles Edward, there was no general rising against him. They found numbers were gathering round. They gave London a good fright. The king's guards were sent out to Finchley to defend London, and troops from other quarters gathered menacingly round Charles Edward's line of march. When on December 5 the Highlanders reached Derby, they were exposed to an attack from forces far superior to their own ; and, further progress being hopeless, they turned back. The king had made ready to leave England if necessary; and it is said that on Black Friday—as it was called—the Bank of England cashed cheques in sixpences, in order to delay payment as long as possible.

16. **Falkirk and Culloden. 1746.**—Charles Edward won one more victory. On January 17 he defeated Hawley—a general as

---

[1] The character of Baillie Nicol Jarvie in Scott's 'Rob Roy' conveys much instruction on this point.

incompetent as Cope—at Falkirk. The Duke of Cumberland, however, advanced into Scotland with an army of 8,000, whilst Charles
Edward (who retreated to Inverness) had now but 5,000 with him.

Hogarth's 'March to Finchley,' 1745.

Cumberland was not a great general, but he had some knowledge
of the art of war. His men, moreover, were well drilled, and the
advantage of superior training soon became manifest. On the

morning of April 16, Charles Edward tried to surprise Cumberland
on Culloden Moor. The Highlanders arrived too late in the field
for a surprise, but they charged as vigorously as at Preston Pans.
They broke the first line of the enemy, but the second line held

The Rt. Hon. William Pitt, Paymaster of the Forces, afterwards Earl of Chatham:
from a painting by Hoare.

firm, and they were broken in turn. Cumberland slaughtered his
now helpless enemies with unrelenting cruelty, and gained for himself the name of the Butcher, which he never lost. The wounded
were dragged from their hiding-places and shot, and a building in

which twenty disabled Highlanders had sought refuge was burnt to
the ground with the wretched fugitives inside it.   Charles Edward
himself wandered long amongst the mountains.   Though a heavy
price was set on his head, not a Highlander would betray him.   At
one moment, when escape seemed impossible, a young lady, Flora
Macdonald, dressed him as her maidservant, and thus carried him
off in safety.   At last he succeeded in making his way back to
France.   His later life was aimless, and he sank into drunkenness.
He did not die till **1788**, and his brother Henry, who had become a
Cardinal, survived till **1807**.   Henry was the last descendant, in
the male line, of the House of Stuart, though there are descendants
of Henrietta, the youngest daughter of Charles I., still living,
amongst whom the most conspicuous is the present King of Italy.

17. **The Pelhams and the King. 1745.**—The Pelhams made
use of the struggle in Scotland to press for Pitt's admission to the
ministry, and, on the king's refusal, resigned office.   George II.
ordered Granville (see p. 739) to form a ministry, but Granville
found it impossible to gain the support of a majority in the Houses,
and in forty-eight hours he gave up the task.   The Pelhams were
reinstated in power, bringing Pitt with them.   It was the first
thorough acknowledgment by a king that he was powerless in the
face of Parliament.   It is true that the majority commanded by the
Pelhams was secured by unblushing corruption ; but there was as
yet no popular sentiment opposed to that corruption to which the
king could appeal.

18. **End of the War.   1746—1748.**—The war on the Continent
still continued.   The French overran the Austrian Netherlands,
but were checked in Italy, whilst the English were successful at
sea.   At last, in **1748**, a general peace was made at Aix-la-Chapelle,
every power restoring its conquests with the exception of Frederick,
who kept Silesia for Prussia.

19. **End of Henry Pelham's Ministry.   1748—1754.**—The remainder of Henry Pelham's ministry was uneventful.   In **1582** Pope
Gregory XIII. had set straight an error which had grown up in
the Calendar, and the new Gregorian Calendar had by this time
been adopted by most European powers.   England, however, had
long objected even to be set right by a Pope, and in the eighteenth
century the almanac was eleven days wrong.   What was really,
for instance, September 11 was known in England as September 1.
In **1751** an Act of Parliament ordered that eleven days should be
dropped out of the calendar, in order to make the reckoning correct.
Large numbers of people fancied that they were cheated out of

eleven days' pay, and mobs went about, shouting, " Give us our eleven days." In 1754 Henry Pelham died. The new constitutional doctrine that England was governed by the Cabinet, and that the Cabinet could retain office irrespective of the king's goodwill if it could secure the support of Parliament, was now fully established.

Books recommended for the further study of Part VIII.

MACAULAY, Lord.   History of England.   Vols. iii.–v.

STANHOPE, Lord.   Reign of Anne.

————————————— History of England from the Peace of Utrecht. Vols. i.–iv.

HARROP, R.   Bolingbroke.

PARNELL, Colonel.   War of the Spanish Succession.

STEBBING, W.   Peterborough.

LECKY, W. E. H.   History of England in the Eighteenth Century. Vols. i. ii.

MORLEY, J.   Walpole.

BALLANTYNE, A.   Lord Carteret.

MAHAN, Capt. A. T.   The Influence of Sea Power upon History. Chapters iv.–vii.

PART IX

THE FALL OF THE WHIGS AND THE RISE OF THE NEW TORYISM. 1754—1789

CHAPTER XLVII

NEWCASTLE AND PITT. 1754—1760

LEADING DATES

Reign of George II., 1727—1760

Newcastle Prime Minister	1754
Beginning of the Seven Years' War	1756
Ministry of Devonshire and Pitt	1756
Coalition between Pitt and Newcastle	1757
Conquest of Cape Breton	1758
Capture of Quebec	1759
Conquest of Canada	1760
Death of George II.	Oct. 25, 1760

Formation of the East India Company	1600
Death of Aurungzebe.	1707
Clive's Defence of Arcot	1751
Battle of Plassey	1757
Battle of Wandewash	1760

1. **Butler, Wesley, and Whitefield. 1736—1754.**—In religion as well as in politics everything savouring of enthusiasm had long been scouted, and in polite society little of moral earnestness was to be found. There had, indeed, been much discussion as to the truth of Christianity, and for a long time there was a steady growth of opinion in favour of deism. Latterly, however, there had been a strong reaction in favour of Christian doctrines. Their noblest advocate, Butler, whose *Analogy* was published in 1736, writing as he did for educated men, appealed to the reason rather than to the heart. The task of moving the masses fell into the hands of John

Wesley, who had in his youth striven to live a pious, beneficent life at Oxford, where he and his followers had been nicknamed Methodists. In 1738, Wesley came to believe that no real Christianity was possible without conversion, or a supernatural conviction of salvation. That which he believed he taught, and his enthusiasm gained him followers, in whom he kindled zeal equal to his own. Wesley was a minister of the Church of England, and in that Church he wished to abide ; but the clergy counted him as a madman, and, in 1739, he was obliged to gather his followers elsewhere than in churches. Whitefield, a born orator, whose views were very similar to those of Wesley, preferred to preach in the open air. He stirred the hearts of immense crowds, as many as twenty thousand sometimes coming to hear him. At Kingswood, near Bristol, the colliers flocked to him in multitudes, their tears flowing down in white streaks over faces blackened with coal-dust. Wesley was, however, the organiser of the movement, and gathered into congregations those who had been converted, teaching them to confess their sins one to another, and to relate in public their spiritual experiences. There was no room for such enthusiasm in the Church of that day, and, much against his will, Wesley was compelled to organise his congregations outside the Church. What he and Whitefield did had a value, apart from their system and teaching. They reminded their generation that man has a heart as well as a head, and that the cultivation of the intellect is not all that is necessary to raise human nature above brutality ; and thus they stirred to higher and purer thoughts thousands of their countrymen who were sunk in inertness and vice. As a matter of course they were persecuted, and men of intelligence and position thought it well that it should be so.

2. Fielding and Hogarth.—In literature and art, as well as in religion, a new life was making itself manifest. Fielding, in his ' Tom Jones ' and ' Joseph Andrews,' has been styled the creator of the modern novel in its portraiture of living humanity. Hogarth was undoubtedly the originator of an English school of painting. Both Fielding and Hogarth were often coarse in expression, but their tendencies were moral, and their work robust and vigorous.

3. Newcastle, Pitt, and Fox. 1754—1755.—In politics, too, the time of drowsy inaction was coming to an end. " Now," said George II., when he heard of Pelham's death, " I shall have no peace." Newcastle was, indeed, appointed First Lord of the Treasury and was regarded as Prime Minister in his brother's place, but Newcastle had not his brother's capacity for business, and, besides that, he was not in the House of Commons. He must choose some one to lead the House of Commons, and there were three persons on whom his choice might fall : Murray, Pitt, and Henry Fox. Murray, who was the greatest lawyer of the day, had no ambition except that of becoming Chief Justice, and was disqualified by his professional turn of mind from occupying a political post. Newcastle objected to Pitt as too opinionated, whilst Fox seemed just the man to suit him. Newcastle and Fox both loved corruption, but whilst Newcastle loved it for the sake of the pleasure of exercising patronage, Fox loved it for the sake of its profits. Fox was the ablest debater of his day, and might have risen high if he had not preferred to hold unimportant but well-paid posts rather than important posts of which the pay was less. He now refused Newcastle's proposal that he should lead the House of Commons, because Newcastle insisted on keeping the secret-service money—in other words, the money spent in bribing men to vote for the government—in his own hands. Fox truly said that it was impossible for him to ask members for their votes unless he knew whether they had been bribed or not. Accordingly Newcastle appointed Sir Thomas Robinson to lead the House. Robinson was a diplomatist, who having been long absent from England, knew nothing about the ways of members. Pitt and Fox, agreeing in nothing else, joined in baiting Robinson. Whenever he made a mistake they ironically took his part on the ground that he had been so long abroad that he could not be expected to know better. Robinson threw up his post in disgust, and, in 1755, Fox abandoning the conditions on which he had formerly insisted became Secretary of State with the leadership of the House of Commons.

4. **The French in America. 1754.**—In 1754, when Newcastle succeeded his brother as Prime Minister, there was already danger of a war with France. In North America France possessed Louisiana, at the mouth of the Mississippi, and Canada, at the mouth of the St. Lawrence. Between the two was a vast region, at that time only inhabited by Indians, who used it for purposes of hunting, and sold furs to the French Canadians. France, which already possessed a line of scattered forts between Canada and Louisiana, claimed the whole of the region to the west of the Alleghany Mountains as her own. On the other hand, there were now thirteen English colonies, and the colonists were beginning to find their way westward over the mountains, especially at the head of the Ohio river, refusing to be penned in by the French forts beyond the Alleghanies. Between the English and the French colonists

fighting began in 1754. The contest then begun was one for the possession of the basin of the Ohio, though the possession of that would ultimately bring with it the power to colonise the far vaster basin of the Mississippi and its affluents. Therein lay the answer to a further question, as yet unsuspected, whether the English or the French was to be the predominating race in America and in the world of the future. Great Britain was once more drifting into a war which, like the war with Spain in 1739, would be one for mercantile and colonial expansion. The difference was that, whereas in 1739 she was matched with the decaying monarchy of Spain, she was now matched against the vigorous monarchy of France. The Family Compact uniting Spain and France had as yet caused little real danger to England. As France had shown no signs of supporting Spain in America in 1739, Spain showed no signs of supporting France in 1754.

5. **Newcastle's Blundering. 1754—1756.**—Newcastle was not the man to conduct a great war successfully. In 1754, hearing that the French had established a fort called Fort Duquesne, at the head of the Ohio valley, he sent General Braddock from England to capture it. In 1755 Braddock, one of those brave, but unintelligent officers of whom there were many in the British service, falling into an ambuscade of French and Indians, was himself killed and his troops routed. Newcastle could not make up his mind whether to fight or not. It was finally resolved that, though war was not to be declared, Hawke was, by way of reprisal for the capture of British shipping, to seize any French ships he met with. Naturally, when Hawke carried out these instructions, the French regarded the seizure of their ships as an act of piracy. Meanwhile George II. was frightened lest Hanover should be lost if a war broke out, and, by his direction, Newcastle agreed to treaties giving subsidies to various German states and even to Russia, in return for promises to find troops for the defence of Hanover. Against this system Pitt openly declared himself. " I think," he said, " regard ought to be had to Hanover, if it should be attacked on our account ; but we could not find money to defend it by subsidies, and if we could that is not the way to defend it." Behind Pitt was the rising spirit of the nation, eager to enter on a struggle for colonial empire, but not wishing to incur loss for the sake of the king's German electorate. Legge, the Chancellor of the Exchequer, a close ally of Pitt, refused to give the money needed to pay a subsidy to Hesse, and both he and Pitt were dismissed from their offices. Newcastle had an overwhelming majority in both Houses, but so helpless was he that in 1756 he

actually asked the king to bring Hanoverian and Hessian soldiers to England to save it from a French invasion.

6. The Loss of Minorca. 1756.—The weakness of the Government weakened the hands of its officers. In 1756 a French fleet and army assailed Port Mahon, in the island of Minorca, which was still a British possession. Admiral Byng set out to relieve it, but, though he was brave, he was deficient in energy, and, finding the French ships more numerous than his own, thought it prudent to withdraw without serious fighting. Before long the whole of Minorca fell into the hands of the French. Port Mahon and Gibraltar were the two ports on which English maritime operations in the Mediterranean could be based, and it is therefore no wonder that there was a howl of indignation in England at the loss of one of them. The popular theory was that Byng had been bribed to avoid fighting. The charge was utterly false, but so many bribes were taken in those days that it cannot be said to have been unreasonable. Byng was brought home to await his trial.

7. Beginning of the Seven Years' War. 1756.—After this, war was at last declared. What might have been the result if England and France had been obliged to fight it out alone, it is impossible to say. France, however, had other enemies than England. Whilst England had only a sea frontier, France had a land frontier as well, and, therefore, whilst England was able to throw her main strength into a struggle for mastery on the sea and for the acquisition of colonies, France threw her main strength into her efforts to become predominant by land, and consequently neglected her navy and her colonies. She now, at the very time when England was ready to challenge her power in America, embarked on a war in Europe which was alone sufficient to occupy her energy. This time she forsook her old policy of hostility to Austria, and joined with Austria, Russia, and the German states to attack and dismember Prussia. The war which was thus begun in 1756 is known as the Seven Years' War.

8. Ministry of Devonshire and Pitt. 1756—1757.—So strong was the feeling aroused by Newcastle's incompetence that his own subordinates were frightened. In October, 1756, Fox resigned, and no one could be found to fill his place. Murray would give no help to the ministry, and was allowed to become Chief Justice, with the title of Lord Mansfield, under which he is known as one of the greatest of English judges. Newcastle, helpless and frightened lest the mob which was raving for the hanging of Byng should want to hang him too, also resigned. The Duke of Devonshire

became First Lord of the Treasury, with Pitt as Secretary of State
and practically Prime Minister. At once Pitt took vigorous
measures for the prosecution of the war. Money was raised, and
men levied. It was not, however, merely by his energy that
Pitt differed from the former ministers. Newcastle relied on
a Parliamentary majority acquired by influence and corruption ;
Pitt had confidence in the nation and in himself as well. " My
Lord," he said to Devonshire, " I know that I can save this nation
and that nobody else can." He understood how to inspire the confidence which he needed. He sent out of England the Hanoverian
and Hessian troops which had been brought over to protect the
country, and passed a Bill for re-organising the national militia.
He even raised regiments in the very Highlands, out of the men
who had been the most vigorous enemies of the House of Hanover,
knowing that the Highlanders had fought under Charles Edward
far more because they were poor than because they reverenced
the House of Stuart. On the other hand, he moved for a grant
of 200,000*l*. for the protection of Hanover. It seemed as if Pitt
was about to fall back on the policy of Carteret. There was,
however, this difference, that whereas with Carteret the war on the
Continent was alone thought of, with Pitt intervention on the Continent was regarded as subsidiary to the great colonial struggle
on which England was now embarked.

9. **Pitt's Dismissal. 1757.**—Pitt was the most popular man in
England, but he had only a scanty following in the House of Commons, and he was disliked by the king on account of his former
declamations against payments for the sake of Hanover. Whilst
he was in office Byng was brought to trial and condemned to be
shot as a coward, which he certainly was not. Pitt pleaded for
Byng's life with the king, telling him that the House of Commons
was favourably disposed. " You have taught me," was George's
reply, " to look for the sense of my people in other places than the
House of Commons." Byng received no pardon, and died bravely,
having been guilty of no more than an error of judgment. Soon
afterwards the king dismissed Pitt. At once there was an outburst
of feeling in his favour. " For some weeks," wrote a brilliant
letter-writer of the day, " it rained gold boxes." The reference
was to the boxes in which numerous corporations sent the freedom
of their respective cities or boroughs to Pitt.

10. **Nature of Pitt's Popularity. 1757.**—Pitt's popularity, though
wide-spread, was not like that by which a popular statesman is
supported at the present day. It was not a popularity amongst

the nation at large, of which the majority could not at that time either read or write, or appreciate a political discussion. Pitt's enthusiastic admirers were to be found amongst the merchants and tradesmen of the towns. These were the men who had built up England's commercial prosperity by their thrift and honesty. Amongst them the profligacy, the drunkenness, and the gambling which disgraced polite society found little place. They had borne long with Newcastle and his like because times had been quiet, and the Government, scandalous as it was, never harassed English-men in their business or their pleasure. Now that times were dangerous they called for Pitt—the Great Commoner, as they styled him—to assume power, not because they were conscious of his latent capacity for statesmanship, but because they knew him to be even ostentatiously uncorrupt. To the end of his life Pitt called himself a Whig, but his hostility to a system of government in which patronage was distributed to those who could bring most votes to the Government, without regard to merit, led him to place himself in opposition to Newcastle, and ultimately led to his es-trangement from the great Whig families. By opposing power derived from popular support to power based on parliamentary connection, he introduced into constitutional struggles an element which had long been left out of account, and thus became (though unintentionally) a precursor of the new Toryism which, in the hands of his son, broke the power of the Whigs.

11. **Coalition between Pitt and Newcastle. 1757.** — The middle class in the towns formed, at this time, the most vigorous element in English society ; but it disposed of few votes in Parlia-ment. The great majority in the House of Commons sought for loaves and fishes, and as they knew that incompetency might hope for reward from Newcastle but not from Pitt, they steadily voted as Newcastle bade them, even after he had ceased to hold office. Newcastle, however, could not make up his mind whether he wished to resume office or not. He was too fond of the lower sort of power to share it willingly with any colleague whose in-telligence was greater than his own, and too timid to grasp authority at a time when it was dangerous to its possessor. Ac-cordingly, he long vacillated between acceptance and refusal, and for eleven weeks there was no ministry at all. At last an admirable arrangement was made. A coalition was effected between New-castle and Pitt. Newcastle was to be First Lord of the Treasury to manage the business of patronage, and Pitt was to be Secretary of State to manage the business of politics and war. Both were

satisfied ; Newcastle gave to Pitt the Parliamentary majority which he wanted, and Pitt took on himself the responsibility which Newcastle shunned. Fox got a lucrative appointment without political influence, and in a few years made himself enormously rich.

12. **Military Disasters. 1757.**—When Pitt took office in combination with Newcastle things were going badly. In America, French reinforcements were poured into Canada, and an attempt made by Lord Loudon, the British commander, to take Louisburg, a strong fortress which guarded the French island of Cape Breton, failed signally. In Germany, the king of Prussia, Frederick the Great, after overrunning Saxony in the preceding year, now, in 1757, attempted to overrun Bohemia. After winning a battle at Prague in May, he was disastrously defeated at Kolin in June, and driven out of the country. A French army, in the meanwhile, entered Hanover and defeated the Duke of Cumberland at Hastenbeck ; after which Cumberland signed the Convention of Closterseven in September, leaving Hanover in the hands of the enemy. " Here is my son," said George II. of him when he returned to England, " who has ruined me and disgraced himself."

13. **Pitt and Frederick the Great. 1757–1758.**—Pitt set himself to remedy the mischief, as far as he could. His plans for military action were often faulty, but he had indomitable courage, and an almost unique power of inspiring others with courage. Boldly throwing aside the traditions of the century, according to which appointments in the army and navy were given to men of good birth, or of families whose favour would bring votes in Parliament, he chose commanders for their merit. Every young officer knew that Pitt's eye was on him, and that he would be promoted if he conducted himself well, even if he were poor and friendless. A new spirit was breathed into both services. Before Pitt could achieve anything, Frederick's military genius had given him the mastery over his enemies. In November the King of Prussia smote down the French at Rossbach, and in December he smote down the Austrians at Leuthen. Pitt at once saw that a close alliance with Frederick was necessary if England was to maintain her struggle with France beyond the Atlantic. In 1758, therefore, he repudiated the Convention of Closterseven, which had not been brought into a binding form, gave a subsidy of 700,000*l.* a year to Frederick, and sent 12,000 English soldiers to join the Hanoverian army in defending Hanover. The commander of this force was Prince Ferdinand of Brunswick, one of the best of Frederick's generals. In June the Prince defeated the French at Crefeld.

Frederick had, in the meanwhile, driven back the Russians at Zorndorf, but late in the year was beaten at Hochkirch by the Austrians.

14. **Fighting in France and America.** **1757—1758.**—Both in 1757 and in 1758 Pitt sent expeditions to harass the French at home. In 1757 an attempt to take Rochefort failed through dissensions amongst the commanders. One expedition, in 1758, destroyed some French ships and stores at St. Malo, whilst a second did some damage at Cherbourg, but was driven off with heavy loss in the Bay of St. Cast. In America Pitt made a great effort to gain his ends. He dismissed the incompetent Loudon, and appointed Abercrombie to command in chief, placing under his orders young men whose ability and energy he had noted, of whom the most conspicuous was Wolfe, who had distinguished himself in the abortive attempt on Rochefort. England's superiority at sea now told heavily in her favour. In the course of 1758 Louisburg and Fort Duquesne were taken, though Abercrombie was repulsed at Ticonderoga. In America the British troops, supported as they were by the colonial militia, far outnumbered the French. France was so fully occupied in Germany that she was unable to send more than scanty reinforcements to the Marquis of Montcalm, the commander of the French army in Canada, who had, therefore, to defend the French possessions in America against heavy odds.

15. **The Campaign in Canada.** **1759.**—Pitt planned a serious attack on Canada for 1759. Abercrombie, having failed at Ticonderoga, was discarded. Three armies were to be brought from distant points to meet before Quebec, the fortified capital of Canada. Amherst, who replaced Abercrombie, was to capture Ticonderoga and Crown Point, push up by way of Lake Champlain, and approach Quebec from the south. Prideaux and Johnson were to capture Fort Niagara and approach it from the west. Wolfe was to sail up the St. Lawrence and to approach it from the east. The idea that three armies, separated by vast and thinly populated regions, could be brought to co-operate at a given time was essentially faulty. In fact, though the western army captured Niagara and the southern army captured Ticonderoga and Crown Point, neither of them got near Quebec that year. Wolfe found himself, with his troops, alone at the meeting-point on the St. Lawrence. The position of Quebec is exceedingly strong, lying between two rivers, the St. Lawrence and the St. Charles. Behind it rise the Heights of Abraham, which are easily defensible, as it has steep cliffs on the river sides. Around the defences of the town Montcalm

A view of Cape Diamond, Plains of Abraham, and part of the town of Quebec and the river St. Lawrence; from an engraving in the Map Department of the British Museum, taken from a drawing by Lieutenant Fisher.

". . . Cape Diamond, on which stand the citadel and fortifications of Quebec, constitutes the most prominent feature in the landscape. The Plains of Abraham . . . form part of a ridge of land of which the cape itself is the extremity. The town is, for the most part, built on the opposite side of this promontory. The view is taken from the opposite side of the river, about two miles above Quebec."

manœuvred with admirable skill ; and though Wolfe landed his
army, he could neither pass his adversary by nor compel him to
fight. The season was growing late, and it seemed as if the
British general would be forced to return home without accomplishing his task.

16. **The Conquest of Canada. 1759—1760.**—The St. Lawrence,
as it flows by Quebec, is a broad and navigable stream, and Wolfe,
re-embarking his troops, moved his ships up the river past Quebec,

Wolfe : from the painting by Schaak in the National Portrait Gallery.

hoping to be able to achieve something from that side. Though
he had but little hope, he resolved to make one desperate attempt.
Placing his men in boats at night he floated with them down
the river. Gray's *Elegy* had been recently published, and Wolfe
repeated some of its lines to his officers. " Now gentlemen,"
he said, " I would rather be the author of that poem than take
Quebec ! " His boats were steered for a point at which there was
a zig-zag path up the cliff which edged the Heights of Abraham.
It was so narrow that the French had taken no special pre-

cautions to guard it, and when a few English soldiers reached the top the French sentinels ran off in surprise. The whole British force had time to draw itself up on the plateau of the Heights of Abraham before Montcalm was ready to meet it. In the battle which ensued Wolfe was killed. As he lay dying he heard an officer cry, " See how they run ! " Wolfe roused himself to ask, " Who run ? " When he heard that it was the enemy he gave orders to cut off their retreat, exclaiming, as he fell back in the arms of his comrades, " God be praised !—I will die in peace." Montcalm, too, was sorely wounded in the battle, and died on the following day. Quebec surrendered, and in 1760 the whole of Canada submitted to the British.

17. **The War in Europe ; Naval Successes.   1759.**—In 1759, the year in which Quebec was captured, the French threatened to invade England. Pitt let loose upon them three admirals. Rodney bombarded Havre and destroyed the boats in which the invading army was to cross the Channel. Boscawen defeated off Lagos in Portugal a fleet which was on its way from Toulon to protect the crossing. Hawke, a seaman of the highest quality, blockaded another fleet at Brest, till it broke out in a storm. Hawke, however, pursued it, and caught it up off Quiberon Bay. Conflans, the French admiral, took refuge amongst the rocks and shoals which guard the mouth of the river Vilaine. Hawke dashed after him, though a gale was blowing. His pilot remonstrated with him at the risk he was incurring. " You have done your duty," replied Hawke, " in this remonstrance ; you are now to obey my orders and lay me alongside the French admiral." A complete victory was the result.

18. **Progress of the War in Germany.   1759.**—In Germany things went hard with Frederick. Hemmed in by enemies on every side he struggled on with unabated heroism, but with almost continued ill success. The time seemed approaching when Prussia and its king must succumb, borne down by mere numbers ; yet the end of 1760 saw Frederick with sadly diminished forces, yet still alert and hopeful of relief, though he knew not where to look for it. Prince Ferdinand and his British and Hanoverian army at least did him good service by warding off the blows of the French. In 1759 the Prince inflicted on a French army at Minden a defeat which would probably have been decisive but for the misconduct of Lord George Sackville, who, being in command of the cavalry, refused, in spite of distinct orders, to charge at a critical moment.

A naval engagement: defeat of the French off Cape Lagos, August, 1759 : from a picture by R. Paton.

19. **The East India Company. 1600—1698.**—The super-abundant energy of the English race, for which Pitt provided an outlet in America, made itself also felt, without assistance from the home Government, in Asia. The East India Company, an association of private merchants, was constituted by a charter from Elizabeth in **1600**, for the purpose of trading in the East. Its most important commerce was for some time with the spice islands of the Eastern Archipelago, but its trade in that quarter was ultimately ruined by the Dutch. In India itself, on the other hand, its

Officer with fusil and gorget.
1759.

factories were secured from violence by the protection of the Great Moguls, the descendants of the Mahomedan conquerors of Northern India, who had at one time fixed their capital at Agra, and at another at Delhi, and who had strengthened their power by a policy of toleration which enabled them to obtain military support from Hindoos as well as from Mussulmans. At the end of the seventeenth century the East India Company held three posts in India. By the permission of a ruler of the Carnatic it had, in **1639**, acquired a piece of ground on which Fort St. George and the town of Madras were built. In **1668** Charles II. made over to the Company Bombay, which he had received from Portugal on his marriage with Catharine of Braganza. In **1686** the Company acquired from the Mogul a piece of ground on the Hoogly, on which it built Fort William, in **1696**, round which the town of Calcutta speedily grew up.

20. **Break up of the Empire of the Great Mogul. 1658—1707.** In the meanwhile, Aurungzebe, whose long reign extended from **1658** to **1707** (that is, from the year of the death of Cromwell to the year of the union with Scotland), weakened the Mogul empire, partly by departing from the tolerant policy of his predecessors, and thus alienating his Hindoo warriors by attacks on their religion, and partly by an extension of conquest in the Deccan, or Southern India, whereas the earlier dominions of his predecessors had been confined to the north, properly known as Hindustan. Aurungzebe

provoked a reaction against his Mahomedan empire in his own lifetime, and the Hindoo chieftain Sivaji founded a powerful Hindoo
state amongst the Mahrattas of the highlands of the western
Deccan.   When Au-
rungzebe died, in 1707,
his vast empire fell to
pieces. His lieutenants
were known as Subah-
dars, or viceroys, under
whom were Nawabs or
governors of smaller
districts.   Both Subah-
dars and Nawabs, and
even Hindoo Rajahs,
who had hitherto been
allowed by the Great
Mogul to rule in de-
pendence on himself
over territories which
their ancestors had
governed as sove-
reigns, now raised them-
selves to practical sove-
reignty.   Yet they con-
tinued to acknowledge
nominally their de-
pendence on the feeble
successors of Aurung-
zebe at Delhi, just as
a king of Prussia or an
elector of Bavaria no-
minally acknowledged
the supremacy of the
Emperor.   Each ruler
quarrelled and fought
with his neighbour, and

Uniform of Militia, 1759.

the Mahratta armies gained post after post, and the Mahratta
horsemen plundered and devastated far and wide.

21. **The Mahratta Confederacy. 1707—1744.**—The Mahratta
power seemed likely to become predominant in the whole of India,
when it was threatened with disintegration in consequence of the
decadence of the House of Sivaji, as marked as the decadence of

the Moguls. After an interval of anarchy, power was grasped by an official known as the Peishwah, who ruled at Poonah, and who—though a descendant of Sivaji was always counted as the nominal sovereign—practically controlled the forces of what now became the confederacy of the Mahratta chieftains. Whether the Mahratta power would, under any circumstances, have mastered the whole of India, it is impossible to say. It was checked by the existence of a French settlement at Pondicherry and of an English settlement at Madras. Both these places were on the coast of the Carnatic, and consequently far removed from the centre of the Mahratta power. There were still Mahomedan rulers in that part of India who were the enemies of the Mahrattas, and whose disputes amongst themselves offered advantages to a European who might strengthen himself by taking part in their quarrels. Dupleix, the French governor of Pondicherry, was the first to perceive this, and was also the first to enlist native soldiers, who came to be known in England as sepoys, and to drill them to fight after the European fashion.

Uniform of a Light Dragoon, about 1760.

22. **La Bourdonnais and Dupleix. 1744—1750.**—When war was declared between France and England in **1744**, the French force in the East was superior to the English ; but the French, unfortunately for them, had two commanders, La Bourdonnais, governor of the Isle of France—now known as the Mauritius— and Dupleix, governor of Pondicherry. In **1746** La Bourdonnais captured Madras, but Dupleix hampered his move-

ments and drove him to return to France, where the Government, instead of giving him the honour due to him, threw him into prison. In 1748 Dupleix, who was as able as he was unscrupulous, successfully defended Pondicherry against an attack from the British, who were now supported by the arrival of a fleet. In 1748 the Peace of Aix-la-Chapelle compelled him to surrender Madras ; but it did not compel him to refrain from pushing his fortune further. The Subahdar of the Deccan, the Nizam-ul-Mulk (whose successors are known by the title of Nizam, which they have derived from him), died in 1748, and left rival claimants to his power. Dupleix sent French sepoys to support one of the claimants, whilst the English sent English sepoys to support the other. The French candidate defeated his rival, and was installed as Nizam, whilst Dupleix was himself appointed governor of the Carnatic from the river Kistna to Cape Comorin, by his own puppet the new Nizam. The native Nawab of the Carnatic was subordinated to him. The English settlement at Madras seemed to be incapable of offering further resistance to the French.

23. **Dupleix and Clive.** 1751—1754.—The English were still traders, not warriors, but amongst the clerks in Madras was a young man of twenty-five, Robert Clive. He early showed his undaunted bravery. Having accused an officer of cheating at cards, he was challenged to a duel. His antagonist walked up to him, held his pistol to his head, and bade him withdraw the accusation. " Fire ! " cried Clive. " I said you cheated, and I say so still, and I will never pay you." The officer threw down his pistol, saying that Clive was mad. In 1751, when Dupleix, paying no attention to the treaty of peace which had been signed in Europe between England and France, threatened Madras, Clive, having volunteered as a soldier, was sent to seize Arcot, the capital of the Nawab of the Carnatic, who was dependent on Dupleix Clive carried with him a force of sepoys, and as he approached Arcot continued his march, though a violent thunderstorm was raging. The garrison of Arcot was so astonished at his fearlessness in facing the storm that they fled in a panic, leaving the place in his hands. Shortly, however, a vast force of the native allies of France laid siege to Arcot, and Clive and his men were all but starved. So complete was the ascendency which Clive had gained over his sepoys that when they discovered that all the provisions except a little rice had been exhausted they begged that he and the few Englishmen with him would take the rice. As for themselves, they would be content with the water in which the rice

had been boiled. Before the siege, Clive had sent to Morari Rao, a Mahratta chief, for aid. The Mahratta held aloof till he heard of the brave defence of Arcot. " I never thought till now," he said, "that the English could fight; since they can, I will help them." Morari Rao came to Clive's help, and Clive gained one success after another. So fearless was he that he became known amongst the natives as Sabat Jung (the daring in war). In 1753 he returned to England, having established English supremacy in south-eastern India. In 1754 Dupleix went back to France, only to suffer the same ill-treatment which had been the lot of Le Bourdonnais.

24. **The Black Hole of Calcutta.** 1756.—Clive was the servant of a trading company, and his successes were not won like those of Wolfe, a few years later, by the support of the British Government and the valour of a British army. In 1755, when a war with France was imminent, the East India Company sent him out as the governor of Fort St. David, near Madras. When he arrived in 1756 he heard bad news from Calcutta. Surajah Dowlah, the Subahdar of Bengal, knowing that the English merchants were rich, seized all their property and thrust 145 Englishmen and one Englishwoman into a room measuring only eighteen feet by fourteen. In a space so small, many would have been suffocated even in an English climate. Under the scorching Indian sun few could expect to live. The prisoners called for water, and, though some was brought, the skins which contained it were too large to pass through the bars of the window. The prisoners struggled madly for the smallest drop, trampling one another down to reach it. All through the day, and through the night which followed, men were dying in agony. When morning came the doors were thrown open, and of the 146 who entered, only twenty-three staggered out alive.

25. **The Battle of Plassey.** 1757.—Clive hastened to Bengal to avenge this outrage. He had now with him a regiment in the king's service, and his whole army consisted of 900 Europeans and 1,500 sepoys. On June 23, 1757, he won a great victory at Plassey over 50,000 men of Surajah Dowlah's army. Clive mingled treachery with force, and had won over Surajah Dowlah's chief officer, Meer Jaffier, to promise to desert his master. Meer Jaffier, however, doubting on which side victory would fall, held back from the ful-filment of his promise till Clive's men had all but won the victory. Meer Jaffier was installed as Subahdar of Bengal, though, in con-sequence of his virtual dependence on the Company, he and his

successors are usually known by the inferior title of Nawab. In
return for his promotion he was compelled to pay large sums of
money to those who raised him to power. Clive received as his

The third Eddystone Lighthouse ; built by Smeaton in 1759.

share more than 200,000*l*., besides a grant of land worth 27,000*l*.
a year. Long afterwards, when he was called in question for his
part in despoiling Meer Jaffier, he told how he had walked through
the treasure-house of the Subahdar at Moorshedabad, where gold

3 D 2

and jewels were piled on either side. " I am astonished," he added, "at my own moderation." .

26. **The Battle of Wandewash and the capture of Pondicherry. 1760—1761.**—Around Madras, in the meanwhile, the French, under Lally, began a fresh struggle for supremacy ; but in **1760** Colonel Eyre Coote gained a signal victory at Wandewash, and Pondicherry surrendered to him early in **1761**. The predominance of Englishmen over Frenchmen in India was thus secured. As yet the English did not undertake the actual government of any part of the country. Nominally, the native rulers around Madras retained their powers ; but they derived their real strength from the support of the armies which the English had organised mainly out of native soldiers. As far as Bengal was concerned, the government continued to be exercised nominally by Meer Jaffier, the Company only receiving from him the zemindary of the district round Calcutta—that is to say, the right of collecting the land-tax, and of keeping the proceeds upon payment of a quit-rent to Meer Jaffier as subahdar. In point of fact, however, the officials of the Company had everything their own way.

27. **Death of George II. 1760.**—In all that had taken place George II. had little part, except so far as he had given up all thought of resisting ministers with whom he was dissatisfied. " Ministers," he once said, " are the king in this country." On October 25, **1760**, he died suddenly. He was succeeded by his grandson, George III., the son of Frederick, the late Prince of Wales, a young man of twenty-two, whose character and training made it unlikely that he would be content to be thrust into the background as his grandfather had been.

CHAPTER XLVIII

THE BREAK UP OF THE WHIG PARTY. 1760—1770

LEADING DATES

Reign of George III., 1760—1780

Accession of George III.	Oct. 25, 1760
Resignation of Pitt	Oct. 5, 1761
Bute's Ministry	1762
The Peace of Paris	1763
Ministry of George Grenville	April 8, 1763
The Stamp Act	1765
Ministry of Rockingham	July 10, 1765
Repeal of the Stamp Act	1766
Ministry of Chatham	July 29, 1766
Grafton Prime Minister	1767
American Import Duties	1767
The Middlesex Elections	1768-9
Lord North Prime Minister.	1770

1. **Character of George III. 1760.**—George III. had been
educated by his mother the Princess of Wales in the principles of
Bolingbroke's *Patriot King*. From her he had learned that it
was his duty to break down that coalition of the great Whig
families which ruled England by means of the corrupting influence
of wealth. "George, be a king," were the words which she had
dinned into his ears. He came to the throne resolved to overthrow
the Whig party connection by setting his own personal authority
above that of the great Whig borough-owners, and to govern, in the
interest of the whole nation, by ministers who, having been selected by himself, would be contented to carry out his policy and
to act at his dictation. To a certain extent his intentions resembled those of Charles I. Both were well-meaning and desirous of
governing in the interests of the nation; but the political situation of
the eighteenth differed much from that of the seventeenth century.
Charles I. defied the House of Commons, whereas George III.
knew that it was necessary to have the House of Commons on his
side, and he knew that it could only be gained by a lavish employment of corruption. Personally, he was simple in his tastes, and
strictly moral in his habits ; but in pursuit of his political aims he

employed men of the vilest character, and recklessly lavished places and gifts of money on those whose services he required. He seems to have thought that, as the House of Commons chose to put itself up to sale, it was better that he rather than Newcastle should be its purchaser.

2. The Fall of Pitt. 1761.—George III. and Pitt joined in detesting the yoke of the Whig families; but they differed as to the remedy for the disease. George III. aimed at crushing them by the exercise of the powers of the Crown; Pitt, by appealing to the people for support. The king's first object, therefore, was to get rid of Pitt. Pitt had raised enemies in the Cabinet by his arrogance, and even amongst his friends there was a growing feeling that all necessary objects of the war had been accomplished. In **1761** Pitt was ready to make peace with France, and was only pursuing his conquests in order to obtain such terms as appeared to him to be reasonable. In June, **1761**, there were fresh English successes, and France would probably have submitted to Pitt's terms, if Charles III., who had recently become king of Spain, had not renewed the Family Compact, knowing that the vast colonial empire of Spain was endangered by the predominance of England in North America. Pitt, having secret intelligence of what had happened, urged the Cabinet to declare war on Spain at once. The Cabinet, however, regarding him as a firebrand, refused to follow him, and on October 5, Pitt resigned office.

3. Resignation of Newcastle and the Peace of Paris. 1762—1763.—Pitt was justified by the event. Spain declared war as soon as she thought it convenient to do so; she was, however, utterly unprepared for it. In **1762** one English expedition reduced Cuba and another reduced Manilla, whilst Spanish commerce was swept from the sea. Pitt got all the credit because it was known that he had foreseen the struggle and had made the preparations which had proved successful. In the meanwhile, the ministry was hopelessly divided. Alongside of Newcastle and the Whigs were new ministers who had been introduced by George III. In May, **1762**, Newcastle was driven to resign, and was succeeded by Lord Bute, the nominee of the king. Peace negotiations had for some time been carried on, and on February 10, **1763**, the Peace of Paris was signed. England regained Minorca in the Mediterranean, whilst her possession of Canada, Nova Scotia, and Cape Breton, besides that of Senegal and of several West Indian islands, was acknowledged by the French. Spain ceded Florida to England and acquired Louisiana from France, receiving back again the other colonies which she had lost. In India, France received back the towns which had been taken from her, but she could not regain the influence which had passed from her, and England thus retained her predominance in India as well as in America. Frederick complained bitterly that England had abandoned him ; yet he suffered little loss in consequence. His enemies gave up their attempt to destroy him, and almost at the same time that peace was signed by England with France and Spain at Paris, he signed the peace of Hubertsburg, which left him in full possession of his dominions. The result of the Seven Years' War was briefly this, that the British race had become predominant in North America, and that the Prussia of Frederick the Great maintained itself against all its enemies.

4. **The King and the Tories.** 1762 - 1763.—In placing Bute in office George III. made his first attempt to break the power of the Whigs. He had already gathered round him the country gentry whose ancestors had formed the strength of the Tory party in the reign of Anne, and who, now that Jacobitism was extinct, were delighted to transfer their devotion to a Hanoverian king who would lead them against the great landowners. They were joined by certain discontented Whigs, and out of this combination sprung up a new Tory Party. Parties vary in their aims from time to time without changing their names, and the new Tory Party ceasing to regard the Dissenters as dangerous, no longer asked for special legislation against them. The principle which now bound the Tories to the King and to one another was their abhorrence of the Whig connection. They constantly declaimed against the party system, generally holding it to be better that George III. should give office to such ministers as he held fit, than that ministers should be appointed at the dictation of the leaders of a parliamentary party.

5. **The King's Friends.**—The principle upheld by the Tories was so far legitimate that Parliamentary parties in those days were not, as is now the case, combinations of members of Parliament holding definite political opinions and constantly appealing for support to the large masses of their countrymen by whom those opinions are shared. The plain fact was that they were composed of wealthy and influential men who, by the possession of boroughs, gained seats in Parliament for men who would vote for them whether they thought them to be right or wrong, and who, if they could obtain office, gained more votes by the attraction of the patronage of which they had the disposal. George III., therefore, if he wished to gain his ends, had to follow their example. He consequently

resolved to rely on members of Parliament known as the king's friends, who voted as he bade them, simply because they thought that he, and not the Whig Lords, would, in future, distribute honours and patronage. In this way George III. deserted the part of a constitutional king to reap the advantages of a party leader, being able, no doubt, to plead that the Whigs had ceased to be a constitutional party and had established themselves in power less by argument than by the possession of patronage. George's attempt to change the balance of politics could not, however, succeed at once. Bute's ministry did not last long. He was a Scotchman, and at that time Scotchmen were very unpopular in England, besides which there were scandals afloat, entirely untrue, about his relations with the king's mother, the Princess of Wales. Mobs insulted and frightened him. He had not sufficient abilities to fill the post of a Prime Minister, and being, unlike Newcastle, aware of his own defects, on April 8, **1763**, he suddenly resigned.

6. **The Three Whig Parties. 1763.**—By this time the king had no longer a united Whig party to contend against. The bulk of the Whigs, indeed, held together, and having selected Lord Rockingham as their leader in the place of Newcastle, had in many ways gained by the change. It is true that Rockingham was not a man of much ability, and was so shy that he seldom ventured to speak in public ; but he was incorruptible himself, and detested the work of corrupting others. Those who followed him renounced the evil ways dear to Newcastle. What these Whigs gained in character they lost in influence over a House of Commons in which many members wanted to be bribed, and did not want to be persuaded. A second party followed the Duke of Bedford. Bedford himself was an independent, though not a very wise politician, but his followers simply put themselves up to auction. The Bedfords, as they were called, understanding that they would command better terms if they hung together, intimated to those who wished for their votes that they would have to buy all, or none. A third party followed Pitt's brother-in-law, George Grenville. Grenville was a thorough man of business, and quite honest ; but he had little knowledge of mankind. He had quarrelled with Pitt because, whilst Pitt thought of the glories of the war, he himself shrank from its enormous costliness, the national debt having nearly doubled during its progress, rising to more than 132,000,000*l.* He had, therefore, after Pitt's resignation and Newcastle's fall, supported Bute, and, now that the king was compelled to choose between Rockingham, Bedford and Grenville, he naturally selected

Grenville as Prime Minister, as having seceded from the great Whig connection.

7. **Grenville and Wilkes. 1763—1764.**—At first the king got on well with Grenville, as they were both inclined to take high-handed proceedings with those who criticised the Government. John Wilkes, a member of the House of Commons, blamed the

The Gift of Mr Henry Grey

Silver coffee-pot belonging to the Salters' Company, 1764.

king's speech in No. 45 of the *North Briton*. The king ordered the prosecution of all concerned in the article, and Lord Halifax, as Secretary of State, issued a warrant for the apprehension of its authors, printers, and publishers. Such a warrant was called a general warrant, because it did not specify the name of any particular person who was to be arrested. On this warrant Wilkes was arrested and sent to the Tower. On May 6, however, he was discharged by Pratt, the Chief Justice of the Common Pleas, on the ground that, by his privilege as a member of Parliament, he was protected from arrest, except for treason, felony, or breach of the peace. Not long afterwards Pratt declared general warrants to be illegal, though there had been several examples of their use. In November, **1763**, the House of Commons, urged on by the king and Grenville, voted No. 45 of the *North Briton* to be a libel, whilst the House of Lords attacked Wilkes on the ground that in the notes of an indecent poem called *An Essay on Woman*, of which he was the author, he had assailed Bishop Warburton, a member of that House. Wilkes, indeed, had never published the poem, but its existence was betrayed by Lord Sandwich, one of the Bedford party, who had been a boon companion of Wilkes, and whose life was as profligate as Wilkes's own. On January 19, **1764**, the House of Commons expelled Wilkes on account of No. 45, and on February 21, in the Court of King's Bench, a verdict was recorded against him both as a libeller and as the author of an obscene poem. Attempts having been made to get rid of him by challenging him to fight duels, he escaped to France and was outlawed by the Court.

8. **George III. and Grenville. 1763—1764.**—Wilkes became suddenly popular because of his indomitable resistance to a king who was at that time unpopular. George III. had shown strength of will, but as yet he had been merely striving for mastery, without proposing any policy which could strike the imaginations of his subjects. All officials who voted against him were dismissed, even when their offices were not political. George III. was as self-willed and dictatorial as Grenville himself, and soon ceased to be on good terms with the Prime Minister. In September, **1763**, Grenville, to increase the number of his supporters in the House of Commons, admitted the Duke of Bedford and his followers to office, but Bedford soon made himself even more disagreeable to the King than Grenville. George III., weary of his ministers, made overtures to Pitt to come to his help, but for a long time they remained without effect, and much as he now disliked both Grenville and Bedford he was compelled to keep them in office.

9. **The Stamp Act. 1765.**—One measure indeed of Grenville's secured the warm support of the king. Since the late war, not only was England burdened with a greatly increased debt, but it had become desirable that a large military force should be kept up for the defence of her increased dominions. The army in America amounted to 10,000 men, and Grenville thought that the

colonists ought to pay the expenses of a force of which they were
to have the chief benefit—especially as the former war had been
carried on in their behalf. If it had been possible, he would have
preferred that the money needed should have been granted by
the colonists themselves. It was, however, extremely improbable
that this would be done. There was no general assembly of the
American colonies with which the home Government could treat.
Each colony had its own separate assembly, and experience had
shown that each colony, even when it granted money at all, was
always unwilling to make a grant for the common service of the
colonies as a whole. Each, in fact, looked after its own interests ;
Virginia, for instance, not having any wish to provide against a
danger threatening Massachusetts, nor Massachusetts any wish to
provide against a danger threatening Virginia. Grenville accordingly
thought that the only authority to which all the colonies would bow
was that of the British Parliament, and, in 1765, he obtained without
difficulty the assent of Parliament to a Stamp Act, calculated to
raise about 100,000*l.*, by a duty on stamps to be placed on legal
documents in America.

10. **The Rockingham Ministry. 1765.**—Before news could
arrive of the effect of the Stamp Act in America, the king had
been so exasperated by the rudeness with which Grenville and
Bedford treated him that, much as he disliked Rockingham and
the old Whigs, he placed them in office until he could find an
opportunity of getting rid of them as well. The new ministers
were weak, not only because the king disliked them and intrigued
against them, but because they refused to resort to bribery, and
were therefore unpopular with the members who wanted to be
bribed. Nor had they any one amongst them of commanding
ability, whilst Pitt, whom Rockingham asked to join him, refused
to have anything to do with the old Whigs, whom he detested
as cordially as did the king.

11. **The Rockingham Ministry and the Repeal of the Stamp
Act. 1766.**—Before Parliament met in December, news reached
England that the Americans had refused to accept the stamped
papers sent out to them, and had riotously attacked the officers
whose duty it was to distribute them. The British Parliament, in
fact, had put itself into the position occupied by Charles I. when he
levied ship-money (see p. 523). It was as desirable in the eighteenth
century that Americans should pay for the army necessary for their
protection as it had been desirable in the seventeenth that Englishmen should pay for the fleet then needed to defend their coasts.

Americans in the eighteenth century however, like Englishmen in
the seventeenth, thought that the first point to be considered was
the authority by which the tax was imposed. If Charles I. might
levy ship-money without consent of Parliament, he might levy
other taxes in the same way, and would thus become absolute
master of England. If the British Parliament could levy a stamp
duty in America, it could levy other duties, and the Americans

Edmund Burke : from a painting by Reynolds in the
National Portrait Gallery.

would thus be entirely at its mercy. The Rockingham ministry
drew back from the prospect of a struggle with the colonists, and,
at its instance, the Stamp Act was repealed early in **1766**, though
its repeal was accompanied by a Declaratory Act asserting the
right of the British Parliament to tax the colonies as well as to
legislate for them.

12. **Pitt and Burke. 1766.**—In taking this course the Rockingham ministry was supported by Edmund Burke, who now entered
Parliament for the first time, and who was the greatest political

thinker of the age. As Pitt, too, applauded the repeal of the Stamp Act, Rockingham made fresh but unsuccessful efforts to induce him to combine with the ministry. Yet, though Pitt and Burke agreed in disliking the Stamp Act, their reasons for so doing were not the same. Pitt held that the British Parliament had a right to impose duties on American trade, for the sake of regulating it—in other words, of securing a monopoly for British manufactures—but that it had no right to levy internal taxes in America. Burke, on the other hand, detested the very idea of claiming or disclaiming a right to tax, holding that in all political matters the only thing worth discussion was whether any particular action was expedient. America, according to him, was not to be taxed, simply because it was not worth while to irritate the Americans for the sake of any sum of money which could be obtained from them. This was not the only point on which Pitt and Burke differed. Burke wished to found government on a combination amongst men of property honestly and intelligently seeking their country's good, and using the influence which their wealth gave them to fill the benches of the House of Commons with men as right-minded as themselves. Pitt, on the other hand, distrusting all combinations between wealthy landowners, preferred appealing to popular support.

13. **The Chatham Ministry. 1766—1767.**—There was this much of agreement between George III. and Pitt, that they both disliked the Rockingham Whigs, and, in July, 1766, the king dismissed Rockingham, created Pitt Earl of Chatham, and made him Prime Minister with the office of Lord Privy Seal. Chatham formed his ministry by selecting men of all kinds of opinion who were willing to serve under him. Before the end of the year his health broke down, and his mind was so completely deranged as to render him incapable of attending to business. In 1767 the Duke of Grafton, being First Lord of the Treasury, became nominally Prime Minister, but he was quite incapable of controlling his subordinates, and the Chancellor of the Exchequer, Charles Townshend, a brilliant, unwise speaker, had everything his own way.

14. **American Import Duties. 1767.**—Although the Stamp Act had been repealed, the irritation caused by its imposition had not died away in America, and the authority of British Acts of Parliament was set at naught by the colonists. In 1767 Townshend obtained from Parliament an Act imposing on America import duties on glass, red and white lead, painters' colours, paper, and tea. The produce was estimated at 40,000*l.*, and was to be em-

ployed, not in maintaining an army to defend the colonies, but in paying their judges and governors, with the object of making them dependent on the Crown, and independent of the public opinion of the colonists. From the point of view of the British Parliament, the colonists were like unruly children, who required to be kept in order. In America, on the other hand, the new duties were denounced as an attempt to govern America from England. Not only did people agree together to avoid the consumption of articles subject to the new duties, but attacks were made on the revenue officers who had to collect the money, and whatever violence was committed against them, juries refused to convict the offenders. On September 4, **1767**, before further steps could be taken in England, Townshend died. His successor as Chancellor of the Exchequer was Lord North, who was inclined to carry out Townshend's policy. In reality, however, the king was himself the head of the ministry.

15. **The Middlesex Election. 1768—1769.**—Though before the end of **1768** Chatham recovered his health, he felt himself helpless, and formally resigned office. In that year there was a general election, and Wilkes, reappearing from France, was elected in Middlesex. His election was a token of a wide-spread dissatisfaction, not so much with the taxation of America as with the corruption by which the king had won Parliament to his side. In February, **1769**, the House of Commons expelled Wilkes. He was then re-elected, and the House replied not only by expelling him again, but by incapacitating him from sitting in the House during the existing Parliament. When an election was again held, Wilkes was again at the head of the poll, but the House declared his opponent, Colonel Luttrell, to be duly elected, though the votes for him had been very few. A grave constitutional question was thus raised. George Grenville and the Rockingham Whigs agreed in asserting that nothing short of an Act of Parliament passed by both Houses could deprive the electors of their right of choosing whom they would as their representative, though they admitted that the House might expel a member so chosen as often as it pleased. To this doctrine Chatham, who had now recovered his health, gave his warm support. It seemed as if it would be impossible for the ministry to hold out against such a weight of authority and argument.

16. "**Wilkes and Liberty.**" **1769.**—The opponents of the court on the question of the Middlesex election had on their side two dangerous allies—a libeller and the mob. The libeller, who called

himself 'Junius,' was probably Sir Philip Francis. He attacked
with malignant bitterness the king and all his instruments. The mob,
actuated by a sense of the unfairness with which Wilkes was treated,

George III. in 1767: from a painting by Allan Ramsay in the
National Portrait Gallery.

took his part warmly. "Wilkes and liberty" was their cry. At the
time of the Middlesex election '45' was freely chalked up on the
doors of the houses, in allusion to the condemned number of the

North Briton. Noblemen most hostile to Wilkes were compelled to illuminate their houses in honour of his success at the poll, and the grave Austrian ambassador was pulled out of his carriage and '45' chalked on the soles of his boots. In June, Wilkes, having surrendered to take his trial for the publication of No. 45 and the *Essay on Woman* (see pp. 769, 770), was committed to prison, whence, on May 10, an enormous crowd strove to rescue him, and was only driven off after the soldiers had fired and killed five or six persons. Wilkes was, in June, sentenced to fine and imprisonment as a libeller, but the citizens of London, as enthusiastic in his favour as the crowd, chose him as Alderman whilst he was still in prison. The badness of his character was forgotten, and his pertinacious stand against the Court was alone remembered.

17. **Lord North Prime Minister. 1770.**—When Parliament met, in January, 1770, Chatham, now again in full possession of his powers, took up the cause of Wilkes, maintaining that the House of Commons had no right to place Luttrell in his seat. The very sound of his voice dissolved the composite Ministry. Those who had entered it as his followers rallied to their leader. Pratt, who had become Lord Chancellor with the title of Lord Camden, was dismissed. The king, finding that no notable lawyer agreed with him as to the right of the House of Commons to disqualify Wilkes from being elected, persuaded Charles Yorke, an eminent lawyer and a hitherto devoted follower of Rockingham, to accept the Chancellorship, although in so doing he would have to argue against his own settled convictions. Yorke, tempted by the greatness of the prize, accepted the offer, but he was unable to bear the reproaches of his friends, and, for very shame, committed suicide. Grafton resigned office, and other ministers followed his example. The king then made Lord North First Lord of the Treasury, and gave him the position of a Prime Minister, though the title was still held to be invidious, and North himself objected to have it used in his own case. North was an able man, skilful in the management of public affairs, and honestly a supporter of strong measures against Wilkes and the Americans, and he fully adopted the principle that the king was to choose his ministers and to direct their policy. If North could maintain himself in Parliament, the new Toryism, of which the dependence of ministers on the Crown was the leading feature, would have won the day.

CHAPTER XLIX

THE STRUGGLE FOR AMERICAN INDEPENDENCE. 1770—1783

LEADING DATES

Reign of George III., 1760—1820

Lord North Prime Minister	1770
Cargoes of Tea thrown into Boston Harbour . . .	1773
Beginning of the American War	1775
Declaration of Independence	1776
Capitulation of Saratoga	1777
War with France	1778
Burke's Bill for Economical Reform	1780
Capitulation of Yorktown	1781
Second Rockingham Ministry	1782
Shelburne Ministry	1782
Peace of Paris	1783

1. **North and the Opposition. 1770.**--The opposition, seemingly strong, was weakened by a conflict of opinion amongst its leaders. Chatham declared for Parliamentary reform, suggesting that a third member should be given to each county, as the freeholders, who at that time alone voted in county elections, were more independent than the borough electors. Burke and the Rockingham Whigs, on the other hand, objected to any constitutional change as likely in the end to throw power into the hands of the ignorant. The violence of mobs since Wilkes's election no doubt strengthened the conservative feeling of this section of the Whigs, and, at the same time, made strongly in favour of the Government, because in times of disorder quiet people are apt to support the Government whether they agree with it politically or not. North was well fitted to take advantage of this state of opinion. He was an easy-going man, who never lost his temper and never gave unnecessary offence. At the same time, he was an able party manager, and, though not a great statesman, was a sensible politician. With the king at his back, he had at his disposal all the engines of corruption by which votes were gained, and though members of Parliament had for some time ceased to sell their votes for ready money as they had done in the days of Walpole and Newcastle, they still continued to sell them for pensions,

offices, and especially for sinecures. Moreover, North had the advantage of sharing in the king's strong feeling against the conduct of the Americans. Public opinion in England was turning more and more against the Americans, and, for the first time in his reign, George III. found support for his policy in public opinion.

2. **North and the Tea Duty, 1770.**—Only two courses were open to the British Government :—the one to treat the Americans

Lord North : from an engraving by Burke, taken from a
painting by Dance.

as a virtually independent people, allowing them to tax themselves and to govern themselves as they pleased ; the other to compel them to obedience by military force. It is hardly strange that Englishmen were not wise enough to accept the former alternative. They did not perceive that the colonists, in refusing the payment of taxes imposed by others than themselves, had a proper foundation for constitutional resistance, whilst they did perceive that the American resistance was not altogether carried on in a constitutional manner. In Massachusetts, especially, all who were concerned in the collection of the import duties were treated with contumely. Soldiers were insulted in the streets. An informer was tarred and feathered. Lord North was, indeed, sensible enough to perceive that Townshend's import duties roused unnecessary irritation, especially as the net income derived from them was less than 300*l.* He induced Parliament to repeal all the duties except that of 3*d.* a pound on tea ; but he openly acknowledged that he kept on the tea-duty, not because anything was to be gained by it, but simply to assert the right of England to tax the colonies. In America a sullen resistance continued to be offered to this claim, becoming more and more defiant as time passed on.

3. **The Freedom of Reporting. 1771.**—In Parliament Lord North gathered strength. George Grenville having died in **1770** and Bedford early in **1771**, the followers of these two leaders resolved to support the Ministry. So, too, did Grafton, who had lately resigned office rather than oppose Chatham, and Wedderburn, an unscrupulous lawyer who had professed the strongest opposition principles, but who now sold himself for the office of Solicitor-General. The combined Opposition was reduced to a hopeless minority. Yet, even thus, though unable to influence the American policy of the Ministry, it was, on one occasion, able to bring about a valuable reform at home. The House of Commons had long been jealous of the reporting of its debates and of the comments of newspapers on its members. In February, **1771**, Colonel Onslow, a member of the House, complained that a newspaper had called him ' little cocking George,' and a ' paltry, insignificant insect.' The proposal to summon the printers to the bar was resisted by obstructive motions from both the followers of Rockingham and the followers of Chatham, and when it was at last carried time had slipped by, and it was found difficult to catch all the printers. One of them, named Miller, was arrested in the city by a messenger of the House, but the messenger, in turn, was arrested and brought before the Lord Mayor and two aldermen—one of whom was Wilkes —who put the messenger in prison for infringing the city charter by making an arrest in the city without the authority of its magistrates. The House of Commons, prudently leaving Wilkes alone, sent the Lord Mayor and the other alderman to the Tower, where they were royally feasted by the city till the end of the session, after which time no imprisonment, by order of either House, can be enforced. The Opposition had gained its point, as since that time no attempt

has been made to stop the reporting of debates. It was the freedom of reporting which ultimately enabled Parliamentary reform to be effected without danger. Only a people which is allowed to have knowledge of the actions and words of its representatives can be trusted to control them.

4. **Continued Resistance in America. 1770—1772.**—In America resistance to the British Government rose and fell from year to year. In 1770 some soldiers at Boston fired, with deadly effect, on a crowd which threatened them, and this ' Boston massacre,' as it was called, so exasperated the townsmen that the governor had to withdraw the troops. Lawlessness spread, as is usually the case when a government has lost the support of public opinion. The revenue officers were subjected to outrage, and, in 1772, a small vessel of war, the ' Gaspee,' was captured and burnt.

5. **The Boston Tea Ships. 1773.**—The people of New England, though they had agreed to avoid the use of tea, found it difficult to abstain from so pleasant a beverage, and in 1773 Lord North struck a bargain with the East India Company to carry a large quantity to Boston. When the tea ships arrived, a meeting of the townsmen was held, and, after a vain attempt to persuade the governor to send them away, a number of young men, disguised as Red Indians, rushed on board in the dark, broke open the chests with tomahawks, and flung the whole of the tea into the harbour.

6. **Repressive Measures. 1774.**—When the news of this violence reached England, it was evident to all that either the British Parliament must abandon its claim to enforce the payment of the tea duty or it would have to maintain its authority by force. Burke pleaded for a return to the older system under which Great Britain had been respected for so many years. " Revert," he said, " to your old principles . . . leave America, if she have taxable matter in her, to tax herself. I am not here going into a distinction of rights, nor attempting to mark their boundaries. I do not enter into these metaphysical distinctions. I hate the very sound of them. Leave the Americans as they anciently stood. Be content to bind America by laws of trade ; you have always done it. Let this be your reason for binding her trade. Do not burden them with taxes ; you were not used to do so from the beginning. Let his be your reason for not taxing. These are the arguments of states and kingdoms. Leave the rest to the schools, for there only they may be discussed with safety." The king, Lord North, and Parliament, thought otherwise. They saw that there was anarchy in America, as far as English law was concerned, and they con-

Distribution of His Majesty's Maundy by the Sub-almoner to His Majesty in the Chapel Royal of Whitehall: from an engraving by Basire after a drawing by Grimm, 1773.

ceived it to be their duty and their right to bring it to an end. In 1774 was passed the Boston Port Act, prohibiting the landing or shipping of goods at Boston ; the Massachusetts Government Act, transferring the appointment of the Council, or Upper House, together with that of all judges and administrative officers, from a popular electorate to the Crown ; and another Act forbidding public meetings without the leave of the governor. In order to keep down resistance, a soldier, General Gage, was sent to be governor of Massachusetts.

7. **The Congress of Philadelphia and the British Parliament. 1774.**—The American colonies had always been divided amongst themselves. The four which made up what was popularly called New England—Massachusetts, New Hampshire, Connecticut, and Rhode Island—had been founded by the Puritans in the seventeenth century, and still retained the democratic character then impressed upon them. It was expected in England that the other nine colonies, where different habits prevailed—New York, Pennsylvania, New Jersey, Delaware, Maryland, Virginia, North Carolina, South Carolina, and Georgia—would take no part in the struggle, if one there was to be. These colonies, however, were frightened lest the British Parliament should alter their constitutions as it had just altered that of Massachusetts, and, in September, 1774, a congress, attended by deputies of all the colonies except Georgia, met at Philadelphia under the name of the Continental Congress. Though this Assembly had no legal powers, it had popular support, and it directed the stoppage of all importation from and exportation to Great Britain till the grievances of the colonies had been redressed. There was no sign of any wish for separation, and there is reason to believe that those amongst the colonists who called themselves Loyalists, and would have clung to the connection with Great Britain in spite of all that was happening, formed at least a third of the population. The majority, however, including all the most active spirits, was determined to resist unless concessions were granted. In the meanwhile, preparations for resistance were made, especially in New England ; officers were selected, and ' minute men '—so called because they offered to fly to arms at a minute's notice—were enrolled in great numbers.

8. **Lexington and Bunker's Hill. 1775.**—Both in America and in England illusions prevailed. The Americans thought that the British Parliament would repeal its obnoxious measures, if only the American case were fairly represented to it, whilst the British

Parliament continued to regard the power of resistance in America as altogether contemptible. Hostilities began without any deliberate purpose on either side. On April 18, **1775**, a small British force, sent from Boston to seize some arms at Concord, drove off on its way a small party of American volunteers at Lexington. On its return, on the 19th, it found the hedges and walls by the roadside lined with a superior number of volunteers, and only effected its retreat with heavy loss. After this all New England sprang to arms. On May 10 Ticonderoga was seized, and the command of Lake Champlain gained, whilst on June 16 about 1,500 insurgents entrenched themselves at the top of Breed's Hill, a height divided from Boston by the Charles river. On June 17, an English force was twice repulsed in an attempt to gain the position, and only succeeded on the third attempt after the ammunition of the Americans had been exhausted. The fight is usually known as the Battle of Bunker's Hill, a neighbouring height on which no fighting actually took place. The affair, taken by itself, was not of great importance, but it showed how well Americans could fight behind entrenchments, and how capable they were of developing military qualities unsuspected by the British generals.

9. **Conciliatory Efforts. 1775.**—After blood had been shed conciliatory efforts were less likely to be successful. An offer to abandon the British claim to tax any American colony which would provide for its own defence and its civil government had been made in March by Lord North, but it was not known in America till after the conflict at Lexington, and was then summarily rejected. On May 10 a second congress was held, at Philadelphia, and as it was attended by delegates from all the thirteen colonies, it assumed the style of 'The Congress of the United Colonies.' On July 8, the Congress set forth terms of reconciliation in a petition known as 'The Olive Branch Petition,' but its offers proved as unacceptable in England as Lord North's had been in America.

10. **George Washington in Command. 1775.**—Congress, whilst offering peace, prepared for war, and commenced raising an army in its own service, to replace the troops which had hitherto been raised by the separate colonies, and, on June 15, two days before the capture of Breed's Hill, appointed George Washington commander of this so-called Continental army. Washington was a good soldier, who had fought with distinction in the Seven Years' War, and was especially skilled in military organisation. His

moral qualifications were even higher than his intellectual. He was absolutely unselfish, and possessed of infinite patience. Never were such qualities more needed. The adverse criticisms of English soldiers were, to a great extent, justified by the American volunteers. They were brave enough, but they were unwilling to submit to the discipline without which an army cannot long exist ; and it sometimes happened that whole regiments, having enlisted for a certain time, would insist on going home when that time expired, even from the presence of the enemy. Washington's subordinate officers, too, constantly quarrelled with one another, whilst each one considered himself a far better soldier than the commander-in-chief.

11. **Progress of the War. 1775—1776.**—In the autumn of 1775 the war languished. An American army attempted to over-run Canada, but the Canadians, being Catholics of French descent, had no love for the New England Puritans, and the enterprise failed disastrously. Gage, who commanded the British army in America, was not a vigorous soldier. His successor, Sir William Howe, was equally remiss, and, on March 16, 1776, evacuated Boston. Yet it was not altogether the fault of these two commanders that they did nothing. So little had the British Parliament expected resistance that it had allowed the numbers of the army to sink to a low ebb. In 1774 the whole of the king's forces did not exceed 17,547 men, and when, in 1775, an attempt was made to raise them to 55,000, it was found impossible to obtain the required number of men in Great Britain. In despair the Government had recourse to a bargain with some German princes for the sale of their subjects. In this way 17,742 unhappy Germans were sent off, like so many slaves, to serve George III. in re-conquering America.

12. **The Declaration of Independence and the Struggle in New Jersey. 1776—1777.**— Nothing did more to alienate the Americans than this attempt to put them down by foreign troops. The result was the Declaration of Independence voted by Congress on July 4, 1776. The United States, as they were now to be called, disclaimed all obedience to the British Crown. They had still, however, to make good their words by action, and during the remainder of the year they were distinctly inferior in the field to their adversaries. On September 15 Howe occupied New York, Washington having been compelled to draw off his insubordinate soldiery. The plundering and violence of the American troops alienated a great part of the population, and in December Washington was driven out of New Jersey by Lord Cornwallis. The

Somerset House—South face of Central Block ; built by Sir William Chambers, 1776–1780.

men deserted in shoals, and the inhabitants of the country through which they passed showed no inclination to assist them. Congress fled from Philadelphia to Baltimore. Washington saw that, unless he could inspire his troops with the ardour of success, his case was hopeless, and on Christmas night he dashed at Trenton, where he surprised the Germans in the midst of their revelry, and carried off 1,000 prisoners. On January 2, 1777, he defeated three British regiments at Princeton. The men of New Jersey rallied round Washington, and New Jersey itself was recovered. The constancy and generalship of Washington had stemmed the tide.

13. **French Assistance to America. 1776 — 1777.** — If Great Britain had had to deal only with the Americans, it could hardly have failed to wear out their resistance, considering how large a part of the population longed for peace rather than for independence. Its own population was 8,000,000, whilst that of the United States was less than 2,000,000. A nation, however, which attacks a people inferior to itself in strength must always take into account the probability that other states, which for any reason bear a grudge against her, will take the part of her weaker enemy. In 1776 France, burning, in the first place, to revenge her defeat in the Seven Years' War, and, in the second place, to break down the British monopoly of American commerce, lent, underhand, large sums of money to America, and gave other assistance in an equally secret way. "All Europe is for us," wrote the American diplomatists who negotiated with France. "Every nation in Europe wishes to see Britain humbled, having all in their turn been offended by her insolence." French volunteers of good birth, of whom the most noted was Lafayette, crossed the Atlantic to take service under Washington.

14. **Brandywine and Saratoga. 1777.** — Such help was insufficient. On September 11, 1777, Howe defeated Washington on the Brandywine, and, pushing onwards, occupied Philadelphia. The vastness of the country, however, fought for the Americans better than their own armies. Whilst Washington was vainly attempting to defend Pennsylvania, Burgoyne, an English officer of repute, was coming down the valley of the Hudson from Canada, hoping to join Clinton, who was to come up the valley from New York. He never reached Clinton. Though he pushed on far, his troops dwindled away and his provisions fell short. The Americans occupied every post around his diminished army, and on October 16 he was forced to capitulate at Saratoga.

15. **The French Alliance with America, and the Death of**

Chatham. 1778.—The British disaster at Saratoga encouraged the French Government, and, on February 6, **1778**, France openly allied herself with America. Lord North offered to yield anything short of independence, and begged the king to relieve him of office and to appoint Chatham. George III. refused to admit Chatham except as North's subordinate. Chatham, though he declined this insulting offer, opposed, on April 7, a motion by one of the Rockingham Whigs for acknowledging the independence of America, and thus practically gave his support to North. He was ready to give way on all the points originally in dispute, but he could not reconcile himself to the abandonment of the colonies, and he firmly protested against 'the dismemberment of this ancient and most noble monarchy.' As he spoke his voice failed him, and, on rising to make a second speech, he fell back in a fit of apoplexy. On May 11 he died. With many faults, he stands forth amongst the greatest figures in English history. He had not merely done great things—he had inspired England with confidence in herself.

16. **Valley Forge. 1777—1778.**—French help was offered to America none too soon. In the winter of **1777—78** Washington's army at Valley Forge was almost destitute. Pennsylvania had little sympathy with him in the struggle, and Washington himself spoke of it as an 'enemy's country.' For three days his soldiers had no bread, and nearly 3,000 men were unfit for duty because they were 'bare-footed and otherwise naked.' Numbers deserted, and the distress increased as winter wore on. When spring arrived the result of the French alliance was clearly seen. In June the British evacuated Philadelphia, and in July a French fleet appeared off the American coast. Yet the operations of **1778** were desultory. The unwillingness of the Americans to support their army was so great that, at the end of **1778**, Washington was almost as despondent as he had been at the beginning of the year.

17. **George III. and Lord North. 1779.**—Each side saw its own difficulties, and, in **1779**, every statesman in England was to the full as despondent as Washington. Lord North himself thought it impossible to re-conquer America now that France was her ally. George III., with a determination which, when it succeeds, is called firmness, and, when it fails, is called obstinacy, declared that he would never yield or give office to any man who would not first sign a declaration that he was 'resolved to keep the empire entire, and that no troops shall consequently be withdrawn from America nor independence ever allowed.' To the king's resolute will North reluctantly submitted, though in June **1779** Spain allied

herself with France and America against Great Britain. North again and again offered his resignation, but the king forced him to retain office.

18. **The French in the Channel.** **1779.**—The hour of French vengeance had come. Early in 1779 a French naval squadron seized the British possessions in Senegal and on the Gambia, and in the summer of the same year a combined French and Spanish fleet sailed up the Channel, which the British fleet did not even venture to meet. For the first time since the battle of La Hogue the French navy was master of the sea. The fact was that the circumstances under which the French navy now appeared at sea were different from those under which it had suffered defeat in the Seven Years' War. In the first place, Louis XVI., who had been king of France since 1774, had paid special attention to the navy, and had both increased the number of his war-ships and had done his utmost to render their crews efficient. In the second place, he abandoned the policy which had been pursued by every ruler of France since the days of Richelieu, and which consisted in throwing the whole strength of the country into territorial aggression on its land frontier, thus weakening its ability to engage successfully in naval warfare. The new king, by keeping at peace with his neighbours on the Continent, was thus enabled to struggle with better chance of success against England, the old maritime rival of France.

19. **English Successes in America.** **1779—1780.**—In America the British had still the upper hand, as far as fighting was concerned. In Georgia, the English beat off an attack by the Americans at Savannah, though the latter were supported by a French fleet under D'Estaing, who had previously reduced some of the West India Islands. On May 12, 1780, Sir Henry Clinton took Charleston, and after his return to New York, Lord Cornwallis, whom he left behind in command, defeated the American general, Gates, at Camden in South Carolina. It seemed as if the whole of the southern states, where the opposition to Great Britain was not nearly so strong as in the north, would be brought into subjection. The enormous distances which the British had to traverse again told against them. Cornwallis had not men enough to hold the country which he had subdued and to gain new ground as well, and he was driven back as soon as he advanced into North Carolina. Yet, in spite of this failure, the gains of the British were so considerable as to increase the alarm of those Americans who had hoped for a decisive result from their combination with France and Spain. In September,

1780, Benedict Arnold, a general in whom Washington placed complete confidence, plotted to betray to the British commander at New York the forts on the hills round the Hudson. If the plot had succeeded, the struggle for American independence would have been at an end. It was, however, detected, and, though Arnold himself escaped, Major André, the British officer who negotiated with him, was caught within the American lines and hanged as a spy.

19. **Economical Reform. 1779—1780.**—In England there was, as yet, no active opposition to the continuance of the war, but there was a growing dissatisfaction with its apparently endless expense. Towards the close of **1779** the opposition turned this current of feeling against the employment of the patronage of the Crown, by which George III. secured votes in Parliament. They raised a cry, which was fully justified, in favour of Economical Reform, and they gathered large public meetings in their support. The practice of bringing the opinion of public meetings to bear upon Parliament was of recent origin, having sprung into existence in **1769,** during the agitation consequent on Wilkes's election. In **1779** it spread over the country. The signal was given by a meeting at York, presided over by Sir George Savile, a highly-respected member of the Rockingham party. These meetings were everywhere attended by the orderly classes, and were an indication of the dissatisfaction widely felt with a system through which the House of Commons had become a mere instrument in the king's hands. In February, **1780,** Burke brought in a Bill for the abolition of sinecures, the only use of which was the purchase of votes ; and, in a magnificent speech, pleaded the cause of Economical Reform. He put the case in a nutshell when he announced that ' the king's turnspit was a peer of Parliament.' The House was too alarmed at the outburst of popular feeling to refuse to the Bill a second reading, but it rejected its leading clauses in Committee, and the Bill was consequently dropped. In April, however, Dunning, a Whig lawyer, carried a resolution that ' the influence of the Crown has increased, is increasing, and ought to be diminished.'

20. **Parliamentary Reform and the Gordon Riots.**—Though the opposition was united in favour of Economical Reform, which would render the House of Commons less dependent on the King, it was divided on the subject of Parliamentary Reform, which would have made it more dependent on the nation. Burke, with the greater number of the Rockingham party, opposed the latter, but it was supported by Charles James Fox, the son of the Henry Fox

who had been noted as the most corrupt minister of a corrupt
time (see pp. 747, 751). The younger Fox was, in private
life, a lover of pleasure, especially at the gaming-table, thereby
alienating from him the more decorous portion of mankind. Yet,
in spite of this, the charm of his kindly nature gained him warm
personal friendships, and often disarmed the hostility of opponents.
In public life he showed himself early as a ready and fluent speaker,

Charles James Fox as a young man : from an engraving by
Watson from a painting by Reynolds.

always prepared with an answer on the spur of the moment.
He was ever ready to throw himself enthusiastically into all
generous and noble causes, praising beyond measure and abusing
beyond measure, and too deficient in tact and self-restraint to
secure power on the rare occasions when he attained it.

21. **The Gordon Riots. 1780.**—On June 2, **1780,** the Duke of
Richmond called, in the House of Lords, for manhood suffrage and

The Riot in Broad Street in the city of London] on the seventh of June, 1780: from a print engraved by James Heath after a picture by Francis Wheatley.

annual Parliaments. That very day the unfitness of the multitude of those times for political power received a strong illustration. In 1778 Sir George Savile had carried a Bill relieving Roman Catholics of some of the hardships inflicted on them by the law. The cry of 'No Popery' was at once raised, and, whilst the Duke of Richmond was speaking to the peers, a mob, led by Lord George Gordon, a half-crazy fanatic, poured down to Westminster with a petition for the repeal of Savile's Act. Members of both Houses were hustled and ill-used, and for some time the mob endeavoured to burst into the House of Commons. Failing in this, they streamed off, and sacked and burnt the chapels of Roman Catholic ambassadors. The mob, however, loved riot more than they hated Popery. They burnt Newgate and liberated the prisoners. They fell, with special eagerness, upon the houses of magistrates. For six days they were in complete possession of a considerable part of London, plundering and setting fire to houses at their pleasure. Soldiers alone could arrest such a flood of mischief; and when, at last, soldiers were ordered to attack the mob, the riot was suppressed.

22. **The Armed Neutrality. 1780.** — The suppression of the riots in London brought back some support to the king, but the enemies of England abroad were growing stronger. English ships claimed the right of search in neutral vessels on the high seas, and they proceeded to confiscate enemies' goods found in them. They also seized neutral vessels trading with ports of their enemies, which they declared to be blockaded, even when they were not in sufficient force to exercise an effective blockade. A league sprung up amongst the northern states, headed by Russia, to establish an 'Armed Neutrality' for protection against such attacks. This league, supported by France, advanced what was then the new doctrine, that 'Free ships make free goods,' and proclaimed that 'paper blockades'—that is to say, blockades not enforced by a sufficient naval squadron—were inadmissible. The Dutch Republic moreover adopted this view and resisted the right of search when used by the English, just as the English, in Walpole's time, had resisted it when exercised by the Spaniards (see p. 728), and in December, 1780, England declared war on the Republic.

23. **The Capitulation of Yorktown. 1781.**—The campaign of 1781 was looked forward to as likely to be decisive. Cornwallis pushed on to the conquest of North Carolina, and, though his advanced guard was defeated at Cowpens in January, in March he routed an American army under Greene at Guilford. Once more the enormous size of the country frustrated the plans of the English

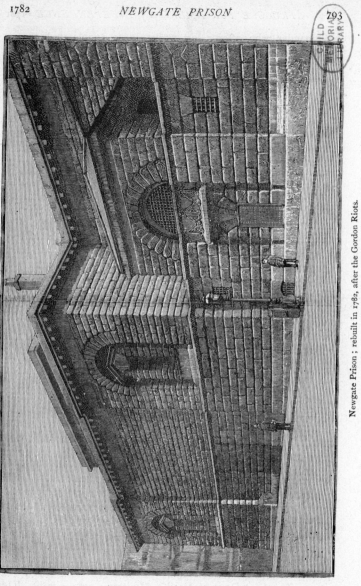

Newgate Prison ; rebuilt in 1782, after the Gordon Riots.

commander, who, after a few weeks, being unable to hold any part of the Carolinas except Charleston, went off to Virginia. The American army was quite unable to inflict a serious defeat on the British in the field. The states themselves left it unpaid and afforded it but scanty means of support. The men deserted in shoals, and those who remained were obliged to obtain food by oppression. "Scarce any state," wrote an American general, "has at this hour an eighth part of its quota in the field. . . . Instead of having the prospect of a glorious offensive campaign before us, we have a bewildered and gloomy one, unless we should receive a powerful aid of ships, land troops, and money, from our generous allies." In expectation of this help the American forces again grew in numbers, so that Cornwallis, though unconquered, was compelled to fortify a post at Yorktown on the shore of the Chesapeake, where, as long as he was master of the sea, he could defy his enemies. The French fleet under De Grasse, however, soon gained the mastery, and blockaded Yorktown on the side of the water, while the Americans blockaded it on the side of the land. On October 19 Cornwallis surrendered, and the American War was virtually at an end.

24. **American success. 1781.**—American Independence had been the work of an active minority, especially vigorous in New England, and in some other parts further south. This minority was always ready to take advantage of every circumstance arising in their favour, and availing themselves of the assistance of the foreign enemies of England. The cause of America was, to some extent, the cause of England herself. The same reasons which made Parliament ready to set aside by an act of power the resistance of the Americans to the payment of a tax to which their representatives had not consented had weighed with the House of Commons when they set aside the repeatedly declared choice of the Middlesex electors. In the one case the British Parliament, in the other case the British House of Commons, insisted on having its way, because it believed itself in the right. The principle of self-government—of the system which acknowledges that it is better to allow a people to blunder in order that they may learn by experience, than to coerce them for their own good—was at stake in both. It seemed as easy to suppress America as it was to suppress the Middlesex electors ; and when England discovered that this was not the case, she learnt a lesson which would teach her in the future how much consideration was due to those dependencies which were still left.

25. **The Last Days of North's Ministry. 1781 — 1782.** — The

news of the surrender at Yorktown reached England on No-vember 25. " O God ! " cried North when he heard it, " it is all over." The king insisted on North's retaining office and pro-longing the struggle. During the next few months Minorca sur-rendered to the Spaniards, and De Grasse's fleet captured one West India island after another. The supporters of the ministry in Parliament deserted it, and on March 20, **1782**, North resigned.

26. **The Rockingham Ministry. 1782.**— Much to his annoy-ance, George III. had to place the opposition in office, with Rockingham as Prime Minister, and to allow the new ministers to open negotiations on the basis of the acknowledgment of American independence. The two most important members of Rockingham's second administration were Fox and Lord Shelburne, the latter being the leader of that section of the Whigs which had fol-lowed Chatham. The king, who hated the Rockingham section as an aristocratic faction, intrigued with Shelburne against the other members of the ministry. As Shelburne disliked Fox personally, the prospect of a united ministry was not encouraging. For the moment, however, the new ministers did plenty of good work. They opened negotiations for peace, and were likely to obtain the better terms, as on April 12 Admiral Rodney gained a decisive victory in the West Indies over De Grasse's fleet. At home, the ministers set themselves to purify Parliament. They carried measures, in the first place, disqualifying revenue officers, who were liable to dismissal by the Government, from voting at elections, and, in the second place, disqualifying contractors from sitting in the House of Commons on the ground that it was their interest not to offend the ministers. Burke's Economical Reform Bill, which had been thrown out in **1781**, was also passed, in a modified form, in **1782**. Though the king still retained sufficient patronage to make him formidable, he would now have less corrupting influence than before.

27. **Irish Religion and Commerce. 1778.**—The Irish Parlia-ment had, for some time, been growing discontented with its subordinate position. It is true that it represented the Protestants only, but its desire to make itself independent had the result of rendering it unusually inclined to conciliate the Catholics. In **1778** it passed a Relief Bill, repealing the worst of the persecuting acts (see p. 686). The leader in this movement was Grattan, who pro-nounced that ' the Irish Protestant could never be free till the Irish Catholic had ceased to be a slave.' In the same year some slight diminution was effected in the restrictions which had been

imposed on Irish commerce, but the outcry raised by English manufacturers was too loud to allow North to concede to Ireland as much as he would willingly have done.

28. **The Irish Volunteers. 1778 — 1781.** — Irish Protestants were, for every reason, warm supporters of the connection with England, but they were hostile to the existing system, because it impoverished them by stopping their trade. They asked for liberty to export what they pleased and to import what they pleased. To gain this they needed legislative independence, their own Parliament being not only prohibited, by Poynings' law (see p. 350), from passing any act which had not been first approved by the English Privy Council, but being bound by a further act of George I. which declared Ireland to be subject to laws made in the British Parliament. The war with France gave to the Irish Protestants the opportunity which they sought. England, bent upon the reconquest of America, had no troops to spare for the defence of Ireland, and the Irish Protestants came forward as volunteers in defence of their own country. At the end of **1781** they had 80,000 men in arms, and with this force behind their backs they now asked for legislative independence.

29. **Irish Legislative Independence. 1782.** — In **1782**, with recent experience gained in America, Rockingham's Government shrank from opposing a movement so formidably supported. At Fox's motion the British Parliament passed an act, by which the act of George I. binding Ireland to obey laws made in Great Britain was repealed, and Poynings' law was so modified as to put an end to the control of the British Privy Council over the making of laws in Ireland. However, the independent Parliament at Dublin—Grattan's Parliament, as it is sometimes called—had two sources of weakness. In the first place the House of Commons was chosen by Protestants alone ; in the second place it had no control over the executive government, which was exercised not, as in England, by ministers responsible to Parliament, but by the Lord Lieutenant, who was appointed by, and was responsible to, the Government in England. Nor were there any constitutional means by which either the two Parliaments in conjunction, or any third body with powers either derived from them or superior to them, could decide upon questions in which both peoples were interested.

30. **The Shelburne Ministry and the Peace of Paris. 1782—1783.** — On July 1, **1782**, Rockingham died, and the king at once appointed Shelburne Prime Minister, who, as he thought, would

The Siege of Gibraltar, 1781: from a contemporary print.

be more likely than any of the other ministers to help him to keep down the Whig aristocracy. Fox, who detested Shelburne, and had for some time been engaged in a bitter dispute with him on the subject of the negotiations for peace, resigned together with others of Rockingham's followers. When Shelburne became Prime Minister the negotiations were far advanced. France and Spain were, however, anxious, before they signed a peace, to regain Gibraltar, which their fleets and armies had been besieging for more than three years. On September 13 a tremendous attack was made on the fortress with floating batteries which were thought to be indestructible. The British, on the other side, fired red-hot shot at the batteries till they were all burnt. After this failure, France and Spain were ready to come to terms with Great Britain. The preliminaries of peace with the United States of America were signed at Paris, on November 30, **1782,** and with France and Spain on January 20, **1783.** The preliminaries were converted into definitive treaties on September 3, **1783.** The Dutch held out longer, but were obliged to yield to a peace a few months later.

31. **Terms of the Treaty of Paris. 1783.**—The treaties with France and Spain restored to France the right of fortifying Dunkirk, which had been taken from her by the Treaty of Utrecht (see p. 699), and to Spain the possession of Minorca, whilst certain exchanges were effected in the West Indies, Africa, and India. In America, Florida went back to Spain. By the treaty with the United States their independence was acknowledged, and their western border was fixed on the Mississippi, beyond which was Louisiana, ceded by France to Spain at the end of the Seven Years' War. (See p. 766.)

CHAPTER L.

PITT AND FOX. 1782 – 1789

LEADING DATES

Reign of George III., 1760 1820

Pitt, Chancellor of the Exchequer	1782
The Coalition Ministry	April 2, 1783
Pitt Prime Minister	Dec. 23, 1783
Pitt's India Bill	1784
Bills for Parliamentary Reform and for a Commercial	
Union with Ireland	1785
Commercial Treaty with France	1786
Insanity of the King	1788
The Regency Bill	1789

1. **The Younger Pitt. 1782—1783.**—Chatham's second son, William Pitt, had entered Parliament in 1780, at the age of twenty-one. He had supported Burke's Economical Reform and denounced the American War. " Pitt," said some one to Fox, " will be one of the first men in the House of Commons." " He is so already," replied Fox. " He is not a chip of the old block," said Burke, " he is the old block itself." Burke's saying was not strictly accurate. The qualities of the younger Pitt were different from those of his father. He had none of the fire of the impetuous Chatham, but he had what Chatham did not possess, unerring tact in the management of men and high sagacity in discriminating between things possible to be done and things which were not possible. When the second Rockingham Ministry was formed, he was offered a post which did not carry with it a seat in the Cabinet, but which brought a salary of 5,000*l.* a year. Pitt, who was a young barrister making a bare 300*l.* a year, refused the offer, and astonished the House by asserting that he 'never would accept a subordinate situation.' He soon asked for a committee to inquire into the need for Parliamentary reform, adopting the views of his father on this subject, in opposition to those of the Rockingham Whigs. When Shelburne became Prime Minister, he made Pitt Chancellor of the Exchequer, with the leadership of the House of Commons.

2. **Resignation of Shelburne. 1783.**—Shelburne's Ministry did not last long. Shelburne never continued for any length of time

on good terms with other men. He was unreasonably suspicious, and his profuse employment of complimentary expressions gave rise to doubts of his sincerity. In the beginning of **1783** most of his colleagues had ceased to attend his Cabinet meetings. It was obvious that Shelburne, with all his ability, was not a ruler of men, and it is almost certain that if Fox had had a little patience, Shel-

Costumes of persons of quality, about 1783.

burne must have resigned, and the way have been opened for a strong and reforming Ministry, in which Fox and Pitt would have played the leading part. Unfortunately, Fox had neither patience nor tact. He formed a coalition with North, and as the two together had a large majority in the House of Commons at their disposal, Shelburne resigned on February 24.

3. **The Coalition Ministry. 1783.**—The king was furious, but for the time, helpless. He regarded North as an ungrateful deserter, and he had more than one reason for disliking Fox. Not only was Fox the most brilliant supporter of the system of Parliamentary connection, which George III. had set himself to break down, but he was personally intimate with the Prince of Wales, afterwards King George IV. The Prince was now living a dissipated life, and the king attributed the mischief to the evil influence of Fox, though the low character of the Prince himself, and the repulsiveness of the very moral, but exceedingly dull, domestic life of the royal family, had, no doubt, some part in the unfortunate result. The people at large were scandalised at a coalition formed appa-

rently for the mere purpose of securing power for Fox and North, who had been abusing one another for many years, and who did not come into office to support any policy which Shelburne had opposed, or to frustrate any policy which Shelburne had supported. Nevertheless, sufficient indignation had not yet been shown to enable the king to dissolve Parliament with a fair hope of success. He was, therefore, after various attempts to avoid yielding, obliged on April 2 to admit the Coalition to office. Fox and North became secretaries of state, and the Duke of Portland, a man of no great capacity, became nominally Prime Minister. During the remainder of the session, Pitt again brought forward a motion for Parliamentary reform, attacking the secret influence of the Crown as strongly as the venality of the electors in the petty boroughs. Fox supported and North opposed him ; after which his motion was lost by a majority of nearly two to one. When the House of Commons met again, Fox laid before it a bill for the government of India.

4. **The English in Bengal.** 1757—1772.—Clive returned to England in **1760**. Before he left India he had obtained from the Great Mogul the grant of the quit-rent with which the Company had to pay for its zemindary (see p. 764), and thus became himself the landlord of the Company. Whatever might be the nominal position of the Company's servants, in reality they were masters of Bengal. They used their power to fill their own pockets at the expense of the natives. After a career of plunder and extortion many of them returned home with enormous fortunes. In **1765** Clive was sent out again to correct the evil. This he endeavoured to do by increasing the scanty pay of the officials, and by forbidding them to engage in trade or to receive gifts from the natives. On the other hand, he obtained for the Company from the Great Mogul, the weak Shah Alum, who nominally ruled at Delhi, the Dewanni, or financial administration of Bengal, Behar, and Orissa, though the criminal jurisdiction was left in the hands of the Nawab · a descendant of Meer Jaffier. Constitutionally this grant of the Dewanni first placed the Company in a legal position in Bengal as administrators under the Great Mogul. In **1767** Clive finally left India. For the next five years everything in Bengal was in confusion. The Company's agents collected the revenue and paid the army ; but they had no authority to punish crime, and the Nawab, who had, was too weak to enforce order. In **1772**, Warren Hastings was appointed governor of Bengal, with orders to put an end to the confusion.

5. **Warren Hastings, Governor of Bengal.** 1772—1774.—
Hastings was a man of the highest ability, and it would have been
well if the Company had given him supreme power to take the
whole of the government of Bengal into his own hands, and to set
aside the pretence of leaving any part of it to the Nawab. The
Company, however, too scrupulous to upset even an evil system
which it found in existence, did not authorise him to do this ; and
though he did immense service in organising the administration
on English principles, he could not prevent considerable confusion
arising from the technical uncertainty of his position. Beyond the
British frontier there was imminent danger. Central India was in
the hands of the Mahratta chiefs. The descendants of Sivaji (see
p. 759) were reduced to obscurity by the Peishwah or hereditary
prime minister at Poonah, whose authority was in turn resisted by
other hereditary officers, by Sindhia and Holkar in Malwa, by
the Bhonsla in Berar, and by the Guicowar in Guzerat. Divided
amongst themselves, these chiefs were always ready to join for
plunder or conquest, and it was their military strength that
was the greatest danger to the Company's government, and, it
must in fairness be added, to the native populations which the
Company was bound to protect. To combat the Mahrattas,
Hastings carried out a policy—originally sketched out by Clive—
of strengthening the Nawab of Oude, in order that he might act as
a breakwater against them in defence of Bengal. The Nawab
gladly welcomed the proffered alliance, and sought to turn it to
account by asking Hastings to support him in annexing Rohilcund,
which was governed by the Rohillas, a military body of Afghan
descent. In 1774 Hastings lent the Nawab English troops, by
whose valour the Rohillas were defeated, whilst the Nawab's own
army followed up the victory by plunder and outrage. Politically,
Hastings had done much, as he had bound the Nawab to his cause,
but he had done this at the expense of soiling the English name by
lending English troops to an Eastern potentate who was certain to
abuse a victory won by their arms.

6. **The Regulating Act and its Results.** 1773—1774.—In 1773
was passed, at the instance of Lord North, the Regulating Act,
which was intended to introduce order into the possessions of the
Company in India. What was needed was to strengthen the
hands of the governor of its principal possession, Bengal, and to
give him control over the governments of Bombay and Madras.
The English Parliament, however, had no experience in dealing
with Eastern peoples, and tried to introduce constitutional checks,

which were better suited for Westminster than for Calcutta.   The
governor of Bengal was to be called governor-general of Bengal,
but there was to be a council of four members besides himself, and
if he was outvoted in the council, he was to be obliged to conform his conduct to the decisions of his opponents.   There was
also set up a supreme court, which might easily come· into conflict
with the governor, as no rules were laid down to define their
separate powers.   The governor-general had authority over the
governors of Madras and Bombay, but it was insufficient to enable
him to dictate their policy.   In 1774, the new Council held its first
sittings.   Its leading spirit was Philip Francis, the reputed author
of ' Junius's Letters' (see p. 782), a man actuated by a suspicious-
ness which amounted to a disease, and who landed with the belief,
which no evidence could shake, that Hastings was an incapable
and corrupt despot.   As two of the other councillors constantly
voted with Francis he commanded a majority.   This majority
thwarted Hastings in everything, cancelled his measures, and set
on foot an inquiry into his supposed peculations.

   7. Hastings and Nuncomar.   1775.—To support Francis, Nuncomar, a Hindoo, came forward with evidence that Hastings had
taken enormous bribes.   This evidence was forged, but the majority of the council supported Nuncomar, hoping to drive Hastings
from his post.   Suddenly Nuncomar was charged with forgery,
and hanged by a sentence of the Supreme Court, over which Sir
Elijah Impey presided as chief justice.   Forgery was too common
a crime in Bengal to be regarded by the natives as highly punishable, and Impey was probably too ready to think that everything
sanctioned by the English law was entirely admirable.   The sentence, however, was so opportune for Hastings, that it has often
been supposed that he had suggested the charge against Nuncomar.   Not only, however, did he subsequently deny this upon
oath, but modern inquirers have generally come to the conclusion
that his denial was true.   He may, however, have let fall some
chance word which induced the accuser of Nuncomar to think that
his action would please the governor-general ; and, in any case,
it was not difficult for a native who wished to stand well with
Hastings, to imagine that the destruction of Nuncomar would be
an agreeable service.   At all events, Hastings's adversaries were
frightened, and no more forged accusations were brought against
him.

   8. War with the Mahrattas and Hyder Ali.   1777—1779.
Gradually, by the death or removal of the hostile councillors,

Hastings regained power. Then came the most critical time in
the history of British rule. in India. Far more important than all
other conflicts in which Englishmen in India were engaged was
the struggle renewed from time to time between the Company and
the Mahratta confederacy. Important as it was to the Company,
it was far more important to the natives of India ; as the victory
of the Mahrattas would bring with it outrage and misery, whereas
the victory of the Company would bring with it the establishment
of peace and settled government. Nevertheless, it would have been
well if the conflict could have been deferred till the Company was
stronger than it then was. Unluckily the Bombay Government
entered upon an unnecessary war with the Mahrattas, and, finding
itself in danger, called on Hastings for help. In 1777, at the time
when the French were preparing to oppose England in America,
they sent an emissary to Poonah to prepare the way for an alliance
between themselves and the Mahrattas. In 1778 came the news
of Burgoyne's capitulation at Saratoga. " If it be really true," said
Hastings, " that the British arms and influence have suffered so
severe a check in the Western world, it is more incumbent on
those who are charged with the interest of Great Britain in the
East to exert themselves for the retrieval of the national loss."
Into the struggle with the Mahrattas, now likely to pass into a
struggle with France, Hastings threw himself with unbounded
energy. His position was made almost desperate by the folly of
the Madras Government, which unnecessarily provoked the two
Mahomedan rulers of the south, the Nizam and an adventurer
named Hyder Ali who had made himself master of Mysore. Hyder
Ali, the ablest warrior in India, threw himself on the lands over which
the British held sway in the Carnatic. " A storm of universal
fire," in Burke's language, " blasted every field, consumed every
house, destroyed every temple." The miserable inhabitants, flying
from their burning villages, were slaughtered or swept into captivity.
All English eyes turned to Hastings.

9. **Cheyt Singh and the Begums of Oude. 1781—1782.**—Money
was the first thing needed, and of money Hastings had but little.
He had to send large sums home every year to pay dividends to
the Company, and his treasury was almost empty. In his straits,
Hastings demanded from Cheyt Singh, the Rajah of Benares, a
large payment as a contribution to the war, on the ground that he
was a dependent on the Company and therefore bound to support
it in times of difficulty. On Cheyt Singh's refusal to pay, Hastings
imposed on him an enormous fine, equal to about 500,000*l*. In order

to ensure payment Hastings went in person to Benares to arrest the Rajah ; but the population rose on his behalf, and Hastings had to fly for his life, though he skilfully made preparations to regain his authority, and before long suppressed the revolters and deposed the Rajah. He then made treaties with some of the Mahratta chiefs, and thus lessened the number of his enemies. The Madras Government, however, continued to cry for support. "We know not," they wrote, " in what words to describe our distress for money." Hastings pressed the Nawab of Oude to furnish him with some, but the Nawab was not rich, because his mother and grandmother, the Begums of Oude as they were called, had retained possession of his father's accumulated treasure, and had enlisted armed men to defend it against him. In 1782 the Nawab laid claim to the money to which he appears to have been rightfully entitled, and in 1782 Hastings lent him the Company's troops to take it from the ladies. They were forced to yield, and Hastings, as his reward, got payment of a large debt which the Nawab owed to the Company.

10. **Restoration of Peace. 1781—1782.**—In 1781, Hyder Ali was joined by some French troops, but the combined force was defeated at Porto Novo by old Sir Eyre Coote, the victor of Wandewash (see p. 764). In 1782 peace was concluded with the Mahrattas, after which Hyder Ali died, and when the French, in consequence of the end of the war in Europe and America, withdrew their assistance, Hyder Ali's son and successor, Tippoo, also made peace with the English.

11. **Hastings as a Statesman. 1783.**—Hastings, by his pertinacity, had saved the British hold on India and had laid the foundations of a system on which the future peace and prosperity of the country depended. Yet that system would have been severely shaken if future governors-general had continued to levy fines limited only by their own discretion, as had been done in the case of Cheyt Singh, or to supply forces to Eastern potentates to enable them to recover their dues as in the cases of the Rohillas and the Begums of Oude. Much as may be said on Hastings's behalf in all these affairs, it can hardly be denied that it would have been better if he could have supported his government upon the revenues of the Company's own provinces, and could have acted beyond the Company's frontier only by agents responsible to himself. That he did not do so was mainly the fault of the weakness of his own official position. Extraordinary expenditure was in most instances forced on him by the folly of the Council

which he was compelled to obey or of the governors of Madras and Bombay who disobeyed his orders. What was urgently needed was the reform of a system which left the governor-general hampered in his authority by those who should have been his subordinates, whilst at the same time it was desirable that he should be made directly responsible, not to a trading company interested in making money, but to the British Government itself.

12. **The India Bill of the Coalition.** 1783.—In 1783 the Coalition Ministry brought in a bill for the better government of India, which was intended to meet only the latter of these two requirements. Though the Bill was introduced by Fox into the House of Commons, it was the work of Burke. Burke felt deeply and passionately the wrongs done to the natives of India, and he proposed to take the government entirely away from the East India Company, giving it to a board of seven commissioners, appointed in the bill itself, that is to say, practically by the ministers who drew up the bill. No member of this board could be dismissed by the King for four years, except at the request of both Houses of Parliament, though at the end of four years the king was to name the commissioners. As the whole patronage of India was placed in the hands of the board, and as the possessor of patronage could always sell it for votes in the British Parliament, the bill made for the increase of the power of the Crown in the long run, though it weakened it for four years. The opponents of the Coalition, however, shutting their eyes to the former fact and fixing them on the latter, bitterly attacked the bill as directed against the power of the Crown. It was an attempt, said Thurlow, who had been Lord Chancellor in Lord Shelburne's ministry, to take the diadem from the king's head and to put it on that of Mr. Fox.

13. **The Fall of the Coalition.** 1783.—Though the bill was strongly opposed by Pitt and others, it passed the Commons by a large majority. When it reached the Lords, the king sent a private message through Pitt's cousin, Lord Temple, to each peer, to the effect that whoever voted for the India Bill was not only not the king's friend, but would be considered as his enemy. As many of the lords were conscientiously opposed to the Coalition, and others needed the king's patronage, the bill was thrown out, on which the king contemptuously dismissed the ministry. Constitutional writers have blamed his interference, on the ground that a king ought not to intrigue against ministers supported by the House of Commons. On the other hand, it may be said that on this occasion the ministers had gained their posts by an intrigue,

and that it was difficult to respect the House of Commons at a time when large numbers of its members were swayed backwards and forwards by hopes of patronage from one side or the other. The only hope of a better state of things lay in the intervention of the nation itself.

14. **Pitt's Struggle with the Coalition. 1783—1784.**—George III., burning to free himself from the Coalition, made Pitt prime minister at the early age of twenty-five. Pitt accepted the position

Costumes of gentlefolk, about 1784.

from the king, and so far adopted what was now the established Tory doctrine, that ministers were to be named by the king, and not by the House of Commons; but he also reintroduced what had long been forgotten, the principle that the constituencies must be appealed to before any final decision could be taken. For weeks he struggled in the House of Commons, refusing to resign or to dissolve Parliament until he could place his opponents at a disadvantage. Fox, with his usual want of tact, gave him the advantage which he required, by opposing a dissolution and the consequent appeal to the constituencies, and by insisting that it was Pitt's duty to resign at once, because he was outvoted in the existing House of Commons. Under these circumstances, Pitt was beaten again and again by large majorities. The nation at large had for some time disliked the Coalition as unprincipled, and it now rallied to Pitt in admiration of his undaunted resolution. Members of the House, who had supported the Coalition merely for the sake of the loaves and fishes, began to suspect that it might be Pitt after all who would have the loaves and fishes to dispense. These men began to change sides, and Pitt's minority grew larger from day to day. At last, on March 8, **1784**, the opposition had only a majority of one. On this Parliament was dissolved. The constituencies rallied to Pitt, and 160 of Fox's supporters lost their seats. They were popularly known as Fox's martyrs.

15. **Pitt's Budget and India Bill. 1784.**—George III., delighted as he was with Pitt's victory, found it impossible to make a tool of him, as he had made a tool of Lord North. Pitt owed his success even more to the nation than to the king, and, with the nation and the House of Commons at his back, he was resolved to have his own way. He soon showed himself to be a first-rate financier, and in his first budget introduced the principle, afterwards largely followed, of reducing customs-duties in order to make smuggling unprofitable. He then passed an India Bill of his own. The Company was to retain all the patronage except the appointment of the governor-general and of one or two high functionaries, so that neither the king nor any other political body would have the disposal of places in India, to serve as an instrument of corruption. As far as the government of India was concerned, it was nominally left in the hands of the directors of the East India Company ; but the despatches in which were conveyed the orders to its servants in India were now liable to be amended by a board of control composed of the king's ministers, power being given to this new board to give orders, in cases requiring secrecy, even without the consent of the directors. This dual government, as it was called, lasted till **1858**. Whilst Pitt avoided Fox's mistake in the matter of patronage, he deprived the Company of its government without the appearance of doing so. He also strengthened the authority of the governor-general over the governors of Madras and Bombay. Without Burke's animosity against Hastings, he saw that Hastings's system was not one of which he could approve, whilst he had little real knowledge of the difficulties by which Hastings had been embarrassed, and therefore failed to make allowances for them. Hastings discovered that he would not be supported by the new minister, and in February, **1785**, he resigned his office and sailed for England.

16. **Pitt's Reform Bill. 1785.**—For the third time (see pp. 799, 801) Pitt attempted to carry Parliamentary reform. He now proposed to lay by a sum of 1,000,000*l.* to be employed in buying up

Society at Vauxhall : from an aquatint after T. Rowlandson, 1785.

seventy-two seats, which were practically in private hands.   If any of the owners refused to sell, the share of the purchase-money which would have fallen to him was to be laid out at compound interest till it became valuable enough to tempt him to close with the increased offer.   The bill was thrown out, and Pitt never again appeared as a parliamentary reformer.   There can be no doubt that he was in earnest in desiring parliamentary reform, as it would have strengthened him against the unpopular Whigs. His proposal of buying up seats, which appears so extraordinary in our own day, was doubtless the result of his perception that he could not otherwise pass the bill, and, when once this offer had been rejected, he must have seen that he could not pass any Reform Bill at all.   Pitt was not one of those statesmen who bring forward particular measures on which they have set their hearts, and who carry them ultimately by their self-abnegation in refusing to take further part in the government of the country till right has been done.   He clung to power, partly for its own sake, but partly also because he believed the Coalition which he resisted to be so un-principled that his own retention of office was, in itself, a benefit to the country.   No statesman of equal eminence ever failed so often to persuade Parliament to adopt his schemes ; but this was chiefly because his schemes were usually too much in advance of the public opinion of the time.

17. **Failure of Pitt's Scheme for a Commercial Union with Ireland. 1785.**—A proposal made by Pitt for a commercial union with Ireland failed as completely as his Reform Bill.   There was to be complete free-trade between the two countries, and Ireland in return was to grant a fixed revenue for the maintenance of the navy, by which both countries were protected.   The Parliament at Dublin assented to the scheme, but in England the manufac-turers raised such an outcry that Pitt was forced to change it, restricting freedom of trade in many directions, and making the Irish Parliament dependent, in some respects, on the British for the regulation of commerce.   The scheme thus altered was rejected at Dublin as giving Ireland less than complete freedom of trade and infringing on the independence of her Parliament.

18. **French Commercial Treaty. 1786.**—Pitt was more success-ful in 1786 with a treaty of commerce with France.   The doctrine, that freedom of trade was good for all countries concerned in it, had been promulgated by Adam Smith in his *Wealth of Nations* published in 1776.   Shelburne was the first minister who adopted his views, but his official career was too short to enable him to give

effect to them, and Pitt was, therefore, the first minister to reduce them to practice. Duties were lowered in each country on the productions of the other, and both countries were the better for the change.

19. **Trial of Warren Hastings.** 1786—1795.—In 1786 Pitt appointed Lord Cornwallis Governor-General of India, and took a wise step in obtaining from Parliament an act empowering him to over-rule his council. Cornwallis was a man of strong common sense, and as he had fewer difficulties to contend with than Hastings had had, he was under no temptation to resort to acts such as those which had disfigured the administration of Hastings. In Parliament, Burke, backed by the whole of the Opposition, called for Hastings's impeachment. Pitt gave way, and in 1788 Hastings's trial began before the Lords in Westminster Hall. Burke and Sheridan, in impassioned harangues, laboured to prove him to

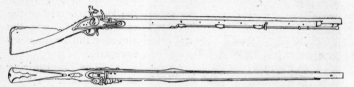

Regulation musket, 1786, popularly known as Brown Bess.

have been a tyrant and a villain. The trial dragged on, and it was not till 1795 that the Lords in accordance with the evidence pronounced sentence of acquittal.

20. **The Regency Bill.** 1788—1789.—In 1765 George III. had been for a short time mentally deranged. In the autumn of 1788 there was a more violent recurrence of the malady. Dr. Willis, the first physician who treated lunatics with kindness, asserted a recovery to be probable, though it might be delayed for some time. Both Pitt and Fox were agreed that there must be a regency during the king's illness, and that the Prince of Wales must be the regent. Fox, however, argued that the Prince had a right to the post, and therefore ought not to be subjected to any restrictions. " I'll unwhig the gentleman for the rest of his life," said Pitt, and argued that it was for Parliament to provide a regent. Pitt carried the day, and a bill was passed through both houses conferring the regency on the prince, but limiting his powers by withholding from him the right of making peers, or of appointing to offices, unless the appointments were revocable by the king if he recovered. By

3 G 2

this arrangement, however, the prince would not be prevented from dismissing the existing ministry and calling a new one to office ; and everyone knew that his first act would be to change the ministry, placing Fox in office instead of Pitt.   Nowadays, if a minister had, like Pitt, a large majority in the Commons, it would be impossible for either a king or a regent to make so sudden a change.   In those days it was easy enough, because many of Pitt's supporters would certainly go over to Fox as soon as he had the patronage of the kingdom in his hands.   Pitt himself knew that it would be so, and as he had amassed no fortune, declared his

readiness to ' take his blue bag again ' and practise as a barrister. The expected change, however, never took place, as, under the wise care of Dr. Willis, the king recovered in the spring of 1789, and the Regency Bill became unnecessary.

21. **The Thanksgiving at St. Paul's. 1789.**— When George III. returned thanks for his recovery at St. Paul's, the enthusiasm of the whole population was unbounded. Something of this popularity was undoubtedly owing to the disgust which had been caused by the recent misconduct of the Prince of Wales, who had heartlessly jeered at the un-

Pitt speaking in the House of Commons : from Huckel's painting in the National Portrait Gallery.

happy condition of his father—speaking, for instance, of the king in a pack of cards as a lunatic—but much of it was the result of genuine delight at the king's recovery. The mass of people could appreciate his domestic virtues, and had no reason to be dissatisfied with his policy. Even if he had gone wrong in the matter of the American War, he went wrong in company with the large majority of his subjects, and for the last five years he had reaped the benefit of the firm and enlightened government of Pitt.

22. **Growth of Population.   1700–1801.**—The country which gave power to Pitt in 1784, and which sustained him in it in 1789, had changed much since the beginning of the century.   Its population was more numerous, its wealth greater, and its intellectual activity more widely spread.   The population of England and Wales was probably about 5,000,000 in 1700 ; about 6,000,000 in 1750 ; and was certainly about 9,000,000 in 1801.   Such growing numbers could not have been fed if there had not been improvements in farming to give them more food, and improvements in manufacture to give them more employment.

23. **Improvements in Agriculture.**— Up to the early part of the eighteenth century, husbandry had been poor, and the necessity of leaving corn land fallow once in three years had made the produce of the soil scanty.   Lord Townshend, after his quarrel with Walpole, encouraged, by his example, the cultivation of turnips, and as turnips could be planted in the third year in which the ground had hitherto been left fallow, the crops were largely increased.   By degrees improvements in draining and manuring were also introduced.

24. **Cattle-breeding.**—In 1755, Bakewell began to improve the breed of sheep and cattle by judicious crossing.   The result was that, before long, a sheep or an ox produced twice as many pounds of meat as before, and that the meat was far more tasty.   Improvements in agriculture and cattle-breeding were possible, because landowners were wealthy enough to enclose waste lands and to make poor lands fit for culture.   In one way, however, the changes effected were not for good.   The small proprietor, who had hitherto to a great extent kept himself free from debt by the domestic manufactures of his wife and daughters, could not afford to lay out the money needed for the cultivation of his land in the new fashion, and was forced to sell it.   Thus gradually small holdings were bought by large landowners, and the work of cultivation fell almost entirely into the hands of hired labourers.

25. **The Bridgewater Canal.   1761.**—Trade, which had been growing steadily during the first half of the century, received an impulse from the invention of a new means of conveyance.   Goods had been conveyed either on slow and lumbering waggons, or, more often, on the backs of pack-horses.   Such a means of transport added greatly to the price of the goods, and made it almost impossible for an inland town to compete in foreign markets with one near the sea.   It happened that the Duke of Bridgewater owned a coal mine at Worsley, seven miles from Manchester ; but

hills intervened, and the expense of carting the coal over the seven miles was too great to make it worth his while to send the coals to Manchester. The duke consulted James Brindley, a millwright in his service, who, though he was without any scientific education, not only advised him to make a canal, but carried out the work for him. There were indeed already canals in existence, but there were none to the making of which the natural obstacles were so great. Brindley's canal passed under hills through tunnels, and over valleys on aqueducts. A famous engineer on being shown a valley which the canal had to cross, asked where the water was to flow. When a spot high up on the hill-side was pointed out to

Lock on a Canal.

him, he said that he had often heard of 'castles in the air,' but he had never before been shown where one was to be built. In **1761** the canal was finished, and many others were before long made in other parts of the country.

26. **Cotton-spinning. 1738.**—In old days, the spinning of thread was mainly committed to young women, who were consequently known as spinsters. In the middle ages and long afterwards the material spun was wool, and Parliament had been so anxious to extend the manufacture of woollen cloth that it even passed an Act directing that all persons should be 'buried in woollen.' Gradually, in the eighteenth century, calico came into

use, and in 1738 the invention of Kay's flying shuttle enabled the weavers to produce double as much as before, thus creating a demand for cotton thread which all the spinners in England were unable to meet.

27. **Hargreaves' Spinning-Jenny.   1767.**—Necessity is the mother of invention, and, in order to provide thread for the weavers, Hargreaves, in 1767, invented the spinning-jenny, which worked several spindles at once, and enabled a single spinner to produce more than a hundred threads at the same time.   By this discovery many persons were thrown out of work, as there was not a demand for calico enough to occupy all the spinners who at first had been needed to produce threads with their hands only. Accordingly, Hargreaves' neighbours broke his machine and obliged him to fly for his life. In the long run, indeed, Hargreaves' invention, like all labour-saving inventions, would, by producing cheaply, create a demand which would increase, instead of diminishing the number of labourers employed in the manufactures ; but it could hardly be expected that uneducated men, threatened with starvation, would look so far ahead.

James Brindley : from the portrait by Parsons, engraved by H. Cook.

28. **Arkwright and Crompton.   1769—1779.**—In 1769 Arkwright took out a patent for an improved spinning machine worked by water-power.   He, too, became obnoxious to the hand-workers, and his mill was burned down by a mob.   He was, however, determined to succeed, and was at last allowed to live in peace.   A yet further improvement was made in 1779, when a poor weaver named Samuel Crompton invented a spinning-machine known as 'the mule.'   When his machine was finished, hearing that a mob was collecting with the intention of destroying it, he took it to pieces and concealed it.

When quiet was restored, he put it together, and began to spin.
Manufacturers came round his house, and peeped through his
windows to discover his secret. Crompton had not enough money
to take out a patent so as to secure the profits of his invention.
He, therefore, told his secret, on the promise of the manufacturers
to raise a subscription for him. They subscribed no more than
67*l.* 6*s.* 6*d.*, and made thousands of pounds by the work of his brains.

Arkwright.

29. **Cartwright's Power-loom.** 1785. — Before Hargreaves
invented the spinning-jenny, no more cotton had been spun
than was required by the weavers. After Crompton invented the
' mule,' the weavers could not make into calico nearly as much thread
as was produced. In 1785, a clergyman named Cartwright patented
a power-loom, which, by weaving by machinery, increased the
number of looms and thus kept the spinning ' mules ' in full work.

30. **Watt's Steam-Engine.** 1785.—There were many other inventions in different branches of manufacture ; but the most important
of all was Watt's steam-engine. For some time steam-engines had
been employed for pumping water out of collieries (see p. 708), but

they consumed much fuel, and therefore cost too much to come into general use. James Watt, a mathematical instrument maker in Glasgow, discovered a way of lessening the cost of fuel, and of making the engine more serviceable at the same time. He entered into partnership with a capitalist named Boulton, and set up works near Birmingham. At first manufacturers distrusted the new engines, and Boulton and Watt only succeeded in inducing them to buy by offering to go without payment if the engines sold did not

Crompton : from a portrait by Allingham.

save their cost in the course of a year. Before long all manufacturers were anxious to get them. " I sell here," said Boulton to George III., when he visited his works, " what all the world desires—power."

31. **General Results of the Growth of Manufactures.**—One great result of the invention of the improved steam-engine was the transference of population from the south to the north. Hitherto the north had been poor and of little weight in the political scale. When the north had taken part in political struggles it had usually chosen the side ultimately rejected by the nation. It fought in the reign of Henry VI. for the Lancastrians ; in the reign of Henry VIII. for the monasteries ; in the reign of Elizabeth for the Papacy ; in the reign of Charles I. for the king ; in the reign of

George I. for the Pretender. Coal, however, existed in many parts of the north; the steam-engine followed coal, manufactures followed the steam-engine, and population followed manufactures. In Sussex, for instance, there was in the seventeenth century a considerable population supported by the manufacture of iron, and it was from this Sussex iron that the railings round St. Paul's were made. By the middle of the eighteenth century, however, the weald of Sussex, on which had once stood the forest which had for some time blocked the way of the South Saxon conquest (see p. 27), had been denuded of its wood, in consequence of the large demands made by the furnaces for smelting iron, and now the industry of iron manufacture moved entirely to the north. At first, indeed, the transfer of labourers to the north was not followed by beneficial results.. The crowds who gathered for work were for the most part ignorant, and always in haste to be rich. There was neglect of sanitary requirements, and those who rose to be masters often wore away the lives of their workmen. As yet, law did not interfere to protect the weak—the women and children—from excessive labour, or to guard against the frequent occurrence of preventable accidents. It was as though a new world had opened in the north, of which Parliament knew so little that it neither desired to regulate it nor even thought of making the attempt.

Books recommended for the further study of Part IX.

LECKY, W. E. H.   History of England in the Eighteenth Century.
    Vol. iii. p. 1—Vol. v. p. 153; Vol. vi. pp. 138–455.
STANHOPE, Earl.   History of England since the Peace of Utrecht.
    Vol. iv. p. 308—Vol. vii.
MACAULAY, Lord.   Essays on Chatham and Clive.
TREVELYAN, Sir George.   The Early Life of C. J. Fox.
MORLEY, J.   Burke : an Historical Study.
RUSSELL, Earl.   Memorials and Correspondence of C. J. Fox.
WAKEMAN, H. O.   Fox.
LEWIS, Sir George Cornewall.   Essays on the Administrations of Great
    Britain, pp. 1–129.
WILSON, Sir Charles.   Clive.
LYALL, Sir A.   Warren Hastings.
TROTTER, Capt. L. J.   Warren Hastings.

PART X

THE CONFLICT WITH DEMOCRACY. 1789—1827

CHAPTER LI

ENGLAND AND THE FRENCH REVOLUTION. 1789—1795

LEADING DATES

Reign of George III., 1760—1820

Meeting of the States-General at Versailles	May 5, 1789
Declaration of War between France and the King of Hungary and his Allies	April 20, 1792
Louis XVI. driven from the Tuileries . . .	Aug. 10, 1792
Proclamation of the French Republic . . .	Sept. 22, 1792
Execution of Louis XVI.	Jan. 21, 1793
Declaration of War between France and England	Feb. 1, 1793
Battle of the First of June	June 1, 1794
End of the Reign of Terror	July 28, 1794
Treaty of Basel, between France and Prussia .	April 5, 1795
Establishment of the Directory	Oct. 27, 1795

1. **Prospects of Pitt's Ministry. 1789.**—The spread of manufacturing industry did much to strengthen Pitt's government, because the wealthy manufacturers were jealous of the landed aristocracy, and, therefore, supported him against the great Whig families. In the beginning of 1789 there seemed to be every prospect that Pitt's tenure of office would continue to be distinguished by a long series of gradual reforms, carried out just so far as Pitt could induce the nation to follow him. Before long, however, events took place in France which shocked the English nation, and produced a temper hostile to reform.

2. **Material Antecedents of the French Revolution.**—The form of government in France had long been an absolute monarchy ; but, though the kings had deprived the nobles and the clergy of all political power, they had allowed them to retain privileges injurious to the rest of the community.   The nobles and the clergy, for instance, who formed the first two estates, paid much lower taxes than the rest of the people, and the Third Estate, which comprised all who were not noblemen or clergymen, bore, in consequence, heavier burdens than ought to have been placed on them.   Many noblemen and clergymen, again, were *seigneurs*, or, as would have been said in England, Lords of Manors, and though the peasants who lived on their estates were often actually proprietors of their own pieces of land, they had nevertheless to pay dues to their *seigneurs* on all sorts of occasions, as for instance when they sold land or brought their produce to market.   The *seigneurs*, too, often treated the peasants harshly by riding over their crops in pursuit of game, or by keeping flocks of pigeons which devoured their corn.   People will sometimes bear injuries from those who render some public service, but in France in the eighteenth century the *seigneurs* did no public service, as the kings had jealously deprived them of the right of taking part—as English country gentlemen took part—in administering justice or in looking after the business of the district in which they lived.   The *seigneurs* and the nobility in general were accordingly hated, in the first place as obnoxious to their neighbours, and in the second place as useless idlers.

3. **Intellectual Antecedents of the French Revolution.**—Discontent only results in revolution when there are found thinking men to lead the oppressed masses, and in France there were thinkers and writers who prepared the way for great changes. Voltaire and several other writers proclaimed the supremacy of human reason.   They called upon kings and rulers to govern reasonably, attacking not only unreasonable and cruel laws, bearing hardly on individuals or injurious to the state and the institutions of civil life, but the practices and doctrines of Christianity itself.   The professors of Christianity in France were certainly open to attack.   Not only were the bishops and higher clergy rolling in wealth and living worldly and sometimes vicious lives, whilst the poor parish priests (*curés*) who did the work were in great poverty, but the bishops cried out for the persecution of Protestants and sceptics, although some of them were themselves sceptics.   On one occasion Louis XVI., who had reigned since **1774,** being asked to name a certain man, who was known to be a sceptic,

as archbishop, replied that an archbishop ought at least to believe in God. Whilst Voltaire and his allies asked that all things should be done by the king and his ministers according to reason, another writer, Rousseau, taught that all had equal rights, and that the people ought to govern themselves, holding that they knew by experience their own needs far better than those who undertook to govern them, and that as the people were always good and just, they would never act tyrannically as kings and priests had too often done.

4. **Louis XVI. 1774—1789.**—The feeling of the French people in general when Louis XVI. came to the throne was hostile not to monarchy but to the privileged orders, namely, the nobility and the clergy. If, therefore, Louis XVI. had put himself at the head of this movement, he would have become a more powerful king than even Louis XIV. Unfortunately, though he was unselfish and well intentioned, he had neither strength of will nor clearness of head, and he allowed the Government to drift into helplessness. Before long he was rushing into bankruptcy, which could only be averted if the nobles and clergy were compelled to pay taxes like the Third Estate. Louis XVI. had not the nerve to compel them to do it, and in **1789** he summoned the States-General, a body answering in some respects to our Parliament, but which had not met for a hundred and seventy-five years. He did this not because he wished to lead his people, but because he did not know any other way of procuring the money that he needed.

5. **The National Assembly. 1789.**—When the States-General met, the work of doing justice upon the privileged orders passed out of the king's hands. Each of the Three Estates had elected its own representatives to the States-General, and those of the Third Estate successfully insisted on all the representatives sitting in one chamber and calling themselves the National Assembly. The National Assembly assumed the right of making a constitution, and when the king feebly attempted to take that work into his own hands, and gave signs of an intention to employ force to make good his claim, the mob rose on July 14 and took the Bastille, a great fortress which commanded the poorer quarters of Paris. Then the peasants rose in many parts of France, burning and sacking the country houses of the *seigneurs*, and, on August 4, the National Assembly swept away all the special privileges of the two privileged orders. From henceforth there was to be in France what there had for centuries been in England—equality before the law.

6. England and France. 1789—1790.—At first the Revolution in France was generally welcomed in England. Englishmen thought that they had before them a mere repetition of the English Revolution of **1688**, and that a Parliamentary Government was about to be set up in France, similar to that which existed in England. It was a complete mistake. The English Revolution had been directed to limit the power of the king. The French Revolution was directed to overthrow the privileges of an aristocracy. The French king became involved in the quarrel by attempting to check the National Assembly, which he distrusted. On October 5 the mob marched upon Versailles, broke into the palace, slaughtered some of the guards, and on the next morning led the king captive to Paris. On the one hand the Assembly made enemies by meddling with the constitution of the Church ; and on the other hand many who had profited by the overthrow of the privileged orders suspected the nobles and the clergy to be intriguing to regain what they had lost, and treated them with harshness and cruelty. The National Assembly busied itself with drawing up a constitution based on abstract principles, whilst it took no account of the necessity of establishing a firm and strong government. It kept the king on the throne, but distrusted him too much to give him real power, and the natural result of such a state of things was the growth of turbulence and anarchy.

7. Fox, Burke, and Pitt. 1789—1790.—In England, each of the great statesmen then living had his own way of regarding the events passing in France. Fox, enthusiastic and impulsive, gave to the Revolution unstinted praise. " How much," he wrote, on hearing of the capture of the Bastille, " the greatest event it is that ever happened in the world ; and how much the best ! " Burke, on the other hand, regarded with disfavour, soon passing into hatred, the destruction of old institutions and the foundation of new ones on general principles. Being unable to perceive how impossible it was, in the existing circumstances of France, to found a government on those old institutions which had so completely broken down, he reviled the National Assembly, with all the wealth of argument and rhetoric at his command. Towards the end of **1790**, he published his *Reflections on the French Revolution*, in which he pointed out, with great sagacity, the danger of all attempts to alter suddenly the habits and institutions of nations, though he failed entirely to suggest any practicable remedy for the evils which existed in France. On May 6, **1791**, there was a complete breach between him and Fox. His dying words, he said, would be, "Fly from the French Revolution!" Pitt agreed with Burke rather than with Fox; but he held that his business was to govern England rather than to denounce France, and he contented himself with hoping that the disorders in France, by weakening that country for a long time, would make the preservation of peace easier.

8. Clarkson and the Slave Trade. 1783—1788.—Cautious as

Pitt was, he shared in some of the generous hopes which filled the mind of Fox. In **1772** Lord Mansfield laid down the law that a slave imported into England becomes free; but the merchants of Bristol and Liverpool were at this time carrying some fifty thousand negroes a year to slavery in the West Indies. On their way across the Atlantic the poor wretches suffered horrible torments, being packed almost as closely as the sufferers in the Black Hole of Calcutta, in nearly as stifling an atmosphere, so that large numbers died on the way. In **1783** a young man named Clarkson gained a prize at Cambridge for an essay on the question whether it was right to make slaves of others, and on his journey home sat down by the wayside to meditate whether the arguments which he used were to be more to him than mere words. He resolved to devote his life to the abolition of the slave trade, and for some years went about the quays at Liverpool, picking up facts from sailors. In **1788** he won to his side some members of the Society of Friends, and published the evidence which he had gathered. Wilberforce, the member for Yorkshire, one of the most pious and disinterested of men, took up the cause, and Wilberforce influenced Pitt.

9. Pitt and the Slave Trade. 1788—1792.—In **1788** a Bill was

brought in by Sir William Dolben, by which means were to be taken for improving the sanitary condition of the vessels carrying slaves. The slave-traders resisted it and argued that the negroes liked being taken from their own barbarous country, and danced and made merry on deck. On enquiry, it turned out that they were from time to time flogged on deck, in order to keep up the circulation of the blood in their numbed limbs, and that what their tyrants called dancing was merely their shrinking from the lash. The Bill passed the Commons, but the Lords so changed it as to make it useless. In **1789** and **1790** Wilberforce urged the Commons to abolish the wicked slave trade entirely, and in **1792** Pitt spoke vehemently in support of the proposal, but the House of Commons refused to accept it. The men of property of whom it was composed thought that the first duty of legislators was to protect property, whether it was property in human beings or in houses and goods.

10. **Rise of a Warlike Feeling in France. 1791—1792.**— In September, **1791**, the National Assembly finished its work on the constitution, and the Legislative Assembly, which, according to the constitution, was to be the first of a series of Assemblies each lasting for two years, met on October 1.   The most influential party in the new Assembly was that of the Girondists, of which the leaders were young and enthusiastic, but utterly without political experience. Many causes contributed to create a warlike feeling.   Crowds of emigrants, French nobles who had left the country either in anger at the revolutionary laws, or in fear lest they should themselves be harshly treated, gathered at Coblentz and held out threats of invasion and vengeance.   It was, moreover, believed in France that the Emperor Leopold II., the brother of the Queen, Marie Antoinette, had combined with the king of Prussia, Frederick William II., to collect troops with the intention of marching on Paris in support of the emigrants.   The Girondists, not doubting that Louis XVI. desired the overthrow of the constitution even with foreign aid, fanned the warlike feeling in the Assembly, in the hope that when war had once been declared the king would lose the confidence of the nation and that the fall of his throne might be effected without a struggle.   They also expected that the war would be short and easy, because they imagined that the subjects of the rulers opposed to them would gladly accept aid from the French armies to win for themselves the equality and popular sovereignty which had been established in France. 'Let us tell Europe,' said one of their orators, 'that if Cabinets engage kings in a war against peoples, we will engage peoples in a war against kings.'   As a matter of fact, neither the Emperor nor the King of Prussia was at this time eager to enter on hostilities with France.   Leopold II., however, died on March 1, and his son Francis, who succeeded him as King of Hungary and Archduke of Austria by hereditary right, and who, some months later, was chosen Emperor as Francis II., resenting the strong language used in Paris, threatened to interfere in France, and on April 20, **1792**, the Assembly retaliated by declaring war against him and his allies, amongst whom the King of Prussia was included.

11. **The French Republic. 1792.**—Burke would have gladly seen England allying itself to Austria and Prussia in the work of crushing French revolutionary principles.   Pitt refused to depart

from his policy of peace. The allies invaded France, and, on August 10, the Paris mob rose in insurrection against the king, who could hardly help wishing well to the invaders who had come to liberate him from bondage. Louis thereupon took refuge with the Legislative Assembly, which suspended him from the exercise of all authority, but, declaring itself incompetent to give a final solution to the question of government, ordered the election of a National Convention to settle it. The Paris mob, hounded on by bloodthirsty and unscrupulous leaders, seized the opportunity when there was no real authority in France, to burst into the prisons and massacre the prisoners suspected of desiring to help the enemy. On September 20 the French army checked the invaders by the cannonade of Valmy, and on the 21st the Convention met and decreed the abolition of the monarchy, thus declaring France to be a republic. On November 6 the French won a victory over the Austrians at Jemmapes, and soon afterwards occupied the Austrian Netherlands, Savoy, and Nice, advanced into Germany, and took possession of Mainz.

12. **Breakdown of Pitt's Policy of Peace.** 1792 — 1793. — The September massacres made Pitt's policy of peace almost hopeless, by the shock which they gave to English public opinion. The subsequent proceedings of the French Revolutionists drove Pitt himself into a policy of war. On November 19, **1792**, the Convention offered its assistance to all peoples desirous of obtaining their freedom, and, on December 15, ordered its generals wherever they were to proclaim the sovereignty of the people and the abolition of feudal rights and privileges. The war was a war not between one nation and another, but between social classes. France, enthusiastic for her new principles, did not neglect her interests. She supported her armies at the expense of the wealthy inhabitants of the countries they overran. She treated the territory of the Austrian Netherlands as if it were her own. In all this Pitt did not find a cause of war, as Austria was at war with France. He remonstrated when France threw open the Scheldt to commerce, which, ever since the 17th century, had been closed by European treaties to please the Dutch who occupied both banks of its estuary ; but he took his stand in resisting a threatened French invasion of the Dutch Netherlands. Whilst the feelings on both sides were growing in hostility, the French Convention condemned Louis XVI. to death, and, on January 21, **1793**, sent him to the scaffold. A thrill of horror ran through England, and on February 1, the Convention, knowing that

III.

peace could not be maintained, and being resolved to pursue its attack on the Dutch Republic, took the initiative in declaring war against England and the Dutch.

13. **French Defeats and the Reign of Terror. 1793.**—When the campaign of 1793 opened, a combined army of Austrians and Prussians advancing in overwhelming numbers drove the French out of the Austrian Netherlands. A force of 10,000 British soldiers, under the king's second son, the Duke of York, joined the victorious allies. At Paris the leading Girondists were expelled from the Convention, and a party known as that of the Jacobins rose to power. The Girondists were so alarmed lest a strong government should develop a despotism that they resisted the establishment of that firm authority which could alone save France from disaster. The Jacobins had no such scruples. In July France was in desperate case. Mainz, Condé, and Valenciennes surrendered, and the Duke of York laid siege to Dunkirk. The Jacobins had to deal with insurrection at home as well as with invasion from abroad. Lyons and Toulon rose against them in the south, La Vendée in the west. They met foreign and domestic enemies on the one hand by calling to arms all the patriotic youth of the country, and on the other hand by a savage system of executions by the guillotine. A Committee of Public Safety directed the government. A revolutionary tribunal judged swiftly on imperfect evidence and with the most violent passion all who were even suspected to be guilty of showing favour to the invaders or to the dispossessed nobility. The Reign of Terror, as it is called, began with the execution of the queen, on October 16. Twenty-two Girondists were executed on October 22, and for months afterwards blood—for the most part innocent blood—was mercilessly shed on the scaffold.

14. **French Successes. 1793.**—It was not the Reign of Terror, but the devotion of her sons, which saved France. On September 8 a French victory at Hondschoote forced the Duke of York to raise the siege of Dunkirk. On October 7 Lyons surrendered. On the 16th, by the victory of Wattignies, the French overpowered the Austrians in the Netherlands, and before the end of the year they drove back both Austrians and Prussians in the country between the Moselle and the Rhine. The army of the Vendeans was destroyed at Le Mans on December 12, and Toulon, which had admitted an English fleet into its harbour, was captured by the skill of young General Bonaparte on the 19th. These successes were due as much to the divisions of the allies as to French valour and conduct. Austria and Prussia had long been rivals, and there

was little real confidence between them even now. In 1772 these two powers, together with Russia, had stripped anarchical Poland of some of her provinces. In 1793 Russia and Prussia were proceeding to a second partition of her territory; whilst Austria was seeking compensation for being left without a share in this new partition of Poland by the acquisition of territory in France. Now that her armies had been driven back, her chance of getting such a compensation was at an end, and her rulers, throwing the blame on Prussia for her lukewarmness in the war with France, began to detest Prussia even more than they detested the French Republic.

15. **Progress of the Reign of Terror. 1793—1794.**—Pitt's mistake had been in thinking that he could take part in a great struggle of principles as though it were merely a struggle for the proper delimitation of States. The French had on their side enthusiasm, not only for their country, but for their own conception of the welfare of humanity. The Governments of Prussia and Austria had no enthusiasm for the old order of things which they professed to support. Even Pitt himself was an example of the impossibility of treating the danger from France as merely territorial. Seeing clearly the evil of the French aggression and the cruelty of the Reign of Terror, he grew to hate the French revolutionary spirit almost as strongly as Burke. It is hardly to be wondered at that it was so. The tyranny of the Reign of Terror became worse and worse. The Convention was dominated by a few bloodthirsty men who sent hundreds to the guillotine, not because they were even suspected of being traitors, but often merely because they did not sympathise with the revolution, or because their condemnation would be followed by the confiscation of their goods. The dominant parties turned upon one another. One party led by Hébert announced itself Atheist, and dressing up women to represent the Goddess of Reason, placed them on the altars of desecrated churches, and danced round them in honour of the principle which they represented. Another party, led by Robespierre, declared itself Deist, and early in 1794 Robespierre sent Hébert and his followers to the guillotine.

16. **Reaction in England. 1792—1793.**—In his growing detestation of these horrors, Pitt was supported by the great mass of Englishmen. In 1792 he refused to accept a proposal for Parliamentary reform, urged in the House of Commons by a young member, Mr. Grey, on the ground that it was not a fitting time to alter the Constitution. In 1793 he was frightened lest the French revolutionary spirit should find its way into England, because a certain number

of persons, regretting their exclusion from all part in parliamentary elections, joined clubs which loudly expressed their sympathy with the French innovations. The danger from such clubs was excessively small, but Pitt and well nigh the whole of the propertied classes dreaded the establishment of a reign of violence in England. In the beginning of 1793, an Act was passed authorising the Government to remove suspected foreigners, and late in the year a Treasonable Correspondence Act was passed to throw obstacles in the way of persons seeking to give assistance to the French, with whom England was by that time at war. No exception can be taken to these measures. It was, however, unjustifiable that the Government, fully supported by judges and juries, should authorise not only the prosecution, but the harshest punishment of persons guilty merely of using strong language against the king or the institutions of the realm. Amongst the sufferers was a bill-sticker who was imprisoned for six months for posting up an address asking for Parliamentary reform, and a man named Hudson who was sentenced to a fine of 200*l.* and two years' imprisonment for proposing a toast to 'The French Republic.' In Scotland Thomas Muir was sent to transportation for fourteen years for exciting to sedition and joining an association for obtaining universal suffrage and annual parliaments. "The landed interest," said the judge who tried the case, "alone has a right to be represented ; the rabble has nothing but personal property ; and what hold has the nation on them ?"

17. **End of the Reign of Terror. 1794.**—On July 28 the Reign of Terror in France came suddenly to an end by the execution of Robespierre. The course of the war in the spring of 1794 had been wholly in favour of France on land, and on June 26 a great French victory over the Austrians at Fleurus was followed by the complete evacuation of the Austrian Netherlands by the allies. It was little to counterbalance this that Lord Howe gained a victory, usually known as the Battle of the First of June, over a French fleet near the mouth of the Channel. France was no longer in danger, and France being safe, it was impossible for the Terrorists again to acquire control over the Government.

18. **Coalition between Pitt and the majority of the Whigs. 1794.**—In England one effect of the Reign of Terror had been to sweep away the differences between Pitt and the majority of the Whigs. Following Burke, the latter had for some time been voting with Pitt, and in 1794 their leaders, the Duke of Portland, Lord Fitzwilliam, and Mr. Windham entered Pitt's Cabinet. Fox and Grey with a

scanty following continued in opposition, partly because, though they loathed the bloody scenes in France, they thought that England ought to remain at peace ; partly because they held that the best way to meet French revolutionary ideas in England was to push on internal reforms.   Before the end of the year the violent proceedings in the English law-courts received a check by the refusal of juries to convict Horne Tooke, Hardy, and Thelwall, who were accused of seditious practices.   They were no doubt acquitted because

Uniform of Sailors about 1790.

ordinary Englishmen resumed their usual habit of distrusting government interference, as soon as the irritation caused by the Reign of Terror was at an end.

19. **The Treaties of Basel. 1795.**—French conquests did not come to an end with the Reign of Terror. In January 1795 a French army under Pichegru overran the Dutch Netherlands and established a Batavian republic on a democratic basis. About the same time there was a third and final partition of Poland, in which Austria, Prussia, and Russia all shared. Prussia had no more to gain in Poland, and on April 5, being unwilling to help Austria to make conquests in France, she concluded peace at Basel with the French Convention. On July 12 Spain, following the example of Prussia, also signed a treaty of peace at Basel.

20. **The Establishment of the Directory in France. 1795.**—Pitt

failed to appreciate the real difficulties of the war on which he had embarked.   In spite of all the atrocities of the Terror, the feeling in France was so strong against any reaction in favour of the old nobility, that there was not the slightest chance of overthrowing the Republican government by giving aid to the French emigrants. The Count of Puisaye, an emigrant royalist, persuaded Pitt to disembark him and a number of other emigrants in Quiberon Bay, in the belief that the country round would take up the royalist cause. The expedition ended in entire failure.   In October a new constitution was established by the Convention.   The legislature consisted of two councils, and the executive of a body of five Directors. The violent stage of the French Revolution had come to an end, and there were many in England who thought that it would be desirable to make peace with a government which gave some hopes of moderation and stability, especially as the burden of the war had given rise to grave discontent in England.   When George III. drove through the streets on October 29 to open Parliament, he was surrounded by a hooting mob.   A bullet pierced one of his carriage windows.

21. **The Treason Act and the Sedition Act. 1795.**—Pitt could see nothing but revolutionary violence in this outburst.   He carried through Parliament two Bills, one declaring the mere writing, preaching, or speaking words against the king's authority to be treason, and the stirring up hatred against the king's person or the established government and constitution to be a punishable misdemeanour ; the other forbidding all political meetings unless advertised beforehand, and permitting any two justices to disperse them if they thought them dangerous.   Against these Bills Fox spoke with extreme vehemence ; but Pitt's supporters did him more harm than his opponents.   "The people," said Bishop Horsley, " had nothing to do with the laws but to obey them."   The two Bills became law, but public feeling was so set against them that they were never put into operation.

CHAPTER LII

THE UNION WITH IRELAND AND THE PEACE OF AMIENS

1795—1804

LEADING DATES

Reign of George III., 1760-1820

Lord Fitzwilliam in Ireland	1795
Bonaparte Invades Italy	1796
Pitt's First Negotiation with the Directory	1796
Battles of St. Vincent and Camperdown	1797
Pitt's Second Negotiation with the Directory	1797
Irish Rebellion	1798
The Battle of the Nile	1798
The Irish Union	1800
Pitt succeeded by Addington	1801
Peace of Amiens	March 28, 1802
Rupture of the Treaty of Amiens	1803
Resignation of Addington	April 30, 1804

1. **The Irish Government and Parliament. 1785—1791.**—In 1785, when Pitt was aiming at a commercial union with Ireland, he had expressed a desire to make ' England and Ireland one country in effect, though for local concerns under distinct legislatures.' The difficulty, however, lay in the unfitness of the Parliament at Dublin to play the part of a legislature 'for local concerns.' It was in no true sense representative. Three-fourths of the population were excluded as Catholics from sitting in Parliament and from voting at elections. Nor was the Irish House of Commons in any sense representative of the remaining Pro-testant fourth. The number of its members was three hundred, and of these, two hundred were chosen by less than one hundred persons, who controlled the elections of petty boroughs. More-over, as the ministers in Ireland were responsible, not to Parliament, but to the Lord Lieutenant, the Lord Lieutenant could, except in times of great excitement, govern without reference to the wishes of the House of Commons, and whenever it seemed desirable to him to have the House of Commons on his side he could, by a lavish distribution of places and pensions, buy up the votes of the members or of their patrons, as neither had any con-stituents to fear. Usually, however, the Lord Lieutenant who wished

to lead an easy life preferred to govern in accordance with the wishes of the corrupt faction which formed the Parliamentary majority.

2. The United Irishmen and Parliamentary Reform. 1791—1794.—Nowhere were the objections to this state of things felt more strongly than amongst the Presbyterians, who formed a great part of the population of Ulster, and especially of the flourishing town of Belfast, and were excluded as completely as the Catholics from office and from Parliament.   Amongst the upper and middle classes in Ulster, religious bigotry had almost died out, and they had, for some time past, been ready to admit Catholics to the franchise and to put them on political equality with themselves.   Then came the influence of the French Revolution, and, in October **1791**, the Society of United Irishmen was founded at Belfast by Wolfe Tone, himself a Presbyterian.   Its object was to unite Catholics and Protestants by widening the franchise and by opening office and Parliament to all without distinction of creed.   Pitt took alarm, but in **1793**, in order to baffle this extreme demand, he obtained from the Irish Parliament two Acts, the one freeing the Catholics from some of the worst penalties under which they suffered, and the other allowing them to vote for members of Parliament.   As, however, they were still disqualified from sitting in Parliament, the concession was almost illusory, and, moreover, only a minority of seats depended on election in any real sense.   In **1794** a very moderate Reform Bill, proposing the increase of independent constituencies, was rejected in the Irish House of Commons by a decisive majority.

3. The Mission of Lord Fitzwilliam. 1794—1795.—The seceders from the Whig party who joined Pitt in **1794** urged him to strengthen the Irish Government by granting Catholic emancipation and moderate reform, so as to keep in check the revolutionists on the one hand and the corrupt officials on the other.   Pitt consented to send Lord Fitzwilliam, one of the Whig seceders, to Ireland, as Lord Lieutenant, rather because he wished to gratify his new allies than because he personally approved of the change. Fitzwilliam himself understood that there was to be a complete change of system and that justice was to be done to the Catholics ; but he had held only verbal communications with Pitt, and there was probably a misunderstanding between the two statesmen.   At all events, Pitt told Fitzwilliam that not one of the existing officials was to be dismissed except for actual misconduct. With Pitt as, at the best, a hesitating ally, Fitzwilliam's mission was doomed to failure.   Fitzwilliam himself hastened that failure.   He landed in Dublin on January 4, 1795, and, almost at once, in defiance of his instructions, dismissed two of the worst of the officials, one of whom, John Beresford, was popularly known as the king of Ireland from the unbounded influence which he had gained by jobbery. He and the Irish Chancellor, Fitzgibbon, complained to the king that his ministers, in favouring Catholic emancipation, were leading him to a breach of the oath which he had taken at his coronation to defend the Protestant religion, and the king gave Pitt to understand that he would never consent to such a measure. Pitt was, moreover, subjected to pressure from English opinion, where the Catholics were anything but popular, and where any proposal to reform Parliament savoured of the principles of the French Revolution. In these views Pitt to some extent shared, and began to look for the best remedy for Irish difficulties in the constitution of a common Parliament for the two countries, as there had been a common Parliament for England and Scotland since 1707 (see p. 685). Fitzwilliam, whose arrival in Dublin had been welcomed as a message of peace from England, was promptly recalled, and Ireland was once more handed over to a Parliament dominated by place-hunters who, under the pretence of maintaining Protestantism, banded themselves together with the object of gaining wealth and position. " Did I ever give an honest vote in my life ? " is a sentence which is said to have escaped from the lips of a member of this faction.

4. **Impending Revolution. 1795—1796.**—Such an evil system was too provocative to remain long unassailed. In the Irish Parliament, Grattan spoke vehemently in favour of a Bill for Catholic emancipation, but the Bill was rejected. Lord Fitzwilliam's recall was followed by an outburst of violence. The Catholic gentry and middle classes were at that time quite ready to make common cause with the Protestants of their own standing in resistance to any popular movement ; but the mass of Irish peasants had grievances of their own so bitter that it was difficult for a Parliament hostile to their race and creed to govern them. The payment of tithes, especially, weighed heavily on an impoverished population, and was the more deeply felt as the money went to the support of a clergy of a creed hostile to that of those from whom it was exacted. If the Catholic gentry had been allowed to sit in Parliament, they would at least have brought their influence to bear in favour of an amelioration of the lot of the Catholic peasant in this respect. With respect to another grievance, it is doubtful whether the introduction of Catholic landlords into Parliament

would have had any salutary effect.   The landlords themselves for
the most part let their land at a low rent, but their tenants usually
let it out again at a higher rent, and the sub-tenants again let it at a
rent higher still, till in some places 6*l.* was charged as the rent of an
acre of potato ground.   In the lower classes the bitterness of religious
animosity had never been extinguished and blazed up into fierce
hatred.   In the summer of 1795, when hope of obtaining fair treatment from Parliament was extinguished, outrages committed by
Catholics upon Protestants became frequent.   Angry Protestants,
calling themselves Orangemen in memory of William III.,
retaliated, with all the strength of the Government behind them.
Violence and illegality appeared on both sides.   The United
Irishmen took up the cause of the Catholics, and, early in 1796,
sent Wolfe Tone to France, to urge the Directory to invade
Ireland and to establish a republic.

   5. **Bonaparte in Italy.**   1796—1797.—Before the end of 1796
France had reached a position of overwhelming strength on the
Continent.   At the beginning of that year her only serious enemies
were England, Austria and Sardinia.   In the spring, Bonaparte was
sent to attack the Austrian and Sardinian armies in Italy.   " You,"
he told his soldiers, " are ill-fed and naked.   I will lead you into
the most fertile places of the world, where you will find glory and
riches."   He defeated both Austrians and Sardinians, compelled
the king of Sardinia to make peace, drove the Austrians out of
Milan, and laid siege to Mantua their strongest fortress in Italy.
Again and again Bonaparte, with marvellous skill, defeated
Austrian armies attempting to save Mantua.   It was not, indeed,
till February 3, 1797, that Mantua, and with it the mastery of Italy,
passed into his hands; but for some time before that its surrender
had been a mere matter of time.

   6. **Pitt's First Negotiation with the Directory.**   1796.—On October
22, 1796, a British ambassador, Lord Malmesbury, reached Paris
to negotiate a peace.   He asked that France should abandon the
Austrian Netherlands, and should withdraw from Italy.   As Pitt
ought to have foreseen, if he did not actually foresee, the Directory
repelled such overtures with scorn.   Believing that they had
England at their mercy, they struck at Ireland.   On December 17,
a great fleet carrying an army of 20,000 men sailed from Brest
under the command of Hoche, one of the ablest of the French
generals, who had set his heart on winning Ireland from the English.
It was, however, dispersed at sea, and only some of its vessels
reached Bantry Bay, out of which they were driven by a violent

storm before a landing could be effected. The most satisfactory thing about this expedition, from the British point of view, was, that the Irish themselves had shown no signs of welcoming the invaders.

7. Suspension of Cash Payments. 1797.—Pitt was too exclusively an English minister to appreciate the real state of things either in Ireland or on the Continent. His treatment of Ireland was not such as to secure the internal peace of that country, and his treatment of France gave him neither peace nor victory. His main support lay in the extraordinary financial resources supplied by the rapidly increasing manufactures of England (see p. 814). Yet even on this ground he did not escape difficulties. In addition to the military and naval expenses incurred by his own country, he spent large sums upon its allies, and in the year **1796** sent no less than 4,000,000*l.* to Austria. Early in **1797** the Bank of England ran short of gold, and was authorised by the Government, and subsequently by Parliament, to suspend cash payments. For twenty-four years banknotes passed from hand to hand, though those who took them knew that it would be a long time before the Bank would be again able to exchange them for gold.

8. Battle of St. Vincent. 1797.—Success in Italy emboldened France in **1797** to attempt a great naval attack on Great Britain. The Batavian Republic—by which title the Dutch Netherlands were now known—had since 1795 been a dependent ally of France, and since October 6, **1796**, France had been allied with Spain, which, as soon as the excitement caused by the horrors of the Revolution came to an end, was brought back to the French side, by alarm at the preponderance of England at sea. If the French and Spanish fleets could effect a junction, they would be able to bring an overwhelming force into the English Channel, whilst the Dutch fleet was to be employed to convey to Ireland an army of 14,000 men. To prevent this, Admiral Sir John Jervis, on February 16, attacked the Spanish fleet off Cape St. Vincent. His ships were fewer and smaller than those of the Spaniards, but they were better equipped and better manned. Commodore[1] Nelson, disobeying orders, dashed with his own and one other ship into the midst of the enemy's fleet. Two other ships followed him after a while, but still the chances of war seemed to be against him. Yet he boarded and captured, first the ' San Nicolas ' of 80 guns, and then the ' San Josef,' the flag-ship of the Spanish Admiral, of 112. As the swords of the Spanish officers who surrendered were too many for

---

[1] *i.e.* A captain having command of other ships besides his own.

him to hold, he gave them to one of his bargemen, who coolly tucked them in a bundle under his arm. Jervis was made Earl St. Vincent for the victory; but he was so nettled at Nelson's disobedience, that he did not even mention his name in the despatch which was published in the 'Gazette.' Nearer home the main business of the British fleet was to prevent a junction between the French and the Dutch. Admiral Duncan was sent to blockade the Dutch in the Texel, whilst Lord Bridport, at the head of the fleet at Spithead, was expected to look after the French.

9. **Mutiny at Spithead. 1797.**—The plans of the Government were nearly upset by an unexpected mutiny in the fleet. The sailors were paid at a rate settled in the reign of Charles II., though the price of clothes and provisions had risen considerably. They were badly fed, and when they were sick or even wounded, their pay was stopped. Order was kept by constant flogging, often administered for slight offences. The sailors at Spithead finding, after petitioning the Admiralty for redress of grievances, that no notice was taken of their petition, refused to go to sea. On this the Lords of the Admiralty instructed Lord Howe to assure them that justice should be done. Howe was a favourite amongst them, and they agreed to return to their duty. A short while afterwards, suspecting the Admiralty of a design to break the promise given to them, they again broke out into mutiny; but subsequently abandoned their hostile attitude on discovering that the Admiralty had no intention of dealing unfairly with them.

10. **Mutiny at the Nore. 1797.**—A more serious mutiny broke out in the fleet stationed at the Nore to guard the mouth of the Thames, where the sailors asked not merely to have actual grievances redressed, but to vote on the movements of their own ships even in the presence of an enemy, and blockaded the mouth of the Thames to enforce their demands. The mutiny spread to Duncan's ships off the Texel, the greater number of which sailed to join the fleet at the Nore. At one time Duncan was left to blockade the Dutch with only one ship besides his own. With this one ship he kept the Dutch in port, by constantly running up flags to make them think that he was signalling to the rest of his fleet, which they imagined to be just out of sight. In the meanwhile, the Government at home got the better of the mutineers. Parker, the chief leader of the revolt, was hanged, with seventeen others, and the crews submitted to their officers and did good service afterwards.

11. **Pitt's second Negotiation with the Directory. 1797.**—Soon

after the submission of the fleet at the Nore, Pitt made one more effort to obtain peace. Negotiations were held at Lille, but they broke down as completely as the negotiations in the preceding year. Austria had already signed preliminaries of peace with France at Leoben, and as Austria then engaged to abandon its possessions in the Netherlands, Pitt agreed to leave them under French dominion. He was also prepared to surrender some West Indian islands which British fleets had conquered from France, but he would not give up Trinidad, which they had taken from Spain, or the Cape of Good Hope, which they had taken from the Dutch. On his refusal the negotiations were broken off by the Directory. England had the mastery by sea, and France by land. On October 11 Duncan defeated the Dutch fleet off Camperdown, on the coast of Holland, thus putting an end to the projected invasion of Ireland (see p. 835) ; and on October 18 Bonaparte signed peace with Austria at Campo-Formio. The Austrian Netherlands were abandoned to France, whilst the Austrian territories in North Italy were made part of a republic called the Cisalpine Republic, and practically dependent on France. To compensate Austria— as the phrase went—the old Venetian Republic was suppressed, and the greater part of its territory given over to Austria, whilst the remainder went to the Cisalpine Republic. In the partition of Poland, the old governments had set the example of despoiling the weak, and Bonaparte did but carry out their principles.

12. **Bonaparte's Expedition to Egypt. 1798.**—When Bonaparte returned to France the Directory urged him to conquer England, but he preferred to go to Egypt. His vast abilities seldom failed him when he was called on to do what was possible to be done, but there was in him a romantic vein which constantly beguiled him into attempting impossible achievements. He hoped by the conquest of Egypt to found an empire in the East, from which he could hold out a hand to the native rulers of India who were struggling against British authority. Foremost amongst these rulers was Tippoo, the son of Hyder Ali (see p. 805), who had inherited his father's throne without his father's military abilities. Tippoo had in 1792 been defeated by Cornwallis and stripped of half his territory, but he was now burning to revenge the disaster, and hoped that Bonaparte would assist him to do so. On May 19 Bonaparte with a large fleet and army sailed from Toulon, seizing Malta on his way from the Knights of St. John. On his arrival in Egypt he marched against the Mamelukes—a splendid body of cavalry, the Beys or chiefs of which ruled the country under

the nominal supremacy of the Sultan—defeated them at the Battle of the Pyramids, and made himself master of the land.

13. **The Battle of the Nile. 1798.** —On August 1, Nelson—now an admiral—found the French fleet which had conveyed Bonaparte anchored in Aboukir Bay. Instead of following the old fashion of fighting in which the hostile fleets engaged one another in parallel lines; he improved upon the example of breaking the line set by Rodney in 1782. Sending half his fleet through the middle of the enemy's line, he made it take up a position between half of the French ships and the shore, whilst the other half of his own ships placed themselves outside the same part of the enemy's line. He thus crushed part of the enemy's fleet by placing it between two fires before the other part had time to weigh anchor and to come up. The battle raged far into the night. Nelson himself was wounded, and carried below. A surgeon ran up to attend on him. " No," he said, " I will take my turn with my brave fellows." Before long he heard a cry that the French Admiral's ship was on fire. Hurrying on deck, he gave orders to send boats to help the French who threw themselves into the sea to escape the flames. The Battle of the Nile ended in a complete British victory, which, by cutting off Bonaparte's army from France, threw insuperable difficulties in the way of his scheme for the establishment of a French empire in the East.

14. **Bonaparte in Syria. 1799.** —Bonaparte, however, refused to abandon the hopes which he had formed. On January 26 he wrote to Tippoo announcing his preparations to relieve him. In the spring of 1799, Lord Mornington, the Governor-General of India, sent an army under Harris against Tippoo, and on May 4 Tippoo's capital, Seringapatam, was stormed and himself slain. Bonaparte was too far off to attempt a rescue. In February, learning that a Turkish army was coming against him through Syria, he set out to meet it. For a while he was victorious, but he was baffled by the desperate resistance of the Turkish garrison of Acre, which had been encouraged in its defence by an English Commodore, Sir Sidney Smith. On April 11, Bonaparte abandoned the siege of Acre and withdrew to Egypt. There he held his own, but Sir Sidney Smith sent him a file of newspapers to inform him of the events which had been passing in Europe during his absence. So startling was the news, that on August 22 Bonaparte sailed for France, leaving his army in Egypt to its fate.

15. **Foundation of the Consulate. 1799—1800.** —What Bonaparte learned from the newspapers was that a new coalition had been formed against France, this time between England, Austria and

Russia.   The French armies in Germany had been driven across the Rhine, and those in Italy had been beaten in two great battles, one on the Trebbia and the other at Novi, and had been driven across the Alps.   When Bonaparte landed in France, he was prepared to turn the disasters of his country to his own advantage. Though a French General, Massena, had defeated the Austrians

Head-dress of a lady (Mrs. Abington), about 1778 : from the *European Magazine.*

at Zürich in September, Bonaparte represented the policy of the Directory in the worst colours, accused them of ruining France, and in November made himself master of the country by military violence, on the plea that it was necessary to revise the Constitution.   In 1800 he was named First Consul, under which title he exercised absolute authority, though he was still nominally only the first magistrate of the Republic.

16. **An Overture for Peace. 1799.**—One of Bonaparte's first acts after thrusting the Directory from power was to offer peace to England, but his offer was repelled with scorn. Lord Grenville, the Foreign Secretary, in his reply, even went so far as to suggest that the best security which the French could give for peace was the recalling of the Bourbons to the throne. Yet, whatever the Government might say, the country longed for peace. In **1798** Pitt had added to its burdens an income-tax of 10 per cent., and if the war was to go on till the Bourbons were recalled, the prospect before the nation was indeed dreary.

17. **The Campaign of Marengo and the Peace of Lunéville. 1800—1801.**—At the end of **1799** Pitt cherished the hope that the recent successes of the coalition against France would be continued. In **1800** this hope was dashed to the ground. The Coalition itself broke up. The Tzar Paul, who was half mad, was an enthusiastic admirer of Bonaparte, and when he learnt that Bonaparte was in power withdrew from his alliance with Austria. Bonaparte crossed the Alps, crushed an Austrian army at Marengo in Piedmont, and later in the same year another French General, Moreau, crushed another Austrian army at Hohenlinden in Bavaria. On February 9, **1801**, a peace in which the Rhine was formally acknowledged to be the boundary of France was signed at Lunéville. The cry for peace increased in England. The harvest of **1800** was a bad one, and in that year and in the following spring the price of corn rose till it reached 156s. a quarter. If peace was to be had, Pitt was hardly the man to negotiate it, as he was regarded in France as the most violent enemy of that country, where every evil from which it suffered was popularly attributed to 'the gold of Pitt.' It happened, however, that before any fresh negotiation was opened, Pitt resigned office from causes entirely disconnected with the affairs of the Continent.

18. **The Irish Rebellion. 1798.**—Hoche's failure in **1797** (see p. 834) had not been followed by any abatement of violence in Ireland. The so-called Protestant militia and yeomanry, under pretence of repressing insurrection and outrage, themselves committed outrages with impunity, and the regular soldiers even learnt to follow their evil example. In order to procure the delivery of concealed arms, suspected persons were flogged and their houses burnt to the ground. Amongst those who were concerned in these savage actions, Fitzgerald, the Sheriff of Tipperary—'Flogging Fitzgerald,' as he was usually called—obtained an unenviable notoriety. He indeed suppressed by his energy the organisation of

those who were preparing to welcome a fresh invasion by the French, but his energy often showed itself in the form of brutal outrage. On one occasion, for instance, he almost flogged to death a teacher of languages because he found in his possession a note in the French language which he was himself unable to read, but which he took as evidence of complicity with the French Government. Sir Ralph Abercromby, the commander-in-chief in Ireland, was in 1798 driven by the clamour of the officials to resign his office because he remonstrated against this rule of license as injurious to the discipline of the army. The Catholics subject to outrage joined the society of United Irishmen in thousands, and the United Irishmen at once made preparations for an insurrection. The secret was betrayed to the Government and the leaders arrested. Nevertheless on May 21 bands of peasants armed with pikes rose in insurrection, principally in Wexford, and in many places committed horrible atrocities. These atrocities, being usually committed against Protestants, alienated the Presbyterians of the North, who from that time began to take part with the Government. At one time it was feared that even Dublin would fall into the hands of the insurgents, but they were defeated at Vinegar Hill near Wexford by the regular troops under General Lake. In August, a French force of 1100 landed in Killala Bay. The first troops sent against them met them at Castlebar, but ran away so fast that the affair is known as the race of Castlebar. The French were, however, too few to make a long resistance, and on September 9 they surrendered, thus bringing to an end all chance of successful resistance to English authority in Ireland.

19. **An Irish Reign of Terror. 1798—1799.**—Before the defeat of the French, Lord Cornwallis arrived as Lord Lieutenant of Ireland. He was a just man, and was deeply moved by the violence of those who styled themselves loyalists. Magistrates and soldiers vied with one another in acts of cruelty. The practice of torturing prisoners to extort confessions was common, and Lord Cornwallis, who did his best to stop these atrocious proceedings, was exasperated by the light way in which they were regarded in his own presence. " The conversation of the principal persons of the country," he wrote, " all tends to encourage this system of blood, and the conversation, even at my table, where you may suppose I do all I can to prevent it, always turns on hanging, shooting, burning, &c., and if a priest has been put to death, the greatest joy is expressed by the whole company." In 1799 the Irish Parliament passed an Act of indemnity securing against punishment all persons

who had used illegal violence which could in any way be connected with the suppression of the rebellion.

20. **The Irish Union.   1800.**—The Irish Parliament could hardly be left as it was.   In **1795** it might have been possible to reform it ; in **1799**, when the country was torn asunder by bitter hatred, when Protestants had used Parliamentary forms to wreak vengeance on Catholics, and when Catholics, if they were allowed to form the majority in it, would use them to wreak vengeance on Protestants, it was no longer possible.   The easy way of putting an end to the difficulty by uniting the British and Irish Parliaments more and more commended itself to Pitt.   The majority in the Irish Parliament was venal, and Pitt, through the medium of a young

The Union Jack, in use
since 1801.

Irish official, Lord Castlereagh, secured a majority in it, not indeed by paying money directly for votes, but by agreeing to compensate the owners of boroughs at the rate of 15,000*l.* a seat,[1] and by granting peerages and lavishly dispensing patronage as a reward for Parliamentary support. Grattan came forth from the retirement in which he had remained during the late times of trouble, and denounced the Union ; but the Act of Union received the assent of the Parliament at Dublin as well as of the Parliament at Westminster, and after January 1, **1801**, there was but one Parliament for the two countries.

21. **Pitt's Resignation.   1801.**—Pitt no doubt had the most generous intentions. He imagined that the United Parliament would judge fairly and justly between the two hostile Irish parties, and he wished it to win over the sympathies of Irish Catholics, by offering a State maintenance to their priests, by improving the existing system of the payment of tithes, and, above all, by admitting Catholics to office and to seats in Parliament. Having little doubt that he would be able to accomplish this, he had allowed it to be understood in Ireland that he would support a measure of Catholic emancipation.   He soon, however, found that the king would not hear of this proposal, and behind the king was the British nation. On this, he resigned office, and indeed he could hardly do less. Pitt, however, though he was himself out of office, offered his

[1] This was, however, paid whether the owner's nominee voted for the government or not.

assistance in the formation of a ministry hostile to the Catholic claims, over which his influence might be felt, and he probably expected at the time that this arrangement would be of long continuance.

22. The Addington Ministry. 1801.—At the head of the new ministry was Addington, who had been Speaker of the House of Commons, a well-meaning, inefficient man, strongly hostile to Catholic emancipation, and warmly attached to Pitt. Before Addington could settle himself in office, the king's mind, shaken

William Pitt : from the bust by Nollekens in the National Portrait Gallery.

by the excitement of recent events, once more gave way. This time, however, the attack was of short duration, and, as soon as recovery was complete, Pitt assured him that he would never again propose Catholic emancipation during his reign. There are reasons for supposing that Pitt would at this time willingly have returned to office, but the king had already engaged himself to the new Ministers, and Addington had to try his hand at governing the country.

23. Malta and Egypt. 1800.—As far as the war was concerned the arrangements made by Pitt before his resignation were crowned with success. After a long siege, Malta surrendered in **1800**, and on March 8, **1801**, an expedition under Sir Ralph Abercromby landed in Egypt to drive out the French army which had been left

there by Bonaparte. Abercromby was killed, but his troops, after a series of successful operations, finally reduced Alexandria to surrender on August 30, when it was agreed that the whole of the French army should evacuate Egypt. The Egyptian campaign was memorable, as showing, for the first time since the French Revolution, that British soldiers were still capable of defeating the French.

Royal Arms as borne from 1714 to 1801.

**24. The Northern Confederacy and the Battle of Copenhagen.
1801.**—In the North the British Government was no less successful. A Northern Confederacy had been formed between Russia, Sweden and Denmark which, though it did not declare itself directly hostile to England, was intended to resist, as in the days of

Royal arms as borne from 1801 to 1816: the Hanoverian scutcheon surmounted by an electoral bonnet.

Royal arms from 1816 to 1837: the Hanoverian scutcheon surmounted by a royal crown.

the American War, the pretensions of British ships to search neutral vessels in order to take out of them French goods (see p. 792). The Government sent a fleet to break up the confederacy, but appointed Nelson only second in command under Sir Hyde Parker, who was of no note as a sailor. Parker sent Nelson to attack Copenhagen. On April 2, Nelson opened fire upon the heavy batteries which defended the city. After the battle had raged for some time, Parker, believing Nelson to be in danger of defeat, hoisted a signal ordering him to draw off. Nelson, who some years before had lost the sight of an eye in action, put his telescope to his blind eye, and, declaring that he could not see the signal of recall, kept his own signal for close action flying. In the end the Danish batteries were silenced. Nelson sent ashore the wounded

Greathead's lifeboat, 1803 : from the *European Magazine.*

Danes, and when he landed was received with shouts by the people in appreciation of his kindness to the sufferers. Nelson assured the Crown Prince, who acted as Regent in his father's place, that he wished to treat the Danes as the brothers of the English, and an armistice was concluded. Not long afterwards, the war in the North came to an end through the murder of the Tzar Paul. His son and successor, Alexander I., made on June 17 a treaty with England, in which he and his allies abandoned their claim that the neutral flag should protect enemies' goods, thus admitting the right of search claimed by the British Government.

25. The Treaty of Amiens. 1802.—Negotiations with France were in the meanwhile pushed rapidly forward. Preliminaries of peace were signed in London on October 1, **1801**, and a definitive treaty at Amiens on March 28, **1802**. Great Britain abandoned all her conquests beyond the seas except Ceylon and Trinidad, and agreed to restore Malta to the Knights, if its possession by them were guaranteed by the great powers. 'It was a peace which,' as Sheridan, the wit of the Opposition, declared, 'everybody would be glad of, but which nobody would be proud of.' The broad fact of the situation was that France was strong enough to retain her conquests in Europe ; and that the enthusiasm which would alone enable those who had suffered from her aggression to wrest

The old East India House in 1803.

her gains from her was entirely lacking both in England and on the Continent. Pitt may have been right in holding that England ought not to allow France to possess herself of the Netherlands ; but he had totally failed in preventing her from doing it, and in **1802** there did not appear to be the remotest chance that he or any other minister would succeed better in the future. In Parliament and out of Parliament the peace was welcomed with joy. George III., when the preliminaries of peace were signed in **1801**, had taken the opportunity to abandon the empty title of king of France, which had been borne by his predecessors since the time of Edward III., and to omit the French lilies from the royal arms (see p. 844).

26. Rupture of the Treaty of Amiens. 1803.—The Treaty of Amiens had scarcely been signed before the English Ministers began

The old Houses of Parliament and Westminster Abbey, 1803.

to fear that Bonaparte was about to employ the time of peace merely to strengthen himself for further attacks upon their own and other countries. He annexed Piedmont and occupied Switzerland. It is probable, however, that these things would have been passed over in England, if the Ministry had not conceived suspicions that he intended to re-occupy Egypt. They therefore refused to give up Malta to the Knights as they were bound by the treaty to do, first on the ground that no guarantee of its independence could be obtained from the great Powers (see p. 846), and then on the ground that, whatever they might be bound to by treaty, they needed Malta as a security against the danger of a French conquest of Egypt. Bonaparte claimed the execution of the treaty, and on one occasion used most violent language to Lord Whitworth, the English ambassador. He was himself irritated, not merely on the subject of Malta, but because the English Ministers refused to suppress without trial the virulent attacks on himself which were published by the French refugees in England. One of these, named Peltier, was indeed convicted of libel by a jury, but he escaped punishment because France and England were again at war before judgment was pronounced against him. As no compromise about Malta acceptable to both sides could be found, war was recommenced before the end of May **1803**.

27. **The last Months of the Addington Ministry.** 1803—1804. On the outbreak of hostilities, Bonaparte gave reasonable offence to the British nation by throwing into prison about 10,000 British travellers, though it had always been the custom to give time to such persons to leave the country after a declaration of war. As he had no other war on his hands than that with Great Britain, he seized Hanover and assembled a large army at Boulogne to invade England. At once a volunteer army stepped forward to aid the regular army in the defence of the country. From one end of the country to the other some 300,000 volunteers of all classes were busily drilling. Public opinion soon demanded a stronger ministry than the existing one. On May 10, **1804**, Addington resigned. General opinion called for Pitt as Prime Minister at the head of a ministry taken from both parties, so that all disposable talent might be employed in the defence of the nation. The King insisted that Pitt should promise never to support Catholic Emancipation, and should exclude Fox from the new ministry. Fox at once consented to be passed over, but Lord Grenville refused to join if Fox was excluded. " I will teach that proud man," said Pitt, " that I can do without him," and on May 18 Pitt again became Prime Minister, though with but a poor staff of ministers to support him.

CHAPTER LIII

THE ASCENDENCY OF NAPOLEON. 1804—1807

LEADING DATES

Reign of George III., 1760—1820

Pitt's Second Prime Ministership . . Napoleon declared Emperor of the French } .	May 18, 1804
Battle of Trafalgar	Oct. 21, 1805
Battle of Austerlitz	Dec. 2, 1805
Death of Pitt	Jan. 23, 1806
Death of Fox	Sept. 13, 1806
Battle of Jena	Oct. 14, 1806
The Berlin Decree	Nov. 21, 1806
Treaty of Tilsit	July 7, 1807
Orders in Council	Nov. 11, 1807
The Milan Decree	Dec. 17, 1807

1. **The Napoleonic Empire. 1804.**—There was scarcely an Englishman living in 1804 who did not regard Napoleon as a wicked and unprincipled villain whom it was the duty of every honest man to resist to the death. This conception of his character was certainly not without foundation. He had no notion of allowing moral scruples to interfere with his designs, and whenever his personal interests were concerned he knew no rule except that of his own will. Having nearly been the victim of an attempt at assassination by a party of Royalists, he avenged himself by kidnapping the Duke of Enghien on the neutral territory of Baden and having him shot, simply because he was a kinsman of the Bourbon Princes, the brothers of the late King. In his dealings with foreign states he took whatever seemed good to him to take, and his seizure of Piedmont was but the forerunner of other annexations. Yet, regardless of morality as he was, Napoleon was not more regardless of it than the statesmen who had partitioned Poland, and he had at least an intellectual preference for good government. He gave to France an excellent administration, and also gave his sanction to the code of law drawn up by the jurists of the Republic, which was now to be known as the Code Napoleon. He also took care that there should be good justice in his courts between man and man. Hence, exasperating as his annexations were to the great sovereigns of Europe, they were not popular grievances. A country annexed to France, or even merely brought, as most of the German

states now were, under the influence of France, found its gain in being better governed.   On May 18 Napoleon was declared here-

The King in the House of Lords, 1804: from *Modern London.*

ditary Emperor of the French.   His power was neither more nor less absolute than it had been before.

2. **A Threatened Invasion.   1804—1805.**—Neither the French
Revolution nor the French Empire was to be resisted by governments acting without a popular force behind them ; and in 1804 it
was only in England that the government had a popular force
behind it, and could therefore oppose to Napoleon a national
resistance.   Every day that saw a French army encamped at
Boulogne strengthened that resistance.   Napoleon was, indeed, so
certain of success that he ordered the preparation of a medal
falsely stating itself to have been struck in London, as if the
conquest of England had been already effected.   Strong as Pitt
became in the country, he was weak in Parliament.   Before the
end of 1804 he was reconciled to Addington, who entered the
ministry as Viscount Sidmouth.   On April 6 a vote was carried which
led to the impeachment, on a charge of peculation, of his old friend

Napoleon's medal struck to commemorate the invasion of England : from a cast in the
British Museum.

Henry Dundas, now Lord Melville and First Lord of the Admiralty.
Ultimately Melville was acquitted, and there is no reason to think
that he was guilty of more than neglect of the forms needed for
guarding against embezzlement ; but Melville's necessary resignation
was a sad blow to Pitt.

3. **The Trafalgar Campaign.   1805.**—Napoleon's plan for the
invasion of England was most skilful.   He was aware that boats
laden with troops could not cross the Channel unless their passage
could be guarded against British ships of war, but as the king
of Spain was now on his side against England, he had three fleets
at his disposal, two French ones at Toulon and Brest, and a
Spanish one at Cadiz.   He thought that, though not one of these
was separately a match for a British fleet, yet that the three
combined would at least be strong enough to hold the Channel

Hyde Park on Sunday, A.D. 1804 : from *Modern London*

long enough to enable him to get his army across. Consequently, the Toulon fleet, escaping by his orders from that port, made its way to Cadiz, and picking up the Spanish fleet there, sailed along with it to the West Indies. As Napoleon expected, Nelson, who commanded the British Mediterranean fleet, sailed to the West Indies in pursuit of the French and Spanish fleets. Whilst Nelson was searching for them, they, in accordance with Napoleon's

Lord Nelson : from the picture by Abbott in the National Portrait Gallery.

instructions, were already on their way back to Europe, where they were to drive off the British squadron blockading Brest, and then, combining with the French fleet which had been shut up there, to make their way up the Channel and hold the Straits of Dover in irresistible force in Nelson's absence. Part of Napoleon's expectation was fulfilled. Nelson indeed sailed to the West Indies with thirteen ships after the enemy's fleet, which numbered thirty. Not finding them there, he sailed back in pursuit. They, however, reached the Bay of Biscay before him, and were there attacked by Sir Robert Calder, who happened to meet them with fifteen British ships. Two Spanish ships were taken, and the rest of the fleet was so terrified that it betook itself to Cadiz.

4. **The Battle of Trafalgar. 1805.**—England was saved from invasion, but it was Napoleon's pride which completed her triumph. Though the French sailors had been too long blockaded in various ports to be efficient seamen, he insisted on his admiral's putting again to sea. With a heavy heart the admiral obeyed orders, and on October 21 Nelson fell in with him off Cape Trafalgar. Nelson gave the signal of " England expects every man to do his duty." In the battle which followed, the French and Spanish fleets were almost entirely destroyed, but Nelson fell mortally wounded by a shot from a French ship. Never again during the war did a French or Spanish fleet venture to put out from harbour, or had a British navy to contend for the mastery over the sea. Yet, so deeply was Nelson honoured in England, that when the news of the triumph arrived, it was doubtful whether joy for the victory or sorrow for the loss was the greater.

5. **The Campaign of Austerlitz. 1805.**—In 1805 there was strife on land as well as at sea. In April the foundations of a third coalition against France were laid by an alliance between England and Russia. Napoleon defied it by annexing Genoa to France, and by converting the old Cisalpine Republic, which had been named the Italian Republic in 1802, into a kingdom of Italy of which he was himself the king. Austria joined the coalition, and in August Napoleon, knowing that by Calder's victory his scheme for the invasion of England had failed, marched his army off from Boulogne to attack Austria and Russia. His enemies had no time to combine against him. An advanced force of Austrians about 40,000 strong was at Ulm on the Upper Danube. The main Austrian army was still around Vienna, whilst the Russian army was slowly advancing to its aid. On October 14 Napoleon compelled the Austrians at Ulm to capitulate. On November 11 he entered Vienna, the Austrian army having retreated to join the Russian. On December 2 he signally defeated the two armies at Austerlitz. The Russians fell back on their own country. On December 6 the Emperor Francis signed the Treaty of Pressburg, abandoning Venetia to the new kingdom of Italy, and Tyrol to Bavaria.

6. **Pitt's Death. 1806.**—Pitt, worn out with work and anxiety,

did not recover the blow. " How I leave my country !" were the last words spoken by him. On January 23, **1806**, he died. In modern times he is chiefly respected as the enlightened financier and statesman of the years of peace. His resistance to France, it is thought, was weakly planned, and his management of the war disastrous. In his own time he was regarded as ' The Pilot that weathered the storm.' If he failed in his military efforts against France on the Continent, where he had but governments to oppose to a nation, he made England safe by the impulse which he gave to her power at sea. " England," he once said in replying to a toast at the Guildhall, " has saved herself by her exertions, and will save Europe by her example." Such words forms Pitt's best epitaph. He showed what could be done by a nation conscious of its strength, and resolute not to bow to the dictates of a despotic conqueror.

7. **The Ministry of All the Talents. 1806.**—Pitt's death left the king no choice but to take Fox as a minister. A ministry known as the Ministry of All the Talents was formed out of various parties. Lord Grenville, who had been Foreign Secretary at the end of Pitt's first ministry, became Prime Minister, bringing with him an air of respectability of which the Whigs were in want, whilst Fox was Foreign Secretary, and a place was even found for Sidmouth, the leader of the stiffest Tories. Fox did his best to bring the war to an end by opening a negotiation with France, taking advantage of the confession of a man, in all probability an agent of Napoleon himself, that he intended to murder the Emperor of the French. Fox, however, soon discovered that Napoleon was too slippery to be bound by treaties. At one time the French Emperor offered to restore Hanover to the King of England, and at another time he drew back and offered it to Prussia. Even Fox became convinced that a continuance of the war was unavoidable. He was himself suffering from dropsy, and had not many weeks to live ; but, though unable to give peace to his country, he had time to signalise the close of his career by moving a resolution for the abolition of the slave trade (see p. 823), as far as British ships and colonies were concerned. Fox died on September 13 ; and though the slave trade was not abolished by law till after his death, he lived to know that all real difficulties had been surmounted. Whether, if he had held office for a longer term, he would have been distinguished amongst practical statesmen, it is difficult to say. It is true that he was not an originator of new schemes of policy ; but a minister may be none the worse for that, if he has the tact and skill to secure the acceptance of the schemes of others. Fox's main defect was his want of power

to forecast the temper with which his words and acts would be received, and he thus frequently, as in the cases of the coalition with Lord North (see p. 800) and of the Regency Bill (see p. 811), made himself unpopular, much to his own surprise. The generous warmth of his disposition, and his hopeful sympathy with all good and great causes, give him a high place amongst British statesmen.

8. **The Overthrow of Prussia.   1806.**—The spring and summer of **1806** had been spent by Napoleon in remodelling Germany. He united the middle-sized states of the south into a confederation of

Fox : from his bust by Nollekens in the National Portrait Gallery.

the Rhine, practically under his own authority, to support France against Austria and Prussia.   On August 6 Francis II. abandoned for ever the futile title of Roman Emperor which had come down to him from the Cæsars, and was thenceforward known by the new title of Emperor of Austria which he had given himself in **1804.** Napoleon placed his brother Joseph on the throne of Naples, and though a British force landed in the Neapolitan dominions and defeated the French invaders at Maida, it could not save the mainland, and the English Government had to content itself with keeping Sicily for the Spanish Bourbon, Ferdinand I., who still called himself King of the Two Sicilies. Somewhat later Napoleon made another of his brothers—Louis—king of Holland. Neither in Italy nor in the smaller states of Germany was there any feeling of offended nationality goading on the populations to resist changes which brought with them more active government and better administration. Prussia, however, still maintained her independence, and when, after offering to her Hanover, Napoleon, in the course of his negotiation with Fox, turned round and offered to restore it to the King of England, the long patience of the King of Prussia, Frederick William III., was exhausted. War between Prussia and France was declared ; but the Prussian State and army were both completely inefficient, and on October 14 two Prussian armies were not merely beaten, but absolutely destroyed as military organisations, at Jena and Auerstadt. The Prussian State crumbled away, and before the end of November Napoleon was in military possession of the greater part of Prussia.

9. **The End of the Ministry of All the Talents. 1807.**—Russia came to the aid of the now diminished Prussia. On February 8, 1807, a drawn battle was fought at Eylau. The Tzar Alexander I. anxiously looked to England for aid, thinking that if an English army were landed on the coast of the Baltic, Napoleon would be obliged to detach part of his forces to watch it, and would thereby be weakened in his struggle with Russia. The Ministry of All the Talents, however, had no capacity for war. They frittered away their strength by sending useless expeditions to the Dardanelles, to Egypt, and to Buenos Ayres, leaving themselves no troops for the decisive struggle nearer home. On March 24 they were expelled from office by the king, because, though they agreed to relinquish a project which they had formed for allowing Catholics to serve as officers in the army and navy, they refused to promise that they would never under any circumstances propose any measure of concession to the Catholics. On March 25, the day after their resignation, the royal assent was given to a bill for the abolition of the slave trade. The new Prime Minister was the inefficient Duke of Portland, who had been the nominal head of the Coalition Ministry in 1783 (see p. 801). The ablest members of the new Cabinet were Lord Castlereagh, who had managed the Irish Parliament at the time of the Union, and the brilliant George Canning, who had been one of the staunchest of the followers of Pitt. The remainder of Portland's colleagues were narrow in their views, and all were pledged to resist Catholic emancipation. A dissolution of Parlia-

III.

3 K

ment took place before long, and it was found that the constituencies supported the king and the new ministry. The reaction against the principles of the French revolutionists was still so strong that it was difficult to obtain a hearing even for the most necessary plan of reform.

10. **The Treaty of Tilsit. 1807.**—Canning, who was Foreign Secretary, would readily have sent to the Baltic the forces which his predecessor had refused to the Tzar. Before, however, they could be got ready, Napoleon defeated the Russians at Friedland on June 14, and on the 25th he held an interview with the Tzar on a raft on the Niemen. Alexander was vexed at the delay of the English, and the first words he uttered to Napoleon were, " I hate the English as much as you do." The Treaty of Tilsit, signed between France and Russia on July 7, was the result of the conference. By a secret understanding, Russia was allowed to conquer Finland from Sweden, and as much of the Turkish dominions as she could get, whilst all Europe west of the Russian border was delivered over to Napoleon. He erected a new kingdom of Westphalia for his youngest brother, Jerome, and gave a great part of Poland, under the name of the Grand Duchy of Warsaw, to the Elector of Saxony, whom he had recently converted into a king. The confederation of the Rhine was extended to include all the German states except Austria and Prussia. The weight of Napoleon's vengeance fell heavily on Prussia. Not only was her territory much reduced, but she was forced to support French garrisons in her fortresses, and was compelled to pay enormous sums of money to France, and to limit her army to 42,000 men. Hitherto the people of defeated states had been, on the whole, better off in consequence of their defeat. The Prussians were far worse off, and, therefore, the treatment of Prussia by Napoleon for the first time brought against him popular ill-will.

11. **The Colonies. 1804—1807.**—Whilst Napoleon was establishing a dominion over the western and central part of the European Continent, Great Britain made use of her dominion of the sea to enlarge her colonial possessions. No one at that time thought much of the establishment in 1788 of a settlement of convicts in Botany Bay, or what afterwards came to be known as New South Wales. The two points at which British ambition aimed were the security of the sea route to India and the extension of the production of sugar in the West Indies. The first design was satisfied in 1806, by a second and permanent occupation of the Dutch territory at the Cape of Good Hope ; the second, in 1804, by the taking from the Dutch of the territory on the mainland of South America,

afterwards known as British Guiana, and by the capture of West India Islands which had hitherto been held by the French and Dutch.

12. **The Overthrow of the Mahrattas. 1802—1806.**—Since the destruction of Tippoo Sahib in 1799, Lord Mornington (see p. 838), recently created Marquis Wellesley, had discovered that Sindhia, one of the Mahratta chiefs, had a large force organised by a Frenchman, Perron. He therefore attempted to introduce a subsidiary system, compelling native rulers to pay the expenses of troops under British officers which could be used against them if they were not submissive. In 1802, the Peishwah having been driven from Poonah by Holkar (see p. 802), Wellesley entered into a compact to restore him on condition of his agreeing to a subsidiary treaty. Two other great Mahratta chiefs, Sindhia and the Bhonsla, who was Rajah of Berar, joined Holkar against the English, and in 1803 Wellesley sent against the confederacy his brother Arthur Wellesley. On September 23, 1803, Arthur Wellesley at the head of 4,500 men defeated Sindhia's 30,000 at Assaye, whilst Lake defeated Perron's force on August 29 at Alighur, and after various successes crushed Sindhia himself on November 1, in a hard-contested battle at Laswaree. On November 29 Wellesley again defeated the united forces of Sindhia and the Bhonsla at Argaum. On this, both chiefs made their submission, ceding territory to the English, and to the allies of the English, the Nizam, and Shah Alum, who held nominal rule at Delhi as the Great Mogul. Holkar, who was again joined by Sindhia, held out till January 1806, at one time gaining no inconsiderable successes, though all three, Sindhia, Holkar, and the Bhonsla, were in the end compelled to submit.

13. **Wellesley's Recall. 1805.**—In 1805, before Holkar had submitted, Lord Wellesley was recalled. His wars had been expensive, and the East India Company never liked expense. No one now doubts that Wellesley was right. The Mahratta chiefs were freebooters on a large scale, and freebooting was incompatible with the peace and civilisation which it was the glory of British statesmen to introduce into India. Wellesley, when he landed in 1798, found the British occupying certain portions of India. When he left the country in 1805, almost the whole of the South had passed under British administration, what are now the North-Western Provinces had been annexed, and the military predominance of the Mahrattas had been brought to an end.

14. **The Continental System. 1806—1807.**—In the meanwhile Napoleon, hopeless of overpowering Britain at sea, attempted to

subjugate her in another way. On November 21, **1806,** soon after his victory at Jena, he issued the Berlin Decree, closing all European ports under his influence—that is to say, almost all the ports from the Vistula to the Adriatic—against British commerce. All British ports were declared in a state of blockade, though Napoleon could not watch any one of them with a single vessel, and all goods coming from Great Britain or her colonies were to be destroyed. On November 11, **1807,** Great Britain retaliated by Orders in Council declaring all ports of France and her allies to be in a state of blockade, and all vessels good prize which attempted to enter them unless they had previously touched at a British harbour. To this, on December 17, **1807,** Napoleon replied by the Milan Decree, declaring all neutral vessels liable to seizure if they touched at any British ports before attempting to land their cargoes in any part of Europe under the control of France. The Berlin and Milan Decrees together established what is known as Napoleon's Continental System.

15. **Effects of the Continental System. 1807.**—Ultimately the effects of the Continental System were most injurious to Napoleon. As the British fleet controlled the sea, no colonial goods could be obtained except through British vessels. A gigantic system of smuggling sprang up, and the seizure and destruction of British goods only served to raise the price of those which escaped. Sugar, coffee, and calico grew dear, and the labourer soon discovered that, in consequence of the Continental System, he had to pay more for the coffee which he drank and for the shirt which he wore. A strong feeling opposed to Napoleon manifested itself for the first time amongst the conquered populations.

16. **The Bombardment of Copenhagen. 1807.**—At sea Englishmen were almost as high-handed as Napoleon by land. They searched neutral vessels for goods destined for France, confiscating them in accordance with decisions of their own admiralty court in a fashion which would not be tolerated now. Shortly after the Treaty of Tilsit Canning learnt that Napoleon meant to seize the fleet of Denmark, which was at that time neutral, and to employ it against Great Britain. A British fleet and army were sent to Copenhagen, and the Crown Prince of Denmark (see p. 845) was asked to deliver up the Danish fleet on a promise that it should be restored at the end of the war. On his refusal, Copenhagen was bombarded till at last the Danes gave way. The fleet was surrendered, and the British Government, on the plea that it had been driven to use force, refused to be bound by its offer to restore the ships ultimately

The taking of Curaçao, 1807.

to their owners.. There were many in England who found fault with the whole proceeding, and even George III. seems to have been very much of their opinion. Speaking to the gentleman who had carried to the Crown Prince the message asking him to give up the fleet, the old king asked whether he found the prince upstairs or downstairs. " He was on the ground floor, please your Majesty," was the reply. " I am glad of it for your sake," said the king ; " for if he had half my spirit, he would have kicked you downstairs."

CHAPTER LIV

THE DOWNFALL OF NAPOLEON.   1807—1814

LEADING DATES

Reign of George III., 1760 –1820

The Establishment of Joseph Bonaparte in Spain	. 1808
Battle of Vimeiro	. Aug. 21, 1808
Battle of Corunna	. Jan. 16, 1809
Napoleon's War with Austria	. 1809
Battle of Talavera	July 27-28, 1809
Defence of Torres Vedras	. July 22, 1812
Napoleon's Invasion of Russia	. 1812
Battle of Salamanca	July 22, 1812
Battle of Vittoria	. June 21, 1813
Napoleon driven out of Germany	. 1813
First Restoration of Louis XVIII.	. 1814
War with America	. 1812—1814
Battle of Waterloo	. June 18, 1815
Second Restoration of Louis XVIII.	. 1815

1. **Napoleon and Spain. 1807—1808.**—Napoleon had been gradually maturing designs against Spain. The king, Charles IV., was too witless to govern, and the queen was living in adultery with Godoy, an unprincipled favourite who ruled the kingdom. The heir to the throne, Ferdinand, despised his father and hated Godoy. Spain, indeed, had been most subservient to Napoleon, and had sacrificed her fleets to him at St. Vincent and Trafalgar, but even Godoy discovered that Spain received all the loss and none of the advantages of the alliance, and began to show signs of independence. Napoleon resolved to bring Spain entirely under his control, and in October **1807**, in order to procure the entry of his troops into the country, signed a treaty with Spain, by which France and Spain

were to make a joint attack on Portugal, and to cut it up into three parts, one of which was to be given to Godoy. Napoleon then stirred up Ferdinand against his parents, and on this Godoy, not knowing that Napoleon had a hand in the matter, obtained from the king a proclamation announcing that he intended to bring his son to justice. Napoleon, partly on the pretence of attacking Portugal, and partly on the pretence of protecting Ferdinand, sent 80,000 men into Spain, and in February 1808 placed Murat, his brother-in-law and his best cavalry officer, at their head.

2. The Dethronement of Charles IV. 1808.—On March 17 a Spanish mob rose against Godoy, and the old king, Charles IV., abdicated in favour of his son. Before long, however, he repented and declared his abdication invalid, whilst Ferdinand insisted that it was in full force. Napoleon, to whom both father and son appealed for support, invited them to Bayonne, where he forced them both to abdicate. In the meanwhile Murat had entered Madrid. On May 2 Madrid rose against him, but the insurrection was put down with great cruelty. Napoleon fancied that all resistance was at an end, but before the end of May the Spanish people, town by town and village by village, rose in a national insurrection against the French, without any one part of the country having previous communication with another. Except in his relations with England, Napoleon had hitherto had to deal with the resistance of governments and armies. He had now to deal with a people inspired with hatred of a foreign conquest. It is true that the Spaniards were ignorant and backward, and that they had no trustworthy military organisation ; but for all that, they had what neither the Germans nor the Italians as yet had, the spirit of national resistance.

3. The Capitulation at Baylen. 1808.—In June Napoleon got together a certain number of Spaniards at Bayonne who, by his directions, chose his brother Joseph, hitherto king of Naples, to be king of Spain, after which Napoleon sent Murat to replace Joseph at Naples. Napoleon also urged his generals to put down the resistance of the peasants. They pressed forwards victoriously, but one of them, Dupont, pushing on too far, was obliged, on July 19, to capitulate at Baylen in the Sierra Morena. Joseph had to fly from Madrid, and the whole French army retreated behind the Ebro.

4. Battle of Vimeiro and Convention of Cintra. 1808.—In the preceding winter a French army under Junot had invaded Portugal, and had occupied Lisbon, though the whole of the royal family escaped capture by sailing away to the great Portuguese colony of

Brazil.   Portugal and England were old allies, and partly in order to deliver Portugal, partly in order to support the resistance of Spain, the British ministry, urged on by Canning, sent an army to resist Junot.   The British Government gave the charge of it to Sir Arthur Wellesley, the best soldier in their service, the victor of Assaye and Argaum (see p. 859).   Indian service, however, was in those days little regarded, and two old officers of no distinction, Sir Henry Dalrymple and Sir Harry Burrard, were sent after Wellesley to take the command over him as soon as they could arrive in Portugal.   Meanwhile, on August 1, Wellesley landed in Mondego Bay.   On August 21 he completely defeated Junot at Vimeiro.   Burrard, who arrived just as the battle was beginning, was enough of a gentleman to let Wellesley remain in command till it was fought out, but he superseded him as soon as it was over, and in spite of Wellesley's pleadings, refused to follow up the enemy.   Junot got safely into Lisbon, and on August 30 was allowed by a convention signed at Cintra to return with all his army to France.

5. **Sir John Moore's Expedition and the Battle of Corunna. 1808—1809.**   In November 1808 Napoleon entered Spain in person to stem the tide of disaster.   The Spanish troops were patriotic, but they were ill-commanded and undisciplined.   Napoleon drove them like sheep before him, and, on December 4, entered Madrid. The British army in Portugal was now commanded by Sir John Moore.   The Convention of Cintra had been received with indignation in England as improperly lenient to the French, and Wellesley and his two official superiors had been recalled to give an account of their conduct in relation to it.   Moore, who was an excellent general, had been ordered to advance to the assistance of the Spaniards, when Napoleon burst into the country.   Deceived by false intelligence, and believing that the Spaniards would fight better than they did, Moore pushed on, reaching Sahagun on December 23.   He there learnt that Napoleon was already hurrying back from Madrid to crush him.   Moore was therefore forced to retreat, but he so skilfully availed himself of the obstacles on the route as to give Napoleon no opportunity of drawing him to a battle.   On January 1, 1809, Napoleon, thinking Moore's destruction to be a mere matter of time, turned back, leaving the French army under the command of Soult.   On January 16 Moore had to fight a battle at Corunna to secure the embarkation of his men. He was himself killed, but his army was completely victorious, and was brought away in safety to England.

6. **Aspern and Wagram. 1809.**—Napoleon had been recalled from Spain by news that Austria was arming against him. A war between France and Austria was the result, and after the indecisive battle of Aspern, fought on May 21 and 22, 1809, the French gained a victory at Wagram on July 6. On October 14 the Treaty of Vienna was signed, by which vast territories were cut off from the Austrian Empire. The treaty was followed by a marriage between Napoleon and the daughter of the Emperor Francis, Napoleon having divorced his wife Josephine on a flimsy pretext, his real motive being that she had borne him no children. The English Government were not idle spectators of this war. Canning had taken in hand the war in Spain.

7. **Walcheren and Talavera. 1809.**—Whilst the result of the campaign in Austria was still uncertain, Castlereagh sent out an expedition to seize Antwerp, in the hope that, if it succeeded, it would compel Napoleon, who was still struggling on the Danube, to send part of his army back. Unfortunately, the command of the land forces sent out was given to Lord Chatham, the eldest son of the great Chatham, who had nothing but his birth to recommend him, and the command of the fleet to Sir Richard Strachan, an officer of no great distinction. Though the expedition did not sail till July 28, three weeks after the defeat of the Austrians at Wagram, there was still a chance that a successful blow at Antwerp might encourage the Emperor of Austria to prolong the struggle. The commanders, however, took Flushing and did no more. Time was frittered away in senseless disputes between the general and the admiral, and Antwerp was put in a good state of defence before they could resolve how to attack it. According to a popular epigram,

> The Earl of Chatham, with his sword drawn
> Stood waiting for Sir Richard Strachan ;
> Sir Richard, longing to be at 'em,
> Stood waiting for the Earl of Chatham.

Whilst admiral and general were hesitating, the troops were left in the low isle of Walcheren, where a fever broke out which swept away thousands, and so weakened the constitutions of those who recovered that few were fit for active service again. When the news of failure reached England, Canning threw all the blame on Castlereagh. The two ministers both resigned office and then fought a duel. The Duke of Portland, the Prime Minister, broken in health, also resigned, and died shortly afterwards. He was succeeded by Perceval, a conscientious but narrow-minded man. Wellesley was sent back to Portugal. Marching rapidly northwards from Lisbon, he drove Soult from Oporto. Having

The Court of King's Bench in 1810: from Pennant's 'Some Account of London.'

thus cleared his left flank, he returned to Lisbon and then pushed up the valley of the Tagus, intending to co-operate with a Spanish force in an attack on Madrid. At Talavera Wellesley met a French army under Marshal Victor, and though the Spanish general gave him no assistance, he completely defeated the French on July 27. Other French generals threatened to cut off his retreat, and he was obliged to fall back on Portugal. Wellesley had indeed learnt the lesson that Spanish armies could not be depended on, but otherwise he had gained nothing by his victory. The French forces in the Peninsula were too overwhelming to be overpowered as yet. Wellesley was rewarded for his skill with the title of Viscount Wellington.

8. **Torres Vedras. 1810—1811.**—In 1810 Napoleon made a great effort to drive the English out of Portugal. Though he did not go himself into the Peninsula, he sent his best general, Marshal Massena. Wellington had now under his orders, besides his English troops, a number of well-trained Portuguese commanded by an Irishman, Marshal Beresford. Even with this addition, however, his force was too small to meet Massena in the field, and, in order to have in reserve a defensible position, he threw up three lines of earthworks across the peninsula which lies between the Tagus and the sea. The first was intended to stop Massena for a time ; the second to form the main defence after the first had been abandoned ; the third to protect the British embarkation, if it were found necessary to leave Portugal. Wellington, who, whilst these lines were being constructed, was some distance in front of them, drew back slowly as Massena advanced, so as to prolong the French invasion as much as possible. Massena's army was accordingly half-starved before the ' Lines of Torres Vedras' were reached, as Wellington had ordered that the crops should be destroyed and the cattle driven off. Yet Massena pressed on, fancying that the English were making for their ships, as the hatred borne to the French by the Portuguese was so deep-seated that not a single peasant informed him of the obstacle in front of him. At Busaco, indeed, Wellington turned on the French army and checked it for a time, but his numbers were not sufficient to enable him to continue his resistance in the open field, and hence he continued his retreat to the first line. Massena did not even attempt to storm it. Week after week he looked helplessly at it whilst his own army was gradually wasted by starvation and disease. More than 30,000 French soldiers perished, though not a single pitched battle had been fought. At last Massena ordered a retreat. Wellington cautiously followed, and by the spring of 1811 not a Frenchman remained in Portugal.

9. **The Regency and the Assassination of Perceval. 1811—**

1812.—Whilst Wellington was struggling with the French, old George III. ceased to have further knowledge of joy or sorrow. The madness with which he had from time to time been afflicted, settled down on him in **1811**. The selfish and unprincipled Prince of Wales took his place as Regent, at first under some restrictions, but after a year had elapsed without any prospect of the king's recovery, with the full powers of a sovereign. It was expected by some that he would place his old friends the Whigs in office ; but he had no gratitude in his nature, and the current of feeling against reform of any kind was now so strong that he could hardly have maintained the Whigs in power even if he had wished to do so. Perceval was well suited for the Prime Ministership at such a time, being as strongly in favour of maintaining the existing state of things as the dullest member of Parliament could possibly be. His ministry, however, was not a long one. In **1812** he was shot dead by a lunatic as he stepped into the House of Commons. His successor was Lord Liverpool.

10. **Napoleon at the Height of Power. 1811.**—In the meantime Napoleon had been proceeding from one annexation to another. In May **1809** he annexed the Papal States ; in July **1810**, the kingdom of Holland ; in November **1810**, the Valais ; and in December **1810** the coast of Germany as far as Hamburg. The motive which impelled him to these extravagant resolutions was his determination to enforce the Continental System in order to ruin England. England was not ruined, but the rise of prices caused by Napoleon's ineffectual attempts to ruin her increased the ill-will of the populations of the Continent, and strengthened the popular resistance to which he ultimately fell a victim.

11. **Wellington's Resources. 1811.**—It was upon the certainty of a general resistance to what had now become a real tyranny that Wellington mainly calculated. Wellington had, however, on his side other elements of success. His English troops had proved superior to more than equal numbers of Frenchmen, not because they were braver, but because they had more coolness. He had therefore been able to draw his men up in a long line only two deep, and could yet count on them to baffle the heavy columns with which the French were accustomed to charge, by pouring into them a steady fire as they approached. Moreover, as the French generals were in the habit of quarrelling with one another, it was possible to defeat one before another could make up his mind to bring up his forces to the help of his rival. The Spaniards, too, though their

armies were bad, made excellent *guerillas*,[1] shooting down French stragglers and taking every advantage of the ground. So dangerous did they make the roads, that when an important despatch was sent to France it had to be guarded by 1,000 horsemen. The French armies in the field perceptibly decreased, in consequence of the necessity of detaching large bodies against the *guerillas*.

12. **Wellington's Advance. 1811 — 1812.** — In spite of these advantages the difference of numbers against Wellington was still very great. Yet on May 5, **1811**, he held his own against Massena at Fuentes d'Onoro. On May 16 Beresford defeated Soult at Albuera, whilst earlier in the year, on March 6, Graham had defeated Victor at Barrosa. For all that, Wellington was unable to retain his advanced position. Massena was indeed recalled from Spain by Napoleon, but two other marshals, Marmont and Soult, joined to resist the English, and Wellington was obliged to retire to Portugal. Before long, however, the two marshals having separated, Wellington resolved to attack the two strong fortresses of Badajoz and Ciudad Rodrigo which barred his way into Spain. Ciudad Rodrigo fell on January 19, **1812**, and Badajoz on April 6. In storming the latter place the slaughter of the British troops was tremendous, as Wellington, knowing that, if he delayed, Soult would be upon him with superior forces, had not been able to wait till all fitting preparations had been made. When at last the soldiers burst in they raged madly through the streets, committing every species of cruelty and outrage. The capture of these two fortresses not only secured Portugal against invasion, but also made it possible for Wellington to conduct offensive operations in Spain.

13. **The Battle of Salamanca. 1812.**—Wellington's task after the capture of Badajoz was lightened by the withdrawal of some of the best of the French regiments from the Peninsula. At the end of **1810** the Tzar Alexander had withdrawn from the Continental System, and it was chiefly on this account that, in **1811**, Napoleon prepared for a war with Russia. In the spring of **1812** his preparations were approaching completion, and troops were recalled from Spain to take part in the attack on the Tzar. In June Napoleon crossed the Niemen to invade Russia, and, in the same month, Wellington crossed the Coa to invade Spain. On July 22 Wellington completely defeated Marmont at Salamanca, after which he entered Madrid in triumph. He pushed on to besiege Burgos,

---

[1] *Guerilla* is a Spanish word meaning primarily a little war, and so is applied to peasants or others taking part in a war on a small scale.

but the French armies from the south of Spain gathered thickly round him before he could take it, and he was compelled again to return to Portugal. The campaign, however, had not been in vain, as the French, in order to secure the north against Wellington, had been obliged to abandon the south to the Spaniards.

Grenadier in the time of the
Peninsular War.

14. **Napoleon in Russia. 1812.**— Whilst Wellington was gaining ground in Spain, Napoleon, at the head of 450,000 men, entered Russia. Of this force the main army, consisting of 380,000 under his own command, was to fall upon the Russian army, and after destroying it, to dictate peace to the Tzar. The Russian army, however, being far inferior in numbers, retreated, whilst Napoleon's dwindled away from desertion or weariness after each day's march. It was not till he reached Borodino, almost at the gates of Moscow, that he was able to fight a battle. Of the 380,000 men whom he had led over the Niemen he now had no more than 145,000 at his disposal. He defeated the enemy, indeed, in the bloody battle which ensued, but the Russians steadily retreated without confusion, and when Napoleon entered Moscow, on September 14, he waited in vain for any sign of the Tzar's submission. He found Moscow almost entirely deserted, and on the second night after his arrival the city was in flames, having been set on fire by the patriotism of its governor, Rostopchin. It was impossible to feed an army in a destroyed town in the frosts of winter, and on October 19 Napoleon started in retreat with the 100,000 men which were all that were now left. The country through which he had to pass had been stripped on his outward march, and he had made so sure of victory that he had provided no stores in view of a retreat. On November 6 the frost came

down on the doomed army. The remainder of the retreat was one long misery. Poor frozen wretches were left behind every morning, and weaklings dropped out to perish every day. Fighting, too, there was ; and in the end a bare 20,000, of whom probably no more than 7,000 belonged to the original army, staggered out of Russia.

15. Napoleon driven out of Germany and Spain. 1813.—In 1813 Prussia, hitherto crushed by French exactions, sprang to arms, and allied herself with Russia. Napoleon put himself at the head of a new army to replace the one which he had lost. So great had been the loss of life in his wars, that he had now to content himself with levying boys, as all those who should now have been the young men had been made soldiers before their time and had for the most part perished. Yet so great was Napoleon's genius that with this young army he defeated the Russians and Prussians in two battles, at Lützen and Bautzen. The defeated armies looked to Austria for aid. Metternich, however, who now governed Austria as the Emperor's minister, feared that if Napoleon were completely beaten, the Tzar would become too powerful, and he therefore, instead of at once joining the allies, asked Napoleon to make peace, by giving up his hold on Germany, but keeping the rest of his dominions. As, however, Napoleon would not yield a jot, Austria joined the allies against him. Napoleon won one battle more at Dresden ; then the commanders of his outlying troops were beaten, and he was himself crushed at Leipzig, at what is known in Germany as the Battle of the Nations. By the end of 1813, so much of his army as still held together was driven across the Rhine. In Spain Wellington was no less successful. On June 21 he overthrew King Joseph at Vittoria, and in the autumn the remains of the French army was forced back out of Spain, and was struggling for its existence round Bayonne.

16. The Restoration of Louis XVIII. 1814.—In the early part of 1814 Russians, Prussians, and Austrians entered France. Napoleon, who opposed them with scanty numbers, was for a time even victorious by dashing first at one part of their army and then at the other. At last, however, his power of resistance came to an end. On March 31 the allies entered Paris. On April 3 Napoleon abdicated and was allowed to retire to Elba. Wellington, who had been made a duke after the battle of Vittoria, had in the meanwhile occupied Bordeaux, and on April 10, not knowing of Napoleon's abdication, he defeated Soult at Toulouse. Louis XVIII., the brother of Louis XVI. who had been guillotined (see p. 825), became king of France, granting a constitution, known as the Charter. French people had become so weary of war and despotism, that they welcomed the promise of peace and constitutional liberty.

17. **Position of England.** 1814.—The position of England was now exceedingly strong. Not only had her wealth, acquired by her manufactures, enabled her to supply the continental governments with vast sums of money, without which it would have been impossible for them to carry on the struggle, but her own army in Spain had powerfully contributed to the success of the allies, by keeping no less than 300,000 French soldiers away from the decisive conflict in Germany and the north-east of France. That she was able to accomplish this had been, to a great extent, owing to her supremacy at sea. Wellington's troops were well supplied, because vessels from all parts of the globe could arrive safely in the Peninsula with provisions for them, whilst the French had to rely on stores conveyed with difficulty across hostile territory. England's mastery over the sea enabled her to make good her claims to the retention of most of the colonies which she had acquired during the war, though she abandoned Java and the Spice Islands to the Dutch, and some of the West India Islands to the French. This time, however, there was no talk of abandoning the Cape of Good Hope, which was an admirable naval station on the way to India and the East.

18. **War with America.** 1812—1814.—Too much power is never good for man or nation, and just as Napoleon provoked enemies by his Continental System, so did England provoke enemies by her Orders in Council (see p. 860). The United States as a neutral nation was aggrieved by the action of the British Government in stopping American vessels from trading with the Continent, unless they first put into British ports, and also by the search exercised on board them by British cruisers, and by the dragging out of deserters who had forsaken the British for American service. In 1812, indeed, the Orders in Council were repealed, but it was then too late to avert war, which had already been declared by the United States. The American navy was composed of very few ships but these were larger and better armed than British ships, nominally of the same class. British captains were so certain that they could take whatever they tried to take, that they laid their ships alongside of American vessels much more powerful than their own. The result was that one British ship after another was captured. The tide was turned by Captain Broke of the 'Shannon,' who courteously invited the captain of the American

frigate the 'Chesapeake' to come out to fight in the open sea. This time the two vessels were on an equality, and Broke, boarding the 'Chesapeake,' took her after an action lasting no more than fifteen minutes. The operations on land made no real impression on the vast American continent. There was much fighting on the Canadian frontier, and in 1814 a large number of the soldiers from the late Peninsular army— an army which, according to Wellington, could go anywhere and do anything—were sent out to America. Washington was taken, and the capitol and other public buildings destroyed—contrary to the usual practice of civilised warfare—in revenge for similar burnings on a smaller scale by the Americans in Canada. The Americans were merely stung to more vigorous resistance, and the British troops were compelled to retreat. A British flotilla on Lake Champlain was overpowered. An attack on New Orleans was baffled. On December 14, 1814, a peace was signed at Ghent, putting an end to this unhappy war.

19. **The Congress of Vienna. 1814—1815.**—It was a hard matter to settle anew the boundaries of European states after the disturbances caused by French annexations. In 1814 a Congress met at Vienna to decide such questions. So far as its decisions were influenced by any principle at all, they rested on the ground that a strong barrier must be set up against a renewal of French aggression. Not only was the frontier of France driven back almost to that which had existed in 1792, but the old territories of the Dutch Republic and the Austrian Netherlands were united under the Prince of Orange as king of the Netherlands. Large districts on the Rhine, henceforth to be known as Rhenish Prussia, were united to Prussia. The King of Sardinia not only received back Savoy and Nice, but acquired the strip of land which had once been under the Genoese Republic. In all else there was a scramble for territory, in which the great Powers were of course the most successful. The Tzar got Poland, though it was kept separate as a constitutional kingdom from the rest of Russia. Prussia got half of Saxony, in addition to her new territory on the Rhine. Austria got Lombardy and Venetia. Italy was again divided into separate states, and was thus really placed under the power of Austria ; whilst the German aspirations after nationality were only nominally satisfied. There was to be a German Confederation, and deputies of the rulers of the states composing it were to meet at Frankfort ; but the powers of this Confederation were extremely restricted, and Austria and

III.   3 L

Prussia were too jealous of one another to allow it to work harmoniously to any good end.

20. **The Hundred Days. 1815.**—In France, the restored Bourbon monarchy soon gave deep offence, by favouring the nobles and clergy, and by showing hostility to the ideas which had become prominent under the Republic and the Empire. Before long Louis XVIII. became widely unpopular. Napoleon watched the movement with pleasure, and, escaping from Elba, landed on the coast of France. The soldiers sent to capture him went over to his side, and on March 21 he reached Paris and was again Emperor of the French. The short reign which followed is known as 'The Hundred Days.' He offered to the allies to remain at peace, but they refused to listen to him, believing that he only wanted to prepare for war, and that the longer they waited the more difficult it would be to suppress him. All four Powers, therefore, England, Prussia, Austria and Russia, prepared for a fresh struggle, but Austria and Russia were far off, and an English army under Wellington and a Prussian army under Blücher were in the Netherlands before the other two allied armies were ready. The English occupied the right and the Prussians the left of a long line in front of Brussels.

21. **The Waterloo Campaign.**—On June 15 Napoleon crossed the frontier. His plan was to beat the Prussians first, and then, driving them off towards Germany, to turn upon the English and to overwhelm them with superior numbers. On the 16th, whilst he sent Ney to keep in check the English at Quatre Bras, he defeated the Prussians at Ligny, and detached Grouchy to follow them up, so as to keep them from coming to the help of Wellington. On the 18th he ,attacked Wellington himself at Waterloo. Wellington, knowing that the Prussians intended, in spite of Grouchy's pursuit, to come to his help, and that his own numbers were inferior to those of Napoleon, had to hold out against all attacks during the early part of the day, without attempting to deliver any in return. He was well served by the tenacity of his mixed army, in which British soldiers fought side by side with Netherlanders, Hanoverians and Brunswickers. The farm of Hougoumont in advance of Wellington's right centre was heroically defended. In vain the French columns charged upon the British squares, and the French artillery slaughtered the men as they stood. In vain, too, the French cavalry dashed against them. As the men dropped their comrades closed their ranks, fighting on with sadly diminished numbers. At last a black line was seen on the horizon, and that black line was the Prussian army. Napoleon taken in flank by the Prussians made one last

desperate charge on the English squares. Then Wellington gave the order to advance. The French army, crushed between two forces, dissolved into a flying mob.

22. The Second Restoration of Louis XVIII.—The allies followed hard upon the beaten enemy and entered Paris in triumph. Napoleon took refuge in the ' Bellerophon,' an English ship of war. By the decision of the four great Powers he was removed to St. Helena, where he was guarded by the English till his death in 1821. Louis XVIII. was restored to the throne of France, and Europe at last enjoyed the peace which it had longed for. The French territory was restricted to the limits of 1792. A heavy fine was also imposed upon France, troops belonging to each of the four Powers being left in occupation of French fortresses till the money was paid.

CHAPTER LV

ENGLAND AFTER WATERLOO. 1815—1827

LEADING DATES

Reign of George III., 1760—1820
Reign of George IV., 1820—1830

Abolition of the Income-Tax	. 1816
Suspension of the Habeas Corpus Act	. 1817
The ' Manchester Massacre ' and the Six Acts . .	. 1819
Death of George III. and Accession of George IV.	Jan. 29, 1820
Peel Home Secretary	. 1821
Canning Foreign Secretary	. 1822
End of Liverpool's Prime Ministership . .	Feb. 17, 1827

1. The Corn-Law and the Abolition of the Property Tax. 1815—1816.—When the war came to an end there was a general expectation in England that peace and plenty would flourish together. Contrary to expectation, the first years of peace were marked by deep agricultural and manufacturing distress. In 1815 Parliament, at that time almost entirely filled with landowners, passed a corn-law forbidding the importation of foreign corn, unless the price of wheat reached 80s. a quarter. The law was, however, inoperative, because the price of wheat, instead of reaching 80s., fell steadily. The cessation of expenditure upon war had thrown large numbers of men out of employment, and there was, consequently, less money spent in the purchase of food. The fall in the price of

corn injured landowners the more because it had been excessively
high in the last years of the war, and they had consequently
spent money in reclaiming from the waste a great extent of
land just good enough to produce sufficient corn to pay expenses
when corn was very dear, but not good enough to produce
sufficient corn to pay expenses when corn was cheap.   In 1816
a bad harvest came, which added to the losses of the agriculturists.   In such a time of distress the burden of the war-taxes was
sorely felt, and in 1816 the House of Commons insisted on the
abolition of the income-tax (see p. 840), which had been imposed
by Pitt only for the duration of the war, and the Government was
obliged, much against its will, to abandon it.

2. **Manufacturing Distress.   1816.**—In 1816 a bad harvest sent
up the price of corn, but did not improve the condition of agriculturists, as they had but little corn to sell.   The return of high
prices for food seriously affected the condition of the artisans in
the manufactories, who were at this time suffering from other causes
as well.   In the war-time England had had almost a monopoly on
the Continent for its wares, because few men cared to build factories
for the production of wares, when they might at any time be burnt
or destroyed by a hostile army.   This danger was now at an end,
and as foreign nations began to increase their own produce, the
demand for English goods diminished.   The want of employment
for labour which had diminished the demand at home for food
also diminished the demand at home for manufactures.   In 1816,
accordingly, there was widely spread manufacturing distress in
England.   Bankruptcies were frequent, and thousands of workmen
lost their employment.

3. **The Factory-System.   1815—1816.**—There was no public
system of education for the poor, and the artisans had no means of
learning what were the real causes of their misery.   The factory-
system, which had grown up since the introduction of improved
machinery, had spread discontent amongst the workers.   Manufacturers, anxious only to make money, were careless of the lives
and health of their workers, and there was no law intervening to
secure more humane action.   London parishes often sent off waggon-
loads of pauper children to the cotton mills in Yorkshire and
Lancashire in order that they might be relieved of the expense of
maintaining them, and the unfortunate children were frequently
compelled to work, even at the age of six, fifteen or sixteen hours a
day.   Grown-up men and women found much of their work taken
from them by the labour of the children, who were practically

slaves, and they themselves, if they got work at all, had to
labour for exceedingly long hours for exceedingly small wages.
When, as in **1816**, large numbers failed to get any work whatever, the starving multitude threw all the blame on the employers.

4. **The Radicals. 1816—1817.**—Towards the end of **1816** riots
broke out in many places, which were only put down by soldiers.
In many places the rioters directed their violence against machinery,
to the existence of which they attributed their misery. Some men
of better education laid all the blame upon the existing political
system which placed power entirely in the hands of the rich, and
called for complete and 'radical' reform, sometimes asking that
it should be effected by violence. These men were, in consequence, styled ' Radicals,' and were looked upon as inspired—as
indeed they were—with the ideas of the French Revolutionists.
In December, **1816**, there was in London a riot, known as the 'Spa-
fields riot,' which was, however, repressed without difficulty. In
the beginning of **1817** a number of secret committees were formed,
and the most extensive changes demanded.

5. **Suspension of the Habeas Corpus Act. 1817—1818.**—
The Government was frightened. Its leading members were Lord
Liverpool, the Prime Minister, Lord Castlereagh, the Foreign
Secretary, and Lord Sidmouth, the Home Secretary, who had
been formerly Prime Minister as Mr. Addington (see p. 843).
They had all been engaged in combating the French Revolutionary
ideas, and, when they saw these ideas making head in England,
they could not think of any way to deal with them other than
forcible repression. They had sufficient influence to carry through
Parliament Bills for the suspension of the Habeas Corpus Act
till the following year, and for the prevention of seditious meetings,
the penalty of death being imposed on those who being engaged in
such a meeting refused to disperse. The Government ignored
the part which physical distress played in promoting disturbances.
In Manchester, indeed, the dissatisfied workmen contented themselves with the simple expedient of marching in a body on foot to
present a petition to the Regent, and as each petitioner took with
him a blanket to keep himself warm, the expedition has been known
as the ' March of the Blanketeers.' The Blanketeers were, however, stopped on the way, and never even approached the Regent.
There was a talk afterwards of a rising in arms, but such designs,
whatever they may really have been, were frustrated by the arrest
of the ringleaders. Only in Nottinghamshire did they actually

Waterloo Bridge: opened June 18, 1817, built by Rennie.

lead to violence. There a certain Brandreth, at the head of a party, seized arms, and shot dead a man who opposed him. Happily in **1817** there was a better harvest. The price of corn fell, and trade revived. Work was again to be had, and the spirit of insubordination was quieted for a time. On March 1, **1818**, the Habeas Corpus Act again came into force, and has never since been suspended in England.

6. **A Time of Prosperity. 1818—1819.**—The return of prosperity was not confined to England. So marked were the peaceful tendencies of France that in **1818** a congress of the four Powers whose soldiers occupied French fortresses was held at Aix-la-Chapelle, and it was resolved to withdraw the garrisons. In England, in **1819**, Mr. Peel, a rising member of Parliament on the Tory side, recommended the resumption of cash payments by the Bank of England (see p. 835), and, so much improved was the financial position of the Government, that a Bill embodying his suggestions was carried, and in **1821** the Bank of England ceased to refuse to change its notes for gold.

7. **Renewal of Distress. 1819.**—The prosperity of **1818** had given rise to speculative over-production of manufactures, with the result that more goods were produced than were needed by consumers. Production was therefore limited in **1819**, and there was again great distress amongst the artisans. Large numbers of those who suffered had come to the conclusion that their condition would never be improved till power was placed in the hands of the masses by a sweeping measure of Parliamentary reform. Their cause had been advocated in the press by Cobbett, the author of hard-hitting, plain-spoken pamphlets, calling for a complete transference of political power from the landowners to the masses. This remedy for the evils of the time was supported on the platform by Hunt, usually known as ' Orator' Hunt, who, whilst stirring up his audiences to violence, took care to keep his own person out of danger, and in Parliament by Sir Francis Burdett, whose advocacy of a universal suffrage met with few supporters in the House of Commons.

8. **The ' Manchester Massacre.' 1819.**—To support these views a vast meeting of at least 50,000 gathered on August 16, **1819**, in St. Peter's Field in Manchester, where an address was to be delivered by Hunt. The magistrates ordered the arrest of Hunt in the midst of the vast crowd of his supporters. A party of mounted Yeomanry, attempting to effect his capture, was soon broken up, and the isolated soldiers were subjected to jeers and

insults. The magistrates then sent Hussars to support the Yeomanry. The Hussars charged, and the weight of disciplined soldiery drove the crowd into a huddled mass of shrieking fugitives, pressed together by their efforts to escape. When at last the ground was cleared many of the victims were piled up on one another. Five or six deaths was the result, and the number of wounded was considerable. The 'Manchester Massacre,' as it was called, opened the eyes of many whose hearts had hitherto been callous to the sufferings of the discontented artisans. Men hitherto content to argue that social and economical difficulties could not be solved by giving power to the ignorant masses began to criticise the ineptitude of the magistrates, who might have avoided all violence by arresting Hunt either before or after the meeting, and to ask themselves whether a system could be justified which led to the dispersal of meetings of peaceable citizens by armed soldiers.

9. **The Six Acts. 1819.**—The Government, on the other hand, took a harsh view of the conduct, not of the magistrates, but of the crowd. " Every meeting for Radical reform," wrote a distinguished lawyer, " was not merely a seditious attempt to undermine the existing constitution and Government by bringing it into contempt, but it was an overt act of treasonable conspiracy against that constitution of Government, including the king as its head and bound by his coronation oath to maintain it." Lord Eldon, the Lord Chancellor, and Lord Sidmouth, the Home Secretary, warmly supported this view of the case, and, as soon as Parliament met, six measures, usually known as 'The Six Acts,' were rapidly passed. Of these some were harmless or even beneficial. The harshest was the one directed against public meetings. With the exception of such as were summoned by official persons, 'all meetings for the consideration of grievances in Church and State, or for the purpose of preparing petitions . . . except in the parishes . . . where the individuals usually reside,' were forbidden. To prevent any attempt to introduce inflammatory appeals from celebrated persons brought from a distance the presence of strangers at these local meetings was prohibited.

10. **Death of George III. and the Cato-Street Conspiracy. 1820.**—On January 29, 1820, George III. died. As the new king, his son George IV., had for many years been acting as regent, the change was merely nominal. The same ministers remained in office, and the same policy was pursued. The attempt to make difficult the free expression of opinion gave rise to secret con-

spiracies, and there were undoubtedly many discontented persons
in the country ready to use violence to gain their ends.   A certain
Thistlewood, with about thirty other persons, proposed to murder
the whole Cabinet when assembled at dinner on February 23.   The
conspiracy was betrayed, and the conspirators, who met in a loft
in Cato Street, were seized, and their leaders executed.   For a time
the 'Manchester Massacre' was forgotten, and many who had felt

George III. in old age : from Turner's mezzotint.

for the victims of the soldiery now execrated all reformers as
supporters of assassins.

11. **Queen Caroline.   1820—1821.**—In 1795 George IV. had
married Caroline of Brunswick.   From the beginning he had treated
her shamefully, and the pair were separated after the birth of an
only child, the Princess Charlotte.   In 1816 this Princess, the
heiress to the throne, was married to Prince Leopold of Saxe
Coburg, and in 1817 she died in child-bed.   She had been very
popular, and hopes had been entertained that when she came to

reign she would establish at Court a purer life.   Her death accordingly caused a general gloom.   When George IV. came to the throne attention was publicly called to his degrading vices. To his wife, who had been leading an indiscreet and probably a discreditable life on the Continent, he refused to allow the position or even the title of a queen.   In 1820, when she returned to meet any charges that might be brought against her, she received a most enthusiastic greeting from the populace, the general feeling being that, even if her conduct had been as bad as her husband said, his own had been so base that he had no right to call her in question.   The ministers, indeed, introduced into the House of Lords a Bill to dissolve her marriage and to deprive her of the title of queen, but the majority in its favour was so small that they had to abandon it.   The queen's popularity, however, deserted her when she accepted a grant of money from the ministers who had attacked her, and in 1821 she died.

12. **The Southern Revolutions. 1820—1823.**—In Spain Ferdinand VII., and in Naples Ferdinand I., had been ruling despotically and harshly.   In 1820 the armies in both countries rose against the kings and established the same democratic constitution in both.   Metternich, the Austrian minister, called on the great Powers of Europe to put down what he held to be a pernicious example to all other countries.   Russia and Prussia supported him, and, meeting in congress at Troppau, called on England and France to join them against the Neapolitans.   Louis XVIII., on the part of France, attempted to mediate, and though Castlereagh, the English Foreign Secretary, warmly disapproved of revolutions, he protested against Metternich's view that the great Powers had a right to interfere to suppress changes of government in smaller states.   In 1821 the congress removed to Laibach, and an Austrian army marched upon Naples.   The Neapolitan army ran away, and the Austrians restored Ferdinand I.   A military revolution which took place in the kingdom of Sardinia was crushed at the same time. In 1823 a French army entered Spain and restored Ferdinand VII. Both at Naples and in Spain the restored kings were vindictively cruel to those who had driven them from power.

13. **Castlereagh and Canning. 1822—1826.**—Castlereagh did not live to work out the policy which he had announced in the protest laid by him before the congress of Troppau.   In 1822, in a moment of insanity, he committed suicide.   His successor was George Canning.   There was no great difference in the substance of the policy of the two men.   Both had supported the doctrine of

national independence against Napoleon, and both were ready to support it against the allied Powers whose union was popularly, though incorrectly, known as the Holy Alliance. Castlereagh, however, was anxious to conciliate the great Powers as much as possible, and confined his protests to written despatches, which were kept secret ; whereas Canning took pleasure in defying Metternich and openly turned him into ridicule in the eyes of the

George IV. : from an unfinished portrait by Lawrence in the National Portrait Gallery.

world. Castlereagh was accordingly detested in England as the supporter of the Holy Alliance, whereas Canning soon became popular as its opponent. He allowed, indeed, the French army to enter Spain in 1823, and had no thought of dragging England into a war ; but in 1824 he acknowledged the independence of the Spanish colonies in America, after it had practically been accomplished by the exertions of the colonists. " I have called," he said boastfully, "a new world into existence to redress the balance of the old." Such claptrap revealed the lower side of his character ; but in 1826 he showed that he could act promptly as well as speak foolishly. A constitutional government having been established in Portugal, Spain, backed by France, threatened to invade Portugal. Canning at once sent British troops to secure Portugal, and the danger was averted.

14. **National Uprising in Greece. 1821—1826.**—The object of the revolutionists in Spain and Italy had been constitutional change. An almost simultaneous rising in Greece aimed at national independence. The Turkish government was a cruel despotism, and in 1821 there was a rising in the Peloponnesus or Morea. Turks and Greeks were merciless to one another. The Turks massacred Greeks, and the Greeks gave no quarter to Turks. The Greeks had the advantage of a well-equipped shipping, and could hold their own at sea. In 1822 two great Turkish armies were sent to conquer the insurgents in the land, but one was driven back by the defenders of Missolonghi in Ætolia, the other was starved out and perished in the mountains of Argolis. The Sultan Mahmoud appealed for help to Mehemet Ali, the Pasha of Egypt, who had practically made himself almost independent of the Sultan, and Mehemet Ali sent to his help an Egyptian army under his own adopted son Ibrahim Pasha. In 1824 Ibrahim conquered Crete, and in 1825 landed in Peloponnesus, where he did his best absolutely to exterminate the population by slaughtering the men and sending off the women to be sold into slavery. In 1826, whilst Ibrahim was wasting Peloponnesus, the Turks captured Missolonghi, and in 1827 they reduced the Acropolis of Athens. Canning had all along sympathised with the Greeks, but Metternich opposed him in all directions. Canning accordingly turned to Russia, where Nicholas had succeeded his brother Alexander I. in 1825, and in 1826 he and the new Tzar came to an agreement that Greece should be freed from the direct government of the sultan, but should be required to pay him a tribute.

15. **Peel as Home Secretary. 1821—1827.**—Whilst Canning won credit for the ministry by a popular direction of foreign affairs, Peel—who had succeeded Sidmouth as Home Secretary in 1821—won credit for it by his mode of dealing with domestic difficulties. When he came into office a deep feeling of distrust existed between the rich and the poor. The rich were in a state of panic, fearing every political movement amongst the mass of

their fellow-countrymen as likely to produce a renewal in England of the horrors of the French Revolution. The poor, on the other hand, attributed the misery resulting from economical causes, or even from the badness of the weather, to the deliberate machinations of the rich. What was wanted at that time was, not to bring classes into more violent collision by attempting to reform Parliament in a democratic direction, but to soften down the irritation between them by a series of administrative and economic reforms, which should present Parliament as a helper rather than as a contriver of fresh methods of repression. Peel was, of all men, the best fitted to take the lead in such a work. He had no sympathy with hasty and sweeping change, but he had an open mind for all practical improvements. Sooner or later the force of reasoning made an impression on him, and he was never above avowing—what with some people is the most terrible of confessions—that he had changed his mind.

16. **Criminal Law Reform. 1823.**—The reform of the criminal law had long been advocated in vain by two large-minded members of the House of Commons, Sir Samuel Romilly and Sir James Mackintosh. As the law stood at the beginning of the century no less than two hundred crimes were punishable by death. Anyone, for instance, who stole fish out of a pond, who hunted in the king's forests, or who injured Westminster Bridge, was to be hanged. Sometimes these harsh laws were put in force, but more often juries refused to convict even the guilty, preferring rather to perjure themselves by delivering a verdict which they knew to be untrue than send to death a person who had merely committed a trivial offence. Again and again the House of Commons had voted for an alteration of the law, but the House of Lords had obstinately refused to pass the Bills sent up to them with this object. In **1823** Peel brought in Bills for the abolition of the death penalty for about a hundred crimes, and the House of Lords at last gave way, now that the abolition was recommended by a minister.

17. **Huskisson and the Combination Laws. 1824—1825.**—Reforms were the more easily made because the distress which had prevailed earlier was now at an end. In **1821** a revival of commerce began, and in **1824** and **1825** there was great prosperity. In the struggle which had long continued between master-manufacturers and their workmen, the workmen had frequently combined together in trades-unions to impose terms upon the masters, and had attempted to enforce their demands by striking work. Combinations between workmen were, however, illegal till

in 1824, at the instance of Joseph Hume, a rising economical reformer, and with the warm support of Huskisson, the President of the Board of Trade, the laws against combinations were repealed, though in 1825, in consequence of acts of violence done by the workmen against unpopular masters, a further act was passed making legal all combinations both of

Lord Byron: from an engraving in the British Museum
from a painting by Sanders.

masters and men, if entered on for the purpose of fixing wages, but illegal if entered on for any other purpose.

18. **Robinson's Budgets. 1823—1825.**—This attempt to give freedom to labour was accompanied by steps in the direction of freedom of trade. Robinson, the Chancellor of the Exchequer, supported by Huskisson, employed the surplus given him by the

prosperity of the country to reduce the duties on some imports.   It was but little that was done, but it was the first time since Pitt's commercial treaty with France that a government showed any signs of perceiving that Englishmen would be better off by the removal of artificial difficulties in the way of their trade with other nations.

19. **The End of the Liverpool Ministry. 1826—1827.**—Though the ministry was in name a Tory ministry, it was far from being united on any subject.   Some of its members, like the Chancellor, Lord Eldon, continued to detest all reforms, thinking that they must ultimately lead to a catastrophe ; whilst other ministers, like Canning, Peel, and Huskisson, were in favour of gradual reforms, though there were some particular questions on which even the reformers were not in agreement.   So discordant a ministry could hardly have been kept together but for the tact and easy nature of its head, the Earl of Liverpool, who allowed the ministers to argue against one another in Parliament even on important subjects.   On February 17, 1827, Liverpool was incapacitated from public service by an attack of apoplexy, and it was by that time evident that the two sections of the Cabinet would not be able to serve together under any other leader.   Whatever differences there might be about details, the main difference between the two sections can be easily described.   On the one hand, the unprogressive section not only disliked the idea of changing institutions which had proved themselves useful in past times, but also shrank from giving way to increased popular control over Parliament, or to any violent popular demand for legislation.   On the other hand, the progressive section, though hardly prepared to allow the decisions of Parliament to be influenced by popular pressure, was yet in some sympathy with the popular feeling on subjects ripe for legislation.

20. **Burns, Byron, and Shelley.**—As usually happens, the strong opinions which prevailed amongst politicians were reflected in the literature of the time.   Burns, the Ayrshire ploughman, whose first verses were written in 1775, was in full accordance with the precursors of the French Revolution in his love of nature and his revolt against traditional custom, and too often in his revolt against traditional morality.   The often-quoted lines

> The rank is but the guinea's stamp,
> The man's the gowd for a' that,

show the same contempt for class distinctions as inspired the writings of Rousseau.   Whilst, however, Rousseau looked to the good sense of the masses to remedy the evils of the time, Burns turned hopefully to the work and sturdiness of individual men to heal the evils caused by the inordinate value placed on social rank. The honour paid to the free development of individual character was, in fact, the characteristic of the English and Scottish

Sir Walter Scott: from a painting by Colvin Smith.

revolt against existing order, as opposed to the honour paid by the French Revolutionists to the opinion of the community. Byron, whose first poems were printed in **1806**, but whose first great work— the first two cantos of *Childe Harold*—appeared in **1812**, embodied this form of revolt in his works as well as in his life in a very different fashion from that of Burns. Breaking loose himself from moral restraints, he loved to glorify the characters of those who set at defiance the order of civilised life. In **1824** he died of fever at Missolonghi, fighting for Greek independence. Shelley, whose poems range from **1808** to his early death by drowning in **1822,** had a gentler spirit. All human law and discipline seemed to him to be the mere invention of tyrants, by which the instinctive craving of the soul for beauty of form and nobility of life was repressed.

21. **Scott and Wordsworth.**—On the other hand two great poets, Scott and Wordsworth, upheld the traditions of the ancient order of society. Scott's first great poem, *The Lay of the Last Minstrel,* appeared in **1805.** In **1814** he deserted poetry for the writing of the Waverley Novels. His mind was filled with reverence

for the past life of his country, and this he set forth in verse and prose as no other writer has done. Yet Scott's works may be quoted in support of the doctrine that no considerable movement of thought can leave its greatest opponents unaffected, and the better side of the revolutionary upturning, its preference of the natural to the artificial, and of the humble to the exalted, inspired the best work of Scott. His imaginative love for the heath-clad mountains of his country, and his skill in depicting the pathos and the humour of the lowly, stood him in better stead than his

Wordsworth at the age of 28 : from a portrait by Hancock in the National Portrait Gallery.

skill in bringing before his readers the chivalry and the pageantry of the past. As it was with Scott so it was with Wordsworth whose first poetry was published in **1793.** The early promise of the French Revolution filled him with enthusiasm, but its excesses disgusted him, and he soon became an attached admirer of the institutions of his country. It was not this admiration, however, which put the stamp of greatness on his work, but his open eye fixed, even more clearly than Scott's, upon the influences of nature upon the human mind, and a loving sympathy with the lives of the poor.

22. **Bentham.**—In politics and in law the same influences were felt as in literature. As the horror caused by the French Revolution cleared away, there arose a general dissatisfaction with the existing tendency to uphold what exists merely because it exists. The dissatisfaction thus caused found support in the writings of Jeremy Bentham, who busied himself from **1776** to his death in **1832** with suggestions of legal and political reform. Like Voltaire and the French encyclopedists, he asked that legislation might be rational, and he sought a basis for rational legislation in the doctrine of utility. Utility he defined to be 'that property in any object whereby it tends to produce benefit, advantage, pleasure, good, or happiness, or to prevent the happening of mischief, pain, evil, or unhappiness to the party whose interest is considered.' The object which Bentham desired, therefore, has been summed up in the phrase ' the greatest happiness of the greatest number,' and though in pursuit of this Bentham and his disciples often left out of sight the satisfaction of the spiritual and emotional parts of man's complex nature, they undoubtedly did much to clear away an enormous quantity of mischievous legislation. It was in a kindred spirit that Romilly, Mackintosh and Peel urged on the modification of the criminal law, and it was hardly likely that a movement of this kind, when once begun, would be soon arrested.

Books recommended for the further study of Part X.

LECKY, W. E. H. History of England in the Eighteenth Century. Vol v. p. 154-Vol. vi. p. 137 ; Vol. vi. p. 456-Vol. viii.

MASSEY, W. A History of England in the Reign of George III. Vol. iv.

MARTINEAU, HARRIET (MISS). History of England, A.D. 1800-1815.

——————————————— A History of the Thirty Years' Peace. Vol. i.-Vol. ii. p. 125.

WALPOLE, SPENCER. A History of England from the Conclusion of the Great War in 1815. Vol. i.-Vol. ii. p. 158.

LEWIS, SIR GEORGE CORNEWALL. Essays on the Administrations of Great Britain. Pp. 129-432.

NAPIER, SIR W. F. P. History of the Peninsular War.

BRIALMONT, A. Life of Arthur, Duke of Wellington, translated from the French, with emendations and additions by the Rev. G. R. Gleig.

PART XI

THE GROWTH OF DEMOCRACY

CHAPTER LVI

CATHOLIC EMANCIPATION AND PARLIAMENTARY REFORM
1827–1832

LEADING DATES

Reign of George IV., 1820–1830
Reign of William IV., 1830–1837

Canning Prime Minister	April 10, 1827
Goderich Prime Minister	Aug. 8, 1827
Battle of Navarino	Oct. 20, 1827
Wellington Prime Minister	Jan. 9, 1828
Repeal of the Test and Corporation Acts . . .	1828
Catholic Emancipation Act	1829
Death of George IV. and Accession of William IV. . .	1830
Lord Grey's Ministry.	1830
Introduction of the Reform Bill . . .	March 1, 1831
The Reform Act becomes Law . . .	Jan. 7, 1832

1. **Questions at Issue.** **1827.**—During the latter years of Liverpool's Prime Ministership two questions had been coming into prominence : the one that of Catholic emancipation by the admission of Catholics to Parliament and to offices of state ; the other that of Parliamentary reform, with a view to diminish the power of the landowners over elections to the House of Commons, and to transfer at least part of their power to enlarged constituencies. Of the leading statesmen Wellington and Peel were opposed to both the proposed changes ; Canning was in favour of Catholic emancipation, but opposed to Parliamentary reform ; whilst the Whigs, the most noteworthy of whom were Earl Grey in the House of Lords, and Lord Althorp and Lord John Russell in the House of Commons, were favourable to both.

3 M 2

2. **Canning Prime Minister. 1827.**—Before Liverpool left office a resolution in favour of Catholic emancipation was defeated in the House of Commons by the slight majority of four, and almost immediately afterwards Canning, who had spoken and voted for it, was appointed Prime Minister. Seven of the former ministers, including Wellington and Peel, refused to serve under him. On the other hand he obtained the support of the Whigs, to a few of whom office was shortly afterwards given. The Whigs had been long unpopular, on account of the opposition which they had offered to the war with France even whilst Wellington was conducting his great campaigns in the Peninsula ; but they had now a chance of recovering public favour by associating themselves with domestic reforms. There can hardly be a doubt that Canning's ministry, if it had lasted, could only have maintained itself by a more extended admission of the Whigs to power. Canning's health was, however, failing, and on August 8 he died, having been Prime Minister for less than four months.

Canning : from Stewardson's portrait.

3. **The Battle of Navarino and the Goderich Ministry. 1827.**—Canning was succeeded by Goderich, who had formerly, as Mr. Robinson (see p. 886), been Chancellor of the Exchequer. His colleagues quarrelled with one another, and Goderich was too weak a man to settle their disputes. Before the end of the year news arrived which increased their differences. On July 6, whilst Canning still lived, a treaty had been signed in London between England, France, and Russia, binding the three powers to offer

mediation between the Turks and the Greeks, and, in the event of either party rejecting their mediation, to put an end by force to the struggle which was going on. Instructions were sent to Codrington, the admiral commanding the Mediterranean fleet, to stop supplies coming into Greece from Turkey or Egypt, but to avoid hostilities. On September 9 a fleet composed of Turkish and Egyptian ships, laden with men and supplies, reached Navarino, close to the ancient Pylos, in the south-west of Peloponnesus. Codrington arrived two days later, and was afterwards joined by French and Russian squadrons. The combined fleet compelled the Turkish and Egyptian fleet to remain inactive. On land, however, Ibrahim (see p. 884), who commanded the army transported in it from Egypt, proceeded deliberately to turn the soil of Peloponnesus into a desert, slaying and wasting as he moved. On October 20, the allied admirals, unwilling to tolerate the commission of such brutalities, entered the Bay of Navarino, in which twenty-two centuries before Athenians and Lacedæmonians had contended for the mastery. A gun was fired from a Turkish ship, and a battle began in which half of the Egyptian fleet was destroyed, and the remainder submitted. The victory made Greek independence possible. There can be little doubt that Canning, if he had lived, would have been overjoyed at the result. Goderich and his colleagues in the ministry could not agree whether Codrington deserved praise or blame. There were fresh quarrels amongst them, and, on December 21, 'Goody Goderich,' as the wits called him, went to the king to complain of his opponents. George IV. told him to go home and take care of himself. It is said that on this the Prime Minister burst into tears, and that the king offered him his pocket handkerchief to dry them. On January 9, 1828, Goderich formally resigned.

4. **Formation of the Wellington Ministry. 1828.**—The Duke of Wellington became Prime Minister, and Peel again became Home Secretary and the leading minister in the House of Commons. The new ministry, from which the Whigs were rigorously excluded, was to be like Lord Liverpool's one, in which Catholic emancipation was to be an open question, each minister being at liberty to speak and vote on it as he thought fit. Those who supported it, of whom Huskisson was one, were now known as Canningites, from their attachment to the principles of that minister. It was, however, unlikely that the two sections of the ministry would long hold together, especially as the question of Parliamentary reform was now rising into importance, and the Canningites showed a disposition to break away on this point

from Wellington and Peel, who were strongly opposed to any change in the constitution of Parliament.

5. Lord John Russell and Parliamentary Reform. 1819—1828.—The cause of Parliamentary reform had suffered much from the sweeping nature of the proposals made after the great war by Hunt and Sir Francis Burdett (see p. 879). In **1819** the question was taken up by a young Whig member, Lord John Russell, who perceived that the only chance of prevailing with the House of Commons was to ask it to accept much smaller changes than those for which Burdett asked, and thought that, whilst it would not listen to declarations about the right of the people to man-hood suffrage, it might listen to a proposal to remedy admitted grievances in detail. In **1819** he drew attention to the subject, and in **1820** asked for the disfranchisement, at the next election, of four places in Devon and Cornwall : Grampound, Penryn, Barnstaple and Camelford, which returned two members apiece, and in which corruption notoriously prevailed. His proposal, accepted by the Commons, was rejected by the Lords. In a new Parliament which met later in the same year Lord John proposed to disfranchise Grampound only, and to transfer its members to Leeds, thus touching one of the great political grievances of the day, the possession of the right of returning members by small villages, whilst it was refused to large communities like Birming-ham and Leeds. The House was, however, frightened at the idea of giving power to populous towns, and in **1821**, when the Bill for disfranchising Grampound was actually passed, its members were transferred, not to Leeds but to Yorkshire, which thus came to return four members instead of two. A first step had thus been taken in the direction of reform, and Lord John Russell from time to time attempted to obtain the assent of the House of Commons to a proposal to take into consideration the whole subject. Time after time, however, his motions were rejected, and in **1827** Lord John fell back on his former plan of separately attacking corrupt boroughs. In **1827** Penryn and East Retford having been found guilty of corruption, he obtained a vote in the Commons for the disfranchisement of Penryn, whilst the disfranchisement of East Retford was favourably considered. As this vote was not followed by the passing of any act of Parliament to give effect to it, it was understood that Lord John would make fresh proposals in the following year.

6. Repeal of the Test and Corporation Acts. 1828.—In **1828**, after the formation of the Wellington Ministry, before the question of the corrupt boroughs was discussed, Russell was successful in removing another grievance. He proposed to repeal the Corporation Act (see p. 585), and the Test Act (see p. 607), so far as it compelled all applicants for office and for seats in Parliament to receive the Communion in the Church of England. By this means relief would be given to Dissenters, whilst Roman Catholics would still be excluded by the clause which required a declaration against transubstantiation and which Russell did not propose to repeal. Russell's scheme was resisted by the ministers but accepted by the House, and it finally became law, passing the House of Lords upon the addition of a clause suggested by Peel requiring a declaration from Dissenters claiming to hold office or to sit in Parliament or in municipal corporations that they would not use their power ' to injure or subvert the Established Church.' It was thus made evident that Peel could not be counted on to resist change as absolutely as Sidmouth could have been calculated on when the reaction against the French Revolution was at its height. He was practical and cautious, not easily caught by new ideas, but prompt to discover when resistance became more dangerous than concession, and resolutely determined to follow honestly his intellectual convictions.

7. **Resignation of the Canningites. 1828.**—The ministry had been distracted by constant squabbles, and at last, in May, 1828, Huskisson and the other Canningites resigned, the ministry being reconstructed as a purely Tory ministry. The Tories were in ecstasies, forgetting that their leaders, Wellington and Peel, were too sensible to pursue a policy of mere resistance.

8. **The Catholic Association. 1823—1828.**—The main question, on which the Tories took one side and the Whigs and Canningites the other, was that of Catholic emancipation. That question now assumed a new prominence. In Ireland Catholic emancipation was advocated by Daniel O'Connell, who was himself a Roman Catholic, and was not only an eloquent speaker whose words went home to the hearts of his countrymen, but also the leader of a great society, the Catholic Association, which had been formed in 1823 to support Catholic emancipation. In 1824 the Catholic Association became thoroughly organised, and commanded a respect amongst the majority of Irishmen which was not given to the Parliament at Westminster. O'Connell's words sometimes pointed to the possibility of resistance if Parliament rejected the Catholic claims. In 1825 Parliament passed an act to dissolve the Association. The Irish were, however, too quick-witted to allow it to be suppressed by British legislation. They dissolved the Association, but started

a new one in which the question of Catholic emancipation was not to be discussed, though the members naturally thought the more about it. In Parliament itself many who had voted for the dissolution of the Association voted for Catholic emancipation, and, in **1825**, a Bill granting it passed the Commons, though it was rejected by the Lords.

9. **O'Connell's Election.** **1828.**—In **1828** Vesey Fitzgerald, member for the county of Clare, was promoted to an office previously held by one of the Canningites, and had, consequently, to present himself for re-election (see p. 674). O'Connell stood in opposition to him for the vacant seat. All the influence of the priests was thrown on his side, and he was triumphantly returned, though it was known that he would refuse to declare against transubstantiation, and would thus be prevented by the unrepealed clause of the Test Act (see p. 890) from taking his seat in the House of Commons.

10. **Catholic Emancipation.** **1829.**—When Parliament met in **1829** it was discovered that the Government intended to grant Catholic emancipation, to which it had hitherto been bitterly opposed. Wellington looked at the matter with a soldier's eye. He did not like to admit the Catholics, and had held the position against them as long as it was tenable. It was now, in his opinion, untenable, because to reject the Catholic claims would bring about a civil war, and a civil war was worse than the proposed legislation. He felt it, therefore, to be his duty to retreat to another position, from which civil order could be better defended. Peel's mind moved slowly, but it moved certainly, and he now appeared as a defender of Catholic relief on principle. To show his sincerity, Peel resigned his seat for the University of Oxford, and presented himself for re-election in order to allow his constituents to express an opinion on his change of front ; and, being defeated at Oxford, was chosen by the small borough of Westbury. A Bill, giving effect to the intentions of the Government, was brought in. The anger of the Tories was exceedingly great, and even Wellington had, after the fashion of those days, to prove his sincerity by fighting a duel with the Earl of Winchilsea. The king resisted, but the resistance of George IV., now a weak old voluptuary, was easily beaten down. The Commons passed the Bill, throwing open Parliament, and all offices except a few of special importance, to the Roman Catholics, after which the House of Lords, under Wellington's influence, accepted it. The Bill therefore became law, accompanied by another for disfranchising forty-shilling freeholders

Apsley House, the residence of the Duke of Wellington : from an engraving of 1829.

in Ireland. These freeholders had been allowed to vote as long as their votes were given to the landlords ; their votes were taken from them now that they were given to the candidates supported by the priests.

11. **Death of George IV. 1830.**—Catholic emancipation was the result of the spread of one of the principles which had actuated the French Revolutionists in 1789, the principle that religious opinions ought not to be a bar to the exercise of civil or political rights. It was—as far, at least, as Great Britain was concerned—not the result of any democratic movement. The mass of Englishmen and Scotchmen still entertained a strong dislike of the Roman Catholics, and it has often been said, perhaps with truth, that if Parliament had been reformed in 1829, the Emancipation Bill would have been rejected. The position of the ministers in the House of Commons was weakened in consequence of the enmity of many of their old supporters, whilst the opposition, composed of Whigs and Canningites, was not likely to give them constant support. In the course of 1830 the Whigs chose Lord Althorp as their leader, who, though he had no commanding genius, inspired confidence by his thorough honesty. Before the effect of this change appeared George IV. died unregretted on June 26.

12. **William IV. and the Second French Revolution. 1830.**—The eldest surviving brother of the late king succeeded as William IV. He was eccentric, and courted popularity by walking about the streets, and allowed himself to be treated with the utmost familiarity by his subjects. Some people thought that, like his father, he would be a lunatic before he died. A new Parliament was elected in which the Tories, though they lost many seats, still had a majority ; but it was a majority divided against itself. Events occurred on the Continent which tended to weaken still further the Wellington ministry. In France Charles X., having succeeded his brother Louis XVIII., became rapidly unpopular. Defying the Chambers, which answered in France to the Parliament in England, he was overthrown in July 1830 by a revolution which placed his distant cousin, the Duke of Orleans, on the throne. Louis Philippe, however, instead of taking the title of King of France, which had been borne by the preceding kings, assumed that of King of the French, as a sign of his adoption of a merely constitutional authority. He was, in fact, to be to France what William III. had been to England. Such a movement in a neighbouring nation could not fail to influence Englishmen, especially as there was a feeling now spreading in England in some respects analogous to

that which existed in France. Charles X. had been deposed not
merely because he claimed absolute power, but because he did so
in the interests of the aristocracy as opposed to those of the middle

William IV.

class, and in England too the middle class was striving to assert
itself against the landowners who almost exclusively filled the two
Houses. The lead was taken by the Birmingham Political Union, and
all over the country demands were made for Parliamentary reform.

13. **The End of the Wellington Ministry.** 1830.—In the House of Lords, when a new Parliament was opened in November, Lord Grey—who as Mr. Grey had urged the necessity of reforming Parliament in the early days of the great French Revolution (see p. 827)—suggested to Wellington that it would be well to bring in such a measure now. Wellington not only refused, but added that if he had to form for the first time a legislature for the country 'he did not mean to assert that he could form such a legislature as they possessed now, for the nature of man was incapable of reaching such

The Duke of Wellington : from a bust by Francis in the National Portrait Gallery.

excellence at once ; but his great endeavour would be to form some description of legislature which would produce the same results.' After this his ministry was doomed. On November 15 it was defeated in the House of Commons by a combination between the opposition and dissatisfied Tories, and Wellington at once resigned. He had done good service to the state, having practised economy and maintained efficiency. In London his ministry made its mark by the introduction, in 1829, of a new police, in the place of the old useless constables who allowed thieves to escape instead of catching them. The nicknames of ' Bobby' and ' Peeler' which long attached themselves to policemen had their origin in the names of Robert Peel, by whom the force was organised.

14. **Lord Grey's Ministry. 1830.**—Lord Grey became the head of a ministry composed of Whigs and Canningites. Amongst the former were Lord John Russell, Lord Althorp who led the House of Commons, and Viscount Melbourne, a man of great abilities and great indolence of temperament, of whom it was said

Earl Grey : from a figure in Hayter's Reformed Parliament in the National Portrait Gallery.

that his usual answer to proposals of reform was, ' Can't you let it alone?' Amongst the latter was Lord Palmerston, another Canningite, who had long been known as a painstaking official of considerable powers, but who now for the first time found a position worthy of them by becoming Secretary for Foreign Affairs. Brougham, a stirring but eccentric orator, was made Lord Chancellor to keep him from being troublesome in the House of Commons. To Lord John Russell an inferior office was assigned, and he was not made a member of the Cabinet, but, in consequence of the services which he had rendered to the cause of Parliamentary reform, he was entrusted with the task of bringing before the House of Commons the Bill which the new Government proposed to introduce on that subject.

15. **The Reform Bill. 1831.**—The Reform Bill was brought in by Russell on March 1, 1831. He had an easy task in exposing the faults of the old system. Old Sarum, which returned two members, was only a green mound, without a habitation upon it. Gatton, which also returned two members, was only a ruined wall, whilst

vast communities like Birmingham and Manchester were totally unrepresented. The proposal of the ministry was to sweep away sixty small boroughs returning 119 members, and to give only one member apiece instead of two to forty-six other boroughs nearly as small. Most of the seats thus placed at the disposal of the ministry were to be given, in almost equal proportions, to the counties and the great towns of England ; a few being reserved for Scotland and Ireland. In the counties, the franchise or right of

Viscount Melbourne : from a figure in Hayter's Reformed Parliament in the National Portrait Gallery.

voting which had hitherto been confined to the possessors of a freehold worth 40s. a year, was conferred also on persons holding land worth 10l. a year by copyhold, or 50l. a year by lease.[1] In the boroughs a uniform franchise was given to all householders paying rent of 10l. a year.

16. **The Bill Withdrawn. 1831.**—The Tories were numerous

---

[1] The copyhold is so called because it is a tenure of which the only evidence is a copy of the Court Roll of a Manor. It is a perpetual holding subject to certain payments. Leasehold is a tenure for a term of years by lease.

in the House of Commons, and opposed the Bill as revolutionary.
Many of them shared the opinion of Wellington, who believed that
if it passed the poor would seize the property of the rich and
divide it amongst themselves. In reality, the character of the voters
in the counties would be much the same as it had been before, whilst
the majority of the voters in the boroughs would be the smaller shop-
keepers who were not in the least likely to attack property. The
second reading of the Bill,[1] however, only passed by a majority of
one, and a hostile amendment to one of its clauses having been
carried, the Government withdrew the Bill and dissolved Parliament in order that the question might be referred to the electors.

17. **The Reform Bill Re-introduced. 1831.**—In times of excitement the electors contrived to impress their feelings on Parliament, even under the old system of voting. From one end of the
country to the other a cry was heard of ' The Bill, the whole Bill,
and nothing but the Bill.' The new House of Commons had an
enormous Whig majority. The Reform Bill, slightly amended, was
again brought in by Russell, to whom a seat in the Cabinet had
been at last given. In the course of discussion in the Commons a
clause, known as the Chandos clause from the name of its proposer,
was introduced, extending the franchise in counties to 50*l.* tenants at
will. As these new voters would be afraid to vote against their
landlords for fear of being turned out of their farms, the change was
satisfactory to the Tories. Yet, after the Bill thus altered had passed
the House of Commons, it was, on October 8, rejected by the House
of Lords.

18. **Public Agitation. 1831.**—The news of the rejection of the
Bill was received with a torrent of indignation. Meetings were
everywhere held in support of the Government. In the House of
Commons Macaulay—a young man afterwards the historian of the
reigns of James II. and William III.—urged the ministry to persist
in its course. " The public enthusiasm," he said, " is undiminished.
Old Sarum has grown no bigger, Manchester has grown no
smaller. . . . I know only two ways in which societies can be
governed—by public opinion and by the sword. A government
having at its command the armies, the fleets, and the revenues of

---

[1] A Bill before either House is read a first time in order that the members
may be enabled to see what it is like. In voting on the second reading members
express an opinion whether or no they approve of its general principle. In
committee it is discussed clause by clause, to give the House an opportunity of
amending it in detail ; and a vote is then taken on the third reading to see if
the majority of the House approves of it in its amended form. It is then sent
to the other House, where it goes through the same process.

Great Britain might possibly hold Ireland by the sword ; . . . but to govern Great Britain by the sword, so wild a thought has never occurred to any public man of any party. . . . In old times, when the villeins were driven to revolt by oppression, when a hundred thousand insurgents appeared in arms on Blackheath, the king rode up to them and exclaimed, 'I will be your leader,' and at once the infuriated multitude laid down their arms and dispersed

Lord Palmerston : from a seated figure in Hayter's Reformed Parliament in the National Portrait Gallery.

at his command.   Herein let us imitate him.   Let us say to our countrymen 'We are your leaders.   Our lawful power shall be firmly exerted to the utmost in your cause ; and our lawful power is such that it must finally prevail.'"   It was a timely warning. Outside Parliament there were men who thought that nothing but force would bear down the resistance of the Lords.   The Birmingham Political Union (see p. 899) held a meeting at which those who were present engaged to pay no taxes if the Reform Bill were again rejected.   At Bristol there were fierce riots in which houses were burnt and men killed.

19. **The Reform Bill becomes Law.   1831—1832.** — On December 12, **1831**, the Reform Bill was again, for a third time, brought into the House of Commons.   On March 23, **1832**, it was passed, and the Lords had then once more to consider it.   On April 14 they passed the second reading.   On May 7, on the motion of Lord Lyndhurst, who had been Chancellor in Wellington's ministry, they adopted a substantial alteration in it.   The ministers at once asked the king to create fifty new peers to carry the Bill, in the same way that the address on the Treaty of Utrecht had been carried by the creation of twelve new peers in the reign of Anne.   The king, who was getting frightened at the turmoil in the country, refused, and ministers resigned.   Wellington was ready to take office, giving his support to a less complete Reform Bill, but Peel refused to join him, and Lord Grey's Government was reinstated, receiving from the king a promise to create peers if necessary.   On this Wellington, unwilling to see the House of Lords swamped by fresh creations, persuaded many of his friends to abstain from voting.   The Bill met with no further obstacles, and, on June 7, became an Act of Parliament by the Royal Assent.

20. **Character of the Reform Act.   1832.** — In its final shape the Reform Act absolutely disfranchised forty-one boroughs and took away one member from thirty others.   Thereby, and by its alteration of the franchise, it accomplished a great transference of power, in favour of the middle classes in the towns.   Though it did not establish a democracy, it took a long step in that direction.

21. **Roads and Coaches.   1802—1820.** — The advent of the middle classes to power was prepared by a series of material improvements by which they were especially benefited.   The canals made in the beginning of the reign of George III. no longer sufficed to carry the increased traffic of the country.   Attention was therefore paid to the improvement of the roads.   Telford, a Scotchman, taught road-makers that it was better to go round a hill than to climb over it, and, beginning in **1802**, he was employed for eighteen years in improving the communications in Scotland and Wales by making good roads and iron bridges.   The Menai suspension bridge, his best known work, was begun in **1819**.   He and another Scotchman, Macadam, also improved the surface of the roads, which had hitherto been made of gravel or flint, thrown down at random.   Telford ordered the large stones to be broken and

mixed with fine gravel, and Macadam pursued the same course round Bristol. He declared that no stone should ever be used in mending roads which was not small enough to go into a man's mouth. Through these improvements travelling became more easy, and coaches flew about the country at what was considered to be the wonderful rate of ten miles an hour.

22. Steam Vessels and Locomotives. 1811—1825.—The first application of steam to locomotion was in vessels. The first steam-boat in Great Britain, 'The Comet,' the work of Henry Bell, plied on the Clyde in **1812**, and though Fulton in America had made a steam-boat in **1811**, it is almost certain that he derived his ideas from Bell. It was not till later that a steam-engine was made to

Early steamboat : from the *Instructor* of 1833.

draw travellers and goods by land. Of many attempts, none succeeded till the matter was taken in hand by George Stephenson, the son of a poor collier in Northumberland. He had learnt something about machinery in the colliery in which he worked as a boy, and when he grew up he saved money to pay for instruction in reading and writing. He began as an engineer by mending a pumping-engine, and at last attempted to construct a locomotive. His new engine, constructed in **1814**, was not successful at first, and it made such a noise that it was popularly known as 'Puffing Billy.' In **1816** he improved it sufficiently to enable it to draw trucks of coal on tramlines from the colliery to the river. At last, in **1825**, the Stockton and Darlington Railway was opened for the conveyance of passengers as well as goods, and both the line and the loco-

motive used on it were constructed under Stephenson's management. The new engine was able to draw ninety tons at the rate
of eight miles an hour.

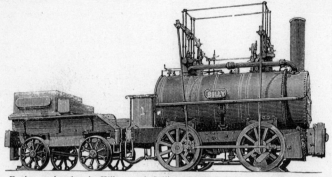

Engine employed at the Killingworth Colliery, familiarly known as 'Puffing Billy.'

23. The Liverpool and Manchester Railway. 1825—1829.—

In 1825 it was resolved to make a railway between Liverpool and
Manchester, and Stephenson was employed as the engineer. In

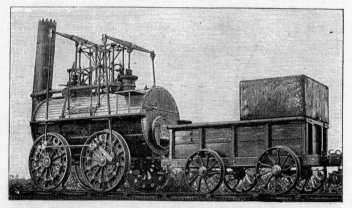

No. 1. Engine of the Stockton and Darlington Railway ; now on a pedestal at
the south end of the new station at Darlington.

1829, when it was finished, the proprietors were frightened at the
idea of employing steam-engines upon it, till Stephenson persuaded
them to offer a prize for an improved locomotive. Four inventors,

St Luke's, Chelsea (an early example of the Gothic revival), designed by
Savage and built in 1824.

of whom Stephenson was one, sent in engines to compete. Stephenson's, which was called the ' Rocket,' was the only one which would move, and finally ran at the rate of thirty-five miles an hour.   After that there was no doubt that Stephenson's was the only engine likely to be of any use.   Unfortunately the experiment cost the life of a statesman.   Huskisson, who had quarrelled with Wellington in 1828 (see p. 895), seeing him in a railway carriage, stepped up to shake hands, when he was himself run over by the Rocket and killed.

CHAPTER LVII

THE REFORMERS IN POWER.   1832—1841

LEADING DATES

<table>
<tr><td colspan="2" align="center">William IV., 1830—1837   Victoria, 1837</td></tr>
<tr><td>Abolition of Slavery . . . .</td><td>1833</td></tr>
<tr><td>The New Poor Law . . . .</td><td>1834</td></tr>
<tr><td>Peel's First Ministry. . . . .</td><td>1834</td></tr>
<tr><td>The Second Melbourne Ministry . . . .</td><td>1835</td></tr>
<tr><td>Accession of Victoria. . . . .</td><td>1837</td></tr>
<tr><td>Resignation and Re-instatement of the Melbourne
    Ministry . . . .</td><td>1839</td></tr>
<tr><td>Final Resignation of the Melbourne Ministry . . .</td><td>1841</td></tr>
</table>

1. **Liberals and Conservatives.   1832.**—Before the end of 1832 a Parliament met, in which the House of Commons was elected by the new constituencies created by the Reform Act.   The Ministerialists were in an enormous majority, all of them anxious to make use of their victory by the introduction of practical reforms.   There was, however, considerable difference amongst them as to the reforms desirable, the Radicals wishing to go much farther than the Whigs.   To conceal, as far as possible, this difference, a new name—that of Liberals—was borrowed from Continental politicians, to cover the whole party.   Their opponents, finding the name of Tories unpopular, began to call themselves Conservatives.

2. **Irish Tithes.   1831—1833.**—One of the first difficulties which the Government had to face was that of Irish tithes.   Catholic emancipation had not made Ireland richer, and there was still in that country a superabundant population, in many parts scarcely able to live and at the same time meet the demands of their

landlords and of the clergy of a Church which was not their own. There was no poor law in Ireland to give relief to the destitute, and many of the landlords were absentees. In **1831** and **1832** the payment of tithes was often refused, and the collectors were sometimes murdered. General outrages also increased in number, and in **1833**, when an attempt was made by the Government to enforce the payment of tithes, only 12,000*l.* out of 104,000*l.* was recovered. The Government was divided as to the proper measures to be adopted. The Chief Secretary [1]—the minister specially entrusted with Irish affairs—was Stanley, a man of great abilities and a fiery temper, who wished to accompany proposals of redress by strong measures for the coercion of those by whom the law was resisted. His policy was described as a 'quick alternation of kicks and kindness.' On the other hand, O'Connell had begun to denounce the Union between Ireland and Great Britain and to ask for its repeal. In **1833** Stanley brought in a Bill for the trial of offenders in disturbed districts by courts-martial. As soon as this had been passed Althorp brought in another Bill to reduce the number of Irish bishops from twenty-two to twelve, and to tax the Irish clergy and apply the proceeds to the extinction of Church-cess, a rate levied to keep the church buildings in good condition. This Bill too became law, but only after the Government had dropped what was called the Appropriation Clause, which was to enable the Government to apply to general purposes the revenue obtained by diminishing the number of the bishops.

3. **Abolition of Slavery. 1833.**—Stanley had made so many enemies in Ireland that it was thought advisable to remove him from his post. He became Colonial Secretary, and was at once confronted with the question of the abolition of slavery in British colonies. For some years Sir Thomas Fowell Buxton, and Zachary Macaulay (the father of Macaulay the historian), had been pleading the cause of the slave. In the West Indies slaves were often subjected to brutal cruelty. To take a few instances : a little slave-girl, having dropped some cream belonging to her mistress, was scolded by her mother, a slave-woman named America. The master of both of them had America flogged with no less than 175 lashes for remonstrating with her own daughter, holding that, as the child was his property, she ought only to have been scolded by himself or his wife. Three slave-women were flogged for crying when their brothers were flogged. Another woman, whose brother was

---

[1] *I.e.* the chief secretary to the Lord-Lieutenant, but practically controlling him, as being responsible directly to Parliament, of which he is a member.

flogged for attending a dissenting chapel, was flogged merely for sighing. When Stanley came into office, new as he was to the details of the subject, he mastered them in three weeks, and carried a Bill for the complete abolition of slavery, though leaving the former slaves apprentices to their late masters for twelve years. The purchase-money given by Great Britain to the slave-owners was 20,000,000*l*. The apprenticeship system was found unsatisfactory and was soon done away with.

4. **The First Factory Act. 1833.**—The abolition of negro slavery was accompanied by an effort to lighten the sorrows of factory children who were kept at work in unwholesome air often for thirteen hours a day. Lord Ashley, who afterwards became Earl of Shaftesbury, took up their cause, and carried a Bill limiting the hours of labour for children under thirteen years to eight hours a day, and for children between thirteen and eighteen to twelve hours a day, though he would himself have preferred a stronger measure. This law was the beginning of a factory legislation which has done much to make England peaceable and contented.

5. **The New Poor Law. 1834.**—The session of 1834 was occupied with a measure of a different kind. The Poor Law, as it existed, was a direct encouragement to thriftlessness. Relief was given to the poor at random, even when they were earning wages, so that employers of labour preferred to be served by paupers, because part of the wages would then be paid out of the rates. The more children a poor man had the more he received from the rates, and in this and in other ways labourers were taught that they would be better off by being dependent on the parish than by striving to make their own way in the world. The consequent increase of the rates had become unbearable to those who had to pay them : in one parish, for instance, rates which had been less than 11*l*. in 1801 had risen to 367*l*. in 1832. By the new Poor Law, passed in 1834, workhouses were built and no person was to receive relief who did not consent to live in one of them. The object of this rule was that no one might claim to be supported by others who was capable of supporting himself, and residence in the workhouse, where work would be required, was considered as the best test of real poverty, because it was thought that no one would consent to go in unless he was really distressed. Afterwards it was remembered that in some cases, such as those of old people who could not work even if they had the will, no such test was required. The strict rule of the law was, therefore, subsequently relaxed, and outdoor relief granted in certain cases.

6. **Break-up of the Ministry.** **1834.**—The ministry had by this time lost much of its popularity. Every piece of successful legislation alienated some of its supporters, and the rapidity of the changes effected by the reformed Parliament frightened many easy-going people. Peel, too, who led the Conservatives in the House of Commons, was growing in favour by the ability, and still more by the moderation, which he displayed. The ministers, too, disagreed amongst themselves. An open rupture occurred when Lord John Russell declared for the right of Parliament to appropriate the misused revenues of the Irish Church to other purposes. "Johnny," wrote Stanley to Sir James Graham, the First Lord of the Admiralty, "has upset the coach." Stanley, Graham, and Lord Ripon —who had formerly been known as Lord Goderich (see p. 892)— resigned together. Further misunderstandings brought about the resignation of Grey, who had been an excellent Prime Minister as long as the Reform question was still unsettled, but who did not possess the qualities needed in the head of a divided Cabinet. He was succeeded by Lord Melbourne, and Melbourne contrived to keep his followers together for a few months. In November, however, Lord Althorp, who was the leader of the House of Commons, became Earl Spencer by his father's death, and it was therefore necessary to find a successor to him. The king, who had long been alienated from the Reformers, took advantage of the occasion to dismiss the ministry. It was the last time that a ministry was dismissed by a sovereign.

7. **Foreign Policy of the Reformers.** **1830—1834.**—Whilst the home policy of the Reform ministry had been weakened by divisions in the Cabinet, its foreign policy had been in the strong hands of Lord Palmerston (see p. 901). In **1830** the revolution at Paris had been followed by a revolution at Brussels, the object of which was not to procure internal reforms but to separate Belgium from the kingdom of the Netherlands, of which it had formed a part only since **1814** (see p. 873). Lord Palmerston's policy was to forward the desire of the Belgians for independence and at the same time to hinder any attempt on the part of France to annex their territory. In this, with the assistance of Louis Philippe the new king of the French, he completely succeeded. In **1831** Leopold of Saxe Coburg, whose first wife had been the Princess Charlotte (see p. 881), was chosen by the Belgians as their king, and married one of the daughters of Louis Philippe. Though the Dutch resisted for a time, they were compelled to relinquish their hold on any part of Belgium. A French army captured from them

the citadel of Antwerp and then retired to its own territory.   The key-stone of Palmerston's policy was an alliance—not too trustful —between the constitutional monarchies of England and France, which was drawn the more tightly because the absolute government of Austria crushed all attempts at resistance in Italy, and the absolute government of Russia put down with great harshness an attempt made by Poland to assert her independence.   To these two monarchies Prussia was a close ally, and Europe was thus divided into two camps, the absolute and the constitutional.

8. **Peel's First Ministry.   1834—1835.**—Sir Robert Peel, having been appointed Prime Minister by the king, dissolved Parliament. In an address to the electors of Tamworth, the borough for which he stood, he threw off the doctrines of the old Tories, professing himself to be a moderate but conservative reformer.   This ' Tamworth manifesto,' as it was called, served his party in good stead. The Conservatives gained seat after seat, and it is probable that, if the king had had a little more patience and had allowed the ministry to fall to pieces of itself instead of dismissing it, the Conservatives would have been in a majority.   As it was, though they had nearly half the House, they were still in a minority.   When Parliament met, February 19, **1835**, it had some difficulty in finding temporary accommodation, as the old Houses of Parliament, in which the struggles of nearly three centuries had been conducted, had been burnt to the ground in the preceding October.   Peel was outvoted from the beginning, but he insisted on bringing in his measures before he would retire, and, at all events, had the satisfaction of showing that he was capable of preparing good laws as well as of giving good advice.   The Liberals, however, were too angry to adopt even good laws when proposed by a minister who had risen to power by the use of the king's prerogative.   They entered into an agreement with O'Connell, known, from the place where its terms were settled, as the Lichfield House Compact, and, having thus secured, by the support of the Irish members, an undivided majority, they insisted on the appropriation of the surplus revenues of the Irish Church to purposes of education.   They carried a succession of votes on this subject, and, on April 8, **1835**, Peel resigned.   He left behind him a general impression that he was the first statesman in the country.

9. **Beginning of Melbourne's Second Ministry.   1835—1837.**— Melbourne again became Prime Minister, and Russell Home Secretary and leader of the House of Commons.   The first great work of the new ministry was the passing of a Municipal Corporations

Bill, providing that corporations should be elected by the ratepayers, instead of being self-chosen as they frequently were. The Tories in the House of Lords, where they had a large majority, tried to introduce considerable alterations in it, but Peel threw them over and accepted the Bill with a few changes, so that it became law without further difficulty. Peel gained in credit by subordinating the interests of his party to those of the country, and the ministry consequently lost ground. Their weakness was exposed by the attitude which they were obliged to assume towards the Lords on another question. The Commons passed a Bill for placing Irish tithes upon the landlord instead of the tenant, adding the Appropriation Clause which they had formerly attempted to attach to the Bill for the reduction of the number of Bishops

Banner of the Royal Arms, as borne since 1837.

(see p. 910). The Lords threw out the clause, and the ministers then withdrew the Bill. Attempts made in later years to get the Bill passed with the clause equally failed, and at last, in **1838**, ministers ignominiously dropped the clause, upon which they passed the Bill through both Houses. A Government with the House of Commons and the nation at its back can in modern times defy the House of Lords. Melbourne's Government tried to defy it with the support of the House of Commons but without the support of the nation. Consequently, though some useful measures were passed, the Lords were able, in the teeth of the Government, to reject anything they disliked.

10. **Queen Victoria. 1837.**—On June 20, **1837**, William IV. died, and was succeeded by his niece the Princess Victoria who was just over eighteen, the time of life at which heirs to the throne come of age. Her dignity and grace won her general popularity, and the ministry, which she was known to favour, regained some popularity and, after the new elections had been held in the autumn, it was, as before, supported by a small majority in the House of Commons.

11. **Canada. 1837—1841.**—The state of Canada at this time caused great difficulties to the ministry. Upper and Lower Canada were independent colonies, the population of the former

Queen Victoria at her accession : engraved by Thompson after a portrait by Lane.

being almost entirely British, and the population of the latter being preponderantly French. In both there were loud complaints of the jobbery and misconduct of the Home Government, but the constitutional arrangements were such that in neither colony was the popularly elected Legislative Assembly able to influence the action of the colonial government, by which the Home Government was represented. The feeling in Lower Canada was particularly bitter, as the French, who were attached to their own ways, resented the pushing, self-satisfied behaviour of English settlers who came amongst them. The Colonial Secretary in England, Lord Glenelg, was not enough of a statesman to find a satisfactory remedy for the grievances of the colonists, and in 1837 a rebellion burst out which was, indeed, suppressed, but which alarmed the Home Government sufficiently to induce it to send Lord Durham out as Commissioner, with full powers to arrange all difficulties, so far as he could do so in accordance with the law. Lord Durham was the ablest man of the Liberal party, but he had no tact, and was excessively self-willed. On his arrival in Canada in 1838, he transported to Bermuda eight persons connected with the rebellion, and ordered that fifteen persons who had left the colony should be put to death if they came back. As both these orders were illegal the Home Government recalled him, but they took his advice after his return, and joined together the two colonies, at the same time altering the constitution so as to give control over the executive to the Legislative Assembly. The union between the colonies, which was intended to prevent the French of Lower Canada having entirely their own way in their own colony, was proposed in 1839 and finally proclaimed in 1841. The new arrangements gave satisfaction to both colonies for the time.

12. **Ireland.** 1835–1841.—The condition of Ireland under the Melbourne Government was much improved, and its improvement was due to the ability and firmness of Thomas Drummond, the Under-Secretary. Hitherto the Orangemen (see p. 834), including in their ranks many magistrates, had had it all their own way in the North, where Catholics, whom they chose to oppress, seldom met with justice. Drummond did his best to enforce the law equally in all parts of Ireland, not only between Protestant and Catholic, but also between landlord and tenant. He thereby exasperated the landlords, whose ideas of right and wrong had hitherto been entirely shared by the Government. On the other hand, he so thoroughly won for himself the goodwill of the Irish Catholics, that O'Connell laid aside for a time the cry for the re-

peal of the Union which he had raised under Lord Grey's ministry. One element of Irish discontent was beyond the power of any government wholly to remove. So rapid was the increase of the population as to bring with it great poverty, and some landlords, finding their rents unpaid, solved the difficulty by evicting the tenants who were unable or unwilling to pay. As there was no poor law in Ireland the evicted tenant had seldom anything but starvation before him, and he often revenged himself by outrages

Lord John Russell: from a painting by Sir F. Grant, in the possession of the Dowager Countess Russell.

and even by murder. In a celebrated letter to the magistrates of Tipperary Drummond announced that 'Property has its duties as well as its rights,' reminding them that in part, at least, the misery in Ireland had arisen from their unsympathetic treatment of their tenants. The magistrates were so angry that they suppressed the letter for a time. In 1838 a Poor Law for Ireland was passed to enable some relief to be given to those who were in danger of starvation, and, in the same year, a Tithe Act became law without the Appropriation Clause, upon which the ministers had hitherto insisted (see p. 914), thus removing one of the chief causes of conflict in Ireland by enacting that tithes should be levied on the landowner and not on the tenant.

13. **The Bedchamber Question. 1839.**—Though Lord Melbourne's government had addressed itself with ability to the solution of most of the questions of the day, it had no longer any popular sentiment behind it, and was obliged to submit without resistance to the mutilation or rejection of its measures by the House of Lords. The Chancellor of the Exchequer, Spring Rice, who was a poor financier, had to announce, without venturing to provide a remedy, that the national expenditure was greater than the national income. The mere fact that the Government found itself baffled, weakened it both in Parliament and in the nation ; and accordingly, in **1839**, the Government resigned. Though Peel, who was summoned to succeed Melbourne, had no difficulty in forming a ministry, he was afraid of the influence which the Ladies of the Bedchamber exercised over the young queen, and asked that the sisters and wives of members of the late Government who held that post should be dismissed. The queen, being unwilling to part with her old friends, refused to dismiss them, and Peel then declined to form a ministry. Melbourne returned to office hoping to be more popular than before, as the sympathy of the country was on the side of the queen.

14. **Post Office Reform. 1839.**—One piece of reform was only unwillingly accepted by the re-instated ministers. One day the poet Coleridge passed a cottage in the north of England as a postman arrived with a letter. A girl came out, looked at the letter, and returned it to the postman. In those days the payment for postage was high, a shilling or two being an ordinary charge, the postage rising according to the distance. The receiver, not the sender of the letter, had to pay for it. Coleridge felt compassion for the girl and paid for the letter. As soon as the postman was out of hearing the girl told him that she was sorry that he had given so much money for a letter which had nothing written inside it. She then explained that her brother had gone to London and had promised that, as she was too poor to pay postage, he would, at stated intervals of time, address to her a blank sheet of paper, which she would have to return to the postman, but the sight of which would let her know that he was in good health. Coleridge told this story to Rowland Hill, an officer in the Post Office, who thought

The new Houses of Parliament: designed by Barry, opened 1852.

it over and asked the Government to reduce the postage on letters between all places in Great Britain and Ireland to a penny. The change, he declared, would be a great boon to the poor, and also in time increase instead of diminishing the revenue of the Government, as the number of letters written would be enormously greater than it had been under the old system. As, in consequence of the large increase of letters carried, the postmen would no longer have time to collect the pennies from the receivers, it would be necessary to charge them upon the senders, and this, Rowland Hill thought, could be done most conveniently by making them buy postage stamps, which had been before unknown. For some time the Post-Office officials and the ministers laughed at the scheme, but public opinion rose in its favour, and, in **1839**, the adoption of the new system was ordered, though it did not come into complete force till **1840**, up to which time there was a uniform charge of fourpence. The system of low payments and postage stamps has since been adopted by every country in the civilised world.

15. **Education.** **1833—1839.**—At the time of the Reform Act general education was at a low ebb. In **1833** Parliament for the first time gave assistance to education by granting 20,000*l.* annually towards the building of school-houses. In **1839** this grant was increased to 30,000*l.*, and its distribution was placed under the direction of a Committee of the Privy Council, called the ' Committee of the Privy Council on Education,' in whose hands the management of public instruction has rested ever since. The Committee was not to teach, but to see that, where public money was employed, the teaching was satisfactory.

16. **The Queen's Marriage.** **1840.**—In **1840** the queen married her first cousin, Prince Albert of Saxe-Coburg, a man of varied learning and accomplishments. What was of more importance, he brought with him affectionate devotion to his young wife, together with a tact and refinement of mind which made him her wisest counsellor. Knowing many things about which Englishmen at that time cared little, he did much towards the development of culture and art in the country.

17. **Palmerston and Spain.** **1833 — 1839.** — The policy of friendship between England and France, which had led to the establishment of Belgian independence (see p. 912), had been continued by Lord Palmerston during the early stages of the second Melbourne ministry. Ferdinand VII. of Spain had for some time before his death in **1833** hesitated whether he should declare as his successor his little daughter Isabella—who, according to old

Spanish law, was capable of inheriting—or his brother, Don Carlos, who claimed in virtue of the so-called Salic law (see p. 232) introduced by the Bourbons. On the side of Don Carlos were the priests, on the side of the child was her mother, and the dying man listened in the end to his wife rather than to the priests. Isabella became queen, and her mother, Christina, regent. The Basque Provinces and the priests and absolutists all over Spain took the side of Don Carlos, and a civil war marked by horrible cruelties on both sides was the result. As Don Carlos declared himself an absolute king, Christina was obliged, in word at least, to profess herself a constitutionalist. Louis Philippe and Palmerston would not interfere directly, but they agreed to interfere indirectly on behalf of Christina and Isabella : Louis Philippe by cutting off the supplies from the Carlists, Palmerston by allowing a British legion of 10,000 men to be enlisted for service against them. The legion fought well, but the Spanish Government did little for it, and it was dissolved in **1838**. The habit of interfering in Spanish quarrels led to a habit of interfering in Spanish politics, and as France and England often took opposite sides in supporting or assailing Spanish ministries, there gradually sprang up an unfortunate coolness between the two. Ultimately, in **1839**, the Carlists were overpowered, and there was no further question of foreign interference.

18. **Palmerston and the Eastern Question. 1831—1839.**—The results of the interference of England in the East were more momentous than the results of her interference in Spain. In **1831** Mehemet Ali, the Pasha of Egypt, sent Ibrahim (see p. 884) to attack the Pasha of Acre. Ibrahim, against whom the Sultan, Mahmoud, sent a Turkish army in **1832**, not only defeated the Turks at Konieh, the ancient Iconium, but crossed the Taurus Mountains into Asia Minor and overthrew the last army which the Sultan could muster. Mahmoud, knowing that Constantinople itself was now at the mercy of the Egyptians, called on the Tzar, his old enemy, for aid. Accordingly, in **1833**, an arrangement was made at Kutaya by which Mehemet Ali stopped hostilities on receiving all Syria and the province of Adana in addition to his own Pashalic. Later in the same year, in reward for Russia's support, the Sultan signed the Treaty of Unkiar Skelessi, by which he bound himself to the Tzar to close the Dardanelles to foreign war ships whenever the Tzar was at war. If this treaty took effect the Russians would be able to train their sailors unmolested in the Black Sea, whilst they would be able to send their fleet out through

the Dardanelles, and to bring it back to a place of safety whenever they pleased. Both England and France disliked this arrangement, but while Palmerston thought that the best remedy was the strengthening of the power of the Sultan, the French Government thought it better to strengthen Mehemet Ali, as being a more capable ruler than Mahmoud. In coming to this conclusion the French were no doubt influenced by the fact that Mehemet Ali employed many Frenchmen in his service. In 1839 the war between the Turks and the Egyptians broke out again, and neither England nor France could remain entirely unconcerned.

19. **Threatened Breach with France. 1839—1841.**—The war was disastrous to the Turks. The army of the Sultan was routed at Nisib. Sultan Mahmoud died before he heard the news, and was succeeded by his son, Abdul Medjid. The Turkish admiral at once sailed off with the fleet under his command, and handed it over at Alexandria to Mehemet Ali. Palmerston insisted that the Egyptians must be driven back, and in 1840, Russia, abandoning the advantages she had gained by the Treaty of Unkiar Skelessi, joined England, Austria, and Prussia in a quadruple Treaty, with the object of enforcing suitable terms on the belligerents. France, left out of the treaty, was deeply exasperated. There was wild talk of avenging Waterloo and reconquering the frontier of the Rhine. The French Prime Minister, Thiers, made every preparation for war. A British admiral, Sir Charles Napier, however, joined by an Austrian squadron, captured Acre, and Mehemet Ali abandoned Syria, receiving from the Sultan in return the hereditary government of Egypt, which he had hitherto held only for his own lifetime. Louis Philippe dismissed Thiers, and placed in office Guizot, a sworn foe to revolutionary projects and revolutionary wars. In 1841 all the powers, including Russia, substituted for the Treaty of Unkiar Skelessi an agreement by which the Dardanelles was closed against the war ships of all nations unless the Sultan himself was at war. Time was thus allowed to the Turks to show whether they were capable, as Palmerston thought they were, of reforming their own government.

20. **Condition of the Poor. 1837—1841.**—The Reform Act of 1832 had brought into power the middle classes, and had been followed by such legislation as was satisfactory to those classes. Little had been done for the artisans and the poor, and their condition was most deplorable. A succession of bad seasons raised the price of wheat from a little over 39s. a quarter in 1835 to a little over 70s. in 1839. Even if food had been cheap the masses

dwelling in great cities were exposed to misery against which the law afforded no protection. Crowded and dirty as many of the dwellings of the poor still are, their condition was far worse early in the reign of Victoria. In Manchester, for instance, one-tenth of the population lived in cellars. Each of these cellars was reached through a small area, to which steps descended from a court, often flooded with stagnating filth. A person standing in one of these areas would, according to the statement of a contemporary writer, 'have his head about one foot below the level of the street, and might, at the same time, without the least motion of his body, touch the window of the cellar and the damp, muddy wall right opposite.' The cellar itself was dark, filled with a horrible stench. Here a whole family lived in a single room, the children lying on the 'damp, nay, wet, brick floor through which the stagnant moisture' oozed up. In Bethnal Green and other parts of the east end of London things were quite as bad. Overcrowding added to the horrors of such a life. One small cellar, measuring four yards by five, contained two rooms and eight persons, sleeping four in a bed. In some parts of the country similar evils prevailed. In one parish in Dorset thirty-six persons dwelt, on an average, in each house. All modesty was at an end under these miserable conditions. In one case—and the case was common enough—a father and mother, with their married daughter and her husband, a baby, a boy of sixteen, and two girls, all slept in a single room. People living in such a way were sure to be ignorant and vicious. They were badly paid, and even for their low wages were very much at the mercy of their employers. In spite of the law against 'truck,' as it was called, employers often persisted in paying their men in goods charged above their real prices instead of in money. In one instance a man was obliged to take a piece of cloth worth only 11s. in payment of his wages of 35s.

21. **The People's Charter. 1837—1840.**—Many remedies were proposed for these evils, but the one which caught the imagination of the workmen themselves was the People's Charter. The six points of the charter were (1) annual parliaments, (2) manhood suffrage, (3) vote by ballot, (4) equal electoral districts, (5) abolition of the property qualification for entering Parliament, and (6) payment for members of the House of Commons. Those who supported the charter thought that, as the acquisition of political power had enabled the middle classes to redress their grievances, the working class would in like way be able to redress theirs. They did not recognise the unfortunate truth that the working class

3 o 2

still needed the political education without which political power is dangerous even to those who exercise it. In **1839** large meetings were held in support of the charter, and at these threats of appealing to violence, if no gentler means availed, were freely used. In **1839** a so-called ' National Convention,' composed of delegates from the workers of the large towns and led by Feargus O'Connor, a newspaper owner, and Ernest Jones, a barrister, sent a monster petition to Parliament. Parliament refused even to take it into consideration, and an increased bitterness of feeling was the result. A riot occurred at Birmingham : houses and shops were sacked, as if Birmingham had been a town taken by storm. The Government repressed these acts of violence by the operation of the ordinary law, without having recourse to those exceptional measures on which Sidmouth had fallen back thirty years before (see p. 880). The last deed of violence was an armed attack on Newport in Monmouthshire. Soldiers, brought to defend the place, fired upon the mob, and killed and wounded many. In **1840** the ringleaders were tried and condemned to death, though the Government commuted the sentence into transportation for life.

22. **The Anti-Corn-Law League. 1838—1840.**—The middle classes were not likely to be tolerant of violence and disorder, but there was one point on which their interests coincided with those of the working men. The high price of corn not only caused sufferings amongst the poor, but also injured trade. This high price was to a great extent owing to the Corn Law, which had been amended from time to time since it was passed in **1815** (see p. 875), and which continued to make corn dear by imposing heavy duties on imported corn whenever there was a good harvest in England, with the view of protecting the agriculturists against low prices. In **1838** an Anti-Corn-Law League was formed at Manchester in which the leading men were Richard Cobden, a master of clear and popular reasoning, whose knowledge of facts relating to the question was exhaustive, and John Bright, whose simple diction and stirring eloquence appealed to the feelings and the morality of his audience. In **1839** Charles Villiers, who took the lead of the Corn Law repealers in the House of Commons, was beaten by 342 votes to 195, but he had amongst his supporters Russell, Palmerston, and most of the prominent members of the Government. It was evident, however, that some time must elapse before a change so great could be accomplished, as the proposal was offensive to the agriculturists, who formed the main strength of the Conservative party. More-

over, the proposal to put an end to the Corn Law had still to make its way, by dint of argument, with the trading and working classes who were interested in its abolition.

23. **The Fall of the Melbourne Ministry. 1841.**—The middle classes had grievances of their own against the ministry. They disliked financial disorder as well as physical violence, and, though the ministry had put down the latter, they had encouraged the former. Every year showed a deficit, and whilst the produce of the taxes was falling, the expenditure was increasing. In **1841** the ministry made an heroic effort to deal with the mischief by a movement in the direction of freedom of trade, proposing that there should be a fixed 8*s.* duty on every quarter of imported corn, whatever its price in England might be, in the place of the sliding scale varying with the price which had been adopted in **1822**. Peel opposed them on the ground that they had shown themselves too incompetent as financiers to be entrusted with the working of so large a scheme. The ministry was defeated in the House of Commons, and, after a dissolution, a new House was returned in which the Conservatives were in a majority of ninety-one. The discredited Melbourne ministry resigned, and Peel had no difficulty in forming a new ministry. There was no longer any difficulty about the Ladies of the Bedchamber. Now that the queen was married and in full enjoyment of the society of a husband whom she loved and trusted, she no longer objected to abandon the company of the Whig ladies whom, in **1839**, she had refused to dismiss.[1]

[1] Genealogy of the principal descendants of Queen Victoria :—

VICTORIA = Albert of Saxe Coburg-Gotha
1819 —   1819—1861

Victoria. 1840 — m. Frederick William, afterwards Frederick III., king of Prussia and German Emperor	Albert Edward, Prince of Wales. 1841— m. Alexandra, dau. of Christian IX. king of Denmark	Alice Maud Mary. 1843 — 1878. m. Louis, Grand Duke of Hesse-Darmstadt	Alfred Ernest Albert, Duke of Edinburgh. 1844— m. Marie, dau. of Alexander II., Emperor of Russia	Helena Augusta Victoria. 1846— m. Prince Frederick Christian of Schleswig-Holstein-Sonderburg-Augustenburg
William II., king of Prussia and German Emperor	Albert Victor, Duke of Clarence and Avondale. 1864-1892.	George Frederick. 1865—	Louise. 1867— m. the Duke of Fife	Victoria. 1868—	Maud. 1869—

Louise Caroline Alberta. 1848— m. the Marquis of Lorne	Arthur William Patrick Albert, Duke of Connaught. 1850— m. Louise Margaret, dau. of Prince Frederick Charles of Prussia	Leopold George Duncan Albert. 1853–1884. m. Helen, a dau. of the Prince of Waldeck-Pyrmont	Beatrice Mary Victoria Feodore. 1857— m. Prince Henry of Battenberg.

CHAPTER LVIII

FREE TRADE. 1841—1852

LEADING DATES

Peel's second Ministry . . . . 1841—1846
Peel's first Free-trade Budget 1842
Peel's second Free-trade Budget 1845
Repeal of the Corn Law 1846
The Russell Ministry . . . . . . 1846—1852
European Revolutions 1848
The first Derby Ministry 1852

1. **Peel's New Ministry. 1841.**—In his new ministry Peel found room not only for leading Conservatives, but also for Stanley, Graham, and Ripon, who had left the Whigs in **1834**, and had since then voted with the Conservatives. Stanley—now Lord Stanley—and Graham were amongst the ablest of the ministers who formed the Cabinet ; though the help of a young minister, Gladstone, who was not a member of the Cabinet, was especially valuable on account of his grasp of economical truths, and of the clearness with which his opinions were set forth.

2. **Peel's First Free-trade Budget. 1842.**—Peel's first great Budget was that of **1842.** He put an end to the deficit by carrying a measure re-imposing, for three years, an income-tax similar to that which Pitt had imposed to carry on the great war with France. He justified his action on the plea that it was necessary, in the first place, to stop the constantly recurring deficit ; and, in the second place, to effect financial reforms which would enlarge the resources of the government. He consequently lowered many duties the main object of which had been the protection of home manufactures or agriculture. So far as the corn duties were concerned, he modified the sliding scale, but refused to effect any distinct reduction. The advocates of free-trade thought he had done too little, and those of protection thought he had done too much.

3. **Returning Prosperity. 1843–1844.**—During the next two years, **1843** and **1844**, Peel's budgets were not remarkable, as he did not wish to take any further step of importance till he had had time to watch the result of the budget of **1842.** The experience gained at the end of three years was in every way favourable, as it showed that manufactures really flourished more now that they had to face competition than they had done in its absence. No doubt

the return of prosperity was partly owing to the good harvests which followed Peel's accession to power, but it was also in a great measure owing to his policy.

4. **Mines and Factories. 1842—1847.**—It would be of little worth to encourage manufactures, if those by whose labour they were produced were to be a miserable, vicious, and stunted population. In 1842, a commission, appointed to examine into the condition of mines, reported that women and even young children were forced to drag heavy trucks underground, sometimes for twelve hours a day. Lord Ashley, foremost in every good work, and who had already alleviated the lot of factory children (see p. 911), induced Parliament to pass a bill which was not all that he wished, but which enacted that no woman or child under ten should be employed under ground, and that no child between ten and thirteen should be employed for more than three days a week. In 1844, Graham passed an Act prohibiting the employment of children under nine in cotton and silk mills ; but it was not till 1847 that, after a long struggle conducted by Lord Ashley, an Act was passed prohibiting the employment of women and children in all factories for more than ten hours a day. The arguments employed in favour of confining these restrictions to women and children were that they could not take care of themselves as well as men, and also that injuries done by overwork to the health of mothers and of young people, seriously affect the health and strength of future generations.

5. **Aberdeen's Foreign Policy. 1841—1846.**—The fall of the Melbourne ministry had been caused nearly as much by its foreign as by its domestic policy. Though Lord Palmerston had succeeded in getting his way in the East without bringing on a war with France (see p. 922), sober people were afraid lest he might sooner or later provoke war by his violent self-assertion. Peel's foreign minister, the Earl of Aberdeen, was always ready to give up something in order to secure the blessing of peace. In 1842 he put an end to a long dispute with the United States about the frontier between the English colonies and the State of Maine on the eastern side of America ; and in 1846 he put an end to another dispute about the frontier of Oregon on the western side. With France, where Guizot was now Prime Minister, his relations were excessively cordial, and a close understanding grew up between the two governments, assuring the maintenance of European peace. The *entente cordiale*, as it was called, was ratified in 1843 by a visit of Queen Victoria to Louis Philippe, at Eu, and by a return visit paid by Louis Philippe to the Queen at Windsor in 1844.

These friendly relations enabled Aberdeen and Guizot to settle amicably a dispute arising out of the conduct of an English Consul at Tahiti, which might very easily have led to war.

6. Peel and O'Connell. 1843.—Each successive ministry was confronted with the problem of Irish government, and soon after Peel came into office the cry for the Repeal of the Union, which had died away during the Melbourne government, was once more loudly raised. In **1843**, O'Connell, instigated by younger men, such as Thomas Davis and Gavan Duffy, pushed the movement on, and predicted that Repeal would be carried before the year was over. He summoned a monster meeting at Clontarf, but before the appointed day the government prohibited the meeting and poured troops into Ireland to enforce the prohibition. O'Connell shrank from causing useless bloodshed, and advised his followers to keep away from the place of gathering. Though no attempt was made to hold the meeting, O'Connell was charged with sedition and conspiracy. Being convicted by a jury from which all Roman Catholics were excluded, he was sentenced to a year's imprisonment and a heavy fine. There were, however, technical errors in the proceedings, and the judgment was reversed in his favour by the House of Lords, or rather by the five lawyers who had seats in the House of Lords, and who alone decided legal appeals in the name of that House. Partly in consequence of the hopelessness of resisting the government, partly in consequence of the satisfaction felt in Ireland at the reversal of the judgment against O'Connell, the demand for Repeal once more died away, and the Irish leader, whose health was breaking, retired from public life, living quietly till his death at Genoa in **1847**.

7. Peel's Irish Policy. 1843—1845.—The main source of mischief in Ireland was to be found in the relations between landlord and tenant. Evictions on the one hand were answered by murder and outrage on the other. To check the latter Peel in **1843** passed an amended Arms Act, forbidding the possession of arms except by special license, whilst, to check the former, he issued, in **1844**, a commission, of which the Earl of Devon was chairman, to inquire into the grievances of Irish tenants. In **1845** he raised, amidst a storm of obloquy from many English Protestants, the government grant to the College of Maynooth, in which Roman Catholics were educated for the priesthood, from 9,000*l.* to 26,000*l.*, and established three Queen's Colleges to give unsectarian education to the laity. In **1845** the Devon Commission reported that in the three provinces of Leinster, Munster, and Connaught the landlords were in most cases unable to make improvements on their land because the law prevented them from borrowing money on the security of their estates ; and that they frequently let their lands to middlemen, who let it out again to tenants at will. Improvements, if made at all, were usually made by the tenant at will, though he was liable to be turned out of his holding without any compensation for what he had done to increase the value of the estate. The consequence was that the tenant rarely made any improvement at all, and that, when he did, he frequently either had his holding taken from him, or had his rent raised in consequence of his own improvements. In Ulster, on the other hand, there had grown up a custom of tenant right, and when a tenant left he received compensation for his improvements from the incoming tenant who took his place. In 1845 the government, finding that Ulster was peaceful whilst the other provinces were not, came to the conclusion that the Ulster tenant-right made the difference between them, and brought in a bill securing a limited amount of compensation to those tenants who made improvements duly certified to be of value. The House of Lords, however, refused to pass it, and for many years no further effort was made to improve the condition of the Irish tenant.

8. Peel's Second Free-trade Budget. 1845.—Peel was more successful in dealing with England. When in 1845 the three years for which the income-tax had been granted came to an end, Peel, instead of remitting it, obtained leave from Parliament to continue it for three more years ; though, as a matter of fact, it was subsequently re-imposed and is still levied to this day. Peel, having received a surplus, employed it to sweep away a vast number of duties upon imports which weighed upon trade, and to lower other duties which he did not sweep away ; whilst at the same time he put an entire end to all duties on exports. The country gentlemen who formed the large majority of Peel's supporters took alarm at a proposal made by him to remove the duties on lard and hides, on the ground that if this were done foreigners would, in regard to these two articles, be enabled to compete with English produce.

9. Peel and Disraeli. 1845.—The country gentlemen could grumble, but they were no match for Peel in debate ; and they were therefore in a mood to transfer their allegiance to any man capable of heading an opposition in Parliament to the statesman whom they had hitherto followed. Such a spokesman they found in a young member, Benjamin Disraeli, who, after attempting to enter Parliament as a Radical, had been elected as a Conservative.

His change of opinion was greater in appearance than in reality, as his principal motive, both as a Radical and as a Conservative, was hostility to the tendencies of the middle classes which he held to be embodied in the Whigs. He now discovered that the same tendencies were also embodied in Peel. Disraeli, indeed, never grasped the meaning of those doctrines of political economy which were in favour with the Whigs, and were growing in favour with Peel, and being moreover a man of great ambition, he seized the occasion to place himself at the head of the malcontent Conservatives, with the less difficulty because, in giving expression to their ignorance, he did not fling away any settled conviction of his own. He was the more angry with Peel because Peel had refused him office. Fixing upon Peel's weak point, his want of originality, he declared that the Prime Minister, having caught the Whigs bathing, had walked away with their clothes, and that under him a Conservative government was 'an organised hypocrisy.'

10. **Spread of the Anti-Corn-Law League. 1845.**—In the meanwhile, the Anti-Corn-Law League was growing in influence. The oratory of Bright and the close reasoning of Cobden were telling even on the agricultural population. The small farmers and the labourers were suffering whilst the manufacturers were flourishing. Peel, indeed, was a free-trader on principle. He believed that legislation ought to make goods cheap for the sake of consumers rather than dear for the sake of producers, and at this time he even believed that the nation would be wealthier if corn fell in price by being freely imported than if its price was raised by the imposition of duties. He still held, however, that it was the duty of Parliament to keep up the price of corn, not for the benefit of the existing generation, but as an insurance for future generations. If Great Britain came to depend for a great part of her food supply upon foreign countries, an enemy in time of war would have little difficulty in starving out the country by cutting off its supply of foreign food. The only answer to this was, that the starvation which Peel dreaded in the future was existing in the present. It was easy to say that the corn laws encouraged the production of food at home to support the population. As a plain matter of fact, the population had increased so rapidly that starvation was permanently established in the country. 'I be protected,' said an agricultural labourer at a meeting of the League, 'and I be starving.' If anything occurred to bring home to Peel the existence of this permanent starvation, he would become a free-trader in corn as well as in manufactures.

11. **The Irish Famine. 1845.**—The conviction which Peel needed came from Ireland. The population was 8,000,000, and half of this number subsisted on potatoes alone. In the summer of **1845**, a potato disease, previously unknown, swept over both islands. Potato plants, green and flourishing at night, were in the morning a blackened and fetid mass of corruption. A misfortune which, in England and Scotland was a mere inconvenience, caused abject misery in Ireland.

12. **The Abolition of the Corn Law. 1845—1846.**—Peel saw that if the starving millions were to be fed, corn must be cheapened as much as possible, and that the only way of cheapening it was to take off the duty. In October he asked the Cabinet to support him in taking off the duty. The majority in it had minds less flexible than his own, and its decision was postponed. In November, Russell, now the leader of the Liberals, wrote what was known as 'the Edinburgh letter' to his constituents, declaring for the complete abolition of the Corn Law. Peel again attempted to induce the Cabinet to follow him, but the Cabinet again refused, and on December 5 he resigned office. Russell, however, was unable to form a ministry, and on December 20 Peel returned to office pledged to repeal the Corn Law. Lord Stanley now resigned, and became the acknowledged head of the Protectionists, who resolved to oppose Peel's forthcoming measure. On the other hand, Russell gave assurances that he and the Whigs would loyally support it. Accordingly, when Parliament met in January **1846**, Peel proposed to bring in a Bill for the abolition of the Corn Law, though three years were to pass before the abolition would be quite complete. On June 25, the Bill, having previously passed the Commons, passed the Lords, and an end was at last put to the long-continued attempt to raise by artificial means the price of bread.

13. **The Close of Peel's Ministry. 1846.**—Peel had done what he could to mitigate the distress in Ireland. He sent Indian corn there to be sold cheaply, and he ordered the establishment of public works to give means of subsistence to the starving population. The old antagonism between landlord and tenant, however, had not ceased, and evicted tenants and those who sympathised with them still had recourse to outrages and murder. Peel brought in a Bill for the protection of life in Ireland. Russell and the Liberals disliked it because it was too stringent. The Protectionists in the House of Commons, led nominally by Lord George Bentinck and really by Disraeli, were glad of any opportunity to

defeat Peel, and on June 25, the day on which the Corn Bill passed
the Lords, the Irish Bill was thrown out by the Commons. On
the 27th Peel resigned office.

14. **The Russell Ministry. 1846—1847.**—Lord John Russell
had no difficulty this time in forming a ministry, and though his
followers were in a minority in the House of Commons, he was sure
of the support of Peel and of the Peelites, as those Conservatives
were called who had voted with their leader for the abolition of

Sir Robert Peel : from the bust by Noble in the
National Portrait Gallery.

the Corn Law. Russell had in **1846** to face a state of things in
Ireland even more deplorable than that which had compelled
his predecessor in **1845** to abandon Protection. In **1846**, the failure
of the potato crop was even more complete than it had been in
1845, and at the same time it was found that the system of public
works established by Peel had led to gross abuses. Thousands of
men who applied to mend the roads made them worse instead of
better, whilst they neglected opportunities of working for private
persons, because the public authorities exacted less work and gave

higher pay than the private employer. Russell did what was possible to check these abuses, and in the session of 1847 he passed a Bill for enabling the guardians to give outdoor relief, which they had been forbidden to do by the Act which in 1838 established a Poor Law (see p. 917). Such a change in the law was imperatively demanded, as in the existing poor-houses there was only room for three out of every hundred starving persons.

15. **Irish Emigration. 1847.**—No poor law, however, could do more than mitigate the consequences of famine, especially as the slow forms of parliamentary procedure delayed the remedy, and as those who had to administer the new law were interested rather in keeping rates down than in saving life. The misery was too wide-spread to be much allayed by any remedy, and such English charity as was added to the relief provided by law was almost as ineffectual. Thousands perished by starvation, and many thousands more emigrated to America, many of them perishing on board ship from disease engendered in bodies enfeebled by previous want of nourishment. Those who reached America preserved and handed down to their children a hatred of the English name and government, to which they attributed their sufferings. By starvation and emigration the population of Ireland fell from 8,000,000 to 5,000,000.

16. **Landlord and Tenant in Ireland. 1847.**—Russell was statesman enough to perceive that the legal relations between landlord and tenant needed alteration, if the deep-seated causes of Irish misery were to be removed. Many of the landlords were hopelessly in debt. Out of a gross rental of 17,000,000*l*. 9,000,000*l*. was mortgaged, and the remaining 8,000,000*l*. was insufficient to provide for the support of the starving poor and to meet the expenses of the landlords. Impoverished landlords were consequently tempted to bear hardly on their tenants. Improvements in the English sense were few, but it often happened that a poor tenant on a wild hillside would erect a fence or clear off the stones from his rough farm, thus making it more productive than before. In too many cases the landlord, or more often the landlord's agent when the landlord was an absentee, pounced down on the struggling improver, and either forced him to pay a higher rent, or evicted him in order to replace him by someone who offered more. The evicted tenant not unfrequently revenged himself by murdering the landlord or his agent, or else the new tenant who had ousted him from his holding.

17. **The Encumbered Estates Act. 1848.**—Russell proposed

to meet the evil by a double remedy. On the one hand he brought in a Bill which became law in **1848** as the Encumbered Estates Act, for the sale of deeply mortgaged estates to solvent purchasers, in the hope that the new landlords might be sufficiently well off to treat their tenants with consideration. At the same time he proposed another measure to compel landlords to compensate their evicted tenants for improvements which the tenants had themselves made, and he would gladly have supported a further measure which he did not venture even to introduce, forbidding the eviction of any tenant who had held land exceeding a quarter of an acre for more than five years, without compensation for the loss of his tenure. English opinion, however, prevented even the Bill for compensation for actual improvements from becoming law ; on the other hand, the Bill for buying out the owners of encumbered estates was readily passed, and was also accompanied by a Coercion Act, milder, indeed, than that which had been proposed by Peel (see p. 931). The Encumbered Estates Act standing alone was a curse rather than a blessing, as many of the indebted landowners had been easy-going, whereas many of the new landowners, having paid down ready money, thought themselves justified in applying purely commercial principles to their relations with the tenants, and exacted from them every penny that could be wrung from men who had no protection for the results of their own industry upon the soil. Those who suffered smarted from a sense of wrong, which in **1848** became stronger and more likely to lead to acts of violence, because in that year the course of affairs in Europe gave superabundant examples of successful resistance to governments.

18. **European Revolution. 1848.**—The year **1848** was a year of European revolution. France expelled Louis Philippe, and established a second republic, based on universal suffrage. In Italy, not only were constitutional reforms forced on the governments, but Charles Albert, king of Sardinia, led an armed attack on the Austrian power in Lombardy and Venice, by which the despotism of the petty sovereigns of Italy had been bolstered up. In Germany, a parliament met at Frankfurt to devise some scheme for uniting in closer bonds the loose confederation which had been established in **1815** (see p. 873), whilst revolutions at Berlin and Vienna led to the adoption of a constitutional system in Prussia and Austria. The demand for constitutional government was everywhere put forth. In France it was associated with socialism ; and an attempt was made to set up national workshops in which every artisan

might find work. In that country, however, there was no aggressive spirit as in **1792**, and no attempt was made to change the frontiers of the State. In central Europe and in Italy, on the other hand, dissatisfaction with existing frontiers was the prominent feature. The peoples were there eager to see real nations, of which the component parts were bound together by the tie of common attachment, taking the place of artificial states the creations of past wars and treaties. Hence the populations of the Italian States drew together in a desire for the expulsion of the Austrians, and the populations of the German states drew together in a desire to give a common government to the German nation. In the heterogeneous Austrian empire, however, the idea of nationality acted as a dissolvent. Austrians, Hungarians, and Slavs, who together formed the vast majority of the population, had no love for each other, and before the end of the year Austria and Hungary were at open war.

19. **Renewed Trouble in Ireland.   1848.**—In Ireland, a number of young men imagined that they could play the part in which O'Connell had failed, and raise up armed resistance against England. One of these, Smith O'Brien, tried to put in practice their teaching by attacking a police station, but he was easily captured, and no attempt was made to follow his example.

20. **The Chartists on Kennington Common.   1848.**—In England the Chartists thought the time had come to gain that supremacy for the mass of the nation which had been gained in France. Their leader, Feargus O'Connor, a half-mad member of Parliament, called on enormous numbers of them to meet on April 10 on Kennington Common,[1] and to carry to the House of Commons a monster petition for the Charter, said to be signed by 5,700,000 persons. The government declared the design to be illegal, as crowds are forbidden by law to present petitions, and called on all who would, to serve as special constables—that is to say, to act as policemen for the day. No less than 200,000 enrolled themselves, whereas, when the appointed day came, no more than 25,000 persons assembled on Kennington Common, many of whom were not Chartists. Those who were Chartists formed a procession intending to cross Westminster Bridge. The Duke of Wellington had posted soldiers in the houses on the Middlesex side of the bridge, to be used in case of necessity, but he left the special constables to stop the procession. This they did without difficulty. There was, however, no attempt to stop the presentation of the petition, which was carried in a cab to the

[1] Now Kennington Park.

House of Commons, and found to bear 2,000 signatures. Many columns of these were, however, in the same handwriting, and some who actually signed it, wrote the names of celebrated persons, such as Prince Albert and the Duke of Wellington, instead of their own. Others called themselves Pugnose, Woodenlegs, Bread-and-cheese, and so forth. For all this there was a large number of Chartists in England ; but, on the other hand, there was a still larger number of persons who were resolved that, whatever changes might be made in the constitution, they should not be brought about by the exertion of physical force.

21. **European reaction.** 1848—1849.—The attempt to change existing European order failed as completely on the Continent as it did in England. In December, 1848, the French nation elected Louis Napoleon Bonaparte, a nephew of the first Napoleon, as President for ten years, on the expectation that he would give to the country a quiet and orderly government. Charles Albert, king of Sardinia, taking up arms to drive the Austrians out of Italy, was defeated by them at Custozza in 1848, and at Novara in 1849. After these successive failures he was forced to abdicate in favour of his son, Victor Emmanuel II., who maintained constitutional government in his own kingdom of Sardinia, whilst the Austrians regained Lombardy and Venetia, and restored the absolute governments in the other Italian states, except in the Papal dominions, where a French army restored the absolute government of the Pope. In Germany the Frankfurt parliament tried to erect a constitutional empire, and was dissolved by force. In Prussia, the King, Frederick William IV., got the better of the revolution, though he established a Parliament which, for the present at least, he was able to control. In the Austrian Empire the war between Austria and Hungary was brought to an end by the intervention of a Russian army in favour of Austria, and the constitution of Hungary was abolished. By the end of 1848 reaction prevailed over the whole Continent.

22. **The Decline of the Russell Ministry.** 1848—1851.—In England the ministry was supported, not merely as the representative of order against turbulence, but also as the representative of free-trade against protection. In 1849 the Navigation Act (see pp. 565, 589) was repealed, and foreign shipping admitted to compete with English. Yet the government only maintained itself by depending on the votes of the Peelites, and in 1850 Peel unfortunately died in consequence of a fall from his horse. Later in the year the Pope appointed Roman Catholic bishops to English sees,

and an excited public opinion saw in this an attack on the Queen's authority.   In 1851 Russell introduced an Ecclesiastical Titles Bill, declaring all acts done by the Roman Catholic bishops, and all deeds bestowing property to them under the new titles, to be null and void.   This Bill alienated the Peelites and advanced Liberals like Bright and Cobden.   In February the ministry resisted a proposal to lower the county franchise, and resigned.   Lord Stanley, however, declined to form a ministry, and Russell and his followers returned to office.   The Ecclesiastical Titles Bill was passed in a

The Britannia Tubular Railway Bridge over the Menai Strait : designed by
Robert Stephenson, opened in 1850.

modified form, but it was never in a single instance put in execution and was ultimately repealed.

   23. **The Great Exhibition.   1851.**—In 1851 people thought less of politics than of the Great Exhibition in Hyde Park, where the produce of the world was to be seen in the enormous glass house known as the Crystal Palace—afterwards removed to Penge Hill. The Exhibition was a useful undertaking suggested by Prince Albert, and it served its purpose in teaching English manufacturers that they might improve their own work by studying the work of foreigners.   Many people thought that crowds of revolutionists, who would come under pretence of seeing the exhibition, would set London on fire.   Others thought that the nations of Europe would

be so knit together by commercial interests that there would be no more wars.

24. **The End of the Russell Ministry. 1851—1852.**—On December 2, 1851, Louis Napoleon dissolved the Assembly, put most of the leading French politicians in prison, and marched soldiers into the streets of Paris to shoot all who resisted him. He then asked the French people to name him President for ten years, with institutions which made him practically the master of the State. The French people, frightened at anarchy, gave him what he asked. In England, Lord Palmerston not only approved of the proceeding, but expressed his approval to the French ambassador, though the Cabinet was for absolute neutrality ; whereupon he was dismissed from office. Early in 1852 he took his revenge by declaring against the ministry on a detail in a militia bill. The ministers, finding themselves in a minority, resigned office.

25. **The First Derby Ministry. 1852.**—Lord Stanley, who had recently become Earl of Derby by his father's death, now formed a ministry out of the Protectionist party, and declared that the question whether free-trade or protection should prevail was one to be settled by a new parliament to be elected in the summer of 1852. The real master of the government was Disraeli, who had succeeded to the nominal as well as to the actual leadership of his party in the House of Commons upon the death of Lord George Bentinck in 1848, and who now became Chancellor of the Exchequer. Disraeli knew well that the feeling of the country was in favour of free-trade, and he astonished his colleagues and supporters by declaring his admiration of its blessings. The elections, when they took place, left the government in a minority. On the meeting of the new Parliament, the first question needing solution was whether the dissensions between Russell and Palmerston, and between the Whigs and Peelites, could be made up so as to form a united opposition, and the second, whether the government could contrive to renounce Protection without complete loss of dignity. The Duke of Wellington had died before Parliament met, and his death served to remind people how he had again and again abandoned political positions with credit, by stating with perfect frankness that his opinions were unchanged, but that circumstances made it no longer possible or desirable to give effect to them.

26. **The Burial of Protection. 1852.**—Soon after the meeting of Parliament, Villiers, the old champion of free trade (see p. 924), brought forward a resolution, declaring the repeal of the Corn Laws to have been ' wise, just, and beneficial.' Those who had once

been Protectionists, shrank from condemning so distinctly a policy which they had formerly defended ; but when Palmerston came to their help by proposing in a less offensive form a resolution which meant much the same as that of Villiers, he was supported by the greater number of them, and his motion was carried with only fifty-three dissentients. Disraeli then brought forward an ingenious budget, which was rejected by the House, upon which the Derby ministry resigned. If Disraeli had not succeeded in maintaining his party in power, at least he had freed it from the unpopular burden of attachment to protection, and had made it capable of rising to power in the future. Before he left office Louis Napoleon became, by a popular vote, Napoleon III. Emperor of the French.

CHAPTER LIX

THE CRIMEAN WAR AND THE INDIAN MUTINY. 1852—1858

LEADING DATES

The Aberdeen Ministry	1852
War between Russia and Turkey	1853
France and England at War with Russia	1854
Battle of the Alma	Sept. 20, 1854
Battle of Inkerman	Nov. 5, 1854
Capture of Sebastopol	Sept. 8, 1855
Peace of Paris	March 30, 1857
Outbreak of the Sepoy Mutiny at Meerut	May 10, 1857
Capture of Delhi	Sept. 14-20, 1857
Relief of Lucknow by Havelock and Outram	Sept. 25, 1857
End of the Indian Mutiny	1858

1. **Expectation of Peace. 1852.**—Since the accession to power of Lord Grey's ministry in 1830, the opinions of Bentham (see p. 890) had gained the upper hand, and the greatest happiness of the greatest number had become the inspiring thought of statesmen. Free trade was regarded, not merely as desirable because it averted starvation, but as uniting nations together in commercial bonds. Nothing was more common in 1851 and 1852 than to hear sensible men predict that the era of wars was past, and that nations trafficking with one another would have no motive for engaging in strife. The fierce passions evoked by the struggles for nationality in 1848 were forgotten, and a time of peace and prosperity regarded as permanently established.

3 P 2

2. **Church Movements. 1827—1853.**—There had, indeed, been signs that it was impossible to bring all men to forsake the pursuit of ideal truth. In **1827** Keble published the first edition of the *Christian Year*, and in the following years a body of writers at Oxford, of whom the most prominent were Newman and Pusey, did their best to inspire the rising generation with the belief that the Church of England had a life of its own independent of the State or of Society, and that its true doctrines were those which had been taught in the earlier centuries of the Church's existence. Their teaching was not unlike that of Laud (see p. 520), though without Laud's leaning upon the State, and with a reverence for the great mediæval ecclesiastics and their teaching which Laud had not possessed. In Scotland, reaction against State interference took another turn. Large numbers of the Scottish clergy and people objected to the system by which lay patrons had in their hands the appointment of ministers to Church livings, and in **1843** no less than **474** ministers threw up their livings and, followed by numerous congregations, formed the Free Church of Scotland. Different as were the movements in the two countries, they had this in common, that they regarded religion as something more than the creature of law and Parliament.

3. **Growth of Science. 1830—1859.**—Other men sought their ideals in science, and though scientific men did not meddle with politics, their work was not only productive of an increase of material comfort, but also permeated the minds of unscientific persons with a belief in natural law and order, which steadied them when they came to deal with the complex facts of human life. The rapid growth of railways, especially after **1844**, the introduction of the electric telegraph in **1837**, and other practical results of scientific discovery, prepared the way for a favourable reception of doctrines such as those announced in Lyell's *Principles of Geology*, the first edition of which was published in **1830**, where the formation of the earth's surface was traced to a series of gradual changes similar to those in action at the present day. Darwin's *Origin of Species*, in which the multiplicity of living forms were accounted for by permanent natural causes, did not appear till **1859**.

4. **Dickens, Thackeray, and Macaulay. 1837—1848.**—The feelings and opinions of the age were, as is usually the case, reflected in its literature. Dickens, whose first considerable work, *The Pickwick Papers*, appeared in **1837**, painted humorously the lives of the middle classes, which had obtained political power through the Reform Act of **1832**; and Thackeray, whose *Vanity Fair* was

published in 1848, lashed the vices of great and wealthy sinners, principally of those who had held a high place in the society of the preceding generations, though he delighted in painting the gentleness and self-denial of men, and still more of women of a lower station. For him the halo of glory with which Scott had crowned the past had disappeared. Amongst the historians of this period, by far the greatest is Macaulay, whose history of England began to appear in 1848, the year in which *Vanity Fair* was published. In him was to be found a massive common-sense in applying the political judgments of the day to the events of past times, combined with an inability to grasp sympathetically the opinions of those who had struggled against the social and political movements out of which the life of the nineteenth century had been developed. As for the future, Macaulay had no such dissatisfaction with life around him as to crave for further organic change. Piecemeal reforms he welcomed gladly, but he had no wish to alter the political basis of society. The Reform Act of 1832 gave him all that he desired.

5. **Grote, Mill, and Carlyle. 1833—1856.**—There were not wanting writers who saw the weak points of that rule of the middle classes which seemed so excellent to Macaulay. Grote's *History of Greece*, which was published at intervals from 1845 to 1856, was in reality a panegyric on the democracy of Athens and, by implication, a pleading in favour of democracy in England. Mill, whose *System of Logic* appeared in 1843, expounded the utilitarian philosophy of Bentham, accompanying his scientific teaching with the expression of hopefulness in the growth of democracy as likely to lead to better government. The man, however, whose teaching did most to rouse the age to a sense of the insufficiency of its work was Thomas Carlyle, whose *Sartor Resartus* began to appear in 1833, and who detested alike the middle-class Parliamentary government dear to Macaulay, and the democratic government dear to Grote and Mill. He was the prophet of duty. Each individual was to set himself resolutely to despise the conventions of the world, and to conform to the utmost of his power to the divine laws of the world. Those who did this most completely were heroes, to whom and not to Parliamentary majorities or scientific deductions, reverence and obedience were due. The negative part of Carlyle's teaching—its condemnation of democracy and science—made no impression. The positive part fixed itself upon the mind of the young, thousands of whom learnt from it to follow the call of duty, and to obey her behests.

St. George's Hall, Liverpool : designed by Elmes, completed in 1859.

6. **Tennyson. 1849.**—The best poetry of the time reflected in a milder way the teaching of Carlyle.   Tennyson, whose most thoughtful work, *In Memoriam*, appeared in **1849**, is filled with a sense of the pre-eminence of duty, combined with a reverent religious feeling and a respect for the teaching of science which was then bursting on the world. The opening lines of *In Memoriam* give the key-note of the teaching of a master who held out the hand to Carlyle on the one hand, and to Keble and Newman on the other.

> Strong Son of God, immortal love
>> Whom we, that have not seen thy face,
>> By faith, and faith alone, embrace,
> Believing where we cannot prove ;
>
> .   .   .   .
>
> Thou seemest human and divine,
>> The holiest, highest manhood, thou ;
>> Our wills are ours, we know not how,
> Our wills are ours, to make them thine.

7. **Turner. 1775—1851.**—The pursuit of the knowledge of the secret processes and the open manifestations of nature, which placed its stamp upon the science and the literature of the time, made itself also visible in its art.   No man ever revealed in landscape-painting the infinity of the natural world and the subtleness of its gradations, as did Turner in the days of his strength, before his eyes fixed on the glory of the atmosphere and the sky lost perception of the beauty of the earth.

8. **The beginning of the Aberdeen Ministry. 1852—1854.**—The Derby Ministry was followed by a coalition ministry of Liberals and Peelites under the Earl of Aberdeen.   At first it seemed as if Parliament was about to settle down to a series of internal reforms.   In **1853**, Gladstone, as Chancellor of the Exchequer, produced a budget which proved generally acceptable, and Russell promised a new Reform Bill which was actually brought forward in **1854**, though by that time circumstances having become adverse to its consideration caused its prompt withdrawal.

9. **The Eastern Question. 1850—1853.**—For some time there had been a diplomatic struggle between France and Russia for the possession of certain holy places in Palestine by the clergy of their respective churches, and though in **1852** the Sultan proposed a compromise, neither party was satisfied.   In the beginning of **1853**, the Tzar Nicholas spoke to Sir Hamilton Seymour of ' the Turk ' as a sick man, and proposed that if he died, that is to say, if the Turkish power fell to pieces, England should take Crete and

Egypt, and that the Sultan's European provinces should be formed into independent states, of course under Russian protection. There can be no doubt that the Christians under the Sultan were misgoverned, and that the Tzar, like every Russian, honestly sympathised with them, especially as they belonged to the Orthodox Church—commonly known as the Greek Church—which was his own. It was, however, also true that every Tzar wished to extend his dominions southward, and that his sympathies undoubtedly tended in the same direction as his ambition. In England the sympathies were ignored, whilst the ambition was clearly perceived, and the British ministers refused to agree to Nicholas's proposal. Nicholas then sent Prince Menschikoff as ambassador to Constantinople to demand that the protection of the Sultan's Christian subjects should be given over to himself, and when this was refused, occupied the principalities of Moldavia and Wallachia with his troops ; upon which a British fleet was moved up to the entrance of the Dardanelles.

10. **War between Russia and Turkey.** 1853—1854.—To avert an outbreak of war the four great Powers, Austria, France, Great Britain, and Prussia, in what is usually called the Vienna note, embodied a proposal, which, if adopted by the Sultan, would convey his promise to the Tzar to protect the Christians of the Greek Church as his predecessors had promised to do in older treaties with the Tzars, and to extend to the Greek Christians all advantages granted to other Christians. With this note the Tzar was contented, but the Sultan urged on by the imperious Sir Stratford Canning, the British ambassador at Constantinople, refused to accept it without alteration, and on the Tzar insisting on its acceptance as it stood declared war upon him. In the autumn the Turks crossed the Danube and defeated some Russian troops, on which the Russian fleet sallied forth from Sebastopol, the great Russian fortified harbour in the Crimea, and on November 30 destroyed the Turkish fleet at Sinope. In England strong indignation was felt ; England and France bound themselves closely together, and, refusing to be held back by Austria and Prussia, entered upon war with Russia in March 1854. In May the Russians laid siege to Silistria on the south bank of the Danube. The siege however ended in failure, and, as a British and French army arrived at Varna, a seaport on the Black Sea, south of the mouth of the Danube, and as the Austrians insisted on the Russians evacuating Moldavia and Wallachia, the Russian army drew back to its own territory, and abandoned any further attempt to enforce its claims by invasion.

11. **Resolution of the Allies.** 1854.—Two courses were now

open to the Allies. They might knit themselves again to Austria and Prussia and substitute a European protection of the Christians under the Sultan for a merely Russian protection, without driving Russia to a prolongation of the war ; or else, breaking loose from their alliance with Austria and Prussia (neither of which was inclined to drive matters to extremities), they might seek to destroy the Russian Black Sea fleet and the fortifications of Sebastopol, in order to take from Russia the power of again threatening the Turks. Public opinion in England was defiantly set upon the latter course. There was exasperation against the ambition of Russia and a determination that the work should be thoroughly done. To the support of this passionate desire to carry on the war to its end, came a misconception of the nature of the Turkish Government. In reality the Turk was, as Nicholas had said, a sick man, and as he would become weaker every year, it was impossible to provide for his guarding his own even if Sebastopol were destroyed. In England the Government of the Sultan was regarded as well-intentioned and perfectly capable of holding its own, if the existing danger could be removed. This view of the case was strongly supported by Palmerston, who, though he was no longer foreign minister, brought his strong will to bear on the resolutions of the ministry. England and France resolved on transporting their armies from Varna to the Crimea. The English force was commanded by Lord Raglan, and the French by Mar hal St. Arnaud.

12. **Alma and Sebastopol. 1854.**—On September 14, the two armies, numbering together with a body of Turkish soldiers about 61,000 men, landed to the south of Eupatoria. They marched southwards and found the Russian army drawn up on high ground beyond the river Alma. There was not much skill shown by the generals on either side, but the Allies had the better weapons, and the dogged persistence of the British contributed much to the success of the Allies. The Russians were defeated, and the Allies wheeled round the harbour of Sebastopol and established themselves on the plateau to the south of the town. There was inside the place a vast store of guns and of everything needed for the defence, and what was more, a man of genius, General Todleben, to improve the fortifications and direct the movements of the garrison. He closed the harbour against the Allied fleets by sinking ships at the mouth, and he brought up guns and raised earthworks to resist the impending attack on the land side. On October 17, the Allies opened a tremendous fire. The British batteries destroyed the guns opposed to them, and the place might perhaps have been taken by assault if the French had done as well. The

French, however, who were now under the command of Marshal Canrobert—St. Arnaud having died after the battle of the Alma—made their magazines of gunpowder too near the surface of the ground, and when one of them exploded, their efforts were rendered useless. The attack had to be postponed for an indefinite time.

13. **Balaclava and Inkerman. 1854.**—The stores and provisions for the British army were landed at the little port of Balaclava. On October 25, a Russian army pushed forward to cut off communication between this port and the British force before Sebastopol. A charge by the Brigade of Heavy Cavalry drove back a huge mass of Russian horsemen. Lord Cardigan, who commanded the Brigade of Light Cavalry, received an order vaguely worded to retake some guns which had been captured by the Russians. The order was misunderstood, and the Light Brigade, knowing that it was riding to its destruction, but refusing to set an example of disobedience, charged not in the direction of the guns, which they were unable to see, but into the very centre of the Russian army. The ranks of the English cavalry were mown down and but few escaped alive. ' It is magnificent,' said a French general, ' but it is not war.' On November 5, the battle of Inkerman was fought, in which the scanty British drove back thick columns of Russians. If the Russians had prevailed, both the Allied armies would have been destroyed. As it was the British held out against fearful odds, till the French came to their help, and forced the Russians to retreat.

14. **Winter in the Crimea. 1854—1855.**—Winter was now upon the armies. It had been supposed at home that their task would be accomplished before the fine weather ended, and no adequate provision for a winter season had been made. A storm swept over the Black Sea and wrecked vessels laden with stores. The soldiers had only tents to keep off the rain and bitter cold, and fell ill by hundreds. The horses, which should have brought stores from Balaclava, died, and it was useless to replace them, because, though large numbers of horses were obtainable, forage had not been sent from home to keep them alive. What provisions reached the camp had to be carried by the men, and the men were worn out by having to spend long hours in guarding the trenches and to fetch provisions as well. Besides, the English Government, having had no experience of war, committed many blunders in their arrangements for the supply of the army. The French were better off, because Kamiesch Bay, where their provisions were landed, was nearer their camp than Balaclava was to the camp of the British.

15. The Hospital at Scutari. 1855.—The sick were carried to a hospital at Scutari near Constantinople, but when they arrived there were no nurses to attend on them, and large numbers died. After a while Miss Florence Nightingale was sent out with other ladies to nurse the sick. It was the first time that women had been employed as nurses in war. Miss Nightingale soon reduced the disorder into order, made the place clean, and saw that the sufferers were skilfully tended. Good nursing at once told on the health of the men, and valuable lives were spared in consequence of the gentle help received.

16. The Palmerston Ministry. 1855.—At home Englishmen looked on the misery in the Crimea with growing anger. They thought that some one was to blame, and as soon as Parliament met, the Government was forced to resign. Lord Palmerston became Prime Minister. It was known that his whole heart was in the war, and that he was a man of strong common sense and resolute character. Matters in the Crimea began to improve, principally because by that time English officials had begun, after numerous failures, to understand their duties.

17. The Fall of Sebastopol and the End of the War. 1855—1856.—During the summer the siege of Sebastopol was pushed on. The British army was in good condition. The French troops were, however, more numerous, and occupied the positions from which the town could be most easily attacked. They had, too, a new commander, Marshal Pelissier, who was more strong-willed than Canrobert had been. The King of Sardinia, Victor Emmanuel, joined the Allies, and in the battle of Trakir [1] his troops took part with the French in driving back a fresh Russian onslaught. After various attempts a final attack on Sebastopol was made on September 8. The English failed to capture the Redan which was opposed to them, but the French stormed the Malakhoff

The Victoria Cross: instituted in 1856.

Tower, and the whole of the fortifications were thereby rendered untenable. The Tzar Nicholas had died in the spring, and his successor, Alexander II., was now ready to make peace. The

---

[1] *Trakir* is the Russian word for an inn.

Russian losses had been enormous, not merely in Sebastopol itself, but over the whole of the empire. There was scarcely a railway in Russia then, and hundreds of thousands of men had perished of fatigue in the long and exhausting marches. In March 1856 peace was made. The fortifications of Sebastopol were destroyed, and Russia promised not to have a fleet in the Black Sea or to re-fortify the town. The Russians abode by these terms as long as they were obliged to do so, and no longer. It was, however, long enough to give the Turks time to improve and strengthen their government if they had been capable of carrying out reforms of any kind.

18. **India after Wellesley's Recall. 1805—1823.**—British hostility to Russia had arisen chiefly from fear lest she should, by gaining possession of Constantinople, cut off the passage to India. Alarm on this score had not been of recent growth. Partly in consequence of a desire to win the attachment of the natives of India as a security against foreign aggression, successive governors-general had, since Wellesley left India in 1805 (see p. 859), devoted themselves to improve the condition of the people, and had for some time abstained from war as much as possible. Their reluctance to appeal to arms had, however, encouraged bands of plunderers known as Pindarrees, supported by the Mahratta chiefs whose power Wellesley had curtailed, but who still retained their independence. In 1817 the Marquis of Hastings, at that time governor-general, began the third Mahratta War (see pp. 804, 859). The Peishwah (see p. 802) abdicated in favour of the British, and the other Mahratta chiefs were reduced to a condition of dependency, and gave no more shelter to robbers. Hastings completed Wellesley's work, by making the power of the East India Company absolutely predominant, and, after 1823, when he left India, there were, indeed, wars occasionally on a small scale, but for some years the chief feature of Indian history was its peaceful progress.

19. **The North-Western Frontier. 1806—1835.**—The suppression of internal disorder did not relieve the Government of India from anxiety lest increasing prosperity within should tempt invaders from without. Secured on the north by the lofty wall of the Himalayas, India, until the arrival of the British by sea, had always been invaded by enemies pouring across its north-western frontier from the passes of the highlands of Afghanistan; and it was from the same quarter that danger was now feared. For some time, indeed, a sufficient bulwark had been erected by the estab-

lishment in the Punjab—the land of the five rivers—of the Sikhs, a warlike people with a special religion, neither Mahomedan nor Hindoo. The Sikhs were strongly organised for military purposes under a capable ruler, Runjeet Singh, who had entered in 1806 into a treaty with the British which to the end of his life he faithfully observed. Under him the Sikhs covered the British territory from an attack through Afghanistan, much in the same way that in the time of Warren Hastings the Nawab of Oude had covered it against the attacks of the Mahrattas (see p. 802).

20. **Russia and Afghanistan.** 1835—1838.—In 1835, when England and Russia were striving for the mastery at Constantinople (see p. 921), the two countries were necessarily thrown into opposition in Asia. In 1837 the Shah of Persia, who was under Russian influence, laid siege to Herat, on the eastern border of his own country. As Herat was on the road to India, Lord Auckland, the governor-general, took alarm, and, even before the siege was actually begun, sent an agent, Alexander Burnes, to Cabul to win over Dost Mahommed, the ruler of Afghanistan, to enter into an alliance with England against Persia, the ally of Russia. Burnes, knowing that soft words would not suffice to gain the heart of Dost Mahommed, offered him British aid in his own quarrels. Auckland, however, refused to carry out the engagement made by Burnes, on which Dost Mahommed, taking offence, allied himself with Russia. In 1838, Auckland sent an expedition to dethrone Dost Mahommed, and to replace him by Shah Soojah, an Afghan prince who had been living in exile in India. Before the expedition started the siege of Herat had been raised by the Persians, and there was, therefore, no longer any real excuse for an attack on the fierce and warlike Afghans.

21. **The Invasion of Afghanistan.** 1839—1842.—Nevertheless the British army entered Afghanistan in 1839, and, reaching Cabul in safety, placed Shah Soojah on the throne. In 1840, Dost Mahommed knowing that he could not carry on a successful resistance in the field, surrendered himself as a prisoner. So peaceful was the outlook that Sir William Macnaghten, who had charge of the political arrangements at Cabul, fancied that all danger was at an end. Suddenly, however, an insurrection broke out, and some of the British officers, amongst whom was Burnes, were murdered. Though the British were taken by surprise, they had still soldiers enough to attack the Afghans with every prospect of success, but General Elphinstone, who was in command, refused to run the risk. On this the Afghans became still more daring,

and, as food was growing short in the British cantonments, Macnaghten and Elphinstone offered to surrender the forts of Cabul to the enemy on condition of being supplied with provisions. Akbar Khan, a son of Dost Mahommed, invited Macnaghten to a conference and shot him dead with his own hand. The British officers then entered on a treaty with the murderer, who engaged to protect their army, if it would immediately return to India.

22. **The Retreat from Cabul. 1842.**—The retreat began on January 6, 1842. Snow and ice lay thickly on the passes over the lofty mountain ranges, which had to be climbed before the plains of India were reached. Akbar Khan did what he could to protect the retreating regiments, but he could not restrain his followers. Crowds of Afghans stationed themselves on the rocks which rose above the track, and shot down the fugitives. With the retreating soldiers were English ladies, some of them with children to care for. To save them from certain death they were surrendered to Akbar Khan, who promised to treat them kindly, and who, to his credit, kept his word. After five days' march, out of 14,500 men who left Cabul, no more than 4,000 remained alive. Each day the butchery was renewed. On the morning of the eighth day only sixty-five were left, and this scanty remnant of a mighty host struggled on to reach Jellalabad in which there was a British garrison. Of these, sixty-four were slain on the way; after which the Afghans, believing that all their enemies had perished, returned in triumph. One Englishman, however, Dr. Brydon, who had lagged behind because both he and the pony on which he rode were too exhausted to keep up with the march, escaped their notice. Fainting and scarcely able to speak, he at last stumbled into Jellalabad, and told the tale of the great disaster.

23. **Pollock's March to Cabul. 1842.**—Jellalabad held out against all the Afghans who could be brought against it. Then General Pollock was sent to retrieve the honour of the British arms. He occupied Cabul, but he had to replace Dost Mahommed on the throne, and to content himself with recovering the British captives.

24. **Conquest of Sindh. 1842.**—Lord Ellenborough, who had succeeded Auckland as governor-general, coveted Sindh, because he wished to control the lower course of the Indus. He brought accusations of treachery against the Ameers who ruled it, some of which appear to have been based on forged letters. He then sent against the Ameers Sir Charles Napier, who, fighting against tremendous odds, defeated them at Meanee. Sindh was annexed,

and its inhabitants, being far better governed than before, rapidly became prosperous and contented.

25. The First Sikh War. 1845—1846.—Runjeet Singh (see p. 949), ' the lion of the Punjab,' as he was called, died in 1839. His succession was disputed, and the Government really fell into the hands of the Sikh army, which raised to power one competitor after another amidst scenes of bloodshed. The governor-general, Sir Henry Hardinge, himself a soldier, had succeeded Ellenborough in 1843. He was anxious to keep the peace, but the mutinous Sikh army was under no restraint, and on December 11, 1845, it crossed the Sutlej and poured into British territory. Never had a British army in India met antagonists so formidable. Yet in two fierce battles, at Ferozeshah and Moodkee, the invaders were repulsed by Sir Hugh Gough, the commander-in-chief. The Sikhs, however, were not disheartened. In January 1846, they were again defeated by Sir Harry Smith at Aliwal, and finally on February 8, their entrenched camp at Sobraon, on the Sutlej, though defended by more powerful artillery than could be brought against them, was stormed by Gough. After these defeats, the Sikhs submitted, yielding the territory between the Sutlej and the Beas.

26. The Second Sikh War. 1848—1849.—In 1848 there was a second Sikh war. On January 13, 1849, Gough—now Lord Gough —met with a check at Chillianwalla, and Sir Charles Napier was sent out to succeed him as commander-in-chief. Before Napier arrived, Gough gained a decisive victory at Gujerat. On this the whole of the Punjab was annexed. Chiefly under the firm and kindly management of two brothers, Henry and John Lawrence, the Punjab was reduced to order and contentment, and the very Sikh soldiers who had been the most dangerous antagonists of the British Government were converted into its most unwavering supporters.

27. Lord Dalhousie's Administration. 1848—1856.—When the second Sikh war was being fought, Lord Dalhousie was the governor-general, and he continued to rule India for eight years, from 1848 to 1856. He was impressed with the advantages which would accrue to the native population by being brought under British rule, and he annexed one territory after another. In his time the Punjab, Sattara, Nagpoor, Lower Burmah, and finally Oude, were brought directly under British authority either by conquest or by the dethronement of the native princes. Lord Dalhousie's intentions were undoubtedly good, but he irritated an

influential class of natives by his entire disregard of their feelings
and prejudices.   Especially was this the case when, as happened
at Sattara, territory was seized, on the ground that the native
ruler, being childless, was without an heir.   The Hindoos, like the
old Romans, regard an adopted son and a real son as standing on
exactly the same footing, and as in the case of the old Romans,
this idea was based on the religious belief that the father needed
a son to perform certain sacrifices for his benefit after death.   When,
therefore, Lord Dalhousie refused to acknowledge the adopted son
of the Rajah of Sattara as his successor, he was guilty, in Hindoo
opinion, of an unjust and irreligious act.   Moreover, Lord Dalhousie alienated, especially in Oude and the North-West Provinces,
an influential class of native gentlemen because the officials
supported by him took every opportunity of depriving them of
certain rights which they claimed over the land, and which they
had long exercised.   Though this was done with the benevolent
intention of sweeping away all middle-men standing between the
officers of the Government and the cultivators, whom they wished
to shield from wrong, the result was none the less deplorable.

   28. **The Sepoy Army.**   **1856—1857.**—In 1856, Lord Canning, a
son of the Prime Minister George Canning, became governor-
general.   By that time some of the dispossessed princes and most
of the offended native gentlemen had formed a conspiracy against
the British Government, which they held to have been unjust
towards them and which in some cases had really been so.   The
conspirators aimed at securing the support of the Bengal Sepoy army,
which had also been alarmed by certain acts in which the Government had not shown itself sufficiently careful of their feelings and
prejudices.   Most of the Sepoys were Hindoos, and all Hindoos
are divided into castes, and believe that the man who loses his
caste is not only disgraced in the present life but suffers misery
after death.   This loss of caste is not the penalty for moral faults,
but for purely bodily actions, such as eating out of the same vessel
as one of a lower caste.   Caste, too, is lost by eating any part of the
sacred animal the cow, and, as a new rifle had been lately served
out, the conspirators easily frightened the mass of the Sepoys into
the belief that the cartridges for this rifle were greased with
cow's fat.   When, therefore, they bit the new cartridges, as soldiers
then had to do, before loading, their lips would touch the cow's
grease and they would at once lose caste.   It was said that the
object of the Government was to render the men miserable by

depriving them of the shelter of their own religion in order to drive them to the adoption of Christianity in despair.

29. **The Outbreak of the Mutiny. 1857.**—In the spring of **1857** there were attempts to mutiny near Calcutta, but the actual outbreak occurred at Meerut near Delhi.   There the native regiments first massacred their English officers and such other Englishmen as they met with, and then marched to Delhi, where they proclaimed the descendant of the Great Mogul (see p. 801), who was living there as a British pensioner, Emperor of India.   Canning did what he could by sending for British troops from other parts of India, and also for a considerable force which happened to be at sea on its way to take part in a war which had broken out with China.   His position was, however, exceedingly precarious till further reinforcements could be brought from England.   His best helper was Sir John Lawrence, who had governed the recently annexed Punjab with such ability and justice that the Sikh warriors, so lately the fierce enemies of the British, were ready to fight in their behalf.   As the Sikhs did not profess the Hindoo religion, there was, in their case, no difficulty about caste.   With their aid Lawrence disarmed the Sepoys in the Punjab, and sent all the troops he could spare to besiege Delhi.   Delhi, however, was a strong place and, as the besiegers were few, months elapsed before it could be taken.

30. **Cawnpore. 1857.**—The mutiny spread to Lucknow, the capital of Oude, where the few Englishmen in the place were driven into the Residency with Sir Henry Lawrence, Sir John's brother, at their head, to hold out, if they could, till help arrived. At Cawnpore, not far off, were about five hundred British women and children, and less than five hundred British men were besieged by one Nana Sahib, who hated the English on account of wrongs which he conceived himself to have suffered at their hands.   After they had endured terrible hardships, Nana Sahib offered to allow the garrison to depart in safety.   The offer was accepted and the weary defenders made their way to the boats waiting for them on the river, where they were shot down from the bank.   Some of the women and children were kept alive for a few days, but in the end all were massacred, and their bodies flung into a well.   Only four of the defenders of Cawnpore escaped to tell the miserable tale.

31. **The Recovery of Delhi and the Relief of Lucknow. 1857.** The mutiny, widely spread as it was, was confined to the Bengal Presidency.   In Lucknow, though Sir Henry Lawrence had been slain, the garrison held out in the Residency.   At last Havelock,

III.   3 Q a brave, pious officer, who prayed and taught his men to pray as the Puritan soldiers had prayed in Cromwell's time, brought a small band through every obstacle to its relief. Before he reached the place Sir James Outram joined him, authorised by the Government to take the command out of his hands. Outram, however, honourably refused to take from Havelock the credit of the achievement. 'To you,' wrote Outram to Havelock, 'shall be left the glory of relieving Lucknow, for which you have already struggled so much. I shall accompany you, placing my military service at your disposal, should you please, and serving under you as a volunteer.' Thus supported, Havelock relieved Lucknow on September 25, but he had not men enough to drive off the besiegers permanently, and Outram, who, after the city had been entered, took the command, had to wait for relief in turn. Delhi had already been taken by storm on September 19.

32. **The End of the Mutiny. 1857—1858.**—Soon after the relief of Lucknow Sir Colin Campbell, who afterwards became Lord Clyde, arrived with reinforcements from England, and finally suppressed the mutiny. In **1858** Parliament put an end to the authority of the East India Company (see p. 808). Thenceforth the Governor-General was brought directly under the Queen, acting through a British Secretary of State for India responsible to Parliament. There was also to be an Indian Council in England composed of persons familiar with Indian affairs, in order that the Secretary of State might have the advice of experienced persons. On assuming full authority, the Queen issued a proclamation to the peoples and princes of India. To the people she promised complete toleration in religion, and admission to office of qualified persons. To the princes she promised scrupulous respect for their rights and dignities. To all she declared her intention of respecting their rights and customs. It is in this last respect especially that the proclamation laid down the lines on which administration of India will always have to move if it is to be successful. Englishmen cannot but perceive that many things are done by the natives of India which are in their nature hurtful, unjust, or even cruel, and they are naturally impatient to remove evils that are very evident to them. The lesson necessary for them to learn is the one which Walpole taught their own ancestors, that it is better to leave evils untouched for a while than to risk the overthrow of a system of government which, on the whole, works beneficently. It is one thing to endeavour to lead the people of India forward to a better life, another thing to drag them forward

and thereby to provoke a general exasperation which would lessen the chances of improvement in the future, and might possibly sweep the reforming government itself away.

CHAPTER LX

ANTECEDENTS AND RESULTS OF THE SECOND REFORM ACT
1857—1874

LEADING DATES

The Second Derby Ministry	1858
The Second Palmerston Ministry	1859
War of Italian Liberation	1859
Commercial Treaty with France	1860
The American Civil War	1861–1864
Earl Russell's Ministry	1865
War between Austria and Prussia	1866
The Third Derby Ministry	1866
The Second Reform Act	1867
The First Disraeli Ministry	1868
The First Gladstone Ministry	1868
Disestablishment of the Irish Church	1869
The First Irish Land Act and the Education Act	1870
War between France and Germany	1870–1871
Abolition of Army Purchase	1871
The Ballot Act	1872
Fall of the Gladstone Ministry	1874

1. **Fall of the First Palmerston Ministry. 1857—1858.**—When the Mutiny was crushed the Palmerston ministry no longer existed. Palmerston's readiness to enforce his will on foreign nations had led him in **1857** to provoke a war with China which the majority of the House of Commons condemned as unjustifiable. He dissolved Parliament and appealed to the fighting instincts of the nation, and, though not only Cobden and Bright, but Gladstone, joined the Conservatives against him, he obtained a sweeping majority in the new Parliament. Curiously enough, he was turned out of office, in **1858**, by this very same Parliament, on a charge of truckling to the French Emperor. Explosive bombs, wherewith to murder Napoleon III., were manufactured in England, and plans for using them against him were laid on English soil. The attempt was made by an Italian, Orsini, and upon its failure the French Government and people called upon the English Government to prevent such designs in future. Palmerston brought in a Conspiracy-to-Murder Bill, the object of which was to punish those who contrived the assassination of foreign princes on English soil. This measure, desirable as it was, was unpopular in England, because

3 Q 2

some Frenchmen talked abusively of Englishmen as protectors of murderers, and even called on the Emperor to invade England. Parliament refused to be bullied even into doing a good thing, and, the Bill being rejected, the Palmerston ministry resigned.

2. **The Second Derby Ministry and the Beginning of the Second Palmerston Ministry. 1858—1859.**—Lord Derby became Prime Minister a second time, and in 1859 Disraeli, who was again Chancellor of the Exchequer and leader of the House of Commons, brought in a Reform Bill which was rejected by the House of Commons. A new ministry was formed which, like Lord Aberdeen's in 1852, comprised Whigs and Peelites. Palmerston was Prime Minister, Russell Foreign Secretary, and Gladstone Chancellor of the Exchequer.

3. **Italian War of Liberation. 1859.**—In 1859, the year in which the second Palmerston ministry took office, a great war broke out in Italy. Italians could have no freedom in their own states as long as Austria held Lombardy and Venetia, because Austrian armies were always ready to help any Italian prince in maintaining despotism. In the kingdom of Sardinia alone, Victor Emmanuel persisted in maintaining a constitutional government in defiance of Austria, and thereby, and by his ingrained honesty of nature, attracted the reverence of all Italians who longed to expel the Austrians and gain political freedom. It was evident that all Italy must be governed despotically or constitutionally, and that constitutional government could not be maintained even in the kingdom of Sardinia unless Austria was driven back, whilst despotic government could not be maintained elsewhere unless Sardinia was crushed. In 1858 Napoleon came to an understanding with Cavour, the statesmanlike Sardinian minister, and in 1859 he led an army across the Alps to support the Sardinians. Tuscany, Parma, Modena, and the northern parts of the States of the Church, drove away their rulers and combined forces with Victor Emmanuel. Napoleon and his ally defeated the Austrians in the two great battles of Magenta and Solferino, after which the Emperor made peace with Austria. Victor Emmanuel and his subjects, who had hoped that the war might be continued till Austria had been entirely excluded from Italy, were grievously disappointed. Napoleon was, however, probably justified in bringing the war to a close, as he had reason to think that, if he continued it, Prussia would take part with Austria against him, and as it was very likely that if hostilities were prolonged his own subjects would refuse to support him. By the peace of Zürich, which put an end to the war, Milan

was given to Victor Emmanuel, but Venetia was left to Austria. The expelled princes were to be reinstated, and all Italian states, including Austrian Venetia and the increased kingdom of Sardinia, were to form a confederation, of which the president was to be the Pope.

4. **The Kingdom of Italy. 1859—1861.**—The Italians of the central provinces, Tuscany, Parma, Modena, and the northern part of the Papal States, refused to accept this absurd arrangement. In 1860 they joined Victor Emmanuel's kingdom, which now began to be known as the Kingdom of Italy. Russell, as Foreign Secretary, did everything in his power to uphold their right to dispose of themselves, and on Savoy and Nice being surrendered to France Napoleon acquiesced in the arrangement, whilst Austria did not venture to provoke a new war by interfering. In 1860, too, Garibaldi, a straightforward and enthusiastic soldier, whose ideal was the union of Italy, invaded Sicily, and in a few weeks conquered both Sicily and Naples, with the exception of the strong fortress of Gaeta. In the meanwhile many Catholics had come from other countries to defend the independence of the Pope, which was visibly threatened. They were, however, defeated by an Italian army, and that part of the Papal dominions which lay between the Apennines and the Adriatic was added to Victor Emmanuel's kingdom. Victor Emmanuel himself came into Southern Italy through his newly-annexed regions, where he was welcomed by Garibaldi. The joint armies laid siege to Gaeta, which surrendered on February 13, 1861. Victor Emmanuel now ruled over all Italy except Venetia, which was held by an Austrian army, and Rome, which, together with the district round it, was secured to the Pope by a French garrison.

5. **The Volunteers. 1859—1860.**—In 1860 Russell brought in a Reform Bill, but the country did not care about it, and even Russell perceived that it was useless to press it. It was withdrawn, and no other similar measure was proposed whilst Palmerston lived. The country, indeed, was agitated about other matters. Napoleon's annexation of Savoy and Nice caused disquiet, and suspicions were entertained that, having succeeded in defeating Austria, he might think of trying to defeat either Prussia or England. Already, whilst Lord Derby was Prime Minister, young men had come forward to serve as volunteers in defence of the country. Palmerston gave great encouragement to the movement, and before long corps of volunteers were established in every county, as a permanent part of the British army.

6. **The Commercial Treaty with France. 1860.**—Napoleon did

not really want to quarrel with England, and before long an opportunity presented itself for binding the two nations together. The Emperor warmly adopted a scheme for a commercial treaty between England and France which had been suggested by Cobden, and which was also supported by Gladstone, who, as Chancellor of the Exchequer, had been completing Peel's work by carrying out the principles of Free Trade. In 1860 was signed the Commercial Treaty, in virtue of which English goods were admitted into France at low duties, whilst French wines and other articles were treated in England in the same way. Between England and France, however, there was this difference : in England the treaty was sanctioned by Parliament as being in accordance with the opinions generally entertained in the country. In France it was put in force by the sole authority of the Emperor in defiance of the opinions generally entertained by the French nation. Consequently, when, at a later time, the power of the Emperor came to an end, France took the earliest opportunity to annul a treaty the value of which she was unable to appreciate.

7. **The Presidential Election in America. 1860.**—In 1860, the year in which the treaty with France was signed, events occurred in the United States of America which pressed heavily on England. In the southern states there were some millions of negro slaves, mostly employed in producing sugar and cotton, whilst in the northern states there were no slaves of any kind. The free states flourished, and the slave states decayed. The slave-owners hoped to improve their position by occupying fresh soil and carrying their slaves with them to cultivate it. The inhabitants of the free states did not yet propose to abolish slavery in the old slave states, which they were unable to do constitutionally, but they asked that slavery should not be tolerated in any new states. In 1860 Abraham Lincoln was chosen President in order that he might enforce this doctrine, on which the slave states declared themselves independent, taking the name of the ' Confederate States.' The free states continued to speak of themselves and of all the other states as still forming the ' United States,' declaring that the confederates had no right to leave the union, and must be compelled to return to it.

8. **England and the American Civil War. 1861-1862.**—A terrible war between the two sections broke out in 1861. English opinion was divided on the subject. The upper classes, for the most part, sided with the South ; the working men, for the most part, with the North. Towards the end of 1861 the Confederate Government despatched two agents, Mason and Slidell, to Europe

in an English mail-steamer to seek for the friendship of England and France. They were taken out of the steamer by the captain of a United States' man-of-war. As it was contrary to the rules of international law to seize anyone on board a neutral ship, the British Government protested, and prepared to make war with the United States if they refused to surrender the agents. Fortunately the United States Government promptly surrendered the men, honourably acknowledging that its officer had acted wrongly, and the miserable spectacle of a war between two nations which ought always to be bound together by ties of brotherhood was averted. When the demand for the surrender of Mason and Slidell was being prepared in England, Prince Albert, who had lately received the title of Prince Consort, lay upon what proved to be his death-bed. His last act was to suggest that some passages in the English despatch, which might possibly give offence in America, should be more courteously expressed. On December 14, 1861, he died. His whole married life had been one of continuous self-abnegation. He never put himself forward, or aspired to the semblance of power ; but he placed his intelligence and tact at the service of the queen and the country, softening down asperities and helping on the smooth working of the machinery of government.

9. **The ' Alabama.' 1862.**—The fleet of the United States had from the beginning of the war blockaded the southern ports, and many English merchants fitted out steamers to run through the blockading squadrons, carrying goods to the confederates and taking away cotton in return. The confederates, who had no navy, were anxious to attack the commercial marine of their enemies, and ordered a swift war-steamer to be built at Birkenhead by an English ship-builder, which, after it had put to sea, was named the ' Alabama.' The ' Alabama ' took a large number of American merchant-ships, sinking the ships after removing the crews and the valuable part of the cargo. Such proceedings caused the greatest indignation in America, where it was held that the British Government ought to have seized the ' Alabama ' before it put to sea, as being in reality a ship of war, which ought not to be allowed to start on its career from a neutral harbour. Some years afterwards England had to pay heavy damages to the United States for the losses arising in consequence of the mismanagement of the Government in allowing this ship to sail.

10. **The Cotton Famine. 1861—1864.**—In the meanwhile great suffering was caused in the north of England by the stoppage of the supplies of cotton from America, in consequence of the

blockade of the southern ports. It was on American cotton that the cotton-mills in Lancashire had almost exclusively depended, and the small amount brought by the blockade-runners was far too little to meet their needs. Attempts were made to get supplies from Egypt and India, but these supplies were as yet insufficient in quantity, and in quality very inferior. Mills were either stopped or kept going only for a few hours in the week. Thousands were thrown out of work, and the cotton-famine caused as much misery as a bread-famine would have done. Yet not only were the sufferers patient under their misfortune, but they refused to speak evil of the northern states, whose blockading operations had been the cause of their misery. Believing that slave-owning was a crime, and that the result of the victory of the northern states would be the downfall of slavery in America, they suffered in silence rather than ask that England should aid a cause which in their hearts they condemned.

11. **End of the American Civil War. 1864.** — In 1864 the American civil war ended by the complete victory of the North. Slavery was brought to an end in the whole of the territory of the United States. The conquerors showed themselves most merciful in the hour of victory, setting themselves deliberately to win back the hearts of the conquered. Such a spectacle could not fail to influence the course of English politics. A democratic government, sorely tried, had shown itself strong and merciful. The cause of democratic progress also gained adherents through the abnegation of the working-men of Lancashire in the time of the cotton-famine. Those who willingly suffered on behalf of what they believed to be a righteous cause could hardly be debarred much longer from the exercise of the full rights of citizenship.

12. **The Last Days of Lord Palmerston. 1865.** —Although Parliamentary reform could not be long delayed, it was not likely to come as long as Lord Palmerston lived. He was the most popular man in England : cheery, high-spirited, and worthily representing the indomitable courage of the race to which he belonged. He was now eighty years of age, and the old system did well enough for him. On the other hand, Gladstone, whose energy and financial success gave him an authority only second to that of Palmerston in the House of Commons, declared for reform. In 1865 a new Parliament was elected. On October 18, before it met, Palmerston died. He had been brisk and active to the last, but there was work now to be done needing the hands and hearts of younger men.

13. **The Ministry of Earl Russell. 1865—1866.** —Russell, who had been created Earl Russell in 1861, succeeded Palmerston as

Prime Minister, and Gladstone became leader of the House of Commons. When the session opened in 1866, the ministry introduced a Reform Bill, with the object of lowering the franchise in counties and boroughs. The majority in the House of Commons did not care about reform, and though the House did not directly throw out the Bill, so many objections were raised, mainly by dissatisfied Liberals, and so much time was lost in discussing them, that the ministry came to the conclusion that the House did not wish to pass it. On this they resigned, intending to show by so doing that they really cared about the Bill, and were ready to sacrifice office for its sake.

14. **The Third Derby Ministry and the Second Reform Act. 1866—1868.**—For the third time Lord Derby became Prime Minister, with Disraeli again as Chancellor of the Exchequer and leader of the House of Commons. It soon appeared that, though the House of Commons cared little for reform, the working-men cared for it much. Crowded and enthusiastic meetings were held in most of the large towns in the North. In London, the Government having prohibited a meeting appointed to be held in Hyde Park, the crowd, finding the gates shut, broke down the railings and rushed in. Disraeli, quick to perceive that the country was determined to have reform, made up his mind to be the minister to give it ; and, as he was able to carry his usual supporters with him, the opposition of the discontented Liberals—through which the Reform Bill of the last session had been wrecked—was rendered innocuous. At the opening of the session of 1867, Disraeli first proposed a series of resolutions laying down the principles on which reform ought to be based. Finding that the House of Commons preferred an actual Bill, he sketched out the plan of a Bill, and then, as it did not please the Houses, withdrew it and brought in a second Bill very different from the one which he had first proposed. Three Cabinet ministers, one of whom was Lord Cranborne (who afterwards became Lord Salisbury), resigned rather than accept a Bill so democratic as the final proposal. Before the Bill got through the House of Commons it became still more democratic. In its final shape every man who paid rates in the boroughs was to have a vote, and in towns therefore household suffrage was practically established, whilst even lodgers were allowed to vote if they paid 10*l*. rent and had resided in the same lodgings for a whole year. In the counties the franchise was given to all who inhabited houses at 12*l.* rental whilst the old freehold suffrage (see p. 902) of 40*s*. was retained. At least in towns large

enough to return members separately, the working-men would henceforth have a voice in managing the affairs of the nation. In 1868 Bills were carried changing on similar principles the franchise in Scotland and Ireland. In England and Scotland there was also a redistribution of seats, small constituencies being disfranchised and their members given to large ones.

15. **Irish Troubles. 1867.**—The year of the second Reform Act was one of trouble in Ireland. The discontented in Ireland were now supported by an immense population of Irish in America, the whole of which was hostile to England, and large numbers of which had acquired military discipline in the American Civil War. A secret society, whose members were known as Fenians, sprang up on both sides of the Atlantic. Many of the military Irish returned from America to Ireland, and in March 1867 a general rising was attempted in Ireland. Heavy snow-storms made the movements of the insurgents impossible, and this effort to bring about a complete separation between Ireland and England was suppressed with little bloodshed. Numbers of Irish, as well those residing in England as those who remained in their own country, sympathised with the Fenians. In Manchester, some of these rescued some Fenian prisoners from a prison van, and in the course of the struggle a shot was fired which killed a policeman. Five of the rescuers were tried in November, and three were hanged. In December, other Irishmen blew down with gunpowder the wall of Clerkenwell Prison, in which two Fenians were confined, hoping to liberate the prisoners.

16. **The Gladstone Ministry and the Disestablishment of the Irish Church. 1868—1869.**—In February 1868, Disraeli became Prime Minister, Lord Derby having resigned in consequence of the state of his health. It had by this time become evident to the principal Liberals that Irish discontent must be caused by grievances which it behoved the British Parliament to remedy. Accordingly, Gladstone proposed and carried resolutions calling for the disestablishment of the Irish Church. Disraeli dissolved Parliament, as he was obliged in any case to do in order to allow the new constituencies created by the Reform Act to choose their representatives. The new Parliament contained a large Liberal majority, and Gladstone became Prime Minister. In 1869 he brought in and carried a Bill disestablishing and disendowing the Protestant Church of Ireland, which was the Church of the minority.

17. **The Irish Land Act. 1870.**—In 1870 the Government attacked the more difficult question of Irish land. An Irish Land

Act was now passed which obliged landlords to compensate their tenants for improvements made by them, and to give them some payment if they turned them out of their holding for any reason except for not paying their rent. Tenants who desired to buy land from their landlords might receive loans from the Government to enable them to become owners of farms which they had rented. The Act had less effect than was intended, as the landlord, being allowed to come to an agreement with a tenant that the Act should not in his case be enforced, had usually sufficient influence over his tenants to induce them to abandon all claim to the benefits which Parliament intended them to receive.

18. **The Education Act. 1870.**—In the same year Forster, who was one of the ministers, introduced a new system of education in primary schools in England. Up to this time the Government had been allowed by Parliament to grant money to schools on condition that a sum at least equal to the grant was raised by school fees and local subscriptions, and that the Government inspectors were satisfied that the children were properly taught. By the new Education Act, wherever there was a deficiency in school accommodation, the ratepayers were to elect a School Board with authority to draw upon the rates for the building and maintenance of as many schools as the Committee of the Privy Council appointed to decide on questions of education (see p. 920) thought to be necessary—which School Boards had authority to compel parents who neglected the education of their children to send them either to the Board School or to some other efficient school. At these schools the Bible was to be read and explained, but no religious instruction according to the principles of any special religious body was to be given in school hours.

19. **The War between Prussia and Austria. 1866.**—Whilst these events were occurring in England great changes had taken place on the Continent. In **1866** a war had broken out between Prussia on the one hand, and Austria supported by the great majority of the German states on the other. The Austrians were completely defeated by the Prussians at Sadowa in Bohemia, though at Custozza they defeated the Italians, who had allied themselves with Prussia. The result was that when peace was made, Venetia was ceded to Italy, whilst in Germany, Hanover, Hesse-Cassel, Nassau and Frankfort were annexed to Prussia, and the whole of the country to the north of the Main formed into a North German Confederation under Prussian supremacy.

20. **War between France and Germany. 1870—1871.**—The

French growing jealous of the success of Prussia, in **1870** the Emperor Napoleon picked a quarrel with the King of Prussia. In the war which followed the whole of Germany sided with Prussia. The German army was thoroughly prepared for war, and had a consummate strategist, Count Moltke, to direct its operations, whilst the French army was in utter confusion. The Germans invaded France, and, after defeating outlying bodies of French troops at Wörth and Forbach, overthrew the main army under Bazaine at Gravelotte. Driving Bazaine into Metz, they left a large part of their force to block him up in the town, whilst they advanced towards Paris with the remainder. On the way, learning that Napoleon was marching to relieve Bazaine, they turned upon him and completely defeated him at Sedan, making both him and his whole army prisoners. On this the Parisians established a Republic, but the Germans pressed on, laid siege to Paris, in the meanwhile forcing the French army in Metz to capitulate. The Republican Government made an heroic resistance, but in March **1871** Paris capitulated and peace was made ; France having to pay a large sum of money and to cede to Germany Alsace and the north-eastern part of Lorraine. Before this the southern German princes had agreed to combine with the northern princes in a new German Empire, and William I., king of Prussia, was proclaimed hereditary German Emperor at Versailles. As France had been obliged to call home the garrison which she had hitherto kept at Rome, the Italian troops entered that city, thus completing Italian unity under the constitutional monarchy of Victor Emmanuel.

21. **Abolition of Army-Purchase. 1871.**—In these wars England took no part. Government and Parliament continued to pay attention to domestic reforms. Hitherto regimental officers in the army had been allowed, on voluntarily retiring from the service, to receive a sum of money from the senior officer beneath them who was willing or able to pay the price for the creation of a vacancy to which he would be promoted over the heads of officers who, though they were his own seniors, did not pay the money. A poor officer, therefore, could only be promoted when vacancies above him were caused by death. A Government Bill for the abolition of this practice passed the Commons, but was laid aside by the Lords till a complete measure of army-reform, which had been joined to the Bill when it was first brought into the Commons, should be produced. Gladstone, taking this to be equivalent to the rejection of the Bill, obtained from the Queen the withdrawal of the warrant by which purchase was authorised, thus settling by a stroke of the

prerogative a measure which he had at first hoped to pass by the authority of Parliament. His action on this occasion lost him the good will of some of his best and most independent supporters, whilst large numbers of Dissenters had been alienated from the Government because the Education Act had not entirely put an end to the giving of religious instruction in schools, and thus relieved them from the fear that the religious belief of the children would be influenced by the teaching of Church of England school-masters and schoolmistresses.

22. **The Ballot Act. 1872.**—All members of the Liberal party, however, concurred in supporting a Bill introduced by Forster in 1872 for establishing secret voting by means of the ballot. The Ballot Act, which passed in this year, made it impossible to know how any man's vote was given, and consequently enabled persons dependent on others for their livelihood or advancement to give their votes freely without fear of being deprived of employment if they voted otherwise than their employers wished. The work of the first Gladstone ministry was in some respects like the work of the ministry of Lord Grey after the first Reform Act. In both cases the accession of a new class to a share of power was followed by almost feverish activity in legislation, in the one case in accordance with the ideas of the middle classes, in the other case in accordance with the ideas of the artisans. In both cases vigorous progress was followed by a reaction. Many who had applauded what was done had no desire to see more done in the same direction, and, as always happens when people are no longer in accord with the ideas of a ministry, they fix angrily on mistakes committed and think of unavoidable misfortunes as though they were intentional mistakes. Some of the ministers, moreover, made themselves unpopular by the discourtesy of their language.

23. **Foreign Policy of the Ministry. 1871—1872.**—The foreign policy of the Government made it unpopular. One result of the great war between France and Germany in 1871 was that Russia refused to be any longer bound by the treaty of 1856 (see p. 948) to abstain from keeping ships of war in the Black Sea, and the English Government, as a matter of necessity, but to its own griev-ous injury at home, agreed to a conference being held between the representatives of the great Powers in London, at which the stipula-tions objected to by Russia were annulled. Another cause of the unpopularity of the Government was its agreement in 1871 to refer to arbitration the claims which had been brought forward by the United States for compensation for damages inflicted on their

commercial marine by the ravages of the 'Alabama' (see p. 960). In **1872** a Court of Arbitration sat at Geneva and awarded to the United States a sum of 15,000,000 dollars, or rather more than 3,000,000*l*. The sum was regarded by many in England as excessive, but, whether this was so or not, it was well spent in putting an end to a misunderstanding between the two great branches of the English-speaking race. Since that time there has been an increasing readiness to submit disputes between nations to arbitration ; but those who admire this course sometimes forget that it is only in some cases that arbitration is acceptable. When two nations are desirous to live on good terms with one another and are only prevented from doing so by a dispute on some particular question of comparatively slight importance, it is not only possible, but in the highest degree desirable, that they should abide by the decision of arbitrators rather than go to war. Questions reaching to the permanent interests of a nation, and still more, questions touching its honour or its very existence, are not likely to be decided by arbitration. In **1872** England could honourably pay an unduly large sum of money rather than go to war. In **1859** the King of Sardinia could not have been expected to submit to arbitration the question whether the Italian nation should be united or divided.

24. **Fall of the First Gladstone Ministry.** **1873—1874.**—In **1873** the ministry brought in a Bill to establish in Ireland a new University which, in order that it might inspire confidence in Protestants and Catholics alike, was to be forbidden to teach the disputed but important subjects of theology, philosophy, and history. This singular Bill being rejected by the House of Commons, the ministers resigned. As, however, Disraeli refused to take office, they continued to carry on the government. In January **1874,** Parliament being dissolved, a large Conservative majority was returned. The ministry then resigned, and Disraeli became Prime Minister a second time. It was the first time since Peel's resignation that the Conservatives had held office, except on sufferance.

25. **Colonial Expansion.** **1815—1874.**—After the great war with France which ended in **1815,** the colonies retained and acquired by England were valued either like the West India Islands because they produced sugar, or like the Cape of Good Hope because they afforded stations for British fleets which would be of the highest value in time of war. There were, no doubt, British emigrants who had left their homes to settle in Canada and Australia, but their numbers were not very great, and at the Cape of Good Hope the population was almost entirely of Dutch origin. Since that

time the West India Islands have decreased in importance in consequence of the abolition of slavery, the throwing open of the British market to foreign sugar, and to defects in a system of cultivation which had been adopted in the time of slavery. On the other hand there have grown up great and powerful communities mainly composed of emigrants from Great Britain, self-governing like Great Britain herself, and held to the mother-country by the loosest possible ties. These communities are to be found in three parts of the globe—the Dominion of Canada, Australasia, and South Africa.

26. **The North-American Colonies. 1841—1874.**—It had been supposed in England that the troubles which had resulted in Canada from the dissensions between the British and French settlers had been brought to an end in 1841 by the legislative union of the two provinces (see p. 916). The British inhabitants of Upper Canada, however, complained of the influence exercised by the French of Lower Canada. To provide a remedy an Act of the British Parliament created, in 1867, a federation known as the Dominion of Canada into which any existing colonies on the North American continent were to be allowed to enter. There was to be a governor-general appointed by the Crown, and a Dominion Parliament seated at Ottawa and legislating for matters of common concern, which was to consist of a Senate, the members of which are nominated for life by the governor-general on the advice of responsible ministers, and a House of Commons, the members of which are elected by constituencies in the provinces in proportion to the population of each province. The parliaments of the separate provinces retained in their own hands the management of their own local affairs. The provincial parliaments of Upper and Lower Canada were separated from one another, bearing respectively the names of the province of Ontario and the province of Quebec. To them were added as component parts of the Dominion Nova Scotia and New Brunswick. Between 1870 and 1872 Manitoba, British Columbia, and Prince Edward Island joined the Dominion. Newfoundland continues to hold aloof. The unoccupied lands of the north-west are placed under the control of the authorities of the Dominion, which thus combines under one government the whole of America north of the territory of the United States from the Atlantic to the Pacific with the exception of Newfoundland and its subject territory of Labrador.

27. **Australasia. 1788—1874.**—The Australasian colonies are divided into two groups, those of Australia and those of New Zealand. The first British settlers in Australia were convicts, who

arrived at Port Jackson in 1788. For many years the colony thus founded under the name of New South Wales remained a penal settlement. The convicts themselves, after serving their time in servitude, became free, their children were free, and there was a certain amount of free emigration from Great Britain. In 1821 New South Wales had a population of 30,000, of which three-fourths were convicts. It had already been discovered that the country was peculiarly adapted to the production of wool, and the number of sheep in the colony rose from 25,000 in 1810 to 290,000 in 1821. From this time success was assured. Other colonies were founded in due course. Van Diemen's Land, afterwards known as Tasmania, was established as a separate colony in 1825. In the same year a small convict settlement was founded under the name of West Australia. South Australia received a separate government in 1836 under a British Act of Parliament passed in 1834. Victoria was separated from New South Wales in 1850. By this time the free population, indignant at the constant influx of British criminals, resisted the importation of convicts so strenuously that in 1851 an end was put to the system of transportation to Australia except in the small and thinly populated colony of West Australia. In that year the population flocked to the newly discovered gold fields, and the attraction of gold brought an enormous number of immigrants from Great Britain. Queensland became a separate colony in 1859. In 1881 the population of the whole of Australia reached 2,833,000. The colonies have not yet combined in any federal system, though it seems likely that they will do so before long. New Zealand, in which the white population reached 489,000 in 1883, has, since 1876, been governed by a single parliament, the seat of which is at Wellington.

28. **South Africa.**—The Cape Colony finally passed under British authority in 1806. In 1820 a stream of British immigration began to set in. The colony was under the disadvantage of having fierce and warlike Kaffir tribes on its north-eastern frontier, and from 1834 onwards a series of wars with the Kaffirs broke out from time to time and taxed to the uttermost the resources of the colony and of the British regiments sent for their defence. Many of the Dutch, who were usually known as Boers or farmers, were dissatisfied with British rule, and in 1835 began a great emigration, which ended in the establishment of the Orange River Free State, the independence of which was finally acknowledged in 1854, the independence of another set of Dutch emigrants in the Transvaal territory having been previously acknowledged in 1852. Since

1843 Natal had been a British colony. In 1871 the discovery of
diamonds at Kimberley attracted immigration, and in 1875 the
population of colonised South Africa was 1,759,000, of which
1,339,000 were in British territory and the remainder in the
two Boer Republics. That which distinguishes the South African
settlements from those in North America and in Australasia is the
enormous preponderance of a native population. The total white
population in 1875 was only 350,000, five persons out of every six
being natives.

Summary of Events, 1874—1885

1. **The Disraeli (Beaconsfield) Ministry. 1874—1880.**—The
Conservative ministry, formed under Disraeli in 1874, contented itself
for some time with domestic legislation. In 1876 troubles broke out
in the Balkan Peninsula, caused by the misdeeds of the Turkish
officials. Servia and Montenegro made war upon the Turks, and in
January 1877 a conference of European ministers was held at Constantinople to settle all questions at issue. Nothing, however, was
done to coerce the Turkish Government into better behaviour, and
as other European powers refused to act, Russia declared war
against Turkey. After a long and doubtful struggle, the Turkish
power of resistance collapsed early in 1878, and a treaty between
Russia and the Sultan was signed at San Stefano, by which the
latter abandoned a considerable amount of territory. Disraeli,
who had recently been made Earl of Beaconsfield, insisted that
no engagement between Russia and Turkey would be valid unless
it were confirmed by a European congress, and a congress was
accordingly held at Berlin. By the Treaty of Berlin, which was
signed in the course of 1878, Roumania and Servia became independent kingdoms, with some addition to their territory ; Montenegro was also enlarged, and Bulgaria erected into a principality
paying tribute to the Sultan : whilst a district to which the name
of Eastern Roumelia was given was to be ruled by a Christian
governor nominated by the Sultan, who was to have the right of
garrisoning fortresses in the Balkan Mountains. Russia acquired
the piece of land near the mouth of the Danube which she had
lost after the Crimean War, and also another piece of land round
Kars, which she had just conquered. The Sultan was recommended
to cede Thessaly and part of Epirus to Greece. The protectorate
over Bosnia and Herzegovina was given to Austria, and, by a

III.　　　　　　　　　・　　　　　　　　3 R

separate convention, Cyprus was given to England on condition of paying tribute to the Sultan and protecting Asia Minor, which the Sultan promised to govern on an improved system.   These arrangements have remained to the present day (1891), except that the Sultan has never garrisoned the fortresses in the Balkans, and that Eastern Roumelia has been annexed by its own population to Bulgaria, whilst the Sultan has only given over Thessaly to Greece, refusing to abandon any part of Epirus.   In 1879 Egypt, having become practically bankrupt, was brought under the dual control of England and France.   In South Africa, the territory of the republic of the Transvaal was annexed in 1877, and in 1879 there was a war with the Zulus, which began with the slaughter of a British force, though it ended in a complete victory.   In Asia there was in 1878 an attempt to check Russia by interfering in Afghanistan.   An impression grew up in the country that the Government was too fond of war, and when Parliament was dissolved in 1880, a considerable Liberal majority was returned.

2. **The Second Gladstone Ministry.   1880—1885.**—Gladstone formed a ministry which was soon confronted by difficulties in Ireland.   There were troubles arising from the relations between landlord and tenant, and a Land League had been formed to support the tenants in their contentions with their landlords.   There had also for some little time been amongst the Irish members a parliamentary party which demanded Home Rule, or the concession of an Irish parliament for the management of Irish affairs.   This party was led by Parnell.   In 1880 the ministry, in which the leading authority on Irish questions was Forster, the Irish Secretary, brought in a Compensation for Disturbance Bill, giving an evicted tenant compensation for the loss falling on him by being thrust out of his holding.   This Bill passed the Commons, but was rejected by the Lords.   In 1881 the ministry carried another fresh Land Act, appointing a land court to fix rents which were not to be changed for fifteen years.   At the same time it carried an Act for the protection of life and property, intended to suppress the murders and outrages which were rife in Ireland, by authorising the imprisonment of suspected persons without legal trial.   In 1881 Parnell and other leading Irishmen were arrested, but in 1882 the Government let them out of prison, with the intention of pursuing a more conciliatory course.   On this Forster resigned.   His successor, Lord Frederick Cavendish, was murdered, together with the Irish Under-Secretary, Burke, in the Phœnix Park, Dublin, by a band of ruffians who called themselves Invincibles.   An Act for

the prevention of crimes was then passed. The Irish members of parliament continued bitterly hostile to the ministry. On the other hand, some at least of the members of the Government and of their supporters were becoming convinced that another method for the suppression of violence than compulsion must be employed, if Ireland was ever to be tranquil. As had been the case with the last Government, foreign complications discredited the ministry. In 1880 the Dutch inhabitants of the Transvaal rose against the English government set up in their territory in 1877, and drove back with slaughter at Majuba Hill a British force sent against them. On this, the home government acknowledged the independence of the republic. The greatest trouble, however, arose in Egypt. An insurrection headed by Arabi Pacha with the object of getting rid of European influence, broke out against the Khedive, as the Pacha of Egypt had been called since his power had become hereditary (see p. 922). France, which had joined Great Britain in establishing the dual control, refused to act, and the British Government sent a fleet and army to overthrow Arabi. The forts of Alexandria were destroyed by the fleet, and a great part of the town burnt by the native populace. Sir Garnet Wolseley, at the head of a British army, defeated Arabi's troops at Tel-el-Kebir, and since that time the British Government has temporarily assumed the protectorate of Egypt, helping the Khedive to improve the condition of the Egyptian people. Farther south, in the Soudan, a Mahommedan fanatic calling himself the Mahdi roused his Mahommedan followers against the tyranny of the Egyptian officials, and almost the whole country broke loose from Egyptian control. An Egyptian army under an Englishman, Hicks, was massacred, and a few posts, of which the principal was Khartoum, alone held out. An enthusiastic and heroic Englishman, General Gordon, who had at one time put down a widespread rebellion in China, and had at another time been governor of the Soudan, where he had been renowned for his justice and kindliness as well as for his vigour, offered to go out, in the hope of saving the people at Khartoum from being overwhelmed by the Mahdi. The Government sent him off, but refused to comply with his requests. In 1884 Gordon's position was so critical that Wolseley, now Lord Wolseley, was sent to relieve him. It was too late, as, before Wolseley could reach Khartoum, the town was betrayed into the hands of the Mahdi, and Gordon himself murdered. The vacillation of the Cabinet, probably resulting from differences of opinion inside it, alienated a large amount of public opinion. In Asia, Russia was pushing on in the direction of Afghanistan, and in 1885 seized a post called Penjdeh. For a time war with Russia seemed imminent, but eventually an arrangement was come to which left Penjdeh in Russian hands. At home, in 1884, by an agreement between Liberals and Conservatives, a third Reform Act was passed, conferring the franchise in the counties on the same conditions as those on which it had been conferred by the second Reform Act on the boroughs. The county constituencies and those in the large towns were split up into separate constituencies each of them returning a single member, so that with a few exceptions no constituency now returns more than one. The ministry was by this time thoroughly unpopular, and in 1885 it was defeated and resigned, being followed by a Conservative Government under Lord Salisbury.

From the time of the passing of the third Reform Act, whichever party may have been in power, the country has been under democratic influence. New questions have arisen—political questions about the relations of one territorial part of the British dominions with another, and social questions about the relations between capital and labour ; but none of these have yet reached the stage at which they justly come within the province of the historian.

Books recommended for the further study of Part XI.

WALPOLE, SPENCER. A History of England from the Conclusion of the Great War in 1815. Vol. ii. p. 159-vol. V.
———————— Life of Lord John Russell.
LE MARCHANT. Memoir of Viscount Althorp, third Earl Spencer.
GREVILLE, CHARLES C. F. Memoirs.
MCLELLAN, J. K. Memoirs of Thomas Drummond.
THURSFIELD. Peel.
MORLEY, J. Life of Richard Cobden.
BULWER, SIR H. L., and ASHLEY, HON. E. Life of Viscount Palmerston.
REID, T. WEMYSS. Life of W. E. Forster.
HAMLEY, GEN. SIR E. The Crimean War.
KAYE, SIR JOHN, and MALLESON, COL. G. B. History of the Indian Mutiny.

INDEX

AAR

AARON, martyrdom of, 23

Abbey lands, the, distributed by Henry VIII., 400; Mary wishes for the restoration of, 422

Abdul Medjid succeeds his father as sultan, 922

Abercrombie, General, repulsed at Ticonderoga, 753

Abercromby, Sir Ralph, resigns his command in Ireland, 841; killed in Egypt, 844

Aberdeen, Earl of, foreign policy of, 927; becomes Prime Minister, 943

Aberdeen, Montrose's victory at, 547

Abhorrers, party name of, 620

Aclea, battle of, 57

Acre, captured by the Crusaders, 161; Edward I. at, 204; failure of Bonaparte to take, 838; taken by Napier, 922

Act of Settlement, the, 622

Addington becomes Prime Minister, 843; resignation of, 848; enters Pitt's ministry and becomes Viscount Sidmouth, 851; see Sidmouth, Viscount

Addison, literary and political position of, 693

Addled Parliament, the, 486

Admonition to Parliament, An, 446

Adrian IV. grants Ireland to Henry II., 152

Adulterine castles, 137

Adwalton Moor, battle of, 538

Aedan, king of the Scots, is defeated at Degsastan, 42

Ælfgar, earl of the Mercians, 90

Ælfgifu, wife of Eadwig, 65, 66

Ælfheah, Archbishop, murdered by the Danes, 82

Ælfred, his struggle with the Danes, 58; his position after the Treaty of Wedmore, 59; gains London, *ib.*; character of his work, 60

Ælfred the Ætheling, murder of, 85, 86

Ælfthryth, wife of Eadgar, 78

Ælla, king of Deira, slave-boys from his kingdom found at Rome, 38

Æscesdun, battle of, 58

Æthelbald, king of the Mercians, 53

ALA

Æthelbald, king of the West Saxons, 57

Æthelberht, king of Kent, his supremacy, 38; becomes a Christian, 39; helps Augustine to set up bishoprics, 40; death of, 41

Æthelberht, king of the West Saxons, 57

Æthelflæd, the Lady of the Mercians, 62

Æthelfrith, king of North-humberland, his struggle with the northern Welsh, 41; defeats the Scots at Degsastan, 42; and the Kymry near Chester, 43; is defeated and slain by Eadwine, *ib.*

Æthelred, ealdorman of Mercia, 60

Æthelred, king of the West Saxons, his struggle with the Danes, 58, 62

Æthelred the Unready, his relations with the Danes, 79; and with the Normans, 80; orders a massacre of the Danes, 81; flies to Normandy, 82; returns and dies, 83

Æthelric unites North-humberland, 41

Æthelstan, reign of, 63

Æthelstan, the Half-King, 73

Æthelwold drives secular canons from Winchester, 68

Æthelwulf defeats the Northmen, 57

Aetius refuses help to the Britons, 26

Afghan war, the first, 949; the second, 972

Afghanistan, invasions of India from, 948

Agincourt, battle of, 302

Agitators, choice of, 554; propose to purge the House, 556

Agreement of the People, the, drawn up by the Agitators, 556

Agricola, campaigns of, 16; forts built by, 17

Agriculture in Eadgar's time, 75; More's views on the decline of, 368; progress of, in Elizabeth's reign, 464; improvements in, 813

Aidan establishes himself in Holy Island, 47; his relations with Oswald, *ib.*; and with Oswine, *ib.*

Aislabie, sent to the Tower, 712

Aix-la-Chapelle (Aachen), peace of, 599, 743; congress at, 879

'Alabama,' the, depredations of, 959; award of a court of arbitration for damages caused by, 966

ALA

Alasco, opinions of, 418

Alban, martyrdom of, 23

Albany, the Duke of, suspected of the murder of the Duke of Rothesay, 295 ; is regent of Scotland, 296

Albemarle, George Monk, Duke of, as George Monk, commands in Scotland, 575 ; effects the restoration, 576 ; created Duke of Albemarle, 580 ; holds a command in the battle off the North Foreland, 592 ; advises Charles II. not to dissolve Parliament, 599

Alberoni, enterprises of, 709

Albert, Prince, marriage of, 920 ; receives the title of Prince Consort, 959 ; death of, *ib.*

Albigeois, the, crusade against, 193

Albin, probable Iberian derivation of the name, 6

Albion, *see* Albin

Albuera, battle of, 869

Alcluyd (Dumbarton), the capital of Strathclyde, 43

Aiençon, Francis, Duke of, Elizabeth proposes to marry, 446 ; entertained by Elizabeth, 454 ; attacks Antwerp, 455 ; death of, 456

Alexander, bishop of Lincoln, 134

Alexander I. (the Tzar) makes a treaty with England, 845 ; looks to England for help, 857 ; makes peace with Napoleon at Tilsit, 858

Alexander II. (the Tzar) succeeds Nicholas, and makes peace, 947

Alexander III., king of Scotland death of, 214

Alexander III., Pope, shrinks from supporting Archbishop Thomas, 145

Alexander IV., Pope, confirms a grant of Sicily to Edmund Crouchback, 197

Alexander VI., Pope, character of, 375

Alford, battle of, 549

Alicante, capture of, 685

Alighur, battle of, 859

All the Talents, the ministry of, formation of, 855 ; resignation of, 857

Allectus asserts a claim to the Empire, 22

Allen, Cardinal, founds a college at Douai, 453 ; plots to murder Elizabeth, 454

Alma, the battle of, 945

Almanza, Galway defeated at, 689

Alnwick, Malcolm Canmore slain at, 119 ; William the Lion captured at, 154 ; dismantled, 296

Althorp, Lord, becomes leader of the Whigs in the House of Commons, 898 ; is a member of Lord Grey's ministry, 901 ; carries a bill reducing the number of Irish bishoprics, 910 ; becomes Earl Spencer, 912

Alva, Duke of, his tyranny in the Netherlands, 443 ; discusses the murder of Elizabeth, 445 ; fails to reduce the Dutch, 449

Ambresbyrig (Amesbury) named from Ambrosius, 34

Ambrosius fights with the West Saxons, 34

ANN

Ambrosius Aurelianus, fights with the Jutes, 27

America, struggle between England and France for territory in, 747

America, North, the British colonies in, resistance to the Stamp Act by, 771 ; import duties imposed on, 773 ; resistance to the duties by, 774 ; public opinion in England turns against, 778 ; repeal of the duties charged on, with the exception of the tea duty, 779 ; resistance to the tea duty in, 780 ; congress of Philadelphia in, 782 ; beginning of armed resistance in, 783 ; meeting of ' the Congress of the United Colonies ' in, *ib.* ; Declaration of Independence voted by the Congress of, 784 ; *see* Canada ; America, the United States of

America, the United States of, assistance secretly given by France to, 786 ; open alliance of France and Spain with, 787 ; British successes against, 788 ; progress of the war in, 792 ; the capitulation of Yorktown ends the war in, 794 ; causes of the success of, *ib.* ; peace made at Paris with, 798 ; war of Great Britain with, 872 ; peace of Ghent with, 873 ; disputes about their frontier with, 927 ; civil war in, 958 ; Mason and Slidell surrendered by, 959

Amherst, General, takes Crown Point and Fort Duquesne, 753

Amicable Loan, the, 372

Amiens, the mise of, 200 ; the treaty of, 846

Anderida destroyed by the South Saxons, 28

André, Major, execution of, 788

Andred's Wood covers the Weald, 27

Angevin kings, Church and State under, 165 ; growth of learning under, 167 ; growth of commerce under, 168 ; architectural changes under, 170

Angles ravage Roman Britain, 24 ; settle in Britain, 28 ; advance gradually, 36 ; *see* Bernicia, Deira, East Anglia, Mercia, North-humberland

Anglesea, *see* Mona

Anjou, Geoffrey, Count of, 131 ; united with Normandy, 137 ; declares for Arthur, 174 ; conquered by Philip II., 176 ; English forays in, 317

Anjou, Henry, Duke of, *see* Henry III., king of France

Annates, first Act of, 388 ; second Act of, 390

Anne, daughter of James II., birth of, 608 ; deserts James II., 645 ; settlement of the crown on, 647 ; accession of, 676 ; influence of Marlborough over, 677 ; gives her confidence to Mrs. Masham, 687 ; dismisses the Whig ministers, 691 ; death of, 700

Anne Boleyn, appears at Court, 380 ; is married to Henry VIII., 389 ; execution of, 395

ANN

Anne of Beaujeu, policy of, 348
Anne of Bohemia marries Richard II., 278
Anne of Brittany is married to Maximilian by proxy, 349; married to Charles VIII., 349
Anne of Cleves married to Henry VIII., 400; divorce of, 401
Annual Parliaments advocated by the Duke of Richmond, 789, 792
Anselm acknowledges Ælfheah to be a martyr, 82; character of, 117; becomes Archbishop of Canterbury, 118; quarrels with William II., *ib.*; his relations with Henry I., 125
Anson, Admiral, sails round the world, 730
Anti-Corn-Law League, the, foundation of, 924; spread of, 932
Antoninus Pius, wall of, 17
Antwerp attacked by Alençon, 455; taken by Parma, 456
Appeals, Act of, 389; provision for the hearing of, 391
Appellant, the Lords, 279
Appropriation clause, the, proposed, 910; dropped, 914
Aquæ Sulis (Bath) subdued of the West Saxons, 35
Aquitaine, Duchy of, passes to Henry II. by his marriage, 137; is given to Richard, 155; divided in language and character from the North of France, 176; intrigues of Philip IV. in, 218; efforts of Philip VI. to gain, 234; ceded to Edward III., 236; the Black Prince made Duke of, 254; resistance to the Black Prince in, 256; almost wholly lost, 257; complete loss of, 320
Arabi, insurrection of, 971
Archers employed at Senlac, 96; armed with the long bow at Falkirk, 221; improperly employed at Bannockburn, 226; effect of, at Halidon Hill, 234; drawn from the yeomen, 236; win the battle of Crecy, 242; are successful at Poitiers, 251
Architecture before the Conquest, 51; Norman, 89; under the Angevins, 170; Early English style of, 207; Decorated and Perpendicular styles of, 247; later development of, 358; Elizabethan, 465; Stuart, 631, 632; in the reign of Anne, 701
Arcot, siege of, 761
Areopagitica, 546
Argaum, battle of, 859
Argyle, Archibald Campbell, Earl of, execution of, 636
Argyle, Archibald Campbell, Marquis of, opposed to Montrose, 547; execution of, 595
Argyle, Duke of, commands against Mar's rising, 705
Arkwright improves the spinning-machine, 815
Arles, Council of, 23
Arlington, Henry Bennet, Earl of, secre-

ASS

tary to Charles II., 599; intrigues against Clifford, 607
Armada, the Invincible, sailing of, 458; destruction of, 462
Armagnac, the Count of, establishes a reign of terror, 303; murder of, 304
Armagnacs, party of the, oppose the Burgundians, 296; relations of Henry IV. with, 299; make war with the Burgundians, 301; insurrection of the Parisians against, 304
Armed Neutrality, the, 792
Army, the, the folk-moot in arms, 33; Ælfred's organisation of, 60; under William I., 104, 106; re-organised by Henry II., 141; its condition under Edward III., 236; the New Model, formation of, 545; attempt of Parliament to disband, 553; choice of Agitators in, 554; gains possession of the king's person, 555; the heads of the proposals presented in the name of, *ib.*; drives out the eleven members, *ib.*; turns against the king, 556, 557; expels members by Pride's Purge, *ib.*; its inability to reconstruct society after the king's execution, 560; overthrows Richard Cromwell, restores and expels the Rump, 575; brings back the Rump, *ib.*; receives Charles II. on Blackheath, 578; paid off, 584; parliamentary control over, 650; reduction of, 667; abolition of purchase in, 964
Army, the Royal, beginning of, 584
Army plot, the, 531
Arnold, Benedict, plots to betray American forts, 789
Arras, congress at, 313; Treaty of, 337
Art in the reign of Anne, 701
Arteveldt, Jacob van, 235
Arteveldt, Philip van, 278
Arthur, legend of, 33
Arthur, nephew of John, descent of, 173; murder of, 174
Arthur, Prince of Wales, marriage and death of, 356
Articles, the ten, 395; the six, 399; the forty-two, 420; the thirty-nine, *ib.*; declaration of Charles I. prefixed to, 512
Arundel, Archbishop of Canterbury, banished, 282; his position under Henry IV., 292; deprived of the Chancellorship, 299; Oldcastle tried before, 300
Arundel Castle taken and lost by Hopton, 542
Arundel, the Earl of, opposes Richard II., 279; executed, 282
Aryans, the, 5
Ashley, Lord, *see* Shaftesbury, Earl of
Ashley, Lord, carries a factory act, 911; carries an act restricting labour in mines, and the labour of women and children in factories, 927
Aske heads the Pilgrimage of Grace, 397
Aspern, battle of, 865
Assandun, battle of, 83

ASS

Assaye, battle of, 859

Assembly of divines, proposal to refer church questions to, 534 ; meeting of, 540 ; declares for Presbyterianism, 543

Asser, life of Ælfred by, 61

Assiento Treaty, the, 696

Assize of Arms, 154

Assize of Clarendon, *see* Clarendon

Association, the, in defence of Elizabeth, 456

Association, the, in defence of William III., 666

Athelney, Ælfred takes refuge in, 58

Athlone taken by the army of William III., 656

Attainder, Bill of, against Thomas Cromwell, 401 ; nature of a, *ib.*, note i. ; against Strafford, 531

Auckland, Lord, his policy in Afghanistan, 949

Aughrim, battle of, 656

Augustine preaches to the men of Kent, 39 ; becomes Archbishop of Canterbury and founds other bishoprics, 40 ; fails to obtain the co-operation of the Welsh bishops, 41

Auldearn, battle of, 547

Aumale, Earl of, surrenders his castles to Hubert de Burgh, 187

Aurungzebe weakens the Mogul empire, 758 ; death of, 759

Austerlitz, battle of, 854

Australia, progress of the colonisation of, 967

Australasian colonies, the, 918

Austria, imprisonment of Richard I. in, 161 ; takes part in the Grand Alliance, 675 ; attacked by Frederick II., 733 ; joins a coalition against Frederick II., 749 ; French declaration of war against, 824 ; makes the treaty of Campo-Formio with France, 837 ; takes part in the second coalition, 838 ; joins the third coalition, 854 ; Francis II. adopts the title of Emperor of, 856 ; joins Russia and Prussia against Napoleon, 871 ; acquires Lombardy and Venetia, 873 ; adoption of a constitutional system in, 934 ; at war with Hungary, 935 ; its army defeated at Magenta and Solferino, 956 ; its army defeated at Sadowa, 963 ; acquires the protectorate over Bosnia and Herzegovina, 970

Austrian succession, war of, 732 ; end of the war of, 743

Avice of Gloucester divorced by John, 174

Avignon, the Popes at, 257

Babington plots the murder of Elizabeth, 457

Bacon, Francis (Lord Verulam and Viscount St. Alban), scientific aspirations of, 474 ; advises Elizabeth as to the treatment of the Catholics, 475 ;

BEA

his conduct to Essex, 478 ; gives political advice to James I., 486 ; his jest on Montague's promotion, 494 ; attacked about monopolies, 495 ; disgrace of, 496

Badajoz, siege of, 869

Badby burnt as a heretic, 298

Badon, Mount, *see* Mount Badon

Bagenal defeated by Hugh O'Neill, 475

Bakewell, improves the breed of sheep and cattle, 813

Balaclava, charges of the heavy and light cavalry at, 946

Ballard takes part in Babington's plot, 457

Balliol, Edward, wins and loses the crown of Scotland, 232, 233

Balliol, John, descent of, 215 ; declared King of Scotland, 216 ; is defeated and surrenders the crown, 219

Ballot, the, introduced into parliamentary elections, 965

Bamborough, Ida's fortress at, 36 ; Mowbray besieged in, 120

Bangor-iscoed, monastery at, 42 ; slaughter of the monks of, 43

Bank of England, the, foundation of, 660

Bannockburn, battle of, 226

Barbadoes, prisoners sent to, 564 ; dissenters sent to, 588

Barcelona, surrender of, 682 ; failure of the French to retake, 684

Barebone's Parliament, the, origin of the name of, 566 ; dissolution of, 567

Barnet, battle of, 334

Baronets, origin of the order of, 494

Barrosa, battle of, 869

Barrow, Henry, a separatist, hanged, 470

Barrow, Isaac, addresses his sermons to the understanding, 598

Basel, treaties of, 829

Basing House taken by Cromwell, 549

Basques, the, Iberian descent of, 5

Bastwick sentenced by the Star Chamber, 521

Bate's case, 484

Bath, *see* Aquæ Sulis

Battle Abbey, site of, 96

Baugé, battle of, 306

Baxter, imprisoned by Jeffreys, 635

Bayeux Tapestry, the, 98

Baylen, capitulation of, 863

Bayonne taken by the French, 320

Beachy Head, battle of, 657

Beaconsfield, Earl of, insists on the Russians laying their agreement with the Turks before a congress, 969 ; end of the ministry of, 971

Bears, performing, 275

Beaton, Cardinal, burns Wishart, 412 ; is murdered, 414

Beaufort, Henry, Bishop of Winchester, becomes Chancellor, 299 ; invites Parliament to support Henry V., 301 ; opposes Gloucester, 308 ; becomes a cardinal, 309 ; continues his opposition

BEC

to Gloucester, 314 ; policy of, 317 ; death of, 318

Bec, Abbey of, 89, 117

Becket, *see* Thomas, Archbishop of Canterbury

Bede, Ecclesiastical History of, 52

Bedford, West Saxon victory at, 35 ; castle of Faukes de Breauté at, 187

Bedford, John, Duke of, brother of Henry V., sent to secure Harfleur, 303 ; Regent of France, 307 ; marries the Duke of Burgundy's sister, *ib.*; defeats the French at Verneuil, 308 ; returns to England, 312 ; death of, 313

Bedford, Duke of, joins George Grenville's ministry, 770 ; death of, 779

Bedingfield, Sir Henry, takes charge of Elizabeth, 423

Begums of Oude, Hastings forces to pay money to the Nawab, 805

Belgians land in Britain, 8

Belgium, independence of, 912

Bellême, *see* Robert of Bellême

Benedict of Nursia establishes the Benedictine rule, 40

Benedictines, monasteries of the, 128

Benevolences invented by Edward IV., 335 ; abolished by Richard III., 342 ; raised by James I., 497

Bengal, Surajah Dowlah's overthrow in, 762 ; Clive returns to, 801

Bensington, Mercian victory at, 53

Bentham, principles of, 890 ; spread of the opinions of, 939

Bentinck, Lord George, nominal leader of the Protectionists in the House of Commons, 931 ; death of, 938

Berengaria marries Richard I., 161

Berlin decree, the, 859

Berlin, treaty of, 969

Bernard du Guesclin, *see* Du Guesclin

Bernicia, formation of the kingdom of, 36 ; is merged for a time in Northhumberland, 41 ; is untouched by the preaching of Paulinus, 46 ; is finally merged in North-humberland, 48 ; maintains its independence after the Danish conquest, 59

Bertha obtains from Æthelberht a disused church, 38

Berwick, Duke of, opposed to Galway in Spain, 684

Berwick, Treaty of, 526

Bhonsla, the, a Mahratta chief, 802 ; reduced to sign a subsidiary treaty, 859

Bible, the, Henry VIII. authorises the translation of, 396

Bigod, Hugh, appointed justiciar by the barons, 199

Bigod, Roger, Earl of Norfolk, resists Edward I., 220

Bill of Rights, the, 656

Birmingham Political Union, the, 904 ; riot at, 924

Bishops, nominated by *congé d'élire*, 391 ; first Bill for removing from the House of Lords, 533 ; impeachment of

BOS

the twelve, 535 ; excluded from the House of Lords, 536

Bishops' War, the first, 526 ; the second, 529

Black Death, the, 248, 259

Black Prince, the, fights at Creçy, 242 ; ravages the south of France, and defeats the French at Poitiers, 251 ; his courtesy to King John, 252 ; is sent to Aquitaine, 254 ; his expedition into Spain, 255 ; taxes Aquitaine, 256 ; loses Aquitaine, 257 ; leads the Good Parliament, and dies, 262

Blackwater, the, defeat of Bagenal on, 475

Blake, defends Taunton, 548 ; appointed to command the fleet, 565 ; sent to the Mediterranean, 571 ; destroys Spanish ships at Santa Cruz, 573 ; death of, *ib.*

Blanche Tache, ford of, 240

Blanketeers, the, march of, 877

Blenheim, battle of, 682

Bloody Assizes, the, 637

Blore Heath, battle of, 326

Boadicea, insurrection of, 15

Bocher, Joan, burnt, 419

Bohemia, outbreak of the Thirty Years' War in, 490

Bohun, Humfrey, Earl of Hereford, resists Edward I., 220

Boleyn, Anne, *see* Anne Boleyn

Bolingbroke, Viscount, carries the Schism Act, 699 ; overpowered by the Whigs, 700 ; escapes to France, and becomes Secretary to the Pretender, 705 ; dismissed by the Pretender, *ib.*; returns to England, 721 ; organises an opposition against Walpole, 722 ; stirs up public opinion against the Excise Bill, 724 ; returns to France, *ib.*; *see* St. John, Henry

Bombay acquired by Charles II., 587 ; made over by Charles II. to the East India Company, 758

Bonaparte, Napoleon, distinguishes himself at the siege of Toulon, 826 ; his campaign in Italy, 834 ; signs the Peace of Campo-Formio, 837 ; his expedition to Egypt, *ib.* ; invades Syria and returns to France, 838 ; becomes First Consul, 839 ; makes overtures to England, 840 : wins the battle of Marengo, and makes peace with Austria at Lunéville, 840 ; continued annexations by, 848 ; becomes Emperor of the French, 858 ; *see* Napoleon I.

Boniface VIII., 220

Boniface of Savoy, Archbishop of Canterbury, 197

Bonner, Bishop, deprived of his see, 416

Booth, Sir George, defeated at Winnington Bridge, 575

Bordeaux taken by the French, 320

Boroughbridge, defeat of Thomas of Lancaster at, 228

Boston, soldiers killed at, 780 ; tea

BOS

thrown into the harbour of, *ib.*; opera-
tions of the British force at, 783 ;
evacuated by Howe, 784
Boston Port Act, the, 782
Bosworth, battle of, 343
Botany Bay, convict settlement at, 858
Bothwell, James Hepburn, Earl of,
career of, 439
Bothwell Bridge, defeat of the Covenan-
ters at, 620
Boulogne, taken by Henry VIII., 405 ;
surrendered by Warwick, 417 ; pre-
parations for the invasion of Eng-
land at, 848 ; French army at, 851
Bourbon, the Duke of, revolt of, 371 ;
death of, 374
Bouvines, battle of, 181
Boxley, destruction of the rood of, 398
Boyne, battle of, the, 656
Brabant, the Duke of, captures Jacque-
line of Hainault, 308
Braddock routed and killed, 748
Bradford-on-Avon, early stone church at,
51
Bramham Moor, defeat of Northumber-
land on, 296
Brandreth, murder by, 879
Breda, declaration of, 576 ; treaty of, 593
Breed's Hill taken by the Americans, 783
Brember hanged, 280
Brentford, Charles I. at, 537
Bretigni, Treaty of, 253
Bretwalda, title of, 44
Bridgenorth, Robert of Bellême's castle
at, 121 ; besieged by Henry I., 124
Bridges, making and repair of, 272, 273
Bridgman, Sir Orlando, declares that
the king's ministers are responsible, 581
Bridgwater taken by Fairfax, 549 ; Mon-
mouth at, 637
Bridgewater Canal, the, 813
Brigantes, the, conquest of, 16
Bright, John, a leader in the Anti-
Corn-Law League, 924 ; opposes a
war with China, 955
Brihtnoth slain at Maldon, 79
Brihuega, surrender of Stanhope at, 692
Brill seized by exiles from the Nether-
lands, 449
Brindley designs the Bridgewater
Canal, 814
Bristol garrisoned by Robert of Glou-
cester, 134 ; stormed by Rupert, 538
Britain, its name derived from the
Britons, 6 ; tin trade opened to, 8 ;
Gauls and Belgians in, *ib.* ; Cæsar's invasion of, 11 ; trade of Gaul with, 12 ;
beginning of the Roman conquest of,
13-17 ; condition of the Roman province of, 19-22 ; emperors specially
connected with, 22 ; Christianity in,
23 ; ravaged by the Picts and Scots, 23 ;
and by the Saxons, 24 ; military divisions of, *ib.* ; end of the Roman government of, 25, 26 ; is deserted by the
Romans, 26 ; its organisation after the
departure of the Romans, *ib.* ; the English conquest of, 27-29

BUR

British Columbia joins the Dominion of
Canada, 967
Britons, the, succeed the Goidels, 6 ; languages spoken by the descendants of,
7 ; habits of, 9 ; religion of, 10 ; introduction of Roman manners amongst,
13 ; increased civilisation of, 21 ; non-
existence of a national feeling amongst,
22 ; ask Honorius in vain for help, 25 ;
the groans of the, 26 ; treatment of, by
the English conquerors, 29 ; are better
treated in the West, 31 ; slight modification of English language by them,
31 ; *see* Kymry
Brittany, its relation with Henry II.,
155 ; Edward III. sends forces to, 240 ;
annexed to France, 349
Broad-bottomed Administration, the,
739
Browne, Archbishop of Dublin, destroys
relics and images in Ireland, 402
Browne, Robert, founder of the Separat-
ists, 470
Brownists, *see* Separatists
Bruce, Edward, invades Ireland, 264
Bruce, Robert, claims the crown of Scotland, 215
Bruce, Robert, grandson of the preceding,
see Robert I.
Brunanburh, battle of, 63
Brut, Layamon's, 207
Brythons, *see* Britons
Bucer, Martin, teaches in England, 416
Buchan, Countess of, imprisoned, 224
Buckingham, Edward Stafford, Duke
of, supports Richard III., 338, 341 ;
executed as a rebel, 342
Buckingham, George Villiers, First
Duke of, becomes Marquis of Buckingham and Lord Admiral, 488 ; accompanies Charles to Madrid, 497 ; becomes Duke of Buckingham, and advocates war with Spain, 500 ; promises
money for foreign wars, 501 ; his
ascendency over Charles I., 502 ; tries
to pawn the crown jewels, 503 ; lends
ships to fight against Rochelle, 504 ;
impeachment of, 505 ; leads an expedition to Ré, 506 ; feeling of Wentworth
towards, 508 ; murder of, 510
Buckingham, George Villiers, Second
Duke of, in favour with Charles II.,
599 ; his sham treaty with France,
603 ; dismissal of, 608
Buckingham, Henry Stafford, Duke of,
execution of, 369
Buildings, improvement in, in Elizabeth's
time, 465
Bulgaria, becomes a tributary princi-
pality, 969 ; annexation of Eastern
Roumelia to, 970
Bunker's Hill, 783
Bunyan writes *Pilgrim's Progress*, 596
Burdett, Sir Francis, advocates uni-
versal suffrage, 879
Burford, West Saxon victory at, 53
Burghley, William Cecil, Lord, as Sir
William Cecil becomes the chief adviser

of Elizabeth, 429 ; urges Elizabeth to assist the Scotch Protestants, 433 ; becomes Lord Burghley and discovers the Ridolfi plot, 445 ; death of, 480

Burgos, siege of, 869

Burgoyne, General, capitulates at Saratoga, 786

Burgundians, party of the, opposed to the Armagnacs, 296, 299 ; are friendly to Henry V., 301

Burgundy, Charles the Rash, Duke of, marries the sister of Edward IV., 332 ; policy of, 336 ; is slain at Nancy, *ib.*

Burgundy, John the Fearless, Duke of, has the Duke of Orleans murdered, 296 ; allies himself with Henry V., 301 ; holds aloof in the campaign of Agincourt, 302 ; makes war upon the Armagnacs, 303 ; murder of, 305

Burgundy, Philip the Good, Duke of, joins the English against the Dauphin, 306 ; allies himself with the Duke of Bedford, 307 ; forms a league with Charles VII., 313 ; inherits territories in the Netherlands, *ib.*

Burhs erected by Eadward the Elder, 62

Burke, Edmund, enters Parliament, 772 ; his views on American taxation, 773 ; opposes parliamentary reform, 777 ; argues against taxing America, 780 ; his speech on economical reform, 789 ; passes a bill for economical reform, 795 ; the author of the India Bill of the Coalition, 806 ; his part in the impeachment of Hastings, 811 ; publishes *Reflections on the French Revolution*, 822

Burley, Sir Simon, executed, 280

Burnet, Gilbert, his conversation with William of Orange, 645

Burns, poetry and opinions of, 887

Burton, sentenced by the Star Chamber, 521

Bury St. Edmunds, foundation of the monastery at, 58 ; death of Svend at, 82 ; meeting of barons at, 181

Busaco, combat at, 867

Bute, Earl of, becomes Prime Minister, 766 ; resignation of, 768

Butler, author of *Hudibras*, 597

Butler, Bishop, writes *The Analogy*, 745

Buxton, Sir Thomas Fowell, pleads for the abolition of slavery, 910

Byng, Admiral, fails to relieve Minorca, 749 ; shot, 750

Byng, Sir George, defeats a Spanish fleet, off Cape Passaro, 709

Byron, Lord, poetry and death of, 888

Cabinet, the, its origin, 660 ; development of, 687 ; strengthened by the withdrawal of George I. from, 704

Cabul, taken by the British, 949 ; retreat of the British from, 950 ; Pollock retakes, *ib.*

Cade, Jack, rebellion of, 322

Cadiz, capture of, 464 ; Cecil's expedition to, 503

Cædmon, poetry of, 52

Cædwalla, allied with Penda, 46 ; is defeated by Oswald, 47

Caen, burial of William I. at, 114 ; stormed by Henry V., 303

Caerleon upon Usk, *see* Isca Silurum

Cæsar, Gaius Julius, makes war in Gaul and Germany, 10 ; twice invades Britain, 11

Caint, the, occupied by the Cantii, 8

Calais taken by Edward III., 243 ; besieged by the Duke of Burgundy, 313 ; loss of, 427 ; Elizabeth's hope of regaining, 436 ; the Armada takes refuge in, 462 ; Cromwell's anxiety to recover, 571

Calcutta, grows up round Fort William, 758 ; the Black Hole of, 762

Calder, Sir Robert, defeats a French fleet, 856

Caledonians, the, wars of Agricola with, 16

Calvin, his work at Geneva, 430

Calvinism influences Elizabethan Protestantism, 430

Cambrai, league of, 363 ; treaty of, 383

Cambridge, the Earl of, execution of, 301

Camden, Lord, dismissed, 776 ; *see* Pratt, Chief Justice

Campbell, Sir Colin, suppresses the Indian mutiny and becomes Lord Clyde, 954

Campeggio, Cardinal, appointed legate to hear the divorce case of Henry VIII., 382

Camperdown, battle of, 837

Campion lands in England, 453 ; execution of, 454

Campo Formio, peace of, 837

Camulodunum, Cunobelin's headquarters at, 12 ; Roman colony of, 13 ; captured by Boadicea, 15

Canada, possessed by France, 747 ; plan of Pitt for the conquest of, 753 ; conquest of, 756 ; abandonment of the French claim to, 766 ; failure of the Americans to overrun, 784 ; discontent in, 914 ; union between the provinces of, 916 ; enters into a federation called the Dominion of Canada, 967

Canning, enters Portland's Ministry, 857 ; sends a fleet to fetch the Danish ships from Copenhagen, 860 ; fights a duel with Castlereagh and resigns office, 865 ; succeeds Castlereagh as Foreign Secretary, 882 ; acknowledges the independence of the Spanish colonies in America, 883 ; sends troops to secure Portugal, 884 ; becomes Prime Minister, 892 ; death of, *ib.*

Canning, Lord, Governor-General of India, 952

Canningites, the, take office under Wellington, 893 ; resignation of, 895 ; join Lord Grey's Ministry, 901

CAN

Cannon, first use of, 242

Canrobert, Marshal, commands the French army in the Crimea, 946

Canterbury, Æthelberht's residence at, 38 ; Augustine preaches at, 39 ; foundation of the archbishopric of, 40 ; murder of Archbishop Thomas at, 150 ; Henry II. does penance at, 153 ; architecture of the choir of, 171 ; disputed election of the Archbishop of, 177

Canterbury Tales, the, 270

Cape Breton ceded by France, 766

Cape of Good Hope, first conquest of, 837 ; second conquest of, 848

Caractacus, defeat and flight of, 13 ; capture of, 14

Carausius claims to be emperor, 22

Carberry Hill, Mary's surrender at, 439

Cardinal College founded by Wolsey, 377, 383 ; *see* Christchurch

Carham, battle of, 84

Carisbrooke Castle, detention of Charles I. in, 556

Carlisle fortified by William II., 119

Carlyle, his *Sartor Resartus*, 941

Carnarvon, Edward I. builds a castle at, 210

Carolina, colonisation of, 629

Caroline, Queen (wife of George II.), her influence over her husband, 720 ; death of, 725

Caroline, Queen (wife of George IV.), separated from her husband, 881 ; failure of a bill for dissolving the marriage of, 882

Carriages and carts, 273

Carteret, Lord, his rivalry with Walpole, 718 ; foreign policy of, 732 ; wishes to combine Frederick the Great and Maria Theresa against France, 736 ; attempts to revive the policy of the Whigs of Anne's reign, 737 ; causes of his weaknesses, 738 ; his fall, 739

Cartwright advocates the Presbyterian system, 446

Cartwright, invents the power loom, 816

Carucage substituted for Danegeld, 162

Cash payments, suspension of, 835 ; resumption of, 879

Cashel, synod at, 152

Casket letters, the, 440

Cassel, battle of, 235

Cassiterides, the geographical position of, 8

Cassivelaunus, resistance to Cæsar by, 11

Castile, intervention of the Black Prince in, 255 ; united with Aragon, 349

Castlebar, the race of, 841

Castlemaine, Lady, uses her influence against Clarendon, 594

Castlereagh, Lord, secures a majority for the Irish Union, 842 ; enters Portland's ministry, 857 ; sends an expedition against Antwerp, 865 ; fights a duel with Canning, and resigns office, *ib.* ; is Foreign Secretary in Liverpool's Ministry, 877 ; protests against Metternich's policy, 882 ; suicide of, *ib.*

CHA

Catalonia, espouses the cause of the Archduke Charles, 684 ; abandoned to Philip V., 696

Câteau Cambresis, peace of, 431

Catesby plans Gunpowder Plot, 483

Catharine of Aragon, marriage of, 363 ; Henry VIII. grows tired of, 379 ; divorce suit against, 382 ; is divorced, 389 ; the sentence of Clement VII. in favour of, 390 ; death of, 395

Catharine of Braganza marries Charles II., 587

Catherine of Aragon married to Prince Arthur, 356 ; marriages proposed for, 357

Catherine of France marries Henry V., 306 ; marries Owen Tudor, 335

Catherine de Medicis, widow of Henry II., king of France, becomes regent, 433 ; takes part in the massacre of St. Bartholomew, 449

Catherine Howard, marriage and execution of, 401

Catherine Parr, marriage of, 401

Catholic Association, the, Act for the dissolution of, 895

Catholic emancipation, proposed by Pitt, 842 ; attitude of parties towards, 895 ; passing of an Act for, 896

Catholics, Roman, laws directed against, 453, 454 ; their position at the end of Elizabeth's reign, 475 ; increased persecution of, after Gunpowder Plot, 483 ; negotiation between James I. and Spain for the relief of, 488 ; tendency of Charles II. to support, 584 ; declaration for the toleration of, issued by Charles II., 587 ; persecuted about the Popish Plot, 616 ; efforts of James II. in favour of, 634, 638, 640

Cato Street Conspiracy, the, 881

Cattle-breeding, improvements in, 813

Catuvellauni, the, position of, 9 ; attacked by Cæsar, 11 ; subsequent history of, 12

Cavour, his negotiation with Napoleon III., 956

Cawnpore, besieged by Nana Sahib, 953 ; massacre at, *ib.*

Caxton, William, establishes a printing-press at Westminster, 358

Ceawlin overruns the Severn Valley, 35 ; defeated at Wanborough, 36

Cecil, Sir Edward, commands the Cadiz expedition, 503

Celibacy of the clergy, early opinion in favour of, 65 ; inculcated at Cluny, 67

Celtic Christianity, influence of, 47, 49

Celts, the, succeed the Iberians in Western Europe, 5 ; are divided into two stocks, 7 ; know their conquerors as Saxons, 29

Ceorls, distinguished from Eorls, 29 ; are the tillers of the soil, 30

Chancellor, the official position of, 127 ; becomes a judge, 260

Chancery, Court of, proposal of the Bare-

CHA

bone's Parliament to suppress, 567 ; reformed by Cromwell, 569 ; nature of the decisions of, 605

Chantries, Act for the dissolution of, 412 ; their income vested in the king, 415

Charles, the Archduke, styles himself Charles III. King of Spain, 682 ; his cause espoused by Catalonia, 684 ; enters Madrid, 692 ; succeeds to his brother's hereditary dominions, 692 ; elected Emperor, 695 ; *see* Charles VI. Emperor

Charles the Great, Emperor, 55, 63

Charles the Simple, king of the West Franks, 63 ; cedes Normandy to Hrolf, 80

Charles Albert, Elector of Bavaria, claims part of the dominions left to Maria Theresa, 732 ; elected Emperor, as Charles VII., 734

Charles Albert, King of Sardinia, attempts to drive the Austrians out of Italy, 934 ; defeat and abdication of, 936

Charles Edward, *see* Pretender, the Young

Charles Martel defeats the Mohammedans, 54

Charles I., intention of the Gunpowder plotters to blow up, 483 ; proposals of marriage for, 488 ; visits Spain, 497 ; is eager for war with Spain, 500 ; negotiation for marriage with Henrietta Maria, 501 ; becomes king and marries Henrietta Maria, 502 ; adjourns his first parliament to Oxford, *ib.* ; dissolves his first parliament and sends out the Cadiz expedition, 503 ; meets his second Parliament, *ib.* ; dissolves his second Parliament, 505 ; orders the collection of a forced loan, 506 ; meets his third Parliament, 508 ; consents to the Petition of Right, 509 ; claims a right to levy Tonnage and Poundage, 510 ; issues a declaration on the Articles, 512 ; dissolves his third Parliament, 513 ; his personal government, 514 ; levies knighthood fines, 515 ; insists on the reading of the *Declaration of Sports*, 517 ; levies fines for encroaching on forests, 523 ; levies ship-money, *ib.* ; imposes a new prayer-book on Scotland, 525 ; leads an army against the Scots, 526 ; consults Wentworth, 527 ; makes Wentworth Earl of Strafford, and summons the Short Parliament, 528 ; dissolves the Short Parliament, marches again against the Scots, and summons the Long Parliament, 529 ; assents to the Triennial Act, 530 ; signs a commission for Strafford's execution, 531 ; visits Scotland, 532 ; returns to England, 534 ; rejects the Grand Remonstrance, 535 ; attempts to arrest the five members, 536 ; fights at Edgehill, 537 ; his plan of campaign, *ib.* ; besieges Gloucester, and fights at New-

CHA

bury, 539 ; looks to Ireland for help, 541 ; sends Rupert to relieve York, 543 ; compels Essex's infantry to surrender at Lostwithiel, and fights again at Newbury, 544 ; is defeated at Naseby, 548 ; attempts to join Montrose, 549 ; sends Glamorgan to Ireland, *ib.* ; gives himself up to the Scots, 551 ; negotiates at Newcastle, *ib.* ; explains his plans to the Queen, 552 ; conveyed to Holmby House, 553 ; conducted by Joyce to Newmarket, 555 ; attempt of Cromwell to come to an understanding with, 555 ; takes refuge in the Isle of Wight, and enters into the *Engagement* with the Scots, 556 ; removed to Hurst Castle, 557 ; trial of, 559 ; execution of, 560

Charles II., as Prince of Wales, possesses himself of part of the fleet, 557 ; lands in Scotland, 563 ; escapes to France, 564 ; offers a reward for Cromwell's murder, 569 ; issues the declaration of Breda, 576 ; restoration of, 578 ; confirms *Magna Carta*, *ib.* ; character of, 579 ; leaves the government to Hyde, 580 ; revenue voted to, 582 ; approves a scheme of modified episcopacy, 583 ; keeps a small armed force, 584 ; retains three regiments on paying off the army, *ib.* ; profligacy of the court of, 586 ; issues a declaration in favour of toleration, 587 ; marriage of, and sale of Dunkirk by, *ib.* ; dismisses Clarendon, 594 ; favours the Roman Catholics, 598 ; thinks of tolerating dissenters, and supports Buckingham and Arlington, 599 ; agrees to the treaty of Dover, 600 ; supports the Cabal, 602 ; extravagance of, 603 ; issues a Declaration of Indulgence, 604 ; goes to war with the Dutch, 605 ; withdraws the Declaration of Indulgence, 606 ; assents to the Test Act, 607 ; dismisses Shaftesbury and makes peace with the Dutch, 608 ; supports Danby, 610 ; receives a pension from Louis XIV., 611 ; is interested in commerce, 612 ; refuses to make war on France, 613 ; threatens France with war, 614 ; dissolves the Cavalier Parliament, 616 ; dissolves the first Short Parliament, 617 ; supports his brother's claim to the crown, against Shaftesbury, 618 ; prorogues the second Short Parliament, 619 ; dismisses Shaftesbury, 620 ; dissolves the second and third Short Parliaments, 621 ; plot to murder, 625 ; death of, 627 ; constitutional progress in the reign of, *ib.*

Charles II., king of Spain, bad health of, 592 ; death of, 671

Charles III., king of Spain, renews the Family Compact, 766

Charles IV., king of France, death of, 232

Charles IV., king of Spain, his relations with his son, 862 ; dethroned, 863

CHA

Charles V., Emperor, as king of Spain becomes the rival of Francis I., 366; vast inheritance of, 369; is chosen emperor, *ib.*; goes to war with France, 371; captures Francis I. at Pavia, 372; liberates Francis I., 374; allies himself with Henry VIII., 405; makes peace with France at Crêpy, 406; defends Mary's mass, 417; abdication of, 426

Charles V., king of France, opposes the English in Spain, 255; summons the Black Prince to Paris, 256; renews the war against the English, *ib.*; avoids a battle, 257

Charles VI., Emperor, dies after leaving his dominions to Maria Theresa, 732

Charles VI., king of France, defeats the Flemings, 278; allies himself with Richard II., 282; loses his senses, 295; disinherits the Dauphin, 306; dies, 307

Charles VII., king of France, as Dauphin, falls into the hands of the Armagnacs, 303; is present at the murder of John, Duke of Burgundy, 305; is disinherited, 306; claims to succeed to the crown at his father's death, 307; his weakness, 309; is helped by the Maid of Orleans, 310; is crowned, 311; consents to a truce, 317; renews the war, 320

Charles VIII., king of France, succeeds to the crown, 348; invades Italy, 352; death of, 354

Charles IX., king of France, accession of, 433; takes part in the massacre of St. Bartholomew, 449; death of, 450

Charles X., king of France, overthrow of, 898

Charlotte, Princess, death of, 881

Charterhouse, the persecution of the monks of, 393

Chartists, the, demands of, 923; violence of, 924; meet on Kennington Common to present a monster petition, 935

Château Gaillard built by Richard I., 165; lost by John, 354

Chatham, Earl of, Prime Minister, 773; illness of, *ib.*; recovers his health, and takes up the cause of Wilkes, 776; resigns office, 774; declares for Parliamentary reform, 777; death of, 787; *see* Pitt, William (the elder)

Chaucer, Geoffrey, his *Canterbury Tales*, 270; influences of the Renascence on, 367

Cherbourg, expedition against, 753

Cheriton, battle of, 542

Chester (*see* Deva) submits to William I., 103

Cheyt Sing, Hastings demands a contribution from, 804

Chinon, Henry II. dies at, 157

Chippenham, treaty of, 59

Chivalry, 235

Chocolate, introduction of, 630

Christ Church, at Canterbury, privileges of, 177; expulsion of the monks of, 178

CLI

Christchurch, foundation of, 377, 383

Christian IV., king of Denmark, Buckingham's overtures to, 501, 504; defeated at Lutter, 505, 506

Christianity introduced into Britain, 23; into England, 39; character of early English, *see* England, the Church of

Chronicle, the, begun under Ælfred, 61; continued at Worcester, 68, 129; completed at Peterborough, 129

Church of England, *see* England, Church of

Churchill, Lord, *see* Marlborough, Duke of

Cinque Ports, the, 218

Cintra, convention of, 864

Cirencester, *see* Corinium

Cistercians, the, introduced into England, 129; decline of asceticism amongst, 167; are fined by John, 179

City of the violated treaty, the, 657

Ciudad Rodrigo, siege of, 869

Clare, Gilbert de, *see* Gloucester, Earl of

Clare, Richard de, *see* Strongbow

Clare, Richard de, *see* Gloucester, Earl of

Clarence, George, Duke of, brother of Edward IV., created a duke, 329; marries Warwick's daughter, and quarrels with Edward IV., 332; put to death, 336

Clarence, Lionel, Duke of, sent to Ireland 265

Clarence, Thomas, Duke of, brother of Henry IV., killed at Baugé, 306

Clarendon, Edward Hyde, first Earl of, as Edward Hyde is one of the leaders of the Anti-Presbyterian party in the Long Parliament, 533; becomes Lord Chancellor after the Restoration, 580: character of, *ib.*; created Earl of Clarendon, 587; is falsely supposed to be bribed, *ib.*; fall of, 594; escapes to France, 595

Clarendon, Henry Hyde, second Earl of, recalled from Ireland, 640

Clarendon, the Constitutions of, 144; the assize of, 146

Clarkson, publishes evidence against the slave trade, 823

Claudius, the Emperor, plans the conquest of Britain, 13

Claverhouse, *see* Graham, John

Clement VII., Pope, forms an Italian league against Charles V., 374; appoints legates to try the divorce suit of Henry VIII., 382; revokes the cause to Rome, 383; gives sentence in favour of Catharine, 390

Clergy, the, *see* Ecclesiastical Courts, England, Church of

Clergy, the country, 633

Clericis Laicos, the Bull named, 220

Clifford, Lord, stabs the Earl of Rutland, 328

Clifford, Thomas, Lord, a member of the Cabal, 602; probable suggester of

CLI

the Stop of the Exchequer, 604 ; resignation of, 607
Clinton, Sir Henry, fails to co-operate with Burgoyne, 786 ; takes Charleston, 788
Clive, Robert, his career in Northern India, 761 ; subjugates Bengal, 762 ; is astonished at his own moderation, 764 ; his return to England and second visit to Bengal, 801
Clontarf, repealers prohibited from meeting at, 928
Closterseven, the Convention of, 752
Cluny, clerical celibacy inculcated at, 67 ; reforms originated at, 107
Cnut, reign of, 83-85
Coaches, improvement in, 633
Coalition Ministry, the, of Fox and North, 800 ; of Pitt and the Whigs, 828 ; of the Whigs and Peelites, 943
Cobbett, pamphlets of, 879
Cobden, a leader of the Anti-Corn-Law League, 924 ; opposes a war with China, 955 ; suggests a commercial treaty with France, 958
Cobham, Eleanor, mistress and wife of the Duke of Gloucester, 315 ; does penance for witchcraft, 316
Coffee-houses, introduction of, 630
Coinage debased by Henry VIII., 409 ; further debased by Somerset, 416
Coke, Sir Edward, takes part in drawing up the Petition of Right, 508
Colchester, execution of the Abbot of, 400 ; reduced by Fairfax, 567
Colet promotes the study of Greek, and founds St. Paul's School, 367
Coligny, murder of, 449
College invents the Protestant flail, 615 ; condemned to death, 622
Colleges, first foundation of, at Oxford, 207
Colman disputes with Wilfrid, 50
Colonial expansion, 966
Colonies founded in Virginia and New England, 489 ; in Carolina, 629
Columba founds a monastery at Iona, 47
Columbus discovers the West Indies, 354
Combination laws, the, modification of, 886
Commerce between Britain and Gaul, 8, 12 ; between England and Gaul, 38 ; under the Angevin kings, 168 ; under Edward I., 211 ; under Edward III., 235, 236 ; under Henry VII., 351
Committee of Both Kingdoms, formation of, 542
Common Pleas, establishment of a separate Court of, 212
Common Prayer, the Book of, beginnings of, 409, 410 ; the first, of Edward VI., 415 ; the second, of Edward VI., 418 ; alterations in, in Elizabeth's reign, 429 ; Strickland proposes to amend, 445 ; generally accepted by the Parliamentary Presbyterians, 586

COM

Commons, the House of (*see* Parliament), finally separated from the Lords, 243 ; struggle of, against unparliamentary taxation, 244 ; importance of the constitution of, 245 ; supported by the Black Prince, 261 ; influence over the elections of, 281 ; proposes to confiscate Church property, 294 ; addressed by Edward IV., 329 ; Wolsey's appearance in, 371 ; made use of by Thomas Cromwell and Henry VIII., 389 ; Elizabeth's relations with, 444 ; Puritanism of, 445 ; growing strength of, 468 ; its tendencies to Puritanism rather than to Presbyterianism, 470 ; attack on monopolies by, 478 ; quarrels with James I., 482 ; anxious to go to war for the Palatinate, 490 ; votes a small supply, 491 : brings charges against Bacon, 495 ; is eager for war with Spain, 500 ; refuses supplies to Charles I., unless spent by counsellors in whom it confides, 502 ; impeaches Buckingham, 504, 505 ; insists on the Petition of Right, 508 ; claims Tonnage and Poundage, 510 : religious ideas prevailing in, 511 ; its breach with the king, 513 ; violent scene before the dissolution of, 514 ; formation of parties in, 532 ; scene in, at the passing of the Grand Remonstrance, 534 ; Presbyterian majority in, 546 ; new elections to, 551 ; a mob in possession of, 555 ; the Agitators propose to purge, 556 ; Pride's purge of, 557 ; declares itself supreme, *ib.* ; constitutes a high court of justice, 558 ; dissolved by Cromwell, 566 ; inquires into the expenditure of the crown, and impeaches Clarendon, 594 ; impeaches Danby, 616 ; the Exclusion Bill in, 617, 621 ; Tory majority in, 636 ; James II. attempts to pack, 641 ; discusses the abdication of James II., 646 ; attacks the Irish grants of William III., 670 ; imprisons the bearers of the Kentish Petition, 675 ; Walpole's determination to rely on, 710 ; corruption in, 714 ; establishment of the freedom of reporting the debates of, 779
Commonwealth, the, establishment of, 561
Communion table, Laud's wish to fix at the east end, 517 ; decision of the Privy Council on the position of, 519 ; removed by the soldiers, 529
Comprehension favoured by some of the clergy, 598 ; attempt of Charles II. to establish, 599
Comprehension Bill, the, is not passed, 651
Compton, Bishop of London, refuses to suspend Dr. Sharp, 639
Compton, Sir Spencer, thought of as Walpole's successor, 720 ; succeeds Walpole and becomes Earl of Wilmington, 731

COM

Compurgation, system of, 32 ; set aside by Henry II., 146, 147

Comyn, John (the Red), slain by Bruce, 224

Con, Papal agent at the court of Henrietta Maria, 521

Concord, attempt to seize arms at, 783

Confederate Catholics of Ireland, the, cessation of hostilities with, 541

Confederation of the Rhine, the, 856

Confirmatio Cartarum, 221

Congé d'élire, provision for the issue of, 391

Congress, of twelve colonies, 782 ; of thirteen colonies, 783

Connaught, proposed plantation of, 528

Conrad III., Emperor, takes part in the second Crusade, 157

Conservative party, the, origin of the name of, 909

Constance of Brittany marries Geoffrey, 155

Constantine takes an army from Britain, 25

Constantine, king of the Scots, allies himself with Eadward, 63

Constantine the Great becomes sole Emperor, 22 ; acknowledges Christianity as the religion of the Empire, 23

Constantinople taken by the Turks, 366

Constantius, the Emperor, 22

Constitutions of Clarendon, 144 ; renounced by Henry II., 153

Continental system, the, 859 ; failure of, 868

Conventicle Act, the, 588

Convention Parliament, the first, 577 ; the second, 646 ; the dissolution of the second, 656

Convocation of the province of Canterbury offers money for a pardon, 385 ; agrees to the submission of the clergy, 386

Convocations of the clergy vote money, 219

Conway, Edward I. builds a castle at, 210

Coote, Colonel (afterwards Sir Eyre), wins a victory at Wandewash, 764 ; defeats Hyder Ali at Porto Novo, 805

Cope, Sir John, defeated at Preston Pans, 740

Copenhagen, battle of, 845 ; bombardment of, 860

Corinium (*Cirencester*), West Saxon conquest of, 35

Cornish, the, derivation of the old language of, 7 ; submit to Ecgberht, 55

Corn-law, the, passing of, 875 ; modification of, 926

Cornwall, insurrection in, 415

Cornwallis, Lord, drives Washington out of New Jersey, 784 ; defeats Yates at Camden, 788 ; routs Green at Guilford, 792 ; surrenders at Yorktown, 794 ; Governor-General of India, 811 ; defeats Tippoo, 837 ; Lord-Lieutenant of Ireland, 841

CRO

Corporation Act, the, 585 ; repeal of, 895

Corporations, remodelling of the, 625

Corunna, battle of, 864

Cotentin, the, sold to Henry, 119

Cotton-famine, the, 959

Cotton-spinning, improvements in, 815

Council of State, the, appointment of, 561

County courts derived from the shire-moots, 141

Courtenay, Bishop of London, supported by the citizens against Lancaster, 263

Covenant, the Scottish National, 525, *see* Solemn League and Covenant

Covenanters, the rise of, 619 ; insurrection of, 620

Coverdale translates the New Testament, 396

Cowper, Lord, becomes Chancellor, 687

Craggs, Postmaster-General, poisons himself, 712

Craggs, Secretary of State, death of, 712

Cranfield, *see* Middlesex, Earl of

Cranmer, Archbishop of Canterbury, pronounces Catharine's marriage to be null, 389 ; is forced to dismiss his wife, 400 ; composes the English litany, 409 ; character and position of, 413 ; wishes to preserve the revenue of the chantries for the poor clergy, 415 ; tries to find common ground with the Zwinglian reformers, 416 ; leaves his mark on the Prayer Book, 418 ; supports Lady Jane Grey, 420 ; burnt, 426

Creçy, battle of, 241, 242

Crêpy, peace of, 406

Cressingham, Sir Hugh, governs Scotland in the name of Edward I., 219

Crimean War, the, origin of, 943 ; course of, 944–8

Crompton, invents 'the mule' for spinning, 815

Cromwell, Oliver, practical sagacity of, 539 ; introduces discipline in the Eastern Association, 540 ; defeats the royalists at Winceby, 542 ; fights at Marston Moor, 543 ; advocates toleration, *ib.* ; accuses Manchester, 544 ; becomes Lieutenant-General of the New Model Army, 545 ; cuts off the king's supplies, 547 ; wins the victory at Naseby, 548 ; reduces Winchester and Basing House, 549 ; proposes to leave England, 554 ; gives instructions to Cornet Joyce, 555 ; attempts to come to an understanding with Charles, *ib.* ; puts down a mutiny in the army, 556 ; suppresses a rising in Wales and defeats the Scots at Preston, 557 ; suppresses the Levellers, 562 ; his campaign in Ireland, *ib.* ; his victory at Dunbar, 563 ; his victory at Worcester, 564 ; dissolves the Long Parliament, 566 ; opens the Barebone's Parliament, 567 ; becomes Protector, 568 ; plots against, 569 ; ecclesiastical arrangements of, *ib.* ; convenes and dis-

CRO

solves his first Parliament, 570 ; establishes major-generals, *ib.* ; foreign policy of, 571 ; calls a second Parliament, 572 ; joins France against Spain, *ib.* ; dissolves his second Parliament, 573 ; makes war against Spain, *ib.* ; death of, 574

Cromwell, Richard, succeeds to the Protectorate, 574 ; abdicates, 575

Cromwell, Thomas, advises Henry VIII. to rely on the House of Commons, 385 ; becomes the king's secretary, and vicar-general, 393 ; attacks the monks of the Charterhouse, *ib.* ; inquires into the state of the monasteries, 394 ; attacks the greater monasteries, 397 ; execution of, 401

Cropredy Bridge, battle of, 544

Crown, the, *see* King

Crown Point taken by Amherst, 753

Crusade, the first, 120 ; the second, 157 ; the third, 161 ; against the Albigeois, 193 ; the seventh, 204

Cuba, reduction of, 766

Cumberland, origin of the name of, 37 ; annexed by William II., 119 ; left to David I., 133 ; regained by Henry II., 140

Cumberland, Duke of, heads the British column at Fontenoy, 739 ; sent against the Young Pretender, 741 ; defeats him at Culloden, 742 ; his cruelty to the Highlanders, *ib.*; being defeated at Hastenbeck, signs the Convention of Closterseven, 752

Cunedda, extensive rule of, 37

Cunobelin, government of, 12

Curia Regis, the, organised under Henry I., 127 ; strengthened by Henry II., 141 ; powers assigned by the Constitutions of Clarendon to, 145 ; orders the appointment of recognitors, 147 ; divided into three courts, 212

Customs on imports and exports under Edward I., 211, 221

Cutha, 35

Cymbeline, original of Shakespeare's, 12

Cynric captures Sorbiodunum, 34

Cyprus ceded to England, 970

DALHOUSIE, Earl of, policy of, as Governor-General of India, 950

Danby, Thomas Osborne, Earl of, as Sir T. Osborne, becomes Lord Treasurer, 607 ; policy of, 610 ; fails to pass a Non-resistance Bill, 611 ; promotes the marriage of William of Orange, 613 ; impeachment of, 616 ; imprisonment of, 617 ; liberated, 626 ; rises in support of William, 645 ; recommends that the crown be given to Mary, 646

Danegeld, levy of, 81 ; abolition of, 143

Danelaw, the, formation of, 59

Danes, the, invade England, 58 ; make peace with Ælfred, 59 ; extent of the settlements of, 62 ; are amalgamated

DES

with the English, 64 ; relations of Dunstan with, 67 ; reappear as invaders, 79 ; conquer England, 81–83 ; settle in Ireland, 152

Darc, Jeanne, delivers Orleans, 310 ; conducts Charles VII. to Rheims, 311 ; martyrdom of, 312 •

Darien expedition, the, 671

Darnley, Henry Stuart, Lord, marries Mary, 438 ; murder of, 439

Darvel Gathern, burning of the wooden figure of, 398

Darwin, his *Origin of Species*, 940

David I., king of the Scots, invades England, 131

David II. (Bruce), king of Scotland, 232 ; takes refuge with Philip VI., 234 ; restoration of, 240 ; taken prisoner at Nevill's Cross, 242 ; restored by Edward III., 252

David, brother of Llewelyn, executed, 140

David, Earl of Huntingdon, 215

David, St., piety of, 42

Davison sends the warrant for Mary's execution, 457 ; dismissal of, 458

De Grasse, Admiral, blockades Yorktown, 794 ; defeated by Rodney, 795

Declaration of Breda, *see* Breda, Declaration of

Declaration of Independence, the American, 784

Declaration of Indulgence issued by Charles II., 604 ; withdrawn by Charles II., 606 ; issued by James II., 640 ; reissued, 642

Declaration of Rights, the, 647

Declaration of Sports, the, ordered to be read in churches, 517

Decorated style, the, 247

Defender of the Faith, title of, 379

Degsastan, Æthelfrith's victory at, 42

Deira, formation of the kingdom of, 36 ; is merged for a time in North-humberland, 41 ; accepts Christianity, 46 ; is finally merged in North-humberland, 48 ; Danish kingdom of, 62, 63

Delhi, siege of, 953 ; recovery of, 954

Denain, battle of, 696

Deorham, battle of, 35

Derby, arrival of the Highlanders at, 740

Derby, Earl of (son of John of Gaunt), opposes Richard II., 279 ; defeats the Duke of Ireland, 280 ; becomes Duke of Hereford, and is banished, 283 ; succeeds to the Duchy of Lancaster, 284 ; and forces Richard II. to abdicate, 285 ; *see* Henry IV.

Derby, Earl of, becomes Prime Minister, 938 ; resignation of, 939 ; Prime Minister for the second time, 956 ; Prime Minister for the third time, 961 ; resignation of, 962

Dermot invites Strongbow to Ireland, 152

Derwentwater, Earl of, beheaded, 705

Desmond, Gerald Fitzgerald, Earl of, insurrection and death of, 453

DES

Despensers, the, 228, 229
Deva, Roman colony of, 14, 19
Devizes, surrender of the castle of, 134
Devolution, the war of, 593
Devonshire, insurrection in, 415
Devonshire, Duke of, becomes First Lord of the Treasury in succession to Newcastle, 749
Devonshire, William Cavendish, Earl of, rises in support of William of Orange, 645
Dewanni of Bengal, Behar, and Orissa granted to the East India Company, 801
Dialogus de Scaccario, 167
Dickens, his *Pickwick Papers*, 940
Digby, John, Lord, his mission to Germany, 497
Diocletian reorganises the Empire, 22
Dispensing power, the, claimed by Charles II., 604; acknowledged by the judges, 639
Disraeli, attacks Peel, 929, 930; the real leader of the Protectionists in the House of Commons, 931; becomes Chancellor of the Exchequer and gives his approbation to Free-trade, 938; resignation of, 939; is again Chancellor of the Exchequer, and brings in a Bill for Parliamentary reform, 956; passes the second Reform Bill, 961; becomes Prime Minister, 962; resignation of, *ib.*; becomes Prime Minister a second time, 966; made Earl of Beaconsfield, 969; *see* Beaconsfield, Earl of
Dissenters the, origin of their name, 585; Charles II. issues a declaration for the toleration of, 587; Conventicle Act against, 588; Five Mile Act against, 590; favour of Charles II. to, 599; reception of the Declaration of Indulgence by, 640; Toleration Act passed in favour of, 651; attacked in the Sacheverell riots, 691; passing of the Occasional Conformity Act against, 695; the Schism Act passed against, 699; partial repeal of acts directed against, 710; repeal of the Test and Corporation Acts affecting, 895
Dissenting Brethren, the five, 543
Divine Right of Kings, doctrine of the, 619
Domesday Book, 111
Domestic life in Eadgar's time, 75
Domfront occupied by Henry, 119
Dominic, St., 190
Dominicans arrive in England, 191
Donald Bane made king of the Scots by the Celts, 119
Dorchester, abandonment of the see of, 107
Dorset, Marquis of, his relations with Richard III., 338
Douai, College at, 453
Dover, treaty of, 600
Drake, Francis, lands at Nombre de Dios, 448; vows to sail on the Pacific

DUT

449; his voyage round the world, 450; (Sir Francis) singes the king of Spain's beard, 458; has a command against the Armada, 460; pursues the Armada, 462; sacks Corunna, and fails before Lisbon, 464; death of, *ib.*
Dramatic writers of the Restoration, 598
Dreux, battle of, 436
Drogheda, slaughter at, 562
Druids, character of the, 10; resist Suetonius, 14
Drumclog, skirmish at, 620
Drummond, Thomas, his career as Under-Secretary in Ireland, 916
Dublin, Danish settlement in, 152; attempt to seize, 533
Du Châtel, Tannegui, murders the Duke of Burgundy, 305
Dudley, *see* Empson and Dudley
Dudley, Lord Guilford, marries Lady Jane Grey, 420; executed, 423
Du Guesclin, Bernard, supports Henry of Trastamara, 255; his mode of fighting with the English, 256
Dunbar, Balliol defeated at, 219; battle of, 563
Duncan, Admiral, blockades the Dutch in the Texel, 836; defeats the Dutch at Camperdown, 837
Duncan II., king of the Scots, 120
Dundee, Viscount, John Graham of Claverhouse, gathers the Highland clans for James II., 652; killed at Killiecrankie, 653
Dunes, the, battle of, 573
Dunkirk, Cromwell wishes Spain to place in his hands, 571; taken from Spain by Cromwell's troops, 573; abandoned by Charles II., 587; France engages to destroy the fortifications of, 696; France regains the right of fortifying, 798
Dunkirk House, 587
Dunning carries a motion against the influence of the Crown, 789
Dunse Law, Scottish army on, 526
Dunstable, marriage of Catharine of Aragon annulled at, 389
Dunstan, character and work of, 65; banished by Eadwig, 67; becomes Eadgar's Minister, *ib.*; his attitude towards the monks, 68; supports Eadward's succession, 78; death of, 79
Dupleix, hostile to Le Bourdonnais, 760; his career in India, 761; returns to France, 762
Dupplin, Edward Balliol's victory at, 234
Durham, architecture of the choir and galilee of, 171
Durham, temporary suppression of the see of, 418; celebration of the mass in the cathedral of, 441
Durham, Earl of, his mission to Canada, 916
Dutch Republic, the, foundation of, 449; abolition of the Stadholderate in, 565; war between the English Common-

wealth and, *ib.* ; peace with, 569 ; first war between Charles II. and, 589 ; military weakness of, 591 ; treaty of Breda with, 593 ; takes part in the Triple Alliance, 599 ; combination of England and France against, 600 ; towns to be taken from, *ib.* ; the second war between Charles II. and, 605 ; resists Louis XIV., *ib.* ; animosity of Shaftesbury against, 606 ; peace made by England with, 608 ; makes peace with France at Nymwegen, 614 ; Marlborough's relations with, 678 ; effect of the war of the Spanish Succession on, 697 ; resists the right of search, 792 ; makes peace with Great Britain, 798 ; receives the name of the Batavian Republic, 835 ; its fleet defeated at Camperdown, 837

Eadgar, reign of, 67
Eadgar, king of the Scots, 121
Eadgar the Ætheling, early years of, 90 ; chosen king, 98 ; is abandoned, 100
Eadgyth married to Eadward the Confessor, 87
Eadgyth married to Henry I., 122 ; is known as Matilda, 124
Eadmund Ironside, 83
Eadmund, king of East Anglia, killed by the Danes, 58
Eadmund, king of the English, 63
Eadred, king of the English, 64
Eadward the Confessor, his life in Normandy, 85 ; is chosen king, 86 ; his relations with Godwine, 87 ; makes William his heir, 88 ; dies, 91
Eadward the Elder, reign of, 62 ; his relations with the Scots, 63
Eadward the Ætheling, death of, 90
Eadward the Martyr, 78
Eadwig, reign of, 64 ; his quarrel with the clergy, 65 ; his marriage and death, 67
Eadwine, king of North-humberland, greatness of, 43 ; marries Æthelburh, 44 ; is converted and slain, 46
Eadwine, son of Ælfgar, becomes Earl of the Mercians, 90 ; is present at Eadgar's election, 98 ; submits to William, 102 ; is murdered, 103
Eadwinesburh, *see* Edinburgh
Ealdhelm as a builder and teacher, 51
Ealdormen, the, are the leaders of the English conquerors, 30 ; preside over the folk-moot, 33 ; growing power of, 73 ; their position under Æthelred the Unready, 79
Ealdred, Archbishop of York, crowns William I., 100
Earl, title of, derivation of, 64
Earldoms under Cnut, 83 ; diminished after the Norman Conquest, 105
Early English architecture, 171
East Anglia, first settlement of, 28 ; growth of, 36 ; comparative weakness

of, 41 ; its relations with Ecgberht, 55; overrun by the Danes, 58
East India Company, the, charter granted to, 758 ; early acquisitions of, *ib.* ; receives the zemindary of the district round Calcutta, 764 ; receives the dewanni of Bengal, Behar, and Orissa, 801 ; North's Regulating Act organising the powers of, 802 ; bill directed by Fox and Burke against, 806 ; Pitt's restrictions on, 808 ; complete overthrow of the authority of, 954
East Saxons establish themselves to the north of the Thames, 28 ; capture London, 35 ; *see* Essex
Easter, dispute on the mode of keeping, 50
Eastern Association, the, formation of, 539 ; Cromwell's activity in, 540 ; Manchester in command of the army of, 542
Ebbsfleet, landing of the Jutes at, 27 ; landing of Augustine at, 39
Ecclesiastical Commission, the, established by James II., 639 ; abolition of, 644
Ecclesiastical courts, jurisdiction of, 106; conflict of Henry II. with, 142 ; attacks on, 385
Ecclesiastical Titles Bill, the, 937
Ecgberht, at the court of Charles the Great, 53 ; becomes king of the West Saxons, and over-lord of the other kingdoms, 55
Economical Reform, bill for, 789 ; passing of a bill for, 795
Edgehill, battle of, 537
Edinburgh, Eadwine builds the castle of, 43 ; occupied by the Scots, 68 ; burnt by Hertford, 409 ; treaty of, 433 ; riot in St. Giles's in, 525 ; Montrose executed at, 563 ; surrenders to Cromwell, *ib.*; the Duke of Gordon holds out in the castle of, 652 ; the Young Pretender welcomed at, 740
Edmund Crouchback, second son of Henry III., named king of Sicily and Naples, 196 ; supposed primogeniture of, 286
Education in the time of Ælfred, 61 ; in the time of Dunstan, 65 ; carried on at Oxford, 167, 207 ; public action of the Melbourne ministry in providing for, 920 ; Forster introduces a new system of, 963
Edward I., appeal of the Knights Bachelors to, 199 ; taken prisoner at Lewes, 201 ; defeats Earl Simon at Evesham, 203 ; takes part in the seventh Crusade, 204 ; becomes king, 208 ; constitutional position of, 209 ; his dealings with Wales, 210 ; finance of, 211 ; judicial reforms and legislation of, 212 ; arranges for a personal union between England and Scotland, 214 ; erects the Eleanor crosses, 215 ; awards the Scottish crown to John Balliol, 216 ; his relations with Philip IV., 218 ; sum-

EDW

mons the Model Parliament, 218 ; his
first conquest of Scotland, 219 ; grants
the *Confirmatio Cartarum,* 220 ; his
second conquest of Scotland, 221 ; in-
corporates Scotland with England, 222;
his third conquest of Scotland, and
death, 224
Edward II., birth of, 210 ; succeeds to
the crown, 224 ; marriage of, 225 ; resistance of the barons to, *ib.*; defeated
at Bannockburn, 226 ; overthrows
Lancaster and effects a constitutional
settlement, 228 ; deposed and murdered, 229
Edward III., accession and marriage of,
231 ; does homage to Philip VI., 232 ;
sets up Edward Balliol in Scotland
and begins war with France, 234 ;
allies himself with the Emperor and
the cities of Flanders, 235 ; encourages
trade, 236 ; is named Imperial Vicar,
237 ; claims the crown of France, 239 ;
wins the battle of Sluys, *ib.* ; marches
through the north of France, 240 ;
wins the battle of Crecy, 241, 242 ;
takes Calais, 243 ; constitutional progress under, *ib.*; restores David Bruce,
252 ; makes peace with France, 253 ;
enters on a fresh war with France,
256
Edward IV., as Earl of March, takes
part in the battle of Northampton, 326 ;
wins the battle of Mortimer's Cross,
and is acknowledged by the Londoners
as king, 328 ; wins the battle of Towton, and is crowned, 329 ; marries
Elizabeth Woodville, and promotes
her kindred, 331 ; allies himself with
Burgundy, 332 ; loses and recovers
the crown, 334 ; invents benevolences,
335 ; invades France, 336 ; puts Clarence to death, 336 ; death of, 337
Edward V. succeeds to the throne, 337 ;
lodged in the Tower, 340 ; deposed,
341 ; murdered, 342
Edward, Prince of Wales, *see* Black
Prince, the
Edward, Prince of Wales, son of Henry
VI., birth of, 323 ; slain at Tewkesbury, 334
Edward, Prince of Wales, son of Richard
III., death of, 342
Edward VI., birth of, 397 ; accession
of, 412 ; precocity of, 419 ; death of,
420
Egypt, Bonaparte's expedition to, 837 ;
the French compelled to evacuate,
844 ; Mehemet Ali's rule of, 884 ; subjected to the dual control of France
and England, 970 ; England assumes
a protectorate over, 971
Ejectors, Commission of, 569
Eldon, Lord, holds that meetings in
support of Radical reform are treasonable, 880
Eleanor of Aquitaine marries Henry II.,
137 ; imprisonment of, 155 ; takes part
with John against Arthur, 174

ELI

Eleanor of Castile, wife of Edward I.,
accompanies her husband on the Crusade, 204 ; death of, 214
Eleanor of Provence marries Henry III.,
192
Eleanor, sister of Henry III., marries
Simon de Montfort, 193
Election petition, the Chippenham,
730
Eleven Members, the, excluded from the
House of Commons, 555
Eliot, Sir John, attacks Buckingham,
504 ; compares Buckingham to
Sejanus, 505 ; his policy compared
with that of Wentworth, 508 ; vindi-
cates the privileges of the House, 512 ;
imprisonment and death of, 514
Elizabeth, daughter of Edward IV.,
proposed marriage of the Dauphin to,
336 ; proposed marriage of Richard
III. to, 342 ; marries Henry VII., 345
Elizabeth, daughter of James I., intention of the Gunpowder plotters to
crown, 483 ; married to the Elector
Palatine, 488
Elizabeth, Queen, birth of, 392 ; her
succession acknowledged, 411 ; sent to
the Tower and afterwards removed to
Woodstock and Hatfield, 423 ; accession of, 428 ; character and policy of,
ib. ; modification of the title of, 429 ;
plays off France and Spain against one
another, 431 ; hesitates to assist the
Scotch Protestants, 432 ; assists the
Lords of the Congregation, 433 ; her
ill-treatment of Catherine Grey, 435 ;
contrasted with Mary, Queen of Scots,
ib. ; hopes to recover Calais by assisting the Huguenots, 436 ; appoints commissioners to examine the case against
Mary, 440 ; detains Mary a prisoner,
and suppresses a rising in the North,
441 ; excommunicated by Pius V.,
ib. ; negotiates a marriage with the
Duke of Anjou, 443 ; her attitude towards the Puritans and towards Parliament, 444 ; the Ridolfi plot against,
445 ; proposes to marry the Duke of
Alençon, 446 ; intervenes in Scotland
on behalf of James VI., 450 ; refuses
to restore Drake's plunder, 451 ; her
treatment of Ireland, 452 ; kisses the
Duke of Alençon, 454 ; plot of Allen
and Parsons to murder, *ib.* ; Throgmorton's plot to murder, 456 ; Babington's plot to murder, 457 ; hesitates
to allow the execution of the Queen of
Scots, *ib.* ; dismisses Davison, 458 ;
her triumph at the defeat of the
Armada, 462 ; allies herself with
Henry IV., 464 ; shows favour to
Essex, *ib.* ; erects the Court of High
Commission, 470 ; sends Essex to
Ireland, 475 ; turns against Essex,
476 ; withdraws monopolies, 478 ;
nature of the work of, 479 ; death of,
480

Elizabethan architecture, 465

Ellenborough, Lord, sends Sir Charles Napier to conquer Sindh, 950

Elmet conquered by Eadwine, 43

Emma marries Æthelred, 81

Empire, the Western, revived by Charles the Great, 55

Empson and Dudley, exactions of, 357 ; execution of, 363

Encumbered Estates Act, the, 934

Engagement, the, between Charles I. and the Scottish Commissioners, 556

England, early social and political institutions of, 29-32 ; contrasted with Gaul, 37 ; commerce with Gaul renewed by, 38 ; Christianity introduced into, 39 ; growing power of three kingdoms in, 41 ; character of the later conquests in, 44 ; political changes in, 45 ; spread of Christianity in, 49 ; influence of Church Councils on the political unity of, 52 ; Ecgberht's overlordship in, 55 ; attacks of the Northmen and Danes on, 56 ; its condition under Ælfred, 60 ; its relations with Scotland, 63, 68 ; development of the institutions of, 69 ; Danish conquest of, 79-83 ; Norman conquest of, 96-103 ; Norman constitution of, 113 ; civil war in, 134 ; pacification of, 137 ; administrative reforms of Henry II. in, 140 ; made tributary to the Papacy, 180 ; military reforms in, 154 ; effect of the reign of Henry II. on, 158 ; constitutional result of the administration of Hubert Walter in, 163 ; growth of learning in, 167 ; growth of commerce in, 168 ; architectural changes in, 170 ; the Barons' Wars in, 200-203 ; architectural and literary growth in, 206, 207 ; complete national unity of, 208 ; completion of the Parliamentary constitution of, 218, 220, 228, 243 ; relieved of tribute to the Papacy, 258 ; social and moral condition of, during the Wars of the Roses, 330

England, the Church of, Wilfrid's influence on, 50 ; parochial organisation of, *ib.*; its close connection with the State, 52; councils of, *ib.*; organisation of, after the Norman Conquest, 106 ; its relations with Stephen, 134 ; and with Henry II., 149 ; result of the Angevin reigns on, 166 ; Papal exactions resisted by, 194 ; payments exacted from, 197 ; temporary Parliamentary representation of the clergy of, 219 ; taxation resisted by the clergy of, 220; social condition of, 236; supports Henry IV., 291; members of noble families in the episcopate of, *ib.*; procures a statute for burning heretics, 292 ; proposal to confiscate the property of, 294 ; relations of Henry VIII. with, 377 ; dealings of Henry VIII. with, 386 ; the clergy acknowledge the king supreme head of, 386 ; becomes more national, 391 ; Parliament acknowledges the king to be

supreme head of, 393 ; Cranmer's position in, 413 ; ecclesiastical changes in, 414 ; issue of the first Prayer Book of Edward VI. for, 415 ; Zwinglian teaching in, 416 ; issue of the second Prayer Book of Edward VI. for, 418 ; reconciled to the see of Rome, 424 ; Elizabeth's settlement of, 429 ; position of, during Parker's archbishopric, 430 ; Presbyterian movement in, 446 ; Presbyterianism adopted by the Assembly of Divines for, 543 ; restoration of episcopacy in, 583 ; proposal to establish a modified episcopacy in, *ib.*; promise of James II. to protect, 634

English, the, origin of the name of, 28 ; nature of their conquest of Britain, 29 ; village settlements of, *ib.* ; division of ranks among, *ib.* ; effect of the conquest of Britain on the language of, 31; early political organisation of, *ib.* ; early judicial system of, 32 ; position of, under William I., 104 ; support William II., 115 ; support Henry I., 124 ; cease to be distinguished from Normans, 155 ; reappearance of their language in literature, 207 ; predominance of their language, 258

Eorls, distinguished from Ceorls, 29 ; their relation to Gesiths, 30

Erse, a Goidelic language, 7

Eskimos, compared with palæolithic men, 3

Essay on Woman, 770

Essex, Arthur Capel, Earl of, suicide of, 625

Essex, Frances, Countess of, divorce and remarriage of, 486

Essex, Robert Devereux, second Earl of, joins in the capture of Cadiz, 464 ; sent to Ireland, 475 ; placed in confinement on his return. 476 ; insurrection of, 477 ; trial and execution of, 478

Essex, Robert Devereux, third Earl of, divorce of, 486 ; appointed general of the Parliamentary army, 537 ; commands at Edgehill, *ib.* ; takes Reading, 538 ; relieves Gloucester and commands at the first battle of Newbury, 539 ; escapes from Lostwithiel, 544 ; resigns, 545

Essex, Saxon settlement in, 28 ; is dependent on Kent, and accepts Christianity, 40 ; relapses into heathenism, 41 ; comparative weakness of, *ib.*

Eugene, Prince, fights in Italy, 680 ; combines with Marlborough at Blenheim, 682 ; raises the siege of Turin, 684 ; attacks Toulon, 689 ; combines with Marlborough at Malplaquet, 690 ; recalled by the Archduke Charles, 695 ; defeated at Denain, 696

Eustace, Count of Boulogne, visits Eadward the Confessor, 87

Eustace, son of Stephen, death of, 137

Evesham, battle of, 203

Exchequer, the, organised by Roger of Salisbury, 127 ; disorganised under

EXC

Stephen, 134; reorganised under Henry II., 140; establishment of a separate Court of, 212

Excise Bill, the, brought in by Walpole, 722; withdrawn, 724

Exclusion Bill, the, brought in, 617; rejected by the House of Lords, 621; lost by dissolution, *ib.*

Exeter taken by William I., 102; besieged by Fairfax, 549

Exeter, Henry Courtenay, Marquis of, executed, 399

Exhibition, the Great, 937

Expenditure of the Crown, parliamentary inquiry into, 593

FACTORY ACT, the first, 911; extension of the, 927

Factory system, the, 876

Faddiley, battle of, 35

Fairfax, Ferdinando, second Lord, defeated at Adwalton Moor, 538

Fairfax, Thomas, third Lord Fairfax, as Sir Thomas Fairfax, is defeated at Adwalton Moor, 538; wins a victory at Nantwich, 542; appointed General of the New Model army, 545; relieves Taunton, 547; commands at Naseby, 548; follows up his successes, 548, 549; reduces the king's army in Cornwall, 550; proposed as commander of the forces retained after the disbandment of the army, 553; as Lord Fairfax, puts down the rising in Kent and takes Colchester, 557; absents himself from the High Court of Justice, 559; refuses to command in the war against Charles II., 563; joins Monk, 576

Falaise, Treaty of, 154; abandoned by Richard I., 159

Falkirk, Wallace defeated at, 222

Falkland, Lucius Cary, Viscount, one of the leaders of the anti-Presbyterian party in the Long Parliament, 533; death of, 539

Family Compact, the, signature of, 725; renewal of, 737; second renewal of, 766

Faukes de Breauté, banishment of, 187

Fawkes, Guy, takes part in the Gunpowder Plot, 483

Felton, John, affixes the Pope's excommunication to the door of the Bishop of London's house, 442

Felton, John, murders the Duke of Buckingham, 510

Fenians, the, 962

Ferdinand I., Emperor, inherits the German territories of Charles V., 421

Ferdinand II., Emperor, loses and regains the crown of Bohemia, 490

Ferdinand V., king of Aragon, marries Isabella of Castile, 349; Italian wars of, 363; conquers Navarre, 364; death of, 366

Ferdinand VII., king of Spain, restored to power by a French army, 882

FOU

Ferdinand of Brunswick, Prince commands in Hanover, 752; defeats the French at Minden, 756

Ferry Bridge, skirmish at, 429

Feudal dues, bargain offered by James I. for, 484; abolition of, 582

Feudality, early forms of, 81; after the Norman Conquest, 104; organised by William I., 113; Flambard's further organisation of, 116; ideas of Edward I. on, 214

Field of the Cloth of Gold, the, 369

Fielding, writes *Tom Jones*, 746

Fifth-Monarchy men, 567; oppose Cromwell, 569

Finchley, the march to, 740

Fire of London, the, 592

First of June, battle of the, 828

Fisher, Bishop of Rochester, opposes the divorce of Henry VIII., 382; sent to the Tower, 392; execution of, 394

Fitzgerald, Flogging, 840

Fitzmaurice, Sir James, lands in Ireland, 452

Fitz-Osbern, William, oppresses the English, 102

Fitzwilliam, Earl, enters Pitt's cabinet, 828; his mission to Ireland, 832

Five Articles of Perth, the, 525

Five Boroughs, the, 62

Five Knights' case, the, 507

Five Members, the, 535; brought back to Westminster, 536

Five Mile Act, the, 590

Flambard, Ranulf, tyranny of, 116; imprisonment of, 122; escapes, 124

Flamsteed, astronomer, 632

Flanders, commercial intercourse with, 211; Edward I. in, 221; alliance of Edward III. with, 235; falls under the control of France, 278

Fleetwood named General by the army, 575

Flemings emigrate to Wales, 128; introduced as weavers by Edward III., 236

Fleurus, Luxembourg's victory at, 657

Fleury, Cardinal, ministry of, 718

Flodden, battle of, 364

Florida, ceded by Spain to England, 766; restored to Spain, 798

Folk-moot, functions of the, 33

Fontenoy, battle of, 739

Forest, Friar, burnt, 398

Forests, the, fines for encroaching on, 523; the king's claims on, limited, 531

Forster, introduces a new system of education, 964; introduces a bill for the use of the ballot, 966; Irish policy of, 971; resignation of, *ib.*

Fort Duquesne, built by the French, 748; taken by the British, 753

Fort St. George built, 758

Fort William built by East India Company, 758

Fotheringhay, execution of Mary Stuart at, 458

Fountains Abbey, 129

Fox, Charles James, supports Parliamentary reform, 789; character of, 790; refuses to serve under Melbourne, 798; coalesces with North, 800; supports Pitt's motion on Parliamentary reform, 801; brings forward an India Bill, 806; his 'martyrs,' 808; his conduct in the debates on the Regency Bill, 811; sympathises with the revolutionists in France, 822; continues in opposition, 828; excluded from Pitt's second ministry, 848; Secretary of State in the ministry of All the Talents, 855; death of, *ib.*

Fox, Henry, becomes leader of the House of Commons, 747; resigns office, 749; accepts a lucrative appointment, 751

Fox, Richard, Bishop of Winchester, minister of Henry VII. and Henry VIII., 363

France, social condition of, 235; miserable state of, 251, 252; friendship of Richard II. with, 282; reign of Louis XII. in, 363; attack of Henry VIII. on, 364; in alliance with England, 366; invaded by Henry VIII., 371; peace with, 374; Mary at war with, 426; recovery of Calais by, 427; civil wars in, 436–443; Philip II. supports the League in, 464; allied with James I., 501; Charles I. breaks with, 506; Charles I. makes peace with, 514; allied with Cromwell against Spain, 572; Danby's policy directed against, 610; war of William III. with, 657; peace made at Ryswick with, 667; grand alliance formed against, 675; war conducted by Marlborough against, 678; decline in the military power of, 682; peace made at Utrecht with, 696; pacific policy of the Whigs towards, 707; recovery of military strength by, 725; takes part in the war of the Austrian succession, 733; peace of Aix-la-Chapelle with, 743; her possessions in North America, 747; embarks on the Seven Years' War, 749; peace with, 766; secretly assists the Americans, 786; openly allies herself with America, 787; her navy master of the sea, 788; her fleet compels the surrender of Cornwallis at Yorktown, 794; makes peace with Great Britain, 798; commercial treaty with, 810; antecedents of the revolution in, 820; calling of the States-General in, 821; progress of the revolution in, *ib.*; rise of a warlike feeling in, 824; declares war against Austria and Prussia, 824; establishment of a republic in, 825; victorious in the Austrian Netherlands, *ib.*; at war with England and the Dutch republic, 826; Reign of Terror in, *ib.*; end of the Reign of Terror in, *ib.*; makes peace with Prussia and Spain, 829; establishment of the Directory in,

830; Malmesbury sent to negotiate a peace in, 834; establishment of the Consulate in, 839; Treaty of Amiens with, 846; renewed war with, 848; establishment of the Empire in, 850; restoration of Louis XVIII. in, 871; restoration of Napoleon in, 874; second restoration of Louis XVIII. in, 875; establishment of Louis Philippe in, 898; supports Mehemet Ali, 922; the *entente cordiale* with, 927; establishment of the second Republic in, 934; Louis Napoleon President of the Republic in, 955; commercial treaty with, 959; German invasion of, 964; third Republic established in, *ib.*

Francis I., king of France, his rivalry with Charles V., 366–369; meets Henry VIII. on the Field of the Cloth of Gold, 369; goes to war with Charles V. about Milan, 371; captured at Pavia, 372; liberated, 374

Francis II., king of France, married as Dauphin to Mary Queen of Scots, 413; accession and death of, 433

Francis II., king of Hungary, afterwards emperor, at war with France, 824

Francis of Assisi, St., 190

Francis, Philip, the probable author of *Junius*, 775; his opposition to Hastings, 803

Franciscans, the, constitution of, 190; arrive in England, 191 ;

Frederick I., Barbarossa, Emperor, supports an anti-pope, 145

Frederick II., Emperor, excommunication of, 194; death of, 195

Frederick II., king of Prussia, claims Silesia, 733; defeats the Austrians at Mollwitz, 734; obtains the cession of Silesia, 735; enters on the second Silesian war, 737; fights in Saxony and Bohemia, 752; defeats the French at Rossbach and the Austrians at Leuthen, *ib.*; fights at Zorndorf and Hochkirch, 753; continues the struggle, 756; complains that England has abandoned him, and makes peace at Hubertsburg, 767

Frederick V., Elector Palatine, marries Elizabeth, daughter of James I., 488; elected King of Bohemia, 490; driven out of Bohemia, *ib.*; diplomatic efforts of James I., in favour of, 496; loses the Palatinate, 497

Frederick, Prince of Wales, quarrels with his father and puts himself at the head of the opposition, 725

Free-trade, Adam Smith promulgates the doctrine of, 810; Pitt's measures in support of, *ib.*; steps taken by Huskisson and Robinson in the direction of, 886

Freemen, gradual disappearance of, 69

French, the, Dukes of, 63; Hugh Capet, king of, 80

French Revolution, the; *see* France

FRI

Friars, the, orders of, 190; arrive in England, 191
Friedland, battle of, 858
Frith burnt, 390
Frobisher holds a command against the Armada, 460
Fuentes d'Onoro, battle of, 869
Furniture, improvement of, in Elizabethan houses, 465
Fyrd, the, a general army of the villagers, 30; Ælfred reforms, 60; comparative disuse of, 69; retained after the Norman Conquest, 106; *see* Assize of Arms

Gaelic a Goidelic language, 7
Gage, General, sent as Governor of Massachusetts, 782; recalled, 784
Gainas, the, settlements of, 28
Gainsborough, origin of the name of, 28
Galway, County, Wentworth punishes the jury of, 528
Galway, Earl of, occupies Madrid, 684; retreats to Valencia, 685; defeated at Almanza, 689; *see* Ruvigny, Marquis of
Gardiner, Bishop of Winchester, sent to Rome by Henry VIII., before he is a bishop, 382; opposes far her innovations, 411; excluded from the Council, 412; sent to the Tower, 414; deprived of his see, 416; made Lord Chancellor by Mary, 421
Garter, the order of the, institution of, 246
Gascoigne, Chief Justice, 299
Gates, General, defeated at Camden, 788
Gaul, trade of Britain with, 8, 12; persistency of Roman civilisation in, 37; renewal of trade with, 38
Gauls arrive in Britain, 8
Gaveston, Piers, favoured by Edward II., 224; execution of, 226
General warrants declared illegal, 769, 770
Geneva, establishment of Calvin's system at, 430
Gentry, the country, 633
Geoffrey, Count of Anjou, marries the Empress Matilda, 131; conquers Normandy, 136
Geoffrey Fitz-Peter, Justiciar, 163
Geoffrey, son of Henry II., marries the heiress of Brittany, 155; dies, 156
George I. proclaimed king, 701; places the Whigs in office, 702; effect of his withdrawal from cabinet meetings, 704; becomes unpopular, 705; dismisses Townshend, 709; death of, 718
George II., accession of, 718; keeps Walpole in power, 719; supports Maria Theresa, 735; defeats the French at Dettingen, 737; laments the death of Henry Pelham, 746; insists on the execution of Byng, 750; death of, 764
George III., accession and aims of, 765; forces Pitt and Newcastle to resign, 766; puts himself at the head of the new Tory party, 767; his

GLA

method of governing, 768; his struggle with Grenville, 770; dismisses Rockingham, and places Chatham in office, 773; makes Lord North Prime Minister, 776; has public opinion on his side against the Americans, 777; resolves to put down resistance in Boston, 780; refuses to admit Chatham to office except as North's subordinate, 787; declares against dividing the empire, 787; attributes the dissipations of his eldest son to Fox, 800; obtains the rejection of Fox's India Bill, 806; his relations with Pitt, 808; mental derangement of, 811; thanksgiving for the recovery of, 812; attacked by a mob, 830; protests against Catholic emancipation, 833; refuses his consent to Pitt's proposals on behalf of the Irish Catholics, 842; short mental derangement of, 843; abandons the title of King of France, 846; insists on the exclusion of Fox from Pitt's second ministry, 848; expels from office the ministry of All the Talents, 857; his remark on the bombardment of Copenhagen, 862; becomes permanently insane, 868; death of, 880
George IV., accession of, 880; separated from his wife, 881; his interview with Goderich, 893; death of, 898
George, Prince of Wales (son of George III.), dissipated life of, 800; bill for conferring the regency on, 811; his misconduct towards his father, 812; becomes Regent, 868; becomes King, 880; *see* George IV.
George of Denmark, Prince, deserts James II., 645
Geraldine rebellion, the, 402
Gerard murders William of Orange, 456
Gerard and Vowel's plot, 569
German confederation, the, 873
German empire, foundation of a new, 964
Germany, attempt of the Frankfurt parliament to unite, 934; dissolution of the Frankfurt parliament in, 936; formation of a North German Confederation in, 963; goes to war with France, 964
Gesiths, the, personal devotion of, 30; their relation to the Ceorls, *ib.*; their name changed to that of Thegns, 31
Gewissas, the, combine with Jutes, 28; *see* West Saxons
Ghent, Jacob van Arteveldt at, 235; Philip van Arteveldt at, 278; pacification of, 450; peace of, 873
Gibraltar, surrenders to Sir G. Rooke, 682; assigned to England by the Treaty of Utrecht, 696; siege of, by the French and Spaniards, 798
Ginkell, General, commands in Ireland, 656
Giraldus Cambrensis, 167
'Give us our eleven days!' 744
Gladstone, as a minister under Peel, 926; becomes Chancellor of the

GLA

Exchequer in the Aberdeen ministry, 943; opposes a war with China, 955; Chancellor of the Exchequer in Palmerston's second ministry, 956; supports the commercial treaty with France, 958; becomes Prime Minister, 962; disestablishes the Protestant Church of Ireland, *ib.*; passes an Irish Land Act, 963; abolishes purchase in the army, 964; foreign policy of the ministry of, 965; resignation of, 966; Prime Minister for the second time, 970; resignation of, 972

Glamorgan, Edward Herbert, Marquis of, his secret mission to Ireland, 549

Glanvile, Ranulf de, captures William the Lion, 154; writes the first English law-book, 167

Glasgow, the Assembly of, 526

Glastonbury, Dunstan, abbot of, 65; proceedings of Dunstan at, 106

Glastonbury, the Abbot of, executed, 400

Glencoe, massacre of, 654

Glendower, Owen, heads the Welsh, 293; decline of the power of, 296

Glevum (Gloucester), Saxon conquest of, 35

Gloucester, Duke of (brother of Edward IV.), *see* Richard III.

Gloucester, Duke of, Humphrey (brother of Henry V.), appointed Protector, 307; marries Jacqueline of Hainault, 308; quarrels with Cardinal Beaufort, 309, 314; his relations with Eleanor Cobham, 315; advocates a war policy, 317; death of, 318

Gloucester, Duke of (son of Queen Anne), death of, 671

Gloucester, Duke of, Thomas, son of Edward III., heads the opposition to Richard II., 279; driven from power, 280; murdered, 282

Gloucester, Earl of (Gilbert de Clare), allies himself with Earl Simon, 200; becomes one of the three Electors, 201; joins Edward against Simon at Evesham, 203

Gloucester, Earl of, *see* Robert

Gloucester, Earl of (Richard de Clare), quarrels with Earl Simon, 199; joins Earl Simon, and dies, 200

Gloucester, raising of the siege of, 539

Gloucester, *see* Glevum

Goderich, Viscount, becomes Prime Minister, 892; resignation of, 893; *see* Robinson, Frederick J., and Ripon, Earl of

Godfrey of Bouillon, 121

Godfrey, Sir Edmund Berry, murder of, 615

'Godly party,' the, 544

Godolphin, Lord, connected with Marlborough, 677; his financial ability, 678; turns to the Whigs, 684; supports the Union with Scotland, 685

Godwine becomes Earl of the West Saxons, 84; supports Harthacnut, 85;

GRE

charged with the murder of Ælfred 86; governs under Eadward, 87; outlawed, 88; return and death of, 89

Goidels, the, a branch of the Celts, 6; languages spoken by the descendants of, 7

Gondomar, Count of, negotiates a Spanish alliance with James I., 488, 490

Good Parliament, the, 262

Gordon, General, murder of, 972

Gordon riots, the, 792

Goring, George Goring, Lord, defeated at Langport, 548

Gough, General, defeats the Sikhs on the Sutlej, 951; becomes Lord Gough, is checked at Chillianwalla, and defeats the Sikhs at Gujerat, *ib.*

Grafton, Duke of, First Lord of the Treasury, 773; resignation of, 776

Graham of Claverhouse, John, attempts to suppress the Covenanters, 620

Graham, Sir James, resigns office, 912; a member of Peel's cabinet, 926

Grammar-schools, foundation of, 419

Granada, conquest of, 349

Grand Alliance, the, signed by William III., 675

Grand Remonstrance, the, 534

Grattan leads the movement for the legislative independence of Ireland, 795; resists the Union, 842

Graupian Hill, the, battle of, 17

Gray, his *Elegy* quoted by Wolfe, 755

Great Contract, the, 484

Great Council, the, composition of, 113; urges William to name an archbishop, 117; summoned to Rockingham, 118; becomes unimportant under Henry I., 126; frequently consulted by Henry II., 141; meets at Clarendon, 144; remonstrates with Henry III., 188, 192; refuses money to Henry III., 194; begins to be known as Parliament, 195; meets at York, 529; *see* Parliament

Great Mogul, the break-up of the empire of, 758

Greece, national uprising in, 884; battle of Navarino fought for the liberation of, 893; acquires Thessaly, 970

Greenwich Hospital, foundation of, 663

Greenwood hanged, 472

Gregorian calendar, the, introduced into England, 743

Gregory I., Pope, finds English slaveboys at Rome, 28; sends Augustine to England, 39

Gregory VII., Pope, his relations with William I., 107

Gregory IX., Pope, demands money from England, 194

Grenville, George, character of, 768; becomes Prime Minister, 769; issues a general warrant, *ib.*; offends George III., 770; carries the Stamp Act, 771; dismissal of, *ib.*; asserts that the House of Commons has no right to

GRE

incapacitate Wilkes, 774; death of, 779

Grenville, Lord, replies to Bonaparte's overture for peace, 840; refuses to join Pitt's second ministry, 848; becomes Prime Minister, 855

Grey, advocates Parliamentary reform, 827; continues in opposition, 828; *see* Grey, Earl

Grey, Arthur, Lord, slaughters foreign soldiers at Smerwick, 453

Grey, Earl, becomes Prime Minister, 901; resignation of, 912

Grey, family of, favoured by Edward IV., 331

Grey, John de, nominated Archbishop of Canterbury by John, 177; unpopularity of, 178

Grey, Lady Catherine, marriage and imprisonment of, 435

Grey, Lady Jane, is proclaimed Queen, 420; executed, 423

Grey, Lord Leonard, becomes Lord Deputy of Ireland, 402; conquers a great part of Ireland, 404

Grey, Sir Thomas, execution of, 301

Grindal, Archbishop of Canterbury, suspension of, 450

Grocyn encourages the study of Greek at Oxford, 367

Grossetête, Robert, Bishop of Lincoln, opposes Henry III., 194, 195; death of, 197

Grote, his *History of Greece*, 941

Gualo, legate of Honorius III., 185

Guerillas, the Spanish, 869

Guiana, Raleigh's voyage to, 489; British, conquest of, 859

Guicowar, the, a Mahratta chief, 802

Guinegatte, battle of the Spurs at, 364

Guise, Francis, Duke of, takes Calais, 427; murder of, 436

Guise, Henry, Duke of, heads the French Catholics, 443; conspires to murder Elizabeth, 454; heads the League, 456; murdered, 464

Guisnes, taken by the French, 427

Guizot becomes Prime Minister in France, 922

Gunpowder Plot, the, 483

Guthrum defeats Ælfred, 58; makes peace at Wedmore, 59; cedes London to Ælfred, *ib.*; extent of the kingdom of, 62

Gwledig, British title of, 26; title thought to have been assumed by Eadwine, 44

Gwynedd under Cædwalla, 46

Gyrth, Earl of East Anglia, 89

Habeas Corpus Act, 617, suspension of, 877; end of the suspension of, 879

Habeas corpus, writ of, dispute whether it ought to show the cause of imprisonment, 507

Hadrian, the Emperor, wall of, 17

Hague, the, conference at, 690

HAS

Hales, destruction of the phial at, 398

Hales, Sir Edward, holds an appointment by the dispensing power, 639

Halidon Hill, the Scots defeated at, 234

Halifax, George Savile, Earl, afterwards Marquis of, supports the Duke of York's succession, 618; persuades the House of Lords to reject the Exclusion Bill, 621; advises Charles II. to summon Parliament, 626; dismissed by James II., 638

Hailey, astronomer, 632

Hamilton, James Hamilton, Duke of, as Marquis of Hamilton dissolves the Assembly of Glasgow, 526; is defeated at Preston, 557

Hamilton family support Mary, 440

Hamilton of Bothwellhaugh assassinates the regent Murray, 441

Hampden resists ship-money, 524; calms the House of Commons after the passing of the Grand Remonstrance, 534; one of the five members, 535; death of, 538

Hampton Court Conference, the, 482

Hanover, George I. anxious to secure, 709; Pitt attacks Carteret for his devotion to the interests of, 738; Newcastle provides for the defence of, 748; Pitt asks for a grant for the protection of, 750; overrun by the French, 752; Pitt's measures for the defence of, *ib.*; seized by Bonaparte, 848; offered alternately to England and Prussia, 855

Harfleur taken by Henry V., 302; secured by the Duke of Bedford, 303

Hargreaves invents the spinning-jenny, 815

Harlech Castle, surrender of, 550

Harley, Sir Robert, comes into office as a moderate Tory, 681; obtains the rejection of an Occasional Conformity Bill, 682; turned out of office, 687; is a member of a purely Tory ministry, 691; recommends the creation of twelve peers, 695; becomes Lord Treasurer and Earl of Oxford, 696; *see* Oxford, Earl of

Harold Hardrada invades England, 94; is slain at Stamford Bridge, 96

Harold, son of Cnut, chosen king by the Mercians, 85; death of, 86

Harold, son of Godwine, earl of the West Saxons, 89; rules England under Eadward, 90; chosen king, 91; his oath to William, 93; marches into the North, 94; defeats Harold Hardrada at Stamford Bridge, 95; defeated and slain at Senlac, 98

Harthacnut, chosen king of the West Saxons, 85; comes to England, and dies, 86

Hastings, battle of, *see* Senlac

Hastings, John, claims a third of Scotland, 215

Hastings, Lord, turns against Richard III., 339; execution of, 340

HAS

Hastings, Marquis of, Governor-General of India, 948

Hastings, Warren, appointed Governor of Bengal, 801 ; his authority diminished by the Regulating Act, 803 ; the execution of Nuncomar happened at an opportune time for, *ib.* ; engages in a struggle with the Mahrattas, 804 ; demands a large contribution from Cheyt Singh, *ib.* ; enforces the payment of money by the Begums of Oude, 805 ; character of his rule, *ib.* ; resignation of, 808 ; impeachment of, 811

Havelock relieves Lucknow, 953

Havre occupied and abandoned by Elizabeth, 436

Hawke, Admiral, sent out against the French, 748 ; defeats the French in Quiberon Bay, 756

Hawley, General, defeated at Falkirk, 740

Hazlerigg, Sir Arthur, one of the five members, 535

Heads of the Proposals, the, 555

Heathfield, battle of, 46

Heavenfield, battle of, 47

Hedgeley Moor, battle of, 331

Helie de la Flêche opposes William II., 121

Hengist, traditional leader of the Jutes, 27

Henrietta Maria, Queen, negotiations for the marriage of, 500 ; marries Charles I., 502 ; a papal agent at the Court of, 521 ; carries abroad the crown jewels, 536 ; urges Charles not to abandon the militia, 552

Henry I. receives no land at his father's death, 114 ; his wars with his brothers, 119 ; accession and marriage of, 122 ; puts down insurrections, 124 ; conquers Normandy, 125 ; his dispute with Anselm, *ib.*; judicial reforms of, 127 ; makes war in Normandy, 129 ; loses his only son, 130 ; death of, 131

Henry II., early career of, 136 ; marries Eleanor, 137 ; character of, 138 ; advances Thomas of London, 140 ; administrative system of, 140-142 ; appoints Thomas archbishop, and quarrels with him, 143 ; draws up the Constitutions of Clarendon, 144 ; persecutes Thomas, 145 ; issues the Assize of Clarendon, 146 ; renews the itinerant justices, and inquires into the conduct of the sheriffs, 148 ; has young Henry crowned, 149 ; uses strong language against Thomas, 150 ; goes to Ireland, 151 ; renounces the Constitutions of Clarendon, 153 ; does penance, 154 ; issues the Assize of Arms, *ib.*; his domestic troubles, 155 ; takes the cross and dies, 157 ; his weakness on the Continent and strength in England, 158 ; literary vigour under, 167

Henry II., king of France, allied with Scotland, 413 ; his attitude towards Elizabeth, 432 ; death of, 433

HEN

Henry III., minority of, 185 ; favours Poitevins under the influence of Peter des Roches, 187 ; marries Eleanor of Provence and favours Provençals, 192 ; frequently renews the Great Charter, 192 ; quarrels with Simon de Montfort, 193 ; surrenders Poitou, 194 ; is opposed by Parliament, 195 ; hopes to make his second son King of Sicily, 196 ; misgovernment of, 197 ; consents to the Provisions of Oxford, 198 ; recovers power, 200 taken prisoner at Lewes, 201 ; last years of, 204 ; progress of the country in the reign of, 206

Henry III., king of France, proposes, as Duke of Anjou, to marry Elizabeth, 443 ; accession of, 450 ; murder of, 464

Henry IV. (*see* Derby, Earl of) claims the throne, 286 ; meets with difficulties, 289 ; leans on the Church, 291 ; rebellion of the Percies against, 293 ; keeps James I. as a hostage, 295 ; suppresses a rebellion in the North, 296 ; quarrels with the Prince of Wales, 298 ; death of, 299

Henry IV., king of France, his succession to the French crown disputed, 456 ; overpowers the League, 464

Henry IV., Emperor, resists Gregory VII., 108

Henry V., career of, as Prince of Wales, 297-299 ; domestic policy of, 299 ; claims the crown of France, 300 ; defeats the French at Agincourt, 302 ; conquers Normandy, 303 ; forms an alliance with the Duke of Burgundy, and is declared heir to the French throne, 306 ; marriage and death of, *ib.*

Henry V., Emperor, marries Matilda, 131

Henry VI., accession of, 307 ; crowned at Westminster and Paris, 312 ; marriage of, 317 ; supports Somerset, 323 ; insanity of, *ib.*; recovery and renewed insanity of, 324 ; second recovery of, *ib.*; attempts to reconcile the parties, 325 ; declared a traitor by Edward IV., 329 ; restoration of, 333 ; murder of, 334

Henry VI., Emperor, his relations with Richard I., 161, 162

Henry VII., as Earl of Richmond, genealogy of, 334 ; invades England, 343 ; defeats Richard III. and becomes king, *ib.* ; supported by the middle classes, 345 ; suppresses Lord Lovel's rising, 346 ; his relations with Brittany and France, 348 ; assailed by Perkin Warbeck, 350 ; sends Poynings to Ireland, 352 ; restores Kildare to the Deputyship, 352 ; secures Warbeck, *ib.* ; effects an alliance with Scotland, 356 ; encourages maritime enterprise, 356 ; fills his treasury, 357 ; his alliance with the Archduke Philip, 358 ; last years and death of, 358

Henry VIII., character of, 361 ; marries Catharine of Aragon, 363 ; foreign policy of, *ib.* ; promotes Wolsey. *ib.* ; favours More, 368 ; meets Francis I. on the Field of the Cloth of Gold, 369 ; has Buckingham executed, *ib.* ; invades France, 371 ; his views on his relations with the Church, 377 ; is named Defender of the Faith, 379 ; thinks of obtaining a divorce, *ib.* ; urges Clement VII. to divorce him, 382 ; demands a sentence of nullity, 383 ; makes a victim of Wolsey, *ib.* ; gains the support of the House of Commons, 385 ; consults the universities, and charges the clergy with being under a *præmunire, ib.* ; obtains from Convocation the title of Supreme Head, 386 ; has no tenderness towards heresy, 388 ; obtains the Act of Annates, *ib.* ; marries Anne Boleyn, and is divorced, 389 ; attempts to suppress heresy, and obtains fresh powers from Parliament, 390 ; sends More and Fisher to the Tower, 392 ; Act of Supremacy in favour of, 393 ; dissolves the smaller monasteries, 394 ; marries Jane Seymour, 395 ; issues the ten articles, and authorises the translation of the Bible, 396 ; deals hardly with the Pilgrimage of Grace, 397 ; begins the confiscation of the greater monasteries, *ib.* ; attacks relics and images, 398 ; presides at Lambert's trial, 399 ; obtains from Parliament the six articles, 399 ; marries and divorces Anne of Cleves, 400-401 ; marries and beheads Catherine Howard, 401 ; marries Catherine Parr, *ib.* ; his government of Ireland, 401-404 ; takes Boulogne, 405 ; makes war with Scotland, 406 ; debases the coinage, 409 ; death of, 411
Henry of Blois, Bishop of Winchester, 131 ; declares against Stephen, 134
Henry of Trastamara, 255
Henry, Prince of Wales, son of James I., intention of the Gunpowder plotters to blow up, 483 ; death of, 488
Henry, son of Henry II., coronation of, 149 ; rebellion of, 153 ; death of, 156
Henry the Fowler, his mode of warfare, 79
Hereford, besieged by the Scots, 549
Hereford, Duke of, *see* Derby, Earl of
Hereford, Earl of, *see* Bohun, Humfrey
Heresy held to be punishable by the Common Law, 419
Heretics, Statute for burning, 292
Hereward, rising of, 103
Herrings, battle of the, 309
Hertford, Earl of, *see* Somerset, Edward Seymour, Duke of
Hexham, battle of, 331
High Commission, the, Court of, erection of, 470 ; its activity in the reign of Charles I., 520 ; abolition of, 531

High Court of Justice, the, proposal to constitute rejected by the Lords, 557 ; constituted by the Commons, 558
Highland Host, the, 619
Hii, *see* Iona
Hill, Rowland, post-office reform advocated by, 918
Hlaford, *see* Lord
Hoche attempts to invade Ireland, 834
Hogarth, paintings of, 746
Hohenlinden, battle of, 840
Holkar, a Mahratta chief, 802 ; induced to sign subsidiary treaty, 859
Holland, province of, its influence in the Dutch Republic, 589
Holles takes part in holding down the Speaker, 514 ; one of the five members, 535
Holmby House, Charles I. at, 553 ; Charles I., removed from, 555
Holmes, Admiral, attacks the Dutch fleet, 605
Holy Alliance, the so-called, 883
Holy League, the, 363
Homildon Hill, battle of, 293
Honorius III., Pope, protects Henry III., 185
Hooker, his *Ecclesiastical Polity*, 472
Hooper, Bishop of Gloucester, refuses to wear vestments, 417 ; receives the bishopric of Worcester, 418 ; speaks of his dioceses as the king's, 420 ; burnt, 424
Hopton, Sir Ralph, commands the Royalists in Cornwall, 537, 538 ; fights on Lansdown, 538 ; takes and loses Arundel Castle, 542 ; is defeated at Cheriton, *ib.*
Horne Tooke, Hardy, and Thelwall, acquittal of, 829
Horsa, a traditional leader of the Jutes, 27
Horses used to carry warriors to battle, 75
Horsley, Bishop, saying of, 830
Hotham, Sir John, shuts the gates of Hull against Charles I., 537
Hough, chosen President of Magdalen College, 641
Houghton, prior of the Charterhouse, execution of, 394
Hounslow, James II. reviews regiments at, 643.
House-carls, 83, 93
Howard of Effingham, Charles Howard, Lord, commands the fleet against the Armada, 460 ; takes part in the capture of Cadiz, 464
Howard of Escrick, Edward Howard, Lord, informs against the Whigs, 625
Howe, Lord, defeats the French fleet on the first of June, 828 ; persuades the mutineers at Spithead to return to their duty, 836
Howe, Sir William, commands the British army in America, and occupies New York, 784
Hrolf, Duke of the Normans, 80

HUB

Hubert de Burgh holds Dover Castle, 185 ; administration of, 186-188
Hubert Walter, administration of, 163 ; death of, 177
Hubertsburg, peace of, 767
Hudibras, 597
Hudson's Bay territory assigned to England, 696
Hugh Capet, 80
Hugh of Lusignan rises against John, 174
Hugh the Great, Duke of the French, 63
Huguenots, the, supported by Elizabeth, 436 ; Buckingham lends ships to fight against, 504
Hull, its gates shut against Charles I., 537 ; besieged by Newcastle, 542
Humble Petition and Advice, the, 573
Hundred Days, the, 874
Hundred Years' War, the, 234
Hundred-moot, the, organisation of, 31 ; judicial functions of, 32 ; gradual decay of, 72
Hundreds, early political organisation of the, 31
Hunt, 'Orator,' attempt to arrest, 879
Huntingdon, David I. holds the earldom of, 132
Huntley, George Gordon, fourth Earl of, overpowered by Mary, 437
Hurst Castle, Charles I. imprisoned in, 557
Huskisson, supports the repeal of the combination laws, 886 ; takes office under Wellington, 893 ; death of, 909
Hwiccas, the, split off from the West Saxons, 36
Hyde, Anne, marries the Duke of York, 6c8
Hyder Ali, makes himself master of Mysore, and ravages the Carnatic, 804; death of, 805

Iberians, the, 5
Ibrahim Pasha, desolates Peloponnesus, 884 ; gains victories over the Turks, 921
Iceni, the geographical position of, 8 ; take part with the Romans, 13 ; roused to insurrection by Boadicea, 15
Ictis, probably identified with Thanet, 8
Ida becomes king of Bernicia, 36
Idle, the, Eadwine's victory on, 43
Images, destruction of, 398
Impeachment of Latimer and Lyons, 262 ; of Suffolk, 322 ; of Bacon, 496 : of Buckingham, Montague, and Manwaring, 511 ; of Strafford, 530 ; of twelve bishops, 535 ; of the five members, 536; of Laud, 546 ; of Danby, 616 ; pardon not to be pleaded in bar of, 617
Impositions, the New, first levy of, 484 : question of the legality of, 505 ; act preventing the king from levying, 531
Inclosures, growth of, 320 ; More's attack on, 368 ; Ket's rebellion directed against, 416 ; cessation of complaints against, 464

IRE

Income-tax, imposed by Pitt, 840 ; removed, 876 ; imposed by Peel, 926
Independents, the, originally known as Separatists, 543 ; driven from the House, and reinstated by the army, 555 ; are unpopular after the Restoration, 584
India, break-up of the empire of the Great Mogul and first settlements of the East India Company in, 758 ; condition of, after the death of Aurungzebe, 759 ; influence of the French in the south of, 760 ; struggle between Clive and Dupleix in, 761; the subjugation of Bengal in, 762 ; struggle with Lally in, 764 ; Clive's return to suppress extortion in, 801 ; Hastings assists the Nawab of Oude to subdue the Rohillas in, 802 ; the Regulating Act alters the government of, *ib.* ; Pitt's Bill for the government of, 808 ; defeat of Tippoo in, 837 ; overthrow of Tippoo in, 838 ; Wellesley's policy of subsidiary treaties in, 859 ; the Marquis of Hastings in, 948 ; the northwestern frontier of, *ib.* ; Afghanistan invaded from, 949 ; conquest of Sindh in, 950 ; the Sikh wars in, 951 ; Dalhousie's annexations in, *ib.* ; the Sepoy army in, 952 ; mutiny of the Sepoy army in, 953 ; end of the authority of the East India Company in, 953 ; the Queen's proclamation to the princes and people of, 954
India Bill, the, of Fox and Burke, 806 ; of Pitt, 808
Ine, his rule in Wessex, 53
Infanta, the, *see* Maria, the Infanta
Inkerman, battle of, 946
Innocent III., Pope, influences the election of Stephen Langton, 177 ; puts England under an interdict, and reduces John to submission, 178-180 ; declares against the barons, 181-184 ; establishes the Friars, 190
Innocent IV. becomes Pope, 195 ; wins over Henry III., 196
Inquisition of the Sheriffs, the, 148
Instrument of Government, the, 568
Intercursus Magnus, the, 351
Interdict, England under, 178
Inverlochy, battle of, 547
Investiture, William I. claims the right of granting, 108 ; Anselm's position with regard to, 125 ; compromise on, 126
Iona, missionaries sent forth from, 47
Ipswich, Wolsey's college at, founded, 377 ; sold by Henry VIII., 383
Ireland, ancient language of, 7 ; Druids in, 10; Christianity introduced into, 47; state of civilisation in, 151 ; partially conquered by Henry II., 152 ; results of the conquest of, 264 ; weakness of the English colony in, 265 ; under Lancaster and York, 346 ; under Henry VII., 350, 351 ; under Henry VIII., 401 ; legislation of Henry VIII. in, 402 ;

IRE

destruction of relics and images in, *ib.* ; conquest of a great part of, 404 ; Henry VIII. named king of, *ib.* ; under Edward VI. and Mary, 451 ; introduction of English colonists into, 452 ; landing of Sir James Fitzmaurice in, *ib.* ; the slaughter at Smerwick, and the Desmond rising in, 453 ; O'Neill's rising in, 475 ; Essex's invasion of, *ib.*; Mountjoy's conquest of, 478 ; plantation of Ulster in, 484 ; Wentworths government of, 527, 528 ; army collected by Strafford in, 529 ; insurrection in, 533 ; massacre in, 534 ; the confederate Catholics in, 541 ; Glamorgan's mission to, 549 ; Rinuccini in, 550 ; soldiers asked to volunteer for, 553 ; Cromwell in, 562 ; Ireton and Ludlow in, 567 ; act of settlement in, 595 ; James II. supported by the Celtic population of, 640 ; struggle between James II. and William III. in, 654 ; penal laws in, 686 ; destruction of the commerce of, *ib.* ; restrictions on commerce in, *ib.*; volunteers in, 796 ; legislative independence conceded to, *ib.* ; Pitt's scheme for a commercial union with, 810 ; defective constitutional arrangements in, 831 ; rise of the United Irishmen in, 832 ; votes given to the Catholics of, *ib.*; mission of Lord Fitzwilliam to, *ib.*; revolutionary outbreak impending in, 833 ; Hoche attempts to invade, 834 ; outrages in, 840 ; rebellion in, 841 ; parliamentary union with, 842 ; struggle for Catholic emancipation in, 895 ; policy of Lord Grey's government towards, 909 ; Thomas Drummond's management of, 916 ; failure of O'Connell's repeal movement in, 928 ; Peel's legislation for, *ib.*; famine in, 931 ; Peel's bill for the protection of life in, *ib.*; public works in, 932 ; emigration from, 933 ; relation between landlord and tenant in, *ib.*; Encumbered Estates Act in, 934 ; Smith O'Brien's attempted rising in, 935 ; Fenian rising in, 962 ; disestablishment of the Protestant Church of, *ib.*; Land Act of the first Gladstone ministry in, 963 ; rejection of a bill on university education in, 966 ; demand of Home-Rule for, 970 ; Land Act of the second Gladstone ministry in, *ib.*; bill for the protection of life and property in, *ib.*; murders by the Invincibles in, *ib.*

Ireland, Duke of (*see* Oxford, Earl of), supports Richard II., 279 ; is condemned to death, but escapes, 280

Ireton draws up *The Heads of the Proposals*, 555 ; in Ireland, 563

Irish grants of William III. attacked by the House of Commons, 670

Irish Parliament, the, summoned by James II., 655 ; represents, under William III., only the English colony, 657 ; passes a bill for the relief of

JAM

Catholics, 795 ; legislative independence granted to, 796 ; sources of the weakness of, *ib.*

Isabella of Angoulême marries John, 174

Isabella of Bavaria, Queen of France, takes part against her son, 306

Isabella of France marries Edward II., 225 ; obtains the deposition of her husband, 229 ; gives power to Mortimer, 231 ; is placed in seclusion, 232

Isca Silurum, Roman colony of, 14 ; martyrdom of Aaron at, 23

Isle of Wight, Jutish settlements in, 28 ; plundered by the French, 234

Italy, the French wars in, 363 ; the French driven from, 364

Italy, Charles Albert fails to drive the Austrians out of, 934, 936 ; war for the liberation of, 956 ; formation of the kingdom of, 957 ; Venetia ceded to, 963 ; Rome united to, 964

Itinerant justices under Henry I., 127 ; under Henry II., 148

Jacobites, the, their action in the last months of Anne's reign, 699 ; attempt a rising against George I., 705 ; form part of the opposition against Walpole, 722

Jacquerie, the, 252

Jacqueline of Hainault, marriage of, 308

Jamaica, conquest of, 572

James I., king of Great Britain (*see* James VI., king of Scotland), becomes king of England, 481 ; imprisons Raleigh, *ib.*; attacks the Puritans at Hampton Court, 482 ; quarrels with his first House of Commons, *ib.*; obtains a legal decision in the case of the *Post-nati*, 483 ; his government of Ireland, 484 ; his financial difficulties, *ib.*; makes Somerset his favourite, 486 ; offers to bargain with the Addled Parliament, 487 ; negotiates a Spanish marriage for his son, 488 ; makes Buckingham a favourite, *ib.*; sends Raleigh to execution, 489 ; watches the development of the Thirty Years' War, and summons Parliament to vote supplies, 490 ; his views on the prerogative, 492 ; sells peerages, 494 ; improvement of the finances of, *ib.*; revokes monopolies, 495 ; sends Digby to Germany and dissolves Parliament, 496 ; raises a benevolence, 497 ; his last Parliament, 500 ; seeks to marry his son to a French princess, 501 ; death of, *ib.*

James I., king of Scotland, kept in custody by Henry IV., 295 ; liberation of, 307

James II., as Duke of York, declares himself a Roman Catholic, 600 ; his conversion known, 607 ; resigns the Admiralty, *ib.* ; marriages of, 608 ;

attempt to exclude from the throne, 617 ; his cruelty to the Scottish covenanters, 620 ; is present at his brother's death, 627 ; accession of, 634 ; first acts of the reign of, 635 ; marches against Monmouth, 637 ; violates the Test Act and prorogues Parliament, 638 ; claims the dispensing power and establishes an ecclesiastical commission, 639 ; his government of Scotland and Ireland, 640 ; issues a declaration of indulgence, *ib.* ; expels the Fellows of Magdalen and tries to pack a Parliament, 641 ; issues a second declaration of indulgence, 642 ; hears of the acquittal of the seven Bishops, 643 ; birth of a son of, 644 ; makes concessions on hearing of William's approach, *ib.* ; attempts to escape, 645 ; embarks for France, 646 ; alleged virtual abdication of, *ib.* ; lands in Ireland, 654 ; is defeated at the Boyne, and takes refuge in France, 656 ; death of, 675

James IV., king of Scotland, invades England, 352 ; marries the daughter of Henry VII., 356 ; killed at Flodden, 364

James V., king of Scotland, policy of, 404 ; death of, 405

James VI., king of Scotland, birth and accession of, 439 ; assisted by Elizabeth, 450 ; becomes the tool of Lennox, 454 ; is captured by Protestant lords, 455 ; becomes king of England, 481 ; *see* James I., king of Great Britain

James (the Old Pretender), birth of, 644

Jane Seymour marries Henry VIII., 395 ; death of, 397

Jaureguy tries to murder William of Orange, 454

Jeffreys enforces the surrender of charters, 625 ; sends Baxter to prison, 635 ; is made Chief Justice, *ib.*; conducts the Bloody Assizes, 637 ; becomes Chancellor, 638

Jena, battle of, 857

Jenkins's Ear, 729

Jerusalem captured by the Crusaders, 121 ; captured by Saladin, 157 ; Richard I. refuses to look at, 161

Jervis, Sir John, commands at the battle of St. Vincent, 835

Jesuits, the, origin of, 436 ; land in England, 453 ; Act of Parliament against, 456

Jews, the, encouraged by William II., 115 ; protected by Henry I., 128 ; massacre of, 160 ; persecuted by John, 179 ; banished by Edward I., 212

Jews' House, the so-called, 170

John, king of England, his misconduct in Ireland, 156 ; leads the opposition to William of Longchamps, 161 ; joins Philip II. against Richard, 162 ; accession of, 173 ; loses Normandy and Anjou, 174 ; appoints an Archbishop of Canterbury, 177 ; quarrels with the Pope, 178 ; submits to the Pope, 180 ; quarrels with the barons, 181 ; confirms *Magna Carta*, 182 ; makes war with the barons, 184 ; dies, 185

John, king of France, defeated at Poitiers, 251 ; brought to England, 252 ; is liberated, but returns to England and dies, 254

John Ball, 268

Jones, Ernest, leads the Chartists, 924

Jones, Inigo, buildings by, 632

Jones, Michael, commands in Dublin, 562

Joseph I., Emperor, succeeds Leopold I., 684 ; death of, 693

Joseph Bonaparte, becomes King of Naples, 856 ; becomes King of Spain, 863

Joyce, Cornet, carries off Charles I. from Holmby, 555

Judicial system of the early English, 31 ; of Eadgar, 72 ; of William I., 107 ; of Henry I., 127 ; of Henry II., 146

Judith accuses Waltheof, 110

Julius II., papacy of, 363 ; character of, 375

Junius' Letters, probable authorship of, 775

Junto, the Whig, formation of, 659 ; break-up of, 669

Jury of presentment, 147

Jury system, the, germ of, 147 ; completed, 321

Justices of the peace, the, origin of, 277

Justiciar, institution of the office of, 116 ; his position under Henry I., 127

Jutes, probably ravage Roman Britain, 24 ; subdue Kent, 27 ; settle in the Isle of Wight and the mainland opposite, 28

Keble, his *Christian Year*, 940

Kemp, Bishop of London, becomes Lord Chancellor, 309

Kenilworth, Earl, Simon's castle at, 199

Kenneth, king of the Scots, receives Lothian from Eadgar, 68

Kenneth MacAlpin unites the Scots and Picts, 63

Kenmure, Lord, beheaded, 705

Kent, foundation of the Jutish kingdom of, 27 ; its inhabitants driven back by the West Saxons, 35 ; Gaulish traders in, 38 ; accepts Christianity, 39 ; is kept by Lawrence from relapsing, 41 ; comparative weakness of, *ib.* ; rising in, suppressed by Fairfax, 557

Kent, Earl of (brother of Edward II.), execution of, 231

Kentish Petition, the, 675

Kerouaille, Louise de, *see* Portsmouth, Duchess of

Ket's rebellion, 415

Kildare, Earl of, supports the Yorkists, 347 ; supports Lambert Simnel, *ib.* ; is deprived of the Deputyship for sup-

KIL

porting Warbeck, 350 ; restored to the Deputyship, 352

Kildare, Earl of, imprisonment of, 402

Kilkenny, meeting of the Confederate Catholics at, 541

Kilkenny, Statute of, 265

Killiecrankie, battle of, 653

Kilsyth, battle of, 549

Kimbolton, Lord, *see* Manchester, Earl of

King, authority of the, origin of, 33 ; effect of the enlargement of the kingdoms on, 45 ; increased importance of, 69 ; limitations imposed by *Magna Carta* on, 182; proposed administrative restrictions on, 195 ; effect of the revolution of 1399 upon, 289

King's Bench, Court of, 212

King's Friends, the, 767

Kinsale, Spanish expedition to, 478

Knights Bachelors, the, appeal to Edward, 199

Knights of the shire first admitted to Parliament, 196 ; later elections of, 200, 201 ; importance of their conjunction with borough members, 245

Knighthood fines, 515 ; prohibited, 531

Knox, John, opinions of, 418 ; urges on the Lords of the Congregation, 432 ; writes *The Monstrous Regimen of Women, ib. ;* organises the Presbyterian Church 434 ; his treatment of Mary, 438

Kymry, the, origin of the name, 37 ; share in the defeat of the Scots at Degsastan, 42 ; are defeated by Æthelfrith near Chester, 43 ; geographical dismemberment of, *ib. ;* in alliance with Penda, 46 ; weakness of, 49 ; *see* Welsh

La Bourdonnais takes Madras, 760

La Hogue, battle of, 653

Labourers, Statute of, 248, 268

Lafayette goes as a volunteer to America, 786

Laibach, congress of, 882

Lake, General, defeats the Irish insurgents at Vinegar Hill, 841 ; his victories in India, 859

Lambert burnt as a heretic, 399

Lambert, Major-General, defeats Booth at Winnington Bridge, 575

Lambeth, ford over the Thames at, 20

Lancaster, Duke of (John of Gaunt), makes unsuccessful war in France, 257 ; heads the anti-clerical party, 260 ; opposes the Black Prince, 262 ; reverses the proceedings of the Good Parliament, *ib. ;* supports Wycliffe, 263 ; takes the lead at the accession of Richard II., 266 ; goes to Spain, 279 ; marries Catherine Swynford, 282

Lancaster, Earl of (Thomas), opposes Edward II., 225 ; execution of, 228

Lanfranc trusted by William I., 88 ; becomes Archbishop of Canterbury,

LEO

106 ; crowns William II., 114 ; death of, 117

Langland, William, 259

Langport, battle of, 548

Langside, defeat of Mary at, 440

Langton, Stephen, chosen Archbishop of Canterbury at Rome, 177 ; allowed by John to come to England, 180 ; produces a charter of Henry I., 181 ; his part in obtaining the Great Charter, 182

Lansdown, battle of, 538

Latimer, made Bishop of Worcester, 390 ; driven from his see, 400 ; sermons preached at Court by, 417 ; burnt, 425

Latimer, Lord, impeached, 262

Laud, Archbishop of Canterbury, character and opinions of, 516 ; becomes Archbishop of Canterbury, and advises the republication of the *Declaration of Sports,* 517 ; wishes that the communion table shall stand at the East end, *ib. ;* conducts a metropolitical visitation, 520 ; unpopularity of, 521 ; imprisonment of, 530 ; execution of, 546

Lauderdale, John Maitland, Earl of, strengthens the king's authority in Scotland, 602 ; his management of Scotland, 619

Lawrence, Archbishop of Canterbury, keeps Kent Christian, 41

Lawrence, Sir Henry, governs the Punjab, 951 ; besieged in Lucknow, 953; killed, *ib.*

Lawrence, Sir John, governs the Punjab, 951 ; sends Sikh troops to Delhi, 953

Layamon's Brut, 207

Le Mans, sieges of, 121

League, the, formed against Henry of Navarre, 456

Legge, dismissal of, 748

Leicester, Anglian settlement at, 36 ; earldom of, inherited by Simon de Montfort, 193

Leicester, Earl of, shares the Justiciar's office with Richard de Lucy, 140

Leicester, Robert Dudley, Earl of, favoured by Elizabeth, 435 ; made Earl of Leicester, 438 ; commands an army in the Netherlands, 457

Leighton punished by the Star Chamber, 514

Leith, surrender of the French garrison of, 433

Lely, Sir Peter, portraits by, 631

Lennox, Esmè Stuart, Duke of, favourite of James VI., 455

Lennox, Matthew Stuart, Earl of, Regent of Scotland, 443

Lenthall, Speaker of the Long Parliament, 536

Leo IX., Papacy of, 88

Leo X., Pope, character of, 375

Leofric, Earl of the Mercians, 85, 90

Leofwine, Earl of the Mercians, 84

LEO

Leofwine, son of Godwine, earl of the shires about the Thames, 90

Leopold I., Emperor, marries the daughter of Philip IV. of Spain, 592 ; death of, 684

Leopold II., Emperor, his attitude towards France, 824

Leopold, Duke of Austria, imprisons Richard I., 161

Leopold of Saxe-Coburg, chosen King of the Belgians, 912

Leslie, David, overthrows Montrose, 549 ; is defeated at Dunbar, 563

Levellers, the, 561

Leven, Alexander Leslie, Earl of, as Alexander Leslie, commands the Scots on Dunse Law, 536 ; becomes Earl of Leven, and invades England, 542

Lewes, battle of, 201

Lewis III. (the Bavarian), Emperor, supports Edward III., 235

Lexington, skirmish at, 783

Leyden, relief of, 449 ; congregation of English Separatists at, 489

Liberals, the introduction of the name of, 909

Lichfield House Compact, the, 913

Lilla gives his life for his lord, 44

Lille, taken by Marlborough, 690 ; negotiations with the French Directory at, 837

Limerick, siege and capitulation of, 655

Limoges taken by the Black Prince, 257

Linacre, promotes the study of Greek at Oxford, 367

Lincoln (see Lindum), settlement of the Lindiswaras round, 28 ; establishment of the see of, 107 ; Stephen taken prisoner at, 135 ; cathedral at, 171, 207 ; stormed by Manchester, 542

Lincoln, Abraham, chosen President of the United States, 958

Lincoln, Earl of, killed at Stoke, 347

Lindiswaras, settlement of, 28 ; possible advance of, 36

Lindsey, Robert Bertie, Earl of, fails to relieve Rochelle, 510

Lindum, Roman city at, 20 ; Anglian settlers round, 28

Lisle, Alice, execution of, 637

Litany, the English, composed by Cranmer, 409

Literature in the reign of Anne, 692

Liveries, see Maintenance and Livery

Liverpool, Earl of, becomes Prime Minister, 868 ; end of the ministry of, 886

Llewelyn, career of, 140

Loch Leven Castle, Mary imprisoned in, 410

Locke, John, his *Letters on Toleration*, 652

Locomotive engines, introduction of, 906

Loidis conquered by Eadwine, 43

Lollards, the, rise of, 269 ; Oldcastle's leadership of, 300

Londinium, see London

LOU

London, early importance of the position of, 20 ; foundation of the bishopric of, 40 ; its commercial position under the kings of Essex, *ib.* ; acquired and fortified by Ælfred, 62, 63 ; attacked by Olaf Trygvasson and Svend, 79 ; after the Conquest, 127 ; supports Stephen, 131, 134 ; submits for a time to Matilda, 135 ; municipal organisation of, 169 ; sends troops to the battle of Lewes, 201 ; Wat Tyler in, 269 ; Jack Cade in, 323 ; Edward IV. in, 328 ; Lady Jane Grey unpopular in, 420 ; provides ships instead of money for the ship-money fleet, 523 ; welcomes Charles I. on his return from Scotland, 534, 535 ; declares against Charles I., 536 ; sends out trained bands to Gloucester, 539 ; attaches itself to the Presbyterian party, 555 ; influences the Whigs in, 622 ; Tory elections in, 623 ; forfeiture of the charter of, 624 ; growth of, 629 ; condition of the streets of, 631 ; restoration of the charter of, 644 ; support given to Wilkes in, 776 ; upholds the Lord Mayor and Aldermen in their contest with the Commons, 779

London Bridge, building of, 272

Londonderry, siege of, 654

Long bow, the, see Archers

Longchamps, William of, appointed a justiciar in the absence of Richard I., 159 ; is banished, 161

Lord, devotion of Gesiths to their, 30 ; is expected to marry, *ib.* ; growth of his jurisdiction, 72

Lords, House of, names the Duke of York Protector, 324 ; decides on his claim to the crown, 329 ; results of the disappearance of the abbots from, 400 ; a bill thrown out for removing the bishops from, 533 ; bishops excluded from, 536 ; refuses to join in constituting a High Court of Justice, 557 ; dissolution of, 561 ; imprisons Shaftesbury, 612 ; discusses the abdication of James II., 646 ; creation of twelve peers to reverse the majority in, 695 ; Peerage Bill introduced to give independence to, 710

Lords of the Congregation, rise against Mary of Guise, 432 ; are helped by Elizabeth, 433

Lorraine ceded to Stanislaus Leczinski, 725

Lose-coat Field, 332

Lothian, cession of, to Scotland, 68, 84

Loudon, Earl of, fails to take Louisburg, 752

Loudoun of Baden commands German forces, 682

Louis VI., king of France, makes war with Henry I., 129

Louis VII., king of France, divorces Eleanor of Aquitaine, 137 ; supports young Henry's rebellion, 153 ; takes part in the second Crusade, 157

LOU

Louis (afterwards Louis VIII., king of France) opposes John, 184; expelled from England, 185

Louis IX., Saint, king of France, surrenders territory to Henry III., 200; mediates between Henry III. and the barons, *ib.*

Louis X., king of France, succeeded by his brother, 232

Louis XI., king of France, succeeds his father, 332; buys off Edward IV., 336

Louis XII., king of France, invades Italy, 354; Italian wars of, 363; marriage and death of, 364

Louis XIII., king of France, negotiates for his sister's marriage, 501; resistance of Rochelle to, 504; besieges Rochelle, 506

Louis XIV., king of France, buys Dunkirk from Charles II., 587; gives a slight support to the Dutch against England, 591; his designs on the Spanish inheritance, 592; signs the treaty of Aix-la-Chapelle, 599; obtains the treaty of Dover from Charles II., 600; invades the Dutch territory, 605; pensions Charles II., 611; is successful in the Netherlands, 613; sends money to Charles II. to prevent the summoning of a parliament, 627; offers financial help to James II., 635; revokes the Edict of Nantes, 638; offers to send his fleet to help James II., 644; accepts the peace of Ryswick, and acknowledges William III., 667; refuses to make war against his grandson, 690; death of, 705

Louis XV., king of France, sickly in his childhood, 707

Louis XVI., king of France, improves the French navy, 788; summons the States-General, 821; distrusted by the National Assembly, 822; dethronement and execution of, 825

Louis XVIII., king of France, first restoration of, 871; second restoration of, 875; attempts to mediate in favour of the Neapolitans, 882

Louis Napoleon, President of the French Republic, 936; named President for ten years, 938; *see* Napoleon III., Emperor

Louis Philippe, king of the French, Charles X. overthrown in favour of, 898; promotes Belgian independence, 912; dismisses Thiers, 922; visits Queen Victoria, 927; dethronement of, 934

Louisbourg, Loudon fails to take, 752; taken, 753

Louisiana, possessed by France, 747; ceded by France to Spain, 766

Lovel, Lord, insurrection of, 345; supports Simnel, and is defeated at Stoke, 346, 347

Lowestoft, battle off, 590

Loyalists, the American, conjectural number of, 782

MAI

Loyola, Ignatius, founds the Jesuit Society, 437

Lucknow, siege of, 953

Lucy, Richard de, joint justiciar with the Earl of Leicester, 140; makes head against young Henry's rebellion, 153

Ludlow, Edmund, in Ireland, 563

Ludlow, break-up of the Yorkists at, 326

Lunéville, peace of, 840

Lunsford, Thomas, Lieutenant of the Tower, 535

Luther, Martin, opposes the Papacy, 377; has a controversy with Henry VIII., 379

Lutheranism, character of, 376, 377; its influence in England, 396

Lutter, Christian IV. defeated at, 506

Luxembourg, Marshal, defeats the allies at Fleurus, 657

Lyell, his *Principles of Geology*, 940

Lynn supports Stephen, 134

Lyons, Richard, impeached, 262

Macadam, improvement of roads by, 905

Macaulay, Thomas B., supports the Reform Bill, 903; his *History of England*, 941

Macaulay, Zachary, pleads for the abolition of slavery, 910

MacIan of Glencoe tenders his oath to William III. too late, 653

Mackay, Andrew, defeated at Killiecrankie, 653; serves in Ireland, 656

Mackintosh, Sir James, advocates the reform of the criminal law, 885

Mad Parliament, the, 198

Madras, building of, 758; taken by the French, 760; restored to the English and secured by Clive, 761

Madrid, journey of Prince Charles to, 497

Magdalen College, Oxford, expulsion of the Fellows of, 641; restoration of the Fellows of, 644

Magna Carta, 182; partially renewed at the accession of Henry III., 185; attitude of Edward I. to, 288

Magnus, king of Norway, 85

Mahdi, the, destroys an Egyptian army and captures Khartoum, 971

Mahmoud, Sultan, asks Mehemet Ali to assist him against the Greeks, 884; death of, 922

Mahrattas, the, rise of, 759; Hastings defends himself against, 802, 804; reduced to submission by Wellesley, 859; reduced to complete dependency by the Marquis of Hastings, 948

Maiden Castle, 4

Maine conquered by William I., 91; failures of William II. in, 121; conquered by Philip II., 176; surrendered to René by Henry VI., 317; the English driven out of, 319

MAI

Maintenance and livery, Statute against, 281 ; increase of, 321 ; measures of Henry VII. against, 345

Maitland of Lethington, William, opposes the Presbyterian clergy, 434

Major-generals, the, 571

Malcolm, king of the Scots, his alliance with Eadmund, 64

Malcolm III., Canmore, ravages England, 103 ; submits to William I., 104 ; death of, 119

Malcolm IV. loses North-humberland and Cumberland, 140

Malmesbury, Earl of, sent to negotiate peace in France, 834

Malplaquet, battle of, 690

Malta, seized by Bonaparte, 837 ; surrenders to the English, 844 ; England engages to surrender, 846 ; England refuses to surrender, 848

Man, Isle of, subdued by Eadwine, 43

Manchester, Edward Montague, Earl of, impeached, as Lord Kimbolton, 535 ; brought back to Westminster, 536 ; becomes Earl of Manchester and is placed in command of the Eastern Association, 542 ; attacked by Cromwell, 544 ; resigns his command, 545

'Manchester massacre,' the, 879

Manfred, king of Sicily and Naples, 195, 197

Manhood suffrage, the Duke of Richmond advocates, 789

Manilla, reduction of, 766

Manitoba, joins the Dominion of Canada, 967

Manor courts, 141

Mansfeld, Count, failure of his expedition, 501

Mansfield, Lord Chief Justice, 749

Mantes burnt by William I., 114

Mantua, siege of, 834

Manufactures, social changes resulting from the growth of, 817

Manufacturers, the distress amongst, 876–879

Manwaring, Roger, impeached, 511 ; receives a good living from Charles I., 512

Manx, a Goidelic language, 7

Mar's rising, 705

March, Earl of, *see* Edward IV.

March, Edmund Mortimer, Earl of, his claim to the crown, 287 ; imprisoned by Henry IV., 291 ; freed by Henry V., 299

March, Roger, Earl of, grandson of the Duke of Clarence, named heir by Richard II., 287

Marengo, battle of, 840

Margaret, daughter of Henry VII., married to James IV., 356 ; excluded from the succession, 411

Margaret of Anjou marries Henry VI., 317 ; gives birth to a son, 323 ; puts herself at the head of the Northern forces, 326 ; defeats the Duke of York at Wakefield, and Warwick at the second battle

MAR

of St. Albans, 328 ; is defeated at Towton, 329 ; is defeated at Hedgeley Moor and Hexham, 331 ; reconciled to Warwick, 333 ; defeated at Tewkesbury, 334

Margaret, sister of Edward IV., married to Charles the Rash, 332 ; protects Lord Lovel, 346

Margaret, the Lady, 334

Margaret, the Maid of Norway, 214

Margaret, first wife of Malcolm Canmore, 119

Margaret Theresa, daughter of Philip IV., marries Leopold I., and renounces the Spanish succession, 592

Maria, the Infanta, proposal to marry her to Prince Charles, 488 ; shrinks from marrying a heretic, 497 ; is courted by Charles, 498

Maria Theresa, daughter of Philip IV., marries Louis XIV., and renounces the Spanish succession, 592

Maria Theresa (Empress), constituted heiress of her father's hereditary dominions, 732 ; attacked on all sides, *ib.* ; cedes Silesia to Frederick II., 735

Marignano, battle of, 366

Marlborough, Statute of, 204

Marlborough, Duchess of, her influence over Anne, 677

Marlborough, John Churchill, Duke of, as Lord Churchill, deserts James II., 645 ; becomes Earl of Marlborough, 657 ; disgraced by William III., 658 ; betrays Talmash, 664 ; placed by William III. at the head of an army, 675 ; his influence over Anne, 677 ; his first campaign in the Netherlands, 678 ; created a Duke, and votes for the Occasional Conformity Bill, 680 ; obtains the dismissal of Rochester and Nottingham, and procures the entry of Harley and St. John into the ministry, 681 ; defeats Tallard at Blenheim, 682 ; turns to the Whigs, 684 ; his victory at Ramillies, *ib.* ; his victories at Oudenarde and Malplaquet, 690 ; blamed for prolonging the war, 691 ; sent to Flanders with inadequate means, and dismissed from his offices, 695

Marprelate Tracts, the, 470

Marriages of heiresses arranged by the lord, 117

Marshal, Richard the, 188, 189

Marshal, William, the, guardian of Henry III., 185

Marston Moor, battle of, 543

Martin, Master, his exactions, 195

Mary I., daughter of Henry VIII., as princess, successively engaged to Francis I. and his second son, 374 ; her place in the succession acknowledged by statute, 411 ; protected by Charles V., 414 ; popularity of, 420 ; is proclaimed queen, 421 ; her feelings and opinions, *ib.* ; wishes to restore the Church lands, 422 ; is married to

INDEX

Philip II., 423; obtains the reconciliation of England to the Roman see, 424; supports the persecution of Protestants, *ib.*; resolves to put Cranmer to death, 425; deserted by her husband, 426; declares war with France, 427; death of, *ib.*

Mary II., birth of, 608; her hand offered to William of Orange, 609; marriage of, 613; finds fault with Danby, 646; the crown offered to, 647; receives the Scottish Crown, 652; illness and death of, 661; Greenwich Hospital founded by, 663

Mary, daughter of Henry VII., marriages of, 364; her place in the succession acknowledged in exclusion of her sister Margaret, 411

Mary, heiress of Burgundy, 336; marries the Archduke Maximilian, and dies, 337

Mary of Guise, Regent of Scotland, her contests with the Protestants, 432; death of, 433

Mary of Modena marries the Duke of York, 608

Mary Stuart, Queen of Scots, birth of, 405; taken to France and married to the Dauphin, 413; assumes the style of Queen of England, 433; returns to Scotland, 434, 435; character of, 437; marries Lord Darnley, 438; being charged with the murder of Darnley, marries Bothwell, 439; imprisoned in Loch Leven Castle, 440; escapes to England, *ib.*; is retained as a prisoner, 441; marriage with the Duke of Norfolk, proposed for, *ib.*; Ridolfi's plot on behalf of, 445; trial of, 457; execution of, 458

Maserfield, Oswald slain at, 48

Masham, Mrs., obtains influence over Anne, 687

Massachusetts Government Act, the, 782

Massalia, tin-trade of, 8

Massena, Marshal, invades Portugal, 867

Massey, Roman Catholic Dean of Christchurch, 639

Matilda, daughter of Henry I., married to the Emperor Henry V., and to Geoffrey of Anjou, 131; claims the crown, 134; fails to maintain her claim, 135

Matilda, wife of Henry I., *see* Eadgyth

Matthias, the Emperor, resistance of the Bohemians to, 490

Maximilian I., Emperor, as Archduke, marries Mary of Burgundy, 337; marries Anne of Brittany by proxy, 348; Italian wars of, 363; death of, 369

Maximus leads an army out of Britain, 25

Mayflower, the, voyage of, 490

Maynard, Sergeant, his answer to William III., 646

Mayne, Cuthbert, execution of, 453

Maynooth taken by Skeffington, 402

Mazarin, Cardinal, makes an alliance with Cromwell, 572

Meanee, battle of, 950

Meaux besieged by Henry V., 306

Medina Sidonia, Duke of, commands the Spanish Armada, 460; is received by Philip II. after his defeat, 462

Medway, the, the Dutch in, 593

Mehemet Ali, makes himself independent, and sends aid to the Sultan, 884; attacks the Turks, and possesses himself of Syria, 921; deprived of Syria, 922

Melbourne, Viscount, is a member of Lord Grey's Ministry, 901; becomes Prime Minister and is dismissed by the King, 912; becomes Prime Minister a second time, 913; resigns and resumes office, 918; final resignation of, 925

Melville, Andrew, insults James VI., 525

Melville, Lord, impeachment of, 851

Menai Suspension Bridge, the, 905

Mendoza sent out of England by Elizabeth, 456

Mercenaries employed on the Continent by Henry II., 142; temporarily brought to England, 153, 155; employed by John, 182

Merchant Adventurers, the, 356

Merchant Gild, the, 169

Mercia, first settlement of, 36; comparative smallness of, 41; unites with other districts under Penda, 46; accepts Christianity, and rejects the supremacy of North-humberland, 48; its relations with Ecgberht, 55; its relations with Ælfred, 60; under Leofwine, 84; under Leofric, 85, 87; under Ælfgar and Eadwine, 90

Mercians, the, distinguished from the Middle English, 36

Merciless Parliament, the, 280

Merton College, foundation of, 207

Metropolitical Visitation, the, 520

Metternich, holds it to be the duty of the great powers to suppress revolutions, 882

Middle English, the, first settlements of, 36

Middle Saxons a branch of the East Saxons, 35

Middlesex election, the, 775

Middlesex, Lionel Cranfield, Earl of, improves the finances of James I., 494; impeachment of, 500

Middlesex, Saxon settlement in, 35

Milan, struggle between Charles V. and Francis I. for, 371

Milan, the Duchy of, assigned to Charles VI., 696

Milan Decree, the, 860

Militia, the, struggle for the command of, 536; the Scots urge Charles I. to abandon, 552

Millenary Petition, the, 482

Milton writes *Comus*, 519 ; writes *Areopagitica*, 546 ; writes a sonnet on the Vaudois, 572 ; publishes *Paradise Lost*, 596

Minden, battle of, 756

Mines, restriction of labour in, 927

Ministerial responsibility, proposal to establish, 195

Ministers excluded from the House of Commons by the Act of Settlement, 673 ; readmitted, 684

Minorca, taken by Stanhope, 690 ; assigned to England by the treaty of Utrecht, 696 ; re-taken by the French, 749 ; regained at the end of the Seven Years' War, 766 ; taken by the Spaniards, 795 ; ceded by England to Spain, 798

Mirebeau, Eleanor besieged in, 174

Mise of Amiens, the, 200

Missolonghi, sieges of, 884 ; death of Byron at, 888

Mohammedanism, origin and spread of, 54

Molynes, Lord, ill-treats John Paston, 321

Mompesson, Sir Giles, flies from the kingdom, 495

Mona (Anglesey) conquered by Suetonius, 14

Monasteries, dissolution of the smaller, 394 ; surrender of some of the greater, 397 ; completion of the suppression of, 400

Monasticism, character of early, 39 ; converts made in England by, 40 ; character of Irish, 47 ; Benedictine, 128

Monk, *see* Albemarle, Duke of

Monks contrasted with Friars, 191

Monmouth, Duke of, proposed as heir to the crown, 618 ; defeats the Covenanters at Bothwell Bridge, 620 ; refuses to take part in acts of violence, 624 ; implicated in a Whig plot, 625 ; rebellion and execution of, 637

Monopolies, the, Elizabeth recalls some of, 478 ; attacked by Parliament in the reign of James I., 494 ; revocation of, 495 ; Act of, 500

Monro, Major-General Robert, holds Carrickfergus, 541

Montague, Charles, one of the Whig Junto, 659 ; restores the currency, 664 ; resigns office, 670

Montague, Chief Justice, becomes Lord Treasurer, 494

Montague, Lord, made Earl of Northhumberland, 331 ; is deprived of the earldom, 333 ; turns against Edward IV., and is killed at Barnet, 332

Montague, Ralph, accuses Danby, 616

Montague, Richard, impeached, 511 ; made a bishop, 512

Montenegro, enlargement of, 969

Montfort, de, *see* Simon de Montfort

Montrose, James Graham, Marquis of, his campaign in the Highlands, 547, 549 ; execution of, 563

Moore, Sir John, killed at Corunna, 864

More, Sir Thomas, writes *Utopia*, 367 ; in favour with Henry VIII., 368 ; is Speaker of the House of Commons, 371 ; becomes Chancellor, 387 ; his displeasure with the Protestants, 388 ; resigns the chancellorship, *ib.* ; is sent to the Tower, 392 ; execution of, 394

Morkere becomes Earl of North-humberland, 90 ; is present at Eadgar's election, 98 ; submits to William, 102 ; is banished, 103

Morley, Bishop, sermons of, 548

Mornington, Lord, Governor-General of India, 838 ; becomes Marquis Wellesley, 859 ; *see* Wellesley, Marquis

Mortimer, Edmund, *see* March, Earl of

Mortimer, Roger, paramour of Queen Isabella, 229 ; governs in the name of Edward III., 231 ; is hanged, 232

Mortimer, Sir Edmund, imprisoned by Glendower, 293

Mortimer's Cross, battle of, 328

Mortmain, Statute of, 212

Morton, Thomas, Bishop of Ely, afterwards Cardinal and Archbishop of Canterbury, gives advice to Buckingham, 341, 342 ; his 'fork,' 349

Moscow, burning of, 870

Mount Badon, British victory at, 28

Mountjoy, Charles Blount, Lord, conquers Ireland, 478

Mountnorris, Francis Annesley, Lord, court-martial on, 528

Mowbray, Robert of, rebellion of, 120

Muir, sentenced to transportation, 828

Municipal Corporations Act, 913, 914

Munster, attempt to colonise, 475

Münster, the Bishop of, overruns two Dutch provinces, 591

Murray, desires to become Chief Justice, 747 ; becomes Chief Justice as Lord Mansfield, 749

Murray, Earl of, is driven into England, 438 ; returns to Scotland, 439 ; becomes Regent, 440 ; produces the Casket letters, *ib.* ; assassinated, 441

Mutinies at Spithead and the Nore, 836

Mutiny Act, the, 650

Mysore, Hyder Ali in, 804 ; Tippoo succeeds his father in, 805

Namur, surrender of, 663

Nana Sahib, grievances of, 952 ; his conduct at Cawnpore, 953

Nantwich, battle of, 542

Napier, Sir Charles, Admiral, takes Acre, 922

Napier, Sir Charles, General, conquers Sindh, 950

Naples, assigned to Charles VI., 696 ; ceded to the son of Philip V., 725 ; Joseph Bonaparte, king of, 856 ; revolution suppressed by Austria in, 882

Napoleon I, Emperor of the French, his

plan for the invasion of England, 851 ; offers Hanover alternately to England and Prussia, 855 ; defeats the Prussians at Jena, 857 ; makes peace with Russia at Tilsit, 858 ; his designs against Spain, 862 ; places Joseph Bonaparte on the Spanish throne, 863 ; invades Spain, 864 ; fights at Aspern and Wagram, 865 ; countries annexed by, 868 ; invades Russia, 869, 870 ; defeat and abdication of, 871 ; returns to France and fights at Waterloo, 874 ; dies at St. Helena, 875

Napoleon III., Emperor, becomes Emperor, 939 ; attempt to murder, 955 ; goes to war for the liberation of Italy, 956 ; annexes Savoy and Nice, 957 ; fall of, 964

Naseby, battle of, 548

Natal, colonisation of, 969

Navarino, battle of, 893

Navarre conquered by Ferdinand of Aragon, 364

Navarrete, battle of, 255

Navigation Act, the, passing of, 565 ; re-enactment of, 589 ; repeal of, 936

Navy, Ælfred's, 60 ; defeats the English, defeats the Spanish Armada, 460–464; equipped by means of ship-money, 523 ; desertion of part of, to the Prince of Wales, 557 ; Blake in command of, 565 ; its contests with the Dutch, 591 ; deterioration in the discipline of, 605

Nelson, his exploits at the battle of St. Vincent, 835 ; defeats the French at the battle of the Nile, 838 ; defeats the Danes at the battle of Copenhagen, 845 ; pursues the French fleet to the West Indies, 853 ; killed at Trafalgar, 854

Neolithic man, 3

Netherlands, the, inherited by Philip II., 426 ; Alva's government of, 443 ; beginning of the Dutch Republic in, 449 ; division into two parts, 450 ; see Netherlands, the Spanish, and Dutch Republic

Netherlands, the Austrian, occupied by the French, 825 ; ceded to France, 837

Netherlands, the Spanish, Alexander of Parma in, 450 ; assigned to Charles VI., 696 ; see Netherlands, the Austrian

Nevill, influence of the family of, 324

Nevill, George, Archbishop of York, deprived of the Chancellorship, 332

Nevill's Cross, battle of, 242

New Amsterdam captured by the English, 589

New Brunswick joins the Dominion of Canada, 967

New England, colonisation of, 489 ; warlike preparations in, 782 ; beginning of resistance in, 783

New Forest, the, making of, 110 ; death of William II. in, 122

New Jersey, Washington driven out of, 784 ; Washington recovers, 786

New Model Army, see Army, the New Model

New Orleans, the British repulsed at, 873

New South Wales, progress of, 968

New York, named after the Duke of York, 589; secured to England, 593 ; occupied by Howe, 784

New Zealand, progress of colonisation in, 968

Newark, death of John at, 185 ; surrenders to the Scots, 551

Newburn, rout of, 529

Newbury, first battle of, 539 ; second battle of, 544

Newcastle, Charles I. at, 551

Newcastle, Duke of, character of, 732 ; succeeds his brother as first Lord of the Treasury, 746 ; his inefficiency in providing for hostilities with France, 748 ; resigns, 749 ; coalesces with Pitt, 751 ; resignation of, 766

Newcastle, William Cavendish, Earl, afterwards Marquis of, commands a Royalist army in Yorkshire, and defeats the Fairfaxes at Adwalton Moor, 538 ; is created Marquis, and besieges Hull, 542 ; besieged in York, ib. ; defeated at Marston Moor, 548

Newcastle-on-Tyne, foundation of, 120

Newfoundland, retained by England, 695 ; refuses to join the Dominion of Canada, 967

Newgate, burning of, 792

Newman, a leader of the Oxford movement, 940

Newport (Monmouthshire), Chartist riot at, 924

Newport, the treaty of, 557

Newton, Sir Isaac, 632 ; assists in restoring the currency, 664

Nicholas, the Tzar, comes to an agreement with England on the liberation of Greece, 884 ; proposes to partition the Turkish dominions, 943 ; goes to war with the Sultan, 944 ; war declared by England and France against, ib. ; death of, 947

Nigel, Bishop of Ely, Treasurer of Henry I., Stephen's attack on, 134 ; is re-appointed Treasurer, 140

Nightingale, Miss Florence, nurses the sick from the Crimea, 917

Nile, the battle of, 838

Nithsdale, Earl of, escapes from prison, 705

No Addresses, vote of, 555

Nonjurors, the, 652

Non-resistance Bill, the, 611

Nore, the, mutiny at, 836

Norfolk, origin of the name of, 28

Norfolk, Duke of, banished by Richard II., 283

Norfolk, Earl of, see Bigod, Roger

Norfolk, resistance to the Amicable Loan in, 372 ; Ket's rebellion in, 415

Norfolk, Thomas Howard, third Duke of, defeats the Scots, as Earl of Surrey, at Flodden, 364 ; opposes Wolsey, 383 ;

NOR

charges Cromwell with treason, 401; wastes the Scottish Borders, 405; condemned to death, 411

Norfolk, Thomas Howard, fourth Duke of, sent to the Tower, 441; is liberated and proposes to marry Mary Stuart, 444; arrested, 445; executed, 446

Norham, award of the crown of Scotland at, 216

Norman Conquest, the, 96–103

Normandy, early dukes of, 80; institutions of, 81; its condition under Robert, 118; pledged to William II., 121; recovered by Robert, 124; conquered by Henry I., 125; conquered by Geoffrey, 136; Henry, Duke of, 137; conquered by Philip II., 174, 176; invaded by Edward III., 240; conquered by Henry V., 303; re-conquered by the French, 320

Normans favoured by Eadward, 87; their style of architecture, 89

Norris, Sir John, joins Drake in sacking Corunna, 464

North Briton, the, 769

North Foreland, battle off, 591

North, Lord, becomes Prime Minister, 776; takes advantage of the division of opinion between Burke and Chatham, 777; feels strongly against the conduct of the Americans, 778; obtains the repeal of all the American duties except that on tea, 779; resolves to put down resistance in Boston, 780; tries to conciliate the Americans, 783; offers to resign office, 787; resignation of, 795; coalesces with Fox, 800; opposes Pitt's motion for Parliamentary reform, 801; passes the Regulating Act, 832

Northampton, Archbishop Thomas called to account at, 145; battle of, 326

Northern confederacy, the, 844

North-humberland, component parts of, 36; united by Æthelric, 41; divided by Penda, and re-united under Oswald, 47; is again divided, but re-united under Oswiu, 48; its relations with Ecgberht, 55; overrun by the Danes, 58; Danish kingdom in, 62, 63; is amalgamated with England, 64; its condition under Cnut, 84; under Siward 84, 87

Northmen, their attacks on England, 56; religion of, 57; *see* Danes

Northumberland invaded by Malcolm Canmore, 119; given to Henry, son of David I., 133; recovered by Henry II., 140

Northumberland, John Dudley, Duke of, as Earl of Warwick, overpowers Ket's rebellion, 416; leads the government after Somerset's fall, *ib.*; becomes Duke of Northumberland, 418; supports Lady Jane Grey, 420; execution of, 421

Northumberland, the Earl of, assists Henry IV., 284; quarrels with Henry

ORF

IV., 293; imprisoned and pardoned, 294; defeated and slain, 296

Northumberland, Thomas Percy, Earl of, takes part in the rising of the North, 441

Norwich, establishment of the see of, 107

Nottingham, Anglian settlement at, 36; seizure of Mortimer at, 232; Charles I. sets up his standard at, 537

Nottingham, Earl of, opposes Richard II., 279; is made Duke of Norfolk and banished, 283; dismissed through the influence of Marlborough, 681; coalesces with the Whigs, 695

Nova Scotia, assigned to England, 696; abandonment of the French claim to, 766; joins the Dominion of Canada, 967

Nuncomar, execution of, 803

Nymwegen, peace of, 615

Oates, Titus, tells the story of the Popish Plot, 615

O'Brien, Smith, heads a rising in Ireland, 935

Occasional Conformity Bill, failure of the Tories to pass, 680; defeat of an attempt to tack it to a land-tax bill, 682; passed, 695; repealed, 710

O'Connell, Daniel, demands Catholic emancipation, 895; refused a seat in the House of Commons, 896; asks for a repeal of the Union, 910; combines with the Whigs to overthrow Peel, 913; drops for a time his demand for repeal of the Union, 916; shrinks from a conflict with Peel, and dies, 928

O'Connor, Feargus, leads the Chartists, 924; summons a meeting on Kennington Common, 935

Oda, Archbishop, advocates the celibacy of the clergy, 65; separates Eadwig and Ælfgifu, 67

Odo oppresses the English, 102; is banished by William II., 115

O'Donnell, Rory, flight of, 484

Offa, king of the Mercians, defeats the West Saxons at Bensington, 53; his dyke, 54

Olaf Trygvasson, 79, 80

Oldcastle, Sir John, burnt as a Lollard, 300

Old Sarum, earthworks of Sorbiodunum at, 34

Olive Branch petition, the, 783

O'Neill, Hugh, defeats Bagenal at the Blackwater, 475; submission of, 478; flight of, 484

O'Neill, Shan, defeat of, 452

Orange River Free State, the foundation of, 968

Ordainers, the Lords, 226

Ordeal, system of, 32; continued by Henry II., 146

Orders in Council, the, 860; repeal of, 872

Ordovices, the, resist the Romans, 14

Orford, Earl of, attacked by the Commons, 670; resigns office, *ib.*; *see* Russell, Admiral

ORL

Orleans, siege of, 309

Orleans, Duke of (the Regent), is on friendly terms with England, 707; guarantees the Hanoverian succession, 708

Orleans, Duke of, Charles, captured at Agincourt, 303; ransomed, 315

Orleans, Duke of, Louis, makes an alliance with Glendower, 295; murdered, 296

Orleans, Henrietta, Duchess of, negotiates the Treaty of Dover, 600

Ormond, Earl of, supports the Lancastrians, 346

Ormond, second Duke of, commands in Flanders, 696; escapes to France, 705

Ormond, Thomas Butler, Marquis of, Lord Lieutenant of Ireland, 542; abandons Ireland to Parliament, 552; returns to Ireland, *ib.*

Osric governs Deira, 48

Ostorius Scapula arrives in Britain, 13; conquests of, 14

Oswald, Bishop of Worcester, 68

Oswald, King of North-humberland, his greatness and piety, 47; is slain at Maserfield, 48

Oswini, his relations with Aidan, 48; is murdered, *ib.*

Oswiu unites North-humberland, 48; defeats Penda, *ib.*; decides for Wilfrid against Colman, 50

Otho, Cardinal, legate of Gregory IX., 194

Otto I., Emperor, 63

Otto IV., Emperor, supports John, 179; defeated at Bouvines, 181

Oude, Hastings seeks its alliance against the Mahrattas, 802; annexation of, 951

Oudenarde, battle of, 690

Outram, Sir James, waives his rank in Havelock's favour, 954

Overbury, Sir Thomas, poisoned, 488

Over-lordship, character of, 38

Oxford, growth of the University of, 167; the so-called Mad Parliament meets at, 198; thronged with scholars, 207; study of Greek in the University of, 367; Parliament adjourned to, 502; headquarters of Charles I. at, 537; Parliament held at, during the Plague, 590; the third Short Parliament meets at, 621; Roman Catholic propaganda of James II. in, 639

Oxford, Earl of, quarrels with Bolingbroke, 699; dismissed, 700; impeached and imprisoned, 704, 705; *see* Harley, Sir Robert

Oxford, Earl of (Robert de Vere), made Duke of Ireland, 278; *see* Ireland, Duke of

Painting, mainly in the hands of foreigners, during the Stuart period, 631

Palæolithic man, 1

Palatinate, the, Spinola's invasion of,

PAR

400; Imperialist invasion of, 496; loss of, 497; failure of the negotiation to induce the king of Spain to obtain the restitution of, 500; attempt to send Mansfeld to recover, 501

Palmerston, Viscount, Foreign Secretary in Lord Grey's ministry, 891; supports the independence of Belgium, 912; maintains an alliance with France, 913; Spanish policy of, 920; interferes in Syria, 922; dismissed, 938; saves the Derby ministry from defeat, 939; is a member of the Aberdeen ministry, 945; becomes Prime Minister, 947; the elections (after his entering on a war with China) in favour of, 955; defeated on the Conspiracy to Murder Bill, and resigns, 956; becomes Prime Minister a second time, *ib.*; death of, 960

Pandulf receives John's submission, 180

Papacy, influence of, in the time of Gregory I., 39; strength of, in the eleventh century, 88; its position in the time of Gregory VII., 107; in the time of Innocent III., 178; Babylonian captivity of, 257; England relieved of tribute to, 258; great schism of, 266; immorality of, 375; legislation against the payment of annates and Peter's pence to, 388, 390

Papal jurisdiction in England, abolition of, 389, 391

Paradise Lost, publication of, 596

Paris, the capital of Hugh Capet's duchy, 80; rising against the Armagnacs in, 304; Henry VI. crowned at, 312; lost to the English, 313; submits to Henry IV., 464

Paris, Peace of, at the end of the Seven Years' War, 766; at the end of the American War, 798

Parker, Matthew, becomes Archbishop of Canterbury, 429; character and position of, 430

Parker, Samuel, Bishop of Oxford, a secret Roman Catholic, 639; intrusive President of Magdalen College, 641

Parliament (*see* Great Council, the), germ of representation in, 180; first use of the name of, 195; scheme of administrative reform proposed in, *ib.*; knights of the shire elected to, 196; relations between the clergy and the barons, 197; insists on the Provisions of Oxford, 197; representatives of towns admitted by Earl Simon to, 201; growth of, under Edward I., 210, 218; Scottish representatives in, 222; acknowledgment of the legislative power of the Commons in, 228; finally separated into two Houses, 244; opposition to the clergy in, 259; Richard II. invites complaints in, 280; relations of Henry VIII. with, 385; relations of Elizabeth with, 444; the Addled, 485; the Short, 528; the Long, 529; formation of parties in, 532; struggles with

PAR

Charles I. for the militia, 536; raises forces against the king, 537; tries to disband the army, 553; its speakers take refuge with the army, 555; dissolution of, by Cromwell, 566; the Barebone's, *ib.*; the first, of the Protectorate, 570; the second, of the Protectorate, 572; Richard Cromwell's, 574; restoration of the Long, 575; final dissolution of the Long, 576; the first convention, 577–584; the Cavalier, 585; supports the Church more than the king, 586; rejects the declaration of Charles II. in favour of toleration, 587; Albemarle resists the dissolution of, 599; opposes James II., 638; James II. attempts to pack, 641

Parliamentary reform, views of Chatham and Burke on, 777; supported by Fox, 789; advanced views of the Duke of Richmond on, 790; Pitt asks for a committee to inquire into, 799; Pitt brings forward a motion for, 801; Pitt's Bill for, 808; advocated by Grey, 827; Hunt and Burdett ask for a sweeping measure of, 879; Lord John Russell supports a moderate measure of, 894; granted by the first Reform Act, 905; Russell proposes to carry farther, 943; Disraeli brings in a bill for, 956; Russell brings in a bill for, 957; Russell's ministry brings in a bill for, 961; Disraeli carries a bill for, *ib.*; a third bill for, carried by agreement between Liberals and Conservatives, 972; *see* Reform Bill

Parma, Alexander Farnese, Prince of, governor of the Spanish Netherlands, 45; gains ground in the Netherlands, 454–456; takes Antwerp, 456; takes Zutphen, 457; hopes to transport an army to England, 459; blockaded by the Dutch, 462; sent to aid the League, 464

Parnell leads the Irish Home Rule party, 970

Parris, Van, burnt, 419

Parsons, Robert, lands in England, 453; escapes, 454

Parsons, Sir William, one of the Lords Justices in Ireland, 533

Parties, Parliamentary, formation of, 532; development of, 610, 628

Partition treaty, the first, 668; the second, 671

Paston, John, attacked by Lord Molynes, 321; domestic life of, 330

Patay, battle of, 311

Paterson, William, suggests the foundation of the Bank of England, 660; originates the Darien expedition, 671

Patrick, St., introduces Christianity into Ireland, 47

Paul, the Tzar, withdraws from the coalition against France, 840; murder of, 845

PET

Paulet, Sir Amias, refuses to put Mary Stuart to death, 457

Paulinus effects conversions in Deira, 46

Pavia, battle of, 372

Peasants' Revolt, the, 268

Pedro the Cruel, 255

Peel, Mr. (afterwards Sir Robert), recommends the resumption of cash payments, 879; becomes Home Secretary, 884; passes bills for the reform of the criminal law, 885; is Home Secretary in Wellington's ministry, 893; agrees to the repeal of the Test and Corporation Acts, 895; defeated at Oxford, 896; carries a bill for Catholic emancipation, *ib.*; introduces the new police, 900; Prime Minister for the first time, 913; refuses to take part against the Municipal Corporations Bill, 914; fails to form a Ministry, 918; becomes Prime Minister a second time, 925; first free-trade budget of, 926; Irish policy of, 928; second free-trade budget of, 929; attacked by Disraeli, 930; abolishes the Corn Law, 931; being defeated on a bill for the protection of life in Ireland, resigns office, 932; public works established in Ireland by, *ib.*; death of, 936

Peerage Bill, the, rejection of, 710

Peers, creation of twelve, 695

Peishwah, the, rules over the Mahratta confederacy, 760; driven from Poonah 859; abdicates, 948

Pelham, Henry, becomes First Lord of the Treasury. 739; death of, 744

Peltier, tried for libelling Bonaparte, 848

Pembroke, Earl of, *see* William the Marshal

Penda defeats Eadwine at Heathfield, 46; splits up North-humberland, 47; is defeated and slain, 48

Penitential system, the, introduced by Theodore, 50

Penjdeh, seized by the Russians, 972

Penn and Venables, expedition of, to the West Indies, 571

Pennsylvania, colonisation of, 629

Penruddock captures the judges at Salisbury, 571

Penry, John, hanged, 472

People's Charter, the, 923; *see* Chartists

Pepys pities dissenters, 588

Perceval, Spencer, becomes Prime Minister, 865; murdered, 868

Percies, the, territorial influence of, 293

Percy, Henry (Hotspur), 293, 294

Perpendicular style, the, 247

Perrers, Alice, 260, 262

Perth, the five articles of, 525

Peter Martyr teaches in England, 416

Peter des Roches influences Henry III. 188; is dismissed, 189

Peter the Great, sends troops to Mecklenburg, 709

PET

Peter the Hermit, 120
Peter's Pence, abolition of, 391
Peterborough, Earl of, his campaign in Spain, 684, 685
Petition of Right, the, 508
Petitioners, party name of, 620
Pevensey, landing of William at, 96
Philadelphia, congress of twelve colonies meets in, 782; congress of thirteen colonies meets in, 783; occupied by Howe, 786; evacuated by the British, 787
Philip I., king of France, makes war with William I., 114
Philip II., king of France, stirs up enmity between Henry II. and his sons, 156; quarrels with Richard I., 161; stirs up John against Richard, 162; supports Arthur against John, 174; wins Normandy and Anjou from John, 175; prepares an invasion of England, 179; wins a victory at Bouvines, 181
Philip II., king of Spain, marries Mary, 423; abdication of Charles V. in favour of, 426; deserts Mary, *ib.*; induces Mary to declare war against France, 427; makes peace with France, 431; proposes to marry Elizabeth, 432; persecutes the Protestants in the Netherlands, 443; annexes Portugal, and shares in a plot for the invasion of England and the murder of Elizabeth, 454; undertakes the invasion of England, 456; claims the English crown, 458; appoints a commander for the Armada, 460; supports the League in France, 464
Philip III., king of Spain, James I. seeks an alliance with, 488
Philip IV., king of France, his relations with Edward I. and with Scotland, 218
Philip IV., king of Spain, receives Prince Charles, and negotiates with the Pope about his sister's marriage, 497; consults theologians, 498; informs Charles of his terms, 500; death of, 592
Philip V., king of France, succeeds in virtue of the so-called Salic law, 232
Philip V., king of Spain, the Spanish inheritance bequeathed to, 671; attachment of the Spaniards to, 682; his claim to the French throne, 707
Philip VI., king of France, succeeds in virtue of the so-called Salic law, and receives the homage of Edward III., 232; protects David Bruce, 234; defeats the Flemings at Cassel, 235; avoids fighting the English, 239; is defeated at Crecy, 242; death of, 251
Philip, the Archduke, birth of, 337; marries Juana, 352; dies, 358
Philip's Norton, Monmouth at, 637
Philiphaugh, battle of, 549
Philippa of Hainault marries Edward III., 231; begs the lives of the burgesses of Calais, 243

PIT

Phœnicians, the, supposed visits to Britain of, 7
Picts, the, ravages of, 23, 26; unite with the Scots, 63
Piers the Plowman, 259
Pilgrim Father, the, 489
Pilgrim's Progress, publication of, 596
Pilgrimage of Grace, the, 396, 397
Pinkie Cleugh, battle of, 413
Pippin becomes king of the Franks, 54
Pitt, William (the elder), opposes Walpole, 728; attacks Spain, 729; declaims against Carteret, 738; his rivalry with Henry Fox, 747; dismissed, 748; becomes Secretary of State, and takes vigorous measures to carry on the war with France, 750; enlists Highland regiments, *ib.*; dismissal and popularity of, *ib.*: political position of, 751; coalesces with Newcastle, *ib.*; encourages men of ability and vigour, 752; enters into an alliance with Frederick, *ib.*; resignation of, 766; refuses to join the Rockingham Whigs, 771; his views on American taxation, 773; created Earl of Chatham, *ib.*; *see* Chatham, Earl of
Pitt, William (the younger), early career of, 799; asks for a committee on Parliamentary reform, and becomes Chancellor of the Exchequer, *ib.*; brings forward a motion for Parliamentary reform, 801; becomes Prime Minister, 807; his struggle against the coalition, *ib.*; obtains a majority in a new Parliament, 808; his financial measures, *ib.*; his India Bill, and his Bill for Parliamentary reform, *ib.*; failure of his scheme for a commercial union with Ireland, 810; consents to the impeachment of Hastings, 811; his conduct in supporting the Regency Bill, *ib.*; strengthened by the growth of manufacturers, 819; thinks that France will be weakened by the Revolution, 823; speaks against the slave-trade, *ib.*: adopts a war policy, 825; fears the spread of French revolutionary principles in England, 828; admits Whigs into his Cabinet, *ib.*; assists French royalists to land in Quiberon Bay, 830; carries the Treason Act and the Sedition Act, *ib.*; his views on the relations between England and Ireland, 831; gives votes to the Catholics in Ireland, 832; sends Fitzwilliam to Ireland, *ib.*; recalls Fitzwilliam, 833; his first negotiation with the Directory, 834; imposes an income-tax, 840; brings about the Irish Union, 842; proposes Catholic emancipation and resigns office, *ib.*; assures the king he will never again support Catholic emancipation, 843; becomes Prime Minister a second time, 848; weak in Parliamentary support, 851; death of, 855

PIU

Pius V., Pope, excommunicates Elizabeth, 441

Place Bill, the, 661

Plague, the, devastations of, 590

Plassey, battle of, 762

Plautius, Aulus, subdues south-east Britain, 13

Plymouth held by a Parliamentary garrison, 538

Poitevins, favour of Henry III. to, 187, 194

Poitiers, battle of, 251

Poitou, John's attack on the barons of, 174 ; submission to Philip II. of part of, 176 ; John attempts to recover, 180 ; Henry III. surrenders, 194

Poland, partition of, 827 ; assigned to Russia, 873

Pole, Reginald, opposes Henry VIII. and becomes a cardinal, 399 ; as Papal legate reconciles England to the see of Rome, 424 ; becomes archbishop of Canterbury, 426 ; death of, 427

Police, the new, introduction of, 900

Polish succession, the war of, 725

Poll-taxes, 267, 268

Ponet made Bishop of Winchester, 416

Poor, the, condition of, 922

Poor Law, the new, 911

Poor priests sent out by Wycliffe, 268

Pope, character of the poetry of, 726

Popish Plot, the, 615

Population, growth of, 813

Port Mahon, excellence of the harbour at, 690 ; taken by the French, 749

Portland, Duke of, Prime Minister in the Coalition Ministry, 801 : enters Pitt's cabinet, 828 ; becomes Prime Minister a second time, 857 ; death of, 865

Portland, Earl of, William III. attached to, 664

Portland, Richard Weston, Earl of, as Lord Weston, becomes Lord Treasurer, 514 ; made Earl of Portland and dies, 521

Porto Novo, battle of, 805

Portsmouth, Louise de Keroualle, Duchess of, betrays the secrets of Charles II., 602 ; extravagance of, 603

Portugal subdued by Philip II., 454 ; French invasion of, 863 ; Wellesley's first landing in, 864 ; return of Wellesley to, 866 ; the French driven out of, 867 ; secured by Canning, 884

Posidonius visits Britain, 8

Post Office reform, 918

Post-nati, the, 483

Power-loom, the, invented by Cartwright, 816

Powick Bridge, skirmish at, 537

Poynings' Acts, 350

Poyntz, Major-General, defeats Charles I. at Rowton Heath, 549

Præmunire, Statute of, 258 ; re-enacted, 282

Pragmatic Sanction, the, 732

PRO

Pratt, Chief Justice of the Common Pleas, discharges Wilkes, and declares against general warrants, 776 ; becomes Lord Chancellor and Lord Camden, 776 ; *see* Camden, Lord

Prayer Book, the, *see* Common Prayer, Book of

Prayer Book, the Scottish, introduced by Charles I., 525

Prerogative, the, opinion of James I. about, 492

Presbyterian clergy, the, prepared to accept a modified episcopacy, 583 ; expelled from their livings, 585 ; proposal of Charles II. to obtain comprehension for, 599

Presbyterian party, the, in a majority in the House of Commons, 546 ; attempts to disband the army, 553 ; negotiates with the Scots for a fresh invasion of England, 554 ; generally accepts the Prayer Book, 586

Presbyterianism emanates from Geneva, 430 ; its organisation completed in France, 431 ; adopted in Scotland, 434 ; attempts to establish, in England, 470 ; feeling in the Long Parliament about, 532 ; adopted by the Assembly of Divines, 543 ; Charles I. urged to establish in England, 551

Press, the liberty of the, 663

Preston, Cromwell's victory at, 557

Preston Pans, battle of, 740

Pretender, the Old, acknowledged King of England by Louis XIV., 675 ; a fraction of the Tory party favours the claims of, 699 ; appears in Scotland to support Mar's rising, 705

Pretender, the Young, his fleet shattered by a storm, 737 ; lands in the Highlands, 739 ; defeats Cope at Preston Pans and marches to Derby, 740 ; returns to Scotland and defeats Hawley at Falkirk, 741 ; defeated at Culloden, 742 ; escapes to the continent, 743

Prichard, Lord Mayor, 624

Pride's Purge, 557

Prime Minister, gradual development of the office of, 716

Prince Edward Island, joins the Dominion of Canada, 968

Printing-press, the, 358

Prisons, condition of, 275

Privilege of Parliament, Strickland's case of, 445 ; Eliot's vindication of the, 512

Privy Council, the, Temple's scheme for reforming, 617

Prophesyings, the, 450

Protectionists, the, led by Stanley, 931 ; vote against Peel's bill for the protection of life in Ireland, *ib.*

Protectorate, establishment of the, 568

Protestants, the English, feeling of Henry VIII. and More towards, 388 ; parties amongst, 413 ; the Marian persecution of, 424 ; local distribution of, 426 ; their position at Elizabeth's acces-

PRO

sion, 423; influence of Calvinism on, 430

Provençals favoured by Henry III., 192

Provisions of Oxford, the, 198

Provisors, Statute of, 258; re-enacted, 282

Prussia, Frederick I. receives the title of King of, 678; succession of Frederick II. in, 732; annexation of Silesia, 735; attacked in the Seven Years' War, 749; takes part in the struggle with revolutionary France, 824; takes part in the partition of Poland, 827; makes peace with France at Basel, 829; overthrown at Jena, 857; ill-treated by Napoleon, 858; joins Russia against Napoleon, 871; gains territory at the Congress of Vienna, 873; adoption of a constitutional system in, 934; repression of the revolutionists in, 936; makes war with Austria, 963; at the head of the North German Confederation, *ib.*; *see* German Empire, the

Prynne, character and writings of, 519; his sentence in the Star Chamber, *ib.*; second sentence on, 521

Public Meetings, origin of, 789

Puiset, Hugh de, appointed a justiciar in the absence of Richard I., 159

Pularoon, refusal of the Dutch to surrender, 589; abandoned by the English, 593

Pulteney, leads a section of the opposition against Walpole, 722; stirs up public opinion against the Excise Bill, 724; refuses office and becomes Earl of Bath, 730, 731

Punishments, early English, 32; mediæval, 275

Puritans, the, aims of, 444; gain influence in the House of Commons, 445, 468; the Court of High Commission directed against, 470; opinions of, at the Hampton Court Conference, 482; unpopular after the Restoration, 586

Purveyance, abolition of, 582

Purveyors, 274

Pusey, a leader of the Oxford movement, 940

Pym differs from Eliot on the method of dealing with the question of Tonnage and Poundage, 512; addresses the Short Parliament on grievances, 529; proposes in the Long Parliament the impeachment of Strafford, *ib.*; his view of Strafford's case, 530; discloses the army plot, 531; is one of the leaders of the party of the Grand Remonstrance, 534; accused as one of the five members, 535; urges the House of Commons to resist Charles I., 540; death of, 542

Pytheas opens a trade-route to Britain, 8

Quadruple Alliance, the, 700

Quebec, Wolfe sent to take, 753; surrender of, 756

RIC

Queen Anne's Bounty, 693

Queensland, established as a separate colony, 969

Quia emptores, Statute of, 212

Quiberon Bay, Hawke's victory in, 756; landing of French royalists in, 830

Quo warranto, writs of, 624, 625

Radcot Bridge, the Duke of Ireland defeated at, 280

Radicals, the demand for reform made by, 877

Rædwald, king of East Anglia, 41; Eadwine takes refuge with, 43

Raglan, Lord, commands the English army invading the Crimea, 945

Railways, introduction of, 906

Raleigh, Sir Walter, takes part in the capture of Cadiz, 464; sentenced to death and imprisonment, 481; loses Sherborne, 486; voyage to Guiana and execution of, 499; his colony in Virginia, *ib.*

Ralph de Diceto, 167

Ralph of Wader takes part in the Rising of the Earls, 110

Ramillies, battle of, 684

Ranulph Flambard, *see* Flambard

Ré, Buckingham's expedition to, 505

Reading taken by Essex, 538

Reading, the abbot of, executed, 400

Recognitions, 147

Recusancy laws, the, penalties inflicted by, 454

Reform Bill, the first, introduced and withdrawn, 902; re-introduced and rejected by the Lords, 903; brought in a third time and passed, 905; passing of the second, 961; passing of the third, 972; *see* Parliamentary Reform

Regency Bill, the, 811

Regicides, the, execution of, 582

Reginald elected Archbishop of Canterbury by the monks, 177

Regni, the, join Aulus Plautius, 13

Regular clergy, the, 65

Regulating Act, the, 802

Reign of Terror, the, 826-828

Reims, College at, 453

Relics, destruction of, 398

Renascence, the, character of, 366; its influence on England, 367; immorality of, 374, 375

Rent, land let for, 321

Reporting, freedom of, established, 779

Representative institutions, *see* Parliament

Requesens, governor of the Netherlands, 449

Retainers substituted for vassals, 281; increase of the number of, 321

Revenue of the crown fixed after the Restoration, 582

Revolution of 1688-9, 646-648

Rich, Edmund, Archbishop of Canterbury, 189

RIC

Richard I., as Duke of Aquitaine, 155; takes the cross, 157; becomes King of England, 159; sells the homage of Scotland, *ib.*; his Crusade and imprisonment, 161; is liberated, 162; his short visit to England, *ib.*; death of, 165

Richard II., proposal to set aside, 261; his minority, 266; meets the insurgents, 268; offers to head them, 269; marries Anne of Bohemia, 278; his favouritism, *ib.*; superseded in his authority by a Commission of Regency, 279; regains power and governs constitutionally, 280; makes an alliance with France, and marries Isabella, 282; makes himself absolute, *ib.*; banishes Norfolk and Hereford, 283; goes to Ireland, 284; forced to abdicate, 285; murdered, 291; alleged re-appearance of, 293; buried at Westminster, 299

Richard III. (*see* Duke of Gloucester) is created a duke, 329; character of, 337; becomes Protector, 338; has Hastings executed, 340; is crowned king, 341; his government, 342; defeated and slain, 343

Richard, Earl of Cornwall, leads the barons against Henry III., 192; deserts the barons, 195; takes part in summoning knights of the shire to Parliament, 196; is chosen king of the Romans, 198; hides himself after the battle of Lewes, 201

Richard Fitz-Nigel writes the *Dialogus de Scaccario*, 167

Richard the Fearless, Duke of the Normans, 80

Richard the Good, Duke of the Normans, 81

Richmond, Duke of, asks for manhood suffrage and annual parliaments. 790

Richmond, Earl of, *see* Henry VII.

Riding on horseback, 273

Ridley made Bishop of London, 416; burnt, 425

Ridolfi plot, the, 444

Rinuccini, Archbishop, arrives in Ireland, 550; leaves Ireland, 562

Ripon, architecture of the choir of, 171

Ripon, Earl of, resigns office, 912; *see* Robinson, Frederick J., and Goderich, Viscount

Ripon, treaty of, 529

Rising in the North, the, 441

Rising of the Earls, the, 110

Rivers, Earl, becomes Lord Constable, 331; imprisoned, 338; executed, 340

Rizzio, David, murder of, 439

Roads, making and repair of, 272, 273; improvement in, 633

Robert I. (Bruce), king of Scotland, allied with Edward I., 223; slays Comyn, and is crowned King of Scotland, 224; defeats Edward II. at Bannockburn, 226; leprosy of, 231; death of, 232

Robert II., king of Scotland, 295

ROM

Robert III., king of Scotland, 295

Robert, Earl of Gloucester, his power in the West of England, 133; declares for Matilda, 134; taken prisoner, and exchanged for Stephen, 135; death of, *ib.*

Robert, Duke of the Normans (father of William the Conqueror), 88

Robert, Duke of the Normans (son of William the Conqueror), incapacity of, 114; rebellion in England in favour of, 115; goes on the first Crusade, 121; fails to overthrow Henry I., 124; defeat, imprisonment, and death of, 125

Robert of Bellême, cruelty of, 119; becomes Earl of Shrewsbury, 121; expelled by Henry I., 124; imprisonment of, 125

Robert of Jumièges, Archbishop of Canterbury, 87

Robin Hood, legend of, 275

Robinson, Sir Thomas, fails as leader of the House of Commons, 747

Robinson, Frederick J., budgets of, 886; *see* Goderich, Viscount, and Ripon, Earl of

Rochefort, failure of an attempt against, 753

Rochelle, Buckingham lends ships to fight against the Huguenots of, 504; siege of, 506; expedition to the relief of, 510

Rochester, foundation of the bishopric of, 40; Odo besieged in, 115

Rochester, Lawrence Hyde, Earl of, advises against the summoning of Parliament, 626; dismissal of, 640; dismissed through the influence of Marlborough, 681

Rockingham, Council at, 118

Rockingham, Marquis of, leads one of the three fractions of the Whig party, 768; first ministry of, 771; dismissal of, 773; second ministry of, 795; death of, 796

Rockingham Whigs, the, Pitt's dislike of, 771; Burke's influence with, 772; take the view that the House of Commons has no right to incapacitate Wilkes, 774; oppose Parliamentary reform, 777; support economical reform, 789

Rodney, Admiral, bombards Havre, 756; defeats De Grasse, 795

Roger, Archbishop of York, crowns the young Henry, 149

Roger, Bishop of Salisbury, Minister of Henry I., 126; quarrels with Stephen, 134

Roger, Earl of Hereford, takes part in the Rising of the Earls, 110

Roger of Hoveden, 167

Roger, son of Roger of Salisbury, 134

Rogers, John, burnt, 424

Rohillas, the, Hastings assists the Nawab of Oude to subdue, 802

Roman Empire, the, establishment of, 12; continuance of, in the East after its destruction in the West, 27

ROM

Romans, the, invasion of Gaul by, 10; invasion of Britain by, 11; commencement of the conquest of Britain by, 12; massacre of, 15; complete conquest of the greater part of Britain by, 17; civilisation introduced into Britain by, 21; end of their rule in Britain, 26; persistency of their civilisation in Gaul, 37

Rome taken by the Duke of Bourbon, 374

Romilly, Sir Samuel, advocates the reform of the criminal law, 885

Romney Marsh divides Jutes from South Saxons, 27

Rooke, Sir George, takes Gibraltar, 682

Roosebeke, battle of, 278

Root and Branch Bill, the, 533

Roses, Wars of the, see Wars of the Roses

Rothesay, Duke of, death of, 295

Rouen occupied by Hrolf, 80; surrenders to Henry V., 304; retaken by the French, 320

Roumania becomes an independent kingdom, 969

Roundway Down, battle of, 538

Rowton Heath, battle of, 549

Royal Assent, the, refused for the last time, 706

Royal Society, the, foundation of, 598

Rump, the, name given to the remnant of the Long Parliament, 565; dissolved by Cromwell, 566; brought back, expelled and brought back again, 575; final dissolution of, 576

Runjeet Singh, allies himself with the British, 949; death of, 951

Rupert, Prince, commands the cavalry at Edgehill, 537; storms Bristol, 538; is defeated at Marston Moor, 543; takes part in the battle of Naseby, 548; surrenders Bristol, 549; holds a command in the battle off the North Foreland, 592; defeated off the Texel, 608

Russell, Admiral, afterwards Earl of Orford, commands the fleet at La Hogue, 658; is one of the Whig Junto, 659; created Earl of Orford, 669; see Orford, Earl of

Russell, Earl, becomes Prime Minister a second time, 961; resignation of, ib.; see Russell, Lord John

Russell, Lord John, advocates Parliamentary reform, 894; obtains the repeal of the Test and Corporation Acts, 895; holds a subordinate office in Lord Grey's ministry, 901; introduces the first Reform Bill, 902; becomes Home Secretary and Leader of the House of Commons, 913; is unable to form a ministry, and supports Peel's abolition of the Corn Law, 931; objects to Peel's Irish policy, ib.; becomes Prime Minister, 932; his dealings with Irish distress, ib.; attempts to improve the condition of tenants in

SAI

Ireland, 933; passes the Encumbered Estates Act, 934; passes the Ecclesiastical Titles Bill, 937; resignation of, 938; joins the Aberdeen Ministry, and promises a new Reform Bill, 943; is Foreign Secretary in Palmerston's second ministry, 956; brings in a Reform Bill, 957; see Russell, Earl

Russell, William Russell, Lord, supports the Exclusion Bill, 617; refuses to take part in acts of violence, 624; trial of, 625; execution of, 626

Russia, interferes for the first time in Western Europe, 709; establishes the 'Armed Neutrality,' 792; takes part in the second coalition, 839; withdraws from the alliance, 840; joins the Northern Confederacy, 844; withdraws from the Northern Confederacy, 845; joins the third coalition, 854; invaded by Napoleon, 869; offers aid to the Sultan, 921; joins England, Austria, and Prussia in supporting the Sultan, 922; proposed partition of the Turkish dominions in agreement with, 943; goes to war with the Sultan, 944; war declared by England and France against, ib.; makes peace with the allies, 948; alliance of Dost Mohammed with, 949; refuses to be bound by the treaty of 1856, 965; overpowers the Turkish army, and submits to the Treaty of Berlin, 969; acquires Penjdeh, 971

Rutland, Earl of (son of the Duke of York), accompanies his father to Ireland, 326; murdered, 328

Ruvigny, Marquis of, serves in Ireland, 656; see Galway, Earl of

Ruyter, De, captures English forts in Guinea, 589

Rye House Plot, the, 625

Ryswick, peace of, 667

Sa, Dom Pantaleon, execution of, 569

Sacheverell, Dr., sermon preached by, 690; impeached, 691

Sackville, Lord George, misconduct of, 756

Sadowa, battle of, 963

St. Albans (see Verulam), architecture of the nave of the abbey of, 171; meeting of a national jury at, 180; the first battle of, 324; the second battle of, 328

St. Andrews captured by the French and recaptured, 413

St. Arnaud, Marshal, commands the French army in the Crimea, 945; death of, 946

St. Bartholomew, massacre of, 449

St. Bartholomew's day, ejection of the Presbyterian clergy on, 585

St. Cast, failure of an expedition to the Bay of, 753

St. Christopher's, England receives the French part of, 696

SAI

St. John, Henry, becomes minister as a moderate Tory, 681 ; obtains the rejection of an Occasional Conformity Bill, 682 ; turned out of office, 687 ; is a member of a purely Tory ministry, 691 ; orders Ormond not to fight, 695 ; created Viscount Bolingbroke, *ib.*; *see* Bolingbroke, Viscount

St. John, Knights of, 157

St. Malo, expedition against, 753

St. Michael's Mount, Henry besieged at, 119

St. Paul's, Old, burnt, 592 ; rebuilt, 677

St. Vincent, battle of, 835

Saladin takes Jerusalem, 157

Saladin tithe, the, 157

Salamanca, battle of, 869

Salic law, the so-called, 232

Salisbury, great Gemot at, 113 ; cathedral at, 207 ; Penruddock captures the judges at, 571

Salisbury, Marquis of, becomes Prime Minister, 971

Salisbury, Richard, Earl of, his connection with the Duke of York, 324 ; takes part in the battles of Blore Heath and Northampton, 326 ; beheaded, 328

Salisbury, Robert Cecil, Earl of, as Sir Robert Cecil, secretary to Elizabeth and James I., 480, 481 ; becomes Earl of Salisbury and Lord Treasurer, 484 ; orders the levy of new impositions, *ib.*; death of, 486

Salisbury, Countess of, executed, 401

San Domingo, Penn and Venables attack, 572

San Stefano, treaty of, 969

Sancroft, William, Archbishop of Canterbury, deprived for refusal to take oaths to William, 651

Sandwich, Earl of, informs against Wilkes, 770

Santa Cruz, Blake destroys Spanish ships at, 573

Saratoga, capitulation of, 786

Sardinia, Kingdom of, conferred on the Duke of Savoy, in lieu of the Kingdom of Sicily, 710

Sarum, Old, 34

Savile, Sir George, presides over a meeting in support of economical reform, 789 ; passes a Bill in relief of Roman Catholics, 792

Savoy, the, burnt, 269

Savoy Conference, the, 585

Savoy, Duke of, persecutes the Vaudois, 572

Sawtre, William, burnt as a heretic, 292

Saxon shore, the defence of, 25 ; overrun by the Jutes, 27

Saxons, the (*see* East Saxons, South Saxons, West Saxons), ravage Roman Britain, 24 ; settle in Britain, 27 ; merge their name in that of English, 28 ; are known by the Celts as Saxons, 29

Say, Lord, beheaded by Jack Cade, 323

SCO

Scheldt, the, opening of, 825

Schism Act, the, passed, 699 ; repealed, 710

Schomberg, Marshal, lands in Ireland, 655 ; killed at the Boyne, 656

Schwartz, Martin, defeated at Stoke, 347

Scotland, kingdom of, formed by a union of Scots and Picts, 63 ; its relations with England under Eadmund, 64 ; its relations with Cnut, 84 ; with William I., 104 ; with William II., 119 ; with Stephen, 133 ; with Henry II., 154 ; with Richard I., 159 ; disputed succession in, 214 ; Edward I. acknowledged Lord Paramount of, 216 ; its league with France, 218 ; twice conquered by Edward I., 219, 221 ; incorporated with England, 222 ; conquered a third time by Edward I., 224 ; independence of, 226 ; first war of Edward III. with, 231 ; struggle between Edward Balliol and David Bruce in, 233, 234 ; accession of the Stuarts to the throne of, 295 ; assists France in its wars with England, 307 ; power of the nobles in, 404 ; Hertford's invasion of, 409 ; Protestant missionaries in, 412 ; Somerset's invasion of, 413 ; the Reformation in, 432 ; the intervention of Elizabeth in, 433 ; Presbyterianism in, 434 ; Mary lands in, 435 ; Mary's government of, 437–440 ; civil war in, 443 ; projected union with, 482 ; Episcopacy and Presbyterianism in, 524 ; introduction of a new prayer book in, 525 ; national covenant signed in, *ib.* ; first Bishops' war with, 526 ; episcopacy abolished by the Assembly and Parliament of, 527 ; the second Bishops' war with, 529 ; visit of Charles I. to, 532 ; solemn league and covenant with, 540 ; sends an army into England, 542 ; its army recalled, 553 ; proposal of a new invasion of England by, 554 ; engagement signed with Charles I. by Commissioners of, 556 ; Charles II. and Cromwell in, 563 ; Restoration settlement of, 595 ; Lauderdale's influence in, 602 ; Lauderdale's management of, 619 ; Covenanters in, *ib.*; rising of the Covenanters in, 620 ; under James II., 639 ; Presbyterianism established in, 652 ; the crown offered to William and Mary in, *ib.* ; pacification of the Highlands of, 654 ; the union with, 685 ; enthusiastic support of the Darien expedition in, 671 ; Mar's rising in, 705 ; disruption of the Church of, 940

Scots, the ravages of, 23 ; abode of, in Ireland, 23 ; renewed ravages of, 26 ; settle in Argyle, and are defeated at Degsastan, 42 ; their relations with Eadward the Elder, 63 ; *see* Scotland

Scott, Sir Walter, works of, 889

Scottish army, the, encamps on Dunse Law, 526 ; routs the English at New-

SCR

burn, 529 ; invades England, 542 ; besieges York, *ib.* ; takes part in the battle of Marston Moor, 543 ; receives Charles I. at Southwell, and conveys him to Newcastle, 551 ; negotiation for the abandonment of Charles I. by, 553 ; returns to Scotland, 553 ; is defeated at Dunbar, 563 ; and at Worcester, 564

Scrope, Archbishop of York, executed, 296

Scrope, Lord, execution of, 301

Scutage, 141

Scutari, hospital at, 947

Sebastopol, siege of, 945 ; reduction of, 947 ; destruction of the fortifications of, 948

Second Civil War, the, 556, 557

Secular clergy, the, 67

Sedan, battle of, 965

Sedgemoor, battle of, 637

Sedition Act, the, 830

Selby taken by the Fairfaxes, 542

Selden, John, takes part in drawing up the Petition of Right, 508

Self-denying Ordinance, the, 545

Selsey, landing of the South Saxons near, 27

Seminary priests, the, 453 ; Act of Parliament against, 456

Senegal ceded by France, 766

Senlac, battle of, 96

Separatists, the, principles of, 470 ; settlement of, in Leyden and New England, 489 ; receive the name of ' Independents, 543 ; *see* Independents

Sepoy mutiny, the, 951–955

Septennial Act, the, 706

Serfs, *see* Villeins

Seringapatam stormed, 838

Servia, becomes an independent kingdom, 969

Settlement, Irish Act of, 595

Settlement, Act of; *see* Act of Settlement

Seven Bishops, the, petition presented by, 642 ; trial of, 643

Seven Years' War, the, beginning of, 749 ; end of, 766 ; results of, 767

Severn, West Saxon conquest of the Valley of, 35

Severus fails in conquering the Caledonians, 19

Seymour, Jane, *see* Jane Seymour

Seymour of Sudley, Lord, execution of, 415

Seymour, William, heir of the Suffolk line, 480

Shaftesbury, Anthony Ashley Cooper, Earl of, early life of, 602 ; policy of, 603 ; supports the Declaration of Indulgence, 605 ; becomes Earl of Shaftesbury and Chancellor, *ib.* ; his invective against the Dutch, 606 ; dismissal of, 608 ; leads the opposition, *ib.* ; supports toleration for Dissenters only, 610 ; declares the present Parliament to be dissolved, 612 ; encourages belief in the Popish Plot,

SIN

616 ; his position similar to that of Pym, 618 ; supports the Exclusion Bill, *ib.* ; indicts the Duke of York as a recusant, 621 ; supported by the third Short Parliament, *ib.* ; the Grand Jury throw out a Bill against, 622 ; Dryden's satire on, 623 ; proposes to attack the king's guards, 624 ; exile and death of, *ib.*

Shakspere, William, teaching of, 474

' Shannon,' the, captures the ' Chesapeake,' 872

Sharp, Archbishop, murder of, 620

Shelburne, Earl of, takes office in Rockingham's second ministry, 795 ; becomes Prime Minister, 796 ; resignation of, 800

Shelley, opinions of, 888

Sherborne taken by Fairfax, 548

Sherfield, Henry, fined by the Star Chamber, 515

Sheridan, takes part in the impeachment of Hastings, 811

Sheriffmuir, battle of, 705

Sheriffs, their position in Eadgar's reign, 73 ; weakened by Henry II., 148

Ship-money, levy of, 523 ; resisted by Hampden, 524

Ships, comparison between English and Spanish, 459

Shires, origin of, 73

Shire-moot, the, 73 ; *see* County Courts

Shore, Jane, penance of, 340

Shovel, Sir Cloudesley, drowned, 689

Shrewsbury, Duke of, becomes Lord Treasurer, 700

Shrewsbury, Earl of, *see* Talbot, Lord

Shrewsbury, Parliament of, 283 ; battle of, 294

Shrines, destruction of, 398

Sicily, the Duke of Savoy becomes king of, 696 ; given to Austria, 710 ; ceded to the son of Philip V., 724 ; retained by Ferdinand I., 857

Sidmouth, Viscount, included in the Ministry of All the Talents, 855 ; is Home Secretary in Lord Liverpool's ministry, 877 ; holds that meetings in favour of Radical reform are treasonable, 880 ; *see* Addington

Sidney, Algernon, execution of, 626

Sidney, Sir Philip, death of, 457

Sikhs, the, allied, under Runjeet Singh, with the British, 949 ; wars with, 951

Silchester, Roman church at, 23

Simnel, Lambert, insurrection in favour of, 347

Simon de Montfort, early career of, 193 ; takes the side of the barons, 195 ; employed in Gascony, 196 ; executes the Provisions of Oxford, 199 ; heads the baronial party, 200 ; wins the battle of Lewes, 201 ; constitutional scheme of, ib. ; killed at Evesham, 203 ; compared with Archbishop Thomas, 204

Sinclair, Oliver, killed at Solway Moss, 405

Sindhia, a Mahratta chief, 802 ; defeated

SIV

and reduced to sign a subsidiary treaty, 859
Sivaji founds the Mahratta State, 759
Siward, Earl of North-humberland, 84, 87
Six Arts, the, 880
Skeffington, Lord Deputy, takes Maynooth, 402
Slave trade, the, carried on by Elizabethan sailors, 447 ; recognised in the Assiento Treaty, 696 ; denounced by Clarkson, 823 ; attacked by Wilberforce and Pitt, *ib.*; abolished, 855, 857
Slavery, agitation for the abolition of, 910 ; abolition of, 911
Slaves preserved alive at the English conquest, 30
Sluys, battle of, 239
Smerwick, slaughter at, 453
Smith, Adam, his *Wealth of Nations*, 810
Smith, Sir Sidney, defends Acre, 838
Solemn league and covenant, the, 540
Solway Moss, defeat of the Scots at, 405 ; Charles I. urged by the Scots to take, 551
Somers, Lord, one of the Whig Junto, 659 ; resignation of, 670 ; dissuades the Whigs from impeaching Sacheverell, 691
Somerset, Welsh driven out of, 53
Somerset, Edmund Beaufort, second Duke of, commands in Normandy, 320 ; supported by Henry VI., 323 ; slain at St. Albans, 324
Somerset, Edmund Beaufort, fourth Duke of, executed, 334
Somerset, Edward Seymour, Duke of, invades Scotland as Earl of Hertford, 406 ; becomes Duke of Somerset and Protector, 412 ; defeats the Scots at Pinkie Cleugh, 413 ; possession of Church property by, 415 ; expelled from the Protectorate, 416 ; execution of, 418
Somerset, Henry Beaufort, third Duke of executed, 331
Somerset, John Beaufort, first Duke of, commands in France, 317 ; kept from court by Suffolk, 318 ; dies, 320
Somerset, Robert Carr, Earl of, favourite of James I., 486 ; disgrace of, 488
Somerset House, building of, 425
Sophia, the Electress, favours the Whigs, 699 ; death of, 701
Sorbiodunum (*Old Sarum*), the stronghold of Ambrosius, 34
South Africa, progress of, 968
South Australia established as a separate colony, 968
South Saxons, the, first conquests of, 27 ; destroy Anderida, 28
South Sea Bubble, the, 711
Southwell, Charles I. surrenders to the Scots at, 551
Southwold Bay, battle in, 605
Spain, union of the kingdoms of, 349 ; growth of the monarchy of, 354 ;

STA

resources of, 426 ; maritime power of, 447 ; authority of, in the West Indies challenged by English sailors, *ib.* ; navy of, 459 ; English attacks on, 464 ; sends an expedition to Kinsale, 478 ; its alliance sought by James I., 486 ; attack of Raleigh on the colonies of, 489 ; sends troops to occupy the Palatinate, 490 ; protest of the Commons against an alliance with, 496 ; visit of Prince Charles to, 497 ; eagerness in England for war with, 500 ; money voted for war with, 501 ; expedition against Cadiz in, 503 ; Charles I. makes peace with, 514 ; Cromwell makes war on, 571 ; question of the succession to, 592 ; war of the Spanish succession in, 682 ; her conflict with England in the West Indies, 726 ; war with, 730 ; joins France against England at the end of the Seven Years' War, 766 ; allies herself with France and America, 787 ; makes peace with Great Britain, 798 ; its fleet defeated off Cape St. Vincent, 835 ; Napoleon's interference in, 862 ; resists Napoleon, 863 ; Napoleon appears in, 864 ; Wellesley's advance to Talavera in, 867 ; Wellington's advance to Madrid and Burgos in, 869 ; the French driven out of, 871 ; revolution against Ferdinand VII. in, 882 ; death of Ferdinand VII. in, 920 ; civil war in, 921
Spanish succession, the, claimants to, 667 ; thrown open by the death of Charles II., 671 ; war of, 675
Spencer, Henry, Bishop of Norwich, leads an expedition to Flanders, 278
Spenser, Edmund, his *Faerie Queen*, 473
Spinning, improvements in, 814
Spinola, Ambrogio, invades the Palatinate, 490
Spithead, mutiny at, 836
Spurs, battle of the, 364
Stadholder, office of, 449 ; abolition of the office of, 565
Stafford, William Howard, Viscount, execution of, 621
Stainer, Admiral, captures a Spanish fleet, 572
Stair, the Master of, John Dalrymple, organises the massacre of Glencoe, 654
Stamford Bridge, battle of, 95
Stamp Act, the, passed, 771 ; repealed, 772
Standard, battle of the, 133
Stanhope, Earl, death of, 712 ; *see* Stanhope, General
Stanhope, General, takes Minorca, 690 ; surrenders at Brihuega, 692 ; takes the lead after the Whig schism, and becomes Viscount and the Earl Stanhope, 709 ; *see* Stanhope, Earl
Stanley, Lord, joins Henry VII., 343
Stanley, Mr., afterwards Lord, his policy as Chief Secretary for Ireland, 910 ; becomes Colonial Secretary,

STA

ib. ; carries a Bill for the abolition of slavery, 911 ; resigns office, 912 ; a member of Peel's cabinet, 926 ; resigns, and becomes a leader of the Protectionists, 931 ; succeeds to the Earldom of Derby, 938 ; *see* Derby, Earl of

Stanley, Sir William, deserts Richard III., 343 ; execution of, 351

Star Chamber, Court of, organisation of, 347 ; its sentences in the reign of Charles I., 514, 519, 521 ; abolition of, 531

States-General, the French, meet during John's captivity, 252

Statute of Wales, 210

Steam-engine, the, improved by Watt, 816 ; introduction of the locomotive, 906

Steam-vessels, introduction of, 906

Stephen, accession of, 131 ; makes peace with the Scots, 133 ; quarrels with the barons, *ib.* ; quarrels with the clergy, 134 ; death of, 135

Stephenson, George, introduces locomotive engines, 906 ; appointed engineer to the Liverpool and Manchester Railway, 907 ; adoption of his locomotive, 909

Stigand, Archbishop of Canterbury, 89

Stillingfleet aims at comprehension, 598

Stirling, Wallace's victory at, 221

Stoke, battle of, 347

Stone implements, 1-4

Stop of the Exchequer, the, 604

Stow-on-the-Wold, surrender of the last Royalist army at, 550

Strafford, Thomas Wentworth, Earl of, as Sir Thomas Wentworth, his policy contrasted with that of Eliot, 508 ; brings in a bill to secure the liberty of the subject, *ib.* ; becomes Lord Wentworth and President of the Council of the North, 514 ; becomes Lord Deputy of Ireland, 527 ; created Earl of Strafford, and advises the summoning of the Short Parliament, 528 ; does not advise the prolongation of the second Bishops war, 529 ; collects an Irish army, *ib.* ; is impeached, 530 ; Bill of Attainder against, *ib.*; execution of, 531

Strathclyde, formation of the kingdom of, 43 ; is not dependent on Ecgberht, 55 ; its relations with Eadmund, 64

Stratton, battle of, 538

Strickland moves for an amendment of the Prayer Book, 445

Strode, William, one of the five members, 535

Strongbow in Ireland, 152

Stuart, family of, inherit the throne of Scotland, 295 ; last descendants of the House of, 743

Submission of the clergy, the, 386

Subsidiary treaties, 859

Succession, Act of, 392

Suetonius Paullinus, campaigns of, 14-16

TAL

Suffolk, origin of the name of, 28

Suffolk, Charles Brandon, Duke of, marries Mary, sister of Henry VIII., 364

Suffolk, Michael de la Pole, Earl of Chancellor of Richard II., 278 ; driven from power, 279 ; condemned to death, 280

Suffolk, Thomas Howard, Earl of, 486

Suffolk, William de la Pole, Earl of, arranges a truce with France, 317 ; presides over the government of England, 318 ; impeached and murdered, 322

Suffolk line, its title to the succession, 410 ; Elizabeth's feeling towards, 435 ; William Seymour, the heir of, 480

Sunderland, Earl of, becomes Secretary of State, 687 ; takes the lead after the Whig schism, 709 ; resignation of, 712

Supremacy, Act of, 393 ; Elizabethan Act of, 429

Supreme head of the Church of England, title of, conferred by Convocation on Henry VIII., 386 ; abandoned by Elizabeth, 429

Surrey, Earl of, governs Scotland in the name of Edward I., 219

Surrey, Henry Howard, Earl of, execution of, 411

Surrey, Thomas Howard, Earl of, minister of Henry VIII., 363 ; the commander at Flodden, *see* Norfolk, Duke of

Sussex, conquest of, 27, 28 ; weakness of, 41 ; accepts Christianity, 49

Sussex, Thomas Ratcliffe, Earl of, Lord Deputy of Ireland, 452

Sutlej, the, battles on, 951

Svend attacks London, 79 ; returns to Denmark, 80 ; invades England, 81 ; death of, 83

Sweden takes part in the Triple Alliance, 599

Swegen, son of Godwine, misconduct of, 87 ; death of, 88

Swift, career of, 693 ; political influence of, 694 ; writes *The Drapier's Letters*, 718

Swynford, Catherine, marries John of Gaunt, 282

Syria, acquired by Mehemet Ali, 921 ; restored to the Sultan, 922

Tacking, successful in the case of a bill on Irish forfeitures, 670 ; rejected by the Commons in the case of an Occasional Conformity Bill, 682

Talavera, battle of, 867

Talbot, Lord, defeats the Burgundians, 313 ; becomes Earl of Shrewsbury, 320 ; defeated and slain, 323

Tallages levied by Edward I., 221 ; abolished by Edward III., 243

Tallard, Marshal, defeated at Blenheim 682

TAN

Tangier acquired by Charles II., 587
Tasmania becomes a separate colony, 968
Taunton, siege of, 548
Taxation, *see* Danegeld, Customs
Taylor, Rowland, burnt, 424
Tel-el-Kebir, battle of, 971
Telford, improvement of roads by, 905
Templars, the Knights, 157
Temple, Lord, canvasses the House of Lords against Fox's India Bill, 806
Temple, Sir William, negotiates the Triple Alliance, 599; advises the reform of the Privy Council, 617; failure of his scheme, 620
Tennyson, his *In Memoriam*, 943
Terouenne, 364
Test Act, the, passed, 607; a second, 616; violated by James II., 638; Sunderland and Stanhope think of repealing, 710; Walpole resists the repeal of, 716; partial repeal of, 895
Tewkesbury, battle of, 334
Texel, the, Rupert defeated off, 608
Thackeray, his *Vanity Fair*, 940
Thames, the, early ferry over, 20
Thanet, probable identification of Ictis with, 8; Jutes established in, 27
Thegns, how distinguished from Gesiths, 31; their devotion to their lord, 44; growing military importance of, 69
Theodore, Archbishop, his influence on the Church of England, 50; assembles the first Church Council, 52
Thetford, removal of the see from, 107
Thiers supports Mehemet Ali, and prepares for war with England, 922
Thirty Years' War, the, beginning of, 490; end of, 564
Thistlewood proposes to murder the cabinet, 881
Thomas of Canterbury, St., destruction of the shrine of, 398
Thomas of London (Becket), Chancellor, 140; being appointed Archbishop of Canterbury, resists Henry II., 143; takes refuge in France, 145; returns to England, 149; is murdered, 150
Throgmorton's conspiracy, 456
Thurlow, Lord, his saying about Fox's India Bill, 806
Thurstan, Archbishop, leads the levies at the battle of the Standard, 132
Tiberias, battle of, 157
Ticonderoga, Abercrombie repulsed at, 753; taken by Amherst, *ib.*; taken by the Americans, 783
Tilsit, the treaty of, 858
Tin, Phœnician and Greek trade in, 8
Tinchebrai, battle of, 125
Tintern Abbey, 129
Tippermuir, battle of, 547
Tippoo, succeeds Hyder Ali, and makes peace, 805; defeated by Cornwallis, 837; defeated by Harris and slain, 838
Tithes, proposal of the Barebone's Parliament to abolish, 567
Tithes, Irish, difficulty of collecting, 910

TRA

Todleben commands the Russians at Sebastopol, 945
Togidumnus, death of, 13
Toleration, Cromwell's advocacy of, 543; Charles II. proposes to adopt, 583; Charles II. issues a declaration in favour of, 587; tendency of sc ence to promote, 598; Locke's letters on, 652
Toleration Act, the, 651
Tone, Wolfe, founds the United Irishmen, 832; sent to France, 834
Tonnage and Poundage, nature of, 509; claimed by Charles I. in spite of the Petition of Right, 510; Act preventing the king from levying, 531
Torbay, arrival of William III. in, 644
Torrington, Earl of, Arthur Herbert, defeated at Beachy Head, 657
Tory party, the, origin of the name of, 620; reaction in favour of, 622; elects officers in the city, 623; gains a majority in the Common Council, 624; supports William III., 656; political ideas of, 672; its aims in the reign of Anne, 691; foreign policy of, 692; twelve peers created from, 695; its position after the Treaty of Utrecht, 699; loses power at the death of Anne, 702; principles of, at the accession of George III., 767; secures office under Lord North, 776; rises to power under Pitt, 808; coalesces with the majority of the Whigs, 828
Tostig, Earl of North-humberland, 89; driven from his earldom, 90; allied to Harold Hardrada, 94; killed at Stamford Bridge, 96
Toulon, attack by Eugene and Shovel on, 689
Toulouse, battle of, 871
Touraine conquered by Philip II., 176
Tournai, 364
Tourville, Count of, defeats the English and Dutch off Beachy Head, and makes himself master of the Channel, 657
Town, the, 693
Towns, growth of, 62, 72, 168; condition of the outskirts of, 191
Townshend, Charles, places duties on imports into the American colonies, 773; death of, 774
Townshend, Lord, becomes Secretary of State, 703; dismissed by George I., 709; re-admitted to office, 711; improves the cultivation of turnips, 813
Townships, early political organisation of, 31
Towton, battle of, 329
Trade, *see* Commerce
Trafalgar, battle of, 854
Trakir, battle of, 947
Transition from round-arched to Pointed architecture, 171
Transvaal Republic, the, foundation of, 969; annexation of, 970; acknow-

TRA

ledgment of the independence of, 971

Travelling, modes of, 273

Treason Act, the, carried, 830

Treasonable Correspondence Act, 828

Treasons, Act creating new, 392

Treasons, Statute of, 250

Trent, the Council of, 436

Trent, the Anglian occupation of the Valley of, 36

Tresilian, Chief Justice, hanged, 280

Triennial Act of Charles I., the, 530 ; repealed, 588

Triennial Act, the second, 661

Triers, Commission of, 569

Trimmer, origin of the name of, 618

Trinobantes, the geographical position of, 8 ; side with Cæsar, 11 ; submit to Cunobelin, 12

Triple Alliance, the, 599

Troppau, Congress of, 882

Troyes, the Treaty of, 306

Tudor, Owen, marries the widow of Henry V., 335

Tulchan bishops, the, 524

Tumblers, 275

Tunis, Blake sent against, 571

Turin, Eugene raises the siege of, 684

Turkish dominions, the proposal of Nicholas to partition, 943

Turks, the, uprising of the Greeks against, 884 ; defeated by Ibrahim Pasha, 921 ; welcome aid from Russia, *ib.* ; Syria restored to, 922 ; at war with Russia, 944 ; are overpowered by Russia, and submit to the Treaty of Berlin, 969

Turner, landscape-painting of, 943

Turnham Green, the militia of the city resist Charles I. at, 537

Tuscany, Duke of, Blake sent against, 571

Tyndale, William, translates the New Testament, 396

Tyrconnel, Earl of, *see* O'Donnell

Tyrconnel, Richard Talbot, Earl of, Lord Deputy in Ireland, 640

Tyre in danger, 157

Tyrone, Earl of, *see* O'Neill, Hugh

Ulm, capitulation of, 854

Ulster, plantation of, 484 ; insurrection and massacre in, 534

Undertakers, the, 487

Uniformity, Elizabethan Act of, 429 ; Restoration Act of, 585

Union with Scotland, 685 ; with Ireland, 842

United Irishmen, Society of, foundation of, 832 ; prepares for an insurrection, 841

United States, the ; *see* America, the United States of

Universities, growth of, 167 ; consulted on the divorce of Henry VIII., 385

Unkiar Skelessi, treaty of, signed, 921 ; abandoned, 922

Urban II., Pope, supported by Lanfranc, 118 ; preaches a Crusade, 120

VIN

Uriconium, *see* Viriconium

Utopia, 367

Utrecht, union of, 450 ; treaty of, signed 696 ; its effect on international relations, 697

Valence, William de, resists the Provisions of Oxford, 199

Valentine takes part in holding down the Speaker, 514

Val-ès-dunes, battle of, 88

Valley Forge, destitute condition of the American army at, 787

Vandevelde paints marine subjects, 631

Van Dyck, portraits by, 631

Vane, Sir Henry, the younger, produces evidence against Strafford, 530 ; negotiates the Solemn League and Covenant, 540 ; brings in a Reform bill, 566

Vaudois, the, Cromwell intervenes in favour of, 572

Venetian Republic, the suppression of, 837

Venice, League of Cambrai formed against, 363

Venner's plot, 584

Vere, Sir Horace, defends the Palatinate, 490

Verneuil, battle of, 308

Vernon, Admiral, takes Porto Bello, and fails to take Cartagena, 730

Verrio paints ceilings, 631

Verulamium, Roman city at, 19 ; martyrdom of St. Alban at, 23

Vestments, ecclesiastical, Hooper's rejection of, 417 ; Puritan resistance to the use of, 444 ; Whitgift's opinion on the propriety of, 468

Vicar, meaning of the term, 129

Victor Emanuel II., King of Sardinia, afterwards King of Italy, maintains constitutional government, 936 ; joins the allies in the Crimean war, 947 ; supported by the French in the war for the liberation of Italy, 956 ; becomes king of Italy, 957

Victoria, accession of, 914 ; refuses to dismiss Whig Ladies of the Bedchamber, 918 ; marriage of, 926 ; visits Louis Philippe, 927

Vienna, congress of, 873

Villa Viciosa, battle of, 692

Villages, arrangements of, 75

Villeins, the, uncertain origin of, 31 ; increase of, 69 ; position of, after the Norman conquest, 102 ; partial commutation of the services of, 168 ; effect of the Black Death upon, 248 ; insurrection of, 268 ; take refuge in towns, 275 ; land ceases to be cultivated by, 320, 321

Villiers, Charles, moves the repeal of the Corn Law, 924 ; moves a resolution approving of the Corn Law, 938

Vimeiro, battle of, 864

Vinegar Hill, defeat of the Irish insurgents at, 841

VIR

Virginia, colonisation of, 489
Viriconium, Roman colony at, 14
Vittoria, battle of, 871
Volunteers, the Irish, 796 ; the English, 848, 957
Vortigern establishes Jutes in Thanet, 27
Vote of No Addresses, 556

WAGRAM, battle of, 865
Wakefield, battle of, 328
Walcheren, expedition to, 865
Wales reduced by Harold, 90 ; Flemish settlement in, 128 ; conquered by Edward I., 210 ; marches of, *ib.*; supports Richard II., 285
Walker, Obadiah, Roman Catholic Master of University College, 639
Wallace, William, rises against Edward I., 221 ; execution of, 222
Waller, Sir William, defeated at Lansdown and Roundway Down, 538 ; takes Arundel Castle and defeats Hopton at Cheriton, 542 ; fights at Cropredy Bridge, 544 ; resigns his command, 545
Wallingford, Treaty of, 137
Walls, the Roman, 17
Walpole, Sir Robert, resigns office, 709 ; opposes the repeal of the Test Act and the passing of Peerage Bill, 710 ; resolves to rely on the Commons, not on the Lords, *ib.* ; re-admitted to office, 711 ; becomes First Lord of the Treasury, 712 ; his method of managing the House of Commons, 714 ; his doctrine of ' Quieta non movere,' 716 ; his rivalry with Carteret, 718 ; continues in power under George II., 720 ; his breach with Townshend, *ib.* ; brings in an Excise Bill, 722 ; withdraws the Excise Bill, 724 ; is unwilling to go to war with Spain, 728 ; characteristics of the sections of the opposition against, *ib.* ; hopes to end the quarrel with Spain by negotiation, 729 ; end of the administration of, 730 ; made Earl of Orford, 731
Walsingham, Sir Francis, Secretary to Elizabeth, 457
Walter Map, 167
Waltheof, Earl of Northamptonshire and Huntingdonshire, 90 ; is beheaded, 110
Wanborough, Ceawlin defeated at, 36
Wandewash, battle of, 764
War-band, the, composed of Gesiths, 30
Warbeck, Perkin, insurrection of, 350-352 ; execution of, 354
Wardship, nature of the lord's claim to, 116 ; results of the system, 330
Wars of the Roses, origin of the name of, 324 ; state of society during, 330
Warwick, Earl of, opposes Richard II , 279 ; banishment of, 282
Warwick, Earl of (son of the Duke of Clarence), imprisonment of, 343 ; execution of, 354

c.

WES

Warwick, Richard Beauchamp, Earl of, regent in France, 313
Warwick, Richard Nevill, Earl of (the King-maker), influence of, 324 ; retires to Calais, and comes back and defeats the Lancastrians at Northampton, 326 ; estranged from Edward IV., 332 ; is reconciled to Queen Margaret, 333 ; restores Henry VI., and is defeated and slain at Barnet, 334
Warwick, Earl of, *see* Northumberland, Duke of
Washington, burning of the Capitol at, 873
Washington, George, appointed commander of the Continental army, 783 ; his difficulties, 784 ; driven by the British out of New Jersey, *ib.* ; regains New Jersey, 786 ; defeated on the Brandywine, *ib.* ; winters at Valley Forge, 787
Wat Tyler, insurrection of, 268, 269
Waterloo, battle of, 874
Watt improves the steam-engine, 816
Wealth of Nations, The, publication of, 810
Wedderburn becomes Solicitor-General, 779
Wedmore, Peace of, (the so-called) 59
Wellesley, Marquis, his subsidiary system, 859 ; *see* Mornington, Lord
Wellesley, Sir Arthur, his victories in India, 859 ; defeats Junot at Vimeiro, 864 ; returns to Portugal, and drives Soult out of Oporto, 866 ; defeats the French at Talavera, 867 ; created a Viscount, *ib.* ; *see* Wellington, Viscount
Wellington, Viscount, afterwards Duke of, defends the lines of Torres Vedras, 867 ; elements of the success of, 868 ; takes Ciudad Rodrigo and Badajoz, 869 ; defeats Marmont at Salamanca, and enters Madrid, *ib.* ; becomes Prime Minister, 893 ; supports the Catholic Emancipation Bill, 896 ; fights a duel, *ib.* ; resignation of, 900 ; takes measures against the Chartists, 935 ; death of, 938 ; *see* Wellesley, Sir Arthur
Welsh, the, speak a language derived from that of the Britons, 7 ; origin of their name, 31 ; adopt the name Kymry, 37 ; defeated by Æthelfrith near Chester, 43 ; split up into three divisions, *ib.*; driven out of Somerset, 53 ; their relations with Ecgberht, 56 ; *see* Wales
Wentworth, Sir Thomas, *see* Strafford, Earl of
Wentworth, Thomas Wentworth, Lord, governor of Calais, 427
Weregild, system of, 32
Wesley, teaching of, 746
Wesley, Samuel, sermon by, 642
Wessex, gradual formation of, 28, 34, 35 ; is weakened by internal quarrels, 41 ; accepts Christianity, 48 ; growing

WES

unity of, 53 ; causes of the supremacy of, 55 ; an earldom under Godwine and Harold, 84, 89

West Indies, the, conflicts between English and Spanish sailors in, 447 ; smuggling in, 726 ; ill-treatment of Englishmen in, 728 ; capture of islands in, 859

West Saxons, the, first conquests of, 28 ; defeated at Mount Badon, *ib.*; occupy Salisbury Plain, 34 ; wage war with the men of Kent and with the Britons of the Severn Valley, 35 ; are defeated at Faddiley, *ib.* ; *see* Wessex

West Wales split off from other Welsh territory, 42

Westminster Abbey, consecration of, 91 ; coronation of William I. in, 100

Westmorland, Charles Neville, Earl of, takes part in the rising of the North, 441

Weston, Lord, *see* Portland, Earl of

Westphalia, Peace of, 564 ; erection of the kingdom of, 858

Westward Ho ! 447

Wexford, slaughter at, 563

Wharton, Lord, as Thomas Wharton, is a member of the Whig Junto 660

Whig party, the, origin of the name of, 620 ; has a hold on the city of London, 622 ; misuses its power in the second Convention Parliament, 656 ; William chooses his ministers from, 659 ; supported by Marlborough and Godolphin, 684 ; obtains complete control over the ministry, 687 ; impeaches Dr. Sacheverell, 691 ; disgraced by Anne, *ib.* ; is strong in the House of Lords, 695 ; position of, after the Treaty of Utrecht, 699 ; supported by George I., 703 ; secures a parliamentary majority, and prepares to impeach the leading Tories, 704 ; supports the Septennial Act, 706 ; change in the foreign policy of, 707 ; schism in, 709 ; causes of its strength when led by Walpole, 713 ; divisions in, 722 ; hostility of George III. to, 765 ; divided into three fractions, 768 ; seceders from, coalesce with Pitt, 828 ; enters into relations with Canning, 892 ; chooses Lord Althorp as its leader, 898 ; coalesces with the Canningites, 891

' Whip with six strings, the,' 400

White Ship, the, wreck of, 129

Whitefield preaches at Kingswood, 746

Whitgift, John, Archbishop of Canterbury, opinions of, 468 ; the High Commission Court under, 470 ; compared with Hooker, 472

Whitworth, Lord, violent language of Bonaparte towards, 848

Wilberforce denounces the slave-trade, 813

Wilfrid supports Papal authority, 50

Wilkes, John, arrested for an article in the *North Briton*, 769 ; condemned as

WIL

the author of an indecent poem, and expelled from the House of Commons, 770 ; escapes to France, *ib.* ; returns to England, and is elected for Middlesex, 774 ; expelled from the House, and declared incapable of sitting in it, *ib.* ; supported by the mob, 775 ; takes part as an alderman in the imprisonment of a messenger of the House of Commons, 779

Wilkins, Bishop, aims at comprehension, 598

William I. (the Conqueror) declared heir of Eadward the Confessor, 88 ; his rule in Normandy, *ib.*; claims the crown from Harold, 91 ; lands at Pevensey, and defeats Harold at Senlac, 96-98 ; crowned at Westminster, 100 ; progress of his conquest, 101-103 ; devastates the Vale of York, 103 ; subdues Hereward, and receives Malcolm's submission, 104 ; his method of keeping English and Normans in subjection, 104-106 ; his relations with the Church, 106-110 ; suppresses the Rising of the Earls, 110 ; lays waste the New Forest, *ib.* ; has Domesday Book prepared, 111 ; receives oaths at Salisbury, 113 ; death of, 114

William I., Prince of Orange, Stadtholder of the Dutch republic, 449 ; Jaureguy's attempt to murder, 454 ; murdered by Gerard, 456

William II. (Rufus) is crowned King of England, 114 ; is supported by the English against Robert, 115 ; character of, *ib.* ; his treatment of Anselm, 117 ; his quarrels with his brothers, 118 ; his relations with Scotland, 119 ; suppresses Mowbray's rebellion, 120 ; last years of, 121 ; is murdered, 122

William II., Prince of Orange, death of, 565

William III., Prince of Orange, defends the Dutch republic, 605 ; is offered the hand of Mary, daughter of the Duke of York, 608 ; at the head of a continental alliance, 609 ; marriage of, 613 ; invited to England, 644 ; lands at Brixham and marches on London, 645 ; arrives at Whitehall, 646 ; the crown offered to, 647 ; chooses his ministers from both parties, 649 ; receives the crown in Holland, 652 ; permits the destruction of the Highlanders of Glencoe, 654 ; dissolves his first parliament, 656 ; defeats James II. at the battle of the Boyne, *ib.* ; deprives Marlborough of his offices, 658 ; defeated at Steinkirk and Neerwinden, *ib.* ; places the Whig Junto in office, 659 ; his grief at his wife's death, 661 ; takes Namur, 663 ; trusts the Dutch more than the English, 664 ; plot for the assassination of, 665 ; compelled to reduce the army, 667 ; signs the first Partition Treaty, 668 ; opposed by the House of Commons, 670 ; signs the second

WIL

Partition Treaty, 671 : appoints a Tory ministry, 672 ; forms the Grand Alliance, 675 ; death of, 676

William IV., accession of, 898 ; dismisses the first Melbourne ministry, 912

William, son of Henry I., wrecked, 129

William Clito, son of Robert, 129

William Longbeard, 169, 170

William of Malmesbury, 129

William of Newburgh, 167

William the Lion, king of Scotland, acknowledges himself to be a vassal of Henry II., 154 ; frees himself from vassalage, 159

Williams, John, Archbishop of York, impeachment of, 535

Winceby, fight at, 542

Winchelsey, Archbishop, 221

Winchester, secular canons driven out of, 68 ; burial of William II. at, 122 ; Stephen chosen king at, 131 ; taken by Cromwell, 549

Windham enters Pitt's cabinet, 828

Winnington Bridge, Booth defeated at, 575

Winwæd, the battle of, 48

Wishart, George, burnt, 413

Witenagemot, the, constitution of, 45 ; discussion on the acceptance of Christianity in, 46 ; constitutional powers of, 74 ; becomes the Great Council, 113 ; *see* Great Council, the

Witt, John de, Pensionary of Holland, 589 ; negotiates the Triple Alliance, 599 ; murder of, 605

Wolfe, General, sent against Quebec, 753 ; death of, 756

Wolfe Tone ; *see* Tone, Wolfe

Wolseley, Sir Garnet, defeats Arabi at Tel-el-Kebir, 971

Wolsey, Thomas, Cardinal, rise of, 363 ; magnificence of, 364 ; supports a policy of peace, 365, 366 ; comes into the House of Commons, 371 ; becomes unpopular on account of the Amicable Loan, 372 ; secures his position by an alliance with France, 374 ; aspires to the papacy, 375 ; is named legate *a latere*, *ib.* ; his views on Church reform, 376 ; founds two colleges, 377 ; fails to persuade Henry VIII. to abandon Anne Boleyn, 380 ; is appointed legate to try Henry's divorce, 382 ; fall of, 383 ; death of, 384

Women, education of, in the Middle Ages, 65

Wonderful Parliament, the, 280

Wood's halfpence, 718

Worcester, battle of, 564

ZWI

Worcester, secular canons driven from, 68

Wordsworth, poetry of, 889

Wren, Sir Christopher, buildings by, 632

Wriothesley, Lord Chancellor, excluded from the Council, 412

Wroxeter, *see* Viriconium

Wulfhere maintains the independence of Mercia, 48

Wyatt, Sir Thomas, rebellion and execution of, 423

Wycliffe, John, his doctrines, 261 ; summoned before an ecclesiastical court at St. Paul's, 262 ; sends out 'poor priests,' and renounces transubstantiation, 266 ; retires, and dies, 269

Wykeham, William of, deprived of the Chancellorship, 260 ; restored to the Council, and again dismissed, 262

YARMOUTH supports Stephen, 134

York (*see* Eboracum) submits to Harold Hardrada, 95 ; taken by William I., 102 ; devastation of the Vale of, 103 ; massacre of Jews at, 160 ; Charles I. at, 537 ; siege of, 542

York, Archbishop of, his right to crown a king questioned, 149

York, Archbishopric of, founded, 46

York, Duke of Edmund (son of Edward III.), joins Henry IV., 285

York, Duke of, second son of George III., commands in the Netherlands, 826

York, James, Duke of, *see* James II.

York, Richard, Duke of (father of Edward IV.), is regent in France, 313 ; governs Ireland, 319 ; first Protectorate of, 323 ; second Protectorate of, 324 ; driven to Ireland, 326 ; claims the throne, 327 ; defeated and slain, 328

York, Richard, Duke of (son of Edward IV.), lodged in the Tower, 341 ; murdered, 342

Yorke, Charles, suicide of, 776

Yorktown, Cornwallis capitulates at, 794

ZEMINDARY of the district around Calcutta granted to the East India Company, 764 ; Clive receives the quit-rent for, 801

Zulu war, the, 970

Zürich, treaty of, 957

Zutphen, death of Sir Philip Sidney at, 457

Zwingli, teaching of, 390

Zwinglianism, spread of, in England 399 ; Cranmer's attitude towards, 416'

Spottiswoode & Co. Printers, New-street Square, London.